St Kilda

Church, Visitors and 'Natives'

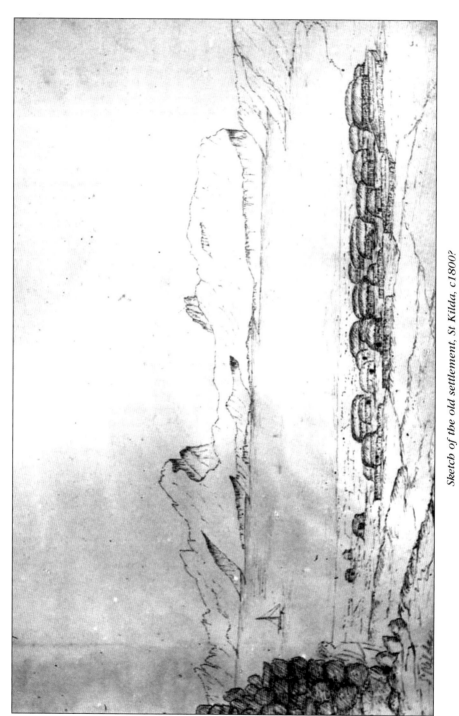

Sketch of the old settlement, St Kilda, c1800?

St Kilda

Church, Visitors and 'Natives'

Michael Robson

The Islands Book Trust

ISBN 0-9546238-4-3

Published by The Islands Book Trust,
10 Callicvol, Port of Ness, Isle of Lewis, HS2 0XA
Telephone +44 (0) 1851 810681
Email info@10callicvol.com
Website www.theislandsbooktrust.com

Published 2005

Printed by Nevisprint Limited, Fort William

CONTENTS

PART IV
New missionaries and a new church

ILLUSTRATIONS

All photographs by F W L Thomas were taken in or around 1860

ACKNOWLEDGEMENTS

I am grateful to many people and their families whose individual contributions have been most valuable in assisting me to write about St Kilda. I have been particularly helped by many of the former 'natives' of St Kilda and, of course, am especially indebted to Rob Fairley for allowing me to use his painting on the cover of the book. Any omissions from the following are my own fault:

Dorothea Abbott, John Ballantyne, Malcolm Bangor-Jones, Alasdair Beaton, Elizabeth Bray, Maureen Byers, Hugh M Cartwright, Alison Cox, Raymond Eagle, David Fowler, Graham E Langmuir, Bill Lawson, John Angus McCusbic, Fraser Macdonald, Iain Gordon Macdonald, John Macdonald (Luskentyre), Nancy Macdonald, John Mackenzie (Lochcarron), Willie Maclean (North Uist), John Mackillop, Calum Macleod (Berneray), Finlay and Norma Macleod, Morag Macleod, Calum Macneil, Chrissie and John Macqueen, Ewan Macrae, Elizabeth Marr, John Marsden, Donald Meek, Helen Murchison, Eileen Petterssen, Marion Richardson, John Trinick, David Wilson.

No less than to these I am greatly appreciative of the willing assistance and researches on my behalf of archivists, librarians and other keepers of records etc. in many institutions and repositories. These include:

Blair Castle, Columba House (Scottish Catholic Archives, Edinburgh), The British Library, City of Edinburgh Council (Central Library), The Clan Donald Centre, University of Edinburgh Library (Special Collections), The Free Church College (Edinburgh), The Highland Council Archives (Inverness), The Mitchell Library, National Archives of Scotland, National Library of Scotland, National Trust of Scotland, New College (Edinburgh), The Public Record Office, Renfrewshire Council Library Headquarters (Paisley), The Royal Society (London), South Ayrshire Council Carnegie Library, UK Hydrographics Office, University of Strathclyde Library, Western Isles Libraries (Stornoway).

The Islands Book Trust is grateful for support towards the publication of this book from Awards for All, Western Isles Enterprise, Comhairle nan Eilean Siar, the Scottish International Education Trust, and Rhea Banker and other members of the Book Trust through donations.

FOREWORD

I have no doubt that this is one of the most important books ever written about St Kilda. That is no small claim when one considers that there have probably been more books on St Kilda per square mile than any other island, a tribute to the perennial fascination which St Kilda, its dramatic landscape and small isolated community, has held for the outside world ever since Martin Martin visited in the seventeenth century.

That fact itself demonstrates the problem. Almost every book written about St Kilda shows the island from the outside, often based on considerable ignorance, prejudice, and the most fleeting of acquaintances. Many simply repeat the received wisdom from earlier writers so that a comprehensive mythology has arisen, usually featuring a poor and simple people living in poverty under the malign influence of successive evangelical Presbyterian Ministers, whose role was to enforce Sabbath observance to the detriment of the islanders' social and economic needs.

Michael Robson has looked beyond the mythology by critically examining original records which have not hitherto been used, particularly those left by the Churches, whose Ministers, missionaries, and teachers played a pivotal role over several centuries as intermediaries between the St Kildans and the outside world. His key insight is that everybody involved with St Kilda had their own agenda, from Martin Martin onwards, and their views need to be interpreted in this light. While this was obviously the case with the Church, it was equally true of visiting tourists and journalists, whose penchant for sensationalising, romanticising, and simplification was as strong in the nineteenth century as it is today.

Did the outsiders succeed in changing St Kilda? There is no simple answer to that question, but there is certainly evidence that the efforts of the post-Reformation Church drove underground many of the traditional beliefs, stories, and songs of the islanders. But some of the Ministers, contrary to myth, were both interested in the traditional culture of the St Kildans, and devoted much effort to improving social life on the island, for example Neil Mackenzie's involvement in the planning of the new village, and Angus Fiddes's role in reducing the high infant tetanus death rate.

Whatever judgement may be made about the ultimate impact of the Church, the more powerful influence leading to a change of social attitudes and expectations on the part of the islanders was that of tourism and journalism. These were the forces which led the St Kildans to embrace new values and become dissatisfied with their lives. If anything, the Church tended to act as a restraining influence on these major changes which eventually led to the evacuation.

Does the experience of St Kilda hold lessons for other small and remote communities? Possibly, through its example of how closer communication and interaction with a more powerful outside world can make small communities vulnerable to competition and cultural takeover. As Michael Robson brings out, while St Kilda attracted a disproportionate amount of attention from outside writers, its objective conditions were in some respects more favourable than other rural communities in the Highlands and islands at the time. For example, housing conditions were certainly better than in many areas from the 1830s onwards, while St Kilda despite substantial emigration did not experience clearance in the nineteenth century and was less seriously affected by the potato famine than many areas. What marked out St Kilda was its difficulty of communications for much of the year, and the fevered attention and so-called help of outside agencies.

The Islands Book Trust is very pleased to publish this genuinely new account of St Kilda to mark the 75th anniversary of the evacuation of the island. While the views of the Gaelic-speaking islanders on their often dramatic history may never be known, perhaps Michael Robson has come as close as it is possible to do through this dispassionate and detailed account of how St Kilda was subject to all sorts of attempts to convert its way of life, and was eventually changed for ever.

JOHN RANDALL
Chairman
The Islands Book Trust

August 2005

PROLOGUE

ONE day in 1883 Donald MacDonald, crofter in St Kilda, was asked about his life in the island, about crofting, fishing and taking birds from the cliffs. Also put to him were questions of a rather different kind which, as a man with an ancestry stretching back over many St Kilda generations, he might have been expected to be able to answer.

> 'Are you acquainted with the history and traditions of the island?'
> 'I am not very skilled in these things', he replied, 'but I have heard some of them'.

For him history was tradition.

> 'In the oldest history that is written about St Kilda, there is mention made of a cross upon which the people were accustomed to take an oath. Have you ever heard of that?'
> 'I never heard of that'.
> 'Does that man sitting behind you know?'

It seems that Donald then turned round and spoke with the man behind him.

> 'We cannot say anything about the oath, but there is a cross cut upon the rock at Boreray, the steep island over there.'
> 'But my inquiry was about a movable cross which would be held up by a party taking the oath, and it was either of gold or silver?'

More conversation perhaps, and then:

> 'We never heard of it.'[1]

On occasions when in Boreray for sheep or birds Donald MacDonald will have seen the cross 'cut upon the rock' there, and perhaps he imagined it to be like another cross cut into a stone built into his own house. Each of these crosses belonged to a time long forgotten, meaning little and with no story attached to them. But they were visible, whereas the 'movable cross' was no longer so. It had been mentioned two hundred years earlier, by Martin Martin in his book *A Late Voyage to St Kilda*, and since then it had disappeared or been destroyed.[2]

Probably no inhabitant of St Kilda had read Martin's account and knowledge of this cross had evidently not survived in any tradition heard by Donald MacDonald.

His ignorance of the 'movable cross' did not mean that Donald was poorly acquainted with the traditions of the island. Oral tradition being very different from written history was equally, if not more so, at the mercy of personal decisions, changes in attitude, new convictions and the abandonment of ancient custom. There were too influences from 'outside' that could cause breaks with the past in the interests of what some called 'improvement', and even the destruction of a golden or silver cross could be considered progress by those of, say, a different religious persuasion.

To many of the communities in the Hebrides of Donald's day the store of tradition was almost the sum of the knowledge that was either useful or of interest to them. It guided their daily occupations and it filled many a half-lit hour of a winter evening. But it was not safe from loss or from scorn. Donald MacDonald was one of those island people, from Islay to Lewis, who by 1883 were known and admired by Alexander Carmichael. While living in Uist Carmichael gathered much, and yet perhaps only a fraction, of that stored cultural world and he had no patience with those who scorned or dismissed Hebridean and Highland tradition: 'I went much among the very poorest of the people, among a people whose pinched features betrayed their poverty, yet during nearly seventeen years in Uist I was never once asked for charity... Yet, these are the people so often misrepresented, and sometimes so cruelly maligned by men who do not know them.' He knew their love of song, of story, and of the associations with familiar places; but he was depressed by the decline in these affections, for which he saw several reasons. 'The oral lore of the old Highland people is rapidly dying out with the old people themselves. There is an essential difference between the old and the young people. The young people are acquiring a smattering of school education in which they are taught to ignore the oral literature which tended to elevate and ennoble their fathers.' Education was of course not the only external influence: 'They had labour songs, with which they accompanied themselves in rowing, shearing, spinning, fulling, milking, and in grinding at the quern. If they sing less now, their silence is due to repression from without.'[3]

Education could itself be repressive, and so could religion. It might quite justifiably be thought that Donald MacDonald had no recollection of the 'movable cross' because of the changes in religion since the period of its use, changes which had educated the St Kilda people away from it and its significance. Some, including Carmichael, have seen religion, especially in more recent forms, as an agent of loss, penetrating the private and inner realms of traditional knowledge. As one who loved those realms and the people who cherished them, Carmichael was saddened by their apparent fading and by the state of mind that had taken over:

'Is there no minister of religion courageous enough, philanthropic enough, far-seeing enough to come to the rescue of these interesting people and bring them out of their slough of despond, out of their windless, waveless, tideless, motionless doldrum into which erroneous seamanship led them and wherein they exist, and back again to their many sports, wholesome functions and joyous pastimes of their fathers. If not, the time may come when these highly endowed men and women shall discover for themselves that religious dogmas are dry husks and that labour without recreation is wearisome.'[4]

More than a century has passed since those words were written, St Kilda has been emptied of its people, and religion can be viewed in a different light. When, in 1883, Rev. John MacKay, Free Church Minister in St Kilda, was himself questioned, some of his answers revealed the limiting effects, if not repression, of the doctrines brought to the people by evangelical religion, but as one answer hinted these effects were not as sweeping and total as has on occasions been claimed.

'Are they all able to read?'
'Yes, they are.'
'They can read Gaelic every one of them?'
'Perfectly well, and commit portions of Scripture to memory.'
'Is there anything else they commit to memory besides portions of Scripture?'
'Nothing.'
'Nothing, in the way of songs?'
'Nothing. Nothing whatever - the Psalms of David and the New Testament.'
'They have no poets of their own?'
'No poets or poetry of their own.'
'Or no recollection of one?'
'Well, perhaps they may have, but I don't hear.'[5]

It may be impossible now, and perhaps always was, to share the feelings and daily concerns of the ancient community in an island long deserted as it struggled to survive over centuries, but sometimes small windows are found opening upon a vanished way of life. To pursue the story of religion and of other external influences bearing upon a people who were so often a captive audience at the mercy of those who came to tell them what to believe or do is to get closer at least, just as listening to tradition can be to hear a voice from the heart. The story is inevitably a long and varied one, haunted throughout by two endlessly repeated phrases which would have meant much to Alexander Carmichael; it is the story of 'the poor people of St Kilda' in that 'remote and interesting island.'

PART I

PAGAN ROOTS AND PRIESTLY ECHOES
St Kilda before 1700

FROM the earliest times St Kilda (Hirt[a], Hiort etc.) could be seen from the Sound of Harris as a distant part of the Outer Hebrides rather than as a different place on its own, isolated by remoteness and way of life. Nevertheless, its high peaks on the horizon, its name and its reputation all had, and still have, a variety of significance for the inhabitants of the main chain of islands from the Butt of Lewis to Berneray (Barra Head) who must have been aware from the beginning of occupation, whenever that was, of its peculiar advantages and dangers.

The arrival of the Irish or Columban church, with connections to islands such as Eigg, Boreray and Pabbay between Uist and Harris, and perhaps to Barra and islands to the south, opens the story. It leads on to the visits and settlement of the Norsemen, their relationship to the communities already long established along the whole west coast of Scotland, with links to Orkney, Shetland, Faroe and Iceland as well as to their 'home' country of Norway. St Kilda traditions, apparently associated with monk and viking sailors and settlers, survived as part of the cultural inheritance of the people there, as they did in other islands. This had no less an impact than that of the requirements of mediaeval rulers, landowners and lairdships which to a great measure controlled the daily lives and social structures of those in the far-off but evidently important possession of *Hirtha*.

The Catholic forms of religious worship also became a natural part of St Kilda life, presumably introduced and certainly maintained by priests sent to the island by the church and proprietors. Although by the sixteenth century there was no regularly residing priest, memories of one and of what he had taught and practised lived on as a tradition well after the Reformation. When Martin Martin visited in 1697 his main concern as a protestant was with the embodiment of just that tradition in the shape of 'the Impostor', of whose behaviour Martin so much disapproved. The removal of 'the Impostor' heralded the introduction of presbyterian teaching in 1705 and a new period of religious transition.

CHAPTER 1

Columba and Moluag, Norsemen, Rocabarraidh,
and early proprietors

NOT far from the site of Sir Norman MacLeod's residence in Berneray, at a
place called Tobhta nan Craobh and near Tobar mòr Mhicleòid, stood a
dwelling occupied at one time by Mary MacLeod, Màiri nighean Alasdair Ruaidh,
who is said to have been born at Rodel in Harris around 1615 and became well
known for her songs or poems. She also stayed a while in Pabbay where lived
her brother Neil MacLeod and where she may have composed her song *Crònan
an Taibh*, the Croon of the Ocean. From either of these islands, green and sunlit,
she could have enjoyed those moments which are recollected in a song of hers
called *Pòsadh MhicLeòid* and which belong to a peaceful summer day in the
Sound of Harris:

'Mi 'nam shuidh	'As I sat
Air chaolas ronach	above a seal-haunted strait,
M'aghaidh air Hirt	Looking towards Hirt
Nan ian gorma..'	of blue birds..'

If from her vantage point Mary did gaze out westwards to those distant
grey peaks unexpectedly breaking the great expanse of the ocean horizon she
would probably also have seen the occasional fulmar or line of gannets, 'blue
birds' of Hirt, over that intervening sea called on an old map *Cheules Yrt*, that is,
Caolas Hirt or the Sound of Hirt. She would have seen ships under sail; and, had
she been able to look far back through time, she would have made out longships
passing from Iceland and Norway through that forty miles wide 'Sound', and,
before them, the curachs of adventurous holy men from Ireland or Iona.[6]

That old map, sketched out before 1600 and published a little more than
fifty years later, may seem an unlikely source for detailed information about
isolated Atlantic islands, but it covers the Hebrides and most of the west coast
of the Scottish mainland from 'The Mull of Kyntyr' to Assynt in Sutherland. It
shows islands as small and remote as Rona, the Flannans and Heisgeir, but for
some reason it does not include Hirt, in spite of the fact that in reality this island
group was considerably larger and better known than these others. However,
on at least one of the published copies an unknown hand made corrections.
The Latin words for North and South in the margins needed to be exchanged as
they had been printed in reverse position; and near the extreme western border
of the map, out from *Valay, Bernera* and *Papa*, past *Cheules Yrt*, beyond *Helskyr
Egach* and *Havelskyr na meul*, the same mysterious person inked in an island
and wrote below it 'dow Hijrtach', signifying Hirt.

These two words, entered on a map perhaps three or more centuries ago,
the ink brown with age, challenge the imagination. They convey a feeling of

discovery, as if someone had just come across a lonely, unsuspected land in the west. They suggest a traveller, irritated by the omission of an important name and entering it in the wide open space available. And they sound sombre, filled with experience of the gloomy place to which they applied. Perhaps the person who wrote them meant all this; or perhaps, knowing of the island's existence and nature, he merely copied the appropriate Dow Hijrtach, already printed on the map to indicate the dangerous rocks west of Colonsay on which a lighthouse was built long afterwards.

Hirt certainly had through the ages a reputation for hardship, poverty and gloom. A really difficult and miserable situation in Tiree would lead people to say, 'O, b'fheàrr leam gu robh mi ann a' Hiort', 'Oh, I'd rather be in Hirt', the extreme example of difficulty and misery. From Ness in Lewis to Vatersay and the other islands south of Barra mothers have for generations threatened children who were being a nuisance with 'Teich air falbh a Hiort' 'Get away to Hirt', 'Nach robh thu an t-Hirt', 'I wish you were in Hirt', or 'Cuiridh mi Hirt air mun mairt thu', 'I'll put you to Hirt on a cow's back'. These and similar expressions, some of them less polite, are still known today and all add up to the conclusion that Hirt has never been anything other than a dreadful place in popular belief. This is probably what 'dow Hijrtach' meant, wherever it was used, even though Mary MacLeod, sitting in the sun and listening to the seals, might have thought very differently. [7]

There is a widespread inclination among all sorts of people to look upon Hebridean placenames as if they have a meaning that could be expressed in English. Many indeed can be so translated. But the origin and meaning, in English, of Hirt are not immediately evident, and as a consequence the name has been the subject of much theorising and discussion. If it were accepted as deriving from Norse then more than one possible 'meaning', however unlikely, could be proposed. After all, many of the nearer islands in the Sound of Harris, including Berneray, Boreray, Coppay, Shillay and Pabbay, have names that are of Norse origin, so why not Hirt? Gaelic seems a less likely source. However the larger islands of Lewis, Harris, Uist, Skye and possibly Barra, have names which are not necessarily derived from Norse or Gaelic, and this may be the case with Hirt. Certainly Norwegian crews and settlers filled the land and the edge of the sea with names of their own, but there is no reason why much older names should not have survived in their own right or by adoption, in spite of widespread Norse 'rejection'. In fact it has been observed that 'Most of the Hebridean names in the sagas appear to be adaptations of earlier (Celtic) names, even though they give the impression of being Norse: *Bòt*, Bute, *Myl*, Mull, *Hirtir*, St Kilda, etc. etc.' And even Lyohùs, Lewis, which 'sounds and looks like a Norse settlement name' may, in spite of its Norse appearance, 'go back to a long forgotten Celtic ancestor.'[8]

Though now known by names of Norse origin the islands in the Sound of Harris were inhabited long before the arrival of viking and other ships from the north, though if they had older names, as they must have done, these have also been 'long forgotten'. Some of the earlier inhabitants were undoubtedly monks of the Celtic church, straight from Ireland or from bases on the west coast of the Scottish mainland and elsewhere in the Hebrides. Their presence is often indicated or implied by placenames. North of Brusda in Berneray is the site of an ancient church called Cill Eiseam on a soft grassy level between rocky outcrops. It could be approached through Cachaileith na Beatha, the gate of life, which led into an area held to be a sanctuary. Another church on this island was dedicated to Columba. Across the channel in Vallay, close to the shore of North Uist, were 'Three Chappels, One Dedicated to *St. Ulton*, and another to the *Virgin Mary*' and 'Two Crosses of Stone, each of them about 7 Foot high, and a Foot and a half broad'. On nearby Boreray at some time there lived someone known as *Mack-vanish*, the son of the monk, and this island must have been of great religious importance in early days, especially as containing a burial ground where a few incised stones still survive:

> 'The Burial place near the Houses, is called the Monks-Field, for all the Monks that dyed in the Islands that lye Northward from *Egg*, were buried in this little Plot, each Grave hath a Stone at both ends, some of which are 3 and others 4 Foot high. There are big Stones without the Burial place even with the Ground, several of them have little Vacuities in them as if made by Art; the Tradition is that these Vacuities were dug for receiving the Monks Knees when they prayed upon 'em.'[9]

Some of these churches or chapels were built in mediaeval times rather than in the sixth or seventh century, but monks occupied the islands, perhaps along with native populations, before the Norsemen arrived around 800. The Norse in the Hebrides borrowed the Irish term *papi* for a Celtic priest or hermit and attached it to some of their own words when naming islands and certain places where presumably monks or hermits were living: Paible, in North Uist and in Taransay, from *Papbyli*, priest's dwelling; Papadil in Rum, from *Papadalr*, priest's glen; and *Papey*, priest's island, occurring in at least four different locations in the Outer Hebrides, and near Skye, as Pabbay. In the Sound of Harris the island of Pabbay has the remains of two churches, close together, in the old settlement of Baile na Cille, one of them called Teampull Mhoire, the other Teampull Mo-Luaig. And eastwards nearer to the shore on top of a little hill are the traces of the MacLeod stronghold called now Seana-Chaisteal, the old castle, in the township lands of Baile Lingaidh.[10]

*

Monks and priests, solitary or in small communities, looked out from the Sound of Harris islands, from Uist, from Harris, from Lewis and even from Barra, and in clear air saw the hills and rocks of Hirt. If they were possessed of a good, ocean-going curach, they could pick a suitable day and make the crossing comparatively easily, although always having to allow for currents, tides, fogs, and sudden changes in wind and weather. Some of them had made longer journeys before and were skilled seafarers after the manner of Brendan from Kerry who may have landed at Hirt in the course of his voyages around the year 560, and like Colum Cille, Columba, who reached Iona at much the same time. Such men sought a 'secret, retired, secure retreat in the ocean, far apart from mankind', and for them Hirt could have been a very appropriate destination, though a determined hermit might have preferred Boreray, towering up in great cliffs four miles from the main island of Hirt, or the equally threatening Soay to the west.[11] At any rate little churches or chapels were built in Hirt at an unknown period and not all at the same time.

A man devoted to the idea of a solitary religious life, perhaps on a remote island for the summer season, could be deterred from landing if he saw that someone else was already in residence or if there was competition. A spirit of friendly rivalry might have given rise to the tradition regarding Lismore in Lorn:

'Columba and Moluag agreed to row together to the island and that the first to land should retain possession. They started together each with his crew of twelve clerics chanting their psalms as they rowed their coracles and as Highland boatmen still sing their iorraim songs when rowing.
'When nearing the island Moluag lifted his axe and cut off the little finger of his left hand and throwing it ashore before him exclaimed -

"M'fhianuis air Dia 's air daoine
M'fhuil is m'fheoil air bharr an
A Chaluim chairdeil chaoimh."

["My witness be to God and men
My flesh and blood are on the land
Thou well beloved Columba."]

'Columba commended the devotion of his brother missionary and turning aside the bow of his boat did not land. The following dialogue is alleged to have occurred between the brethren before parting -

Calum-cille	Sliosmor mar ainm an eilean
Moluag	Ma's a sliosmor gu'm bu slios tarbhach
Calum-cille	Slocach, cnocach, creagach
Moluag	Brioghar, mioghar, preasach
Calum-cille	Faobhar a chloiche bhos a chionn
Moluag	A goimh foipe
Calum-cille	Fearna mar chonnadh da
Moluag	Gabhail mar a choingeal da

[Columba	The great plain be the name of the island
Moluag	If great the plain great be the fruit
Columba	Pitfull, knollfull, rocky
Moluag	Fertile, sweet, bushful
Columba	Be the edges of its rocks uppermost
Moluag	Be their venom under
Columba	Alder be its fuel
Moluag	To kindle like the candle.]

'The place where Molluag landed in Lismore is still called Port Moluag. Immediately above are the grass grown ruins of a cell or oratory built on the spot where Moluag threw his finger.'

An alternative tradition is less complimentary to Moluag and emphasises Columba's good nature. Having agreed that the one who was first on land would have possession of the island, they set off on their race. As the boats came in to the rocks Columba jumped ashore. 'Moluag was disappointed that he himself did not succeed and said in depreciation of the island - The sharpest side of the rock uppermost', whereupon 'Calum cille' replied 'May it not be venomous.' Moluag then said 'may there be no fuel but green alder', and Columba answered 'may it burn like a candle'. Thus thwarted in his 'evil wishes' Moluag resolved to make another effort to win possession and cut off a finger which he threw 'from the shore to the soil above, calling on God and Calumcille to witness that his flesh and blood mingled with the earth of the island.' Columba generously admitted this and so the dispute came to an end.[12]

Associations with early Christian figures like Columba and Moluag have persisted, sometimes in half-legendary tradition, sometimes where there are visible remains such as a ruined building, a well or a stone cross. Places and structures often have a powerful and moving atmosphere; Applecross in its bay below the mountains has still the air of the sanctuary it became after Maelrubha (Maelrubai) arrived from Ireland in 673 and founded the monastery of 'Apur Crossan', and Tobar Che in Taransay remains as a reminder that Columba himself and other holy men put their blessing on wells as if they were as sacred as crosses and graveyards. Sanctuary-like areas of ground have also been blessed. A graveyard in Barra or in the islands to the south was known by the usual term Cladh, but it might equally be known as Beannachadh, blessed ground, as in Beannachadh Bhrianain at Borve, Beannachadh Chaluim Chille in Mingulay, and just Beannachadh in Vatersay. The windswept and rocky headland southwest of Gallan Head on the west coast of Lewis 'is known as Am Beannachadh, and has always been considered a holy place'; and although Beannachadh has been apparently used for the little stone building, generally called a chapel, on Eilean Mor of the Flannans, the word is traditionally, and perhaps more correctly, applied to the ground on the western headland of that island where there are remains of small stone-built cells. Dedications to Columba in Mingulay, Brendan at Borve in Barra and Maelrubha at Cladh Maolrithe near Borve in Berneray, Harris, do not mean that these people of the sixth or seventh century themselves went to the islands, though of course they may have done, but their names and reputation survived in tradition and continued to be treated with respect and even veneration. More than six hundred years after the death of Moluag in 592 a man called Gillemoluag was dean of Lismore, and a century later in the mid 1300s Amy MacRuari, wife, or the 'discarded and ill-used wife', of John, Lord of the Isles, caused to be built, according to tradition, Eaglais Chaluim Chille, the church dedicated to Columba standing now in ruins upon a small island in Loch na Cille at Balivanich in Benbecula.[13]

How and when religious tradition came into being is no more possible to determine than when dedications were chosen and used. Brendan may have landed in Hirt, where a chapel was dedicated to him, but no one can at present be certain that he did. The name and reputation of Columba came to Hirt and were attached to another chapel through its dedication but again it is not known when that happened. And even supposing that these two famous men, among other monks, did reach Hirt with their learning and monastic customs, who in the mysterious dusk of an evening came out of the shadows to greet them and learn from them?

*

Just before 800 the Norsemen came to the Hebrides and so began a lengthy period during which peaceful conditions never prevailed generally in the islands for more than a year or two. Plunder, settlement, piracy, farming, paganism and Christianity mixed together, perhaps none of them new but finding themselves more frequently recorded. Connections were established and broken and re-established between the western islands and lands to the north, Orkney, Iceland and Scandinavia, and inevitably different traditions were introduced. Local leaders, part Celt, part Norse, emerged as rulers within small 'kingdoms', asserting independence or expressing loyalty and paying taxes to greater figures elsewhere. In the early 870s a 'great viking' called Onund with three companions and five ships 'well manned' once again crossed 'west beyond the sea' to plunder in the Hebrides:

'..and when they came to the Barra isles, they found a king there, who was called Kiarval: he also had five ships. They opened battle with him, and there was a hard fight. Onund's men were the most vigorous people. Many fell there on both sides; and it ended so, that the king fled with one ship. There Onund and his men took the ships and much treasure as well, and they stayed there for the winter.'[14]

It is not known whether this king, or perhaps another further north in Uist, laid claim to the distant Hirt, nor whether any Norsemen on viking expeditions, eager to find 'treasure', gave much attention to a remote island that may have seemed unattractive to would-be settlers. Possibly holy men still lived there, just as the Norsemen were to discover when they went to Iceland: '..before Iceland was inhabited from Norway, there were there the men whom the Norwegians call *papar*; these were Christian men, and it is believed that they had come from the west beyond the sea, because Irish books, and bells, and croziers, were found [left] behind them, and many other things besides, so that one might know that they were Westmen'. Similarly, what was said rather earlier of the Faroe islands might well apply to Hirt also: 'Some of these islands are small; nearly all alike are separated by narrow channels; and in them for nearly a hundred years hermits have dwelt, sailing from our Scottia (Ireland). But just as from the beginning of the world they were ever uninhabited, so now, because of those robbers the Northmen, they are empty of anchorites, though full of innumerable sheep, and very many kinds of sea-birds.' [15] Whether Hirt was empty at this time or not Norsemen met the Christian hermits and communities in the Hebrides, slaughtering some of them for their valuable possessions and being eventually in a manner converted by others.

A number of settlers in Iceland were Hebridean Norse who had been baptised before they left but whose Christian convictions varied in depth: 'some of them held Christianity well till their death day, but it seldom passed to their descendants; so that some of their sons built temples, and sacrificed.' Among the settlers were two men known as Helgi the Lean and Orlyg the Old. Helgi was religiously in two minds, a condition which was no doubt far from uncommon. 'Helgi was called Christian, and yet was very mixed in his beliefs; he was baptized and professed faith in Christ, but he vowed to Thor for sea-journeys and difficult undertakings.' Orlyg on the other hand had perhaps been more thoroughly educated in Christian ways for he was fostered by the supposed Bishop Patrick of the Isles who helped to prepare him for his venture to Iceland, supplying him with timber to build a church, a book of gospels, an iron bell, a gold penny, 'and consecrated earth to lay under the corner-posts, and to have it as consecration, and for the sake of hallowing [the church] to Columcille.' It was said of Orlyg's descendants that 'they believed in Columcille although they were unbaptized.' Another Iceland settler, Halldor the Red, also dedicated a church there to Columba. [16]

There could be differences of religion within one family. By 880 men like Bjorn, son of Ketil Flatnose who asserted chieftainship in the Hebrides, might refuse to accept Christianity themselves but they did not necessarily kill those who did, Bjorn stayed two winters in the islands with his Christian brother and sisters and was ill at ease until he moved on to Iceland. He 'became aware that they had another religion; and he thought it a paltry thing that they should have forsaken the old faith, to which their kindred had clung.' As with the religion of

Columba and Moluag, some elements of the 'old faith' of the Norsemen entered the body of tradition inherited by later generations of the people who lived in even the remotest Hebridean islands.[17]

*

Some traditions, like some placenames, derived from an uncertain and very distant past. Brendan, who became known as 'the voyager', sailed into the ocean in search of 'the Land of Promise', in the course of which he and his crew celebrated Easter on the back of a whale which served as a temporary island. The land which he journeyed to discover seemed to be part real, part imaginary, a dream perhaps but one that could materialise into ordinary life, much like the strange land out in the ocean which in the Hebrides was called Rocabarraidh, 'a beautiful green island under the sea about a day's sail due west of Barra, from which taciturn men and maidens and hornless scallop-eared (corc-chluasach) dun cows occasionally came to visit their friends in Barra and by whose mysterious inhabitants belated Barra fishermen have often been hospitably entertained.'[18] Although Barra was possibly the main source of information the people living on Pabbay, a few miles to the south, also met with the inhabitants and cattle from that distant 'green island', and it was a mason at Carnan in Uist, Duncan MacLellan, known as Donnachadh Ban, who in 1872 told the story of Rocabarraidh, otherwise called Iola nam miola mora, the fishing bank of the great sea creatures, or Iola nam muca mara, the fishing bank of the whales.

> 'A man came to Barra once, and no one knew who he was or whence he came. He married and three sons were born to him. He and his three sons were always fishing, and however many came home empty they would come with the sgoth full of fish. This was a source of wonder and displeasure to the other boats and they decided to follow the old man wherever he went, and follow him they did.

> 'On a day of days the old man said, "I am now an old man, and it is time for me to return home to Rocabarri, and you will come with me." "What place is that?" asked the lads. "It is a charmed island out in the ocean. Nothing can be seen except the sea, but there is an island there all the same. Come with me, lads, and stay there while you live." "We shall not indeed go with you, father. Although you are our own father we are not going to any charmed island of the sea with you." "Well, whether you come or don't come, I must return and you make ready to take me home. But we will spend one more day fishing yet before I leave and I will show you the best fishing bank in the ocean. Place every barrel and hogshead you can find into the sgoth." The lads did that and they set off.

' "Are n't we silly," said the other boats, "to come home completely empty, while the old man and his three sons come home every day they go out with [their boat] full to the thwarts." And they followed the old man.

'The old man gave directions to his sons and they went straight out into the ocean. They carried on until they lost sight of land, and they threw out the anchor stone. The other boats followed them. They caught as much fish as they could lift. "Are you seeing any mark in the ocean, lads?" asked the old man. "No," they replied. A short time afterwards he requested one of the lads to have a look. "I see nothing," said the lad, and everyone laughed mockingly at the old man. "Look out," said the old man to another of the lads, "and look right round the ocean to see what you can see." "I see nothing," answered the lad. "I shall have a look myself now," said one of the lads, " and I shall search standing up."

' "I see nothing," he said, "but I seem to see on the horizon breaking seas as if the sea were breaking on a sunken rock."

' "It is time to flee," said the old man. "This is Iolla nam Muca-mara, and today is the first day of the year and they come here every first day of the year to breed and play, and pity the man who meets them when they come. Cut the cable and don't wait to lift the anchor stone at all." The cable was cut, her sail set, and she made off. They beckoned the others to come away, but they laughed mockingly at them, thinking they wanted to take them away from the fishing when they were catching as much as they liked.

'The whales were seen coming, churning the ocean into foam in the air, hundreds and hundreds of them. They drowned, broke and killed the other boats, in the turning of a hand's palm. They carried on without turning, pausing or retreating, after the old man, and when almost at the sgoth he shouted for a hogshead to be thrown out. The whales attacked it until they splintered it and off again they set after the old man. Och but what have you, but they threw out hogshead after hogshead, until out went the cargo that the old man had ordered to be placed in the boat. The old man and his three sons reached land after much trouble and danger but nothing was ever heard of the rest.

'The next day after that the old man said, "Now I am grown old, and I must return home to the charmed island itself. I have taught you, my sons, the best fishing bank in the ocean, and although yesterday we experienced trouble and disorder you do not need to fear it. The whales will not come to cause annoyance on the fishing bank except on the first day of the year. Take note of the first day of the year and of the directions I gave you on Iolla nam Muca-mara. Come home with me today and we shall go away again."

'They departed and set out towards the ocean. "Steer now," said the old man, "west south west, and keep open the gap in Beinn Bhearnarach of Barra." They kept on and on until at least one of the sons said, "Are n't we fools, father, going out this distance into the western ocean in search of land where neither land nor earth was ever heard of nor ever will be." "Foolish indeed we are," said every one of the brothers, "and it is time now for us to turn back." "There is land right enough," said the old man, "and we are now near it. This is Rocabarrai, a charmed island under the sea where the young men were. The young men and those who came with them to take possession of the island thought there was no land there at all. But there was indeed and they were sailing above it, but the people of the island placed a charm on their eyes and they could not see it. But the island is there for all that and we are at it now. Look out and try to see a small stretch of the ocean calm and peaceful, and three large billows going to one side." "We see that," said every one of the lads. "Give her a slight pull over towards it, and you will put me out there." "We cannot put you out, father, on the back of the ocean when we do not see a bit of land." "You throw me out, my sons, where you see the three waves, and I will be without delay at the home of my childhood and you will return to Barra to your own home."

'the sons threw the old man overboard and he made for home on Rocabarrai the green isle of the sea, and they returned home to Barra.'[19]

The Rocabarraidh of the tradition was never confused with Hirt but it was out in the same great ocean and there was in the nineteenth century still a belief in Uist that occasionally land could be seen out beyond Hirt 'and that it would be Rocabarra'. At this same period Mor MacLean, wife of a crofter at Borve in the west of Barra, 'This bright intelligent woman', said that Hirt could be 'seen from the top of Beinn Tangaval and that in an exceptionally clear day Rocabarraidh can be seen from the same place. The first is in a line with Rudh Thangavail and the second in a line with Rudh Ghlinne.' Hirt was often visible, Rocabarraidh when it appeared was 'seen in the long long distance like a ship under sail.'[20]

A neighbour of Mor MacLean, Donald Macpherson, 'aged 83 years hale of mind and of body save for rheumatism from which he was confined to bed', was one of several old people in both Barra and Tiree who asserted that there was an association between Rocabarraidh and 'Macneill of Barra of the long ago'. MacNeil was said to have rent rights over Rocabarraidh, though what he received was unknown, and that he used to go there from time to time. When the direct line of MacNeils of Barra died out it was believed that an heir would come from the green isle and claim the 'ancient heritage'. There is no such record of a link between an early MacNeil and Hirt although a connection could have existed in the latter days of the Norse rule over the Hebrides.[21]

*

In spite of the violence inflicted by Norsemen on some of the monastic communities in the islands Christian church organisation in the Isles re-emerged in the later eleventh century in the time of Godred Crovan, King of Man (1079-1095), but most prominently when his son Olaf the Red established a bishopric of Man and the Isles under the notorious Bishop Wimund, a Skyeman, in 1134. Commonly called 'of Sodor and Man', it was closely linked with the isle of Man, centre of government for the Hebrides until the time of Somerled. There may well have been north and south divisions of so extensive an area for administrative convenience, and in 1387 there were two separate lines of bishops for Man and the Isles. In the later fifteenth century, following the apparent close of the base at Skeabost, the bishops of the Isles seem to have been without a cathedral since in 1498 a request was brought to the pope that he would allow the abbey on Iona to be erected as the bishop's seat until the 'principal kirk' in Man became available.[22]

In the course of these years religious organisation in the Hebrides was as complicated as the political control under the Norse and their successors, the Lord of the Isles. When in 1156 a group of islands, possibly extending from the north of Uist to Islay, was 'permanently relinquished' by King Godred of Man to the lords of Argyll, Somerled and his sons, the foundations of the Lordship of the Isles were laid, and theoretically, if not in practice, Hirt would have come under their control along with Uist. Latterly the diocese of the Isles became closely associated with the Lords of the Isles, who were patrons, and around 1430 the bishop was Angus, son of Donald, Lord of the Isles. This was all markedly different from the situation in the diocese of Argyll, which though erected about 1189 after separation from the existing see of Dunkeld, possibly at the instigation of one of Somerled's sons, seems to have had little connection with the Lordship. The cathedral of Argyll was on Lismore, an island not included in the Lordship.[23]

The area covered by the diocese of the Isles extended from Rona north of Lewis to the isle of Man but while early monastic or bishopric centres may have established lesser chapels or churches in some of the districts within their sphere of influence it is likely that parishes did not take a recognisable form until after 1200. Eventually the parishes in the diocese included one in Barra, five in Uist, one in Harris, four in Lewis and eight or nine in Skye; and from some of the islands, among them Rona and those south of Barra from

Vatersay to Berneray, the bishop derived income apart from whatever revenues were received from ecclesiastical foundations.[24]

John, first Lord of the Isles, held Skye and Lewis, together with other islands and the mainland districts of Morvern and Ardnamurchan, in 1336. After obtaining dispensation from Rome in June 1337 he married his cousin Amy MacRuari through whom he acquired the MacRuari lands of Garmoran, which comprised the mainland districts of Moidart, Morar, Arisaig and Knoydart, and certain islands to which these districts had been added to form an extended possession reaching westward from the bounds of Moidart to the Outer Hebrides. The islands were Eigg, Rum, Uist, Benbecula, Barra, and probably Hirt, though it was not mentioned at this time. If included, Hirt would probably have been considered part of either the parish of Barra or one of the five parishes of Uist - Sand or Kilcolmkill, Kilpheder, Kilmuir or Kilmorie, Howmore and Benbecula, the last mentioned having a church with yet another dedication to Columba. There was a sixth church in Uist, that of the Holy Trinity at Carinish, otherwise called Teampall na Trionaid, around which a parish never formed, and perhaps several more as for instance at Kildonan and those on the west coast destroyed by the encroaching sea.[25]

In March 1372 King Robert II granted to John, Lord of the Isles, a charter of lands which had been in the latter's possession some thirty years previously, and in January 1373 he confirmed John's own grant of them, probably in 1346, to his son Ranald, first of the line called after him the 'Sliocht Ragnaill' or race of Clanranald. Ranald thus came to possess not only the larger Garmoran, in which was the island variously called in these charters 'Heryce', 'Hyrte' and 'the island of Hert' but also further mainland districts such as Lochy, Kilmallie and Locharkaig in Lochaber. It is therefore reasonable to assume that the ownership of Hirt passed from the MacRuari family to that of Clanranald, which means that association with Uist at least continued for some years more.[26]

In June 1427 Alexander, Lord of the Isles, granted the island of Barra and the lands of 'Baegastallis', the two parts of Boisdale in Uist, to Gilleownan 'son of Roderick son of Murchard Makneill'. The MacNeils had probably been in possession for many years, perhaps without title but holding in return for services to the MacRuaris and then Clanranald or the Lord of the Isles. Two centuries later the MacNeils were still owners of Barra: 'The Inhabitants theroff are verie antient Inhabitants and the Superior or Laird of Barray is called Rorie McNeill'. This 'Rorie', Roderick MacNeil, may have been of some significance in the history of Hirt. He claimed, according to the account of the early seventeenth century, that he was at the time when it was composed 'sex or sevin score of years' of age and in his youth, which at that rate would be about 1500, he picked up tales from seafaring men - 'hearing from skippers that oftymes were wont to travell to ane Illand which the Inhabitants of the Illand alledged this McNeill and his predecessors should be their Superiors, which Illand is sein oftymes from the tope of the mountaines of Barray.' Having frequently heard this Rorie 'fraughted a shipe but nowayes could find the Illand'. Driven eventually to the west of Ireland he plundered some cattle and came home with them.[27]

The story is a reminder of the tale of Rocabarraidh told by Donnachadh Ban at Carnan. But the 'green isle' below the waves is hardly likely to have had inhabitants with whom skippers could talk about MacNeil's supposed ownership, nor would it be seen often from Barra hills. It is therefore possible that the island in question was Hirt, and that its inhabitants, being in a neglected state, were remembering an ancient attachment to the MacNeils of Barra. However by 1600 any connection with the MacNeils that Hirt may have had had long been replaced when a different family became hereditary lairds.

The ownership of Hirt is a curious subject. It may be wondered why an isolated island out in the ocean should have appeared alongside great tracts of the mainland and large islands in charters to and by the Lords of the Isles. Was it of perhaps strategic importance to some leading Hebridean figure like MacNeill as 'the best stronghold of all the islands'? Was it of economic significance to its owner - or just a remarkable place? When and why the MacLeods of Harris and Dunvegan acquired Hirt remain virtually unanswered questions, but their interest in it cannot have arisen just because they could see it from Pabbay. It was reported in 1549 that Hirt 'perteinit to Macloyd of Haray of auld'. If this meant for more than one or two generations then it was perhaps odd that an island specifically named as belonging to the Lords of the Isles in the fourteenth century should have been omitted from the charter of 1498 by King James IV to Alexander MacLeod, son and heir of the late William son of John MacLeod of Dunvegan, of 'lands commonly called Ardmanach in Herag of Lewis, with all the small islands pertaining to the said Ardmanach'. These lands had been held from the Lord of the Isles as superior and, as with the MacNeils, the MacLeods had no doubt been present perhaps for centuries.[28]

The supposed connection between Hirt and Uist might suggest why Hirt was not mentioned by name in the charter of 1498. It might also suggest that, so far as possession was concerned, an arrangement, perhaps informal, had been reached between the Lord of the Isles and MacLeod long before the charter and before their descendants were involved in an extended dispute over the ownership of North Uist and Harris in the early 1500s. An account of the early MacLeods, the 'Siol Tormod' of Dunvegan, states that until 1493 when the Lordship was finally forfeited they held much of their estate from the Lords of the Isles. 'Harris… belonged at an early period to the Macruaries of Garmoran …, under whom the chief of Siol Tormod appears to have possessed it', and after the forfeiture became the object of rival claims although the MacLeods appeared to be in full control. This would seem to be an unlikely time for Hirt to be transferred from MacDonalds to MacLeods, and consequently it may be best to accept the mid or later seventeenth century history of the MacDonalds, which says that Godfrey, son of John first Lord of the Isles and Amy MacRuari, gave the lands of Boisdale to MacNeil of Barra and gifted Hirt to the Laird of Harris. Godfrey died about 1390; from him were descended the MacDonalds of North Uist called 'Siol Ghorraidh'.[29]

Some knowledge of the rivalry between the MacDonalds of Uist and the MacLeods of Harris could have survived in a tale of Hirt which is a mixture of traditions. MacLeod of Harris and Dunvegan and MacDonald of Skye and North Uist both claimed an equal right to the island: 'The two men met and both decided to get two boats built by the same boatbuilder, both boats to be of the same size. They then cast lots for the boats and sailed off with them, in a race... The boat's crew which arrived there first and kindled fire ashore, would decide who was to be the proprietor ..' The MacLeods won. To this, other versions added the cutting off a finger or hand, as in the similar competitions for Rona, Skye, and of course between Columba and Moluag for Lismore. As for the kindling of fire this may be derived from a Norse method of claiming land, as when in Iceland fire was carried on an arrow:

> 'There was a man called Onund the Sage, who took possession of land above Merkigill, including the eastermost valley. When Eirik was going to take possession of the valley to the west, Onund cast the divining rod to find out when Eirik would set out to make his claim. Onund got in first, shot a tinder-arrow [tundroru] across the river to claim the land west of it, and made his home between the rivers.'[30]

From this arrow of flame might come the name of Sron an Tinntinn on Rona, the headland where the winner of the race lit the decisive fire.

CHAPTER 2

*Dugan and Fearchar Mor, the medieval church
and chapels, land division*

IN December 1886 Kenneth Campbell, a native of Skye and resident in
Oban, gave a talk about Hirt where two years previously he had been teacher.
His talk was naturally enough based for the most part on his own experience and
on what he had learned from the people while there. He began by saying that the
island or island group was 'called by the natives Hirst' but by strangers 'St Kilda'.[31]

Map-makers mostly of the sixteenth century were apparently responsible
for introducing two new names for Hirt, the first by adding a letter to extend
it into Hirta or, by adding two, Hirtha, the second by producing from
somewhere a mysterious Skilder which quickly became St Kilda and in that
form was adopted by people who either did not speak Gaelic or did not wish
to use the ancient and correct name. Out of the considerable discussion there
has been on the matter of map versions the only firm conclusions seem to be
that there was never a 'saint' called Kilda and that in any case 'St' has no place
in any of the Hebridean island names.[32] The placename St Kilda, probably the
result of mistake and misunderstanding, has never troubled Gaelic-speakers,
nor did it particularly concern Kenneth Campbell even though he used it as a
matter of course when addressing his audience and even though he was soon
dealing with the distant past:

> 'One is not long in St Kilda before he discovers some ruins of interest to
> antiquarians. Besides the remains of an ancient fort or Dun there are or
> have been several under-ground houses, 7 temples and an altar, the latter
> being still well preserved. One is led to hazard the opinions that either the
> St Kildans of a former age were very devout or, what I am more inclined to
> believe, that St Columba or at least some of his disciples established
> themselves on the island. The fact that at the present time there is a piece
> of ground called "Leob Challuim Chille" goes to strengthen this opinion.'

Campbell found that the inhabitants were 'entirely ignorant of the
subject', and could tell him little about such distant times. 'If you ask them
who built those places, the invariable answer is "Papanaich a ghraidh, droch
dhaoine a ghraidh." ' Such disapproval of the people long ago meant that even
if some tradition had survived it might not have been disclosed very easily.
Nevertheless questions arising from the existence of ruins must have
occurred to Campbell's interested mind. Who were the people who had
occupied the underground houses? Who had worshipped in the 'seven
temples'? Who had defended themselves in the fort? How had they reached
the island from across the dangerous ocean? What had happened to them, and
were they ancestors of any of those who now, in 1886, condemned them?

The arrival of holy men from Barra, Uist, or Pabbay seems rather less unlikely than a decision by one of the bishops of the Isles to have a church founded in Hirt to serve an island community, yet inhabitants of some kind there were long before the first mention of Hirt in historical records. Whether there was continuity from an early Celtic settlement to a later Gaelic one, as much in religion as in any other aspects, remains unknown, but the teacher Kenneth Campbell had a theory that there was, that something had lasted from the age of itinerant monks to his own day:

> 'Were it the case that a monastery had ever been there one would perhaps look for something in the customs of the present inhabitants that had been derived from these monastic times. I have at least rightly or wrongly fancied that I had discovered something of this kind. First of all unlike their neighbours in Harris or elsewhere the St Kildans never go in winter to bed before two or three A.M. Again when they want to sleep without putting off their clothes, they go on their knees in the attitude of prayer, place their hands on their brows and then rest them on the ground, which suggests to an observer the idea of penance of some sort.'

Imagined grey figures moving in silence through the dark remoteness of Hirt in its distant past are scarcely different from the dream-like people of Rocabarraidh, but the remains of ' temples' and of underground dwellings are more solidly substantial, able to survive beyond many human lifetimes and to bridge the centuries. Their definite, visible presence long after the period of their original purpose meant that they became locations to which events preserved only in tradition were, perhaps justifiably, attached. The traditional story most often told by the people of Hirt in recent times, concerning the slaughter of almost the entire population of Hirt by fire and smoke, is an example of the association between a dramatic episode and a particular structure or place. Kenneth Campbell gave a brief outline in the course of his talk:'One mournful tale tells how two villains planned the destruction of all the rest on the island and succeeded, by enticing them into one of the temples where with one exception they were all smothered to death. The two conspirators were however afterwards brought to justice and left to starve on one of the adjacent islands'. This was not quite an accurate summary but Campbell may have been reluctant to dwell on such a topic, even though he was pleased to record that in spite of their disapproval of ancient 'Catholic' churches the islanders 'do have some traditions of a time subsequent to the buildings' of those 'evil men'. There is no doubt however that the actions of the 'two villains' were a good deal more evil than the religious persuasion of monks and priests.

The story introduces perhaps the most important of the old 'temples'.

Long ago, there were two men in Hirt called Dugan and Fearchar Mor.

Some people said they had come from the mainland in a boat which they rowed with oars of iron:'They landed and said that they were taking command of the island, and the St Kildans, they could not say anything'. In good weather these two used to row to the Flannan Islands to kill sheep, and on one occasion a sailing ship tried to arrest them without success, even though the boat with the iron oars was full of stolen animals being taken back to Hirt. Nothing else is told of the daily lives of these men or of how they got on with the rest of the islanders.

But on a fine day Dugan and Fearchar went to the hill called Oiseabhal to gather heather, and they reached the top. Suddenly they began to shout, first from the hill top, then as they came hurrying down, calling out that there were loingeas cogaidh, warships, in the kyle of Boreray and that everyone should take refuge in the chapel of the Trinity: 'teichibh teichibh do Teampall na Trionaid'. And this the people did, in great alarm, for it was customary to hide in the chapel when danger threatened.

The two men came down from Oiseabhal with their bundles of heather and placed them against the doors of Teampall na Trionaid. They set fire to the bundles so that soon the building filled with smoke and those trapped inside were choked to death.

Believing that they were now the only inhabitants of the island Dugan and Fearchar left the chapel. But not everyone had perished there. A girl of fifteen, or, as some said, a grown woman, had managed to avoid the fate of the rest because she had been out on a hillside and never reached the chapel. On seeing what happened she crept away and hid in a cave below Ruabhal, opposite the island of Dun, from which she made a visit to the village in the night time to take away corn, a quern mill, and the means of making a fire in the cave. After some time had passed the fire nearly betrayed her presence to Dugan and Fearchar. They were out on the Dun catching puffins when one said to the other: 'Friend, friend, I get the smell of fire here'. 'Oh,' replied his companion, 'it is only the fire that we left behind us', and they went on with their hunting.

At length a boat with supplies came to Hirt and the two men walked to the shore to meet it, 'thinking that no one was on the island but themselves'. They told the boat crew that everyone else had died of disease and that they were the only survivors. At that moment the woman, who had waited until she thought it safe, came along from her cave to where the boat was, crying out: 'Thainig Dia! Thainig Dia!', 'God has come! God has come!' Dugan and Fearchar thought of killing her but it was too late. She told her story, and the men were seized immediately and taken on board.

The boat left and sailed over towards Boreray. Fearchar Mor was 'put out on to Stac an Aramair among the birds'. He did not enjoy the thought of being marooned in such a place so he jumped into the sea and tried to swim after the boat, 'but they left him there to drown, and quite right too'. Dugan was taken to Soay where he had to manage as best he could. It is said that, with Soay being bigger than Stac an Aramair, he was able to remain alive there for years, looking across to the deserted island of Hirt and eating sheep and birds. His bones were found in the cave where he had lived, called Taigh Dhugain, with a dirk stuck in the ground beside them. 'His ribs are there still; I myself have handled the ribs'.[33]

Among the old church buildings of Hirt, though not the earliest, Teampall na Trionaid seems to have held first place. About 1860 it was remembered that 'Trinity was the name of a temple which stood where the burial-ground is now. Some of the inhabitants remember seeing it; it had two doors, and the roof was covered with green turf.' If its grassy appearance gave it an underground look it would be possible in the retelling of the Dugan and Fearchar story for the church to become confused with a subterranean structure at least as old nearby and this might explain why in one version the church was indeed underground with a doorway so narrow 'that you could not get in unless you entered sideways'. Even so a turf-covered Teampall na Trionaid, in the midst of a burial-ground, resembling in position the monastic cell and chapel on Rona, stood close to the dwellings of the small island 'village'.[34]

In his talk Kenneth Campbell said that there were seven chapels or churches in Hirt, and this receives some support from a seventeenth century account which he had probably not seen. The account stated that 'Ther are Six Chapells here', and then gave their dedications: 'the first is called Christs Church, the 2nd St Columbs, the 3rd St Peters, the 4th St Johns, the 5th St Clemens, the 6th St Briannes'. These were not necessarily all on the main island of Hirt, but at least three of them were. Teampall na Trionaid might have formed the seventh 'temple', but it was apparently the same as Christ's Church for among dedications in both Scotland and England Christ and Trinity have been 'convertible terms', that is to say, interchangeable, and the alteration of the name from one to the other does not mean the introduction of a new place of worship. In 1697 'Christ Chappel' was situated near the settlement and 'covered and thatched after the same manner with their houses', a roofing which did not change much over the centuries of the building's existence.[35]

The occurrence of 'Trinity' or 'Trionaid' in a dedication is not common in the Western Isles, yet the most important religious building in North Uist was Teampall na Trionaid at Carinish; and though the dedication to Christ, for which 'Trionaid' seems to have been the alternative, is just as unusual, Cladh Chriosd in Pabbay, Barra, and Teampall Chriosd at Bailesear, only a short distance from Carinish, show that Hirt was not alone. On the other hand dedications to Columba were abundant throughout the Hebrides and in many parts of the Highlands, the name usually appearing as 'Calum Cille' as for instance in Tobar Chaluim Chille, Columba's Well, in North Uist. Brianan or Brendan, commemorated at 'St Briannes', the sixth 'temple' in Hirt, was almost as frequent in island dedications including a chapel in Tiree and a well at Borve in Barra. There was a belief in Hirt that 'Cailleach Rhuaibheall' as the solitary surviving woman was known hid from Dugan and Fearchar Mor in the church dedicated to Brendan and not in a cave. The three churches, Teampall na Trionaid or Teampall Chriosd, Teampall Chaluim Chille and Teampall Bhrianain, were evidently still in reasonable repair in the late 1690s, all constructed in the same manner and all with 'churchyards belonging to them'. Each of the three lay east and west, with an altar at the east end.[36]

Incised cross in the wall of an 1861 house ('no.16'), St Kilda

Altar near summit of Soay, St Kilda

Of the other three (or four) churches little is recorded. Dedications to Peter were widespread in the Outer Hebrides, ranging from Teampall Pheadair in the north of Lewis to Cille Pheadair in South Uist, but those to John are few, and Clement is to be found in only three or four places, one of them being Rodel in Harris where Tur Mor Chliamain once served as the parish church. No certain traces of the three survive and even the sites are unknown, but one could have been the chapel of uncertain dedication said to have been on Boreray. In 1862 it was remarked that this building, presumably like all the other churches, was of hewn stone, and 'Euphemia Macrimmon remembers seeing it'. No walls remained, the stones having been removed and reused in constructing storage huts.[37]

Apart from the churches and situated in wild and exposed places were the altars, built like cornered cairns. There is nothing to explain why any of them deserved the name of altar nor to determine whether, if indeed they had a religious purpose, they were used by priest or people. There was 'an altar in Boreray, and another on the top of Soay'; the second still stands, a curious, partly-fallen little square structure of stone slabs. Another altar was also said to have stood on the hill of Hirt called Mullach Sgar. Away from Hirt altars were scarcely to be found, but in South Uist there used to be 'one in Coire an t-Sagairt on Hecla, another in Sgalavat called the Altair'. Also in Coire an t-Sagairt were 'earth houses' called 'Taigheana Talmhuin' and 'shelves' - perhaps small terraces on the slopes - known as 'Sgeilpichean'.[38]

Tradition offers only a faint and broken pathway through time to the days when these sacred buildings were serving their original purpose. As centuries went by the ancient churches and altars of Hirt, remarkable for their number, lost some of their life and meaning, even though three of them at least continued to play a part in the day-to-day existence of the island people. Hirt was not alone in its loss. Throughout the Hebrides and western mainland districts early churches fell into decay. In July 1382 it was reported that 'the chapel of St Columba in the parish of St Congan', possibly at Uig in Skye or in Knoydart, had collapsed to the ground on account of its great antiquity; and even the monastery of Iona, 'situated in the Isles among the wild Scots', was in 1421 said, perhaps with some exaggeration, to be almost destroyed by continuous wars. One reason for decline was poverty, there being insufficient means to sustain priests and of course to keep buildings in repair, and Hirt, on the utmost edge of the Scottish kingdom which itself was described in 1421 as being 'at the ends of the world', was more likely than most islands to suffer neglect. The wonder is that three rather than one of the old churches were still visible, and even in use, long after 1600.[39]

Teampall Chriosd, Teampall Chaluim Chille and Teampall Bhrianain, in particular the first, were places of worship for people living in Hirt, but who these people were is also a mystery. In Rona there was an 'ancient race' with names taken from the natural world, from the stars, moon and sun. The inhabitants of Hirt in the 1500s were, like those of Rona and no doubt of many other small islands, 'simple creatures' whose names and origin no one saw fit to record, and who lived far out amid 'the mane Ocean seais'. How often they made use of the old churches remains unknown, but they came to lack the regular care and guidance of a resident priest and from time to time had to take religious duties upon themselves. It was not that they had little regard for religion but that they were uneducated in it. In 1549 the people of both Hirt and Rona were described by Donald Monro, Archdeacon of the Isles, as 'scant learnit in ony Religion', not as irreligious.[40]

Donald Monro was the son of Alexander Monro of Kiltearn in Easter Ross and Janet MacLean who was the daughter of Farquhar MacLean, probably Bishop of the Isles in the mid sixteenth century. In 1526 Donald was presented to the vicarage of Snizort in Skye and Raasay, in the diocese of the Isles, and in 1548 he was appointed Archdeacon of the Isles. His duties then included supervision of all the parish clergy within the bounds of the diocese, a task made a little easier by gaining the acquaintance with the islands which he acquired in the course of an extensive tour in 1549. At the Reformation in 1560 the old diocese was divided between the new districts of Ross and Argyll. Donald Monro then became minister of Kiltearn and was subsequently active on behalf of the reformed church.[41]

For all his wide-ranging travels in the Hebrides Monro may have found Hirt and Rona too remote for a personal visit and have relied for his information on sources in more accessible places. In his description of all the islands he had surprisingly little to say about religion, being more concerned with economic aspects such as whether an island was inhabited and if so whether it was agriculturally productive, so that the state of religion generally in the Hebrides could well have been not much different from that in Hirt. Once each year around midsummer a boat went out to Hirt taking with it 'sum chaiplane to baptize bairns thair', and if no chaplain could go 'thai baptize thair bairns thameselfis'. This had been the situation twenty years earlier when a short notice of 'Hirtha' mentioned that in June 'ane preist cumis out of the Lewis in ane bait to this Ile, and ministeris the sacrament of baptisme to all the barnis that hes bene borne in the yeir afore'; and when he had completed this task and said mass the priest received the teinds of all the island produce and returned home. There had apparently once been rather better provision, for according to an account of about 1595 a priest had actually resided in Hirt: 'In auld times thai sustenit ane auld Priest or Clerk continuallie amangis thame, to schaw and tell to thame the halie dayis to be keipit in the yeir'. This old priest, retired and perhaps not well qualified, may have achieved very little but his presence alone suggested greater attention to religious matters than was possible when a short annual visit from a chaplain was all that the islanders enjoyed. The contemporary position in 1595 was not greatly different from that in Donald Monro's time as Archdeacon forty or so years earlier:

'Anes in the yeir ane Priest or Minister cumis to thame and baptizes all the bairnis born amangis thame sen his last being thair, and celebrattis mariage to the parteis desyrand, and makes sic uther ministration of the Sacraments to thame as he thinkis gude, and gifis thame sic directionnis as he wills thame to use and keip for ane yeir thaireftir; and gadderis payment of thair teinds (qlk thai pay maist thankfullie and justlie of ony people) and departs qll the next yeir agane'.[42]

Apart from the baptisms and marriages the visiting priest's most important activity, and one which had considerable effect upon the circumstances of survival in Hirt, was the collection of the teinds or tenth parts of the various kinds of island produce This was one way by which the church, or, if he had acquired right to them, the landlord, could make money, for when the teinds were brought to the mainland or perhaps to Skye they could be sold. From the islanders' point of view the gathering of the teinds must have been just like the collecting of the rent, both being paid in kind. The boat that took out the priest or chaplain in the 1540s also took the landlord's 'Steward' or his deputy, and the two men, after a stay of some length to conduct their business, each left with dried mutton, birds, feathers, seals, and other customary contributions. Monro's mention in 1549 of 'Mccloyd of Haray his Stewart' seems to be the earliest reference to this official, and it was from the steward that the Archdeacon heard something of Hirt and of how, 'the commons of the town baith men, women and bairns' became 'deid drunkin, so that thai could nocht stand on thair feit', when the steward arrived and mixed up a malt concoction. Getting the people drunk by making a kind of powerful whisky and letting them have as much as they wanted no doubt made collection of the rent and teinds a great deal easier.[43]

Since he made the journey with the steward the visiting priest would probably have spent most of the year at some conveniently nearby Hebridean church such as St Clement's at Rodel. That he 'cumis out of the Lewis' is at first sight a clue to his usual residence, but these words could be misleading as the name 'Lewis' could have included Harris at that time and appears once to have been applied, for some administrative purposes, to a much wider area than that island alone. The account of 1595 records an ancient division of all the Hebrides into four groups, and to 'the Ile of Lewis' were annexed the isles of Uist, Barra, Harris, Rona, Pabbay in the Sound of Harris, Heisgeir, 'Collismown' [Causamul] and Hirt. It happens to note too that the island closest to Hirt, Heisgeir, was 'possest evir be ane gentillman of the Clandonald', and that one of this clan, 'the principall man of the north end of Wyist', went once a year to Causamul and killed seals there, adding therefore to the impression that possession of Hirt in these earlier years was very much a borderline affair between the MacDonalds and the MacLeods.[44]

The sixteenth century accounts of Hirt contain brief information on a few other aspects of life on Hirt. They agree that landing was difficult owing to the 'stark and verie evill' seas and rocks; they remark on 'infinite fair scheippis' with long tails and big horns that are found there; and they all comment on the great number of birds, on which and on the eggs 'thay leif for the maist pairt of thair fude'. But little is said of the human inhabitants themselves, 'simple creatures' whatever that may mean, generously ready to pay their teinds without argument, and described as 'a poor barbarous people unexpert' because they made no use of weapons and supplied no men to take part in wars or military exercises. Nothing was said about houses or about the cultivated land; but a little later, perhaps in the early seventeenth century, it was stated that the main island of Hirt was 'accounted five pennie Land', that 'ther are ten families', and that 'Their ordinarie way of divyding their Land is one half penny to every familie.' The system of division extended to the cliffs: 'The Rocks also are devyded such and such on every half pennie, and there is a kinde of officer left by the master of the Land, who Governs in his absence, and so Regulates that the Best Climbers and the Worst are mixed togither, that so none of the Land be unlaboured, that is that all the shelvs of the highest rocks be searched for eggs.' The division of land into pennylands, or in practice into half pennylands, indicates a deliberate arrangement, comparable with but not the same as the limitation on population in Rona; it was not by any means a method of division restricted to Hirt, but it implies that at some point in the past a decisive step had been taken regarding the way in which the island would be occupied and perhaps involving deliberate settlement. From small beginnings perhaps the people living in Hirt in 1600 formed a peaceful though struggling community, deserving no condemnation nor possibly the curiosity which led Monro and other writers, as well as mapmakers, to produce descriptions and versions of the place out of all proportion to its very modest size and importance.[45]

Monro wrote of the steward, representative of MacLeod of Harris and Dunvegan, as if he were already a familiar figure in the story of Hirt. It is hardly likely that he was merely a rent-collector on behalf of a landowner unwilling or unable himself to endure a tedious sea journey. The title certainly carries with it a management or farming interest intended to make the position worth having, and even in the early days of MacLeod possession the stewardship may well have been hereditary. Advantages would have had to outweigh the inconvenience involved, to the extent that the MacLeod chief would originally have felt it appropriate to bestow the position on a close relative, perhaps as a favour or reward. In the absence of records it is difficult to be sure who the stewards were before the seventeenth century, but a return to Màiri nighean Alasdair Ruaidh and her family will be helpful.

There is a tradition that Mary MacLeod was born not at Rodel but in the Sound of Harris island of Pabbay, with which her family was so closely connected. Her brother Neil, known as Niall mac Alasdair Ruaidh, resident and farmer in Pabbay, was steward of Hirt in the mid seventeenth century. It is possible that he was the first of the family to be steward, but just as the description Ruadh was handed down through the generations of these MacLeods so too may have descended the stewardship. Mary and Neil could recount their ancestry back to William, fifth chief of MacLeod, and as the MacLeods of Harris had an ancient stronghold on Pabbay their relatives, the family of Alasdair Ruadh, second son of Norman, son of the fifth chief, might have been given land on that island and the care of Hirt at an early stage of their history.[46]

CHAPTER 3

Seventeenth century ownership and rivalry,
Coll Ciotach, Irish missionaries

A N Act of Parliament passed in December 1597 was one of several important and harsh steps taken by King James VI to bring the leading figures in the Highlands and Islands under firm control and to improve the condition and profitability of the 'barbarous natives' in those parts of the country. Landowners were expected to produce their title deeds on 15 May 1598, to ensure that rents to the crown would be properly paid, and to guarantee their own and their clansmen's good behaviour. Failure to comply in any respect meant inevitable forfeiture of estates. As a consequence MacLeod of Harris lost his lands of Harris, Dunvegan and Glenelg, and the MacLeods of Lewis were similarly deprived of Lewis and Trotternish in Skye. The king then made grants of all these areas to that company of Lowland gentry who became known as the Fife adventurers and they began their efforts to colonise in Lewis. A year later a special commission of 'Lieutenandry' over those islands and Highland districts that were considered to lie in Invernessshire was given to the Duke of Lennox and the Earl of Huntly, the latter a Catholic at a time when neither the old religion nor episcopalianism were much in favour. By 1600 the Earl had become the Marquis, and in June 1601 his responsibility was specifically defined by a new commission of lieutenancy and justiciary as covering the more northerly isles of the Hebrides apart from Lewis and some adjacent mainland areas. The Marquis was recognised as being 'of guid experience and maist able be powar and force to reduce the North Ilis of this realme to his Hienes obedience.' Those parts listed as falling within his guardianship were 'Sky, Hereis, Hert, Uist, Skalpa, Rum, Canna, Rasa, Eigg, Iland Tyrum and Arissag', and he was also to control 'sic disorderit clannit men of the Hielandis nixt adjacent to the saidis Ilis as sall plainlie and avowedlie tak pairt with the saides disobedient Ilismen aganis the said Lieutenant.' The king was especially concerned about 'Rory McLeud of Dunvegane, alias McCleud of Hereis', against whom the Marquis promised not to use his commission until after 10 August 1601 when MacLeod was to appear before the king 'to render his obedience to his Majesty, and find surety for his future behaviour and for payment of the King's rents due by him for his lands.'[47]

All this meant very little to the people in Hirt whose lives were untouched by events in distant Edinburgh although they may have been disturbed by the quarrel between MacLeod and the MacDonalds which flared up again at the same time. The MacDonalds went to Harris, killed many of the inhabitants and took away their cattle, while the MacLeods visited North Uist in a less successful attempt to commit the same sort of plunder there.

Whether this violence had any effect on Hirt is unknown; if not, it may at least have prevented rent collection for a year or two. The Marquis of Huntly was told not to get involved.

In the spring of 1607, however, new conditions were proposed under which the Marquis was to 'quiet' the northern islands and ensure that 'a constant and suir rent' would be paid annually by them to the crown. Huntly asked, among other things, that 'a securitie ... be maid to him of the Ilis of Ust, Eg, Canna, Rume, Barra, Rasa, and Hirtha, with all the rest of the North Ilis, except the Sky and the Lewis.' There was discussion of the terms and report to the king for his views. When the royal response came it contained the order that Huntly should bring his service to a conclusion within a year by slaughtering all 'the barbarous people of the Isles'. Fortunately the whole undertaking came to nothing, chiefly because some influential and powerful 'Presbyterians' disapproved of any increase in the power of a Catholic Marquis.[48]

The next stage of the king's campaign was the commissioning of Andrew Knox, Bishop of the Isles, to survey the islands. He set off in July 1609 and almost immediately met the chief leaders of the island clans in Iona where they accepted and bound themselves to observe nine laws known as the Statutes of Iona. One of the principal matters of concern was the poor state of religion in the islands and its consequences for the condition of the people. Bishop Knox had already informed the king of 'the present estate of thais folkis now void of the trew knowledge of God' and of their ignorance of law and order, and the king had announced 'the cair we haif of planting of the Gospell amang these rude barbarous and uncivill people.' To a large extent his greatest care was to lay hands upon the rents owing to him by the island landowners, though he claimed that debt was the outcome of allowing part of the country 'to be possessed with suche wild savageis voide of Godis feare and our obedience.'[49]

The introduction attached to the first statute made it plain that the rebellious and feuding habits of the island people flourished in the absence of 'all dewtie to God and of his trew worship.' There was a lack of Protestant ministers and the few who laboured in the islands were treated with contempt. The statute therefore required the chiefs to make sure that ministers present and future were 'reverentlie obeyit', that they were properly paid, and that 'rwynous kirkis' were repaired. Education of youth in 'the knowledge of God and good letters' was also judged to be of great value, and those gentlemen of sufficient wealth and standing were ordered to place the eldest child, male unless there were no boys, in a lowland school where he would be taught 'to speik, read and wryte Inglische'. By signing the bond associated with the statutes the assembled island leaders, including 'Rorie McCloyd of Hareiss' but not MacNeil of Barra, undertook to profess the reformed 'trew religioun', being 'the onlie and undoubtit treuth of God', to maintain loyalty to the sovereign and obedience to acts of Parliament, and to assist in the apprehension of any of their number who failed to observe the obligations in the bond. The costs involved in paying ministers their stipends, repairing churches, and educating children on the mainland had all to be borne by the chiefs themselves.[50]

Following the forfeiture of his estate in 1598 Roderick MacLeod of Harris and Dunvegan appears to have continued in possession of the lands in practice, the king taking no direct action against him. Nevertheless titles to different parts of the estate were granted as nominal rewards to people who had as a rule no connection at all with the Hebrides. The so-called Fife adventurers acquired the majority, and a charter of October 1607 shows that three of them, James Lord Balmerino, James Spens of Wolmerstoun and Sir George Hay of Nether Liff, then shared the lands and barony of Glenelg, the lands of Harris with the lands and castle of Dunvegan, the lands of Duirinish, and other lands in Skye and Lewis with all the small islands around them. Hirt was not among these small islands as it had been the subject of a separate grant to one Thomas Ker who was thereafter called Sir Thomas Ker of Hirt or Hirth. This extraordinary knighthood, meaningless and probably entirely unknown to the people of the island, was conferred in 1600. In November of that year news sent to England from Scotland contained the information that 'The King made 3 knights, my Lord Seton 3 and Sir Robert Kerr 2, whereof Thomas Kerr that did the great service against Argyll was one, to whom the King has given the Isle of Hirtha.' Sir Thomas then served, along with Spens of Wormiston and Hay of Netherliff, as king's justice and commissioner in Lewis. On 7 March 1610 the king granted to Ker a charter of the island called Hirta, with three islands adjacent, said to lie about 60 miles out in the sea from the north-west part of Uist and 'Halkster' - probably Heisgeir; but this charter's effectiveness, if any, was short-lived as within four months Roderick MacLeod received a royal pardon for misdemeanours that included murder, plunder and arson, and in April 1611 the estate forfeited thirteen years previously was returned to him by a further charter from the king.[51]

From the commissions and charges of this period, as well as from the Statutes of Iona, there emerged two views of the people in the Hebrides which in one form or another lasted into comparatively recent times. The first was that, in speaking a language that was not English, in having customs of their own, and in resisting government measures to 'improve' them, the people were ignorant and barbaric, clear evidence for which appeared in their quarrels and feuds; and the second was that political control of the islanders could be exercised or at least effectively supported through the teaching of the reformed presbyterian religion. Though seldom perhaps touched by the upheavals of the times, Hirt was to feel the effects of both views for many years to come and on occasions to experience more immediately the impact of unrest centred elsewhere.

In the years up to 1615, following the departure of the unsuccessful Fife adventurers and the loss of Lewis by the MacLeods to the MacKenzies of Seaforth, the greatest disturbance in the islands occurred chiefly in and around Islay, where branches of Clan Donald sought to recover some of their lost power. Instances of the Protestant eagerness to suppress the old Catholic faith were not unusual. 'Sence my cuming heir,' wrote Archibald Campbell of Glencarradale, bailie of Kintyre, 'I fand owt a number of images whiche I hawe caussit to be bruntt: the religion that the cuntrie pepill hes heir amongst them is Popishe for thair is newer a minister in the wholle Ille except wan poore man that the bishop did leaue heir.' And when the strongholds of Dunnyveg and Lochgorm were besieged in February 1615 a Catholic MacDonald called Coll Ciotach, Coll the left-handed, of Irish birth but brought up in Colonsay, escaped in the night and took to a life of wandering and piracy.[52]

Early in March 1615 Coll captured a vessel and pressed into his own service several of the crew, among them a man called Robert Williamson. Towards the end of the month Coll and his men reached North Uist which was then in the possession of Domhnall Gorm Mor of Sleat, with whom Roderick MacLeod of Harris was still contesting the ownership of North Uist and of Sleat and Trotternish in Skye. Coll was hospitably received in Uist by Domhnall Gorm Mor's wife Marjory and his nephew and heir Domhnall Gorm Og, later Sir Donald MacDonald, who provided Coll's party with supplies and, aided by the MacLeans of Boreray, hereditary bailies of North Uist, persuaded Coll to go to Hirt, out of what seems to have been spite against Roderick MacLeod. They also sent two men as 'pilots' to take him there. The story of what then happened is well recorded in two documents, that containing information supplied by Robert Williamson who was examined on the subject on 13 May 1615, the day after he escaped from Coll, and a letter from MacLeod to Lord Binning written on 18 June 1615.[53]

Williamson described how he had been a 'labourer' and 'wrought in the boat'. Before reaching Uist they had called at Islay, Colonsay, Mull and Canna, from which they had sailed on to Uist where they spent eight days. Then they went to Hirt, to which Williamson referred as 'Isle Art', landed there and 'took great store of barley, and some 30 sheep for their provision.' According to Williamson Coll and his crew spent a month in Hirt, where they found 'but 10 men and 10 women inhabiting', a number strangely suited to the ten half pennylands. Looking out from the island Coll could see Boreray clearly, only four miles away, and made up his mind to go there. 'From Art they sailed to another island called Burribaugh, which is six miles from Art, of some half a mile in compass.' The place was daunting: 'there is noe dwelling thereon, but only is a rocky streinght where Coll had a purpose to keepe himselfe, for it is of such streynght as not to be gayned but by famine.' There were examples of such pirate refuges which he could follow, one of the latest being the island of Berisay at the Atlantic edge of Loch Roag in Lewis where Neil

MacLeod had held out for three years. But Coll, probably unable to land, had to turn away and go back the route he had come by North Uist, Canna, Mull and Iona.

As the injured landowner Roderick MacLeod reacted angrily, particularly because he had recently been injured in a different manner when he fell off his horse as he was entering Stirling and broke two ribs. He had gone south to visit his children who were at school in Glasgow, and while he was away Coll Ciotach had 'come to the north Illes'. In his letter MacLeod told Lord Binning how Domhnall Gorm's wife, Domhnall Gorm Og, and the MacLeans, 'clann Neill vaine the speciall tenents of north Wyest', had moved Coll 'to pass to a yle of myne called Hirta, a day and a night sailing from the rest of the north yles far out in the ocean sea, and to that effect derected two of the tenents of north Wyest to be there guyd and pylat there for they wer vnknowen thame selues there ...' On reaching the island, said MacLeod, perhaps with some exaggeration, 'they slew all the beastiall of the ylle both kowes and horses and sheepe and took away all the spoolyee of the yle, onlie reserved the lyves of the enhabitants thereof. And when all wes done they returned to North Wyest againe, where they randered their guyde and pyllats agane, and' - and this was the final insult - 'gave to the inhabitants thereof all and whole the spoyle of my yle.' There was no mention, then or later, of the sufferings of the islanders in Hirt as a consequence of Coll's visit.

*

There being no abrupt transformation from one religion to another in the islands ministers were as sparsely scattered after the Reformation as priests had been before and a general adherence to the old faith remained among the people. The poor man left by the Bishop in Islay was perhaps typical, and he can be imagined caught in the uncertain world of religious transition, as might have been 'Malkome Persone of the Herie' [Harris] who in September 1571 led the hand of Norman MacLeod of Dunvegan at the pen. He was the first of the MacPherson ministers in Harris, the 'Makcolme Makpherson' who in 1566 was granted the parsonage and vicarage of St Bryde in Harris, but there is no sign that he held any responsibility for Hirt, which was possibly still linked with South Uist or else unattached to any parish, old or new.[54]

Here and there were other men like MacPherson, adventuring into the wilderness on behalf of the reformed church. The areas in which they laboured were not yet fully integrated into a pattern of Protestant parishes, nor were they always recognisable portions of the pre-Reformation parish system either. When Bishop Thomas Knox, son of Andrew, reported on the state of his diocese in 1626 he said that Rum, Eigg, Muck and Canna formed now part of the two combined parishes of Strath and Sleat in Skye, the whole being served by one minister, Neil MacKinnon. There were two other ministers and a reader in Skye, two ministers in Lewis, and the whole of Uist was supposed to be in the care of 'ane verie auld man callit Donald Macmillen'. John MacPherson, minister of Harris, had charge of Barra also, 'with the fyve little Ylandis nixt adjacent to it' known as the Bishop's Isles, but there was little likelihood of his being able to reach these southern outliers of his 'parish', and though it has been stated that Barra and its lesser isles were once Protestant this appears to have been a false conclusion drawn from the theoretical attachment to Harris. In any case, by the middle of the century MacPherson, 'Preacher of the Herries', was failing to fulfil his duties even at home; in May 1656 he was suspended for 'scandalous carriage and unchristian conversation', a year later he was accused of celebrating marriage between excommunicated persons and under threat of deposition, and in May 1661 he was deposed for similar offences and considered 'a man inattentive to his character and duty.'[55]

Few Protestant ministers, some of them inattentive, attempting to supply the supposed needs of people living amid great tracts of Highland mountains and on scattered Hebridean islands, inevitably meant opportunities for the reappearance of Catholic priests and missionaries. Many of the 'natives' of these areas were, it has been said, left alone 'to pray and to believe as they wished, without priest or minister', and being without guidance and direction they 'clung to the beliefs and practices of the catholic faith, the memories of which grew more blurred and indistinct as the years passed by.' In northern Lewis the people were keeping the church called Teampall Mholuaidh in good repair in 1630 but, apparently lacking both priest and minister, arranged their own form of 'devotions' and held merry meetings with 'dancinge and dalliance' twice a year. In Hirt, more likely than most islands to be without pastoral guidance, the inhabitants, still 'a simple people', were at this time 'much given to Keeping of Holy dayes, having severall little Chapells, wher sometymes they watch whole nights, making merry togither with their offerings.' The 'kinde of officer', governing the island in place of the owner and steward, 'when any couple is to be maried, brings them to one of their Chapells, and administers ane oath to them so they are maried'. As for baptism now, 'Their Children, when they come to the age of fyfteen or sixteen, come with the master of the Isle to the Hereishe Islande and are there baptized.' For the most part, however, the religious condition of Hirt throughout the seventeenth century remains a matter of speculation; if, as was believed, 'a Minister goeth there in summer' on occasions, it was equally possible for a Catholic missionary to do so on others, but the community was left to its own ways of praying and believing year after year, and it is events in other islands that suggest what might have happened in Hirt during this period.[56]

If, after years of exclusion and resistance following the Reformation, Catholic priests had been available somewhere revival of the old religion would have been possible. None were in the islands, and help in this regard had to come from a country with which Hebrideans had an ancient connection, though not always a friendly one. The MacNeils of Barra went on raids to Ireland in the 1590s, but some of their people joined in more peaceful expeditions there, such as those who went 'by boat into Mayo to offer at Knockpatrick - a superstitious practice', but also an important scene of pilgrimage. It was from Ireland in the 1620s that missionaries came to work in places that promised them some chance of success.[57]

About 1618 an Irish Jesuit found people in Islay and Colonsay who had never seen a priest, information of the sort that was to promote developments over the next few years. Two Franciscans, Patrick Brady and Edmund McCann, were sent on mission to Scotland in 1619, the latter, with the greater fluency in Gaelic, heading for the Hebrides. The hostility aroused among Protestants by McCann's missionary success forced him to leave for Ireland for a while, and late in 1620 he was arrested and spent two years in prison. This led to further appeals for Irish Franciscans who spoke Gaelic 'to come to the help of the catholics in the Highlands and the Isles'. There were twenty volunteers, but eventually only four were chosen - Edmund McCann, who was willing to take the risk of returning, Paul O' Neill, Patrick Hegarty and Cornelius Ward, all of whom arrived in July 1624 from County Antrim.[58]

Before they departed on their dangerous task the missionaries were told that Coll Ciotach, then in Colonsay, was a good Catholic and could help them with information and directions; 'another leading man in the Hebrides is Roderick MacLeod of Harris, who is a catholic', and the missionaries could find out from Coll how to contact MacLeod, 'who, fervent catholic that he is, will attend to their needs and give them whatever instructions they might want'. They were also told how to conduct themselves, and some indication was given as to what they might be paid. Should circumstances be convenient Ward would be allowed to listen to sermons preached by non-Catholics, for by attending to what the minister said in the morning he would be able to correct the errors later the same day.[59]

The Franciscans endured many hardships in the course of their work. Hegarty, for instance, spent days hiding in caves, living for long periods on butter, cheese and water, and when in Islay might have been captured 'but was saved by a band of thirty catholics'. Mass could not be said without bread and wine, which had to come from Ireland or Lowland Scotland for the island people 'are so poor that they cannot give anything to the missionaries, and the missionaries cannot accept anything in case they might be considered avaricious'. In order to avoid their enemies and capture they sought permission to use money, ride horses, leave off 'the religious habit', and retire every now and again for relief and rest to some quiet corner in Ireland. The country they were working in, mainland and island, was difficult to live in, almost inaccessible, and 'the inhabitants have a greater taste for military exploits than for food and are content with fare which would be scarcely sufficient for other people when fasting'. Furthermore the inhabitants were distinct from other Scots:

> ' .. with the exception of some of the Irish, there is nobody near them who knows their Gaelic tongue; thus, just as the people there are cut off from others by the sea, so they differ from others in language also, with the result that only those Irish priests who had a sound knowledge of Gaelic could be chosen to go on the mission; the missionaries state they wholeheartedly undertook the mission at the command of the pope, and they feel that they have carried out the task imposed on them to the best of their ability; they consider themselves as following in the steps of Saint Columba, as it was he and his eleven disciples from Ireland first brought the light of faith to these districts; the isle of Iona, which was famous in ancient times for its monastery of Saint Columba, bears witness to this ... the people of the Hebrides are proof of this too, as they have a great devotion to Saint Columba and venerate him as their patron and apostle ..'[60]

Cornelius Ward further reported that in the northern Highlands the progress of the Catholic faith was hindered by 'the numerical strength of the ministers and their boldness', the fear that Catholics had of being discovered and penalised, and the severe laws against Catholics, whereas to the south and in the islands where, even though they had not seen a priest or minister for sixty years, some of the people had memories of Catholicism uninfluenced by 'the errors of the new religion', life was a little easier. But whatever place he was in Ward saw that the want of necessary facilities - wheat for bread, books, pyxes, chalices, rosaries, vestments, and crosses - was a serious disadvantage, and that people long separated from the custom of the old religion were liable to be put off the return to it if certain regulations stood in the way. The recovery of the Catholic faith in the islands depended upon a relaxed approach as much as upon the noticeable presence of the priest.[61]

Neil MacKinnon, the Protestant minister of Strath, Sleat and the Small Isles, was none too pleased when in the summer of 1625 Ward arrived in Eigg, said mass to a great crowd, and converted 198 of MacKinnon's adherents. The minister came with soldiers in the night intending to kill or capture Ward, but leading men on the island, only just recovered to the former faith, gathered together 'and threatened the minister and his soldiers with death unless they left the island immediately'. The angry MacKinnon vowed revenge, but Clanranald came to terms with him, giving him a third of the teinds of the island 'on condition that he would never again molest the catholics there or their priests'. Ward continued his work on Eigg, and an old woman of eighty, who remembered having seen in her youth mass celebrated there and in the neighbouring isles, was somewhat disapproving of Ward's form of the mass until she was set at ease by his explanation.[62]

Paul O'Neill, who had been 'labouring in the territory of MacLeod of Harris and in adjacent districts' for well over a year, and who had been seriously ill, joined Ward in Eigg, during which time the latter met Clanranald, then visited three villages in Rum, and returned to Canna 'where St Columba was held in great veneration'. Ward crossed over to South Uist where, he was told, there had been no priest for about one hundred years, and where, hearing that a Catholic priest had landed, a large crowd assembled, 'some anxious to learn about the faith, some merely curious'; and leaders here, invited to be present, 'promised to accept the faith if they found Ward's arguments more convincing than those put forward by the ministers'. As in other places the listeners were in a dilemma, for acceptance of the Catholic belief, which they understood would bring salvation, meant the probability of imprisonment and ruin if they admitted it publicly.[63]

It was now October 1625, and one day Ward received an invitation from Clanranald's uncle, Ranald MacDonald, 'a staunch defender of catholicism'. Ward, O'Neill and the still active Patrick Brady met in Ranald's house to discuss the mission. Afterwards O'Neill and Brady left to visit MacLeod of Harris, while Ward responded to a request from 'a gentleman' in Barra to baptise a child. While in that island he also converted or 'reconciled' a large number, including MacNeil of Barra's sister, and on his way back to South Uist he converted two people living in the island of Fuday where, according to tradition, had been the last Norse-speaking community in the Barra isles. A minister in North Uist is supposed to have often warned the people not to allow 'a popish priest' into the island, but Ward arrived safely and was soon at work. When he left 'there were only fourteen who remained loyal to the minister'.[64]

However accurate or approximate these descriptions of missionary activity may have been, they all show island communities in a state of religious uncertainty, swayed one way or the other by persuasive speakers and strong personalities. Cornelius Ward, at the beginning of 1626, was about to encounter one of the most flexible individuals, moving his loyalties according to circumstance. Back in South Uist Ward held further meetings and at one converted a Protestant minister called Ranald MacDonald and his two brothers. This Ranald, believed to be a son of Clanranald, made it known that he would like to study for the priesthood, so he went away south with Ward, on to Ireland, and at last to the college at Louvain in Belgium. He moved to Douai with letters of commendation, but the superiors there 'refused to accept a Calvinist minister whom ..Ward had converted to catholicism', and it would appear that at this stage the attempt to produce one native-born, Gaelic-speaking priest for the islands failed. Ward persisted, though nervously. He asked that Ranald be provided 'with a place in some establishment where he can study cases of conscience and controversy for two years'. He was afraid that if no place was granted Ranald would go home, 'return to his former religion and be the occasion of drawing some of the recent converts in the Highlands and the Isles away from catholicism'. Perhaps a dispensation could be allowed for Ranald so that he could be 'promoted to orders' which would no doubt keep him in the faith. In January 1627 a testimonial signed by the rector of the Irish College at Louvain stated that Ranald MacDonald was a former Calvinist minister converted two years previously and that for some months he had been living at the college where he had shown himself to be of upright character, attentive to his studies, 'rather well versed in the humanities', and likely to 'work zealously at the evangelization of souls in Scotland'. Considering these and other qualities it was thought that he would 'do much fruitful work', especially as he would when a priest 'enjoy the patrimony of a well-born relative in Scotland' - presumably Clanranald. So Ranald completed his course, became a priest, and in 1629 Ward, trusting in the success of his convert, tried to bring him back to his home country. Unfortunately as he was passing through London Ranald was arrested and put in gaol, and Ward too was soon a prisoner himself. After only a few days, however Ranald was released and by a circuitous route reached Uist.[65]

CHAPTER 4
Irish missionaries and Protestant resistance

The labours of the Franciscan missionaries took their toll of the health and courage which had enabled them over the years to achieve considerable success. Paul O'Neill withdrew in 1626, Hegarty went to Antrim in 1631, Brady continued his work on the mainland, mostly in Sutherland, for a total of eighteen years, and Ward, liberated after two years in prison, came back to the Hebrides. McCann disappeared into the unknown until emerging once more in Armagh in 1640. Eventually, in 1637, the heroic Ward ceased his efforts, partly because of lack of support from authorities on the continent. Financial contributions were minimal and irregular, the necessary permissions and supplies were slow in coming, and conditions imposed were unrealistic. While for a time in the reigns of James VI and Charles I a Catholic revival had seemed possible the new system of bishops agreed in 1610, which gave them a powerful administrative role and led to the combination of two old dioceses into that of Argyll and the Isles, meant that the lives of the missionaries were constantly under threat from the fiercer opposing ecclesiastics, and then, in the year after Ward gave up, the National Covenant was signed, the presbyterian church acquired greater authority, and hostility to both Catholics and Episcopalians increased.[66]

Back in 1618 the guardian of St Anthony's College at Louvain had written a letter saying that 'a very great number of Gaelic-speaking Scots are blind concerning the true faith or have strayed from it, not through any malice of their own but through sheer ignorance, as they had nobody to impart the teachings of the church to them; for a long time no one has been found who would go to Scotland to instruct these people, and, consequently, they are half-pagan in as much as very many of them have never been baptized ..' Nineteen years later he might have felt rather happier about the situation in some Hebridean and west mainland districts, but while the missionaries achieved a great deal the lack of resident priests meant that the marriages, baptisms, administering of sacraments and so on could not be conducted on a regular basis. Ward's visit to the Bishop's Isles in 1637, where no priest had been since the Reformation, was not followed up by sustained pastoral care, and while there and in other places crowds had attended his presence, much as happened at Protestant revival meetings two centuries later, the enthusiasm was temporary and soon faded. Though 'the traditions of their fathers' had by no means been forgotten and affection for the 'true faith' and the mass persisted, the people in many of the islands were without religious teaching for most of the time unless a Protestant minister had been settled. Out in the Atlantic ocean Hirt may have experienced a fleeting visit from a priest and perhaps from a minister but the inhabitants can have heard little of events involving church and government. Instead they held onto traditions, customs and beliefs which may have been a strange mixture out of the pagan and Christian past.[67]

In 1638 the General Assembly of the Church of Scotland erected the Synod of Argyll and the Isles, with a territory extending from Rona and Lewis to Kintyre and including mainland Invernessshire districts on the west coast. Effectively replacing previous episcopal authority the Synod's organisational task was enormous, and for many years the remoter islands, left largely to their own devices, were scarcely touched by any attempt to substitute Protestant teaching for their older loyalties. The continuance of the Catholic faith in South Uist under the Clanranald MacDonalds and in Barra under the MacNeils may have had some influence on the religious attitudes of the people in Hirt, especially while MacLeod appeared to be Catholic also.

The Synod was only one of three possible levels of kirk hierarchy below the General Assembly. Responsible for the moral and spiritual well-being of a very large tract of the Highlands and all the Hebridean islands it found that the presbyteries in Argyll could be formed without too much trouble but that those further away in wilder parts could not establish firm boundaries or more than a limited number of parishes with adequate ministers and kirk sessions. There were even fewer manses and glebes, and so extensive were the more northerly presbyteries it proved almost impossible for all members to attend meetings. In these circumstances the Synod was bound to feel that remnants of Catholic religious practice and of the cultural world that accompanied it would linger and, with the aid of missionaries, recover their former vigour.

An unusual building high above the St Kilda 'village', possibly Taigh an Triar (House of three)

The early presbyterian church was therefore seriously worried about a return to what it considered a faith of superstition and even barbarism. It took steps where possible to remove everything that might encourage that return. Persecution of missionaries and priests from Ireland was but one method of blocking the Catholic tradition. Another was the destruction of objects, including buildings, of Catholic inspiration. In 1641 the General Assembly ordained 'all idolatrous images, crucifixes, pictures of Christ to be demolished and removed' from kirks, chapels, and 'other public places', and in accordance with such instructions the Synod of Argyll, in 1643, felt bound to correct the situation in Barra. One of the ministers of the Skye presbytery, Martin MacPherson, reported that there were 'two Idols kept by McNeill of Barra in his private Chappell called Our Lady and her Babe trained up in their Apparel and Ornaments'. Since the Synod had determined the year before that all ministers in its 'province' should bring information in on 'all idolatrouse monuments within their paroaches to the which the vulgar superstitiously resorts to worship, to the end the same may be demolished', it must be assumed that Martin MacPherson was doing just that. Having listened to him the Synod resolved 'that McNeill should be written to, desiring him to deliver the idols to Mr Martain to be destroyed'. MacNeil may have taken no notice of the letter. Many regretted this form of anti-Catholic behaviour, thinking it mere vandalism, and the Protestant minister of Kirkhill, Inverness, later in the century, wrote sadly of the loss of records and of fine old religious buildings 'in the fury of our confused Reformation, whose over heasty actions in these behalfes hath left us a want of many truthes which otherwayes we might have had ..' Every now and again in the future the impulse to destroy was to emerge as part of religious conviction, and many more 'truthes' were lost in this way.[68]

Another of the Synod's concerns in its first years was adequate church administration in the isles when the structure was incomplete. The presbytery of Skye covered not only all the Skye parishes and the Small Isles but also the whole length of the Outer Hebrides, yet 'it is universally regretted by the ministers of the Isles that very few or none of them has constitute Sessions The Gentlemen and Heritors of the Country refusing to give their concurrence to the Exercise of kirk discipline'. Some churches were vacant, and the obstructive landowners were, at least in the case of MacLeod of Harris, Clanranald and MacNeil of Barra, able to turn a blind eye to any sign of Catholic intervention. In the absence of the required 'discipline' various beliefs and practices stemming from some distant period of antiquity were likely to be retained, and ministers like Martin MacPherson had to be on the lookout for more than 'idols':

'Because it is a common Custom in some of the remotest parts within this province of ignorant poor women to howle their dead unto the Graves which commonly is called the Corronach, a thing unseemly to be used in any true Christian Kirk where there is preaching and profession of the comfortable Resurrection of the dead Where fore and for the restraining thereof It is ordained that every Minister both in preaching and Catechising endeavour to inform them how unseemly to Christians and offensive to God to others the like practice and carriage must be ..'[69]

Then to prevent further instances of the practice the ministers were told to make its unseemliness widely known and to indicate that punishment would follow unless it was given up. Those 'found guilty of the said Corronach' would have to 'stand on Sunday in the Church', and if they still continued 'it is ordained that some of them be jogged and made Examples to the rest'. If this too was insufficient the matter would have to be represented by an Act of Session to the Marquis of Argyll, who, in his capacity as justice general of Argyll and the Isles, 'has promised to take order with the same'. Similar procedures and perhaps worse penalties awaited the 'witches Sorcerers, Charmers, palmisters, Jugglers, Second sighted Diviners Soothsayers, necromancers, consulters with Spirits and such like' of whom the Synod in 1649 appointed several ministers in the parishes 'to take tryall'.[70]

People who, judged from a Protestant standpoint of the time, fell into one or more of these categories, were known, directly or indirectly, to Cornelius Ward who reported instances of visions and other unusual events, 'which helped to draw the people of the Hebrides to catholicism'. When O'Neill, Brady and Ward met in South Uist before dividing forces 'a man who lived six miles away saw them in a vision clothed in the whitest of clothes and surrounded by light as they approached the isle of Barra, where he then was'. He then saw two bidding farewell to the third. On another occasion, when Ward returned to Barra, the same man told him how a woman saw two armies near the shore, one in shining dress with a leader more splendid than the sun, the other 'evil and squalid-looking', led by a man coloured black with a 'fearful countenance'. On enquiry the woman was told that the first army was of converts, led by Christ, the second of the unconverted led by the devil. Blasphemy featured in some instances. In one a staunch Protestant farmer at Carinish in North Uist spoke blasphemously of 'sacred images', especially a wooden statue of the Holy Trinity in the church nearby, when Ward was present. The farmer then had a vision in the course of which the devil appeared to injure his side. The pain woke him, his wife discovered that his side was lifeless and blackened, and a Catholic neighbour advised that he should be laid before the statue of the Trinity in the church, 'where he was to withdraw all the blasphemies and profess the catholic faith'. This he did, and soon recovered. Stories of this kind were quite common and helped to convince the Synod that its worries over the state of remote areas were justified.[71]

It was almost inevitable that before long the Synod would become interested in Ranald MacDonald who had returned to work in Uist in 1629. Any shelter he received from relatives did not compensate for the conditions in which he usually lived and laboured, so that in 1637 it was reported by Ward at first hand that Ranald 'was compelled, because of persecution, to reside in a very remote district, and he supported himself with his hands and feet by tilling the land, and by fishing and gathering shellfish ..' Ranald confined himself most of the time to Uist where he visited islanders to strengthen them in their faith and occasionally administer the sacraments to them in secret. But he was afraid he would be unable to continue as he was receiving no financial support, the people, who had to pay teinds to the Protestant church, having nothing to give him. In 1642 he was brought before the Commissioners of the General Assembly in Edinburgh, having been apprehended by order of the Marquis of Argyll. He was examined 'upon his errors and profession' and found 'so grossly ignorant' that no 'acknowledgement and confession' by him could be accepted 'untill he be bettir informed'. His 'ignorance' was not in general but of reformed presbyterian doctrine, so that he was ordained 'to study diligently to understand the errors of his bygone profession, and to this effect to read some bookes and treatises as may give him information thereannent ..' When he had done so he was 'to give out of knowledge and conscience ane ample and sincere confession of all his errors' to the Synod at its next meeting. He would be 'tryed and examined' there as well, and dealt with in such a manner as would bring him 'to the acknowledgement and renunciation, privat and publict, of his errors, and for publict satisfaction to the kirk, for the scandall and offence that his lyfe, profession and practice hes given thereby'. Ranald was also instructed to compose and sign a confession, deliver it to the Moderator of the Assembly, and place himself in the care of the presbytery of Edinburgh who would 'take such course with him dureing his abode with them as they shall think convenient…'[72]

Ranald appeared before the Synod of Argyll in May 1643. He was asked whether he had studied books and treatises as he had been told, and Martin MacPherson testified that he had. The signed confession was produced, but 'being examined upon the particular heads of supremacy, the worshipeing of images, the number of the sacraments, purgatory and invocation of saints', conceived as being all standard elements of the Catholic faith, 'he was fund not to be strongly grounded in his profession, neither very able to cleare himselfe to the satisfaction of others that he was resolved of his doubts as he alleadged ..' So three ministers were given the task of 'educating' him. Within a day or two they reported that they had 'brought him a great way on' and that it seemed he had never had much knowledge of the old religion or much affection for it. Ranald had said to them that in renouncing 'his own religion' to begin with he had been moved by his need for a means of living and now regretted his action. He was willing to confess all before the congregation on Sunday and to declare to the people 'the vanity, idleness and unprofitablenes, yea and ridiculousenes of the superstitiouse ceremonies and worshipe of the church of Rome'. This undertaking appeared to satisfy the Synod.[73]

The former minister was now held to be no longer a priest. However the upheavals of the civil wars that immediately followed in the 1640s drew him into support of the royalist side represented by the Duke of Montrose and, in the Highlands and islands, by Alasdair MacDonald, son of Coll Ciotach. In May 1650 the Synod ordained 'Ranald Mc Ranald, who hes diverse tymes before jugled in his religion and profession, and now since the late rebellion is become apostate and a preist, to be sumarily excommunicat be the presbyterie of Sky'. Twenty-five years previously Ranald had been a minister; then he was converted by Ward and became a priest; in 1643 he gave up the priesthood and was accepted as a Protestant again; and around 1646 he abandoned the Protestant world and became a priest once more. At its next meeting in October 1650 the Synod reckoned that his conduct for the second time deserved the attention of the justice for Argyll and the Isles:

> 'Considering That Ranald Macdonald Sometime Professed Papist Priest after making of his recantation and Embracing the true Protestant religion and swearing and Subscribing the covenant having made apostacy and desertion from the truth and being also in the late rebellion and therefore Excommunicate And that notwithstanding thereof he is Still labouring to pervert poor ignorant people in the parts where he haunts in the Isle of Uist and other parts of the farr Isles to the dishonor of God and ruin of poor souls Therefore The assembly doe most Seriously recommend to the Lord Marquiss of Argyle as justice of these bounds to be pleased to See a course taken with the said Ranald and ordains an extract thereof with a Letter from this Assembly to be sent to his Lordship for this purpose.'[74]

In April 1651 the Synod appointed a letter to be written to the Marquis concerning Ranald MacDonald, again called priest but only a day or so later 'sometime preist', and Mr Duncan McCalman, 'sometime minister at Ardnamurchan', both of whom were still 'excommunicate' for having taken part in the 'rebellion'. Of Ranald thereafter nothing more seems to be recorded, but McCalman was 'deposed and excommunicat' for his behaviour.[75]

*

The presbytery of Skye, having at first objected to being attached to the Synod of Argyll, agreed to join, although its members were rarely able to attend Synod assemblies and were often entirely absent. The main reasons for non-attendance were the problem of travel, the troubles of the times and the lack of decent communication. The nine presbytery ministers present in May 1642 included five from the Outer Hebrides - Farquhar Clerk, Stornoway, Murdoch mc Huistonne, 'Minister at Lews', John MacPherson, Harris, Angus MacQueen, North Uist, and Martin MacPherson, South Uist. For all these men to attend presbytery and Synod meetings meant a long and difficult journey by sea and land, and so reluctant were they to make it that the presbytery often met with only Skye representation, while the Synod agreed to allow the presbytery to come in summer only and the minister 'at Lews' to come as he may. All this was accompanied with great difficulty in obtaining up-to-date news of what was happening in the 'farr Isles' with regard especially to the

47

implementation of the new 'true' religion and resistance to the old.[76]

It was therefore some time before the Skye presbytery could inform the Synod of a further papist threat. In October 1650 Vincent de Paul, in a letter to Rome, requested facilities for two priests, Dermot Duggan or Dugan and Francis White, both Gaelic-speaking Irishmen, to go as missionaries to the Highlands and Hebrides where, since the departure of the Franciscans, the people were again in danger of losing the faith. These two 'Vincentians' left for Scotland disguised as merchants late in the same year and arrived at the beginning of March 1651. On the way they met Angus MacDonald of Glengarry, also in disguise, who went home with them.[77]

Dermot Duggan eventually made his way to Uist where Clanranald and his family welcomed the priest, but the laird and the tenants had been without religious direction in recent years and some of the latter had forgotten how to make the 'Sign of the Cross'. Like his missionary predecessors Duggan suffered great hardships. 'Money is scarce in these parts', he wrote, 'and we accept nothing from the people .. My poverty is increased because of the fact that I need two men, men I pay. One helps me to row the boat when I go from island to island and to carry the vestments and Mass requisites overland .. I have taught the other man to serve Mass and to help in the teaching of the Pater, Ave and Credo.' At best he had one meal a day, sometimes went whole days without eating, and occasionally enjoyed the luxury of a little beer or whisky. The island people, Duggan thought, lacked fishing skill, 'being naturally lethargic and not industrious'.[78]

By 1654 Duggan had been to Skye where MacLeod and the people on his estate had come for instruction and the sacraments. He had also visited Barra:

> 'With the coming of spring I went to another island called Barra where the people, so fervent and so eager for instruction, delighted me. One needed only to teach the *Pater, Ave* and *Credo* to one young child in each village and a few days later all in that village knew them, grown-ups as well as little ones. The leading persons on Barra, among them the young Lord with his brothers and sisters, were reconciled with the Church. I hope to reconcile the old Lord when I go there again. The son of a minister has become a Catholic; he is well known to the Barra people, who are greatly edified by his fervour.'[79]

The mere presence of Catholic missionaries, rather than the long-term effects of their labour, was enough to upset the Protestant authorities. At the summer Synod assembly of 1656 the presbytery of Skye reported 'the sad condition of several places in the Isles in respect of Poppery creeping in amongst them by three several seminary Priests, viz., Frances Whyte and Draimid o Morgan [Dermot Duggan] … and one father John Macdonald ..' The meeting responded by telling the presbytery to deal with Catholic lairds like the Clanranalds and MacNeil of Barra to persuade them of their errors, and the assistance of MacKenzie of Seaforth, Sir James MacDonald of Sleat, and some others, including interestingly MacLeod of Harris and Dunvegan, was sought in 'repressing the forsaid infectione'. But Duggan at least never felt any effect of such remote measures, and in May 1657 prepared to sail from South Uist to an island beyond Barra which has been identified as Hirt, 'then still unreached by Protestant ministers', but which appears to have in fact been Pabbay, one of the Bishop's Isles and described in a short account of Duggan's last days:

'There still remained an island named Pabba … which he had not visited. It was a wild and weird place. The inhabitants were not attached to any heresy, but they were totally without instruction. Father Dugan hoped to bring numbers of them to the practice of religion. He had his preparations made for setting out to Pabba on May 10th 1657, but his strength failed him. He fell ill and died in the Island of Uist on 17th of the same month. The people amongst whom he ministered long mourned his loss; they revered him as a Saint, and gave his name to the chapel where his remains were laid to rest.'[80]

The chapel, or rather an old graveyard, was called Cladh a' Ghugain, though whether Duggan was indeed buried there is uncertain. There is also said to be a hill pass in Barra known as Bealach a' Ghugain, and with an unwarranted stretch of the imagination it seems possible that the story of Dugan and Fearchar in Hirt was invented later by some eager Protestant to pour scorn on a priest remembered affectionately by either the people of that island or those of Barra and South Uist. In these latter islands 'The poor islanders, young and old, wept for him as for a father'.[81]

*

Even in Skye, the seat of the presbytery, 'Priests, Jesuits and Papists' were going about among the people in 1655, and though such reports were perhaps exaggerated to scare other Protestants, as the reports of priests may have equally exaggerated the success of the missionaries, the Synod had to take notice of them. In 1656 it had to postpone a visitation arranged to 'the north Isles' for 'trying the condition of those bounds who are like to be Infected with Poppery', and instead decided to go to Lochaber, Ardgour, Sunart and Ardnamurchan, these districts being altogether 'desolate of the ordinances' and 'in no less danger than the Isles'. Over the remaining forty years or so of the seventeenth century the position did not change much, with Protestant ministers, rather like missionaries themselves, still struggling with wild parishes often of a size far beyond their capacity to look after, and lonely, exhausted and poorly supported priests doing their best to maintain the faith in at least the traditionally Catholic areas. Among the latter were Father George Fanning, an Irish Dominican, who would not have been able to exist in Barra had he not found a home with MacNeil, and Francis White who for many years after the death of Duggan was the only priest in the Highlands and islands and died there in January 1679, having among other achievements established a school in Barra intended to teach boys who, if they were sent away for their education, might never return 'after they have tasted the delights of Italy, France or Flanders'. From 1681 there were up to ten priests on mission in the Highlands and islands, including John Cahassy [Casey], James Devoyer [Dwyer], Patrick Carolan [O'Carolan] and Cornelius Con [Coan, Conn], who roamed about in the north attending to the needs of individual families or small communities as best they could. Whether any of them reached Hirt before the 1690s is doubtful.[82]

The Synod of Argyll, as the principal body responsible for the progress of the Protestant church on the west coast, had in 1690 concerns similar to those of half a century earlier. The rents once received by bishops had passed to the crown, but were now granted to the Synod to be bestowed 'upon erecting of English schools for rooting out the Irish language and other pious uses'. The Irish language, that is, Gaelic, was associated, in the government's thinking, with Jacobites, barbaric natives adhering to the Catholic faith, and obstacles to government control, and consequently was judged to pose a threat matching that of 'popery'. The money allocated to pay parish ministers but, in the absence of incumbents, not taken up, otherwise called 'vacant stipends', was again available for bursaries to assist divinity students to attend schools and colleges in Glasgow. But even though, with the help of some landowners, schools existed before 1700 in some of the islands they were few and far between and often temporary, and there was no flow of Gaelic-speaking graduates into a church that was opposed to Gaelic. The Catholic missions may have faltered for lack of priests who spoke Gaelic, but they were not troubled by the language problem which already confronted Protestant ministers and teachers, who were being encouraged to promote and use English in communicating with people who did not understand it or, for nearly all the time, hear or see any signs of it.[83]

Communication between ministers was possible at presbytery and Synod meetings as well as in the ordinary circumstances of daily life by letter or chance encounter, but the missionary priests, forced into concealment and secrecy, had a much more difficult time. Occasionally two of them worked together, as when Con and Casey toured through the islands probably in the summer of 1686, but often they worked alone, relying on Catholic households to give them shelter. When in Lewis Con lived in Aignish with MacKenzie of Kildun, and while there he confronted local ministers. 'The ministers of the island,' he wrote, 'claimed they would kill me, and having met three of them against me we informally discussed the principal points of the faith. In the end they left ashamed.' Like his colleagues Con needed a rest sometimes and an opportunity to talk with other priests, so he took refuge at Gordon Castle, a safe haven. There too was James Dwyer, who had been in the Sleat district of Skye, and the two of them discussed their recent activities. This was in May 1687, after which respite Con returned to Lewis and Uist and Dwyer went back to Skye and neighbouring mainland districts where Casey joined him. The latter was particularly impressed by the eagerness of people everywhere to ensure that their children were baptised:

> 'They are even afraid of temporary misfortunes if there are unbaptised
> children in the family, which means that many of our catholics have strong
> and healthy children baptised by laymen when the priest is far away, an
> abuse of the permission they were given to baptise dying children. We have
> come across some poor old men who have been employed to baptise
> children when there was no priest or minister in these rough lands. These
> old men, not being aware of the true form of baptism, make use of a
> superstitious rhapsody [incantation?] with demented ceremonies. They put
> salt in the water and place the child in a goatskin. The father or the mother
> is outside the door of the house; the old man being inside and holding the
> child on the threshold asks the mother from what illness she wished to
> preserve the child by the holy waters of baptism, and what good fortune
> she would wish for him. When he has the reply, he puts the water on the
> child saying - I baptise you for your father and mother, for your spouse and
> [?] child, for all your relatives and friends, and I guarantee and preserve you
> from such and such illnesses and misfortunes etc.'[84]

Meeting in Inveraray with only the ministers and ruling elders of nearer
presbyteries being anything like regular attenders, the Synod of Argyll, unable
to improve lines of communication, felt at times particularly frustrated by the
lack of first-hand, recent information from the Outer Hebrides. At its June
assembly in 1695 which was held at Bracadale during a 'visitation' to Skye, it
had in mind 'the Desolat condition of the Isles' and planned a further 'visitation'
for the following year. Meeting therefore at Clachan Sand in North Uist in July
1696 the visiting party heard disturbing rumours. One was that Mr Alexander
Couper, late Episcopal incumbent in North Uist, had 'intruded himself' into the
charge by a 'paction' with 'Mr Allan Moryson', former Episcopal incumbent at
Clachan Sand but 'now at Nesse in Lewis'. Many Episcopal ministers had been
evicted after the revolution of 1688-1689 but there were still several in the
islands, as elsewhere, and agreements or 'pactions' between them of this kind
aroused suspicion. Another rumour may also have reached the Synod party
either when at Clachan or after it had moved on. Members stayed in Berneray
for the night of 28 July, in Ensay for the night following, and came to Rodel in
the afternoon of 30 July where they were storm-stayed for a day or two. At any
of these places the rumour could have been reported from direct knowledge
of its source, and it could have been discussed at the meeting held in St
Clement's church at Rodel on Sunday 1 August.[85]

Early next morning, at 4 o'clock, the group sailed for Skye and in mid
afternoon arrived at Monkstad ['Muggustet'], where Flora MacDonald and her
crew were to bring Prince Charles Edward fifty years later. While in Skye a
member could have reported the rumour to Dunvegan, for it concerned
curious and worrying events in Hirt.

CHAPTER 5

Martin Martin, John Campbell and the 'Impostor'

I N 1696 Roderick, nineteenth chief of MacLeod, was a young man, consumptive and with only three years to live. Stories relating to Hirt may not have interested him greatly but since a rumour was as likely to have been brought by the steward or one of the boat's crew as by a Synod member he could have left any initial response to one of his managers, such as the steward himself, if not to the church. However a close companion, Martin Martin, his former tutor, seems to have been ready to take immediate action. On Roderick's death Martin wrote: 'A Consumption brought him Low as a Skeleton of which he died the 24 Instant. He was the kindest freind I had on earth, he was overjoyed to see me here [Fortrose], and declared often that death only could separat us and that herafter we should have but one purse.' Such intimacy would have allowed Roderick to place full confidence in the intelligent and educated Martin.[86]

Martin Martin was a member of a Skye family belonging to the district of northern Trotternish. He was brother to Daniel or Donald Martin, at one time Protestant minister in North Uist, and had another brother, John, who farmed at Duntulm and at Flodigarry. In 1686 he was tutor to a MacDonald of Sleat at Armadale ['Armindill'] and since Roderick MacLeod's father, known as Iain Breac, was married to one of that family it was possibly through that connection that Martin obtained his post at Dunvegan. In 1694 or 1695 he was asked to supply information on the islands to the Royal Society and in December 1695 wrote from Dunvegan: 'Be pleased to deliver the Inclosed remarks to the Viscount Tarbat ... I have dir[ected] another Copy of them to Doctor [Sloan] ... one of the greatest virtuosos of the royall Society.' It seems that the Viscount 'obleidged me to send all my observations to the Royall Society ..[87]

Sir George MacKenzie of Tarbat, first Earl of Cromartie, was one of the original Fellows of the Royal Society and the author of contributions to its transactions. His varied pursuits included natural history, support for Catholic, Episcopal and presbyterian religions, and historical research. At some point, possibly in the 1690s but perhaps as far back as 1680, he received 'from intelligent persons dwelling in the place' an account of the islands of Hirt and Rona, and this was passed to Sir Robert Sibbald, collector of information along the lines of MacKenzie's interests. The 'intelligent persons' could have been Martin Martin and John Morison, 'indweller' in Bragar, Lewis, in which case 'that place' would be no more precise a location than 'the Hebrides'. By this time Hirt was often written Hirta, a form of the name used in the 'MacKenzie' account, which described the sheep, the ewe-milk cheese 'which my Lord Register [MacKenzie] saith pleaseth his tast better then Hollands Cheese', the lack of salt, and bird-catching on the cliffs. 'The Island of Hirta', begins the account, 'of all the Isles about Scotland lyeth farthest out into the sea, is very mountanous, and not accessible but by climbing'; with which remarks another anonymous note is entirely consistent: 'No access to Hirta but at one place, wher the boat is heased up, loading and all, by the Inhabitants - there be some 60 families there'.[88]

Whether or not Martin had sent a brief account of Hirt to MacKenzie it was preceded some years earlier by 'A Description of the Island Hirta Brought in by Sir Robert Moray' and published in 1678 in the Royal Society's Transactions. This description, perhaps dating from much earlier in the century, was available to Martin and provided fuller details than had previously been recorded. It mentioned three of the islands in the group, *Hirta*, *Soa* and *Borra*, explaining at length how the people landed at *Borra* and on *Stacka Donna* to get birds and eggs. Its comments on ten families - not sixty - , chapels, making merry, 'keeping of holy dayes', marriages conducted by the 'officer' and baptisms in Harris have already been noticed.[89]

During the first weeks of 1696 Martin contemplated an expedition for the purpose of making further 'observations' but 'The badness of the season and the accident befallen my leg, Conspired to retard my progress', forcing him to curtail what he had proposed. In spite of this however, 'I'm resolved shortlie for the long Isle', and in two months he indeed reached the Outer Hebrides. Writing in June of that year he expressed his concerns on the state of religion:

'I am Latelie Come from the Long Island where there is not one minister to preach. I am uncertain as to the parson of Harries. this presents a fair opportunity for the popish priests who will not lose time at Such a junture - a short Space might dispose the Comon people for poperie or atheism. The Contempt of Baptism, and Sponsors or Gossops as they call them here inclines them the more to poperie for they will have there Children Christened tho by a Layman.'[90]

The landlord or his steward and representatives of the Synod of Argyll may have agreed together on the measures to be taken to deal with what they saw as a major problem in Hirt, for the 'visitation' to the island that took place in the summer of 1697 had the appearance of a combination of laird and church. The former was represented by his good friend Martin Martin and the latter by John Campbell, Episcopal minister in Harris. In 1670 a John Campbell, minister of 'St Clementes in Heris', served as a witness to an undertaking by John MacLeod of MacLeod, Iain Breac, and it has been said that the John Campbell who went to Hirt with Martin was his son and presumably therefore also minister at St Clement's. The Harris parish was still linked to Catholic Barra, ministers in Uist being responsible for the intervening islands, and Hirt was not within the bounds of Campbell's or anyone else's parish. Being at Rodel, however, with the annual steward's boat normally leaving from a place nearby, perhaps Pabbay itself but also possibly from Obbe, Rodel or Ensay, Campbell, living under the patronage and on the estate of MacLeod, was the natural choice to visit the island on behalf of the Protestant church. He was supposed to have been there before though perhaps only once.[91]

When at last he returned from Hirt Martin Martin wrote and published in 1698 an account of his visit with Campbell. It had a lengthy title:

> 'A Late Voyage to St. Kilda, the Remotest of all the Hebrides, or Western Isles of Scotland. With a History of the Island, Natural, Moral, and Topographical. Wherein is an Account of their Customs, Religion, Fish, Fowl, etc. As also a Relation of a late IMPOSTOR there, pretended to be Sent by *St. John Baptist.*'

The name 'St Kilda' was thereby introduced as a replacement for Hirt, as if Martin thought it was more suitable for the educated, reading public and members of the Royal Society, to whose president the book was dedicated, than the real name used by the inhabitants and other Gaelic-speaking communities. Possibly to display his learning he seems to have chosen 'St. Kilda' from the maps, some of them over a century old and one copying another, made by people having little or no first-hand acquaintance with the areas covered, with the result that the island or island group of Hirt has become widely and popularly known by what must be an entirely fictitious name.

The preface to his book states that the author's 'great desire to propagate the Natural History of the Isles of Scotland, makes him relate, without any disguise, the several particulars that fell under his accurate Observation'. This and later remarks in the preface show that Martin had the Royal Society very much in mind as he wrote, and while 'Natural History' covered a wide range of topics it could not be said that it comprehended any motives of religious enquiry that may have encouraged him to visit 'the Remotest of all the Hebrides'. The adventure to Hirt with John Campbell surely presented itself therefore as a fine opportunity to inform the world about a remarkable and largely mysterious place, the nature of which was discovered by Martin 'from his own particular Observation, or else from the constant and harmonious Testimony that was given him by the Inhabitants ... a sort of People so Plain, and so little inclined to Impose upon Mankind, that perhaps no place in the World at this day, knows such Instances of true primitive Honour and Simplicity; a People who abhor lying Tricks and Artifices, as they do the most poisonous Plants, or devouring Animals'. An island with a false name and certainly no devouring animals but with its 'simple' people was thus described for the first time to entertain the intellectual curiosity of remote figures like the president of the Royal Society.

What made the book even more appealing was the voyage itself; made 'in an open Boat, to the almost manifest hazard of his life,' claimed Martin, 'since the Seas and Tides in those Rocky Islands are more inconstant and raging than in most other places.' For centuries open boats had run the dangers of Caolas Hirt, from the violent tides and currents of the Sound of Harris to the white-topped swells of the ocean rising into the cliffs of Hirt, but now Martin, having made several previous attempts to visit the island without success, was able to describe the journey out of vivid personal experience.

So, with 'the Laird of *Mack-Leod* heartily recommending the Care of the Inhabitants of *St. Kilda* to Mr. John Campbel, Minister of Harries', Martin found the way of fulfilling an ambition which the present steward of the island had aroused in him 'by his Description, and the Products of the Island.' The two men went on board at Ensay on 29 May 1697 and left 'at Six in the Afternoon'. They sailed with the help of a gentle south-east wind but almost immediately 'Mr Campbell observing the Whiteness of the Waves attended with an extraordinary Noise beating upon the Rocks, express'd his Dislike of it, as in those Parts a never-failing Prognostick of an ensuing Storm'. The crew disagreed, saying that in summer 'excessive heat' was sometimes predicted in this way. They therefore continued out of Caolas Sgaire towards Pabbay despite increasing signs of bad weather, and after trying in vain to row into the shelter of Haisgeir were forced to 'make the best of our way for St. Kilda'. After sixteen hours out of sight of land the crew were utterly weary and discouraged, concluding from the flight direction of birds that the boat was well off-course, but they all cheered up greatly when someone saw Boreray looming to the south: 'this was a joyful Sight, and begot new Vigor in our Men, who being refresh'd with Victuals, low'ring Mast and Sail, rowed to a Miracle'. While they were 'tugging at the Oars', Martin and Campbell poured whisky into them, 'whose borrow'd Spirits did so far waste their own, that upon our Arrival at Borera, there was scarce one of our Crew able to manage Cable or Anchor'. After sheltering from a storm for two nights and a day in the lee of Boreray, during which 'our men laid aside all hopes of life', they rowed across to Hirt in calm weather and landed safely on 1 June.[92]

Martin and Campbell were carried ashore on shoulders, 'All of us walking together to the little Village where there was a Lodging prepared for us, furnished with Beds of Straw, and according to the ancient Custom of the place, the Officer, who presides over them (in the Steward's absence) summoned the Inhabitants, who by concert agreed upon a daily Maintenance for us'. Almost immediately the visitors, with prior information to guide them, set to work on their most important task, not the gathering of details about island life but an investigation into the subject of rumour, the activities of the person subseqently called the 'IMPOSTOR', one of the most interesting individuals in the history of Hirt.

*

'After our Landing, the Minister and I (according to our first resolution) examined the Inhabitants apart by themselves concerning the New pretended Religion delivered to them by their False Prophet.'[93]

Ruairidh Mòr, big Roderick, was a curious and indeed remarkable character. He was a native of the island, 'a Comely well-proportioned Fellow, Red-hair'd, and exceeding all the Inhabitants of St. Kilda in Strength, Climbing, etc.' He was a poet or bard, though he could not read or write, and was 'also endued with that rare Faculty of enjoying the Second Sight, which makes it the more probable that he was haunted by a Familiar Spirit'. He had never been away from the island, 'all his Converse being only with the Steward's Retinue, who were as ignorant of Letters as himself'. He was in fact in most respects a typical islander and seems to have been as genuinely sincere as the rest.

When he was eighteen years old Roderick went fishing on a Sunday, something Martin said was otherwise unknown although in the religious circumstances of Hirt at this time there would be no reason for Sunday fishing to be forbidden. On his way back home, according to his own story, Roderick met a man 'in Lowland Dress', wearing a cloak and hat. He was so surprised he fell on the ground 'in great disorder', whereupon the man announced that he was 'John the Baptist immediately come from Heaven with good Tidings to the Inhabitants of that place, who had been for a long time kept in Ignorance and Error'. When Roderick answered that he was not worthy of the task assigned to him 'John the Baptist' said 'he would instantly make him capable of his Mission', and gave him instructions 'in which he so mixed the laudable Customs of the Church with his own Diabolical Inventions' that the ignorant people could not tell which was which.

In writing of Roderick and his story Martin coloured everything with the language of religious hostility, of which 'impostor' is the outstanding example. One of a people who abhorred 'lying Tricks and Artifices' Roderick was made to seem full of such devices in order to impose his rule upon his neighbours. His experiences and his teaching suggest a man who sought to assume the role of religious pastor in the manner of the Catholic priests of old but who, because no priest had arrived for more than a century or at least none who had stayed for more than a few days, lacked the training and the knowledge to provide an authentic Catholic service. As a consequence Martin was able to ridicule him and treat him as if he were an offender against the 'true religion' claimed by the two visiting inquisitors. In attributing to Roderick 'a Familiar Spirit' Martin was of course himself guilty to a degree of what he considered one of the impostor's faults.

Roderick's respect for John the Baptist would have been entirely acceptable to the Franciscan and Vincentian missionaries of fifty years previously, as would his second-sight and his proneness to visions. The commands he received from John included a strict Friday fast covering all food and even tobacco 'which they love dearly'. The people were told that some of their dead were now saints in heaven, acting as advocates on behalf of the living, and that the anniversary of each such saint was to be celebrated by the person for whom the saint was advocate. The celebrations were to take the form of a liberal entertainment of meat, birds and other dishes, a festival for the neighbours at which the 'priest' Roderick would be the chief guest, with a share sent to his wife and children. Various penances were to be imposed which in Martin's description sound like tortures, of which one was standing in cold water as long as Roderick required. Every family was, for some purpose, to kill a sheep on its own threshold with the blunt edge of a caschrom and not with a sharp knife.

Martin also stated that Roderick 'imposed' his own peculiar religious instructions. He forbade the traditional use of 'the Lord's Prayer, Creed, and Ten Commandments', and instead of them 'prescribed Diabolical Forms of his Own'. He offered up 'Prayers and Rhapsodical Forms', perhaps like the 'superstitious rhapsody' and strange ceremonies reported by Casey ten years before, and he used 'several unintelligible Words' in his 'obscure Prayers' of which he did not know the meaning himself for he had received them from John the Baptist and merely delivered them to his hearers. One of his words was 'Phersichin', verses, which, Martin said, was not known in Hirt 'nor in the North-West Isles, except to such as can Read the Irish Tongue'. This indicates that Roderick had learned 'Phersichin' most probably from someone who was acquainted with a literary source, someone like a missionary priest. A more familiar Catholic invocation was 'a Devout Hymn, which he called the Virgin Mary's, as sent from her', and which he taught to women, 'always in a private House, or some remote place where no Eye could see them but that of Heaven'. What was meant by a private house is not clear since all the houses in the 'village' of 1697 or earlier were so close to each other that many of them touched their neighbours. The hymn was supposed to be 'of such Merit and Efficacy' that its repetition would ensure the safe delivery of a child. Martin claimed that Roderick was paid a sheep by every woman who learned the hymn. Even two hundred years later many hymns to the Virgin Mary were still sung or recited in the Outer Hebrides, especially in Uist and Barra, some of them seeking the safety of the mother about to give birth, and an unsuccessful appeal was made for Roderick's version from anyone who happened to know it.[94]

'The Place and Manner of Teaching this Hymn', Martin noted, only too ready to shed the worst possible light on Roderick, 'afforded him a fair opportunity of Debauching the simple Women; and this some of their number acknowledged to the Minister and me upon Examination'. It is quite likely that the women were just anxious to please the visitors by telling them what they wanted to hear, but if Roderick did in fact 'debauch' any of his neighbours he was evidently no different from the priest Cornelius Con or indeed several

Protestant ministers in more 'civilised' mainland districts. Martin himself also said that he had been told how strangers had landed and attempted 'to Ravish their Women, a practice altogether unknown in St. Kilda, where there has not been one instance of Fornication or Adultery for many Ages before this time', which would seem to contradict what he said of Roderick, but he was inclined to picture the rest of the islanders as models of morality and as a consequence he made Roderick look as if he did not really belong to the community at all. However Martin's description of the people's virtues is so extreme as to verge on nonsense, and the reality must have been markedly different:

> 'The Inhabitants of St. Kilda, are much happier than the generality of Mankind, as being almost the only People in the World who feel the sweetness of true Liberty: What the Condition of the People in the Golden Age is feign'd by the Poets to be, that theirs really is, I mean, in Innocency and Simplicity, Purity, Mutual Love and Cordial Friendship, free from solicitous Cares, and anxious Covetousness; from Envy, Deceit, and Dissumulation; from Ambition and Pride, and the Consequences that attend them. They are altogether ignorant of the Vices of Foreigners, and governed by the Dictates of Reason and Christianity, as it was first delivered to them by those Heroick Souls whose Zeal moved them to undergo danger and trouble to plant Religion here in one of the remotest Corners of the World'.[95]

Simple and in some ways innocent the people of Hirt may have been, but living in the utmost poverty, struggling to survive by climbing on cliffs for food, and subject to often violent weather and long isolation, they could hardly be seen as enjoying 'the sweetness of true Liberty' and 'free from Solicitous Cares', while 'Reason and Christianity' were far from guiding their lives.

Roderick was also accused of having tried 'to alter the common way of Burying' by facing the dead to the south instead of the east, making an example with deceased members of his own family. He went in for incantations, 'long Rhimes, which he called Psalms', and these he sang out 'at his Rhapsodical Preachments'. And he persuaded women that if they 'complied with his New Revelation' they would go to heaven riding on white horses. 'These and many more Ridiculous things, he imposed upon the People'. But, adopting a different attitude towards him, his behaviour in all these respects may not seem nearly so ridiculous.

Rhapsodies, whether in Hirt or in Skye or on the mainland, might have had a Catholic ancestry, or perhaps origins in pre-Christian times, descending through generations as part of a tradition that survived into the twentieth century. His other practices, among them the setting aside of a small piece of ground as an area sacred to John the Baptist with penalties for trespassing upon it, are recognisable as remnants of a half-understood, half-forgotten old faith to which a Ward or a Casey might have 'recovered' the people. A more sympathetic attitude towards Roderick would have led to a gentler treatment than he in fact received.

Although John Campbell was supposed to have visited Hirt before it seems he had done nothing to counteract Roderick who, according to Martin, had 'continued for the space of several Years … to delude these poor innocent well-meaning People'. This is surprising, since Roderick achieved a fair measure of success and his claim to inspiration was no doubt as convincing as a visiting minister's. Eventually however 'his villainous design upon the women' during his private hymn lessons was found out because one woman, the wife of the officer and one of his first converts, proved 'so Heroically Virtuous' as to reveal his intentions to her husband. The latter concealed himself 'in another room' and suddenly appeared at the vital moment to accuse Roderick of being clearly an impostor. Thrown into confusion Roderick admitted some offence and asked pardon of the officer who told him he was 'a Notorious Deceiver' and 'set on by the Devil'. Roderick however was held in great regard by the islanders and succeeded in getting the officer, who may have found in him an unwelcome rival in authority over the people, 'to patch up a Friendship with him'.

In later times the people of Hirt were said to be given to sudden quarrels and impetuous reconciliations, as well as being very hospitable, devoted to rumours, and ready to believe more or less anything they were told. Perhaps this was the case in 1697 and a condition of remote and isolated living. At any rate, in spite of the agreement between Roderick and the officer, stories began to circulate, and it was said by Martin that Roderick's own father, 'who was reputed a very Honest Man' but whose previous dealings with his son are unknown, told him 'that he was a Deceiver, and would come to a fatal end'. It would have been useful if Roderick's ancestry and family were certain, since it is possible that with his red hair and poetic talent that he might have been related to the steward of the time and therefore to Mairi nighean Alasdair Ruaidh. However there is an air of invention about Martin's account of Roderick which makes it difficult to accept what he wrote at face value, and the predictions of an unknown father may have been introduced merely to add to the condemnation of the 'impostor'.

The same doubts surround the incident involving Roderick's supposed cousin. Martin said he was called 'Muldonich, alias Lewis'. This man has something legendary about him. The name 'Muldonich', signifying a religious figure, possibly a monk, occurs oddly as an island off Castlebay in Barra, and far to the north in Sula Sgeir where according to tradition 'a man of the name of Muldona[c]h' lived for five or six weeks and died. A dwelling on Sula Sgeir occupied by this person was known as 'Tigh Muldonich', reckoned to mean

'Ludovick's House', and 'Ludovick' translates as 'Lewis'. In Martin's story Lewis had a ewe with three lambs, all of which were seen feeding on the ground sacred to John the Baptist. Lewis refused to kill the animals according to the rule, declaring that such slaughter as an act of worship would be both ridiculous and unheard of in the Hebrides as a religious practice. Roderick threatened heavenly punishment, Lewis persisted in refusal, and when nothing happened to him the people began to have 'less Veneration for the Impostor than before'.[96]

In the end it was supposed to have been a Harris boy called John who initiated Roderick's downfall; perhaps here too Martin wished to make fun of his belief in John the Baptist. One night, while Roderick was holding a meeting, John, who with his father was staying in Hirt for a year and helping to mend the boat, chanced to enter the house where Roderick was preaching. In the dark interior he listened to what went on and afterwards told his father all that he had heard. The father in turn told the steward when he arrived, and the latter, being much concerned at the news, took Roderick away with him and sent him to Skye. Here the 'impostor' stood before Iain Breac at Dunvegan and was ordered not to preach any more on pain of death. This both shocked and disappointed Roderick for he had been of the belief that MacLeod was wanting to hear him preach and would probably become one of his followers. In a dazed state he returned to Hirt, only to face, in due course, strict examination by Martin and Campbell.

The two visitors performed their duties of enquiry as if their victim was being examined before a kirk session though the task took up a large proportion of the three weeks they were in Hirt. When the investigation was over Roderick appeared to accept the truth of what had been recorded about him, and then went to church, presumably Teampall Chriosd, where, after a service conducted by Campbell, he made his confession to those present. Prayers were said for 'this poor Wretch', and everybody, including all the other island inhabitants, went out to the sacred piece of ground with Roderick in the lead. He was ordered to pull down part of the wall he had built round the ground, and when after about an hour he and the people helping him had finished the assembled company was made to scatter the stones 'up and down in the Field, lest their Posterity might see such a Monument of Folly and Ignorance'. Rebuke followed:

'We Reproved the Credulous People for complying implicitly with such Follies and Delusions as were delivered to them by the Impostor; and all of them with one Voice answered, That what they did was Unaccountable; but seeing one of their own number and stamp in all respects, endued, as they fancied, with a powerful faculty of Preaching so fluently and frequently, and pretending to Converse with John the Baptist, they were induc'd to believe his Mission from Heaven, and therefore complied with his Commands without dispute, and the rather, because he did not change their Laws of Neighbourhood'.

In the presence of Martin and Campbell they now expressed regret and hoped that God would pardon their error. A 'happy' conclusion had been reached: 'They are now overjoyed to find themselves undeceived, and the Light of the Gospel restored to them, as it was as first delivered to their Ancestors by the first Christian Monks, who had gone thither to Instruct them'. Thus one of the few instances of independent action on the part of an islander came to nothing and its possibly fascinating consequences remain a subject for mere speculation.

Whatever the form of the Gospel, if any, brought to Hirt around 700, religion in the island at the approach of 1700 was not the same as it had been nor had it yet assumed any new shape. Although the Catholic church had been as near to a direct successor of the early Irish monastic religion as there was, it became in due course a claim of the Protestant churches that they were the true followers of the Columba missionaries. But as Martin and Campbell prepared to leave the island they were bound to abandon the population to its undirected, indefinite state, in which faint versions and other marks of old and new faiths mixed together along with superstition of a different kind, legend, and the legacy of the 'impostor' who innocently practised his beliefs at the spiritual crossroads where the new country was about to begin.

*

Roderick, the so-called 'impostor', departed Hirt with the minister of Harris and Martin Martin in the late summer of 1697. He was delivered to the servants of the steward on the island of Pabbay where he was kept 'in Custody in order to his Trial'. Later he was removed once more to Skye, 'made Publick Confession in several Churches', and was ordered never to return to his home. As the boat taking him away from his birthplace was hidden by the ocean swell it was as if the people on the island looked upon the dying of a faded and broken world. There was darkness even in his going. When on the way out to Hirt that boat had been caught in bad weather at Boreray the despair of the rowers had apparently been heightened by their belief 'that all this Misfortune proceeded from the Impostor ... who they believed had employed the Devil to raise this extraordinary Storm against Mr Campbel, Minister, who was to counteract him'. And when the party left towards the end of June the islanders, said Martin, tried to prevent them from taking Roderick on board, not because they knew that they might never see him again, but because it had been noticed that whenever he had been employed by the steward to journey to or from Pabbay the boat he was in was always beset by storms. Roderick had apparently been one of the crew when the steward's boat was driven to Rona: 'the Steward's Wife, and all his Crew making their reflections upon these Dangers since the discovery of his Imposture, could never be prevailed upon to receive him again into their Boat'. These remarks are obviously a contradiction of Martin's other statements on the impostor's superstitious beliefs and on his never having been out of the island.[97]

There was indeed something rather hypocritical about Martin's dealings with Roderick. The latter's curious religious forms were dismissed as ridiculous, yet the belief of the islanders that his presence in a boat could influence the weather was described in all seriousness, and throughout the rest of Martin's writing superstitious practices which might seem far more ridiculous were presented without condemnation. This, and the separate section in the book, sets the 'impostor' enquiry firmly apart from the general account of life in Hirt and emphasises the importance of the religious or church aspect of Martin and Campbell's visit.

*

Three surviving religious buildings were, in 1697, still in reasonable repair, and inside one of them, Teampall Chriosd, was a brass crucifix 'not exceeding a Foot in length' which lay on the altar. The figure of Christ was attached: 'the Body is compleatly done, distended, and having a Crown on, all in the Crucified Posture'. Here too was a sign of superstition so far as the Protestant church was concerned; while held 'in great Reverence' this object of devotion was not worshipped in itself but was brought into use on special 'Occasions of Marriage, and Swearing decisive Oaths, which puts an end to all Strife'. It was an instrument of law in Hirt as well as of religion. In 1883 Donald MacDonald had never heard of it, so perhaps John Campbell had suggested that it should be destroyed.[98]

If the population of Hirt in 1697 was correctly stated at 180 then it is not surprising that Teampall Chriosd alone could not accommodate all the inhabitants. Apart from Roderick there was no one to take services unless Campbell from Harris or some other minister or priest had come out on a visit, which seems to have happened only very rarely. So on Sunday mornings the islanders gathered in the graveyard, 'fenced in', as it was, 'with a little Stone Wall', and there 'devoutly say the Lord's Prayer, Creed, and Ten Commandments', this being the full extent of the ritual. It was also 'an ancient Custom delivered down to them from their Ancestors' that they should cease labour at noon on Saturday until Monday morning, and being Christians 'much of the Primitive Temper, neither inclined to Enthusiasm nor to Popery', they observed the custom faithfully. Ceasing labour however did not mean abstaining from recreation over the same period. They believed in 'the Holy Trinity', 'a State of Future Happiness and Misery', and that everything was determined by God. But setting Christianity aside, 'They have a Notion, that

Spirits are embodied; these they fancy to be locally in Rocks, Hills, and where-ever they list in an instant'; and they venerated certain wells. The mixture of religious and non-religious behaviour was clearly seen in the celebration of certain festivals, including Christmas, Good Friday, Easter, St. Columba's Day, and Michaelmas or All Saints, at the last of which, like many communities in the islands, they held 'an Anniversary Cavalcade'.[99]

Should a priest or minister appear in Hirt his main task was to ratify or repeat the ceremonies carried out in his absence by the islanders themselves. This was especially evident in the case of marriage and baptism, for which the crucifix and often the local officer were needed. According to Martin, when two people wished to marry the officer called all the people to Teampall Chriosd, where, after enquiring 'if there be any lawful Impediment' and hearing no objection, he asked the couple if they were willing to live together 'in Weal and Woe, etc.' On their agreeing to do so he then requested them to confirm their promise publicly before God by setting the right hand on the crucifix and swearing fidelity. Celebrations then followed. As for baptism, when a child was born the parents summoned the officer or any of their neighbours to conduct the ceremony, while another neighbour, possibly a close friend or relative, was appointed to be 'Sponsor' or 'Gossip', in Gaelic 'goistidh'. The parent 'holding up the Child, he that acts the Minister, Inquyres the Childs name and thereafter sayeth I Baptize yow AB to your father and mother, in the name of the father, the son and holy Ghost'. Then the sponsor took the child into his arms, as did his wife who was 'banaghoistidh' - godmother.[100]

The relationship of the 'goistidh' to the parent was a very close one, for, as Martin described it, 'there is a Friendship between the Parent and the Sponsor, which is esteemed so sacred and inviolable, that no Accident, how cross soever, is able to set them at variance; and it reconciles such as have been at Enmity formerly'. When Roderick and the officer were reconciled the latter 'condescended to be the Impostor's Gossip, i.e. Sponsor at the Baptism of one of his Children'; and that Dugan and Fearchar could refer to each other as 'goistidh' suggests either that they were so linked after a baptism or, more probably, that the bond between them was comparable with that between parent and sponsor. The custom seems ancient, and while familiar in a Catholic context may go back to a pre-Christian age for it has been considered equivalent to 'blood-brothering', and Martin noted that 'When there is no opportunity of being Sponsor to one another, and it is necessary to enter into Bonds of Friendship at Baptism; the Inhabitants of the Western Isles, supplied this Ceremony by Tasting a drop of each other's Blood'. The blood was 'commonly drawn out of the little Finger'. This custom was not associated with baptisms only for Martin added that 'ancient Leagues of Friendship' in the islands were ratified in this manner and 'Religiously observ'd as a sacred Bond', anyone violating it being henceforward 'reputed unworthy of all honest Mens Conversation'. The word 'goisteachd' has been more recently explained as 'spiritual kinship'. A state achieved even in youth when one young man put his blood on another's knuckles and said 'I have done "goisteachd" to you', which meant that the two of them were friends for evermore and that nothing would separate them. In general 'goisteachd' could not be established between a boy and a girl for it would mean that one did not like the other. 'Goisteachd' excluded marriage.[101]

An accompaniment to marriages in Hirt, and probably to most festivals and ceremonies there and in other islands, was the merry-making on which Martin also commented. The visitors in June 1697 may have themselves enjoyed such celebrations: 'Mr Campbell, the Minister, Married ... Fifteen Pair of the Inhabitants on the Seventeenth of June, who immediately after their Marriage, join'd in a Country Dance, having only a Bagpipe for their Musick, which pleased them exceedingly'. The number of couples may indicate either that John Campbell was neglectful of this duty on a previous visit or else that he never visited at all, but it might also indicate a recent settlement, which could help to account for the difference between the ten families earlier in the century and the size of the population noted by Martin.[102]

Songs were part of the merry-making, and Roderick was not the only bard in Hirt: 'There are some of both Sexes who have a Genius for Poetry, and are great admirers of Musick: The Trump or Jewish Harp is all the Musical Instrument they have, which disposes them to Dance mightily'. But they must have had 'a Bagpipe' unless this instrument was brought by one of the steward's men or unless Martin was once again contradicting himself. Màiri nighean Alasdair Ruaidh would not have been out of place in an island where the women 'Sing and Jest for Diversion, and in their way, understand Poetry, and make Rhimes in their Language'. They sang too when waulking cloth, 'one of their Number acting the part of a Prime Chantress, whom all the rest follow and Obey'. There was nothing barbaric about this, nor were the inhabitants of Hirt exceptional. Those who gathered in Eoropie, Ness, at 'Hallowtide' came out of the old church into fields 'where they fell a drinking their Ale, and spent the remainder of the Night in Dancing, and Singing etc.' And more generally in Lewis Martin learned that 'several of both Sexes have a Gift of Poesy, and are able to form a Satyr or Panegyrick ex tempore, without the assistance of any stronger Liquor than Water to raise their Fancy. They are great lovers of Musick; and when I was there they gave an account of 18 Men who could play on the Violin pretty well, without being taught ..' A kind of song accompanied funerals in Hirt, comparable perhaps to the howling of women which met with the disapproval of the Argyll Synod; the people of Hirt 'bewail the Death of their Relations excessively, and upon those Occasions make doleful Songs, which they call Laments'. This mourning could be carried to extremes, and when the news of the death of Iain Breac reached them 'they abandoned their Houses, Mourning Two Days in the Field'. A similar response may have greeted the death of the steward, whose fate, like that of MacLeod, was supposed to be heralded by the appearance on the island of a cuckoo.[103]

The steward of Hirt, with what was called his 'Retinue' of convalescents and servants, was in the island at the same time as Martin and Campbell, although the two parties had travelled separately. June - often about the middle of the month - was the usual time for his annual visit in his 'Birlin, or Galley', and it is not impossible that the population figure given by Martin included his company: 'The Steward's Retinue consist of Forty, Fifty, or Sixty Persons, and among them, perhaps, the most Meagre in the Parish are carried thither to be recruited with good Chear; but this Retinue is now retrenched, as also some of their Ancient and unreasonable Exactions'. It would seem that these 'exactions' were a survival of the once widespread custom known in some places as 'conveth', the obligatory hospitality provided as a service to a king or other leading figure. Although treated as a sort of rent several 'exactions' were still expected in Hirt in the 1690s. On arrival the steward and his party were given all the milk available 'in a Treat'. A second 'Treat' was supplied on St Columba's Day. Throughout his stay until well into August he lived 'upon the Charge of the Inhabitants', which seemed 'long enough' to a people who had to devote most of their resources to maintaining the visitors, each providing amounts measured 'with regard to their respective Proportions of Lands and Rocks ..' The continuation of the practice could have been maintained as a tradition among stewards, who in the seventeenth century at least were successive members of the same family.[104]

The steward in 1697, Alexander MacLeod, farmed in Pabbay, Harris, where he held the lease or 'tack' of Baile na Cille, and was also said to be tenant of land in Skye. Each summer he set off on the hazardous voyage to Hirt to collect rents in kind, for which he 'pays Yearly to his Master an Acknowledgment of the various Products of this Isle'. His father was Norman and his grandfather Neil, brother of Màiri nighean Alasdair Ruaidh. Both Norman and Neil were, it is supposed, stewards of Hirt and tenants of Baile na Cille, thus providing a continuity which strengthened the long association of Hirt with Pabbay.[105]

Martin also referred to 'The Stewards Deputy', his representative in Hirt, who 'is one of the Natives, and stays always upon the place; he has free Lands, and an Omer of Barley from each Family; and has the honour of being the first and last in their Boat, as they go and come to the lesser Isles or Rocks'. This 'deputy' was the officer, whose few acres were allowed him in return for his service. Each year he received special gifts which must have re-established his standing on the island and confirmed his position of authority. The steward gave him 'the Bonnet worn by himself upon his going out of the Island', while the steward's wife 'leaves with the Officer's Wife the Kerch, or Head-dress worn by herself' and 'an Ounce of Indigo'. In 1697 the officer was 'Donald Mack-Gill-Colm', who shares with 'the impostor' the distinction of being the first islander to be known by name. Originally, wrote Martin, the officer was elected by the people of Hirt, 'but now the Stewards have the Nomination of him absolutely'. He evidently believed himself to be a cut above the rest of the islanders. 'The officer made a good figure Sunday after our Arrivall having a Cravat and a Coat in the Fashion, with breeches wide at the knee'. There was good reason for his conceit, since he had various important duties, including service as 'President over them in all their Debates', managing with the aid of the crucifix and a system of drawing lots if necessary the allocation of land and cliff, conducting marriages, settling disputes, reporting offences to the steward, and on rare occasions representing the people to the landlord. When there was disagreement between the people and the steward over the condition of their wooden measuring vessel the issue was put by the steward to Martin and Campbell, but the islanders would not accept anything other than a decision from MacLeod, so the officer was deputed 'as Envoy (according to the Ancient Custom) to represent their case', with the boat's crew acting as a check upon him lest 'his Dependance upon the Steward might be apt to bias him'. The decision to send the officer 'was the result of a General Council, in which the Master of every Family has a Vote, since every Family pays this Officer an Amir of Barly per Annum, to maintain his character'.[106]

A curious ritual took place when the steward and his deputy entered into argument, which the latter was bound to do in certain circumstances:

'he is obliged always to dispute with the Steward for what is due to any of them, and never to give over until he has obtained his Demand, or put the Steward into such a Passion, that he gives the Officer at least Three Strokes with his Cudgel over the Crown of his Head; after these Three Strokes he has done the utmost that is required of him by their Ancient Customs. I enquired of the Officer (who told me this passage) what if the Steward give him but One Blow over the Crown, he answered, That the Inhabitants would not be satisfied if he did not so far plead as to Irritate the Steward to give both a Second and a Third Blow; I had the farther curiosity to enquire of the Steward himself if he was wont to Treat the Officer in this manner; who answered, That it was an Ancient Custom, which in his short time he had not had occasion to practise, but if he should, he would not confine himself to the Number of Three Blows, if the Officer should prove Indiscreet'.

In spite of running the risk of more than three blows on the head the officer had to show his appreciation not only of his appointment but also of the allowance of land and the presents of bonnet and kerch:

'The Steward has a large cake of Barly presented to him by the Officer at every Meal, and it must be made so large as shall be sufficient to satisfy Three Men at a time, and by way of Eminence it is baked in the Form of a Triangle, and furrowed Twice round; the Officer is likewise obliged to furnish the Steward with Mutton, or Beef, to his Dinner every Sunday during his Residence in the Island'.[107]

All in all, the impression of life in Hirt conveyed by the records of the time is that at the beginning of the eighteenth century ancient custom and ritualised ways of dealing with most events constituted the manner in which it was conducted. For everyone apart from the officer and his wife dress was of a standard kind with no marked individuality or variations, from the linen headdress worn by women to the circular brass buckle with which they used to fix a plaid on the chest. Probably there was nothing unique to Hirt about clothing except for the gannet-neck footwear, the inhabitants of Pabbay going about in similar style, although 'the Buckle antiently worn by the Steward's Wives were of Silver, but the present Steward's Wife makes no use of either this Dress or Buckle'. An equally formal and ancient custom was the islanders' supposed readiness to be hospitable and self-sacrificing towards strangers. When the Lowland crew of a ship that came into the bay in 1696 behaved badly this charitable attitude must have been as sorely tested as on many previous occasions, for instance when Coll Ciotach landed in 1615; and suspicion of the unknown seems naturally to have been a lasting feature of exposed, isolated and kindly communities in the remoter parts of the Highlands and Hebrides.[108]

*

When the Synod members arrived in Skye from Harris in August 1696 they dealt with certain matters in that island. They admitted Mr Martin MacPherson to the charge of 'Sleat and Strathuaradale with the Isles Rum Egg Canna and Muk' and sought to revive the lapsed presbytery of Skye which was newly erected in the early autumn. Having originally departed on the 'visitation' journey with worries about 'the desolate conditiones of the Isles of the Hebrides and adjacent parts both continent and other Islands, and how they are pestered with traffequeing Jesuits', the members seem to have heard and done nothing to dispel these fears, and on 4 June 1697, as Martin and Campbell were beginning their work in Hirt, the Synod issued a general instruction to all ministers 'to make Search if there be any that uses witchcraft, charmes, Spells, divinations, bone reading, familiar Spirits, seeking and giving responses'. If they found any of these 'abominations' going on they were to 'processe' the offenders 'ecclesiastically' or 'delate them to the civill Magistrat'. In addition each minister was to preach against and 'open up the nature of these horrid evills'. Had it been already reported, which it probably had been, the case of Roderick called 'the impostor' would have proved a convenient example.[109]

At this time too those ministers who had served as Episcopal incumbents during the years of Charles II's reign and were so doing at the revolution in 1689 were meant to have decided between resigning their charge and accepting restored presbyterianism. Some who refused to do the latter were in places deprived of their livings, but others, especially in remoter or very strongly Episcopalian districts, were allowed to continue, although there was an increasing presbyterian view that both Episcopal ministers and roaming Catholic priests posed a threat as being allied to the Jacobite movement. At its meeting in June 1697 the Synod heard that Mr John Fraser Episcopal minister in Tiree and some others wished to be received into the presbyterian 'ministerial communion', but owing to stormy weather the Skye presbytery had still 'had no accesse to Summond Mr Alexander Cooper intruder in north uist nor Mr Alan Morison intruder in Nesse in Lewis'. These two, whose presence had caused concern the previous year, were 'intruders' because they were or had been Episcopalians, and John Campbell at Rodel would now have been considered an 'intruder' as well.[110]

There was not much that could be done about Alan Morison, who remained an Episcopal 'deserter' from North Uist and 'intruder' in the parish of 'Nesse and Cladich' in June 1699. Having in mind 'the greatnes of the charg of Nesse and Cladich, and that some relicts of Heathenisme and Popery ignorance and prophanity are there abounding' and knowing 'the vast distance that parioch is from any Supply the great number of Souls within the said parioch the discontiguity of the towns the danger of the inrods of the Priests with other weighty consideratiounes', the Synod decided to allow to Mr Alan the year's stipend, for he was better than nothing, especially as both he and Cooper, and perhaps Campbell, were willing to accept presbyterian qualification if the weather would only allow them to attend the Synod's assembly. Although storms may have provided an excuse for no change and non-attendance, at least Morison and his like were rather better than popery.[111]

Nevertheless the Synod assembly in June 1699 understood that North Uist, being remote from supply of ministers, even though Cooper was apparently still there, was 'Lyable to the inroads of the priests, and in hazard to run to poperie and heathenism'. There was evidently nothing exceptional about North Uist in this respect, for the same threat had been envisaged in 'Nesse and Cladich' and presented itself to presbyterian authority in many more islands and districts of the west coast. The presbytery of Skye found it difficult if not impossible to counteract papist intervention even in nearby islands and cannot have devoted much time or thought to the isolated population of Hirt after the removal of Roderick. Furthermore the presbytery did not know what to do with Roderick after he was brought to Skye for processing 'ecclesiastically'. So in the late summer or autumn of 1700, three years after he had been taken from Hirt, a letter was sent by the presbytery to the Synod asking for help, and on 19 October the Synod gave consideration to that letter, 'this day presented to them', from their Skye brethren,

> 'representing that there are severall priests come from Ireland to the northern Isles, perverting the people, and that there is one Mcinaish, now in their presbyterie, professing his repentance for deludeing the people of Saint Kilda, and alledging that John the Baptist useallie appeared to him, and that he was John the Baptists preacher, desireing to know what method to take with him as to the church censure'.[112]

The Synod did not know what to do with Roderick either. As regards 'the Deluder Mackinnaish', its commissioners to the General Assembly had been told 'to consult what method to take with him'. While the rest of the Roderick story remains as yet unknown, the name of 'Mcinaish' or 'Mackinnaish' indicates that he was a son of Angus, but it still does not allow a precise identification of his ancestry.[113]

The invaders from Ireland, on the other hand, were not treated as a matter for the General Assembly but for 'Brigadier Maiteland' and his troops at Fort William, to whom an order had already been sent 'for suppressing priests and their abbettors', among them the Catholic Bishop Thomas Nicolson, born in Aberdeenshire, who was now the most significant. In the summer months of 1700 Bishop Nicolson, emerging from the shelter provided for him by the Duke of Gordon, made his own courageous 'visitation' through the Catholic Highlands and islands, landing in Eigg, Rum, Canna, South Uist and Barra, and seeking to rescue the people in these and other places from the dangers of presbyterian influence. He and the priests who were busy in the same areas were constantly at risk of being apprehended and imprisoned by the Brigadier's men, but they appear to have found protection among numerous sympathisers who gave their support in spite of various acts and dictates against papists by the Privy Council, the General Assembly and other lesser Protestant authorities. Rumours that 'The pope pays each priest five pounds sterling for each proselyte he makes' were counterbalanced by measures taken against priests, Jesuits and trafficking papists which included rewards for seizing them, banishment and even death. For instance, 'If any person be found in any Meeting where there is any Altar, Mass-Book, or other Instruments of Popish Superstition, and shall refuse to purge ... it shall be sufficient Ground ... to Banish, under any Certification ... even to that of Death'. Neither the altar nor the crucifix in Hirt was any longer to be tolerated, should anyone happen to remember they were there or read Martin Martin's book.[114]

The possibility of enlisting a powerful arm of the civil law such as Mr John Campbell, brother to the Earl of Argyll and 'justiciar depute', to supplement the efforts of Brigadier Maitland against the papists and adherents like 'Lauchlan mackhearlich vic finguon, in Keanuachdarach Scalpa', who assaulted the parish minister Martin MacPherson, added a sense of potential effectiveness to the threatening pronouncements of the Protestant kirk in its attempt to deal with those of whom it disapproved, but it did not greatly ease the difficulties of tracking them down and of finding means of daily religious supervision in the remote places they frequented. Hirt, now often called St Kilda, was a likely retreat, it was imagined, for itinerant priests and other dangerous characters, its innocent population all too ready to yield to their influence and persuasions, but it was not the only community at risk. There were isolated corners of the mainland just as prone to the teachings of 'Romish Missionaries'. The activities of Roderick had after all been successful, and 'The gross Ignorance of the People in those parts, together with some late Endeavours to reduce the Inhabitants of the Isle of Hirta, or St. Kilda, into a State of Heathenism' made it necessary, not that they should be provided with 'such Treatises as prove the Truth of the Christian Religion', as was suggested, but that since they could not read anyway they should have the personal attention of a willing and industrious Protestant set of missionaries instead.[115]

Hirt was believed by some to be linked to the parish of Harris under John Campbell and like all the islands in the Outer Hebrides to come within the bounds of the presbytery of Skye. This would have meant that Campbell was responsible for keeping out the priests, as he had been, in part, for getting rid of Roderick. However the church authorities knew differently:

> 'The Synod considering that Saint Kilda or Hirta has no minister and that it is a pendicle of no parioch; resolves to address the Lords of Plantation, for a fond [i.e. fund], either to setle a minister in the said Hirta; or to adjoine the same to Harres or North uist: and till a Distinct minister be gotten to Saint Kilda, that the Lords aforsaid grant a fond, for a constant catechist, who can teach the children to read, and instruct the people in the fundamentalls of relligion'.[116]

Almost as an afterthought there was added:'(Let such as revise this book, bring in the consideration of Saint Kilda, to the Generall assemblie.)' It was in this way that the General Assembly, with little understanding of the implications, was launched into a sea of problems every bit as unpredictable and hazardous as the tides and weathers of Caolas Hirt. Its task was to introduce a 'constant catechist' prepared to cut himself off from the 'civilized' world and to devote himself to establishing 'the true Protestant religion' among a people whose customs and beliefs and traditions would be utterly strange to him. With his appointment a new era in the history of Hirt would begin and the island would become a focus of interest among those whose ignorance of life there was at least as great as the often-mentioned ignorance of the islanders. Could such a brave catechist be found?

[1]   NC (Evidence) Vol.II p.873

[2]   Martin (1698) p.84

[3]   A Carmichael: 'Grazing and Agrestic Customs of the Outer Hebrides' in NC (Report) Appendix A pp.460, 473, 482

[4]   CWC no.126

[5]   NC (Evidence) Vol. II p.869

[6]   Watson (1965) pp. xiv, xv, xvii; Matheson (1953) pp.11-25; MacKillop p.148; Watson (1965) pp.6-7 cf. Berneray saying: 'Irt nan caorach ghorma' [MacKillop p.156]; Map: 'Aebudae Insulae sive Hebrides' in J Blaeu: Atlas Novus Amsterdam 1654.
      Alexander Carmichael [CWC no.465] noted in 1872 that 'North Uist is Known among Western Islanders as Caolas Ioirt (the land on) "the Sound of Ioirt" or St Kilda', but his understanding that the name applied to North Uist may be mistaken.

[7]   W J Watson: The History of the Celtic Place-Names of Scotland Edinburgh & London 1926 pp.98-99. In 1896 John MacKenzie, factor for St Kilda, stated that in Skye 'mothers say to their children when they are troublesome, "If you don't be quiet, I'll send you to St Kilda"' [Kearton p.18]. Neither this nor the story of Lady Grange seems in itself to be strong enough evidence for concluding that 'the progenitors of the St. Kildans were undoubtedly transported from Skye by the Chief of MacLeod for various offences' [Kearton p.18]. In Raasay children were told 'Teich le t-anam gu Crodhlinn', while in the Outer Hebrides they were also once threatened with Barbadoes and Halifax in New England [the late William Matheson]. An example from a political setting occurred in October 1885: 'Addressing the electors on Saturday in the Kirkhill district, Mr Fraser-Mackintosh said his friend, Mr Campbell, had asked him…what was to be done with Sheriff Ivory? - (laughter and applause, and a voice, "Send him to St Kilda.") ' [HN Vol. III no.108 2 November 1885]

[8]   A B Taylor: 'The Norsemen in St. Kilda' in Saga Book Viking Society for Northern Research, University College, London 1967-1968 Vol.XVII Parts 2-3 pp.116-144; Palsson (1996) p.314; Palsson (1996/2) pp.22-23

[9]   MacKillop p.150. A sculptured stone from the burying ground at 'Cill aiseam', located incorrectly, it seems, in 'Bearnaray, Barra', was sent to the former National Museum of Scotland by Alexander Carmichael [CWC NO.457]. Martin (1703) pp.67, 68

[10] Palsson (1996/2) p.18; Munro (1981) pp.17-19; Morrison (1989) p.149

[11] J Marsden: Sea Road of the Saints: Celtic Holy Men in the Hebrides Edinburgh 1995 pp.165-184

[12] CWC no.231 (e), no.106 (2 September 1870). In a letter of 19 April 1892 to Carmichael John Stewart, Bachuil, Lismore, added some further Gaelic lines, but 'all the old people who had interest in folk lore are gone - and so very little can be gathered in Lismore now' [CWC no.382]. In some versions Columba and Moluag were said to be brothers. A more detailed account of Moluag's connection with Lismore is given by I Carmichael [Lismore in Alba pp.35-66].

[13] ESSH Vol. I p.35 (quoting Irish Life of Columba - Stokes's Three Homilies); CWC no.368; RCAHCM p.17 no.63; ESSH Vol. I p.95 (quoting Annals of Tigernach); Cowan (1995) p.136; CWC no.362. The church is called Teampull Chaluim Chille in RCAHCM [p.99 no.339]. Nearby is Tobar Chaluim Chille.

[14] ESSH Vol. I pp.320-321 (quoting Gretti's Saga)

[15] ESSH Vol. I pp.340,341 (quoting Landnamabok and Dicuil's account of Thule)

[16] ESSH Vol. I pp.342-344 (quoting Landnamabok)

[17] ESSH Vol. I pp360-361 (quoting Landnamabok, Eyrbyggia Saga)

[18] D O' Donoghue (edit.) : Lives and Legends of Saint Brendan the Voyager Reprint Felinfach 1994 pp.25-29; CWC no.465

[19] CG Vol. II p.293 (Note on 'Iol, iola'). Also from Uist came verse about the green isle:
                    'Thainig Rocabarra ris,
                    Thainig e ris an dara uair,
                    Thig crioch air an t-saoghal
                    'Nuair thig Rocabarra ris a rithis' [CWC no.138]

[20] CWC no.138

[21] CWC nos.138, 465

[22] Cowan (1995) pp.129-131

[23] D E R Watt: 'Bishops in the Isles before 1203: Bibliography and Biographical Lists' in IR Vol. XLV no.2 (Autumn) 1994 pp.112-113

[24] Cowan (1995) p.140

[25] Munro (1986) p.208 A3; B Webster: Regesta Regum Scottorum Vol.VI The Acts of David II, King of Scots 1329-1371 Edinburgh 1982 pp.114-115 no.73; Cowan (1967) pp.16, 83, 107, 109, 179; Munro (1986) pp.28-29 no.18

[26] Munro (1986) p209 A6; RMS Vol. I (1306-1424) p.147 no.412, p.201 no.551; Munro (1986) pp.10-11 no.7; RMS Vol. I p.189 no.520. There has been doubt over whether 'Heryce' and 'Hyrte' denoted Hirt or Harris [Munro (1982) pp.16-19] but it seems certain that Hirt was intended.

[27] Munro (1986) pp.34-35 no.21; RMS Vol. II (1424-1513) p.485 no.2287 (Confirmation dated 12 November 1495); MGC Vol. II pp.179-180. This Roderick MacNeil was known as 'Ruairi an Tartair', and the island he could not find has been identified as Rocabarraidh [J L Campbell (edit.): Tales from Barra Told by the Coddy Edinburgh 1960 pp.32-33]

[28] W F Skene (edit.): John of Fordun's Chronicle of the Scottish Nation Reprint Felinfach 1993 Vol. I p.40; Munro (1961) p.78; Munro (1986) pp.227-228 A51; RMS Vol. II p.514 no.2420 (15 June 1498)

[29] Gregory pp.72-74; MacPhail Vol. I p.25

[30] N Macdonald: The Morrison Manuscript - Traditions of the Western Isles by Donald Morrison, Cooper, Stornoway National Society Daughters of Founders and Patriots of America 1975 pp.286-287; H Palsson & P Edwards (trans.): The Book of Settlements (Landnamabok) Winnipeg 1972 p.91

[31] CWC no.395

[32] E.g. A B Taylor: 'The Name "St Kilda"' in Scottish Studies Vol.13 (1969) pp.145-158. 'Hirtha' occurs in the early sixteenth century account by Boece [PHB]

[33] J Macinnes: 'A Folktale from St Kilda' in Scottish Studies Vol.5 Part 2 (1961) pp.215-219; Thomas (1874) pp.704, 708-709. Also versions from, among others, the late Rev. Donald J Gillies and the late Rev. Donald Ferguson, both of St Kilda.

[34] Thomas (1874) p.704

[35] Sibbald Adv MS 33.3.20 Description of the Islands 'taken from severall manuscripts, and the Relations of thes that Lived in them or frequented them' p.40; J M MacKinlay: Ancient Church Dedications in Scotland (Scriptural Dedications) Edinburgh 1910 pp.44-45; Martin (1698) p.83

[36] J M MacKinlay: Ancient Church Dedications in Scotland (Non-Scriptural Dedications) Edinburgh 1914 pp.36-55, 65-70; Martin (1698) pp.83,88

[37] Thomas (1874) p.705

[38] Thomas (1874) p.705; CWC no. 58 A p.183

[39] C Burns (edit.): Calendar of Papal Letters to Scotland of Clement VII of Avignon 1378-1394 SHS (Fourth Series Vol.12) Edinburgh 1976 p.79; E R Lindsay & A I Cameron (edits.): Calendar of Scottish Supplications to Rome 1418-1422 SHS (Third Series Vol.23) Edinburgh 1934 pp.264-265, 164, 267-269, 276

[40] Munro (1961) pp.77-78 Traditions and customs associated with certain places and objects in the island suggest continuity of belief from early, even pre-Christian times. These are indicated by placenames and occasional brief descriptions. For instance, Tobar a ' Chleirich, the clerk's well, may derive from a pre-Reformation, Catholic age, as might Tigh an Triar, but Tobar nam Buaidh, well of virtues, and the Liani-nin-ore,' that is to say the plain of spells, exorcisms, or prayers' (MacAulay pp.88-89), could preserve pagan elements from a much older period.

[41] Munro (1961) p.11 etc.

[42] Munro (1961) p.78; PHB pp.88-89. Boece refers to 'The last and outmaist Ile...namit Hirtha'. Sibbald Adv MS 31.2.6 p.24; also W F Skene: Celtic Scotland: A History of Ancient Alban Edinburgh 1880 Vol. III Appendix III The Description of the Isles of Scotland c.1595 p.432. Here Skene replaces 'In auld times' with 'In all times' but, since this would, in the circumstances, not make sense, the manuscript must surely be correct. Sibbald Adv MS 31.2.6 p.24 cf. Adv MS 33.3.20 p.50 'In Ancient tymes they kept a priest' etc.

[43] Munro (1961) p.78

[44] Sibbald Adv MS 31.2.6 pp.22, 24; Skene (1880) Vol. III Appendix III pp.428, 431

[45] Munro (1961) p.78; PHB p.88; Sibbald Adv MS 31.2.6 p.24; Sibbald Adv MS 15.1.1 Description of Hirta f.217. This is the account brought in by Sir Robert Moray. Martin, writing nearly a century later, noted further subdivisions of land: 'Their Arable Land is very nicely parted into Ten Divisions, and these into Subdivisions, each Division distinguished by the Name of some

Deceased Man or Woman, who were Natives of the Place..' (1698 p.28). If each of the ten lots of land had been subdivided once into equal parts the resulting twenty lots would correspond closely to the number of families present around 1800, but soon after Martin's visit there appear to have been about 30 families which would probably have meant a threefold or fourfold division of the ten lots, at least for a period. See Part IV p.274 and n.12 for further comment.

[46] Watson (1965) p.xvii. It is even claimed that most probably she was born at Ullinish in Skye. Matheson (1953) provides details of Mary MacLeod's family [see n.6].

[47] Gregory pp.286, 293; RPC Vol. VI (1599-1604) p.256

[48] RPC Vol. VIII (1604-1607) p.341; Gregory pp.314-315

[49] Gregory p.330; CRA pp.112-115

[50] CRA pp.115-118

[51] RMS Vol. VI (1593-1608) p.719 no.1981; CSP Vol. XIII (1597-1603) Part 2 pp.737-738 no.586 20 November 1600; MacKenzie (1903) p.217; RPC Vol. VII pp.84-90; RMS Vol. VII (1609-1620) pp.95 no.259, 168-169 no.458. The Sheriff Court Records of Aberdeenshire contain two references to Ker. On 21 May 1610 'Sir Thomas Kar of Hertho Knicht factour and uptaker' of the Marquis of Huntly's 'leiwing' [living] was recorded as having performed a service for 'the said nobill lord'; and on 3 October 1611 John Ker was served as heir to 'Sir Thomas Ker of Hirtha, knight, his father' [D. Littlejohn (edit.) Records of the Sheriff Court of Aberdeenshire New Spalding Club Vol. II (1598-1649) Aberdeen 1906 pp.157, 164]

[52] MacPhail Vol. III pp.185-186

[53] Calendar of the State Papers of Ireland (1615-1625) pp.57-59 no.103; MacPhail Vol. III pp.241-242. This gives no doubt a more accurate version of MacLeod's letter than that in BD Vol. II (1700-1920) pp.53-55. R Black: 'Colla Ciotach' in TGSI Vol. 48 (1972-1974) p.210; D Stevenson: Alasdair MacColla and the Highland Problem in the Seventeenth Century Edinburgh 1980 pp 42-43

[54] BD Vol. I pp.214-215; OPS Vol. II p.377

[55] CRA pp.122-125; SA CH2/557/2 p.118; Fasti Vol. VII p.189

[56] Giblin p.vii; Robson (1997) pp.58-59; Sibbald Adv MS 15.1.1 f.217

[57] MacKenzie (1937) p.193, quoting 'Calendar of State Papers (Irish Series) 1591' p.400. 'Knockpatrick' is now recognised as Croagh Patrick

[58] Campbell (1955) p.655; Giblin p.x

[59] Giblin pp.24, 26, 30

[60] Giblin pp.23, 33-37, 48

[61] Giblin pp.55-57

[62] Giblin pp.63-64

[63] Giblin pp.66-69

[64] Giblin pp.72-74; J L Campbell (edit.): Tales from Barra Told by the Coddy Edinburgh 1960 p.30

[65] Anson p.24; Giblin pp.90, 97, 104, 112, 144

[66] Giblin pp.xi-xii

[67] Giblin pp.15, 171-175. EUL Rev. Colin Campbell Collection MS 3097.12 Letter, copied by Campbell, containing 'Ane Accompt of some heathenish and superstitious rites used in the Isle of Lewis given by a freind to Mr alan Morisone Minister of Ness 15 Aprill 1700' (signed 'Your loving cousine J Morisone At Bragar'). For Rev. Alan Morison see pp. 51,68 The account was in general anticipated by the Synod of Argyll in 1699 (see p.68). Among the festivals celebrated in Hirt that of St Brendan was on 27 May, that commemorating St Columba on 16 June, being 'in the calendar' 16 May and 9 June respectively - a matter discussed briefly by MacAulay (p.76).

[68] Anson p.35; SA CH2/557/1 p.79 25 May 1643; MacTavish Vol. 37 p.68. Martin MacPherson was at this time already minister in South Uist and therefore nearest to Barra. For an account of him and his family - D MacKinnon: 'The MacPhersons of Skye' in The Scottish Genealogist I. 2-3 pp.26-34, also III nn.171, 217. MacTavish Vol.37 p.45; SA CH2/557/1 p.79; W MacKay (edit.): Chronicles of the Frasers - The Wardlaw Manuscript entitled 'Polichronicon seu Policratica Temporum, or, The True Genealogy of the Frasers'. 916-1674 by Master James Fraser SHS (Vol. XLVII) Edinburgh 1905 p.506

[69] SA CH2/557/1 p.85 (May 1643), pp.71-72; Campbell (1975) pp.86-87. See also n.106 (Sibbald).

[70] SA CH2/557/1 pp.71-72, 197 (10 October 1649)

71 Giblin pp. 83-85

72 Giblin pp.174-175; MacTavish Vol.37 pp.69-70

73 MacTavish Vol. 37 pp.71-72. Mr Lachlan Frazer was ordained to give 'the thrid pairt of his yeares rent of the kirk of Snisort to Ronald mc Ronald, sometyme preist, for his maintenance this yeare' [MacTavish Vol. 37 p.74].

74 MacTavish Vol. 37 p172; SA CH2/557/1 pp.243-244 (16 October 1650): the printed version of this passage [MacTavish Vol. 37 p.185] differs in rather more than spelling.

75 MacTavish Vol. 37 p.184, 199. McCalman was 'deposed and excommunicat' for 'his joyneing in rebellion with Alexr. mc Donald' (i.e. Alasdair MacColla).

76 MacTavish Vol. 37 pp.33, 114-115; SA CH2/557/2 p.133

77 Purcell pp.43-44

78 Purcell pp.46-47

79 Purcell p.49

80 MacTavish Vol. 38 pp.121-122; SA CH2/557/2 p.148; Purcell p.49; Campbell (1955) p.656; Blundell pp.3, 26; C MacKenzie: Catholicism and Scotland London 1936 pp.123-124, quoting Duggan's letter of 5 May 1657. J L Campbell (2000 p.7) took the view that Duggan intended to go to Hirt, but there is insufficient evidence for this conclusion. Nevertheless it is possible that Hirt rather than Pabbay was his planned destination.

81 Purcell pp.49, 51

82 SA CH2/557/2 p.95 (9 May 1655); MacTavish Vol.38 p.121; SA CH2/557/2 p.147 (28 May 1656); Blundell pp.8, 10, 12-13; Purcell p.57; F A Macdonald: 'Irish Priests in the Highlands: Judicial Evidence from Argyll' in IR Vol. LXVI no.1 (Spring 1995) p.18

83 D Mackinnon: 'Education in Argyll and the Isles 1638-1709' in Records of the Scottish Church History Society Vol.6 (1938) pp.50-51

84 CA BL1/100/2 Letter (in French). Con went on: 'At this time I came to the mainland to obtain some help from our superiors according to their promises…' Also BL1/99/1 Letter from Casey ('Jean Cahassy'), and BL1/99/2 Letter of 19 September 1687. Gordon Castle was a safe haven where priests occasionally assembled for conference. Campbell (1975) pp.80-81

85 SA CH2/557/14 (6 June 1695), (1696). The progress of the visitation can be followed according to the dated entries in the minutes. According to Fasti [VII p.191] Cooper was 'intruded' in 1692, 'submitted to Presbyterianism' in June 1699, and was drowned in August 1706. Martin (1703) received information from 'Mr Alexander Cooper present Minister of North-viest' (i.e. North Uist) [p.112]

86 DP MS 1389 f.74

87 DP MS 1389 f.73 Letter of 10 April 1686. The word 'governor' is used often in place of tutor as in Sir Robert Sibbald's letter to Sir Hans Sloane of the Royal Society of 29 December 1698. This letter shows Martin's links with both the Society and the map-maker John Adair:
'I must recommend to your favour the Bearer my friend Master Martine, who hath been at great paines in making a description of the Isle of Sky (the biggest of our West isles) and some other of the isles. It heth him coast much paines and expense, and John Adair instead of rewarding him as he promised, heth treated him scurvily. I shall intreat yow to employ your friends to gett him some incouragement and reward from the Court. He was borne in the Isle of Sky, was Governour to the Chieffs of the Clans in these isles and heth that interest and favour with them, they will doe for him what they will doe for no other, their Language is his Mother Language, and he is well acquainted with their maners and customes and is the person here most capable to serve the Royall Society in the accounts of what relateth to the description of these Isles.'
[EUL Dc.8.35 ff.5-10 Letters preserved in the British Museum (MS4060) and copied from the originals]
DP MS 1389 f.84 Letter of 14 December 1695

88 Sibbald Adv MS 33.3.16 f.16 Sibbald's sources list, including '[John] Morison Indweller in the Lewis by the procurement of my friend Mr Colin Mackenzie brother to the Earl of Seaforth', and 'Mr Martin MacMartin' who wrote for Sibbald 'a description of the Hirta or St Kilda with the isles adjacent to it'. Sibbald Adv MS 33.5.15 pp.26-27; MGC Vol. III pp.28-29; W R MacKay: 'Early St Kilda: A Reconsideration' in NQS no.26 (April 1985) pp.13-19 and (August 1985) pp.17-21; MGC Vol. III p.94

89 Philosophical Transactions of the Royal Society of London Vol. 12 (1678) pp.927-929; PRO SP9/17; Sibbald Adv MS 15.1.1 [see n.45 above]

90   <u>DP</u> MS 1389 f.85 Letter of 19 March 1696, and f.86 Letter of 25 June 1696. On 1 August 1696 Martin wrote of his 'Observations' in the islands and of the 'Curiosities' he had found there 'in the Course of my short Travels in *Skie Harries* South and North Uist and some Isles'. [<u>RS</u> LBC 11(2) pp.160-161]. The punctuation of '*Harries* South and North, *Uist*' seems to need the above correction.

91   <u>RPC</u> 3rd Series Vol. III (1669-1672) pp.647-648 (1 & 15 May 1670 Bond of Caution by John McCleod of that Ilk. Campbell could of course have represented MacLeod. It seems possible that the supposed two John Campbells were in fact one and the same. Martin (1703 p.95) described how 'Mr John Campbell, the present Minister of <u>Harries</u>, told me that his Father being then Parson of *Harries* and Minister of *Barray*' visited Berneray (Barra) with his wife. In 1698 'Herrys' and 'St Killda with the pendicles' were linked under the name of 'Mr John Cambell', but this was an arrangement for convenience rather than a recognised parish unit [<u>Kirkwood</u> Kirk. 3.2 p.27 'An Account of the Parishes in the Highlands']. His association with the Royal Society seems to have been the principal reason for Martin's visit to St Kilda. On 4 September 1697 he wrote to the Society Secretary: 'My Curiosity led me to venture to the length of St. Kilda, 20 Leagues beyond the Western Isles, 'tis a place alltogether unknown to the world, which oblidged me to write a Natural and Moral Description of it, which must needs be very acceptable to all of your Genius. It fills 5 Sheets of paper.' [<u>RS</u> LBC 12 pp.344-345]. Charles Preston followed this on 27 October 1697 with a letter of his own to the Secretary: 'I have met frequently with Dr Sibbald and Mr Martin who informs me he has Lately travelled thorough some of the western Isles as Scay, Lewis hareys, hirta and St Kilda and has made severall curious observations of the natural products of those Isles but more particularly of St Kilda which Island it seems is undescribed by Buchanan or any other author.' [<u>RS</u> EL. Pi.101]

92   As regards the names Martin's observation when writing of the Flannan Islands is of interest: 'It is absolutely unlawful to call the Island of *St. Kilda* .. by Its proper *Irish* Name **Hirt**, but only the High Country' (1703 p.17). It has been said, incorrectly, that Martin and Campbell travelled with the steward to St Kilda [e.g. <u>MM</u> Section Three p.205]

93   The following account of Roderick is based chiefly on the last section of Martin's book. Other sources are noted. Popular trivialisations of Roderick and his activities have appeared in subsequent writings, usually hostile in tone and generally inaccurate - e.g. 'A St Kilda Religious Impostor' in <u>OT</u> 11 October 1902.

94   W MacKenzie: 'The Gaelic Incantations and Charms of the Hebrides' in <u>TGSI</u> Vol. XVIII (1891-1892) pp.116-122; <u>CG</u> Vol. III pp.2-23

95   Martin (1698) pp.89, 131-132. 'The women are of good pure Complexions and thought Beauties, they live long, they are much given to Vocall Musice, are very Chaste and never Branded with Fornication or adultery' [<u>Sibbald</u> Adv MS 33.3.20 p.41]

96   An interesting note on 'Maol Domhnaich' is in <u>CG</u> Vol. VI pp.104-105. The name was applied to a male child before baptism. 'For a natural child, however, baptism was not always to be got, in which case the temporary name remained, occasionally for life. When the father of the child failed to provide for it and the mother was poor, the woman got a dole from the Church funds…' In Skye and Argyll a natural child raised on Church doles was called in English 'Ludovic'. It is also noted that 'Ludovic' or Ludovick was 'the general equation in English for the name Maol Domhnaich' and that in Lewis this 'has now been reduced to Louis'. For Sula Sgeir see Robson (1997) pp.46-47. In the earlier eighteenth century 'a notable old Seer, one Evander MacMhaoldonich', was 'a domestic' in the Campbell family on the island of Scalpay (Harris) [<u>TI</u> pp.60-62]

97   Martin (1703) p.289; Martin (1698) p.9

98   Martin (1698) p.84. Of the three chapels 'the first closse upon the Town call'd Christs church. a litle one with ane alter upon the East end, the door is very low, one must bow almost to the ground, befor he doe enter it it heth a litle yard wher they bury, fenced and Keep't very clean' [<u>Sibbald</u> Adv MS 33.3.20 p.54]

99   Martin (1698) pp.82-84; <u>Sibbald</u> Adv MS 33.3.20 p.59 - 'they observe for Anniversaries St Michaels day Christmass and good fryday'. First hand experience of such a blended inheritance in Lewis forms the basis of the remarkable account sent by John Morison, of Bragar, to Rev. Alan Morison, minister in Ness, in April 1700. The contents illustrate the kind of religious conditions which must have prevailed in Hirt during the seventeenth century. For example:

'I have seen Mc Torcal Vc Varrish go about the Lewis with the crosse Molruy, putting it thryce about every every ones head and rubbing the cristall stones in it to ther eyes. The like adoration was performed to Flanan in Uig, and generally to all dedicated kirks wherof there are about 24 in [the] countrey, but none of them at present roofed, save one in Stornway'. See n.67 EUL Colin Campbell Collection MS 3097.12

[100] Martin (1698) pp.90-91; Sibbald Adv MS 33.3.20 p.59. It has been pointed out however that goistidh was not godfather but god-sib, and that the parents of the baptised child and those who held it at baptism called each other goistidh and bana-ghoistidh [Campbell (1958) p.144]

[101] Martin (1698) p.109; Campbell (1958) p.144; CWC nos.63, 239,244. Buchanan described the custom as generally practised [pp. 168-169]. After baptism itself, 'the parents present the child to some neighbour, and call him gosti, or god-father; and after kissing and blessing the child, the gosti delivers the infant to the mother, and ever afterwards looks upon himself as bound not only to be careful of that infant, but also very much attached to the parents. They call one another gosties during life. This name becomes more familiar to them than their own Christian names... if they had formerly been at variance, by this simple union they became reconciled to one another.'

[102] Martin (1698) p.90

[103] Martin (1698) pp.73, 111, 123; Martin (1703) pp.14, 29; Martin (1698) p.112; Sibbald Adv MS 33.3.20 p.62 - 'upon the newes of the Late Mackleods death, they did abandon their houses morning and evening, crying two dayes'.

[104] Martin (1698) pp. 12, 92, 93. The steward was said to have made 17 June his usual time for travelling to Hirt [Sibbald Adv MS 33.2.27 f.361 ('A shorte Surway of the Vesterne Iyllands... Lyinge in the Deucalidonian Sea')]. cf. Sibbald Adv MS 33.3.20 p.59. The 'retinue' included 'some of the most meagre in Harris' who 'recover merveillously in Hirta'.

[105] MM Section Three pp.202-206; Martin (1698) p.92

[106] Martin (1703) p.290; Martin (1698) pp.99, 100 - 'the Chamberland comes in the Summer to exact their rents, he deputeth ane officer who determineth differences in his absence' [Sibbald Adv MS 33.3.20 p.41]; Sibbald Adv MS 33.3.20 p.62; Martin (1698) pp.94-99. In the 'Council', it was also said, 'all arived to the years of discretion have a vote' [Sibbald Adv MS 33.3.20 p.60]

[107] Martin (1698) pp.96-98. Some resemblance may be imagined between the officer's cake and that called 'St Michael's cake' made in various other Hebridean islands.

[108] Martin (1698) p.110

[109] SA CH2/557/3 pp.768-769 (3 June 1697), 753 (13 June 1696), 771

[110] SA CH2/557/3 p.771

[111] SA CH2/557/3 pp.822-823 (13 June 1699)

[112] SA CH2/557/3 pp.822-823 (10 June 1699), 873 (19 October 1700)

[113] 'Mcinaish' may of course be understood as the surname Macinnes. It is interesting to find people of this name mentioned as 'Clann mhic 'ille Threubhaich' in the Boisdale district of South Uist, descended it is said from a 'Gille treubhach' who 'lifted the poetess Mairi Ni' n Alasdair Ruaidh.. over a stream in Smerclete'. One of the family visited St Kilda in search of food. He was given a hostile reception, and his boat was about to be sunk beneath him when he asked if there were any kin of 'Iain Mor Mac 'ille Threubhaich' on the island. 'Apparently there were, as his boat was filled with sea fowl' [A MacLean:'Notes on South Uist Families' in TGSI Vol. LIII (1982-1984) p.499]. Could the 'Clann Mhic 'ille Riabhaich' mentioned by MacAulay (p.263) as one of the two 'true native' surnames of St Kilda but derived from South Uist really be Macinneses and descended from the 'Impostor'?

[114] Anson pp.99-100; Kirkwood Kirk. 3.8 'A List of Papists in the Highlands'; Collections and Observations methodiz'd; concerning the worship, discipline, and government of the Church in Four Books Edinburgh 1709 pp.191 etc.

[115] SA CH2/557/4 pp.8-9 (13 June 1701); Kirkwood Kirk. 3.9 'An Account of a Design to erect Libraries In the Highlands of Scotland' etc.

[116] SA CH2/557/4 pp.9-10 (13 June 1701). That St Kilda was part of no parish contradicts the statement in Fasti (Vol. VII p.188) that the 'parishes' of Harris and Hirt were united 'not later than the sixteenth century, but most likely before that'. There seems to be no firm evidence that the island was ever itself a parish.

PART II

EXILE AND MISSION
Alexander Buchan in St Kilda

It was already apparent that practical matters such as the system of land holding and rent payments as well as religious persuasion deeply influenced feeling, tradition and assumptions in St Kilda. The departure of the Caithness catechist Alexander Buchan for that distant and little known destination in the autumn of 1704 and his arrival there in the following summer marked a move away from what came to be called 'the old faith', by then an attachment to a mixture of beliefs and customs derived from many very ancient sources, to a whole new and entirely different blend of protestant and political concepts. These were reflected in the set of instructions given to Buchan as guides to his intended work. They took hold only gradually and perhaps never completely. One probably unforeseen result was the beginning of much greater dependence by the population on the 'outside world'.

This dependence could first be seen in Buchan's own life and difficulties in St Kilda. His activities as catechist, teacher, and later as minister were in accordance with the expectations of his employers, the remote Edinburgh-based SSPCK. Between him and that section of the established church there were enormous problems of communication and of knowing what was going on in each place. The island 'natives' accepted or more often rejected his efforts, as is made clear in his letters. It is evident from what he wrote that life was nowhere near as 'utopian' as some have made out. The harsh conditions and the periodic but too rarely explained 'disasters' were described and endured by Buchan and his family, as were his own privations resulting from lack or shortfall of pay and the failure of his masters to appreciate what he had to put up with and what conditions in general were like. The reaction of the islanders to his circumstances and labours reveals a good deal of their approach to an existence of poverty and hardship.

Through his letters and 'little book' Buchan, protestant missionary in St Kilda for over 20 years and as heroic a religious figure as any of a different kind that had gone before him, an immediately personal view of the inhabitants and their customs was given for virtually the only time in the history of the place until after 1900. However, the book which for so long has gone under his name is only his in part, and that part a considerably earlier record of his experience than the date of its eventual publication in 1727 would suggest.

CHAPTER 1

Alexander Buchan leaves for St Kilda

FAR away in Caithness in December 1701 the kirk session of Thurso appointed a catechist to serve the parish. His name was Alexander Buchan.[1]

Although it has been stated more than once that Buchan was a native of Aberdeenshire and an army veteran this is not correct and probably arises from confusion with another of the same name. He was in fact born in the Caithness parish of Halkirk, was 'Lawfully descended of honest parents', and, apparently in the early part of his career, was 'Catechist in this place' for several years, 'behaveing himselfe Christianlly and Soberly a laborious Instructer of our youth and Peopell, Searching much into, and Conversant with the Holly Scriptures from his youth, free from any Church Censure or Scandall, haveing a Circumspect Tender and exemplary behaviour in every Step as suitable to his Character'. From Halkirk he moved to Argyleshire, possibly at the beginning of 1694, and became schoolmaster for a year at Ederline in the parish of Kilmichael, Glassary. He then spent two years as teacher in the isle of Jura, where among his pupils there might from time to time have been children from 'the Small Isles of Scaraba Luinga Garvelich and Elachanive, which are Remote parts of the parish of Jura'. James Campbell, minister at Kilbrandon, estimated in 1729 that 'Garvelich and Elich na naomh', owned by John McLachlan of Kilbride, 'a bigotted Prelatist', contained about six families or thirty catechisable persons.[2]

After a year as catechist in the isle of Mull Buchan seems to have made the journey back to Caithness and to his appointment in Thurso, the kirk session there later testifying that he 'did live in this our parish of Thurso for about the space of three years, where he officiated in the Station of a Catechist'. As in Halkirk he gave sufficient proof of his ability and talents, behaved 'Christianly Soberly and Inoffensively', and remained free from all public scandal.[3]

As a fluent Gaelic speaker or, as his daughter was to put it, a 'master of the Irish tongue', and clearly a devoted Protestant, Buchan was seen to be well qualified for a post in the Highlands and islands and more particularly, in the Synod of Argyll's opinion, for that of 'constant catechist' and teacher in St Kilda.[4]

The General Assembly made slow progress towards taking up the Synod's idea and in responding positively to it. The problem was in the main a familiar and worldly one. Who would pay Mr Buchan anything in St Kilda if he went there? It was decided to start him off with a sum, and in the last days of July 1704 he was paid 200 merks 'for his encouragement in going to St Kilda' and given a suitable supply of books at a cost of £13.4s. On 1 August members of the Assembly Commission gave somewhat overdue consideration to the matter because 'it is referred to them by the General Assembly to send one to the Island of Hirta alias St Kilda, to Instruct the people there in the grounds of the Christian, Reformed Protestant Religion, and to teach the people there the Shorter Catechism, by goeing from house to house, and to Lay Down effectual methodes for that end'. The Commission, knowing their man, had already received 'ample and sufficient testimonialls in [favour]s of Alexander Buchan a person formerly Imployed in the [capacity?] in some other places'. Some of their number therefore examined him and found him 'qualified to undertake that work'. Buchan feeling himself 'under more than an ordinary Call to go thither' and being very willing to undertake the task proposed, 'The said Comission did and hereby doe Nominate comissionate and appoint the said Alexander Buchan forthwith to go to and reside in the said Island of Hirta alias St Kilda, and there to Instruct and Catechise the Inhabitants therof in the grounds and principles of the Reformed protestant religion, In maner and conforme to the particular Instructions given him by the said Comission thereanent, hereby prohibiting him to Baptise or Exercise any other part of the Holy function of the Ministry, But to keep closs by his Instructions in all poynts as he will be answerable'.[5]

The 'Instructions' which the Commission had drawn up set a pattern for both Buchan himself and the ensuing imposition of Protestant religion upon the islanders. There were twelve paragraphs:

'1. There being no Minister in the said Island of St Kilda, and the people there deprived of the means of Christian knowledge, and seing yow are sent upon a publick service for promoting the knowledge of God and of Christ in that place It is seriously recommended to yow, that yow Sincerely and without reserve devout yourself to serve God in that matter, and for this end Labour to have the saving knowledge of God in Christ and the holy aw and fear of God and Love to him, and faith in your heart, that you may be truely religious yourself, and in order to this be frequent and fervent in prayer and diligent in reading the Holy Scriptures, and make them your Counsellours.

2. See that in all your conversation you be prudent and Circumspect, Blamelesse and harmelesse commending holyness by word and work to these with whom yow converse Phil. 2 14.15.16., endeavour to Keep yourself and family from all Vice especially these that abound in that place and do what yow can to disgrace Sin and commend holyness.

3. endeavour to have a wise and convinceing behaviour, be not too familiar and open, yet not sullen or morose, but be humble and Holy very kind and Courteous that the people there and all may see yow seek their good, and not your own advantage.

4. When yow converse with the Comon people shew them the evill

and danger of Ignorance and Vice, and in a kind and Loving maner offer them your help and be conscienteously carefull to Instruct them in the principles of the protestant Reformed religion, and these who can read endeavour to perswade them to Learne the Shorter Catechism by heart, But as to Young ones that cannot read teach them some Questions and answers concerning God, the Creation, our Souls, our sin misery, and redemption by Jesus Christ, what he is and hath done and Suffered, what we should doe to be saved, teach them the ten Comands, the Beleif and Lords prayer, what Baptism is, and signifieth the Covenant of Grace, and what was promised, what we are bound to, The evill of Sin, and anent Death, Judgment, and the state of men and women after this in heaven or hell, And this yow are to doe by going from house to house, and otherwayes as occasion offers.

5. When yow are in any of their houses all Night, entertain them with conference to the effect above mentioned, read the Scriptures, or any other good Book yow have and pray with them, and Excite them to private prayer themselves and in their families.

6. On the Lords day when there is not a Minister in the Island, if yow can get some of the people gathered together in any convenient house or place yow may praye with them sing psalms, read the scriptures in the Irish Langwadge, especially the Gospells, psalms and Epistles, and yow may read any other good book such as Mr Guthries tryall of a saveing Intrest in Christ or any other book given yow by the Commission Synod or Presbytery in Argyleshyre.

7. frequently Visit the Sick and such as are under affliction, endeavour first to informe yourself as to their soules case and what their former conversation [?] and then speak freely prudently and faithfully to them as yow find their case requires, and pray with them.

8. Do what yow can to remove any prejudice yow may Find among the people, against the present establishment of this Church and State in this Nation and shew the people their Duty to their Superiours.

9. But in all this yow are to remember that yow are not to be esteemed by yourself or others as doing this by Vertue of any pastorall office, and you are not to presume to Baptise or exercise any other part of the Ministeriall function and yow are to subject yourself to the Synod of Argyle and presbytery of the bounds to whom yow are frequently to give an account of your Diligence and Successe, and from whom yow are to receive farther Directions and Instructions from time to time as they shall Find it needfull.

10. When children and young ones come to yow, encourage them, and shew them the advantage of Learning, and take much pains on them, that their profiteing may encourage others, take up a School and

begin your meetings in your School in the morning and end it in the evening with prayer.

11. Studie patience, and be not soon angry, But be meek and humble, and be not given to unnecessary Debates.

12. Be very careful of the Books now Comitted or hereafter to be Comitted to Your care that they may be preserved for those who succeed yow in the forsaid Service and faill not when Occasion offers to write to the Moderator of the Comission or General Assembly and give account how matters goes with yow.'[6]

Stirred no doubt by Martin Martin's recent books on St Kilda and the Hebrides to a limited awareness of the 'Ignorance and Vice' supposed to be flourishing in the island and apparently convinced that certain vices were abundant there the Commission in, for example, instruction 8, showed itself resolute in seeking to introduce the Protestant 'truth' at the expense of previous or existing religious custom and practice, and this meant that every aspect of daily life in St Kilda would be affected. Education was judged to be of the greatest importance to the success of the programme, so that Buchan's school, along with the 'good books' committed to his care, was to be an instrument of propaganda as much as, if not more than, a place to learn to read and write. The people spoke nothing but Gaelic and the Commission evidently expected Buchan to interpret many of the books which were of course written in English. With little if any awareness of what real life in St Kilda was like the Commission had adopted almost a standard approach towards the mission, expecting Buchan to achieve virtually the impossible, even down to the protection of books in hopeless conditions, and forbidding him, according to rules for non-ministers, to carry out the two familiar and necessary ceremonies of baptism and marriage. Of course, no amount of imagination could have brought into a comfortable Edinburgh meeting room the true picture of existence on St Kilda, and the distinction between Buchan's immediate experience of the place and the ideal aims of the Protestant Church underlies all the subsequent correspondence and disagreements. As for the islanders, little did they realise the nature and degree of the religious onslaught prepared for them in the 'Instructions'.

It must have been a relief to find anyone willing and able to fill the post of catechist in St Kilda and it is not entirely clear why Alexander Buchan was so ready to do so. He had a wife and two young children but in his future employment no definite source of income, yet, 'finding himself then necessitate, as it were, to go to them by more than an ordinary call of providence', off he went into virtual exile from the relative comfort and congenial company on or nearer to the mainland. To these and other circumstances the church authorities appeared to give scarcely a thought.[7]

Having established the rules governing Buchan's work and being of the opinion that 'he may be very usefull in that Island of Hirta or St Kilda', the Assembly Commission decided to inform the Synod of Argyll about developments by sending along with him a letter of recommendation to two ministers in Argyll, Daniel McKay and Daniel Campbell, who would then communicate the message in the letter to the rest of the 'brethren' at a meeting of the Synod. In the same letter the Synod was asked to write to 'the Laird of McLeod', proprietor of the island, requesting him to provide Buchan with every encouragement, including 'a viaticum' of £100 scots to help him get to St Kilda, and proposing 'that he be despatched thither with all diligence before the Season be over'. Since it was already August the season for travelling out into the Atlantic was nearly over anyway and the matter was of some urgency. The brethren of Argyll were to give all the help they could in the despatching of Buchan who was to take with him the appropriate literature, though how the volumes were to be kept free of damp, mould, smoke and mice on the island is as much of a mystery as what use Buchan and the islanders would make of them.[8]

So in the autumn of 1704 Buchan set out for St Kilda and, passing through the Sound of Harris, he reached Pabbay at the beginning of November, far too late in the year to continue the voyage to his ultimate destination. He therefore had to spend the winter in the steward's island where he practised his catechist's duties and learned something of the situation to which he had been appointed. While in Pabbay he wrote twice at least to the Moderator of the General Assembly in accordance with instruction 12, and like most of his letters these first efforts bear the marks of the hazards through which island correspondence had to pass. Damp stained, partly illegible and with bits missing, the two letters from 'pappa', full of anxiety and apprehension, are similar in content. The earlier is the more difficult to read but, even so, the more informative. It appears to have been written about three weeks after his arrival at Pabbay following a 'tedious' and troublesome journey, and he was now having to live there 'at my own expences with out anie help'. He had learned that as most of the inhabitants of 'hirta' were very poor, surviving on birds, eggs and fish, he could not expect any help from them either. Moreover he could not look forward to greatly improved conditions, the winter being past, when he eventually landed on St Kilda, since 'the best of them hath no bread in sumer but the stewarts familie, and they say that I must by my food and rayment once a year from the stewart whils I live ther'. Perhaps MacLeod, who 'lives at Saint Johnston and wil not come home til march or beltan', would allow him 'some of his f[er]me for bread to my familie'; but should he be fortunate enough to have bread he would not be supplied by the people with butter, cheese or milk, 'for they have litl of it to themselves'. If nothing at all was available then he would have to return with the steward at the end of the latter's stay around Lammas, the beginning of August.[9]

Of equal concern to Buchan was his salary, for if no money reached

Pabbay by 'beltan', the first day or so of May, when the steward prepared to leave for St Kilda, he would be without any means of making purchases until the summer of the following year. With this worry hanging over him as well Buchan occupied himself for the present by seeing to the religious welfare of the Pabbay people, who gathered before him on Sundays to hear him 'read a discourse out of mr wa[tso]n to them in irish', and to listen to him as he prayed and sang psalms. In addition, 'daylie I go in to the Stewarts familie for prayers becaus he hath fourty [do]mesticks and a great familie'. Yet his concerns for the future seemed to outweigh everything else. Obstacles and dangers presented themselves in reality and to his imagination as he gazed, on the few clear days, at those sharp peaks on the distant horizon, and the prospect of life on St Kilda seemed all the more dreadful as the day approached when he would have to go there.[10]

Buchan came to realise that since he was not ordained he could not baptise any further children he might have while in the island, and he would rather leave than accept that situation. He knew that the inhabitants 'lived and died under ther own baptisms and mariages' except when a minister 'remarried and rebaptized' some of them, but various stories about ministers did nothing to encourage him. He had heard that 'the last minister that was ther lived a month ther on his own expences and his men and [was] driven eight days with a storm out in the ocean out of sight of all land'. Furthermore he remembered how 'some ministers told me they would not venter to go ther for a thousand pounds and tarrie on[e] year'; and he had been told that 'this severall centurries no minister was ther but tuo times and on[e] of thes in bringing out the impostur'. What sort of place was it out of which came such a dark figure as the 'impostur'?[11]

The second letter from Pabbay was shorter but no less nervous:

'at Pappa the 1 of Januarie 1700:5

this is to acquaint your godly wisdom that I have arived hear the first of november last. I bless god for it though not only with expences and dificulties but with dan[g]er of my life not once or twice. the inhabitants of this island comes to me on the Sabbath always and I read a discours to them out of mr watson and prayes and singes psalms tuice with them and they are very glade of it. the stewart saith and his men that go yearly to hirta that the place is so poor that they can give me no help but fouls and eggs upon which they almost live themselves both in time of plentie and penury and the journey hath exhausted the most part of my money or I came hear and I have no houshold plenishing neither can they of hirta help me and their hou[s]es are very little and they keep all the dung they make in the year in their fire houses with all the intralls of the fouls. the stewart saith he will give me his oun hous in winter without plenishing mckloud is in the low countrey. I know not whither he will give help or trust me the first year. I intreat your godly wisdom to write to him concerning me as ye think fit. if money fail to come to me at the first of may and that a method will not be laid for a Livelihood to my familie I must return at Lames with the stewar[t] contrar to my design which is to hand down religion to posteritie. I hope your wisdom will take to your serious consideration my condition for nothing moves me to go ther but to invit sinners to close with christ on his oun terms and to lay out my self for the edifiing of the bodie of christ in improving time and talent thorow the suplie of the Spirit of christ Jesus I buy all necessars heer at the countre rate. send me an ansuer with mckouds post with the first occasion. no mor at present but rests your godlie wisdoms servant and weell wisher in the Lord allexander buchan'[12]

CHAPTER 2
Buchan begins work and finds difficulties

A T last the beginning of May 1705 arrived and Buchan, apparently without
having yet received any funds, expected the steward's boat would leave
from Pabbay any day. But it was midsummer when he arrived in St Kilda, as
he described in a letter of 16 July, in which he tried to indicate that he was
already responding to his instructions:

'at hirta the 16 of July 170:5

> this is to aquaint your godly wisdom that I have arived safe at this
> place the 20 of June and I have goten but tuo boys to learn as y[e]t for
> they think I wil go away the next year becaus my money is exhausted
> and mccleud gave no orders to see well to me and no man spoke or wrot
> to that effect and he can compell them to give me nothing but eldin and
> wild fouls, for on[e] farmers family els where destroy more bread then
> the five and tuentie that are here. they have the same wild smell that the
> wild fouls on which they live hath so that I must go betueen them and
> the wind. Saturday they leave of[f] labour at tuel but men and women
> and children wer[e] sporting and gaming when I came her Sunday and
> I examin Saturday allways three or four families and gathers as manie as
> possible to hear. they ar mightie ignorant of the true god in his
> uncommunicable attributs especially and of christ in his naturs and
> offices or mans misery by nature original and atual sin the spirituallity of
> the law the evil of sin Judgmen[t] to com heaven or hel. they venter
> salvation on a little morality. som say thers tuo god others a great and litle
> but I take pains eneugh and ther hearts are like the nether milston or like
> flint. on the lords day we begin at nine and leavs of[f] at on[e] or tuo
> acloake. after salmes and prayers I read a chapter out of the gospel and
> gives them the chur[c]h opinion of it and if anie thing be obscur I pass
> that and speaks mos[t] to that which is manifold and necessar for
> salvation and reads a discours out of mr watson again and gets the drift
> of it be heart friday becaus I examin a saturday from tuel til four acloak.
> quis hominen crevit was the method was taught them when rodrik the
> impostur wad [i.e. was?] deposed who is alive y[e]t and leprous like
> manie of his prosolits that I canot visite for fear and lest they would say
> I hade a new religion and that the substance of what I taugh[t] formerly
> migh[t] be understood from henc by subquestions and having the ocean
> of the scriptures befor me I labour to make them understand what they
> have by ratrym. the stewart hath trusted me a years provision of all
> things nessesar. I hope your godly wisdom wil encourage me to this

work in sending me again mayday a competencie to mantain my familie honestly for this year and the next and write to mckloud concerning me. no more at present but rest your wisdoms servant

Allexander Buchan

and write to me with Mckclouds post for they say Ile get tuo other boys and send me four new testaments with the money for I have but catechising and proverbs. I am content to receiv what further instruction iyle get from your wisdom or the sinod of arguil'[13]

This letter, which was presumably taken away by the steward early in August, draws attention to a number of things about life in the island which clearly struck Buchan during the first weeks there. There was the smell of the people, the recreation on Sundays, the belief in two gods, and the continued acceptance of what Roderick had taught. Only two boys had begun to learn something at the 'school' which Buchan had opened, other people having little faith in a man with no money who might not stay for long. It was all an unpromising field for the efforts of a catechist who was supposed to launch a convincing account of 'the true god in his uncommunicable attributs' and carry out the instructions given him.

The Synod read the letter at a meeting in October 1705 amd sent it on to the General Assembly Commission. Unknown to Buchan the Synod had taken up the question of his pay in May while he was still in Pabbay and appointed Rev. Daniel McKay to approach the Commission for money to maintain the 'Catechist in Hirta' over the ensuing years. The Commission in turn wrote to MacLeod and to his steward asking for an advance of what was 'necessar for transporting and mantaineing him there', to which 'the Laird of mackLeoud' replied with a promise 'to advance gratis' a sum for these purposes. McKay reported these moves to the Synod's October meeting, and the Synod, perhaps realising that Buchan would be unlikely to receive any money for at least eight months, instructed Rev. Dugal Campbell to write in its name to the catechist 'to exhort and encourage him in his work'. It was the first of many such letters. [14]

In spite of the repeated call for some form of salary and the assistance of the two ministers no regular method of payment had been organised by the beginning of June 1706 when the Synod asked Sir James Campbell of Auchinbreck to write another letter to MacLeod reminding him of the catechist on St Kilda. At the same time Daniel Campbell, senior, was to communicate with the Commission to like purpose in the hope that it would at last 'Lay down a method for his mantainance pro futuro'. The presbyteries within the bounds of the Synod were also approached with a view to their ensuring that all those kirk sessions and others who had not yet 'given in their

Collections for the Catechist of Hirta' would pay in the same immediately to Daniel Campbell at Kilmichael of Glassary.[15]

In the meantime Campbell had written to the Moderator of the General Assembly commenting on a letter he had received from Buchan and outlining the content:

'Alexander Buchan Catechist in Hirta Sent me the inclosed Directed for the moderator of the assemblie, which I coppied over, and sent the authentick, and the coppie inclosed that it might be the easier read: He wrot ane ample account to me of his circumstances, which he Desired me to Communicat to the Synod of argyle. I think it not amiss to informe the venerable assemblie of some passages in his Letter as followes. He complaines that for a mean dyet in thirty merks he payed for himself and his wife six score of marks, that he buyes everie thing at a dear rate; they give him nothing for nought, no not a vessell to carrie water to him, or a drop milk to his tender young one. He intreats the Laird of McLeoud be written to by the assemblie to cause his Stewart order foules and eggs for him, and some victuall and vessell and salt to Salt his Solen geese, which they feed on mostly if not alwise without salt; that he sayes he cannot endure the smell of the foules, nor people, nor can he stay scarcely to pray within their houses, because of the smell of their rotten unsalted foules, and their guts, they mix with their ashes, una cum hominum urina, to make gooding or manure for their Land. He sayes they are so frugal in this point, that if one be in his neighbours house, he comes home to his own ho[use] ad exonerandam vesicam to mix with his own ashes. He sayes they a[re?] readie to seek butter, linen, tobacco, threed, plaisters etc from him gratis, and believes those that sent him Should mantain him. He sayes there is fyve and twenty familes there, and that fyve and twenty bolls will [gaine?] them in the year, and that they pay fy[f]tein bolls of barley of rent. I think the assemblie should pay McLeoud for this barley and order it for the Catechist. He sayes the[y] [e]at old withered foules unsalted, and fat, with which he would Scund[er] [to?] grease his Shoes with. He adds that he payes twenty pennies for every pint of milk to his two babbies, but now that he has not a farthing to buy anie more, and that he cannot get a Drink of whey without giveing thrice the worth of it of tobacco for it. He cannot get salt to make a water caddell, (or Drink of Brochan as they call it there) but must make use of salt water. He sayes anie money that must be given him must be at him, or mackleouds Stewart there first of may, otherwise ther will be no passage there [this?] year. He adds (for I writ in the order of his own letter) that he is straitned for want of fireing, and severall accomadations, that he has non but God to

Complaine to, and that he incourages himself in the Lord, that he must hire one to fetch him peats, which must be taken down through precip[ices?] from high mountaines; the person that carries the burden, must hurkle down on one of his hips all alongs, and if he miss his ho[ld?] he must goe the way of all fish in to the ocean. He wri[tes?] that he calls them on the Lords day from nyne to two, and agane about [?]. He catechises from 12 to four acloack on Saturday. He write [?] obedient to hear catechiseing and the word, but complaines of the hardness of their hearts, and Longs much for a daye of Gods power among them. He Sayes that he instructs them to know mans Sin miserie and impotence by nature, their need of Cal and that hinders from Comeing to Christ, and from what, and in what manner he must Come to Christ, etc. He sayes the people has ane awfull Deference to him, though he gets nothing from them, but on the contrare they expect from him. He intreats that McLeoud be dealt with to cause his Stuart allow him the milk of a cow or two he designes to buy, because the Stuart has all the milk of the cowes in Hirta in Summer and Harvest dureing his abode for his own use. He thinks it hard to want milk, and harder to buy cowes and not be allowed their milk, and with macleouds patent he writes that the inhabitants tells him, though he were the Duke of Hamiltun he must not have his own Cowes milk during the Stuarts abode in Hirta. He adds manie moe historical accounts to[o] tedious to transcribe. I wrot a full Letter with Directions to him how to carrie. Our moderatour in name of the Synod wrote also to him. By the premises it appeers that the Catechist of Hirta has out [of] a zeal to Gods glorie and the Salvation of Soules, undertakein a task, that many would shrink at. He is in great straits. He got 200 m[er]ks two year agoe and has now nothing but what he taiks on tick. He has neither riches, nor pleasure, nor aire, nor spoil, nor converse, nor hop of preferment, to allure him to stay in Hirta. On the Countrere he wrestles with wants, has no converse, nay nor correspondence with the rest of mortals save 25 ignorant families that never almost went out of that Isle. He has a bad unwholsome dyet. He has a wife and two young ones to provide for, yet if the general assemblie will lay down a way for a competencie to mantaine him he is Satisfied to Stay to teach Schollers, Catechise and instruct the people. I humblie think it will be worth the assemblies while to order a fund for his mantanence. This is ane outfield of Gods vineyeard. As it will be for gods glorie, so it will be for the Commendation of the presbyterian government, that in their tyme and by these means, this ignorant people neglected in former ages was brought in to Ch[ris]t. It will be needfull to order Some good books, paper and ink or materialls to make it with pen-knifes, to be sent him to instruct the people and teach youth to read and write. The zeall of the venerable assemblie is alwise so conspicuous in planting vacancies, and propagateing the Gospell, that it will be superflous, to use arguments to prompt them to such a pious designe as this is, and therefor it is hoped they will c[on]tribut cheerfullie and liberallie and tymeously for the end above written. I beg pardon for takeing up so much of your pretious tyme, which I did out of Zeall to the propagation of the Gospell'.[16]

However the year went by without any sign that either the Commission, which had been so ready to set out the fine words of his 'Instructions', or the other sources had produced anything to support Buchan in a practical way. The Synod did what it could to remedy the situation at its meeting in March 1707: 'Nothing being got done at the Commission this Last season as to the Isle of Hirta, it is recommended to such members as are going to the Assemblie to Represent the case of that Isle, and of the Catechist there, to the Assemblie, or to any others at Edinburgh they shall see propper'. There was no self-righteousness in this. Mr Alexander Campbell told the meeting that he had a letter, apparently from Buchan himself, showing that the catechist had received nothing as yet either from the Commission or the Synod, and there is no evidence that MacLeod as proprietor had contributed. In addition therefore to their message to the Assembly the Synod desired Mr Daniel Campbell, senior, to show what had come in from the presbyteries by way of collections.[17]

At this point Alexander Buchan, now two years in St Kilda without pay, took the opportunity of the steward's visit in the summer of 1707 to write another letter reporting his activities and hinting the possibility of his enforced departure in the year to come. He remarks that, though he might be able to leave, the islanders, 'poor slaves', would not be able to do so even if they wanted to.

'at hirta 170 & 7 the 10 of Jun

right reverend
sir

I have given your godly Wisdom a very good account of my proceedings and dealings with this poorre remote people especially on sabbath days and days of exammination and when the lords hand was heavy in this place the first harvest I came here and how I visited eight or nine familys dayly and was wholly imployd in prayers to god from hous to hous and how I took a promise of every man to worship god in his family and of evry soul that [ ]e to the years of discretion to seek god in secret and what pregnant directions I gave them what to pray for and particularized the graces of the Spirit and gave them the marks of saving grace and how from Sabbath breaking and many exorbitances and enormitys they the poor people in generall turnd to lament after the lord and cry mightyly to god [?] to seek in to the fountain of christs blood for salvation which looks like a god glorifiing and enjoying work tho the instrument be weak poor and contemptible. I bless god my conscience doth not reprove me for want of zeal or diligence but they will not be compeld to Duties be me having no man to strengthen my hands the boys all hath learned to the morall law be heart of the assemblys catechism I read some every sabbath out of the confession of faith before psalms prayers and a chapter explained with the annotations help holding forth always their misery by nature and need of christ and what a fulness and abillity and willinnes is in him to save if discouragments from without or from within might [have] persuaded me from incouraging my self in the lord my god I had neither come or stayed here some tender hearted weeps when they hear threatings of my removing from them and say they will cleave to me as ruth to naomie but tho I go they poor slaves dare not go and can do no service work thats worth els where but I labour to encourage them that men cannot take away their god from them

'I wrote to your godly [wisdom?] that ther was some teen payed here yearly of lambs and wooll and butter and chees. ther is teen payed to the stewart yearly and I think it might help forward so good a work as this and it would keep back the third part of what items and receits I gave to mcklouds tutor I rather have it then fourty or fifty merks yearly becaus such things as it is the worst pennyworth for which I gave receits for evry tuo pennyworth I received since I came to hirta neither [it?] will I get the lend of any houshold plenishing for a day or a year without extraordinary payment and likwis the grinding my barley and casting and wining and leading my peats from top of great hy and stay mountains the difficlest place I think in the world to get a days work or any thing to borrow and now let [thes?] receits I gave wherof I sent a memorand to your wisdom be cleared of to mckclouds tutor who they tel me was angry the last year for writing concerning me and got no ansuer. I cannot stay longer then the next summer here unless there [be?] certainty for an honest livelyhood, during my abode here which is till my lord call me to an acount if your wisdom be pleasd to keep me here allways to teach and explain the truths of god I and the tuo boys thats learning needeth books for they have abusd my english bible and I have nothing to read nowe but bibles and the annotations I had but litl I was off through them having no good convers with my betters I am likeways despised becaus your wisdom hath not written to me as weel as I am for poverty and want of authority. it grieves me to the heart to hear how supperstitiously the sacrament of baptism is prophaned among this i[g]norant people. no more at present but rests your wisdoms obedient and faithful servant in christ

Allexander Buchan

the tuo boys that ar reading [are?] getting the catechism in english and irish be heart and some men [are?] learning the irish catechism be heart'[18]

Certain 'brethren' duly attended the Assembly and towards the end of July 1707 reported that they had addressed that body 'in Wryte' on the subject of the neglected catechist, that the Assembly had 'remitted the Address' to its Commission, and that the Commission was thinking about it. The Synod suggested to those of its members who were also members of that Commission that they should 'keep them in mynd of the said Address'. The next day, on his stating that he had only received 40s sterling of what had been determined for Buchan and had used the money in accordance with the catechist's wishes, Daniel Campbell was asked to submit a list of those who had not paid their proportions to him, but this was all that was achieved and the next meeting was not till October. It looked as if Buchan, in his isolation, was going to be without any financial assistance or reward for three years in a row, and it must have seemed to him that his needs, if not his existence, were being entirely ignored.[19]

Not surprisingly therefore both Buchan and, given their methods of trying to raise money, the Synod lost patience. Mrs Buchan, otherwise Katharine Campbell and apparently daughter of Rev. Daniel Campbell, left the island at Lammas, the beginning of August. She was pregnant and may have wished to give birth in more pleasant conditions that those in St Kilda but she was also in pursuit of the money so long sought by her husband. She attended the Synod meeting on 11 October 1707 when she was asked to give an account of 'their Circumstances there'; and she produced a letter from her husband, probably that written on 10 June, but unfortunately her own story was not included in the minutes of that meeting. However the Synod appointed Daniel Campbell senior, Dugald Campbell senior, and James Boes to be a sub-committee with a remit to consider the letter and 'bring in an overture thereanent' at the next meeting some months ahead. It was also decided that the several presbyteries should 'look after' those who were still defaulters in payment to the collection for Buchan, and all such outstanding sums should be sent to Daniel Campbell without delay. The lack of funds and at least the hint in the letter that Buchan might leave left no doubt in anybody's mind that the situation was becoming desperate, and the Synod was determined to deal with those who did not pay up: 'the blame and loss of the said Catechists Leaving Hirta (as he threatens to do) shall ly at the door of every recusant, and besides that the Synod will take course with them otherwayes'. Almost overlooked at this stage, but not quite, was the death in October 1707 of John Campbell, 'Episcopal Incumbent in Harries' and Martin's companion to St Kilda ten years before, whose widow, Anna MacKinnon, received an overdue payment to her husband in June 1709.[20]

On 25 February 1708 Daniel Campbell, Kilmichael of Glassary, wrote a covering letter for Mrs. Buchan to take to George Meldrum, professor of divinity at the University of Edinburgh. It expanded on points raised by Buchan in his last communication:

'The bearer Cathrine Campbell is spouse to Alexander Buchan Catechist of Hirta. She came about Lambas last from Hirta, in order to apply for a mantainance to her husband, and a fund to pay what meall and barley he took for the mantainance of his wife and young ones. it was michaelmas er she won my Length. I have mantained her since, she not being able to travell in winter to Edinburgh, being brought to bed in November last: she has now gone to address the Commission and others ministers and good christians for a fund to pay what they ow of meal and barley as aforsaid, and to be a mantenance pro future her husband was resolved to come himself for the forsaid ends, but when he came to the shoar in order to boat, the men of the place, did with cryes and teares beseech him, not to leave them. Therfor he sent his wife to the maineland. And now she being to address the Commission I knew non to whom I might direct her to ag[ent?] her effair that was fitter or readier to assist then your self. I hop therfor you will deall with the Commission if sitting, or with your general session, or brethren, or the managers of the publick money the Queen bestowes on the Church for a fund to pay what she tells is owing for meall and barley and to get a fixed yearly Sallarie named to him, and to deall with the Commission that they send necessr practicall books to Hirta and books and paper to teach the children with. Ther are 15 bolls barley payable to the Stuart of Hirta. if the Commission would yearly pay to Mr Alexander Mcleoud advocat the price of the barley he might transmitt it to the Stuart. I hop that some present subsistance will be given her in hand, and that the Commission will consider what will be necessar to mantaine himself, wife, and three children. I can assure, if he leave that place (which he must doe, if he be not suplyed with the necessars of humane life) that it will not be easie to get another to Supply the place. all things are dear there. he has no sowing, not so much as a kale yeard. he payes for the lend of everie household utensile he wants. the poor people rather expects Supply from him than to give him anie help. he has brought them to some

Length of knowledge and to worship God in their families. they conveen each Saturnday at twelve for Catechiseing till six at night. he spends the whole day in explaineing the fundamentalls out of the Larger and Shorter Catechism and Confession of faith and reading and explaineing the scriptures and exhorting them suteablie. it were a pitie not to encourage him. Perhaps a kingdom will not afford but few or non that would out of pure Zeall be content to undergoe such hardship and want as he [does?]. I think privat Christians and ministers and sessions should contribut for this end rather than the poor man be contrarie to his Zealous inclination forced to leave a poor starveing people so desireous of the Gospell and I hope you will be instrumentall to that effect, and to dispatch her back. if she overtake not the boat about May day, She may miss passage this year. The thing required is soe much for Gods glorie, and the good of poor neglected Souls, that I know ther is no need of arguments. a true information is enough. I dealt with our Synod for him, but we have no vacancie and what we have of the Bishoprents is disposed of by the Lords for Stipends and augmentations, and cess etc. that not 300 lib. remaines ther was a collection appointed of three merks each minister of which I as yet received 24 lib. scots for which I count with the bearer. money is so scairce here we cannot get to bear our expences at Judicatures. The officer of the place marries the people which lessens Alexander Buchans authoritie. I think the Commission may send him ane allowance to marry. The people Baptises their own children. if a fund were fixed for his constant abode there I think he might be ordained minister of that place to prevent such disorders, and a letter might be writtin to the brethren of argyle Synod to send the brethren of Sky nixt Summer [to] ordain him. I can promise, some preaches that has not his knowledge nor zeal. He does rebuke in publick on the Lords day such as commit publick sins, and keeps g[ood?] authoritie and leads a strict examplarie life. it will but [divert you?] a little to informe that the people since his comeing are become so Zealous of Discipline and of keeping the Sabbath and to see Discipline execut with [im]partialitie that one Lords Day Alexander Buchans wife haveing discovered that [a] litle one she left to keep her house with some other litle ones in tyme of Divine service did open her meal chist and steall some of it, did be the little ones she left keeping the house thinking it a work of necessity al which they conceiled such offence, beleiveing this a gross breach of the Lords day that they would not submitt to discipline anie more, unless Mr Buchan would publickly nixt Lords day in face of congregation rebuke his wife for the foresaid deed. whatever he thought of the Lawfullness or necessitie of what his wife did, for prudent ends he complyed with the peoples humour, which has gained him much respect and authoritie. I doubt if anie minister in

Edinburgh or elswhere would doe the like. I fe[el?] by this tyme I wearie your patience. Pray doe what can be done [for] the releif and encouragment of this poor man and deal with Mr McLeod advocat to write to the stuart to trust Mr Buchan the said 15 bolls.'[21]

The Commission would pay the cost, said Campbell, and receive some help from kirk sessions and brethren.

In her address to the moderator and members of Commission of the General Assembly Mrs Buchan gave a brief account of her reasons for being present on the mainland. She had now lived three years in St Kilda. She had left the island about Lammas, there 'being no passage to or from Hirta but in Summer', had stayed in Skye until the end of September, and had then gone to 'Glassrie' where she was 'brought to bed' in November. Her husband had received only the initial 200 merks in three years and had been forced to take meal and barley from the steward on trust. He was also forced to pay for everything for housekeeping, including the loan of pots and other vessels. Out of charity he was 'induced to aliment for the most pairt two boys which he taught to read there (for their parents would not keep them at School, though he taught gratis, unless he thus helped himself to aliment them, thinking they oblidged him in sending their children to be taught'. From all this, she said, 'it appears my husband cannot continue Longer there, (and there is litle hope, that another will expose himself to such povertie and want and hardship as he has endured there to succeed him in his office) unless there be a fond advanced to pay what meall and barley he took on trust allreadie, and a method laid Doune for a yearlie Subsistance there'. Nothing was to be had for nothing in St Kilda.

In these circumstances Mrs Buchan was come to seek assistance from the Commission 'and other ministers and charitable Christians'. She asked that the steward be paid what is owing to him, that a fixed salary be settled on her husband, that Alexander MacLeod advocate be requested to write to his half brother John MacLeod of Contullich, now tutor to the infant Norman MacLeod of MacLeod, and to the steward of St Kilda, for an allowance of 15 bolls of St Kilda barley for which Alexander MacLeod should be paid, and that some 'practicall books' for her husband's use in teaching should be sent. As time was getting on she made known her wish to catch the steward's boat soon to leave and so avoid spending another year away.[22]

Having received Daniel Campbell's letter of 25 February 1708 from Mrs Buchan George Meldrum was busy writing to various people at the end of March. One letter went to John MacLeod of Contullich:

'We doubt not But you know, how on the sad account of the inhabitants of St Kilda's living without all manner of Instruction, The Generall Assembly, or its Commission, some yeeres agoe sent one Alexander

Bucchan there as a catechist, to teach the people the principles of Religion, and Learn children to read, and they gave to him some money to bear his charges to that place, and for his Subsistence for some tyme, Being hopefull the Laird of MacLeud, would take some course for his provision and Indeed on our application to the late Laird of MacLeud and by your Worthy Brother Mr Alexander his mediation the Laird did most generously promise to provyde for his Subsistence while there which made us secure and him the more neglected by us. Bot now we are informed, Mr Bucchan hath been much straitned, and tho we were Informed the Inhabitants there have no use for money among themselfs he can neither have Barley nor Milk without money, and at as Dear a Rate as at Edinburgh and when he had no money was oblieged to give tickets for it nor can he have the Lend of pot or pan or gett fewell brought to him without money So that it is a wonder that he continueth there under such hardship, and if he came away and Left them we would hardly gett any to undertake Such hardship and toyle. We are Refreshed to hear of the Successe he hath among them, as to the Instruction of same, and engaging them to worship God in their familyes and to sanctify the Lords Day, and they seem to have a Love to Mr Bucchan, and desire of his Continuance among them, so that when he designed to come here to represent his case, they hanged on him, and with teares besought him not to goe, whereupon he stayed and sent his wyfe.

'Bot it grieveth me to hear that [severall?] send their children to Learn to read, and think he is oblieged to them, if they send their children to Learn, and that the officer marryeth them and they baptize their own children. There is a Design, of ordayning Mr Bucchan a Minister, that these things may be orderly done and he have the more authority among them.

'Sir we doe humbly represent these things to you, and earnestly recommend them to your Consideration and are hopefull you will in compassion to the Soules of that people, Doe what may be in your power, and proper for you for Mr Bucchans provision and encouragement in his Labours for their Instruction, which will be for the honor of God, and a mean to procure a Blessing on your pupill, the Laird of MacLeud, and to Bring the Blessing of God on yourself and your Family.

'Yet we humbly Intreat that what is written, may not be Interpreted or made use of as a complaint from Mr Bucchan, lest it occasion worse treatment afterward, when he hath no occasion to complayn to you.

'Other particulars we referre to your Brothers Letter, who hath promised to write to you. only one thing we adde, as our earnest Request, that you would in your Wisedome, use the fittest Method, to obliege them to send their children to School. We have sent some Bibles and good Bookes to Mr Bucchan and catechisms for children, tho there is difficulty to carry them so farre, and therefore they are the fewer.'[23]

Meldrum had also sent a letter to the 'pupill' Laird of MacLeod, perhaps aged about two, regarding Buchan, 'desiring that you would be pleased to give him encouragement, that he may not be forced to leave the place and the work so happily begun'. The writer then urged the matter forward further: 'we are sensible of your kind return to the Commission on Mr Alexander McLeods Letter to you, shewing that you will ecnourage the Catechist, so long as he stayeth there, of which we hope you will be mindful. He writes they subject themselves to him, and pay him respect, which we do in a great measure impute to his having your Countenance, and it is expected you will not be wanting in giving order to your steward concerning him ...' Then there was Buchan himself, whose letter of 10 June 1707 had at last reached Meldrum's attention along with Daniel Campbell's on 18 March 1708. Meldrum explained to Buchan that when his wife reached Edinburgh neither the General Assembly nor its Commission was in session and as waiting for such meetings to take place would have meant her losing the boat home the matter was put to a meeting of the 'Committee for Propagating Christian Knowledge', the members of which 'were much refreshed with the account of your Labours'. He then told the catechist what other correspondence there had been, that 'we were indeed afflicted with your straites', but that he was encouraged in his work, that 400 merks were to be paid to Mr Alexander MacLeod to be sent to the tutor, John MacLeod of Contullich, for Buchan's use, and that some books had been given to Mrs Buchan to bring back with her: 'we have not detayned your wyfe, but dispatched her with all possible diligence, and provyded some money of privat charity for defraying her expense while here, and to help her on her journey'. The Committee would report to the General Assembly or its Commission at the next meeting, but in the mean time 'there is a desyn to ordayn you a minister that you may have the more authority and that Baptism, and Marriage may be the more orderly administrat'. Meldrum had also written to Daniel Campbell to urge him to cause the Synod of Argyll to recommend that the presbytery of Skye should carry out the ordination and that if this was not done the Assembly itself would order it. At the same time, still on 29 March 1708, Meldrum sent a note to Nicol Spence, secretary to the Committee for Propagating Christian Knowledge, asking what books had actually been sent for Buchan and indicating that two 'Irish Bibles' should be supplied for the two boys who could now read as well as two English bibles 'in privat charity'. There were additional instructions also: 'Cause transcribe and send to me the letter read on Friday to the Tutor and end the effeyre with Mr Alexander MacLeud, and mind him to write to his Brother, that Alexander Bucchan may have two kines grasse free and provision of house [free?] when the Steward cometh there ... and if possible the Tutor would give him the Tithe [i.e. teinds] payed there'.[24]

While Meldrum was busy writing these letters the problem of remuneration for Buchan was placed before the presbytery of Edinburgh and discussed at length. The presbytery was informed of 'the circumstances of Alexander Buchan, sent by the Commission of the General Assembly to the Island of St Kilda, or Hirta, for instructing the poor people there in the knowledge of Christ, and how useful he has been in that place, and that the funds designed for his encouragement have not been made effectual, so that he was obliged to send his wife hither to represent his case, seeing he could not come himself.' All ministers, kirk sessions and other Christians within the presbytery's bounds were recommended to contribute sums sufficient in total to enable Buchan to stay on the island 'for propagating the knowledge of Christ there, and rooting out the pagan and popish superstitious customes so much yet in use amongst that people, for want of ministers to Instruct them'. Presumably the city of Edinburgh and its neighbourhood was more capable of producing funds than the impoverished areas of the north and west.[25]

Meanwhile Alexander Buchan himself was having to await the return of his wife for any news relating to their possible future welfare. In May 1708 the Synod of Argyll was still struggling to complete its record of contributions for the catechist and had to recommend to the presbytery of Lorn that its collection should be given to Daniel McNeill, the young minister in Morvern. At about this time Mrs Buchan reached home and was able to cheer up her husband immensely with the account of her adventure to the mainland, the letters she brought, and of course the new baby, so that when Buchan wrote his annual report in July he sounded quite optimistic:

'At hirta the 17 of July 1708

Right reverend

Sir this is to aquaint your godly wisdom that your commity and the reverend and Pious mr meldrum their diligent and zealous proceedings hath refreshed my soul [and?] strengthned my hands a litle in the work of the lord which was interwpted much by reason of the troubles that befel me. I read a sentence always on the lords day first out of the confesscion of faith and makes the heads of religion as plain [as?] I can and after psalms and prayers a chapter explaining most [w?]hat is to their edification with the help of diedatys annotations who helps me to understand the scripturs better then formerly [where?] sin is threatned and exhort to shun that sins that they may escape the Judgments threatned and to do the dutyes theirin [that?] they may be counted worthie in christ to obtain the promises of free grace in christ to the elect and I read a sermon out of Mr Watson and after psalms and prayers again they dismis and when the day is long I read and pray in the afternoon again. some boys hath learned the assemblys catechism the length of baptism [and?] all that came to discretion might have learned it all if will [and?] memory would allow them and such as will not do it I teach them quis hominen creavit and from thence mans misery by nature the covenants their conditions and differences their need of a gracious change and an interest in christ and what he did and suffered and what [?] is to god the father and to his elect and will be to his [enemis?] for [?] what fulnes is in christ of light life grace and spirit and love [?] Penitent siners his readines willingness and ability to save from sin and wrath to come his natures and offices and relations to his chosen and what wil come of siners with out christ I teach them the [ten] comandments the belief and the lords prayer. four men in hirt could not repeat the commandments right when I came here but se[verals?] had some broken halfes of them. if anny perish it is not for want of fair and timous warning tho in weakness yet in sincerity and faithfully which I pray earnestly that christ may be magnified therby others be found in him and with him then I [have?] my design ansuered of weel by weak [?] strong means [?] god be glorified I care not who will be the instrument and if [a ?] better then I cannot be goten especially an able minister I [am?] content to live alwa[y]s a mean soloitary life here for the glory [of] our Lord Jesus christ till he remove me by death and pray and [hope] he will send abbetter when I am rotten in my grave. I would think it a sin to be ordained where abbeter might be had and run [?] without sending and speaking without being commanded but for necessity here I am content to be cloathed with authority that I may exercis discipline and pul doun what I can of satans stron[g]est pillars that upholds his kingdom by takeing oaths of all in generall by ministers in my presence that they will never learn charms [?] or witchcraft or observe superstition they or their seed which I hope god may and will bury with the old generation and that baptizm and mariag may be duly administered and the sabbath more sanctified and god more glorified when I will get more respect and audience in the lord and no other ends will permit me to accept of imposition of hands to which effect I am content to be examined on all the essential heads and principles of christian religion no other tryals am I qualified for becaus I always read and studied but as a privat christian. my wife brought me the most part of houshold plenishing and timber to build a chamber and bibles to the boys and got some books for my self. send me a body of divinity or some good book that fallows a method of preaching for the lords day. the stewart is civil discreet and kind in all his dealing with me and hath caused the natives help me home with my elding with which I was much troubled this time bypast carrying it on my oun back tho I have a dayly hired servant for want of a horse to help us which work I bless god for it neither my predecessors did or caused ther servants do and it would be dear if I had given wages for it. the tutor of mckloud was kind to my wife likways as this good orders came from him and hired a boat and men thirty milles of sea on his oun expences to bring my wife to the ferry where she hired a boat and men for fifty five merks and payed five and tuenty in hand and I gave a receit to the men to be paid at martimes or allowed in payment by the tutor for tuenty pounds scots. I beseech your godly wisdom to pay mckloud yearly for what I give receits that the gentle man do not ly out of the use of his mony having many things to do with his mony for himself and others. I have three young babes and a servant dayly and wee pay them ther wages when they come to us that they may be cloathed and wear it [if?] in our oun service

I remain your wisdoms faithful and obedient servant in Christ

Allexander Buchan

The presbetery of Sky hath vacancy and several preaching places all of them and some have several ferrys to cross to go and preach and catechis places distant by reason of sea and some by reason of wildernes and it is expensive to come here or go from this place with a boat and nine or seven sufficient sailers at least none in the isles would hardly ventur or come so sheap as the men of pappa did for they ar aquaint with the sea from their youth at hirta'

Buchan also listed acquisitions in 1708 for which he had given receipts, that is, acknowledgements of goods required. They included ten bolls [of barley?], twelve stones [of oatmeal?], six wedders, sixteen merks for a milk cow, sixteen merks for 'cloath and Linings and shoos', 'tuo grots for Lits', thirty merks 'for fraught be allowed his tenents that came to hirta with my wife', and sixteen pence for a pound of tobacco.[26]

His letter repeated his conviction that his success as a teacher of religion and reading in the island depended on his holding a position there which would gain more respect and attention than it had done so far. This would be achieved, he felt, if he received a regular salary and if he were enabled to marry and baptise, for all of which he would need to be ordained as a regular minister. Nothing of this was to be settled for another two years.

CHAPTER 3

Buchan prepares to be ordained to St Kilda

The existence in 1708 of a General Assembly Committee for Propagating Christian Knowledge may have owed a good deal to the 'small number of pious and public-spirited citizens of Edinburgh' who, in 1701, had 'thought proper to form themselves into a society for the reformation of manners, for the purpose of labouring in the dreary and dark regions of their own country, where a high northern latitude, a surly climate, a stubborn sterile soil, civil oppression and a gloomy religious superstition presented a melancholy and afflicting picture of accumulated human misery'. [27] The words caught on, the Edinburgh presbytery using them in its reference to Buchan's work in St Kilda, and in 1709 the Society in Scotland for the Propagating of Christian Knowledge, the SSPCK, was granted its founding charter. One of its chief aims was to prevent the Highlands and islands from falling universally back into the hands of Catholics, who, along with Episcopalians, were increasingly associated with Jacobite, and consequently anti-government, political activities. It was soon to be among this Society's responsibilities to deal with the problem of 'the Catechist of Hirta'.

In spite of the assistance given by George Meldrum and others in the spring of 1708 no lasting practical improvement in conditions took place and Buchan's spirits sank back to such an extent that in the summer of 1709 he seems to have left the island twice, the second time in August when the steward departed at the end of his annual visit. He was therefore prepared to spend a year away in pursuit of a solution to the difficulties he had experienced. But this was not his only reason for leaving.

His letter of 1709, heavy with description of his religious labours, hinted at the possibility that he might not return to St Kilda at all, except to fetch away his family:

'at Hirta

Right reverend
Sir

this year in may last I had occasion to go to Sky and came back again with the same boat of hirta the brethren being at the sinod I wanting fraught and provision to give for a boat and men to com to hirta I have come again with the stewart to see what your godly wisdom will Judge to do in this work for your lords glory. I continue the sabbats exercises as I began. all the youth hath learnd the assemb[l]ys catechism be heart and repeats it by cours each Lords day immediatly when we are done with the last prayers and psalmes which cost me much pains night and day or [er?] they could move their questions. all the aged and maids will not give that much pains, therfor I teach four families each Saturday when they are at home and the absent on the lords day or [er?] the people all dismis on god in his person and attributs mans end in creation and misery by nature the evil of sin among [a mans?] god christ in his natures offices relations the covenants the terms and promises and threatnin[g]s therof the marks of saving faith and saving repentance a conformity to christ in life death and resurrection heavenly mindednes the trysting place in mercy and hiding place from wrath the receiving whole christ in all conditions and regeneration. I particularis the graes and gives dire[c]tions what to pray [for?] of a day of the power of god a suing of omnipotent power a saving cast of Jehovahs arm heart holines the power of godlynes the on[e] thing needfull a saving interest in christ and him above all things and what he did and suffered is doing and will for His elect. I was eight and fourty nights with moon light at family visitations. I went out at day set and came home at supper time [a lords?] night about always I teach them also the ten commands the lords prayer and gives marks if god or the divil be their father and I teach and examine every family apart on their heads I name [...d] and exhorts them to cleav to the lord with ful purpos of heart and to perfume their houses with prayers as they gave their hand and promise to me in gods name the first year and to lay siedge to heavens gate with strong crys and groans and to take it by a Holy violenc in taking up the cross and following christ to Heaven thorow manifold temptations and tribulations subduing within and renouncing without our selves and others whatsoever com[e]s in competition with the glory of god and what religion may cost us and what will come of graceles and christles persons in eternity. I met with such ignorant expressions as I read in doolitel and wors, when I cam here. I bless god for it I am not ashamed who will hear me examin[e?] some good inclined people here the others never come half that length. th[e] tutor hath refreshed my soul in giving order to the people to obey me in the lord according to the ruls of gods work in sabbath sanctification and in taking an oath of the [   ] may pull doun thes strongest pillars that support satans kingdom and that it may be buried under the head of the chief servants the scol master and hipodidasciolus he hath here for at her I level my moian with god and men I bless god her children are father and mother write a line to the tutor and thank him. he likwis makes every hous in hirta bring home six burden of peats to me yearly brevity will not allowe me to write what I would make knowe to your godly wisdom of my procedings on al the heads of what I teach if an able minister were goten I would leave this litl foundation to rais the burlind if not I rather live a poor solitary life in it then leave them in gros and thick darkness again and I think shame to write or tell al my straits. I never knew among friends what a family was. the tutor hath but ten bols of barley to give me here. it is litl enewgh for my wife and four children and servant that grinds it. if I be here I will need either oatmeal for pottadge or barley for drink. I took eight merks worth of land this year to gett some fouls and eggs not being able to buy them. ther will grow a bol of black meal on it with a good year and half therof must be given the man that goeth in danger of egs and fouls in the rocks. the peats is dear to me likewise far to carry and troubles my oun person much with servile work and diverts me much from my book. the people hath refuse to bring home to me so much of my peats as was ordered by the tutor except so many of them as I was able to give a large allowance of provision to and to their contentment by reason of their poverty and necessity in sumer and harvest in seeking the fouls of weel the day they get none of when they get more or less of them. Right reverend Sir my straits have been such in hirta that I was nessessitat to come in person very much contrar to my inclination to address your godly wisdom in order to lay doun an effectual method to pay what debts I have contracted for maintaining my self and my familie hitherto 381 merks as also to provide me a yearly competent maintainance if the church think fit to continue me in hirta otherwise absolute nesessity wil force me to leave that place and veryly it is the zeal I have for the glory of god and the salvation of thess poor souls that were litl better then heathens when I came first amongst them first moved me to go there and ther after under great straits to continue going there and if I had respect to wordly ends I might turn to be catechist where I lived better formerly amongest all my oun people yet tho living there separats me from the rest of mankind I am content to return and continue providing the church setle a yearly pension on me of tuo hundred pound Scots which is but a mean maintainance in such a dear place wher nothin can be had without money and it will but scarcely provid me and my family in a very mean dyet and habit while I live and it will [no?]t lcave my wife and children but beggars when I die [?]herfor I expect you wisdoms will encourag me yourselves [and?] deal with the commitee for propagating christanan knowled[ge] [fo?]r the same end for no place stands mor in need of propagating knouledge then hirta I hope your wisdoms will lay doun such a sure and effectuall method of paying to me yearly what cellor[ie] ye think fit to give me that neither I or my wife be oblidg[ed] to come out of hirta to seek the same which did and will [take?] us near a years time at each voyage their being no pass[ag]e to or from hirta but in summer and such needless [ted]dious and dan[g]erous voyages by sea and Journeys be land will put me and my wife to great trouble and the church [to?] expences and the people to be deprived of the means [of?]

instruction too long which I pray and hope to be prevented. [I?] pray that the lord of the vineyard may send forth mor labo[ur]ers and blesse thair labours with more aboundand success. [I?] rest

Right reverend
your wisdoms
unworthy servant in christ

Allexander Buchan'[28]

On this occasion Buchan took with him the two boys, Finlay MacDonald and Murdo Campbell, who had been his regular and perhaps only pupils since he opened the 'school' in 1705. He made directly for Argyll, where he met Daniel Campbell, then clerk to the presbytery of Inveraray and moderator of the Synod, and after a brief stay went on to Edinburgh, carrying with him his own letter as a 'representation' and one of 13 September 1709 written by Campbell in support:

'Killmartin September 13 1709

    R Reverend

The Bearer Alexander Buchan, Catechist of Saint Kilda or Hirta, has bein these fyve yeares in Hirta, instructing the people Sabbath and week dayes, conforme to the Commission given him for that effect, by the Commission of the Assemblie. His paines has not bein without Success, for the People begin all to pray in Secret, and the bulk of them, to worship God in their families: They have also made a considerable advance in Knowledge. He could get non to engadge to learn to read but two boyes quhom he took with him to Edinburgh that they might not in his absence forget quhat they formerly Learned but by being still in his companie might improve more and more. The boyes can read tollerablie and answer quhen examined on the assemblies catechism prettie well.

'He has Laboured under verie greivous circumstances all the [while?] he had not so much as a cow till Lambas Last he bought one, nor consequently a Drop milk to give his young ones, but quhat he bought, he had not a grain of oat meall, but only barley meall all the tyme quhich neither aggrees with his wife nor children: for anie Liqor save water, he had non to take in health or sicknes: he was oblidged to carrie peates on his back, from the topes of great mountaines and precipices: he had neither great plentie, and as litle varieties of food, and though the place abounded with eggs and fowles, he must purchase all with money he made use of. All he got these five yeares was 200 merks quhen he went their and 400 merks allowed him the Last year, with quhat the magistrats and ministers of the good town [?] did kindly give his wife. he has contracted about four hundred merks of Debt to the Stewart of Hirta for barley meall and other necessars for food and rayment, and now he can get no credit unless former Debts be first payed. And had he stayed ther this winter, he had not to mantaine himself and familie to march nixt, and could not expect suply till the first of June quhen the Stuart comes there yearly. The Last year quhen he got some suply to mantaine him, the People reverenced him and stood in aw. But quhen they saw he was reduced to his former straits they changed their behaviour: He was oblidged to give a boll of barley to the mother of one of the boyes to allow him to stay at schooll: All quhich oblidged him to come to the maine Land, to address the Commission, and other church Judicatories for a fund to pay quhat he is resting, and a yearly Pension to mantain himself and his familie in caice the Church think fitt to continue him there. It adds to his greivous circumstances, that they not only marrie by the officer of the Iseland to the Lessening of his Authoritie, but that the People baptise superstitiousely as followes. they goe thrice with the child about the fire, and at each tyme Dippes the child thrice in the ashes, and then a man that must not speak Dureing the action fetches in water, in quhich salt and a knife is put, with quhich they baptise, and then throwes the rest of the water about ane immoveable stone, and all he can Doe cannot oblidge them to quit this superstition. but quhen he reproves them they desire himself to administer baptisme to them, or else not to find fault.

'Our Presbyterie are very sensible, that nothing but the Zeal of God would move the bearer to goe to, or continue in Hirta, for we know that he had a more comfortable way of Liveing as catechist in Caithnes formerly, among his acquaintances, quhere he had plenty of all outward comforts. and that if he Leave Hirta he may still have more affluence of the necessars of this Life elsquhere - though his sallarie should be small yet a small Sallarie is better in a civilised place quhere things are cheap, and quhere Good people give gratuities, then thrice so much sallarie quhere a chappin of whey or creel full of peats cannot be had [without?] money. Upon the wholl, it is our unanimous oppinion that the [Reverend?] Commission should give all incouragement to Mr Buchan, and Lay Down a method to pay quhat he owes, and setle a yearly pension of two hunder libs. scots on him Dureing Life, for it puts him to great trouble to be oblidged to come to Edinburgh to receive it or to seek it. His wife was a year on the Last voyage er she returned to him, and payed Fyftie five merks and provision to the boat men for passage at her returne, and now he cannot returne till may nixt. therefore the Sallarie to be allowed would be advanced to Mr Alexander McLeoud advocat, who will transmitt the same to Mr Buchan, that he and his wife may [continue?] in Hirta, and not put themselves to trouble or church to charges [in?] comeing to the maine Land for their mantainance anie more: Moreover we find that the Commission wrote to our Synod and we by [thir?] Directions to the Presbyterie of Sky to ordain Mr Buchan minister of Hirta a year agoe. But the Brethren of Sky are so Discontiguous, that they meet seldom, and in the summer Season they are so throng with Communion[s?] and visitations that they cannot goe to Hirta for his ordination, nor though he came to them in winter they cannot meet but seldom, nor had he [a ?] to mantain himself among them. Therefore we humblie think, that the Commission might appoint the brethren of Edinburgh to ordain him, that he may be in capacitie to marrie and baptise and exerce some Discipline quhich will capacitat him to Doe some more good in the place, and we think that the exer[c]ise of his ministrie should be restricted to Saint Kilda onlie as also that the two boyes be provided for at school quhill Mr Buchan continues at Edinburgh, quhich will be till march nixt for then he must return in order to wait for ane occasion of a Boat to Herries quhere he must continue till the stuart goe in the Latter end of may or first of June. One of the boyes Murdoch or Mordecai Campbell is fatherless haveing nothing to sustain him, the other is sone to the officer of the Isle. If a bursarie or some fund were given for two or three yeares to the fatherless boy, he is most hopefull though his countenance promise Less, he might doe some good in Hirta quhen Mr Buchan Depairts this Life. But we fear [that if] they be keept in the maineland they will not incline to returne to Hirta and therefore if the church think fitt to cause him only Learn English, and were better to send him home with Mr Buchan and board him with himself, but if they designe more Learning for him in order to succeed Mr Buchan a highland bursarie or some other fund might be allowed him to stay at Edinburgh. Mr Buchan had and has thir boyes to mantaine since he left Hirta till he returne and had not a farthing to [carrie him in the rod?], but a litle he got from us. Therefore it will be necessar a method be Laid down to mantain him and the boyes at Edinburgh till his returne in March nixt. If anie of the Libraries sent from England be undisposed of, it will be necessar one be given Mr Buchan - and that it consist of practical books, yea that ministers gift him such usefull books as they can spare, for he can borrow non[e] in Hirta, and therefore we think it will be most aggreeable to the mind of the Donnours that a librarie of the English books be given him.

'We think quhen you examine the boyes and gets a fuller account from Mr Buchan of his paines and success you will conclude that this work is of the Lord, and that it were a pitie that it should not be carried one, and that it will be scandalous to the national church to suffer such a work to fall to the ground for La[c]ke of incouragment, and veryly few will be fand willing or able to undergoe such hardships as Mr Buchan has allready suffered, and yet most suffer by continuing in Hirta, quhere he has not a Phisician in sickness, nor converse in health, nor access to see freinds, quhere he is separat in a manner from mankind, and therefore we hope you will take the premises to serious consideration, and see to his ordination and mantainance, for without both he will signifie Litle there, and since a man of pairts and learning will not be gotten to that place, we think Mr Buchan may if ordained be useful there, and if after some knowledge taught the People they be now left Desolat, we fear they will be worse than formerly. This is written and subscrived at appointment, and in the name and presence of the Presbytery of Argyle by

Right Rd
Your wisdomes
Humble and unworthie servant and fellow Labourer Daniel Campbell Clerk to the Presbytery

P.S. Mr Buchan got not a farding from the parents of the two boyes to carrie their expenses in this voyage.

We expect your wisdomes will address the Committee for Propagation of Christian Knowledge for incouragment of Mr Buchan.'[29]

On 22 October 1709 Daniel Campbell followed up his letter with a testimonial, certifying that Buchan had resided since the beginning of 1694 'for the most part in our bounds except some time we hear he was Catechist in Caithnes'. All but one or two of the ministers within the Synod's bounds had 'personal converse and acquaintance of him', and 'after inquirie made in open Synod concerning his life Conversation and diligence ... it was found by the unanimous voices of all the Synod that he behaved himself piously and Soberly and unofensivly and that he had a savourie edifying deportment in all the respective places of his abode amongst us and that he was truely painfull and dil[i]gent as schoolmaster or Catechist'. In view of his character and success 'this Synod judges that he is a person fit to be continued as Catechist in Hirta or to be employed any where else in the Highlands in that office', and there was no reason why he should not be ordained minister of 'Hirta' as envisaged, 'his ministrie being restricted to that place'. The Assembly Commission had already recommended his ordination but 'his Distance from us and difficultie of passage to and from Hirta' had prevented both Synod and presbytery of Skye from carrying it out.[30]

The Committee for Propagating Christian Knowledge, having considered this information, came to the opinion 'that he should be referred to the presbytery of Edinburgh to be tried in such manner as they shall think fittest in order to his ordination, and if it shall be thought fit after tryals to ordain him that his Ministry be restricted to Hirta or some of the remote Islands where the Irish Languadge is used ... under the inspection of the Synod of Argyle or presbytery of the bounds'. The matter was also to be 'seriously recommended to the Honourable Societie for propagateing Christian knowledge as soon as they can .. fall upon some way to provide a way for Mr Buchans Maintainance'.[31]

No doubt pleased at the thought of transferring to the SSPCK a responsibility which had always caused it trouble and which had seemed in some ways a burden that no existing branch of the Protestant church's organisation was suited to bear the Synod brought its immediate concern to a conclusion on 24 October 1709 at the time when Daniel Campbell wrote his testimonial. It suggested too that Buchan should be paid a sum of £40 scots out of the funds designed for Harris and left unused since John Campbell's death, 'partly for Charity and partly in Satisfaction of what he can demand from the Synod for his sallary while he was schoolmaster in Jura'. Outlying dues like that underlined the fact that Buchan 'suffered much for his good affection to the Church and State'. Inadequately rewarded while in Jura he spent nearly five years in St Kilda living in the harshest of conditions with hardly any financial support and as a substitute for a minister but without the authority of one. Now all was up to the SSPCK.

CHAPTER 4

The SSPCK is formed and Buchan is ordained with new instructions

THE SSPCK had been deliberately formed as a missionary body to cater for the spiritual needs, as they were envisaged by the Society members, of remote communities in 'the Highlands and Islands of Scotland and Forraign Parts of the World'; not that there were no needs nearer home, for, as the Society felt, 'it is matter of great Grief and Sorrow of Heart, that even among them who profess themselves Christians, there should be in many parts such Ignorance, Error and Corruption in Doctrine, Worship and Practice, that it is no easy thing to find Christian Religion in the midst of professed Christians'. What was judged as error and corruption obviously depended on the point of view of those who used the words, but the SSPCK, like other religious organisations and individuals, was not short of conviction in its own beliefs. There was no room for compromise with Catholicism, the continuing presence of which in places where the presbyterian kirk had not yet established an all-pervading influence meant that the SSPCK treated St Kilda as if it were a small, barbarous colony in Africa or America, ready for rescue from a religious wilderness before it fell into the wrong hands. The people for whom Buchan had been originally instructed to care, and for whom he came to have an affection which had nothing much to do with his instructions, were supposed to be inclined towards pagan and superstitious customs, vice and barbarity, a prey to their own 'popish' inheritance and traditions. According to his daughter in after years Buchan found them on his arrival to be ignorant and 'much given to idolatry'. It is evident therefore that the general remarks in the initial 'Proposals' upon which the Society's work was based applied to the island as much as anywhere else:

> 'There are also sad Complaints, that in diverse of the Plantations in America, there is great want of the means of Knowledge, and Pastors to teach them. Yea even at home in Scotland now North Britain, in some places in the Highlands and Islands, by reason of Barbarity and Ignorance, many are little better then Infidels, and in many places Popery spreadeth, to the great Grief of such as love the Truth; Yea some places were never reformed from Popery …'[32]

The instructions given to Buchan in 1704 were quite consistent with such sentiments, and the Society's approach followed familiar lines. Founded upon a claim to possession of 'the Truth' it depended to some extent also on the inability or unwillingness of most people to recognise that the inhabitants of St Kilda and other remote places might not be barbaric and that they might have beliefs and customs at least as valid as those which were already, or to be, imposed from without.

On 27 October 1709 the Committee of the General Assembly which could be said to have initiated the SSPCK received Buchan's 'representation', asked him about his work and success, and heard him catechise the two boys he had brought with him.

Satisfied with this but disturbed to find that Buchan had still not been paid it turned the matter over to the Society and to the Synod of Lothian and Tweeddale, the latter being expected to persuade its presbyterians to contribute funds as the presbytery of Edinburgh had done to make up Buchan's missing 'salary'. As a consequence the Society dealt with the 'representation' at the beginning of January 1710. Members learned about 'the State of that Island and the Success he has had amongst the people there, and how he was necessitat to Leave them for want of Subsistance'. The usual step was taken in passing consideration on to a committee with a recommendation 'to do what they can for his Subsistence and Encouragement to continue in that Place', and in early March the committee reported that Buchan 'is not in a capacity to go back and continue there Except some assureance be given that he will be taken care of', which, it might be thought, had been obvious for some long time. However it also reported that it had given some attention to this point and had reached the rather unsatisfactory conclusion that he should be told that as soon as the Society was able to it would indeed 'take care of him'. Buchan, whose activities during these winter months are not recorded, was called in to the meeting to hear this decision. Perhaps unconvinced he gave another account of his circumstances, whereupon the Society 'Desired him to return to his Work in Hirta as Soon as he can and for his Encouragement the General meetting appointed that a letter be written to the Tutors and Curators of the Laird of McLeod to allow the said Alexander Buchan a Subsistence untill the Societie be in case to take care of him'.[33]

So Buchan was persuaded and agreed to return, even though he was not in very good health. The letter to the Tutors and Curators reminded them that St Kilda belonged to their pupil, the new young Laird, that Buchan was very useful in the island, and that the late Laird had been very encouraging to him and, if he had been spared, 'would have prosecute his pious intention of giving all due Encouragement to the Instructing of the Inhabitants of the said Island in the Knowledge of the Reformed Christian Religion'. The approval of Buchan by the tutors was commended to them, and, since 'he is prevailed with to return to the said Island in order to reside there and continue to Instruct the Inhabitants thereof in the principles of Religion and vertue', they were asked to assist him, to ensure that the people there treated him with 'due respect and obedience', and to supply him with 'a suitable and competent allowance' for himself and family until the Society could do so. They were told: 'yow need not fear to give him Credit'.[34]

Certificates testifying to his good character as a catechist having been received from Halkirk and Thurso in late December 1709, and Daniel Campbell having pointed out that 'this being a national concern' the Synod of Argyll was afraid that if nothing was done 'other nationall churches will sadlie reflect on our church, and that the poor Soules in Hirta will perish for Lack of knowledge', the presbytery of Edinburgh duly ordained Alexander Buchan as minister in St Kilda in St Giles's church on 15 March 1710. The service was attended by Alexander MacLeod, advocate, and by the two boys from the island, Finlay MacDonald and Murdo Campbell. In this way both landlord and community were represented. After the ordination money was apparently donated by a wide variety of people; a Major Le Blanc and George Buchan, clerk to the Commission of Teinds, contributed towards a fund for building a manse in St Kilda, many 'other charitable Christians' gave money and books, and 'diverse Members of the Society did contribute out of their own Pockets'. On 22 March the Edinburgh city council, which had received a petition from Buchan, 'minister of St Kilda', told its chamberlain to pay him £40 scots 'for defraying the expences of his journey to the said Island for propagating the Christian knowledge there', and 'appointed Thomas Dunbar present deacon of the Taylors to make and provide a suit of cloaths for him out of the cloath in his custody belonging to the Good Town ..' A week later the Society commissioned Buchan to be 'one of their Schoolmasters' and drew up another set of 'Instructions how to carry'.[35]

All this time Buchan himself became ever more bemused at the events which had overtaken him. He had been made 'a Minister of the Gospell for the use of that Island and other Remote places' even though 'I am very unworthie of being Imployed in that holy function and unfitt both in body and mind'. He had been given a new suit but still no money. Nevertheless, in obedience to the call and trusting to receive some pay eventually, he resolved 'to return to Hirta and cast myself upon the Lord'. It was a big risk, he knew. 'My tyme cannot be Long in this World, the fatigue and badness of my diet has brought me Low, and I am concerned for haveing some Persons bred up to succeed me in that Place'. His concern was partly induced by the knowledge that few other people would be prepared to stay in St Kilda and undergo all the privations which he had himself endured, for which reason he had hopes that a suitable successor might be found out of the island population; 'seing it is not easy to prevaill with Strangers to go there I have been at some pains to Instruct Finlay McDonald and Murdo Campbell two of the natives of that Island whom I have been Intertaining and Learning since August [1705] when I went first to the Isle'. Having brought these two with him he then 'keept them at School for Reading writting and Musick upon my own charges and I must acknowledge the great charity of severall good people in this City'. Now that he was going back he was no longer able 'to breed these boyes' but wished to see his aims fulfilled through their continued education in grammar and 'other Learning' so that one at least might be able to succeed him. He therefore petitioned that 'if one Hundred merks were bestowed on them in the year I hope it would go a great Length to maintain them at the Grammar School in Skye'. He requested the Society's consideration and approval of the idea, for 'I thought it my Duty to use all proper means to have the Gospell continued in that Place after I am dead and gone and it will ease my mind that I have Left this before yow'. Buchan promised also to deposit a catalogue or list of all the books he had received with the Society's secretary and, in accordance with the twelfth of his original instructions, to 'preserve them in the Island for the use of my Successours'.[36]

The Society's reaction was theoretically what Buchan might have wished but once again unpromising in practice. While willing to give 'encouragement' in the usual manner and 'to concurr for helping to Educat Finlay McDonald and Murdo Campbell in order to their being Serviceable to Instruct the Inhabitants of hirta or other remote Islands', the Society was unable to allocate any capital to this purpose and a long time would elapse before sufficient interest had accumulated. Those present at the meeting unanimously resolved to contribute again out of their own pockets and to recommend to absentees and others that they should do so as well. Finlay and Murdo therefore faced an uncertain future at this stage, and though their subsequent fate is not recorded in any detail it is certain that they went back home with their minister, probably to spend the rest of their lives in the island.[37]

At its meeting on 13 April 1710 and with a vivid recollection of the two boys the Society turned its attention to education. In so doing it followed the tenth instruction of 1704 with thirteen more which to some extent were adaptations of the original dozen. The members now knew well that the poor people of St Kilda had lacked anyone 'to Instruct them in the principles of the Christian Reformed Protestant Religion' and to teach them to read until the arrival of Alexander Buchan, and they knew too that there was 'no Setled maintinance for one in his Station' there. They had heard of the difficulties he faced in a community where, according to the Protestant church, 'Errour Superstition and Ignorance abounds'. Now that Buchan was ordained and had produced 'ample Certificates' of his qualifications and of 'his Life and good conversation' from 'other places where he hath resided from his Infancie', the meeting, aware of his readiness to return, now authorised him 'to Erect and keep up a School in the Said Island and to teach the Inhabitants thereof to read Especially the holy Scriptures and other good and pious books, as also to teach writting Arithmetick and such lyke Degrees of Knowledge and to use Such means for Instructing the People in the Christian Reformed Protestant Religion as may be proper'. The Society had in mind that adults as well as children would attend.

Along with these ambitious aims came the new set of 'Instructions', which showed how the Church conceived the role of combined minister and schoolteacher. The Protestant religion together with the approved kind of education would in total chase away the shadows of the past:

1. 'Yow are to return to Hirta and according to your Commission given by the said Societie Erect a School there and Deall with the Inhabitants of that Island especially the younger Sort to come to yow to Learn What yow are required by the said Commission to teach'.
2. Those who came to the school should be encouraged and shown the advantage of learning. Great care should be taken to let the benefit gained by those attending encourage others to join in.

3. School was to begin every morning and end every evening with prayer. Lying, cursing, swearing and other immorality among the youth should be suppressed and there were to be 'privy Censures for that effect in the School'. In other words the pupils were to inform on each other in private.
4. When days were short there was to be one meeting of the school, but when long there were to be two - 'if yow find the Children can be so Long Spared by their parents'.
5. Buchan was conscientiously to instruct in religious principles, the Confession of Faith and the Longer and Shorter Catechisms. Those who learned to read were to acquire the Shorter Catechism by heart, while the others were to be taught questions on God, the Creation, the preciousness of immortal souls, their sins and misery and redemption by Jesus, what Jesus had done for them, what they should do to be saved, the ten commandments, the Lord's Prayer, the meaning of baptism and the nature of the Lord's Supper, the Covenant of Grace, the evil of sin and the sins that abound - including 'the evil of useing Charming and other Superstitious customs', the Judgment to come and their future state in Heaven or Hell.
6. In going from house to house the teacher was to commend what was good and virtuous, reprove vice and idleness, pray with and in the family, and teach them to pray on their own. He was to show them how to sanctify the Lord's Day and how to behave during divine worship.
7. 'When yow converse with the Comon people Shew them the Evill and Danger of Ignorance and Vice and offer them your help'.
8. 'Be not morose or sullen, nor too familiar and open but kind and Courteous of a wise and gaining conversation that they may See yow are Sent for their good and not your own profit nor any gain from them'.
9. The conduct of the teacher was to be careful. He was to put vice and immorality to shame and flight, but commend religion to the conscience.
10. In school the teacher was also to teach the pupils to read English and to write it. Those who profited by these were to teach others, and all were to observe their duties to their superiors.
11. The teacher was to be restrained in attitude, patient, meek, humble, slow to anger, and 'not given to unnecessary debates'.
12. 'Be carefull to Instruct Murdo Campbell and Finlay McDonald', and encourage them to be useful in the island.
13. Finally, as before, Buchan was instructed to look after the books and not to forget to report to the Society 'how matters go with you'.[38]

And with these exhortations filling his mind Alexander Buchan, in the early summer of 1710, along with his books and the two boys, voyaged back through the Sound of Harris and across the surging sea to his life, and death, in St Kilda.

CHAPTER 5

Buchan's 'Litle book', progress and disasters,
Mrs Buchan and children go to Edinburgh

When Buchan went out to the mainland in August 1709 he had a purpose other than securing ordination and overdue payment. He took with him the manuscript of what he called 'his Litle book'.

This book was about his island home, but it was written not so much in imitation of Martin Martin, whose works may have been the inspiration, but rather with the intention of raising funds to support the education of Murdo Campbell, hitherto his best and almost his only pupil. He left the manuscript in the care of an acquaintance, probably in Edinburgh, in the hope that once it appeared in print it would earn the necessary money. Having heard nothing as to its fate by 1711 he wrote to find out what was happening. 'He desires to know,' the SSPCK heard, 'If his Litle book of the discription of Hirta, which he left with Mr James Hart, be printed, and intreats that the third part of the money therof may be sent to him, to be given to Murdo Campbell to keep him at the Grammar School, and he declares that he is resolved to give him thirty merks of the Three hundred merks [£200 scots] yearly that the Society has allowed him, with any other help he can give him, to train him up at Schools to fit him to Succeed him'. There was no other way, Buchan stated, by which Murdo's education could be furthered, 'Because the natives will Let none of their children come to School that can work, unless he will maintain them all the while'. As a consequence Buchan had a houseful of children: 'he maintains Eight or Nine poor orphans in his family, and teaches them English, which they can only Learn in his house'. But nothing had been done by way of the publication desired, and it was to be another sixteen years before the manuscript was, in a manner, printed.[39]

The children and parents in the 'village' of St Kilda lived within an oral tradition of learning rather than a literate one of reading and writing, and the move expected by the SSPCK from the first to the second could not have been greater. It was equivalent in many ways to the change expected from the old, traditional religious life to the new Protestant world, and neither could be accomplished overnight. The remaining twenty years of Buchan's life were not enough to achieve such transformations, even supposing there had been no resistance, and more than one islander would have questioned the Society's intentions given the opportunity. The people of St Kilda were not all so unintelligent as to be unable to challenge what Buchan had been instructed to do. As it was they had priorities in the business of survival which put the 'school' into the background and may have made the skills of reading, writing, arithmetic and 'music' acquired with some success by Murdo Campbell and Finlay MacDonald seem like harmless amusements for which they would take no responsibility.

A
DESCRIPTION
OF
Saint KILDA;

Giving an Account of its

SITUATION,	Adjacent ISLANDS,
EXTENT,	Ancient LAWS and
SOIL,	GOVERNMENT,
PRODUCT,	RELIGION,
BAYS,	CUSTOMS, and late
ROCKS,	REFORMATION.

By the Rev. Mr. ALEXANDER BUCHAN
late Minifter there.

Printed in the Year, M, DCC, LII.

Title page of possibly the fourth edition (1752) of the book bearing
the name of Alexander Buchan as author

Early in 1711 the Society had agreed that a salary of £200 scots (£16.13s.4d sterling) would be paid out of interest on funds to Buchan during his continued ministry and teaching in the island, although conveying the money to him was almost as big a problem as finding it. A letter had arrived from their 'Catechist and Schoolmaster in St Kilda', containing an account of his progress and the promised catalogue of the 'library' there. The books may have broadened the mind of the minister but it cannot be imagined that they were of much use to the people, children or adults. Two more letters came from Buchan in 1711, written no doubt during the summer when they could be taken away by the steward, and were discussed by the SSPCK in March 1712, yet another illustration of the difficulty of communication and the time taken to deal with pressing matters and respond. Buchan had been ill and although 'somewhat recovered' he was evidently still of the view that he might not live much longer. He was, however, able to given an account of his diligence at work. He wrote of how he had decided 'to Leave the houses and accomodations he had built, and all the plenishing thereof, and his other moveables, to Murdo Campbell, the best inclined and most hopefull of his boys that he is educating, or to any other that Shall Succeed him as Catechist, and that if he could get the five pounds Sterling promised him, he would sufficiently provide him and his successors in all necessaries'. He also made here his enquiry about his intended book.[40]

Somewhere not too far from the group of 'village' huts stood now 'the houses and accomodations' which Buchan had built with the aid of the financial contributions towards a manse that he had brought back with him in 1710. Perhaps he had purchased the help of some islanders and had been able to add wreck timber and driftwood to the materials needed, but the end product cannot have been very substantial. The buildings would have to accommodate the minister and his increasing family, the library assembled in 1710, and possibly the schoolroom which might have served some religious purposes as well as daily education. That Buchan felt all this belonged to the SSPCK or to the posts of minister and teacher rather than to himself is clear from his wish to leave everything to his successor, but his family may have been a little disappointed to find that not even any of the 'moveables' were destined for them.

*

Norman, Laird of MacLeod and born in 1706, was a minor for most of the years during which Buchan remained in St Kilda. In the course of his minority the Laird's affairs were managed by John MacLeod of Contullich as tutor and by Contullich's 'natural brother', the advocate Alexander MacLeod, who had served previous lairds in the same capacity. There is frequent reference to the tutor and to Mr Alexander in the SSPCK records, chiefly because they were concerned in matters relating to St Kilda and inevitably in the circumstances of Buchan's life there.[41]

Contullich's accounts for 1712 refer to a 'remarkable Disaster in the Island of Borera' and to the ensuing poverty 'occasioned by the said Disaster'. The St Kilda boat was lost and had to be replaced, the tutor allowing 146^1/$_2$ merks for this purpose, and because the islanders were so impoverished by the event they were relieved from paying rent for two years.[42] The lack of a boat meant that there was no means of reaching Boreray or Soay, with their accompanying rocks, and a severe shortage of birds inevitably followed. In his letter of 24 June 1712 Alexander Buchan briefly conveyed some feeling of what the loss signified to the inhabitants. He also explained at length what steps he had taken to carry out his latest instructions.

'very reverend Sir

'I have been much aflicted with the state of this poor peopl who lost their boat this year. when they breaks the Sabbath I cause them stand in sackcloat dipped in the filthiest gutter in the toun, and I exhort them as weel as I rebuke them, and they pay the value of half a merk every on[e] to the poor, if they have goods, the fyns are sixteen pence. the greatest fyn I took was tuo merks from the officers wife and she gave a compleint to my wife to get the sackcloaths clean, and I gave the poor the value theirof. any that curs or swear by the ewil on[e] or renting of the rocks pays a half merk and I parted the corn all I got for fyns this year with my oun hand to the poor becaus of the scarcity of food I would not trust to my [?] the parting. every widou that had a child I gave her child as much as her self. the officers wife commanded tuo women to kill a dog on the lords day she being a delinquent formerly for Sabbath breaking and tuic[e] or thried for cursing and the most wicked. I caused them both to stand in sackcloath dreeping doun black gutter and rebuk her publickly as weel as them, and she payed the value of a merk for the tuo women to the poor tuo girles went out with the rocks this year seek fouls and taking sheep for want of men, all the males being storm stead eleven months in borrara eight mils distant to the north east. It is my constant and earnest Prayer to god to glorifie his wisdom by my foolishness and his Power by my weaknes and his all sufficiency by my unsufficiency for tho this work be glorious its great and dangerous. it [is] no light thing to be instrumental to bring any of Jacob to christ and if they be not better that they may never be wors provided for having no less of the means of grace and that all that will teach or preach crist her may be of Publick Spirits gracious hearts and liberal hands above and not beneath only in the lord not seeking their oun but the profit of many that they may be saved and that a proud rich officer may never reign over a poor despised minister and since I am afraid and the best inclined that another man wil not come so far of to do as I do and live as I live in hirta I striving by gods help to take away the reproach of poverty from all my succeeding teachers. I cannot get any to learn to read only the officer who is richer then ten of his neighbours permits his youngest son to get som[e?] lessons. his riches and power and influence is much to gods dishonor and the contempt of the gospel. this is to aquaint your wisdom of my burden of position. the lord in mercy grant that non of his servants meet with the like for I am busie at the [thron?] to that effect as I am concer[n]ing my self daylie at the thron about the generations to come that they may Prais the Lord beging many favours and mercies for them and their teacher. if I were of som mens spirit I would leave the ministery to the officer with his office and as mr Spence knows it to no purpos to your wisdoms to write to maklowd to that effect for I am thought better of now for tuenty sheep I have and three or four kous then I am for my ministery books and the graces of gods holy spirit. the oficer hath upwards of tuo hunder sheep and mor then tuenty cows and he ay exalts himsel and [cryes?] he'el live and dy rich

'he said to my face befor all the land he would never honor [ane?] god or man and all the kindnes I shewed his son he took it to be done out of abundance of respect to him self for being officer and being rich. I have peac in summer when the bailie is present; all the other three quarters he reigneth and his wife and they proclaim they are the bailis deputs and have the authority and word of the Laird and that non can com in competition with them and were it not for fear of mckloud I could not get a fyn from delinquents to the poor. the bailie allows to take fyns from delinquents. som say I am providing for my soul and not for my familie. I am repairing the buildings this year with mor timber I get for nough[t] from a worthy gentlman of my acquaintanc rory mckcloud of [mothertoun?]. I could give no mor to murdoch campbel this year but ten merks worth of the goods I received that his friends might give him time to read some every day. if I get the thirty merks I sought yearly of my salary I shall endeavor to put him and all that will teach in hirta in kous and sheep which will be much to gods glory and the honor of the gospel and comfort of the begars I have ordered the old cloaths of my sheep I leave here to be given to the poorest orphans that will be in hirta knowing the poor wil never depart from the [gate?]. the lord water your wisdom labour with his great rich and effectual blessing and grant that all his sent servants may not complain of labouring in vain and may have a Joyful acount to giv christ on day as I am busie praying earnestly to that effect day by sam. your wisdoms debitor in love and all thankfulnes for the kindness of the lord ye have shewed to me and this poor place. I rest your wisdoms obedient servant in Christ

Alexander Buchan
at hirta the 24 of Jun 1712'⁴³

Among the several memorable sentences in this letter perhaps the most striking is that which records the marooning of all the St Kilda men on Boreray for eleven months. That they apparently all survived reduced the degree of the 'Disaster' a little but their experience was no less dramatic in its impact on the women left at home than the loss of the boat. The deprived families could easily picture the plight of the men on Boreray in the middle of winter, assuming that they knew they were there and not drowned, and in having to do men's work in the spring of 1712 it seems from what Buchan wrote that 'the poor tuo girles' fell from the cliffs when pursuing birds and sheep. The accident was not the first at Boreray, however. Martin had described a similar occasion and how communication was possible:

> 'All the Men in the Isle, having gone to the Isle *Boreray* for purchase, the Rope that fastened their Boat, happened to break, and by this unlucky accident, the Boat was quite lost, and the Poor People confined in the Isle, from the middle of *March*, till the latter end of *May*; without so much as a crust of Bread, but they had Sheep, Fowl and Fish in abundance. They were at a loss, how to acquaint their Wives and Friends, that all of them were alive; but to effect this, they kindled as many Fires on the top of an Eminence, as there was Men in Number; this was no sooner seen, and the Fires counted than the Women understood the signal, and were so overjoyed at this unexpected News, that they fell to labour the Ground with the Foot-spade, a fatigue they had never been accustomed to; and that Years product of Corn, was the most plentiful that they had for many Years before. After the Stewards arrival in the Isle, about the end of *May*, he sent his Galley to bring home all the Men confined in the Isle, to their so much longed for *St. Kilda*; where the mutual Joy between them and their Wives, and other Relations was extraordinary.'[44]

Buchan said very little in his letter about the disaster because he knew that the General Assembly and the SSPCK limited interest in the island to the religious and teaching labours of the minister there, to the payment of his salary, and to the supply of books. Other aspects were considered to be the responsibility of 'the Tutor', MacLeod of Contullich, 'who is concerned in that place', and Buchan was told 'that when he has any grieveances to Complain of, he may lay the same before the Tutor of McLeod, who had promised to redress the same, and to cause that all due encouragement be given to him'. The advocate Alexander MacLeod had the task of conveying payment to the minister. The sum of £200 scots from the SSPCK was continued, but in 1713 a total of £600 scots or 900 merks arrears was owing as pay while Buchan in turn owed 760 merks to 'the Laird of Mcleod', an indication that in the absence of three years' worth of salary, the whole period since his ordination, Buchan had received money via the Laird's managers on credit. Arrangements had been made by the Society that each year the salary should be given to

Alexander MacLeod, either to recompense him for what amounted to loans or to hand on to the steward for taking to the island. In 1713 the Society determined that the sum due should be passed to Alexander MacLeod and that letters should be written to the tutor and to 'the Baillie of Hirta', asking them to continue to encourage the minister 'in his work in that Island'.[45]

It was also a possibility that the Synod of Argyll, given its personal links with the Buchans, might still play some part in assisting the St Kilda minister, but in August 1711 this body had distanced itself further from the problem of the island by writing to Buchan that henceforth he should 'fix a Correspondence' with the presbytery of Skye as the appropriate and nearest source of help and advice. The early minutes of this presbytery's meetings are missing, except for a fragment from 1712 which happens to note, among other business, a letter received from Buchan saying 'that he wanted of the allowance given unto him by the Synod'. Although 'the respective Brethren', including members from North Uist and other parts of the Outer Hebrides, were to be informed of this communication, the lack of the records leaves the outcome unknown. It appears that neither the Synod nor the presbytery gave any further support to their most lonely outpost.[46]

Over the next few years even SSPCK support over and beyond salary seemed to diminish. The Society had other things to think about, for apart from the 'one who officiats as minister and Schoolmaster in Hirta, alias St Kilda', there were teachers to be paid at sixteen other schools, including Snizort in Skye and Glenelg 'in the remote Highlands'. The Jacobite rising of 1715 came as a reminder that there was an ever present threat to its 'good works' in so many places. When 'a very long letter … Consisting of four sheets of paper' arrived from Buchan towards the end of 1714 and gave 'an account of how matters stand with him' it aroused little response other than a continuation of salary, and a few months later the only point of concern was the realisation that he 'has never yet Sent any list of his Schollars or account of their progress at his School'. He was promptly asked to do so, although it would probably be a year until he received the request. But at a meeting on 1 March 1716 members of the Society committee contemplated submitting an application for a financial contribution from the Royal Bounty funds 'In order to Erect more Schools in the Highlands and Islands where popery and Ignorance does so much abound, It being certain that the poor people in these places have been the unhappy tools of the Late Rebellion, and of much trouble to their nighbours'. St Kilda was probably protected to some extent from the feared reversion to 'popery' by its remoteness and inaccessibility, and by Buchan himself, but among the Catholic districts Barra and South Uist were not all that far away, and a glance at history showed that the St Kilda people could quite easily be made 'tools' by any persuasive and seemingly authoritative leader. And since Buchan could not reply quickly to the Society's enquiry on the state of the school what was going on there became something of a worry.[47]

By June 1716 a total of 25 schools had been founded by the SSPCK, yet this fell 'far short of answering the great necessity of the vast and Large bounds of the

Highlands and Islands where Schools are wanting, and the poor people brought up in ignorance, and thereby are proper tools to their popish and Jacobite heads of Clanns and others for carrying on their wicked and Rebellious projects for overturning our present happy establishment ..' The Society had often received from presbyteries and ministers 'Lamentable accounts' of these remote areas with their huge, unorganised parishes. It had heard and believed 'that many of the heads of Clanns, Especially popish ones, do discourage learning in their Countreys, Because it would draw off the people from that unlimited Subjection to them'. In such a situation the Society saw its aim of teaching religious principles and the fundamentals of learning in the Highlands and islands as identical with that of 'reduceing these Countries to order' and of 'making them usefull to the Common wealth'. This could be done by showing that duty to God was accompanied by duty to 'King and Countrey', and implied of course 'unlimited Subjection' to a different authority from that about which it complained.[48]

The native Gaelic speech was in itself seen as an enemy of the state and had been treated as such for a long time. The people of St Kilda, like those elsewhere in the islands and in a large area of the mainland, had to put up with the consequences, although this would depend on the willingness or ability of the teacher to conduct his activities in English. The intention was clear enough: 'rooting out their Irish language ... has been the care of the Society so farr as they could, For all the Schollars are taught in English and none are allowed to be Masters of the Societie's charitie Schools, but Such as produce Sufficient Certificats of their piety knowledge and Loyalty ..' The Society even referred to the process of 'Civilizing the Highlands' which would be accomplished through methods that included 'by time wearing out the Irish'.[49]

As witnessed by its attempts to communicate with Alexander Buchan the SSPCK, that useful instrument of the establishment, could do little to prevent the gap between aims and intentions in Edinburgh and practice in St Kilda from remaining a wide one. The Laird of MacLeod might have been some kind of bridge across the space but in 1717 he was a boy of about ten without decided loyalties in relation to the Jacobite cause, while his agent of business, Alexander MacLeod, and the latter's nephew, Roderick MacLeod, were Jacobite sympathisers with projects of their own in mind, and each had sisters married to Catholic lairds including Clanranald and MacNeil of Barra. For all the encouragement that Contullich and Alexander the advocate may have given Buchan in St Kilda there is no sign that they did anything to promote enthusiasm there for learning and loyalty to the government or for that matter to persuade the inhabitants to pay much heed to their teacher and minister. Whatever his qualifications and however great his commitment to the Society's aims Buchan would have experienced a remarkable lack of success and even of ordinary conversation if he had adhered strictly to the English language in a place where no one except members of his own family understood it. There were indeed many reasons why the doubtful value of the Society's purposes was not immediately appreciated by the St. Kilda community and why the people were shielded from the full impact of its missionary programme.

It was all very well for the Society to talk about the usefulness of schools, but how effective would the educating and 'civilizing' process be if hardly anyone attended them or if attendance was only occasional and perhaps quite rare? With parents often frustrating the teacher by keeping children off to do seasonal work, or because the weather was bad, the Society found it difficult to know whether a teacher really had anyone to teach. The long silence that followed the Society's enquiry about the school in St Kilda did not help. On 15 May 1717 the management committee reported 'That for these tuo years bygone, or thereby they have had no accompts what Mr Buchan is doing at Hirta'. Two years without such information was likely to result in the witholding of salary. However there was some news of his work as minister; during the summer Buchan wrote again to the presbytery of Skye, which in turn forwarded its views to the SSPCK at the beginning of September. The message was that he 'has been very Successful in his work, and has given the Sacrament of the Lords Supper once … and that the people are desireous to have it again'. The presbytery suggested that flour and wine should be sent to the island, along with the standard 'encourageing Letter'. In preparing its reply the Society noted another, more important event that promised to produce the information needed not only about the school but also about circumstances in general. Mrs. Buchan had 'come to Toun' again.[50]

*

Katherine Campbell, Mrs. Buchan, reached Edinburgh by way of Argyll, where she again called on Daniel Campbell, minister at Kilmichael of Glassary. She then made for the city, and at the beginning of November 1717 the Society found itself having to respond to one supplication or petition handed in by her 'in her husbands name', another in her own, and a letter in support, dated 3 October, from Daniel Campbell. The supplications revealed a good deal about the realities of life faced by the Buchan family in St Kilda, and, to some extent, by the people to whom Buchan ministered. In the first he stated 'that he has only four Schollars beside his oun Children' in the school, 'the poverty of the place and people hindering them to send their Children to School except in Stormy weather, when they cannot be otherwayes Imployed.' Of his own six children, Buchan said, 'the eldest being a girle, teaches the catechisme to all the girles in the Island upon Saturdays and Sundays afternoon, being the only time they can Spare, and that he himself is always present to help her'. For her part Mrs Buchan, evidently a strong personality and ready with the sort of domestic complaints which her husband might not have wished to make himself, wrote of the mundane problems which added daily to their distress. She described how, in spite of his diligent attention to duty as minister and schoolmaster, her husband 'Labours under many discouragements both as to Spritualls and temporalls'.

He was a lonely figure, 'haveing no minister or experienced Christian to Converse with, and give him advice in his many difficulties'. As someone expected to bring 'order' to the community he was unable to make much progress, for 'through want of a Magistrat to assist him in discipline, his hands are very much weakened that way'. At home in his own house he was living in poverty and no longer looked after any island children. His household consisted of ten people; Buchan himself and his wife, their six children, and a maid servant and nurse, the last, according to Mrs Buchan, being a person 'whom She is obliged to keep, her oun milk having gone from her by the change of her diet'. The family had also 'to hire the natives to Grind their meall in quirns, cast and Lead their peats, herd their few Cattle, thatch their oun house and do other services', work which in mainland parishes was normally carried out for the minister by the various tenants and other inhabitants as a free service. As a result of expenditure on these necessities the Society's allowance of 300 merks 'is every year exhausted Long before the Stewart come to the Island, and they are put to the borrowing, which exposes them to disdain and reproach'. They were, in addition, 'forced to wear Shirts of plaiding and other Such things which exposes them to contempt'. Their only bread was made from old barley, 'the Country affords no Liquors but water', their few cows were not 'Sufficient to affoord them milk and whey', and they had but 'Six weathers allowed them in the year by the Chamberland in part of their Three hundered merks'. It would appear from all these observations that instead of holding the respected and influential position of a minister in a more conventional situation Mr Buchan, and his family, were almost as badly off as the majority of 'the natives'.

The purpose of both supplications was to secure some sort of remedy for what was considered a very unsatisfactory position. Authority was undermined by inadequate living standards, and without authority little or nothing could be achieved. The Buchans asked the Society to add another hundred merks a year to the previous allowance, some of it in money but 'in part therof to allow them tuo bolls oatmeall, and a boll of peese to be put up in barrells at Neill McCallums house in Glasgow, to be sent to them yearly with the boats of Harreis'. They also requested 'tuenty ells of Course Linnen at eight pence the yard, and eight ells at Sixteen pence the yard', presumably for shirts. Mrs Buchan had brought with her two lists of books, one noting those for which her husband no longer had any use, the other setting out books which he would like to have, and in her petition she asked for the latter to be despatched to the island with 'some competent number of Irish psalm books, and Bibles both English and Irish for the use of the children, and Such as can read'. Then there was the matter of the landlord and how, apart from sending letters, he or his agents might help. Mrs Buchan suggested a letter should be sent to the Tutor, and to his son Roderick, 'Baillie of Harreis', recommending them to exert their authority over the people and thereby 'to give her husband all Suteable encouragement for Strenthening his hands in discipline'.

The MacLeods could also encourage the minister by 'obligeing the natives to pay him the ordinary dues for marriages and Baptismes, which he once possesst but is now deprived of, And ... to help cast and Lead her husbands peats as is usuall in other places'. Finally she wished that a copy might be sent to her husband of whatever was written about him to the 'Tutor' and 'Baillie', so that he might be able to show the people in St Kilda what the Society ordered to be done for him.

The SSPCK committee paid due attention to these petitions and though willing to respond favourably to them concluded that first of all 'Mr Buchans successe both as minister and Schoolmaster Should be particularly enquired into, and what's the reason that he has so few Schollars'. That the number of his own children should be greater than the total of native 'scholars' seemed odd, and the need for books in Gaelic may have struck some committee members as out of line with the task of suppressing that language. The decision they took was as follows:

'The Society ... Laid it upon the Reverend Ministers and Ruling Elderes members of this Society, who are also members of the Commission of the General Assembly, to move in the said Commission, That they would write a Letter to the Presbytery of Sky, Desireing them to send a minister of their said Presbytery next Summer to visite the Island of St Kilda, and enquire into the carriage of Alexander Buchan Minister there, and Successe in his Labours amongst the people there, and to assist and Joine with him in administring the Sacrament of the Lords Supper to such of the Inhabitants as they find in a Condition to partake of that ordinance, And that because of the distance of the Said Island, and that there is no Correspondence therewith but by The Laird of Mcleods Chamberland and officer, who are ordinarly both illiterat men, wherby no certain accounts can be had of the State of the people there or of the said Mr Buchans Success and behaviour among them.'[51]

During the early weeks of 1718 further information was received confirming Mrs Buchan's report that 'the people of Hirta are not forward to send their children to School'. In the circumstances this is hardly surprising, but the Society naturally had the achievement of its own aims to worry about. If so few of the island children were being taught to read, then was it worth keeping Buchan in St Kilda? The place was after all exceptionally difficult to deal with, although like Foula and Fair Isle it appealed strongly to the missionary instincts of the Society. After deliberation the secretary wrote 'to the Tutor of McLeod and others concerned in that Island to take more care in obligeing people to send their Children to Mr Buchan to be taught, and also to see that he have all due encouragement, and be not extortioned as to the pryce of necessaries furnished to him'. Otherwise, the Society threatened, 'he will be removed and sent elsewhere'.[52]

By the time this letter was sent, in March 1718, Mrs Buchan had spent nearly five months on the mainland. Apart from her supplications she had brought with her from St Kilda her eldest daughter, Jean, who in after years remembered that on their way they had been 'shipwrecked upon the Mull of Cantyre'. When they had left Argyll for Edinburgh Daniel Campbell requested that the Society give them something by which they 'may be Subsisted untill Summer next, that they return home'. On presenting the supplications Mrs Buchan repeated this request, saying too that she would like her daughter to be kept at a school until May 1718 when they would 'catch the occasion of the Stuarts boat' and go back to the island. The Society listened to the appeal and linked it to the matter of the salary. An additional sum of 100 merks was added to the existing 300 merks, but it was not thought that Buchan should expect anything on account of baptisms, which were now within his powers as minister. Were there any arrears of salary? Mrs Buchan said that little or nothing was still owing to her husband, 'effects to the value therof being got from the Laird of McLeods Chamberlands'. The SSPCK committee, finding that 'letters of Credit' had been sent to 'the Tutor' in favour of Buchan, did not feel the need 'to medle with advanceing any of the old Sallary', or to produce any more money to support mother and daughter. However, it advised Mrs. Buchan to leave the girl on the mainland, and members would 'speake to some school mistress to teach her'. The members would also try to produce from collections sufficient to cover Jean's board for a year, but if they were unsuccessful and no other way to maintain her could be found part or all of the extra 100 merks would have to be used.[53]

Mrs. Buchan left for Glasgow on the first stage of her journey home, having with her the new books for her husband and, apparently, the 100 merks with which she would buy 'necessaries' at a rate cheaper than that at which they were charged by the steward of St Kilda. She had left her daughter behind her, 'to have her breeding gratis in the trades hospital' and boarded at £15 scots per quarter, which amount would take up nearly all the additional salary. But it would seem that the Buchans saw no future for their children, if they survived, in their island home.[54]

Jean Buchan was looked after by Mr and Mrs William McEwen in Edinburgh while her education progressed. From time to time sums were paid to Mrs McEwen for the girl's keep, and on 1 October 1719 £6 scots was added to the usual quarterly instalment of £15 scots to help Jean buy clothes. The problem of how to find the money remained. In July 1718 the SSPCK management committee had asked those of their number who were ministers or members of kirk sessions to approach their parishes in the hope 'that Something may be got from them for paying the said Jean Buchans Board'. Perhaps these appeals had some success, since when the Society gave consideration to Jean's circumstances in June 1719 it heard that after 'being Left here without any provision for her boarding' help had come in the form of 'Some private Collections', but these had now all been spent. One solution suggested was to see if interest from the Viscountess of Kenmure's mortification, a bequest gifted to the Society by the King because it was supposed to be for the maintenance and education of the poor children of ministers, could be used to support Jean, but after investigation the committee discovered that it could not draw upon this source because the girl was not attending any of the Society's charity schools. Even so it 'thought it was necessary that She Should be seen to', and proposed that another 100 merks should be added to Alexander Buchan's salary for a year or two, so that he might himself be able to maintain and educate his daughter. The proposal was implemented immediately, and for a short while it looked as though everything was under control and that Buchan was taken care of. The Contullich accounts for 1720 seem to bear out the improved salary for they include a sum of 550 merks 'paid to Alexander Buchan Minister of Herta for which he has drawn two Bills upon the Thesaurer of the Society ... payable for MacLeods Behoof to Roderick MacLeod of Contullich' who was the bailie or factor of Harris. Whether or not this apparently satisfactory situation was real it was certainly short-lived.[55]

*

The presbytery of Skye's reaction to the request that they find a minister or two to visit St Kilda in the summer of 1718 is not known because of the lack of its minutes, but no minister went there, in 1718 or in the summers that followed. In a letter read by the SSPCK committee at the beginning of 1719 Buchan reported that he had administered the Sacrament for a second time on his own and that he had many more communicants than on the first occasion. The school was also reviving; he said 'that he had Seven Children and a Servant Lad, that he is teaching to read', that five of 'the Natives' and three of his own children could read the bible, and 'that there are two Young ones whom the Parents have promised to Send to School'. The Society was pleased at this news and asked for yet another encouraging letter to be sent to him, 'recommending to him to be at all possible pains in having the Inhabitants of that Island taught to read the Holy Scripture, and other good Books', of which there was clearly a plentiful supply. Since no news from Skye had come, the presbytery was asked whether a visit had been made to St Kilda in accordance with earlier recommendations, but as this brought no recorded answer it appears that the idea was thereafter laid aside.[56]

That things were not as satisfactory in St Kilda as they might have appeared became evident within a year or so when Mrs Buchan made her third expedition to the mainland, travelling to Edinburgh by the familiar route. This time she brought with her another letter from her husband and two more daughters who were to be educated in Glasgow. In December 1720 the SSPCK committee learned from the letter that Buchan wished 'Baillie Murdo' to be given 100 merks for the education of these two children, and upon a quick look at the accounts it found that there was more than enough owing to the minister to pay both that sum and one bill at least of those due to MacLeod's 'factors and doers'. Mrs. Buchan no doubt reached Argyll in the summer of 1720 but it was 1 June 1721 when the Society received an indication of her purposes in coming from the management committee. She described once more 'her husbands Circumstances in that place and their bad accomodation, and how needfull it is that She have Some money to furnish meal and other necessaries to carry home with her'. She said that their only food there consisted of 'barley meal and meal of black oats, sea fowells and fish', and that 'for Cloaths and other things furnished them by these who serve under the Laird of McLeod, they are obliged to pay very dear for the same ..' As a result of this plea the committee had reviewed the whole story of payments to Buchan over the years and noted that in total his salary had amounted to £2000 scots with only 50 merks unpaid. The treasurer was told to remit this sum immediately to Mrs Buchan and to include £100 scots in advance. Further, the 100 merks of additional money granted at the end of 1717 was to be conveyed to the Glasgow town clerk, Mr Alexander Finlayson, 'to be paid to these who keep two of the said Mr Buchan's daughters at Glasgow', and as regards the second 100 merks allowed for a limited period in August 1719 all that was due was already paid to Mrs McEwen for boarding Jean Buchan. Since Mrs McEwen now claimed that without an increase in the allowance she could not go on looking after Jean the Society's treasurer was instructed to pay her 25 merks a quarter, that is, an additional £1.13s.4d per instalment, until he received orders to the contrary. By the time the Society ratified these arrangements in June 1721 Mrs Buchan was already back in St Kilda, learning of developments while she had been away.[57]

The hazards of life in the island and the difficulties arising from lack of means of communication in emergency were apparent in Alexander Buchan's letter to the SSPCK written on 22 July 1721, though it was 4 January 1722 before the contents reached the Society's general meeting. The significance of the bad news contained in the first few lines was perhaps lost on members who were more interested in the later information about progress in religious instruction and education, and little attention seems to have been paid to Buchan's personal troubles 'at Hirta'. They heard that 'he had Last year Sent a Letter giving an account of the great mortality that had been there'. This letter had been lost so that no one knew of the suffering soon enough to do anything about it. Neither the cause nor details of the consequences found a place in the minutes of the Society, other than that 'the sad case of the people had Scattered the School'. There were however 'twenty yet alive that can read the Bible, and other four that were Learning in the proverbs, besides Some who began to Learn and went back'. Managing as best he could Buchan was still frustrated by an old obstacle to progress in school, and reported that 'there is a great aversion among the Children to Learning, and the parents and friends are not encouraging thereto'. The Tutor and the steward had therefore failed to impress sufficiently strongly upon the people the need for attendance and in their absence Buchan had to do his solitary best. He pointed out that 'he is not to blame for the paucity of Schollars' and that to compensate a little for the inadequate numbers he had taken into his care an orphan who might prove a useful assistant:'there is a poor boy both fatherless and motherless that came of his own accord to the School whom [he] had maintained in food and Rayment for two years and he proposed twenty or thirty merks to help to maintain him for he assists in teaching the School and reads the Bible well and the Catechism every Sabbath afternoon to the Children, and he and other of the natives can read the Irish psalm book'. With the threatened but as yet unmaterialised visit of ministers from the presbytery of Skye in mind Buchan claimed that 'all the young men that marries', and the young women, had to be able to repeat the catechism by heart, and that 'the generality of the people do answer as well as he had seen Illiterate people do, whereof they will give prooff when the Ministers come to visite the place'. Finally, as in 1710, he expressed fears about his own future: 'he says he is failing much this year, and thinks he is drawing near his end and Seeks Some Catechisms'.[58]

In response the Society merely noted that the poor boy should be given an annual allowance of 20 merks for so long as was thought necessary and told its secretary to write to Buchan 'to take care of the Instruction of that boy in order to qualifie him to be usefull in that place'. As it turned out none of the boys of whom Buchan had high hopes became his successor and there is nothing known about what happened to them. His labours evidently still met with resistance among the majority of the islanders who struggled on from day to day more concerned with the task of survival than with what they may have seen as time-consuming incidentals which had little application to their essential activities. Disasters and mortality left hardly any space for education. Religion may have fared better, since its relationship to disaster is more obvious. Yet in spite of hostility something of what Buchan was trying to achieve entered, though it did not greatly alter, the cultural and spiritual tradition of the community.[59]

In 1722 the Laird of MacLeod was 16 years old and his affairs were still managed by the Tutor, John MacLeod of Contullich, and Mr Alexander MacLeod, advocate. John MacLeod had three sons. The eldest was Roderick, who for a short time succeeded his father in the lands of Contullich, was qualified as an advocate, and in due course became factor for the Laird until replaced by two Skye gentlemen, Donald MacLeod of Talisker and Roderick MacLeod of Ullinish. His younger brother, second son of John of Contullich, was also called John and as an advocate as well was engaged by his uncle Mr Alexander to share the responsibility of the Laird's legal business. He is better known as John MacLeod of Muiravonside. The third son was Donald, known first by his lands of Unish at the tip of Waternish in Skye and later as 'the old Trojan' of Berneray. All of these distinguished members of the MacLeod clan were in some way connected with St Kilda and, except for Donald of Talisker and Roderick of Ullinish, with the island of Berneray.[60]

In his capacity of Bailie of Harris Roderick MacLeod of Contullich wrote to the SSPCK in March 1722 to ask for 550 merks owing to him following his payment of that amount in salary to Buchan. He said that if he was not in receipt of the sum promptly no further 'advances' would go to the minister on St Kilda who would then be obliged to leave. Two months later a request from MacLeod of Ullinish sought 'express orders' for the advance of money and other necessaries to be sent to Buchan. Ullinish explained 'the diligence he had used' to get the people of St Kilda to send their children to school, an action which, alongside his concern for payments to Buchan and the presence of his name in the Harris estate accounts of 1725-1726, suggests that he may then have held the position of factor or bailie. The variety of MacLeods involved in dealing with Buchan at this time confused the Society's treasurer who was not sure where he should send money. In December 1722 the sum of 200 merks drawn by Buchan on the Tutor for provisions was overdue for payment to the Tutor's son John, but the treasurer refused to pay because he understood that it was payable to the Tutor himself. However one acted for another in this complicated administration and at the beginning of 1723 the treasurer was told to remit the money to the younger John.[61]

Securing his salary either in money or in provisions as and when he could Alexander Buchan was not given any further help by the MacLeods except indirectly through the very limited control they exercised over the people of St Kilda. Neither the Laird's managers nor the presbytery of Skye were involved financially with the education of the minister's children, and the participation of the SSPCK only came about through its role as provider of his salary. It was for this reason alone that the Society kept an eye on some of his daughters and sons.

In the spring of 1723 Jean Buchan was thought to be fit for service and ready to leave the care of Mrs McEwen. Anything still due for her board would be cleared and a half year's allowance given to her for clothes when she found a job. The Society was not then relieved of its involvement in this respect, for as soon as Jean secured a place in service she was replaced educationally by her brother George who was sent to the mainland during the summer of 1723 and appeared before the SSPCK's committee in the autumn. He had been given letters from his father to various gentlemen of the Society, including Dr Dundas, Mr or Major Leblanc, Mr George Buchan and Mr Nicol Spence, but on the way one of the several John MacLeods then concerned with St Kilda had taken them all from him. The Society was hesitant over which John MacLeod this was but asked Mr Alexander Macleod to write to the correct one for the letters. The minutes of 21 November 1723 recorded that 'George Buchan a young boy son to Alexander Buchan in Hirta came to the Committee, and Shewed that his father had sent him hither to be educated'. Perhaps seeing in George an illustration of the effectiveness or otherwise of his father's teaching the committee, 'having heard him read and discoursed him, and considering that one hundered merks of his Fathers Salary was formerly bestowed on Jean Buchan who is now at Service and has not that allowance', was of the opinion that the money should be applied to his education 'till a Burse be provided for him', and that he too should be boarded with the McEwens. The amount that his father received in salary therefore did not change.[62]

In spite of the steward's efforts Buchan continued to complain of the poor attendance at his school and of how those who had attended 'with their Staying from School forget their Learning'. Irregularity was seasonal as he pointed out, for 'though the Baillie compells them to come to School in Summer, yet when he Leaves the place they forsake the School, and he gets but few Schollars in winter'. Since outdoor work was greatly restricted in winter Buchan could not plead that as an excuse for the children's absence, and the Society, lacking any impartial evidence, was never very clear as to the truth of the situation. It had figures for 1721 which seemed to show that there were 20 boys and 4 girls at the school, but what might be correct at one moment was inaccurate the next and it is unlikely that the Society ever knew, far less kept up with, the reality of Buchan's position as teacher. In May 1724 he was requested 'to be more exact in sending the names of his Schollars and an exact accompt of their proficiencie', yet even if he had responded immediately the information would have been long out of date by the time it reached Edinburgh. There had also been a hardening of attitude respecting the native language, for Buchan was instructed not 'to Learn any to read the Bible in Irish but in English', and it is interesting to find that this order may have been accidentally provoked by the minister himself, who, being anxious about the education of his son George, wished 'that he may keep his Irish, seing he may come to make use thereof'.[63]

Disasters, mortality and the reluctance of the people hindered progress in education but the introduction of new religious habits went on with less difficulty. Daniel Campbell's son James Campbell, who became minister of Kilbrandon, received a communication from 'Mr Buchan at Hirta' in 1724 and with it a letter to the Society which Campbell, after transcribing it 'for more easy reading', forwarded with his own comments. At the end of April 1725 the Society learned from it that 'notwithstanding of the great Ignorance Superstition and Immoralitie of the people of that place, Yet now from the Least to the greatest they have the Shorter Catechism by heart, and not only know the principles of Christianitie, but make wonderfull advances in the way of Godliness'. Buchan claimed to have taught over the years more than 60 people to read, many of whom had died, 'and blessed be God, that by the Bounty of the Societie, he had been enabled to be an Instrument of good in the Remotest and most uncivilized Corner of his vineyeard'. He looked for further encouragement to himself and his 'poor Children', and James Campbell supported his wish that those of his own children on the mainland who were old enough, that is, Jean and her two sisters, 'may have the management of sending him necessaries from Glasgow which would be had at easier rates than what the Baillie or Stewart of Hirta does'.[64]

For years Buchan had made his now familiar complaint that the steward's charges for essential goods were excessive, and one way of overcoming this problem on three occasions had been for Mrs Buchan, during her visits to the mainland, to purchase meal, clothing and any other items that could be conveyed to the island without too much trouble. Now that the three daughters were old enough to help and 'may be doing for themselves' they could readily buy the 'necessaries' and send them to St Kilda, but they needed a proportion of their father's salary to do so. The Society responded to Buchan's wish and Campbell's support by sending more books to the minister and asking him not to draw through MacLeod's representatives anything over 200 merks of salary money so that it could allocate the remaining 100 merks to the maintenance and assistance of the four children staying in Edinburgh and Glasgow. If the children, and more especially Jean, cared to use any part of this sum for the cheaper and better wares needed that was up to them. Meanwhile the SSPCK treasurer went on paying George Buchan's board out of the extra 100 merks initially allowed in 1719 for maintaining Jean and then continued for her brother.[65]

With financial matters arranged in this way the Society turned its attention in 1726 to a piece of unfinished business almost ten years old. Perhaps members had forgotten that in 1717 the presbytery of Skye had been asked to send 'a minister or tuo' to visit St Kilda and find out what was really happening there by way of teaching and catechising. They now heard that no visit had ever occurred, and that their management committee was still without an independent account of 'the Carriage, diligence and Success of Mr Buchan'. All that they had been going on were accounts from Buchan himself. The request to the presbytery had not been 'obeyed', and now that church organisation in general was being improved it seemed the right time to pursue the matter and select someone 'who may go and come with the Stewart', see what Buchan was doing, preach to and catechise the people, and carry out 'other ministerial dueties'. The visit that eventually took place happened to coincide with a momentous stage in the story of the island.[66]

CHAPTER 6

*Popery and the Protestant concern, Daniel Macaulay finds
disaster and inspects Buchan, Buchan dies and his wife
goes again to Edinburgh*

MR James McKenzie, minister of the parish of Laggan in Invernessshire, was upset over the growth of 'popery' in his neighbourhood and on 28 April 1726 wrote to the General Assembly about it:

> 'That amongst the number of popish priests that travell up and downe thorough Lochchabber ther is on called McDonald who has been very Instrumentall in seduceing that people and having given the finishing stroake to a protestant Interest in that Countrey has somtyme agoe made inroads unto my parish being next adjacent, who by his industrious practices together with his relation to the people about Loch Laggan has obtained such a footing amongst them that he really has gained much ground there And has actually perverted severall Families. He frequentlie baptises, Marries and publickly says Mass And has arived to such a degree of Impudence as even to threaten the most Considerable heads of Families ther with the loss of the Duke of Gordons Favour in case they stand in his way.'

The impudent and industrious McDonald was now moving into Badenoch.[67]

McKenzie's letter is an example of the sort of information that came in and disturbed the Protestant church during the period between the Jacobite risings of 1719 and 1745. The Catholic faith, and the possibility of its widespread revival, remained a source of anxiety to Protestants through most of the eighteenth century. In the 1720s there were areas of the north and west beyond the control of any of the several different bodies which might have exercised moral, spiritual and, less directly, political authority. In 1725 the SSPCK, one of these bodies, was joined by another grandly entitled group, the Committee of the General Assembly for the Reformation of the Highlands and Islands of Scotland and for managing His Majesty's Bounty for that end. Members of one were often to be found as members of the other, and it was the intention of both to continue to counteract 'popery', with the SSPCK concentrating upon education as a means of doing so while the Royal Bounty committee directed its funds towards the support of catechists and itinerant preachers. In Buchan's case the burden of the salary could be shared. The achievements of the two inevitably overlapped, and sometimes duplicated rather than complemented the efforts to the same end of the more local and conventional hierarchy of Synod, presbytery and kirk session. Yet in spite of all its missionary intentions and the backing from government the Protestant church was unable to prevent the Catholic areas from remaining Catholic and the people of St Kilda from retaining much of their ancient cultural inheritance.

On the whole daily religious supervision was lacking in extensive mainland districts and in islands such as North Uist and Harris, where the services of one minister were insufficient because of the nature of his parish or were irregularly provided long after they were available on a continuous basis in St Kilda. The equally if not more isolated community on Rona, north of Lewis, would perhaps have attracted a Buchan of its own if it had survived after 1700, although cost and the self-limiting size of the population would probably have meant that even the SSPCK would have left it to the occasional visit of a minister from Ness or Barvas. The words 'desolate condition' as used by the Synod of Argyll in 1695 later appeared repeatedly in application to the circumstances in much larger and more accessible islands, where failure or inability to organise an adequate Protestant parochial system meant that the contributions of the SSPCK and the Royal Bounty committee were at least as important as they were in St Kilda.

A comment on the early days of the SSPCK was made in its annual report issued at the beginning of 1759. Such reviews of the Society's history were not unusual at that time, and of course they followed the last Jacobite rising. 'When this society was first erected', it was said 'the condition of the inhabitants of the highlands and islands of *Scotland* was extremely melancholy. In the more remote corners, the only religion was Popery; and even in the counties less remote, ignorance prevailed greatly'. In the reigns of the brothers Charles II and James VII, this account went on, no genuine attempts were made to 'reform' these areas nor to bring to them instruction in 'the true religion'. On the contrary, where 'Charles had no religion at all, *James's* religion was Popery', and from the history of those reigns it appeared that there were efforts, 'which proved too successful, to retain the highlands, in their former errors, wildness and barbarity'. As a consequence ignorance of 'true religion' was accompanied by idleness, false liberty, 'disaffection to the revolution-settlement, and our happy constitution in church and state'. Instead of a Protestant clergy ministering to people won over already to 'reformed' Christianity, 'those very assiduous creatures the Romish priests, who compass sea and land to gain one proselyte', went about ceaselessly with zeal and bigotry to bring those same remote populations back to an understanding of what Protestants called the errors of popery and false principles of government. Therefore the Society set out with 'a design to remedy these evils' by introducing missionaries and erecting schools in the distant corners most in need of instruction and reform. There was no admission of the possibility that its opponents might then and later have used much the same words to describe the behaviour of the reformed church, nor seemed there to be any realisation of that fortunate ability in the people of St Kilda and elsewhere to sustain in the imagination a world which is not obedient to immediate doctrine, education, or passing fashion.[68]

There were many obstacles in the way of Protestant success, not just mountains, lochs and sea, but barriers of belief and custom which were formidable to those ministers who sought to defeat rather than give place to the strengths of an ancient and deeply established culture. 'The Society met with great discouragements at their first attempts - Especially in the heart of the *Highlands*, and remote corners or Islands, where heritors were *Papists*, or disaffected to the established government, and the poor people had then no taste of the benefit of learning, so that when schools were settled among them, few or none could be got to attend the same …' St Kilda was not alone in its unwillingness to send children to school, nor in resisting what might well have been called the 'zeal and bigotry' which condemned faith and traditions cherished for centuries. 'Several places could be condescended on, where the inhabitants were idolatrous, superstitious and ignorant, living without the knowledge of God, knew not so much as the creed or ten commandments, but given to charms, only using the Lord's name in spells and diabolical practices'.[69]

These difficulties did not only confront the SSPCK and the Royal Bounty committee. Among its many concerns in August 1717 the Synod of Argyll had in mind 'the Lamentable Condition of the parish of Harries'. No one seems to have been minister there after the death of John Campbell in 1707 until about 1713 when Aulay MacAulay was admitted to the charge. Within a short time of his settlement Mr Aulay came to realise that many of the more remote parts of the parish were too difficult to reach frequently or even at all, and in 1717 he wrote, probably in the first instance to the presbytery of Skye, 'Craving the dissjunction of the Islands of Pabba and Bernera from the said parish, and the annexing of them to the parish of Northuist'. When the request reached the Synod members agreed to give it due consideration but in the end did nothing, possibly because they already had under discussion a more important reorganisation.[70]

For a long time it had been evident that the presbytery of Skye was an insufficient link between the Outer Hebrides and the Synod, particularly since Barra and South Uist with their adjacent lesser isles formed a principal haven of the Catholic faith. The SSPCK sent out a message to all presbyteries in 1718, seeking from them lists of papists, priests, Jesuits, 'apostats from the true Religion', and so on, and in 1723 received a memorial which referred to priests travelling freely about in South Uist, Benbecula, Rum, Eigg, and other usual districts including Moidart where they still sought to 'propagat their poyson'. By this time the Society's 'charity schools' were its main weapon of resistance to the papist threat, the earliest being that in St Kilda, which island, so it was said in 1719, appeared to be at last in a Protestant parish - 'the parish of Lewis'. The idea that Lewis contained only one parish and that St Kilda was part of it may have revealed the extent of the Society's ignorance of the islands but it also indicated the lack of defined parish limits, a matter to which the Synod had to devote some time.[71]

The outcome of deliberations was first a decision reached in 1723 whereby Lewis was to consist of four parishes. This was followed in 1725 with a further act reducing the bounds of the Synod of Argyll by erecting the new Synod of Glenelg, which was to consist of four presbyteries, including Gairloch, Abertarff, Skye and the new presbytery of 'Long Island' formed of 'the whole parishes in Lewis, Harries, North and South Uist and Barra and Small Islands adjacent with Hirta'. This new presbytery was normally to meet at 'Rowdall in Harries and Balallan in Lewis'. Representation from the 'Long Island' at the Synod of Glenelg's first meeting in July 1725 should have consisted of Mr Daniel Morison, Stornoway, Mr Aulay MacAulay, Harris, Mr John MacLean, North Uist, Mr Colin MacKenzie, Lochs, and 'Mr Alexander Buchan minister St Kildah', but inevitably the last-mentioned was absent, and it was up to the rest of the assembly to deal with, among other matters, the 'desolate condition' of the four Lewis parishes. Nothing in the minutes made it clear to which parish, if any, the island of St Kilda belonged, the SSPCK continued in the belief that it had some attachment to Lewis, and for at least another ten years anyone who thought about a possible connection and put the question to presbytery or Synod would probably not have been given a satisfactory answer.[72]

Meanwhile the General Assembly was considering how the Royal Bounty fund might be best employed. The sum of £1000 sterling had been made available, at a time when 'Popery and Ignorance did increase and prevail in several places in the Highlands and Islands', in order 'to encourage Itinerant Preachers and Catechists to go to these parts'. The distribution of this annual royal grant had been entrusted to the Assembly, which appointed a committee, among the early members of which were William Morrison, minister in Tiree and Coll, and Daniel MacAulay, minister of Bracadale in Skye. This committee would find qualified persons 'of a pious Life and Conversation, Prudent, of undoubted Loyalty to His Majesty and competently skill'd in the Principles of Divinity, and in Popish Contraversies' to serve in the remoter areas; and it would consult with presbyteries regarding these appointments and associated business. A preacher would receive a maximum pay of £40, a catechist £25.[73]

Daniel MacAulay, descended from the Brenish family in Lewis and related to Aulay, was more than a committee member. Before the end of 1725 he had responded positively to the General Assembly's instruction to go on mission. The Royal Bounty committee knew that he 'had very Zealously and to good purpose exerted himself against popery, and had publick debates with priests and other papists, and wrote an account thereof'. He was therefore thought suitable to visit the Catholic islands of Rum and Canna, while Kenneth Bethune of 'Kilmore' parish in Trotternish was to take on Eigg and Muck. The two ministers were to stay in their respective mission stations for three months and would be allowed £4 a month each. It appears that their task was carried out as planned although MacAulay was none too happy about it. He wrote letters 'Shewing his Fears that the Missions to the Popish Countrys will have little Effect, Except that the Missionarys will be in better Case to inform where the Stops to a Reformation do ly'. He was unable to have any effect himself among the people of Canna 'Because they would not hear him, being under the influence of Priests, and popish Managers, and dare not hear a Protestant Minister preach or pray'; but in Rum with its Protestant owner things were rather more satisfactory. Another letter from MacAulay, who was at the time first moderator of the Glenelg Synod, was uneasy about things in general, 'Holding forth the Lamentable State of their bounds, and Craving more Missionaries'.[74]

*

The resolution reached by the SSPCK committee on 3 November 1726, taking into account the Skye presbytery's former failure and that St Kilda 'Lyes now in the new Erected presbytery of Long Island which is fully planted', was to renew attempts to send a visiting minister on mission to the island. The committee therefore recommended to its convener, Dr Dundas, who was also a member of the Royal Bounty committee, to move at a meeting of the latter, and if need be in the Commission of the General Assembly, that one of the ministers from the presbyteries of Long Island, Gairloch or Skye, all in the Synod of Glenelg, be sent the following summer to St Kilda at the Royal Bounty's expense. A week later, on 11 November 1726,

> 'Doctor Dundas from the Society of Christian Knowledge Did Represent the Circumstances of Alexander Buchan Minister and Schoolmaster in Hirta and how Straitn'd he and his Family are, in that Remote Island, by reason of the smallness of his Sallary, and also Shewed that the forsaid Society Judged it needful and very agreeable to the Design of his Majesty's Bounty a Minister one or more be sent to Visit Hirta, Preach to the People there, and Catechize them and also to enquire into Mr Buchan's Doctrine and Conversation, and his Usefulness in that place and Report'.[75]

After reference to a sub-committee it was finally agreed that Buchan should have his allowance of £10 sterling or 200 merks for one year, and that suggestions for sending missionaries 'to Hirta and other Remote Islands next adjacent thereto' should be presented, each missionary minister having £12 per quarter 'besides their Fraught' or travel expenses. Within three weeks it was stated that sums were available for preachers and catechists, but that as all vacant kirks had been 'planted' there was no demand for probationers. Further,

> 'Considering the discouragements that the said Alexander Buchan is under having no Legal Settlment or Stipend there, so that he is only a Missionary, and is said to be much in debt, The Committee appoints the Cashier to pay to the said Alexander Buchan, or in his Absence, to his wife, now here, The Sum of Ten pounds Sterling for this Year's Service. Secondly Agrees That the Reverend Mr Daniel McAulay, Minister of Braccadale in Skye, be sent to Visit St Kilda … and Report'.[76]

Given his position and experience MacAulay was the natural choice for the task. He was to have £18 to cover his expenses and to be sent a letter 'desiring him to prepare for his Voyage Against the beginning of Aprile Next, And in his Coming and going thither, He is appointed to preach Catechize and perform other Ministerial Dutys in the Remote Islands belonging to the Presbytery of Long Island'. His remit as 'missioner' was reported to the SSPCK committee on 5

January 1727, and consideration was immediately to be given as to 'what orders will be fit to be sent with that occasion to Alexander Buchan and what Books will be necessary to be sent thither'. The presbytery of Long Island had by then already received two boxes of books, one of which was for St Kilda. By mid March the committee had sent a copy of Buchan's original instructions along with a letter to MacAulay so that, on his arrival, he might note how the instructions were being observed and 'what is proper to be done for the good of that place'. Since 'Hirta Lyes at a very great distance from any other place' and had communication only once a year the committee's treasurer was told to present communion elements to Mrs Buchan, who had come to Edinburgh on her latest visit probably with her son Dougal, for her to take back with her, and to pay her what was due of her husband's salary. In the event Buchan was supplied with communion elements, some pay and more books, but no visiting minister arrived in the summer of 1727.[77]

Everybody expected Daniel MacAulay to leave in early May or within the next four weeks, but towards the end of the month the Royal Bounty committee was able to tell its SSPCK colleagues that MacAulay 'has Excused himself from going to Hirta this year' and was nominated instead to go with Mr Archibald McQueen, minister of Sleat, on mission to South Uist and Barra and deal with the gentlemen and people there to advance the interest of 'the True Religion'. The SSPCK wanted to know whether, if he was not going this year, he would go next, but the Royal Bounty committee was unable to say and was still unsure in October when the Long Island presbytery wrote to 'desire that a Minister may be timeously sent to Hirta' or that it be asked to arrange for one, and that his expenses, whatever they might be, should be given to the presbytery to use if nobody else went.[78]

MacAulay and MacQueen returned from their expedition to the 'Long Island' none too pleased but not deterred. MacQueen complained that 'he had been Expos'd to great Hazard, and Charges', as he had been previously when on a similar mission in the bounds of Gairloch presbytery, and that the lairds in South Uist and Barra were papists, so that he felt no success would be obtained in future, especially while 'Swarms of Priests are allow'd to Reside among them'. Even so, he was prepared to go back there. MacAulay did not get home till mid December 1727, 'having been Stoped by a violent Storm and Contrary winds' and further detained by sickness.

But on 1 February 1728 he was sufficiently recovered to be 'preparing for his voyage to Hirta' and he wrote to ask for some money, 'it being very Scarce there', to cover his expenses. He requested that the £18 formerly allowed for the purpose should be advanced to him and transmitted with 'Donald McDonald of King's Barrow' [i.e. Kingsburgh, in Skye]. The Royal Bounty committee accepted this arrangement.[79]

The next members heard of Daniel MacAulay was on 25 July 1728 when their clerk read a letter from him. It carried remarkable news of another great disaster in St Kilda:

'Dear Sir

'It seems when my Reverend and Worthy Brethren appointed me to go in mission to Hirta, they had under Consideration that Old men, being, by the Course of Nature nearer their End, than Young men, it was less inconvenient to hazard their Lives; I went to and came from that Isle with an Unusual adventure, having much Work on my hands at my Return in attending my parish and the Synod. I was the first that ever Ventured to Sail out of [i.e. to?] Hirta, in an Open Boat with a South west wind. I had a Stout and Clever Boat and Sufficient Crew, and above all, the Remarkable Conduct of Divine Providence; upon my dropping Anchor near the place of landing in Hirta and waiting an Opportunity of landing on the Rock, called the Sadle, The Baillie of Hirta's Brother with the Crew of his Boat running down from the houses in order to receive me; Surpriz'd me with the Lamentable account of the depopulation of that place by the Small pox, for, of the twenty one Familys which were there, Only Four Remain, which bear the Burden of Twenty six Orphans left by the other Seventeen parents, being cut off, by the forsaid Disease, the Escape of some of the few who live is owing to a Remarkable Act of Divine Providence; For, about the fifteenth of August last three men, and Eight boys were left in the Rock called Stackriarmin, in Order to Catch a Loadning of Young Solan Geese, which is the Chief product of Hirta, but while they were there, the Inhabitants, who were fit to bring them out of that Rock were cutt off, by the small pox, so that the forsaid Eleven persons continued in the said Rock untill the thirteenth of May at which time they were relieved by the Baillie's Brother but before I went to Hirta, They were sent to the Isle Soa, where they remained while I was at Hirta so that I could see none of them.

'I employ'd Mr Buchan to Preach, the Subject of his Discourse was Genesis Fourty Ninth, and tenth, last part of the Words Unto Him shall the gathering of the people be. He followed Exactly the pamphlet on that Subject called The Gathering of the People to Shiloh, he is pretty well read in the Scriptures, but otherways of low Qualifications, and his Stock of Prudence is not very large, but tho' he cannot say that he was brought up at the feet of Gamaliel, Yet I think he may say, he determined to know nothing among them, but Jesus Christ, and Him Crucified; In a word, he is fitter for that, than any other place I know. After Sermon I called Mr Buchan, and the three heads of Families who were there, as also the Baillie's Brother, the particulars of my Enquiry was as Follows -

'1st I asked, if they had any Complaints against Mr Buchan their Minister? To which they Answered, They had none. 2. Whether the Sacrament of the Lord's Supper was administred there? They Answered. It was, in August last, and I asked of the Baillie's Brother, whether he thought it was done regularly? He answered, he thought it was, in the same Manner as in Harris and other parts of our Bounds. 3. I asked whether Mr Buchan was Diligent in Catechising? It was answered, that he had a General Catechizing twice a year, but continually Catechiz'd the young ones when they were not absent. 4. I Examined whether he Visited their Families? It was answered, he did frequently and sometimes employ'd some of them to pray in his hearing. 5. I asked what Number lived of these he taught to read? Answered only two. 6. I asked whether the present Baillie Exacts more of the People than his Predecessors? It was answered rather less.

'I proposed the following Questions to Mr Buchan. 1st Whither he had any Complaints against his Flock? He answered, he had None. 2 Whether he had any Complaints against the Baillie? He answered, None, but afterwards he told me privatly, that the Baillie Exacted Extravagant Rates for the little salt and Tobacco he gave them, but I did not find this Complaint so well grounded, for tho' he should take some more than was taken in Our Bounds, it is not to be admired when we consider, with what Charges and Difficultys, and Danger he goes to and comes from that Isle, for as he can get no Sufficient Crew for that voyage, but the Inhabitants of one Isle in the Harris, so, to my Certain Knowledge, Each of the Crew he took from that Isle had ten Merks from him and I could not get them Cheaper. 3 I examined both him and them whether he Exacted any Church Fines? I found he Exacts none. 4 I examined whether they were given to Superstition as formerly? I found they were not. 5 I asked what Gratuity he had from the Superiour? Answered, The Grass of two Cows.

'Among Several Mistakes I found in Mr Martin's Account of that Isle, This was one When he says, that the Inhabitants had Conceived Prejudices against Lowlanders, for I am Confident they have no Prejudice against any Christian people. I never met with a more affectionate and kind people, and as in Christian Knowledge, they are not inferiour to their Equals in our Bounds, so they far exceed them in piety, Charity and Discretion Particularly in Courtesy, or the Common Modes of Civil Behaviour. Twixt Harvest and Winter last Seventy Seven died of the small pox, and three of other Diseases. All that Remain alive are Nine Men, Ten Women, Fifteen Boys and Eight Girls.

'I took a view of all the Books in Mr. Buchan's Custody, I found the most of them in very Bad Case, Yea, useless*.... He had no Press, and such of those as were not shut up in a Chist, lay Scattered in Moist Places through his house.

'I am Dear Sir Your affectionate and humble Servant'[80]

*For list of books – see Appendix to this Part.

Daniel MacAulay's reference to 'Several Mistakes' in Martin's book about St Kilda is a reminder that throughout the recorded history of the island mistakes have been made which introduce an element of uncertainty regarding even the most factual statements. For instance, in MacAulay's own account it is not easy to relate the number of orphans, twenty six, to the number of surviving children given later in the letter, some of the latter presumably being members of the four families remaining after the small pox had struck. Nevertheless it must be accepted that MacAulays's letter is the closest it is possible to come to the true situation and that out of a population in, say, July 1727 of about 122 only 42 were left, 11 of whom had escaped the disease by being isolated on 'the Rock called Stackriarmin'.[81]

Misfortunes of one kind or another were a familiar feature of existence in St Kilda, fatal illness occurring quite often. In 1697 Martin learned that 'The Small-Pox hath not been heard of in this Place for several Ages, except in one Instance, of Two of the Steward's Retinue, who not having been well recovered of it, upon their Arrival here, infected One Man only'. He mentioned also a few ailments apart from the cough and cold regularly brought by strangers; one was 'a Spotted Fever .. confin'd to one Tribe, to whom this Disease is, as it were, become Hereditary'. Still applicable in certain areas of the Hebrides, the word 'Tribe' signified an extended family including quite distant relations, although in St Kilda the range of connection was necessarily more confined. Then there was the 'great mortality' recorded by Buchan in his lost letter of 1720; this was no doubt the result of disease and may have seen the fall of the population from Martin's high figure of nearly 200 to the level which was to be further lowered by the small pox infliction of 1727-1728.[82]

Neither the Royal Bounty committee nor the SSPCK made much comment on Daniel MacAulay's news although the latter noted that the school in 'Vatternish', Skye, was greatly depleted 'by reason of the Death of Children by the Small Pox, and Great Dearth in the Countrey'.[83] However, James Campbell, minister of Kilbrandon, wrote twice early in 1729 giving, in his first letter of 3 January, a sympathetic appreciation of Buchan's plight based on a recent communication from St Kilda. 'The Inclosed which came from Mr Buchan Pastor of St Kilda, contains Such a Lamentable account of the desolateness of his Parish, as well as the Extreme poverty, of his own private Circumstances, that I hope you'l use your wonted diligence in Laying his Clamant Case both before the Society .. and the Committee for managing the Royal Bounty'. Campbell then said that he would try to explain Buchan's circumstances by interpreting his letter 'which if you are not well acquainted with his writing and stile you'l Scarce .. be able to understand'. The interpretation followed:

'He informs me, That McLeod's Chamberlain in the Harris is very much disoblidged at the Bailzie of Hirta who for Severall years bygone has [accept?]ed of Mr Buchan Bills upon the Society whereas they are not pay'd up according to the allowance made for the maintenance of his

Family besides the Education of his Children. The yearly allowance is three hundred merks of which for these Six years bygone he received only fourteen hundred merks So that he wants three hundred merks preceeding this Current year for which he drew Bills upon the Society in payment to the Bailie of Hirta who Supplies his Familie yearly to the Extent of the said allowance. If it be said, that his Children got payment, he asks why he shou'd be sent thither to a poor and now desolat Island Separated from the rest of Mankind … where he is at so great a distance from his Friends as that they can Contribute nothing to his Relief, and that for this year he has nothing to live on but three Cows and ten Sheep together with three bolls meal and four Stones Cheese the Baillie has given him upon trust, and that to Compleat his other miseries, the Small pox which never enter'd into that Island before has Swept away all the natives both Men and women together with Children Save the number of fifty yet remaining, So that thro want of either money or victual if he continues there must inevitably Starve, and if he come away is afraid that Sea Sickness and the Infirmitie of old age will carry him off.

'This together with other Complaints of unkind usage and pious Concern for the Settlement of a Stipend, not so much for himself as his Successor is the substance of his Letter but if you Judge it proper to Lay his own Letter before the Society I think it may prove a more moving Address that if drawn up in a better form'.[84]

Certainly those earlier letters from Buchan that have survived, individual in 'writing and stile' and stained with transport and time, are moving enough, forlorn messages from a writer in some damp corner amid mortality great and small.

On the second occasion Campbell added a note dated 27 March 1729 to a letter written two weeks earlier:

'After writing the Inclosed yours of the 8th of February came to hand wherein you Inform me of the Societies displeasure against Mr Buchan for negligence, and unreasonable Complaints. But I am far from believing many things that are Said of poor old Mr Buchan, because I am told there are some Ministers in the Presbyterie of Long Island who would be glad to have him turn'd out of his Living to make way for a favorite and the great Mortality which happen'd in St Kilda has Swept away (as I am told) the one half, or more, of the Inhabitants So that among those who died, it cannot be Supposed but there were a greater number of readers than what you mention besides that I hope you'l endeavour to Represent what a Change the Infirmities of old age will make in the Diligence, and Labours of the greatest Men, And it wou'd be next to a piece of Crueltie, to reduce him to Starve, when unable to go about so much as to ask Charity after having Spent his Life in that desolate Corner'.[85]

Nichol Spence, associated with several austerely religious bodies, was evidently not prepared to be as immediately charitable as Campbell whose letters to him were, if not free of mistakes, at least accurate in their depiction of Buchan's circumstances in St Kilda. As reluctant to spend or provide money as had been the Catholic authorities for whom Cornelius Ward was apparently no less devoted a missionary than was Buchan for the Protestant church, General Assembly, Synod, presbytery, SSPCK and Royal Bounty committee may well have been restrained by limited funds, but they were never very willing or able to understand the human predicaments in which remote and isolated catechists and teachers were placed. They sometimes seemed to grasp only half the information that reached them. It was curiously unsympathetic of the presbytery of Long Island, which in its location should have known better, to report in 1726 to the new Synod of Glenelg that Alexander Buchan, who was of course absent from the Synod assembly, 'did not attend any of the Meetings of his Presbyterie', and unfair of the Synod to censure him for his non-attendance. These meetings were held at a time and at a distance which meant that the impoverished St Kilda minister had no chance and no means of reaching them. Perhaps there was an excuse for the Synod, which acted out of ignorance and two years later had to correct its earlier mistake. On 19 June 1728 Daniel MacAulay was home from his mission to St Kilda and able to put a clear and up-to-date picture to the meeting:

'The Synod Inquired at Master Daniel McAulay who had been sent Missionary to Saint Kilda, about the state of the people in that Isleand and about the Faithfulness and Diligence of Master Buchan their Minister; Master McAulay gave a very Satisfying Account of Master Buchan, and reported that for his old age and other Reasons he could not attend Church Judicatories: The Synod having considered the said Report did Excuse Master Buchan for former absences and Dispense with his not attending Judicatories for time to come'.[86]

*

One of the main reasons why in the 1720s Buchan was so poor was the allocation of part of his salary to pay for the education of his children on the mainland. Jean had been boarded in Glasgow from early in 1719 and had been joined there by a younger sister. George Buchan then arrived in 1723, followed soon afterwards by his brother Dougal, and on 4 January 1728 the SSPCK heard from a letter written just before the invasion of small pox in the early autumn of 1727 that Buchan was about to celebrate 'the Sacrament of the Lords Supper' and that he had already sent on her way his youngest daughter Christian to be boarded with her sisters and given an allowance of 50 merks out of his 300 merks salary. Rev. William Miller, however, had spoken with a Mrs. McIlwraith in Edinburgh who had promised to take Christian to her house and educate her for six months. If Christian pleased her she would keep her until she was capable 'to do for herself' free of any burden. So Mr Miller handed over Christian to Mrs McIlwraith and the SSPCK conveyed its thanks to her for her kindness. It turned out to be a fortunate arrangement, and after six months or so with her 'teacher' Christian was found to have been treated with great kindness, to be 'in very good cloathing', and to have 'profited as much with her as She could have done in any School in this City'.[87]

In the meantime Alexander Buchan, never in very good health while in the island, was also concerned about the boys George and Dougal and what might become of them. So too, for slightly different reasons, were the people of St Kilda:

> 'The Inhabitants are in great Fear lest that, upon their present Minister's Decease, they will not soon be provided of another; and to prevent this, he, at their Desire, is breeding his two Sons at Schools in Edinburgh that if they ever be in a Capacity, and do incline to the Ministry, one of them may be imployed there … And Mr. Buchan has been very much obliged to that religiously inclin'd, and publick-spirited Gentleman, Dr Alexander Dundas, Preses to the Committee of the Society, who has not only been a Physician to these poor Children, but in Place of a Father'.[88]

When Mrs Buchan came to Edinburgh during her stay on the mainland over the winter of 1726-1727 she placed the two boys in the care of a schoolmaster called James Dewar, whose submission to 'the Committee for Reformation of the Highlands and Islands of Scotland' in July 1727 drew attention to their poverty. He stated that 'Upon the 27th of February George, and upon the 7th of March, in this instant Year, Dougal Buchans foresaid, were, by their Mother, settled with me Underscriber, for Bed, Board and Washing, at 10¼£ Sterling Money Yearly for both'. Mrs Buchan paid eight months' worth of keep for Dougal 'before her off-going to Hirta' and told Dewar 'that when this time for Dougal expired, or when any thing for either of them was needed' he would get more money from 'Mr Dundas of Philpston, Advocate', out of the Royal Bounty proportion of her husband's salary. This would cover Dougal's board and 'maintain both in cloathing or other necessaries as far as it would go'. He therefore now requested 'supply' in advance since both were 'void of Cloathing, as having neither Body-cloaths, nor Breeches that can cover their Nakedness, nor Shoes nor Stockins'. An allowance was necessary so 'that they be not left destitute'.[89]

Although Dewar received some money it did not seem to make much difference to the clothing problem. In the summer of 1728 he represented to the SSPCK committee that the boys were 'altogether destitute of clothing' and that their shirts were 'past all mending'. He requested payment for their board and a crown for each of them for washing and dressing their 'Linnens', but the SSPCK passed the whole matter over to the Royal Bounty committee to see what sum was owing to Buchan so that a subtraction could be made of the necessary amount.[90]

It was at first thought that Dougal should be apprenticed to a wright, but this idea was quickly replaced when the SSPCK committee paid some attention to his father's circumstances in St Kilda. After hearing Daniel MacAulay's sad tale it formed the opinion 'That it would be a great hardship upon the poor people there, now in their dismal Circumstances to take Mr Buchan from them, and seeing The [Royal Bounty] Committee ... have continued his Salary as a Minister for One Year, They agreed That his Salary as Schoolmaster be likewise continued with him for that time, And they Considering that Mr Buchan is now old, and that few will go there to succeed him, were of opinion that Dougald Buchan his Son now here, be bred to be Schoolmaster in that Island'. So Dougal was intended to replace his father in St Kilda, for Alexander Buchan, by 1727, 'is now come to a good Age, and cannot live long, considering his Toil and Food'.[91]

George Buchan, on the other hand, was not destined to be either schoolmaster or minister. The two boys appeared before the SSPCK committee on 5 September 1728, and when members had 'discoursed' them the treasurer and Rev. William Miller were appointed to meet with them and Mr Dewar and consider what employment would best suit George, 'Seeing it is said, He has not a Sufficient Capacity for Letters'. It would also be decided 'How they shall be provided in Cloaths'. Four books - 'a Watt's Grammer, An Arithmetick Book, a Copie Book and a Musick Book' - were to be inflicted on Dougal 'towards his Assistance in Learning for the end proposed by the General Meeting'. A month later the shirts had been bought, but the brothers were still 'altogether destitute of body cloaths', and the treasurer, looking for money to pay for some, was told to get from the Royal Bounty committee cashier 'the money allowed by the Committee ... to Mr Buchan and employ it that way'.[92]

It was now George's turn to have his future planned as 'an apprentice to some employment as his Capacity will come up to'. In the spring of 1729 the SSPCK committee, having previously received a letter from Alexander Buchan seeking an addition to his salary, care and education for his boys, and that a 'settled ministry' be established in St Kilda, requested Mr Miller to do his best to obtain a 'Burse' for George Buchan from the town council of Edinburgh, and still thought that the most suitable fate for Dougal would be to send him out to St Kilda 'to keep a school under his father'. Money to pay him would amount to 100 merks, to be found by the SSPCK which held the view that since 'he has learn'd so few in the Island to read' Mr Buchan should have no more salary from them, and that the 300 merks salary as minister should as before come from the Royal Bounty fund, 'the Society to be free of any more Salary for that Island except the said hundred Merks yearly for the Schoolmaster'. A letter would be sent to Alexander Buchan informing him of all this, and 'shewing him, That if the People there will not be taught to read, the Society's allowance will be withdrawn'. Dougal, whose future as teacher seemed therefore to be doubtful, was to have a sum for his journey and for some clothes; and his immediate response was to ask that 'the Society may allow him a big Coat'. This the Society agreed to do. James Campbell having written in March 1729 on Buchan's behalf the Royal Bounty committee, 'Finding that many named to be Employ'd upon the

Fund of the Royal Bounty did not obey whereby there is a Considerable Excrescence', had no difficulty in agreeing to pay out of this surplus £16.12s sterling, approximately 300 merks, for one year from 1 November 1728. But in 1729, before anything further was done for the boys, James Dewar asked the SSPCK committee to remove them from his care at the end of the current quarter, 20 August 1729, and put them to some other teacher, since he could not keep them any longer himself. He also requested board wages due on 20 May past. The SSPCK treasurer had to discuss the matter with the Royal Bounty committee and so Dewar had to continue his care, especially for Dougal who, destined then for St Kilda, had fallen sick and 'missed the occasion of going thither this Summer'.[93]

The SSPCK treasurer persuaded Dewar to keep the boys while the Society tried to decide what to do about them. In October the 'proficiency' of each boy was to be tested and a month later, after consultation with Mr Watt, professor of humanity, George Buchan was assigned to 'the Bajean Class'. Dougal's career remained uncertain until late December 1729 when a letter from his eldest sister, Margaret, of whom next to nothing seems to be recorded, informed the SSPCK that a 'Mr Niel Buchannan', merchant in Glasgow, was willing to take Dougal on as his apprentice to serve on board a ship for five years without any pay. The Society, giving up the notion of employing him as his father's successor in teaching, found 'That the Boy inclines most to a Seafaring Business, and is averse from what was formerly proposed about his teaching a School in Hirta, and besides that by reason of the late Mortality there, there are few to be taught'. It therefore approved of the apprenticeship and agreed to allow Dougal 40s sterling for 'buying of Seacloaths and other necessars'.[94]

At the same time the Society, in considering withdrawal of Alexander Buchan's allowance as teacher, had 'taken notice … That three of his Daughters are now come to Such age and are so educat that they may provide for themselves, as they are at present doing at Glasgow'. As regards the fourth and youngest daughter, Christian, 'The Reverend Mr Miller shew'd the Committee that Mistress McIlwraith in this City had taken her into family, and both now and for some time past had seen well to her'. Mrs McIlwraith, one of a no doubt prosperous merchant family in Edinburgh, could afford to be generous and in addition to looking after Christian she had just sent five guineas to the Society 'to be bestowed for mentaining Poor Scholars, Buying Books, Or to be added to the Society's Stock'. Presumably therefore she was able to continue her care of the girl without too much trouble. It must have seemed that by the autumn of 1729 the Society at least had almost cleared itself of responsibility for payments to the Buchan family. But then it was discovered that most of the discussion over the previous seven or eight months had been irrelevant and a waste of time, for news came in that Alexander Buchan was dead.[95]

*

145

The SSPCK was not the sort of body to minute an appreciation of Buchan's self-sacrificing labours in St Kilda. Business-like as ever its committee decided on 30 December 1729 that the 40s allocated to equip Dougal could come 'out of any Salarys that may be due to his Deceased father', and if nothing was due then perhaps the Royal Bounty committee would give the money out of what might be owing to his father as one of its missionaries. This could have proved a satisfactory solution for Dougal but it did not see the end of claims by surviving Buchans on the funds of the two committees. In the main these took the form of petitions by Mrs Buchan.

She first petitioned Lord Louden Campbell, a commissioner to the General Assembly, for a small aliment. Her husband had preached the gospel in St Kilda for 24 years and had received 'a very small Stipen', but 'now is dead, and left me Destitute and six young Children of whom three is uncapable of any service, and I myself aged sixty am not able to doe for myself or Children'. On 27 February 1730 she submitted a petition to the SSPCK in which she pointed out that since her deceased husband had been raising 'a numerous growing Family' the allowance paid to him and 'the liberal helps' received from 'Good People' in general were scarcely enough to support his family and educate the children, so the petitioner was left 'destitute'. She asked that the Society would 'interpose with the Barons of Exchequer' for a small yearly sum out of charity.[96] All members were recommended to assist her in this application, and a petition from her, backed by the SSPCK, to the Barons was not long in being presented:

'The Petition of Kathrin Campbell Relict of the deceas'd Mr Alexander Buchan Minister of the Gospel in the Remote Island of Hirta alias St Kilda [Humbly Sheweth]

'That the petitioner's husband having got Information of the Sad State of the Inhabitants of the foresaid Island of Hirta, which lyes about Sixty Leagues from any other Inhabited Land, and where the grossest Ignorance and most foolish Superstition was to be found, and that they had been imposed upon by an Impostor, to committ Devilish Practices, He did in the year 1703 offer his Service to that Place and was sent thither as a Catechist by the Commission of the General Assembly with an Allowance out of their Publick Fund, and sometime thereafter returned with tuo of the Natives to this Place, and was ordain'd by the Presbytery of Edinburgh, and when the Society for Christian Knowledge was erected, They granted him An Allowance to teach a School in the foresaid Island, and his family increasing, the same was augmented for his Encouragment to continue there, And by the Blessing of God on his Endeavours these poor people were brought a considerable length in the Knowledge of the Protestant Religion, and were baptised, and at last the Sacrament of the Lord's Supper was administrat to them, But of late the Inhabitants of that Island were, in the Providence of God, trysted with great Sickness and Mortality, And the Petitioner's husband

146

dy'd among the rest in February 1729, So that there are now only about Twenty five Persons left alive in that Place, And the Petitioner being left with Six fatherless Children was necessitat to come to this Place to Shift for a Livelyhood, And now She finds That the foresaid Society can give none of their funds in Charity, But only for promoting the design of the Royal Letters Patent And the Members of the foresaid Society thinking me a very proper Object of His Majestie's Charity I was advised by them to represent my Circumstances thus to Your Lordships.

'May it therefore Please Your Lordships In consideration of the Premises to Ordain the Petitioner to be put upon His Majestie's Charitable Roll of Pensioners in order to help to Subsist me and my fatherless Children And We shall ever pray for His Majestie and Royal Family and for Your Lordships'.[97]

The remainder of the Buchan story lies almost entirely in the accounting of small sums allowed to his family. Remnants of money due to the minister were still sought by its members for a year or two more. In June 1730 new clothes were asked for George Buchan but nothing was supplied by the SSPCK which considered that no part of the salary for which it had been in latter years responsible was still outstanding. However in March 1731 the Society reviewed the financial position, finding that since his entry to its service on 13 April 1710 to his death in February 1729 Alexander Buchan's salary, with two increases, had amounted to £422.4s.5⅓d sterling, of which only £397.14s.9¼d had been paid, so that there was still due about £24.9s.8d. It was thought proper to devote this amount to support George's further education by giving it out in small proportions quarterly, George being presently 'at the College in this City', with a view to his being fitted to succeed his late father as the island teacher. Thus the intentions for George and Dougal had, apparently, again been reversed.[98]

Mrs Buchan and the other children were told that there was nothing for them out of the salary money. Jean wrote to ask for an allowance of at least £5 sterling of the balance due her father and of what might be due from the Royal Bounty to purchase the 'Sea Cloaths' for Dougal and to pay for his 'Portarrage' and navigation lessons during his apprenticeship, money which she and her sisters were unable to provide themselves. She suggested that this sum could be deposited with Provost Murdoch in Glasgow, one of the owners of the ship in which Dougal was serving, but the SSPCK, adhering to its resolve that all the remaining salary should go to George, refused her request and left any more helpful response to the Royal Bounty committee. A month later the latter body discovered £9.3s owing to Alexander Buchan and allowed this amount to her. When, observing the SSPCK's terms, Jean asked for something with which to buy clothes for George the Society gave her 30s.[99]

As late as August 1733 it was complained to the SSPCK, perhaps by Rev.Miller, that the Buchan children were 'molesting' Mrs McIlwraith with unsigned letters containing 'Calumnious and Injurious Reflections and Indecent Expressions which they repeat to herself in her presence'. What the reason was for these is not at all clear but as a consequence the Society committee stopped any more payments of the money assigned for George until 'a particular warrand' was given for that purpose. Eventually, in June 1734, the committee approved payment of £1.18s.11d sterling to George in completion of all claims that might be made by the children, and with this the none too happy tale of Alexander Buchan and his years in St Kilda might be brought to a close.[100]

Those years were a time of severe trial. They are the period of transition from a fading older world to the beginnings of a new. To Buchan fell the task of introducing to a remote island changes of religion and attitude, the impact of which can only be learned from future events and the writings of ministers and others over the next two centuries. The experience of St Kilda in this regard must have been shared by island and mainland communities elsewhere, but the remote and lonely scene of Buchan's labours was exceptional and heightened the difficulties and miseries that he suffered, sometimes as a result of a distant and unfeeling administration which was itself the victim of ignorance and belated, hazardous communication. In spite of all it is hard to picture Buchan as anything but heroic in his devotion to what he considered his duty, and it is well to remember words that he wrote back in 1710, words that resound through the long story of missionary visitors to that 'outfield of Gods vineyeard':

> 'the Island of Hirta has been much upon my heart and I have denied my Self the Ease and other Worldly accommodations I might have had elsewhere to serve the Intrest of the Gospell in that Place, and I bless the Lord not without some success'.[101]

1   Kirk Session Minutes, Parish of Thurso CH2/414/1 p.332 (10 December 1701), p.336 (2 July 1702)
2   Fasti Vol. VII p.193; GA CH1/2/31 ff.492, 488; D Budge: Jura –an island of Argyll Glasgow 1960 p.105; GA CH1/2/59 f.198. In his letter of 3 January 1729 to Nichol Spence James Campbell said that the Synod of Argyll had joined 'Garvelich and Elich na naomh', formerly in the parish of Jura, to his own parish of Kilbrandon, but he could only go there in summer [GA CH1/2/59 ff.162-163]. It would appear that Budge's statement that Buchan was at Ederline in 1699 and in Jura in 1700-1702 cannot be entirely correct. See also D MacKinnon: 'Education in Argyll and the Isles 1638-1709' in Records of the Scottish Church History Society Vol.6 (1938) p.53 (source lacking).
3   GA CH1/2/31 ff.488, 494
4   Buchan (1818) p.3; J L Campbell (2000 pp.12-28) gives an unsympathetic and hostile account of Buchan and his career in St Kilda.
5   GA CH1/2/25/2 ff.159, 162. For books see appendix to Part II. GA CH1/2/24/2 f.251; Buchan (1727) p.42
6   GA CH1/2/24/2 f.166 (1 August 1704), CH1/2/4/2 pp.166-167 Draft instructions
7   Buchan (1818) p.51. Buchan's offer to serve in St Kilda was made in 1703, the year in which Martin's second book [A Description of the Western Islands of Scotland], was published.
8   GA CH1/2/24/2 f.167. The 'Irish bible' sent among the books may have been a copy of Robert Kirk's second edition (1690) of Bedell's Irish bible (1685); for an account of the background to these works – V E Durkacz: The Decline of the Celtic Languages Edinburgh 1983 pp.18-23
9   GA CH1/2/24/2/4 ff.243-244. Buchan's letters have been so tightly bound into the volumes that many words cannot be read.

10 GA CH1/2/24/2/4 ff.243-244
11 GA CH1/2/24/2/4 ff.243-244
12 GA CH1/2/24/2/4 ff.249-250 – 'addressed to Rt Rev Moderator and Reverend… of General Assembly'
13 GA CH1/2/31 f.475:'eldin'= fuel,'ratrym' is possibly 'rotrym', perhaps learning by heart or rote. A footnote in Daniel Campbell's hand reads:'Ther is no wax in Hirta to seal Letters with'.
14 SA CH2/557/4 pp.119, 130, 139
15 SA CH2/557/4 pp.145, 152
16 GA CH1/2/31 f.477 Buchan's letter, containing the many 'historical accounts', seems unfortunately to be missing.
17 SA CH2/557/4 pp.234 (21 March 1707), 242 (28 March 1707)
18 GA CH1/2/31 ff.479-480:'teen'= teind,'stay' ('hy and stay mountains') = steep.
19 SA CH2/557/4 pp.252-253 (23-24 July 1707)
20 SA CH2/557/5 pp.18-19 (11 October 1707), 23 (14 October 1707), 3; DC Section 1/852; Morrison (1967) p.324: 110 merks paid 'to Anne Campbell Relect of Mr John Campbell minister of Harries'. Mr John Campbell had died insolvent.
21 GA CH1/2/31 f.468
22 GA CH1/2/31 ff.481-482. Mrs Buchan's 'address' seems to have been written for her by Daniel Campbell
23 GA CH1/2/31 f.472 (26 March 1708)
24 GA CH1/2/31 ff.483, 487 (29 March 1708), 471 (29 March 1708)
25 PE CH2/121/6 pp.357-358 (24 March 1708). See also extract, in the form of a document possessed by Robert Johnston Esq., given by permission as a footnote to the printed Anniversary Sermon to the SSPCK by Rev. Robert Gordon on 5 June 1823 and published that year [SSPCK GD95/13/108 p.39]. Contributions were to be given to Mrs Buchan.
26 SA CH2/557/5 p.43 (20 May 1708); GA CH1/2/31 ff.484-486
27 M MacLeod:'Gaelic in Highland Education' in TGSI Vol. XLIII (1960-1963) pp.308-309
28 GA CH1/2/31 ff.490-491
29 GA CH1/2/31 ff.497-498
30 GA CH1/2/31 f.488
31 GA CH1/2/31 f.489
32 SA CH2/557/5 p.82. The SSPCK noted in June 1721 that prior to 15 April 1711 Buchan's only pay came from collections and from the pockets of its members [GD95/1/2 p.157]
33 SSPCK GD95/1/1 Proposals; Buchan p.3
34 SSPCK GD95/10/19; SSPCK GD95/1/1 pp.41, 52-53
35 SSPCK GD95/1/1 pp.57-58
36 GA CH1/2/31 ff.492, 494, 496. Daniel Campbell's certificate (f.496) also testified that Buchan had been on 'Hirta' for five years and was of good character; that 'his Labour had good Success'; and that he was willing to return to settle and instruct in the island, even though it was 'remote from Suply' and few would go there. He seriously recommended to the Committee for Propagating Christian Knowledge and to the General Assembly that a fund or 'yearly competent portion' should be allowed, to enable Buchan to continue. Buchan (1727) p.41; Fasti Vol. VII p.193. There is reference to a Mr James Leblanc, merchant, 6 September 1704 [Roll of Edinburgh Burgesses and Guild Brethren 1701-1841 (SRS)], and to Major James Leblanc's marriage 26 July 1725 [Register of Marriages for the Parish of Edinburgh 1701-1750 (SRS)]. The latter's testament is also recorded [Edinburgh Commissariot – Register of Testaments 1801-1800 p.159]. H Armet (edit.): Extracts from the Records of the Burgh of Edinburgh 1701-1718 Edinburgh & London 1967 p.190; Buchan (1727) p.41
37 SSPCK GD95/1/1 p.58
38 SSPCK GD95/1/1 p.58
39 SSPCK GD95/1/1 pp.62-65. These instructions may be interestingly compared with Bishop Gordon's 'Rules' for the Catholic seminary at Scalan, Glen Livet [J Watts: Scalan: The Forbidden College, 1716-1799 East Linton 1999 pp.47-51].
40 SSPCK GD95/1/1 p.157. See Buchan's letter of 1709 (p.101-104 above) for what seems to be a reference to writing his book. James Hart was probably the minister of Old Greyfriars, Edinburgh. The SSPCK committee said it would enquire about the book 'and give orders about it' [GD95/1/1 p.157 (6 March 1712)].

41 SSPCK GD95/1/1 pp.114 (7 June 1711), 123-124 (31 July 1711) – for books see appendix to this part, 157. At this meeting on 6 March 1712 the SSPCK treasurer was instructed to speak to Mr Leblanc, merchant, and George Buchan, clerk to the committee for plantation of kirks etc., already known as contributors of funds for Buchan, asking them to send money promised to the missionary to enable him to continue his work in St Kilda [GD95/1/1 p.157].

42 R C MacLeod: The MacLeods – Their History and Traditions Edinburgh N.D. [1929] pp.24-25; Morrison (1979) pp.97-140; Grant pp.383-387

43 Morrison (1967) p.332

44 GA CH1/2/33/2 ff.141-142

45 Martin (1703) p.286. Martin also wrote (p.293): 'they told me that some years ago their Boat was split to pieces upon the West side of Boreray isle, and they were forc'd to lay hold on a bare Rock, which was steep, and above twenty Fathom high; notwithstanding this difficulty, some of them climb'd up to the top, and from thence let down a Rope, and Plads, and so drew up all the Boats Crew, tho' the climbing this Rock would seem impossible to any other except themselves'.

46 SSPCK GD95/1/1 p.208 (5 November 1713); SSPCK GD95/2/1 p.307 (2 April 1713); SSPCK GD95/1/1 p.157. At Buchan's wish a sum of £10 scots was allowed for books in 1713 'for the use of the poor Schollars in Hirta' [SSPCK GD95/2/1 p.344 (16 October 1713)].

47 SA CH2/557/5 p.123; PS CH2/330/1 p.9 (11 April 1712)

48 SSPCK GD95/1/1 pp.230 (3 June 1714), 254-255; GD95/2/2 p.76 (9 June 1715); GD95/1/1 p.288

49 SSPCK GD95/1/1 pp.293-294. Seen from a different point of view the SSPCK's mission 'was to destroy the language, superstition, disaffection and indolence that Whig Scotland saw as the way of life of the Highlander' [J Watts: Scalan: The Forbidden College, 1716-1799 East Linton 1999 p.42] The destruction of the Gaelic culture might have been included.

50 SSPCK GD95/1/1 pp.293-294

51 SSPCK GD95/2/2 p.198 (5 September 1717)

52 SSPCK GD95/2/2 pp.202-204 (4 November 1717); GD95/1/1 pp.347-349 (7 November 1717); GD95/10/127 (7 November 1717)

53 SSPCK GD95/2/2 p.220 (22 March 1718)

54 Buchan (1818) p.4; SSPCK GD95/2/2 pp.202-204 (4 November 1717); SSPCK GD95/1/1 pp.347-349 (7 November 1717)

55 SSPCK GD95/2/2 p.221 (3 April 1718)

56 E.g. SSPCK GD95/2/2 pp.241, 252, 309, 320, 345; SSPCK GD95/1/2 p.48 (4 June 1719), p.67 (13 August 1719); Morrision (1967) p.341

57 SSPCK GD95/1/2 p.38 (20 March 1719); GD95/2/2 p.260 (13 January 1719)

58 SSPCK GD95/2/3 p.28 (8 December 1720); GD95/1/2 pp.157-158 (1 June 1721); GD95/2/3 pp.50 (17 March 1721), 57 (6 April 1721)

59 Further letters were 'lost' in 1725 [SSPCK GD95/2/3 p.395 (14 July 1726)]; SSPCK GD95/1/2 pp.196-197 (4 January 1722) and GD95/2/3 p.90 (7 December 1721)

60 SSPCK GD95/1/2 pp.196-197

61 Grant pp.392-393; Morrison (1979) p.50

62 SSPCK GD95/2/3 pp.117 (18 April 1722), 125 (21 June 1722), 155 (14 December 1722), 167 (10 January 1723)

63 SSPCK GD95/2/3 pp.182 (26 March 1723), 227 (21 November 1723); also GD95/1/2 p.265 (2 January 1724)

64 SSPCK GD95/2/3 p.210 (27 June 1723); GD95/1/2 p.187; GD95/2/3 p.256 (7 May 1724) – letter from Buchan of 5 August 1723

65 SSPCK GD95/1/2 pp.330-331; GD95/2/3 p.302

66 E.g. SSPCK GD95/2/2 p.260 (13 January 1719); GD95/1/2 pp.330-331; GD95/2/3 p.252 (2 April 1724) Memorial given in by three daughters.

67 SSPCK GD95/1/2 pp.399-400 (3 November 1726)

68 GA CH1/2/53 f.179

69 SSPCK GD95/13/24 pp.59-63

70 SSPCK GD95/11/2 A Short State of the [SSPCK] 1732 pp.25-27

71 SA CH2/557/5 p.208

72 SSPCK GD95/1/1 p.354 (2 January 1718); GD95/10/77; GD95/1/2 pp.76-77

73 SA CH2/557/5 p.303 (14 August 1723); SG CH2/568/1 p.2 Act erecting the Synod of Glenelg and Presbytery of Long Island – see also p.1, and p.11 (10 July 1725).

74 RB E412/1 Act of General Assembly 17 May 1725

75 Fasti Vol. VII p.166; GA CH1/5/52 Register of the Committee's Proceedings pp.14, 10, 53-54, 59. A receipt for Rev Donald McQueen requested payment to 'Mr Daniel McAulay', minister at Bracadale and commissioner to the General Assembly, of the sum of £100 scots 'as the fourth quarter of the Sallary' allowed to McQueen by the Royal Bounty committee for the first year of his mission to the isles of Rum, Muck, Eigg and Canna (MacAulay received the money 23 May 1727) [EUL Laing MSS II 484/4 no.110].

The dangers of a mission were experienced by Archibald McQueen and Norman McLeod, ministers in the presbytery of Skye who were sent into the bounds of the presbytery of Gairloch in 1725. They were still there in February 1726. They had laboured in several vacant parts 'and travelled from house to house instructing Such as did receive them notwithstanding of what opposition distress and difficulties they have met with from disaffected persons, Severitie of the Season and roughness of the bounds they being even in time of Divine worship Barrocaded in the Church and made prisoners therein and after their Escape therefrom in another Paroch had their lodgeing Set on fire upon them under Silence of night Tho providence did prevent the dismall effects of so barbarous a Design'. Such sufferings 'might dishearten any but persons of zeal and Resolution'. The two men attended a Gairloch presbytery meeting in hazard of their lives, 'there being So great a storm and deep snow as there was no travelling Through these high mountains Spacious deserts and many rapid rivers...without manifest hazard To their persons they being obliged to travell all along on foot' [EUL Laing MSS II 484/3 no.251 (16 February 1726) Certificate of presbytery of Gairloch]

76 SSPCK GD95/1/2 pp.399-400 (11 November 1726); GA CH1/5/52 p.142 (11 November 1726)

77 GA CH1/5/52 pp.145-146. Another minister was to be sent to the parishes of Barra and South Uist 'to deal with Papists for their Conversion' (p.145).

78 SSPCK GD95/1/2 pp.408-409 (5 January 1727), 428 (16 March 1727); EUL Laing MSS II 484/3 no.257 A direction to Mr John Dundas of Philipston that he should pay Alexander Buchan minister and schoolmaster 'in the Island of Hirta alias St Kilda as a Missionary to that Island or to his wife she being on the place' – i.e. Edinburgh - £10.

79 GA CH1/5/52 pp.203-205. The minister of Sleat is more usually called Edmund McQueen [Fasti Vol. VII p.175; GA CH1/5/52 p.255]. SSPCK GD95/1/3 p.7 (1 June 1727); GA CH1/5/52 p.237 (26 October 1727)

80 GA CH1/5/52 pp.255 (7 February 1728), 265 (28 February 1728)

81 GA CH1/5/52 pp.338-341 (25 July 1728); CH1/5/51 pp.339-341; SSPCK GD95/1/3 pp.71-72 (6 August 1728) letter from D MacAulay to SSPCK; SSPCK GD95/2/4 pp.98-99 (26 July 1728); GA CH1/5/71 Scroll Minutes of Royal Bounty committee 25 July 1728.

82 In one copy of the letter [GA CH1/5/51 pp.339-341] the name of the stack is given as 'Stack n' armin'; and subsequently the words introducing the questions were 'the particulars of my Enquiry were as Follows.'

83 Martin (1698) p.75

84 SSPCK GD95/1/3 p.91 (6 November 1728)

85 GA CH1/2/59 ff.162-163

86 GA CH1/2/59 f.198 (11 March & 27 March 1729). On 11 March Campbell wrote to show the necessity of continuing Buchan in St Kilda. The Royal Bounty committee was in funds so it allowed another £16.12s sterling as salary for a year from 1 November 1728 [GA CH1/5/71 p.71 (10 April 1729)]

87 SG CH2/568/1 pp.15, 23 (6 July 1726), 35 (19 June 1728)

88 SSPCK GD95/6/1 pp.18, 132, etc.; GD95/1/3 p.37 (4 January 1728 – letter of August last); GD95/2/4 (7 December 1727); GD95/2/4 pp.98-99 (26 July 1728)

89 Buchan (1727) p.43

90 GA CH1/2/55 f.407

91 SSPCK GD95/1/3 pp.71-72 (6 August 1728); GD95/2/4 pp.80-81 (10 June 1728)

92 SSPCK GD95/2/4 p.51 (11 January 1728); GD95/1/3 pp.71-72 (6 August 1728); GD95/2/4 pp.98-99 – Here the record reads 'Mr Buchan is become very old' and 'Everyone will not go there'. Buchan (1727) p.43

93 SSPCK GD95/2/4 p.106 (5 September 1728), pp.109-110 (3 October 1728)

94 SSPCK GD95/2/4 p.164 (20 March 1729); GD95/1/3 pp.134-135 (5 June 1729); GD95/2/4 p.171 (3 April 1729), p.177 (23 April 1729); GA CH1/5/52 p.447 (10 April 1729) – Campbell's letter of 11 March 1729; GA CH1/5/51 p.447; SSPCK GD95/2/4 p.200 (3 July 1729); GD95/1/3 p.146 (7 August 1729); GD95/2/4 p.171

95 SSPCK GD95/2/4 pp.220 (4 September 1729), 226 (3 October 1729), 237 (3 November 1729), 248 (30 December 1729 – 'the Bajean Class' at Edinburgh University); GD95/1/3 pp.134-135 (5 June 1729)

96 SSPCK GD95/1/3 p.328. Mrs McIlwraith had made previous donations to the Society.

97 GA CH1/2/62 f.4. It is not clear how many children the Buchans had. Jean Buchan said that there were thirteen [Buchan (1818) p.4], but Mrs Buchan several times mentioned six, the names of five being recorded. It is possible of course that some died in infancy on the island, though this would probably have been a matter for comment in a letter or petition. SSPCK GD95/2/4 p.260 (27 February 1730); GD95/1/3 p.186 (2 April 1730)

98 EUL Laing MSS II no.488 Petition for Kathrin Campbell To The Right Honourable The Barons of Exchequer, certified: 'We do humbly Certifye the truth of the Petitioner's Case to be as above Represented and the same is humbly offerr'd by Us at the Desire and Direction of the Society for Propagating of Christian Knowledge in the Highlands' – signed by James Campbell, William Hamilton and John Dundas. With note: 'Charity Rd 5th June To be Consider'd at a proper time'. Mrs Buchan's mention of about 25 survivors may indicate that the smallpox continued into 1729, claiming her husband and further reducing the population from the numbers recorded by Rev. Daniel MacAulay a year earlier.

99 SSPCK GD95/2/4 p.285 (12 June 1730), p.348 (9 March 1731)

100 SSPCK GD95/2/4 p.368 (25 March 1731); GA CH1/5/53 pp.94-95 (22 April 1731); SSPCK GD95/2/4 pp.379, 384 (21 May 1731)

101 SSPCK GD95/2/5 p.106 (23 August 1733), p.152 (13 June 1734)

102 SSPCK GD95/1/1 p.58

Appendix to Part 2

Books supplied for St Kilda

26 July 1704   Books to be given to Alexander Buchan to take with him:

Mr Mathew Pooles annotations on the holy Bible, his dialogues, his Nullity of the Romish faith
Mr Watson and Vincent on the Catechism
Mr Guthries tryall of a Saveing Intrest of Christ
the Bible; psalms; Confession of Faith and Catechisms in the Irish Language

2 August 1704   Buchan acknowledges receipt of books except Pool's annotations, 'judged by the Commission not needful to be sent to St Kilda'

[NAS CH1/2/25/2 f.159]

2 August 1704   Account – 'Mr John Blair for the Catechist that went to St Kilda to Alexander Henderson Watson's body of divinity - £10; Guthries Interest – 8s; Pooles Nulity - £1.4s; his dialogues – 12s; Confession of faith – 8s; Vincent's Catechisme – 12s. Total: £13.4s.

[NAS CH1/2/25/2 f.162]

3 July 1710   Letter from Alexander Buchan, 'Catechist and Schoolmaster in St Kilda', giving an account of his success and management in the island, and including a catalogue of books in 'the library' there as follows:

'Catalogue of books in Hirta'
Mr Watson and Mr Vincent on the Assemblys Catechism; Dolitle on the Assembly's Catechism; Flavell on [the] same; Confession of Faith; Mr Gutries trial of a Saving Interest in Christ; Mr Mathew Pooll his Nullities on the Romish faith; - his dialogues; Leighton on the Creed; The Miror of Martyrs; Jeremie Dyke on the Sacrament; The Childs guide; Ferriers body of divinity; The Righteous Branch; Heart Humiliation; Mr Andrew Grays works; Exposition on the first five chapters of Ezekiel; Episcopacie Examined; Flavells works; Perkins works; Pooll on the old and new Testament; Diodates annotations on the old and new Testament; The nature and necessity of Restitution; a Cordial for Christians; Closet prayer a Christians duty; The new Covenant a Saints portion; Spiritual Refyning or Treatise of Sin; Exposition on the Second of Amos; The Sum of Sacred divinity; Exposition on Hebrews; The world conquered, or believers victory; Exposition on James Epistle; Alarm to unconverted Sinners; The doctrine of the old and new Testament; Wedderburn on the Covenant of Grace; A discovery of the child of God, under Seeming wrath; A Patern of Catechetical doctrine; The work of Robert Hakies; Sacramental Sermons by Mr Webster; A Reply against Mr Gilbert Brown priest; The almost Christian discovered; Exposition on the first of Amos; A guide to Godlyness; The Christian's dictionary; The Tryal and triumph of faith; Matrimonial Honour; A Brieff Exposition of the Prophesie of Obadiah, Jonah, Micah, Nahum, Habbakuk and Zephaniah; A breiff Instruction in the worship of God; A Treatise of Justification; Soul persuading Inducements Leading to Christ; The blessedness of Death to the Godly; The Saints Legacies; The Christians Schollar in Rules and directions; Lectors on Christs Passion, Resurrection and Assencion; Christs certain and Sudden appearance to Judgment; A Call to delaying Sinners; The Spiritual warfare; A guide to the true Religion.

[NAS GD95/1/1 pp.123-24 31 July 1711]

PART III

THE BEGINNINGS OF ROMANCE
St Kilda imagined by the 'Outside World'

Old house in Boreray

Following Buchan's death in 1729 a sum was bequeathed in 1734 which enabled the SSPCK and Royal Bounty Committees to employ Roderick Maclennan in St Kilda.

The coming of Maclennan as minister coincided, to his misfortune, with that of Lady Grange. His rather unhappy career included supposed disgrace when in St Kilda and controversy when he moved on to Sutherland, Caithness and the island of Stroma. His varied life bears some resemblance to that of Buchan with its sometimes difficult relationship to the island communities where he served and showed the limitations of the church organisations that employed both of them as well as the inadequacies of the system which governed missionary provision to remote places.

Maclennan was immediately followed in St Kilda by the first missionary of the name of Macleod to be appointed. The sequence of Macleods, probably five of them and the majority originating in Skye, covered a period of a little over eight decades, and it was during the second of these that Kenneth Macaulay, author of the next book about St Kilda, made his brief visit of inspection and research. The story of the Macaulay family, more particularly of Kenneth, and of the Macleods, illustrates the problems arising from the increased distancing of SSPCK and other mainland concern for the missionaries. Meanwhile there was a growing emergence of commercial and tourist interest of a 'romantic' nature in St Kilda, and this in turn had its impact upon the people who began to sense that they had a curiosity value not limited to the investigations by the church into their spiritual state.

In the absence of effective contact, regular educational and religious provision, and political and administrative reasons for thinking of them as useful to Britain, the people of St Kilda held onto traditional entertainment like dancing, songs and stories stemming from far older times. They were treated as if they were a band of primitive 'savages' who, together with the wild island they occupied, came to be worthy of including in travel routes of those in search of the remarkable and 'sublime'. A widening gap between what they knew themselves to be and what others 'outside' imagined them to be was clear after the publication of Kenneth Macaulay's book, if not long before.

CHAPTER 1
'Buchan's' book and its authors

IN 1727 there appeared a small volume called *A Description of St.Kilda - The Most remote Western Isle of Scotland.* According to the introduction it was published by 'an Inhabitant' of the island but no author's name was given. The work was republished in 1733, again in 1741 when the copies were being sold by Alexander Buchan's daughter Jean, and there were several later editions which, in place of the introduction, contained a preface apparently added by Jean and various other alterations. Most of these latter changes were minor adjustments of spelling and punctuation, some of which were intended to clarify but really gave a different sense to particular phrases; small but significant differences also appeared, as, for example, in replacing 'his predecessor' with 'his predecessors' and 'Mr. Martin's two Books' with 'Mr. Martin's Book'. More importantly two lengthy passages in 1727 were omitted and much less interesting material introduced instead.[1]

Though the author's name was not present in 1727 subsequent editions included it, and so the book came to be accepted as written by Alexander Buchan. There are however grounds for believing that he was neither the author of a large part nor the instigator of publication. Various sentences in the book refer to Buchan as if he were not connected with its production at all: for instance, it was remarked of the islanders' 'Cloth Hoase' that 'some knit upon Weirs since their present Ministers Wife went there'; and a ceremony involving use of the crucifix was one of several superstitious practices 'done away since Mr. Buchan their Minister came among them'. Later in the book nearly six pages were devoted to a description of Buchan's association with St Kilda up to the time when 'now, he has sent another Son [Dougal] to Edinburgh to be bred'. The passage begins with the time Buchan 'came from Thurso in Caithness to Edinburgh, to offer his Service to that Place', and the writer, identifying himself only as 'I', is clearly not Buchan himself. In short, there can be little doubt that essentially the publication is an extended and 'improved' version of the 'Litle book of the discription of Hirta', the manuscript of which Buchan brought to the mainland in 1709.[2]

Bearing in mind that the manuscript was completed by 1709 it may properly be wondered whether information in the published work relates to that earlier period rather than to the mid 1720s or 1727. In addition, Jean Buchan's eventual preface is also questionable. She said that her father had 'erected an eldership and kirk session, with other steps of reformation and order', but this may be only an elaboration upon the unknown writer's note in 1727 that 'Mr. Buchan several Years ago, got a Kirk-session constitute at Hirta, which exercises Discipline'. There seems to be no mention of either elders or session in the SSPCK records and if they existed it can only have been in the simplest form. The preface also places Buchan's death a year too late, and it refers to thirteen Buchan children, a number that conflicts with that given in her petition by the mother. Again it is possible that a hand other than Jean's was involved in composing her preface or in putting it into print.[3]

Much of the book consisted of extracts from Martin Martin's work, which had given wide publicity to the episode of Roderick the 'impostor' and helped to make the words 'ignorance and idolatry' conventional among Protestant writings of the time and later. However there was an earlier instance than Roderick in the volume of 1727, a curious and confused tale deriving from events in the previous century and probably recorded by Buchan himself. He had heard from 'the Natives, and others more concerned in this Affair', that not long after 1600 'there happened to be One in St.Kilda, who went under the Name of a Popish-Priest; but was so ignorant, that he was not capable to teach them the Repetition of the Lord's Prayer, the Creed, and Ten Commandments, aright; yet was this nominal Priest it seems skilful enough to teach these poor ignorant People, who then might receive any Impress, Superstition and Idolatry, by giving them Beads, Images, Observing of superstitious Days, Erecting idolatrous Monuments, etc. among them'. This form of religious teaching, fairly unexceptional from a Catholic standpoint, continued for many years until, in 1641, 'Coll Mackdonald, alias Ketoch', fleeing for his life after defeat in battle, arrived in St Kilda. On his approach the inhabitants ran away to hide 'into a Cave in some remote Corner of the Island'. Having shown that 'he had no hostile Design against them' Coll 'lived in Safety and Quietness with them for the Space of three Quarters of a Year', during which time he asked the people about their religion, rebuked the ignorant priest, and, 'being himself a bigotted Papist', corrected errors and re-established the islanders 'in their superstitious and idolatrous Practices'. It was decided that the priest need not be deposed. 'And this was all the Religion they had till the Year 1697, when Mr John Campbel Minister of Harries (and Mr Martin) came to them'. So much for the unhistorical dismissal of the past.[4]

As for more recent times Buchan was again probably the author of remarks on Campbell and Martin. He said that they were in St Kilda for only twenty days, and, with some caution, that Campbell 'did doubtless good among them' by disapproving of their 'superstitious and idolatrous Kind of Worship' but when he also 'threw down severals of their Statues and Altars' the islanders 'were highly offended, and did upbraid him therefore', saying that 'some sad Judgment would befal him for his so Doing, so wedded were they to these Abominations'. The different hand must surely have written that throwing down 'Monuments of Idolatary' in practice was not sufficient, for 'the spiritual Ones which were erected in their Hearts were not touched, as their present Minister, Mr Alexander Buchan found at his first settling there among them'. What happened after 1704 was then outlined by the same mysterious contributor.[5]

Buchan seems also to have been responsible for comments on the steward or bailie of St Kilda. According to the first edition of 1727 the steward 'at present is one called John Mack-Leod, and lives all the Winter in another Isle called Paba, with his Family, and such as he is pleased to take along with him'. The difficulty here lies in the words 'at present' since they do not necessarily mean the year 1727. If Buchan wrote them they could signify some moment before 1709; but if, as is probable, the book was brought up to date for publication, then they would apply to the later time. Unfortunately records that might have provided confirmation one way or the other appear to be lacking. It is claimed, perhaps with good reason, that John was the son of Alexander MacLeod, the 'allister mc tormod vic Neill' who in the 1680s and 1690s held the greater part of 'kirketoune' (Baile na Cille) in Pabbay and who was presumably of the Clann Alasdair Ruaidh. Certainly the ancient connection between Pabbay and St Kilda persisted until at least 1772 when John's son, also Alexander, gave up his lease of St Kilda and prepared to emigrate. Another of John's sons is reckoned to have been Neil who became minister of Kilfinichen in Mull. The story of how a steward of St Kilda and his wife, with a crew that may have included Roderick the 'impostor', were driven by a storm to Rona, and of how a son who became a minister in Mull was conceived in that island, has been naturally thought to relate to John MacLeod and Neil, but it is argued that Alexander, believed to be John's father, was the steward in question irrespective of the minister son. In the absence of definite dates and ages it is not easy to decide which version is correct.[6]

The circumstances of the steward's annual stay on St Kilda and relations between him and the island people were described in 1727 in such a way as plainly to indicate the burden which he and his 'retinue' placed upon a community with few and limited resources:

'.. during their Abode in the Island, the Natives are taken up in climbing the Rocks cat[c]hing Fowls, and taking Eggs; and the Steward disposes of such Merchandise as he takes along with him, and receives therefore of the Product of the Island. They pay the Value of 20 Pence for the Peck of Salt, and the like for a Pound of coarse Tobacco, and so proportionally for other Things; and, by reason of their great Distance and Poverty, no other but the Steward and his Retinue ever comes to that Place; and seldom or never does any of the Natives come out of that Island, so that 'tis little they can know of the World, and upon many Accounts are much to be pitied: They are in a Manner Prisoners, yea worse, all Things being considered; Prisoners in other Places have the Advantage of Visits from Friends, and Converse with them, and Christian Comfort in their Distress, and other Assistance, which that poor People have not for the greatest Part of the Year, except when the Steward and his Followers come among them to demand his Rents, viz. Down, Wool, Butter, Cheese,

Cows, Sheep, Fowls, Oil etc. And they look upon that visit as no great Advantage to them, seeing they are kept in continual Trouble while the Steward is among them, and they very much grudge what he carries away with him, and that they must all the Year be toiling for Others ..'

There is an element of firsthand knowledge in this passage, however altered it may have been from Buchan's own words. Buchan too would have known that though the islanders were not unique in so having to toil they were not aware that any other community was taxed to the same extent and that the exactions were therefore bound to seem more onerous. When the passage appeared in the editions of 1774 and 1818, both of which stated that Buchan was the author, it was differently presented, and the notion of 'prisoners', together with some of the emphasis placed on the harshness of the steward's demands, was omitted.[7]

The book is therefore a mixture of three different contributions, those of Martin by quotation, of Buchan and of the unknown third party. Two further paragraphs may help towards an identification of the last-mentioned, suggesting as they do that he might have been a minister interested in St Kilda who would know details not provided by Buchan himself, possibly also a member of the SSPCK committee with some advance knowledge of the way things were going to be after Buchan's death or departure. 'O that the Lord would put it in the Heart of some piously, and charitably inclined Persons, to mortify a Fund, for a fixed yearly Stipend to a Minister in that Place, to continue the Gospel there!' With an eye to the future he continued: 'This would be truly a charitable Deed, and would not fail of a Reward'. If this were to happen, he hinted strongly, the Society 'might be prevailed with to continue a Salary for a School-master', since the work of a minister is 'a sufficient Task of itself' (and probably paid for by the Royal Bounty committee, though he did not say so) without the added burden of teaching, reading and writing. Moreover the support of the landlord was essential:

'None can subsist in this Island, without the Favour and Countenance of the Laird of McLeod, and the Steward; and Mr Buchan gives Thanks for the Kindness he has had from the Managers of that Estate, during the Minority: And now, that the Representative of that ancient Family is near the Years of Majority, it is not to be doubted, but he will go on to encourage the Promoting the Knowledge of Religion among that People, as his Predecessor did, not only the Head of that Family, but almost the whole Name of McLeod have been Asserters of the Protestant Religion, and against Popery; and will give Orders that Mr. Buchan meet with all Encouragement in Hirta'.[8]

With these words the purpose of the publication in 1727 becomes clear.

No longer, by many years, intended as a means of earning money to support the studies of Murdo Campbell, the book was aimed at securing more practical assistance from the landlord and the other sympathetic MacLeods. Much was made of Buchan's supposed gratitude to 'charitable Persons' of various kinds and of his desire 'to bless the Lord, that raised up that noble Societty', the SSPCK. Help was needed to maintain Buchan and his successors in St Kilda, especially since, 'if he were gone, 'tis to be feared few will go, upon so small an Allowance, to reside in that Island'. The message, it will be seen, did not go unheeded.[9]

A second, perhaps less obvious aim of the book was to record some of Buchan's successes in St Kilda. These included the abandonment of the 'superstitious Custom' of touching the crucifix when swearing an oath and of similar declarations while laying hands on the officer's 'Durk' as well as the crucifix during marriage ceremonies. Funerals had become a blend of Buchan success and tradition:

> 'Their Manner of Burying their Dead of old was thus, viz. When One dies, they give a Cry through the whole Island, that all the People at Work, whether in Field or Mountain, may thereupon come home. And indeed they seem to have a great Regard for the Dead, they all abstaining from ordinary Work till the Corps is interr'd, which they keep out of the Ground but for one Day only. The Time of the Funerals, the Gentlemen and Commonality are entertain'd with a good deal of Civility; These concerned with the Corps giving them what the Isle affords, and their Circumstances can allow; and also, friendly Compliments sett to the Houses of those that watch the Corps, and make the Grave. At Interring the Corps, they are so mindful of Mortality, Judgment and a future Life, that they all draw to a Side, take off their Bonnets, and the Poor their Caps made of Cloth, and say Prayers; therein humbly craving, That the Lord would prepare them for that State. The which may serve for a sharp Reproof to (and, if not taken and duly improven, will be a Witness against) many, who, notwithstanding of their better Education, and having by the Gospel been taught better Things, yet act far otherwise, and much more discommendably, at such Occasions. They esteem the Grave, where the Corps of the Dead is to be interr'd, so sacred a Bed, that they set a Person at each End of it, that no Dog, Cat, or other Brute-creature, approach to, nor cross over the same. After Prayers, a Snuff-box or two goes round the Best-respected; and the Poor get only a Penful or two in their Palms, especially if in Haste to be away.
>
> 'The Women also have a superstitious Custom, when they meet with any cross Providence, That they go ordinarily to the Grave-stone of their Husband, or nearest Relation, and there weep and howl. But now they, as

also the Men, are much reformed from this and their other foolish and mimical Observances, since they have been blessed with a Gospel-minister of their own: Upon these Occasions, he would go to them, and give them the Substance of the 5th of the Romans, or what was found fittest for the Purpose; so that now, seeing the Madness of these their foolish Ways, they have much abandoned them, and come to a better Mind. The Foresaid says, He never saw them make a Grave or bury their Dead on the odd Day of the Year. Also, out of a groundless (tho' superstitious) Fancy that their Children will live by Baptizing them on Saturday, they did it all then; yet they see it has not the wished-for Effect: Which Custom is now also done away. Also, lately, the Minister having approached the Grave nearer than his usual, he espied one of the Tenants using some superstitious Motions, which he took not heed to, until he took up a Spade, and lifted as much Earth of the Grave, as would fill a Child's Hand or Fist, and then did spit a little in the Grave, and threw in the little Quantity of Earth he had on the Spade into the Grave; all which he did the 2d or 3d Time. All the Reason he had from him or others was, That they are obliged to do it for Antiquity or Custom's Sake'.

Judged from the Protestant way of thinking perhaps the greatest 'success' was the mere presence of a missionary on the island, particularly one who had managed to teach many to read and write; 'and, which is most to be regarded and prised, their Esteem of, and Love to Religion, does appear from their Desire of Knowledge'. No less important, in their way, were the two successes of Mrs Buchan in the island; she taught some of the people to 'knit upon Weirs' and she brought a cock and hens - 'a Wonder to the Inhabitants, who had never seen any before'.[10]

For some time before 1727 the islanders had become fearful of what would happen if Buchan left them. The book came out at around the same time as the small pox reached the community, and the disease probably lasted until early 1729 when Alexander Buchan was perhaps among its final victims. Now he was indeed 'gone', but so were most of the 'poor people' of St Kilda. Few were left to wonder what would happen to the legacy of his teaching and to ask who would replace him.

CHAPTER 2

Catechists, preachers and counteracting 'popery'

IN districts or islands like Moidart, Lochaber, South Uist, Eigg and Rum, and even within 'the vast Bounds of the Presbytery of Gairloch' the familiar 'Ignorance and Barbarity' were believed still to abound in 1730. These were the symptoms, to Protestants, of flourishing popery. It was understood that zealous papists were preventing Protestant teachers and missionaries from carrying out their work, as indeed zealous Protestants were trying to do where priests were active, but it was not as straightforward as that. The two religious persuasions were sometimes mingled together to the confusion of church authorities. 'Considering the Restless Endeavours of papists, the Influence of Popish Heretors, who succeed to Heretage notwithstanding the Law to the Contrary', and that some Protestants were taking managerial positions such as factors on papist estates, it was surprising - to the Royal Bounty committee at any rate - that not more people had become Catholic. But 'It is much to be lamented that protestants of these Countrys are so far from discouraging the Wicked designs of the Papists, that many do Support them therein, and are Tools to them, and Concurr together, in their Opposition to his Majesty's Government'. For their part Protestants on the Clanranald estate were asked not to employ papists in management, while 'The Popish people', being 'Generally very ignorant' and forbidden to listen to Protestant ministers, were 'depriv'd of the Means of knowing the truth ..'[11]

A Protestant document dated 29 May 1714 described the situation in the Catholic Highlands and islands. In Rum, Eigg, Canna and presumably Muck, the people, 'all popish', kept a priest and paid tithes or teinds to him. In South Uist and Barra, with the 'adjacent Lesser Isles', there were two thousand papists, with 'six priests and a mendicant friar still resideing and officiating among them'. One priest lived with MacNeil of Barra, another with the MacDonald lairds of Clanranald and Benbecula. 'They have their respective paroches where they ordinarily reside and officiat as if formally fixed and countenanced by authority, and it's said they are duly maintained from abroad.' On the mainland there were two priests 'that frequent the Braes of Lochaber and Glengarrie, and sometimes go to Knoidart and Morhirr, who have perverted the most part of the people of the braes of Lochaber ... They have infested a great part of the paroch of Kilmanivoig, They haunt also the braes of Locharkaig in the paroch of Kilmalie and are like to over run all that County, if not speedily and effectually prevented.' Since St Kilda was associated with South Uist in some way it is of interest that the priests of that area had their 'respective paroches', to one of which the island could have been traditionally attached.

To counteract this so-called threat the Protestant church relied upon zealous men like Buchan and MacAulay. Reporting in 1726 to the General Assembly on its first year's achievements the Royal Bounty committee said that it had despatched twelve ministers on mission, twenty-one itinerant preachers and eighteen catechists, to places 'where their Services were most wanted'. These were places in which parish ministers alone were insufficient or where there were no ministers at all. The committee was pleased to be able to claim that the missionary ministers had had some success, even though it was clear that in the Catholic districts, 'where Ignorance does most abound', their labour was particularly hard, for 'the Restraining of the Growth of Popery and promoting of the Knowledge of God ... is a Work of time'. On this as on several other occasions the committee complained of how papists were obstructive: 'When the Ministers are in one Corner of the Parish, the Priests take Care to be in another, Ready to Visit Sick Persons to Marry and Baptise, and fail not then to take oaths of them, Never to hear protestant Ministers Pray or Preach'. It was up to the itinerant preachers and catechists to labour in parts which the ministers themselves had little or no opportunity to visit and to ensure that they were always seeking to be one step ahead of the clever papists.[12]

Catechists in particular, as in Buchan's case, were expected to stay in one place if possible for then they would be more effective in their work. Over a period the shorter catechism could be taught, and 'the Longer they Remain among a People, and the more Intimate and Familiar they are with them', the better able they would be 'to do good'; and, in some places, 'in Winter nights in houses and in Summer in the Shealls, the People may be Receiving Instruction with little diversion from their work'. A pattern of distribution emerged in the islands. Each of the eight parishes of Skye would have a catechist, to whom £2 a year would be allowed to help maintain him. This was a low sum, but there were no papists in Skye itself and the work was therefore easier. The catechist in Muck and his colleague in Canna would have £7 each, for here papists were numerous and liable to hinder and interrupt. In the Outer Hebrides there were to be catechists or preachers in four principal islands: Donald Morrison in Stornoway, John Morrison in Barvas, John Morrison in Harris, Allan MacLean in North Uist, and John MacLeod in South Uist. A certificate of approval for the latter from the presbytery of Long Island, dated at Scarista in Harris 11 March 1726 and signed by Aulay MacAulay, parish minister, sets out the conditions under which an appointment of this kind was made:

'Master John McLeod Probationer who was nominated and appointed by the Committee for mannadgeing the Kings bountie as itinerant preacher in the Isles of South uist and Barra in place of Mr Daniel [alt.Donald] McLeod former missionarie thereto, did produce before our Presbitery a sufficient Testimoniall from the Presbyterie of Sky, of his

163

orthodoxie, pietie, literature, prudence and other necessarie qualifications for that work, and particularly of his being skilled in the popish controversies, Lickwise a certificate from a justice of peace of his Loyalty and good-affection to his Majesties person and Government having qualified in terms of law whereupon the Presbiterie did assign the said Mr John McLeod as missionarie to the Isles of South Uist and Barra where he entered as such upon the first of March, where he behaves himself to the satisfaction of the Presbiterie; and approbation of the people there ...'[13]

In 1728 a slightly more generous arrangement was made to compensate for the large and scattered nature of parishes in the Outer Hebrides. Considering extensive parish bounds and the trouble and expense involved in attending presbytery meetings it was decided that to increase the number of ministers and others 'and for assisting to Carry on the Reformation, an Itinerant Preacher be sent to Bara, and South Uist, and that he be Ordain'd, and because he is to Expect nothing from the Papists, But what they will make all vivers as dear, as they can, to him and he will be at great Expences there, That therefore his allowance be Thirty pounds Sterling for the year'. There would also be two catechists for South Uist and Barra, at this time one large Protestant parish, who would receive £15 sterling each; North Uist and Harris would each have one catechist at £8 sterling , and 'the four Parishes in the Lewes' would have 'Four Catechists at Five pounds each, Living being Easier there, than among Papists'.[14]

In due course cooperation between the SSPCK and Royal Bounty committees developed along lines already established for St Kilda. On 26 June 1729 the combination of duties of catechist and schoolmaster was confirmed as meaning that one man carrying out both would have an improved salary of around £20, paid in equal shares by the two bodies. However even this sensible arrangement could not ensure the desired level of provision and there were from time to time lengthy vacancies. A letter from the presbytery of Long Island in June 1730 reported that neither South Uist nor Uig had enjoyed the services of a catechist since the previous November, and although proposals for an appointment were made the Royal Bounty committee concluded that Uig at least should for a while contine to be without a catechist. Soon afterwards it was noted that Harris had no catechist as there was a 'Charity School' there, this presumably being thought sufficient in itself.[15]

Protestant ministers and missionaries of whatever sort were at this time frequently pessimistic about their circumstances, as Alexander Buchan had been in St Kilda. In August 1728 Donald MacNeil of Vatersay, cousin of MacNeil of Barra and apparently a convert to the Protestant church prior to 1727, wrote from an otherwise thoroughly Catholic setting a letter 'shewing that a

Popish Bishop with five more priests were lately in Bara, and South-Uist visiting and confirming their people'. This activity on behalf of the old faith can hardly have come as a surprise to Protestants but the news heralded, as usual, increased claims upon the limited resources of the SSPCK and its companion body. Threats of spreading 'Popery' meant inevitable demands for support to be given to already hard-pressed missionary ministers, preachers and catechists whose salaries if increased and whose numbers if extended would further drain limited funds.[16]

Without support, however, the cause of the continuing 'Reformation' in the remote north-west could easily be seen as forlorn if not hopeless. In parishes of great extent, even those far away from traditional Catholic influence, Protestant ministers lacking assistance in their isolation became depressed. This feeling is apparent in a letter from John MacLeod, who, after a short season as preacher in South Uist and Barra, had moved up to Lewis as minister of Uig. He was writing at the end of December 1726 when the gloom of his situation was probably at its deepest. When initially on his way from Skye to South Uist he had, ominously, lost most of his books. After a while 'he was put on it by the Presbytery of Long Island to accept of the Charge of Uig a very Difficult Post, wherein he thinks there was not a Minister since the Reformation'. To describe his position in Uig as very difficult seems to have been an understatement, for 'a Stranger can Scarcely Conceive the Inconveniencys he labours under'. MacLeod declared that he needed 'Sympathy and Assistance'; as a matter of daily concern 'he is in great danger when travelling in that parish, and hath neither Kirk, Manse, nor Gleib, and is put to great hardship, So that in all appearance he cannot live long there'.[17]

It was in the nature of the need for them that catechists often found themselves in lonely and wild places. The parish minister might be expected to occupy a more central location, where, if not at first, eventually there would be a manse and glebe as well as a church; but the catechist, and the itinerant preacher, were likely to be labouring at the extremities or on the fringes of the parish and in places such as remote glens among mountains and smaller islands which the minister could not be expected to reach on a regular basis. Mr Daniel MacAulay who had visited Rum on mission around the beginning of 1726 had discovered that there 'the Reformation goes on Successfully by the Zeal of their Worthy Superior Hector McLean of Coll', so that where three years previously there had been only a handful of Protestants now 'there is only one little family, and some Silly women … Continuing under Antichristian delusion'. The Royal Bounty committee was thus pleased to report to the General Assembly in May 1726 that as a result of the intervention of 'a Protestant Minister' and of Hector MacLean, 'a Gentleman zealous for the Protestant Religion', together of course with 'God's Blessing on their Prudent Endeavours', the people of Rum had been 'brought over', leaving only the very few staunch 'papists'. By 1728 there was a catechist on Rum, a John McArthur, paid from the Royal Bounty fund, 'who, in the Minister's absence reads Prays, and Sings Psalms, with the People on the Lords Day and Catechizes, and wants not Zeal for the Protestant Interest, But is not master of the Prudence and good Temper which is necessary to his doing good among that people, who are yet in a great Measure, Ignorant, and some of them Addicted to the Old Superstitious Customs'. In a letter of July 1728 McArthur, in a position not unlike that of Buchan, wrote that 'it is Dear living in that place, and that he is under Discouragements But that he Continues Dutiful and Submissive, untill it be thought fit to Order his post to some other place, where he may have more Satisfaction, Yea, though it were to Hirta'. The Royal Bounty committee replied 'admonishing him to take heed to himself, and to Carry as becomes, otherwise he will be Removed', and the presbytery of Skye was told to keep an eye on him. The parish minister Daniel McQueen, who was resident in Skye, was 'obliged Constantly to keep a Boat, and Crew in Order to his travelling from Island to Island', although his stipend was insufficient to cover this expense 'among a disaffected People from whom he can Expect no kindness' and so he seldom visited. It was observed by Daniel MacAulay after his mission there before going to St Kilda that the people of Rum did not like MacArthur who was clearly not suited to that island. Nor was Allan MacLean, who in 1729 considered that a proposal 'of banishing me to Rume is a sufficient punishment' for a past 'importunity'. MacLean had a big family of eight 'weak' children and no substance or ability to provide for them 'in such a barren and remote Isle' situated 'in the very midle of the popish Islands'. He would, it seems, have preferred to stay in Tiree.[18]

The committees in Edinburgh had no difficulty in offering their employees sympathy and encouragement nor - since they could simply withdraw salaries - in ordering them about, but positive assistance, all very well in theory, was not usually something that could be put into practice tomorrow. Many administrative problems hindered progress, one of the most serious being a lack of suitable people to send out as missionaries, preachers and catechists. It was one thing to hear or even to decide that a minister or preacher should be sent to Barra 'to deal with Papists for their Conversion, and to Confirm, and instruct the protestants there', but quite another to find a man who could speak Gaelic and who would not disappear after a few days in post. In the spring of 1727 the General Assembly was informed that there was 'a greate Scarcity of Preachers having the Irish Language, and Such of them as were sent in Mission, were soon called, and Settled in vacant Parishes, so that the Committee were Necessitate to send Catechists to some places, that preachers were design'd for'. Moreover, even if Gaelic-speaking preachers were appointed, it appeared that some had failed in their duties; they 'had not been punctual in going from house to house, visiting and Catechizing on week days as well as Preaching on the Lord's days', while 'some who had been nam'd, and had got a Quarter's Allowance, had not obey'd, and others who had been Employ'd had not fulfill'd the whole time Appointed'. Although the advantages of a long stay had been recognised, catechists and preachers alike were liable to move on with or without the permission of those distant authorities which had commissioned them, and since the money to pay them was always scarce the committees quickly learned that extreme caution was necessary when it came to responding to requests for their services from needy parishes.[19]

The effect of the intervention in Rum of Hector MacLean of Coll did not go unnoticed by the committees. It showed them that the influence of landowners could be of the greatest importance when it came to religious loyalties, but it could not always be relied upon. In 1726 the Royal Bounty committee had to admit that when 'Colin McKenzie of Kildin a Papist in the Lewis', one of the few, 'brought a Popish Schoolmaster thither, where few papists were formerly, and Protestants put their Children thereto', it was a bad sign, for Colin was closely related to the landowner. In the southern half of the Outer Hebrides the landowners were rather hesitant over their faith. Spending time away on the mainland could suggest new social and religious possibilities to lairds of remote islands. 'Mackniel of Bara was once thought in a fair way of Coming off from Popery and when at Edinburgh some Years ago did hear Protestant Ministers, But when he came home to his Priests, he returned to the Profession of Popery'. Ten years later, towards the end of 1737, when Barra had been made a separate Protestant parish, there came news that Roderick MacNeil of Barra, as strong a Catholic as ever, 'threatens to Disinherite Margaret McNiel his Eldest Daughter who has lately Embraced the Protestant Religion', and that 'She and the Lady Bara who are protestants have been necessitate to leave the family'. In spite of this domestic disturbance Roderick MacNeil was carefully educating three other children 'in principals of Popery', and any chance there might have been of making him alter his religion had faded away. Meanwhile Benbecula and South Uist, along with the islands of Eigg, Muck and Canna, and mainland districts opposite, had long been in the possession of Clanranald and Glengarry MacDonalds, but here there had been perhaps more hopeful changes, since in 1726, 'the present Glengarry is Protestant and Mr Alexander McKenzie of Delvin[e] Younger a Protestant did lately purchase the forfeited Estate of Clanrannald'. The best way, from a Protestant point of view, was to arrange that people like MacNeil of Barra and MacDonald of Benbecula were approached by distinguished Protestants in the hope that they might be brought to their senses; for instance, Alexander MacLeod, advocate, and John MacLeod, also advocate, through their married female relations, were both 'friends to the Laird of Bara' and might be expected to have some influence upon him. In the end, whatever the attachment of the lairds, the people of Barra, South Uist and other places remained mostly Catholic, and it became clear that the isolated Protestant, Donald MacNeil of Vatersay, was right when he said that any loss of ground by the local priests would ultimately depend upon 'the diligence of the protestant Ministers'.[20]

One other means of control and inducement therefore recommended itself to the Protestant committees. In an atmosphere of lurking Jacobite danger they could turn to the potential use of force. One of the first tasks of the Royal Bounty committee had been to write to various Protestant landowners and to General Wade as commander in chief of his Majesty's forces in Scotland, requesting them to give all the protection they could to the missionaries, especially those ministers who like Daniel MacAulay of Bracadale, ventured out of their own secure parishes to ill-provided districts such as Eigg, Lochaber and Knoydart. Whether or not this protection was given is not certain, and there is no evidence that the several appeals directed to General Wade and, before him, to Brigadier Maitland, were very successful, but the threat of military backing was there to be used by the Protestant ministers. It was accepted by everyone that the influence of a proprietor, whatever his religion, could be of crucial importance, but it was rarely predictable. When Patrick Nicolson travelled within the wild and rough bounds of the Synod of Glenelg for six weeks during the summer of 1728 he found many people ignorant and rather hostile to the 'present establishment'. As a consequence ministers there were 'exposed to daylie fatigue and danger', while 'their ministrie are much despised, ordinances not attended on in many places, nor their Characters much regarded'. Yet as 'the Generality there are naturally sagacious, and somewhat religiously inclined', a more just view of the ordinary people than that which held them to be barbaric, so they may be 'easily brought to a better temper' and to attend Protestant services. What held them back for the time was that they were 'miserably managed and so much under the Influence of their Masters and Leaders; who are more absolute within their litle territories than most princes in Europe'.[21]

On reading Nicolson's account the Royal Bounty committee naturally had a 'due concern for and a sincere sense of the melancholy circumstances of these remote Corners', but the main message was that if 'Masters and Leaders' were converted their followers would follow. More extreme opinions were put to General Wade in a memorial of the same 1728 summer. It was stated that it should be obvious to anyone acquainted with the area 'that the gross Ignorance and Extreme Indolence and Idleness of the Meaner Sort of people keeps them poor, and their Spirits low, and in Consequence makes them Yield a Blind Obedience to the Commands of their Superiours without Regard to Religion, Law or Reason, to which Causes are to be attributed the Multitudes that followed the Disaffected Nobility and Gentry in the late Rebellion'. Neither deeply-rooted beliefs founded in ancient religion and tradition nor the effects of poverty upon the spirits and energies, physical and mental, of a struggling people seemed to be appreciated by the Protestant church, which considered that its kind of religion would provide a sure remedy, for if the people were instructed 'in the Principles of Religion and in Methods of Virtue and Industry, They would soon become peaceable Useful and Loyal Subjects'. It was therefore requested, in this appeal to the General, that Popish priests be banished from the country, that children of Popish parents should be educated in the Protestant religion, that Protestant judges should be appointed to cover every parish, that new parishes be erected, and that encouragement be given to new 'Collonies of Protestants to Settle in Popish Countrys and Islands'.[22]

All these concerns - Catholic threat, intermixing of Catholic and Protestant people through marriage and employment, the problems of Protestant ministers, preachers and catechists, the lack of funds, the uncertain religious allegiances of landowners - hovered in the background when in 1730, after news of Alexander Buchan's death and of the latest disaster in St Kilda, the committees in Edinburgh were compelled to contemplate what to do next about that distant and sombre outpost of missionary labour.

CHAPTER 3

*Finding Buchan's replacement, Roderick Maclennan in Lochaber and
St Kilda where he meets Lady Grange, Maclennan leaves St Kilda*

T HE parishes of Kilmonivaig and Kilmallie in the Braes of Lochaber formed
a largely Catholic area, in the first of which at least, according to a Royal
Bounty committee report of 1727, 'the People are most Barbarous and Cruel
their Minister is not in Safety to Reside among them They having under Cloud
of Night besett his house, and with Guns or Pistols, fir'd in at his Windows'.
From such surroundings the minister of Kilmallie, James Gilchrist, wrote to
the committee which considered his letter on 10 November 1727. He said
'That there is a pious young man, nam'd Mr Roderick McLennan' in the
district, who, having been examined by a Synod was found qualified to be a
catechist, and the writer therefore asked that a salary be provided. The
committee could hardly refuse, and on 14 December MacLennan
acknowledged receipt of £3 as his pay for serving as cathechist within the
bounds of the presbytery of Abertarff from 1 November 1727 to 1 February
1728. It was agreed that he should work as catechist 'for the Parish of Laggan
and Braes of Lochaber' which would have meant moving into the parish of
Kilmonivaig but he remained in Kilmallie, living at 'the foot of Glenlaoy',
otherwise called 'Bunlaoi', where the river Loy flows into the Lochy a few
miles from Fort William.[23]

Roderick MacLennan is supposed to have attended King's College,
Aberdeen, and the University of Edinburgh around 1720, but this is doubtful,
and the place of his birth is unknown. He was evidently a Gaelic speaker. It
appears that he remained at 'Bunlaoi' for a year or two and then may have
gone for a brief spell to Mull, being replaced in Kilmallie by another young
catechist called Charles McArthur, perhaps a relative of John McArthur in
Rum. In 1726 John Skeldoch, the endangered minister of Kilmonivaig, had
requested a first payment for Charles McArthur and Alexander Cameron, who
kept schools at 'the old Castle of Inverlochy' and 'Katalich more in Dauch in
cassie' respectively. MacLennan was back in 1730 when it was noted by the
Royal Bounty committee that he was to be employed at 'Glenlaoi' in the parish
of Kilmallie in place of Charles McArthur. On 11 June 1730 the SSPCK
committee heard that MacLennan, formerly schoolmaster in Kilfinichen in
Mull, was to return to Kilmallie as schoolmaster and catechist, and a receipt
for salary from him was dated at Bunloy 12 June 1730. The following
September it was agreed that he should continue in 'Glen laoy' and would still
receive £5 from each committee as his yearly wage.[24]

In the spring MacLennan wrote to the Royal Bounty committee from
Maryburgh (Fort William):

'Very Reverend Sir

I continue still at Bunlaoi in the parish of Kilmalie as Schoolmaster jointly Employed discharging my office as the Lord assists me. Since I came from Edinburgh I hope Sir you Remember that I was Recommended to you by the Synod of Glainelg the preceeding year, It was for want of fonds and not of Good will that I did not attend the profession the last session. Charles Mcarthur writes to Master Gilchrist minister of Kilmalie, that he designs to leave Edinburgh at whitsunday in order to be schoolmaster at Bunlaoi. I hope Sir you shall recommend me to some corner in the north where there is cheaper living, unless the Reverend Committee and Honourable Society did augment my Sallary to fifteen pounds sterlin in the corner where I serve now. I should Reckon it my honour to be useful in some corner of the world by saving souls. If you know not of any other Encouragment that offers at present, If you design to send any to the Island of St Kilda this year, providing due encouragement be given, I am willing to accept of it, I Conclude this being all at present Sir from

Your humble servant and well wisher

Post. Reverend Sir you shal excuse any slip or defect in the write, being in hast.'[25]

On discussing the matter, and accepting that MacLennan 'shewed his readiness of going to any other place - even to St Kilda - to serve the Interest of Religion', the committee decided that since McArthur was already 'provided' MacLennan should stay where he was 'till farder orders'. McArthur had been recently appointed by the SSPCK, on 16 March, to be schoolmaster in the 'Appin-Glenco' district and, to improve on his SSPCK salary of £4 a year, wished to be made a catechist there as well by the Royal Bounty committee, 'providing the Sallary formerly allowed him be not diminished when he is going to a very wild place where living is exceeding dear'. The committee allowed the plea and paid him £6.[26]

The most demanding vacancy and probably the most difficult to fill was that at St Kilda, where there had now been no catechist, teacher or minister for two years. The knowledge that since the fatal epidemic in 1727-29 there had been very few people there may have taken away any sense of urgency from the search for a successor to Buchan, but by 1731 the population had greatly increased and the welfare of souls was again a matter of concern. The unusual proposal put forward in 1727 and 1728 'that some Collonies of Protestants be Settl'd in the Countrys of Moror, Arisaig, Moydart, Bara, and South Uist' as a means of counteracting papist prevalance could possibly have had some bearing upon the revival of the St Kilda community. Whether or not the state of the island while without Protestant pastoral care and without many inhabitants suggested to the SSPCK or the Royal Bounty committee that it was at the mercy of the priests, who might even set up a colony of their own, the idea of transporting people to fill the almost empty settlement certainly entered the mind of authority somewhere, and within a short while there was a more numerous band of islanders. The new arrivals did not all come at once, for the repopulation took place in stages, and the Protestant church at least was interested in the migration. On 13 March 1730 the Long Island presbytery wrote to the SSPCK committee requesting 'That Regard might be had to the People of Hirta, Which Island by the yearly transporting of People to it, will soon be populous again, and the Gentleman concerned in the management of it had before the Presbytery obliged himself to cause the Children attend the School, and to be easy and just to any Person who shall be sent thither'.[27]

The record of this deliberate transportation raises many questions. It is not known whether the renewed island population was to be fixed at a certain level, nor whether those people introduced consisted of families or individuals. Were the sexes evenly balanced or was there a preponderance of men to assist in establishing life once more? There seems to be no information on whether the migrants went voluntarily or under compulsion, on relationships which might include connections with former or surviving islanders, on religion, and on where they came from. Above all, perhaps, it may be wondered whether this sort of movement had happened before in similar circumstances, and why, given the conditions and reputation of life in St Kilda, trouble should be taken to repopulate such a difficult island. Answers to only two of these questions may be suggested. On the basis of later surnames Skye, Uist and Berneray in the Sound of Harris have been indicated as the places of origin; and as with the attempted repopulation of Rona after about 1700 the main purpose in re-establishing a permanent and sufficient settlement seems to have been to continue the economic value of the island to its tacksman, if not to the landowner. It therefore becomes possible to envisage the St Kilda community of the eighteenth century as being similar to, though far larger than, that of Rona; it depended upon the steward or tenant resident in Pabbay much as Rona's few people depended on the tenant of Swainbost in Ness, and its contributions of produce were important enough for the steward still to spend up to two months or more on the island each summer. Distance and the need to survive gave each group of island dwellers the appearance of at least modest independence, but as with any cluster of cottars on a farm this was indeed more superficial than real. With the example of Rona in mind it might have been reasonably supposed that some settlers in St Kilda would derive from Baile na Cille in Pabbay.[28]

The presbytery of Long Island's letter of March 1730 went further than the mere mention of 'any Person who shall be sent' to St Kilda. It recommended 'one Donald Morison who they write is a Serious Man and well qualifyed in all Respects as likely to have Success there ..' However the SSPCK committee delayed consideration of a possible appointment for a year, spending rather more time on the fate of Alexander Buchan's widow and children than on his replacement, until on 8 July 1731 there was received a further letter from the same presbytery stating that 'the Island of Hirta is now pretty well peopled'. The letter expressed concern at seeing 'the Young dy unbaptized and the aged in danger of falling off to Heathnish darkness and Superstition'; and it urged that the Society encourage 'Some proper person' to go to 'Hirta' as soon as possible.[29]

At much the same time the Royal Bounty committee received similar communications. The presbytery of Long Island wrote on 1 March 1731 proposing 'That Daniel Morison be sent to Hirta, that place being again peopled'. It said, as it had done previously to the SSPCK, that 'the Baillie of that place promises all due Encouragement' to the person sent there. But as it happened Daniel or Donald Morison was not the only candidate, for in June 1731 the Synod of Glenelg, which of course included the presbyteries of both Long Island and Abertarff, gave consideration not only to 'the desolate condition of the Island of St Kilda … for want of Gospel ordinances since the death of Mr Buchan' but also to the representation from the presbytery of Abertarff that Roderick MacLennan, who had been catechist and schoolteacher within its bounds for several years, was a fit person to be entered on trials in order to be licenced and ordained as Buchan's successor. The Synod therefore asked that 'a Speedy method may be fallen upon for settling a Minister in St Kilda Lately depopulated, but now fully planted', and put forward 'Mr Rory McLennan Student in their bounds'. There was no immediate response; and on 26 August 1731 the Royal Bounty committee decided that 'the providing of Hirta by Daniel Morison as Craved by the said presbytrie, or by Mr Rory McLenan as the Synod of Glenelg desires, be delayed till another dyet'. So a further year passed without a Protestant representative in the island.[30]

The Royal Bounty committee paid Roderick MacLennan, still catechist at 'Bunlaoi', his quarterly salary of £1.5s throughout 1731 and on till May 1732. Meanwhile the Synod of Glenelg's attention to the state of St Kilda increased, and, having heard nothing from the relevant committees, it wrote in again towards the end of June 1732 to express the island's plight. Using words borrowed from an earlier communication from the presbytery of Long Island the Synod asked once more 'that some Person be sent to instruct the Inhabitants of St Kilda in danger of falling back to Heathnish darkness', and the Royal Bounty committee's reaction was to refer the case to a sub-committee in the hope that 'if the Funds will bear, one may be sent thither for the Ensuing Year'. But the ensuing year from July 1732 to July 1733 came and went with very little progress, except for a decision that MacLennan was to be sent there in preference to Morison, perhaps because he had worked in a district where Catholics were numerous and therefore had experience of a people living under a 'Heathnish' shadow.[31]

The salaries of catechists at 'Bunlaoi', 'Bellaloyn' and 'Glenroy' had been withdrawn by the summer of 1733 and re-allocated to posts elsewhere. This meant that Roderick MacLennan was no longer employed in Kilmallie parish, and as he does not seem to have moved to some other west Highland area he may have spent time finishing his studies and preparing for his St Kilda venture. On 26 July 1733 the SSPCK committee remitted to its companion body a further request from the anxious Synod of Glenelg that a missionary be sent to St Kilda 'until Mr Rory McLenan, probationer, whom they recommend, be settled there'. Again the matter was passed to the sub-committee, but in addition a letter was addressed to Alexander MacLeod, advocate, asking him to 'deal with' the Laird of MacLeod as proprietor in order to make him provide adequate accommodation in St Kilda and otherwise give positive encouragement to 'such person as shall be sent to Instruct the Inhabitants'.[32]

Between 1725 and 1730 Alexander Macleod and the Laird were in dispute and not on good terms, and there is no sign that they did deal with each other later. However Alexander already had intentions of becoming a benefactor, as he may have conceived it, to the people of St Kilda, and in December 1733, when apparently in a state of poor health, he asked his nephew John MacLeod, also advocate and later laird of the estate of Muiravonside on the Stirlingshire river Avon, to write to the SSPCK committee and let members know of a surprising and generous proposal. Mr John's letter, before the committee at its meeting on 25 December 1733, assured the SSPCK that his uncle 'had had the Disconsolate Condition of the Inhabitants of St Kilda, very much at heart, ever since the death of Mr Buchan'. So much concerned was he that he had 'executed a Deed, perpetually Mortifying to any Minister who shall happen to be settled there, the Sum of Three hundred merks yearly, Or such other Annual Sum, as shall by Law effeir and Correspond to the Capital Sum of Six Thousand merks, on condition nevertheless, That the Society shall give such additional Encouragement out of their Funds, as may in Conjunction with the above Mortified Sum, Invite and determine any person to be admitted Minister, to fix and settle amongst these poor people'. Mr John MacLeod made it clear that his uncle's wish was to ensure the prompt appointment of a minister in St Kilda by adding 'That if Mr McLenan, or any other person by the Recommendation of the Presbytrie of Long Island, shall be found duly qualified by the Society, and shall by such additional Encouragement, as they shall judge reasonable to give, be once fixed and Established Minister in the Isle of St Kilda, Mr McLeods Intentions towards founding and perpetrating a Work so pious and necessary stand fixed'. The initial sum of 300 merks, or whatever interest was derived from the capital, was to be paid to the Society's treasurer at the first term, Martinmas or Whitsunday, following the new minister's arrival in St Kilda.[33]

The SSPCK committee lost no time in responding to this most welcome windfall. Since it corresponded so closely with the words of the wish expressed in the book published six years earlier and republished in 1733 the mortification may perhaps have not been so surprising after all. Here was the pious and charitable person looked for, providing a fund to support a minister! With some tact the Society immediately suggested that it would recommend to the presbytery of Long Island, or that of Skye, that Mr Roderick MacLennan, student of divinity, should be put through his trials with a view to his being licensed and ordained as soon as possible and that he, or, less probably, some other suitable person, should be employed as minister in St Kilda with an annual salary of not more than 500 merks. It also arranged for letters of thanks to go to the two MacLeods without delay. The chance of having a minister paid, at least in part, from someone else's resources was not to be missed.[34]

The sum assigned by Alexander MacLeod, whose former Catholic loyalties had apparently faded away, was intended to cover the salary of MacLennan, or another, in his capacity as minister and catechist, thus incidentally freeing the Royal Bounty committee of any responsibility for paying him. But the St Kilda missionary also acted as schoolmaster, and here the SSPCK continued to play its part in promoting the principles of the reformed religion. There was at first some uncertainty and even disbelief among members over the exact terms of the mortification, and early in 1734 John MacLeod had to reassure the Society that the capital amount made available by Alexander was indeed to stand fixed in perpetuity. On hearing this the committee concluded that a salary to Roderick MacLennan of 450 merks per annum would be appropriate.[35]

On 29 April 1734 Daniel MacAulay, still minister of Bracadale, on a visit to Edinburgh, told the SSPCK committee clerk that the presbytery of Skye had taken MacLennan 'on tryals' with a view to 'his Repairing to St Kilda', and that probably this procedure would now be over. Another report from MacAulay three weeks later indicated that MacLennan, 'designed as Missionary for St Kilda', was a licensed preacher and undergoing 'tryals for Ordination'. He could not undertake the voyage to his remote station without 'an advance of money', so the committee authorised payment of a half year's salary, 225 merks, to MacAulay, who would hand on the sum to MacLennan on his setting out for the island, perhaps even as he went on board the boat from Skye to Harris or Pabbay. On 5 June 1734 the presbytery of Skye noted that it had ordained Roderick MacLennan as minister for St Kilda, and so almost immediately he journeyed out to a place where, on stepping ashore, he found himself participating in extraordinary events which lay outside normal missionary duties.[36]

*

The sad story of Rachel Erskine, commonly called 'Lady Grange', is well known. She was abducted from an Edinburgh lodging-house one night in January 1732 and nine months later was taken to Heisgeir, 'a Poor Miserable Island' as she called it, where she was kept a prisoner for nearly two years. Eventually, on 14 June 1734, there arrived a 'sloop' or 'Galley' with the steward of St Kilda, then John MacLeod, on board. She said he was tenant to the Laird of MacLeod 'in a place they call the north town' in the parish of Harris, and that though the sloop belonged to him the 'manager' of it was his brother Norman. They were both 'very rud and hurt me sore'. By them she was removed to St Kilda which she thought even worse than Heisgeir:

'when I came into the Island I found it as I dreaded a very desolate barren miserable spot no body in it but the Natives of the place John and his Brother stay'd some days but wou'd by [no] means discover by whose Orders he acted ... I'm sure he left me in a miserable Condition there being no Provisions left me but what the Island afforded and no body to assist me but an ill natured Man who understood a little English and Explained to others what I wanted he not only was surly but half witted he having one day taken out his Durk to kill me ...'[37]

Exactly a century later a tourist party was landed at St Kilda, and one member, by going 'up to the village', was able to visit 'the ruins of the hut in which the celebrated Lady Grange spent seven years'. He was led to this now romantic site 'by a grandson of the native, Finlay McDonald, who attended her in her exile'. The house was about 20 feet long by 10 wide, and like the rest at that time was 'divided in the centre by a partition of rude loose stone'. On one side, he was told, Finlay sat every night, on the other Lady Grange, who never slept. The guide said that she learned Gaelic quite well and 'took pleasure in listening to the native tales and romances of Finlay'. She went for solitary walks, fell asleep during the day, and was provided with a seat of twisted straw which Finlay made for her and which in the end she took away with her, leaving 12s in silver to the maker. And now the thought occurs that looking after this unhappy woman would have been a suitable and interesting task for Alexander Buchan's pupil, Finlay MacDonald, who went to Edinburgh with his teacher and Murdo Campbell in 1709 and twenty years afterwards survived the smallpox.[38]

Another account of Rachel Erskine's adventures was published in 1846. It contrasted with that of only eight years earlier and may have been based on information intended to show that her confinement in St Kilda was quite comfortable:

'We learn … some particulars of her history during this period from the testimony of those who had a charge over her. If this is to be believed, she made incessant efforts, though without effect, to bribe the islanders to assist in liberating her. Once a stray vessel sent a boat ashore for water: she no sooner heard of it, than she despatched the minister's wife to apprise the sailors of her situation, and intreat them to rescue her; but Mrs Maclennan did not reach the spot till after they had departed. She was kind to the peasantry, giving them from her own stores; and sometimes had the women to come and dance before her; but her temper and habits were not such as to gain their esteem. Often she drank too much, and whenever any one near her committed the slightest mistake, she would fly into a furious passion, and even resort to violence. Once she was detected in an attempt during the night to obtain a pistol from above the steward's bed in the room next to her own: on his awaking and seeing her, she ran off to her own bed.'[39]

That the steward shared her dwelling seems at first sight unlikely, as too the reference to her 'house or cottage' as being 'tolerably well-furnished', but since Buchan's Finlay was apparently the officer's son, it is possible that he in turn became officer with a better than average dwelling.

The arrival of Lady Grange at St Kilda in mid June 1734 coincided almost to the day with that of Roderick MacLennan and his wife, but she seems to have got there first. She remarked that at first there was nobody in the island but the 'natives', and she wrote that 'the Society [SSPCK] sent a Minister here I have given him a much fuller account then this and he wroit it down'. What may be that more detailed version of her experiences conveys the impression that she had already been in St Kilda for some time when 'God in his good providence who in all my Distresses has taken Care of me for which I have great reason to Bless and Praise him so ordered it that there came to the Island a Minister and his Wife to whom I am infinitely obliged to'. The words of Lady Grange at the time appear to be the only indication that Roderick MacLennan was married and that it was his wife who helped Rachel to survive:

'for had it not been for the care she took of me I shou'd have dyed for Want for there was no provisions sent me but two Pecks of flower and such as the place can afford such as Milk, and a little Barley knocked, and that forced from them by threatning the people being miserably poor and much oppressed: I have no body to serve me but a little highland Girl and the Minister or his Wife is obliged to explain to her; he is a very serious devout Man and what time he can spare he is so good as to come and see me. I am not sure whose hands this may fall into, but if I'm dead I beg my friends may be kind to this good man and his wife for they have preserved my life and made it as comfortable as possible …. I gott the

Minister to write the Account how I was stolen and by whom that he might acquaint my friends, he wou'd not give me paper to write myself but said he would do all in his power for me when he left this Island and went to Edinburgh he wou'd not venture to carry this paper with him but I gave him a letter to you and two other of my friends that they might know where I was but he being threatned with his life hindred him either of goeing to Edinburgh or writing about me since he came back to this Island he sent me word by his Wife he had burnt the Letters I had given him he is in such a terrour for his life and his Uncle and some other Ministers were so angry for the care and Concern he had about me that he desired his Wife she wou'd gett this paper that it might never come to light wrote by his hand since I could not gett so much paper as to write so full an Account as this I thought it no sin to deceive her so burnt [two?] papers before her and told her now to tell her husband to be easy'.

About February 1741 'Captain William Gregory with his sloop Arabella' was sent to fetch Lady Grange away from St Kilda. 'This ship proceeded no farther than the harbour called the Horseshoe in Lorn (now, we believe, the seat of the thriving young town of Oban), where the master quarrelled with and set on shore Mrs Maclennan, his guide. Apparently the voyage was not prosecuted, in consequence of intelligence being received that the lady had been removed to another place, where she was kept in more humane circumstances'. Various claims have been made as to the identity of this other place, ranging from Harris to Assynt. Writing in 1841 Archibald Clerk, minister of Duirinish parish in Skye, dismissed some 'very romantic and fabulous accounts' of Lady Grange's sufferings and himself provided 'particulars .. stated to us on authority which deserves regard'. According to his version of events after St Kilda Lady Grange spent some of the time in Uist and some in Skye. However a letter of 26 November 1763 from Charles MacSueen to Norman MacLeod of MacLeod shows that she was in Harris from early autumn 1741 to the following spring. 'Consider with yourself', wrote MacSueen, 'what Guest I brought from Harrish in March 42 or by whose orders I kept her seven months and who wrote me in September 42 to deliver her to Rory macNeil ..' MacLeod must also have instructed MacNeil to look after her, since accounts were submitted to him by Rory for her board which cost around £30 a year. On 12 May 1745 MacNeil wrote from Trumpan in Waternish to MacLeod: 'These are to inform you that the first in this Familie departed this life about 3 of the Cloak fryday last being the tenth instant; which puts me to no Small trouble in thir hard times when I cannot get any Sort of Eatables to Buy, yet I will doe in it what I can, ... and seeing you left me no written orders wher or how to burie her in caice She Should happen to die in this house .. I hope to see her decently interred Wednesday nixt ..' The burial, so it is said, was at Trumpan.[40]

Once Roderick MacLennan was settled as missionary in St Kilda he became automatically a member of the presbytery of Long Island, which body had preferred Donald Morison when the appointment was as yet undecided. Although presbytery meetings at Scarista were closer than those held in Skye this made little difference to his ability to attend, and he soon found that, in addition to the awkward presence of Lady Grange, he was faced with the same difficulties as had surrounded Alexander Buchan. He remained discontented throughout the years of his stay in the island.

During the first few days of 1735 the treasurer of the SSPCK spoke with Mr John MacLeod of Muiravonside about his uncle's mortification, there having been some delay in doing so since Mr John was 'for the most part out of Town', and told him that MacLennan had been sent to St Kilda the previous summer 'for Instructing the Inhabitants' with a half year's salary in advance. The benefactor, Alexander MacLeod, after a long and eventful life, died on 10 March 1735, and the news was reported to the SSPCK by his nephew a week later. Mr John MacLeod enclosed to the Society the deed of mortification dated 29 May 1733, the terms of which then became clear. In general Alexander MacLeod's estate was left to John of Muiravonside, 'my Eldest Brother's son'; but knowing 'that the Island of Hirta alias St Kilda does for the present and has for some time past wanted the means of the Knowledge of God, and the principles of the Christian Religion', and having in mind the parish of Harris, certain parishes in Skye, and the parish of Glenelg, all of which were so extensive that the ministers needed what help they could get, he had decided to leave money for maintaining a teacher in St Kilda and catechists 'in other parts of the Laird of McLeod's Country'. He therefore mortified 12000 merks to the Society, of which he had been a founding member. The interest, 350 merks per annum on the capital sum of 7000 merks, was to be used for supporting a catechist in Harris, its small islands, and St Kilda, the catechist being bound to reside in Harris except in summer when he was bound to go to St Kilda with the steward of the island, to stay for as long as the steward was there, and during that time 'to use his outmost diligence in Instructing and Catechising the Inhabitants'. The sum of 250 merks, being the interest on the remaining capital of 5000 merks, was to be used for a catechist in Skye and Glenelg. 'And in Case it shall happen that the forsaid Society … shall in Compassion to the saids Inhabitants of Hirta and towards their more Effectual and permanent Instruction in the means of salvation, think it proper hereafter as it is highly expedient by an additional Encouragment from themselves to find out and settle a proper person for a Constant minister or Catechist within the said Island of Hirta', Alexander MacLeod mortified a further 2000 merks, making a total of 14000 merks, with a design that 300 merks as the interest on 6000 merks should go to the man in St Kilda and that 400 merks as the interest on 8000 merks should help to pay the catechist in Harris and the catechist in Skye and Glenelg. Mr John MacLeod, failing whom MacLeod of MacLeod, was to have the right of presentation to these positions, and if either failed to nominate someone within six months of a vacancy the right was to pass to the SSPCK. There was no mention in Mr John's communication of any decision that subsequent catechists or ministers would have to bear the surname of MacLeod, and nothing had stood in the way of appointing one called MacLennan.[41]

As a consequence of the mortification now fully understood the SSPCK was able annually to pay Roderick MacLennan a salary of £25 or 450 merks, 300 of which derived from the legacy. Although he had received payment more recently MacLennan wrote in a letter read on 6 July 1738 that he had not yet had any salary instalment for the period May to November 1734, for which it might be thought the original advance of 225 merks was supposed to serve. He also complained that the Laird of MacLeod had refused to assist him with the provision of a house and cows' grass, and that 'his Steward of the Isle gives him no Encouragement'. The Society continued MacLennan through 1738 and 1739, but in the autumn of the latter year had another letter from their 'minister and schoolmaster' in St Kilda, written at 'Kilmorie' in Skye on 29 August, a date indicating that MacLennan had left his charge with the steward's departure some weeks earlier. The letter stated that the number of inhabitants was now seventy, of whom fifty were 'catechisable' persons, and a list of the scholars who occasionally attended school was enclosed. Though he had contemplated staying until 1 November MacLennan had in fact departed at the end of July, 'being much Discouragement [i.e. discouraged] by the harsh Treatment his Family met with from the Steward in so much that he intends not again to return thither, and Craves to be Employed by the Society Elsewhere'. Accustomed to hearing that catechists had deserted their stations the Society was none too pleased at this latest instance. It arranged that the contents of the letter should be notified to Mr John MacLeod and that the treasurer should not pay MacLennan any more salary. It also resolved that if MacLennan did not return to St Kilda then he would be dismissed from the Society's service and a replacement for him would be found. If on the other hand he agreed to go back the following summer he would be found employment during the intervening months of winter and spring within the bounds of the presbytery of Long Island.[42]

Roderick MacLennan did not return and a search for someone else was necessary. On 21 August 1740 Mr John MacLeod of Muiravonside put forward Alexander MacLeod, schoolmaster at Eynort in the parish of Bracadale, to be appointed as minister in St Kilda, and the Society agreed to see that he was taken on trial, licensed as a preacher, and ordained minister of the island - the usual process. These duties were given to the presbytery of Skye which in February 1741 wrote that the task was begun and that when ordained Alexander would have to leave for St Kilda in April or May with the steward or else have to wait another year. There was therefore no time for him to meet the SSPCK in Edinburgh, and, dispensing with this formality, the committee told him to go at the first opportunity, his salary to remain that of the Bracadale teacher until he was ordained, after which it would rise to the accepted 450 merks for a St Kilda minister. Alexander MacLeod was thus hurried out into a different presbytery, and to an island so far away that the SSPCK at least now imagined it to be a parish on its own, including in a list of 'Charity Schools' St Kilda, in St Kilda parish, presbytery of Long Island.[43]

CHAPTER 4

Maclennan's later career in Sutherland, Caithness and Stroma

AS it happens the declining career of Roderick MacLennan can be followed
a little further. He was rumoured to have disgraced himself in St Kilda.
The SSPCK wrote to MacLeod of MacLeod in December 1740 to ask that help
be given to whoever might succeed as missionary there, and MacLeod replied
in March 1741. He assured the Society that 'nothing shall be wanting on his
part towards the Encouragement of any that shall be sent to preach the
Gospel in the Island of St Kilda', but at the same time he complained of
'certain malicious and vile practices whereof Mr Roderick MacLennan late
Minister there had been guilty which are vouched by Documents in the hands
of Mr John MacLeod Advocate'. This made the SSPCK committee look back at
a memorial personally delivered by MacLennan when he came to Edinburgh
and considered on 4 December 1740. It contained an account of his
'settlement' in St Kilda with certain 'Discouragements' he met with there, and
proposed 'Certain Expedients proper for Removing Grievances and
Encouraging any Person whom the Society may send thither'. Mr John
MacLeod of Muiravonside had promised to use his influence with the Laird of
MacLeod in remedying any such difficulties, and it was probably in response
to Mr John's efforts that the Laird communicated with the SSPCK.[44]

After its inspection of MacLennan's memorial the SSPCK committee
arranged for a group of four members to meet with Mr John MacLeod to
discuss matters arising from it, and in August 1741 it was reported that the
'documents' concerning MacLennan had been examined. There is some
indication that these papers were intended to destroy MacLennan's
reputation. In particular a 'precognition', which had been taken by Donald
MacLeod of Berneray, baron bailie of Harris, in the island of 'Tarronsay' on 24
October 1740, contained declarations by various people in St Kilda 'touching
several Immoralitys, whereof Mr McLennan is said to have been guilty when
there'. Some mystery surrounds these supposedly incriminating records, and
their present location, if they still exist, is unknown, but it appears that they
were seen by the editors of Chamber's Edinburgh Journal in 1846, when their
content, or at least the content of two of them, was briefly set out:

> 'There lies before us a warrant, signed … [by] Normand Macleod … The
> document is dated at Dunvegan, February 17, 1741, and proceeds upon
> a rumour which has reached the writer, that a certain gentlewoman,
> called Lady Grange, was carried to his isle of St Kilda in 1734, and has
> ever since been confined there under cruel circumstances. Regarding
> this as a scandal which he is bound to inquire into (as if it could have
> hitherto been a secret to him), he orders his baron-bailie of Harrish,

Donald Macleod of Bernera ..., to proceed to that island and make the necessary investigations. Before us also lies the original precognition taken by honest Donald, six days thereafter, when the various persons who had been about Lady Grange gave evidence respecting her. The general bearing of this testimony, besides establishing the fact of her confinement as a prisoner, is to the effect that she was treated well in all other respects, having a house forty feet long, with an inner room and a chimney to it, a curtained bed, arm-chair, table, and other articles; ample store of good provisions, including spirits; and plenty of good clothes; but that she was addicted to liquor, and liable to dreadful outbreaks of anger. Evidence was at the same time taken regarding the character of the Maclennans ... It was Mr Erskine's interest to establish that they were worthless persons, and to this effect strong testimony was given by several of the islanders, though it would be difficult to say with what degree of verity'.[45]

The intention of the documents seems to have been to show that, so far as the Laird of Macleod's involvement was concerned, the plight of Lady Grange and the treatment she received in St Kilda had not been nearly so bad as many believed. In order to do this successfully it was necessary to assert strongly that her living conditions in the island had in fact been quite comfortable, and to make out a case against the MacLennans who had brought away information from her to the contrary. Certain inhabitants of St Kilda had therefore to be 'persuaded' to declare that Lady Grange had been well looked after and that the minister and his wife had been immoral rogues whose evidence was consequently entirely unreliable. Whatever the truth, Roderick MacLennan never really recovered his credibility as a missionary, and the unfortunate coincidence of his stay on St Kilda with the 'imprisonment' there of Lady Grange blighted his life thereafter.

A 'representation' from the SSPCK committee to the General Assembly's Commission was immediately drawn up, describing first the Society's connection with St Kilda in outline:

'That whereas the Inhabitants of Hirta alias St Kilda live in the remotest Island belonging to the Church and Country, and are by their great Poverty quite disabled from maintaining a Minister and Teacher among them, for the Instruction and Salvation of their precious Souls; Therefore this Society did among the first and Earliest Instances of their Christian Charity, make provision for the Supply of that poor Ignorant People, and for many years maintained the deceast Mr Alexander Buchan as their Minister and School-Master, after he had been tried licensed and Ordained for that effect, by the Reverend Presbytery of Edinburgh

'And whereas Mr Alexander MacLeod Advocate, of pious Memory, Legated and Mortifyed to this Society, Six Thousand Merks as a perpetual Fund towards the Maintainance of a Minister and Schoolmaster in the foresaid Island, Therefore the Society after Mr Buchan's death, proceeded once and again to supply the said Vaccancy, in the terms of the said Mortification, First with Mr Roderick McLennan, tried Licensed and ordained by the Presbytery of Sky, and afterwards with Mr Alexander McLeod in like manner ordained by the said Presbytery for the said Effect, and present Incumbent in the said Island

'And whereas it appears by a Precognition of John McLeod Stewart of the said Island and others, taken by Donald McLeod of Berneray, Baron Baillie of Herris at Taransay upon the twenty fourth of October last, and lately laid before the said Directors; That there is a *fama Clamosa*, Charge or Report against the said Mr McLennan for several offences, alleadged to have been committed by him, during his Incumbency, in the said Island, such as Cursing Swearing Stealling and Stricking, together with other Gross miscarriages unbecoming his Station

'And whereas the said Island, where these offences are alleadged to have been committed, are in the Bounds of the Presbytery of Long Island, and the said Mr McLennan has of late resided and according to the best Information of the said Directors, does presently reside within the Bounds of the Presbytery of Edinburgh ...'

Therefore the Commission was asked to order an enquiry, judgement and direction to the Society for the future should the same thing happen again, 'when a person of no greater Abilities, no better Education than whats necessary, for a Mission to Hirta, is ordained for that Station, does after some time, desert that Station, upon pretence that the Climate is disagreeable and enjurious to his health, and yet without any Sentence of the Church, loosing him from that Station, pretend to carry his Ministerial office and Character along with him, to any other place he pleases to preferr thereto'. The SSPCK was clearly annoyed and wished to know what should be done and whether it or the presbytery should do it.[46]

Still in Edinburgh, Roderick MacLennan was called before the SSPCK committee in June 1742, denied that he was guilty of any charge brought against him, and insisted that as accusations were made in his absence they were malicious and invalid. The Society must have quickly realised that it was going to be excessively awkward and expensive to bring witnesses away from St Kilda, and since MacLennan was no longer in its employment and had in a manner been already condemned it decided to tidy up the affair by concluding that he and his activities were now none of its business and so withdrew its representation.[47]

Where then did, or could, MacLennan go? He had been ordained, like Buchan and Alexander MacLeod, specifically for St Kilda, and with an unfortunate reputation at best to carry with him he had little chance of continuing as a minister anywhere. But, perhaps wishing to avoid central and western districts for a while or being advised to do so, he somehow obtained the support of the SSPCK's companion body, the Royal Bounty committee, disappeared from Edinburgh, and early in 1743 reappeared in Sutherland, where in March the presbytery of Tongue took notice of his arrival: 'there is one Mr Roderick Maclennan, an ordain'd minister, lately of St Kilda, came to our Bounds in Capacity of an itinerant missionary from the Committee for Reformation of the Highlands'. Irrespective of his past and of his qualifications he could be put to use in that wide and often wild area. The presbytery appointed him to supply the parish of 'Edderachilis' for the next few months until it could consider his fate again. 'Mean Time, in regard the said missionary is a Stranger to us, he is order'd, being upon the Place, if he can overtake it in the Intervall, to preach in the Parishes of Tongue and Durness, he having preach'd already in the Parish of Farr, agreeably to his Letter of Mission, Since the twentyeth of February last'. It is doubtful whether he ever went to Eddrachilles, for in August 1743 he was told to supply Farr in place of the minister, William Henderson, who was himself settled in Eddrachilles. MacLennan was not settled in any place but for the time being he received an annual salary from the Royal Bounty of £20, not much less than his allowance in St Kilda.[48]

Before long the Presbytery of Tongue formed a rather brutal opinion 'of the insufficiency of Mr Roderick McLennan missionary minister in their Bounds, for his work, that he is unacceptable to the People, useless in his Station, and that there is a necessity of removing him to Some other Place'. This criticism of him was not necessarily fair for it seems to have relied in some measure upon information derived from the ill-tempered John Skeldoch, minister of Farr, who had been an old enemy of Roderick MacLennan when both were in Lochaber, whose manse, perhaps not surprisingly, had been attacked by people with guns and pistols, and who, under a cloud of his own, had been forced to move to Sutherland. The problem remained, however, of what to do with MacLennan, and the Royal Bounty committee took time to decide. A possible solution was provided when in late November 1743 a letter arrived in Edinburgh from the ministers of Thurso and Reay in Caithness. They described to the committee the large bounds of their own parishes and of the equally extensive parishes of Halkirk and Latheron, all of which areas surely had a better claim to the assistance of a missionary minister than the parish of Farr. It was also mentioned that MacLennan had lately been assisting at the administering of the sacrament at Thurso, 'where his performances were Satisfying to all the Hearers', even those of the parish of Farr who attended. The trouble was, said the ministers, that he was unacceptable to Mr Skeldoch; but, disregarding the latter's 'missive' to them of 22 November, they would like to employ him. The committee accepted this proposal and changed the appointment from Farr to the four Caithness parishes, continuing the £20 salary. It also wondered whether, given his conduct, Mr Skeldoch should have the help of any more missionaries.[49]

The altered arrangement did not come into being as planned. MacLennan remained as itinerant in Farr for several months and was then informed by the Royal Bounty committee that he was to be itinerant minister and catechist not in Caithness but back in Lochaber, where he would replace Duncan MacPherson who had been assigned to the presbytery of Mull. But shortly afterwards, on 13 August 1744, the committee returned to the original idea, which now formed part of a wider reshuffle of missionaries. Duncan MacPherson was to go to the parish of Ardnamurchan from Lochaber, 'in which Station Mr McLennan in respect of his peculiar Circumstances is thought will not be So usefull as in another place'. The committee, 'after reasoning', agreed that it would not be 'expedient' for him to go to Lochaber and resolved that he should be employed in Caithness after all. Murdo MacLennan would fill the Lochaber vacancy, and James Dunbar would move from Caithness to Strathdon where Murdo had been working. This would leave space in Caithness for Roderick MacLennan. The scheme was approved and confirmed at the end of August 1744.[50]

Unfortunately the appointment of Dunbar to Strathdon was found to be a mistake. On 6 November 1744 the presbytery of Caithness minuted that Mr Roderick MacLennan was to be 'itinerant' in place of Dunbar who had gone to 'Corgarph' within the presbytery of Alford, Aberdeenshire. MacLennan would serve in the parish of Wick and adjacent parts of the parishes of Latheron, Halkirk and Thurso. However, on 31 January 1745 the Royal Bounty committee noted that James Dunbar was unsuited to Strathdon since he was 'wanting the Irish language' and should therefore stay in Caithness, while MacLennan, who had evidently arrived in Caithness, was 'also of use in his Station, particularly where the Irish Language is Spoke'. Both men were to continue where they were, provided 'that they always preach in places other than the Parish Churches or where the minister[s] of the Parishes Do or Should themselves officiate'. Each was of use in that part of Caithness where his native language predominated.[51]

It then happened that a conveniently fatal accident occurred in the island of Stroma in the Pentland Firth. Stroma belonged to the parish of Canisbay in Caithness and in 1744 a Mr George Gibson was catechist there, paid by the Royal Bounty committee. On 25 September that year Gibson died 'by a Casual fall over the Rocks of Stroma' and the Caithness presbytery, apart from requesting that the half year's salary due in November should be paid to his widow and children 'who are in mean circumstances', came to a conclusion regarding his successor. In the presbytery's view 'Master Roderick Maclennan can be of no use in the parish of Wick and adjacent parts of the parish of Latheron in regaurd that he cannot Speake the English Language so as to be well understood by the people', nor could he be of any great use 'in the extremities of the other large parishes where the Irish Language is Spoken because his Gift of preaching is generally unacceptable to the people'. It was therefore suggested that MacLennan be appointed to succeed Gibson in an island 'where the Inhabitants are not numerous and probably be easiely pleased to have a minister att hand to baptise theire Children without crossing the Sea'. The fact that the Stroma people would be unlikely to understand MacLennan's English did not seem to matter; the island was obviously a convenient 'station' for an unwanted catechist. The Royal Bounty committee duly accepted that he should 'officiate' there but could not produce any extra money for his 'additional encouragement'.[52]

For much of 1745 Roderick MacLennan remained in Caithness, though the presbytery was empowered by the Royal Bounty committee to send him over to Stroma as often as it wished. In fact the committee must have looked for ways to employ him permanently there, for by August both it and the presbytery had obtained the agreement of the SSPCK to place him on the island as catechist and schoolmaster with salaries of £10 and £8 for the respective duties. Whether he was successful or not was hard to say. After a 'visitation' during the summer of 1746 by the presbytery moderator and another minister it was reported that 'they had called together some of the people of the Island and enquired them how they did not send theire Children to school and that they asked Mr McLenan how there was no School, to which both He and the people answered that the povertie of their circumstances and other hardships that they laboured under made it impracticable for them to spare their Childrens Labour'. To MacLennan poverty and lack of attendance in Stroma can have seemed little different from conditions in St Kilda; in Stroma it was 'the Severity of their Services' that weighed upon the inhabitants, and perhaps this burden too was not unlike that of the steward's demands made of the St Kilda community. Lack of a school raised doubts as to whether that part of his salary contributed by the SSPCK should be paid to MacLennan, and on hearing from its representatives after their visitation the presbytery thought that Stroma was perhaps not challenging enough for the missionary's admittedly questionable abilities. He had catechised the people, preached to them every Sabbath, and visited the sick, while 'his affection to the Government', an important point especially just after the latest Jacobite rising, 'is well known'. So in the belief that someone who could merely read and write and who could be employed for £4 or £5 would be sufficient to teach and catechise on the island at suitable seasons the presbytery proposed to the Royal Bounty committee that 'they transport Mr McLenan with their first convenience to some place where he may be more useful', although there would be no objection if the committee chose to leave things as they were.[53]

No change was made, and the presbytery, which had hoped that MacLennan would be transported to a locality outside its bounds, endured another ten years of uneven reports from the detached and often inaccessible piece of Canisbay parish. In the summer of 1748 MacLennan's salary was reduced by £2.5s, and in discontent he wrote the following year to the SSPCK stating his persistent lack of success in Stroma and offering to serve instead as itinerant minister and teacher back in the parishes of Thurso, Reay and Halkirk. The Society asked the presbytery to look into the situation, and the Royal Bounty committee sent a similar request for 'a Distinct account of Mr Mclenans Dilligence with the causes of his want of Success' so that it might be considered whether the money assigned to Stroma could be better used. The presbytery's reply stated that the advanced season delayed discussion of these communications and prevented a visit to the island, 'access to it being very uncertain excepting only in the summer months, and tho the visitors might get into the Island in a fair Day even in the Winter or Spring Seasons, they might happen to be detained in it for many Days'. But since it already had a thorough knowledge of conditions on Stroma and of the causes of MacLennan's lack of 'success' the presbytery was able to explain the position there which MacLennan himself had described accurately enough:

> 'The people labour under great Discouragments by theire Hard Service, and Mr Mclenan has not that prudence, Gentleness of Temper and Forbearance that is necessarie to soften and gain them so as to make the best that can be made of them in theire present circumstances nor has he the Talent of wining theire affections when he happens to preach to them'.[54]

The SSPCK received this information and after some thought decided that 'Mr Rorie' as he was still commonly called should be transported from Stroma to the mainland parishes as he had proposed. The ministers of Thurso, Reay and Halkirk had written to the Royal Bounty committee actually asking that MacLennan be appointed itinerant minister and catechist in their parishes, presumably because he would be useful in the Gaelic-speaking districts, and so the committee also favoured his transportation, his salary to remain at the existing combined sum of £15.15s. MacLennan was therefore assigned to his new duties even though five years previously he had been judged unsuitable for them, and it was not long before he was in trouble once more.[55]

The Caithness presbytery expressed its dissatisfaction with 'Mr Rorie' in

September 1751, but this time there was some confusion. On the one hand the presbytery, in a letter to the Royal Bounty committee, stated that having 'frequently hinted to the Committee that Mr Roderick McLean [i.e.MacLennan] is unacceptable to people of all Ranks', and having received repeated enquiries as to his usefulness, 'We reckon it our Duty to inform you in plain words that in our opinion he is not usefull and therefore ought not to be continued or if continued his Sallarie should have been dimin[i]shed in place of being augmented', especially since 'we are credibly informed that the Man does not Stand in need of it'. And the presbytery, its patience clearly exhausted, went further in saying that were it not for the real regard it had for the committee it would be bound to complain to the General Assembly about the misapplication of the Church's funds. However, contrary to this bluntly hostile view, the Royal Bounty committee had also to deal with another letter from the ministers of Thurso and Halkirk which asked that MacLennan be continued.[56]

The committee questioned the inconsistency of the letters, and from the presbytery's answer it emerged that MacLennan had never properly left Stroma, so that having failed to attend his stations in the mainland parishes he could not be given the certificate necessary for him to obtain his salary. According to the presbytery it was 'faintly said for him' that he might have been indisposed, but he himself never complained of any such problem during the eight months that he was absent. Though the parish of Reay formed a large proportion of the area MacLennan was supposed to serve, the minister there, knowing 'Mr Mclenan's Infirmitys', never put him to work. The presbytery acknowledged that the Royal Bounty committee had done everything it could to assist him, perhaps because 'he is grown old in theire Service', and consequently it had itself sought to tolerate his 'weakness' so far as it could, but in spite of the easiness of his charge in Stroma he had never come up to expectations:'he is with all his other Defects very Negligent and Lazie'. He had now withdrawn again to the island 'where we are told he intends to continue att a small Farm which he has taken in Tack and is under his wifes Direction. Tho he is unfitt to bear the Fatigue of Teaching he may be of some use in the Island by Baptizing and marrying the Inhabitants when they can not get over to the Continent'. The presbytery would have no objection if the committee continued him there with a 'moderate' allowance of £6 to £8 yearly, although both bodies 'have been often reproached since this man came amongst us for throwing away the publict money'. Once again Roderick MacLennan was employed as schoolmaster and catechist on Stroma with a salary of £2 from the SSPCK and £10 from the Royal Bounty committee, and his allowance for the mainland work was of course withdrawn. The minister of Canisbay, James Brodie, was charged with the task of telling him all this.[57]

The request from Thurso and Halkirk that MacLennan should be continued on the mainland, over which the Royal Bounty committee had been concerned in 1752, had been answered without any need for committee action. The minister of Thurso died, the minister of Halkirk regretted that he wrote in support of MacLennan, and the minister of Reay had not been much involved in any case. It was therefore possible for the presbytery to act in unison when dealing with Stroma, and for the next few years there was little to say about either the place or its teacher and catechist. Another visitation of the school in the spring of 1753 found that 'there are Three Children who attend that School Dayly, and there were other Five who came there on the Day of visitation, and are said to attend now and then, which Children Two of them only were reading on the Bible Five on the New Testament, and one on the Proverbs, all of them read tollerably well'. Reluctantly it seems, the visitors admitted that the position was satisfactory: 'The People being enquired about the Schoolmasters Dilligence, declined saying much on that Subject, only they acknowledged, it better than Formerly ..'[58]

The end of Roderick MacLennan's strange career was in sight in 1754, when the SSPCK learned that its schoolmaster in Stroma was in 'peculiar Circumstances' though it paid and continued him. The following year the presbytery of Caithness wrote to the Society proposing that a Mr John Tulloch should go to the school in Stroma, 'which thro the Infirmities of Mr McLennan who presently officiates there, has been as good as Vacant for several years'. Tulloch's allowance would, it was suggested, be £20, half of which could be paid to MacLennan until he was otherwise provided, the teacher's salary alone being therefore restored to £10 or £12. Soon after this idea was put forward, however, a further visitation of the Stroma school was made in early July 1755, a report from the presbytery moderator Brodie of Canisbay and the clerk David Dunbar, minister of Olrig, being presented at the Society's committee meeting in August. A difficulty lay in what appeared to be a sustained though modest improvement at the school. The meeting had in mind the words 'as good as Vacant', but the two ministers who had been to the island reported that 'Mr McLennan is as dilligent and Active as can be Expected ... within these twelve moneths he has become very acceptable to the people, and .. there is a promising prospect of the usefullness of the School there, where twenty two Children attend for ordinary'. With this information the Society could not accept the presbytery's recommendation and decided to ask the local sheriff depute to enquire into the circumstances of education on Stroma.[59]

It may be that certain members of the Caithness presbytery were heavily prejudiced against MacLennan, whatever he did. At various stages of his thirty years of life as a missionary it became clear that ministers no less than other men could be malicious, underhand and vindictive. On the other hand MacLennan probably did have faults that annoyed colleagues and church authorities. Perhaps Brodie and Dunbar were either exceptionally sympathetic or entirely deceived by what they found at the Stroma school in

1755. Another inspection planned for May 1756 was postponed because Brodie had learned 'that the Bad state of Mr McLennan's health for a considerable time has rendered him unable to do the duties of his office and that there are few if any Children presently taught there which Renders a Visitation unnecessary at this time'. Later in the same year a lengthy account of the failing MacLennan was recorded by the presbytery, which had found all missionaries within its bounds satisfactorily in attendance,

'Excepting only Mr. Roderick McLennan in the Island of Stroma who for about Ten months past has continued under an Indisposition that unfits him for teaching or being otherwise useful in his Station. His Disorder is rather Foolishness than fury but he is so timid jealous and fearful that he cannot be prevaild with to grant Receipts for bygane Sallaries and these indeed are much wanted for his Appetite is stronger and he needs more Subsistence than when he was in Health, and we cannot understand that the Savings are such as can support him and his family. What we wou'd with all humble Submission propose to the Society and Committee is that they wou'd be pleased to accept his son Daniel's Receipts for the Sallaries due to the Father But if this is not agreeable we leave it to the Wisdom of the Society and Committee to prescribe any other method for granting Discharges to the Committee's Cashier and to the Society's Treasurer and we shall endeavour to follow their Directions. Far be it from us to wish that the Society and Committee wou'd discharge Mr McLennan out of their Service without making some Provision for his future Support, And upon Their known Compassion we do chearfully cast him still. What we wou'd further request is that in case private Application is made in favours of any Person to fill up Mr McLennan's Station the Presbytery may be first acquainted, as the Missionary at Stroma wou'd need to be a person of Prudence and Discretion'.[60]

The conclusion reached by the SSPCK on 3 February 1757 was that MacLennan should be dismissed, ceasing his service at the end of the coming April, and that Daniel's receipt for any salary then due would be acceptable. The presbytery was asked to look for a successor. At the stated time poor 'Mr Rorie', once in St Kilda and kind to Lady Grange, either guilty of indiscretions and imprudence or much maligned by enemies, was dismissed into oblivion, and in his place was supposed to come William Morison from the charity school at Ratagan in the district of Kintail, where there were 'but few' scholars and no parochial provision. The presbytery of Caithness, having at last got its way, was pleased to hear from the Society that Morison was to be transported from Ratagan to Stroma where he would be 'employ'd as Schoolmaster and Catechist ... with Six Pounds from the Society and as much from the Committee in Place of Mr Roderick McLennan ..' Morison soon arrived in

Caithness 'and we have desired him to repair to his Station with all convenient Speed'. A parting shot from the presbytery contained no sign of generosity:

> 'We cannot but inform the Society anent Mr McLennan's Case that he is still bad and disordered in his mind. He has been long in the Service, and will in all probability in a short time hence be in a miserable Condition, destitute of Bread for himself and his Family'.[61]

CHAPTER 5

The Macaulay family, their attempt to betray
Prince Charles Edward and their involvement with the next
missionaries to St Kilda, Alexander and Donald Macleod

OF the earlier MacAulays in western Lewis the best known is Domhnall Cam, whose exploits in the first years of the seventeenth century were the subject of many a tale. He had three sons, the eldest being Angus, tacksman of Brenish, who along with his brother William was killed at the battle of Auldearn in 1645. Angus himself had sons, one of whom was Dugald or Donald, also of Brenish. Dugald was the father of Aulay MacAulay who became minister of the parish of Harris. The contemporary minister of Bracadale, Daniel MacAulay, who visited Alexander Buchan in St Kilda in 1728, was descended of the same Brenish family and would appear to be the Donald MacAulay mentioned in the Morrison collection of traditions.[62]

Aulay MacAulay, born about 1670, was ordained to Tiree and Coll in 1704 and moved to Harris in 1713. He was moderator of the Long Island presbytery in 1725 and 1726 and remained in his Harris charge for the rest of his life. In January 1729 his brother Donald was catechist in the home district of Uig, Lewis, in place of John Stewart who had left the previous Whitsunday; and Donald was himself succeeded after only one year by Donald MacLeod. From Aulay, Daniel and Donald there spread out a network of MacAulay ministers serving many parishes in the western Highlands and islands, and related to them was Zachary MacAulay, factor for the Lewis estate in the early eighteenth century.[63]

There was a tradition that Aulay MacAulay was sixty years of age when he married. According to this story he went to Lewis to ask a young lady to marry him and she refused. While he was in the house of one of the Morrison ministers at Barvas a child was born and the old nurse, placing the baby in Aulay's arms, told him that she would be his wife. About twenty years later this child, Mary Morrison, became Aulay's wife, and they had six sons and two daughters. One of the daughters married a Kenneth MacIver, the other, Isabella, never married. Four of the sons were said to have become ministers. Though his age may be questioned, Aulay's late marriage need not be doubted.[64]

Based at Scarista, Aulay MacAulay added to his income by taking the tenancy of the farm of 'Meikle Borrow' [Big Borve] on the west side of south Harris. He held these 'Two pennies three farthing lands' in 1724 at a money rent of £60.3s.4d, with a further sum of £14.13s.4d as teind payment, and a 'victuall' rent of two bolls of meal, two stones of butter and three wedders. The rent of St Kilda at this time was sixteen bolls of 'bear'. By 1735 Rev. MacAulay was tenant of 'Meikle and Middle Borrows' for double the rent of his previous single farm, while the rent of St Kilda was now £86.13s.4d. All three Borves, 'Meikle, Little and Middle Burrows', were tenanted together in 1754 when the minister was Aulay's son Kenneth, who paid in total £333.6s.8d, a sum which comprised the value of the old 'victuall' amounts now converted to money and which was £27.15s.6⅔d in sterling. St Kilda, let as usual with 'a penny of Kirktown, Linga and Northtown' in Pabbay, was rented at £133.6s.8d or just over £11 sterling.[65]

It was said of Aulay MacAulay, presumably in his younger days, that he went to Pabbay to deliver a sermon one Sabbath and was then marooned by storms so that in fact he 'preached there seven successive Sundays'. Life in Pabbay was apparently very cheerful while he was on that island for 'They had a dance there every night and enjoyed themselves much'. Under normal circumstances, however, he remained at home in Scarista, the extent of the parish with many places difficult to reach making more than enough demand on his time and energies. In the 1730s, if not earlier, he was given the help of an itinerant preacher but had to pay £5 out of his salary towards the maintenance of this man. Having a large number of children to provide for, 'Mr Aulay' wrote in 1740 to say that he had decided 'to be no further obliged to give five pound to the Itinerant Preacher' in his parish 'in Respect of the Circumstances of his Family', but in spite of this declaration the assistant's allowance seems to have been continued a little longer and no doubt therefore outlying districts and some lesser islands were still occasionally visited.[66]

One of Aulay's sons, Kenneth, supposed to have been born in 1723, may have assisted his father in or about 1740; and in May 1742 the presbytery of Long Island, soon to be disbanded, requested that Kenneth should be employed as schoolmaster and catechist in Harris, to which the Royal Bounty committee responded favourably some months later. On 17 June 1741 the Synod of Glenelg had agreed that the presbytery of Long Island should be divided, and in the summer of 1742 it was replaced by two new presbyteries, of Uist and of Lewis. It was therefore to the presbytery of Uist, the bounds of which included Harris and all of the Outer Hebrides southwards with St Kilda, that the Royal Bounty committee wrote to state that Kenneth MacAulay could take up his dual role at Scarista with a salary of £6 jointly paid by the committee and by the SSPCK. There was some delay, but when the presbytery of Uist let it be known in October 1743 that the present minister of Harris, 'aged upwards of Seventy years, valetudinary, and having the burden of a numerous Family', was not capable of serving a 'most discontiguous' parish where there were eight places of worship 'at a great distance from each other', Kenneth MacAulay seems to have come into action, if only for a short while. After less than two years Kenneth's brother, John MacAulay, was appointed itinerant preacher in the parish of Harris, and Kenneth gave up his work as schoolmaster and catechist. It probably made little difference to Aulay MacAulay which of his sons helped him.[67]

In May 1749 Aulay was 'by old age and Infirmities rendered incapable of discharging any part of his office', so an itinerant was all the more important. The minister of Laggan parish in mainland Invernessshire tried to secure Kenneth's help for his district instead of Martin Macpherson who had gone to the Isle of Bute, and the Royal Bounty committee agreed to this plan; but a renewed plea from the Uist presbytery for help to the Harris minister who was ready to give £6 'to either a Helper or minister for officiating in his Spatious and discontiguous Parish' encouraged Kenneth MacAulay to stay with his father. It seems that South Uist and Harris were linked together at this time when it came to the placing of catechist and itinerant preacher, and when John MacAulay was appointed to Harris it may well be that Kenneth went off to work in South Uist. By 1746, however, John was fixed in South Uist. Since their father was still minister in Harris Kenneth then seems to have worked between the two areas, spending rather more of his time in Harris where his help was more greatly needed. The Royal Bounty committee received in 1749 a letter from MacLeod of MacLeod 'describing the Situation of the Parish of Harris both as to its Extent and abounding with Papists'. Since there were no papists in Harris the last part of this remark was intended either to lend urgency to the need for a helper or, more probably, was meant to apply to the 'situation' in South Uist, and the words were followed by a repeated mention of Aulay's infirmities and a call for a £10 allowance for an assistant to him. No funds were then available, but early in 1750 when the presbytery of Uist asked permission to employ Kenneth MacAulay as missionary to both South Uist and Harris the Royal Bounty committee agreed to allow this after Lauchlan MacLean, a probationer working in Uist, had moved to Barra. With Aulay MacAulay now 'almost confined to his own House' Kenneth could be devoted entirely to Harris, and in 1751 he was 'transported' from South Uist as 'Settled assistant' to his father in the capacity of itinerant minister and catechist.[68]

In the meantime John MacAulay, said to have been born in 1720, had become a minister. In June 1743 the Synod of Glenelg wrote to the Royal Bounty committee expressing its concern over Protestant provision in South Uist where two priests and two 'Popish Scholmasters' were active. It asked that Mr John MacAulay, probationer, should be employed as missionary there, an appeal that seemed to meet with some success as in May 1744 the presbytery of Uist proposed that John MacAulay and Lauchlan MacLean, both probationers, should be continued as missionaries in South Uist and Harris. This time the committee replied that John should spend half the forthcoming year in South Uist and the second half in Harris, for there was no money to support a second missionary. This was the time when there seemed to be no vacancy for Kenneth MacAulay. However when it was proposed to settle a certain Neil Macleod as minister of South Uist the idea aroused opposition and the presbytery decided - perhaps under the influence of 'Mr Aulay' - that John MacAulay should be chosen instead. The presbytery appealed to the General Assembly regarding the settlement of John in South Uist, but it was not until May 1746 that the Assembly, which had previously stood in the way of the presbytery's decision, admitted him as minister there.[69]

This was the period of the '45 rising and of Prince Charles Edward's fugitive adventures in the Outer Hebrides. Already connected with South Uist and perhaps wishing to further his own career by demonstrating loyalty to the government John MacAulay allowed himself to be involved, and his behaviour entered tradition in Uist and Harris. As regards his settlement in opposition to

Neil MacLeod it was said that 'Macaulay was disliked in South Uist and all were glad when he left. He had no tolerance. One MacLeod who was missionary in Benbecula [Bracadale?] was the choice of Clanranald and of the people but Mr Macqueen minister of North Uist and Mr Macaulay minister of Harris and father of John Macaulay the presentee managed to change the place of meeting of the presbytery and appointed him to the parish. The change caused delay and the presentation lapsed to the Presbytery. The case was carried to the General Assembly but the Presbytery managed to retain their position'. John added further to the hostility against him when it became known that he tried to betray the prince. He sent a message to his father in Harris that the prince was heading in that direction, and Mr Aulay passed on the news to relatives in Stornoway which appeared to be Charles Edward's destination. However Aulay discovered that the prince was sheltering in the house of Donald Campbell, tacksman of Scalpay, Harris, so he and several friends went to capture him. They reached Scalpay 'in the grey dawn of the morning', and Campbell asked them why he was receiving such an early visit. 'When Mr Campbell understood the purpose for which Mr MacAulay and his friends came he rose and [girded?] his sword and declared that the first man who touched the Prince be he parson or priest lay or cleric would have his skull cloven to the chin on the spot. Addressing Macaulay he said "On principle I am as much against the Prince and the arbitrary power of his family as you are and I would fight him in the open field but by all that is sacred if any man or combination of men were to touch [him] in his now forlorn condition and under my roof [I] would defend him to the last. And I would advise you Mr Aulay to go home and to let the poor Prince alone because were you to betray him not all the waters of the ocean would wash the bloodstain off you and your descendants'.[70]

The house of the tacksman of Scalpay, Donald Campbell, who in 1746 sheltered Prince Charles Edward and defended him from Rev. Aulay Macaulay. (c1860)

So Aulay MacAulay went away. He had no parochial responsibility for St Kilda, but, as it happened, the island was not quite untouched by the repercussions of the Jacobite rising of this time, and other remote but inhabited islands also briefly felt its effects. In a letter of 12 June 1746 General John Campbell, then at Tobermory, wrote setting out his intentions regarding the hunt for the Prince. 'I am to sail this evening for Moydart where Colonel Campbell Commands, having left 100 men at Strontian. I had either send the Colonel or goe my Self with 300 men and two of the Sloops to Visit St Kilda where I am inform'd some people of fashion have retired'. The information was in fact exaggerated and misleading, as the journal of Donald Macleod makes clear. The government forces believed that the prince 'had set sail from the continent for St Kilda, being a place so remote that no suspicion would be readily entertained of his being there'. General Campbell arrived as intended a few days after sending his letter, and when his ships came in sight 'the greater part of the poor inhabitants ran off to the clifts of their rocks to hide themselves, being frighted out of their wits at seeing such an appearance coming towards their island'. About 100 men were landed and enquired of those they met about the prince, but the 'poor creatures' were quite bewildered, having no idea what the visitors were talking about. Soon the island was left in peace and those in hiding could safely return to their houses.[71]

At the end of September 1746 General Campbell briefly outlined 'the Expedition I undertook in Quest of the Younger Adventurer'. He had travelled 'Round and through what is call'd the long Island', landing troops in most parts, and then visited Skye. 'I look't inn at St Kilda which in the Map is lay'd down to be 20 Leagues to the Westward of the Harris and North Uist, but I think it is not so much ..' He explained that he had requested 'the Furnace Sloop and a Folkstone Cutter' of Commodore Smith, along with 'the arm'd Wherries I had fitted out before his Arrival', and Smith had consented, but as the voyage was 'not much out of his way' he had also decided to accompany Campbell 'with two 40 Gun Ships to take care I was not pick't up by a French Privateer'. Smith's attendance and his supply of provisions were appreciated: 'In short he was Zealous and like a father to me, ply'd off and on St Kilda till the Search was made. And gave Orders that any of the 20 Gun Ships I mett at Sea should be at my disposal'.[72]

On 2 July 1755 the Synod of Glenelg learned from Kenneth MacAulay that John had been 'transported from South-Uist to the parish of Lismore'. He was no more liked there than he had been in his previous island home, and further stories were told about him and his family. When in Uist he had married Isobel MacNeil and had a son Hector, but Isobel had died young, and now in Lismore he married again, this time Margaret Campbell, daughter of James Campbell of Invereasragain in Benderloch. It was said of her that she 'was a capable, handsome woman and as much liked as her husband was disliked throughout the Land of Lorn'. Some explanation was given for this view of him:

'Macaulay's personal character was good … but he was so dogmatic and intolerant and so utterly anti-Jacobite that he made himself utterly disliked'. Those who worked with him confirmed these unwelcome characteristics:

> 'The parish clerk of Mr John Macaulay was known as Calum mor cleireach - Big Calum the clerk. He lived to a great age. A man called John Black, usually called Iain ruadh piobair - Red John the piper - was married to the daughter of this church officer. He described John Macaulay as a capable excellent man but … bold froward stiff obstinate headstrong proud authoritative - all [were] wrong he alone [was] right. A class fellow of Lord Macaulay said that he wished he were as cocksure of anything as John Macaulay was of everything.'[73]

John MacAulay left Lismore in 1765 and his departure was somewhat embarrassing. He was unhappy about leaving 'and the last day he held service there he announced that if the congregation wished he would remain. The congregation remained silent. Then he announced that if any three members asked him to remain he would remain. There was no response. Then any two members but there was no reply. Then any one member but not even one member of the congregation rose.' MacAulay was due to go to Inveraray by sea, but when the ship by which his effects would travel arrived at Appin there were more difficulties. 'He could get no one to help him with the removal of his furniture. The people boycotted him as they did his grandson at Corran. They would not ferry across his carriage. All the men about the ferry house disappeared as if by magic leaving Macaulay pacing up and down the quay fuming and scolding and raging after the manner of a madman.' Eventually a solution was found: 'The people of Lismore would not help Macaulay to send his things to the vessel which was to carry them to Inveraray. At last [his wife] went out among the people and they readily came for her for she was much beloved and respected.'[74]

So ran the traditions relating to an island minister who, spending about ten years in each of three parishes, was unpopular wherever he went. From Inveraray MacAulay moved in 1774 to Cardross, in the presbytery of Dunbarton, where he died in 1789, leaving a large number of sons and daughters who all seemed to do well in life. Among them was Zachary, whose name, handed down through MacAulay generations, was a biblical rendering of Sgair or Sgaire, surviving still among certain members of the clan. Zachary was the father of Thomas MacAulay the historian, the grandson of John MacAulay, who was apparently involved in an incident at the Corran ferry across Loch Linnhe. According to tradition Lord MacAulay, when preparing his *History of England*, made a tour through the Highlands, meeting, as he said, with little courtesy and less hospitality throughout his journey:

'He came from Fort William to Corran. Some person at Fort William chalked upon the back of his carriage - "Macamhlaidh ogha Judais" - Macaulay grandson of Judas. He came to Corran with a view to visit Loch nan Uamh from which Prince Charlie left. The hotel keeper and his men turned out to ferry the horses carriage and owner. They noticed the inscription. First a man went away for thole pins to replace broken ones. Then another man went away in search of the man of the thole pins. When he came back he found that one oar was broken and needed replacing. The time was passing and Macaulay was fuming and he left for Bailechaolais storming at the people as he left.

'At Caolas nan con much the same scene was inacted with the result that Macaulay returned to Fort William in a towering passion. Had he crossed at Baile chaolais he meant to see the scene of Colin Campbells murder the scene of the massacre of Glencoe and Lismore the parish of his grandfather where his own father Sgaire Macamhlaidh had been born.

'Lord Macaulay took his revenge upon Highlanders in his history'[75]

In place of John MacAulay on Lismore came Donald MacNicol, 'who was as much liked as his predecessor was disliked'. MacNicol gained a wide reputation as a learned and literary man who, among other pursuits, assembled much Highland lore and wrote a commentary on Dr Johnson's Journey to the Hebrides.

*

Alexander MacLeod, schoolteacher and missionary in St Kilda from the late spring of 1741, was the first of a sequence of MacLeods there extending into the third decade of the next century. How efficient and conscientious they were cannot be precisely known but there is every sign that they may not have achieved very much in the way of educating the islanders either at school or in religion. Alexander was paid on the usual half-yearly basis, the total annual salary amounting still to £25 sterling or 450 merks. It was as always difficult to obtain news from the island and the SSPCK sometimes thought that it was handing out six months' worth of pay to a person either no longer in his station or perhaps no longer alive. Receipts were often much overdue, and in April 1743 it was noted 'that its doubtfull whether the said Mr McLeod be on Life' or has carried out his duties, with the result that payment of the latest instalment due was withheld until evidence was received 'of his officiating in his Station'. However a report came by way of the presbytery of Uist that all was well and Alexander was continued without any further hesitations until 1748. At this point a letter from the Presbytery brought another rumour to cause concern. Information had reached Harris that the minister in St Kilda was not keeping the school, 'And as they have no Access to know what he is doing' the presbytery members 'cannot Certify his Service'. It was therefore proposed that the SSPCK should stand the cost of sending one of these members out to St Kilda to report 'how far Mr McLeod answers the Design of the Society in sending him thither'. The Society's committee, faced with what was a familiar problem of communication, agreed that either the presbytery of Uist or that of Skye should nominate someone to carry out this mission, but meantime Alexander MacLeod would be continued, whether he was present and at work or not; and because the Society lacked the funds to send anyone to inspect in the immediate future he was left to carry on in one way or another undisturbed.[76]

During this period another link between St Kilda and the Protestant church emerged in the form of Neil MacLeod, challenger for the role of settled minister in South Uist, who is said to have been the second son of John MacLeod, steward and tenant of St Kilda, and to have been born in 1729, probably in the island. But this date at least may well be incorrect if he was indeed the Neil MacLeod, probationer in 1736, of whom Aulay MacAulay wrote on 19 November that year with a request that he be appointed itinerant preacher in the parish of Harris. MacAulay's proposal was refused as a John Logan, itinerant preacher in Jura, had already been appointed, but early in 1737 and before he could take up this new post Logan died, and John MacLennan, itinerant preacher in the parish of Kilmallie and perhaps related to the unfortunate Roderick MacLennan in St Kilda, was told to supply Harris from 1 August 1737. This did not appeal to MacLennan who 'represented the Inconveniency of travelling into that Distant Place in respect of his Bodely Constitution, but is willing to Serve the Committee any where else nearer to the place of his nativity'. The Royal Bounty committee then appointed Neil MacLeod to Harris after all, providing him with a salary of £15 to which a further £5 from Aulay MacAulay would be added in accordance with the obligation he had undertaken in March 1736.[77]

The presbytery of Skye wrote to the Royal Bounty committee in 1743 asking that 'Mr Niel MacLeod' be made itinerant preacher in Bracadale, 'the minister of Harris having a Son of his own' - probably Kenneth - 'Licensed that can help him'. Consequently the committee, as ever exercising careful control over its limited funds, assigned Neil to officiate six months in Bracadale and six months in Snizort, parishes in which both ministers were 'aged'. In 1744 there was some intention of settling Neil as minister of South Uist, and perhaps at this time he served for a short while in Benbecula, but there was the MacAulay opposition to contend with, and it appears that Neil Macleod was compelled by circumstances to continue in his two Skye parishes for another year. Then funds were withdrawn and the salary for a missionary preacher in Bracadale and Snizort ceased to be available. The presbyteries of Uist and Skye, having held a joint meeting 'to take the Tryals' of Neil MacLeod, still probationer but also still in mind for possible minister of South Uist, wrote to the committee in October 1745 to say that it was their unanimous opinion that he was unfit to be settled in 'that Popish Parish' and recommended that he be employed again as a missionary in 'Some Protestant Parishes'. The MacAulays had won; and Neil, who then seems to have been unemployed, may have stayed in St Kilda during at least a part of 1746.[78]

Aware that Neil MacLeod might be looking for a charge of some sort the presbytery of Abertarff sent him an invitation to become missionary in the extensively 'Popish' parish of Laggan, and on 4 February 1747 wrote a letter to the Royal Bounty committee informing it of this development. The committee wished 'to know whither the said Mr Niel be the Same Person who was presented Some years ago to be minister of South Uist, and upon tryal was found not qualified'; and the minister of Kilmallie replying with information 'whereby it appears that Mr Niel McLeod … is the same Person', the committee did not approve of the intended appointment and refused to employ and pay him. Thereupon Mr Neil remained in Skye where the presbytery sought permission in 1748 to place him in the vacant parish of Bracadale as successor to the recently deceased Daniel MacAulay. Nothing appeared to come of this, and in June 1752 the Synod of Glenelg announced that Neil MacLeod, 'a deserving young Man' within the bounds of the Skye presbytery, was to be taken on trials. He may then have worked for a while in Moidart, but in May 1756 he was presented to the parish of Kilfinichen in Mull and became a settled minister at last.[79]

Forty years later, in June 1798, Murdoch Mackenzie, nephew of the Murdoch MacKenzie who during the 1750s surveyed western waters for the production of charts covering the island and mainland coasts, enclosed with a letter of his own a curious account he had discovered:

'Since the receipt of your favour of the 31st ult. I have looked over my late Uncle Murdoch's Papers, and found the enclosed description of St Kilda. I fancied it to be much more worthy of your acceptance than I now find it is; for exclusive of its deficiency in information, it wants the subscription of the Gentleman who sent it to my Uncle. I think I have heard my Uncle say, that his name was Macleod or Maclean (I now forget which) and that he occasionally officiated as Clergyman to that Island. I believe my Uncle's enquiries were more directed to the extent and form of these Islands than to other matters; for I have heard him say, that those three Islands were the only parts of all his Surveys which were not actually surveyed by him: for when he was surveying the neighbouring Coast, it was in the time of war; and as the Enemies Privateers very frequently cruized of[f] these Islands it was not safe to go there in the Surveying Sloop, nor were her Boats adapted to land on the shore of St Kilda …'[80]

The account, unsigned and undated, to which MacKenzie referred could have been written by Neil MacLeod in or about 1757 when he was established in Mull. The introductory paragraph explains that the description was composed in response to enquiries from the elder, surveying Murdoch:

'I have received yours of the 22nd December, and as I am heartily willing to improve the little acquaintance I had the pleasure to contract with you when you were last in this country, I take the opportunity of the bearer to trouble you with such particulars relating to St Kilda as you desire to know, so far as I can recollect them: indeed the account I give you will be far from being so minute and uncircumstantial as I wou'd incline, for I have not been in that Island since the year 1746, when I was just from the grammer school, and did not then take any pains to inform myself of any circumstances about that place further than what I could not help observing or hearing in it; for I had not then the least notion that I shou'd have a call of this nature to write any about it: all I can at present recollect shall be freely communicated to you notwithstanding'.

The hills of the 'three Islands', he said, were similar in height to those in Mull except for 'Benmore' - a natural comparison for a minister at Kilfinichen to make - and his other memories were of aspects which could be expected to have impressed him. He recollected the great cliffs of St Kilda, the hauling up of boats 'upon a certain rock which has a sloping descent towards the sea', the houses, the arable land, the middens, and above all the birds and how they were caught. About twenty families were living there. Not far out into the ocean good fishing banks could probably be found, and 'I make no question but great shoals of cod and Ling are upon these banks because they are got in very deep water near the rocks'. The possible development of fisheries had helped to launch MacKenzie on his surveys, and fish might well be a major ingredient of St Kilda produce, but the writer was not acquainted with such important things as prices and quantities:

'I intend soon to see my friends in Harris from whence I shall write more particularly on this subject. This much however I shall venture to assure you of that if gentlemen from your city shou'd be pleas'd to attempt a discovery of banks about that I[sland], those who are now in possession of it wou'd give them all the assistance in their power'. [81]

These observations on a potential industry were in line with government interest in the subject, and within a year or two another minister, John Walker, was planning an expedition as far as St Kilda to report on marine as well as agricultural circumstances and resources.

At the beginning of April 1754 the SSPCK management committee discussed a communication from the presbytery of Uist. Among other matters raised was the familiar difficulty of communication with St Kilda. It was stated yet again that 'tho' the Presbytery from year to year Certify the Minister of St Kilda's Service, they have no access to know anything about him, but what he is pleased to write himself, so that it is only upon the Credite of his own Letter that they do Certify him, there being no Fund allowed for any person to go to that Remote Island'. This reminded the committee of the suggestion made by the presbytery in 1748 that the Society should pay the expenses of a minister to visit the island. Now six years had gone by and nobody had been chosen to make the voyage. The emotional intensity which had been a feature of the Buchan days had gone, relations between St Kilda and the SSPCK in Edinburgh were distant, occasional, even rather casual, and the urgent spiritual needs of the poor islanders had somehow become less pressing. The committee, showing some ignorance of geography, now suddenly took a more than usually positive step. 'Judging that the Presbytery of Skye is more contiguous to the said Island than that of Uist, and that it will be more Convenient for one of their number going there, as they may take the opportunity of going along with the Laird of McLeod's Factor, which one from the Presbytery of Uist Cannot do', the members agreed to pay the 'necessary Charges' of a representative chosen by the Skye presbytery, though they emphasised that such a visitor should 'be as moderate in his Expence, and as particular in his Report as possible'. Only if the factor or steward now lived in Skye rather than Pabbay could it be argued that the presbytery of Skye was more 'contiguous'.[82]

The SSPCK secretary told the respective bodies of the decision, but no reply had been received by the next committee meeting on 6 June and no action had been taken. At this meeting a petition from John MacAulay, then still in South Uist, was considered. MacAulay reported that 'the minister of St Kilda is now Dead' and requested the Society's attention to the state of that island. He asked that it 'lay down some certain Regulation with respect to the person to be Employed as Minister and Schoolmaster there for the Future'. As he was present at the meeting himself he was able to give the committee an account of the death of the minister, Alexander MacLeod, and expressed his own opinion on the subject of 'a proper person' to visit the island. Possibly as a result of further conversation with MacAulay the Society changed its former view and now decided 'that it is more Convenient to Send one from the Presbytery of Uist than from Skye'. It must have been realised that the Macleod territory of Harris lay within the bounds of the presbytery of Uist and that the most sensible choice of person would be one from either Harris or Uist. No doubt MacAulay suggested one. However members delayed the choice itself, recommending first of all that MacAulay should give in 'a memorial in writing anent the visitation of that Island in time Coming' and ordering a letter with this information to be sent to Mr John MacLeod of Muiravonside with whom by his uncle's deed of mortification the right of presentation now lay.[83]

Late in September 1754 Mr John MacLeod put forward Donald MacLeod, catechist in the parish of Bracadale, to be minister of St Kilda in place of Alexander MacLeod. The SSPCK immediately wrote to the presbytery of Uist asking for the particular time of the late minister's death so that it could work out matters of salary, and it wrote to the presbytery of Skye for its opinion of Donald MacLeod and his qualifications. No answer to either enquiry came within the next month, but one from Skye arrived in November, declaring that Donald MacLeod was in every way worthy to assume the duties of St Kilda minister. The presbytery was therefore given the task of taking him 'on trials' and ordaining him to the island.[84]

Although the Society had wanted to know the general state of St Kilda, the death of Alexander MacLeod and the ensuing vacancy removed for the time being the necessity for a visitor to go there and of course left the islanders without instruction either in religion or in reading and writing. A moderate element of haste was apparent in the search for a successor, and by early April 1755 the Skye presbytery had examined and ordained Donald MacLeod to be minister, catechist and teacher. It sought official approval of his appointment and proposed that he should be given part of his predecessor's outstanding salary to cover the expense of transporting himself and his family to his station and of purchasing some books to take with him. The deceased Alexander MacLeod's widow had been allowed her late husband's pay to 1 April 1754, so there was a sum available for helping Donald MacLeod, whose position in Bracadale was to be filled by another Alexander MacLeod, an elder in the parish. The Society was now liable to confuse one MacLeod with another, especially if called Alexander, and it was soon to have the same difficulty with MacAulays.[85]

A commission to St Kilda was granted by the Society to Donald MacLeod on 5 June 1755, though he had already left for his remote charge. Like his predecessor Donald was a native of Skye, and although a stranger to St Kilda he met with the approval of the island's owner. It has been thought that he remained in his post for over twenty years, but during whatever period he was there the Society heard scarcely anything from him by way of an acccount of his work or a description of the state of the island. It turned out that his attendance to his duties was neither regular nor, in some people's minds, in the least adequate. Indeed the ease with which presbyteries pronounced some missionaries entirely worthy of appointment calls into question their judgement and the genuineness of their concern for the communities to which they sent men like Donald MacLeod. Synods too, and even the SSPCK, cannot escape responsibility for the inadequacies of the system.[86]

Suspicion as to Donald MacLeod's behaviour and diligence may have been aroused less than a year after he took up his charge. On 14 July 1756 the SSPCK committee heard a petition from the new minister of Harris, Kenneth MacAulay, who set out the difficulty which the presbytery of Uist experienced in securing adequate certification of the St Kilda minister's good service, 'which they can have little access of knowing by reason of the great Distance of that Island from the main Land'. The presbytery was anxious to revive the idea temporarily dropped at the time of Alexander MacLeod's death that 'a proper person' should be sent out to St Kilda 'to Examine the people, [and] Enquire into their Situation and Knowledge', and that this person's expenses should be met by a special allowance from the Society. This time there was an immediate and firm response. The person was chosen, and within the next fortnight was approved by Mr John MacLeod of Muiravonside who confessed that he had 'never yet understood from proper authority what Effects the Employing of a minister there has produced'. This person was naturally and it might be thought inevitably Kenneth MacAulay.[87]

A view of Tarbert c1860 with the smithy (thatched, below the road), a shop to the left, the slated inn, and in the distance the Free Church manse. The latest cottages on St Kilda were about to be built.

CHAPTER 6

*Kenneth Macaulay goes to St Kilda, in conjunction with
John Macpherson writes a book for the SSPCK, and Johnson
and Boswell comment on both authors and book*

KENNETH MacAulay was well suited to the task of enquiring into
conditions on St Kilda which the SSPCK entrusted to him. One
qualification was the knowledge he already possessed of the St Kilda people,
acquired not from visits he had made but when boats came in from St Kilda
to Harris. A member of the presbytery of Skye and close acquaintance of
MacAulay was Dr John MacPherson, who lived at Ostaig and who, while
minister of the parish of Sleat, gained a reputation for considerable learning.
Letters from Ostaig greeted MacAulay as 'Bausie' and showed a casual interest
in his affairs, including his occasional contact with those inhabitants of St
Kilda who braved the hazards of the voyage to Harris in order to sell produce,
collect supplies, and perhaps to see relatives. MacPherson used to make an
annual request of MacAulay.'Tell the St Kilda people', he wrote on 26 February
1755, 'to send next Summer to me what will be another Bed of feathers and
as good as the Last. My Complements to them, especially as Mr Neil belongs
to them'.[88]

In the summer of 1756 and more or less at the same time as he submitted
the petition to the SSPCK on behalf of the presbytery of Uist Kenneth
MacAulay made a trip to Lismore, presumably to call on his brother John who
had been transported there from South Uist almost exactly a year before. It
would have been possible for him to pay a visit to Ostaig on the way out or
back and to speak with MacPherson about the forthcoming expedition to St
Kilda, news of which, although not yet ratified by a general meeting of the
Society, would have reached Skye and Harris shortly after the committee
meeting in mid July. MacPherson's interest in St Kilda was not confined to
feathers for beds since he was probably already planning what he called in a
later letter to MacAulay 'My Essay on the antient inhabitants of N[orth]
B[ritain] and Ireland', to which he hoped to add 'the Miscellaneous History of
St K.' Since he had no intention of going to this remote part of North Britain
himself he can only have expected to gather the material of his 'History' from
the few earlier works and from whatever MacAulay could discover.[89]

MacAulay was therefore likely to have had at least two aims when he
agreed to be 'the proper person' who would check on the state of St Kilda. He
would carry out the wishes of the SSPCK, and, with the Society's approval, he
would gather information about the island on behalf of himself or John
MacPherson, or perhaps both, with a view to publication. MacPherson had
brought his own interest in the island to the attention of the SSPCK on 28 July
1756 when a petition from him seeking the allocation of part of the recently

'vacant salary' of St Kilda to Alexander MacLeod's widow was received and considered. The 'vacant salary', thirteen months' worth, amounted to £27 sterling, of which £10 had been given to Donald MacLeod to cover his travelling expenses. In response the Society decided on applying another £10 to the support of the widow and her family. Earlier it had been agreed that MacAulay should have £6 towards his travel costs and a promise of more on his return so long as he was careful to limit his expenditure as much as possible, but it was not made clear at the time whether the sum of £6 would come out of the £27 total.[90]

The Society too had an interest in the literary possibilities of MacAulay's visit and report. On 18 November 1756 the management committee announced that 'as they have never got an exact account of the Island of St Kilda' they had asked Kenneth MacAulay not only to go to the school there to find out 'what progress the Missionary stationed there is makeing' but also to produce such a 'full and true Account' in accordance with 'a particular memorandum' to be sent him by the committee. This memorandum contained headings and questions to guide the visitor in what he was to observe and record, and it meant that whatever ambitions John MacPherson might have the minister of Harris was bound to submit to the Society some piece of writing in fulfilment of his instructions.[91]

Although Kenneth MacAulay was ordained and admitted as 'assistant and successor' to his father Aulay in 1752 both were treated as ministers in Harris thereafter, the church authorities being fully aware that Aulay was no longer capable of carrying out his duties but also being either unable or unwilling to retire him. Kenneth knew by July 1756 that he was to go to St Kilda, but by then the year was too advanced for him even to contemplate a journey of such risk, and if he had thought of going with the steward then the latter was most probably on his way home in July. Instead of a remote island therefore Kenneth found himself in Skye that year. The Synod of Glenelg, considering the need for encouraging 'some promising young men from the Highlands' to enter the ministry, appointed him and five more including John MacPherson to meet at Broadford 'to concert such measures for the Encouragement of Students having the Irish language' as might be forwarded by the presbytery commissioners at the General Assembly. The Synod's commissioners turned out to be MacAulay and MacPherson, who had achieved the highest and third highest parish collections - £10 and £6 - for the students, and these two invested £100 out of a total £139.6s.5d in the Corporation of Bakers in Glasgow. As regards St Kilda nothing happened in 1757 either, other than another request for feathers from Dr MacPherson, but on 7 June Kenneth MacAulay, attended a meeting of the SSPCK management committee in Edinburgh, at which he said that the instructions given him had been so late in reaching him that he had been unable to travel to St Kilda the previous year and the £6 allowed him for his expenses would not even pay for the boat passage alone. At this point he still was planning to visit the island in the course of that summer and the committee agreed on £12 as an allowance for the meantime. However the season passed without the intended expedition, and MacAulay had to wait until calmer weather returned the following year. Perhaps too he was occupied in looking after his aged and failing father. In July 1758 the Synod recorded that Mr Aulay had died since its last meeting, which would have been before 2 June 1758 when Kenneth left his house and set out at last on his brief but memorable adventure.[92]

*

Although it was early June the boat that took MacAulay to St Kilda was not the steward's. It was hired by the minister at his own expense and had a crew of ten men. He took with him 'Severall Small presents', which he was 'obliged to distribute among the Inhabitants of the Island' on his arrival, and, as he put it, 'loosed from Harris' on 6 June for what proved to be a very wet and stormy crossing: 'To me it was matter of astonishment that a vessel so small and frail, a six-oared highland boat, could have struggled for any time against such enormous billows, without either being overset or dashed to pieces'. They had put in to Haisgeir where the crew made an 'unnecessary acquisition' of 'incredible numbers of wild fowl eggs', especially unnecessary when going to St Kilda, and left the vicinity of the rocks at 10 o'clock at night, so that after more than six hours battling with the bad sea and weather they must have reached the island some time the following morning. Later the SSPCK heard that they had 'made St Kilda on the Sixth, and returned on the Sixteenth'.[93]

MacAulay wrote to the Society on 8 August 1758 to report the success of his visit, but added that during the seven or more weeks since his return he had been 'so hurried' that he had not had time 'to draw out the Different Remarks he had made, so as to answer Certain Queries, which he was appointed to answer'. He promised that he would supply the 'full account' as soon as possible. As for his expenses, he was ready to refer them to the Society, being of the opinion that nothing less than £30 in all would be adequate. He had of course received £12 in advance, and the SSPCK committee decided to delay consideration of the remainder until MacAulay's account of St Kilda was sent.[94]

In writing of the 'hurried' nature of his life after his return to Harris Kenneth MacAulay was being far from straightforward. On 4 August he married, probably in Skye, Penelope, daughter of Alexander MacLeod of Drynoch, an event which may have distracted him from his writing. Even so, the account, based on notes made during his ten days or less on the island, was started promptly enough, and the first version was complete by the spring of 1759. In July he crossed to Skye again and went to see John

MacPherson in Sleat. MacPherson told a friend: 'Kenneth was here till about three daies ago. We read his History of St Kilda tete a tete. The Subject is truly curious - but to Say the truth handled [in] a careless way. If that Essay is to be published Some one ought Surely to retouch it'. That person should be, Dr MacPherson thought, himself, though he claimed that he did not much enjoy writing because his legs and feet became 'almost congeal'd into Ice'. With these remarks he introduced the future controversy over the authorship of the eventually published work on St Kilda.[95]

With the physical disadvantages tolerated John MacPherson proceeded with the retouching of MacAulay's original 'Essay'. 'But after all', he wrote, 'as my friends are not a little interested in this thing, and as Mr Smollet takes the matter so much to heart, I will undertake to do what I can ..' He would need five or six weeks for it: 'You will perhaps Say - Why so much time when I have no more than a Small pamphlet to revise. I answer that the Subject may possibly lead me into the large field of our Scottish Antiquities and perhaps tempt me to Some litle Remarks in the Critical and Etymological way etc. etc. How far my Imagination may carry me, I am not just now able to determine or foresee … Ask your Friend, whether he will give me leave to ramble a little, or whether he chuses to confine me to the Text of my author. You will observe that the Parson of Harris is to answer for all my lucubrations, or in other words, to publish all under his own name, If the paper shall ever make any Sort of appearance in the World'. From all this it can be concluded that MacAulay's own writings were neither very respectable nor very long, being no more than an essay or small pamphlet. Mr Smollet, convener of the SSPCK, evidently wanted something of greater literary importance.[96]

If it had been left alone MacAulay's simple narrative might have been no bigger than the little book of 1727 which also appeared to have two minister authors, one to provide the information gained from firsthand experience, the other, more learned, to adjust the work for publication. In MacAulay's case both ministers might have felt that it would then have lacked the size and show of literary skill which would make it impressive as a report to the SSPCK and as a book of general public interest. At any rate MacPherson persisted in his belief that ramblings or 'lucubrations' would ornament the work and began the task with vigour. But by December 1759 he had made little progress, having been held up at various stages and especially when his house went on fire: 'The History of St Kilda gives me now a good deal of pain. I had written out ten large Sheets before my house was destroyed and these perished in the flames. Since that time it was not in my power to do any thing in that way, and the Carpenters I have now employed are So confoundedly Slow that I have not a place where to lay a chair, If I should resume this business. But the greatest misfortune of all is a cold in my legs of which I am never free but when I roam about.' By great good fortune, on the other hand, MacAulay's manuscript survived for MacPherson to re-touch.[97]

Before the end of the year MacPherson resumed his labours, often finding himself 'insensibly drawn away into degression'. As he admitted, 'To confine myself to the Text of St Kilda I am neither able nor willing'. Consequently he rambled on, though he did have the sense to realise that if he were to 'take it into my head to engage in a critical discussion of Such questions as these, were the Old Caledonians from Germany or Gaul originally, Was Ireland peopled from Scotland, or were the Old Scots from Ireland', some members of the SSPCK at least would 'exclaim against Kenneth and the whole performance'. Even so the work dragged on for three years, during which the Society became increasingly impatient on two counts. It wanted to see the finished description of the island, and it grew less and less pleased with what it heard of Donald MacLeod, minister and schoolmaster there.[98]

*

One of the main problems about Donald MacLeod was that he was frequently not in St Kilda. He was certainly on the island when MacAulay visited but that may have been more by coincidence than intention, although the delay of two years between the instructions given to MacAulay in 1756 and his journey to St Kilda in 1758 gave time for a warning indication of an imminent inspection to reach MacLeod. A communication from the presbytery of Uist in March 1759 asked the SSPCK to pay the year's salary due to the minister of St Kilda in spite of his departure from the island the previous August, 'which he was under an absolute necessity of doing, by reason of his bad State of health, and Circumstances of his family'. Though he had been absent all the following autumn and winter, 'and Cou'd not Return before the month of April, as all Communication with that Island, During the winter Season is impracticable', the Society committee agreed to pay the salary to him upon the production of 'a Certificate of his returning to the Island of St Kilda'.[99]

When at last it was available to them in the summer of 1761 the members of the SSPCK management committee found 'from the Report of Mr Mcaulays visitation that McLeod minister of St Kilda gives very bad attendance on his office being but Seldom and for Short times on the Island'. This was of course the situation in 1758 when the 'visitation' was made and nothing had changed since then, so MacAulay was told 'to Speak to the Presbytery of Wist and Desire they may enquire into the reasons of Mr McLeods bad attendance and to Certify him that if he does not attend better other methods will be used'. The threatening tone of 'other methods' was for the time being backed up by an instruction to the Society's treasurer not to pay MacLeod's salary without specific order from the committee, and the president was to speak to Mr John MacLeod of Muiravonside on the subject. In February 1762 Donald MacLeod submitted a claim for the salary due to him on 1 May the preceeding year but payment was refused until the certificate of good attendance appeared.[100]

The unpaid missionary must have become more than a little anxious about his money. A petition on his behalf, recommended by MacLeod of MacLeod, was before the SSPCK committee on 22 February 1763. It gave an outline of Donald MacLeod's appointment and subsequent activities. Ordered to St Kilda in the spring of 1755 'he repaired thither in the Month of May that Year, and continued to Discharge his Duty to the utmost of his ability till the month of September 1759, when he was siezed with the Gravel and a Rupture in the Groin which confined him to his Bed for the Greatest part of that Year'. The story so far did not quite fit the information previously supplied by the Uist presbytery and by MacAulay but it still showed MacLeod's difficulty in attending properly to his duties. The petition continued with further details of his troubles:

> 'That tho' he had no access to relief from Medicine, he continued in the Island till the end of August 1760, when the Grieveous complecation of the Distempers he laboured under obliged him to leave it, in hopes of procuring some Relief from the Advice and Prescriptions of [a] Physician, which by the blessing of God gave him relief, and finding his Pain abate somewhat in the month of March, he resolved to return to his Charge, and accordingly in the Month of April 1761, he performed the Voyage and Journey with a Great deal of Pain and Danger, and considerable Expence; That notwithstanding he was the most of the time of his Residence in St Kilda confined to his Bed, he remained there untill the month of September thereafter when finding his Ailments dayly Encreasing he was necessitate to leave it a second time, and notwithstanding his Earnest desire of returning hither, Yet his miserable State of Health always on the decline has rendered it hitherto impossible for him, being always confined to his Bed by the Exquisite Pains that are the constant Attendants of his Ailment'.

The petition concluded with a request that in view of 'the low condition' to which the lack of two years' salary, as well as situation and health, had brought the minister and his numerous family the Society would order payment of what was due and empower him 'to look out for a Helper to whom he will Chearfully allow as large a Proportion of his Salary as to the Society shall seem fitt'.[101]

Donald MacLeod had gone home to Bracadale for his 'relief' and for treatment by a surgeon in that district called Norman Stewart. Two certificates, one from the minister and kirk session of Bracadale parish and the other from the surgeon, confirmed at least part of the account given in the petition, with the result that the SSPCK committee decided to inform Mr John MacLeod of Muiravonside, the patron, that one year's salary would be paid immediately but that the second year's would be delayed until Donald MacLeod found 'a Proper Person', approved by Mr John MacLeod, to be his assistant. In reply Mr John MacLeod urged a reconsideration of the SSPCK's decision regarding the salary, desiring immediate payment of both years' dues 'And promising that he would Co-operate with the Committee for carrying the Pious intention of his Uncle the Donor into full execution'. The committee reacted favourably, and asked Donald MacLeod to look out for 'a Proper Assistant ... whose Character and Qualifications must be Reported to the Committee and Mr John McLeod the Patron, for their Approbation'. A month later the committee at its meeting on 20 April 1763 read a letter from Mr John MacLeod of 'Tulliscar' [Tallisker], informing it that Donald MacLeod had now found 'a Helper' who appeared very suitable. This was none other than Alexander MacLeod, who had succeeded Donald as catechist in the parishes of Bracadale, Duirinish and Glenelg. The letter therefore asked the committee to write to the presbytery of Skye with a request that it enter 'the said Alexander McLeod upon Trials ...'.[102]

The 'Trials' were accordingly passed, and on 23 June 1763 the Society heard from William MacLeod, minister of Bracadale, on behalf of his presbytery, that Alexander MacLeod had been ordained assistant minister and catechist of St Kilda and instructed 'to repair to that Island without loss of time'. Mr John MacLeod had given his approval, as did the SSPCK committee, and Donald MacLeod was allowed the second year's salary. It appears that thereafter Donald, though officially minister at St Kilda, remained in Skye, and that Alexander MacLeod carried out all duties in the island, where he was perhaps still catechist in 1780.[103]

*

Meanwhile the production of Kenneth MacAulay's report had been the other principal concern of the Society as regards St Kilda. At the end of 1759 John MacPherson was still struggling with his 'improvements', and after another year or so with no satisfactory conclusion reached MacAulay lost patience. Though he did not fall out completely with MacPherson it can only have been after some discussion that in the summer of 1761 he went off with a manuscript version of the account, probably in part 're-touched', to present to the Society. The management committee met on 8 July:

'Mr Kenneth Mcaulay who was Some time ago appointed by the Society to visit the Island of St Kilda being now present gave in the Report of his visitation with a History of that Island which he prepared in Consequence of the Instructions given to him for that purpose by the Committee and some members having already read the History the report of the visitation was now read and the Committee agreed that for

Mr Mcaulays trouble and Expence in the said visitation and preparing the foresaid History he have the sum of forty guineas including Twelve pound formerly paid him, and Mr Mcaulay having Signified his desiring of having the Benefite of printing the said History and bringing it to the Country in order to make some amendments on it before printing The Committee agreed thereto But appointed the Clerk to keep a Copie of the History and to employ as many hands as are necessary to Transcribe it'.[104]

Only a week later, on 15 July 1761, Kenneth MacAulay began on the next stage of his career as minister of the parish of Ardnamurchan. His departure from Harris, and from the presbytery of Uist, might well have reduced his interest in St Kilda at this vital stage, but he was determined to publish his 'History' and now that the SSPCK had a copy he could not delay much longer. MacPherson's intentions too added to the urgency. MacPherson, with whom the original of MacAulay's account had apparently been left, had become so pleased with his own 'lucubrations' that he had decided to make the 'History' part of a long work of his own in more than one volume. He wrote to MacAulay at Ardnamurchan on 5 April 1762 to tell him: 'I have drawn out a new and a much fuller Edition of the first volume … As to St Kilda I know not yet whether it shall make a part of the 2nd volume as I may perhaps have material enough without it. If I use any freedoms with it, nothing shall be done without your advice and consent and depend on it, no injury shall be done to your character.' MacAulay did not like the idea of his *History of St Kilda* being swallowed up by MacPherson's *Critical Dissertations on the Ancient Caledonians*, so he asked for the original manuscript back and received it safely. After this MacPherson occasionally wondered how 'St Kilda' was getting on.[105]

The SSPCK management committee wrote to MacAulay in February 1763, urging him to publish the 'History' without delay, otherwise, 'if he fails to do it soon, the Society will Publish the Copy in their Possession'. MacAulay, in response, declared to the committee 'That the not Publishing his Account of St Kilda has been owing to many unforseen Accidents, but that he is determined to be in Edinburgh in May next in order to have it Published'. In June rather than May he informed the Society that 'he was immediately to Sett about the Publication of his Account of St Kilda' but previous thereto he wished to know if the committee would purchase any copies for the use of the Society. The committee, which had already allowed 40 guineas by way of expenses and to cover costs of preparing for publication, had also come to an agreement with MacAulay that a member of the Society would write a preface and that some printed copies would be donated to the Society, so it declined to contribute any more. Instead MacAulay was given a further ultimatum which stated that the Society's copy would be printed if his own work was not published by the time of the SSPCK Anniversary Meeting which would be held as usual in January.[106]

January 1764 came and went without a book, but the Society's copy did not appear in print either. Then, in the early summer, *The History of St Kilda* by the Rev. Mr. Kenneth MacAulay at last was published. It was immediately examined by the SSPCK committee which had waited so long for this promised event. It found no preface by a member but this drew no comment, perhaps because an agreement had subsequently been reached with the author over the form of the introduction. What did upset the committee, which referred to a printed copy of the book at the meeting on 6 June 1764, was a serious fault in the title page. The members observed with some annoyance that 'the Society is thereby described in such ambiguous terms that Strangers into whose hands the History may come, cannot distinguish whether the designation belongs to the Society in Scotland or the Society in England'. MacAulay was therefore to be instructed 'to Cause the Title Page of his History to be Cancelled, and to Cause Print a New Title Page, describing the Society here more Particularly - And Certifying him that in case he refused to Comply with the Society's Demand, they will be under a necessity in Justice to themselves to Cause Insert in the English Newspapers an Advertizement explaining the above mistake'. In the event no such drastic steps were taken and following MacAulay's reply the committee agreed 'to stop any further procedure in that matter'.[107]

There is no obvious reason why the Society should have changed its mind, particularly when it might have noticed that the second paragraph of the introduction, in which MacAulay outlined the circumstances of his visit and his motives in writing, repeated the fault in the title page. If written by MacAulay himself rather than by MacPherson, it revealed a minister of quite different character from Buchan and MacLennan, one who, like many of later generations, stood apart from the people and gave himself an air of superiority, with airs and graces that he imagined might make him acceptable among a polite mainland public:

'It is hardly necessary, I presume, to inform the publick, that the Society for propagating Christian Knowledge, take a peculiar concern in the people of that island. Animated by a primitive zeal, and a disinterested benevolence of the most exalted kind, they have been for above half a century back continually employing men possessed of a competent share of knowledge among these our domestic Indians, with the strictest orders, enforced by proper encouragements, to instruct them carefully in the great truths of our holy religion, and to give the younger sort some tolerable notion of the English tongue. Sollicitous to know whether the persons so employed have been diligent or useful, the Honourable and Reverend Gentlemen, who compose that respectable body, found it necessary to send some of the Highland Clergy upon a mission to the place; and as I was at that time settled in a parish, which is the only part of the world that maintains any kind of intercourse with St. Kilda, their commission fell to my share. To catechize the natives with a consciencious exactness, to preach among them as oft as I could without a manifest inconvenience, and to see into the state of the charity school there, were my principal instructions: Another was, to collect all the observations I could make that might in any degree be thought worthy of being communicated to the Public'.[108]

Possibly the committee found the compliments paid to the Society so flattering and the observations on life in St Kilda so interesting that it chose to forget about the fault of which it had complained. Soon it was a matter of looking at the reviews, which on balance were just. Much of the book found favour but there was a strong disapproval of sections on 'Augurs and Auspices' (chapter 9) and on 'the first inhabitants of Hirta' (chapter 14), both of which showed evident signs of John MacPherson's contribution. The former was described as 'trifling beyond all conception, by his ridiculous application on every occasion, of classical and antient learning to so uninteresting a subject'. MacPherson, commenting on the book's reception in yet another letter to MacAulay, sought to defend himself: '... but after all That mercenary partial and Scurrilous Critics have said, there will be some found who may think the history of St Kilda not an absolutely bad performance'. He must have been deeply offended by some of the critical remarks since they were directed against parts of the 'History' that were almost certainly not by MacAulay, but his defensive words suggest that he tried to shift responsibility for inadequacies, if there were any, away from himself to the named author.[109]

As with the little book of 1727 and books of much more recent date it is necessary in the case of MacAulay's work to exercise caution. Information and attitudes may not reflect reality nor help in bringing the reader closer to the subject. In the *History of St Kilda* there are passages that may derive from a minister who was never nearer St Kilda than Barra and which reduce the immediacy of details emerging from MacAulay's personal though limited experience. As in 1727 Martin Martin reappears as a source, sometimes at length, and there are many classical references which again most probably come from MacPherson. These aspects do not prevent the work from being used as a source itself but they mean that a proportion at least cannot be taken at face value. Nevertheless there is much that can. As a minister on a short mission with specific instructions to catechise, preach, examine whatever school there was, and collect observations of a more general kind, MacAulay will have been busily occupied over his nine or ten days, and those original descriptions and remarks which form a substantial part of the book and give the impression of genuine experience must be the result.

MacAulay was of the opinion that St Kilda was 'now in some manner a pendicle' of Harris, but it was still not part of the Harris parish and there is no sign that a Harris minister in this period ever went there to fulfil his parochial duty. His visit was therefore entirely owing to the SSPCK and his report probably reflected this, but his published book showed a far wider range of interest. One of its most useful aspects was its pursuit of topics covered in earlier accounts, as for example the ecclesiastical buildings. In MacAulay's day the three 'temples' or chapels shown by Martin on his map of St Kilda were still visible though perhaps all were suffering from neglect: that dedicated to Columba had 'neither altar, cross or cell within its precincts'; Brendan's chapel had 'an altar within, and some Monkish cells without.'; and 'the largest church .. was dedicated to *Christ*', was built of dry stone, 24 feet long and 14 feet wide, and 'was in former times the principal place of worship in the isle'. Burials continued there. In addition to the altar in Brendan's chapel four more still existed, one of them on top of the hill called Mullach Geal. Other subjects of religious or superstitious devotion such as sacred wells and the Clach na Gruagach also caught MacAulay's attention. In association with two of the old chapels the festival days of Brendan and Columba were celebrated in St Kilda on 27 May and 16 June; this did not prevent ordinary daily work from being carried on, and on these occasions all the milk collected was presented to the steward or the officer for him to distribute in equal amounts to every islander.[110]

The presence of a resident minister on St Kilda, MacAulay said, might be thought to have a controlling influence through 'advice and remonstrances'. But this was not the case:

> 'as the minister is himself in some degree a prisoner, as his living here with any comfort, and his enjoying the very necessaries of his su[b]sistance, depend so much on the steward's friendship, it may be convenient for him to look on with a prudent taciturnity, if he intends to continue long in the place. I add further, that any one who undertakes to exercise the sacred function in this remote and uncomfortable little diocese, may be very reasonably thought a person of no great authority or influence'.[111]

Donald MacLeod, missionary minister in St Kilda at the time of MacAulay's visit, was described in the *History* as 'a man of sense, virtue and piety: But the precarious state of his health, disables him from doing all the service he would incline, and will probably in a little time render him absolutely unfit for that station'. MacAulay did not have a high opinion of his teaching or of that of his predecessors: 'It will hardly be expected, after all the pains employed by a succession of ministers, whom the world may probably rank in the lowest class of public teachers, that the St.Kildians can have the exactest notions of the Christian institution'. In fact the people had very little notion of Protestant principles, retaining some element of ancient faith partly because the presence of poorly educated and barely qualified teachers since Buchan had been so erratic and ineffective. Alongside rituals at wells and stones, 'The belief of a destiny, or an unavoidable resistless fate, is one of the strongest articles of their creed'; and quite in line with this the people had become 'devout' in more orthodox Protestant behaviour, attending 'divine worship very regularly' and strictly keeping the Sabbath.[112]

MacAulay met one of the two granddaughters of Roderick the 'impostor' and naturally had nothing good to say of her or of her ancestor. She was supposed to have inherited the faculty of second sight but when on being asked about it she 'disclaimed all pretensions to this gift' he concluded that, in keeping with her 'scandalous and wicked' personality, she had lied. In the matter of character estimation MacAulay, in this instance at least, is no sound guide since it may be supposed that his religious persuasion biased him, but it is of interest that some of Roderick's family had survived the small pox.[113]

If Roderick was one of those whom MacAulay called 'the true natives of St Kilda' then he would presumably have been a member of one of the two 'tribes' whose posterity avoided fatal disease and disaster until the time of MacAulay's visitation. Their 'sir-names' were recorded in the *History* as *Mac Ille Mhoirre*, identified by the author as Morrison, and *Mac Ille Rhiabhich*, the latter apparently claiming a connection with Clanranald and South Uist. The words 'true natives' may denote inhabitants of the island who were there before the small pox epidemic, and their descendants, while those who were not 'true natives' would therefore most likely be the people who came, or were descended from migrants who came, to St Kilda about 1730 to fill the space left by the recent dead. In the absence of regular and thorough Protestant teaching a blend of new, old, native and non-native traditions and religious beliefs could have become established over the subsequent years, and there is no good reason to think that the introduction of people from Skye or Berneray would necessarily have brought the St Kilda community into a less 'barbaric' or more up-to-date world. It was, after all, in Skye during the early years of the nineteenth century that 'An event occurred ... which, from the wildness, extravagance, and imprudence that marked its origin and progress, had at the time every appearance of being hurtful to the interests of religion'. This was the emergence of 'a sect .. headed by a poor illiterate woman named Flora Macpherson', a kind of female Roderick and known not as 'the impostor' but as 'the Prophetess':

'her errors were embraced by a considerable number of the people, - her wildest reveries were looked upon as divine illuminations; - some of the most serious and best disposed were seduced by her imposing appearance, and viewing her in the light of one divinely inspired, the people considered it incumbent upon them to place the most unbounded confidence in every thing that dropped from the lips of one whom they believed gifted with supernatural endowments. Without entering into the detail of her peculiarities, suffice it for the present to say, that the distinguishing traits of her character were roaring, violent convulsions, high pretensions to inspiration, and communication with the Saviour, by which she pretended to have acquired a controuling influence over the actions of her fellow-creatures, and to have arrived at a knowledge of their present state and future destiny.'[114]

There were many other features of island life as MacAulay saw it which were noticed in his book. He had something to say about the power and excessive demands of the steward or factor; and he remarked that 'The present steward's brother, who is a clergyman of our church, and a man of learning and veracity' (quite probably Neil MacLeod, now minister in Mull) had told him how he had seen the spread of the 'boat cough' on three occasions when his father, the previous steward, visited the island three times within the space of two months. The story of the small pox was told; in MacAulay's version numbers of survivors were not quite consistent with those given by Daniel MacAulay at the time - 'of twenty-one families, four grown persons only remained, and these had the burden of twenty-six orphans to support'. The 'extraordinary kind of sickness' which caused the deaths of infants was also described, but not for the first time. A new disaster was added which took place in 1759, an illustration of the fact that MacAulay's book incorporated material that did not derive from his 'visitation'. Nineteen men left for Boreray in the island's only boat on 6 October. Ten landed, nine tried to return home; but for three days there was a gale which forced the boat to shelter 'under the lee side of one of the high rocks' until, desperate with cold and hunger, 'they made for the bay'. Here, in trying to land on the beach, three men were washed away, six swept ashore, and the boat was broken to pieces. The ten men on Boreray spent the winter in an underground dwelling called Taigh Stallir and survived on birds and sheep until rescued by the steward the following June. The loss of the only boat again meant nothing but deep distress. Agriculture, antiquities, birds and houses were also among the subjects of MacAulay's observations.[115]

It is not difficult therefore to distinguish the essential MacAulay from the rather superfluous MacPherson in the course of the *History*, yet it entered popular tradition that the real author was MacPherson. When in the summer of 1773 Samuel Johnson and James Boswell reached the island of Skye they learned that MacAulay had merely collected the information while MacPherson had put it all in order, dressed it up in 'appropriate' language, and provided commentaries and reflections. Some years later another writer was told that 'Dr Macpherson was certainly the author of the book which goes under McAulay's name', and John MacCulloch, who should have known better, stated in his work on the Highlands and islands published in 1824 that 'Macaulay wrote a voyage to that St Kilda which he never saw'.[116]

The journey made by Johnson and Boswell in Scotland only nine years after the publication of the '*History*' brought them into direct contact with several of the ministers involved. By that time MacAulay had moved to Cawdor near Nairn where he was admitted as parish minister in November 1772. Johnson and Boswell had breakfast in Nairn one morning in late August the following year and as Johnson recollected 'went forward to the house of Mr Macaulay, the minister who published an account of St Kilda'. Although Johnson himself made no further comment on MacAulay, Boswell recorded the occasion more fully. ' "We'll go", said Mr Johnson, which we accordingly did'. They were received at the 'remarkably good manse' by Mrs MacAulay, 'a MacLeod of a very good family', and waited for nearly three hours until the minister returned from distributing communion tokens. When he at last arrived 'Dr Johnson thanked him for his book, and said "it was a very pretty piece of topography." McAulay did not seem much to mind the compliment. From his conversation, Dr Johnson was persuaded that he had not written the book which goes under his name. I myself always suspected so; and I have been told it was written by the learned Dr John McPherson of Sky, from the materials collected by McAulay. Dr Johnson said privately to me, "There is a combination in it of which McAulay is not capable." ' He added also in private that MacAulay 'is a coarse man'. Later Boswell, who considered that their host was kindly and generous, grew afraid that Johnson and MacAulay would openly quarrel, and it appears that Johnson was subsequently even more rude about the minister since Boswell noted when they were at Talisker that his companion   said: 'There is Macaulay - the most ignorant booby and the grossest bastard'. Nevertheless MacAulay gave his guests 'a good hospitable dinner, and as we were to get a route from him for our tour among the western isles, we agreed to stay all night'.[117]

On their way to Skye the travellers were joined at Glenelg for breakfast by 'Mr MacLeod of Drynoch, to whom we had a letter from Kenneth Macaulay', Kenneth being MacLeod's son-in-law. They visited 'Corrichatachin' near Broadford where lived the MacKinnon family who were to have their own associations with St Kilda. Here Johnson glanced at John MacPherson's *Critical Dissertations*, and later, when at Greshornish, was rude about that as well, observing that 'you might read half an hour, and ask yourself what you had been reading: there were so many words to so little matter, that there was no getting through the book'. Boswell agreed, being 'disgusted by the unsatisfactory conjectures as to antiquity' in it, and both had to be restrained when they met Dr MacPherson's son, Martin, who had followed his father as minister of Sleat. Boswell remarked on a Latin ode written by Dr MacPherson when he was in Barra, which island had struck the minister as 'the most western isle of Scotland, except St Kilda', a barbaric 'Thule' which made him long for the comparatively civilised world of Ostaig. Whatever his part in the composition of the *History* MacPherson evidently had no sympathy with its subject.[118]

Unlikely as it may seem, classical learning was not unknown in the missionary's simple dwelling in St Kilda. On the evening of 20 October 1773 Johnson and Boswell arrived in Mull where they were welcomed by the minister of Kilfinichen, Neil MacLeod. According to Johnson Neil was 'the cleanest-headed man that he had met with in the Western Islands'. He told them that he had lived for some time in St Kilda, 'under the tuition of the minister or catechist there', and that he had read the Latin classical authors Horace and Virgil for the first time on the island. 'The scenes which they describe', thought Boswell, 'must have been a strong contrast to the dreary waste around him'.[119]

Kenneth MacAulay died in March 1779, the controversy over his part in the book still undecided. In course of time one unsuccessful attempt was made to prove that he was in fact the principal author; his nephew, Aulay MacAulay, who was a clergyman near Leicester, intended to republish the *History* with notes to show that it was 'altogether his uncle's composition', but he died before he could carry out his purpose.[120]

CHAPTER 7

More Macleod missionaries, Rev. John Walker raises new economic and 'romantic' themes, and Harris and St Kilda have a change of owner

THE arrival of Alexander MacLeod in St Kilda as assistant minister and schoolteacher in place of the ailing Donald MacLeod is a little known episode in the history of the island. Far from serving twenty or so years there Donald's occasional presence must have amounted to not much more than five or six years, after which Alexander seems to have been properly resident, at least for the rest of the 1760s. His work in St Kilda meant rather more to the inhabitants than the publication a year after his coming to them of MacAulay's *History*, a remote event, news of which probably took a long time to reach the island.

At the same period and similarly unknown to the islanders yet another minister was busy exploring the north-west of Scotland for scientific as much as for religious reasons and showing an interest in St Kilda. This was John Walker, incumbent in the parishes of Glencorse and Moffat, who travelled in the Highlands in 1761 and in the Hebrides in 1762. His interest then was chiefly geological, but in 1764 three commissions brought him back to these areas with rather different purposes. A joint request from the General Assembly and the SSPCK for an account of the state of religion and education in the Highlands and islands led to reports submitted in 1765, while a commission from the Commissioners of the Annexed Estates resulted eventually in the Report on the Hebrides of 1771. A later outcome was the two volume *Economical History of the Hebrides and Highlands*, written by Walker probably for the Board of Agriculture and published in 1808, four years after his death.[121]

Walker was a 'moderate' minister of the established church and was strongly opposed to Catholicism which he felt tended to reinforce an undesirable attachment to ancient custom and traditional ways. The Catholic areas therefore did not meet with his approval as regards either religious faith or agricultural advancement: 'Even the progress of the arts of industry will be prevented, as Popery prevails. For the Balefull influence of the Popish religion, wherever it is generally professed in the Highlands, is visible, even in the face of the Country. There, not only the morals and manners of the People, but the very Soil, is more rude and uncultivated. The Popish inhabitants ... become peculiarly averse, to every innovation, that tends to promote industry, or improve the country.' The connection between the Protestant religion and innovation, agricultural and industrial, was made within the ranks of the SSPCK, and in a sermon preached by Robert Winter in April 1788 the dual role of the Society, which already was associated with spinning schools and farms, was pointed out: 'Its leading object is to propagate Christian knowledge in the

Highlands and Islands of Scotland. And in subordination to this, a second object is to encourage among the poor inhabitants of that remote and uncultivated part of Great Britain, such an attendance to agriculture and manufactures, as will render them industrious and useful, and consequently happy ..' Holding them back from this projected state of contentment was the dreaded 'Popery', 'a rough and narrow scheme, so little calculated for the good of mankind, that it breathes the reverse', nowhere more so than in Britain where 'it is totally inconsistent either with the peace or prosperity of the kingdom'. The two 'rebellions' of 1715 and 1745 on behalf of a 'Popish pretender' did not mean that the Society had been unsuccessful, but they showed 'the necessity of having the highlanders reformed one way or other', and the Society's way, the best one, was through schooling which 'melts them down into voteries of peace, and things that make for it'. In 1788 Winter repeated the view held by the SSPCK at its foundation eighty years earlier: 'experience has long proved, that nothing so much tends to prevent the baleful effects of ignorance, superstition, and vice, as early religious education'. The Society had done much to provide such (Protestant) education, but there were still wide tracts of the north where there was work to do. 'It will not therefore appear surprising,' said Winter, 'that popish emissaries have been both diligent and successful in spreading among this before benighted people, their false and pernicious tenets. And though much good has been done in counteracting their attempts by this extensively useful Society, continued exertions are necessary to confirm the advantage already obtained.' Financial contributions, he concluded, would be welcome.[122]

Like many of his Protestant predecessors and contemporaries, and many in succeeding generations, Walker was of the opinion that 'morals and manners' could be thought inadequate not necessarily because people behaved in an immoral or uncivilised way but because their behaviour did not conform to a certain Protestant code. If he had managed to visit St Kilda while on tour he would have taken with him several preconceptions of this kind, including an aversion to the 'pernicious tenets' of Catholicism, hostility towards 'ignorance' and 'superstition', and an inclination to make the islanders happy by getting them to be 'industrious and useful'. This latter approach has not been confined to Walker or to the eighteenth century, for it has been in evidence ever since, its accompaniment being the view that if the people of the islands do not appear 'industrious and useful' they must be lazy. Whether or not this accusation is justifiable it comes from strangers often lacking in sympathetic understanding, and with this in mind it may be necessary to call in question the remark made of Walker that 'There can have been few men so well qualified to undertake a survey of the Hebrides in 1764.'[123]

Sponsored by the General Assembly, the SSPCK and the Board of Annexed Estates, John Walker prepared to set off on his latest tour in the summer of 1764. He was urged by Thomas Pennant, a Welsh naturalist and Fellow of the

Royal Society soon to be a visitor to the Highlands himself, to pay 'a thorough attention to the zoology of the western Isles', and especially to enquire about certain birds and sheep, including a peculiar kind of sheep 'in the Isle of Hirta' rumoured to have 'horns as large as those of oxen'. So with a busy programme ahead of him Walker left from Greenock, crossed to Ireland, and then made his way by Islay and the Inner Hebrides to Barra and South Uist which he reached at the end of July. Over two full weeks he continued northwards through Benbecula, North Uist and the Sound of Harris islands, and after Harris reached Stornoway on 16 August. He then turned his attention to Skye and the mainland and so never ventured to St Kilda. The nearest he came to the island was the attempt to arrange for a boat to take him in 1762, and, judging from a letter written to him when he was on Berneray by John Ritchie 'on Bord of the Cumbra Whirie' at Lochmaddy, it was fortunate that he did not take the only chance of a voyage:

'Dear Sir

'Yours at Seven a clock Received and for ansor this Deay Eight Days Coming oup this way I meat with a hard Gell of North East wind which obleadged mi to Berr away for Canna the Whirie meacking so much water I Lead hir on the Ground In Canna and found a Great Meney Neals Started by the Strean of being on the Rock She still Continous Leck and I am of openon onfit to Go to St Kilda at this Seson of the year but I should be sorie to be the stop of your seaing St Kilda if you think proper to ventor In the Whirie I will taik my Chance My Complements to Mr Anderson.
I am
Dear Sir your Most Obedient Humble Servant
P.S. If you ar Determined to Go you most fiend the pilot as Duncan is not aquanted.'[124]

Walker must consequently have relied upon information supplied by others for inclusion in his Report on the Hebrides. The section in the Report which deals with St Kilda has little to say about the place and is chiefly of interest as conveying the writer's attitude. It speculates on the potential value of the 'Cod Banks' around the island and in the vicinity of 'the little solitary Island called Rocca' - Rockall - 'which lies about 50 Leagues westward of Barra'. It reports that 'two Wherries fitted out for the Cod Fishery' sailed from Greenock the previous April 'To make Trial of these Banks', paid for with an allowance from the Trustees for Fisheries and Manufactures. In addition a brig sailed from Campbeltown at its own expense 'upon the same Design'. The vessels from Greenock chose a route round the Butt of Lewis, and in May 'reached St Kilda after a very bad tedious Passage, in which, one of the Wherries had a Suit of new Sails torn to pieces'. The experience of rough weather did not deter them from remaining there while they 'made Trial of the Fishing about that Island', and it was lack of success that sent them home in June. The master of the brig told of the sea depths and other conditions and though 'upon this Station he caught only 3 dozen of Cod' he admitted that they were 'the largest and finest he had ever seen'. Walker, who from his reading believed that cod should be very numerous in this location, excused their absence by stating the 'well known' fact that 'the Cod is a Fish which frequently shifts its Quarters'. So far as Walker was concerned a reason for St Kilda to take its place in the developing commercial world had to be found: 'This small and remote Island can never promise to be of any Importance to the Publick except in the way of Fishery; but it has been judged that in this way, it might be a place of considerable moment'.[125]

Walker put all his other comments on St Kilda into only two paragraphs of an introductory sort, but in doing so added a new and important descriptive word to the stranger's vocabulary. St Kilda, already a subject of curiosity and literary extravagance, was now romantic: 'This remote and romantick Island lies out in the Atlantick, to the westward of all the Hebrides.' Why was the word used, and what attitude did it reflect? The rest of the observation, also conveying a sense of seabound mystery, of a different world alone in the west, is reminiscent of the Brendan tales of old and heralds that popular sentiment of the nineteenth and twentieth centuries which made it virtually impossible for an outsider in later times ever to see or to write of St Kilda simply as one of the Hebrides and as a place where people lived a poor and harsh life.

Indirectly the process of separation from reality had begun with the first written commentary on the island, but with the SSPCK and MacAulay's book it had taken a stride forward. Now again in Walker's Report even the few pieces of supposedly 'factual' information were expressed without any real concern for their human implications. In the main they were statistical and were presented to satisfy curiosity as well as to indicate fishery potential. The size of the principal island alone, computed from the distances between extremities, was given as 3840 acres, almost twice the actual land area of the whole group. The rent of 200 merks apparently paid to the proprietor had interest as being equivalent to less than a penny sterling per acre, but since neither the actual quantity, nor the nature, of the acreage played a part in the calculation the information was meaningless. Remaining statistics related to population and the events which had influenced it during the eighteenth century - the small pox epidemic, the occurrence of tetanus, the former prevalence of 'leprosy'. The disappearance of the last had coincided with the recent availability of salt on the island, 'but it would require more particular Information, to be certain that the Extirpation of the Desease was entirely owing to this Cause'.

The number of inhabitants in St Kilda at this time varied slightly from

224

report to report. MacAulay's figure, representing the position in 1758, was 88, while Walker's for 1764 was 90 though in his 1771 Report it appeared as 92. In a communication from Murdoch MacIver, catechist in Harris, in 1771 the numbers of 'catechisable' persons were supplied for the Harris area; on Ensay there were 55 in 9 families, on Killigray 45 in 7 families, on Berneray 215 in 53 families and on Pabbay 150 in 32 families. 'St Kilda lays from Pabba Eighteen Leagues Distance where there are 19 families, and the Minister, Containing about 100 Souls'. Walker was struck by the increase in the population of St Kilda since the time of the small pox and formed the opinion that 'the People of St Kilda are 4 times more numerous than they were 38 years ago', and that the number would have risen even higher were it not for the loss of children. His notion that after the small pox there were only 18 left on the island is incorrect, and he did not take fully into account the transportations of the early 1730s, so that his reckoning as to the rate of population increase cannot be accurate.[126]

After a journey which lasted seven months and two days John Walker reached home and in mid December 1764 wrote from his manse in Moffat to Lord Kames outlining his achievements and intentions. Among his observations were some general conclusions about the Highland people:

'I was very much struck at the vast extent of the Highland Parishes, and at the great Numbers of People cut off by their distant Situation or by Lochs, Arms of the Sea, Rivers or Mountains, from their Parish Churches and from Schools, and entirely destitute of all the means of Christian Knowledge. I constantly observd, that wherever the People have Access to Publick Worship and the Ordinances of Religion, there, they are more regular in their Morals, more civilizd in their Manners, and more industrious, than their Countrymen who are remote from these advantages.

'There are many considerable Tracts of the Country peopled only with Papists, and there the Country is the least improvd and the Inhabitants the most slothfull of any. For all the old Customs, are connected in their Minds, with the old Religion, which makes them peculiarly averse to every Innovation that tends to promote Industry or improve the Country.'[127]

Whatever the value of Walker's surveys all that can be said here is that they had little immediate effect upon the inhabitants of unvisited St Kilda, except that the erroneous impression of the island already in existence on the mainland was if anything strengthened and the developments which he thought desirable were to have their impact, for better or worse, on the people in years still some distance into the future.

John MacLeod of Muiravonside died in 1771 and was succeeded by his son Alexander, also an advocate and ardent Jacobite, who met Johnson and Boswell on Raasay in September 1773. Boswell wrote of him as 'Mr MacLeod of Muiravonside, best known by the name of Sandie MacLeod, who was aide-de-camp to the Prince in 1745, and remained eighteen years in exile on that account'. At a dance in Raasay House, according to Boswell, Sandie 'made much jovial noise, but was too violent for my nerves'. This was typical, for Sandie, 'who has at times an excessive flow of spirits, was, in his days of absconding, known by the name of McCruslick, which it seems was the designation of a kind of wild man in the Highlands'. Now in the 1770s 'McCruslick' had the responsibility of patronage in respect of the missionary minister of St Kilda, about which place he would have learned much from his father and from other relations in the Berneray family.[128]

Other important changes occurred during this period around 1770, and like the succession of Sandie MacLeod they too had a bearing upon the fate of St Kilda. In 1769 or within the next few years the Harris estate lands were as usual rented out to principal tenants or tacksmen for up to almost four decades. Among the tacksmen were Campbells who held the valuable islands of Scalpay, Ensay, Killigray and in part Taransay, as well as other large areas, and Alexander MacLeod, son of John MacLeod and tenant of St Kilda with Lingay, Northtown and a pennyland of Kirktown all in Pabbay. Alexander was now known as factor or steward of St Kilda but was apparently none too satisfied with his farming life in the islands and had emigration in mind. This may have been because rents were greatly increased in 1769 and the inclination to emigrate was widespread and well-known. As for St Kilda's proprietor, MacLeod of MacLeod was deeply in debt and consequently unlikely to ease the rent burden.[129]

MacLeod of MacLeod sought to repay £3000 by applying to Captain Alexander MacLeod, of the Berneray family also, who was the wealthy owner and captain of the *Mansfield*, a ship engaged in the East India trade. The captain was interested in purchasing Harris from a man who he knew was financially in trouble, and the possible sale of that estate was being discussed in 1770, a year when the sharp fall in cattle prices added to everyone's troubles. On 21 December 1771 William Fraser W.S. wrote from Edinburgh to Rev. John Walker to say that 'The Laird of MacLeod by the advice of his freinds in order to clear off the family debts has come to a resolution to Sell off the Barony of Harries and St Kilda, and for that purpose to advertyse it in the English and Scots papers'. Since there had never been 'any regular Survey' of the barony and its islands there was a lack of accurate, first-hand information to put in the advertisement, and so Fraser used an extract from Walker's report, which was then found to contain several inaccuracies. The urge to sell was strengthened by the severities of the ensuing winter which forced people of Skye and elsewhere, who had no bread nor seed to sow, to eat the carcases of cattle which were dying around them.[130]

Norman MacLeod of MacLeod died in 1772 and was succeeded by his grandson, another Norman, who sought to clear the debts he inherited. Correspondence on the subject of Harris continued, during which the main contender for purchase was Sir George Strickland and a participant was Rev.Kenneth MacAulay whose local knowledge was thought to be of use. Some reluctance to sell at all was natural, and John MacLeod of Talisker advised against it: 'I think its worth while to delay parting with so ancient a possession', and 'besides were it sold at this period it is more than probable the greatest part of the Inhabitants woud Emigrate, and God knows how far their example woud infect others - that dangerous spirit it is our bussiness to discourage as much as possible ..' Moreover, he added, 'I am told the late Factor of St Kilda is Just now takeing some stepps that indicate his intentions of going away - his name is Alexander MacLeod one of the Tennants of Pabbay in Herries, you may remember to have seen him at Dunvegan'. Whether or not MacLeod was able to remember his factor, in 1773 Alexander tidied up his affairs in St Kilda and Pabbay, his 'Effects left on the Island of St.Kilda' being accepted by the landlord as part payment of rent arrears and the produce of the island received by him as equivalent to the rent due. The remaining sum of £17.18s.2d was made over to the landlord, Alexander renounced his tack, and emigration followed.[131]

The remoteness of the owner from parts of his estate allowed him to plan for a military career abroad and to retain a sentimental interest in his property, leaving others to cope with the immediate and pressing management problems. The younger Norman MacLeod of MacLeod had by October 1775 commissioned lawyers to sell Harris after all, although negotiations with Strickland and with Captain Alexander MacLeod were protracted. 'The Island of St Kilda which is part of the Barony of Harries', wrote Norman, 'is very inconsiderable in value: but I have a very strong passion to retain it, on account of its curiosity. If, therefore, you find that you can keep it out of the sale, without injuring the price unreasonably, I wish you to do it: but I do not wish to stop the sale on its account, or to give a very large deduction for it'. At this stage Norman, as would-be seller, was finding Captain Alexander 'really the hardest man I ever met with', but there was little he could do to avoid disposing of Harris to him in the end, in spite of Sir George Strickland's sustained interest. In April 1776, while Captain Alexander, having offered £15000, was biding his time, Strickland was wondering whether St Kilda was available or not, and was told that it was now not for sale as MacLeod 'wishes still to keep it rather than to accept of even a proportional price for it'. But at the same time and in the same letter he was also told that 'it shall still be your's on paying £500 of additional price'. The matter was concluded three years later when Captain Alexander succeeded in his bid to purchase, and after four more years he settled in Harris with ideas on how, among other things, to develop Rodel.[132]

One of the new owner's main projects for Harris related to fishing:

'He fitted out a fine cutter, sounded the coast, and found a bank half way between Harris and Sky, where many boats have caught cod and ling. In August, 1785, he made a trial of the banks of St. Kilda, which lies fifty-four miles west from the nearest land of the Long Island. He sounded thirty miles round the former in every direction, and believes these banks to extend still farther, being yet very little known. In June, 1786, he sent out a stout boat, with expert fishermen, to make another trial of these banks. They met with great success, and he recommends a small bay on St. Kilda, (the only one on that coast) as a place worthy of public notice, both on account of the fisheries and general navigation'.

The master of the cutter also reported 'that they observed the whales plowing their way through the shoals of herrings that were passing to the south, between the Long Island and St. Kilda'. Commercial value may have been seen in the whales themselves, but the chief interest lay in the scarcely tapped herring shoals out at sea as opposed to those that came into the lochs.[133]

The possibility of exploiting the fish in the ocean off St Kilda had been considered in 1735 by the writer of a curious tract who reflected also on the nature of the place and its community. 'This Litle mainland and its Small adjacent Islands', he wrote, 'is an excellent Epitome of the whole world and … we have a view of it as being possesed with a few poor, Ignorant, and Indolent people who by their poverty Ignorance and Simplicity are not at all or but very little either serviceable or hurtfull to the Rest of Mankind'. If the islanders were to become 'serviceable' then they could usefully be 'Employed about and Live upon the fishing', and between fishing and fowling 'the Number of people who posibly Could Live on the product of this Island by Land and Watter Will be about 5000'. Further absurd ideas were presented, but in the end 'the want of a harbour in the Island Ruins our whole Scheme'. The piece can hardly be taken seriously, yet the notion of a fishery base in St Kilda lingered on, a subject to be taken up from time to time as in the case of John Walker's report which in turn played a part in the sale of Harris and St Kilda to Captain Alexander MacLeod. However, the commercial implications were always envisaged as a means of promoting the national or at least the landowner's interest and had very little bearing on the living conditions of the St Kilda residents who were probably unaware of and certainly unable to react constructively to proposals of that kind, even when related to their 'small bay'. In the event the people experienced nothing more than industrial attitudes towards them, and it was to be more than a century before they had a slipway, never mind a harbour.[134]

When Alexander MacLeod of Pabbay gave up the tenancy of St Kilda he was succeeded by William MacNeil who in 1776 was £54.10s.3d in arrears, the rent at that time being £20. This MacNeil family is of uncertain origin though it may have come from Trumpan or Dunvegan in Skye. In 1769 a tack of the lands of 'Roudel' and of those called 'the Bay of Sunsbay' [i.e.Finsbay] was held by William and Rachael McNeil, and it appears that the MacNeil connection with Rodel and St Kilda survived for many years. William's son Roderick MacNeil seems to have taken over St Kilda and, like previous tenants, to have lived in Pabbay, although a letter of 2 November 1801 in which he styled himself 'Roderick McNeil, St Kilda' was sent from 'Roudle' and, relating as it did to trading between Harris and Stein in Skye, suggested that he had wider interests. Perhaps by that time his brother Norman, said to have been known as 'Tarmad Hiort', had succeeded as tenant. By 1779, when Harris was sold, St Kilda had a new owner, a new patron, and a new steward or tenant.[135]

*

Somewhere in the 1770s the SSPCK lost track of what the missionary situation in St Kilda really was. On 2 November 1780 the Society noted that 'Some difficulties having occurred in ordering payment of the Salary to Alexander McLeod Catechist at St Kilda, the Committee appoint the Clerk to write to the Minister of Harris to inform the Society whether the said Alexander MacLeod regularly resides and officiates in his Station in St Kilda; And faithfully discharges the duties of that Station'. The minister of Harris, John MacLeod, was also to be told that until he sent 'a particular authenticated account' of these matters the Society would not pay any instalments of salary to Alexander. An immediate answer was required. On receiving these demands John MacLeod took them to the presbytery meeting on 14 December. The presbytery of Uist was at least more up to date than the Society with news from St Kilda and understood the enquiry to relate not to Alexander but to Angus MacLeod, son of Donald MacLeod formerly in the island. Angus was now none too young himself. His father is said to have died around 1775 and it was perhaps then that Angus took over from Donald's substitute Alexander, possibly without the sanction of either the Society or Sandie MacLeod of Muiravonside. Payments were made to Alexander until 1770 without doubt as to who received them, but thereafter the position is uncertain, the Society being likely to have become confused between many Alexander MacLeods.[136]

Several details from Angus MacLeod's career have been put forward, though with questionable reliability. He is supposed to have studied law in Inverness, to have married Margaret MacKinnon from Strathaird in Skye, and to have become a small farmer in South Uist. He may have been living with his father in St Kilda just before the latter withdrew since his son Lachlan is said to have been born in the island in 1762. An appointment as catechist in South Uist in 1768, if a fact, may indicate that he took up a life in the church when farming in that island, and it seems that he was transferred from Uist to St Kilda. By 1780 he had probably been in that 'Station' for a few years. In replying to the Society's letter to John MacLeod the presbytery, 'considering that they have always sent regular certificates of Mr MacLeods attendance, resented with just indignation the Societies want of candour in giving ear to vague and malicious reports in prejudice to their veracity and ordered Mr John MacLeod to draw up a spirited answer setting this matter in a proper light'. It appears from the terms of the presbytery's comments that Angus MacLeod had occupied his post long enough for 'regular certificates' to have been submitted, yet there was possibly confusion here too over which Mr MacLeod was the subject of concern.[137]

Mr John MacLeod sent off his 'spirited answer', testifying to the residence and attention to duty of Angus MacLeod in St Kilda, and on consideration the Society's management committee at its meeting of 1 February 1781 allowed payment of salary. Thereafter nothing happened in St Kilda to arouse the concern of the several distant authorities for three or four years. The Protestant church continued its anxious interest in the religious and moral state of the Highlands and islands, especially in those districts where 'Popish Missionaries' were having some success in 'establishing the Romish superstition and in making converts' and where the few Protestant missionaries were often 'ill instructed and little qualified to answer the subtle arguments, and combate the artifices of Priests trained up for the purpose of perverting the ignorant'. St Kilda would have been one such district naturally, but it seems that the priests were busy elsewhere and Protestant attention was concentrated on those places known to be already Catholic, more particularly South Uist, Barra, and the 'popish part' of the great parish of Ardnamurchan. The SSPCK proposed to set up some small libraries in 'the sequestered parts of the Highlands' as well as some of the islands in order that 'true religion' should be helped along by appropriate books made readily available. Since there was a larger number of 'papists' in South Uist and Barra than anywhere else in the islands the books for those destinations would be promptly conveyed there 'by Barks or Sloops which go commonly twice in the year for Kelp to these Islands'; but if the books were like those sent to St Kilda they would scarcely have appealed to disaffected Gaelic-speaking inhabitants and probably have been left to moulder away unused.[138]

It was not only the presence and influence of priests that worried the Protestant authorities in respect of the islands, for in places not much less remote than St Kilda and falling definitely within the bounds of an established parish there was still inadequate provision. In March 1785 the presbytery of Uist viewed 'with sincere regret the deplorable state of Religeon in the islands of Bernera and Pabba in the parish of Harris, and the district of Sand in the parish of North Uist, which being remote and discontiguous to the principal places of worship in their respective parishes are ... in a great measure deprived of the benefit of Gospel ordinances'. This was the situation in spite of the efforts of hard-working parish ministers, and the presbytery resolved to petition the Royal Bounty committee, requesting that the two islands and district in question should be made a mission station and that a salary be provided for a missionary. This did not happen, but the circumstances are a reminder that as long as the missionary minister and teacher in St Kilda carried out his duties properly there were in fact places less well supplied than even that island as late as the end of the eighteenth century.[139]

Doubt was not long in reappearing, however, over whether the St Kilda missionary was indeed looking after his charge as the SSPCK and conscientiousness required. In the course of 1785 Angus MacLeod himself admitted that he was not able to do so. He communicated with John MacLeod of Harris parish, the presbytery clerk, making known to him 'the great decline of his health as well as a decay of his faculties, owing to old age and infirmities, which he finds severely creeping upon him', and asking the presbytery to consider his position. Perhaps the members would recommend to the SSPCK the appointment of his son Lachlan as his assistant and successor? He sent the same message to Alexander MacLeod Esq. of Harris, and on 7 July 1785 a petition from Captain Alexander was studied by the Society's committee. Since Angus MacLeod was now 'unable properly to discharge his duties' the petitioner recommended the son Lachlan, who, it was claimed, had been satisfactorily educated and for some time past had assisted his father. The committee waited for the usual documentation from the presbytery of Uist before appointing Lachlan.[140]

A letter from John MacLeod on behalf of the presbytery was before the committee on 5 April 1786. It repeated the content of Angus MacLeod's own communication to the presbytery the previous summer and of Captain Alexander's petition, and the SSPCK committee wrote back consenting to the arrangement so long as 'the young man' was licensed as a preacher. The presbytery, dealing with the matter in November 1786, welcomed the Society's approval of its proposal but objected strongly to the licensing which it thought remarkably lax and casual: 'it is an unprecedented thing to license a man to preach the Gospel without a liberal education'. A renewed application was sent to the Society in favour of Lachlan MacLeod, seeking to have him appointed to St Kilda in the usual way by 'trials' and ordination, and stating that although he as yet lacked the necessary education 'they can see no reason why he should not be settled there in the same manner with his predecessors, he having the suffrages of the people, the proprietor, the patron and the clergy, and being at the same time as well qualified as most of his predecessors have been'. The Society now felt that the most appropriate step would be for Lachlan MacLeod to go to Edinburgh to be examined by the Society's directors before they gave authority for his appointment.[141]

The meeting of the presbytery of Uist on 5 December 1787 was attended by 'Mr William MacNiel of St Kilda' as the representative of the Harris kirk session. Members present gave attention to 'that part of the Society's scheme which respects the proposed settlement of an assistant and successor to the Missionary Minister of St Kilda'. They unanimously disapproved of the resolution to call Lachlan MacLeod to Edinburgh and set up a committee to compose a letter 'urging in the strongest terms the unexpediency of this measure'. In addition this committee, which included William MacNeil and the minister of Harris, John MacLeod, was to inform the presbytery of Skye as to what had been decided. Before concluding the meeting also addressed a matter of morality. A Harris gentleman called 'Kenneth Hossag' had committed the 'abominable sin' of adultery for the fourth time. The presbytery found 'his present delinquency peculiarly aggravated by the circumstances of its commission in the island of St Kilda, among a simple innocent people, to the hazard of corrupting their morals, and perverting their native sentiments of honour and chastity; it being a crime till now unknown in that remote island'. A similar offence by one John MacCuish, 'said to have been committed in the island of St Kilda some time in Summer or Harvest last', was dealt with on 6 March 1788 at a presbytery meeting at Rodel. MacCuish declared he was not guilty but the presbytery did not believe him. Eventually the two offenders confessed. All this went to show that moral guidance from a missionary was necessary even in St Kilda where visits by the steward's party were not without their unexpected risks and where the 'natives' were perhaps not so innocent as was claimed.[142]

A letter from the Uist presbytery read by the SSPCK committee on 1 January 1789 announced the death of Angus MacLeod, 'late Catechist of St Kilda', and reported that his son Lachlan, who had already been officiating as catechist there, was licensed and ordained by the presbytery of Skye in consequence of a presentation to the mission by Norman MacLeod of Berneray, cousin and successor as patron of Alexander of Muiravonside, on 13 November 1788. The committee was none too sure how to respond, for Lachlan had evidently not been to Edinburgh for his examination, and it therefore adopted the usual method in such uncertain circumstances of letting the letter 'lie' while the members reminded themselves of procedure and, in this case, of the contents of the old deed of mortification with which they were less than familiar. They found that MacLeod of Berneray had indeed the right of presentation, but that the Society had the sole responsibility for trying and examining a missionary destined for St Kilda and for dismissing him if he neglected his duties. However the Society accepted Lachlan MacLeod's appointment in June 1789, by which time he had been many months in post.[143]

In spite of its long association with the island the Society's understanding of the conditions under which the missionary to St Kilda was employed seems to have become very limited and at best vague. When a letter from Lachlan MacLeod was read in October 1790, 'praying to be allowed his Salary as Missionary, for the year 1788, tho' he had not then entered upon his office, having been unavoidably prevented from doing so', it was necessary to write to Rev. John MacLeod in Harris to ascertain the facts. MacLeod, who was evidently judged by the Society to be the most responsible churchman in the presbytery and who in 1797 was thanked 'for his great attention in superintending the Society's Schools in the Western Isles', testified to the truth of Lachlan's letter, and at the beginning of 1791 the long-awaited salary payment was allowed. Lachlan MacLeod seems therefore to have been settled in St Kilda without the Society's full knowledge of what was happening.[144]

*

In November 1782 John Buchanan was appointed missionary in Harris to assist the parish minister. He was well settled not far from Tarbert when John Knox visited the island in 1786 and admired the developments begun by the proprietor, Captain Alexander MacLeod. Knox reached Scalpay and then 'sailed up East Loch Tarbert, accompanied by Mr. Buchanan, a clergyman near that place'. He then viewed the few fishermen's huts that formed the 'small village' of Tarbert, and since Buchanan had 'to marry a couple at the end of one of the bays' the visitor decided to attend both the ceremony and the dance that followed. Buchanan himself seems to have enjoyed the few opportunities available to him for entertainment, but within three years his indulgence caught him out when he became the subject of a powerful rumour which had spread throughout Harris, was 'injurious to his moral character', and undermined his standing as missionary. He was supposed to have committed 'the sin of Uncleanness' with Catharine Bain, 'a servant woman at Loskintyre in Harris'. The following summer, 1790, he was accused of 'having had carnal commerce' with a lady of Tarbert called Ann MacLeod. The presbytery listened to witnesses, noted many details, and after much discussion and many meetings dismissed the delinquent from his post on 31 December 1790.[145]

Rev. John MacLeod, a key figure in these proceedings, then turned to writing the statistical account of his parish, and John Buchanan, who considered the minister and William MacLeod, Luskentyre, whom he called 'our little tyranical country Surgeon', to be his chief enemies, set to work on his book *Travels in the Western Hebrides*, in which he sought to take his revenge by attacking the local tacksmen in general and more particularly by placing in a bad light the two men whom he saw as the leaders of the move to expel him. His prejudices call into question the reliability of his account; he goes to some length in contrasting the attitudes and actions of the tacksmen and wealthier tenants with the situation of the ordinary people who lived in poverty and suffered helplessly the hardships inflicted upon them, his aim being to show the former in as unfavourable a manner as possible.

In a chapter devoted to St Kilda Buchanan drew extensively on Martin and MacAulay for his information but did not fail to state that in contrast to supposedly less burdensome times in the past 'their present master having forgot his former insignificance, has assumed all the turbulant pride of a purse-proud pedagogue, to keep them under'. This master was presumably William MacNeil, who in the later 1760s had been employed by the SSPCK as teacher and catechist in Pabbay and then in Harris, though Buchanan referred to the landlord when he exclaimed: 'How cruel and impolitic does the heritor of this isle behave to these brave men'. As for the St Kilda minister, Lachlan MacLeod, he was inferior to the mere Harris missionary:

> 'Their clergyman is illiterate, farther than his little knowledge of the English language. At St. Kilda he studied his divinity from his father, who was a poor man that failed in his circumstances, being a farmer and mechanic in Uist, before he was clothed with the character of a minister, and was sent to officiate among those people; in which capacity he continued till his death opened the vacancy for his son, who was judged qualified to explain the English Bible into Galic'.[146]

Buchanan remarked on the salary paid to the St Kilda minister, explaining how it was composed of the MacLeod mortification - 'to be given to any name-sake, who can anwer the above purpose' - and of a contribution from the SSPCK; but 'no man of letters would be buried from the world for such a small sum'. The 'illiterate' Lachlan was doing what he could however: 'He acts up to this duty to the best of his knowledge'.[147]

Travels in the Western Hebrides contains descriptions of island conditions and customs which may be accurate enough, but perhaps the main interest of the book lies in its author's own approach to what proves to be his experience in Harris rather than his journeys, theoretical and actual, to other islands. Since he was not an impartial writer Buchanan's statements, full of insinuation, tend towards entertaining exaggeration, as in his comments on presbytery meetings which 'are for the most part held at public houses' and turn out to be 'for the most part, scenes of riot .. attended only by young people of both sexes, who delight in frolic'. Presbytery assemblies in Lewis, however, were more sober affairs for 'a greater decency of character begins to prevail here among the clergy than in the other isles'.[148]

Though there is no sign that he ever went to St Kilda himself, Buchanan wrote rather like a visitor to that island, giving a superficial description and a range of information discovered by hearsay from knowledgeable individuals he happened to meet. Not long after this book was published Lachlan

MacLeod was to encounter on the St Kilda shore the first of a long line of well-to-do visitors touring north in their sailing ships and yachts, and a new era in the history of the island had begun, brought into being perhaps by a combination of earlier works, including Martin, MacAulay and Buchanan, romantic curiosity and philanthropic interest. The islanders were to fall victim of other people's version of them and their ways, and the missionary minister was always in the front line of the reception afforded the stranger reaching the landing rock.

CHAPTER 8

'Tourist' visitors begin to arrive, Clarke, Brougham and Robert Campbell of Shawfield, all met by Rev. Lachlan Macleod, the last Macleod missionary

IN the summer of 1797 a young Sussex gentleman, Edward Daniel Clarke, set off to explore the north with the much younger Berkely Paget, son of Lord Uxbridge, to whom he was tutor and companion. Clarke was acquainted with Thomas Pennant, with whom he communicated on his forthcoming expedition, Pennant pointing out to him that there were parts of the country and particular objects which 'had either escaped his own notice, or had not been within the compass of his plan' on his own tour. Neither Pennant nor Johnson and Boswell had visited 'that range of insular territory, extending from the point of Oreby in Lewis, to Barra Head'. So at Lord Uxbridge's request a 'revenue cutter' was made available for transport in dangerous seas and letters of introduction were sent to 'the most distinguished persons in Edinburgh' who would produce essential information 'on every subject'.[149]

Clarke and Paget reached Edinburgh on 30 June and embarked on the cutter at Greenock. After a varied journey through the more southerly isles, including calls at Mull, Iona, Tiree, Coll and Rum, they reached Barra and stayed with 'the Great Macneil' on the night of 29 July. Early the next morning Clarke was summoned hastily 'as the wind was favourable for St. Kilda, and the weather extremely fine'. He was filled with excited anticipation, for he could see that 'Our long concerted project was now likely to take place, after innumerable difficulties, some real and others imaginary, which had been artfully opposed to interrupt it'. The journal which Clarke was keeping took on life and vivid enthusiasm as this ultimate goal was at last approached.

Fog and 'a very heavy rolling sea' seemed to add greatly to the height of the cliffs which loomed over the cutter. The visitors were eager to land and impatiently asked Mr Ritchy, presumably the captain, 'to order out the long boat', which he did. As the six rowers urged on the boat Mr Ritchy shot a fulmar, 'the first we had seen', and then they passed through what seems to have been the channel between the main island and Dun into the bay. 'The reader will perhaps imagine', noted Clarke, 'what my emotions were, as I approached the shore, and beheld the little colony of St. Kilda.' The people were seen, apparently in great confusion, 'some running towards the hills, others on the tops of their huts, pointing with great earnestness towards the boat'. Friendly waves from the new arrivals brought the majority quickly down to the sea's edge, and soon Clarke was ashore, making what became the conventional opening move by anyone landing in that remote 'little colony': 'I shook hands with all of them, and began to distribute my little parcels of tobacco and snuff.' What surprised him and his companions was that one of the 'natives' was 'a good-looking young man' who spoke 'in broken English' to them, asking them who they were, where they came from, and why they were in St. Kilda. 'Some of them, more advanced in years, desired our young friend, in Gaelic, to ask how we knew the name of the island to be St. Kilda.' Clarke said that he had learned it from books, at which the young man was a little astonished for he did not know of any book that mentioned the island and indeed they had no books of any kind. Clarke's authors were Martin and MacAulay, the latter being someone the people remembered from forty years previously.

As they all walked towards the houses Clarke could not resist asking the young man how he had picked up English. 'Our minister taught me', was the answer. Clarke evidently knew nothing of a minister. 'Oh, yes!' said the English-speaker, 'MacLeod is our minister; here he comes.' And there was Lachlan MacLeod, standing before the strangers.

> 'The minister, who was only distinguished from the other natives by wearing a hat, instead of a bonnet, or cap of wool, seemed full as much alarmed as the rest, and hastily inquired who we were, and whence from? Being informed, he told us a general panic had seized the people, who took us at first for French or Spaniards. And what induced them to expect either of those nations at St Kilda? said I. "Oh, it is a whim the steward puts into their heads, sir," said he, "to prevent them from going to the Long Island, as they might then enlist for soldiers, and he would lose his tenants; but he need not fear this, for they are too much attached to the island to leave it. But I was myself," continued he, "a little alarmed, thinking you might probably belong to some privateer." '

Pirate ships or privateers were a not uncommon sight in the years around 1800 and the people of St Kilda, like those of Rona who on occasions received unwelcome visitors from strange ships, had good reason to be afraid of more or less any vessel that appeared on the horizon. The steward, MacNeil, would therefore have found it easy to dominate them with threats of the French or Spaniards, yet another instance of the way in which the inhabitants of remote and isolated islands could be influenced by some knowing outsider.

The next stage of Clarke's visit was again to become established as the customary practice of yachtsmen and tourists. He asked Lachlan MacLeod to take him 'into several of their huts', just as if he were going to investigate the living conditions of an African or American tribe in the interests of science. The occupants did not much like this, being still distrustful and rather afraid, and they were upset even more when 'one of our party indiscreetly fired a gun at one of the Solan geese'. Women screamed, men gathered round the minister, 'and a general alarm once more prevailed, which was not easily dispelled'. Entry to the 'huts' was forbidden until Clarke was the only stranger left on the island, so the party went to see what the inside of Lachlan's 'hut' was like. This they found 'differed from the rest only in having two chairs, and a couple of bedsteads, and a bare earth floor, instead of a covering of peat ashes and heath' - a brief glimpse perhaps but the first look into the dwelling used by missionaries in St Kilda, possibly the very one Alexander Buchan had built long ago, and it impressed Clarke as being a poor home for a minister and his family:

> 'His wife and mother were introduced to us, who with himself and three small children, resided in that wretched abode. It is true he might be called king of the island in the absence of the tacksman, but his throne is the throne of wretchedness, and misery his court. His father preceded him in the office of minister to St Kilda, which he held during sixteen years. The present minister has been with them ten, and it is from his instructions that two or three of the inhabitants have derived a slight knowledge of English'.

The rest of the group left to rejoin the cutter and wait aboard while weather permitted for Clarke to complete his explorations. 'I remained among them alone, and with no other object than curiosity.' He was welcomed into the houses and quickly rid himself of his remaining tobacco before making a close examination of the smoke-filled interiors. Later he added to his journal a description of the people, their appearance and dress, their dogs, the haphazard nature of the 'village', and the cough and cold brought by strangers and more especially by the steward and his company. He learned that the young man who had spoken in English to him had been married only a few days earlier, just before the steward had left; 'he expressed a wish that I had been present upon the occasion', for in that case, he said, 'you would have seen the whole island dancing, and the whole island drunk'. The drink was whisky, brought in quantity by the steward, 'and, when he comes, we dance and sing merrily'. 'And don't you dance during the rest of the year?' asked Clarke. 'Not so much; when the steward comes, we dance all night, and make a fine noise altogether.'

Lachlan MacLeod confirmed that marriages were delayed until the steward's arrival, which was 'the jubilee of the year'. With him came not only 'spirituous liquors' but also 'a total change of diet', though MacLeod did not explain what this change was. He was in no doubt that 'The return of this period is the only gleam of sunshine which cheers the long and gloomy night of their miseries'. The people welcomed the sunshine ecstatically: 'they rejoice, they drink, they dance, their spirits are elevated, they become heated, they expose themselves to the humid influence of an atmosphere, constantly impregnated with fogs; their mode of diet is totally changed, and the consequence is very natural, that out of twenty-two families, the greatest part of them are afflicted with a violent cold and cough'. Clarke gave his views on the subject to the minister 'but nothing could alter his opinion', which was in effect a belief in 'the old miraculous tale' of how the smell of fresh air coming from the steward's clothes caused the cough.

The 'second sight' was accepted as a matter of course in the island as it was elsewhere. 'Even the minister was not without credulity', and Clarke was introduced by him 'to two men who were particularly visited by these appearances'. Did he wonder whether they were related to the family of Roderick the 'impostor'? Probably not. But Clarke was not inclined to believe in 'native' tradition, and so he again tried, unsuccessfully, to convince Lachlan MacLeod that there was a different explanation. However the visitor and the minister, unlike some of their successors, were each unusually tolerant in their approach to established ways of thinking different from their own, and Clarke was impressed by islanders who were apparently 'far more intelligent than I had any reason to expect'. His opinion of the minister's attitude is revealing of his own and and Lachlan's open-minded responses:

> ' .. it is not easy, neither is the task attended with any pleasing consequences, to root out old prejudices by new systems of faith, especially when the advocate on the side of reason has numbered fewer years over his head than the advocate for superstition. Their humble and unassuming pastor modestly declined the contest; placidly reminding me that former ages possessed a faculty of this kind, which no young theorist had found presumption to dispute: and ended with an assurance that in the isle of Pabba, instances of this kind had occurred, and frequently transpired even during the present day, which had neither been accounted for, nor denied. I must, however, do the minister of St. Kilda the justice to acknowledge, that to general superstition he was a declared enemy, and had neglected no means in his power which might conduce to the happiness or improvement of his people. With regard to this particular instance, his belief of second sight was not so much founded on any instance attached to St. Kilda, as on some marvellous tales he had heard, perhaps from men to whom he had looked up for instruction, respecting the island of Pabba, with whose inhabitants he had no intercourse, and whose prophets he knew only by report.'

Clarke's curiosity extended to antiquities, although in the short time he had he learned little about those on St Kilda. The minister and all the able-bodied men in the 'village' took him along to look at the remains of 'St. Brianan's chapel', then nothing more than a 'Circular pile of stones, very little larger than one of their common huts'. They pointed out 'a broad stone, on which the saint used to read mass to their ancestors', but they knew no other tradition about the place. Having mentioned the supposed 'house of the druids' on Boreray, about which he had read in the books by Martin and MacAulay, Clarke was assured by the minister that these authors were mistaken and that it was merely 'a Roman Catholic chapel, used to say mass in at no very remote period'. This was possibly one of the seven, or six, chapels of St Kilda rather than the structure in which Clarke was interested and which Martin had called 'Stallir-House' - 'it is all Green without like a little Hill, the Inhabitants there have a Tradition that it was Built by one Stallir, who was a Devout Hermit of St.Kilda; and had he Travelled the Universe he could scarcely have found a more Solitary place for a Monastick Life'. MacAulay heard a story about this underground dwelling which he called the 'greatest artificial curiosity' in St Kilda. A man called Staller was supposed to have rebelled against the steward in early times and resorted with his sixteen supporters to Boreray where he built a strange house which MacAulay described:

> 'The house is eighteen foot high, and its top lies almost level with the earth, by which it is surrounded; below it is of a circular form, and all its parts are contrived so, that a single stone covers the top - If this stone is removed, the house has a very sufficient vent. - In the middle of the floor is a large hearth. Round the wall is a paved seat, on which sixteen persons may conveniently sit. Here are four beds roofed with strong flags or stone lintels, everyone of which is capable enough to receive four men. To each of these beds is a separate entry; the distances between these different openings, resembling in some degree so many pillars'.[150]

However questionable in detail, MacAulay's description may give a generally true outline picture of the building, but the rest of his information about it is quite conjectural and there was evidently confusion as to whether Stallir's house was different from the structure described and whether one or the other was on Boreray or Soa. The problem for visitors like Clarke was the inaccessibility of the island on which the house was situated, and few apart from the islanders themselves ever saw it. Sixty-five years after Lachlan MacLeod dismissed it so casually tradition about it was still strong and associated it with the race for possession of St Kilda, in which the participants had developed into Colla Ciotach and his brother 'Gilespeig Og or Young Archibald':

> 'Coll and his brother used to war with each other. Coll resided in the Dun, and Archibald in a large house, built under ground in Boreray. The house is called Tigh a Stalair, after the name of him who built it. It was built on stone pillars, with hewn stones, which it was thought were brought from the point of the Dun. It was round inside, with the ends of

long narrow stones sticking through the walls round about, on which clothes might be hung. There were six croops or beds in the wall, one of them very large, called Rastalla; it would accommodate twenty men or more to sleep in. Next to that was another called Ralighe, which was large, but rather less than the first. Next to that were Beran and Shimidaran, lesser than Ralighe, and they would accommodate twelve men each to sleep in. Next to that was *Leaba nan Con*, or the Dog's bed, and next to that was Leaba an tealich, or the Fireside bed. There was an entrance [passage] within the wall round about, by which they might go from one croop to another without coming into the central chamber. The house was not to be noticed outside, except a small hole on the top of it, to allow the smoke to get out and to let in some light. There was a doorway on one side (where they had to bend to get in and out) facing the sea, and a large hill of ashes a little way from the door which would not allow the wind to come in. Bar Righ was the name of the door. The present inhabitants of St Kilda [c1860], when in Boreray fowling, or hunting sheep to pull the wool off them, … used to live in the house until about twenty years ago, when the roof fell in. Some of the croops are partly to be seen yet'.[151]

There may be a touch of myth, exaggeration and even invention about 'Tigh a Stalair' but, like the visible remains of the dwellings on Rona and of the wall on the eastern slope of Biraslum by Vatersay, it calls to the imagination with its hewn stones and its mysterious names. And from its floor, as from the floor of Teampall Sula Sgeir, a shaft was said to descend through rock to the sea far below.

The pattern for tourist visits in the late nineteenth century, already set in part by the distribution of tobacco and other gifts and by investigation of the houses, reached its third and final stage when Clarke walked along the cliff edges and shot 'an Ailsa cock' - possibly a puffin. Immediately an islander went down the cliff and retrieved the wounded bird, much to Clarke's amazement. The shot amazed the people who 'began to caper and dance, talking with great earnestness to one another, and making signs as if they were shooting themselves, looking all the while as wild as a party of Indians. I more than ever regretted that I had not brought a few fireworks'. Clarke contemplated launching a small balloon but lacked the time, so Lachlan MacLeod told the people about it and they were very eager to see what promised to be 'a fine contrivance .. to take their birds from the rocks'. Within a few minutes, however, the visitor, who wanted to spend the night on the island, was being treated to a display of fowling on the highest cliffs. It was the climax of his own and of the future tourist's St Kilda adventure.

As previously arranged a gun was fired to summon Clarke back from the hill and call him on board. The island men were again alarmed by the noise, the women fled from their houses, and Clarke tried to calm everybody. He refused to obey the instructions from the cutter, sending a message that he was determined to stay ashore. When his decision was made known the people rejoiced; 'they kissed my hands, running sometimes before, and sometimes after me, saying, "Come, we dance and sing; you eat and drink!" ', and they all entered the minister's 'hut' where 'some of the oldest and most respectable of the inhabitants, assisted by the minister as interpreter, thus opened the history of their grievances'.

Unfortunately at this point the journal extract stops and the grievances remain unknown. It resumes with remarks on the birds of Borera and the towering rocks beside it. Edward Daniel Clarke and his party had left St Kilda, sailing north east towards Lewis and making out the Flannans on their way to Loch Roag and the Butt.

*

Earlier in the summer of 1797 the moderator of the presbytery of Skye, William Bethune, wrote to the SSPCK to ask that Lachlan MacLeod should have his salary increased, but an excuse was found in the terms of the old mortification and the application was refused.[152] So long as he was carrying out his duties the Society showed little interest in the St Kilda minister and his circumstances in the island, so that the only variations to normal routine were provided by the occasional unexpected visitor of the Clarke kind. One such event occurred in August 1799 when an expedition intending to go to Iceland organised by John Joseph Henry, 'an excellent and enterprising man of large fortune in Ireland', ran out of time when in the Hebrides and treated St Kilda as if it were the true purpose of the voyage. On reaching Stornoway on 14 August Henry Lord Brougham, one of the party, wrote in a letter of how the St Kilda 'natives' mistook their ship for a French privateer and were about to retreat into the hills when the ship's boat reached the shore and eventually reassured them. Then two boats came out, 'one belonging to the place and ours besides, but both manned by savages'. Alarmed by this the visitors prepared to defend themselves, but they soon discovered that these 'natives' were friendly and were led by 'their priests, without whom nothing would induce them to venture near us'. They gave Lachlan MacLeod a drink on board, finding 'him and his compatriots in a state of ignorance truly singular'. Nothing was known of the war with France, though news of it could have been brought to them by the steward who now came twice a year; 'but we were told that he carefully conceals every event from them .. in order to keep up their alarms, which, we found, he turns to good account'. The simplicity of the 'savages' amused Brougham and his friends who concluded that the people of St Kilda could be easily led to believe more or less anything and that they already lived in dread of an invasion.[153]

After the rowers had been promised a dram 'the song arose, extempore in composition and far from unmusical in execution', and soon the ten explorers were landed safely. They were led along to 'the town' where they entered the minister's house: 'A more wretched hovel never sheltered beast from the storm than this; and yet it is the only thing tenantable in the island, except the tacksman's'. There they met Lachlan's wife and mother, and then Brougham and some others, with their provisions, made for 'the other house' and on the way were 'surrounded by many of the savages'. This was not surprising, as 'I always make a point', said Brougham 'of landing in full uniform', and 'command over the stores and servants gives me vast dignity and patronage'. He then carried out the expected distribution to each 'native' of 'a ration of tobacco and a dram - their two greatest prizes, though neither had been in the island for two and a half years' - presumably when Clarke came with his gifts. 'We then drank tea and fine milk till three in the morning', when most of the party went to sleep, but Brougham 'sat up with the clergyman, whom I instantly put under the question, and talked over on all topics (insular ones) till near five o'clock, when we sallied forth to view the island in four different parties, the priest with us'.

They looked with curiosity on the 'village'. 'Nothing in Captain Cook's voyages comes half so low. The natives are savage in due proportion; the air is infected by a stench almost insupportable - a compound of rotten fish, filth of all sorts, and stinking sea-fowl'. They saw clothes, brooches, ropes, fish-hooks and other articles, thought the thread and horn spoons 'infinitely coarser and more clumsy, and made in smaller quantity and less variety, than those which navigators have found in any of the Pacific islands, New Holland in the south excepted'. The marks of poverty and the natural inability of the islander to understand the language and the behaviour of the condescending strangers were interpreted by Brougham as evidence of the primitive savagery which he had expected, if not hoped, to find: 'A total want of curiosity, a stupid gaze of wonder, an excessive eagerness for spirits and tobacco, a laziness only to be conquered by the hope of the above-mentioned cordials, and a beastly degree of filth, the natural consequences of this, render the St Kildian character truly savage.' They showed too, so the visitors thought, 'the leading trait of furtivity of disposition', which was manifested in their readiness to remove anything that the party left lying around. Brougham lost his 'boat-cloak' for a while but on going into 'the suspected house' and waving his drawn sword he retrieved it. 'The only mortals among the present inhabitants whom we found in any degree civilised above the brutes, were the priest and his family', but Brougham had no sympathy for the minister's financial ambitions as he told Lord Robertson: 'If in the course of your calls you ever see Mr Kemp (who corresponds with him once in an olympiad), pray give Mr Lachlan McLeod's respects to him, and tell him that he complains grievously of his short allowance. This will make me quit of my promise to him; - to say the truth, I think he has quite enough, unless that it requires some bribe to keep a man in St Kilda'.

The strangers enjoyed 'a cheerful breakfast', and heard divine service 'performed audibly and fluently by our host in his kitchen, his only church … The savages stood round and the priest performed in a corner. He read, sang, and spoke in Gaelic'. However unsympathetic, this description of a service in St Kilda seems to be the first since Alexander Buchan reported his activities in his letters, and it would appear that none of the ancient churches was still capable of being put to use for meetings of any kind. At this point, however, Brougham's own version of the event ceased. Further detail was recorded in an account by another member of the group, apparently Robert Campbell of Shawfield, who wrote at greater length but in an equally unpleasant and pretentious tone not only of the service but also of St Kilda in general.

> 'About 8 o'clock next morning we all assembled in the Parson's kitchen to breakfast upon the provisions brought from the ship, for, alas! the Parson's larder could not have furnished a meal for one half of the party…

> 'This being sunday, immediately after breakfast the Bellman, if he may be so called, was sent to summon the inhabitants to church, which he did by retiring to the end of the house, and emitting a kind of a piercing howl, which he had borrowed from some of the seals which frequent the neighbouring rocks. In a few minutes the whole congregation was assembled in the Parson's kitchen, men, women and Children. The parson himself was seated upon a large bag of feathers, with a barrel of oil before him by way of reading desk - the psalm being read out, the whole party proceeded to sing it, accompanying it with every species of gesticulation and grimace, the melody was not a little heightened by the snoring of some of the party, which enraged the Bell man so much, that getting up, he struck one of them over the back with a species of boat hook, which he carried by way of mace or badge of Office. With this exception the whole of the service was conducted with the utmost decency'.[154]

Campbell had landed in Glen Mor where he met half a dozen of the 'natives', among them Lachlan MacLeod, who was distinguishable from the rest by his ability to speak English and by the largeness of his beard. When they reached the 'cluster of bee-hives' which passed for the 'village' the minister went home and changed into 'as decent a set of canonicals as ever graced an episcopal pulpit'. Campbell himself and five islanders went off in the ship's 'jolly boat' to collect the rest of the visitors, while those already ashore began to explore the island. On returning from their tour they saw near the 'village' on the west side 'the ruins of an ancient church dedicated to Christ … where they still continue to bury their dead, altho' it has long been abandoned as a place of worship'. And to add to the solemnity of that first evening, with its cries of seabirds, wave roar along the beach, and sunset light, they discovered all the island women gathered at the end of the minister's house and gazing out to sea: 'They spoke not, they moved not, they looked not around; but ever and anon shaking their heads, they emitted a species of half formed musical note, which, even while we did not understand, inspired a kind of melancholy sensation.' What were they doing? 'We enquired of Mrs. McLeod the cause of this extraordinary appearance, which she informed us was in consequence of the long delay of the boats, and that the women whose fathers and husbands were gone off to the vessell, fearing they would never return, were now listening for their groans in the air, which they declare they always hear, previous to the death of any of the islanders.'

Those of the visitors already on the island reassured the women, gave them some presents, and later on proposed a dance:

'We accordingly all retired to the Steward's house, as being the largest in the island, where we soon mustered to the number of about Sixty, of which only four besides ourselves were of the male sex. These kinds of meetings are what constitute their chief happiness - there seated in a large circle, they listen to the tale of other times recited by some of their number, the few luxuries they possess are handed round, and for some moments they forget the niggard hand of providence, and the barbarous oppression of an unfeeling master'.

In the absence of a musical instrument now, 'they are in the habit of dancing to their own voices, the whole assembly joining in chorus during the time of reeling', and an instance of this took place at the very beginning when eight women danced 'a sort of Cotillon, singing at the same time', while all the other women joined in the song at intervals, their men enlivening the whole by a species of extatic yelp, which added spirit if not harmony'. Campbell, Brougham and company took part in the dancing, and 'Between the different dances, the women sung us a number of songs, the subjects of which … are in general elegiac; but as they also make a point of commemorating the arrival and manners of every stranger that visits …, we looked forward with pleasure to the hopes of being handed down to posterity in the artless verses of these children of nature'. The dance coming to an end after midnight with no appearance of the men, everyone retired to the houses, but it was not long before it was found that 'about twenty of the male savages', together with the remainder of the visitors, had taken over the steward's house and were reviewing the dangers they had survived in reaching land.

The service in the minister's kitchen was brought to an abrupt close by the firing of a gun on the ship as a signal to depart:

'so bidding adieu to these hospitable islanders, we proceeded to the shore, in order to launch one of their boats, which after a considerable degree of difficulty we accomplished. We then all got into her and after a most severe pull of two leagues, the sea running very high, we reached the brig, when we found our worthy captain in a state little short of insanity on account of our long delay. The Parson had intended to stay aboard of us for some time, but the wind blowing fresh of[f] shore, which rendered their return very precarious, he was obliged to put off, when filling our sails, we bad a long adieu to the weather-beaten cliffs of St Kilda.'

CHAPTER 9

The close of Lachlan Macleod's life in St Kilda

CAPTAIN Alexander MacLeod, proprietor of the Harris estate including St Kilda, is said to have died in 1790. He was succeeded by his son Alexander who was first known as Alexander MacLeod and later, using his mother's surname, as Alexander Hume. For much of his time he was an absentee laird and in 1804 he sold St Kilda to Lt. Col. Donald MacLeod of Auchagoyle, understood to be a son of Alexander MacLeod, missionary to St Kilda in the 1740s, and his wife Barbara MacPherson. In 1811 Colonel Donald was said to be 'in every sense of the word a blessing to the inhabitants', having reduced, perhaps by suspending the tacksman system, the oppressive demands for rent, and having given 'two stout boats' to assist the islanders in making a living. Further help in this line was expected from 'A young man of knowledge and enterprise from Edinburgh', an anonymous and rather mysterious figure, who 'has taken a part of the lands in lease, and bound himself to build a good house, and to improve the island in various ways, especially by teaching the inhabitants the best mode of turning to account the staple production of the place, which is wild fowls and their feathers or down'. This young man may have been Colonel Donald's son, John MacPherson MacLeod, who followed his father as owner, but his proposed improvements do not seem to have materialised.[155]

In the Scots Magazine and Edinburgh Literary Magazine for December 1814 there appeared an article by Lt. Col. Donald MacLeod, who had died the previous year. It was entitled 'Notices on the Present State of St Kilda' and described the product of seabird feathers, as if taking up the young man's idea. Of the feathers 140 stones now composed 'the only rent' received by the proprietor. The great number of birds, many of which 'may be cured and used as a nourishing and savoury diet, upon the main land of Britain', suggested that the fish stocks nearby must also be abundant and that fishing could be very rewarding. As it was 'The Islanders sitting on the rocks with the most clumsy tackle, catch cod, sea carpe, lythe, or darkwhelen, all of a large size, as well as various other kinds of fish'. However, Donald being dead, any commercial value in birds and fish would have to be discovered and exploited by his son.[156]

So far as the missionary minister in St Kilda was concerned the change of ownership made little difference and his situation did not greatly improve. He was still living in very poor conditions and using his kitchen as a meeting place. He received his salary of £25 for the period of 1 May 1800 to 1 May 1801 rather later in the latter year because the SSPCK declined to allow payment until the directors authorised it since 'the attestation of Service bore that Mr McLeod had been absent from the beginning of June to the latter end of April owing to his being obliged to go to Inverness to establish his Wife's titles to some lands in the West Indies which was not got accomplished till September when the Season did not permit him to have access to the Island'. The directors, 'without meaning to give any Indulgence to Absentees from their duties and Stations', accepted that in this case there were special circumstances and consented to payment. Probably they did not realise that Lachlan Macleod was already reluctant to spend winters on the island.[157]

The matter of property in the West Indies was evidently tidied up successfully, for in 1811 Lachlan and his wife came to an agreement with Neil MacLeod of Gesto, to whom the minister was quite closely related. Neil directed an offer of £200 sterling to 'Mr Lauch[l]an McLeod Missionary Minister of St Kilda and his wife Marion MacLeod alias MacLean', for certain possessions:

[Dear Sir]

'Your joint letter of this date [8 November 1811] offering me, the Estates and Property left to Marion MacLeod alias McLean one of you, and Spouse of the other by the last will and testament of her deceased brother Alexander MacLean of the Bahama Islands, with all the Produce of Said Estate, and slaves therein or belonging to the said Alexander MacLean at the time of his death, with the Buildings etc.'[158]

It seems to be a fact therefore, however curious, that for a few years the minister in St Kilda, through his wife, was an owner of slaves in the Bahamas.

Lachlan MacLeod also had other interests which took him away from his island 'Station'. In September 1803 the SSPCK heard from him that he had felt obliged to leave St Kilda and go to Harris with his family for the winter 'on account of want of feuel and a scarcity of provisions'. Unable to return before the spring of the following year he nevertheless resolved to do so then, 'when a better prospect of living may open'. Along with his letter came one from John MacLeod, minister of Harris, who referred to 'his belief of the good reason Mr Lachlan MacLeod had for leaving St Kilda'. The Society directors told their secretary to write to Lachlan asking him to come to Edinburgh for the winter and there attend 'the Divinity hall' and such other classes as he might think suitable for his 'improvement', his salary being allowed him along with some extra funds to pay for his accommodation in the city. But apparently Lachlan did not like the idea of going to Edinburgh and some weeks later wrote 'apologizing for not complying with the desire of the directors ... on account of bad health'. Again the Harris minister supported the excuse, which the directors accepted, but not long afterwards changed his mind and on 2 December 1803 wrote of the presbytery's annoyance at Lachlan's absence, particularly as it appeared that he had another job:

'As to the Minister of St Kilda I have neither seen nor heard anything of him. Our intention in sending for him is certainly good and I would willingly hope that his being here if he does come will not be to inflame his vanity as you suspect but rather the reverse - to convince him how little he knows - how much he had to learn and to put him upon a plan of improvement - but the Session is advancing fast and if he does not make haste he will lose much of the benefit that may result from his coming. I am very doubtful how far we shall be vindicated to ourselves for allowing him his salary while he is employed in a different part of the country and in an employment quite distinct from that to which he ought to devote himself in the Service of the Society. Surely he does not get a salary for teaching a School in Sky. This will attract the Attention of the Directors who are by no means satisfied with the reasons of absence from his charge which he assigns. If the people want food in winter they will probably labour under a still greater scarcity in the spring. Had he come here in order to his improvement and acquiring a greater fitness for his duty the apology of absence might on that account have been sustained - but as to teaching a school in Skye I fear there will be a difficulty in finding it a good one'.[159]

When the spring of 1804 arrived Lachlan MacLeod sought payment of his salary to enable him and his family to go back to the island they said they had been forced to leave 'on account of the scarcity of provisions', and a sum due to 1 November 1803 but withheld was to be paid 'with certification that if he does not now return to his Charge no more salary shall be paid him'. Nothing was said about how the islanders fared when 'provisions' were scarce.[160]

Lt. Col. Donald MacLeod was not only proprietor of St Kilda; he was also a member of the SSPCK and as such had an interest in Lachlan MacLeod's religious if not material welfare. In 1807 he reported that the missionary was 'extremely ill provided with books and cannot afford to purchase them', so he suggested that a sum be made available for the purchase of a book supply, and since this was considered 'an useful and important object' there was no difficulty in finding the money. The SSPCK secretary was given the task of buying the books, and when some had been acquired they were sent out to St Kilda, it having been decided to add the rest later. Rather more than half of the assigned £25, a year's salary for the minister, was spent on forty serious and solemn works which, like their predecessors in the St Kilda 'library', cannot have had much appeal to the minister and little if any at all to the island people. Within the next three years Lachlan MacLeod was pleased to receive at least two special allowances of £5 each to help him through 'difficulties', and the proprietor, who offered £10 a year if the Society would add £25, assisted in securing the welcome addition of the £5 instalments to a salary that had not changed for generations. From the present state of its funds the Society claimed that it could not contribute an extra £25.[161]

In spite of these small benefits Lachlan MacLeod was growing weary of his St Kilda charge and not just in winter. Late in 1811 he wrote 'complaining much of the people of that Island' and 'stating that he had come with his family to the Island of Skye' once more. Having spent, on and off, over twenty years in St Kilda as catechist, minister and teacher, and perhaps an even greater proportion of his lifetime, he clearly needed a change of scene and offered 'various applications and proposals' to the Society directors. On 5 August 1812 he wrote again, from Dunvegan, but the directors were not pleased with him. They 'disapprove highly of Mr McLeods having left his charge without permission' and ordered him to return immediately without any allowance for expenses. However, since 'Mr McLeod may have grounds of complaint from the bad state of his house, and the inattention of the people of the Island to his comfort', the Society agreed to apply to the proprietor for his assistance in 'putting the Mission house in a proper state of repair'. He was also asked 'to use his influence with his Tenants to perform the services incumbent on them, and in general to do what they can to render Mr McLeod's situation as comfortable as possible'. For his part, Lachlan MacLeod was told 'to use his best endeavours in every proper way, and especially by fidelity and diligence in the discharge of his duty as minister, to cultivate a good understanding with the people of his charge'. To give his 'wretched hovel' as grand a name as 'the Mission house' hints at the growing, though familiar, inadequacy of the Society's management of the St Kilda mission, and the indications of differences, or at least failings, in the relationship between minister and people, reminiscent of Buchan's years, may reflect the wider neglect of a community's welfare, of which the established church now stood often accused, as well as the lack of attention paid to the struggle for survival which was a constant aspect of existence on St Kilda. These circumstances may suggest that, so far as religion and education were concerned, in St Kilda as elsewhere there was scope for a new, more devoted missionary of an evangelical persuasion.[162]

His absences meant that Lachlan missed a number of interesting visitors to the island. In the summer of 1800 a visitor who may have been Sir George MacKenzie of Coul came away with a collection of songs which he put in the hands of 'an excellent Gaelic scholar', Rev. Alexander Campbell of Portree. They had apparently been gathered together by Lachlan MacLeod himself, as another writer recorded:

'It is a singular fact, that in the Island of St Kilda, the women are the only composers of poetry, and few of them are incapable of relating their joys and sorrows in a species of verse, which is far from being rude. I saw, in the possession of Mr Campbell of Sky, two MS volumes, one of 80 and the other of 70 pages, containing entirely these songs, collected by the present Missionary of St Kilda. Many of them were very difficult to be read, from the inaccurate orthography of the transcriber, whose knowledge of the language was but imperfect'.

Remarks were made on four of the songs. There were two elegies, one by Christian Campbell, 'a young Woman, whose Husband, soon after their Marriage, fell over a Rock and was Drowned', the other by Rachel Maciver, 'a Widow, on the melancholy occasion of her only Son's being lost in the Isle of Soay'. The other two songs were believed to have been composed only a short while before the visit in 1800, one of them, 'a Love Song', by Marion Gillies of St Kilda, being an outcome of the presence on the island in 1799 of Brougham and company and, in particular, Robert Campbell. The remaining song was a lament, 'composed by a disconsolate Father, from under whose foot, while catching Solan Geese, along with his two sons, a piece of rock gave way, and killed one of them'.[163]

During 1812, when the minister was in Skye, more strangers arrived. The wealthy Sir Thomas Acland and his wife Lydia came from Devon, the latter being supposed the first female visitor ever to land on the island. Though spending only a short time there Sir Thomas 'was shocked by the islanders' poverty, and spoke earnestly with them before sketching their wretched huddle of thatched huts .., and returning to his boat with a firm promise to come again'. How he 'spoke earnestly with them' without a knowledge of Gaelic is a mystery, but perhaps one or two of the people could manage a conversation in English. In the same year there landed someone with an interest in geology who, eighteen years later, supplied an article on St Kilda to the Edinburgh Encyclopaedia. By that time he had lost his rock specimens, but he had evidently acquired some useful information about the island. There were at the time of his visit 24 families, containing 40 males and 57 females. The missionary placed there by the SSPCK was 'instructed to act also as schoolmaster, although it is feared, the natives are not much troubled with his lessons'. Even so, the inhabitants had distinctive qualities:

'The people of St. Kilda never connect themselves by marriage with those of the Long Island; and few of them ever leave their native spot even for a short time. They seem to be endowed with talent for music and poetry; many of them, both men and women, composing songs with great facility, and exhibiting imaginations of no despicable cast. When they dance, all the party sing; and the tune goes round, every one singing a portion and stopping, while the next takes it up instantly where the other left off. This has a singular effect; but it appears greatly to enliven the dance'.[164]

*

Lachlan MacLeod did not return to St Kilda in 1812, and he could always claim that nothing had been done to make his house habitable. On 26 December he requested permission to remain in Skye through the winter until March or April 1813, and to be allowed some additional financial help. Although Rev. MacDonald, moderator of the presbytery of Skye at the time, had earlier sent a letter possibly explaining Lachlan's presence, the Society was only too aware that he had left his mission without asking or obtaining leave and without saying what he was intending to do, so his request met with a refusal. But the determined missionary remained in Skye and in February 1813 wished to know whether anything had yet been done to make 'the Mission house' comfortable enough to live in. He also stated that he and his family could not continue to live on an inadequate salary. There were risks involved for either side when an increase was considered. On the one hand the minister might achieve nothing but greater hostility towards him among members of the Society's committee. On the other the Society, which could use the threat of no increase, or possibly no salary at all, to silence a pestering applicant and even to get rid of him, had to bear in mind that there might be genuine reasons for allowing an increase and that if a minister did indeed leave as a consequence of refusal there might be no one willing to replace him. On this occasion Lachlan MacLeod, now perhaps aged around fifty, was allowed £10 as a temporary measure, while the Society secretary was to inform the Skye presbytery that it should urge him to reside 'on his Mission', otherwise he would get no salary.[165]

The next few years were no less irregular when it came to the minister's presence on the island. Receipts for the latest half-year's pay and a temporary supply of £10 were sent by Lachlan's son Angus in late November 1814, when the SSPCK took the opportunity to note that grants of such 'supply' on two previous occasions 'with a view to relieve the pressures under which he then laboured' were not to be treated as if they were the first of more to follow. But, 'in respect of the necessities of Mr McLeods family still stated to be urgent and the extreme inconvenience which in his remote situation might possibly result from refusing payment', the Society authorised an 'indulgence' of £10 and declared that it was not to be granted in future. Each claim for salary had henceforward to be accompanied by a 'certificate of service'. The remark by MacCulloch that in 1815 the minister's salary stood at £35 is misleading in that it implies a salary increase instead of a temporary 'indulgence'.[166]

In fact MacCulloch's account of his visit to St Kilda at midsummer 1815 is neither very accurate nor much of an improvement on the unsympathetic descriptions by Brougham and Campbell. All three adopted the manner of a superior and educated tourist from the civilised world come to investigate an extraordinary, primitive community living within the bounds of Britain. The manner has persisted, as apparent in attitudes towards the church as in views of ordinary everyday work. Interspersed among the facetious remarks and irrelevant generalisations, however, MacCulloch provided observations of some value.

'On approaching the landing place', he wrote, 'where a crowd of people was ready to receive us, a tall and matron-like female figure advanced before the rest, with an air of mixed dignity and command, hailing us with the words "Friends or enemies".' This was evidently Marion MacLean, the minister's wife, whose courage 'We could not but admire' since she apparently took the visitors for hostile Americans. Once accepted as 'friend' MacCulloch, followed 'by all the male population down to the age of six', made his way towards Conachair, which he climbed in order to find out the height of the island's highest point. He also walked to other places of interest and collected odd pieces of information. Of three chapels 'extant in Martin's time' he learned that 'the very obscure traces of two still remain', but there was no church and the people now had 'to worship in their storehouse', which will have been better adapted for the purpose than the minister's kitchen. Though his wife, without children, was present, Mr Lachlan was once again away from his charge, and MacCulloch found his absence 'a serious impediment to my political enquiries'.

There was no school, 'and not one of the inhabitants could read'. This may have been an exaggeration, but the observation confirms the impression that since about 1740 the SSPCK's contribution to the missionary's salary had not been specifically aimed at rewarding his role as teacher. Evidently some effort was made by Lachlan and probably his predecessors to maintain a very basic form of education, but none of them seems to have suppressed popular traditions and superstitions or tried to restrain or prevent the resurgence of religious beliefs and practices that had prevailed before Alexander Buchan sought to control them. But MacCulloch discovered that superstitions and songs were not forthcoming. 'All the world has heard', he said, 'of St. Kilda music and St. Kilda poetry, just as all the world has heard of the musical and poetical genius of the Highlanders, of this land of poetry, and spirit of poetry, and poetic imagination ..' In St Kilda, however, he heard neither music nor song, and superstitions were not available for the asking; the islanders were not prepared to perform on demand to satisfy idle curiosity.

After noticing some features of the old settlement MacCulloch and his friends made for the shore: 'the boat was launched down the rock as it had been drawn up; and, with the cheers of the whole island, we embarked to plough once more the deep'. They sailed away through the brief June night past Boreray and into a calm Sabbath day, so calm that MacCulloch was 'obliged to take to the boat and to row for the Flannan islands', on which he landed. On board or in the years that followed he had time enough to invent an entirely unreal image of life on St Kilda which became a popular concept among those who had never been to the island or any other of the smaller Hebrides:

'it is delightful to find one green place in this dreary world of islands where want is unknown. I trust that St.Kilda may long yet continue the Eden of the Western Ocean. It is a state of real opulence. Their arable land supplies the people with corn, their birds with game, and their cattle with milk …

'If this island is not the Utopia so long sought, where will it be found. Where is the land which has neither arms, money, law, physic, politics, nor taxes; that land is St. Kilda …

'Well may the pampered native of the happy Hirta refuse to change his situation. His slumbers are late, his labours are light, and his occupation is his amusement, since his sea fowl constitute, at once, his food, his luxury, his game, his wealth, and his bed of down. Government he has not, law he feels not, physic he wants not … His climate is mild and his island is green; and … the stranger who might corrupt him shuns its shores. If happiness is not a dweller in St.Kilda, where shall it be sought'.

Of course St Kilda had no experience of 'real opulence' and was used to taxes of a kind. It had been governed by special laws. Its climate was one of salt winds and violent storms, and the 'sea fowl' had to be captured at extreme risk to life. It might well have seemed that 'the spirit of romance appears still to dwell in the clouds and storms that separate this narrow spot from the world'; but MacCulloch was nearer the mark in saying that 'it vanishes at the rude touch of investigation'. And the corrupting stranger had already reached that 'remote and solitary' island shore more than once.

*

Lachlan MacLeod, like other missionaries in St Kilda, was not the only regular absentee among the SSPCK's employees. The problem extended from one side of Scotland to the other. In 1817 the parish minister of Harris, Alexander Bethune, complained that Alexander Ross, catechist there, was not residing on the island, although a few months later he did appear and was 'officiating in his Station'. Ross's case was that because of 'the backwardness of the Heritors to provide the requisite accommodations' he had been unable to move his family to live in Harris and so he himself made regular visits, once or twice a year, and remained there three or four months at a time. He lived near Beauly, which, though on the east coast not far from Inverness, enabled him to reach Harris more easily than he could from Assynt.[167]

Lachlan spent the autumn and winter of 1817 in Harris. Comments about him and meetings with him during these months were recorded quite frequently by William MacGillivray who was staying with his uncle at

Northton in Harris and kept a journal from August 1817 to April 1818. 'The only company we have had of late', wrote MacGillivray on 1 September 1817, 'was Master Lachlan Macleod, Minister of Hirta - a pleasantish, flattering, weak man - much addicted to drinking, and Mr Degraves, a smart little Englishman who has undertaken to secure the Northtown sands'. In the case of 'Master Lachlan', he added later, the title was little more than amusing, for 'Master' was properly attached to qualified parish ministers whereas 'Lachlan is no regularly reared clergyman, but a sort of holy lecturer and catechist'. He went on to describe the missionary in some detail:

> 'He has left St Kilda for want of accomodations in a domiciliary way, and does not intend to return till these be furnished. His salary however appears to be regularly paid. He is a short robusteous fellow with a black coat and white wig, plays a little on the fiddle, violin I mean, not the Scottish fiddle, though perchance he may occasionally, i.e. by way of amusement take a scrape of it with a long bow, keeping time with his mouth, and prolonging and dulcifying the conclusory notes of each stave with a spirited exhalation or rather efflation through the nostrils, very much like the grunting of a hog. Master Lachlan takes snuff also, smokes tobacco, and he would leave not "the devil a drop" - albeit, nevertheless, furthermore, also, as Donald McKenzie says, he is not a bad fellow, though apparently a weak man.'

While in Harris Lachlan lived at Strond, to which place MacGillivray went one day in November 1817 'and procured some sermon books from Master Lachlan's wife'. From time to time the missionary preached at services in the parish church at Scarista and told stories about St Kilda, not all of which were to be believed without question.[168]

Norman MacLeod of Berneray, who had succeeded his cousin Alexander MacLeod of Muiravonside as patron of St Kilda, died in 1803 and was himself succeeded by his nephew Alexander Hume, owner of Harris, so that for a while the landlord of Harris was the presenter of ministers to St Kilda if such changes occurred. For most of the period after 1803 until the sale of Harris in 1834, there were no changes, but by 1817 Alexander Hume's estate had been inherited by his son Alexander Norman MacLeod, and it was to him that Lachlan MacLeod wrote at this time stating 'the extreme hardships his family had sustained from the circumstances which he details'. Contacting the SSPCK Alexander Norman proposed that he would, as successor to the patronage of St Kilda held formerly by the MacLeods of Muiravonside, 'convey to the Society the right of Nomination to the Mission'. This he hoped would help to introduce a means whereby the Society would find it possible to relieve the missionary of some of his hardships. The idea needed some thought and so inevitably a small subcommittee was formed.[169]

At its meeting on 6 August 1818 the Society had before it a receipt for £7 from Lachlan MacLeod, 'to defray the expence of freight of a vessel for carrying his family from Skye to St Kilda'. Although complaints from the missionary had been received earlier in the year, the SSPCK directors had no hesitation in paying, being 'Impressed with the hardship sustained by the Missionary at St Kilda', and instead of expressing disapproval of him turned their attention to the offer made by MacLeod of Harris. They 'resolved that if a satisfactory conveyance of the right of nomination to the Mission shall be granted to the Society … they will make a more suitable provision for the Missionary than he at present enjoys'. In effect the offer meant that if accepted the Society would have total control over the appointment of a missionary and over the financial resources, including the old mortification, from which he would be paid.[170]

The state of the St Kilda mission was reviewed in 1819, and a draft form of the patronage conveyance was approved. In the summer Lachlan MacLeod again left the island and came to Portree, from which he submitted a further application for financial assistance which was considered in December of that year. The application proved to be a turning point in Lachlan's career. On 11 July 1820 it was given due and full discussion by the SSPCK directors who were convinced from information that had reached them at various times 'that Mr McLeod has for a long time been extremely inefficient in that station; and therefore judge that in order to prepare the way for an arrangement more calculated to improve the Inhabitants of that Island, it would be proper to place Mr McLeod on the superannuated List, to retain his present salary of £25, on condition that he shall remove himself and family from the Island and that his receipt of Salary shall always be accompanied with a certificate of character from the Minister of the Parish in which he resides'. This proposal was to be put to Lachlan and should he agree the directors 'will afterwards judge of the measures that may be most expedient for affording a useful Missionary or Catechist to the Island of St Kilda'. Nothing would be done however until negotiation concerning patronage was concluded.[171]

Unaware at first of what was being planned for him Lachlan MacLeod repeated complaints about his situation. To some extent these were justifiable, as his house was scarcely habitable, there was no proper place for either religious worship or for teaching, and necessities of everyday existence such as fuel and food were often inadequate. But his position was soon made clear to him. The SSPCK secretary wrote on 2 March 1821 to indicate the terms of the proposal and Lachlan replied, expressing his willingness to resign 'as soon as he is put in possession of a deed securing his present salary for life in a formal way'. He also sent a receipt for £7 to cover the expense of his 'freight' back from St Kilda to Skye. The Society agreed to give him 'a satisfactory document' as soon as he submitted his resignation properly, and before future payments of salary certificates of service would have to be provided by the presbytery of Uist, to which the secretary had already written with details of how Lachlan was 'to retire with his present Salary of £25 for life and to reside wherever he might choose'. The presbytery was pleased to cooperate 'in any measure proposed to ameliorate the moral and Religious instruction of the inhabitants of St Kilda'.[172]

It was just over a year before Lachlan Macleod sent in his formal resignation as requested. Previously he had written enclosing a certificate in his favour from several inhabitants of the island and expressing his willingness to return to St Kilda if so desired. He then received the assurance he wished regarding his salary, and on 19 March 1822 at Rodel he committed himself at last to leaving his lonely station for ever: 'I have taken your proposal into my most serious consideration, and as I have the fullest reliance on your honour and the good faith of the Society, I now resign my charge as Missionary Minister of St Kilda into your hands and do hereby accept of the terms offered to me in your letter of 2nd of March 1821'. The directors of the Society were 'highly gratified with this unqualified resignation' and undertook to pay the £7 for a passage from St Kilda to Harris as well as to continue the salary. Thus ended forty years of work, intermittent at times, in the Society's remotest station.[173]

The choice of residence for his retirement may have been 'the house of Roderick MacGillivary, farmer at Baile in the Island of Berneray'. Once or twice the Society heard from him. Towards the end of 1822 he wrote to say that 'most of the books furnished by the Society for the benefit of the inhabitants of St Kilda were entirely destroyed by the dampness of the house which contained them'. Receipts or enquiries relating to salary instalments were sent regularly, but on 12 April 1832 Rev. Roderick MacLean of South Uist pursued the subject on his behalf, and on 29 August of the same year Rev. Finlay Macrae reported from North Uist that Lachlan MacLeod, formerly missionary at St Kilda, had died on 23 August, and that the remaining half-year's salary should be paid to Alexander McCuish to whom Lachlan had given the receipt now enclosed. There was also a letter from Roderick MacGillivray at Berneray announcing the same news and asking that the salary due should be paid to him as Lachlan was lodging in his house at the time of his death and that he had been at the expense of the funeral. The SSPCK judged that payment of funeral expenses constituted a prior claim and asked for an account to be sent so that reimbursement up to the amount of the salary due could be made. Any balance of salary left over could be argued over between the claimants provided no other creditor appeared. Finlay Macrae responded by asking that the salary sum should be sent to him for division between McCuish and MacGillivray, but the Society said the funeral cost must be met first of all. MacGillivray stated that the expenses amounted to £14.18s, the whole of which, though more than the half year's salary, he wished to receive. He was told that he was not the only person making a claim and as the expenses given in his letter seemed large in the circumstances a detailed account was necessary. When this came in February 1833 and showed that the total was in fact £15.0s.2d the salary sum of £12.10s was remitted to MacGillivray, and no more was allowed. That McCuish received anything seems unlikely.[174]

A tradition recorded many years later may give the cause of Lachlan's death and concluded with yet another St Kilda mystery:

> 'Mr Lachlan was for many years minister in St Kilda. After coming from St Kilda when dining with MacLeod of Bearnaray in the Sound of Harris he was choked with a piece of beef. He told Macleod of Bearnaray that boys - perhaps girls also - were digging in taigh an Stallair in Boraraidh near S.Kilda and in their upturning they came upon a curious "stone". They brought home the stone from Bororay to St Kilda. The "stone" was a parchment manuscript of the Gospels now become hard and solidified like stone. The minister said that the letters were like Hebrew - old Celtic. What became of the M.S. no one knows. Probably the M.S. belonged to the anchorite who lived in [the] lonely spot'.[175]

1 Buchan (1727); e.g. Buchan (1818)
2 Buchan (1727) pp.18-19, 29-30, 39-44
3 Buchan (1818) pp.3-4; Buchan (1727) p.42
4 Buchan (1727) pp.36-37
5 Buchan (1727) pp.37-38
6 Buchan (1727) p.24; MM Section Three p.205 (All sections of this work, while a useful guide, lack sources and are not entirely reliable); DC Section 2/487/8, 12, 15 (1698), 16 (1701); Robson (1991) pp.28-31; MacDonald (1975) pp.287-290; MM Section Three pp.205-206
7 Buchan (1727) pp.23-25. Later editions still comment on the harshness of the steward's demands [e.g. Buchan (1818) pp.31-32].
8 Buchan (1727) pp.43-44
9 Buchan (1727) p.43
10 Buchan (1727) pp.9, 18-19, 29-30, 33, 34-35
11 RB CH1/5/52 pp.10, 182, 186
12 N M Wilby: 'The "Encrease of Popery" in the Highlands 1714-1747' in IR Vol. 17 (1966) pp.93-94; RB CH1/5/52 pp.71-81 (10 May 1726), 186 (Report 28 April 1727)
13 RB CH1/5/52 pp.188 (Report 28 April 1727), 201 (20 May 1727), 206; EUL Laing MSS II 484/3/241
14 RB CH1/5/52 pp.303-304 (State of the Presbytery of Long Island 30 May 1728); also CH1/5/71 p.4 (30 May 1728)
15 RB CH1/5/52 pp.484-490 (Overtures); RB CH1/5/53 pp.15-16 (25 June 1730), 42 (30 September 1730)
16 SSPCK GD95/2/4 p.115 (Letter 26 August 1728, Minutes 24 October 1728); RB CH1/5/52 p.256 – Here Donald MacNeil is called 'the next Protestant Heir to McNiel of Bara' and is said to be keen to advance the interest of the 'true religion'; J L Campbell & C Eastwick: 'The MacNeils of Barra in the Forty-Five' in IR Vol.17 (1966) pp.82-90. Donald MacNeil was cousin of MacNeil of Barra and apparently converted to the Protestant church prior to 1727. He was eager that the SSPCK should establish a school in Barra, and in 1734 was still a promoter of the Protestant cause [GA CH1/5/53 p.306 (28 February 1734)].
17 RB CH1/5/52 pp.160-161 (Letter 26 December 1726, Minutes 10 March 1727)
18 RB CH1/5/52 pp.53-54 (Letters from Daniel MacAulay 31 March 1726), 79 (10 May 1726).

James Coutts was 'to take up a School' in Rum in 1726 but never actually did so [SSPCK GD95/1/2 pp.366 (10 March 1726)]. RB CH1/5/52 pp.345, 362 (Letter from Daniel MacAulay 7 September 1728, Minutes 15 November 1728); GA CH1/2/59 f.150

19 RB CH1/5/52 pp.145-146 (Minutes 30 November 1726), 179, 180 (28 April 1727)

20 RB CH1/5/52 pp.78, 76; RB CH1/5/53 (Minutes 24 November 1737). A letter from the presbytery of Long Island mentioning 'the Laird of Bara's intention to deprive his Daughter of her portion on account of her Embracing the Protestant Religion' was read earlier on 28 July 1737 [GA CH1/5/53 p.483]. RB CH1/5/52 p.76; M McHugh: 'The Religious Condition of the Highlands and Islands in the mid-eighteenth Century' in IR Vol.35 (1984) pp.14-15; RB CH1/5/52 p.100 Report of the Sub-Committee on the State of the Highlands and Islands 1 June 1726; SSPCK GD95/2/4 p.115 (see n.16 above)

21 RB CH1/5/52 p.10; EUL Laing MSS II 484/6/495 (31 July 1729). Patrick Nicolson's 'Communication' was dated 27 August 1728.

22 RB CH1/5/52 pp.346-350 (Memorial to General Wade 1728)

23 RB CH1/5/52 pp.185-186, 243 (Letter 20 October 1727); EUL Laing MSS II 484/4/176; RB CH1/5/52 p.301 (Minutes 30 May 1728); GA CH1/5/71 p.3; EUL Laing MSS II 484/6/499 (10 November 1729). On 30 January 1729 it was noted of Roderick MacLennan that his 'first year was out the beginning of November last', i.e. November 1727 – November 1728 [CH1/5/71 pp.48-49]. It was then agreed that he would again receive £12 for the succeeding year 1728-1729, although he had asked for £15 which was thought reasonable.

24 Fasti Vol. VII p.193; RB CH1/5/53 p.20 (25 June 1730); GA CH1/2/53 ff.180, 182 (Letters to Nicol Spence, SSPCK secretary, from John Skeldoch April/May 1726, 8 July 1726); SSPCK GD95/2/4 p.281; EUL Laing MSS II 484/3/394 (12 June 1730); RB CH1/5/53 p.145 (15 September 1731). In the interim, while MacLennan was away in Mull, Peter King served in Kilmallie parish from 1 November 1729 to 1 August 1730 and seems to have been still in the parish from 1 August to 1 May 1731 [RB CH1/5/68 pp.20, 27].

25 GA CH1/2/64 f.187

26 RB CH1/5/53 p.93 Minutes 22 April 1731

27 It was noted that in Martin's time the population did 'not ordinarily exceed 200' in 27 families, and that in the writer's day [prob. Buchan c.1709] there were 30 or 33 families [Buchan (1727) pp.4, 8]. Mrs Buchan in her petition said that there were only 25 people left after the small pox and other disasters (see Part II n.98). RB CH1/5/52 p.187 (28 April 1727); SSPCK GD95/2/4 p.279 (Letter 11 June 1730)

28 Lawson (St Kilda and its Church) pp.19-21; Lawson (1981) pp.38-43

29 SSPCK GD95/2/4 pp.280, 396

30 RB CH1/5/53 pp.128-129; SG CH2/568/1 p.80 (16 June 1731); RB CH1/5/53 pp.125-127, 140

31 RB CH1/5/68 pp.27, 33, 38: SG CH2/568/1 pp.97, 112; RB CH1/5/53 p.217 (27 July 1732, letter 24 June 1732)

32 RB CH1/5/53 pp.268-269 (26 July 1733), 269, 271; SSPCK GD95/2/5 p.102

33 Morrison (1979) pp.101-105. This article lacks sources and is not always reliable. SSPCK GD95/1/3 pp.384-385 (3 January 1734) ; GD95/2/5 pp.126-127 (25 Dec 1733, letter 17 Dec 1733)

34 SSPCK GD95/1/3 pp.384-385

35 SSPCK GD95/1/3 p.390 (Minutes 5 April 1734)

36 SSPCK GD95/2/5 pp.145 (29 April 1734), 146-147 (21 May 1734); GD95/1/3 p.396 (6 June 1734); SG CH2/568/1 p.120 (5 June 1734). The presbytery of Skye reported that it had ordained Roderick MacLennan to be minister at St Kilda. There must have been some impression, given to the presbytery of Long Island, that MacLennan had gone to his station earlier: 'Hirta or St Kilda An Island on the West of Northuist, Mr Roderick Mclennan Minister and Schoolmaster sent thither 7 February 1734' [SSPCK GD95/1/4 p.24 (3 June 1736)].

37 D Laing: 'An Episode in the Life of Mrs Rachel Erskine, Lady Grange' etc., in PSAS Vol. XI Part II (1876) pp.595-608; also 'Lady Grange, in Edinburgh, 1730' etc., in PSAS Vol. XII Part I (1877) pp.312-313. EUL Laing MSS II 201; R W Seton –Watson: 'The Strange Story of Lady Grange' in History Vol. XVI pp.12-24; DC Section 4/149 Letter (11 February 1741) from Thomas Hope, Edinburgh, to the Laird of MacLeod.

38 MacLean pp.46-47

39 Chambers (1846) p.147

40 R W Seton – Watson: 'The Strange Story of Lady Grange' in History Vol. XVI (1931) p.22;

Chambers (1846) p.147; <u>NSA</u> Inverness-shire pp.325, 333-335; <u>DC</u> Section 4/153. The letter was written in anger after MacLeod had 'banished' MacSween's brother out of his 'country' and had 'banished me and my son yesterday'. It would seem that MacLeod's involvement followed upon his receipt of Thomas Hope's letter. <u>DC</u> Section 4/151

41 <u>SSPCK</u> GD95/1/3 pp.410-411 (7 November 1734); GD95/2/5 p.183 (9 January 1735); GD95/10/134 (30 April 1735); GD95/2/5 pp.199-204 (17 March 1735). The actual deed was in the hands of the Society by 31 January 1735. GD95/1/3 p.426

42 <u>SSPCK</u> GD95/2/5 pp.331. 381, 297-298, 392, 448, 260-461

43 <u>SSPCK</u> GD95/2/5 pp.492, 505; GD95/6/1 Vol. 4 p.75; GD95/2/6 p.11; GD95/6/1 Vol. 4 p.75 (payments in April 1741 to Alexander MacLeod); GD95/1/4 p.89

44 <u>SSPCK</u> GD95/2/6 p.18 (2 April 1741); GD95/2/5 p.515 (4 December 1740)

45 <u>SSPCK</u> GD95/2/6 pp.18, 29 (2 July 1741); GD95/1/4 p.270 (25 November 1741); Chambers (1846) pp.147-148

46 <u>SSPCK</u> GD95/2/6 pp.32-33; GD95/1/4 pp.289-290

47 <u>SSPCK</u> GD95/2/6 p.80; GD95/1/4 pp.289-290

48 <u>PT</u> CH2/508/1 p.301. In the summers of 1742 and 1743 MacLennan was not on the SSPCK's payroll [<u>SSPCK</u> GD95/2/6 pp.89, 154]. <u>RB</u> CH1/5/54 p.210

49 <u>RB</u> CH1/5/54 p.225 (27 October 1743, letter 25 August 1743). Disagreeable reports of Mr Skeldoch, minister at Kilmonivaig, reached the presbytery of Abertarff during 1726 and on 14 September that year the presbytery warned him to be prudent and cautious in his speech and behaviour. On 14 August 1734 the presbytery noted that Skeldoch had moved to Farr [<u>PA</u> CH2/7/1 pp.36, 114]. <u>RB</u> CH1/5/54 pp.231-232

50 <u>RB</u> CH1/5/54 pp.267, 270, 286-287

51 <u>PC</u> CH2/47/4 f.200; <u>RB</u> CH1/5/54 pp.357, 305

52 <u>RB</u> CH1/5/54 p.305; <u>SSPCK</u> GD95/2/6 p.261; <u>PC</u> CH2/47/4 f.200

53 <u>PC</u> CH2/47/4 ff.203, 214; <u>SSPCK</u> GD95/2/6 pp.261, 304; <u>RB</u> CH1/5/54 pp.367, 377, 428

54 <u>SSPCK</u> GD95/2/6 pp.530, 604; <u>RB</u> CH1/5/55 p.38; <u>PC</u> CH2/47/4 f.235

55 <u>SSPCK</u> GD95/2/6 p.638; GD95/2/7 p.12; <u>RB</u> CH1/5/55 p.134-135

56 <u>PC</u> CH2/47/4 f.257; <u>RB</u> CH1/5/55 p.220

57 <u>PC</u> CH2/47/4 ff.265-266, 274

58 <u>RB</u> CH1/5/55 pp.227-228; <u>PC</u> CH2/47/5 pp.5, 12, 29-30, 48; <u>PC</u> CH2/47/4 f.278

59 <u>SSPCK</u> GD95/2/7 pp.217-218, 298, 313

60 <u>PC</u> CH2/47/5 pp.58, 74-75

61 <u>SSPCK</u> GD95/2/7 pp.425-426, 453. Morison had previously been at 'Nisburn a Corner of the Parish of Applecross' in or about 1745-1746 and was paid £5 by each of the respective committees [GD95/2/6 p.294]. <u>PC</u> CH2/47/5 p.86

62 MacDonald (1975) pp.179-183

63 Fasti Vol. VII p.189; <u>RB</u> CH1/5/52 pp.55, 409; <u>RB</u> CH1/5/53 pp.15-16

64 <u>CWC</u> no.155. Aulay's wife has been given as Margaret, daughter of Kenneth Morrison, minister of Stornoway [Fasti Vol. VII p.189].

65 <u>DC</u> Section 2/487/19, 20, 22, 28, 29. The rent of £86.13s.4d for St Kilda suggests that the Pabbay lands were included within this sum.

66 <u>CWC</u> no.215; Morrison (1989) p.149; <u>RB</u> CH1/5/53 p.462; <u>RB</u> CH1/5/54 p.39

67 <u>RB</u> CH1/5/54 p.117; <u>SG</u> CH2/568/1 p.241; <u>RB</u> CH1/5/54 pp.160, 210, 228-229, 312-313; <u>SSPCK</u> GD95/2/6 pp.118, 155, 205

68 <u>RB</u> CH1/5/55 pp.62-63, 70, 91-92, 106, 124-125, 174-175, 196, 257

69 <u>RB</u> CH1/5/54 pp.198, 258-259, 308-309, 312-313, 406

70 <u>CWC</u> no.155, no.217 p.3, no.170. Carmichael noted [no.170] that 'When in Scalpay for six nights on his way to Stornoway the Prince was visited by MacLeod and the writer has a cup out of which the Prince and MacLeod drank to one another. It was given to me in 1890 by the descendant of an old and faithful follower of MacLeod.' The cup was made of horn, about the size of a wine glass, plain and simple with no ornamentation.

71 <u>Campbell of Stonefield Papers</u> GD14/93; H Paton (edit.): <u>The Lyon in Mourning or a collection of speeches letters journals etc. relative to the affairs of Prince Charles Edward Stuart by the Rev Robert Forbes – 1746-1775</u> (SHS Vol. XX) Edinburgh 1895 Vol. I pp.162, 328

72 <u>Historical Manuscripts Commission 11th Report Appendix Part IV</u> The MSS of the Marquess of Townshend p.361 Postscript to letter of 30 September 1746. An account of the search for Prince Charles Edward in St Kilda is given in J Fergusson: <u>Argyll in the Forty-Five</u> London 1951

pp.218-220. Captain George Anderson kept a journal of the expedition to the Outer Hebrides, in which he wrote: 'The 19th [June] we came near St Kilda, and landed part of our troops, and some sailors, but after searching the island found nothing but the miserable inhabitants whose aspect, dress, and sentiments, sufficiently denote their remote situation and the little commerce they have had with the continent. At St Kilda we parted with the Commodore who made for his renevous off Barra head.'

73 SG CH2/568/2 p.44; CWC no.155. It has also been stated that Margaret's father was Colin Campbell of Inveresregan [Fasti Vol. III p.336]. CWC no.226. For a detailed account of Lord MacAulay and his ancestors see T M Murchison: 'Lord Macaulay and the Scottish Highlanders' in TGSI Vol. XLIII (1960-1963) 1966 pp.89-131, where the saying is attributed to Lord Melbourne. However I Carmichael gives the father as James Campbell and the saying as Lord MacAulay's [Lismore in Alba pp.142-146].

74 CWC no.155

75 CWC no.226. Zachary is supposed to have been born in 1768, three years after his parents had left Lismore [Fasti Vol. III p.336].

76 SSPCK GD95/6/1 pp.93, 119 etc.; GD95/2/6 pp.35, 138, 494, 516. In a list of SSPCK schools of 1748 that at St Kilda was said to have 18 boys and 10 girls [GD95/11/2]. A consideration of the state of the SSPCK in 1748 noted that many of the children who had benefitted from instruction were 'living in the most remote and dark Corners of the Country, where otherwise the Rays of the Sun of Righteousness had never yet reach'd, particularly in the lonely Islands of St Kilda, Foula, Fair Isle, etc.' [GD95/11/2 p.56]. At the same time 'Popery or Paganism', between which 'the Difference is not extremely great', had been reduced following the '45 rising, but 'these very assiduous Creatures, the Priests, are again buzzing about, and doing all they can, to regain their former Place in the Hearts and Houses of their deluded People' [GD95/11/2 p.57].

77 MM Section Three pp.216-217; RB CH1/5/53 pp.462 (the writer's name is incorrectly given as Mr Daniel MacAulay), 469, 478-479; RB CH1/5/54 p.83. The inconsistency of dates may mean that there were two Neil MacLeods at this time.

78 RB CH1/5/54 pp.204-205, 308-309, 351, 370

79 RB CH1/5/54 pp.460, 481-482; CH1/5/55 p.21; SG CH2/568/2 p.22

80 Chalmers Adv. MS 21.1.5 f.224

81 Chalmers Adv. MS 21.1.5 ff.183-185

82 SSPCK GD95/2/7 pp.186-187; GD95/1/4 pp.543-544

83 SSPCK GD95/1/4 pp.543-544

84 SSPCK GD95/2/7 pp.243, 257; GD95/1/4 pp.550-551; EUL Laing MSS II 484/1 f.65 Presentation of 26 September 1754 by John MacLeod of Muiravonside in favour of Donald MacLeod catechist at 'Braccadale' to be minister of St Kilda vacant by the death of Alexander MacLeod. In a letter of 8 November 1754 in answer to one sent by the SSPCK committee regarding the qualifications of Donald MacLeod the presbytery of Skye expressed the opinion that MacLeod was sufficiently qualified in every way to be minister there. The committee therefore asked the presbytery to take him on 'tryals' and commission him to be preacher and catechist in St Kilda [EUL Laing MSS II 484/1 f.62].

85 SSPCK GD95/2/7 pp.294, 318; GD95/1/4 pp.555, 568

86 SSPCK GD95/1/4 p.568

87 SSPCK GD95/2/7 pp.384, 393-394

88 ML ff.26, 36, 42

89 Powell pp.46-47

90 SSPCK GD95/2/7 pp.393-394, 384

91 SSPCK GD95/1/4 pp.595-596; GD95/2/7 p.384

92 SG CH2/568/2 pp.18, 57-58, 71; SSPCK GD95/2/7 pp.448, 537-538; SG CH2/568/2 p.86

93 MacAulay pp.5-9; SSPCK GD95/2/7 pp.537-538. Some publications have stated that MacAulay spent 'several months on St Kilda, 1758-59', but this is clearly incorrect [PB p.417].

94 SSPCK GD95/2/7 pp.537-538

95 Fasti Vol. IV p.439; ML f.60

96 ML f.60

97 ML f.64

98 ML f.64

99 SSPCK GD95/2/8 p.18

100 SSPCK GD95/2/8 pp.102, 109

101 SSPCK GD95/2/8 pp.148-149

102 SSPCK GD95/2/8 pp.153-154, 167

103 SSPCK GD95/2/8 p.177. It is perhaps more likely that Alexander MacLeod had left St Kilda by the early 1770s and that he was confused thereafter with his successor, Angus MacLeod. There is reference to Angus, Donald MacLeod's son, as missionary and schoolteacher in the island in 1774 [GD95/11/2 Account of the Society 1774 Appendix p.29]. See n.136 below.

104 SSPCK GD95/2/8 p.102; GD95/1/5 p.30

105 ML ff.67-68

106 SSPCK GD95/2/8 pp.148-149, 160, 180; GD95/1/5 p.30

107 SSPCK GD95/2/8 pp.255, 263-264; GD95/1/5 p.83

108 MacAulay pp.ii-iii

109 Powell p.50, quoting Critical Review XVII (May 1764) p.370; ML f.75

110 MacAulay pp.21, 69-101

111 MacAulay p.274

112 MacAulay pp.241-243

113 MacAulay p.240

114 MacAulay pp.262-263; D R[oss]: 'Thoughts on the Beneficial Effects of Gaelic Schools, and on the Present State of Religion in the Isle of Skye' in The Edinburgh Christian Instructor No. LXXXII (May 1817) Vol. XIV no.V pp.281-287. Donald Ross was minister of Kilmuir parish in Skye.

115 MacAulay pp.192-208. MacAulay also wrote [pp.40-41]:
'Another mighty discouragement is, that the steward will always have it in his power to monopolize the whole trade of this island...or..to ingross every thing it produces, excepting what is necessary to keep the people alive; or to render them fit for labouring, rather for another than for themselves: Nor is it an easy matter to redress this grievance. So peculiarly unhappy is the place in its situation, that the inhabitants must...to the end of time, be wholly at the mercy of some one person, who may swallow all the small commodities this island can afford; and rule the whole community with a rod of iron, unless restrained by honour, conscience, or an uncommon share of humanity.'

116 Powell p.44; J W Croker (edit.): Boswell's Life of Johnson Second Edition London 1835 Vol. IV p.122 n.2; MacCulloch (1824) Vol.III pp.168-169

117 Johnson p.51; PB pp.86, 89; Boswell p.126; PB pp.86 n.5, 215, 86

118 PB p.113; Boswell pp.247, 179, 329. For this MacPherson family see n.155 below and Part I n.68.

119 Boswell pp.423-424; PB p.339 n.11

120 Powell p.46

121 McKay (1980) p.2

122 McKay (1980) p.4; A Sermon preached at Salters Hall 7 April 1788 by Robert Winter before the Correspondent Board in London of the [SSPCK] London 1788 pp.29-30 [SSPCK GD95/13/56]. Ministers themselves conducted their own agricultural pursuits, an interest later condemned by evangelicals. In July 1796 the Synod of Glenelg reviewed a request from the presbytery of Uist that synod meetings should be altered from the first to the third Wednesday of July, as the ministers of the two Outer Hebrides presbyteries had 'an arduous task' to attend the present Synod meetings because the cattle fairs were held at the same time – in Uist the week before Synod, in Lewis the week after; and 'from the distance of their Parishes from the seat of Synod, being no less than a hundred miles, and contrary winds frequently happening, they were under the necessity of either neglecting their duty to Synod, or materially suffering in their interest from attending the Synod and losing the sale of their cattle.' The request was granted. [SG CH2/568/3 pp.83-84].
Sermon 1 January 1759 and Report on the state of the Society [SSPCK GD95/13/24 pp.59-63]

123 McKay (1980) p.5. Walker's remarks on the people of Iona, of which Neil MacLeod was minister, are of interest in this context:
'...They are Professed Protestants, but being entirely destitute of the means of Knowledge, and having no School they are left in such a State of Ignorance, as in a Christian Country is really deplorable. For of the 200 Inhabitants, there is not one, who can either speak English or read the Scriptures, though their little Island was for many Centuries one of the chief Seats of Religion and Learning in Britain.

'They are all of the lowest Rank, under a Gentleman of the name of Campbell who rents the Island, but they are a civil inoffensive People. They are apparently in great Poverty, and yet are happy in having to supply all the wants with which they are acquainted. Entirely excluded from all Intercourse with the Rest of Mankind, they enjoy the mere necessaries of Life, with Peace and Contentment, and have always been remarked, as being of a soft and gentle disposition.

'They have all of them a remarkable Propensity to whatever is marvelous and supernatural. Every Person has the traditional History of Columba, with numberless Legends, which have been handed down from his monkish Seminary. They are famous for the second Sight; full of Visions seen either by themselves or others; and have many wild and romantick notions concerning Religion and invisible things. Though they know not what Popery is, the Vestages of it they suck in with their Milk, which appear in many of their Opinions and Practices.'

One of these practices was 'to carry the Corpse with great Reverence, round the whole Buildings' of the ruinous Abbey at a funeral. Neil MacLeod was trying to abolish it, but as an imaginative people, 'Their un-limited Veneration for Antiquity, supplies the Place of Truth, in the most marvelous and frightfull Legends, and their Slender Acquaintance with Religion, is but the Parent of that Superstition, which can only be remedied, by a more perfect Knowledge of divine Things.' [McKay (1980) pp.140-141]

124   EUL Laing MSS III 352/1 Letter from Thomas Pennant to John Walker 21 April 1764, and letter from John Ritchie to John Walker 8 August 1762.
125   McKay (1980) pp.59-60
126   GA CH1/2/113 f.303
127   EUL Laing MSS III 352/1 Draft letter from John Walker to Lord Kames, Moffat 10 December 1764
128   PB pp.132-133
129   DC Section 2 487/32 Rental of the Barony of Harris; Grant p.497
130   Grant pp.496-497; DC Section 1 466/20 Draft Advertisement; BD Vol. II p.10 no.32
131   DC Section 4 394 Letter 23 November 17? ; DC Section 1 466/28
132   DC Section 4 682/2 Letter 16 October 1775; Section 4 682/1 Letter 12 September 1775, Section 1 382/50 Letter from Sir George Strickland to Rev. Kenneth MacAulay 28 April 1776, Section 1 382/51 Letter from W Dick to Sir George Strickland 8 May 1776.
133   Knox pp.160-161
134   Chalmers (2) ff.169-172
135   DC Section 2 485/47/2, 485/50; Section 1 466/36 Inventory of Tacks, mostly 6 September 1769. According to A Morrison William MacNeil was the son of Roderick MacNeil, innkeeper and vintner at Dunvegan, the same as Roderick at Trumpan [Morrison (1969) p.17]
136   SSPCK GD95/2/9 pp.350-351. Payment was made to Donald MacLeod for the year ending 1 May 1765, and for the following year to Alexander MacLeod. Continued annual payments to Alexander persisted until at least 1 May 1769 [GD95/6/1 Accounts Vol. 6 (1759-1769)], and apparently he was paid salary due to Martinmas 1780 [GD95/6/2 Accounts Vol.2 (1779-1797) p.7] but see n.103 above.
137   Fasti Vol. VII p.194. An Angus MacLeod succeeded William Hay as schoolmaster and catechist at Bornish, South Uist, about 1754 [RB CH1/5/78 Scheme of Missionaries 1754-1755]. PU CH2/361/1 p.83
138   SSPCK GD95/2/9 pp.366, 436; PU CH2/361/1 p.89. On 4 July 1778 the Synod of Glenelg expressed concern over 'the alarming progress' of 'the popish religion' within its bounds, and over 'the arts and industry practised by the professors of that religion to gain proselytes' and 'the dismal situation into which at different times their audacious attempts brought the nation, to the almost utter subversion of our happy constitution, both in church and state together; likewise calling to mind the noble stand which our ancestors made to stem the torrent of this superstitious inundation.' In an account by 'a learned and worthy clergyman' there was reference to 'Popish' practices: 'I believe it is true that they worship saints who have been long since expunged from the Romish Kalendar; and I am sure St Barr is not worshipped any where on the face of the globe but in the Island of Barra; nor is St Michael's day so eminently celebrated with a general cavalcade as in South Uist, where the people, after eating St Michael's cake, baked with milk and the yoke of eggs, ride sun-ways round the chapel of St Michael, every man carrying his wife behind him, and every young man his mistress.' [SSPCK GD95/11/2 A Summary Account of the Rise and Progress of the Society Edinburgh 1783

pp.34-35],A St Michael's cavalcade was once enjoyed on St Kilda and many other Hebridean islands [Martin (1698) p.85 etc.]

PU CH2/361/1 p.119

PU CH2/361/1 p.123; SSPCK GD95/2/10 pp.88-89

SSPCK GD95/2/10 pp.116, 149; PU CH2/361/1 p.129

PU CH2/361/1 pp.138-141, 146, 150

SSPCK GD95/2/10 pp.216, 224, 244; PU CH2/361/1 pp.151-152; PS CH2/330/2 p.39. The presbytery, which had found Lachlan 'upon the whole sufficiently qualified to officiate in holy things in the station to which he is presented', sustained the presentation by Norman MacLeod of Berneray, 'male heir of Mr MacLeod of Muiravonside and consequently Patron of the Mission to St Kilda in the Parish of Harris', and 'ordain'd him so that he may be further enabled to administer all the ordinances of the Gospel in the foresaid Island only'. The ordination took place at 'Rhenitra' in northern Skye, with Rev. Malcolm MacLeod, Snizort, as presbytery moderator.

SSPCK GD95/2/10 pp.350-351, 363; GD95/1/6 p.46

PU CH2/361/1 p.96; Knox pp.169, 172; PU CH2/361/1 pp.155-156, 163-230

Buchanan p.119; SSPCK GD95/6/1 vol.6 pp.80, 98, 123 – for payments to MacNeil; Buchanan pp.135, 143. For an account of Buchanan's years in Harris see A MacLean's 'Foreword' in the reprint of Travels in the Western Hebrides Isle of Skye 1997

Buchanan pp.143-144

Buchanan pp.223-224

Unless otherwise stated the source for what follows is W Otter (edit.): The Life and Remains of Edward Daniel Clarke (2 vols. London 1824 Vol. I pp.277-282, 341-368).

Martin (1698) pp.42-43; MacAulay pp.54-55. MacAulay could have seen 'Staller's house' for himself when on Boreray [pp.116-119].

Thomas (1874) pp.704-705. Some of the names were recorded about 1812: in Boreray 'is to be seen what is called Staller's House. It is built on four pillars, and between these are recesses, each distinguished by its name, viz. Simmidran, Bearran, Ralli, and Raistalla. The whole is roofed with stones, and covered with earth' [EE Vol. XII p.451].

SSPCK GD95/2/11 p.283

Letter to Robert Lundie, Manse of Kelso, from Henry Brougham 23 July 1799 NLS MS 1675 ff.194-195; [Brougham]: The Life and Times of Henry Lord Brougham – by himself (2 vols.) Edinburgh & London 1871 Vol. I pp.91-108

Robert Campbell of Shawfield: Journal – 'An Account of the Island of St Kilda and Neighbouring Islands, Visited August 1799' NLS MS 3051

MM Section Two p.80. The existence of a second Alexander MacLeod, substitute as minister for Donald MacLeod in St Kilda, might have suggested that the proprietor of the island after 1804, Lt. Col. Donald MacLeod, was his son, rather than the son of Alexander in St Kilda in the 1740s. There is however reference in 1763 to Barbara MacPherson as 'relict of the deceased Mr Alexander MacLeod, late minister of St. Kilda', and an interesting story is told about her. Barbara recounted how the St Kilda people had a particular kind of second sight, considered a forerunner of their approaching end. 'Some months before they sicken, they are haunted with an apparition resembling themselves in all respects, as to their person, features or clothing: this image (seemingly animated) walks with them in the fields in broad daylight; and if they are employed in delving, harrowing, seed-sowing, or any other occupation, they are at the same time mimicked by this ghostly visitant.' Barbara said that when visiting a sick inhabitant she asked if he had seen this ghost. He said he had, and 'to make further trial, as he was going out of his house on a morning, he put on straw-rope garters, instead of those he formerly used, and having gone to the fields, his other self appeared in such garters'. The sick man died and Barbara no longer questioned the truth of the presages. [TI pp.8-9]
Since Lt. Col. Donald MacLeod's son was John MacPherson MacLeod it is probable that Donald's parents were the first Alexander and his wife Barbara MacPherson. From the same source [p.17] comes a mention of 'Florence MacLeod' as 'spouse to the present minister of St. Kilda' – in 1763, presumably therefore the unwell Donald MacLeod. According to this source Florence's mother, Elizabeth MacLeod, lived in 'Pabbay in the Harris' where she employed 'a domestic girl' born in St Kilda. See also D MacKinnon: 'The MacPhersons of Skye' in The Scottish Genealogist I. 2-3 p.28, where unfortunately sources are lacking. J MacDonald: General View of the Agriculture of the Hebrides or Western Isles of Scotland Edinburgh 1811

pp.817-818

[156] [D] McLeod: 'Notices on the Present Sate of St Kilda – by Lieut. Col. McLeod, the Proprietor' in Scots Magazine and Edinburgh Literary Magazine December 1814 pp.912-913

[157] SSPCK GD95/2/12 pp.171-172

[158] DC Section 1 489/1 Agreement. On 9 March 1812 Neil MacLeod wrote on the matter to James Grant, provost of Inverness:

'As Lord Provost of Inverness I beg you will pardon me for transmitting to you a deed of the sale of a property in the Bahama Islands (by Mr Lauchlan MacLeod, minister of St Kilda, and wife) to me – to this property Mr Lauchlan and his wife made up their tytle some years before the Provost of Inverness, and which I suppose will be found some way recorded there and I think 1800 or 1801'.

The letter continues with legal technicalities. Enclosed with it is a letter of 17 March 1812 on the same subject to Grant from Lachlan MacKinnon, 'Corrychatachan', Skye [Warrand of Bught Papers GD23/6/494].

[159] SSPCK GD95/2/12 pp.304, 319; GD95/3/2 p.426 Inland Letter Book 1794-1805

[160] SSPCK GD95/2/12 pp.334-335

[161] SSPCK GD95/2/13 pp.129, 150, 239, 298, 322; GD95/1/6 pp.351, 467-468. At least two letters of this period from the SSPCK to Lachlan MacLeod relate chiefly to books and to Lachlan's own unsuccessful literary efforts:

a. 28 July 1810

'Rev. Dear Sir I am favoured with your letter of 23rd June. The Reasons which you assign for not forwarding your certificate of service along with your receipt for your last year's salary will I doubt not be sustained by the Directors. I fear you have misunderstood Col. McLeod's information with regard to the £4, which he got to transmit to you, as it was only a temporary supply, not a permanent addition to the salary.

'I am glad that the Books which were sent by order of the Directors came safe to hand; and I doubt not you will derive much advantage from the writings of these excellent authors. I approve very much of your translating some of the Sermons into Gaelic; it is an improving exercise to yourself, and may prove useful to others. The Sermons which I would particularly recommend as best adapted for this purpose, are the Village Sermons by the Rev. George Burden. Were you to send a few specimens of your translations of these Sermons next year, I would shew them to Gentlemen qualified to judge of their merits, and to decide how far it might be advisable to think of publishing them.

'I have only to add my best wishes for your personal comfort, and success in your labours among your people.'

b. 8 September 1812

'Rev. Sir, I have received your letter of 8th August, which together with your former communications, has been duly considered by the Directors. Their Resolution is continued in the Extract from their Minutes of 3rd current, which you will find on the other side. I have only to add that I hope you will take care of the Books which were sent some time ago, for the benefit of the Missionary of St Kilda; and give the necessary orders for their being put in a situation where they may not receive injury in consequence of the present bad state of the Manse.

'I received the MS which you sent me some time ago, containing the translations of some of Mr Burden's Sermons; but the Gentlemen to whose judgement they were submitted, did not think them fit for publication.'

[SSPCK GD95/3/3 Inland Letter Book 1806-1814 pp.131-132, 281]

[162] SSPCK GD95/2/13 p.371. Consideration of this letter was delayed till Lt. Col. MacLeod 'came to Town'. GD95/2/13 p.414

[163] J.L[eyden]: 'Specimens of the Poetry of St Kilda' in Scots Magazine Vol. 64 pp.976-977; 'St Kilda Poetry' in The Edinburgh Magazine and Literary Miscellany March 1818 pp.241-242. Alexander Campbell, minister of Portree, was married to Margaret, daughter of William MacLeod of Luskentyre. He was killed in a fall from the top of a stair in 1811. See n.161 for Lachlan MacLeod's literary interest.

[164] Acland pp.49-50. The sketch was of 'the main square', one of several watercolour and pencil sketches done by Sir Thomas in and around St Kilda and published by Quine (1988). EE Vol.XII pp.450-452 – the anonymous contributor wrote: 'It may be supposed, that these are contemporaneous veins of felspar; but, to the best of the writer's recollection (his specimens

having been lost) at the distance of eighteen years, these veins contain quartz as well as felspar'.

[165] SSPCK GD95/2/13 pp.435, 445. On 1 December 1812 'The Presbytery [of Skye] wrote a strong letter to the [SSPCK] in favour of Mr Lachlan McLeod Minister of St Kilda, recommending to them, to grant him some addition to his Salary, which in the present times is very inadequate to the maintenance of his family and also, to use their good offices with Coll. McLeod, the present Proprietor of St Kilda, to have Mr Lachlan's dwelling house repaired' [PS CH2/330/2 p.274]. The presbytery moderator was Rev. Coll MacDonald now of Portree parish.

[166] SSPCK GD95/2/14 pp.57-58; MacCulloch Vol. III p.178. The following paragraphs are from the same source [pp.170-196].

[167] SSPCK GD95/2/14 pp.237-239, 256

[168] R Ralph (edit.): William MacGillivray: A Hebridean Naturalist's Journal 1817-1818 Stornoway 1996 pp.32, 38, 64 etc.

[169] SSPCK GD95/2/14 pp.239, 241-242. The only appointment of a minister to St Kilda in the period 1803-1834 was that of Neil MacKenzie who arrived in 1830.

[170] SSPCK GD95/2/14 pp.239, 260

[171] SSPCK GD95/2/14 pp.356, 397. It appears that the resignation of Lachlan MacLeod was a prerequisite to the transfer of the right of nomination and increase of salary. In 1822 'The Directors having, for a considerable period, had reason to believe that the situation of these islanders was in different respects truly deplorable, regretted to find that they did not possess the means of affording adequate and effectual relief.' The resignation opened the way for the SSPCK to fulfil its intention to increase the salary and to take steps 'for sending a well qualified person to that interesting Mission'. [GD95/11/11 Society Report 1821-1822 pp.55-57]

[172] SSPCK GD95/2/14 pp.423, 488; PU CH2/361/2 p.16

[173] SSPCK GD95/2/14 pp.504, 548-549

[174] MM Section Three p.277; SSPCK GD95/2/14 p.579; GD95/2/17 (10 May 1832 Letter 12 April 1832), pp.94, 106, 109, 121

[175] CWC no.170

PART IV

NEW MISSIONARIES AND
A NEW CHURCH
John Macdonald and Neil Mackenzie
in St Kilda

The line of Macleod ministers in St Kilda ended with the enforced retirement of Lachlan Macleod in 1821.

All had been out of contact with the SSPCK for most of the time and frequently absent from their charge, so that the islanders had lacked a consistent religious and teaching provision for about three quarters of a century.

It fell to the Presbytery of Uist to try to find a replacement for Lachlan, while the philanthropic groups in Edinburgh and other cities or larger towns became ever more concerned about the educational plight of St Kilda. A teacher was found whose main task was to enable his pupils to read the Gaelic bible, and the SSPCK supported four visits by the evangelical minister John Macdonald. The efforts of this exceptional churchman led to the construction of a manse and church, and the introduction followed, after a gap of ten years, of the next resident minister, Neil Mackenzie, in 1830.

The new buildings completed, there was at first difficulty in finding a minister to occupy them, but Mackenzie duly arrived and within a few years was receiving tourists from the 'steamers' and yachts that began to call. In spite of the brief presence of these strangers Mackenzie himself felt the cultural and intellectual deprivation inherent in a prolonged stay in St Kilda. Yet he kept in touch with some of the developments in the 'outside world' and assisted, along with a new factor, in the rearrangement of land lots and the introduction of houses with limited furnishings. He prided himself also with securing the abandonment of certain native traditions and was pleased to report that the people had undergone a remarkable religious revival.

With Macdonald's visits and during Mackenzie's fourteen years as minister it became clear that even more than before St Kilda was subject to outside influences not just on religious attitudes and customs but on the cultural heritage and on daily circumstances. According to some accounts the increased interest of the outside world, with its complete lack of understanding of remote Hebridean life, created tales of undesirable traits such as greed and petty dishonesty, and helped to broadcast questionable images of island conditions. Perhaps this had long been the case to a lesser degree, but now there developed a division of concern in which the fate of a person's soul, seemingly more important than the necessary self-sufficient means of survival, was balanced against the expectation of outside assistance and goods to make that survival possible.

CHAPTER 1

Finding a teacher and trying to find another minister

LACHLAN MacLeod was still in the course of retiring when, on 12 December 1821, the members of the presbytery of Uist resumed their deliberations on the vacancy in the St Kilda mission. They 'deeply deplore the state of the people, for want of religious instruction, and are surprised, that no steps have yet been taken to supply them with an instructor'. What they had in mind by way of instruction was a task for sharing between a missionary and a teacher, and so long as it was largely religious in content this could mean that as formerly one man only was needed. However such a man would have to be more attentive to his duties than it appeared Lachlan MacLeod and the earlier generations of his family had been, and he would probably have to be better educated, as the presbytery, aware of developments in more privileged districts than St Kilda, expected a great improvement in the teaching side of the work. It was resolved to communicate with the SSPCK on the subject and to 'recommend that any person appointed to said Station, shall be required to teach English writing and Arithmetic, with the reading of the Gaelic Language, together with his other official duties, and to add to the allowance now given, an additional Salary, equal to what is generally granted to Schoolmasters on the Society's Scheme, in order to make the Missionary of St Kilda at the same time more comfortable and useful'.[1]

Until provision of this kind was achieved the people of St Kilda would no doubt retain those beliefs, traditions and even practices that stemmed from an older, partially Catholic world and that had not been eradicated by a sequence of Protestant missionaries who appeared to lack the vigorous and constant zeal that would have been necessary. Indeed ministers like Donald MacLeod and his grandson Lachlan quite possibly found no difficulty in accommodating and perhaps actually enjoying some of the island's 'superstitious' customs. In the circumstances the islanders of 1820 might have struck Alexander Buchan as little different from those he knew a century and more earlier, even though their ancestry might have lain in Skye or Uist.

The presbytery of Uist may not have realised in December 1821, or if it did it perhaps did not approve of the fact, that a month earlier a teacher had been sent to St Kilda. This was Alexander MacKenzie, employed by the Society for the Support of Gaelic Schools, the sole object of which body was 'to teach the Inhabitants of the Highlands and Islands, to read the Sacred Scriptures in their Native tongue'. Schools were to be 'circulating', moving on after a year or so from one place to another, although in the case of St Kilda MacKenzie taught there until 1829 when he was removed during the summer. His remit, to teach Gaelic only, would not perhaps have satisfied the presbytery although members could hardly have objected.

The Edinburgh Society for the Support of Gaelic Schools (ESSGS) was founded in 1810 and other societies were formed in Glasgow, Dundee and Inverness over the next decade.[2] From its annual report of 29 November 1811 the ESSGS learned that in Harris only 100 people out of a population of 3000 could read English, in North Uist only 200 out of 4000, while 'in the remote glens, or subordinate islands of almost every parish, few or none can be found who know even the letters!' The nature of the country alone dictated the need for circulating schools as stationary establishments in the wilder areas could only be reached by those living near them. The inaccessibility of St Kilda may have accounted for the continuance there of the ESSGS teacher for eight years.[3]

Urgent need was expressed at the beginning for 'an Elementary Book' with the help of which Gaelic speakers could learn how to read and write in their own tongue. Through 'the generosity of a Member of the Institution' 3000 copies of the *First Book for Children in the Gaelic Language* were printed, some being sent in response to requests to Farr in Sutherland, to Mull, and to St Kilda. Three schools were in action by the end of 1811, the first at Badantarbet in the Aird district of Coigeach. The minister of North Uist, James MacQueen, was not alone in thinking that a school should begin in the autumn, for 'the people will be at their sheallings till the 12th of August'; and others thought that harvest should be over first. Teaching could then continue through the winter until about the middle of April when the busy outdoor season began. Although he may have been absent one or two winters MacKenzie seems to have attended to his class on St Kilda on much the same lines.[4]

St Kilda was not the only island to have been without a distinct Protestant teacher hitherto. In 1820 it was reported that Boreray in the Sound of Harris had a population of around 160 'souls, *who seldom or never hear a sermon*' and 'have no Teacher of any kind'. Taransay, with nearly 200 people, 'never had a school', and in Scarp where there were about 20 families 'there is not an individual … that can read'. So at the same time as MacKenzie went to St Kilda for the ESSGS Donald Munro went to Taransay and John Shaw to Scarp, each for not much longer than a year to try to rescue the inhabitants from illiteracy in their own language; but by 1824 there was again no teacher in Taransay and Shaw had gone off to Renigadale. The Scarp islanders secured James Fraser to carry on, teaching Gaelic and English: 'They are very poor and have no money; but they have agreed to give this teacher a little of the produce of their small farms to support him and his family.' The Harris estate factor, Donald Stewart, said of Scarp: 'I do not suppose they have heard above three sermons for the last ten years.' By comparison St Kilda, from an established church point of view, had done rather well.[5]

The owner of St Kilda played no part in the provision and support of either minister or schoolteacher at this stage, although according to John

MacCulloch, writing of his visit in 1815 when there was, as he stated, no school and not one person who could read, the island was under the direct management of 'its very liberal proprietor'. So far as a teacher was concerned MacCulloch was later to pride himself that directly or indirectly he had helped to achieve the appointment of Alexander MacKenzie, although in 1824 he did not know whether English was to be taught. Practical assistance to teacher or missionary was expected from the St Kilda tacksman, but after the departure of the MacNeils in 1804 no one seems to have occupied that position until perhaps 1818 or 1820 when Murdo MacLellan, tacksman of Scalpay, added St Kilda to his 'possessions'.[6]

The way for Alexander MacKenzie was prepared by an anonymous visitor to St Kilda, possibly in the summer of 1821 when the process of 'retiring' Lachlan MacLeod had already begun. On 8 September 1821 this unknown person sent to the ESSGS useful information which encouraged its directors to think of the island as a suitable place for one of their schools:

'I visited St.Kilda, in order to ascertain the state of Religion in that remote Island. I consider it an important station for a Gaelic school; as among a population of about 110, there is none that can read but one person. There are 58, between Males and Females, who might attend: of these there are 31 Boys, and 27 Girls, from 5 to 16 years of age; the rest consist of 3 young Men, and 12 young Women, who would willingly attend, as they are single.'

When the idea was put to the islanders 'they seemed very much inclined to have such an Institution among them', and both they and the tacksman, with whom the visitor may have travelled, 'faithfully promised to furnish the necessary accommodations for any proper person that may be sent among them as a Teacher'.[7]

Much discussion was still taking place at this time regarding the duties of a missionary for the districts of Sand and Sollas in North Uist and the neighbouring islands of Boreray, Berneray and Pabbay. The 'accommodations' required for him were 'a house (consisting of at least two apartments and a Kitchen), a garden, a Cow house, a Cows grass in Summer, and ground Sufficient to furnish provender for her during the winter, and that peats for fuel shall be cast and driven to his house free of expence'. As for St Kilda, 'Mr Murdoch Maclellan, who is the present Tacksman of the place, and likewise of Scalpa in Harris, promises to give all the assistance in his power to make the Teacher comfortable, by erecting a building which will serve both as a Dwelling-house and a School-house; likewise, a patch of ground, the grazing of 2 or 3 cows, as many sheep as he pleases, and fuel for the whole year'. There was therefore not much difference between the conditions offered for a missionary in North Uist and those proposed for a teacher in St Kilda, and the unknown correspondent recommended to the ESSGS the sending of a teacher to the islands as soon as possible. He also suggested that the teacher should be allowed 'a few pounds more salary than the rest' because 'there cannot be a more destitute place in Britain, being shut up from having any intercourse with their fellow creatures'. Books too would have to be supplied free as the people were too poor to pay for them, and 'they have not a coin in circulation among them'. In a short while Alexander MacKenzie was on his way to this destitute and isolated station.[8]

Although employed by a religiously-minded body, MacKenzie was a teacher, not a missionary. Following the departure of Lachlan MacLeod the tacksman Murdo MacLellan, who lived in Scalpay, sent a letter in March 1822 to the SSPCK, 'giving a deplorable account of the religious and moral state of [the] island, in consequence of the want of a Clergyman, and praying that the Society would either authorise a Mr John Bethune who lives near him to visit the Island, or appoint some other clergyman either for stated or occasional residence'. He added that he was accustomed to visit St Kilda twice a year, in May and August, and that 'no other opportunity of direct intercourse occurs during the year'. John Bethune had recently been itinerant minister in the islands of Rum and Canna and had just been appointed to 'the Mission of Harris' by the Royal Bounty committee, but the SSPCK, while appreciating the 'zeal' which MacLellan's letter demonstrated, could not take action as promptly as the tacksman evidently wished for only a short period had elapsed since Lachlan MacLeod's resignation. The Society promised, however, that no time would be lost 'in prosecuting so far as depends on them those measures which the exigency of the case demands'.[9]

Almost immediately, indeed, the SSPCK secretary wrote to Rev. John MacDonald, minister of the parish of Urquhart in Easter Ross, asking him to recommend a person qualified to undertake the St Kilda mission. No answer was received, and so the secretary wrote again, this time with a request that MacDonald should himself visit the island when the tacksman went out in August:

'The object of this communication is, to call your attention to the Mission of St Kilda; certainly a very interesting object, and a case which presents strong claims on the attention of the friends of religion in the Highlands. Despairing, from the shortness of time, to be able to send a minister to the island before August, I now state that I am authorised by the Directors to make a proposal to you, which, from your well known principles, and feelings of love to our common Lord, and to the souls of men; and from your habits of itinerating, I should incline to think would not fail to be agreeable to you. It is, that you yourself shall take a trip to St Kilda, along with the tacksman, in the month of August. The necessities of the islanders are urgent in the extreme. And I should think that the cry of their distress must be heard as loud in the ear of a zealous evangelical minister, as that of the men of Macedonia by Paul - "Come over and help us." I leave it to your own heart to make up an argument on the case, which I doubt not you will feel as irresistible. You go at the expense of the Society. The time is short; and, if no minister goes with the tacksman in August, the poor St Kildaites must be destitute of spiritual instruction for another year.'[10]

Should MacDonald refuse he was asked to invite 'one of his Brethren' whom he judged suitable to go instead. Two letters returned in July 1822, the first suggesting a young man called Murdo Campbell for the mission, and the second stating that owing to family circumstances a personal visit by MacDonald to St Kilda would most likely not be possible. However Murdo Campbell did not go, and John MacDonald did, thereby introducing a new and somewhat disturbing period in the island's story.[11]

*

Why should the St Kilda mission have been 'a very interesting object'? Elsewhere in the Hebrides there were equally interesting and deserving islands, none of which received the same particular attention. It has already been justly said that St Kilda was not in a category of its own, but one of the Hebrides like Pabbay or Scarp. Yet object of attention St Kilda certainly was, especially after the publication of Martin's *Voyage* and MacAulay's *History*. Various easy and no doubt correct answers to the question are possible, ranging from the island's remoteness, scenery and even 'atmosphere' to the mysterious community in need of 'civilising', but another aspect is also worth consideration. If the Catholic church of old had helped to preserve and perpetuate an established way of life with ancient customs, traditions and beliefs, singing, dancing and telling of stories, then the Protestant mission, associating these things with a 'barbaric' and 'savage' people, sought to bring about an overdue change by publicising its concern for the moral state of this isolated and 'primitive' group, desolate because it lacked the light of 'truth'. To achieve the change and development it thought desirable not only in St Kilda but also in many areas of the Highlands and islands it was to the advantage of the Protestant church that St Kilda should be held up as 'a very interesting object'.

Change seems always to be an important and contentious matter, and is often introduced by some outside influence. At times when that influence was strong St Kilda's people were almost as helpless as they were in the face of the natural and accidental disasters that sometimes overtook them. On the one hand the simple, poor islanders, hospitable, uneducated and easily persuaded, were organised, and re-organised, by actions of the landlord, the steward and his deputy, rather than by the various kinds of church denomination, and their existence seems to have been long regulated according to allotment of land and cliffs. It is possible that the division of the more fertile ground at an early stage into five penny lands meant occupation by five families, and that the subsequent subdivision, perhaps nearly as early, into ten half penny lands related to the reported ten men and ten women of around 1610-1620. Again, if John MacDonald was correct, the further subdivision into farthing lands would have meant about twenty families, which was approximately the number through most of the eighteenth and nineteenth centuries. It is quite likely that these arrangements were responses to the demands of a population at a level set by the requirements of the landlord or steward, for whose benefit the size of that population was maintained, or, after disaster, restored. Only when, after 1804, the steward or tacksman system became fitful or went into temporary decline did the adjustment of population cease to be important in that way. No one thought of transporting people then, and numbers came to depend on natural causes or the inclinations of the islanders. On the other hand, the same poor people of St Kilda found themselves, from Buchan's time onwards, at the mercy of a church which, though at one stage linking its missionary activities with material progress, concerned itself primarily with their spiritual and moral condition. Outside influence of this kind was never more distinctly apparent than in 1822 when the SSPCK's call for an evangelical preacher was answered by the minister of Urquhart.[12]

Much of what is now generally known about John MacDonald stems from the book about him by John Kennedy of Dingwall, a rather hollow and repetitive work that gave popular currency to the description of MacDonald as 'The Apostle of the North'. In this and in his other well-known book, *The Days of the Fathers in Ross-shire*, Kennedy gave a great deal of space to proclaiming the virtues of evangelical preachers in language that contained colourful high-sounding phrases of little meaning except when revealing what the author considered the inadequacies of those who belonged to different religious persuasions. In all this Kennedy may have been a leading figure but he was not unusual, for writers of the nineteenth century within the evangelical tradition were numerous and like one another in style.

Kennedy had no kind feelings for 'Popery', which had once held sway over all the Highlands and islands. Seemingly unaware that his condemnations could be applied to his own doctrines, he declared that 'the priesthood had been content to rule the people, without attempting to teach them. His ignorance and superstition made the rude Highlander all the more manageable in the hands of the clergy, and they therefore kept him a heathen'. Thus when the Reformation arrived it found this Highlander 'as Popery had left him, an utter heathen in ignorance, a very fanatic in superstition, and, in his habits, a lawless savage, rioting in the wild excitements of the chase, in the perilous adventures of plundering raids, and in the fierce combats of rival clans and chieftains'. Episcopal incumbents around 1700 were almost as bad, being 'in opposition to the cause of the Gospel'. And those ministers of the eighteenth and early nineteenth century church who, in Kennedy's opinion, lacked evangelical fervour, the so-called 'moderates', were but 'stipend-lifters of the Establishment' who gave too much attention to worldly matters and too little to the care of souls.[13]

The admired, exemplary figures among evangelicals, going back to seventeenth century Easter Ross, were distinguished by their inward spontaneity. 'Deep impressions of their utter impotence under the power of sin, as well as of their utter inexcusableness under its guilt, with a distinct recognition of the necessity of regeneration and of the sovereignty of grace, distinguished the experience of the awakened'. Pastoral care and common humanity seemed to be of little importance. 'They were not much given to the formalities of stated visiting. It was not their habit to cross a certain number of thresholds every year. They did what was better for themselves and their flocks, for they visited them often in spirit, as they went to carry them on their hearts to the footstool of mercy. They obtained a more thorough knowledge of the views and feelings of their people from one course of catechising, than they could from the perfunctory visiting of a lifetime'. In claiming the attention of an audience the ability to speak well was all important: 'The power of the pulpit was paramount .., and the people became, to a great extent, plastic to its influence. The preachers could mould the opinions and habits of their hearers, without any counteracting influences, besides such as invariably operate, to distort the impression which they desired to produce'. Words such as 'unction' and 'unctuous', neither of them very attractive in meaning, were used along with 'grace', 'excitement', 'conversion' and so on, to characterise the work of these men, all of whom relied heavily on an appeal through the emotions. The extent to which listeners broke down in tears or fainted seemed to be a measure of the preacher's success. When John MacDonald attended his first communion at Urquhart in or about 1813 'Few eyes were tearless … The excitement at last was very great, the groans and outcries of the stricken ones sometimes drowning the voice of the preacher'. These were considered the signs of an 'awakening', as at Ardeonaig beside Loch Tay, when a sermon 'was accompanied with an extraordinary outpouring of the Spirit. Some cried out; others were melted into tears; while many laboured in vain to suppress their feelings'. The meeting place was then 'no other than the house of God and the gate of heaven'. And in case the response might, by some unwise people, be considered mere hysteria ministers contrived a more acceptable explanation, as at Dornoch communion when attended by many young converts from Tarbat: 'When the service was over the linen cloth was as wet with their tears as though it had been taken out of the sea.' Was this a mark of genuine conversion? Mr Stewart of Portmahomack had gone along 'to see for himself if it was only a time of sensational and emotional excitement or if it was a real awakening to spiritual conviction and concern'. Hardly an impartial enquirer, Mr Stewart decided, without providing evidence, that it was the latter.[14]

For some the experience of 'awakening' proved too much. An old man at Geanies, wrote Kennedy, had been looked after by his daughter. But 'She was one of the awakened, and in her excitement her reason was touched'. As a consequence she was kept at home tied to her bed. However a person not brought to the point of asking 'What must I do to be saved?' could meet as unhappy a fate, and become the object of yet another instance of that familiar device, evangelical prophecy. Kennedy's father is supposed to have predicted: 'There is a sinner in this place, very ripe for destruction, who shall this night be suddenly summoned to a judgement-seat.' Next morning, so the story went, flames were seen to be leaping from the dwelling hut of 'a woman, notorious for immorality', where were found later only 'the charred bones of its miserable tenant'. A merciless, uncharitable streak could appear in the evangelical's behaviour and pronouncements.[15]

CHAPTER 2

John Macdonald, evangelical.

JOHN MacDonald was aged about 43 when he visited St Kilda in 1822. He was born in the parish of Reay in Caithness where his father had been a catechist. As a boy he learned to play the bagpipes and had the set with him at King's College, Aberdeen, until increasing spiritual devotion led him to abandon his musical interests and eventually to chop up the pipes with an axe. In the autumn of 1805 he went on what Kennedy called 'an Ossianic tour throughout the North-west Highlands' at the request of Sir John Sinclair to find out to what extent traditions of the Fingalians survived in the Highlands and whether Ossian's poems were still remembered. His small manuscript collection of nine items was discovered about 1870 in the Advocates Library, Edinburgh, and made use of by J. F. Campbell in his *Leabhar na Feinne*. When crossing through the hills southwards from Assynt to Loch Broom MacDonald was guided by a little girl 'just entering her teens', to whom the only thing he is known to have said on parting was the sombre quotation: 'Remember now thy Creator in the days of thy youth, while the evil days come not, nor the years draw nigh, when thou shalt say, I have no pleasure in them.'[16]

Returning from this excursion MacDonald became a missionary in Caithness until in 1807 he was presented to the Gaelic Chapel in Edinburgh by the SSPCK. In this new setting 'his preaching now became instinct with life. It was searching and fervent, as well as sound and lucid. Knowing the terror of the Lord, as he knew it not before, he warned sinners in Zion with such faithfulness and power as excited the wonder and the awe of his hearers'. His manner of delivery had noticeable impact: 'Chanting occasionally as he spoke, he added greatly to the effect of his preaching on Celtic sensibility.' Six years later he was translated to the parish of Urquhart, where he lived at Ferintosh and from which he made frequent evangelical expeditions that inevitably brought him into conflict with his church authorities. In 1818 his case came before the General Assembly, which in due course instituted a rule asserting, among other things, 'that the conduct of any minister of the Church who exercises his pastoral functions in a vagrant manner, preaching during his journeys from place to place, in the open air, in other parishes than his own, or officiating in any meeting for religious exercises, without the special invitation of the minister in whose parish it shall be held, and by whom such meeting shall be called, is disorderly …' Such meetings were to be discouraged, and, if held, reported to the next Assembly.[17]

Not put off by this rebuke John MacDonald maintained his support for the evangelical side of his church. On 5 August 1822 he repeated to the SSPCK his reasons for not being able to go to St Kilda, but on 22 August he was able to report that family circumstances which had hitherto prevented his going were now 'removed' and he planned to leave in a day or two, evidently with Murdo MacLellan who a month previously had expressed his pleasure at the prospect of a minister, at that time possibly Murdo Campbell, visiting the island at the Society's request.[18]

John MacDonald left home on 26 August 1822 and reached Skye by way of the manses at Lochcarron and Lochalsh and the ferry of 'Kylaken' three days later. He was then detained by bad weather but enjoyed staying with Rev. John Shaw, minister of the parish of Bracadale. The latter was enthusiastic and wished to go with MacDonald at least as far as Harris; and so on 4 September, 'after a rather disagreeable and tedious passage', they arrived by 'the packet' from Dunvegan at Rodel where they were met by Donald Stewart, the Harris estate factor. Ten days went by before Murdo MacLellan put in an appearance, during which period MacDonald began a journal. He was not idle while in Harris. He and his companion paid a visit to a fellow minister, Mr Bethune, at Borve, where they were received 'very kindly'. Bethune was pleased to hear that MacDonald at least was going to St Kilda, which, though he believed it to be in his parish, he had never seen at close quarters. Mindful of the Assembly's rule about itinerant preaching MacDonald noted in his journal that Bethune gave him 'full permission to discharge .. all the duties of a clergyman in St Kilda' and requested him to preach in Harris. Bethune had the church at Rodel in his charge as well as that at Scarista, and MacDonald chose Rodel as being 'more destitute in point of religious advantages'. During the sermon, delivered on Sunday 8 September, 'The people were very attentive, and some in tears'. A lecture was given in the evening, and probably on both occasions one of the audience was John Morrison, known as Ian Gobha, the religious bard of Harris.[19]

On Tuesday 10 September Shaw and MacDonald, having received 'a kind invitation from Mrs. Campbell, who has the island in lease', went to Killigray, where, on a clear, fine evening, they stood and had 'a peep of St.Kilda', with its hills blue in the distance. 'Immediately my heart seemed to be transported thither'. The clarity of St Kilda, as often, heralded rain and wind which kept the two visitors another day on Killigray, and gave MacDonald the opportunity to address the thirty or forty inhabitants 'on the great concerns of eternity'. The weather improved on Friday 13 September and MacLellan arrived in Rodel. He stayed for only an hour and then left for Ensay, 'where he had some business to transact the following day'. Shaw said he was returning home at this point, so MacDonald was alone when he caught up with MacLellan at Ensay on the Saturday evening about eight o'clock. He found the tacksman ready to sail for St Kilda early the next morning if weather permitted, but this plan met with some opposition from the minister for it would mean voyaging out on the Sabbath. MacLellan admitted the difficulty; 'But, on weighing all circumstances, particularly the lateness of the season, and the precarious state of the weather, it appeared to be rather a measure of necessity; and my scruples were abated by the consideration, that by setting sail at an early hour, we had the prospect of reaching St. Kilda in time to assemble the people for public worship.' Thirty people on Ensay were then given a lecture before everyone went to bed.

The boat left Ensay at 4.30 a.m. in a moderate southerly wind, but when past Pabbay and out into the ocean the wind increased to become 'rather squally'. The top of the mast broke 'and down came the sail and all about our ears'. After initial panic it was realised that the remaining portion of mast would carry all the sail that the boat could then bear, and in this way they mounted 'the billows, which now ran mountains high', and reached St Kilda. The strong wind forced them to shelter in the bay below Glen More, and, leaving the crew with instructions to move round to the usual landing place as soon as possible, MacLellan and MacDonald managed to get ashore and walked over to the houses.

Alarmed at first by the sight of strangers appearing on the hill the people started to take flight in all directions until they discovered that one of the figures approaching was the tacksman. John MacDonald was introduced and greeted enthusiastically. 'Mr.McLellan and I then entered the house where the late Missionary resided, and which is at present occupied by a Gaelic teacher lately sent to the island.' No special accommodation had been provided for Alexander MacKenzie after all, but the missionary's old dwelling, which 'consists of a pretty large room with two concealed beds and a kitchen', provided the cramped space into which they all had to fit.

After a little refreshment MacDonald announced his intention of preaching and that worship would begin at six that evening. 'Word soon spread - for the houses being all built in a cluster, a cry, which served as a church bell, was heard over the whole town; and at six, we all met in the School-house, which is also the only barn in the place, and a sort of common property. It was sufficient to accommodate the inhabitants, who, I believe, were all present.' The service concluded the Sabbath, people dispersed to their houses, and presumably the two most recent arrivals and the Gaelic teacher then worked out who would sleep on the floor.

Since the islanders were fully occupied with their harvest and in dealing with the tacksman, MacDonald realised that he could not ask them to assemble before the evening, so he spent his first whole day there in wandering about and talking to them as they worked. 'Finding the people thus employed, I entered on some familiar conversation with them, in order to become a little acquainted with their views and habits, particularly in regard to religion. Found that they are fond of receiving and relating news. Endeavoured to gratify them as much as I could; and they, in return, entertained me with all the little tales of their island.'

There is nothing unexpected in what he learned, for their reaction, the interest in 'news', the telling of 'the little tales', could be that of some people in remoter Hebridean communities today. But MacDonald had a motive which persuaded him to set aside these natural responses, and, in spite of his experience as an 'Ossian' collector, to attribute next to no importance to their news and stories, even though they were basic elements of the island's traditional life. His real purpose was to secure 'readier access to their minds' and 'with better effect to introduce, now and then, something about religion'. They listened carefully, agreed readily, but said little - 'which I imputed to a degree of bashfulness at this early stage of our acquaintance'. It is hard to imagine the past inhabitant of St Kilda ever having been 'a lawless savage, rioting in the wild excitements of the chase' but easy to see him in 1822 as 'plastic' to the influence of the pulpit and subject to the moulding of his opinions and habits by a determined and fervent preacher. The islanders were after all the supremely captive audience, at the mercy of whoever wished to persuade them one way or another.

After sermon on the evening of Monday 16 September John MacDonald explained to the people the purpose of his mission and hoped they would all agree, attend worship regularly, and accept what they were told. They all said they would. 'I told them farther, that during my stay among them, I meant to preach every day, besides catechising, and performing such other duties as might be necessary.' Meetings would begin at an hour that suited them but he thought 6 p.m. would be convenient. They agreed to assemble at any hour he chose. This programme was indeed followed until Friday 27 September when, after eleven days on the island, the tacksman's party left.

In addition to the evening services and the catechising there were the daytime conversations on religious topics. At first MacDonald found their views on religion 'rather defective, and in many important points extremely inaccurate', although they had some awareness of fundamental principles consistent with those for which MacDonald was looking: 'They seem to have a sense on their minds of a Supreme Being, who superintends and governs all things; and they admit also that they are sinners, and merit his displeasure. But they appear to have no correct views as to the method, either of obtaining his favour, or of being qualified for enjoying him.' To the question 'What must I do to be saved?' they had only incomplete answers. When men went to Boreray for gannets MacDonald spoke to the women in the fields and was surprised to find 'that they could repeat many of the questions of the Shorter Catechism, although they understood little of the meaning of them'. Apparently the questions had been handed down through generations and remembered by frequent repetition. He asked them if there was anyone on the island 'distinguished for religion', to which they replied that there was no one at present who could be called 'remarkable in that way' but that a few years ago there had been 'a young man of singular piety' who did scarcely anything other than pray and read the bible. He had died aged only 19 or 20. If he could not come across anybody to talk to during the day MacDonald went for longer walks and on one occasion 'took a trip' in one of the island's two boats, along with 'my kind friend Mr. McLellan', to Boreray where he was astonished at the sheer number of the gannets. On the way back they tried to catch some fish, but without success.

The sermons were planned in such a way as might stimulate spiritual progress. The first dealt with 'the angel's message to the shepherds', the second dealt with sin, the third with 'man's natural state under the law, as being under the curse'. The people listened attentively, and on the third occasion 'some were evidently impressed'. After the trip to Boreray the sermon involved reference to 'the Redeemer's sufferings', at which some were so deeply impressed that 'there was something like a melting under the word'. The following day MacDonald preached on 'the manner of becoming interested in the righteousness of Christ' and noticed, with appropriate satisfaction no doubt, that 'some, both old and young, were affected even to tears; and among others, an old man upwards of sixty years of age'. Still more were affected by the sermon on 22 September, the Sabbath, 'and at one time almost all were in tears', including two children aged about 11. The sermon over MacDonald baptised a child of John Ferguson who was the only person among the islanders who could read 'to any purpose' and whose child was the only one needing baptism as two others had died since Lachlan MacLeod had left.

The long-term effects of John MacDonald's intensive course of thirteen sermons, much catechising and 'repeated conversations' remain doubtful. One morning Alexander MacKenzie, the Gaelic teacher, saw an islander 'earnestly at prayer in the fields', a thing previously unknown to him. MacDonald himself felt that the emotional response accompanied by tears might be a good sign but could also be 'of short duration', for soon after the end of the Sunday morning service he saw small groups standing about and showing no obvious signs of concern about what they had just heard - 'a general decay of impression marked almost every countenance'. He was hoping for evidence of serious, inward contemplation, but apart from the occasional individual leaning on a wall 'as if musing over something' he saw little sign of it. He was however better pleased by certain aspects of behaviour later on. The enthusiasm with which a few 'stout active young men' repaired the roof damaged by the wind so that evening worship could take place greatly encouraged him. And when he announced that he was preaching for the last time and 'they all began to weep' the scene 'quite overcame me'. As he was preparing himself to leave he reckoned that he had been reasonably successful: 'a few, at least five or six, appear to be under serious impressions; while the general body seem to feel more than an ordinary concern about their eternal interests'.

John MacDonald also completed three more practical tasks. He listed those books gifted by the SSPCK to the 'church' of St Kilda which had been left there by 'the late Missionary' and were in a poor condition. There were 56, most of them damaged by damp and water, and these were put in the charge of Alexander MacKenzie. He listed too the island population, made up of 51 males and 57 females. On another day he 'examined the Gaelic School lately established … in the presence of Mr. McLellan, and of the parents and friends of the children'. Scholars present numbered 44, and not all were in fact children, for of 26 males six were aged between 20 and 40, three of these being married, and similarly six of the 18 females were between 20 and 30 years old. Progress, in his view, was 'truly pleasing' for the school had only been in action just over three months and even those older pupils who had been able to attend less often than the children were able to read psalms. MacDonald had frequently felt frustrated at the inability of the inhabitants to read the bible, but now it seemed as if they might soon be able to do so. 'All of them discover a great degree of eagerness to learn; and the appearance they made was such as did great credit to the talents, fidelity, and diligence of the teacher.' It presumably also did credit to the intelligence of the learners.[20]

Alexander MacKenzie was considered to be of much value to the community because of his readiness to give 'the best religious advice'. In the absence of a missionary he read from the bible on Sundays. His presence was appreciated by the people who 'cannot sufficiently express their obligations to the Gaelic School Society, for the benefit thus conferred upon them … "God bless them," say they, "for remembering us; and He will bless and reward them."' The touching gratitude of the islanders showed how pleased they now were that someone elsewhere, apart from the tacksman, should think of them in their ministerless plight.

The tacksman's crew had brought the boat round from Glen More after two nights in the bay there. It was then, as was customary, hauled ashore above high tide. On the morning of 27 September it was launched again and the visitors prepared to leave. It was an impressive experience for John MacDonald, and with imagination the scene, which in a different age had been Alexander Buchan's experience also, can be movingly pictured. All the poor people of St Kilda came down to the sea's edge, crying out and tearful as they shook hands with the departing company. Some from that little cluster on the shore climbed up the steep slope above and watched the boat disappear in the distance. 'During the greater part of the way', wrote MacDonald in his journal, 'I could scarcely get the poor St. Kilda people out of my mind; and felt as if connected with them by a most endearing tie, and as bound to carry them on my spirit. The Lord preserve them and provide for them in his good time.'

The boat safely reached Ensay with a favourable wind. The next day MacLellan took MacDonald on to Scalpay where Mrs MacLellan, 'who is nothing behind her husband in friendship and hospitality', welcomed him. Eventually he arrived in Skye and returned home by much the same route as he had used at the start of his adventure. MacLellan refused to make any charge for conveying MacDonald to and from St Kilda and for feeding him the whole time. 'This circumstance', said his guest, 'I am confident, will not escape the notice of the Society'.

At its November meeting in 1822 the Society resolved to thank Murdo MacLellan for his generous assistance.[21]

*

John MacDonald added a 'Report' to his 'Journal'. By way of explanation he wrote to the SSPCK on 26 October 1822 to say that he had visited St Kilda as requested and that he had 'a short journal of his Travels and a report of the state of things in the island', both of which he would be willing to present to the Society. The report provided some descriptive details of the island and its people but sought to concentrate on religious matters, about which he had heard a little from the inhabitants. He was told that 'they were Roman Catholics till upwards of a century ago, (I suppose about the revolution 1688,) when the Protestant religion was introduced among them, and has ever since been the religion of the island; that down from that period they had a succession of ministers or missionaries connected with the church of Scotland, but of whom, with the exception of the last two, the late missionary and his father, they now know nothing but the name'. To the question 'What must I do to be saved?' MacDonald had found that 'acceptance by *works* and not by *faith*' was the general response, and 'This, alas! it is to be feared, is a way of thinking on the subject by no means confined to St.Kilda. It is the creed of many who enjoy superior advantages to these poor people, and who sit under the Gospel from day to day, but who do not believe its record. It is the creed of our fallen nature, and a creed which nothing less than a day of divine power will wrest from deluded man'. The people were not unusually ignorant of religious truth, however, and they were not opinionated. 'I believe them, on the contrary, to be tractable, willing to be instructed, and open to conviction, when the truth is fairly represented to them: - a circumstance which must be encouraging to the missionary whose lot it may be to labour among them'. What they needed was a good man to lead them out of 'almost habitual indolence' into becoming 'savingly acquainted with that Gospel, which teaches its true subjects to be "diligent in business, fervent in spirit, serving the Lord!"' MacDonald did not doubt that, 'without interfering with the prerogative of a landlord or tacksman, a prudent missionary, by his advice and example, might effect much in this way, as well as in more important respects'. If such a missionary had 'a sensible judicious wife' all the better, for she would take a constructive interest in 'the females' and 'would in every respect be an acquisition to his own comfort'.[22]

Certain characteristics and what he considered moral, or immoral, behaviour also received MacDonald's comments. He found that the people gave due regard to the Sabbath - but 'I suspect that the proper spiritual sanctification of it is utterly unknown among them'. Drunkenness was now almost a thing of the past on St Kilda because the means of getting drunk were not available; and 'incontinence or unchastity is seldom heard of, except (shameful to say) when strangers come among them'. Isolation obviously had its advantages in these respects, but 'I wish I could say the same with regard to other vices, particularly swearing'. This was only 'too prevalent' on the island; 'common expressions, such as, by the soul, by Mary, by the book, (I suppose in allusion to the custom of taking one's oath over the Bible,) and, what is worse, by the sacred name, seem to be quite familiar with them on every occasion. The evil of this, I endeavoured as much as I could, to point out to them, and, I hope, not without some effect.' The islanders were also, said MacDonald, guilty of 'little low cunning', lying, and dishonesty, 'if they could but escape detection'. Some apparently were hot-tempered and liable to fight on a sudden impulse. Part of the trouble was, in the writer's opinion, the absence of any 'decidedly religious character' to serve as a model Christian example to the rest.

It is curious that John MacDonald, having searched out some Ossianic fragments, should have paid so little attention to St Kilda traditions. 'The people of St. Kilda', he reported, 'have scarcely any tradition among them relative to their origin or history, further than that their forefathers came originally from the Western Isles, particularly Uist and Harris ..' At the same time, perhaps without being aware of the implications, he noted one or two features of the islanders which might have indicated a strong leaning towards learning by tradition. Apart from the handing on from one generation to the next of the Shorter Catechism questions in the way that a lengthy tale might have been transmitted from father to son in any Hebridean community there was also the matter of scriptural knowledge on the island. MacDonald thought it confused, imperfect and inaccurate, but he made a further, more perceptive and interesting comment: 'It is, besides, rather of a traditional and theoretical than of a scriptural and practical character. So much is this the case, that the greater number of them are apt to consider the bare knowledge of the facts of Scripture, or rather the talent of recollecting and relating them, as all that is requisite to constitute the character of a true Christian.' No doubt there were some individuals on St Kilda whose acquaintance with the scriptures earned them the respect paid to storytellers of another kind, and perhaps, on occasion, the two experts were one and the same person.

In the end, of course, John MacDonald was most concerned about the future of the St Kilda people in relation to what he believed to be religious truth. It was essential that a missionary be sent there to safeguard this future. If 'a man of a truly apostolic spirit, (and no other than a person of this description, whatever his qualifications otherwise may be, will either suit St.

Kilda, or be reconciled to his situation in it,)' were indeed to go there, then he would be received 'with open arms' and treated with 'the utmost respect and attention'. The main obstacle to the fulfilment of this ideal was the want of 'accommodations', none as yet having been built. The house occupied by Lachlan MacLeod was neither available nor 'in a condition to admit of such alterations and repairs as would make it comfortable for a missionary to dwell in'. MacDonald had seen 'no old edifices' other than '*Christ's Church*, near the village, and situate in the burying-ground', and 'St. Brianan's, a little above the bay, on the S.W. side'. Both were in ruins and could not therefore be used for meetings. This meant that there was 'no house of worship' on the island, so that 'the people assembled in a barn, which is common property, and which, were it otherwise suitable for the purpose, cannot at all times be commanded'. Therefore, before a missionary could be sent something would have to be done by way of providing appropriate buildings, a project which could not be achieved overnight. Nothing 'costly or elegant' was needed, MacDonald reassured his SSPCK readers, just 'what is comfortable and commodious', a plain, slated house, built of stone and lime: '40 feet long, and 12 or 14 feet broad, containing two rooms and a closet, together with an outer kitchen, and a place for a cow'. This would be enough for the missionary to live in. The 'church' could be '30 feet long by 15 broad'. Stone was at hand, but other materials would have to be brought to St Kilda. No such facilities had been offered to Lachlan MacLeod and those before him, but they were now to be treated as absolute requirements for his successor.

CHAPTER 3
A new church and a new manse planned

THE SSPCK directors felt 'a deep sense of gratitude' to John MacDonald for visiting St Kilda, and determined that his Journal and Report should appear in print. At the beginning of 1823 the Ecclesiastical Sub-Committee of the SSPCK was given the task of revising and preparing them for publication. They had been clearly written for this end and closed with indications as to how the money for the cost of the 'accommodations' might be raised. The report put forward the tacksman of St Kilda, Murdo MacLellan, as 'the fittest of any' to undertake the building work because he had his own boat and because he already went to the island annually. As he would be 'most reasonable in his demands' regarding payment an appeal to 'the benevolent public' for funds should be made, and 'the Christian philanthropy for which our country is distinguished, while it extends its beneficent influence to every quarter of the globe, will "not forget to cast a pitying eye" on St. Kilda'. And soon the people of St Kilda, already recipients of small presents from visitors, would become used to money spent on them by distant organisations and individuals.[23]

In 1823 there was expectation that Parliament would shortly allocate money for building additional churches, with manses, in remote or very large parishes where the inhabitants had difficulty in reaching an existing church. An approach to this possible source was apparently suggested by J Alexander Norman MacLeod, proprietor of Harris and patron of St Kilda, but the SSPCK secretary replied that no parliamentary grant had yet been made and that it looked as though 'public liberality' might provide the only solution. There had already been some help. Mr. Robert Simpson had written in April 1821 that the Highland Missionary Society would be able to give some support if the transfer of patronage to the SSPCK was completed, and in July 1822 the SSPCK was awarded a contribution of £50 from the Missionary Society to be applied to the St Kilda mission. By letter of 28 May 1823 Rev. James Robertson, Slamannan, subscribed a guinea towards the same purpose. Further assistance came with sermons.[24]

The anniversary sermon at the SSPCK's June meeting in 1822 was preached by Rev. William Thomson of Perth and followed, when eventually published, by an appendix containing MacDonald's journal and report. A year later, on 5 June 1823 Rev. Robert Gordon delivered the sermon, giving it a special purpose with a concluding section:

> 'there is one object connected with the present plan of the Society's operations, to which, from the peculiarly interesting circumstances of the case, I would .. for a moment solicit your attention. I allude to the state of the small island of St Kilda, the inhabitants of which are at

present destitute of the means of religious instruction, and, but for the aid of the Christian public, are likely to remain in that condition.'

Gordon referred to the visit of John MacDonald, 'a most active, intelligent, and pious minister', whose report was 'already before the public', and he then outlined the circumstances of the island people who were so poor that they could not afford 'to provide religious instruction for themselves'. Church and manse were wanting, and since the constitution of the SSPCK did not permit funds to be expended in that way the only hope lay in 'the liberality of their Christian brethren'. Meanwhile 'the helpless, and hitherto but half instructed inhabitants, on whose behalf I would most earnestly solicit your aid, are looking with imploring anxiety to their richer and more enlightened brethren, for those means of religious knowledge which they cannot procure for themselves'. There was a good possibility that a missionary would be 'permanently established among them ... and it remains for the friends of the truth to determine, whether they shall be left as sheep without a shepherd, or whether there shall be sent to them a spiritual pastor'. Gordon asked that the work of previous missionaries in 'this remote, but not on that account less interesting island' should not be allowed to go to waste, and appealed at length for charitable donations. A collection was then made at the church door, the Society directors having resolved to put the money towards 'a fund for the erection of a place of worship, and a house for a missionary'.[25]

With the publication of the appeals by John MacDonald and Robert Gordon St Kilda became the subject of wide general interest. An extraordinary meeting of the SSPCK committee was held on 12 June 1823 in order to decide on exactly what if any steps should be taken to find the money 'while the attention of the public had been called to the necessities of the inhabitants of that Island'. The treasurer was already able to announce that collection and donations amounted to £101.7s.6d, and by early 1824 the sum had reached £169.11s. But money was not the only problem.[26]

The SSPCK secretary was asked at this same meeting to find out from Mr Henry David Hill, lawyer and Edinburgh agent for the proprietor of St Kilda, Mr John MacPherson MacLeod, whether Mr MacLeod would be willing to make available ground for the intended buildings, for a garden, and for grazing to one or two cows. And how much fuel would he allow to the missionary? Within a week there came a reply from Hill, answering some of the questions. Mr MacLeod had hoped an application would be made for a sum from the government grant, but from the fact that St Kilda was let to one tacksman and from 'the peculiar occupation by the people in the Island' a grant seemed uncertain if not unlikely. However the SSPCK might assume that it could have the use of all the land the present buildings occupied, although this cannot have amounted to very much.[27]

A sub-committee appointed by the SSPCK directors to push forward the proposals for a St Kilda church and manse was due to report progress on 17 July 1823 but in view of a statement made after a meeting of 'certain Gentlemen in Edinburgh who have taken an interest in the welfare of the Inhabitants of that Island' it was judged unnecessary to do anything other than to present the statement itself. It began as follows:

> 'The state of the Inhabitants of the Island of St Kilda has of late excited considerable attention. Their remote and secluded situation - their almost entire want of the institutions and advantages of civilised life - and their inability, partly from poverty, and partly from the smallness of their number, to do any thing for themselves - have produced an interest in their favour, and a desire to do something to ameliorate their condition: particularly to furnish them with the means of Moral and Religious Instruction.'

John MacDonald's journal and report, and Robert Gordon's powerful sermon, were acknowledged to have been the main agents in bringing together another anxious and philanthropic group to join the various societies and other bodies concerned to introduce what they considered the obvious benefits of mainland, 'civilised' life to the island. Because of its remoteness and seclusion St Kilda still drew all the attention, even though other island, and mainland, communities were equally impoverished and deprived, and of course it was widely taken for granted that what was going to be introduced would without question be beneficial.

The statement went on to outline yet again the terms of the old Alexander MacLeod mortification drawn from mention in SSPCK reports.

> 'From the same reports it appears also, that the Reverend Lachlan McLeod ... had lately retired on a Pension from the Society, to the full amount of his Salary; that the Society, anxious to place the Mission on a more respectable footing, had entered into a negociation with J. A. Norman McLeod Esqr. of Harris, on whom, as the representative of Alexander McLeod Esqr., the right of nominating the Missionary had devolved; - that Mr McLeod had agreed to convey to the Society the right of nomination, on the single condition of their becoming bound to raise the Missionary's Salary to £50: - and that the Society having, through aid received from the Highland Missionary Society, been enabled to undertake that obligation, they are now ready to send a Minister to St Kilda.'[28]

The interested 'Gentlemen in Edinburgh' held their meeting on 9 July, with a banker, Thomas Allan, as chairman. It was resolved 'that measures shall be immediately adopted' to raise the necessary money for the 'accommodations' through subscription. The sum required was put at £400, and when this was obtained the subscribers would appoint a committee to join with the SSPCK directors or representatives in applying it to the intended purpose. With collections, donations and subscriptions all coming in and John MacDonald busy in the north looking for money from similar sources a Committee of Subscribers was quickly formed and converted into a 'St Kilda Committee', made up of the secretary, treasurer and two ministers - Messrs Dickson and Ross - from the SSPCK and representation from the Subscribers. In November 1823 the SSPCK directors were hoping that funds would soon be available for 'erecting a Chapel and Mission house in St Kilda' so that 'a permanent Missionary for that interesting although distant colony' could go there promptly. They were anxious 'that the necessary funds should be provided in such time as to enable them to enter into contracts for the work in the course of the winter, that the buildings may be erected in summer. In the mean time a correspondence is carrying on with the proprietor of the Island (who is at present abroad) as to granting ground for these buildings, and the other necessary accommodations for a Missionary, and the Directors have no doubt of their wishes in this respect being complied with, from the interest expressed by the Proprietor before he left this country, and his great anxiety to get a Missionary established there under the Society'. The idea that building could be carried on and completed in the summer to come proved to be over optimistic.[29]

*

In the spring of 1824 John MacDonald, who had already sent in a sum of £60.9s.4½d which he had collected, had to interrupt his work 'in the North' so that he could make a second visit to St Kilda. When in the previous July the SSPCK had thought that some 'proper person', certainly a clergyman, should go that year MacDonald was the obvious choice, but later in the month he had written to say that having been long absent from his parish on evangelical tours he was 'extremely doubtful' whether he would be able to go and he had not found anyone else willing to do so - 'indeed as he understood the Tenant did not intend to visit the Island again this season, he doubted if it would be practicable for any clergyman to go there unless the tenant was there at the time'. In the event no one went to renew the islanders' religious enthusiasm in 1823. But at the end of that year MacDonald wrote to the SSPCK to ask whether he would have to visit St Kilda in 1824 and the secretary told him that 'in all probability he would be required to do so'. The assembling of funds by the St Kilda Committee was an important reason for making another journey there as a published journal and report would help in encouraging donations, and in March 1824 Murdo MacLellan, in a letter from Scalpay, happened to propose 'that a Clergyman should visit St Kilda this season'. Furthermore the moment when the erection of a church might start seemed quite close. MacDonald had collected another £70, the St Kilda Committee reported that the subscription total now stood at £380, and Robert Stevenson, member of the SSPCK as well as being a 'civil Engineer and Superintendant of the Northern light houses', had offered to visit St Kilda himself and provide the Committee with 'a plan and specification of the building which might be required'. The SSPCK directors were however as cautious as ever, deciding that no construction work could possibly begin during the summer or indeed at any point in 1824 and therefore requesting that John MacDonald make a second visit at any time that suited him. On 2 April MacDonald announced that he was willing to set out at the beginning of May and travel as before with the tacksman.[30]

Again John MacDonald kept a journal covering his journeys and stay on the island. He left home on 2 May and arrived in Skye by much the same route, with nights spent at the manses of Lochcarron and Lochalsh. He had breakfast at 'Corry' near Broadford with the MacKinnons on 4 May and then preached to a large gathering at Sconser where he was surprised to meet up with 'my old fellow-traveller to St Kilda, and tacksman of that island, Mr Murdoch McLellan', who said he had come to Skye to meet him and take him to Harris in his own boat. Also at Sconser was the new minister of Bracadale, Roderick MacLeod, who was on his way to the General Assembly in Edinburgh. Thursday 5 May was spent at Bracadale, and the following morning MacDonald made his way to Dunvegan in the company of James MacDonald of Kingsburgh. As Murdo MacLellan was going first to Scalpay MacDonald intended to cross to Rodel with 'the Harris packet' but this boat was undergoing repairs so James MacDonald 'offered to send me to Harris in his own vessel'. In this way MacDonald safely reached Rodel, where he stayed the weekend with the Harris estate factor Donald Stewart and his wife, whom John MacDonald surprisingly called his 'old friends'.[31]

MacDonald's fondness for the Stewarts is surprising because few in Harris during the 1820s can have called the factor a friend. William MacGillivray, writing in April 1818, did not like Donald Stewart, calling him 'a wretch', 'a man of mean part and conscious of his ignorance', 'a great lump of a fellow', and a great blusterer among his vassals', and 'a coward'. Nearly seventy years later John MacLeod, a crofter and fisherman at Ardhasaig north of Tarbert, described how Stewart had been responsible for clearing the people from the whole of the west side of Harris, and Alexander Carmichael heard that he had even ploughed an old burial ground at Seilebost. Rodel, to which John MacDonald came in 1822 and again in 1824 and where he preached, had just been cleared and a certain desolation must have been obvious. 'Who was Stewart?' John MacLeod was asked. 'He was a native of Appin, and he came first to this country as a shepherd to the Park in Lewis, and from the Park in Lewis he came here.'

On Sunday 8 May 1824 MacDonald preached again at Rodel at the request of the parish minister. 'The congregation were very much affected, many were in tears; and I trust some good has been done.' This was in the morning, and in the evening, after sermon, 'Many were bathed in tears'. The minister of Harris, Alexander Bethune, was happy to see the visitor once more on his way to St Kilda, 'that remote part of his clerical dominions', and readily gave the necessary permission for work by an itinerant minister from the mainland.[32]

The tacksman appeared in the afternoon of Wednesday 11 May 'in his fine barge-rigged boat for St Kilda'. MacDonald was very glad to see him, 'and even the boat which conducted me formerly to that island, and which was now to be my vehicle a second time, occasioned a sensation in my mind which I cannot define'. Once more MacDonald had to cross to Killigray, from which island he was collected by MacLellan on 12 May, and on this occasion they called in at Pabbay, 'which is the nearest land to St Kilda, and generally the point of departure for it'. As the day was 'far gone' any idea of proceeding straight on into the Atlantic was given up, and they decided to spend the night where they were, taking up 'our quarters at a venerable old gentleman's, Mr Macneil, late tacksman of St Kilda, whom of course I was happy to fall in with, and whose hospitality and kindness, and agreeable conversation, reminded me of "other days" in the Highlands of Scotland'. In Pabbay there was a school 'supported by the Education Society, which is doing well', and inevitably a sermon was called for. Three hundred islanders gathered at six o'clock in the evening 'and a more interesting set of faces I never saw'.

Also returning to St Kilda with Murdo MacLellan was the teacher, Alexander MacKenzie, who had been away for almost a year after leaving the island with the tacksman in June 1823. He had been some time at home and in visiting friends in Skye, and in spite of several attempts he had failed to make the journey back to his charge before the winter set in. In his absence the scholars seemed to maintain the skills they had learned without too much difficulty.

The party left Pabbay about 8 o'clock on the morning of Friday 13 May and reached St Kilda about eight hours later. John MacDonald was overwhelmed, and perhaps flattered, by the welcome:

'We had no sooner appeared in sight than the people flew down to the shore to meet us, and stood in a body on the shelving rock on which we were to land, to receive ourselves and our little bark. We had no sooner effected a landing … than they all pressed around me, and grasped my hand each in his turn, when I thought they would have wrung the very blood out of it. Few words passed for a minute or two, but tears trickled from every eye. I was overcome myself; at last, silence was broke - "And," says one here and there, "This is a surprise." - "This is more than looked for." - "We little expected to see his face again; - (for they addressed themselves to one another). - God bless him for this visit - He will bless him, whatever becomes of us." After I could speak, for (God knows) my heart was full, I told them, I came once more to see them, at the request of the Society in Edinburgh, who took an interest in their welfare. - "*Many, many* blessings on the head of the Society, for their attention to us, and for sending you among us." '

The emotional appeal that this and other such passages of the journal would have had to members of the St Kilda Committee and other potential donors may easily be imagined.

Three hours later, the tacksman's boat having been unloaded and hauled ashore, everyone made for the barn and a service of prayer and praise brought the day to a close. Over the nineteen days that followed before completed business and a fair wind enabled the visitors to leave MacDonald's programme was much the same as his previous one in 1822, although this time he introduced a more demanding religious timetable: 'besides meeting for sermon once a-day, as formerly, we should also meet for an exercise, somewhat resembling family worship'. This 'exercise' he thought should be in the morning, and when this was proposed everybody agreed, saying 'We can easily manage our other business; and what is every thing else to this?' So each day while MacDonald was in St Kilda the people gathered at 7 o'clock in the morning to listen to his lecture for two hours, and then they met again in the evening at six o'clock to hear the sermon for a further two hours. The minister's concentrated assault on the emotions of his captive congregation, begun in 1822, evidently achieved at least a measure of its purpose, for by the end of the first Sabbath, 15 May, he noticed with satisfaction that a new mood seemed to have developed: 'Both during the day and the evening the people appeared much affected, and discovered a greater degree of solemnity and composure, (something like a visible sanctity,) in hearing the word, than I have hitherto observed'. On the same day he saw the children assemble in a kind of Sunday school to read the Scriptures and to 'sing the praises of God with their teacher'. Further signs of his success followed. He was pleased to see some of the islanders mark special places in their bibles 'as if with a view to examine them after going home'; answers to questions put to them 'regarding man's guilt and depravity, and the method of acceptance with God, were, upon the whole, scriptural and correct'; and when he pointed out to them how the Sabbath ought to be observed, and 'the great evil of indulging in carnal and worldly conversation, and certain practices connected with the business of the week, particularly baking their bread, and carrying their potatoes or other vegetables from the field on that day', they responded with tears in their eyes, and confessed their guilt with respect to these habits in which they now saw the evil. 'With God's help, we are resolved to avoid them in future.' The next Sabbath was quite different - 'No levity, no giddy conversation, no disposition to meet in parties during the intervals of public worship, every one retired to his house, and seemed to court secresy'. Private devotion took over in several of the squalid hut dwellings, and 'a more than ordinary degree of solemnity and sacred decorum marked their conduct during the whole day'.

In what was left by way of working hours while MacDonald was present ordinary island tasks were carried out. Sheep 'fleecing' took place close to the cliffs, houses were thatched, men went to Boreray for eggs, women milked cows and sheep twice a day, and quantities of feathers, barley and surplus 'articles of produce' were brought to the tacksman either as payment of rent - this chiefly in feathers - or in exchange for goods and 'articles of husbandry' which had been carried by the tacksman in accordance with the community's wishes and needs. MacDonald watched some of the 'fleecing': 'The animals are driven together to a precipice on the summit of a high perpendicular rock, and are there hemmed in on all sides, by the men and their dogs, till every one of them is got at, and stripped of its fleecy mantle.' He saw one sheep fall about 300 feet 'headlong into the sea ... and completely disappear'. On Saturday 28 May Murdo MacLellan and MacDonald examined the Gaelic school, where there were 57 pupils, among them as usual 'several grown-up and married persons, at least 16 or 18', and, as on the previous occasion, MacDonald sent a modified extract from his journal for that date to the Gaelic Schools Society after he got home.

The tacksman had finished his business in the island by the afternoon of Friday 27 May, but it was the following Wednesday evening before the boat could leave. Again the departure was upsetting to everyone. A final service was held in the barn where 'The scene was peculiarly affecting'. The people then all went to the shore 'and amidst tears and cries' MacDonald shook hands with them. The voyage turned out well; towards ten o'clock next morning the boat arrived at 'Caolis' in North Uist where lived Captain MacNeil, 'a near relation of Mrs McLellan', and soon after midday MacDonald was on his way from 'Caolis' to Berneray where he addressed a company of around 200 people. More preaching and lecturing took place in Scalpay, Tarbert, and many miles across the hills and moors at Uig in the far west of Lewis, until at length on the evening of 15 June the minister returned to his own house in the parish of Urquhart.

*

News of John MacDonald's second mission to St Kilda was welcomed by the SSPCK on 1 July 1824, when another 'very favourable account of the Island' was given in a letter also 'expressing in high terms the kindness and attention of the Tacksman'. MacDonald wrote:

'I may here observe in general, that the people were extremely glad to see me back again, and the more so that they little expected it when we parted formerly. That they readily listened to my instructions twice a day (at 7 in the morning and 6 in the evening) for 19 days successively, That I have reason to believe that not a few among them have derived benefit from them - some I trust are asking the way to Zion, and the greater part of them has made considerable improvement in point of religious knowledge and morals. I was pleased particularly to find that the Sabbath is strictly observed by them, and that the worship of God is set up regularly in almost every family. It was inexpressibly pleasing to me to hear at a certain hour in the Evening the voice of praise and of prayer to God ascend from almost every family in the island.'

Cordial thanks were accordingly sent to the minister for his important work and to Murdo MacLellan for 'the generous and handsome manner' in which he had assisted the Society's missionary. Though it was wanted without delay for publication as an appendix to Dr McGill's anniversary sermon, already 'in the Press', MacDonald's journal was late in coming as he was busy with parish business after his return, and it was well into 1825 before it appeared.[33]

On the day that John MacDonald left St Kilda, 2 June 1824, the secretary of the SSPCK received a communication from John MacPherson MacLeod's agent, H D Hill, enclosing another from Mr Rickman, 'Secretary to the Commission upon the Parliamentary fund for the erection of churches in the Highlands'. Rickman suggested that a renewed application for the St Kilda church and manse might be worthwhile, and Hill wished to know whether the Society 'would be willing to concur in such an application by representing the urgency of the case'. The Society directors authorised their secretary to concur. John MacDonald wrote on 27 August to say that Sir James MacKenzie of Scatwell might be worth contacting with regard to possible government aid for the St Kilda mission, but it seems that nothing came of either this or whatever further steps were taken by Hill. In December 1824 Murdo MacLellan, ever eager to push things along, offered to contract for the buildings on the island at £20 lower than any other person, and in the early months of 1825 the Society considered both this and a letter from John MacDonald containing 'Specification and Estimate of the Buildings at St Kilda by Mathieson and Macdonald both residing at Conan Bridge near Dingwall'. These proposals were to be placed before Robert Stevenson for his opinion, but if he saw them he made no immediate response.[34]

No mission to St Kilda was undertaken in 1825, and the first news from the island that year was received by the ESSGS in a letter from its teacher there, Alexander MacKenzie, dated 11 July. He reported that 49 were attending school, of whom 6 were reading 'the Guide', 36 'the Testament', and 7 the bible. Another 9 had left the school five months previously, 'being able to read fluently'. The benefits of the interest shown by the ESSGS were then indicated,

MacKenzie evidently acting as temporary missionary as well as teaching:

'on Sabbath the Scholars meet at 8, and dismiss at half past 10, and again at half past 3, and dismiss at 5. All the inhabitants meet at 12 for religious instruction, without the exception of a single individual, unless prevented by sickness or some other necessary cause, and continue together till 2; and they meet again in the evening at 6, and dismiss at 8. The Rev. John Macdonald's acceptable visits to us, and his pious and laborious labours of love while here, will not soon be forgotten.

'You may easily understand that much good has been done for the poor people of St Kilda; and many of those clouds which formerly overshadowed their mental powers are now dispelled, and the people who sat in darkness have seen some certain measure of light.

'Some of them say, that the result of your bounty to the poor inhabitants of this destitute land will be had in grateful remembrance to the latest posterity. Their own prophetic way of expression is: *Cha bhi muinntir Hiort gu deireadh an t'saoghail cho aineollach sa bhà iad, do bhrì, gu bheil iad a'faotainn comais focal naomha Dhe a leubhadh anns a chainnt a thuigeas iad.* - That is, "The people of St Kilda shall not, to the end of the world, be so ignorant as they were; because they are receiving ability to read the sacred Word of God in the language they can understand." May God, in his infinite mercy, grant that their prophetic wishes may be accomplished.'

Much, however, remained to be done and MacKenzie, in conveying the thanks of the people to the ESSGS, also stated their earnest request that 'in tender compassion to them, in their necessitous and destitute condition, you would grant the continuance of the School for some time longer'.

In another letter, written only a week later 'as Mr McLellan, the tacksman, is detained by contrary winds', MacKenzie drew the attention of his employers to 'some circumstances peculiar to this place'. He first pointed out that the islanders were 'generally employed in fowling, from the beginning of April to the latter end of October', for they had to pay most of their rent in feathers, and that this occupation 'must be a very material hindrance to improvement', perhaps because they therefore rarely attended school during this period. Similarly cattle-herding kept some of the children from being present through the middle of the day. A third 'hindrance' might have been rather surprising to the ESSGS committee:

'The houses are thatched with great quantities of straw; and in the month of May, when the barley begins to cover the ground, they uncover their houses, and spread the inside of the thatch on the field, to improve their small crop. They have neither vents nor chimneys for the emission of the smoke; only some small openings at both ends of the house to enable them to traverse safely through it, consequently the greater part of the house is darkish, though surrounded with the dazzling splendour of the meridian sun. This must be a great disadvantage to the most industrious student.'[35]

Any student will have found it difficult to practice reading in the gloom of the interior, but the fact that MacKenzie held 'a night School' from the beginning of November till the beginning of March indicates that some study was possible by fulmar oil light.

Education everywhere at this time was largely of a religious kind except perhaps at the parish schools, and more often than not comment on the teaching or examination by visiting clergymen was confined to religious matters. In 1822 when Alexander MacKenzie opened his school in St Kilda reports came in to the impartial ESSGS on its schools in other islands. Improvements in behaviour, increased ability to read, and gratitude to the body that had instituted the schools were among the main topics, but Gaelic, the language through which these things were achieved, came in for little attention by visitors. Two clergymen of different denominations, along with two Gaelic School teachers from the parish of South Uist, attended the examination of the Gaelic School in Barra. Rev. Alexander Nicolson, established church minister, remarked chiefly on progress in reading the bible, the new testament, the psalm book and the *Guide to Reading*; while Rev. Angus MacDonald, Catholic priest, commented similarly, but also took evident pleasure in hearing Gaelic being used, and recorded that 'Several parents were present, who felt the most gratifying sensation on hearing the Divine Word read in their own language by their children'. Both men approved of the teacher's efforts, but Angus MacDonald showed a wider sensitivity to the situation:

'In confirmation of the Teacher's attention to his charge, I understand he keeps Sunday Schools for such as choose to attend, to prevent any violation of the Sabbath, and check immorality. As a pastor of souls, I have cause to be satisfied with his conduct and assiduity in promoting the good of his pupils, and hope the Society [ESSGS] may be pleased to continue him, if it be his own desire. As a Catholic clergyman, I return thanks to the Society for their liberality of sentiment, set forth in their instructions to their Teachers, in confining these instructions to teaching alone, abstracting from controversial points, and giving trouble to such as are of a different persuasion, at same time affording equal advantage of education. As a true Highlander, my gratification is still increased, from a consideration of the encouragement given, to the revival of a primitive language, which has scarcely a rival. It is rare to find, if at all, a language which expresses the most sublime sentiments and ideas, still intelligible to the lowest peasant, its charms and beauties are only known and admired by those who possess it.'[36]

Evangelical sincerity and a certain perception there may have been in St Kilda's own missionary examiner, John MacDonald, but he expressed neither interest in nor admiration for the ancient and rich language used by him in his lectures and sermons and by the simple people who listened to what he said. On the other hand the SSPCK now showed a limited and practical interest in Gaelic, probably encouraged by the success of the Gaelic Schools. This was a complete contrast to their view of the language a century earlier and, in its origin and purpose, markedly different from the affectionate understanding shown by Rev. Angus MacDonald. In October 1825 a unanimous opinion was given that the attitude towards Gaelic in SSPCK schools should be changed: 'Although the people appear to be in general reluctant at their children learning Gaelic, and are more anxious that they should be taught English, yet .. injury is done by yielding to them in this respect, and .. the English can never be efficiently taught except through the medium of Gaelic, which is the language in which the people think and carry on their daily communication with each other.' This was a far cry from the imposition of English and condemnation of Gaelic as a sign of barbarity, ignorance and inclination towards popery that had been SSPCK policy when Alexander Buchan was in St Kilda. Of course in that island as in many other places less remote English had never secured a place, and what the SSPCK was now saying, 'that in all those districts where the Gaelic language is in general used, it should be made an imperative regulation, that the Gaelic should be taught in the first instance', was in part an admission that most probably Gaelic had always been the medium employed by a teacher or missionary who wanted to achieve anything. Perhaps the only difference was that until the ESSGS schools appeared Gaelic had not actually been taught to native Gaelic speakers.

As a consequence of this resolution a new set of instructions for SSPCK teachers was contrived, these including a requirement for more precise and regularly kept records of scholars and their progress, the learning of catechism questions and answers as of old, the learning too of psalm verses and scripture passages each day, the teaching of Gaelic as proposed, and the establishment of a 'Sabbath Evening School both for ordinary scholars and for any people who choose to attend'. Once Alexander MacKenzie had left, St Kilda had no SSPCK teacher, but the new guidelines most probably influenced the approach taken by later churchmen, ministers and catechists, who attempted to continue education on the island through the mid nineteenth century.[37]

CHAPTER 4

*Plans and arrangements for the buildings and
John Macdonald continues his visits*

ROBERT Stevenson, who did not visit St Kilda for work on site, submitted a report on the proposed church and manse on 13 March 1826. Annexed to it were the specification and a sketch plan. The design had been discussed with John Tawse, secretary to the SSPCK, and with Thomas Allan the banker, and was drawn 'upon a scale corresponding as nearly as may be with the very limited nature of the fund, amounting it is believed only to £600'. The church was intended to have room for about 100 'Sitters', and 'for a time part of it may perhaps be occupied as a School house'. The missionary's house was to be built 'contiguous' to the church, 'and with a view to conveniency in this exposed situation, a private communication is formed between the dwelling house and the Church'. There were only four rooms, 'with other conveniences', in the house. Seating in the church was to be forms, for 'every thing is conceived in the same style of economy'. Since it was difficult for a missionary to bring larger moveable furniture with him, 'the bulky and mighty articles' were to be provided.[38]

In calculating expenditure Stevenson assumed 'gratuitous services in some instances', that the tacksman would convey materials in his boat at moderate cost, and that the islanders would assist in landing and moving these materials up from the shore. 'He is further confident that when the Lighthouse Ship in the course of her proper voyages to Harris can be rendered usefull, the Lighthouse board will as in similar cases, be disposed to allow the vessel to carry passengers or materials for such a work.' As regards the building operations, he did not think that they should be undertaken by contract because since the work was 'small' and 'the natural difficulties of the place' were great there would not be much chance of 'persons of respectability' being willing to participate at a low price. Inspection of a contractor's progress would be very expensive, 'although without such Inspection the whole fund might be expended in Works which in so exposed a situation would in all probability be so imperfect as in a few years to render the buildings untenable.' Stevenson considered it better to find 'a young man of good character and moderate expectations' who would act as working foreman.

Timber, already cut, should be transported from Greenock, where the reporter's friend, Quinton Leitch, merchant and shipping agent for the Lighthouse Board, would cheerfully help because of his 'regard to the Church' and 'his well known patriotic and benevolent disposition'. Leitch's 'acquaintance with seafaring business' would ensure that he would 'execute matters of this kind in the best manner'. Certain articles of furniture would be of the category 'supplied to Lighthouses and Barracks', while since the SSPCK 'can have no very regular establishment at St Kilda' and the missionary may be frequently changed some of the articles would be fixtures, 'or at least such as can be easily taken charge of' and 'extremely difficult if not impossible' for the missionary to take to or from the island at his own expense.

Stevenson proposed that the work should not start until the summer of 1827, and that only the working foreman should go to the island in 1826 in order to prepare the way by examining local materials and deciding on what would have to be shipped out. The lighthouse vessel could take him as far as Harris in May, and then he could go on to St Kilda with the tacksman 'at little expense to the Church fund'. It was also suggested 'that the Missionary who is to undertake this charge should at the same time visit the Island, and be otherwise identified with the proposed operations'. The final recommendation was that the SSPCK or the St Kilda Committee should ensure that 'a systematic body' exist properly to manage the whole business.

Details of dimensions, materials and construction were given in the lengthy specification, from which the description of the pulpit will serve as an example:

'the Pulpit shall be of an Octagonal form measuring 3 feet 6 inches in height and 3 feet in width on the floor inside measure; the framing to be 1½ ins. in thickness and 4 inches in breadth; finished at top edge with a moulding or cope 3 inches in breadth and a back board measureing 18 inches in length by 12 inches in breadth and 1 inch thick supported in a sloping direction by two brackets; One of the sides of the Pulpit to form a door which is also to be pannelled like to the other sides and hinged with broad tailed Edge-Hinges. The Pulpit seat of the above to be of the same breadth and thickness with the other seats in the Church. The sole or floor shall be elevated 4 feet above the floor of the Church, and that of the Pulpit shall be accessible, both from the body of the Church and from the Minister or Missionary's house by a flight of steps measureing each 9 inches as shewn in the said Plan.'

The St Kilda Committee was studying Stevenson's submission, including the plan, in early April 1826, and a month later everything was laid before the SSPCK meeting on 11 May. John MacDonald, happening to be in Edinburgh, was asked to attend and provided 'many valuable hints'. Now that plans were well forward, though not yet at the stage of final arrangements, it seemed that buildings might be complete by the summer of 1827 and that there was every chance of a 'stated pastor' being soon in action. After remitting the subject to a subcommittee the meeting asked MacDonald if he would revisit St Kilda within the next few weeks and he replied that he was willing to do so - because he had such an interest in 'the inhabitants of that distant island' and was anxious to further the Society's work. The SSPCK directors considered that 'it is mainly to the exertions of that benevolent individual, that the Society are indebted for the funds which have been raised', MacDonald having recently sent in £104.4s.11d collected after sermon in various places in the north. The inmates of the Blind Asylum paid £5.10s to him, being savings from their earnings set aside 'that the poor Inhabitants of St Kilda may soon enjoy the same blessings with which they themselves are so highly favoured'.[39]

MacDonald had hoped to voyage with the tacksman in July, but on 20 September he wrote to say that as 'the Revenue Cutter' could not be 'procured' in 1826 he intended to postpone his visit till the following spring. When Alexander MacKenzie was writing his annual letter from St Kilda to the ESSGS on 15 June 1826 he was of the impression that 'our worthy friend Rev. Mr McDonald, is expected to visit this Island soon', and for that reason merely said that he had two classes in which there were 13 males and 22 females and had kept a night school through the winter. 'As to our religious attendance, we continue the same as formerly, with this acceptable addition that the heads of families not only pray in their closets, and with their families, but the one third of them take the occasional privilege of praying publicly in our small congregation on Thursday and other evenings, and they are qualified to do it with some degree of acceptance.' The teacher's letter was brief, partly because he imagined that John MacDonald would take away another from him and partly because 'I like better to be reported than to make reports'.[40]

In spite of his inability to reach St Kilda in 1826 the ESSGS received a letter from MacDonald dated 18 January 1827 containing an account of the examination of the St Kilda school as if he had been there himself. It opened with statements that did not sound as if they related to that particular island: 'After having examined the more advanced classes among them, on the general principles of christianity, and particularly the leading doctrines of the gospel, on all of which they gave me much satisfaction, I confined my examinations to the chapter which they had just read'. The rest of the description consisted almost entirely of questions put to children and their replies, all of which conveyed little apart from illustrating the conventional method used to persuade an easily-led group into accepting and giving required responses. When John MacDonald was holding one of his morning services back in 1824 he realised that, unusually, the listeners were not understanding him: 'I seemed to myself to have forgotten that I was addressing not strong men but babes. I immediately checked myself, and endeavoured to bring my subject down to the level of their capacities'. Now in 1826 the St Kilda people, young and old, were still 'babes' being 'educated' towards particular religious ends.[41]

The account of the school examination in MacDonald's letter to the ESSGS was uncharacteristic of the writer and seemed more like a quotation from some other examiner, such as the tacksman or possibly even the teacher. It made the usual plea for the school to be continued until a missionary was appointed, which event was not expected to be delayed much longer. Far away in distant Edinburgh the preparations for establishing the 'accommodations' for that missionary were proceeding slowly.

In September 1826 Murdo MacLellan in Scalpay sent to the SSPCK his offer to build 'the Chapel' in St Kilda for £550. He clearly hoped for a prompt answer, but on 18 January 1827 John MacDonald was writing to say that 'Mr McLellan of St Kilda' was eager to know whether his offer had been accepted. The Society directors had decided either not to heed Stevenson's advice or to interpret it widely as they resolved to have the work carried out under contract, and on receiving MacDonald's letter they gave the St Kilda Committee the task of getting construction started 'suitably to the funds which have been collected'. MacDonald continued as an intermediary between the Society and MacLellan, for certainly by March 1827 there was no doubt that use would be made of the tacksman's services. The SSPCK secretary reported to a meeting of the committee on 5 April 1827 'that he had this morning received the draft of the Building Contract for the Church and House of St Kilda from Mr Alexander MacKenzie, Builder in Stornoway, approved of by him and Mr McLellan ... who were willing to undertake the Building on the terms of the Contract'. The Society treasurer was immediately authorised to sign the contract and to return it for the signatures of the contractors and their cautioners. Thereupon the contract was signed by all parties and in June Murdo MacLellan wrote from Scalpay 'holding out the prospect of the whole work being finished this season'. Again this was too optimistic, especially as MacLellan himself, a key figure, was preparing to leave Scalpay and to give up the tenancy of St Kilda.[42]

The other suggestion by Robert Stevenson that the missionary intended for St Kilda should visit along with a 'working foreman' in order that he be associated with the buildings in the minds of the people depended for its fulfilment on the existence of a missionary in that position. There was no such person in 1826 and 1827. The idea, however, may have fostered the wish that someone, preferably John MacDonald, should go. MacDonald after all had said that he would be willing to do so in the spring of 1827, means of travel having failed him in the previous year. Use of the 'Revenue Cutter' envisaged for 1826 signalled the beginning of a change in the usual arrangements for reaching the island, made necessary anyhow by MacLellan's plans for moving. There was too a difference in the patterns of estate management which may at some point have influenced MacLellan when reflecting upon his existing situation. Lachlan MacKinnon of Corry in Skye was now principal factor for John MacPherson MacLeod, proprietor of St Kilda, and Murdo MacLellan was at this point called 'the Subtacksman', a position that may have meant less advantage in being the tenant of St Kilda. By April 1827 it was known that MacKinnon was keen to accompany MacDonald on the latter's third mission to the island, and as the SSPCK secretary had been told by them that they would be ready to depart early in the month he had applied to the Inspector General of the

Coast Guard for the use of 'the Government Cutter'. The inspector, Captain Knight, complied with this request 'most politely', and the cutter was ordered to collect the two men at Portree, which it did on 5 April. 'They were unable, however, to effect a landing on the island, from the weather being too stormy, and were obliged to put back, without having attained the object in view.' The next opportunity for the voyage did not come until June, and that was too late for Lachlan MacKinnon.[43]

*

John MacDonald and his second son were at Corry on 14 June 1827, but here they found that Lachlan MacKinnon was not well and could not accompany them after all. The factor, nevertheless, wrote to Murdo MacLellan to tell him 'that although his health will not admit of his visiting St Kilda at present, as far as he is concerned, any measure Mr MacDonald and Mr. McLellan may adopt for the comfort and accommodation of the Clergyman to be settled there, shall meet with his hearty concurrence'. The MacDonalds therefore went on alone and on 18 June were at Lochmaddy where they were 'waiting .. for a fair wind to proceed to St Kilda'. At this stage they were being transported by 'his Majesty's Revenue-Cutter, the Swift, Captain Beatson master', and had met the captain at Loch Bracadale on the evening of 16 June so presumably left Skye from there. In the morning of 19 June 'we got fairly out of the sound of Harris, and were scudding our way across the billows of the Atlantic, till we reached within about fifteen miles of St Kilda, when, on a sudden, owing to a tremendously heavy gale, which sprung up quite a-head of us, we were obliged to put back to Harris'. Forced to shelter there for several days they had to give up hope of reaching their destination in the *Swift* because Captain Beatson 'found that the time allowed him for the expedition had expired'.[44]

Disappointed, and having nowhere to stay, John MacDonald thought of 'taking a trip to the island of Lewis' where he would take part in the communion at Uig on 24 June. He and his son then left Harris for several days of preaching in various places where there were showers of 'divine influences' and 'much weeping', and came to Scalpay in the evening of Wednesday 27 June. MacDonald later wrote in his journal:

> 'I had scarcely sat down when I began to mention to Mr McLellan how vexed I was, and how sadly disappointed, at being obliged to return home then, a second time, without being able to see the poor people of St Kilda. I had not, however, gone through with the one half of my tale, when he interrupted me by saying, he felt for my situation, and was disposed, notwithstanding that it was highly inconvenient for him at present to do so, (having his cattle to remove to South Uist, to a new farm he had taken there,) to accompany me in his own boat to St Kilda;

and that if Mr Stewart, Harris's factor, who had taken his present place into his own hands, would allow these cattle to remain a few days longer on the island, that he would set off with me to-morrow, wind and weather serving.'

John MacDonald was most grateful for this act of generosity, wrote to Stewart himself, and in return heard that 'in consideration of the object I had in view, my request was granted.' But wind and weather did not serve, and MacDonald spent much of his time preaching to 'perishing souls' whose opportunities to hear the word were 'like angel visits, .. "few and far between"'. He was still in Scalpay on 5 July, having also preached in Tarbert and spent evenings 'addressing the people of this neighbourhood, who assembled regularly after work-hours to hear sermon'. That day they were able to set out soon after noon and against a contrary wind they reached as far as Ensay where they spent the night. The day after they made Pabbay, where again 'we took our quarters with Mr McNeil, once tacksman of St Kilda, and a gentleman remarkable for Highland hospitality'. Sermons followed, and MacDonald examined the Pabbay school which was 'supported by the Inverness Society', that is, the Inverness branch of the Society for the Education of the Poor in the Highlands. 'The school-master seems to do credit to his profession, and to be a blessing to the people, in promoting their moral and religious improvement.'

At about 3 o'clock on the morning of Saturday 7 July they left Pabbay, but because the wind was variable and the weather 'foul and hazy' they took 24 hours to make the crossing to St Kilda, arriving at the same hour of the morning on Sunday when the people were asleep - 'the little town was hushed in silence, and not a vestige of smoke was to be seen'. But one man in the midst of his duty 'guarding the corn from the cattle' saw the boat come in, gave the alarm, and soon the visitors were welcomed ashore enthusiastically. Off they went to the houses, and at 8 o'clock the tireless MacDonald gathered the people for worship. He preached in 'the forenoon', and again in the evening. Another invasion of religious doctrine had begun; 'and it gratified us much to hear Mr McK., the Gaelic teacher (who is still continued with them,) say that there were several hopeful characters among this class. "And should but one soul be converted," says he, "it were worth coming fifty times to St Kilda for it." '

John MacDonald examined the school as a matter of course and found that Alexander MacKenzie was busy with 53 scholars, including 20 females and some married men. Several of those attending were 'as old as 40 and upwards.' The minister was delighted to learn that 'the Saint Kildaites have them now in every house who can read the Word of God to them', and wished that kind friends would send some valuable and appropriate books such as Boston's *Fourfold State*, Bunyan's *Pilgrim's Progress*, Doddridge's *Rise and*

Progress and Dyer's *Christ's Famous Titles* for the people to enjoy reading. There would have to be enough books for equal distribution over about twenty families in order to prevent jealousy, for 'There is no place in which little jealousies are more apt to break out, than where there is no distinction of rank - no superior, and therefore no inferior, - in short, where *liberty and equality* reign - and if they do so any where on earth, it is in St Kilda'. Another pleasure was to be told by the teacher that seven or eight young men under 20 and four or five married men met together for prayer and reading the scriptures once a week. 'I said immediately in my heart, *God bless the lads!*'[45]

Services were held frequently as before. After sermon on the first Monday MacDonald baptised four children, all that survived of those born since 1824; and on Tuesday 10 July after the evening service there was a marriage. The bridegroom, who was the brother of the pious young man of whom MacDonald heard on his first visit, pleased the minister with his remark to some of the company 'who proposed that they should have a reel at the dance' which, according to custom, was to follow the wedding. 'Cha mhaith an cleachdamh sin air an t-searmoin a chuala sinn,' said the bridegroom - 'That would not be a good practice after the sermon we have heard.' Another example of piety was the old man, mentioned by MacDonald in his previous journals, who had been 'affected even to tears' in 1822, had thereafter gone blind, and in 1824 felt that he was 'by nature a lost sinner'. His name, a reminder of others so called long ago, was Finlay MacDonald, and he was well over sixty years old during the period of MacDonald's missionary visits. 'He appears really to feel the power of the truth,' observed MacDonald in 1827, 'and, as I am told, to have no relish for any thing so much as conversing about the Scriptures, and hearing them read to him.' Finlay was something of an exception to the principle upon which the evangelical preacher relied, that 'the season of youth is the time when impressions of truth are most easily made on the mind'.

Although it was originally intended that John MacDonald and Lachlan MacKinnon should 'fix upon the site for the buildings', by the time the former and Murdo MacLellan reached the island work had already begun. After a successful address at 9 o'clock on Monday morning which reduced some listeners to tears, 'Mr McLellan, my son, and I, visited the buildings intended for a place of worship and mansion-house for a missionary'. They were pleased to find that 'the work was going on with spirit'. Eight active young men, 'quite expert at their business', were fortunately also 'men of correct and regular conduct', which was 'of no small consequence to the morals of the people of St Kilda'. As far as they could see the site seemed to be well chosen, 'as well indeed as if we ourselves had been on the spot at the time'. It was about 400 yards from the houses and 'a little above that part of the shore where the only landing place is'. MacDonald thought that the fact that the manse being prepared for the missionary, the walls of which were nearly finished, would be some distance from the dwellings of the inhabitants 'will certainly conduce much to his comfort'.

The foundation stone of the church was laid on Wednesday 11 July 1827, and John MacDonald offered up a prayer on the occasion. This was succeeded by 'a few hints of advice' to the people which were greeted 'with feelings of joy on their part approaching to ecstacy', and 'On every face you could see the tears trickling down', including those of 'the youths, and even little children'. The nature of the ground had compelled a change in the site for the church so that instead of joining the manse at right angles 'it is placed in a line with it', and in order 'to afford the Missionary the pleasure of eyeing the Atlantic from his parlour .. I have ordered a window to be struck out in the western gable of the house'. Two days afterwards MacDonald and MacLellan marked out an area of land for the missionary's glebe. 'Corry, who is factor to the proprietor, having given authority to Mr McLellan to act for him in that business', the two men spent a morning 'looking over the lands, or rather straggling *crofts* around the village', and decided on a portion of them lying about the church and manse and to a large extent separated from the rest of the 'village' ground. The area was bounded by the shore and by 'the bottom of a steep hill', and amounted in all to approximately four acres, nearly all arable. Some temporary boundary marks were pointed out to the people 'that they might know what was to be the property of their future missionary', and permission was given to them to work the land until that gentleman appeared. Firmer, more evident boundaries would eventually be necessary, and some deduction in their rents would have to be allowed to compensate the people for loss of land. 'It is to be hoped, however, that the proprietor, who has generously given the land, will give instructions to his factor or tacksman to make every due and reasonable consideration to the people on this account.' During the year 1830-1831 the SSPCK allowed £4 for 'damage sustained by the tenants of St Kilda in building a Church and Manse on the Island'.[46]

The stay on the island this time was quite short. On Saturday 14 July, less than seven days after their arrival, the tacksman and his crew, with islanders to help, loaded baggage, feathers and other produce on board the boat, 'which had lain all the while at anchor, that, in the event of our departure taking place either at the commencement or conclusion of the Sabbath, there might be as little interference of worldly matters as possible with the sanctity of that day'. MacDonald was delighted that MacLellan had made this arrangement. 'Works of necessity,' the minister declared, as if creating the rule on the spot, 'are allowable on the Sabbath; but it is to be feared there are many who account as works of necessity what are not so.' The crew roused everybody early on the Sabbath morning, 'the wind blowing pretty fair for Harris', but MacLellan, whose 'pressing business' meant that he should return home as soon as possible, agreed to delay departure until at least the evening, so as to allow time for appropriate sermons and worship. The wind miraculously fell during the day to a perfect calm as if by the design of 'Providence', and then revived at about 5 o'clock in the afternoon. 'We stepped into the boat: at seven we were under sail.' Left behind were the inhabitants of St Kilda, gathered on the shore after the Sabbath services during which almost all, including old Finlay, had been weeping once more.

The boat reached Pabbay after twelve hours on the open sea, and here some of the crew were put ashore. The next call was at Ensay, then Rodel, and finally Scalpay was reached about 11 in the morning. 'Thus Providence so ordered it, that Mr McLellan was home just in time to attend to a cattle market .. at Tarbat, in the neighbourhood' on Tuesday 17 July. MacDonald went with MacLellan to the market but 'felt the day hang heavy upon me, and was quite out of my element'. After nearly a week in Scalpay MacDonald father and son crossed to Dunvegan along with MacLellan's cattle, called to see how 'Corry' was, and were back at the Manse of Urquhart on Friday 27 July. Three days later John MacDonald announced his return in a letter to the SSPCK, in which he remarked that after getting home 'I found all here well, only my friends began to be seriously apprehensive about me having taken upwards of six weeks to a trip which I expected to have accomplished in three.' He continued with some general observations regarding progress of every kind on the island:

'I shall transmit you a Journal of my proceedings as soon as I can possibly get it transcribed … I may .. observe that the people received me with no less enthusiasm at this time than on former occasions. That they seem to be making increasing improvements in religious knowledge and morals, and are inexpressibly happy at the prospect of having a Missionary settled among them, and cast an eye frequently on the prognostics of this desireable privilege in the buildings which are now going on in the vicinity of their little village. I may also observe that during the eight days I had been among them I preached to them always twice and sometimes thrice a day, that I married a couple, and baptized four children. I trust the word preached has not been without effect and particularly among some of the young people, of whom I entertain promising hopes, but what the extent of this effect is, "the day alone shall reveal".

'Mr McLellan and I marked out some land for a Glebe… In regard to the buildings, I must say, that so far as they are carried on, the work seems to me to be solid and substantial. The sites are as eligible as any that could be fixed upon. The Mason work of the Missionary's house was almost finished before we left the island, and the foundation of the church was laid in our presence. I assembled the people on the occasion, addressed them, and prayed with them, all standing round the foundation stone. Many of them seemed considerably affected even to tears, but they were tears of Joy. The scene I must own was interesting. The workmen expect that the buildings will be roofed in by the middle of Autumn.'

The Society appreciated this letter, sent their thanks to John MacDonald and Murdo MacLellan, and once again looked forward to being able to send out a missionary in the following summer, this time 1828, 'to labour stately among these distant but interesting Islanders'.

As most of the materials had been sent to St Kilda in early summer 1827 the contractor, Alexander MacKenzie of Stornoway, had thought that the buildings would be finished in August, but though the weather did not much hinder them the workmen, as MacDonald reported, still had plenty to do in the autumn when they had to leave to avoid being marooned for the winter. It was believed in Edinburgh that the manse was then 'nearly finished' and that the church walls were 'ready for the roof'. Work would begin again as soon as it was possible to go to the island in the spring and no doubt everything would be completed by the beginning of summer.[47]

*

On the day of the marriage in St Kilda, 10 July 1827, the contractor, Alexander MacKenzie, enquired about payment of the second instalment to cover works so far. Reports from Robert Stevenson accompanied these works, beginning with one on 'the necessity of forthwith sending an Inspector to the Island to attend to the due execution' thereof. A suitable person had been found. John Skethway, builder in Leith, 'who has had some experience in this way', offered to go under certain conditions - 'if from the day I leave here you promise to pay me 25s per week until the 1st of November, and from that date to the 1st of February 18s and then to rise again to 25s per week, with expences paid out to St Kilda and back again to Edinburgh'. Stevenson consulted with Tawse and they agreed to accept the offer but reduced the payments to 22s weekly from 'tomorrow', 11 July 1827, when Skethway was due to depart, until Martinmas, and then, in the event of continued services, 15s to March. 'If after this you are still wanted, your wages will rise again' to 22s. The difference of 3s between what Skethway asked and what he would be given would be paid if his conduct as inspector was approved at the end of the contract. There was some initial difficulty in settling with him but this was overcome and he left Edinburgh as planned on 11 July for Troon whence he sailed, with locks and hinges for the buildings, in the cutter belonging to the Commissioners for the Northern Lights in the company of Mr Slight, Stevenson's 'Superintendant'. On 27 July the SSPCK directors, having assented to these arrangements, heard that the cutter had arrived at St Kilda, and authorised their treasurer 'to pay the expence of the locks, hinges etc. which by the contract were to be furnished by the Society'.[48]

On 4 August 1827 Skethway, hoping for an early completion date, wrote 'that the Walls of the Manse are built, and that the Church is 3 feet high above the area, and that he thinks, if the weather is good, the work will be finished in the end of October'. The contractor in Stornoway made the same prediction. Stevenson's report of 7 August was perhaps not quite so up to date but it gave a more detailed account of events:

'the Reporter has the satisfaction of stating that the Lighthouse vessel in passing the Island of St Kilda on the 15th [July] had an opportunity of landing Mr John Skethway the Inspector of the Works, and his Apparatus, along with Mr Slight … when they found that the Rev. John Macdonald had left the Island but a few hours before their arrival, but the weather being thick and hazey they passed each other without having been aware of it.'

Mr Slight found everything going on 'in a proper manner'; the manse walls were 'nearly to their full height' but nothing had been done to the church, although of course the foundation stone had been put in place. This was contrary to the terms of the contract under which both buildings were to be constructed at the same time, but since John MacDonald had sanctioned both this 'deviation' and the extra gable window there was to be no complaint. Slight continued with the cutter to Stornoway where he inspected 'the Joiners work of the Manse and Church now preparing by Mr MacKenzie', and found it almost completely satisfactory, so that all in all Stevenson considered MacKenzie 'now entitled … to receive the first and second instalments of the Contract price'.[49]

According to the next Stevenson report, of 17 November 1827, the building work had been suspended for the season owing to the want of materials, but the contractor deserved his fourth instalment. Skethway had returned to Edinburgh and there was no reason why the sum of £15.12s, less the advance of £12 allowed when he set out in July, should not be paid. Stevenson was of the rather cautious opinion that the contractor had on the whole 'manifested a dispositon to do justice to the work', while the inspector had 'done his duty to the best of his ability'. As to the next steps to be taken:

'It will be necessary for the Committee to keep in view, that the articles of Household Furniture already specified - and others which may appear to have been omitted - such as Church Bell, and the necessary appendages of the Pulpit etc. will require to be provided against the Spring of the ensuing year, when it is hoped that a convenient opportunity for landing these articles, and for making the ultimate inspection of the Works will occur.

'The Reporter also begs thus early to bring under the notice of the Committee, that the Manse being nearly ready for possession, and as the Church is expected to be finished by the term of Lammas [1 August] next - the sooner that a Minister can be appointed to this peculiar charge, the better.'[50]

The outcome was that the SSPCK's ecclesiastical subcommittee was told 'to look out for a suitable person to be appointed as Missionary in that island'; but no obvious candidate was in sight and it took about two years to find one.

In the course of 1828 construction work on St Kilda was completed. Alexander MacKenzie, the contractor, wrote to Robert Stevenson on 4 June 'intimating that the Buildings at St Kilda are finished, and wishing an Inspector to go and inspect the works'. After this it was a matter of paying the balance of the fifth instalment and tidying up the accounts. John MacDonald was awarded a sum of £50 in acknowledgement of all his services on behalf of the Society, and in March 1828 H D Hill forwarded a copy of a letter from the island proprietor approving all the developments and recommending a renewed application to the parliamentary commissioners overseeing the establishment of new Protestant churches in various parts of the Highlands and islands. Four were built at this time in the Outer Hebrides, at Cross and Knock in Lewis, at Trumisgarry in North Uist, and in Berneray, Harris. St Kilda, if proposed, was again turned down. On 6 November 1828 the SSPCK directors, satisfied at the completion of building on St Kilda, hoped that a missionary would be sent out to that 'distant island' in the spring - a forlorn expectation as it turned out. Meanwhile they felt that there was a continuing need for public support:

'It is well known that the funds by which the expence of these buildings has been defrayed, was obtained by collections made chiefly by the Rev. Mr. Macdonald and contributions by individuals. The greater part of that fund was taken charge of by a Committee of Gentlemen who entered warmly into the object, and to whose disinterested services the Directors consider themselves under peculiar obligations. The balance of that fund, on the buildings being finished, was paid over to the Society by Thomas Allan Esqr., Banker, Treasurer to the Committee.

'But although the buildings are now finished, there are still many articles necessary for the comfort of any clergyman who may be appointed to the station for which the balance of the fund is quite inadequate to provide. It is hoped however that the christian public, when inform'd of the circumstance, will not be backward in contributing the means that are requisite for rendering his situation in so remote and sequestered an island as comfortable as possible.'[51]

Towards the end of the year a legacy of £60 from Miss Mary Milne of Aberdeen 'for instructing the poor in the island of St Kilda' materially helped the need expressed and enabled the directors to focus their attention on the search for a missionary. John MacDonald, ever willing to assist, applied himself to that task also, looking in the north for the yet undiscovered man who would be the first official occupant of the new St Kilda manse.[52]

CHAPTER 5

Neil Mackenzie discovered, appointed,
and introduced by John Macdonald

ST Kilda, so often described by the SSPCK as 'that interesting island',
attracted donations and concern because of its romantic appeal to the
many people who looked upon it from a distance with curiosity, and during
the nineteenth century its 'poor people' became rather better off than the
equally and perhaps even more poor inhabitants of other, far less remote
places. But the appeal did not extend to potential ministers and teachers who
would have to go and live there, and in January 1829 the SSPCK had to
acknowledge the fact: 'The Directors have not yet been able to nominate a
Missionary for St Kilda, the peculiar situation of that island and the
circumstances of the people renders it somewhat difficult to get a person
willing and at the same time qualified for so important a charge.' They hoped
to find one soon so that he might 'go out to that island early in summer',
especially as there were now excellent 'accommodations' ready and waiting.[53]

By the end of February 1829 the 'Ecclesiastical Sub Committee' of the
SSPCK believed that a suitable candidate had been discovered: 'The
Committee having met for the purpose of recommending a person to the
Directors to be appointed Missionary for St Kilda beg leave to report their
opinion that Mr Peter Davidson appears to them in every respect peculiarly
well qualified for that important station.' Davidson was a preacher not yet
ordained, but having received several testimonials in his favour the directors
approved the nomination and sought to arrange the necessary ordination.
They 'have every reason to hope that they have been fortunate in the
selection they have made' and the presence of a 'stated Missionary' seemed to
be a welcome inevitability. Because it was so difficult to call together the
members of the Uist presbytery for the exceptional ordination meeting the
moderator, Finlay Macrae in North Uist, did not doubt that 'the other members
would concur with him in opinion that it was more eligible that Mr
Davidson's ordination should take place in Edinburgh or Lanark than in Uist'.
The watchful John MacDonald wanted a meeting with Davidson in
Edinburgh, and on 28 May 1829 Davidson wrote from New Lanark, where he
was living, to ask about visiting St Kilda with the tacksman during the
summer. He hoped that MacDonald would go with him. It seems unlikely that
he did go out to the island, but either what he saw or what he learned must
have changed his mind as on 1 December he sent a letter declining the
appointment.[54]

A few weeks later Dr Daniel Dewar, minister of the Tron church in
Glasgow and later principal of Marischal College, Aberdeen, recommended to
the SSPCK another possibility for St Kilda but in mid January 1830 he had to

advise that this person too declined going and that he was unable to find anyone else. John MacDonald was similarly unsuccessful but offered to return to the island for a fourth visit in the summer if this was considered necessary. The Society directors, fearing that Davidson's resignation 'may be attended with serious inconvenience to the inhabitants of that remote island, unless some suitable person for that situation should soon occur', felt that no time should be lost in filling what they saw as a 'vacancy', and greeted MacDonald's proposal with some relief. They thought he should go if a satisfactory missionary was not found beforehand, 'and even if a young man was got to go out there to give the people religious instruction for one year, … they would be greatly obliged by Mr Macdonald accompanying him to perform the other ministerial duties to the inhabitants which a young preacher cannot perform.' In March the directors were still trying to locate a 'proper person', and in May things were looking rather desperate when a message came from Dr Dewar. It appeared that he had managed to persuade the man he had originally approached, a Mr MacKenzie, to consider the post in St Kilda. MacKenzie, 'a licentiate of the Presbytery of Kintyre', who was, according to Dewar, well qualified and willing to undertake the duties of the missionary in spite of the fact that he had already been appointed by 'the Glasgow Society' to go to Canada, came to Edinburgh and was introduced to the Ecclesiastical Subcommittee, members of which he had previously so impressed with 'his piety and devotion' that there was no hesitation on the part of the directors in appointing him to St Kilda. As with nearly every missionary appointment to the island over the centuries there appeared to be no alternative anyway and the man who showed some willingness to go was virtually certain to be sent.[55]

MacKenzie was appointed 'missionary and catechist' to St Kilda on 13 May 1830 and was to receive the new salary level of £50 and allowances for 'outfit' as had been fixed for Peter Davidson the previous year. The SSPCK secretary then stated to the directors 'that it was of great consequence that Mr MacKenzie should if possible go out this summer, and this could only be done, if he was ready to go out with the tacksman who sailed early in June.' This meant that trials, ordination and preparation had to be completed 'with all speed' inside three weeks, and the secretary, along with Dr Dickson, minister of St Cuthbert's, Edinburgh, had the task of providing 'the necessary articles of standing furniture which it was formerly agreed should be sent to that station, and also such books as might be thought useful and necessary to be sent out there for the use of the Missionary'. They were also to give any further help appropriate, and to pay MacKenzie a half year's salary at his departure in addition to a sum for his 'outfit'. The committee of the Edinburgh Bible Society was asked to supply bibles for the islanders, and Dr Dickson was to apply to the Highland Missionary Society for the £50 formerly promised and to be forthcoming on the entry of a missionary to his remote charge.[56]

Haste was of prime importance. In accordance with a request from the SSPCK the presbytery of Glasgow ordained MacKenzie at a specially-called meeting on 5 June, and ten days later the new missionary sailed from the Clyde to join up with John MacDonald and Murdo MacLellan in or near Harris. When the SSPCK met again on 1 July, which as it happened was the day when MacKenzie and his companions left on the final stage of their journey, there was no recent information on progress but everyone hoped 'that before this time, Mr Mackenzie has arrived on the island, and has entered upon his sacred and important charge'. But the secretary was able to read a reply from H.D.Hill in response to his letter written 'to secure the ground of the Glebe, Church, and Manse'. After preliminary references to previous correspondence Hill wrote: 'that there may be no obstacle to the immediate settlement of the New Missionary, I can have no hesitation in engaging for Mr MacLeod, that he shall have the use of the ground as marked out by Mr Macdonald and Mr McLellan, as well as the stance of the Chapel and Manse, and that these shall be continued to the Society while the Mission lasts. I shall not fail to make the necessary exception of all such in any new lease of the Island that may be granted, which will not however be for a year to come, as Mr. McLellan is to continue in possession till Whitsunday next [1831].'

The other steps taken to prepare for MacKenzie's departure had also met with success. Dr Dickson collected 'a variety of Books' which were bound, catalogued, marked as SSPCK property 'for the Mission house at St Kilda', and despatched. Gaelic bibles and testaments 'for the use of the inhabitants', Gaelic catechisms and 'a quarto Bible, bound, and with a suitable inscription for the pulpit there', were all sent, and a quantity of furniture was transported under the management of Mr Leitch of Greenock from Leith to Greenock on 29 May following an application to Robert Stevenson for his advice on suitable items. The furniture too was 'safely shipped in the same vessel with Mr Mackenzie'.

The half year's salary and £20 'outfit' money, paid immediately after his ordination, were spent by MacKenzie on provisions, and by 15 June he had scarcely left himself enough to pay the expense of passage for himself and his furniture to Harris. The SSPCK committee was evidently in a benevolent mood now that it had resolved the difficulty of finding a missionary, for, having the idea that MacKenzie might need to buy a few sheep on the island, it authorised Dr Dewar to pay the travel expenses, so enabling the missionary to keep what was left of his earlier allowances 'for his own use'. Then, perhaps aware that its generosity was both out of character and a little rash, the committee excused itself by noting that it had done everything possible to make the missionary comfortable but had tried to do so 'with every attention to economy', and, regretting the heavy expense, it hoped that 'from the quality of the articles that have been furnished, no similar expence will again be required for a great number of years'.[57]

*

Neil MacKenzie, born in Glen Sannox, Arran, about 1795, came of a family that may have originally lived in Wester Ross. He married Elizabeth Crawford, daughter of a builder in Kilwinning, and while his own language was Gaelic it is unlikely that his wife knew much, if any at all, until she arrived in St Kilda, where, according to her son James, she 'taught the female portion of the population something of the art of housekeeping, of the management of their young children, of the importance of proper cooking and other sanitary matters, and of the virtues of soap and starch'. James proved to be not the most accurate of recorders and probably exaggerated when describing the beneficial contributions of his parents to island life, but it was noted in 1832 that Mrs MacKenzie was teaching the girls to sew.[58]

John MacDonald once again kept a journal describing his visit to the island and this time the introduction of the long-awaited missionary. He was at the Bracadale manse in Skye the day before MacKenzie left Greenock and was looking forward to meeting him in Harris. 'I rejoiced in spirit,' he wrote, 'to think that the Lord had thus provided for the poor people of that place, as I trusted, "a pastor according to his own heart, and who should feed them with knowledge and understanding" - for such a character Mr MacKenzie, by all accounts, appeared to be.' Indeed Mr MacKenzie's character made it look as if MacDonald's own presence might be superfluous but he explained that since it had been uncertain whether a missionary could be ready in time and the islanders had not seen a clergyman for three years a visit from him, 'or some other person', was required. A touch of perhaps understandable self-importance is recognisable in MacDonald's attitude towards St Kilda, for which place he had long felt a special responsibility. In the circumstances prevailing in late June 1830 MacKenzie was supposed to need MacDonald's guidance:

> ' .. it was highly desirable, (and it appeared so to the Society and to myself,) that I should accompany him thither; see him introduced to the people, and settled among them .. I may add, besides, (and I trust I shall be forgiven when I do so,) that a certain feeling of attachment to the people - formed and increased by my former visits to them - and an anxious desire to see them once more - perhaps for the last time in this world - contributed much towards determining me to undertake this *fourth visit* to St Kilda.'[59]

MacDonald had heard some time before from Murdo MacLellan of his intention to leave for St Kilda about the middle of June and of how he would be happy to take the minister again in his own boat. So he travelled to Skye by way of intermediate manses at Kinlochluichart and Plockton and by boat from Plockton to Broadford. At Corry he stayed with the family of 'my late worthy friend' Lachlan MacKinnon who had died over two years previously, then moved to Bracadale where, as he found no boat going to Uist or Harris, he 'consented to remain over Sabbath, and to preach for the Rev. R. McLeod'. Having spent Monday 14 June with MacLeod and his wife, 'with whom I had much Christian conversation', he was impatiently waiting for a packet boat to Uist when he was offered a lift there from Loch Bracadale by William MacNeil from North Uist whose own vessel was preparing to sail. That afternoon he reached Benbecula and immediately 'made for Mr Duncan Shaw's, factor to the proprietors of Uist, and brother to my late worthy and lamented friend, the minister of Bracadale'. Two days later Shaw took MacDonald in his horse-drawn gig to Milton in South Uist to which the MacLellans had removed from Scalpay in 1827. Milton was much less convenient as a starting point for St Kilda but the tacksman was seeing out his lease of the island and was ready to leave whenever the weather, then very unsettled, improved. While he waited MacDonald learned that both the Protestants and far more numerous Catholics of South Uist seemed 'to be buried in ignorance, and to rest quietly in the stillness of moral death', and as 'In these circumstances, it would be highly criminal in a servant of the Redeemer not to occupy, nay, to seize every opportunity which came in his way for addressing immortal souls' he set about preaching in order to rescue at least some souls from sinking for ever 'into unutterable perdition'. Two young female Catholics were soon in tears at one meeting. 'Why should we not love the souls of Catholics as well as Protestants, and do them all the good we can? Alas, that so often we should treat them as if they were a people of a different species from ourselves!'

John MacDonald was still at Milton on Wednesday 23 June when Neil MacKenzie was somewhere in Harris. The weather was unrelentingly cold and stormy, valuable time was passing and MacLellan regretted that the delay, a degree of ill health, and the approach of important cattle markets would prevent him from going on the voyage. However he would be quite willing for the boat and crew to take out MacDonald who was determined to fulfil his mission: 'St Kilda still lies before me; and I long to see its poor inhabitants.' On Friday 25 June the boat left, while MacDonald, to whom it had been suggested by MacLellan that he should 'journey by land as far as North Uist' and meet the boat at Pabbay, parted tearfully from his hosts and rode to Duncan Shaw's house in Benbecula that night. The following day he continued to Trumisgarry where he preached on the Sabbath, and on Monday he crossed to Boreray where again he preached in a 'government church' before being ferried over to Pabbay. Here the St Kilda boat had just arrived; 'and it gave me inexpressible pleasure to find that the missionary of St Kilda was aboard … having been taken in at Roudel, in Harris, where Mr McLellan's men were directed to call for him. The feelings excited in my mind at the very sight of him it is not easy to describe. I seemed to myself to see, in him, the messenger of peace, and the dawn of a better day to St Kilda.'[60]

In Pabbay lodging was provided in the house formerly occupied by William MacNeil, 'for many years tacksman of St Kilda', and now by his son Major John MacNeil, 'who, to the politeness of the soldier, joins the hospitality of the Highlander'. William MacNeil lived with his son Roderick at 'Kyles Berneray', the 'Caolis' or Kyles where John MacDonald had met the MacNeil family at the end of his second mission to St Kilda in 1824. Now Major John was ready to join the party going to the island although he had no official connection with the place. While in Pabbay MacDonald again examined the school there; it was supported, as he said, by what he called 'the Inverness Education Society' and was well taught by a Mr Noble. After 'addressing a few words of exhortation to the scholars' he then assembled the inhabitants for a service: 'Pabbay is another needy spot - far removed from the means of grace; so much so, that the inhabitants seldom or never can hear sermon. Oh, may some Society think of their case!'[61]

Eventually, on the last day of June, the weather eased, and in the afternoon John MacDonald, Major MacNeil, Mr Bethune - a tutor in the MacLellan family, Neil MacKenzie with his wife and baby, and Mrs MacKenzie's mother and sister, all went on board and set out for St Kilda, which they reached at around 4 o'clock next morning, the hour being one when, as in 1827, nearly all the islanders were asleep. Not a dog barked; but someone saw the boat come into the bay and soon the usual crowd gathered above the shore and energetically greeted MacDonald. Pious words were exchanged, and the MacKenzie group looked on their new home and neighbours with wonder.[62]

*

In a moment or two time moved on again. 'Mr McKenzie, who, with his female friends, had been all this while standing at a little distance from us, gazing, and gazed at occasionally, was at last introduced to them as the minister appointed for them by the Society.' MacDonald naturally proposed a service in the church, so everybody marched off to the new building which stood ready for its inauguration, and when the short meeting was over and a sermon promised for the afternoon MacDonald and his 'fellow-travellers' entered the manse, inspected the rooms, and sat down 'to rest and refresh us, after the fatigues and fastings of the voyage'. Exulting in the sight of a real church on the island, MacDonald allowed himself to visualise a future for the buildings 'in which, there was reason to hope, his Gospel would be preached, and his ordinances administered for generations to come' and to which 'not a few of the inhabitants, perhaps, from age to age, down to a remote posterity, may trace the means, under God, which had been blessed to their souls for salvation'. Surely, he thought, neither the Society, nor the public, nor he himself had any reason 'to repent what they have done for St Kilda'. And he thought too of the visitor such as Clarke or MacCulloch who had already put in an appearance:

'Here, too, the *strangers* who may be prompted by curiosity, or pleasure, to visit the island, will find a suitable retreat after the tossings of the ocean, and in the manse of St Kilda, a comfortable lodging place, while he chooses to remain on the island.' Whether in fact there was reason for anyone to repent what had been done for St Kilda can only be judged by its effects upon the people over long years, and by setting it against what was not done; but some kind of verdict may lie in the fate of the island before 'remote posterity' was reached, when, after only two or three generations, church and manse stood empty beyond the end of a line of deserted houses falling rapidly into decay.

The next ten days were devoted to a programme in which there was little surprising. The tutor, Mr Bethune, acted as clerk for the absent tacksman and received contributions of rent in feathers, barley, cheese and so on. This business was finished by the evening of the sixth day and both Bethune and MacDonald were eager to depart as soon as possible. But the weather did not permit; on 8 July there was 'a perfect hurricane' with the sea 'all in commotion', columns of spray rising to a great height and everything 'awfully grand and sublime' in the storm's fury. These conditions prolonged the stay and added opportunities for MacDonald to preach and pray. This he did on most weekdays about 5 o'clock in the afternoon, and there were three services on the Sabbaths. One of the first tasks was to land the furniture provided for the missionary, convey it to the manse, and then to haul up the boat, 'which it took them two hours to get fairly placed beyond the sea-mark'. The visitors all lent a hand in sorting out the furniture and fitting up the rooms. 'While we were employed at this work, it was rather amusing, though by no means surprising, to see the gazings and astonishment with which the people viewed and narrowly inspected every part of the furniture, as an assemblage of materials which they had never seen before, and which certainly presented a striking contrast to the species of furniture in use among themselves.' They were astonished at the variety and puzzled by the purpose of many articles, including a set of bed curtains, and an old man, in MacDonald's opinion, 'very sagely remarked, "Och, sirs, you wonder at these fine good things, but who ought to get such things, but the messengers and people of God? Is it not said, that *all things are theirs*?" "True," said I.' Nothing could have contrasted the 'outside' world with that of St Kilda more vividly than that furniture. The effect must have been enormous. Quite suddenly, after a sequence of missionaries who, like the islanders themselves, had lacked all home comforts, a decent house and an adequate meeting place in which to carry out their labours, 'accommodations' beyond the people's dreams had arrived - but only for the new minister as the messenger of God for whose work God's temple had been built. Respect for him must have redoubled when the bed-curtains were unwrapped.

There was now no school to be inspected as Alexander MacKenzie had left and there had been no missionary at work for three years, yet for some reason an improvement 'in point of knowledge', presumably biblical, seemed to have occurred, or at least it was reported by John MacDonald: 'there seems to be more of the love of the truth among them, and more openness of heart to receive it, than I had discovered on former occasions. I speak generally. There are many exceptions, of course. But to a considerable part of them this observation will apply. The result is, that I find it easier to speak to them, and that the truths addressed to them, seem to sink insensibly, and without apparent obstruction, into their hearts.' There is no doubt that MacDonald knew how to use the right words, whatever they might amount to. Tears were as usual abundant. Old blind Finlay MacDonald, who 'holds out steadfastly in the ways of the Lord', wept copiously. There were three particularly emotional incidents. One was on the first Sabbath, 4 July, when Neil MacKenzie was inducted and officially began his ministry. To John MacDonald this was 'the most important and delightful day I ever spent in St Kilda'. MacKenzie preached at the forenoon service, with MacDonald attending 'rather as a critic than as a humble hearer'. The sermon turned out to be 'plain, practical, and impressive', and MacDonald was happy that 'the poor people of St Kilda should have such a person for their spiritual guide'. Everyone seemed satisfied and when MacDonald addressed the congregation for the second time in the evening and spoke of how, with a church, bibles and minister the Lord had been 'mindful' of the community 'many burst out into sobbing and weeping'. Afterwards the five survivors of seven or eight children born since 1827 were baptised, along with Neil MacKenzie's 'infant'. A second moving event took place on 6 July when there was a marriage, but neither this nor the induction could quite measure up to the scenes that accompanied MacDonald's final sermon and his departure.

On Saturday 10 July the wind had gone down and the sea was quieter, but MacDonald and the tacksman's clerk had no intention of leaving at such a time: 'we have made up our minds (however inviting the weather may happen to be,) not to move now till after the Sabbath - it being certainly not desirable, whenever it can be avoided, to *set out* on a journey on the Lord's holy day.' So 'the poor people' wandered about watching to see what would happen and 'appeared quite sad and downcast, whenever we talked of setting off', but when 'we announced to them our resolution to remain, they all felt quite happy'. The Sabbath arrived, MacKenzie preached in the forenoon, MacDonald at the early morning and evening services. The people seemed to like MacKenzie's sermon, and the 'critic' noted his views in his journal:

'Mr McKenzie is certainly not *seen* at first sight; but he grows upon acquaintance; naturally shy, unobtrusive, and of a retiring disposition, he appears to a stranger to have very little *in* him; but upon further acquaintance, one is soon agreeably disappointed, and discovers him to be a man of mind, and of general knowledge - a man, too, of prudence, piety, firmness of principle, and mildness of disposition - qualities which it well becomes every minister of the gospel to possess; but which are peculiarly fitting in the Missionary of St Kilda.'

It was however the evening service that proved to be, according to the journal, the climax of the day and indeed of the visit. His purpose, MacDonald said, was to fix the attention of the people upon the cross, 'nay, to shut them up to this glorious object'. He told them that this was 'the great end of my ministrations among them', that he believed it would be MacKenzie's, and that with this in view he would leave them and, 'in all probability, see them no more'. On hearing these concluding words the whole assembly was overwhelmed with weeping, including MacDonald himself.

Outside the church islanders and departing minister seemed to be quite overcome.

Next morning, in good weather, the boat was launched and loaded. Weeping was abundant once more, and MacDonald, comparing himself to Paul, *'prayed with them* on the shore' before setting off. He left with the people's 'thousand blessings on the Society, who had done so much for them, and had now sent them the word of life'; and in response to their repeated implorings that these feelings should be passed on he promised to 'communicate their good wishes to the Society'. The boat reached Pabbay the same evening; though 'but newly off the sea' MacDonald preached there for nearly two hours; and on Tuesday 17 July he began a prolonged journey home by way of the manse at Trumisgarry and Lochmaddy to Dunvegan, thence to Bracadale and, after preaching at the head of Loch Sligachan, to Corry. He was back at the Urquhart manse on Friday 23 July, writing up his journal and preparing it, like the others, for the eyes of the SSPCK members who would no doubt be impressed by the fine sentiments and reassuring accounts of the spiritual condition in which he had left the people of St Kilda, where 'the marked improvement .. in *religious knowledge* and *moral conduct* - not to speak of the *saving* and *practical* acquaintance with the truth' must surely please both the Society and 'the Christian public'.

The day after MacDonald left Pabbay the MacKenzies' infant son Nathaniel died 'of cold'.[63]

CHAPTER 6

Neil Mackenzie meets visitors and reflects on life in St Kilda

THE MacKenzie group stood on the shore watching John MacDonald, Major MacNeil and Mr Bethune, with their Pabbay crew, retreating into the misty billows of the Atlantic. Mrs MacKenzie's mother and sister were to leave with the tacksman after his autumn visit, which, if he managed to make it, would probably be his last, but she and her husband were now to face an isolated and uncertain life in a strangely different world for an unknown length of time. It was mid July 1830.

John MacDonald, whose own visits to the island never amounted to much more than two weeks, expressed an understanding of the new minister's inner response to his charge:

> 'I should state, indeed, that Mr McKenzie feels quite happy in his new situation. He has often expressed himself so to me. He views it as that which the Lord has designed for him, and in which he is to occupy, while the Lord continues him in it. "I know not," says he, "why one might not be happy here, provided he is satisfied that the Lord has sent him hither … Besides, one has retirement here, and opportunities for meditation, prayer, and improvement in various respects .. And as to temporals", says he "having food and raiment, we should be therewith content." These observations of his pleased me much; and I said immediately within myself, *this is the man for St Kilda.'*

Since true happiness stemmed from God, and since 'Joseph was happy in prison, Daniel in a den of lions' and 'Paul among barbarians', there was no reason why MacKenzie should not be happy in St Kilda where it was now believed there were no prisons, no lion's dens and no barbarians. The old idea that the islanders were prisoners and barbaric was, temporarily at least, set aside. Moreover Neil MacKenzie had 'a suitable helpmate in his wife', who would 'enhance his personal comforts' and 'in her sphere .. co-operate with him in promoting both the spiritual and temporal interests of the people'. She was, MacDonald said, 'Affable, mild, and condescending in her manners', had already 'gained much on the people', and, 'could she but speak their language, (which I hope she will soon be able to do,) she appears to be every thing else they could wish'.[64]

The SSPCK read a letter from John MacDonald in the second week of August 1830 which briefly reported the success of his fourth and final visit and promised that his journal, when properly prepared, would be submitted as soon as possible. It came within the next two months and on 11 November was given to Dr Dickson and the secretary to see to printing and publication.

At the same meeting the directors of the Society recognised their 'deep obligations' to MacDonald 'for all his kind services in regard to St Kilda'; on each of the four missions 'he has been subjected to great personal labour, fatigue, and inconvenience - and although to him the success of all his labours and services must be the best reward, yet the Society ought never to forget, as the inhabitants of St Kilda never can forget, that it was from the interest he took in the Island, from the means which he by his individual exertions in a great measure procured, and from the valuable information which he furnished, that there is now erected on this western island of the Hebrides, a house of God, and that there is among the people an ordained Minister, to conduct their devotions, to instruct their minds, and to point out to them the way which leadeth to everlasting life'. Gratitude was also expressed to Murdo MacLellan for his 'obliging and ready assistance' over the past decade and as a reward he was sent a copy of the Society's edition of 'the quarto Gaelic Bible'. In 1832 John MacDonald was presented with a handsomely bound copy of 'Bagster's Folio Polyglot Bible' suitably inscribed, at a cost of £10.18s.[65]

In August 1830 Neil MacKenzie wrote his first letter to the SSPCK from St Kilda. He told of his arrival and his satisfaction with the place so far, and with the people, but mentioned the dampness of the manse, especially in wet weather. In September he wrote again, asking that repairs to his house should be ordered, and it is likely that both letters were taken away, as were Mrs MacKenzie's mother and sister, by Murdo MacLellan, who had managed to make his early autumn visit and reported that when he left the island MacKenzie was in good health and 'much esteemed by the people'. The condition of the manse about which MacKenzie complained seems to have been at variance with the picture of fine new 'accommodations' drawn by John MacDonald, and while it had probably been unoccupied for more than two years, which certainly cannot have helped, repairs were definitely needed. The necessary work was carried out by Mrs MacKenzie's father, James Crawford, although by the time it was undertaken and completed another four years had passed.[66]

The problem of how to know the real or true situation in St Kilda, which had always confronted the SSPCK and indeed everyone else who had had to deal with the island from somewhere far distant, remained unresolved, and not only because of minimal communication and remoteness. Much also depended on the accounts of the place given by those who did manage to get there, including 'the apostle of the north', each of whom saw things in his own way according to his preconceptions. Those who lay claim to possession of 'the truth' often expose themselves to contradiction, and while the claim might be accepted at the time a different point of view might not be long in emerging. John MacDonald, who seems to have felt a genuine affection for the islanders and to have preached with conviction, may have deceived himself and written journals the rather to please the SSPCK directors and the

'Christian public' than to record actuality. He declared that the 'poor people' of St Kilda 'seemed to melt' under his spiritual onslaught, that they were 'deeply impressed', and that, on his leaving for the last time, they said: 'the present is a more sorrowful parting than any we ever had.' Perhaps he was right. But Neil MacKenzie's experience was very different.[67]

When MacDonald first came to the island in 1822 he found no one who could be called 'a decidedly religious person'. This was after more than a century of Protestant missionaries. Eight years later, after many sermons and much weeping, MacKenzie found that 'things were even worse. Not only was every moral obligation disregarded, but they seemed to have no idea that they were doing anything wrong. For any effect which religion had upon their lives they might just as well never have heard of such a thing as a moral law.' As for the 'eloquent and powerful sermons' of 'my friend Dr. McDonald', their effect was but superficial. The people listened apparently with 'great attention'; but MacKenzie soon discovered 'that they were only charmed by his eloquence and energy, and had not knowledge enough to follow or understand his arguments.' MacKenzie was aware of his own limitations in this respect:

> 'Notwithstanding all my labours and prayers, I could not see for several years any real spiritual fruit. They acquired much knowledge of the facts and doctrines of Christianity, but it did not seem to enter into their hearts or do much to influence their lives. Open and gross sins were getting less frequent, but it was only in a very few cases that the heart seemed to be at all touched, or that there was awakened any real anxiety about the salvation of their souls.'[68]

The hearts of the people were perhaps still allied to the island, to its ancient traditions, and to the essential business of trying to survive. Evangelical teaching must at first have seemed as alien an imposition as other curious fashions such as those brought by tourists in the 1880s or the presumption that life on St Kilda ought to be like life in 'civilised' places on the mainland. And MacKenzie believed that the islanders were capable of deliberately deceiving MacDonald, for like 'the simple, kindly, primitive people whom they were, they were always anxious to please visitors by confirming any opinion which they [the visitors] chose to express'. They were also, in MacKenzie's view, much more aware than the visitor of later times gave them credit for and were able, as it were, to fight back: 'Encouraged by the amazing credulity of the ordinary tourist, the natives have got to be very successful in imposing upon them. The tourist comes with a certain idea in his mind as to what the native is like, and would be disappointed if they did not find him like that; this the natives have been shrewd enough to discover and turn to their own profit.' Judged from this, less complimentary angle, men like John MacDonald were spiritual tourists.[69]

Visitors of a tourist kind were a feature of Neil MacKenzie's years in St Kilda.[70] On Tuesday 31 May 1831 there stepped ashore George Clayton Atkinson, aged 23, with his brother Richard. A second brother, Isaac, had been left behind in Skye. The Atkinsons were from near Newcastle. George was especially interested in natural history, collected specimens, and in 1829 became a founder member of the Natural History Society of Newcastle upon Tyne. The party had set out on 16 May by steamship for Edinburgh, and on the way the helpful captain steered close to flocks of birds on the water to enable Isaac with his 'double barrel gun' and George with his rifle to fire at them, but 'we did no execution .. as there was nothing rare enough to be desirable'. In Edinburgh George met someone called MacGillivray - in fact William MacGillivray the naturalist - who gave him an introduction to his brother, 'a young surgeon, gone for the vacation to his home in the Island of Pabbay'. This was fortunate, as George was thereby put in contact with the very place where help in getting to St Kilda was most likely to be found. Armed also with an introduction supplied by a Mr Hutton George called upon 'Mr Allan the Banker', no doubt Thomas Allan of the St Kilda Committee and 'the only man I ever met with who had been there'. Curiously Mr Allan said he had hardly one acquaintance 'among the islands'. The next stage of the journey was by coach to Glasgow, and a conversation with Mr MacKinnon, 'the Colombian consul', who provided a further introduction to his mother, still at Corry. The Atkinsons were clearly on the right trail.

Their good fortune continued on their way north to Portree. Travelling with them on the *Maid of Islay* was a 'Colonel MacNeil', probably the Major John MacNeil who had accompanied the MacKenzies to St Kilda the year before. Colonel MacNeil was an uncle of William MacGillivray and his brother, or rather half brother, Donald MacGillivray, the surgeon who was going home to Pabbay. Donald had been making for Rodel by means of 'the Sloop Rhoderick of Greenock' but his vessel called at Portree and there, on the morning of 26 May, George Atkinson went aboard the *Roderick* and 'delivered my introduction to MacGillivray in bed'. As the sloop was taking an indirect route by Stornoway Donald MacGillivray joined George and Richard Atkinson and an artist, Edward Train. They hired a boat with two of a crew and had a rough, spray-soaked voyage, during which Train 'whistled and sang, told stories and made remarks, till it became very squally when he laid himself on a seat, wrapped as to his head in a plaid, and making a final request that we would take care of his hat, spake but little'. They covered the distance from Rudha Hunish, the north point of Skye, to Rodel in three hours.

At Rodel they found Colonel MacNeil, who had come by the packet boat from Dunvegan and 'was on his way to Pabbay to recruit'. In Harris and the nearby islands 'all the inhabitants seem known to each other and his being so was of advantage to us, as I know he urged the people to be kind and attentive to us, and suggested to John McDonald some days after, to take blankets in the boat to St Kilda.' Donald MacGillivray was even more helpful, being equally well known as 'the Doctor' and acquainted with the right people: 'I can not conceive any one more likely to be of use to us: St.Kilda he says will be easily attained, as the Tacksman goes about this time on his half yearly visit.' In the event, however, the Atkinsons found a different means of journeying to the island. Train did not risk the open ocean.

Having time to spare they went to Scarista to see the minister's son, 'Mr Bethun'. The reason was sporting rather than ecclesiastical. They found him 'a truculent athletic-looking fellow', but he came out with them to shoot birds, a favourite occupation of George and 'Dick', though the latter seemed to prefer fishing. The next day being Sunday 29 May they climbed Roineval above Rodel and were just able to see St Kilda in the hazy west. The start of a fishing expedition on Monday was delayed because Donald MacGillivray was always reluctant to get out of bed in the morning and when he was up and about there were, in Harris, numerous calls for his medical attention. As there was 'some situation now vacant in N. Uist, for which he intends to offer himself', he told his companions that he would not be able to go with them to St Kilda, but suggested that as a favourable east wind was blowing they should leave as soon as possible. George Atkinson considered that 'it is a good piece of temporal economy to sail during the night if the weather be fine, so we got a boat 18 feet in the keel belonging to John McDonald of Coshlatter [Coishletter near Leverburgh] who with two others constituted our crew, and embarked at 9 for the island of St Kilda.' The Harris people were not able to understand why anyone should wish to go 'on a rather uncertain voyage from curiosity about the inhabitants and productions of a small island', and their amazement led George to think that the journey might be more difficult than he had imagined.[71]

The skipper of the boat, John MacDonald from Coishletter, had added pillows, five bottles of whisky, a cask of water, and a bag of oatmeal to the blankets recommended by Colonel MacNeil. There was straw to sleep on, and, towards the bow, a peat fire in an iron pot. Without delay 'we went merrily on our way' through the night, with one of the two 'junior boatmen', John MacLeod, singing *The St Kilda Wedding* 'all the way over', and landed 'comfortably and tolerably easily' at 11 o'clock next morning. The boat was unloaded and then hauled ashore by men, women and children to 'a particular cry from one of their party, the words of which meaning "here with her altogether", were "Hoy sho wallosho, wallosho, wallosho".' This would appear to be George's version of 'uile an seo'. The usual pattern of events began when Neil MacKenzie met the visitors on the rocks and led them to the manse, where he introduced his wife who 'has not one word of Gaelic' and consequently no one to speak with except her husband. They had a cup of tea and then climbed with MacKenzie to the top of Conachar, the highest point of the island, from which they watched two islanders descend the cliff a little to fetch them puffin and fulmar eggs. 'During this walk, the minister gave us a most interesting account of the morals of the inhabitants', as well as providing other information, on all of which George Atkinson relied heavily for the contents of his journal and of an article printed in the *Transactions of the Natural History Society of Northumberland, Durham and Newcastle.*

The Atkinsons spent the night in the manse, which became the lodging generally enjoyed by the occasional visitor for it was more comfortable and less unsavoury than the houses in the 'village'. On 1 June they went to Boreray with twelve islanders in 'the native boat' and returned with two young falcons taken from the nest there. Irrespective of the fact that two more young birds had been left untouched, George fired at the parent falcons screaming overhead but missed. After a second night with the MacKenzies a successful bargaining over tobacco with 'the only one who has any english', John Ferguson, as interpreter, proved sufficient to persuade a group of men to go to Stac Biorach and climb 'infinitely the most difficult rock' in St Kilda: 'its ascent is never made but for some weighty consideration in general to gratify the proprietor or his friends, but in this case to obtain a little Tobacco of which they then happened to be destitute.' George and Richard had scarcely any of this valuable commodity but what they had was better appreciated than on the occasion when 'a gentleman who came in his yacht and lay in the bay a fortnight … gave them three Guineas for their day's labor'. When they reached the rock no one was keen to climb it, but for the honour of the island two young men, Roderick MacDonald and John MacDonald, accepted the challenge and did so successfully. Afterwards the Atkinson brothers, their crewman John MacDonald, and Neil MacKenzie landed at the mouth of Glen More and walked back over the hill, John seizing the moment to say that he and his companions wanted to go home the next day. George Atkinson thought this was because they 'had not fared very sumptuously' as regards accommodation. In fact they left the same evening, and George's attempt to say 'goodbye' in Gaelic, rendered by him as 'Slan leave ullah', so impressed the people that there was 'a display of feeling, which was the most gratifying I ever remember to have witnessed'. In the course of the night the breeze fell to a dead calm, so the crew had to row while the brothers 'lay snugly enveloped in straw and blankets' and went to sleep. In the morning they had a breakfast of oatcakes, whisky and water, blew and packed a variety of wild birds' eggs, fed the two young falcons on bits of 'some fowls brought for the purpose', fired at 'shoals of Dogfish', and took a turn at rowing. A thick mist then covered everything and after some danger near the rocks of Haisgeir they found their way to Berneray in the Sound of Harris with the help of George's compass. Reunited with the artist Edward Train who had remained in Harris the trio continued homeward by way of Raasay and Corry.[72]

With the records left by visitors from Martin Martin onwards there is always the problem of what to believe. George Atkinson thought that the inhabitants of St Kilda were good-looking, generally healthy, and 'in a curiously primitive state of Integrity and simplicity'. But whether this was true or not is difficult to determine from such comments; for instance, Neil MacKenzie described two murders, whereas Atkinson said that 'Murder ..., from the impossibility of escape, and the absence of the usual causes of incitement, is unknown in their traditions'. Similarly, the minister remarked that theft 'was only limited by their opportunities, and if the thing which it was possible to steal belonged to the proprietor, it was all right'; but Atkinson merely observed that dishonesty was 'very nearly' unknown. It might be imagined that after a stay of not much more than two days Atkinson would be the more likely to be mistaken, as many, often from yachts calling in, who visited for only one day frequently were, and that MacKenzie with about a dozen years to look back on would be correct, but the latter's recollections are not always accurate and may be misleading. The conclusion must be that impressions and even blunt statements cannot always be immediately accepted. Atkinson, like others, was of the opinion that the people of St Kilda were 'kind and hospitable in the highest degree; observe the most scrupulous regard for truth; and are obliging and attentive to strangers to a most pleasing extent'. They may have been, but exaggeration is possible, and MacKenzie thought otherwise.[73]

Some of Atkinson's comments were of a more objective kind and less dependent upon fleeting observation and hearsay. He noted that all matters of importance in island life were 'managed and arranged by a common assembly of the male population' which 'convened on the roof of a house somewhat larger than the rest in the middle of the village'. This probably meant that the top of the house wall served as seating or standing space for the men while they talked. The 'single heavy ships boat' was jointly owned by the community; it had six oars, a home-made sail of wool, and was used in fine weather for the journey to Boreray. He also mentioned, incorrectly, that MacLeod of Harris was the owner of the island, but more accurately noted the visits of the tacksman who generally set out from Pabbay as 'the Pabbah boats and men are better adapted for the purpose'. There were remarks on Taigh Stallair - 'the Stal house' as Atkinson called it, climbing techniques, the birds which were the main prey, and the time spent on Soay, along with his brother, the minister, and 'a dozen of the natives', in search of shearwaters' nests. While on the sea by Boreray the minister 'earnestly dissuaded us from using our fire arms', because startled birds flying over the boat would make a mess of 'a good coat or hat'.[74]

Though impressed with the cliff scenery of St Kilda the Atkinsons, when looking back on their adventure, concluded that most of what they had seen in the Outer Hebrides could not match the splendours of Skye. Harris was 'not worth a visit from the ordinary tourist', while St Kilda itself 'except to the ornithologist is not worthy of a journey, for though even sublimer and more uncommon than any of the scenes in Sky, the difficulty of attaining to it - tho' generally very much exagerated - renders a special visit, scarcely worth while.' However they duly acknowledged the help and hospitality of the MacKenzies: 'with the tractible and unsophisticated materials he has to work on, his task must be a pleasing and gratifying one, and most sincerely do I hope he may be of benefit to his little flock both in a spiritual and temporal view.'

*

The year 1831 was a minor watershed in the story of St Kilda. It saw the end of John MacDonald's major contributions to the SSPCK's fund in aid of the island and in May Murdo MacLellan ceased to be tacksman. The Society was appreciative of a sum of £84.1s remitted by MacDonald who had collected it in varying amounts from places where he preached ranging from Port Glasgow to Comrie and Muthil; and a new system of sending instalments of stipend had to be arranged when MacLellan, who had been willing to take them, no longer visited his remote 'farm'. The tenant or tacksman replacing him was Donald MacDonald, in business at Lochinver, whose application on 3 May 1833 to the Society for the salary to 1 May then due to MacKenzie appears to show that he had also taken over the responsibility for delivery. In November 1833 the builder James Crawford sent MacKenzie's receipt for a half year's stipend, which in addition to indicating that Crawford had been busy on repairs to the manse also suggests that receipts and payments might be carried by another closely connected visitor.[75]

In the summer of 1831, less than three weeks after the departure of the Atkinson brothers, Mrs MacKenzie gave birth to two daughters, baptised Mary and Jane on 20 June, but these infants died of 'Chincough' in August when 'about 6 weeks old'. She was pregnant again when she and her husband left the island in spring 1832 for a three month stay on the mainland visiting friends. This was her first 'holiday' away, and Neil MacKenzie took the opportunity of writing to the SSPCK secretary from Glasgow on 25 May. His letter was in effect an 'annual' report covering almost two years:

'When on my way to St Kilda, from the accounts of those who visited it, and the books I read that described the state of the Inhabitants, I could not tell what to think or believe with certainty. Some described them as ignorant and simple in their manners, yet upon the whole a very moral people - others as ignorant cunning and immoral. From what I saw of their manners and learned of their practices and knowledge, I was at first ready to embrace the former opinion, however different from the general observation that ignorance and immorality produce each other. In the course of time however, several circumstances occurred which tended much to develope their true character, and I found that both accounts are partly true, and partly erroneous. Their knowledge of the world, and what is far more important, of the religion of Christ, was extremely deficient and incorrect. Of the world beside the name they know nothing correctly, except their own island, and Harris and Uist. Their acquaintance with moral and religious truth was neither correct nor extensive. It was a custom with them I understand to commit to memory the ten commandments, the creed and the Lord's prayer, all which they used as a prayer. They also learned the Shorter Catechism, and since the School was introduced among them, by reading the scriptures, and the exhortations of the Schoolmaster they acquired a confused knowledge of our most holy faith. Their morality however specious corresponded with their knowledge.'

So much for the achievements of John MacDonald and Alexander MacKenzie. There then followed some of Neil MacKenzie's own views of the people and of his teaching:

'We have on St Kilda in miniature, almost all the vices which disfigure the moral aspect of Society in large towns. The description which the word of God gives of mankind in general, fits us. On the other hand they have some good qualities which are not found in a different stage of Society. The teachableness of their disposition and their desire to hear the truth are well known. The means which at first we used to meet their desire and enlighten their minds were described in a former letter. After some trial I found it necessary to alter a little my plan. Experience taught me that the Catechetical method is well adapted to communicate knowledge to an ignorant people. I changed therefore the service of Wednesday into a catechetical exercise. Finding the females also more ignorant than the men, I set the first Monday of every month apart for them, and to excite them to prayer, I caused the heads of families to pray in rotation after the Wednesday Service, and the young men in commencing the Sabbath School. Besides this, I divided the village into three divisions, and appointed three of the most intelligent and pious men to spend a night in every week in teaching the shorter catechism, and praying with the people, and another night in reading the Scriptures to those in his own division that cannot read. The success which attended our labour is very conspicuous. Their desire for Bible knowledge is increased, the value of spiritual things is better estimated and their morals greatly improved. They do not think any service too tedious, nor the time ill spent, which we spend in church. The time that used to be spent in relating their own and their fathers exploits is now generally spent in searching the Scriptures, or in relating the discoveries which they made in the Bible. Their holidays, wakes and vain diversions are changed, vain songs, dancing etc. are discontinued. Upon the whole their habits are greatly changed and much to the better. We trust that perhaps a few have tasted of the joys of salvation, at least we have a good hope that that is really the case.'[76]

While the MacKenzies were away on the mainland an admiralty ship approached the island on 12 May 1832. Perhaps there was more than one. The St Kilda 'natives', always nervous when seeing what might prove a danger to them, may again have taken cover among the rocks. But the ship was a survey vessel, possibly H.M.S. *Pike*, with Captain Vidal in command, and on board was a Mr W. H. Church, who painted views of St Kilda from about three miles out to the south and again from the east. Survey ships were to return thirty or so years later; but the presence of one in 1832 heralded the imminent arrival of various other strangers within the next decade, including the first tourist party on board a 'steamer'.

When he arrived home with his family on 22 June 1832 Neil MacKenzie immediately began keeping his own journal of events in St Kilda. It lasted until at least the end of May 1833, at which point the SSPCK directors thought it appropriate to print extracts, 'not only as showing the nature of the Missionary's labours, but as communicating some curious information of the manners and customs of the inhabitants of that island'. To some extent these extracts repeated part of the content of his letter in May 1832, but they showed that the minister had wider interests than might have been expected of a man approved by John MacDonald and of one who had suppressed where he could some of those 'manners and customs'. Neither in his daily dealings with the people nor in his journal did he confine himself to religious matters, and in spite of his professed hostility towards them he had a keen awareness of island traditions, about which he wrote at some length. He also showed a greater concern for everyday things and ways by which life might be improved. When he came back in June 1832 MacKenzie spent a day delivering 'articles which they desired me to bring for them, and things sent by friends in Glasgow'. These included 'a hand-bell to call the people to worship, medicines, spoons, razors, cotton cloth, ribbons, sheep-shears, thread, needles, caps, and other dresses'. They were, in MacKenzie's eyes, of immediate value, either in ordinary, practical instances like the sheep-shears, sent by 'a humane lady in Glasgow', which, he hoped, would mean the end of plucking the wool from the animal, or more generally 'for the purpose of exciting a spirit of activity and cleanliness'. The response to these items, gift or otherwise, was an uncontrolled gratitude which, MacKenzie thought rather unsympathetically, a stranger would have found amusing: 'Some gave vent to their feeling in thankful expressions, wondering at the goodness of those who never saw them; others were so overjoyed that they could not utter a coherent expression, but exclaimed in Gaelic, "O meat, and drink, and clothes!" - an odd, but very common expression here; some were uneasy till they could get home to show what they had got to their friends, scarce believing that it was theirs; one man was really leaping for joy.' Once the excitement had passed, however, the various articles, apart from the bell and perhaps the dresses, stood a good chance of being left aside and forgotten. In removing fleeces 'all my reasoning with them on the cruelty of their mode of taking the wool off the sheep, and the advantage of using shears, could not prevail on one of them to use them'. Having resolved that setting a good example was the best way of bringing about change, Mackenzie determined 'that they shall shear a few sheep that I have, and thus when they see that we can get the wool off them better, that more wool grows on them by cutting it, and that they keep it much better, I am persuaded myself that they will follow'. The exhibition apparently made no difference.[77]

The 'curious information' contained in the journal included descriptions of fowling, the ropes used, the birds, harvesting, drying barley at the kiln, 'sooting' the freshly-sprouted barley with old thatch, and turf cutting. Passages of a religious content were also present; these were not nearly so extensive as in MacDonald's accounts, but their frequency is unknown since reference can be made only to the extracts. In November 1832 MacKenzie was still pursuing the 'Catechetical' method, his programme of catechising families being added to the usual Sabbath and Wednesday meetings. The missionary concentrated upon trying 'to familiarise them with the historical parts of the Bible', perhaps because he felt they would find it easy to substitute them for, or add them to, the 'historical parts' of their familiar island traditions. In the same way he also introduced them to 'the principal individuals mentioned' in the bible, and set exercises one week with questions thereon the next - on 22 November 'We have been these two weeks past considering the history of Moses'. Bible history and personalities were evidently to replace the tales of their fathers which had been handed down and re-told over generations.

What particularly attracted MacKenzie's interest seems to have been those emotional times when the inner nature of the islanders was likely to be disclosed, as at marriages, funerals, story-telling, and, of course, farewells. In describing these moments and events the minister betrayed conflicting attitudes within himself. On the one hand he was clearly intrigued, even fascinated, by what he saw and heard on these and similar occasions; on the other, as missionary minister, he felt compelled to condemn and disapprove. The contrast is apparent in his entry for 4 December 1832 when he 'went to the village':

'The people, that is, the men, were, according to a bad custom they have, which consumes much precious time, leaning against the walls of their houses in an open place near the centre of the village. According to another custom, they all shook hands with me, and, after inquiring for their health, I entered into conversation with them. One of them, among other things, said that one of his neighbours, naming the man, saw a vision, or had an instance of what is called the second sight. The man who ought to have seen that sight, being questioned, affirmed, that coming out of his own house one evening, he saw a great number of men seemingly carrying a corpse wrapped in funeral clothes; and some days after that, a woman, who was confined by a nervous disorder, died, and was carried out the way he saw the vision moving. Wishing to know their opinion, I said nothing, but seemed surprised. This encouraged them to proceed with their imaginary stories. Another man declared, that previous to the death of his own son, he saw in the day time a great number of his friends from the Harris meet him below the garden, in the way they carry their dead to be interred, carrying something. Also, that he was ordered by Mr McLellan to keep a fire, before we came, occasionally in the manse; and in doing that one day, a man whom he knew not came in, and would not let him either to the fire or windows; and in consequence of that fright, he did not venture to put any more fire on in the manse, nor come alone into it till we came hither. Another man then said, that two men, whom he named, long ago were going to the hill to catch sheep, when they heard a noise like a woman churning in the side of a hillock. One of them exclaimed, "Woman, give me a drink;" and to his great surprise a woman came out, carrying in her hand a dish of milk, which the one who asked it refused, but the other took it. She said to the one who refused her milk, that he would not long survive for thus mocking her; and accordingly he died in his own house that night.'

MacKenzie's reaction to the confidence placed in him by those who told him these incidents is of interest. He did not hesitate to retell the stories in his journal, then to dismiss them, and, lastly, to counteract them with what some might call 'equally ridiculous' tales of his own:

'These, and many other stories equally ridiculous and fanciful, were related, and many seemed to believe them; and all wished to hear my thoughts on the subject. I took occasion thence to enlarge on the folly and absurdity of believing such reveries; and, with an eye to the same thing, explained that part of the answer to the question, "What is God?" "God is a spirit." I told them in the simplest manner what is a spirit, and what is not; that there are three spiritual existences, namely, the Supreme Spirit God, angels. and the souls of men; that the Supreme Being differed from all other spirits, in being infinite, eternal, and unchangeable in all his attributes; whereas angels and souls of men are but limited, changeable, and created beings. I observed also, that some of the angels had trespassed against God, and so become evil spirits ..'

MacKenzie no doubt thought that he was fitting a Christian and superseding version of the spiritual world into a traditional island framework for better understanding, but it may be easily imagined that the islanders, a little confused, found it more understandable and quite consistent to remain loyal to their second sight and other 'reveries'.

*

Hoping that they 'would not be so credulous in future', Neil MacKenzie claimed some success in his attempt to change the customary form of celebrating Christmas and also the new year which was still considered to fall on 12 January. He felt that he had managed to suppress the accompanying festivities: 'Formerly they were accustomed to spend the first day of the year in out-door play, and the night in dancing', but 'What was deemed superstitious or foolish were laid aside, and the time spent in a more rational and Christian way.' There were indeed such moments when the missionary must surely have recognised that he was seeking to undo a way of life and thinking profoundly different from his own, although he probably did not fully understand the significance of his efforts or have much idea of the consequences. Gradually an ancient world, not peculiar to St Kilda alone, was being dismantled, and MacKenzie, with his 'temporal' as well as 'spiritual' introductions made his distinctive contribution to the process as John MacDonald had done to a lesser degree before him. The St Kilda people were far from being exceptional in their traditions, but they had maintained an element from distant, early days and by their isolation certain features were given unusual prominence.

Marriage and death, like birth and baptism, presented their special challenges to a missionary who was employed to bring the people into line with a form of religion which for a time at least had no place for what it saw as superstition, the waste of 'precious time', excessively emotional farewells and needless handshakes in the morning. Several generations later there was less space for the spiritual teaching that had been a means of undermining St Kilda's accumulated inheritance. A marriage, relatively harmless to any one worried about superstition, was reported in detail to the SSPCK directors, and so too was the funeral on 28 July 1832 of a seven weeks old child, the seventh or eighth of those who had died soon after birth since the MacKenzies came to the island in 1830. The lengthy description of funeral customs provided by the minister covered those which he believed were superstitious and therefore undesirable as well as the measures he took to prevent their continued survival.

The conditions fostering a disease 'like the croup' which destroyed the infant children were set out first of all:

'The dampness and foulness of the air of their houses may contribute, if they be not the principal causes of this disease. Their houses are built in a very wet place, and the dampness is increased by their pouring continually all the water used in their houses on the composition with which the floors are covered. The houses are also very cold, and for some time the only covering of the infant is a piece of bare cloth wrapped round it.'

Not only children suffered. Contrary to George Atkinson's remark on the healthy state of the islanders, MacKenzie said that 'much sickness and mortality prevail, and there are few who do not suffer from stomach complaints, nervous disorders, and dysenteries ... It is painful to see a poor creature languishing under the power of disease, lying on the floor with nothing but a little straw and a dirty blanket, all day alone in the house, with a bottle of water or whey at his head.' In the event of death the relatives who seemed to pay no regard to the invalid 'mourn excessively'; and MacKenzie went on to describe with a minister's concern what seems like a timeless ritual retained from some remote past:

'As soon as it is thought that the sick person is dying, all the inhabitants leave their work, and crowd to the house, to bewail his death, and bid him a long farewell. Meanwhile, the near friends, in the most impassioned manner, and in a kind of measured language which they sing or chaunt, addressing themselves to the dying man, say, "Farewell with you; farewell with you for ever; the blessing of all your friends is with you, and their good wishes!" or similar expressions.'

Again the contradictions are apparent in MacKenzie's account. His interest in the islanders' behaviour is limited; his opinion of it has to be a religious one. 'Oh, what cold comfort,' he exclaimed, 'to a soul about entering into the presence of its Judge! how ill-placed such an address! how unbecoming in those who should be comforting their friend with the heart-cheering consolations of the gospel!' Yet the people's farewell, their inconsolable crying and wailing which moved MacKenzie to say 'Who on such an occasion could refrain from tears?', and their recovery to seeming 'nearly as cheerful as ever' contained an age-old realism which compared favourably with the minister's otherworldly solution.

The funeral routine involved preparation of food, watching the corpse in the house, and, in the close community, an interval from work, nothing greatly different from procedure today. The coffin, 'well tied on two sticks', was carried sunwise or deiseal, 'in the course of the sun round the gardens, with which the group of houses which form the village are surrounded, though they should go through their corn'. This custom was then usual throughout the western Highlands and islands on many kinds of ceremonial occasion. The filling of the grave after burial was then followed by eating the prepared meat and bread at the graveside, the closing stage of a sequence which MacKenzie, interested and sympathetic as he was, sought to alter:

'In this part of their customs there are some things superstitious and others that are wasteful. I have therefore endeavoured to change what I conceived to be so. First I try to impress on their minds to be kind to the sick, not to come in crowds to the house to disturb them with their talk, or distress them with the heat; but to visit one after another, to keep the house quiet, to show as much attention as they can to them, and to soothe their minds with sympathy and kindness, particularly to take every opportunity of reading to the sick select scripture passages, to pray for them and with them, and as their strength admitted, to draw their minds to things spiritual and eternal. Secondly, to moderate their grief, and not to mourn as those who have no hope. Thirdly, not to sit in bands with the dead at night, but (if it is deemed necessary to watch at all) that two are sufficient for that purpose, and that they ought not to burden their friends with unnecessary trouble or expense; but to spend the night in reading the Bible and good books, and in prayer. Fourthly, never to mind in what direction they go to the grave - on no account to destroy any part of their corn when they could go to the burying-ground by another way, though it should not be in the course of the sun; and by all means to discontinue the practice of killing any sheep or cows for a feast that was unnecessary and indecent, or to put themselves to any expense except in dead-clothes and a coffin.'[78]

*

In all aspects, from wool-plucking to funerals, MacKenzie realised that habits which had prevailed for centuries were not easily contradicted. 'It is very difficult,' he wrote, 'next to impossible, to change any part of their practice which has antiquity to san[c]tion it. In any of their debates it is enough, they think, to make out that such or such a custom, or that such or such a thing has been affirmed by their forefathers, to settle any point in dispute.' He also knew that 'To change the habits of such a people must be the work either of time or grace. If the latter takes place, we may expect great things in a short time, for with God all things are possible.' If not, then perseverance in rebuking the people would, in his view, eventually wear them down and the superstitious practices would be given up.

The 'slavish attachment to what obtained formerly in their own native place' was not of course unique to St Kilda, for it existed all over Scotland wherever there were reasonably undisturbed rural communities, and

MacKenzie was one of many with ideas for improvement who complained about adherence to old ways. Usually tradition and custom predominated in farming, but in St Kilda MacKenzie took particular exception to the persistance of what he saw as immoral practices such as stealing the property of the tacksman. 'Any thing of that nature I would not look on with indifference, nor delay showing its awful criminality.' But in general he had made good progress in reducing 'the spirit of pilfering', one of his more useful achievements in his opinion.

After less than three years of trying to introduce changes that he believed to be beneficial, Neil MacKenzie sensed that the island was changing him. On 21 August 1832 he climbed Conachair in beautifully fine weather and from the top gazed out over the great expanse of ocean that surrounded his little world. He could see the long extent of hilly land from Lewis to Barra on the eastern horizon. Round the shoulder of Boreray were the Flannans, 'like cows in a distant meadow'. Sounds of the island reached him: 'The lowing of a solitary cow, the bleating of sheep at the folds, the barking of dogs in the village below me, and the ceaseless screaming of the various tribes of sea-fowls feeding their young, seem to give a life to the scene around me, and draw my attention from contemplating the vast expanse of water, and the ample dome above me, and to fix it on the little spot of earth to which I am attached.' He was small and isolated, an insignificant speck in creation. And on 28 May 1833, in the last entry of his journal, he expressed for the benefit of the SSPCK directors the change wrought by St Kilda in his state of mind, his words emphasising the distance between his own way of thinking and that of the island people:

'In a place like this, where there is no intelligent society, a person is apt to lose instead of improving the power of communicating his ideas. I felt this in a very sensible degree when I went to the mainland last year. I could not express my thoughts with so much propriety and energy as I was wont to do. But, what is still worse than that, for want of the stimulus and the many opportunities of informing the mind by newspapers, magazines, new works of every kind, and instructive conversation, the powers of the mind are not constantly kept on the alert, nor directed to many important topics to which intercourse with intelligent society would lead them.'

Alexander Buchan had endured both inadequate 'accommodations' and exile from this form of 'intelligent society' for around 25 years. Many of his successors had perhaps chosen to be periodically absent from their 'station' rather than suffer the same fate. Probably no minister in St Kilda, keen to replace traditional lore with biblical stories and scripture readings, ever wondered whether the associations with places such as sacred wells, the telling of tales and singing of songs, the dances and the festivals, had anything to do with preserving and developing the 'powers of the mind'. For the missionary events and visitors brought some excitement and the more numerous strangers of the earlier nineteenth century to some extent compensated a man like MacKenzie for the lack of communication which he regretted. After 1830 the minister, always at the shore to welcome the new arrival and usually the host at his manse, enthusiastically greeted a diverse collection of visitors, tacksman, tacksman's agent, yachtsman, fisherman, and tourist. They all brought news and an otherwise unavailable opportunity for 'instructive conversation'. At the end of 1833 the invasion was about to begin.

CHAPTER 7

The first steamers, the Aclands, the rebuilding of the
'village' and the visit of Drs Macleod and Dickson

O N 21 July 1834 a ship called *Glenalbyn*, Daniel Mathieson 'Commander',
elegantly furnished and reputed to be the first 'steam vessel' ever to call
at St Kilda, set out from Glasgow and 'performed a most extensive, varied and
magnificent voyage'. Rounding the Mull of Kintyre, it called at Oban where it
took on more passengers, Tobermory, Staffa, Iona, again at Oban, passed
through the Caledonian Canal to Inverness, returned to Oban (for yet more
passengers), and on 26th July returned to Tobermory. Special attractions such
as the Spar Cave in Skye and 'Loch-Appin' – 'one of the most splendid views
imaginable' – a romantic place 'celebrated in a note by Sir Walter Scott, to his
poem of the "Lord of the Isles" ', led on to 'Lochbraccadale' in the west of Skye
where there came aboard 'some young geologists', one of whom was
apparently T Jameson Torrie, who a few days later after the visit to St Kilda,
wrote from Portree to his mother in Edinburgh, giving a brief account of his
adventure so far:

> 'We arrived here this Morning safe and sound after a most prosperous
> voyage to St Kilda and Stornoway in the new steam boat the Glen Albyn.
> As I mentioned we were to do in the letter I wrote from Isle Oransay we
> proceeded on Saturday across the island to Macalister's cave and after a
> very long walk succeeded in getting to the Inn at Broadford the same
> night. We were occupied till the following Wednesday evening in
> examining the neighbourhood of Broadford, - and then recrossed to the
> Western part of the island, where there are no inns of any description,
> and where we were therefore obliged to trust to the hospitality of the
> farmers, who in reality are the gentlemen of the country. We were most
> kindly treated at the homes [houses?] of two of them; and arranged our
> plans so as to suit the time the steamer was expected to touch at Loch
> Bracadale a wild inlet of the sea in the North West of Skye; but from
> accidental circumstances she was a day later of coming, and we had
> therefore to put up with some hardship and uncertainty, till when we
> had almost given up hope the vessel made its appearance on Sunday
> morning, and by dint of hard running down the banks of the loch we
> reached it just when she was again starting. We were all exceedingly glad
> to get on board both because we were anxious to see St Kilda, and as we
> were pretty well knocked up by the fatigues we had endured amongst
> the mountains. We reached St Kilda about 12 O'clock on Sunday night,
> but did not venture to anchor that night as there was no one on board
> who was acquainted with the landing place. Next morning however
> proved favourable and we landed about 4 O'clock after previously

rousing the inhabitants by firing cannons from the vessel. The excitement and astonishment produced by our appearance were great as no Steam vessel had ever before landed passengers on the island; and we were soon surrounded by the whole population amounting at this time to 93 persons. The clergyman showed us the lions of the place, and the people were most anxious to show us every thing the[y] thought could interest us and equally so to see the wonders of the vessel, more especially the ornaments and mirrors of the cabin. Altogether the appearance of the natives, the island, and the animals upon it - together with the interest attracted to the first visit of so large a party to so desolate and distant a spot - and also the uncertainty there was for some time of our being able to land at all made the trip a most curious one. The number of passengers on board the steamer was very considerable - not less than 50 or 60 but they were chiefly from Glasgow or Inverness except Sir John and Lady Ord who were in Edinburgh last winter, and a few young Englishmen and foreigners. From St Kilda we again returned through the intricate passage of the Sound of Harris and arrived at Stornoway in Lewis about 10 o'clock on Monday night - but again sailed for this place at 1 and arrived about ½ past 6 this morning.'[79]

The 93 inhabitants were, according to a report, members of 21 families and formed a population which had never increased for a century. Having been woken by the firing of the two cannons most of the people 'issued from their dwellings like flocks of bees' and fled to the steepest rocks, but one, 'more courageous than the others', slowly came back, approached the manse and then led the rest of the 'natives' to the beach where they met the visitors. Some general impressions among the latter included the comment that the people married very young, inevitably with near relatives which accounted for 'the apparent deterioration of the race'. 'The clergyman's duties', it was noted, 'appear to be strictly confined to religious matters', but 'magisterial duties' fell to a ground officer who spoke English, was mainly in charge of collection of feathers as rent, seemed 'rather intelligent', and exercised a considerable degree of authority. The houses were 'collected close to each other, with very narrow passages between, and form a circle', at one side of which the ground officer 'has a bench erected, where he holds courts once a week, and dispenses justice liberally'. A house on its own, 'remote from the others, has a lock on the door, (the only one amongst the natives,) where young couples are placed in upon being married, and the door locked upon them for 24 hours; there are also several other houses at a distance, where the inhabitants store their feathers'.[80]

Another member of the party, much more critical in his account, was shocked by 'the state of the forlorn islanders'. To mainland Britain in general St Kilda, if heard of, was a half-real place, where primitive inhabitants lived on birds caught on immense cliffs, a subject for romantic poetry and humorous comment, but among actual visitors much depended on expectations; the more understanding or sympathetic shared with ministers like John MacDonald and Neil MacKenzie a genuine concern, but this anonymous, layman tourist of 1834 gave the impression that it was 'a national humiliation and disgrace that a people situated almost at our own doors should have been so utterly neglected.' When the party landed it was itself the object of curiosity and wonder, and 'The dresses of the ladies … called forth exclamations of surprise and delight.' Souvenirs in the shape of dogs, cheese, 'brooches' and other island products were bought, and the 'considerable shrewdness' shown in bargaining was thought to prove that the people were 'not deficient in natural capacity, however wanting in cultivation'. The group of irregularly clustered 'huts' which formed the 'village' impressed only with its squalor and the cultivation was 'deplorable', but the manse and church were 'respectable buildings' and the clergyman 'a very respectable man'. Intelligence there was, it seemed, but 'Civilisation' was lacking. 'Like all semi-barbarians,' this tourist went on, on the basis of at most a few hours' acquaintance, 'they are subject to prejudices, and strongly attached to old customs'. They were - to his disappointment - contented with their filthy and stinking hovels, and being 'semi-barbarous', as he concluded from his brief experience, 'their sources of emotion are few, but the emotions themselves vivid and strong'. It was high time that Britain, already 'sending missions of instruction and of mercy to the farthest limits of the world', paid some attention to an island 'so near her own shores, and owing allegiance to her own sovereign', and ensured that the degraded and barbaric conditions were removed. The proprietor too, with the help of 'other active friends of benevolence', could, with a 'very little effort', quite easily 'rescue these unhappy people from their physical and moral lethargy'. People just as 'unhappy' on other islands received no comment.

As the *Glenalbyn* prepared to leave several of the St Kilda men came aboard to look with amazement on the ship's fittings and machinery. Then they had to go ashore, and the steamer's departure evoked some perceptive remarks:

> 'At length the party took leave of that simple-minded and warm-hearted little community, with feelings of deep interest and commiseration, hoping that the visit might be remembered in their annals as the commencing point in an era of improvement. Yet they could not altogether suppress their fears, that if a visit to St Kilda should become a common occurrence in parties of pleasure, it might unfortunately happen, that the vices of civilised life would be imparted to them sooner than its virtues and its blessings.'[81]

The corrupting stranger was always a threat.

St Kilda was still recovering from the *Glenalbyn's* cannon firing when a two-masted schooner converted to a steam yacht, 'adorned with a vast number of flags', entered the bay one evening in September 1834. This was *The Lady of St Kilda*, with Captain Moresby in command, on her maiden voyage round England and Scotland. The owner, Sir Thomas Acland, was aboard, and so too was the piano belonging to Lady Lydia, after whose adventure to the island in 1812 the yacht was named. Such a large ship was well-furnished, and among the facilities was a tray holding sketching materials which hung from the cabin roof. Sir Thomas again made 'a pictorial log' of the voyage, this time mostly pencil sketches, and when he landed he distributed gifts among the islanders and met and talked for a while with Neil MacKenzie, 'resident minister', who must have had vividly in his mind the comments on the 'village' settlement made only five days earlier. Sir Thomas saw that no improvement in conditions had been achieved over the last twenty years and before leaving decided to award a prize for significant improvement. Rev. MacKenzie recorded details:

'Sir Thomas and his lady, willing to confer a more lasting mark of their favour on the inhabitants of this island, or rather his benevolent mind being excited by their miserable homes, left with me twenty sovereigns, to help them to build new houses, as soon as they could get their ground lotted. To hasten them, it was given them on condition that they should build within two years. If they do not build in that time, I am to apply the money to any purpose I may think useful. Were a few gentlemen to follow this generous example, a fund could be raised by the natives themselves, sufficient to build in St Kilda neat cottages. One or two hundred pounds, I believe, would cover all expenses. Wood for roofs, small glass windows, and a mason to help them to build houses, are all that is required to render them comfortable. Were the ground once lotted, some would endeavour themselves to build better dwellings, while others would follow the filthy customs of their forefathers.'[82]

The dwellings in the old 'town', of unknown antiquity, may have struck visitors as primitive and squalid but they were not exceptionally poor. Conditioned as they were by the nature of the island, by weather and by isolation, they could be compared with the homes of cottars in other parts of the Hebrides and elsewhere, but they attracted special note and concern because St Kilda did. Had strangers shown as much interest in Scarp or even Harris and Lewis they would have found similarly dark 'hovels' huddled together in a seemingly haphazard way but giving each other shelter and a sociable comfort. When Rev. Daniel McAllum, a kind of John MacDonald of the far north, travelled to Shetland on his evangelical trip in June 1822 he and his companion had to retreat out of bad weather:

'we saw the inside of a Shetland hut. It had two apartments. That into which we were introduced, had a fire on the floor, but no chimney, and the smoke eddied near the opening in the roof, as if reluctant to sally forth. The bedsteads were wooden recesses at the further end of the apartments, where all sleep together, the household and the stranger. On this subject it is to be observed, that it is nowhere the practice to have only one couch. There is one bed for the parents, another for the females, a third for the males. When pressed for room by the visitation of a stranger, if a man, one or two of the men retire with him, and sleep in the barn; if a female, one or two of the girls do the same thing … Little or no furniture is to be found in their habitations.'[83]

The St Kilda house interiors were made particularly uncomfortable by the practice of storing refuse on the floor, and just outside the door, in preparation for using it as a manure. 'Like the people of some of the islands nearer the mainland, the natives of St. Kilda are very dirty in their persons; and a very indifferent nose may be sensible of their approach. Their huts are cleaned but once in the year, from the filth which is carefully accumulated in them, and which is preserved for enriching their fields. The straw is also removed from the roofs of the huts every spring, and spread upon the arable land.' Other writers went into more detail about this habit of hoarding rubbish:

'Their method of preparing a sort of manure, to them indeed of vast use, proves that they are very indelicate. After having burnt a considerable quantity of dried turf, they spread the ashes with the nicest care over the floor of that apartment in which they eat and sleep. These ashes, so exactly laid out, they cover with a rich friable sort of earth; over this bed of earth they scatter a proportionable heap of that dust into which peats are apt to crumble away: this done, they water, tread, and beat the whole compost into a hard floor, on which they immediately make new fires very large, and never extinguished till they have a sufficient stock of new ashes on hand. The same operations are repeated with a never-failing punctuality, till they are just ready to sow their barley; by that time the walls of their houses are sunk down, or, to speak more properly, the floors risen about four or five feet high.

'To have room enough for accumulating heaps of this compost one above another, the ancient St Kildans had ingenuity enough to contrive their beds within the linings of their walls; and it was for the same reason they took care to raise these walls to a height far from being common in the other Western islands.'[84]

341

The cluster of houses had stood for many generations in the wet area of ground near the well Tobar Childa, but it seems to have been the accumulated 'filth' rather than the site to which Neil MacKenzie most objected, since, having less 'delicacy' himself, he remarked that the 'rich friable sort of earth' really consisted of 'many things far worse' than ashes and dirty water, this making 'a visit to a parishioner' in early spring unpleasant as well as 'quite an adventure'. The living apartment was by that time almost filled with the heap that now did for the floor, and, if the parishioner was unwell in bed, it was necessary to approach with caution: 'Carefully creeping along in the almost total darkness you made your way to the top of the steep slope which led down to the bed opening. Down this you went head foremost, nothing visible above but your legs, while you spoke and prayed.' John MacDonald, whose visits occurred after the manure had been applied to the fields and before much more had been saved up, will have missed the unusual excitement of this pastoral duty, and the house abandoned by Lachlan MacLeod as inadequate was of a different kind. MacDonald's own remarks on the dwellings were therefore rather less dramatic than MacKenzie's:

> 'Their houses, or huts, are all exactly of the same form and dimensions, and in internal appearance also completely alike. They consist of but one apartment, in which the family is accommodated at one end, and the cattle at the other. The walls contain their beds, and places for their stores, for which purpose they are generally six or seven feet thick. No chairs or tables are to be seen; wooden stools and even stones being made to supply their place. The ashes are never carried out of the house, nor even removed to the part of the room appropriated to the cattle, but are spread every morning under the feet of the inmates, in order as they call it, to help the manure. The floor, thus raised in the course of the season, to a considerable height, is reduced to its proper level only once a-year, when the whole matter so accumulated is conveyed to the fields. I reasoned with the people on the impropriety of this habit, chiefly on the ground of its being injurious to their health and comfort, but to little effect, long custom having reconciled them to it.'[85]

It is no wonder then that MacKenzie, as sensitive to the smell as Buchan had been a century and more earlier, approved of Sir Thomas Acland's donation, although it seems to have been the prospect of the prize rather than his own persuasion that induced the islanders to take some sort of action. Building better houses was not however immediately possible. If the settlement was to be moved, where would it go? Any change of site would be likely to mean the loss of cultivated land or good pasture, most of which was held in common by the inhabitants. In addition, giving up the old houses would be a departure from 'long custom' and the benefits discovered in the course of a well-established way of life.

It was necessary first therefore to plan how the new settlement would be set out or 'lotted', and it is likely that this was done by the tacksman in conjunction with the minister. There were plenty of examples on the mainland and in the islands of the rearrangement of old farm 'towns' into separated smallholdings or 'crofts', and in St Kilda the pattern was followed whereby the better land rising from the shore to the foot of the hills was divided into lots, one for each family, 'so that each might build upon his own portion'. The proprietor, John MacPherson MacLeod, apparently agreed to this without hesitation, and the task of division or lotting was appropriately given to the tacksman or tenant, Donald MacDonald.[86]

MacDonald, whose ancestry lay in Heisgeir and Griminish, North Uist, had been given the tenancy of St Kilda for one year from Whitsunday 1831 at a rent of £55. The circumstances were explained to H D Hill by MacLeod's factor in Skye, probably MacKinnon of Corry: 'Mr McLennan (the last tenant) threw up the Island shortly after Whitsunday, and I did not think it advisable to make any attempt to make him keep it, considering how far he is already behind. I set it to a neighbour of mine, Mr. McDonald of Scalpay, at the same rent, and I hope he will not have the same difficulty in realizing it.' From then on MacDonald held the island on a yearly basis without any rent alteration, but as something of an entrepreneur he was none too popular. In 1790 he bought the Tanera fishing station near Ullapool and the station of Culag at Lochinver, where it appears he had one or two fishing vessels. He became known then as a fish merchant and curer and as the 'extensive and enterprising sheep-farmer' who also had 'a manufactory, for the preserving of butchermeat, fish, and vegetables' in Lochinver. In 1837 when, having succeeded his father, he was called MacDonald of Skeabost rather than of Tanera he purchased the British Fisheries Society land at Lochbay in Waternish, Skye, where 'Mr Macleod of St Kilda' was one of the local proprietors. It has been said that Donald MacDonald had a brother James who lived in Stornoway and possessed a boat known as the *Rover's Bride*, in which Donald or his representative used to sail to St Kilda.[87]

According to Neil MacKenzie's recollections Donald MacDonald, 'the father of Mr MacDonald, lately tenant of Kingsburgh, but now of Seaport [i.e. Skeabost] in Skye', came to St Kilda to divide the land, but the islanders were not satisfied with the division he made, 'each thinking that the other's share was better than his own'. Consequently MacKenzie persuaded the people themselves to fix upon portions of ground, making them as equal as possible, and then to assign them by a form of drawing lots. This was done successfully, and in due course a house, without wall beds and floor manure, was built on each lot, although this took some time as many were reluctant to start on such a radically new venture. In 1838, some three years after building began, a number of the old oval-shaped houses still stood as always 'all in one confused cluster', but there were 21 new houses in which the former bed 'cave' as it was called did not exist and here and there a few of 'their most ancient houses', nearly circular and with bed spaces in the thickness of the walls, survived like little green hills, giving the impression at least that, in some cases, they were 'almost entirely underground'. Thus at this time it seems that three stages of dwelling were simultaneously in existence, and as the latest buildings were occupied one or two of their predecessors remained in use as the homes of solitary women and widows while the rest were demolished. A visitor in 1838 remarked that 'in the widows' houses there is but one circular apartment, like a pig-stye', while Neil MacKenzie remembered that when the new houses were built all the oval ones were removed 'except one small one in which dwelt a widow'.[88]

Another reason for the slow beginning to the new 'village' was the unwillingness of anyone in St Kilda to be different, 'no man being allowed, or at least encouraged, to outstrip his neighbours'. However, as soon as one 'spirit bolder than the rest' decided to begin construction others followed, and encouragement was given by the minister who set an example by working energetically himself on the project. This was probably not earlier than the summer of 1835 as MacKenzie was in Edinburgh previously, and in November H D Hill stated that the minister, possibly taking advantage of the lotting, 'was demanding more pasturage etc. than was agreed on'.[89]

In May 1837, with the erection of new houses well forward, the SSPCK secretary thought that 'sundry small articles of hardware would be of great use in the Island of St Kilda', and proposed, when an opportunity should arise, 'to send out a few things of this description'. The idea was approved and £5 allowed for the purpose, but the purchase and transport of the goods had to wait till the summer of 1838 when MacKenzie, after an interval of three busy years, again left the island. He was in Glasgow and then Edinburgh in June and returned to Glasgow at the beginning of July to be ready for the journey home which he made by the steamer *Vulcan*. While in Edinburgh he gave the SSPCK 'a most favourable report' of progress in St Kilda, and, as he had 'many things to provide for his family', he was supplied with a sum comprising all stipend arrears owing and the half year's stipend to November 1838. In Glasgow he bought 'furnishings to St Kilda' which included tables, chairs, bedsteads, kitchen dressers, stools and crockery, all being 'means of comfort formerly unknown in the Island'. The money for these things had apparently been raised by Rev. Dr Norman MacLeod of St Columba's, Glasgow. Further expenditure also proved possible on educational material, for in his report MacKenzie had spoken of how 'several of the inhabitants were now not only able to read Gaelic but had also been learning English' and 'were at the same time learning writing and Arithmetic', though there was a great lack of suitable stationery. The SSPCK directors were therefore very pleased to instruct their secretary to release £5.10s.6d for spending on paper, pencils, knives, slates, scissors and so on 'to encourage the people in the prosecution of their studies'. Orders were given for a supply of books in English and Gaelic, and MacKenzie was presented with 'a Copy of the Christian Herald as far as hitherto published'.[90]

Satisfaction was also expressed at the news of religious improvement, 'not only in Christian Knowledge and information but in their morals and habits'. Since many of the islanders could now read Gaelic they could read the bible, and the advance in moral behaviour was a consequence, the SSPCK believed, 'of their advancement in Religious knowledge and the power of Divine truth upon their minds'. Many customs 'to which they had been formerly addicted' and which were considered vices had been abandoned, 'and their former filthy habits were giving place to those of greater cleanliness and order'; indeed 'improvements in civilization, cleanliness and order, kept pace with their improvement in education, religious instruction and knowledge', so that those who were most religiously inclined in heart and mind were also the cleanest. Several people 'had attained so much knowledge of Divine truth and given such evidence of its practical influence on their lives that Mr MacKenzie was anxious to have an opportunity of administering the Sacrament of the Lords Supper to them', and therefore wished to have the assistance of none other than John MacDonald of Urquhart. The directors hoped the latter would be willing to participate.[91]

The 21 new houses were soon to be furnished with the articles from Glasgow. At the same time repairs were again needed on the church and manse where the glass in windows had been broken in many places and slates were missing. The church itself had to be roughcast to protect it from the severe weather. For these purposes the Society secretary told MacKenzie to consult James Crawford over what work would be essential, and to buy window glass, slates, nails and lead, together with 'a few barrels of lime'. And to complete the list of contributions to buildings Dr Dickson, a minister with a great interest in the island, 'ordered for the use of the St Kilda Mission' on behalf of the Society a baptismal basin, a plate, and a communion cup on which were inscribed the words: 'Gifted by the Society in Scotland for Propagating Christian Knowledge to the Church of St Kilda'.[92]

*

Materials for the repairs having been provided by a Mr Neil McGregor in Glasgow at the cost of £26.14s.4d, and all items acquired by MacKenzie being safely stored on board, the *Vulcan* left the Broomielaw at 2 o'clock in the afternoon of 25 July 1838. Among the passengers were Neil MacKenzie, Drs Dickson and MacLeod, and Lachlan MacLean, already author of a small book on Iona and about to set to work on *Sketches of the island of St Kilda*. The ship, which 'furnishes not only the comforts but the *luxuries* of life', crossed first to the coast of Ireland for a view of the Giant's Causeway, then moved north to Iona, Staffa and Skye. At Lochmaddy the brig *Corsair* was preparing to leave with emigrants for Cape Breton, an unwelcome sight: 'I advised Dr Macleod to go; he said his feelings could not stand it; and indeed it was a heart-rending scene. If he *had* gone, it would have marred his pleasure for the future part of the voyage.' A visit was paid to Lochmaddy inn where the party met the emigration agent and a medical gentleman called MacLeod, and was served by, 'to me a living curiosity, a black fellow of a waiter, who spoke and sang in Gaelic!'[93]

On Saturday 28 July they drew near St Kilda. At Boreray and Stac Lee 'our cannons belched at intervals' in an attempt to scare the gannets into the air, but few took off. There followed 'the cracks of a grove of rifles' and some gannets were killed. 'I know not,' said MacLean, 'whether this sort of sport is consistent with a well regulated mind.' But he himself tried shooting and missed. A large cannon was fired as the *Vulcan* arrived in the bay, and 'natives', who had obviously been watching a display of absurd noise and foolish purpose, ran barefooted down the slopes of Oiseabhal like a flock of frightened goats. When the first boat from the ship touched the shore MacLean 'leaped out with great facility, and ran up to welcome Mrs McKenzie', apparently before Mr MacKenzie could do so. One of the islanders, Donald MacKinnon, 'the sub-tacksman', presumably the equivalent of the old ground officer or a constable, took MacLean away 'up the village' on his tour of the buildings, including the ruins of Lady Grange's dwelling, and especially to a hut in which were 'two live solan geese in their wild state, and full grown'. These birds were presented to MacLean and looked after rather carelessly. Meanwhile some hardier passengers bathed from the beach.[94]

In June 1833 MacKenzie had applied to the SSPCK for financial assistance to run a school in the island but had been refused and so had persisted on his own. He began a Sabbath school, 'attended by both young and old', and since few could then read he opened 'a day school', which MacLean and his guide visited in 1838: 'On our way we entered the academy or schoolhouse. It is a new building of one apartment, about nine feet by eight, where the clergyman, as a free-will offering instructs a few. It has one window looking towards the bay, with canvass for glass, and a wooden tube, of about three inches square, thrust through the roof by way of a chimney, or ventilator.' By 1841 the school seems to have been conducted in part of the church.[95]

At some point, probably on the day of arrival, MacLean heard Dr MacLeod preach to the islanders and thought the service 'most impressive'. The audience could not have been more devoutly attentive as they listened to the sermon, during which MacLeod 'wrestled with a fervour and unction' which 'convinced us that God was present in St Kilda'. Weeping broke out again. Old men were in tears and of the women two or three young ones, MacLean thought, 'would break their hearts - they grieved as a mother grieves for an only son'. The next day being the Sabbath, communion was celebrated as Neil MacKenzie had wished, though John MacDonald was not present. At 8 o'clock in the morning Drs MacLeod and Dickson, along with a Mr Stewart and MacLean, 'went ashore with a view to examine the young communicants', all of whom were above the age of forty. In the church 'one of the natives' led prayer, his neighbours being all assembled. His voice was firm, his delivery appropriately slow, his manner solemn and expressive, and his Gaelic carefully chosen; 'prayer seemed to him not a matter of rote, but the emanation of a mind imbued with the *spirit* of prayer'. The prayer meeting ended, and in came the three ministers. MacKenzie read out the names of fifteen people considered fit to receive the sacrament who were to stay behind and be questioned on scriptural subjects and Christian doctrine. At the examination their highly satisfactory answers were slow and clear. One old man whose name was not included in the list of those thought 'worthy of the table' pursued the ministers to the manse in a state of great distress, and was admitted.[96]

Portrait of Rev. Norman Macleod, who visited St Kilda with Rev. Dr Dickson in 1838

About 11 o'clock, after breakfast, Dr Dickson, who in travelling to the island had worn 'a short Macintosh, knee-breeches, silk stockings, and a fur-cap pulled over his ears' and who may now have appeared in more solemn dress, went to the shore in order to go out to preach a sermon to those still on the *Vulcan*. MacLean, who claimed to have disappeared behind a large stone in order 'to jot down something', emerged just in time to see Mr Stewart struggling with 'a large black object in the water'. The object was 'the worthy Dr. Dickson' who had lost his balance when one leg was in the small boat and fallen. As a result he did not preach on the *Vulcan*; instead he changed clothes and wore trousers that did not fit.[97]

Some time about noon Neil MacKenzie swung his hand bell, the 'natives' trooped off to church, some with Gaelic bibles, and Dr MacLeod preached the 'action sermon'. Dr Dickson presented the communion cup and other 'sacred utensils', and then 'served a table in English' to Mrs MacKenzie, her father James Crawford, and one or two others. Neil MacKenzie took over and administered the sacrament to the chosen, who for such a solemn occasion wore rather better clothes than usual. The service lasted until 4 o'clock. Another service followed at 6.30 that evening, Dickson taking one in English on the steamer, MacLeod preaching in Gaelic in the church. MacLean stayed on board to hear Dickson, hardly able to believe that he was not dreaming the whole experience. When he was attending to Dr MacLeod's first sermon in the church he was of the same mind: 'There is something in the very name of St Kilda that is romantic: remote and solitary, the spirit of poetry seems to dwell in the waves and the storms that separate it from the rest of the world.' Could he really be sitting in the church on St Kilda? Now, on the *Vulcan*, 'I could scarce convince myself, for a while, that the scene was a reality'.

The evening service over the visitors went ashore again and met Dr MacLeod coming down to the beach 'quite spent', the 'natives' after him all in tears because he had said he must be leaving and would not return. Late that Sunday evening, with the firing of another gun, the *Vulcan* steamed away.[98]

*

Although he gave much space in his *Sketches* to some St Kilda history taken from earlier books, and relied heavily on what Neil MacKenzie told him, Lachlan MacLean was an observant, lively visitor and recorded a mixture of historical and contemporary detail. Like others he commented on dress - the barefooted men wore 'wide shapeless trousers resembling those of the Barra-men' - and noticed how the back of the waistcoat between the shoulders was uniformly in tatters from 'lounging the half of their time with their backs against the houses, talking of this one and that one's feats in the rocks.' He saw many a small thing from the men's big toes to the women's brooches, and he examined the patchwork woollen sail of the island's boat, the 'Lair-dhonn' or

'Brown Mare'. He looked at a few piles of loose stones in the burial ground, apparently all that remained of Teampall Chriosd. Dr MacLeod, he said, distributed 47 bedsteads at the rate of two per house and one each to the poor widows, 24 chairs, 21 stools, 21 tables, 21 dressers, 21 glass windows, and various pieces of crockery. Since there were 21 new houses it might be concluded from this that all a widow received was the bedstead and perhaps a dish or plate. The barrels of lime and the slates were destined for the necessary repairs to church and manse and for an extension to the latter. MacLean then came to two conclusions. He suggested that there should be, in spite of recent developments, an entirely new village of chimneyed houses: 'It would really be charity to give the natives something to do - they are, I must confess, passing indolent.' And he reckoned 'that government ought to instruct one of their revenue cutters who, at any rate are slumbering at anchor, or cruising at will like strayed comets, to touch once in six months at St Kilda'.[99]

Dr Dickson and Dr MacLeod returned to the mainland with very different ideas arising from their interest in the religious state of the community. Dickson's accident led to the temporary renaming of that part of the St Kilda coast as 'Dickson's Bay', matched inevitably by the equally temporary 'MacLeod's Bay' off Glen More for his colleague, but the unfortunate soaking did not sour his recollection of the visit. He said afterwards that he had found the St Kilda mission in 'a very prosperous condition', that he and Dr MacLeod had 'administered the Lord's Supper' to the people, and that 'he had admitted to the ordinance several individuals with whose fitness to be received as communicants he was much satisfied'. In fact the entire occasion was 'altogether most interesting and delightful'. The SSPCK was left in no doubt that their missionary in the island was a success.[100]

After a year in which work on the manse extension and probably the repairs to the church had been carried out under the supervision of his father in law MacKenzie decided on another visit to the mainland and in the spring of 1840, by some unrecorded means, he crossed from the island and arrived in Edinburgh, where, at a meeting of the Society on 7 May, he was allowed his next half year's salary and was told he would be supplied with more books for the use of the St Kilda people. He gave 'a most gratifying account of the advancement of the inhabitants .. not only in Christian knowledge, but as a necessary consequence their improvement in the general morals, and the habits of civilized life'. The people were so grateful to the Society that many of them, lacking money, had delivered sheep, feathers and 'woollen materials' as donations to the Society's funds, the value of which had amounted to £2.17s.2d which MacKenzie had paid to the treasurer. 'The sum though small in itself, is like the widows mite of high value, and this first contribution from these remote islanders to the spread of Christian Knowledge, must be received by the Society as the best evidence of the people being awakened to the value and importance of Christian instruction, and as an anxiety on their part to contribute towards its extension.' It was also reported 'that Mr MacKenzie with the assistance of his father in Law had at his own expence built a small room for a library adjoining the Manse, and he had also built a Byre, and some other offices; that the latter of these had not been roofed in, but they were so essential for the comfort of himself and his family that he was to endeavour to get them completed'. This was all greatly different from the days when the failure to provide adequate 'accommodations' had discouraged Lachlan MacLeod and the ill-supported missionaries before him; now the Society was quite ready to cover the cost of these extra buildings, for 'the addition and repairs' were 'for the permanent benefit of the Mission'.[101]

MacKenzie was back in St Kilda in time to meet John MacGillivray, member of the 'Cuvierian Natural History Society' and especially interested in birds. John was most probably the son of William MacGillivray and would therefore have spent most of his childhood in Edinburgh, so that, being distant from his relations in the Hebrides, he shared the vague and romantic notion of St Kilda as 'some remote and barren island, "placed far amid the melancholy main," tenanted by myriads of seafowl, and the abode of a race of men living in a state of primitive simplicity'. Possibly only eighteen years old he was eager to see the island about which he must have heard so much, and on 29 June 1840 he left 'Borneray' [Boreray or Berneray] and crossed over to Pabbay in search of a boat. Having found one of a suitable size and a crew with it he set off about midday. After passing Haisgeir the boat was overtaken by fog and rain, so that, lacking a compass, 'our situation became rather unpleasant'. Further on and still troubled by the fog MacGillivray and his boatmen were feeling rather lost when suddenly they 'fell in with a large yacht belonging to the tacksman of St Kilda, who was on board, and, like us, on his way to that island'. This can only have been Donald MacDonald, going out to extract rents from his subtenants. For a while the wake of the yacht - perhaps the *Rover's Bride* - was followed, but soon the fog obscured everything. MacGillivray's boatmen began to lose hope 'and told dismal stories of boats leaving for St Kilda that had never since been heard of, and of others that had been several nights at sea, or glad to take shelter under a rock for a fortnight, as happened once to Mr McNiel, a former tacksman'.[102]

The wind rose, the fog cleared, and strenuous rowing brought them about midnight into the St Kilda bay where were the tacksman's yacht which had just arrived and 'the Prince of Wales gun-brig'. A boat from the latter took MacGillivray ashore and he spent the rest of the night in one of the 'huts'. He then stayed four days, exploring the island as thoroughly as possible. He made hasty notes on the scenery, the wells 'Tobir na slainnte' and 'Tobir na h'oige', on the damage done by violent gusts of wind, on geology and vegetation, and on the people. Neil MacKenzie, 'the worthy minister of the island', accompanied him on his walks and informed him on the more interesting features and occurrences. As always the houses attracted attention, 'no longer the miserable hovels congregated together in a confused mass' but now 'very neatly built in the ordinary way' and 'in regular order' with one gable end 'touching upon a well-paved footpath'. Because of this change, achieved with ' the praiseworthy exertions of their most excellent minister' and 'encouraged by the proprietor', the people 'are now better lodged, clothed, and fed, than are the great mass of the population throughout the Hebrides'. Even so, the old accusation of 'extreme laziness' was repeated, though 'more than compensated for by their cheerful disposition, religious principles, and great hospitality'. The only flaw seemed to be that 'intercourse with strangers has created many artificial wants and previously unknown luxuries, as well as encouraged an avaricious spirit, shewn by the value they place upon the articles offered for sale to strangers'.

John MacGillivray, impressed by the great cliffs and by the work of the 'birdcatcher', had time to watch the typical kind of demonstration put on for visitors:

'When exhibiting before strangers, which they are easily induced to do, they generally choose for the display of their agility a precipice about 600 feet in height, overhanging the sea, at a short distance from the village. One of them will then suspend himself about mid-way down the cliff, and, striking his feet against the rock, shoot himself out some ten or twelve feet more, rebounding from it several times, and increasing the distance with each rebound; performing this, and many similar feats, with all the agility of a professional performer upon the tight rope.'

A breeze favourable for the return journey suddenly sprang up, and at noon on 4 July MacGillivray with two 'St Kildians' left in a 'small leaky boat' which was for a while towed along by presumably the Pabbay boat until, in fog and rain, they were abandoned and then lost their way. After a stormy night of rowing a landing was made on Shillay where they breakfasted on 'brackish water and raw limpets', and eventually they persuaded their 'frail vessel' across to the safer haven of Pabbay.

The dangers experienced by George and Richard Atkinson and John MacGillivray in their scarcely sufficient craft, and even by the tacksman in his fairly regular crossings, were by no means unusual and they were taken for granted by the people of St Kilda, of Pabbay, and of other islands to whom such hazards were part of life. But while the risks remained for island inhabitants MacGillivray was one of a dwindling band of adventurous voyagers, for big steam yachts and steamer services were beginning to provide the fashionable means of visiting the Hebrides and of calling in at St Kilda. Soon even the church was to visit in its own vessel.

CHAPTER 8

James Wilson calls in with the Fishery Board, a religious revival shakes the island, and Mackenzie unexpectedly leaves

IN the 1830s a different kind of adventure was being faced by the established church. Evangelical ministers, of whom there were many, were disputing the control over what they considered entirely spiritual matters by landlords and civil courts and were approaching the point of separation. Neil MacKenzie in St Kilda, no doubt learning on his visits to Edinburgh and Glasgow of the latest developments, seems to have had sympathy for the evangelical cause, and in any case had been guided by 'the most prominent Church of Scotland evangelical', John MacDonald. Soon churchmen were to be launched on the voyage, full of its own risks and dangers, that followed the Disruption and birth of the Free Church in 1843.[103]

On 3 May 1841 John MacDonald wrote to the SSPCK, stating that 'he has been requested by the Minister of St Kilda to visit that island this summer, and to try to get a Ruling Elder to come along with him as he wished to make two or three Elders, never as yet having had a Session'. MacDonald, who had continued his itinerant preaching after his last mission to St Kilda in 1830, proposed that the SSPCK secretary, John Tawse, should accompany him and that they should go in August, which suggestion the Society directors approved and authorised the secretary also to inspect all the SSPCK schools near Inverness and along the coast of Sutherland. The journey to St Kilda was not made, for as a disappointed MacDonald explained at the end of July 'the Sloop he expected to get to St Kilda could not be got till the end of August or beginning of September which would be too late in the Season'. He therefore thought it best to defer the visit till the summer of 1842. Tawse, however, managed to complete his task around Inverness. The 'Sloop' had been offered by the St Kilda tacksman and may therefore have been the 'yacht' followed by John MacGillivray the previous summer.[104]

With major ecclesiastical issues looming over it the SSPCK turned its attention from John MacDonald and concentrated its interest in St Kilda upon the matter of the repairs supposed to have been carried out on the church and manse. James Crawford had sent a receipt for £20 but the Society secretary refused payment until 'Mr Crawford should specify more particularly the work for which the charge was made', this being necessary as MacKenzie himself when in Edinburgh early in 1840 had been given a sum 'equal to what was now asked' and intended to cover the expense of all the repairs. In return there came a more specific account, 'which amounted to more than the sum asked but Mr. Crawford agreed to restrict the claim to £20 as he had mentioned that sum to Mr Mackenzie'. There also came a letter from MacKenzie himself, rather indistinctly making out that the £20 given him was for building his 'library' and a byre, and for materials, whereas Crawford's charge was for repairing the roof and walls of the church, and for plastering and repairing the roof, walls and two rooms of the manse. Opportunity had been taken of Crawford's presence on the island to get the work done and so avoid the expense of 'getting over other tradesmen'. Rather reluctantly the Society agreed to pay because, from MacKenzie's letter, it appeared that the repairs had indeed been carried out, but it would have preferred to have had the independent confirmation of John MacDonald and John Tawse. Concern over such business detail disguised involvement in 'disruption' issues.[105]

*

Cheering news was received on 4 November 1841 when James Wilson, a member of the SSPCK committee and brother of Professor John Wilson known as 'Christopher North', reported that during the recent summer he had been to St Kilda. He said that 'he had in corresponding with his family, transmitted to them some account of what he had witnessed during his visit to that remote and interesting island, and as any information respecting that distant field of the Society's labours might be gratifying to the Meeting, he would if it were agreeable to them, read such extracts of his correspondence as he thought might be interesting to them'. This idea being most acceptable, Wilson then submitted 'a detailed and animated description' of the island and of 'the manners and customs of the Inhabitants', after which Dr Dickson, familiar as many people were with previous accounts of 'manners and customs', thanked him and moved that Wilson be requested 'to furnish the Society with the Manuscript of the details now read' for printing, like the journals of MacDonald and MacKenzie, in the appendix to the annual sermon.[106]

James Wilson was born in Paisley in 1795 and died in 1856. In early youth he showed an interest in natural history and the collection of specimens. He made a continental tour in 1816, contributed articles to Blackwood's Magazine, and went to live at a house called Woodville in the Morningside district of Edinburgh. He contributed articles also on angling, ornithology, and other subjects to the Encyclopaedia Britannica and spent three summers botanising among the hills of Forfar and Sutherland. In the later 1830s he 'interested himself in territorial churches, and in efforts for improving the dwellings of the poor'. His particular involvement then was with 'the White Herring Fishery Board', for 'he was anxious that all should be done which proprietors or a government can do, to lessen the dangers, and augment the productiveness of this great branch of national industry'. So in the company first of Sir Thomas Dick Lauder and then of the Hon. Bouverie F. Primrose he spent much time at sea 'in order to examine stations, quays, and harbours'. Thus the greater part of the 1841 summer was taken up by a voyage on 'the government cutter the Princess Royal', under Captain Stewart, which lasted from 17 June till 12 September and included the call at St Kilda. His letters describing his tour were revised as a continuous narrative and published late in 1842 under the title *A Voyage round the Coasts of Scotland and the Isles*.[107]

Wilson, and Dick Lauder the Board secretary, saw St Kilda early on 2 August 1841. A fortnight later he wrote to his friend Miss Sym in Glasgow from Stromness:

'Altho, we have had a good deal of bad weather and of contrary winds during our voyage we have also met with our own pieces of good fortune. For example after being detained for several stormy days in and about the Eastern shores of the island of Barra, we had an excellent run from Barra Head to St Kilda, and a couple of very clear quiet days during our examination of that so seldom visited island. Its character I think has been greatly misconceived or erroneously expressed by those who have given us any accounts of its nature and aspect. Instead of being a dark solitary cliff surrounded rock, it forms, with its dependencies, a magnificent mountain range, steep enough assuredly in many places, yet presenting at least two beautiful embayed harbours, in one or other of which a safe landing may be affected in all ordinary weather. The one in which we landed receded gently upwards towards the sloping hills, and with its still waters might have passed for a portion of a Lake in Peebleshire, rather than as the dangerous and almost inaccessible haven of the farthest british Isle. Indeed whether it is a british isle or no I can scarcely say, for little attention is paid to it by any one, and it certainly derives no advantage from its connection with the Kingdom of Great Britain and Ireland, and the Town of Berwick upon Tweed. No intimation had been sent to it regarding the recent Census, of which the Minister (for there is a Minister) had never heard altho' I think that some record of a people living so far "amid the melancholy main" would have been interesting as data for ascertaining the rate of diminution or increase. The increase seems to have been very slight for several years, not but what people are born as well as die there, but the children are very subject to croup in very early life, and many of them die about the ninth day.'

He went on to mention his 'crack (in Gaelic)' with an old lady aged 83, and to remark that there were other elderly people. He sympathised with the minister, Neil MacKenzie, three of whose children were buried in the island graveyard. 'He is a pious, sincere simple minded man, much attached to his people, as they to him, and greatly devoted to all their interests whether spiritual or temporal.' The walk to the 'village' produced information on birds, and the demonstration of fowling differed from that witnessed by MacGillivray only because it was viewed from below:

'The natives gave us an example of their daring skill as cragsmen. One man stands upon the very verge of a cliff 700 feet high, and lets down his companion by a rope. The latter descends most merrily, singing and dancing in the air, and pushing himself out in vast bounds with his feet from the surface of the perpendicular rock. It would have been a fearful and almost unjustifiable sight had we not known that it was their accustomed vocation, and that scarcely an accident had happened in the memory of the present generation. But to us who were in a boat below, and saw the small black specks above us, dangling over the black abyss, like spiders suspended by their webs, and knew that they were doing this merely for our amusement, the spectacle, at least on its commencement, was somewhat alarming. However after each man had swung about over many a horrid chasm and had caught and thrawn the neck of a few unoffending sea-fowl, he was drawn up hand over hand, as the sailors say, by his companion and landed as lightly as a Lark on the summit of the cliff from which he had thrown himself.'[108]

Before leaving the island Wilson 'collected from the minister many curious particulars regarding the people, their history and habits', but Miss Sym was, it now seems unfortunately, spared the details.

On 18 December 1841 Wilson sent to the Society secretary a letter containing a 'general sketch' of his observations at St Kilda. This 'brief communication' was really an expanded version of his letter to Miss Sym. As promised it was printed with three illustrations done in 1838 as an appendix to the Society's annual sermon, and appeared also as a slim volume under the title *St Kilda* and perhaps intended for private circulation. The additional information it contained related to activities over the two or three days spent on the island, and the sequence of events is typical.[109]

Landing from the cutter's 'row-boat' Wilson was welcomed by 'several of the natives'. The boat was hauled ashore, and soon the minister appeared: 'we descried a person of the better class making his way towards us. He gave us the right hand of fellowship with great cordiality, and we found, as we had supposed, that this was the Rev. Neil Mackenzie ... a pure-minded, simple, sincere, kind-hearted, pious man, as we firmly believe, from the impression which our subsequent intercourse with him produced upon us all'. They all walked 'upwards towards the village', looking at the feather store, the manse and the church on the way. Part of the church near the pulpit appeared to be used as 'a writing school', and it was discovered that 'The good minister is teacher and writing-master .. as well as priest, and seems to leave nothing untried to ameliorate the condition of his flock, whether by enlightening their spiritual darkness, improving their worldly fortunes, or .. raising them in the scale of thinking beings'. MacKenzie's reward for this good work was not so much in money as in the 'confiding and unbounded affection' of the people.

When at 'the so-called village' they looked into the houses, the majority of which contained two rooms; but 'there are smaller single tenements for widow women and old maids'. Fuel was distinctly in short supply, 'and the minister said he always rejoiced when the long and lightsome days arrived, as it was so often dark and cheerless in winter, from the want or scarcity of fire'. As for the spiritual fires within, MacKenzie stated that the people were 'a very moral race', that many were 'under very serious religious impressions, and were becoming more so', and that there were about twenty communicants out of the population of nearly one hundred. Twenty more were being instructed and prepared for 'that sacred ordinance'. Older men were able to pray fluently and always conducted a form of public worship when the minister was away.[110]

After the 'little tour' Sir Thomas Dick Lauder invited MacKenzie to go aboard the cutter and enjoy a cruise round the island group. He accepted gladly, and Mrs MacKenzie was told not to expect him back that night. As she had children to look after she was not invited. On the *Princess Royal* the minister was well entertained. 'He ate heartily of several unaccustomed articles, and with an undisguised and almost youthful relish which it was delightful to look upon. The curry-soup and pancakes were thought surprising, - the porter was swallowed, though deliberately, - the wine and liqueurs were almost entirely avoided.' The reason given for avoiding the drinks was that he had been so long without them he did not want to acquire a taste for them again since they were not available on the island. 'When pressed after dinner to take another glass of wine, he said, "If you please, I would rather just speak a little more," meaning thereby to express his pleasure in conversing about many things which were of course as dead letters to those among whom he had sojourned for nearly twelve long years.' The minister's presence on board was widely appreciated, for 'Though probably not a person of finished education, he is yet well informed and intelligent, and assuredly possesses that without which knowledge is vain, the fear of God'. He amused them as they circled the inhabited island with stories of its people, and after a night at sea sent a note ashore to his wife asking her to get some 'natives' to put on the demonstration of bird-catching. The islanders were supposed to be worried that the intention was to kidnap MacKenzie and take him off to America - in which case they would go too.

The second day was spent around Boreray where 'one of our great guns' was fired close beside Stac Lee in order to scare the gannets into the air. In the evening the cutter returned to 'Dickson's Bay' where MacKenzie was landed. As he left for the northern isles Wilson reflected on the minister's isolated life, closing his letter to Tawse with religious sentiments greatly at odds with reality. The minister may well have been glad of the myriad 'fowls of the air' around him, but he could hardly dismiss thoughts of what to eat, drink and wear in such a place.

In Wilson's *Voyage* the description of St Kilda formed the first two chapters of the second volume and contained some new information, more elaborate commentary, and a survey of former writers about the island. There were different illustrations, one of them a map attributed to Sir George MacKenzie of Coul who had been to St Kilda 'early in the present century'; but basically the wording and content were those of the letter to Tawse. In this work, however, Wilson wrote of such features as the graveyard wall, recently built at Neil MacKenzie's instigation, 'the debris rather than the ruins of the ancient chapel of St. Mary' within the enclosure, the corn-drying kiln, the island produce, rents and prices, and the tacksman arrangement. And he told the story of how the minister, about eighteen months previously, had gone on board a mysterious ship that had been dodging about for ten days, and of how he and his companion islanders had been entertained by the armed crew to 'sundry foreign wines'.[111]

Wilson's view of the St Kilda tacksman amounted to a general criticism of a system under which he felt the proprietor and the subtenants were both losers. 'It seems to be thought that the proprietor obtains a very small rent from the tacksman, but that the latter gains a large proportional profit from the people.' Possibly the lease of the island was 'but a small matter' to 'so enterprising and extensive a dealer as Mr MacDonald of Loch Inver', and Wilson reckoned that 'it would certainly be better for these poor people to have no tacksman, but to make the minister the factor, ..and accountable'. Part of this idea had already occurred to the proprietor, since on 10 December 1841 it was stated that MacDonald was to give up possession of the island at Whitsunday 1842. Correspondence between proprietor and tacksman raised questions which it required expert legal opinion to settle. The main issue seemed to be the tacksman's wish to collect rent arrears. There was no difficulty in deciding that 'if the sub-rents demanded from the inhabitants of St Kilda be clearly fixed by usage' the tacksman had a legal right to them, and it appeared that there was no proper evidence to show that any arrears had been abandoned, even though MacDonald had not hitherto demanded them. However, from the delay in asserting his claim it seemed that the tacksman had lost his right to treat as security the goods of those in debt to him. If he had not he would have been able to sell the stock and other possessions of the islanders for payment of the rents. If any settlement in his favour was to be made MacDonald would have to produce 'a proper state specifying the names of the subtenants and the sums alleged to be due by each' before he could reasonably pursue an action in the sheriff court. The legal expert, Thomas MacKenzie, of India Street in Edinburgh, concluded that 'if Mr McLeod is desirous to protect the poor people of St Kilda from the oppressive legal proceedings threatened by McDonald' the sensible thing to do was to pay the arrears claimed and at the same time give MacDonald due warning that his lease, not a written one, was at an end. This solution seems to have been adopted, and in 1842 the landlord, not adhering

Norman MacRaild, St Kilda agent or factor for John Macpherson Macleod 1842-1871

quite to the suggestion Wilson was about to publish, appointed an agent of the name of MacRaild to deal with St Kilda from Whitsunday onwards.[112]

*

Like the Roman Catholic priests evangelical preachers were fond of tracing their doctrinal ancestry back to the era of Columba and the roving monks from Iona and Ireland. Extreme condemnations of the Catholics, however, left no room for a recognition that the two persuasions had anything in common, and books celebrating the virtues of evangelicalism went in for exaggerated statements which distorted the nature of tradition and frustrated any genuine attempts to approach the truth. According to one author the mediaeval church was corrupt, 'sinking into the state of moral and spiritual degeneration of which the Highlands and Islands contain so many crumbling and warning monuments'. In the northern and western isles of the seventeenth century the mediaeval church having collapsed had left nothing 'except a mixture of nature-worship, Norse religious customs, and wild orgies connected in some cases with the name of Maolrubha, the great Celtic missionary, who by that time had become a mythological person'. In St Kilda the 'impostor', Roderick, 'became an incarnation of evil'. Hostility towards the Catholic communities in the islands persisted, and

358

even in 1840 the SSPCK felt that the so-called 'Small Isles' south of Skye, especially perhaps Eigg and Canna, were in need of help; 'the circumstance of the Inhabitants .. being under the influence of the Roman Catholic Priests, and being in all the ignorance and darkness and superstition of the Roman Catholic Religion' made the necessity extremely pressing. Rev. John Kennedy, described by another minister only a few years later as 'impulsive and credulous to a high degree' yet an authoritative and much admired figure among evangelicals, used similar language in his biography of John MacDonald when condemning not Catholics but Protestant, 'moderate' ministers: 'If a few of them were contiguous in a district preserved from the intrusion of enthusiasts, fearing no Church censures, and feeling no restraint from the public opinion which their own influence had chiefly formed, they lived as do those who care not though all should see the brand of evil on their brow.' Examples of those so branded were given; one was a great cattle-dealer at a market, another the leading dancer at a wedding, a third the toast-master at the farmers' dinner - 'and if the last to slide off his chair at the drinking bout, it was because he was more "seasoned" than the rest'. Such a 'moderate', with his worldly interests, preached from a borrowed sermon and sent his listeners to sleep; 'in gluttony and ungodly jesting he and they together would spend the Sabbath evening'.[113]

Against Catholics and 'moderates' the evangelical preachers felt they had a special mission, in which no half measures seemed to exist. 'There were outlying districts,' Kennedy wrote, 'on the mainland and in the Western Isles, never before visited by evangelical preachers, and where people remained in a state of heathenism … There were cries to heaven from many spots in the midst of the desert for the visits of an evangelist.' John MacDonald was one of those who answered the call, but there were others, only a little less prominent, who also sought to bring about 'awakenings' and self-awareness. Almost universally evangelical preaching was the means of awakening people to an awareness of their sinfulness, and the most common symptom of this knowledge was the emotional response to the realisation. John MacDonald, having preached at Rothiemurchus in September 1835, recorded in his journal: 'Duke of Bedford, the Marchioness of Abercorn etc., in church. Felt liberty notwithstanding the presence of such personages, because I felt as in the presence of God, and felt that these were but fellow-worms.'[114]

Whether the Duke or Marchioness felt they were worms is not known, but the 'poor people' of island communities, struggling to survive in wretched conditions, probably had no difficulty in doing so. The emotional response to which they were worked by stirring language was almost inevitable. When sustained to the point of achieving not only a continued consciousness of sin but also a devotion to reading the bible, an eagerness to attend services and meetings, and a rejection of other occupations apart from labouring for a living, the 'awakening' became a 'visible reality'.

In the early decades of the nineteenth century revivals were abundant.

What John MacDonald described as the 'purest' instance took place in Uig, Lewis, after Rev. Alexander MacLeod came to the parish. Huge crowds gathered. 'From neighbouring districts people came to Uig to hear and see, and returned home wounded and broken in spirit. In 1828 the whole island seemed to be moved with one great and powerful emotion.' An eyewitness told how 'at all hours, from eight o'clock at night till one in the morning, he had passed by and overheard persons engaged in prayer. Along the ridges of the moor, by stooping so as to catch the figures between the eye and the clear margin of the horizon, dim forms might be discerned, either alone or two or three together, kneeling and pouring out their wants at the footstool of mercy.' Elsewhere similarly remarkable scenes were recorded. After John MacDonald had preached at Invermoriston, 'The place was like a battlefield strewn with the dead and dying'; at Tobermory 'Again and again the entire congregation was swept by a tide of spiritual emotion which left no one untouched'; and 'A shower of blessing fell on Oban in the autumn of 1841'. Such 'showers' could come as if from nowhere. 'At Lismore, on 12th of January 1843, a great work of grace began. The agent used was a young man who could scarcely speak a word of English. He began to hold meetings for prayer, and to exhort the people about the state of their souls. Two of the most ungodly characters in the island were thus awakened.' Revivals, above all, resulted often in conversion, as in the case of John Morrison, Ian Gobha, of Harris.[115]

For all their isolation neither the St Kilda people nor their minister could remain unaware of these spectacular events. Both will have heard of and perhaps met John Morrison and other enthusiasts in Harris and its lesser islands. As was evident, revivals were catching, one leading to another. Ministers influenced each other; a convert at Moulin near Pitlochry where Alexander Stewart led a revival was John Shaw, subsequently at Bracadale and the friend of John MacDonald. Neil MacKenzie must surely have heard a great deal of good evangelical news during his visits to the mainland, and he may have been excited by the thought of being involved in a campaign to bring spiritual truth to a land of darkness:

> 'The awakenings that took place throughout the north, almost simultaneously, in districts far removed from one another, during the first two decades of the century, did more for the moral and intellectual development of the people than it is possible now to compute. With the exception of the districts of Moray, Easter Ross, and Sutherland, the land was held in the deadening grip of the black frost of moderatism. With two or three conspicuous exceptions every pulpit, from Mull of Kintyre to Cape Wrath along the western shores, and every pulpit in the islands, without exception, was without the light of the living gospel of the grace of God at the close of the 18th century.'[116]

This was a verdict long afterwards, but it presented, from a certain point of view and in the sweeping, familiar phrases, the situation which evangelicals sought to change and the success which they claimed to have achieved.

*

On 6 July 1843 committee members of the SSPCK were interested in an extraordinary letter from Neil MacKenzie, dated at St Kilda on 24 May 1843. It contained 'a detailed account of a remarkable revival among the inhabitants of that remote and sequestered Island'. The secretary judged it appropriate to place a summarised version and commentary in the minutes:

'The particulars of the case are all very interesting, but in general it may be stated that Mr Mackenzie observing with regret some symptoms of religious declension appearing among his people, changed his mode of preaching, dwelt on the difference between real and counterfeit religion, the nature and evidence of true godliness, and the necessity of divine influences and after a faithful exhibition of divine truth, and a close application thereof to the heart and conscience, most powerful impressions were produced, the minds of his hearers melted into unusual tenderness, the tears gushing like a fountain. The administration of the Sacrament being announced for the second Sabbath of October last, to prepare the minds of his people for that solemn service, he preached from Luke 22.44, dwelling at considerable length on the sufferings of Christ, their multiplicity, intensity, and the ends they answered in the economy of salvation - the consequence was, that the same melting began to manifest itself the feelings of not a few being much excited, both strong men and feeble females sobbing aloud, their hearts like to break, the excitement being so great that he could not be heard. Spiritual things seem to absorb their whole soul, their very language is altered, an awful solemnity pervading all their intercourse. And on the communion Sabbath 8th October, the commotion increased to that degree that the whole congregation became so agitated that they could not contain themselves, some cried with vehement energy, some fainted, others sobbed, and the children participated in the distress of their parents. Mr Mackenzie could not go on with his discourse, the precentor could not sing, so that he had to do it himself. When he went through the service of the first table, such a sense of unworthiness was experienced by the Members that they could scarcely be induced to approach the table, the communicants all in tears, and some scarcely refraining from weeping aloud. The effect of this revival is powerfully exhibited in their character and conduct, great desire of solitude and retirement for the purposes of devotion, to steal away at night to get a retired spot to pray, is deemed a luxury, scarcely a wall, old building, a large Stone, that is not made a place of prayer - great delight is also

361

experienced in the means of grace, in short their own language is, "We are as if in a new world." [117]

Far away on the mainland there were thought to be two opinions on such responses to evangelical preaching. Some claimed that 'revival' was divine power manifest; others held that it was 'something like mesmerism' or 'mere excitement occasioned by the violent preaching of terrorising doctrines on the one hand, and the ignorance and credulity of a certain class of people on the other'. Mesmerised or not the community in St Kilda, already with a reputation for credulity, was clearly of a sudden transformed; and the SSPCK, pleased with the contents of the letter, 'trust that Mr Mackenzie will have the satisfaction of seeing the spiritual nature of these impressions proved and exhibited in their sanctified fruits and effects in the subsequent life and conversation of that interesting people.'[118]

All this happened at the very time when the church in Scotland was itself transformed by the Disruption and formation of the Free Church only a few weeks before MacKenzie's letter was read. Tactfully therefore the Society secretary sent one copy of the letter for insertion in the Missionary Record of the Free Church and another to be entered in the Missionary Record of the established Church of Scotland. He may have thought, in the confusion and uncertainties of the time, that the St Kilda minister, freshly invigorated by his own 'revival', would be likely to join the Free Church, and that therefore the future support of the island mission was in doubt. MacKenzie's letter had almost suggested as much, written as it was only six days after roughly 470 ministers had left the Church of Scotland.[119]

In fact the letter had been re-written following a 'casualty' at St Kilda.'The vessel by which this is sent, ' MacKenzie explained, 'came here more than a week ago. Expecting her to sail next day, or the day following, I put all my letters on board. A gale of wind came on, and the vessel filled so far with water, as to wash the portmanteau out of a bed into which it had been thrown, and so they got wet and soiled.'The letter was really a continuation of notes sent the previous year in which he had begun 'a description of the physical character and state of the natives of this place'. Now he went on with that description, remarking on their small stature, similarity of feature, strength, and inclination when walking 'to follow one another like sheep'. The women in particular 'very soon get an old appearance', and in general 'they seem to be slow in coming to maturity'. Although he had assisted in getting the houses re-sited and built on a different plan, he wrote, only five years later, that 'Their houses, food, and clothing, are of the worst kind'.[120]

MacKenzie then moved to their 'Spiritual state' and quoted from 'a journal kept from time to time' in order to describe the process of the revival. His language seemed to have been borrowed from John MacDonald: 'Many a troubled meeting we had during this season. To describe some of these, (though not so extravagent as might be expected from so powerful an awakening) is impossible. The general cast of them was weeping aloud, - crying for mercy with such pathos and energy as beggars description - women frequently fainting, - some rolling themselves on the floor of the church; a few crying in the language of praise.' But however enthusiastically satisfied at the effects, MacKenzie was also able to take an objective view of them:

> 'The symptoms that exhibit themselves to a spectator are generally as follow. First, the person affected seems to be labouring under an uncommon oppressive weight, the whole frame greatly excited. During this time the individual so affected seems to be powerfully restraining himself from crying; at last he bursts out with a violent outcry, which continues for a longer or shorter time, according to the effect of the discourse upon him. When it begins to subside, it is followed by great trembling, and if attempting to speak, chattering of the teeth, accompanied with great weakness and absorption of mind. I inquired of a very intelligent man how he felt inwardly. He said, when the truth drew powerfully his attention, that on a sudden his whole frame became as if about to give way, feeling a cold trembling all over his body, being eased a little by crying out; that this continued for a time, and gradually passed away. After it, he felt as if all his joints had been powerless, accompanied with trembling. He remarked, that when thus affected it was highly painful. The portions of divine truth which affect them most are those which relate to the sufferings of Christ, the evil of sin, the coming of the Son of God to judgment, and the pains of the place of misery; but particularly the feelings of the saints under darkness, desertion, or conviction of sin.'[121]

Perhaps before the 'revival' and certainly after it began the minister held meetings every day in the week except Saturday and Monday. On the Sabbath the meeting started at 6 o'clock in the morning and continued all day, 'except two intervals for breakfast and dinner'. No programme of later years was quite as intense as this. A whole way of life was changing. 'All the peculiar vices of the place have disappeared - I hope not for a time, but for ever, at least I wish it to be so .. If these effects continue, and the fruits be like the blossoms, a truly great reformation will take place in this remote and formerly dark corner.' This was MacKenzie's verdict on what was happening, and he wrote like a different man, one caught up in a 'disruption' of his own. Even the SSPCK seemed to be carried away beyond reason by his excitement, earnestly wishing that 'this great work of awakening and revival in the souls of the inhabitants' might be carried on faithfully in this 'interesting spot where, it may be said that, many centuries ago, the light of the Christian religion first dawned upon Scotland , as it was here St Columba landed before he proceeded to Iona ..'

One of the 'vices' that had supposedly disappeared was the talent of St Kilda people, especially women, for music, song and dancing. Since Martin Martin writers about St Kilda had commented on this aspect of the community while at the same time dismissing the islanders as ignorant and lacking a cultural tradition. MacAulay had much to say on the subject:

'The power of music is felt every where... The St.Kildians are enthusiastically fond of it, whether in the vocal or instrumental way: The very lowest tinklings of the latter, throws them into extasy of joy. I have seen them dancing to a bad violin much to my satisfaction: Even the old women in the isle act their part in the great assemblies, and the most agile dancers are here, as well as every where else, very great favourites.'

Singing could be heard at home, among women cutting barley in the fields, and men at the oars generally sang while rowing. Composition of songs was common, the subjects including 'the beauty and accomplishments of their favourites among the fair sex, the heroic actions of their friends, their dexterity in climbing rocks, their superior skill in fishing, their extraordinary vigour, skill and constancy while at the oar, besides the common topics of personal advantages and intellectual merit'. During the 1820s, however, when the islanders were trying to make sense of the sermons of John MacDonald, liveliness began to decline. MacDonald's 1827 journal was rather dry on the subject: 'In regard to music and dancing in St Kilda, I may here observe, that though the people are naturally fond of these exercises, yet as they are not connected with those habits of dissipation and debauchery, which, alas, prevail too much in other places, and which oblige ministers of the Gospel, for that very reason, to lift up their voices against them, they are with them but comparatively harmless amusements.' While, however, MacDonald may have been able to tolerate such 'amusements' Neil MacKenzie, as so often, allowed his religious enthusiasm to contradict his wider interests. Whether it was his influence or a conclusion reached by certain islanders is not certain, but the fundamental tradition embracing music, song, composition, and tales celebrating, among other things, the prowess of ancestors, was set aside - though not perhaps abandoned altogether - and replaced by the new religious domination which some have seen as exactly usurping the place of an ancient culture. James Wilson in 1841 noticed the change:

'The singing of psalms and hymns is even a favourite spiritual recreation of the people, and is resorted to frequently and voluntarily in their own houses, independent of the more formal meetings which may be occasionally called for the express purpose. These spiritual songs may even be said to be of ordinary use almost as the *popular poetry* of the day, and have in a great measure superseded all ordinary vocal music of a worldly character. The Irish melodies are unknown. Dancing is also now regarded by them as a frivolous amusement, and has ceased to be practised even during their more joyous festivals, such as marriage or baptism.'

Yet an undercurrent of the old 'worldly' habit persisted among the people of St Kilda, who, like those of other Hebridean islands, allowed meetings, services, psalms and sermons to occupy much of their waking time. MacKenzie was aware of this, and, some might say hypocritically, had a real interest in trying to preserve the very things which his evangelical activities had helped to drive away. 'Before I left the island,' he wrote much later, 'I got some of them to write out for me much of their poetry and traditions, but, unfortunately, almost all these, and several other collections which I had made of things which had interested me, were lost on the way from St. Kilda to Duror, and could never be recovered.' Twenty songs collected by MacKenzie were nevertheless sent by his son for publication in *The Celtic Review* of April 1906, twenty-seven years after the collector's death.[122]

The extent to which the church, of whatever Protestant kind, was able or wished to suppress song and story in the Highlands and islands may have been exaggerated, and if there was a real loss in St Kilda then Neil MacKenzie, in spite of the pleasure he derived from his evangelical success, may have been partly responsible and equally have regretted it. It has often been claimed that strict, even severe religious discipline demanded the destruction of musical instruments and those accompaniments which were once a source of entertainment, enjoyment and creative opportunity. Alexander Carmichael's account of what he was told in the Ness district of Lewis about weddings, fiddle-playing and dancing may have a large element of truth in it, but there are not all that many precise records to confirm that the church was always hostile. One instance of disapproval at a comparatively early date from Lewis was the condemnation of an event at Shawbost which combined music with 'dissipation and debauchery', the undesirable association of which John MacDonald disapproved:

'The Presbytery being inform'd that a house of several Couples has been built in north Shabost for fiddling, Dancing and other Sports suitable to the dispositions of those who frequent it, and that a vast number of people of both Sexes, and a Fiddler resort to the same, on the Saturday nights, where there are musick, dancing, drinking of Spirituous Liquors, Loose carriage, cursing, and Swearing practised, and where these persons continue so long, that the Presbytery have reason to be persuaded they encroach on the Sabbath. The Presbytery taking the above affair under consideration, with this aggravating Circumstance, that Mr Murdoch Morison by the advice of the Presbytery, having dealt with the bulk of those, who are principally concerned in the Said house to pull down the same, which they unanimously promised to do without loss of time. Notwithstanding said promises, the said house hath been lately repaired and continues to be used as formerly. Therefore the Presbytery did and hereby do appoint the Kirk Session of the Parish of Barves to prosecute the Fiddler, and the other persons concerned irregularily in the diversions of the said house, and appoint Donald MacKy [MacLey?] officer of the Kirk Session of Barvas to Cite the foresaid Persons before the said Kirk Session ..'[123]

This was long before evangelical fervour spread both to Lewis and St Kilda, bringing with it that realisation of sinfulness and desperate need for salvation which in turn led the people to reject what were considered mere frivolous distractions and, it might be said, partly to disinherit themselves. With converts, communion, and devotion to scripture appeared those who, in John Kennedy's words, 'were favoured with more intimate communion with the Lord than the others'. In St Kilda the custom of taking action and decisions in unison did not mean that the community had been without individuals in special positions; for years, perhaps centuries, there had been the steward's deputy, the ground officer, and when in 1830 John MacDonald and Neil MacKenzie marked out the glebe ground they did so in the company of 'two men who are called constables in St Kilda (and have some powers in that way vested in them by the tacksman,)'. The constables may have temporarily replaced the ground officer, and one of them could have been John Ferguson, member of that intelligent and enterprising family on the island and interpreter for George Atkinson in 1831. And now, Neil MacKenzie, in seeking to establish a kirk session and to select communicants, opened the way for a religious organisation that placed certain, especially devoted men of the community above the rest and, should they also be the constables, made them in both a spiritual and temporal sense powerful leaders and directors.[124]

*

The SSPCK's missionary minister in St Kilda left the island again at the beginning of summer 1844 and in the first few days of June paid a visit to the secretary. 'It is four years since he was absent from the Island before, and he found it necessary to come here at present on account of his health.' The reasons he gave for his being unwell were almost welcome: 'The excessive fatigue which he had undergone for these last 18 months the great excitement and anxiety which the state of the religious feelings of the people had occasioned and the personal and mental exertions which he found it necessary to make, materially affected his health, and he found it necessary to leave the Island for a change of air for a short time.' So MacKenzie, his wife - pregnant again - and two children had made their way to Edinburgh and by 6 June were in Arran where they were to spend the short time 'in the hopes that his native air will restore his health, which is even [now] considerably improved'. The secretary suggested that some allowance should be given to cover travelling expenses and that MacKenzie 'before he return to St Kilda should be furnished with such materials as may be necessary to keep the house [i.e. church] and manse in repair, as these could not be got on the Island'. This the directors accepted, authorised a payment of £10 for the expenses, and allowed 'such additional furnishings for the repair of the Manse and Church as may be thought necessary as well as Books for the School and people of the Island'. The secretary received 'a very favourable verbal account of the state of religion among the Inhabitants' in advance of the journal for the past year which MacKenzie was proposing to submit shortly. In the meantime a summary of the progress he reported was considered useful:

> 'It will be recollected, the very interesting account which he transmitted last year of the religious awakening and revival which had occurred in that Island. He left home so unexpectedly that he had not time to prepare his farther notes, but this he is to do during the few weeks he resides at Arran, and transmit them to the Society. In the mean time from the personal communication which the Secretary had with him, it is very gratifying to know that there is no falling off in the religious feeling of the people; there is an abatement in the violence of the manner by which it was marked at its first breaking out, but in other respects there has been none, on the contrary there has been a steady advance - so much so that the feelings - the morals - the habits and the manners of the people seem to have undergone a most complete and a happy change. Their sole delight is now in religious exercises and in secret communion with their God - they are more industrious in their habits, more quiet and orderly in their manner, and more kindly and affectionate towards each other.'

A few examples illustrating the change were given:

> 'There is not a family in the whole Island where family worship is not regularly kept up morning and evening. Many will be seen seeking solitary retirement in the fields at prayer. When a party go to the neighbouring Islands for fishing or bird catching, they have their regular worship, And in the Island itself there are many meetings during the week for prayer and praise, and there is a quietness of manner, a sobriety and seriousness of demeanour even in common conversation that strongly marks the change that has been wrought.'

Thought to be the most striking feature of the altered state of the islanders was 'their confessing openly their former sins'. Any injury or deception of their neighbours, even up to forty years before, was now immediately acknowledged, and they 'do not rest till they have made restitution, although the offence itself was not known or even suspected by the person against whom it was committed'. An enthusiasm for the administration of the sacrament was also evident. This had happened twice over the past year at their 'particular desire', the people themselves providing 'the elements' so that the minister was spared that expense. The islanders also contributed 'such small sums as they could afford' as a sort of sustentation fund, so that when MacKenzie came away he again brought money, this time totalling £6.15s.6d and not the result of selling island produce, as 'a grateful offering from the people to the Society for the blessings they have been the means of conveying to them'.

As might be expected all this was 'very gratifying' once more to the SSPCK directors. They were interested in the fact that though it was more than a hundred years since the St Kilda mission had been established 'yet during all that time there seemed to be little awakening among the people, and little vital religion in the Island'; but it appeared that 'the good seed sown had not been lost' and that 'at a time least expected and without any apparent outward cause, it sprung forth, and is now producing goodly fruit'. The conclusion was that 'Surely this is the doing of the Lord, and it is wondrous in our eyes'. For his part Neil MacKenzie was gratified as well, saying that although the past eighteen months had been 'by far the most laborious' they had also been 'by far the most happy period of his life - and while he frequently in former years felt disheartened and discouraged, his heart is now filled with joy'.[125]

The year of MacKenzie's final departure from St Kilda, like that of his arrival there, has often been given inaccurately. The occasion of it too perhaps deserves reflection. It is curious that he took his family with him when it would seem from what the Society's secretary reported that he had every intention of returning. But this might not have been his intention. He left in a hurry, possibly because someone on the boat that took him away, the new factor perhaps, had brought important news relating to parishes vacant after the Disruption. While still in Arran, or in Glasgow, during the summer of 1844 he received and accepted a presentation by the Crown on 5 July to 'the Government Church' of Duror in the presbytery of Lorn, and by the beginning of September all the preliminary steps had been taken with a view to his induction. The SSPCK secretary wondered why he had not had official notice of the event before then, and consequently of MacKenzie's resignation from the St Kilda mission, but nothing of this had reached the Society by the next general meeting on 7 November when the vacancy in that place was discussed. It was disappointing to learn that MacKenzie, 'who has so long been Missionary there, and laboured with much success among the people', had left so abruptly and 'particularly at a time when from all the recent accounts there had been a great religious awakening'.[126]

The advice of the secretary was that there was no need for an immediate replacement since 'at this season of the year there is no communication with that remote island, as it is only in the summer months that this can be done'. Some relief was felt, because 'There is no situation more difficult from its peculiarities to fill up than this one', and it was left to the directors to work out 'how in the present circumstances of the Society the spiritual wants of the people .. were to be provided for'. Apologetic letters from MacKenzie, dated 15 and 25 November, eventually arrived with news of his appointment to Duror. In them 'Mr MacKenzie also states the provision he had made for the people of St Kilda this winter, and had desired a fire to be kept in the Manse once a week, and both it and the Church regularly aired'. Most of the Society's furniture was 'still in good repair', but there was always a risk of damage by damp, especially to the books. Neil MacKenzie seems therefore to have made provision not for his own return but for a successor; the SSPCK was left with the problem of finding one; and the people of St Kilda, recently awakened, were left once again to worship as they might see fit.[127]

1 PU CH2/361/2 pp.18-19
2 Ansdell p.103
3 ESSGS (1811) pp.5-6. None could read Gaelic.
4 ESSGS (1811) p.7, (1812) p.35
5 ESSGS (1821) pp.48-51, (1824) p.37
6 MacCulloch (1824) Vol. III pp.178, 184-185
7 ESSGS (1822) pp.36-37. The visit may in fact have been made in 1818, if the report in the *Inverness Courier* (quoting from the *Caledonian Mercury*) of 30 July 1818 refers to the same event:

'A Gentleman who recently visited St Kilda, carried with him 12 Gaelic Bibles, to distribute among the poor inhabitants of that place. It will speak volumes to those who are so fond of illuminating the heathen abroad, that out of the 12 Bibles he brought back 11, as he found only one individual, among a community of 110 souls, who could read. We pledge ourselves for the truth of this statement.'

8 PU CH2/361/2 pp.21-30; ESSGS (1822) pp.36-37
9 SSPCK GD95/2/14 pp.548-549; PU CH2/361/2 p.18
10 SSPCK GD95/11/4 p.63 MacDonald Journal 1830; GD95/1/7 pp.211-212
11 SSPCK GD95/2/14 pp.556, 568-569
12 SSPCK GD95/11/12 J MacDonald: Report and Journal of Two Visits to The Island of St. Kilda in the years 1822 and 1824 Edinburgh 1825 p.24 (Report 1822): 'All the cultivated lands lie around the village in scattered and irregular patches; of which each family in the island, about twenty in number, has nearly an equal quantity, - what they call a *farthing-land*, or something about two acres' (see Part 1 n.45). For Journal and Report 1822 see also GD95/11/4 & GD95/11/11. It is persuasively argued that St Kilda's special appeal could well have derived from its status as a port of call for those in fashionable pursuit of the 'sublime' in Scottish scenery, which interest Rev. MacDonald of Urquhart seems to have shared (F MacDonald: St Kilda and the Sublime forthcoming article).
13 Kennedy (1932) pp.71-72, 232; Kennedy (1867) pp.2, 4, 11, 53
14 Kennedy (1867) pp.13, 26; Kennedy (1932) pp.58, 65-66, 342
15 Kennedy (1932) p.342; Kennedy (1867) p.187. In an essay which misleadingly narrows the gap of time between widespread Catholicism and episcopal religion in the Highlands on the one hand and the fervent evangelicalism of the 'Men' there on the other (see Part V p.464 n.70) it has been suggested that the transition for those holding traditional beliefs to their acceptance of evangelical preaching was not as difficult as might be imagined. The 'Men' were given to 'second-sight, visions, prophecy, and a curious propensity to fore-see deaths', all of which were, broadly, recognisable features of a pre-presbyterian era, and so the people found themselves 'going from one mystical supernaturalist and miracle-filled religion to another' [S Bruce: 'Social change and collective behaviour: the revival in eighteenth-century Ross-shire' in The British Journal of Sociology Vol. XXXIV no.4 p.567].
16 Kennedy (1932) pp.18-19; J F Campbell (edit): Leabhar na Feinne Vol. I Gaelic Texts London 1872 pp.xxix-xxx; Kennedy (1932) pp.29-30; Maidment Vol. II p.207
17 Kennedy (1932) pp.31, 36; Maidment Vol. II p.208
18 SSPCK GD95/2/14 pp.576-577
19 This account of Rev. John MacDonald's first visit to St Kilda is drawn from the Journal pp.3-22 [SSPCK GD95/11/4]. Only references to other sources follow. G Henderson (edit.): Dain Iain Ghobha: The Poems of John Morison Second edition 2 vols. Glasgow & Edinburgh 1896 Vol. I p.xxxiv
20 Kennedy (1932) pp.294-296 (Appendix) for list
21 SSPCK GD95/2/14 p.577; GD95/1/7 pp.211-212
22 SSPCK GD95/2/14 pp.576-577. Unless otherwise stated this section is based on MacDonald's 1822 Report [GD95/11/4]. The list of ministers provided is not entirely accurate: Buchan; Roderick McKinnon; Alexander McLeod; Donald McLeod; Alexander McLeod; Angus McLeod 'said to have been settled about 1774', and to have died in 1788; Lachlan McLeod, 'late missionary, and son of Mr Alexander' [Report p.28].
23
24 SSPCK GD95/2/15 p.20; GD95/1/7 p.201 for an account of the mortification; GD95/2/14 p.456 (Letter from R Simpson 13 April 1822); GD95/2/14 p.555; GD95/2/15 p.49
25 SSPCK GD95/1/8 pp.27-28 Reference to William Thomson's Anniversary Sermon, and to copies of MacDonald's 1822 journal being 'thrown off separately' and widely circulated. The journal and report were originally intended to be published along with Thomson's sermon and on 2 January 1823 it was noted that they were 'in the hands of the Sub committee' preparing for publication [GD95/1/7 pp.211-212, GD95/1/8 p.2]. GD95/13/108 pp.36-46 Gordon's Anniversary Sermon; GD95/11/4

26 SSPCK GD95/2/15 p.51; GD95/6/4 Vol. 4 p.4 incl. list of donors and amounts donated.
27 SSPCK GD95/2/15 p.55; GD95/1/8 pp.27-28
28 SSPCK GD95/2/15 pp.69-70
29 SSPCK GD95/2/15 pp.90, 101, 114, 118; GD95/1/8 pp.27-28
30 SSPCK GD95/2/15 pp.63, 74, 129, 141-142, 153-154; GD95/1/8 p.50 'The Committee upon the Chapel of St Kilda' reported a sum in hand of £300-£400.
31 See n.12 above.
32 R Ralph (edit.): William MacGillivray:A Hebridean Naturalist's Journal 1817-1818 Stornoway 1996 p.121; NC (Evidence) Vol.II pp.1172-1173; CWC no.116. Alexander Bethune's belief that St Kilda was part of his parish of Harris is not consistent with the continued records of its attachment to South Uist [e.g. SSPCK GD95/6/4 pp.21-22].
33 SSPCK GD95/2/15 p.162; GD95/1/8 pp.58-59; GD95/2/15 p.172; GD95/11/4 Report 1824 Appendix pp.48-49
34 SSPCK GD95/2/15 pp.160, 183, 212, 217
35 ESSGS (1825) pp.30-31. 'the Guide' was The Guide to Reading. In his 1824 journal (pp.16-17, 27 May) MacDonald described the thatching method: 'During the day, the people were busied in thatching their houses. For the winter half year their huts have generally two coats of thatch; but about this season of the year they remove the lower, by this time sufficiently smoked and sooty, for the benefit of their fields, and lay the other in its place. In October, again, they lay a new cover of thatch over the old; and, in May thereafter, remove the old as formerly; thus repeating the operation every year.'
36 ESSGS (1823) pp.40-41
37 SSPCK GD95/2/15 p.263, 319-322. Being taught English after Gaelic was to be treated as if it were a reward.
38 Stevenson Papers NLS Acc 10706/102
39 SSPCK GD95/2/15 pp.335-338; GD95/1/8 pp.176-178; GD95/6/5 p.4
40 ESSGS (1827) pp.29-30
41 ESSGS (1827) pp.30-31; MacDonald's journal (1825) pp.11-12 [See n.12]
42 SSPCK GD95/2/15 pp.379, 417, 425, 431, 462-463
43 SSPCK GD95/2/15 p.431 and MacDonald's journal (1827) [GD95/11/4 p.129]. Lachlan MacKinnon was also, at one time, an important figure in Lewis where, together with 'Captain Reid and Mr Downie of Lochalsh', all being 'men of good sense, spirit, and perseverance', he had taken steps to introduce sheep-farming on a large scale by stocking an extensive area [Park] with blackfaced sheep, and had 'begun to rear better cattle in Lewis than was ever done before' [J MacDonald: General View of the Agriculture of the Hebrides or Western Isles of Scotland etc. Edinburgh 1811 pp.467, 813. The 'subtacksman' was also called 'the subfactor'. The 'Government Cutter' and the 'Revenue Cutter' were one and the same.
44 SSPCK GD95/2/15 pp.462-463; GD95/2/16 p.6; MacDonald's journal (1827) [GD95/11/4 pp.129-130]
45 ESSGS (1828) p.44. The Inverness Society was also mentioned in 1824 (see p.291 above).
46 SSPCK GD95/6/5 Vol.5 (1826-1840) p.31
47 SSPCK GD95/1/8 pp.234-237
48 SSPCK GD95/2/16 pp.6-9 Locks and hinges were furnished by Mr Edmonstone for £8.18s.10d. Skethway was supposed to keep a journal 'of all your proceedings' in connection with the works.
49 SSPCK GD95/2/16 pp.12-13 Part of MacDonald's 1827 journal was sent in on 30 January 1828.
50 SSPCK GD95/2/16 pp.53-54
51 SSPCK GD95/2/16 pp.151, 100, 210, 219
52 SSPCK GD95/1/8 pp.278-279. After deduction of duty the legacy amounted to £54.10s.
53 SSPCK GD95/1/8 pp.278-279
54 SSPCK GD95/2/16 pp.248, 270, 287, 335; GD95/11/4 1829 p.35 (Appendix to Report)
55 SSPCK GD95/2/16 pp.335, 342-343, 346-347, 357-359; GD95/1/8 pp.311-312, 318, 327-328. MacKenzie 'preferred to offer himself as a Candidate' for St Kilda rather than go to Canada.
56 SSPCK GD95/2/16 pp.357-359. There was however a preference for one called MacLeod. In June 1822 the right of nomination to the St Kilda mission was being conveyed to the SSPCK, 'they having still a special regard to persons of the name of McLeod in terms of the said original mortification' [GD95/1/7 p.201; GD95/11/11 Society Report 1821-1822 pp.55-57].
57 SSPCK GD95/2/16 pp.377-382; GD95/1/8 pp.327-328
58 MacKenzie (1911) pp.3-4; SSPCK GD95/1/8 p.386; A L M Cook's A Family Saga is a description of the MacKenzies largely drawn from J B MacKenzie's work but is also rather inaccurate - e.g. Neil MacKenzie is said to have been 'the first resident Minister at St Kilda', and his first task the supervision of the building of the church and manse there [NAS GD1/980/10 & 11 pp.128-133].
59 See MacDonald's journal 1830 for what follows [SSPCK GD95/11/4 pp.37-64].
60 MacDonald may have meant not Boreray but Berneray where there was a new parliamentary church.

[61] The William MacNeil who brought John MacDonald to Uist from Loch Bracadale was Roderick's son, the elder William, Roderick's father, having died about 1827 [Information supplied by Bill Lawson, Northton, Harris].

[62] In the SSPCK's introduction to extracts from MacDonald's journal it is said that the party left Pabbay 'on the afternoon of the 1st of July', and the same date was given in the first extract:'At 6 P.M. (1st July) we were all on board'. However, the date here is entered by the SSPCK, and arrival at 4 a.m. on 1st July seems to be correct [SSPCK GD95/1/8 pp.335-359]. The opening notes in the St Kilda Parish Register 1830-1851 contain a contradiction:'The Revd. Neil Mackenzie came to this Island July the 3rd 1830' is followed by 'N. Mackenzie came hither as a missionary from the [SSPCK], the first of July [1830]'. The former entry is in a different hand from what follows.

[63] St Kilda Register of Baptisms, Marriages and Deaths (18 July 1830) [Western Isles Libraries, Stornoway: microfilm copy]

[64] See n.59

[65] SSPCK GD95/2/16 pp.403, 419; GD95/1/8 pp.335-341, 358, 369, 380; GD95/6/5 p.33

[66] SSPCK GD95/2/16 p.424; GD95/1/8 p.343; GD95/2/17 pp.60 Letter (10 May 1832) from James Crawford, Glasgow, with estimate of £33.10s for the work, 197 Letters (5 & 29 May 1834) from James Crawford junior - work completed for £45

[67] SSPCK GD95/11/4 1830 Report pp.51, 53

[68] MacKenzie (1911) pp.29, 32-33

[69] MacKenzie (1911) p.28

[70] The following account is derived from G C Atkinson: Typescript copy of MS journal A few Week's Ramble among the Hebrides in the Summer of 1831 and 'A Notice of the Island of St Kilda, on the North-west Coast of Scotland' (Read, January 16, 1832) in Transactions of the Natural History Society of Northumberland, Durham and Newcastle Vol. II (1838) pp.215-225

[71] 'Coshlatter' was described as 'a small village', and the boat was hired for £5.

[72] In 1838 MacLean wrote that over the last eight years only two men had reached the top of Stac Biorach: 'They did it to show their dexterity to an Englishman, and for a quid of tobacco' [MacLean (1838) p.12].

[73] Atkinson wrote:'murder has not been committed within the memory of man, and adultery is unknown' [Atkinson (1832) p.219].

[74] MacLean (1838 p.46) mentioned that the woollen sail was made of 21 patches of varied sizes and shades in proportion to the families and shares of land and rocks.

[75] SSPCK GD95/2/16 p.447; GD95/2/17 p.7. On 13 July 1831 Murdo MacLellan wrote requesting that £11 of MacKenzie's stipend should be paid to H D Hill for goods furnished by MacLellan to MacKenzie. GD95/2/17 pp.137, 166

[76] St Kilda Register of Baptisms, Marriages and Deaths (20 June & 6 August 1831) for baptisms and deaths. SSPCK GD/1/8 pp.384-386

[77] SSPCK GD95/11/4 pp.61-86 Extracts from MacKenzie's journal 1832-1833

[78] CG Vol. II pp.210-211, 262; Vol. VI p.162 'Sunwise Turn' ['Deiseal']. The 'sunwise' course seems to have been a widespread custom [cf. J Watts: Scalan: The Forbidden College, 1716-1799 East Linton 1999 p.171, p.173 n.37].

[79] Letter from T Jameson Torrie, Portree, Skye, to his mother at 'Professor Jameson's', 21 Royal Circus, Edinburgh 29 July 1834 [EUL General 1996/8/8]. On 19 July Torrie had arrived at 'Isle Oronsay' after a sail of two days and a night from Glasgow. He then wrote a letter in which he said:'I shall not be able to write for some time as there is no Post on the West coast of Skye and as it is likely we may go with the steam boat to St Kilda from Loch Bracadale on the West coast' [EUL General 1996/8/7]. Three weeks after Portree he wrote again from 'Loch-Gilp-head', mentioning that 'Another person we met in Lochaber was Donald Gregory in full highland costume, and the chief leader of a new nondescript Antiquarian club called the Iona Club which is to hold its meeting at Fort William next week' [EUL General 1996/8/9 (22 August 1834)].

[80] Report in Glasgow Free Press 2 August 1834. There were also mentions of the distribution of tobacco and cotton handkerchiefs of 'gay patterns', the latter causing some of the 'matrons and maids' to 'shed tears of exultation', funeral customs, house interiors, viewing the steamer, and, on the return journey south, of the whole steamer company, presumably crew and passengers, singing 'God save the King' in Fingal's Cave at Staffa to 'remarkably striking' effect. The pilot required for the outward passage through the Sound of Harris 'although uneducated, displayed much accurate knowledge'.

[81] R Carruthers: The Highland Note-Book or Sketches and Anecdotes New edition Inverness 1887 pp.399-403

[82] Extract from Rev. Neil MacKenzie's Journal 23 September 1834.
The date of Acland's second visit has been given as 2 August 1834, but it would seem from Rev. MacKenzie's journal that it was really on a Sunday in mid September. In addition to the 20

continued on page 381

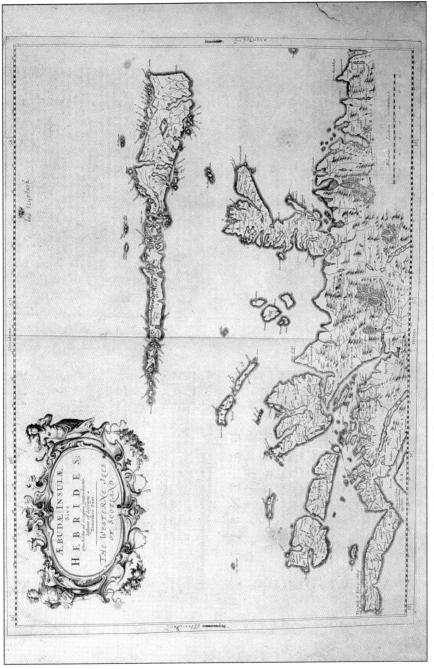

Map of the Hebrides, with 'dow Hijrtach' (St Kilda) entered at top

Pre-Reformation chapel and burial ground at Galson, Isle of Lewis,
perhaps similar to Teampall na Trionaid (Teampall Cbriosd) and burial ground, St Kilda

Farr, Sutherland, (c1825) where Roderick Maclennan served as missionary after leaving St Kilda

St Kilda Peak beari...

St Kilda. Peak bearing NNE

St Kilda approached from the south-east and south-west. (c1832)

H.O. 12 Ma. 32

sland.

H.O. 12 May. 32

An 'outside world' view of St Kilda – 'Doctor Factobend's Recantation in the Bird Basket, St. Kilda' – a caricature illustration (1820)

Front cover of an illustrated brochure advertising the 'Circular Tours'
to the Hebrides by S.S.Dunara Castle and S.S.Hebrides (c1920)

The Bride (Annie Ferguson) and the Bridegroom (John Gillies) 1890

380

sovereigns he also presented to the people 'Bibles, knives, scissors, thread, bed-flannel shifts, snuff, and white flannel in great abundance,' while the minister's 'wardrobe, cellar, library, and pantry,' benefited from his generosity. MacKenzie's response was appropriate:'I believe and pray that the God, whose steward he is, may reward him a hundred-fold. It would be tedious to enumerate the various ways in which the benevolence and endearing kindness of that honourable, during the short time they remained here, were exhibited.' Some of the 'natives' were allowed on board the yacht, 'and Lady Acland, playing on the piano-forte, and her family joining with her in a charming chorus, showed them the power of music.' Lady Acland was particularly interested in the white flannel, wishing that it should be divided so that the most aged and infirm females received two shifts. 'There was enough of it to have given a shift to every married woman; but she chose to divide the shifts in pairs, that the person who would get them should have one while the other was a –cleaning. Her aim was to promote cleanliness.' White flannel surplus to their requirements was left 'for dressing every child with flannels, which lives after this date, till the whole be exhausted'. [Inverness Courier Vol.VXII no.916 17 June 1835]

83   As regards Hebridean dwellings the houses in St Kilda were apparently not exceptionally squalid. 'In Lewis, and some other parts of the range called the Long Island, the tenants houses are mean and filthy beyond all description.' In Lewis too, 'Dwelling-houses, dress, food, and general accommodation, are the most wretched imaginable throughout the whole range of the country district. So vile indeed are the dwellings in general, that we cannot enter upon a description of them. Suffice it to observe, that the houses are cleaned out only once a year, for the purpose of manuring the land with what polluted contents the most Hottentot economy had collected in them during the whole season' [J MacDonald: General View of the Agriculture of the Hebrides or Western Isles of Scotland etc. Edinburgh 1811 pp.89, 812]. MacDonald also refers (p.89) to the 'present Hottentot houses' of a tenant in the Hebrides; and some Lewis natives attending a Stornoway court for offences of 'illicit distillation' in July 1808 appeared to be 'perhaps the most uncouth figures to be seen in Britain' (p.809). [D McAllum]: Remains of the late Rev. Daniel McAllum, M.D. With a memoir London 1829 pp.85-116 (Journal of an Excursion to the Shetland Isles - typescript copy pp.6-7)

84   EE Vol. XII pp.450-452; EB Vol. XI pp.450-452

85   MacKenzie (1911) p.20; MacKenzie (1905) p.402; see n.12 (Report p.25).

86   MacKenzie (1911) p.21

87   A & A MacDonald Vol. III pp.494-499, reference to 'Donald MacDonald of Tanera, son of Skeabost'; HB Case Papers regarding St Kilda tenancy 1841. 'Scalpay' is here the island beside Skye. J Munro: The British Fisheries Society 1786-1893 Edinburgh 1978 pp.96-97, 182; A MacKenzie: History of the MacDonalds Inverness 1881 p.276n; R J Adam (edit.): Papers on Sutherland Estate Management 1802-1816 (SHS) 2 vols Edinburgh 1972 Vol. I pp.xxx-xxxi; NSA (Sutherland - parish of Assynt) p.114; NSA (Inverness-shire - parish of Duirinish) p.341; MacKenzie (1921) p.84

88   MacKenzie (1911) pp.18-19, 21; MacLean p.40; MacKenzie (1905) pp.400,402

89   Wilson (1842) Vol. II pp.33-34; SSPCK GD95/2/17 pp.271, 321. Many years later Alexander Ross, of Inverness, spoke with 'Mr MacKenzie, Fort William [N B MacKenzie, banker], whose father was minister' in St Kilda. MacKenzie told him about the building of new houses in '1830', following the donation by Sir Thomas Dyke Acland, whom he confused with Sir Thomas Dick Lauder. 'On that occasion Sir Thomas offered a premium for each man who could build a house with chimneys and other improvements, and entrusted the Rev. Mr Mackenzie with the money to pay the man who should move first. Mr Mackenzie found the money of little use and not coveted, and he resolved to try tobacco…He offered the first man who should lay a foundation one pound of tobacco, and so a beginning was made. One man built a house and won the prize, next year three more began, and the premium had to be reduced to one-fourth of a pound of tobacco' [Ross (1893) p.82].

90   SSPCK GD95/2/18 pp.26, 172-175, 181-182; GD95/1/9 pp.20-21; MacKenzie (1911) p.22

91   SSPCK GD95/2/18 pp.172-175; GD95/1/9 pp.20-21

92   SSPCK GD95/1/9 pp.20-21; GD95/2/18 pp.181-182. It was stated on 5 July 1838 that 20 houses had been completed [GD95/2/18 pp.172-175].

93   MacLean (1838) pp.25-34. At Skye the passengers were able to see the Spar Cave and Loch Scavaig. Of the emigrants at Lochmaddy MacLean said (p.33): 'Their berths seemed uncomfortable and ill aired - their tale of woe was harrowing to the feelings.' SSPCK GD95/11/4 1838 (Appendix) pp.30-31. Dr Dickson was 'Comptroller of the Society'. The Society expected 'ere long…a detailed account of the state in which these reverend gentlemen found the inhabitants…which, along with a more full description of the scenery, etc. of the island itself, than has been given for more than a century, will, if not published separately, be introduced, in substance at least, into the Appendix to the next Sermon. It will contain also a succinct view of the present intellectual and religious attainments of the islanders, as communicated…in Mr Mackenzie's Journals…compared with their condition, in these respects, when they were last visited by the Rev. Mr Macdonald of Urquhart'. MacDonald was really responsible for introducing

381

the people to the 'precious and saving truths of the gospel…after many years of most distressing spiritual destitution'. The inhabitants were found to be 'in a state of much greater advancement', with 17 out of a population of 92 admitted for the first time to communion, their devotion being 'of the inmost heart', not 'of mere outward solemnity'.

94 MacLean (1838) p.36
95 SSPCK GD95/2/17 p.144; J B M (1911) p.32; MacLean p.39
96 MacLean (1838) pp.41-42, 48-50
97 MacLean (1838) pp.35, 49
98 MacLean (1838) pp.41, 50-51; SSPCK GD95/2/18 pp.181-182
99 MacLean (1838) pp.45-46, 54, 24
100 SSPCK GD95/2/18 pp.181-182
101 SSPCK GD95/2/18 pp.403 (7 May 1840 - MacKenzie is 'at present in town'), 409; GD95/1/9 pp.73-74; GD95/11/4 1840 pp.40-41
102 MacGillivray pp.47-70 for this description
103 Ansdell p.50
104 SSPCK GD95/2/18 pp.518, 541; GD95/1/9 p.97
105 SSPCK GD95/2/18 pp.543-544, 553
106 SSPCK GD95/1/9 p.99
107 J Hamilton: Memoirs of the Life of James Wilson of Woodville London 1859
108 Letter (18 August 1841) from James Wilson, FRSE, MWS, of Woodville, to Miss Sym, Brandon Place, Glasgow [NAS RH1/2/862]. Wilson (1842) pp.49-53 for longer account of the demonstration on the cliffs.
109 SSPCK GD95/13/122 pp.39-53 Letter (3 June 1841) from James Wilson Esq. FRSE to John Tawse Esq. regarding St Kilda, printed as appendix to Robert Elder's Anniversary Sermon.
110 Wilson's 'census' gave a total of 105, including the minister and his family.
111 Wilson (1842) Vol. II pp.3, 63-64. It was said of the versatile Sir Thomas Dick Lauder that he contributed to the book 'by aiding in the supply of materials for a narrative of the voyage in 1842, which was written by Mr Wilson, the naturalist, who accompanied him' [A Biographical Dictionary of Eminent Scotsmen New edition London 1872 Vol. II p.466]. Lord Cockburn was more direct: 'The best part of James Wilson's book called Voyage round the Coasts of Scotland, being the account of St Kilda, is substantially Lauder's' [H Cockburn: Circuit Journeys 1837-1854 Edinburgh 1888 p.290].
112 Wilson (1842) Vol. II p.46; HB - see n.86 above.
113 Mackay (1914) pp.83, 99, 200-201. Romanism, wrote MacKay, was 'a vast conspiracy against the civil and religious liberty of mankind'. SSPCK GD95/1/9 p.69; MacDonald (1902) p.169; Kennedy (1932) p.50
114 Kennedy (1932) pp.53, 165
115 MacRae pp.82-83, 97-98, 65, 53, 93
116 MacRae pp.6, 2-3
117 SSPCK GD95/2/19 p.168; GD95/1/9 p.167. The revival in St Kilda during the autumn of 1842 has been seen as closely related to the excessively emotional outburst in Skye a year earlier, of which a Baptist pastor at Broadford wrote: 'I suppose you have heard what has occurred in the other end of the island. They had the sacrament last week, and I hear that between 12,000 and 15,000 attended, and that hundreds fell down as if they were dead. This usually commences with violent shaking and crying out, with clapping of hands. Those affected were mostly women and children.' [D E Meek: 'Gaelic Bible, revival and mission: the spiritual rebirth of the nineteenth century Highlands' in J Kirk (edit.): The Church in the Highlands (Scottish Church History Society) Edinburgh 1998 pp.127-132]
118 MacRae p.98
119 SSPCK GD95/2/19 p.168
120 SSPCK GD95/11/14 pp.vii-xii (1842-1843)
121 A more extensive and better known account of these 'symptoms' and the effects of 'revival' written by Neil MacKenzie was also recorded [MacKenzie (1911) pp.34-38].
122 MacAulay pp.216-218; SSPCK GD95/11/4 Journal 1827 pp.135-136; Wilson's letter to Tawse p.8 (see n.108 above); Wilson (1842) Vol. II p.24; MacKenzie (1911) pp.32 etc. (to which the article from the Celtic Review was added); The Celtic Review Vol. II Edinburgh 1906 (July 1905-April 1906) pp.327-342
123 CG Vol. I pp.xxix-xxxii; PL CH2/473/1 p.102 (29 November 1759)
124 Kennedy (1867) p.20; SSPCK GD95/11/4 Journal 1830 p.54
125 Fasti Vol. IV p.93; SSPCK GD95/1/9 pp.198-200; GD95/2/19 pp.259-260
126 Fasti (Suppl. Vol.) p.194; SSPCK GD95/2/19 p.300; GD95/1/9 p.206
127 SSPCK GD95/2/19 pp.300, 321-322

PART V

UNCERTAINTY AND EMIGRATION
Departures from St Kilda

In 1844 Neil Mackenzie left for a charge on the mainland probably available to him, as a member of the established church, following the Disruption. During the next eight years the SSPCK could find no regular replacement and instead entered into a period of competition with the new Free Church for the loyalties of the St Kilda people. Each side tried to arrange visits or longer stays by temporary catechists, the SSPCK having some modest success, and each relied on ministers sent on missions of a few days to celebrate marriages, baptisms and communions. Occasional visitors called in, treated themselves to what was by now a standard pattern of sightseeing, and reported with limited accuracy on their experiences.

About a third of the island population emigrated to Australia in 1852. Neither of the church rivals had then produced an answer to the crisis of religion, and until the appearance of Duncan Kennedy , Free Church catechist, in 1853 there was little education. The Kelsall bequest of 1857 initiated a new era of outside interest which accompanied the greater enthusiasm of tourists curious to see one of the most remarkable places in Britain. The bequest offered the possibility of financial aid towards material improvements, including a specially constructed boat landing 'dock'. The latter was organized by the Admiralty's Captain Henry Otter whose survey ship survived a ferocious storm at St Kilda in 1860. It was the proprietor, having eventually given way to the Free Church and allowed it the use of the island church and manse, who chose to stand the cost of constructing the houses in a reshaped 'village' after the storm. The administrator of the Kelsall bequest, the secretary of the Highland and Agricultural Society, made two fact-finding visits and saw to the delivery of a substantial boat, soon to be lost with all on board in crossing to Harris in 1863.

In the course of these dramatic events the division between the spiritual and material welfare of the islanders became more pronounced, and reliance for both on outside agencies increased. As easily persuaded and influenced inhabitants, knowing little beyond what they were told, the people might have all abandoned their home much sooner than they did had they not received aid from mainland sources, and the effects of Free Church doctrine might be seen as either supportive of their ability to endure or as encouraging them to think more strongly of giving up.

CHAPTER 1

Searching again for a minister, and the
Free Church approaches by sea

The presentation of Neil Mackenzie to the church of Duror depended, to some extent at least, upon the influence of Sir Thomas Dick Lauder who had visited St Kilda with James Wilson in 1841 and had been impressed by the minister. In the late summer of 1844 Sir Thomas went on another 'official cruise' which lasted three months. 'My only regret in this matter,' he told Mackenzie in a letter of 4 December 1844, 'is for the poor people of St Kilda, for I cannot conceive how they can do without you. I sailed round every island in the group this last trip, and I was almost thankful that I did so in a tremendous gale of wind and awful sea which prevented my landing, for if I had landed I don't know what I could have said to them, conscious as I felt that I had been the cause of depriving them of their much-loved Archbishop.'[1]

The 'poor people' must indeed have felt abandoned at a high point of their religious enthusiasm, but Mackenzie himself retained an interest in them for some years afterwards. In March 1845 he wrote from Duror to enquire whether anyone had been appointed to succeed him and in April he proposed a catechist to be sent in the meantime since the SSPCK was 'not in a condition' to support a resident minister. Even though he had just moved on to Kilbrandon, after only six months in Duror, he told the Society he was willing to visit St Kilda during the summer 'to dispense ordinances' if it wished him to do so, and the offer was accepted gratefully.[2]

The reason why the Society was unwilling or unable to find an immediate replacement for Mackenzie was not so much a financial one, as might have been expected, but more probably the situation in which it was placed following the Disruption. Many of the teachers, catechists, and, in a few cases, missionaries employed by the SSPCK had joined the Free Church, and as the Society had been associated with the established Church of Scotland since its inception it had, late in 1843, to clarify the legal basis of its powers and duties in relation to those employees who had changed allegiance. Was it to dismiss those of its teachers who had left the establishment? Was it to get rid of some of its own directors who had moved to the Free Church? Was the Society, unaware then of Mackenzie's intentions, entitled to continue in its service 'the Missionary at present officiating at St Kilda, though he should join the Free Church'? And was it bound in future to select for that charge a missionary linked to the established church? The Disruption was to have far-reaching effects on the St Kilda mission.[3]

In relation to St Kilda the difficulties faced by the SSPCK were somewhat eased, first by the missionary's departure in 1844 and secondly by the fact that conditions of appointment had been to an extent determined by Alexander

Macleod's mortification in 1735. 'Nothing is said in the deed of mortification, requiring either the Missionary or Catechists to belong to the Established Church; but they have always been so.' As already noted contrary to popular belief no absolute requirement that missionaries or catechists should be surnamed MacLeod existed either although there was a preference in that direction. By 1845, however, the Society was no longer in an indeterminate state, having resolved to adhere to the established church. It had never appointed more than one person at a time to carry out the duties of teacher, catechist and missionary in St Kilda, and still saw the three roles as the combined tasks of its representative there. That a catechist should now go to the island as proposed by Neil Mackenzie raised the problem not of his responsibilities, nor even of how much he should be paid, but rather of whether he would be sufficient to satisfy the religious needs of the community. Marriages and baptisms would have to be carried out by a minister on mission.

Fortunately for the SSPCK the matter was temporarily taken out of its hands by the proprietor of St Kilda, John Macpherson MacLeod, who, initially at his own expense, arranged for a catechist to go out in order that, until the directors made up their minds, 'the people may not be destitute of spiritual instruction'. With the proprietor's consent Dr Norman MacLeod, visitor to St Kilda in 1838, engaged a Mr Carmichael to stay on the island for a year from May 1845. The presence of this catechist did not remove the need for a minister on mission, but it was not until September 1845 that Neil Mackenzie was able to visit in accordance with his own suggestion and the request of the Society directors. He journeyed with the factor, Norman MacRaild, and remained as long as it took him to 'dispense the ordinances of religion among them'. When he got back to Kilbrandon in the same month he wrote to inform the Society that he had returned and to report on 'the condition in which he found the inhabitants of that Island.' The directors were pleased to have his account, written on 24 September:

'The natives of St Kilda are advancing both in Scriptural Knowledge and in Holiness of life. None of them who had made a profession of religion have fallen away, although the Elders who are mighty in the Scriptures and holy in their lives, doubt the genuiness of the characters of one or two of them, of whose piety we in the judgement of Charity at first deemed new men. Yet none have fallen into open vice. Some have been added to the number of those who made a public profession of religion. I baptized 5 infants and administered the Sacrament of the Lord's Supper to 36 communicants - three of them for the first time - more devoted and feeling communicants I never saw.'[4]

Nothing was said in the report about the islanders' feelings towards their former minister, but he was not deterred from repeating the visit two years later.

The catechist Carmichael completed his year on St Kilda in the summer of 1846, by which time the SSPCK had become even more distracted by the issue of relations with the Free Church. Nevertheless it responded quickly to a letter from Norman MacRaild, who on 21 April wrote to say that he was intending to go to the island at the beginning of May. The secretary asked him to inspect the church and manse while he was there and to arrange for any necessary repairs to be carried out at the Society's expense. MacRaild, who lived at Colbost, about six miles from Dunvegan on the road to Glendale, made his survey and on his return home sent a note of requirements for repairs to the manse which were probably completed some time during the next two or three months. The task of finding a catechist to succeed Carmichael proved more difficult.[5]

The necessity of providing someone to look after the spiritual and educational welfare of St Kilda was given great urgency by the early stages of the battle between the SSPCK and the Free Church. The dispute tended to underline the former's close adherence to the established church, but this was brought about by the demands of the landowner as much as by the natural association of the Society itself. The absence of religious provision after the departure of Carmichael left a space which the evangelical Free Church, spurred on perhaps by the still active John MacDonald, was ready to fill, and it did not wish to miss the opportunity of stepping in. On 5 August 1846 two carefully chosen Free Church representatives landed on the island to speak with the inhabitants. They were Rev. Roderick MacLeod, formerly at Bracadale and then at Snizort, and a 'Mr McLennan', almost certainly the former St Kilda tacksman Murdo MacLellan, who now lived at Milton in South Uist and who could have provided the transport if needed. However they were taken to St Kilda by the Free Church yacht, the *Breadalbane*, having gone on board at Lochboisdale. They spent a day in the island, and it was said afterwards that 'Old Mr Rory turned sick from the stench, on landing'. On the way back MacLellan was landed at Lochmaddy, MacLeod first at Berneray for a short call and then at Loch Snizort.

Roderick Macleod had been an energetic, leading evangelical in the days before the Disruption when perhaps his best known acts, one of which led to a dispute with his church, were to reduce the number of Bracadale communicants from 150 to under 10 by allowing only 'God-fearing consistent Christians' to attend, and to refuse baptism to insufficiently religious families. In 1844 he was the only Free Church minister in Skye. Murdo MacLellan, an enthusiastic supporter of John MacDonald's missions to St Kilda, probably attached himself to the Free Church after the Disruption and would have been a suitably strong companion for Macleod. Together they were likely to have a profound influence upon the St Kilda people, who were ever easily persuaded and in 1846 ready for a message that would refresh their spiritual condition left high and dry after the tide of revival had ebbed. They must already have heard of 'Maighstir Ruairidh' of Bracadale, and of course Murdo MacLellan would have been no stranger.[6]

Much less would have been achieved among the islands and inlets of the west coast, and in St Kilda, by the young Free Church, if it had been without the services of the *Breadalbane*. Called after the Marquis of Breadalbane, the leading Free Church supporter among landowners, and intended specifically to transport ministers to remote spots on the west coast, the yacht was said by Rev. Alexander Beith to be 'a small vessel - of about thirty tons register - schooner rigged, of great sailing virtue, and safe as any sailing vessel could be.' Among some Free Church ministers there was a preference for a steam ship as being more likely to be dependable, but it was the cost of maintenance and the increased availability of steamer services that eventually led to the disposal of the *Breadalbane* in 1853. In the mid 1840s, however, the Free Church benefited greatly from having a flagship to signal its real presence and, as Beith said, supporters felt that 'the *prestige* of such an institution would tell greatly in our favour in the Highland mind generally', while the Missionary Record for September 1845 praised the yacht's success:

'The *Breadalbane* carries the messengers of Christ from island to island, and her blue flag is welcomed in many a creek where hitherto the Gospel has been a strange sound. You can have no idea of the feelings with which these islanders view the good schooner. I will never forget one evening when a party came from a distance, "just to get a sight of the ship," and having examined her snug and comfortable cabin, one of them came to me, and with tears in his eyes said, "I now see the Free Church is determined to send us the preaching of the Cross, and to look after our souls."'[7]

The *Breadalbane*, built of oak in 1844 under the supervision of Robert Brown, had accommodation for six passengers which included an after-cabin, two 'staterooms', and two sofas in the main cabin which could be converted into bunks. The master throughout the ship's short career was Captain McEwan from Rothesay who had the assistance of at least four crewmen. Being exceptionally stable in rough weather the yacht gave ministers who voyaged with her more comfortable journeys than they might have expected, and they were impressed with the interest aroused by their striking interventions from the sea. No island community could have been more interested than that of St Kilda when the *Breadalbane* sailed into the bay with Roderick Macleod and 'Mr McLennan' in 1846.[8]

Later that year, on 12 October, the yacht crossed from Tobermory to Loch Sunart 'to ship a Catechist for St Kilda, according to orders; but he did not come forward.' And on 12 November the intention of visiting the island was given up, it 'being impossible, from lateness of season, now to proceed to St

Kilda'. In all however the *Breadalbane* made four visits there over the years.[9]

It is believed, or claimed, that the people of St Kilda were persuaded to join the Free Church by MacLeod and MacLellan. Certainly the two visitors must have brought news that the inhabitants were lacking proper religious guidance, and in the early autumn the proprietor heard from the Free Church that it was going to send a missionary to the island. He replied, 'declining his countenance to any such appointment, as measures had already been taken for sending out a Catechist there in connection with the Established Church'; and he copied the correspondence to the SSPCK. Three weeks earlier the Society had received a communication from Norman MacRaild who was then in St Kilda and intending to remain there all winter, as if, in the circumstances, he was going to serve as a one-man defence against an attack by Free Church opponents. But it seems that he had help, for in November Rev. Angus Martin of Snizort informed the Society that 'Mr Bethune' was about to leave Skye for St Kilda, perhaps to work as the catechist promised by the proprietor. The failure of the catechist for the Free Church to appear at Loch Sunart in October and the bad weather at the beginning of November were in a sense fortunate since otherwise there might have been an unseemly confrontation between two catechists on the island shore.[10]

The proprietor, John Macpherson MacLeod, may have disliked involvement in controversy but as owner of the island he was the principal obstacle in the way of the Free Church attempt to take over. He and Norman MacRaild were both anxious that the SSPCK should appoint a minister or catechist for longer than one year, and when, in December 1846, MacLeod wrote to request 'the Expences defray'd by him on account of the late Catechist of St Kilda, Mr Carmichael', the sum being £28 and almost twice Neil MacKenzie's costs in going out for his short visit in 1845, the directors authorised payment 'with any farther sum he may have paid in providing the Inhabitants of that Island with a Catechist until a regular minister is settled there, which they hope may be the case early next summer'. As it turned out, no 'regular' minister of the established church was found then or ever again.[11]

*

In 1846 and 1847 the Hebrides and many parts of the Highlands suffered from the repeated failure of the potato crops to such an extent that famine and death by starvation were immediate threats to the population. Free Church ministers on roving mission in those areas saw the reality of the disaster in the remoter districts of the west and a special committee on Highland destitution was set up by the Free Church which was the first body in the country to react positively to the crisis. The yacht *Breadalbane* was pressed into service and was found 'of eminent use' in carrying both deputations of ministers and supplies of meal to stricken communities. St

Kilda, however, was less badly hit, having, particularly in its birds, a greater variety of food resources, and in September 1846 the proprietor wrote: 'we never had a thought of getting any assistance from Government for St Kilda.' He and his factor had just sent off a supply of oatmeal and other goods 'which we hope will carry them through the winter and spring'. Seed for 1847 was also sent. As a consequence the islanders probably saw nothing of the Free Church during the months after the *Breadalbane* put in with MacLeod and MacLellan, but visitors in 1847 would no doubt have brought news of that church's praiseworthy efforts in helping people elsewhere.[12]

One such arrival at St Kilda in 1847 was Neil MacKenzie, making his final trip to the island. The SSPCK directors had asked him if he would go and at the beginning of June he accepted the invitation. The reason now put forward by the Society for the continued vacancy, which it was ever more anxious to fill as promptly as possible, was the difficulty of finding a missionary who could speak and preach in Gaelic, always a problem confronting every form of church since at least the seventeenth century. Now MacKenzie was a useful stopgap, a temporary provider of Gaelic at a time when what Gaelic abilities there were had probably associated themselves with the Free Church. So he made his way to Harris where he joined forces with the established church minister, Roderick MacDonald, who had recently arrived in his parish, and they prepared to leave for St Kilda together.[13]

As has been said earlier the Protestant church had never been quite sure to which parish, if any, St Kilda belonged. There is a general presumption that it was part of the parish of Harris, but it seems that if it ever became a 'pendicle' of that scattered ecclesiastical district that was more by natural association and accident than by deliberate, official attachment. The SSPCK was always uncertain as long as it had to deal with the island, and so too was the Synod of Glenelg. In 1761 the latter body appointed either Rev. Donald MacQueen in North Uist or Rev. Angus MacNeil in South Uist, not being sure who was really responsible even after Kenneth MacAulay's involvement in 1758, 'to certify the Minister of St Kilda' to the SSPCK. And the Society believed that the island might be in any one of at least four Protestant parishes; in 1774 and again in 1822 it 'formerly belonged to the parish of North Uist, but is now part of that of Harris', in 1779-1780 it was part of the parish of Barra, and at the same time, from 1815 or before through to 1852, it was in the parish of South Uist. A guide book published in 1852 stated that 'The Island is annexed to the parish and Island of South Uist'. With islands like Pabbay and Berneray being definitely in Harris parish, and with its proprietor and tacksman connections in the past, St Kilda could quite sensibly be imagined to have the same parochial link, but it may be that the firmest push in that direction came from the SSPCK or General Assembly of the established church in the course of their attempts to defend the island against Free Church incursions. They would have found it useful, in the absence of a settled missionary, to make the nearest minister, of Harris rather than South Uist in that case, responsible for religious provision there. A proper parish minister, even though fifty miles away, could probably visit once or twice a year to administer the sacrament, marry and baptise, so that all that was necessary on the island, at least until a better arrangement could be made, was a resident teacher or catechist to act as guardian and to keep the established church alive.[14]

In the summer of 1847 Neil MacKenzie and Roderick MacDonald, already in Harris, chanced to meet up with two keen ornithologists, Mr W M E Milner and friend, who, after exploring Sutherland, planned to continue their researches in the Outer Hebrides. Passing from Ross-shire through Skye they crossed on 29 May to Stornoway by means of 'Mr Matheson's steamer', probably the *Mary Jane* which had been recently acquired and which, like the *Breadalbane*, was placed by Matheson at the disposal of the Free Church Destitution committee. From Stornoway Milner travelled to 'Ath Lin' beside Loch Seaforth and thence to Tarbert. On 1 June the two men sailed to Rodel, where they thought the people seemed 'very contented, though badly off'. From Rodel they went on to enjoy what they considered to be the far more interesting birds of North Uist until their return to Rodel in order to make themselves ready for the voyage to St Kilda. They were able to hire 'a very comfortable little cutter of forty tons, formerly engaged as the mail-packet between Skye and Harris'. This vessel was 'well manned by an able crew of five men', and it was to start from Obbe. Somehow they were joined by Neil Mackenzie, 'to whose kindness and zeal we were mainly indebted for the great success we met with', and by Roderick MacDonald, 'the clergyman of Harris, in which parish St. Kilda is situated', who was to act as interpreter 'in an island where not a word but Gaelic is understood'.[15]

At 6 o'clock in the morning of 12 June they left with a favourable wind, but not far from their destination they were overtaken by a storm 'and for four hours we were beaten about most helplessly'. Then, by a fortunate chance, they entered the bay of St Kilda and anchored two hundred yards from the shore. The customary investigation of the 'natives' and their habits was soon carried out and recorded in 'a short account of the extraordinary people of that remote island'. Milner said the 'village', a primitive settlement, 'gives one the idea of a number of bee-hives, all thatched, with no chimneys, the smoke escaping through the roof'. Some houses had glass windows, but most were 'very dark and dirty' inside. There were twenty-eight of them altogether, with land attached to the twenty-one occupied by families. The remaining seven were inhabited by 'old maids and widows'. The ornithologists found the people 'hospitable, most anxious to serve us, and, unlike their brethren in the mainland, we had great difficulty in persuading them to take what we considered they were entitled to for two hard days' work among the cliffs and rocks'. Several pounds of tobacco, however, 'delighted them not a little'. On Sunday Neil Mackenzie conducted a service in the church:

'Every human being was there; and the attention to the whole service, lasting near four hours, was wonderful: even during the English service not a word was spoken, neither was there any curiosity shown at our appearance among them. Their affection for their minister seems very great; and his account of them, very much corroborated by what we saw, proves, that though separated by a stormy ocean from the rest of the world, and visited by not more than three or four vessels in the year, they deserve the credit of being the most virtuous, moral and religious people in the British Isles.'[16]

Comments of this kind by visitors before and after Milner have at least one thing in common. Whether complimentary or not they all convey a feeling of distance from reality. Perhaps this was inevitable, given the short period spent on the island by most of those who wrote accounts afterwards. Statements about islanders seem often to be superficial or based on second-hand information rather than on immediate experience. An apparently factual observation such as Milner's reference to 'their annual parliament' can contain a confusion between one event and another, in this instance between daily morning discussions and the meetings held once a year at which areas of the cliffs were allocated. Similarly an impression that, for example, there was no curiosity shown in church is contradicted by other observations on the natural curiosity of a community to whom the appearance of strangers was still an uncommon occurrence, and it is difficult to accept that the islanders were sitting on the rough benches for nearly four hours without a curious interest, well concealed though it might be, in their new companions. It is difficult to believe too that the people were as extraordinary as Milner said they were, when often enough, in dress, custom and behaviour, they were seen to be not much different from the inhabitants of Harris or Uist. Throughout the remainder of the nineteenth century the personal viewpoint of the commentator gave rise to misleading and inconsistent descriptions or opinions.

After three or four days the visiting party left, Neil Mackenzie for the last time. 'Their leave-taking with their minister was very touching: they stood on the rocky shore, in a bright moonlight night, grouped round him, listening with the greatest attention to his parting exhortations for two hours, and when he made the signal for departure there was not a dry eye in the island. So much had this good man made himself beloved, that the people would have obeyed him in everything except leaving their barren rock, to which they are most deeply attached.' If Milner was correct there was no sign here of disapproval for a minister who had left his people too abruptly or for one who, unlike the islanders, had remained attached to the established church. At 5 o'clock in the morning the cutter moved away through a calm sea, reached Obbe late in the evening, and then, passing the Shiant islands and calling in at

Stornoway, took its ornithological passengers on to Lochinver.[17]

Both Mackenzie and MacDonald would have been able to give in to the SSPCK a report on their experiences but apparently neither did, although MacKenzie sent a letter about the mission. Another correspondent was Dr Norman MacLeod who planned to visit the Western Isles in July 1847 and 'expressed a willingness to go to St Kilda, if he could get a Catechist to go with him to remain there'. There was a possibility already in mind, but by early August this had fallen through - or rather an alternative had. 'Mr Urquhart, who had been examined for Urray, was recommended as a suitable person for that purpose, and he had agreed to go, but afterwards by a communication from the Revd. Neil McKenzie, who had been at St Kilda, it was thought, in present circumstances, it would be more suitable to send a schoolmaster rather than a Catechist.' A Mr Robertson of 'Tarksvaig' [Tarskavaig] was selected as a suitable teacher, but members of a committee who had recently visited schools in Skye found him in poor health and he could not go. So Dr MacLeod, who indeed went to the Hebrides, 'was on the look out for a proper person to recommend for teacher in the meantime... but from the last communication from him, it appeared he had not yet been successful.' The SSPCK directors were very disappointed that no minister, no catechist and no teacher had been discovered and left to their secretary the task of arranging with Dr MacLeod and the proprietor for, if possible, a catechist or teacher to go to the island before winter.[18]

On 7 October 1847 the secretary was able to report some success. According to the terms of his remit he had come to an agreement with Peter McEwan in Benbecula that he would go to St Kilda as schoolmaster, catechist or 'Reader', and hoped that he had already 'entered upon his duties'. One of the conditions of the agreement was that the post at the school in Benbecula should be kept open for at least one year so that McEwan might resume work there, but that a substitute approved by the presbytery should be found by McEwan to cover in his absence. The salary demanded by the teacher for his services in St Kilda and the stores required by him during his stay there had seemed to the secretary 'somewhat high and unreasonable', but John MacPherson MacLeod, as proprietor, had immediately undertaken to make up the sum if the Society was unwilling to go 'the length of his full demands'. A letter from Dr MacLeod read on 4 November informed the Society that Peter McEwan had in fact arrived in St Kilda.[19]

Subsequent news was cheering. On his journey out McEwan had been accompanied by Roderick MacDonald, minister of Harris, who had preached twice while on the island at services 'well attended by all the inhabitants'. The new teacher had been well received, and, to the Society, perhaps best of all was the message that 'the Catechist, who had been sent out by the Free Church, had left the Island before McEwan had arrived'. Dr MacLeod also let it be known that the cost of 'fitting out Mr McEwan with provisions and other necessaries', together with £10 for 'the freight of the vessel that carried him out', had been considerable, and that while he would be in Edinburgh within the next fortnight with all the account he would like £30 to be sent to him immediately. The directors were much relieved, greatly indebted to Dr MacLeod, and authorised payment of the £30 without delay, though this left a balance of £16.1s still due. It was paid early in 1848.[20]

Peter McEwan was to remain in St Kilda until summer 1848, combining the work of teacher, reader and catechist. But the Society, which had 'much confidence' in him, considered that this arrangement was 'only partially supplying the wants of this remote Island' and still had in mind a regular missionary to relieve the Harris minister of an awkward responsibility. The directors were of course very grateful to the proprietor who had 'most liberally met the views' they had expressed on McEwan's possibly excessive demands. Milner's opinion of Mr Macleod was also a complimentary one: 'The present proprietor … is most kind and charitable to the people: he sent a large vessel laden with meal in the time of distress, and at the present moment has offered an annual stipend of £100, in addition to £50 previously given, to any clergyman who will undertake the spiritual charge of these poor islanders.' Mr MacLeod, having ancestral connections with St Kilda and its catechists, was extremely anxious to see that the island had missionary supply, but in spite of his generosity no clergyman presented himself for the job.[21]

Nothing more was heard from Neil MacKenzie. In 1852 he left Kilbrandon and spent the rest of his career as incumbent at Kilchrenan. He died in December 1879 in Glasgow, leaving behind him a quantity of miscellaneous notes and observations relating to St Kilda, its antiquities, its songs, and its birds. These were published between 1904 and 1911 by his son James, who became minister of Kenmore parish in 1872. The notes which were assembled as an account of St Kilda could have been written at any time between 1830 and their author's death and were adapted by James to compose a coherent description. This resulted in some confusion of detail, as in remarks on ownership. The sale in 1804 to Lt. Col. Donald MacLeod was said to have taken place 'thirty years ago', which would mean that these words were written in 1834, but at the same time Lt. Col. MacLeod was 'the father of Sir John MacLeod, who is the present proprietor.' As John MacPherson MacLeod did not become Sir John until 1866 the information as a whole must have been put together at different times before it was used by James MacKenzie. Then there was the matter of the murders. The published remarks of Neil MacKenzie on stealing and so on suggest that offences such as theft took place up until he went to the island in 1830; and the general practice of 'concealing the truth' had in the past led to 'the most cruel and brutal extremities against any whom they suspected of giving information'. Contrary to all other observations to the effect that the people were not of a kind to inflict brutalities, MacKenzie illustrated his accusation with two instances of murder, the first of a man called MacLeod, therefore 'a clansman of the proprietor', who was pushed over a rock into the sea, the second of a woman, servant to the steward, who was strangled on the shore between high and low water mark. Although told as if the events were quite recent both these stories seem not much different in atmosphere from that of Fearchar and Dugan; they may be taken from tradition and belong to some ancient time, but from the manner of presentation in James MacKenzie's publication it is not possible to be sure. Nevertheless, in spite of reservations, Neil Mackenzie's notes contain much information about St Kilda corresponding quite closely to the content of his letters and reports to the SSPCK, and with his varied interests he naturally became an authority on most aspects of island life.[22]

*

Dr Norman MacLeod showed by his interest in St Kilda that he was in many respects a successor to John MacDonald. Acknowledging his efforts in 1847 the SSPCK made him an honorary member, for 'it was mainly thro' his great and disinterested exertions, that a Catechist had been procured for that Island this season'. In March 1848 he and the factor, Norman MacRaild, sought from the Society yet another supply of books for St Kilda, and MacRaild said that as he was due to sail on 3 April he would take them with him. The opportunity was missed because the books could not be produced in time, but they were sent about the beginning of May. Two months later a letter from Peter McEwan raised a problem that was also given to Dr MacLeod for his opinion.[23]

Peter McEwan, in St Kilda 'nominally as teacher, but for the purpose also of officiating as Catechist and Reader', complained of the people's unwillingness to be instructed and stated 'that they seemingly had more willingness to hear him occasionally in the church, or at their meetings, than to send their children to School'. The letter was forwarded to Dr MacLeod, 'who had taken such a deep interest in the people of St Kilda', and by way of reply he sent to the Society secretary a letter he had received from the minister of Harris, Roderick MacDonald. MacDonald said that McEwan had earnestly requested him 'to pay a ministerial visit .. this summer', to which he had agreed. Had it not been for 'his other avocations' Dr MacLeod would have been happy to go with him, but instead suggested to MacDonald that he should take with him the minister at the parliamentary church of Trumisgarry in North Uist, Donald MacDonald, 'he being a remarkably pious and good man'. The secretary thought this mission by the two MacDonalds was an excellent plan and wrote to the minister of Harris expressing his approval and adding that his expenses would be paid by the Society. It was hoped that a report would be submitted with ideas on how 'to promote the spiritual welfare of the inhabitants'.[24]

This report came in the form of a long letter from Roderick MacDonald, dated 26 July 1848 at the 'Manse of Harris', and the SSPCK found it a 'very interesting' account:

'Dear Sir,

'Your letter of 3rd instant I received in due course of post, and agreeably to the wishes of the Society, I made arrangements to pay a visit to St Kilda. I hired a vessel and wrote to Mr McDonald of Trumisgarry, requesting him to accompany me, this however he declined to do, as before the receipt of my letter, he had set apart and announced a day for dispensing the Sacrament of the Lords supper in his parish. As I could not after engaging the vessel, put off any time, I was obliged to proceed on my voyage alone, the weather was extremely boisterous, and we were beat back in our first attempt, after being two nights at sea. I however made a second and successful attempt. The trip kept me a whole fortnight from home, and cost me £12, which sum please send to my credit to the National Bank office at Portree.

'I was disappointed to find on my arrival at St Kilda that ten (about the half) of the heads of families were absent "making feathers" in one of the adjoining Islands, without the possibility of having any access to them then, or as it turned out during my stay of four nights in St Kilda, owing to the great difficulty of effecting a landing on such a bold coast as these Islands have, excepting in very fine weather. I preached four times while there, and am glad to say that they all, both old and young, attended on all these occasions. I went prepared to dispense the Sacrament.., but as so many were absent, and especially as those present did not express any wish to partake of that Holy ordinance at that time, I did not like to urge them to such a step farther than impressing on them in my exhortations, the sacred duty of attending frequently on the ordinances of religion.

'I held a meeting with them on the evening of Saturday last, at which time, I read and explained to them letters from their worthy and benevolent proprietor, in which he expresses his great anxiety to promote their temporal and spiritual concerns, and also informing them distinctly that he had no intention of affording the Free Church party any facilities in St Kilda, that the manner in which they treated him and applied for his cooperation, did not deserve or warrant his putting any confidence in them, and that he did not think it was for their benefit to join themselves to any party, in whom he could put no trust, that it was his great desire to get St Kilda made into a parish, provided with an ordained Clergyman, tho' at present, times were not favourable for the accomplishment of such a desirable object.

'I expatiated largely on what has already been done for their good by your Society, in sending and keeping Mr McKenzie in St Kilda for a period of 14 years etc. I assured them of your continued good wishes towards them, your great anxiety to advance their spiritual interests, read and explained to them your letter authorising me to visit them, and convince them of your desire to benefit them, but that of course all the good intentions of their proprietor, and of the Honorable Society, with every effort from these quarters to afford them the means of grace, and to improve them in the most important of all their concerns, would be completely frustrated, unless they would adhere to the established church.

'My attempts to open their eyes and show them their duty, and the course they ought to follow at this crisis, I think were not unsuccessful, for some of the most intelligent and influential of them told me, that they were now tired of "Free church promises", that they saw clearly that it was their duty to follow the established church, but in the absence of the other men, they would not come to any determination. But promised me that by first opportunity (likely in September or earlier) they would write me as to their views, and the resolution they would come to. I have very strong hopes that, unless they are interfered with and misled by artful misrepresentations from the other party, they will unanimously come back to the Church; had they been all at home, I am quite certain this would have been the course they would follow.

'It is rather a difficult matter to send them a teacher that will please them. There must have been great pains bestowed upon them by Mr MacKenzie, they are consequently much more enlightened and better versed in scripture, than from their outlandish situation, people are apt to imagine. I do not think we could have given them a more suitable Catechist than Mr McEwan, but some wicked person prejudiced them against him. In October last when he was sent, I went to introduce him to the people, and at that advanced period of the year, it was not an easy matter to get a boat to go, so we had to take the most convenient, the master of which happened to be a keen and not very scrupulous partizan of the Free Church. I learned the other day at St Kilda that his presence there at the time was far from being favourable to the object of our mission. I did not bring the same person this year, but he went to make some purchases there, before we went, a few days and promised the St Kilda people that Dr McKay is to bring the Free Church yacht on a cruise to St Kilda before the end of this month.

'However Mr McEwan's services at St Kilda were a proof of the interest we take in their concerns, they joined him in worship, and tho' they did not at first send their children to school, they began to do so after a visit paid them by my precentor, a native of St Kilda, and now they attend on Sabbath and week days, such a pious excellent person must do a great deal of good there. Mr McEwan is not much inclined to stop there for another year, but I think he would obey the injunction of the Society, to stop there till next year, provided the St Kildians expressed a wish he should do so. I think he should be asked to stop on these conditions. I should not like to leave the "coast clear" for the other party, if he comes back he should be ordered to do so in the vessel that goes for the factor, this may be 3 or 4 weeks before the year's end, but it will save the freight of a vessel to the Society. I had the greatest desire to stop at St Kilda, until I could see all the people, but the master of the vessel would not stop longer, for my bargain with him was to stop over Sabbath, whatever time we arrived, this he did, and I did not consider it prudent to urge him to stop longer, as after the strain the vessel got during the rough passage we had, she got very leaky, and now he is obliged to run her ashore immediately to get her caulked and repaired.

'I wish there was an ordained clergyman ready to be sent in September, but I am afraid there is not much chance of this; they told me, even before this last trip, that if they got a minister to their mind from the established church, they would again join her, and I have not the shadow of a doubt they would do so, especially at this time. Their great fear is, that if they join our church they will be denied the liberty of objecting to a Minister that was not acceptable to them. I explained to them the law anent the settlement of Ministers in the Established church, that no minister would be forced on a congregation, if they could allege any good reason why he should not be their Minister, and that it was not likely that the people of St Kilda would be more harshly dealt with than the Christian people in other parts, adhering to the church of Scotland, that in this respect they would have more liberty than if they would be of the Free church, notwithstanding the statement of that party to the contrary. They are much afraid of being looked down upon on account of their insulated situation, and very suspicious of being taken advantage of on account of their peculiar relation to the rest of the people of the kingdom. They tell plainly that we on the mainland are of opinion that any minister may do in St Kilda, and they therefore wish to have the power of objecting, which I told them they would have, as above mentioned, in common with all the other congregations of the Church of Scotland.

'I expect to hear from you ere long. I shall write you again as soon as I have any communication from St Kilda. I returned only very late last night, and drew up this hurried report, which I must send by a private hand to Stornoway, perhaps to Glasgow, as we have no regular postal communication with the South from this country at present.'[25]

This letter has been quoted almost in full because no other record has been found which shows clearly the confusing situation in which the St Kilda people were placed by the dispute between the two churches. They had evidently been told things by the Free Church representatives who had visited them which were intended to put the established church in a bad light, and now Roderick MacDonald tried to reverse the position. In the middle of the argument the islanders, more informed on matters of religion but still persuadable one way or the other, were not sure what to believe but increasingly aware that the rest of the world tended to look down upon them as remote, ignorant and of no real importance except as curiosities. An acceptable minister was at least a sign that their existence mattered. As a result of MacDonald's letter Peter McEwan, who seemed to have the respect of the people, was asked to stay for a second winter on the island.[26]

CHAPTER 2

Established church visits, Free Church visits, and
rivalry between them, leading on to emigration

T
HE crisis which Roderick MacDonald saw in St Kilda, matched by that
existing on the mainland, was an outcome of the competition between
the established church and the Free Church for the spiritual loyalty of St
Kilda's community. The opposing factions were at odds over the 'poor people',
who, as ever swayed this way and that by whoever was speaking to them,
were the real victims of the contest, although there were signs, noted by
MacDonald, that they might make their own decision as to which church they
would attach themselves. In addition, would they all decide unanimously, or
would there be divisions of a kind not hitherto known in the island?
MacDonald had met with 'a very warm and hospitable reception from the
people, who treated him with great kindness, and listened to him with great
attention', in spite of their uncertainty and of the attempts made, 'and too
successfully made', to get them to leave the established church. But the
situation was too doubtful for them to be left without someone to keep them,
as the Church of Scotland thought, on the 'established' side, especially as the
Free Church yacht *Breadalbane* was hovering near like some pirate ship
waiting to seize the island if left unguarded.[27]

On 24 August 1848, a month after MacDonald wrote his lengthy letter, the
Breadalbane arrived off St Kilda, having on board a team of Free Church
gentlemen. They went ashore on Friday 25 August but had to leave the next
day before they could conduct communion. After they had gone the factor,
Norman MacRaild, and Peter McEwan each wrote to the proprietor describing
what had happened, and MacLeod then sent the two letters to the SSPCK.
From them 'it appeared that on the 25th of August, a party of the Free Church,
consisting of the Revd. James Noble, late of the Gaelic church here
[Edinburgh], the Revd. Thomas Pitcairn of the Free Church Cockpen and
another clergyman, with Mr Crawford W.S. and Mr [Gunning?] landed at St
Kilda, and having assembled the people in the open air, Mr Noble preached to
them in Gaelic, and after sermon he informed them, that the proprietor of the
Island was willing to give them the Church and Manse for the Free Church,
provided the people were unanimous in joining the Free Church.' This news
must have come as a shock to the proprietor and as something of a surprise
to the islanders after being told so recently by Roderick MacDonald that the
proprietor had no intention of making such a gift. It had all the appearance of
a deliberate deception by the Free Church in order to bring islanders into the
fold, and of course it was not the only instance of such untruth. Mr Pitcairn
followed up Noble with a sort of examination. He 'put various questions to the
people, from the answers to which, it appeared that the people had been

induced, on the false representations of the sentiments of the proprietor, to declare their adherence to the free Church.' Pitcairn spoke in English, but Noble acted as one interpreter, translating the questions into Gaelic, while, surprisingly, Norman MacRaild served as interpreter for the people by translating their answers into English.[28]

The SSPCK could claim to have a more correct and truthful approach because it had the letter from the proprietor himself stating 'that he was never less disposed than he is at present, to let the Free Church get footing on the Island', and that 'the people had been completely misled, when they were falsely informed that he was willing to give the Church and Manse to a Free Church minister, which he was neither disposed to do, nor had he the power of doing'. Mr MacLeod was also rather annoyed with MacRaild: 'he found great fault with the conduct of his factor on that occasion, who had no authority from him, and ought not to have given any countenance to the proceedings'. It is possible of course that the factor either had his own sympathy with the Free Church or else, knowing the minds of the people, felt that the necessity of providing some pastoral care was more important than who provided it. MacLeod concluded his letter to the secretary: 'I trust the Directors will enter into your views and stand firm; if indeed we could get a suitable minister for St Kilda next summer, I should have no fears, but that all would be as we wish them.'[29]

The directors were not pleased to hear of the Free Church attempts 'to mislead the people of St Kilda' and felt bound to support both the established church and 'the sentiments and views of the proprietor'. The trouble was that they could not instantly produce a suitable Gaelic-speaking minister willing to go to the island, a charge which many saw as exile in a place where accommodation was comparatively minimal, where there were only a few people, and which was nothing like a parish living. So they urgently requested 'their Ecclesiastical Committee' to find one. However in the Spring of 1849 they were still without even the possibility of a minister, and it would not be long before Peter McEwan would leave. The proprietor said he was ready to contribute £20 towards the expense of a minister's visit to St Kilda in the summer, but even this did not happen. The Society secretary enquired of both Roderick MacDonald in Harris and Neil MacKenzie in Kilbrandon whether they would visit the island but neither of them was able, or willing, to do so.[30]

Around mid-summer an interesting communication came from Peter McEwan, reporting on the religious situation in the island and on the progress of the children at school over the past year. He said that although 'the most of the people are of the Free Church, yet the whole of them send their children to school; few of the parents come to hear him in the church on the Sabbath, but they all send their children to be taught'. This information was copied to MacLeod, then in London, and the secretary met with him when he arrived in Edinburgh. The proprietor again expressed his great desire that an established church clergyman should pay a visit to St Kilda and decided, with that purpose in mind, to get in touch once more with Dr Norman MacLeod. Correspondence between the secretary and the proprietor continued with regard to the Free Church's intervention, and it was learned 'that a deputation of the Free Church had visited St Kilda in the end of July'. In fact it seems that the visit extended from 7 to 16 July, that those present included Rev. A M McGillivray of Dairsie and Mr MacDonald of Fearn, and that there was communion, wrongly claimed by the Free Church to be the first since the Disruption, on 15 July. The SSPCK heard that the deputation had remained several days and over a Sabbath, 'that 'they preached every day in the open air, married two couples and baptized three children', and that 'on the Sunday they administered the Sacrament of the Lord's Supper, and took their departure on the day following'. All this news was supplied by the factor, MacRaild. At much the same time Roderick MacLeod, now Free Church minister at Snizort, sent to the proprietor what purported to be a copy of 'a Minute of the Free Church Gaelic Committee', dated in the previous January, in which an argument was put forward for a gift of the church and manse in St Kilda to the Free Church.[31]

This argument ran as follows. Since all the people of St Kilda now belonged to the Free Church, the proprietor, John MacPherson MacLeod, should 'either procure for them the use of the present Church and Manse, or .. give them ground on which they might erect a church and a manse for the accommodation of a Free Church minister'. MacLeod liked neither the tone of this communication nor the means by which it had come, and had therefore not acknowledged it. However, 'he had distinctly intimated to the people of the Island, that he could not give the present church or manse for the use of the Free Church, and would not give ground to build a new church.' This latter refusal was because he felt it 'would be absurd in a population, which only amounted to about 100 souls', and he begged the islanders 'to dismiss the idea that he ever could comply with so unreasonable an application, when there was already a church, a manse and an endowment ..' He suggested that it was more sensible for 'such of the people as could not conscientiously worship God in the church already provided for them' to move to 'where they could worship according to their own consciences, and he was willing to give them every reasonable assistance in leaving the Island'. Furthermore he deeply regretted seeing the St Kilda people being 'led away by the folly of vainly and ridiculously imagining that they are themselves competent to judge on any matter about which the two churches differ, instead of humbly and piously contenting themselves with being followers of Christ, and taking the benefit of the endowment and provision of stipend, glebe, manse and church, which under Divine Providence had been made for them by benevolent men, anxious to promote their well-being, both temporal and eternal'. The SSPCK declared that it shared all the proprietor's sentiments and, still hoping to arrange at least 'an early visitation next summer', felt sure that 'when the people see the firmness of the proprietor, and the great and liberal interest he has taken in their welfare, that their eyes will be opened to the delusion practised upon them, and by which they have unfortunately been so much misled'.[32]

The inhabitants of St Kilda were, however, a different community from what they had been thirty years previously. The four visits of John MacDonald, who died in April 1849, and the 'revival' under Neil Mackenzie had planted in them or made them strongly aware of a need for inward comfort. Individuals had emerged as intelligent leaders and remarks to the effect that they were incapable of judging matters for themselves were insulting. Moreover the idea that they should leave their island home if they could not accept the established church had more of a threat than good advice in it, and neither it nor the worldly appeal made by MacLeod through reminding them of temporal benefits such as endowment and glebe could outweigh in their hearts the fact that the established church was failing, if not neglecting, them by not sending a 'regular' minister. When Roderick MacDonald announced in September 1849 that Peter McEwan had gone back to Benbecula it looked as though the Free Church had a clear field in which to achieve its aims in St Kilda.[33]

*

The SSPCK directors were disappointed that McEwan had left 'at this period of the year' and told their secretary to find out whether he was willing to go to St Kilda again. The reply came with a medical certificate to confirm that the teacher had given up his work in St Kilda owing to ill-health, so that the people there were going to be 'all winter without an instructor', but it was hoped that he would be able to return as early in the spring as weather would allow. McEwan said that he was willing to do so, but the year 1850 proved to be a turning point, the island having no representation from the established church at all. Norman MacRaild concerned himself with maintenance repairs to the church and manse authorised by the SSPCK, and the Society once again had to explain that the reason for its inability to provide anyone for the vacancy was the lack of Gaelic-speaking preachers. The Free Church, on the other hand, sent two major figures to the island, Angus MacGillivray who had already been there in 1849 and Thomas McLauchlan, minister of St Columba's Free Church in Edinburgh and a convener of the Free Church Highlands Committee.[34]

It was generally a bad time for the SSPCK in its responsibilities for St Kilda. On 29 August 1850 news was received of the death of Robert Stevenson, who had been admitted a member of the Society in 1806 and served several times as a director. A regular attender at meetings, he had always shown a deep interest in the Society's work and in no direction more positively than in the arrangement and supervision of the erection of church and manse in St Kilda. Soon after he died, the buildings were visited by Norman MacRaild, the factor, who discovered that all was not well with them. A letter from him to the SSPCK about the beginning of November stated 'that he had lately returned .., that the buildings there were much in need of repair, and altho' he had got this partially done before he left the Island, he could not remain longer to get them completed, that the Manse had been broken into during the previous winter, but he had not been able to discover by whom, and the wood in the stalls in the byres and cellar had been carried off.' These were all signs of neglect, matched by the religious decline in the people who 'for the want of a teacher or minister were returning to their old dissolute habits', from which nevertheless 'they might yet be reclaimed if a teacher was sent out to them in Spring'. The search for a minister or a teacher failed as usual, but it was hoped rather than expected that the difficulty might shortly be overcome 'as several Gaelic students have finished or nearly finish'd their preparatory course, and will soon be ready for licence'.[35]

The Free Church, in its early missionary enthusiasm, was more determined and more successful. It viewed the situation in St Kilda quite differently from the established church and the SSPCK. The inhabitants had already shown themselves to be inclined towards the Free Church. They had been neglected by their formerly revered Society in matters of religion and education, and John MacPherson MacLeod was, at the least, unhelpful. There was therefore a pressing need for that remote little community to be given the care they deserved, and so in 1850, at a point when it looked as though the established church was beginning to think of the island as something of an expensive nuisance, MacGillivray and McLauchlan were in a mood not unlike that in which John MacDonald had come nearly thirty years earlier at the Society's urgent request. Their report was similar to one of MacDonald's, fervent but not entirely true.

'To our Church,' they said, 'two things invest the island with deep interest.' These were naturally not the scenery, the birds, the antiquities or the traditions. 'The first is the universal adherence of the people to the principles we hold, an adherence consistent and intelligent, as well as universal. And the next is the usage they have met with, in being hitherto deprived of the benefit of public Christian ordinances for themselves, and in a great measure ordinary education for their children since the Disruption, through the opposition of a hostile proprietor.' This was not fair to MacLeod, who had done what he could to supply religion and education, and whose only offence was his support of the opposite church party, but his refusal to offer the Free Church what it wanted was seen at this stage as the principal obstruction to its progress in the island.

The two ministers then went on to describe their visit. They arrived on the morning of Wednesday 3 July 1850. Of course the people were delighted, expressing 'the greatest satisfaction at receiving another deputation from the Free Church'. They met the elders, perhaps two of them, 'excellent and highly intelligent men' who 'told us that the feelings of the entire community towards the Free Church were unchanged, and that from us alone, could they, holding the principles they did, receive sealing ordinances'. Celebrating the sacrament on the coming Sunday was therefore a welcome proposal, prepared for at a sequence of meetings which began on the evening of arrival with a sermon, continued through Thursday, when there was preaching morning and evening, and Friday which was kept as a fast day with two sermons during the day and one at night, to Saturday when Thursday's programme was repeated. The Friday evening and part of Saturday saw the examination of applicants for communion, seven of them, of whom three were admitted. These were all young people 'who had given evidence of a saving change'. On the Sabbath the first service began at noon, the evening one at seven, and the scene was reminiscent of the 'revival' days. 'The people were much affected during the services, their sobs at one time almost drowning the voice of the speaker. They are a people who have universally a deep reverence for the truth, and many of them seem indeed to have felt its power.' The meetings must have been held outside unless illegitimate use was made of the church.

After Monday's two sermons and concluding address the people were told that 'the Committee for the Highlands had used every means in their power to obtain for the island the permanent means of grace, but hitherto without success. Care was taken to avoid anything like an attack upon their proprietor, to whom they seem grateful and attached; but it was distinctly stated, that until he agreed to give a site for a place of worship the Church could do nothing for them'. They were also warned that 'one of the obstacles which existed to their obtaining a site, as we believed, was, a doubt on the part of the proprietor as to their being Free Churchmen'. Since the existing circumstances were obviously a trial of their faith they were urged to hold firm 'and the Lord would provide'. On leaving this last meeting the islanders declared that there was 'no risk of their falling away from their testimony', for they believed Free Church doctrine was the truth, and this the two ministers accepted for 'They are an intelligent, moral, warm-hearted people', longing anxiously for 'a permanent labourer connected with the Free Church'. So convinced McGillivray and McLauchlan departed St Kilda.[36]

The struggle for the church and manse in St Kilda must be seen in the wider context. Sites for churches and the attitude of landowners had been principal issues challenging the Free Church after the Disruption. Parliament appointed a Select Committee on Sites for Churches (Scotland) which was 'to Inquire whether and in what Parts of *Scotland*, and under what Circumstances, large Numbers of Her Majesty's Subjects have been deprived of the Means of Religious Worship, by the Refusal of certain Proprietors to grant them Sites for the Erection of Churches'. The committee's first report was published in March 1847, and by 1850 most of the problems had been removed, so that the Free Church could think of itself as being in a strong position when arguing against the proprietor's persistent 'hostility' regarding St Kilda.

Another Free Church strength lay in the recognition of its sympathy with the plight of the Highland and Island communities during and after the worst years of the potato blight. The account by Rev. Donald McRae of his visit to Harris in July 1850 vigorously condemned the treatment of ordinary cottars not only in Harris itself and the neighbouring lesser islands but throughout the west. By comparison the 'poor people' of St Kilda did not seem too badly off.

'It has become fashionable, both in the north and south, to denounce the Highlanders as incurably lazy. It is very easy to get up a cry of this kind. And with whom has it originated? Just with their oppressors - those who have driven them from the best of the land, where they could subsist with comfort to themselves and advantage to their superiors, to swamps and rocks along the margin of arms of the sea - places where it is not in the nature of things that they could be otherwise than on the brink of starvation, even after they have put forth the utmost exertion and industry. Let any one take a fair view of the adverse circumstances these poor people have to contend with, and he will certainly not lay the blame on them. In the poor island of Scalpay, where I have formerly seen just one cow-herd and his family, there are now crowded together forty families, driven there by the hand of oppression from the localities where they lived in comparative comfort, and left to fish or to starve as they may.

'I should like to see any four of those who accuse them of indolence, be they northerns or southerns, attempt to row a boat for sixteen long miles without a halt, as did the four athletic lads who conveyed me to the island of Scarp; and I suppose they would, before the third of the distance was passed over, rest on their oars, even at the risk of their skiff being driven against the rocks by the constant surf that prevails on that boisterous coast. The people here have bones and sinews, and every disposition to exert them, and they have a fine moral bearing. They are in every respect a valuable class of men, and such as it is certainly not the interest of the community to see exterminated. They are the victims of oppression, and of calumny, to give some feasible colouring to the oppression.'[37]

Strong language perhaps, but Martin Martin's St Kilda crew who 'rowed to a Miracle' one day at the end of May 1697 would perhaps have appreciated the comments.

In July 1851, while the SSPCK was still striving in vain to find a missionary, Angus McGillivray went back to St Kilda for the third time along with Rev. Sinclair from Kenmore. They found an unchanged community, still in what they considered to be circumstances of great spiritual hardship; and they retold the story of the last thirty years with less than due accuracy. John MacDonald's labours, 'year after year' were 'manifestly blessed'. Neil MacKenzie, unnamed, had laboured on the right lines until the Disruption when he left the island 'and was settled in the parish of one of the outed ministers'. Such an action might have persuaded the people to remain in the established church, but 'without a single exception they adhered to the Free Church', and when MacKenzie, still unnamed, came back to visit them and 'offered to dispense ordinances to them' they refused to receive them at his hands. 'In short', and this was further untrue information, 'their adherence to the Free Church is so decided and manifest, that for the last six years no minister of the Establishment has visited the island, and though a catechist was sent, he soon left the island, and has never returned.' In this way recent history, which included four visits by established church ministers within the last six years and a catechist who stayed two years, was conveniently re-written. At a time of intense religious rivalry some might have thought that misleading untruths from a party laying claim to 'the truth' were excusable.

The main obstacle in the Free Church's path was unchanged:

> 'Whilst the Establishment thus makes no provision whatever for the people, the proprietor refuses to allow the Free Church to supply them with ordinances. The people sent him a petition, begging him either to hand over to them the buildings on the island, or to grant them a site for erecting new buildings; and lately the convener of the Site Committee, through a friend, requested him to lease a piece of ground on which to erect a house for a catechist, but all these applications have been sternly refused. The consequence is, that except once a year, the people never have the gospel preached to them, nor the sacraments administered; and but for the ministrations of their elders, they would be completely destitute of the ordinances of religion during the rest of the year. Such is the case of this interesting people.'[38]

It seems improbable that many of the St Kilda people had heard of something called a petition, but the Free Church evidently saw one as useful in its campaign to alter the mind of the proprietor. At the end of September 1851 MacLeod met the SSPCK secretary and again 'expressed great anxiety for a Missionary being obtained' with the hope that the Society 'would be able to procure one in course of the winter'. His factor had recently returned from the island, having left the inhabitants with sufficient provisions for the winter, 'but relapsing into a most unsatisfactory state from the want of a teacher or missionary', news that will have neither surprised nor pleased his employer. MacRaild also spent £3 on repairs to the church and manse, an annual necessity for unoccupied buildings in a wet and windy climate.[39]

The SSPCK had no success in its search during the winter, and in the spring of 1852 the secretary, Dr Norman MacLeod and the proprietor were once again in urgent communication with each other. On 19 April John Tawse, the Society secretary, wrote to John MacPherson MacLeod in reply to a pressing letter:

> 'I am not surprised at your feeling anxious and even impatient about St Kilda. I can scarcely tell you how anxious I feel for the poor people of that Island, they are seldom long out of my thoughts and I assure you it is from no want either of anxiety or exertion on my part that they have not long since been provided with a minister. The difficulty is to get one. He must have Gaelic - to send one that is not able both to speak and preach Gaelic would be [?] - one might as well send a mute altogether. So great has been the demand for Gaelic Preachers that no sooner do they finish their studies at the Divinity Hall than they are picked up for parish churches or missions at home which they naturally prefer to banishing themselves to so remote an island. I have been in communication with all the divinity Halls on the subject for I have never lost sight of it for one moment. I Have this day again written to Dr McLeod who has perhaps a more extensive acquaintance with Gaelic students than any other person. He feels most anxiously for St Kilda and from having been there he knows the kind of person that would suit. I am sure he will do what he can and I expect to hear from him soon ... I hope something may be done for St Kilda this year.'

At the same time Tawse sent a copy of the proprietor's letter to Dr MacLeod and asked: 'Can you help the poor St Kildites who I fear are every day [retrograding?]?' A negative answer came from Dr MacLeod in the second week of May, and the news was passed on to the proprietor. 'I am sure you will feel as deeply as both he [Dr Macleod] and I do,' said Tawse, 'the little prospect of getting a Missionary for St Kilda at present. All my hopes are disappointed and my worst fears realized for this year.' He had tried to catch a student just finished, 'but they were all secured before they were licensed and are all now provided for'; no amount of anxiety was going to help, and now Principal Dewar at Aberdeen was his last hope.[40]

On 3 June Tawse informed the directors that he had received 'a most pressing letter from Mr McLeod of St Kilda' regarding the appointment of a missionary, that he had 'used every endeavour to secure a proper person', and that Dr Dewar had a possible candidate. But this too came to nothing:

'In this remote Island nothing but Gaelic is spoken or understood, and it is this circumstance that has occasioned much of the difficulty in getting the mission supplied. The Directors expected that at the close of the College Session of this year [1852], the Society would have been able to secure for the Island, the services of some of the Gaelic Students, who they understood would by that time have completed their course of study and be ready for license. In this however the Directors have been disappointed, all the young men that have been licensed have received other appointments, and the Directors regret this the more, as they have every reason to fear, that in consequence of not having a stated minister among them, the Inhabitants of St Kilda are relapsing into that state of ignorance and irreligion, from which they had in a great measure been reclaimed, first by the labours of the late Dr McLeod [i.e. John MacDonald], and afterwards by the stated ministrations of Mr McKenzie... The highly respected proprietor of the Island, Mr McLeod, a staunch friend of the established church, has hitherto resisted every attempt on the part of the Free Church to get a footing on the Island, altho' they have every year visited St Kilda, and been too successful, it is feared, in alienating the attachment of the people from the established church.'[41]

Whatever 'relapsing' had taken place it can hardly have been into 'irreligion' since the islanders were still eager for missionary provision. But the SSPCK could do nothing about it. The proprietor appears to have come up briefly with a possible solution of his own, although the Society secretary, still hopeful at the time that Dr Dewar would secure a student, did not think much of it:

'With respect to your prospective plan, where all others fail, I considered your hinting it to me as being given in perfect confidence and therefore I have told it to no individual whatever, I see great difficulties in the way. The party you refer to would not take the Island. I do not think they either would or could pay any rent for it, and the people I fear, instead of being benefited would be quite the reverse and would be equally neglected as they have been.'

Later sentences in this letter contain dark hints of another, more drastic solution:

'If matters come to the worst, I think the best way would be for Government to come forward, and I think they only require a hint to do so – what a saving it would ultimately be to the Country. But the subject is a painful one.'

In the end Tawse was baffled. 'Surely there is some wise purpose, tho' to us unseen, in leaving these poor Islanders so long without a spiritual guide.'[42]

If the suggestion of Government intervention signified possible evacuation or at least partial emigration aided by the state, then it was not the first time the idea had occurred. The proprietor's notion that supporters of the Free Church might do well to leave the island was but the latest in a line of thought extending from at least the 1770s when the last MacLeod steward of St Kilda emigrated. It would therefore not be surprising if it was the dispute over the religious future of the island that brought 'government' into the picture in the shape of the Highlands and Islands Emigration Society with its offer to organise the people's emigration to Australia. Eight families, consisting of thirty-six inhabitants or about a third of the total population, chose to go, and on 13 November they left the country for ever. For about half their number the voyage was a disaster, many dying from measles contracted on the way and the rest while in quarantine in Melbourne.[43]

A writer in the Glasgow Herald at the time of the emigration said, without sympathy or understanding: 'we think the cause of humanity would be served if [emigration/it?] continued until all the inhabitants were removed from this barren rock'. Certainly more were thinking of leaving. At the beginning of 1853 the SSPCK directors were again unable to fill the vacancy at St Kilda because, as they claimed, 'The demand for Gaelic preachers had been so great both at home and abroad, that no sooner is a probationer licensed than he finds employment in situations more congenial than the remote Island'. They also mentioned, as if the event implied that their search for a missionary was now less urgent or important, 'that the population of the Island has this last year been considerably reduced, in consequence of about one third of them having emigrated last summer, and probably another portion may follow them next summer, but that may depend very much on the accounts received from those who have already left.' When these accounts arrived they were grim enough to remove thoughts of a further exodus.[44]

The established church was evidently unable to ask the parish minister of Harris or any other clergyman to visit St Kilda for a few days, since in all likelihood he would have received no hearing now from a community already leaning heavily towards the Free Church. This would have been a great embarrassment, as would similar treatment of a 'stated missionary' if one had been found. Perhaps this, as much as a lack of qualifications in Gaelic and the isolated nature of the mission, was a deterrent to potential candidates. John MacPherson MacLeod, however, may have detected in the SSPCK's continued failure to produce a missionary more than a touch of unwillingness to do so in the circumstances now prevailing. The Society's secretary had written to Dr

410

Norman MacLeod in April 1852: 'I am not surprised at his getting impatient about his unhappy Island... But unfortunately we cannot make Gaelic ministers.' Then, a few weeks later, he had said to Principal Dewar: 'The excellent Proprietor of the Island has hitherto resisted all the attempts of the Free Church – but his patience has been much tried.' Now that patience and the ability to resist were gone, and the proprietor wrote 'stating that the Inhabitants.. had for several years been without a Minister or religious instructor of any class from the Society, and there being no prospect of the Society sending one, and he believed that they would not now accept of even a regularly ordained clergyman of the Established church, the free church in the long interval, having got a footing in the Island and a hold on the people's affections from their ministrations among them. In these circumstances, and that the Islanders might be regularly supplied with religious instruction, he considered he might be justified in giving up the mission to that church, with the use of the church, Manse etc.' There was some delay, since before any such transaction the proprietor wanted to know what the Society thought about the matter, and 'how far the existing endowment of the mission could be available for the support of a Missionary or Catechist of the Free Church'. Whether the old mortification would be available to the Free Church was a question for the SSPCK's 'Law Committee'; but in the meantime the island, following the emigration and with a population thereby reduced from 110 recorded at the census in 1851 to around 70, could be considered as well on the way to being 'surrendered.. to the Free church'.[45]

411

CHAPTER 3

Duncan Kennedy, Free Church catechist, takes over duty in buildings made available at last by the proprietor and is visited by 'deputies'

THE Edinburgh Society for the Support of Gaelic Schools (ESSGS) sent Alexander MacKenzie to St Kilda as teacher in 1821 and kept him there for eight years. The Edinburgh Society did not consider itself as evangelical and the established church was its chief means of support, so difficulties arose when the Free Church came into being and nearly all the teachers employed by the ESSGS in the north were 'won over' by it. The ESSGS took no part in the disputes that followed but decided 'to pursue the even tenor of its way'. However at the annual general meeting on 9 February 1846, after some attempt at impartiality, the Free Church element secured control and so, according to those who objected, 'the narrow-minded principles of bigoted sectarianism' excluded the established church adherents from the Society. The last teacher to be connected with the Church of Scotland, John MacDonald at Bracadale, was dismissed because he refused to join the Free Church.[46]

As a result of this division the ladies associated with the established church side of the argument, some of whom had no doubt been members of the Edinburgh Ladies Association in aid of the ESSGS formed in 1817 with Mrs Stewart MacKenzie of Seaforth as patroness, now organised themselves into the Ladies Association in Support of Gaelic Schools. Patronesses included the Duchess of Athole, the Duchess of Sutherland, the Dowager Duchess of Roxburgh, Lady Vere Cameron of Lochiel, and others 'of high rank and interest'. Various Edinburgh ladies, with Miss Louisa McNeill of Barra and Miss MacLean of Ardgour, composed a general committee. The interests of the Association were confined to Gaelic-speaking areas and there was specific encouragement given to 'Female Schools of Industry'. Before long support in the form of modest grants was being given to schools at Lochbroom, Glenelg, Kintail, in Barra, and elsewhere.[47]

Not to be outdone in this respect, the ladies of the opposite faction formed the 'Association for the religious improvement of the remote Highlands and Islands in connexion with the Free Church of Scotland', otherwise known as the Edinburgh Ladies Highland Schools Association (ELHSA). Their first meeting was held on 18 December 1850, when the Hon. Augusta Mackenzie, of Castle Street, Edinburgh, was president, and the secretaries were Miss Abercrombie of York Place and Mrs MacLauchlan of Lauriston Place in the same city. The aims of the ELHSA were to increase and support charity schools, to assist promising young men in their studies for the ministry as long as they taught in the schools when students, to provide an agency for counteracting 'Popery', and to supply clothing for the poorest people, chiefly to enable them to attend church and school. A sister association came into being in Glasgow with a special interest in North and South Uist.[48]

Within a year or two there were thirteen ELHSA schools in the islands, four each in North Uist, Skye and Harris, and one in St Kilda. Numerous letters were received from ministers and their wives, catechists and teachers, 'with most affecting details of the destitution of the people, both temporally and spiritually - and the demands for clotheing were most urgent and touching'. In the spring of 1852 a bale of clothing was sent to Renigadale in Harris, the eighty school pupils aged between seven and seventy being the 'more [i.e. most] miserably clothed of all' seen by 'Rev. Mr McDonald Gaelic School Inspector'. A sum of £10 was donated for St Kilda and since 'Rev. Mr MacDougal of Raasay' was going to the island in June he took charge of the money. In due course MacDougall paid his visit in the company of Rev. Roderick MacLeod of Snizort at the very time that the proprietor was deciding to give in to the Free Church, and they examined the ELHSA school there, finding that 'through the instrumentality of the school every child in that remote island above the age of seven years is able to read the Word of God'. Of the population of just over one hundred, this being about three months before the emigration to Australia, forty-three attended for some part of the year, 'so that a very considerable proportion of the whole population availed themselves of the means of instruction with which they were favoured'. Thus well before the full admission of the established church's failure to serve the island either religiously or educationally, the Free Church had supplemented their deputations of ministers with a school which presumably met in the church or manse, neither of which was supposed to be available in 1852. The name of the ELHSA teacher was not recorded in the Association minutes, but was in fact Malcolm MacQueen, one of the St Kilda community.[49]

*

On Monday 30 May 1853 Mary Lady MacKenzie of Gairloch and her son Osgood aged 11, having hired a boat called the *Jessie*, set off on a voyage to St Kilda. They passed the north tip of Skye, crossed to Lochmaddy where they collected a pilot to guide them through the Sound of Harris, and then called at Obbe where they went ashore to visit the Ladies' Flowering Work School established by the Countess of Dunmore, whose son, aged only one year more than Osgood, was the proprietor of Harris. After a rough journey they reached St Kilda and landed on the seaweed-coated rock which served as a kind of slipway and jetty. Lady MacKenzie had heard gloomy stories about the difficulties of landing: 'I was told by the people that the last time the factor came to visit them he was three days before he could land. When at last he did accomplish it, it was by tying a rope round his body and throwing the other end to the people on shore, and waiting till one of the enormous waves went backwards, when he flung himself out and was drawn up on the flat rock, the usual landing-place.' When home again she learned from one of the *Jessie*'s crew that a man met in Poolewe had said: 'the last time I sailed there, when in the service of Macdonald of Lochinver, who had the islands, I was twenty days beating about and round St Kilda in the *Rover's Bride* and never could land at all'.[50]

As the MacKenzies came up the rock the island men gathered round, anxious to learn news of their friends who had gone to Australia, while Lady MacKenzie started to take note of features that caught her interest. She thought that there were 60 people left in the community, although the following year the number was given as 85. Appearance and dress evidently attracted her attention, and she remarked that 'Their persons and houses and everything belonging to them smell of fulmar petrel oil'. She was perhaps a bit put out when she failed to 'notice any of them bow or curtsey at any time'. Although she found the people 'kind and gentle in speech and obliging and friendly in actions', this did not 'prevent them from being keen for money and still more for tobacco'. They would apparently sell anything at a cheap rate for the sake of tobacco. It seems that any ELHSA teacher there had been had given up since none was there when the MacKenzies explored around, and the manse was kept locked except when the factor came and lived in it during the summer visits. In spite of the lack of minister, catechist and teacher, the people worshipped in the church every weekday evening except on Monday and Saturday, and again on Sunday 'before breakfast' and in the evening.

At the time of the Disruption the MacKenzies of Gairloch joined the Free Church. It is therefore not at all surprising that Lady MacKenzie spoke with Rev. James Noble, who was Free Church minister at nearby Poolewe, about his visit along with Rev. Thomas Pitcairn and others to St Kilda in 1848, and was given an account of that deputation's troubles when the *Breadalbane* was overtaken by 'a frightful hurricane' and at last reached Harris with its passengers 'thankfully wondering that their existence was thus preserved'. Perhaps Noble inspired her visit, and she and her son would have found it of great interest to be in St Kilda at the moment when it looked certain that the Free Church was having success in its attempt to win control of the island's church and manse as well as of its people.

The proprietor finally yielded in or about June 1853, and the Free Church's victory was celebrated immediately with the appointment of a catechist, Duncan Kennedy, born in Ardchattan parish, Argyleshire, and working as catechist in Tiree. Following an interview with him in July 1853 John MacPherson MacLeod 'made arrangements of a very favourable character' for his accommodation and the *Breadalbane* yacht, which some of the Free Church Highlands committee members wanted to sell, was assigned to take him out to the island. A deputation consisting of Rev. McGillivray and Rev. Findlater of Lochearnhead was to accompany him. All three men prepared themselves to leave early in August but the yacht was delayed and there was concern that if the journey was not made soon it would be too late. Although there was talk of hiring a different vessel if the *Breadalbane* was not ready by 15 August the party eventually left in the yacht, which set out from Oban on 1 September. Because of unfavourable winds it took them six days to reach their destination.[51]

Angus McGillivray opened his description of the visit tactfully:

> 'The proprietor, Mr McLeod, having, in the most liberal way, handed over to the Free Church, the church, manse and glebe, the Highland Committee appointed Mr Duncan Kennedy to be catechist at St Kilda. We took Mr Kennedy with us in the schooner, and, as the sea was smooth when we got to the island, our first work was to land him and his furniture. The poor people were delighted to see us, and they were particularly gratified by the arrival of the catechist. Nothing could exceed their expressions of gratitude to their landlord for putting the buildings at our disposal, and thus affording them the privilege of having a stated labourer among them.'

Having arrived on a Wednesday the deputation also began to prepare for communion. Thursday was kept as a fast day, with two sermons and the baptism of four children. Then the weather took a hand and spoiled the programme:

> 'The Loch of St Kilda is always an unsafe anchorage, and it is specially so in September during the equinoctial gales. It is an open bay, looking to the south-east, with high rocks on each side … When the wind blows hard from the south-east, it raises a tremendous sea, which no cable can stand, and yet from the high land all round you dare not take up your anchor after it has come on to blow. The wind comes in swirls and squalls, so that you cannot beat out, and you are sure to be driven on the rocks. Our excellent captain knew all this from former experience, having in 1848 snapped his cable and left an anchor in the bay. Finding, therefore, during Thursday night, that the wind was blowing strongly into the bay, and likely to increase, at five o' clock on Friday morning, he took up his anchor and put to sea. In taking this step he did not consult us, but we soon saw the kindness of God in leading him to act as he did. After beating about during Friday and Saturday, on Saturday night it came to blow very hard from the south-east, and at eight o' clock on Sabbath morning, we came to anchor on the Sutherland coast, in the midst of the heaviest gale of wind I ever was out with … Though thus driven off the island, we did not altogether lose our object. We preached to the people,

we baptized their children, and we left a labourer among them, who will, I have no doubt be active and useful.'[52]

In the meantime the SSPCK seemed doubtful as to its continued responsibilities, if it had any. Norman MacRaild applied in May 1853 for materials with which to carry out the next bout of repairs to church and manse, but he would get no answer until it was decided whether maintenance of the buildings was still the responsibility of the Society. There was also the problem of the furniture and other possessions of the Society inside the manse, and MacRaild wondered what was to happen in the event of a Free Church takeover. The secretary told him that nothing would until the mortification question was determined, but he indicated that if no established church missionary was sent the furniture should probably be auctioned.[53]

A year later the question was still unanswered at the time when MacRaild enquired again in the summer of 1854 about what should be done with the SSPCK furniture in the manse, 'the use of the manse having been given by the proprietor to a Catechist of the Free Church'. There being, however, a more definite situation he was authorised to dispose of it at valuation, getting what he could for it, 'but to send the Books to the Society except such as could be disposed of on the island'. Another, lesser battle between the two churches was about to begin.[54]

Aware that all their 'Stations' in the Outer Hebrides could be reached with the help of steamer communication now opened up everywhere except to St Kilda, the Free Church sold its yacht in February 1854 for £410, although it was still available the year after. A visit by the Free Church presbytery of Skye, in the person of Rev. Fletcher of Bracadale, was to go to St Kilda in 1854 but it proved to be impossible to arrange it so there was none that year, and the catechist, who reported favourably on his activities, had to wait longer for his salary. A letter from him came in March 1855 with news that repairs were again needed to the church and manse and that the SSPCK was laying claim to the furniture as the property of the established church. Messrs McGillivray and Findlater were about to sail once more as the annual deputation in the *Breadalbane*; they could therefore take away with them 'some of the less cumbrous articles' noted by Kennedy, and McGillivray would carry out an inspection of both furniture and buildings.[55]

In June 1855 the SSPCK secretary informed Norman MacRaild that there was no longer any reason why the Society should bear the burden of repairs, and 'he thought the least Mr Kennedy, the free church catechist, or his constituents, can do, when allowed to possess the premises, was to keep them in repair for the use of them, or pay a rent equal to what these repairs would cost.' There was no argument about this and the repairs were duly carried out by the Free Church. The furniture and the books, however, were a different matter, and kept the two sides in dispute for another two years.[56]

Duncan Kennedy said that he had a right to retain both furniture and books 'as they did not belong to the Society, but to the person who was in possession of the Manse', whereas MacRaild, who happened to be in the unfortunate position of factor combined with the SSPCK's only means of contact with St Kilda, was expected to remove these items and dispose of them or sell them to the Free Church. The Society advised the factor to tell Kennedy 'that he is in a complete mistake, and that his using and retaining the articles of furniture and Books in the Manse, which he was merely allowed to occupy by tolerance, was an unlawful act'. The articles and books were the Society's property, sent to the island at its own expense for the use of its own missionary, and when MacRaild next visited the island 'he would consider himself authorised to protect the rights and secure the property of the Society'. No one else was entitled even to use these possessions without the Society's consent. In spite of this firm message 'the Free Church Catechist still continued to possess the manse, and refused to deliver up the Books and the furniture' at the time when the factor was due to leave St Kilda towards the end of September 1855, and the issue dragged on into 1857 when MacRaild at last sold the books for 35s, 'which from many of them being in bad condition and old editions he thought was their full value'. Thus the SSPCK severed its final link with St Kilda and an association which had spanned nearly 150 years came to an end. In its place the Free Church assumed undoubted responsibility for the spiritual well-being of the community. Whether it would also look to temporal matters, as Neil MacKenzie had done, on behalf of the 'poor people' no one knew.[57]

*

The intention of the Free Church was to send 'deputies' to St Kilda once a year, and to begin with such visits were as regular as they could be given weather conditions and ministers' commitments. When McGillivray and Findlater were planning their visit in 1855 a letter was sent to the ELHSA 'requesting that some of the Ladies should go in the yacht with the deputation' and should take from the Association some donated bibles, catechisms and 'other useful things for the poor people there'. It is not known whether any lady went; if one did she would probably have spent most of the time at houses and at the 'school' taught by Duncan Kennedy. In 1856 Rev. Alexander Davidson from Manish in Harris tried twice to reach the island. On the first occasion in July the hired boat was forced by the weather to turn back. The second attempt was successful. A vessel called *Cornwallis,* 'going for the factor', left the Sound of Harris on Tuesday 2 September and arrived on Wednesday morning at 5 o'clock. The early stage of the voyage was calm but when they were nearing the island 'the gale was so strong that we were glad to get ashore after a good drenching from the wave on the lic', that is, the *leac* or landing rock. Davidson preached just after he had landed, and as this was again a communion occasion Thursday was a fast day. A 'Fellowship' meeting was held on Friday, 'following the example of the pious fathers in the Highlands'; a 'native' of St Kilda gave out the question and ten of the 'natives' spoke to it 'although wholly unaccustomed to public speaking'. There were 31 communicants on the Sabbath, including three young men and three young women for the first time. 'The St Kilda people,' thought Davidson, 'are very devout in public worship, and there is something peculiarly solemnising in their singing.'[58]

The school was examined. It had about 35 attending, of whom twelve were able to read English at different levels though they had only very limited reading resources, letters of the alphabet and old reports being used for want of more suitable school books. The fortieth chapter of Isaiah in Gaelic was read by 29 pupils, and 14 of them were 'very fair' writers. A praiseworthy showing was made of religious knowledge. At the end of the visit Davidson came away with £3.1s.7¼ d by way of a collection which, being from a place 'where money is so rarely seen', was considered 'truly a large sum'. He also had some suggestions to make. A supply of school books in English was evidently needed for 'the rising generation', and Gaelic bibles and new testaments were equally necessary for everybody. A female teacher to instruct in sewing and other branches of 'female education' was much required, and to enable Kennedy to devote himself to his catechist's duties. 'The services of an industrious and painstaking teacher for a twelve month would do much good among them.' It was almost certainly as a result of these latter ideas that Kennedy's niece Anne joined him in the island the following year.[59]

Davidson returned on Thursday 8 July 1858 after some delay owing to poor weather. 'On my arrival in the island, the leading men, Mr Kennedy, the catechist, and Neil Ferguson, the elder, expressed a wish that the sacrament of the Lord's Supper should be dispensed among them on the first Sabbath; at the same time expressing a regret that the time for giving notice to the people was so short, as many of them were then in the neighbouring rocks and islands catching fowls.' Parties of islanders were in Soay, Boreray and Stac an Armuin, but nearly all managed to reach home by the Saturday.

The sequence of communion days was interrupted surprisingly, not by any unexpected return of bird hunters but by the sudden appearance towards the close of Friday's communion 'exercises' of a boat bearing the established church parish minister of Harris, together with the teacher, catechist, and 'a gentleman from Edinburgh', all of them having come to see 'the natural curiosities of the far-famed St Kilda'. After recovering from their journey the visitors, or most of them, joined in the communion celebration.[60]

The Edinburgh gentleman was Thomas Muir, usually known by his initials as T. S. Muir. He had hired 'a small trading sloop' called the *Fowey* or *Foey* in Stornoway. It had a crew of three men, the skipper Kenneth

MacDonald, John MacDonald and Alexander MacKinnon. At some point the vessel was joined by the three men from Harris, the minister John Norman MacDonald, the parish schoolteacher James Stewart, and, perhaps most interestingly, Donald MacKinnon, a native of St Kilda, who was employed, said Muir, as 'minister's man' and was presumably the catechist in the party. If identified correctly MacKinnon was born about 1805, the eldest son of Ewen MacKinnon and Kirsty MacCrimmon. In 1838 he acted as Lachlan MacLean's guide through the St Kilda settlement when he was 'sub-tacksman'; and in 1877 Donald MacKinnon, 'a native of St Kilda' and 'an intelligent man of about sixty years of age', was 'precentor in the parish church of Harris'. He died in 1883.[61]

For much of his working life T. S. Muir, born in 1802, was bookkeeper to a firm of West India merchants in Leith, but he devoted himself to the study of Scottish church architecture and began publishing books on the subject in 1848. It was stated of him that 'Though possessed of a wide education, and able to mix in good society, Mr Muir became so absorbed in his favourite study as to be latterly a man almost of one idea'. His publisher, David Douglas, in Edinburgh said: 'His enthusiasm in his search for material was persistent. Semi-starvation, stormy seas, and obstacles of many kinds he gloriously endured to keep on his search. His journeys were made alone and on foot during his holidays – all too brief for the object to be crowded into them.' And now he was in St Kilda.[62]

He and his Harris companions had hardly arrived before they were washing themselves in a stream and then being taken to a house where they hoped to cook breakfast. Unable to see what they were doing they were about to give up when the catechist, Duncan Kennedy, 'a worthy man, whose easy hospitality quickly made everything lightsome and fluent', invited them 'down' to the manse. Here they met Kennedy's niece, Anne Kennedy, together with Alexander Davidson and Norman MacRaild. They would have liked to hear from Kennedy 'the story of his life amongst a people so little removed from a state of pure nature', but there was no time for that if they were going to attend communion services and explore the island. In spite of the claims of religious 'ordinances' they gave four islanders 'each a good day's wages' for an hour's demonstration on the cliffs – 'They had *once* got as many pounds as we were offering shillings for doing the same thing for a Lady Somebody, and what was there to hinder us from giving a like sum?' – and naturally Muir had to see the visible antiquities, to which he was introduced by Donald MacKinnon who guided him to the graveyard, 'the Amazon's dwelling', Tobar nam Buadh, and back to the manse where they all enjoyed 'barley-broth, mutton, and friendly glass of sherry'. As Muir concluded, 'we had got our glimpse of Hirt'; and the *Foey* sailed away.

The appeal of St Kilda to Muir's imagination was much less than that of Rona; and on his way back, after a call at Pabbay, he decided that 'Hirt may be the island to look at, but Pabba is the island to dwell in'. Thirty years later, in

419

1888, the intrepid Muir died, and was buried in Greyfriars churchyard, Edinburgh, where the ornamental gravestone can still be seen.[63]

*

The 1858 communion, attended so briefly by Muir and his Harris travelling companions, saw eighteen participate as communicants, some who 'communicated' in 1856 having 'kept back .. from conscientious motives', either because they had not had an opportunity of being present at the services until the Saturday or because they had been busy bringing others from 'the adjacent rocks and islands' while services were in progress. A communion set of cups and plate 'sent, along with other useful articles to St Kilda, by an anonymous Christian friend in Alves', was brought into use on this occasion, and at the end of the Monday service a collection totalling £2.17s.2½d was taken up in support of the Free Church's efforts in 'sending the word of life to perishing souls'. One child was baptised, the 'scholars' of the Sabbath school were examined, and 26 young people of both sexes read very well from the prophecies of Jeremiah. 'A box from Mr Drummond, Stirling, containing many of his own useful publications, together with a large lot of other books, chiefly schoolbooks from kind friends in that neighbourhood', was brought ashore and the whole load distributed among the islanders for their benefit.[64]

More immediately beneficial material arrived in 1859 when Norman MacRaild came out with slates and lime for yet more repairs to the roof of the church and of the manse, the work now being on behalf of the Free Church. After everything was completed the factor reported 'that the houses in St Kilda were in the best order', by which he seems to have meant the Free Church buildings there. However, an even more interesting communication was received a short while after MacRaild's. It was from the Admiralty, and in a way marked the beginning of a new and important phase in the involuntary progress of the island community.[65]

CHAPTER 4

The Kelsall Bequest, the Highland and Agricultural Society,
John Hall Maxwell, Betty Scott, and Captain Otter of the Porcupine

MANY unexpected events are to be found in any island's history but few
were more important to the fortunes of the St Kilda community than
developments around 1860, which were as usual, at least in their early stages,
completely unknown to those upon whom they were to have an impact. It
could be said that they began in the West Indies.

> 'In June 1857, the late Sir James Stuart Menteith Bart. informed the then
> Secretary of the Highland and Agricultural Society of Scotland … that an
> old friend of his Charles Kelsall Esq. of Hythe, near Southampton, had
> died at Nice in January 1857 and that he understood from the law agents
> of his Executors … that the deceased left a legacy to the Highland
> Society of Scotland for the purpose of distribution among the distressed
> inhabitants of some of the Western Islands. From the wording of the Will
> there was some difficulty about deciding whether the Highland and
> Agricultural Society of Scotland was meant, but the Vice Chancellor
> recognised the validity of the Society's claim ..'[66]

The Society secretary in 1857, John Hall Maxwell, noted that Kelsall had
been resident in the West Indies where in 1851, having heard no doubt of the
impoverished condition of the Highland and island people but having little
accurate knowledge of circumstances, he had drawn up his will and inserted
in it a bequest not to the Highland and Agricultural Society but to 'the Society
for the Improvement of the Highlands of Scotland'. The sum of £700, reduced
in the event to just over £602 after legal expenses were deducted, was to be
applied to 'the purchase of such articles and things' as might in the judgement
of the Society's treasurer 'be the most fitting for the Inhabitants of the Island
of Saint Kilda in the Hebrides regard being had to their situation, habits, and
wants'. The trouble was that no society as Kelsall described it existed, and
there was therefore a protracted legal argument between Kelsall's heirs, who
claimed that since there was no such society the bequest must lapse, and the
Highland and Agricultural Society, which asserted that it was the intended
body. A decision was eventually reached in the latter's favour, and the money
was at last remitted to the Highland and Agricultural Society of Scotland
(HASS) in May 1859 when it was deposited with the Royal Bank of Scotland.

Maxwell, as secretary, then had the responsibility of managing the 'Kelsall
Fund'. This was not a straightforward task as he himself remarked: 'The money
having been obtained, its proper and safe application presented the next
difficulty, it being obvious that £700 imprudently expended on a population

so limited in numbers, and so primitive in their wants, as that of St Kilda, might be productive of injurious consequences, not contemplated by the benevolent donor.' So thought was required, and advice from those already immediately concerned with the island. The first contact was therefore with John MacPherson MacLeod, proprietor, 'a gentleman who takes the warmest interest in its inhabitants, and whose knowledge of their position rendered his opinion safe and valuable'. A discussion with both MacLeod and his 'Overseer', Norman MacRaild, followed soon after in November 1859, the essentials of which 'conversation' Maxwell recorded in a memorandum.

He heard that the islanders were not short of food or clothing – 'these necessaries of life they enjoy perhaps in a higher degree than is usually to be met with in the Class to which they belong'. They lacked household furniture but since they had some money of their own and could 'by industry' get more 'it should be an object to induce them to obtain for themselves such articles as are within the scope of their own means'. No help was needed therefore in these directions, nor should any part of the fund be applied to education:

> '..in regard to their condition as to education, there is a Catechist on the Island belonging to the Free Church, slenderly qualified for giving secular instruction, but useful in that respect to the extent of the wishes of the inhabitants, and capable of teaching a little more than they care to learn. Hardly any of them speak English, but they can generally, if not universally, read the Gaelic Bible. They have no desire to make further literary progress; and no course appears to be open by which the Fund at the disposal of the Society or any portion of it could be applied to the purpose of improving their instruction. Indeed were it practicable, which it does not appear to be, to impart to them by means of that Fund a higher Kind of education, it may be questioned whether that would be a right use of it; for there is reason to think that the consequence would be emigration; and it must be remembered that the present object is to increase the comfort and happiness of the existing community, not to break it up by raising the ideas of its members above contentment with its position and to see them replaced from another part of the Hebrides by a set of people morally and socially inferior to them in their present state.'

Had the case for educating the islanders only to the extent of their wishes been approved in earlier days, for example in Alexander Buchan's time, few of them would ever have attended 'school' or learned anything; and the view that improved education would lead to emigration had long ago been expressed by those who wished to preserve the St Kilda inhabitants in their ignorance and to ensure that they did not break free from the control of unscrupulous masters. Now, deprivation, both educational and material, was seen by

Maxwell as advantageous since it helped to maintain on the island a people 'primitive in their wants' and economically undemanding. In both cases, though for different reasons, there was a need to keep the community where it was, but other forces were at work bringing drastic change and inevitably raising questions over what might be considered the nature of 'injurious consequences'.

It seemed to Maxwell that there were only two ways in which the Fund could be properly used. These were 'providing them with better dwellings and furnishing them with the means of hauling up their boats'. Before any step could be taken, however, the first essential was for a representative of the HASS to visit St Kilda, inspect the situation, and report. This duty fell to John Hall Maxwell, who was then faced with the problem of how to reach the island. He thought initially of the Northern Lights Commission's vessel, *Pharos*, and 'sounded several of my friends who are Members of that Board', but without success. The only alternative seemed to be a passage in the sloop which annually took Norman MacRaild, 'the Baillie', from Dunvegan, 'but an incident of recent occurrence made me unambitious of taking such a conveyance, while it ultimately threw in my way one, of a very different character'. This was the moment when the Admiralty, in the shape of the Hydrographic Survey, having written to the Free Church on much the same matter of transport, offered assistance in an undertaking which saw the HASS and the Free Church briefly join forces.

The 'incident' which deterred Maxwell from taking advantage of the factor's sloop had occurred in 1859 and was first reported by the Free Church Highlands committee:

> 'The Committee maintain a godly man constantly on that remote island who acts as Catechist and Teacher, and this year they expended about £60 on repairing the Church and Dwelling house, besides they appoint a minister as Deputy every year to visit the Island, to preach, administer ordinances, and perform marriages. They have to regret that this year although two ministers have been asked to go, neither of them has been able to accomplish it; indeed the Factor for St Kilda and the tradesmen employed by the Committee on repairing the buildings have been detained for weeks on the island by the total loss of the vessel which went for them, and until they were relieved by Capt. Otter, who kindly went in search of them.'[67]

Maxwell also described what he had heard about this unfortunate shipwreck:

> 'Owing to the want of secure anchorage off the Island, the Baillie is compelled to send his vessel back to Skye as soon as he lands, and in four

or five weeks she returns for him and the cargo of feathers - oil - cloth etc., which during that period he has been sorting and packing. Last year the sloop as usual sailed from Skye to fetch him back, but she failed to return, and after a suspense of some weeks, Captain Otter commanding H.M.S. Porcupine and in charge of the Survey of the Hebridean coasts was applied to, and kindly consented to go out in search of the missing vessel. On arriving at St Kilda, he found that she had been wrecked there soon after her arrival, that the Crew were safe, but that they and the Baillie were imprisoned to all appearance for the winter.'

Henry C Otter, whose name appears on many of the Survey charts of the period, was the principal officer of the Survey, then being conducted around the coasts of northern and western Scotland. For some years he commanded the *Sparrow* working along the edges of Sutherland but by 1856 he was on the east side of Lewis and in 1859 he was captain of the *Porcupine*, surveying the coastal waters of North Uist. At the same time Lieutenant, later Captain, Frederick W L Thomas, in the *Woodlark*, was carrying out the survey of the Atlantic coast of Harris and south-west Lewis. Both became deeply interested in the islands while they were in the area and afterwards. They watched and recorded birds, studied antiquities, and commented frequently on the people and their way of life. Otter seems to have had a real concern for the religious state of communities, while Mrs Thomas attached herself to the benevolent activities of the Free Church Ladies Association, particularly when it came to the provision of clothes and appropriate books.

It would seem that Otter had expressed some worry over the lack of communication, religious and otherwise, with St Kilda in 1859. As a consequence of his representation and its own sense of regret the Highlands committee agreed to ask the Free Church presbytery of Skye. 'within whose bounds St Kilda is', to provide a deputy for the spring of 1860, and the committee convener undertook to write to Captain Otter to enquire whether he would 'give a passage in his vessel to a minister in Spring to visit St Kilda'. Otter soon replied that he was awaiting a response from the Admiralty regarding 'the necessity of sending a Government vessel periodically to St Kilda', but, in the meantime, he was willing, if he was in North Uist the following summer, 'to run over with a minister to that Island in May'. The committee thought that Rev. Angus McGillivray should go along then, but when H.M.S. *Porcupine* set out he was not one of the party.[68]

The voyage had more than Free Church 'visitation' as its purpose. John Hall Maxwell was still looking for a means of reaching St Kilda when 'with no small satisfaction I received a letter from Mr McLeod in London stating that Captain Otter was about to return to Portree with his Ship, and being desirous of repeating his visit to St Kilda would be happy to carry me there in the end of May or early in June'. Mr MacLeod, the proprietor, was of course interested in the planned visit by Maxwell, to whom he had written a year previously giving his views on how the Kelsall Fund might be used in support of the islanders and suggesting improvement of dwellings and furniture, along with religious and secular education, medical aid, and the gift of a boat as the most worthwhile objects. Though Mr Macleod himself did not go Maxwell was delighted at the opportunity offered by Otter, and the HASS president, the Duke of Athole, wished to join the expedition. As Maxwell had to keep an appointment at Dumfries on 13 June and as no word of departure arrangements had come by the close of Thursday 24 May time seemed to be running short, but a letter from Otter arrived on Friday 25 May with instructions that Maxwell and the Duke should 'leave Glasgow by the Skye Steamer on the following Monday, so as to join the Porcupine, and sail from Portree in the course of that week'. Maxwell immediately telegraphed the news to the Duke, who travelled to Maxwell's home in Renfrewshire the next day.

*

The Duke of Athole was looking forward to his imminent adventure, and the Duchess, then in London, appeared to have a romantic wish to accompany him. 'I am glad your expedition to St Kilda is coming off soon,' she wrote on 22 May, 'as I think it will be very interesting.' Three days later he heard the news from Maxwell; it contained a slight change of plan, the intention now being to leave on Monday morning by coach and journey 'via Lochgoil and Inverary with a view to catch the Steamer at Oban and thus avoid that ugliest of all points on the west coast - the much dreaded Moill of Cantyre'. The Duke understood that he and the secretary would continue by steamer from Oban to Portree, where 'we are to put up at Capten Otter's House till Friday, when he will be ready to take us over to St Kilda in the Porcupine'. He had heard about the experienced captain: 'He has been I believe for some 10 years on the Trigonometrical Survey of Skye etc.' It was hoped that the party would be back at Portree on Tuesday 5 June, but as it was understood that a landing at St Kilda was only possible in 'a dead calm' this was uncertain.[69]

So the Duke left with high expectations: 'I intend if possible to sleep on shore at St Kilda but Maxwell says he thinks Captin Otter will not allow it as if it came on to blow I could not be got off, but we shall see, and I don't care if I had to rough it for a month or so.' It was also to be a sporting occasion: 'I have a Lancaster Rifle with me, and my big shot gun, so expect some fun among the Solan geese.' What Otter, or anybody else, would have done if the Duke had been forced 'to rough it for a month or so' is not known as no emergency arrangements were made to cover the situation if the Duke's speculation turned into reality.

The two representatives of the HASS met at Maxwell's house, *Dargavel,* a rather sombre looking mansion near Bishopton between Paisley and Greenock and later within the bounds of the Royal Ordnance Factory. They arrived in Oban and were pleased with themselves for having chosen the land route when they heard that the steamer, which came in on the Tuesday afternoon, had 'experienced a shocking passage' from the Clyde. 'The discomfort,' they learned, 'had been aggravated by the insufficiency of the vessel and by the entire absence of the commonest comforts and conveniences.' In spite of these drawbacks they had 'a pleasant passage to Portree where we found the Porcupine moored and we soon were, ourselves, at very comfortable anchorage in Portree House, the residence of Captain Otter, in whose Lady I was agreeably surprised to meet an old acquaintance'. On being told that the *Porcupine* would leave on Friday, 1 June, they spent the whole of Thursday exploring Glen Sligachan and Loch Coruisk.

The Duke found time while at Portree to make some purchases: 'Today I have been [buying] silk neck chiefs and small shawls, brooches, scissors, knives, combs, Teapots India Rubber Galoshes etc. etc. etc. (Tea I brought from Paisley) for the St Kilda people of whom I believe there are some 60, but no one has been there for a year so I do not know how they have fared this winter. I mean to buy some oil (which is ejected from the throat of a bird like a gull when attacked by anything (a <u>Fulmer</u> or <u>Foumart</u> I don't know) also some of the St Kilda sheep and perhaps a Cow.' He was already picking up, probably from Captain Otter, information about conditions in St Kilda, not all of them very promising:

> 'My Gun will be no use, as I fancy they do not like the birds being disturbed. The[y] catch them by noosing them round the neck with a hair at the end of a pole or Rod. We are likely to see all their modes of going to work. We shall also see some marriages, as the Free Church Minister is going with us. This I am sorry for as <u>we</u> would rather not have been mixed up with that set, tho' I see Captain otter is considerably leaning to that side. We are to sail at 7 on Friday morning and expect to anchor off St Kilda some time that night and spend three days there.'

It was therefore when going aboard the *Porcupine* at Portree that the two sets of passengers, HASS and Free Church, came together under the command of Captain Otter, and, as Maxwell recorded, they did not find each other's company too uncomfortable.

> 'As a fellow passenger we had the Reverend Mr Reid, free Church Minister of Portree, whom I may here dispose of as an agreeable gentleman, and a zealous, but tolerant and enlightened church man. His object was to administer the sacrament to the St Kildans, and to bring up the arrears of baptism and marriage, which it might be expected had

accumulated since they had last seen a Clergyman. Mr Reid carried with him a couple of ecclesiastical Aides de camp in the guise of Free Church Elders, one of whom was at once christened Judas by the crew … a long, lanky figure, a lanthorn jawed cadaverous countenance, a mouth destitute of teeth except a couple of fangs, an expression of sanctimony and self satisfaction, a long cloak and a black staple hat, all reminded me of the notorious <u>Men</u>, who exercise so unbounded and tyrannical a spiritual sway over the ignorant people of Sutherland and Caithness.'[70]

While on the subject of religion Maxwell also remarked on practice aboard ship:

'Captain Otter, one of the best of men, labours to disseminate religious principles and feelings among his crew, and, morning and evening, all hands are piped to prayer - on the morning of our departure service was conducted at 8 o' clock by Mr Reid, and consisted of a chapter, a prayer, and doxology, and repeated by him at 8 in the Evening; by that time, however, we were in the open sea, and he was obliged to abandon the attempt to read - for myself I felt it difficult to stand the motion of the Ship, with so many people crowded below decks, and though unwilling to absent myself I was unable, as the weather became worse, to participate in more than the first days services. I should state that these were not held merely because we had a Clergyman on board, they were the practice of the ship, and are uniformly conducted by Captain Otter. He is, besides, a total abstainer from the use of spirits, wine and beer, and labours to win his officers and men to the observance of similar self denial.'

The *Porcupine* departed at 8 a.m., and, rounding the north tip of Skye, crossed the Minch, entered the Sound of Harris and anchored for a short while at Obbe where the Duke got a dozen lobsters 'with a silver hook' and where a pilot, for the rest of the Sound especially, was taken on board. The vessel then made its way through the maze of channels between reefs, sandbanks and small islands, to spend part of the night off Vallay. 'It was not very easy landing at Valay in a small boat,' the Duke of Athole remembered, 'as the sea was running high, and there are a good many breakers and slippery rocks. Here we left the "Growler" a great big clumsy boat which we had towed all the way from Portree', and here too 'An Officer and 8 men were left in her to survey that part of the Coast.' The Duke and John Maxwell both went ashore for a while, and, as the Duke wrote briefly, 'visited a farm, picked up 3 Gentlemen and returned to sleep on board'. Maxwell noted things at greater length as usual:

'We found several gentlemen belonging to Uist waiting to welcome us, and with them proceeded to the Farm House of Valay, where tea had been prepared. I may remark that the Tenants of Uist are among the few remnants of the old Duihne wassel or Tacksman, gentlemen of good blood and descent, well educated, and holding large farms. Captain Mackay whose house we visited was absent with his company of Inverness Militia, but we were hospitably entertained by his mother and his Sister. On re-embarking, our party was reinforced by three of the Uist gentlemen, Mr Macdonald Tacksman of Balranald, Dr Macdonald a medic and also a farmer, and Mr John McD. Factor to the proprietor Sir John Orde by whom the Island was purchased a few years ago from Lord Macdonald. I had expressed to Captain O[tter], a wish that one or two gentlemen, well acquainted with the Hebrides, should give me the benefit of their local knowledge to aid my own judgement regarding the application of Mr Kelsalls bequest, and he had considerately invited the three by whom we were now joined. They proved of essential service, for without their assistance as interpreters we should have found ourselves unable to communicate with the natives.'

The evening had been fine, and Maxwell had enjoyed a first distant glimpse of St Kilda, with Boreray 'floating like a filmy cloud on the clear western horizon'. But when the *Porcupine* left the Sound of Harris soon after 3 a.m. the weather was worsening, and a north easterly gale was blowing as the ship approached the island. Most of the passengers were unable to eat breakfast, the three Uist gentlemen were 'in a very unhappy and helpless state', and only the Duke 'was in a normal state'. In fact 'the worse the weather became the more he did eat'. Maxwell was not impressed by his first view of the St Kilda scene, for to him 'the jagged precipices on our left, the bluff barren mountain to our right, the uncouth looking wigwams before us, the scanty vegetation, the heavy sea outside, and the scurrying mist which veiled the higher portions of the Island combined to produce a singularly wild cold and inhospitable effect'. Of course Maxwell was feeling poorly after the voyage, whereas the Duke, breakfasted and eager to go ashore, was business-like as ever:

'It was a wettish morning and St Kilda's tops were in a mist, but still it was very grand. Captain Otter, Mr Maxwell and I landed, the boat being partly dragged up the shelving rock by the St Kildians who flocked down the stony ground, and set to work shaking us by the hand. We saw nothing at first but men and a few children. We went up and inspected some of the houses, saw a few women and lassies but the most of them were away up in the Glen milking the Cows and Sheep.'

The usual visitors' routine was followed - handshaking, house inspection, and climb to the cliff edge for a demonstration of fowling. The Duke had been pleased to discover that Mr Reid was a local Perthshire man: 'the Free Church Minister who went with us is the Minister at Portree - Mr Reid (from Ballechin) so we got on very well'. The Free Church group landed about 11 o'clock in the morning, and after being greeted announced a prayer meeting for 12 noon. When the bell was sounded to call the people to church no one came because the women were not back from their milking and the men would not attend without them. So the service was delayed until the evening, and the visitors watched the cliff-climbing. Maxwell also had time to ask the resident catechist, Duncan Kennedy, some serious questions. 'How long is it since there has been a Marriage?' 'Nine years.' 'How many marriageable but unmarried pairs may there be?' 'Eight or nine.' 'How many illegitimate births have occurred within the nine years?' 'One - but the woman was herself illegitimate and the daughter of a Stranger.' These matters seem to have been outside the planned scope of Maxwell's HASS duty in the island, but his next task, drawing up a census of the island from information supplied by Kennedy, was much more relevant.

The prayer meeting, which began at 5 o'clock and was intended to conclude at 7, lasted four hours. It was followed by an even distribution of various presents brought to the island, in particular the tea, sugar, tobacco, snuff and clay pipes. In order to do this Maxwell and the Duke went from house to house, accompanied by their interpreters and two seamen who carried the baskets of goods. 'On our return along the row of Houses, we had the satisfaction of seeing each man at his door blowing a cloud from his new pipe.' They then went back on board the *Porcupine* for the night.

The next day, Sunday, 'all the passengers, except the Duke, rose in a very seedy state' and could make nothing of breakfast. 'His Grace' alone ate heartily and was able to 'stomach a long service in the fore part of the vessel'. Reid and the elders, together with the Uist gentlemen, had slept in the manse, and Maxwell and the Duke went ashore again to attend communion in the church, 'all in Gaelic'. Maxwell, not understanding the language, was not present at all the proceedings but described what he saw:

'When the hour for service approached I took up my position at the Church door to see the congregation enter; the men first came down in a body, and the women followed. It may be supposed that to a people of strong religious impressions who had not seen a clergyman for three years, the occasion was a solemn one, and this was strikingly apparent in the deportment of all. Each entered the Church in the deepest silence and with the most reverential demeanour. Women who had been freely chattering to us half an hour before now uttered no word, but approaching the Duke and me, with folded hands, and downcast eyes, each in her turn made a low bow or obeisance and silently glided into the little Church. Presently some of the intending Communicants re-appeared on their way to the catechist's house, which adjoined, to obtain their tokens. We asked one of the women as she returned to show this to us, and it is impossible to describe the solemnity with which she complied or the reverential awe with which she gazed on the token while in our hands, or the deep sigh of relief with which she received it back. As the service was to be a long one, and of course in Gaelic, I would not benefit by it, and, ascertaining about what time the communion would take place, I started on an exploring walk.'

Nothing could better illustrate the influence of the Protestant church, in any of its several evolving forms, than that little scene of the communion token. For a century and a half St Kilda's children had been faced by the incomprehensible questions of the catechist and had given automatic answers if any at all. For a century and a half St Kilda's adult community had been led by preachers whose sermons must often have seemed equally baffling and yet emotionally persuasive. No doubt, long before, the ancient religion had been just as mysterious, mystifying and impressive. And now one of those poor, simple, easily-moved natives gazed with 'reverential awe' on a small, grey, squarish piece of lead lying in the palm of a hand. It might be compared to the 'two Idols kept by McNeill of Barra' which Martin MacPherson was told to destroy long ago, or to the vanished crucifix.

When John Maxwell returned from his walk in the mist among the innumerable 'Store Houses' on the hills above the bay, he 'arrived at the Church before the Communion service had commenced'. His description of the service resumed:

'In addition to the Inhabitants there were the passengers, and the Highland portion of the Crew, and the little building was filled. I managed to get a seat close to the door, and too close to Miss Christie McLeod the Idiot, who insisted on patronising me and offering me a share of her Gaelic Bible which neither of us was capable of reading. Mr Reid, when I entered, was exhorting the congregation preparatory to administering the Sacrament, and the scene was one of no small interest, more particularly in connexion with revivalism. Had he been like too many of his class he could easily have returned to Skye with accounts of the wonders he had worked, and the revival he had stimulated. The work was ready to his hand, but to his credit he would not take advantage of the excitement under which many of these before him labored. He strove on the contrary to calm and soothe them, and did not proceed with the Communion till he had succeeded in doing so. I, of course could not understand him, but his tone and demeanour clearly showed what his object was, and my impressions were confirmed afterwards by the Uist gentlemen. Notwithstanding his creditable conduct, we were in expectation of hearing "the cry" at any moment and of being required to carry out some of those affected. The class who were so corroberated all the most reliable [accounts?] of such scenes. The weaker the intellect, the greater was the emotion. There was none visible among the men - comparatively little among the married women, a few of them were moved, but many of the Girls were bending and twisting their bodies, and groaning piteously. It may seem irreverent to record it but it is perfectly true, that, of all present, my neighbour Miss McLeod was most saturated with revivalism, and had the movement been encouraged by the preacher, she was the first who would have required assistance.'

Towards the end of the service a message came that the sea was rising and that it would be wise to return to the *Porcupine* as soon as possible. Some of the shore party went off again to revisit the houses but while there a boat came in with Captain Otter himself in charge and with difficulty took off Lieutenant Dent who made a safe jump and John Maxwell who was half submerged and had to be pulled out of the water. Meanwhile the minister, the three Uist gentlemen, one or two officers and about fifteen men were left on the island, along with the Duke who wanted to stay there anyway. Some provisions and dry clothes were packed into canvas bags and thrown into the sea to be pulled out onto dry land as quickly as could be managed. That night all but the Duke and Mr MacDonald of Balranald 'slept in and about the Manse' while those on board, apart from Maxwell, attended another service of 'great length' in 'the close atmosphere of the Mens quarters' before retiring to an uneasy sleep. The Duke and Mr MacDonald as interpreter 'went and slept on the floor of one of the Cottagers', thus fulfilling the former's declared ambition although they had to lie, as Maxwell put it, 'in an atmosphere as offensive as peat smoke, and the odour of oil, feathers, and birds could make it'. Even so, 'His grace, whom no roughing nor discomfort can disconcert, was delighted at having accomplished his object. I suspect however that Balranald by no means enjoyed his nights rest, and indeed I believe he kindly ventured into such quarters only out of consideration to the Duke, knowing that without an Interpreter he could not communicate with his hosts.' The house graced by the Duke belonged to Malcolm MacDonald, whose wife, Betty Scott, was an exceptional figure in the island community.

*

Elizabeth (Betty) Scott came from the mainland in the early 1830s, perhaps with Neil MacKenzie, and married Malcolm MacDonald on 20

431

September 1834. It has been said that she came from the parish of Assynt in Sutherland, this information presumably being derived from the census of 1851, in which it was stated that she was born in Assynt, and of 1861 where it was recorded that her birthplace was Lochinver, the settlement in which Donald MacDonald, tacksman of St Kilda from 1831, carried on some of his business. In the former year her age was given as 35, and even though this might be approximate it would place her birth around 1816. There seems to be no record of her baptism in Assynt; but on the other hand Betty Scott, 'a bastard', was baptised on 1 July 1816 in the parish of Lochbroom which borders with Assynt, and she was most probably the Betty who moved to St Kilda as a teenage girl. When baptised this Betty was at Ridorroch, near Ullapool, and her father would very likely have been one of the shepherds who migrated north from the Borders at that period. As a shepherd he could well have lived in some lonely dwelling on the edges of Assynt or struck up a relationship with some girl who did.[71]

In 1835 Malcolm and Betty had the first of their fourteen children, and in 1860, by which time all but two had died, she entertained the Duke of Athole and his interpreter. 'Betty our Landlady was the only one on shore who could speak English; her Family consisted of Husband, son, and daughter, 3 dogs, 1 Puppy and 3 Cats. Our bed, i.e. the Interpreters and mine was some hay and sheets and blankets that had never been used. They wished to give us their beds but we did not wish to turn them out. The daughter slept out at a neighbours.' The Duke got on well with his hostess and sympathised with her in her loss: 'My friend Betty 42 years of age has had 14 children, 5 stillborn 7 dead in 8 or 9 days and 2 now living. Supposed Mothers milk too strong from the Fulmar diet etc.' The two surviving children were Neil, baptised in October 1839, and Ann(e), born about 1841, who was later to become servant or housekeeper in the manse.[72]

After his interesting night the Duke woke to quieter but still misty and wet weather. Maxwell came ashore and the remaining presents were distributed. 'We did our best to observe the strictest impartiality, and to regulate our gifts as far as possible by the numbers and wants of each family, but as we could not give to all alike, all, I apprehend, were not equally pleased. Indeed, I fear, that by the time our [baskets?] were emptied, our primitive freinds had not been improved, and that the Dukes well meant kindness had sown the seeds of a certain amount of greed and envy among them.' Some got tin teapots, and some did not. But whatever sense of injustice there was gave way that Monday to the excitement of two baptisms and a marriage.

One baptism was of an infant daughter in the family of Norman Gillies. 'Mr Reid of course conducted the proceedings in Gaelic, naming the child after Captain Otter's Lady, and after the service was over the eldest child, a girl of 5½ years old, read passages from the Bible with a fluency and accuracy which amazed the minister.' Thereafter the little girl was officially known as Mary Jemima Otter Gillies and lived to marry Finlay MacQueen in 1884, but

Betty (Betsy) Scott and her son Neil Macdonald (c1860)

her mother died in 1863, apparently of tetanus. The wedding was an extremely last-minute affair. When Maxwell had first landed in the island he had been surprised to find that even though there had been no marriages for nine years no one wanted to be married. Now, after the last communion service, Mr Reid was ready to leave, but there were moves afoot to bring about at least one wedding before he did so. There were indeed, according to Maxwell, eight or nine unwedded couples of marriageable age, though whether they were 'couples' wanting to marry was not said. 'The fact is that none of the men can marry till his father, by dying, leaves the coast clear for him. He must have a house and a few articles of furniture - a croft - and a Cow. The present dwellings are so circumscribed in point of room that it would be impossible, under any arrangement however rude, to accomodate a second establishment. There are no means, from want of wood and necessary fittings, to erect more houses; if there were they would be unplenished, for the primitive stock of paternal furniture and utensils is certainly unsusceptible of subdivision. In like manner the crofts are inadequate for one family, and cannot be parcelled. Therefore ...the rising generation must practice celibacy while their fathers are on the scene.' Most young men were, it seemed, in this unenviable situation, but there was one exception, Malcolm Mackinnon, aged about 30, 'whose father was dead, and whose mother was willing to turn out in favor of a bride, and join another old woman in house keeping'. There was, however, a rumour that Malcolm had been the father of the one illegitimate child born, supposedly to a Harris woman, within the past 24 years, and he was therefore shunned by potential wives. Maxwell claimed that he and the Duke, having made some investigation, persuaded Mr Reid that Malcolm was innocent, and on Monday morning Reid restored the young man to 'Church privileges'. This made all the difference, and all Malcolm had then to do was choose a bride. This he did, she accepted, and, as the Duke wrote, 'at 3p.m. on Monday the parties had not made up their minds and by 5 all was over. Rapid work; I placed a neckerchief round the Bride and Bridesmaids necks in Church and kissed the Bride'.

These were the ceremonies attended by the distinguished visitors on their last day at St Kilda. More presents were given on each occasion, and all were joyfully received. Immediately after the wedding the majority of the strangers embarked once more and spent the evening on board the *Porcupine* discussing their experiences, but the Duke, who would have liked to spend another night on the island lingered behind until summoned by Captain Otter who was afraid that with weather worsening again he might have to leave him behind. 'I had to bid them a hasty farewell, dispose of the remainder of my presents, and go on board.' At 5a.m. the ship left, reached Rodel soon after mid-day, and so pleasant was the journey thereafter that the Duke, with happy recollection of his adventure, told his wife: 'I should like to return there with you this year in the beginning of August which is their season for going down the Rocks - they do not like to disturb the birds now as they are sitting.' It seems, however, that St Kilda had no further visit from the Duke or the Duchess.

*

The return from St Kilda brought with it reflection and reminiscence. When the *Porcupine* reached Rodel Rev. Reid and Captain Otter 'passed the afternoon on a missionary expedition'. The Duke went off to shoot seals and was unsuccessful. The Uist MacDonalds made for home, and Maxwell inspected 'the fine old ruins of Rodel Church - once half military half ecclesiastical, now roofless, and celebrated for the sculptured tombs which it contains'. When the vessel arrived at Portree on Wednesday their own expedition 'was wound up in the Evening by a Dinner Party given in the Hotel by his Grace and myself to the Officers and to excellent Mr Reid'.

Maxwell was one of those who, after a visit of only three days, concluded that the inhabitants of St Kilda were fortunate in living an almost ideal life, given the 'class' to which they belonged:

'A philanthropist contemplating a community, limited in number, secluded from the world, deprived of all the aids of Ecclesiastical [and?] judicial establishments, of medical advice, and of all but the barest necessities of life would, at first, counsel their removal to some more civilized and accessible spot. But on closer acquaintance with the people, I apprehend that he would pause ere trusting to their Exodus, and ask whether it would surely tend to the increase of their prosperity and happiness or to the elevation of their moral and religious qualities. Ask the simple Islanders and the response will [be] a prompt and direct negative. They adore their rock; they regard it as their world; they look with a certain suspicion on all beyond it, and many circumstances have concurred to produce this impression. Any act of immorality that has occurred in the Island has proceeded from some one with imported blood ... In short, I found but one family who could have been tempted to emigrate - and that under special circumstances - its commanding officer was not the father but the mother. She had been born in Harris, and could speak English, and moreover the temptation was great - an offer by the Duke of employment and protection. For my part, I think the people are right, and I would be loth to assume the responsibility of moving them. With all their great disadvantages they are the happiest, the most contented, orderly, moral and religious Community, which it has ever been my lot to encounter. It is true that they want many of what elsewhere would be regarded as the necessaries of life, that they are ignorant of its most Common luxuries, that they are wretchedly housed, and are frequently short of vegetable and farinacious food. Still in other respects they are better off than many others in the same class. Their

435

labour is light, their rent is nominal and paid chiefly in kind, they know not the tax gatherer, they are clad in the produce of their own sheep and looms far more comfortably than their neighbours in the Hebrides and West Highland coast, and though their food is peculiar it is generally plentiful for, what with flesh of fowl and sheep, few poor people can afford to gratify Carnivorous tastes to the same extent as they.'

Three months later James Reid wrote to Maxwell that 'the poor St. Kildians suffered much by the late terrific and disastrous storm. Their houses were unroofed, their crops swept into the sea, and their boat broken to pieces'; and three years later Betty Scott and seven young men of the island had all been lost on their way to Harris.[73]

As secretary to the HASS John Hall Maxwell inevitably paid particular attention to those aspects of St Kilda life towards which he had been directed by the hints in the proprietor's letter of May 1859, so his general remarks after his visit followed along the same lines. The people were contented, led an easy existence, and had plenty of food. But he noticed the 'stranger's cold' or 'cough': 'Our own case was one in point. We had no influenza among us, but after our departure it broke out, and nowhere so virulently as in the hut where the Duke and Mr Macdonald slept.' He also commented on the infant mortality, assigning its cause not to 'the unventilated hovels' nor to the diet of the mothers, but, bluntly, to a simple and basic situation: 'in the absence of medical assistance the weakly die, while the strong live'. The problem brought with it, in Maxwell's view, an important advantage: 'In one respect, this loss is providential; did the ordinary proportion of the children according to births survive the Island could not support its Inhabitants irrespective of prospective increase, its resources would be insufficient to maintain the existing families had there been no such losses among them.'

As always with the visitors' accounts of St Kilda and its community there was something unreal, vain and condescending about Maxwell's version of the people's feelings and practices. He can be imagined fitting in an 'expedition' to the island before he had to be back for his meeting in Dumfries, becoming seasick, questioning the catechist, attending services which he could not understand, going into houses with his interpreters, looking down on Mrs Gillies with her baby on a pad of straw, half falling in the sea, getting rather lost in the low cloud that scudded across the island hills, achieving no direct communication with any of 'the natives', and in the end setting on paper, with a view to the application of the Kelsall Fund, what he knew to be the needs of the islanders. But at least he saw the place for himself and made some useful observations, including his 'census' of the population.[74]

On the mainland the Duchess of Athole was not alone in having only the vaguest of notions about the remote island. On 2 June 1860, the day that her husband landed there for the first time, she wrote in a letter to the Duke for him to collect at Portree: 'I like out of the way places. I hear there are only 37 inhabitants and no babies - is that true? and that all the inhabitants catch cold when anyone lands from Britain!' Now the Duke knew better. He had discovered the lack of children and the cold infection for himself, and he wrote that there were '20 Families in all and out of these 124 children have been born 84 of them dead within 8 or 9 days after birth'. He had found that the people were 'very good looking with beautiful large eyes', but when he was there 'They had all got the Influenza from some fishermen from Harris who got there 10 days before us. They always catch cold from open boat parties from Harris but do no[t] fear any other vessels but the open boats. They are a very intelligent people.' In several ways the Duke's sympathy with the poor people seems evident and as he was HASS president this can only have been beneficial when it came to allocating sums from the Fund.

The third principal figure in the *Porcupine*'s adventure to St Kilda in June 1860 was Captain Henry Otter himself. He had been there before, his affection for the people had grown as he got to know them, and he too made comments in the form of a letter to Captain Washington of the Admiralty after the voyage was over. Suggesting the fascination that the island had for him it gave a down-to-earth account which covered nearly all aspects of the visit and indicated what he believed would be sensible improvements to life there.[75]

'On the 1st June the president and Secretary of the Highland [and] Agricultural Society ... having arrived I proceeded with them and Mr Reid, Free Church Minister and 2 Elders to St Kilda, leaving Lieut. Hawes at Vallay with a boat and crew to commence the Survey of the West side of North Uist. I arrived at St Kilda at 10 a.m. next day. On landing I found there had been no communication since my visit last year except a boat from Harris which was then engaged fishing with long lines; she had been fairly successful in Ling, Cod and Turbot and Skate, but the great drawback was the difficulty in communicating with the shore and in hauling up their boat. The only landing place is at the edge of a sloping rock on the N.E. side of the bay which is steep to at low water, and whenever the boats bow touches the shore, the inhabitants lay hold and pull her up above the reach of the sea - but the risk is great and frequently found impracticable - indeed one night whilst there we were obliged to leave a number of our party on shore in consequence.

'The only means of improving the landing would be to clear out an indentation amongst the rocks, which at present is filled with large stones, and erect a crane on the cliff above which is only 30 feet high, and so hoist the boats up above the reach of the sea. I believe this, if found to answer would be one of the greatest benefits that could be conferred on the people, as it would give them much more confidence in visiting the adjacent Islands, would encourage them to prosecute the fishing and enable them to obtain for manure, a limited quantity of seaware which grows upon the rocks.

'The Secretary I believe intends to recommend the Committee of the Agricultural Society to expend £100 for this purpose. The number of people at present on the Island is 83 inclusive of the men of the Harris fishing boat: 16 of them have families out of which no less than 85 children have died chiefly before they were 9 days old. A list of the inhabitants is enclosed. Upon the whole they are well off, each family keeps 1 or 2 cows and a few sheep besides a common stock of several hundred of the latter on Boreray and Soa - but their chief source of wealth and food is the birds which frequent the perpendicular (and to any but a St Kildean) inaccessible cliffs for breeding. Of these the Fulmar is the most valuable and is not found on any other part of Great Britain - like all the genus Procilaria, it produces a quantity of clear pinkish coloured oil which it spits out on any appearance of danger and to prevent this wasteful expenditure of what helps to pay their rent the cragsmen are provided with a long fishing rod having a noose at the end which is dexterously slipped over the unsuspecting Fulmar and after he has been permitted to spit out his rage into the stomach of a Solan Goose ready prepared for the purpose, his neck is wrung and he is then turned to the 3 fold use of providing feathers for the factor, winter food for themselves and grease to enlighten their dark dwellings. This bird only lays one egg and if taken or disturbed seldom produces another, so that each person is very jealous lest their portion of the Cliff should be disturbed in the breeding season. The next bird in value is the Solan Goose which inhabits Boreray, Stack Lee, and Stack an Narnan. The young are taken and salted down for winter food in the same manner as the Fulmar, Puffin, Hawk (Alca Torda) Puffin, Stormy Petrel (3 kinds) and Shearwater which are all found on these islands and used as food.

'I ascertained that about 10,000 Fulmars and between 2 and 3000 Solan Geese were salted down every year - besides those eaten fresh, and yet there is no diminution of their number but rather an increase particularly in the former. These with a little barley meal, potatoes and occasionally salted mutton, form their daily food - nearly the whole of their clothes are manufactured by themselves and generally they are well and warmly clad and shew much good sense in preferring the useful to the ornamental, invariably selecting plain warm woollen shawls to gaudy silk ones when offered their choice by the Duke of Athole. The whole population appears to be deeply influenced by religious feelings and their conduct to be in keeping with it. Whenever the subject of Religion is mentioned, the tone of voice and manner, become most reverential and they spoke of the services of Mr Reid as being most welcome to them.

'Theiving is unknown and there has only been one illegitimate child during the last 20 years. Family prayer is daily held in every house and the greatest care is taken to teach the children to read, one child of 6 read the Gaelic bible with perfect fluency - another of 4 was learning and with the assistance of Mr Kennedy the good Catechist who lives on the Island, the parents find no difficulty in perfecting their children in this essential part of education, but one can write and only one speak English - their Gaelic is said to be very pure and rather resembles that of Harris from which place in all probability the Colony was derived. Only one marriage was celebrated during our stay, the first for 9 years, and two children were baptized, one 9 days old which appeared to be doing well. 'The people are very cleanly in person and manners but their houses are worse than any I have seen in the Highlands - no aperture whatever is allowed for the smoke to escape, the soot lies 2 or 3 inches thick on the rafters and everything is impregnated with it, rendering it nearly impossible to discern any object in the dwelling. This inconvenience is submitted to, in order that the soot may be saved for manure and yearly the black straw from the inside of the roof is pulled out and an additional quantity laid on the top. To each house is attached a barn or store which is erected opposite the door to defend them from the wind and in this is deposited their manure, ashes, and pickled birds.

'It was proposed by the Secretary to build new houses more commodious in size, which proposition gave great satisfaction and they all agreed to put up the walls themselves.

'The quantity of arable land is about 25 acres but their system of agriculture is said to be very defective and much more might be produced by a proper succession of crops and a different plan of manuring. The most difficult thing to obtain is fuel; for this purpose the ground is pared and the turf when dry, stored in narrow houses, built for the purpose. It is said that peat exists in 2 or 3 places but the distance is too great to carry it. The weather was wet and stormy during the 3 days of our stay, and fog hanging over the island prevented my making any observations from the top.

'Tomorrow I propose leaving this to commence the triangulation of the Island of Rum, accompanied by the Seagull.'

Captain Otter's main conclusion as regards improvements related to the landing place and this coincided with Maxwell's opinion that 'the first and most needful article was a sea worthy and well appointed boat', and that a new boat would be wasted if there was no improved landing place. Education and religion could be left to the Free Church. As for new houses, Maxwell considered that the Kelsall Fund was not sufficient in itself to provide the means of erecting them, but he thought 'that much good might be effected by building outhouses for the cattle, and thus increasing the existing accomodation and by inlarging the windows and improving the ventilation'. Moreover the proprietor, while having suggested a boat in the first place and no doubt approving of the necessity for a better landing arrangement, had some reservations regarding the provision and expense of improved dwellings. What emerged at this point from the 1860 'expedition' was a twofold pattern of involvement at St Kilda which was to last as long as the island was occupied by a native population. On the one hand an increased array of outside interest, stemming from the proprietor, the HASS, and from an unpredictable and miscellaneous set of so-called 'philanthropists', took charge of the islanders' material welfare, whether they wanted it or not. And on the other hand the Free Church, principally concerned with matters of spiritual importance, maintained a missionary presence and influence, while at the same time doing what it could to provide some sort of basic education. For a few years Captain Otter acted as a link between material and spiritual branches, and the people of St Kilda, happy to receive gifts of any kind, now looked forward to the arrival of the next yacht or steamer from the 'outside' world as eagerly as they would to the appointment of a new minister. Whether all this would have, or had already had, 'injurious consequences' would soon become clear.

For the present neither the HASS, with its Kelsall Fund, nor the Free Church took any responsibility for dealing with the 'boat cough' or 'stranger's cold' and the dreadful mortality of infant children, and neither body sought to arrange for the 'medical aid' suggested by John MacPherson MacLeod. However both troubles were, like the islanders themselves, made subjects for more serious study, and the days of dismissing the cold as a myth or a foolish piece of native imagination were past. It was not the Free Church which thought that the deaths of infants were a providential form of birth control suited to the size of the island, and after another thirty years it was an individual Free Church minister who took the first, successful steps to eradicate what Neil MacKenzie, entering the loss in his register, called the 'eight day sickness'.

CHAPTER 5
Storms, losses, and disputes

THE year 1860 was an unusually busy one at St Kilda, in that the ordinary round of daily life was interrupted by an exceptional number of unexpected events. Ten days before the *Porcupine's* visit in June the Harris fishing boat had arrived, perhaps not so unusual; then ten days after, there came the *Falcon*, 'a cutter-yacht of twenty-five tons', hired to convey Dr John E Morgan and a friend to the island. The brief call took a now well-worn course, from 'natives' rushing into the sea to haul the small boat ashore and shaking hands to the rather hurried departure under threatening skies. In the manse the visitors met Duncan Kennedy, 'a man of very interesting appearance and address who spoke most feelingly and kindly of the poor islanders'. He was still schoolteacher as well as catechist, took services each Sunday, and kept the new registers of baptisms, marriages and deaths. Morgan also happened to come across Betty Scott, 'smart, energetic, talkative, and shrewd' as he described her, and so he heard the story of the Duke of Athole and the wedding. A few hours later he and his companion were gone.[76]

Another party during the same summer included Lieutenant F W L Thomas, abandoning for the time his survey work, and his assistant, Mr H Sharbau (Sharban?), who had, 'by the courtesy of Captain Otter, an opportunity of visiting St Kilda in 1860'. When there Thomas took possibly the first photographs of islanders, including one of 'Euphemia Macrimmon', who

Euphemia (Effie) MacCrimmon (c1860),
some of whose information about St Kilda was sent to
F W L Thomas, and some recorded by Alexander Carmichael

at an age given incorrectly as 60 was described in 1862 as 'the oldest woman in St Kilda'. He too met Duncan Kennedy and subsequently sent him 'a string of questions .. on points of antiquarian interest', but instead of receiving answers from the catechist he got them from Anne Kennedy, Duncan's niece, who had been on the island, perhaps intermittently, for at least four years helping out as sewing teacher. The letter sent by Anne, dated 9 April 1862, contained traditions of the island which she had been able to collect from a people who, after many years of devotion to a body of biblical stories, might well have put them out of mind. Most of her collection came from Euphemia MacCrimmon, who told of 'a temple in Boreray built with hewn stones', one of which, still in the ground where the temple had been situated, had some writing on it, of an underground house called 'Tigh a Stalair', and of 'Dugan and Ferchar Mor' who destroyed the people in 'Teampull na Trionaid'. The photograph of 'Effy' leads away from the dry present, beyond the years of the Free Church, the revival, and the preachings of ministers to a distant and deep world of knowledge and belief that once filled the minds and imaginations of the inhabitants of Hirt, and was yet part of an old woman's life in the last years on St Kilda of the Free Church catechist Duncan Kennedy and his niece.[77]

It had been agreed by proprietor, HASS secretary and Captain Otter that an improved landing place was essential, and work began not long after the *Porcupine* had left early on 5 June 1860. Lieutenant Hawes, who had been landed on Vallay in order to carry on the survey work in that area, rejoined the ship and in the autumn was at St Kilda on an occasion which led to an 'interesting but painful statement' from him to the Inverness Courier.

Hawes told how on 27 September 'H.M. steam surveying vessel, "Porcupine," … left the Sound of Harris for the purpose of sounding to the westward of North Uist, and in the evening anchored in the east bay of St Kilda, to see what progress some masons employed by the Highland and Agricultural Society had been making in the landing place, and to assist them in the adjustment of some large stones for the protection of their boats when hauled up.' The *Porcupine* remained at the island for several days, and on the evening of 2 October, when 'the weather looked threatening' and the barometer was falling, it steamed round to the north side in order to be sheltered from the sea driven by a strengthening wind.

> 'During the night it blew hard from the S. to S.W., the squalls coming down with great violence from the high land, which falls 1200 feet nearly perpendicular to the sea. About 2 A.M. the following morning the wind fell light, and Captain Otter was thinking of returning to the anchorage, when the ship, then lying with her head inshore, and about a mile distant, was suddenly struck by a hurricane from the N.W., which placed her in a most dangerous position, as the island, from the change of wind, instead of affording shelter, became a lee shore. In vain was the helm put hard-a-port, and the engines turned on full speed; the ship was

on her beam ends, and both engines and helm were powerless. Finding which, the dangerous experiment of turning astern full speed was tried - dangerous because the rudder might go at any moment, or the ship become pooped - but even this seemed to have little effect. The sea was one mass of foam and spray, with a lurid glare all round. The weather paddle-box boat was blown off the box in-board, but fortunately was brought up by the upright davits which are used for hoisting her out. Had this not been the case, the foremost funnel must have gone, and the ship would then have been on fire. All the binnacle lights were either blown out or dashed to pieces, tiller ropes carried away, boats' oars, rudders, and other small things flying about with dangerous velocity in all directions. For two hours the storm raged with unparalleled fury, and although so close as the ship must have been to the island nothing could be seen of it.'

At 6 a.m. the wind began to go down and the crew, who had been afraid of total shipwreck against the unseen cliffs and consequently total loss of life, were relieved to find that the *Porcupine* had 'drifted clear of all the islands'. On returning to the bay the destruction in and around the settlement could be easily seen; only two houses were still roofed, all the corn was blown into the sea, and the boat 'on which they depended both for fishing and bringing sheep from the other islands' was smashed to pieces. As regards the predicament in which the islanders found themselves, the Courier article continued:

'It is a most providential thing for them that the "Porcupine" happened to be about the neighbourhood, otherwise their destitute condition would not have been known for the space of nine or ten months, as there is no communication with the island. As much meat and biscuit as could be spared from the ship was left with them, also some small sails to protect the sick until they can get their houses re-thatched.'

Meanwhile they would have to survive on salted birds and a few potatoes until the *Porcupine* returned after picking up supplies to be delivered by a steamer at Lochmaddy around the end of the month.

Described as 'one of the severest storms or hurricanes ever remembered', the 'tempest' raged all over the north of Scotland and even as far south as Perthshire. The steamer *Clansman* had a narrow escape off the Mull of Kintyre when several tons of water broke the skylight and washed about the saloon. All its sails were 'blown to atoms' except 'the fore-try-sail' which was torn to shreds by a squall off Arran. At Poolewe houses were unroofed and corn sheaves carried off like feathers, and at Stornoway, at the height of the gale in the early morning, the strongest buildings vibrated 'to the great discomfort of the inmates'.[78]

Captain Otter himself wrote to J Hall Maxwell from Lochmaddy immediately after his escape from the 'terrific hurricane' that had so nearly destroyed the *Porcupine*. His account is in similar words to those of Hawes and vividly captures the severity of the storm and the state of the St Kilda people:

'We were lying in the bay on the evening of 2nd when the wind coming in and the night looking dirty I weighed and scarcely got out of the bay before the gale commenced from S and SSW. so I steamed round to the north side of the island and got under the lee - the squalls were terrific but the water moderately smooth - about 3 a.m. it was nearly calm, but the barometer still falling, and I was just thinking of returning to the anchorage when the ship was struck as in a moment with the most violent hurricane I ever experienced. I tried to get her head off shore but the tillar ropes broke, and the vessel lay a log on the water drifting at the mercy of the winds and waves. The high cliff which you remember the bird catchers descending was on our lee and we all felt that either this or Levinish must be the point on which the ship must strike. All that now could be done was the dangerous evolution of turning the engines astern and trusting in Gods mercy. The howling and screaming of the wind was terrific and nothing of land sea or sky to be seen except a lurid glare and every now and then an imaginary outline of those awful cliffs over our heads. The binnacle lights had blown out or were dashed to pieces, the large paddle box boat was lifted up and down as if made of paper and oars spars and everything that could break adrift was flying off to leeward with a dangerous velocity. For two hours the hurricane continued with unabated force when a break in the sky showed St Kilda's Peak bearing north and the ship in comparative safety. It was not until noon that we again obtained an anchorage in the bay and then we found that we were not the only sufferers. It was affecting to see and hear of these poor peoples solicitude for the safety of the ship - they at once saw the dangerous position we must be placed in from the sudden change of wind and tho their houses were knee deep in water the rafters flying about and the roofs blowing away their chief anxiety and prayers were put up for our preservation.

'I enclose a copy of the statement Kennedy sent to me but I am sorry I was so short of provisions that I could only land a few gallons of meal and a barrel of biscuit with a few sails and boats covers to protect the sick until the houses can be rethatched. You are aware there is no heather on the island and the little remaining oat straw if used to thatch their houses will leave their cows without food during the winter. Some bags of bran would I have no doubt [be] very acceptable for this purpose and any thing you can get or send might come here by the Islesman on

444

11th or 18th Instant.

'The harbour had just been finished the previous evening, the crane was erected and large stones moved and a strong breakwater formed to protect the boats from the waves, but the wind lifted their large boat and dashed her upon the very place formed for her protection.'

Otter suggested that in addition to a new boat some bags of potatoes, seed corn and guano fertilizer would be necessary and that things should be sent as soon as possible as the people were in such a miserable state. He made a general appeal: 'I hope the charitable people in the south will enable me to return with some assistance before the end of the month.' [79]

Use of the Kelsall Fund, though seen as an appropriate source, could not be made without some delay, and so the HASS secretary took immediate action of a different kind:

'In these circumstances I sent Captain Otter's letter to the newspaper with an intimation that I was willing to take charge of any money which might be subscribed for the relief of the Island and trusting to the result, as well as knowing that Kelsalls fund was behind me, I at once took the necessary steps to have the supplies forwarded. The appeal to the public was responded to with wonderful alacrity, Money poured in from all quarters. The Duke of Athole not only contributed liberally but induced others to do so, indeed at his instance, the Duke of Hamilton sent me no less than £50. Much was received anonymously from England, and a Committee of Glasgow gentlemen was not only instrumental in raising funds but of the greatest service, in ordering and shipping the necessary supplies. In short, within 10 days after publishing Otter's Letter, I had to insert a notice in the papers requesting that no more remittances should be sent to me, and I had the satisfaction of seeing the Lochmaddy Steamer sail with a cargo calculated to make my freinds at St Kilda richer and more comfortable than they had ever before been.' [80]

So many donations of money and goods came in that when the steamer *Islesman* sailed on 29 October it could not carry all the supplies of provisions and building materials that had accumulated. Apart from the £50 given by the Duke of Hamilton and £10 from the Duke of Athole there were small and great sums from an extraordinary variety of people, including 10s from Merchant Taylors' School in London, £20 from 'a few Scotch Gentlemen' in Dublin, £5 from Lord Burghley in the Isle of Wight, and £10 from Samuel Morley, 'the great warehouseman in London as well known there as Lord Palmerston', who having been to St Kilda himself some 25 years previously and having read in the *Times* of 'the calamity that has befallen the Island' cautiously sent his contribution to a Bank of Scotland branch in Glasgow. The *Islesman's* cargo contained sacks of meal and flour, sacks of potatoes, seed oats, seed bere and seed rye, 2 tons of Peruvian guano, horse-hair for ropes, cordage, twine, roofing timber, straw for thatch, cattle bran, cheese, tea, sugar, tobacco, teapots, 'and a great variety of culinary utensils'. But one thing that is not clear is whether all the gifts from 'benevolent friends in the South' eventually, in one form or another, reached those suffering islanders they were intended to benefit.[81]

The goods conveyed to St Kilda by way of relief were paid for out of the subscription by the public in response to the publication of Captain Otter's letter, and any contribution from the Kelsall Fund was reserved for a different purpose. The effect of the storm upon those individuals and agencies that felt they had responsibility for the islanders' welfare was to concentrate attention once more on the proposals made before it happened. The proprietor took exception to the subscription because he was afraid that everybody would think the appeal had been necessary owing to his own failure to respond. He had the same reason for refusing to allow the HASS to apply any of the Kelsall money to the building of improved houses. On the other hand the existing dwellings, having been so severely damaged, needed to be replaced, and so he took on the task of building at his own expense. The landing place, on which work had already been carried out, and a new boat both seemed suitable objects for the allocation of sums from the Kelsall Fund, and Captain Otter was put in charge of both undertakings. The position was reviewed by John Hall Maxwell in 1863:

'The improvements of the dwellings appeared to me the principal object, but, on mooting that to Mr Macleod the proprietor, I found him most averse to any thing like interference, indeed, to prevent it, he undertook at his own cost to build new Houses. The money advances by me was applied principally in the purchase [of] a large, well appointed, safe boat built on the Clyde under Otters directions, and in an attempt, by means of blasting and building, to form something like a rude Breakwater with a view of enabling the Islanders to avail themselves of the fishing banks in their vicinity, by affording them facilities for disembarking in the event of an unfavourable change of weather. Among other things, an allowance of £10 annually was given to the Catechists Neice to induce her to join him and act as a teacher of sewing.'[82]

The 'other things' included expenses to Maxwell and Otter, some furniture, goods such as tea and horse-hair, in 1869 a bull, and, more immediately, the new boat. This was built early in 1861 by Messrs Darroch and Espie of Glasgow. It was a fishing boat 30 feet over all length, with mast, lugsail and yard, 6 ash oars, 2 boat hooks, anchors and other necessary equipment, costing altogether with freight to St Kilda £50.16s.6d. Everything was arranged by Captain Otter, and the name given to the boat was *Dargavel* in honour of John Hall Maxwell.[83]

Dargavel can be added to the list of alien names, such as 'the Saddle' and 'St Kilda', which surely meant little to the Gaelic-speaking inhabitants of the island. The boat itself however promised to be of valuable service to the people. They had others, but this new and supposedly safe craft seemed to be suitable for journeys as far as Harris or Uist, and perhaps even Skye, since it was sufficiently large and well-equipped. Nevertheless the distance over open sea was great enough to make any venture of that kind, as long ago Martin Martin had discovered, a risky undertaking, and there was now some doubt as to whether the islanders could produce a crew with adequate skill and experience to deal with the dangers that would beset them.

During its first full year of use the *Dargavel* nearly came to grief on the west side of North Uist but for the most part things went well and in 1863, with confidence high, there was a plan to make a similar trip to Harris. The boat left early in April with a crew of seven men. Three of them were married – Angus MacDonald, Donald Gillies and Donald MacDonald; the remainder, unmarried, were another Donald Gillies, Alexander Gillies, Ewen Gillies and Donald MacKinnon. Along with them went Mrs Malcolm MacDonald, better known as Betty Scott, whose purpose in leaving St Kilda is not certainly known although it is sometimes assumed that she was on her way to visit relatives on the mainland. No sign of the boat was ever seen again, and all on board were believed lost.[84]

Some clothes and other goods were cast up at Mealasta on the Atlantic coast of Lewis, and since there was every indication that these had come from the island news of the disaster was taken to St Kilda, so the story goes, by three 'London smacks', and when the skippers came ashore 'they played "quoits" with flat stones, and mocked the poor natives when they gave expression to their grief.' It can only have been a very short time after this that John Hall Maxwell, due to pay another visit to the island, noted what he had heard of the fate of 'his' boat and its passengers:

'.. my voyage acquired an unexpected and melancholy interest under the following circumstances. About the end of April a number of boxes were washed ashore on the Lewis containing cloth feathers oil and other articles which could only have come from St Kilda. There were besides sea birds cured for winter use as is done only in St Kilda; in Uist though no vestige of boat or bodies was cast ashore there seemed but little doubt that the large boat had been lost in an attempt to reach the Hebrides. A letter by a free Church Clergyman in Lewis who had inspected the articles was sent to me and forwarded to Macleod, who at once accepted as certain the catastrophe, and who, apprehending that the people might have been driven by want of meal to attempt the voyage, instructed his agent to take immediate steps to ascertain their condition and to carry out the relief that might be required. At the same time, and in case I should be the first to make the Island, he requested me to take, on his account, as much meal as I could stow.'[85]

Later, while on the island, Maxwell was told much more and came to some conclusions of his own:

'The first question naturally referred to the loss of the boat. They all concurred in representing her as the finest and safest they had ever seen. I fear however she was a fatal gift, and tempted them to undertake a voyage, for which their inexperience as seamen, notwithstanding their Insular position, unfitted them. Her crew consisted of seven men, the pick of the population, and with them was poor Betty Scott, the Duke of Atholes hostess, the best head, indeed the ruling spirit of the Island. All were lost, and not a body was found. There was one circumstance singular, and calculated to impress so simple a race. It seems that once a month, and on the day when Captain Otter made so narrow an escape in the Porcupine [they] held a sort of religious service and it was on that day of the Month that our freinds had sailed. In reply to my inquiries respecting the object of the voyage at so early a period of the year, they pled want of meal, but this I do not credit. In Skye and other parts of the Hebrides the people were in great straights for seed oats, having been obliged to eat the ordinary store; now every Croft at St Kilda had been well sown and was far advanced - real evidence that they could not have been severely pinched, and had not been compelled to turn their Store of Seed into meal. Though they would not admit it, my theory is that they were trying for the first time a free trade voyage. Heretofore all their dealings with the outer world have been conducted through McCraild - Macleod's Baillie, he taking their products and giving in exchange the necessaries they Stand in need of. They have always been jealous of him, and did not hesitate to express a belief that they were <u>done</u> by him. Hence I think that they wished to deal independently of him, and with that object undertook the fatal voyage. The boat contained the various articles they sell - Cloth, feathers, oil, etc., besides salted meat, which forbids the idea of Starvation; the value of the Cargo was estimated at above £100 - a great loss, but trivial compared to that of the best men of the Island. Their apprehensions had been roused by the non appearance of the boat, and the worst fears were realised by intelligence obtained from a vessel which visited them on its way to fish at Rockall. Indeed the calamity was aggravated by the exaggerations with which the tale was told, and received. We found them under an impression that their freinds had landed safely in the Lewis and had there been murdered and Stripped of every thing. I hope I succeeded in dispelling this delusion by quoting the [   ] I have already referred to and by reminding them it was a free Church Minister who had vouched that neither boat nor body, but only bales and boxes had been cast ashore.'

This was really all that was believed and guessed about the loss of the *Dargavel* with all hands, but the whole event was to be brought back to the forefront of memories in which it had never become blurred twelve years later.

*

In the late summer or early Autumn of 1862 Duncan Kennedy wrote to the Free Church Highlands committee 'tendering his resignation', but he was of course unable to leave until the following summer. The committee discussed the matter on 21 October and again in November, concluding on the latter occasion that nothing could be done about a replacement until the spring and agreeing that any proposal for an ordained missionary there would [readily] be considered. On 20 May 1863 a petition from the inhabitants for such a missionary was read along with a request from the Presbytery of Skye and Uist to the same purpose. Nothing was decided at this meeting; but in June Rev. MacColl of Duirinish wrote to suggest that Rev. George Corbett would be a suitable choice and the committee's convener was asked to send a letter offering the post to him. Without hesitation Corbett declined.

The Highlands committee had previously received an application for an appointment from Rev. Alexander Cameron and had resolved to give him one wherever his services were required. Now in the circumstances that had arisen it was decided to make St Kilda, not for the first time, 'a special case', and to offer the mission there to Cameron for six months. This time it was accepted, and before long the new missionary was on his way to his 'exile' in the ocean. Meanwhile Duncan Kennedy, the former catechist, was now regretting that he had resigned his position and was himself seeking another appointment, but the committee was unable to help him.[86]

In May 1863, with Kennedy still on the island and at work, John Hall Maxwell arranged a second visit to St Kilda to see his 'old friends' and to inspect such progress as had been achieved with the help of his own 'small efforts'. Not knowing the catechist's intentions he took with him 'a smart dress' for the sewing mistress, and a barometer and some good snuff for her uncle, these being packed along with a collection of 'presents' which he imagined would be useful – 'for the women tea and sugar, black Kerchiefs for the heads of the married, and the gaudiest bandanas for those of the unmarried, sewing material of all sorts; for the men tobacco and pipes, pocket knives – spades, shovels, and hoes – tools and nails – horse hair for crag ropes – and an abundant supply of lines hooks and fishing gear.' Some medicine, pens, paper, copy books, and a few bibles in English and in Gaelic, were also taken, as were 12 bolls of meal and some salt in case the islanders had run short of these essentials.[87]

449

The party assembled at Dargavel and on 26 May 'drove down to Gourock, a cart preceding us with our luggage, guns and rifles, - a deadly war against every species of marine monster open to bullet or shot having been declared'. The hired yacht, *Mosquito*, made good progress to Lochboisdale, where they met up with Lieutenant Hawes, now in command of the *Shamrock*, a survey 'gun boat', and took on board John MacDonald, 'Otters old pilot'. Maxwell had some sympathy for the unfortunate Lieutenant:

> 'Hause's post is not one to be coveted – his surveying station is on the wild coast between Barra head and the Monach Islands, in a wet and stormy climate, with nothing to break the force of the Atlantic. His ship is almost unseaworthy, an unmanageable tup of a gun boat, all the cranker and worse for the want of weight in guns and stores. He complains he is never dry, and is suffering from Rheumatism. His sole society consists of Maxwell a Masters Mate. We gave him a good breakfast and some newspapers of late date to him, and we left him little envying either his ship or his employment.'[88]

After lingering off Haisgeir so that the guns and rifles could be used on seals there, which in fact proved to be impossible in the conditions, the yacht at last reached St Kilda on 1 June. The scene was again dreary and desolate, partly because of the weather and partly because of the new houses: 'Outside of the shallow bay a heavy sea was tearing – overhead dark clouds were driving – ashore, the upper half of the Island was enveloped in mist – the old crescent of beehive huts had been broken in on, and every here and there a cold hard stone and lime, slated cottage presented itself – while, to make matters more forbidding like, there was no concourse of natives at the landing rock to welcome the Strangers – neither man nor beast, not even one of the innumerable curs, was visible.' The island was in its Sabbath silence, and no one was ready to help unload the supplies.

Maxwell took the yacht skipper, 'Sinclair', ashore with him as interpreter, having instructed him to wear his 'best club uniform' in the hope that 'the blue and gold would impress the natives with his importance should any difficulty be experienced in getting them to work on a Sunday'. It proved very difficult to land as it was impossible to recognise the right spot, and they were just about to give up the attempt and wait for a 'native' to come down from the church 'when one of us spied a ring attached to a rock – which was followed by the discovery of some broken iron work and a mass of large quarried stones heaped in confusion over each other'. This was all that was left of Captain Otter's 'harbour making', of 'the work I had paid for', destroyed by the crashing sea. Here, however, they landed and immediately went up to the church where they found 'Kennedy the Chatecist' at work. Maxwell's account of that part of the service he witnessed provides a rare glimpse of what, to a stranger, such a meeting was like:

'As our arrival was unlooked for, and as the congregation could not see the vessel from the windows, the apparition of five strangers must have taken them all by surprise. Whatever they may have felt, they evinced nothing. When we entered they were singing, and not one of them made a movement, nor otherwise allowed our presence to distract them. The scene was striking - in some respects more so than when I formerly saw them assembled for public worship. Then we had the usual array of Clergymen - Elders - communion table - with a regular service - and all the people specially got up and dressed for it. Now we dropped on them as if from the clouds, in the midst of their primitive prayer meeting - the old Catechist occupying the precentors box - the people in their ordinary attire - most of the women with their babies, an old rudder, or oar, or a big stone serving as a footstool or hassock. We entered when a psalm was being sung. Kennedy read a line in Gaelic, and then the congregation pealed it forth. I am not musical, but some of the party who are were much struck with the wild cadency of the air, at times, indeed, taken with all the features and circumstances of place, case and people, it was a little too much for the nerves. A prayer followed and, then, the effect was overpowering. As Kennedy proceeded most of the women became deeply affected, a long low wail ran through the building; it would subside for a minute - and again its moan would rise, the women wringing their hands, and racking their bodies as if struggling with [?]. Had it been louder, mere weeping or a cry, it would have been less affecting - its very lowness made it the more mournful and plaintive, and the more difficult to resist. Poor people! the Catechist (as Sinclair whispered to us) was alluding to the wreck of the boat, and the loss of their Husbands and Brothers. It was an interesting and touching but a terribly painful scene.'

While listening to these mournful sounds the visitors were unaware that the weather was changing. They could hear the wind rising, and after briefly slipping outside Sinclair said that he did not think the yacht could stay much longer. Maxwell decided he would have to interrupt the catechist:

'On re-entering the Church I found him finishing a Chapter, and before he could break fresh ground, I walked up to his desk - whispered that I had an important communication to make - and that I begged he would close the service as soon as possible. This he very sensibly agreed to, gave a short prayer - and dismissed the congregation, requesting the men at my desire to remain. I then explained through him that I had on board many articles of use and value to them - that it was very unlikely I could remain at my moorings till Monday morning, that a few hours might be the duration of my stay, that without their services and the assistance of their boat, I could not land the heavier things, and that I therefore trusted under the circumstances they would consider it a work of necessity and mercy to themselves to bear a hand although it was the Sabbath day.'

The men were rather surprised at this, but when Kennedy gave his backing they agreed to bring the goods ashore. Maxwell thought that certain circumstances had helped; Kennedy, he reckoned, was looking forward to the tea, sugar, tobacco and snuff which would soon be available, while Sinclair's uniform apparently gave him the authority of an admiral and Maxwell's own dress, especially his 'nicker bockers' and 'scarlet stockings', if not entirely suited to the Sabbath, caused a sensation. So the St Kilda helpers were told to launch their boat, while Maxwell himself returned to the yacht to prepare for loading. Everything was ready and lighter articles were put into the yacht's own boat where they were covered with a tarpaulin. Rain had come on heavily, haste was important, but there was no sign of the boat from the island. Maxwell, losing patience, landed and intended to urge on people whom he now believed were merely lazy. It was at this point, however, that he learned of a situation that may well have had much to do with Kennedy's resignation.

'On landing I ran to Kennedys [to ask] why half an hour had been lost, and not a hand was at the boat, when I was informed that the "<u>other party</u>" would not let her be launched. "The other party"! there had been no "Parties" when I was formerly there. What did he mean? - on which he commenced a narration about a Cow which might have lasted longer than his Church service had my patience permitted him to proceed. I gathered enough to learn that the "Elder" of the Island Neill Ferguson and he had quarrelled about the Sale of a Cow - that each of them had his adherents - that, as a matter of course, the affair had taken a religious complexion - and that the population was divided into two parties, one of which had seceded from the church or rather from Kennedy, and worshipped under the guidance and in the cottage of Neil. This explained what had struck me earlier as a very scanty attendance at the Church Service. Shaking off Kennedy and cutting short his history, I rushed off to discover Ferguson, whom I found surrounded by his freinds, and resolved of course to oppose whatever Kennedy had supported. He was the Elder - he had more men on his side than the Catechist. It would be a deadly sin to launch the boat - besides it was quite uncalled for, as he knew that next morning there would be a fin[e] breeze off shore from the west. In vain, through Sinclair, I argued the religious question - in vain I sought to know Neils means of ascertaining the intentions of Providence in respect to the weather - in vain I hinted at the good things I wished to land - vain even was the proffered bait of giving him an equal say in their distribution as the price of adhesion, and of conferring the whole patronage on his Enemy as a punishment of refusal. No! - every argument was received with a sort of supercilious ultra righteous – conceited refusal. He was the Elder, and he and his men would not permit me or any one to launch the boat. A thought struck me, when on the point of giving up the attempt in despair. "Is the boat yours Neill?" "No" "Was it sent for the common good of the Island?" "Yes" "Who sent it?" "Either Captain Otter or yourself." There I clinched my freind. "I sent it. I shall take posses[s]ion of it, and I shall launch it." Neill and his friends looked very blue, but they did not dare to resist. My volunteers who had been becoming shaky, plucked up – in a few minutes the boat so long battled for was afloat – and in [an] hour every thing was landed.'

Maxwell's troubles were not over. He was in the manse when a call from Sinclair took him to the landing place where, on a bare rock stood perishable articles like salt in the pouring rain. The St Kilda crew who had brought the goods ashore were refusing to take them any further as they considered it would be a sin to carry them anywhere on the Sabbath. The distance to the storehouse was, said Maxwell, a mere 20 yards, and it was only after he and Sinclair had set an example by heaving bags of meal to the dry cover that the islanders decided to assist.

Maxwell then heard more from Duncan Kennedy about 'the causes of the Schism between him and Ferguson'. It had indeed arisen as a result of differences over the cow:

'Kennedy refused to take it, alledging want of the Stipulated amount of fat. Neill responded that there was no such condition and that Kennedy was a liar. He retorted by excluding Neill from the first religious Service – and thereupon Neill hoisted his own spiritual Flag – and the people ranged themselves under the respective leaders. Thus had discord and dis[s]ension succeeded the harmony which struck me so pleasingly on the occasion of my first visit. So far as we could ascertain Kennedy had the largest following among the women, Neill among the men, which rather looks as if the first was in the wrong. Kennedy would have spoken for a week on the point, "he had not refused to take the Cow, but said he would throw it into the Sea, and into the Sea it went", for it was killed pending the dispute and formed part of the cargo of the ill fated boat. One unhappy consequence will probably be – not so much Kennedys leaving the Island, as the loss of his neice who acts as sowing and writing mistress, and who showed us some excellent specimens of the progress which had been made in both by the Children.'

Further attention was also paid to the cold hard cottages, 'Macleods new houses' as Maxwell called them.

'I have already characterised them as any thing but picturesque in comparison with the old ones, and I much doubt if in a winters storm they will be as impervious to the blast. They are common low country cottages with a couple of rooms and some other accommodation - with slated roofs - and good glazed windows. They afford light and air in abundance, blessings unknown in the old abodes, and if kept well they may be made neat, but comparatively they are hard and prim, and when completed, will entirely destroy the unique aspect of the place from the sea. The people say they are cold, and let in water; it may be so, but allowance must be made for their prejudices, and much praise should be accorded to Mr Macleod, for the liberal manner in which he is endeavouring to improve their condition. My fear would be the risk of one of the winter hurricanes unslating a house, and the difficulty of restoring the roof. Captain Otter was very confident that his landing place would resist the force of the sea, and Macleod may find that the old thick walls, and low rounded roof of thatch tied down by heavy stones is more suitable to resist that of the wind.'

Presents were given to Anne Kennedy, and her uncle was left with the task of dividing goods into equal portions for the islanders 'without reference to "the other party"'. Neil Ferguson's weather forecast proved incorrect and with the wind even stronger than it had been on the Sabbath the visiting yacht left as soon as it could on the Monday morning, making for the Sound of Harris and the shelter of Lochmaddy. At the end of the voyage John Hall Maxwell, HASS secretary, returned to his work in Edinburgh after an interesting experience but with no great optimism regarding the measures being taken to improve the lot of the St Kilda people.

*

The dispute between Duncan Kennedy and Neil Ferguson was of greater significance than its apparent cause might suggest. For the second time a division emerged among the islanders, and it became a religious one because the catechist was involved. Neil, one of the exceptionally intelligent and enterprising family of Fergusons, was, it seems, the only elder and had been for at least four years. Holding this position he had evidently acquired a leader's authority over the community, as presumably his father John had done before him, and was able to oppose the 'official' religious guide appointed by the Free Church. With the support of most of the men he could outdo Kennedy and his small group of adherents and behave as if the catechist was away on holiday and he had been left in charge of spiritual matters. Religion, not for the first time, created its own capacity for division, although on this occasion it was more an issue of personality and mundane disagreement than of doctrine, and Kennedy's replacement would not necessarily have to confront an opposing faction.

Alexander Cameron, a probationer, left Glasgow on the first stage of his journey at the beginning of September 1863. His departure coincided, either by accident or by intention, with an article on St Kilda in the Free Church Monthly Record of 1 September, imposingly headed with a picture of a towering rock that may have been intended to represent a particular part of St Kilda such as Levinish but no doubt also served to emphasise the wild and harsh circumstances in which the islanders, and their missionary, struggled to survive. The article began with some inaccurate 'facts' relating to distance, height of the main island, and former population, and it stated that 'owing to emigration, there are only eighty-four people on the island', six more than the number recorded in the 1861 census. There followed some general comments about them, deriving perhaps from a former 'deputy' or from information supplied by Duncan Kennedy:

> 'Having little intercourse with the mainland - at one time never more than once a year - the people are shy and reserved. It is difficult to get acquainted with them; but once you have gained their confidence, they give you it thoroughly. And owing to the same cause, some of their customs are peculiar. For example, everything that concerns their general interests is determined by a kind of senate. The heads of families meet in a certain open space in the middle of the hamlet or village, the proprietor's bailiff - one of themselves - presides, motions are made and seconded, and speeches delivered (all, of course, in Gaelic), and till a majority consents, they won't launch the boat, or commence taking the birds, or laying down their crops. Then, in coming to church, the men and women never come together. The men and boys come first, and take their seats, and the females come a few minutes after; and they retire from church in the same way, the females being the first to leave.'

The writer then launched into an account of St Kilda's religious history. Of the early stages there was little known, but this did not prevent some condemnation of those 'spiritually desolate' times. There were 'the ruins of two Popish chapels' to indicate a former attachment to Rome, though which two was not stated. 'Most likely through the influence of the proprietor, they became Protestants soon after the Reformation; but, like numbers of their countrymen in the Hebrides, they were Protestants merely in name. Ignorance and superstition reigned among them.' The activities of the 'impostor' were then described, Martin Martin being transformed into the proprietor himself when it came to the visit with the minister of Harris that brought an end to Roderick's regime. However, 'though about the end of last century they had a minister for some years among them, this made little difference; spiritual religion was almost wholly unknown'.[89]

Thus was religion in the island before the 1820s both re-written and dismissed. Then along came 'the apostle of the north', John MacDonald, as a result of whose visits 'a blessed change took place'. Assembling the people twice a day during the weeks he was there, 'he expounded to them, in his own clear, vigorous way, the first eight chapters of the Epistle to the Romans; and the consequence was a general awakening'. The islanders may be imagined waking 'from the sleep of ages' on hearing MacDonald expound; at least it is easy to understand why someone forty years later should portray MacDonald's work in that way.

The 1863 article continued to illustrate the process of transformation, though in doing so it omitted the name and extensive influence of Neil MacKenzie altogether. In 1849, it said, a Free Church minister who visited the island that year was impressed with what were called 'facts' that he picked up: 'That, so far as man could judge, the proportion of really converted people among them was large; that their religion was the impress of Dr. McDonald's peculiar manner of stating divine truth; and that when they were told of Dr. McDonald's death, which took place that year, they mourned for him as for their father.' MacDonald's successful efforts in raising money for a church and manse were mentioned, as was the supply of bibles and 'all the religious books that the Gaelic language could furnish'. It was also remarked, incorrectly, that 'an old endowment becoming available for the minister's stipend, a minister was settled among them in 1830'. The endowment of course by that time had been available for nearly a century.

The visiting minister of 1849 – probably Angus McGillivray – dispensed the sacrament only to those who had previously been communicants, whereas the two Free Church deputies who arrived in 1850 – McGillivray and Thomas McLauchlan – 'resolved to admit persons for the first time', and finding that there were 'two admirable elders on the island – men who, for piety and intelligence, would have graced any congregation' – they helped to constitute a kirk session which proceeded to examine the applicants for communion. The inclusion of the elders on the interviewing panel would have increased the importance of the position they held in the community, and the degree of religious conviction which they demonstrated gave them an aura of spiritual superiority in the eyes of the poor islanders. Two examples of the more general 'piety and intelligence' of the people were instanced in the 1863 account, one from an elder who appeared to have read *Pilgrim's Progress*, the other from a 'quiet-looking young girl of eighteen' who remembered a time when she 'was under the curse of God'.

After the handing-over of the manse, church and glebe, but not of the old MacLeod mortification or endowment, to the Free Church there came the Kennedy years, now just concluded, and the petition, written in Gaelic, from St Kilda seeking an ordained minister on a permanent basis. At this point the purpose of the article became clear:

'This, however, cannot be done without an endowment; and at last Assembly the Committee, by their convener, made an earnest appeal to the Church in reference to this matter. We do trust that this appeal will be responded to, and responded to without delay. The proprietor – himself an Episcopalian – has given the buildings and the glebe; the members of the Free Church will surely follow this up by providing an endowment, and thus securing to the people of St Kilda what their heart is set on – an ordained ministry. Let them rest assured that in giving their money to this object, they are giving it to the Lord, and that they are giving the bread of life to those who, though they are the poor of this world, are rich in faith.'

It was therefore no wonder that the island people were said to be enlightened, pious, intelligent and 'rich in faith'; clearly they deserved the sought-for endowment.

Dr Thomas McLauchlan, convener of the Highlands committee, announced the appeal and 'through the disinterested labours of several ladies' a sum of around £180 was collected within a year. But this was far short of what was needed. As a consequence the probationer Alexander Cameron, being conveniently more economical than an ordained minister, was appointed to fill the vacancy, not as it turned out for six months but for a whole year. His journey to St Kilda was managed economically as well, though it took quite a long time. The steamer from Glasgow brought him to South Uist and from there 'he was conveyed… by Captain Otter of the Royal Navy'. It was a week after leaving Lochboisdale on 5 September before he reached St Kilda owing to the storminess of the weather, but the enthusiastic Captain Otter, 'being in the habit of conducting family worship, morning and evening, at which the sailors always attend', filled up some of the time with regular 'religious exercises'. When at last they reached their destination Otter 'showed his interest in the mission and the people, by visiting the sick and doing all he could to render the manse comfortable for the missionary'.[90]

The Highlands committee heard nothing from Cameron about 'his arrival and labours' until July 1864. A letter from him, dated 7 March, was then received, describing what had happened and reporting, among other things, that the people lived happily in 'comfortable structures of stone and lime, and covered above with zinc', the slates having presumably proved inadequate in the conditions. It was also said that during the winter the population had been 'comfortably provided for' as a result of a favourable fishing season in October, the produce having supplemented that of the land. The missionary went on to give an account of the religious regime for which he was responsible.

'Public worship begins on Sabbath at half-past eleven o'clock, and the congregation is dismissed shortly after two o'clock. About an hour afterwards a Sabbath school – superintended by the missionary – is held in the church, the exercises being varied to suit the capacities of the pupils, as old and young attend the Sabbath school in St. Kilda. There is also a weekly prayer-meeting, at which, after praise, prayer, and reading of the Word by the missionary, several of the men engage in prayer, a number of them being in the habit of praying publicly at the meetings. There is also a monthly prayer-meeting conducted in the same manner.'

In winter and early spring weekly 'diets of catechizing', attended regularly, were added to the programme, and since there was no schoolteacher since the Kennedys had left 'the missionary has felt constrained to set apart three days of the week' in winter 'to teaching the youth of the island writing and English reading'. He thought that they learned very quickly, 'their proficiency being on a level with those of the mainland'. In general Cameron found that 'the people are orderly, anxious to attend on and profit by the means of grace, and warmly attached to the Free Church of Scotland; that they feel themselves placed under unspeakable obligation to the Free Church and the Committee for the Highlands, for the privileges hitherto extended to them; and that it is their earnest desire and prayer, that these may be still continued among them'. In view of all this, the committee indicated, a further endowment sum would be most welcome so as to 'secure to the people of this lonely island – what they so much desire – an ordained pastor, who shall, in their own language, administer ordinances and break the bread of life among them'.[91]

However satisfactory it felt the spiritual condition of the islanders to be the Highlands committee saw little need to devote any thought, or money, to the other daily 'bread of life' on which the physical survival of the people depended. This, members could still argue or assume, was the business of bodies such as the HASS and of philanthropic individuals as well as of the proprietor. High infant mortality, lack of medical care, inadequate communication, crop failures, cliff climbing, these meant inevitably a decline in the size of the population and an increasing likelihood of emigration, but it appeared that, in spite of its praiseworthy efforts during the late 1840s, the Free Church was now concerned only with the spiritual state of the people who remained, and in a period of mounting public interest in the curious western colony out in the Atlantic with the economic problems it posed this is neither surprising nor to be criticised. It was however possible for a churchman, of whatever kind, priest, catechist or minister, to show individual initiative in seeking to secure help on behalf of his congregation, and since the eighteenth century at least the missionary at St Kilda had been spokesman when non-Gaelic-speaking visitors arrived. He therefore was in a position to convey information and impressions which may have represented the position in the island in a way quite different from that in which the islanders themselves would have done had they been able to communicate clearly in the foreign English tongue. When the Free Church representative on the island had, after 1850, to write or talk to a Royal Navy captain or a government official he might seem a self-important but knowledgeable figure; what he said could nevertheless be entirely inaccurate and misleading, since often he would see things from his own, religious standpoint and not from that of the 'poor people'.

It is unlikely that the inhabitants of St Kilda were ever a self-sustaining community. In early days the steward had to take to the island both supplies and even families if he was going to continue to profit from the labour and produce of those who lived there. There is no need to suppose that the replenishing of the population only occurred after the smallpox devastation. The entertainment and rents provided for him on his visits may at times have looked like surplus, but the people lived in the utmost poverty and would not even lend a pot or a pan to Alexander Buchan for nothing. When in due course the steward arrangement was replaced by a tenant or factor such as Donald MacDonald and then Norman MacRaild there were no more regular supplies and no more introduced occupants to maintain the community and make inbreeding less probable. Instead the island people had to purchase needed goods through the factor to whom they paid their rents, to rely on the gifts of visitors for any luxury at all, and to perpetuate their numbers from within their own ranks while the majority of their children died a few days after birth. All this meant a dependence on the outside world as great as, if not greater than, it had been in the years of the stewards, and it meant too more frequent thoughts of emigration.

The islanders were deeply attached to their remote home, but some visitors might well have wondered why, when it came to the hardships of ordinary existence, they should remain there. The Free Church Monthly Record itself reported problems in much more accessible places. On 30 June 1863, for instance, the *Forth*, a steamer 'freighted with three hundred and fifty Gaelic-speaking emigrants from the Isle of Lewis', arrived at Derry, its human cargo then to be transferred to the *Elizabeth* for the voyage to Canada. The proprietor of Lewis, Sir James Matheson, had 'generously offered to aid those who intended emigrating', and 'a far greater number than was expected threw up their holdings' for many were in arrears with the rent and since for several years 'the seasons have been most unfavourable in the Hebrides' they 'have become very depressed in their circumstances'. A Derry newspaper commented on these unhappy souls:

'They are all members of the Free Church of Scotland. The men are all far above the average size – rough and stalwart – not very active in their movements, but, seemingly, have any amount of latent bodily power ready to be applied when a fitting opportunity presents itself. The women and children look stout and strong. Their dress is simple, and their manners exceedingly primitive. A deep religious feeling pervades their breasts. On their way from Lewis to Derry they sang their Gaelic psalms ... What a contrast this to the emigration scenes witnessed weekly in Liverpool and London.'[92]

What a contrast too there was between the 'modern' manners of mainland, city populations and the so-called 'primitive' manners of this sad crowd from Lewis, in whose breasts a 'deep religious feeling' perhaps provided a consolation which no action of a proprietor nor such social conscience as the government may have possessed could supply in order to enable them to stay at home. That the little community of St Kilda remained there after losing so many of its number to Australia and in the *Dargavel* may be in part owing to that isolation which had aroused curiosity and sympathy over centuries and its capacity to endure was perhaps prolonged and even strengthened rather than undermined by the teachings of the Free Church. Yet however deeply attached the people were to 'their rock' in the ocean, and however remarkable the inclination of the Protestant church to be bothered with them, the time had come when emigration began to seem ever more probable, and involuntarily the island's representatives of the Free Church found themselves having to deal with the forces that promoted that course of action.

1   MacKenzie (1911) Preface p.4

2   SSPCK GD95/2/19 pp.343-344, 367-368; GD95/1/9 p.223

3   SSPCK Case for the Society in Scotland...and Opinion of Counsel thereon Edinburgh 1843 – with Report 13 June 1843

4   SSPCK GD95/1/9 p.223; GD95/2/19 pp.367-368, 385; GD95/1/9 pp.224-225

5   SSPCK GD95/2/19 pp.456-457, 469-470, 476.

6   Ansdell p.75 (Extract from logbook June-August 1846); NMS File of Notes by Captain F W L Thomas; Ansdell pp.116, 120. For Rev. Roderick MacLeod see R. MacLeod: 'The Bishop of Skye' in TGSI Vol. LIII (1985) pp.174-209. In 1850-1851 MacLellan was still tacksman at Milton and a member of the Parochial Board of South Uist, where, as a Free Church man amid Catholics, he might have been able to give an objective view of conditions among the people [Report to the Board of Supervision by Sir John McNeill on the Western Highlands and Islands Edinburgh 1851 pp.124-125].

7   A Beith: A Highland Tour Second edition Edinburgh 1874 p.169; D MacArthur: 'The Breadalbane 1844-1853 and her work for the Highland Destitution Committee' in TGSI Vol.LV (1989) pp.1-20; T Brown: Annals of the Disruption New edition Edinburgh 1893 pp.653-654 (quoting the Missionary Record September 1845 p.202)

8   MacArthur pp.5-6

9   MacArthur p.13

10 SSPCK GD95/2/19 pp.532-533. It appears that Bethune did not go to St Kilda either.

11 SSPCK GD95/2/19 pp.403-404

12 Letter from 'MacLeod of St. Kilda' to Mr Charles Trevelyan in Correspondence from July, 1846, to February, 1847, relating to The Measures Adopted for the Relief of the Distress in Scotland London 1847 p.38

13 SSPCK GD95/2/20 p.23; GD95/1/9 p.274

14 SG CH2/568/2 p.157; SSPCK GD95/11/2 Account of Society Appendix p.29; GD95/11/3 pp.55-57; GD95/11/11 pp.55-57; GD95/1/7 p.201; GD95/6/2 p.7; GD95/11/14 p.7; GD95/13/121 p.7 etc.; Oliver & Boyd's Scottish Tourist Edinburgh 1852 p.341

15 Milner pp.2014-2017, 2054; MacArthur p.18

16 Milner p.2057

17 Milner p.2057

18 SSPCK GD95/2/20 pp.31-32. William Urquhart was paid £7 for his preparation before being told he would not be going to St Kilda [GD95/6/6 p.29].

19 SSPCK GD95/2/20 pp.39-40

20 SSPCK GD95/2/20 pp.50, 92-93

21 SSPCK GD95/1/9 p.276; Milner p.2058. Of the proprietor Milner wrote further but not entirely correctly: 'His family was originally from St. Kilda; his grandfather was catechist of the island, and the present man bought it a few years ago for £1400.'

22 MacKenzie (1911) pp.6, 30. Some of Neil MacKenzie's collections were lost. One of his daughters, wife of Rev. C A McVean of Killin, also preserved some 'Reminiscences of St Kilda'. She remarked on shipwrecks, on how her father set the broken leg of a sailor, and on the arrival of, probably, the Vulcan steamboat in 1838; it had a brass band on board which terrified the islanders with its music [Seton p.57].

23 SSPCK GD95/2/20 pp.66, 122. The factor's name was minuted as 'Norman Riald' (p.66).

24 SSPCK GD95/2/20 pp.134-135. 'Trumisgarry' was incorrectly minuted as 'Timsgary'. GD95/1/9 pp.301-302

25 SSPCK GD95/2/20 pp.149-152 (paragraphing introduced)

26 SSPCK GD95/1/9 pp.301-302

27 SSPCK GD95/1/9 pp.301-302

28 MacArthur p.15; SSPCK GD95/2/20 pp.164-165

29 SSPCK GD95/2/20 pp.164-165

30 SSPCK GD95/2/20 p.191

31   SSPCK GD95/2/20 pp.217-218; MacArthur p.15. Neil MacKenzie had administered the sacrament in September 1845.

32   SSPCK GD95/2/20 pp.226-228. There was, it is said, a rumour in the island that everybody was 'to be put off the land and sent away' [by the factor?], but that the proprietor had forbidden this:

'When MacEwen [Peter McEwan] came he found the elders carrying on service regularly. He wanted to take the service on an equal footing with the elders. The people resented this. One family kept away from this meeting and then Finlay Gillies..., then MacDonald [Betty Scott's husband]. ... - these three families gathered in our house; then we got double the congregation. At last my uncle Neil came and we went to a larger place – to Roderick Gillies' house – a large room. We were there for nearly six months and all the people except 15 or 16 came there. Among those going to the church were 9 who got the benefit from the minister's glebe and thought MacEwen might have some control over the glebe.

'The factor Norman McRail[d] then came. He was vexed at the state of matters. He threatened to evict any who refused to go [to the church]. In this he overstepped his powers and the owner was opposed to his conduct. A fortnight or three weeks after that MacEwan left and all went back to the church.' [MacQueen pp.16-17]

33   SSPCK GD95/2/20 p.235. Leading figures in the community like the Fergusons were of course easily able to persuade the other people to follow. It was remembered how at this time the father of Ewen Gillies said that 'he reckoned the people had made a mistake in coming out' to the Free Church. Ewen himself was 'one of the principal movers in coming away'. Those who followed had apparently signed for the Free Church, and one said: 'I did not know what I was doing. I saw John Ferguson my brother-in-law signing and I never knew him to make a mistake or do anything bad in his life and I thought I was quite safe in following his example.' The speaker was Malcolm MacDonald, Betty Scott's husband. [MacQueen p.17]

34   SSPCK GD95/2/20 pp.242, 251, 301; GD95/1/9 pp.320, 335

35   SSPCK GD95/1/9 pp.335, 337; GD95/2/20 pp.313, 334

36   HFR Vol. I p.191 Report of a visit to St Kilda by a Deputation from the Committee

37   HFR Vol. I p.267 Report (see n.36)

38   HFR Vol. II pp.82-83

39   SSPCK GD95/2/20 p.395

40   SSPCK GD95/2/20 p.437; GD95/3/5 ff.504, 514

41   SSPCK GD95/2/20 p.441; GD95/1/9 p.367

42   SSPCK GD95/3/5 f.529 (letter 10 June 1852)

43   Richards (1) pp.55-75; Richards (2) pp.129-155; Lawson (St Kilda and its Church) p.25. Malcolm MacQueen seems to be the main source of first-hand information on the St Kilda emigrants' experience. His account includes the following:

'St. Kilda was owned by Sir John MacPherson MacLeod. I remember seeing him on the island with his wife and servants. He was the son of Col. MacLeod and was Chief Justice of Calcutta for 22 years. When we were leaving the island he met us in Glasgow and was speaking to them all till we came to Liverpool. In Liverpool he offered to send them all back to St. Kilda in a steamer and give them all they needed for two years. We told him probably the rest of the inhabitants would come away shortly. He asked what he had better do to retain them. The people were not pleased because the Established Church sent catechists and a schoolmaster while the people belonged to the Free Church. We suggested that the manse and church be given to the people. He replied that he had no power to do that as although built on his land they belonged to the Established Church – but he would see what he could do. We afterwards learned that he purchased them from the Established Church and presented them to the Free Church and the people are now in the Free Church.' [MacQueen p.20]

Regarding the supposed adherence of the people to the Free Church when 'catechists and a schoolmaster' were sent by the 'opposition' MacQueen was not entirely accurate. In addition, like Richards (2), his reference to the proprietor as Sir John is inappropriate since at the time of the emigration the latter was not yet knighted.

For a list of emigrants see Holohan (1986) pp.46-49. Trevelyan was the leading figure in the Highland and Island Emigration Society; John MacPherson MacLeod was a committee member. In a letter of 3 May 1850 Rev. Norman MacLeod revealed the social connections between Society members: 'Sir Charles Trevelyan had a MacLeod party at dinner at his house on Wednesday – MacLeod and his lady, St Kilda – MacDonald, Tormore – young McAulay, General Duncan MacLeod, etc.' [MacLeod (1898) p.256]

44 Richards (1) p.55 (quoting Glasgow Herald); SSPCK GD95/1/9 pp.371-372. Trevelyan wrote in November 1852: 'we expect soon to be called upon to send the rest of the population of the island. They are a singularly primitive people. Of the one hundred and ten souls of whom the population consists only three or four had been on the mainland.' [Richards (2) p.139]

45 SSPCK GD95/3/5 ff.504, 514; GD95/2/20 pp.500-501; GD95/1/9 p.398

46 First Report of the Ladies Association in Support of Gaelic Schools (15 April 1847) pp.4-18

47 ESSGS Seventh Report (1818) p.37

48 ELHSA CH3/1428/1

49 ELHSA CH3/1428/1 26 February 1851, 5 April 1852, 31 May 1852; HFR Vol. III p.208 (1853). Malcolm MacQueen, emigrant in 1852, said that a cousin, Donald MacQueen, was his first teacher, and that a schoolhouse was built 'about a quarter of a mile from the church', to which he and others went for four or five years. The proprietor thought the school should be held in the church and this move was made. MacQueen then mentioned Carmichael and McEwan, 'catechists', the former starting a singing class. In 1851, when he was 'about 22 or 23', the deputies McGillivray and Sinclair arrived, and, according to MacQueen, their main purpose was to appoint a schoolteacher. They interviewed Malcolm Ferguson, Finlay MacQueen, and Malcolm MacQueen himself. Ferguson had apparently been chosen by the community to teach for 9 months about 1845, but now the visitors asked the elders for their preference and Malcolm MacQueen was nominated. 'They took me out to the yacht and I was then examined. They told me that I had to teach English and brought me the English Bible to read, but especially to teach Gaelic. I was appointed and acted as schoolmaster till three days before leaving' [MacQueen pp.16-18]. There would seem to be no doubt therefore that MacQueen was the teacher supported by the ELHSA.

50 For the record of the MacKenzies' visit see MacKenzie (1921) pp.74-95

51 HC CH3/983/1 pp.5, 9, 12

52 HFR Vol. IV pp.129-130 (1854)

53 SSPCK GD95/2/20 pp.508, 514

54 SSPCK GD95/2/20 p.596

55 HC CH3/983/1 pp.33-34, 36-37, 43, 56, 62, 70, 94-95

56 SSPCK GD95/2/20 pp.661-662; HC CH3/983/1 pp.102-103, 115, 142

57 SSPCK GD95/2/20 pp.658, 678; GD95/2/21 p.66

58 ELHSA CH3/1428/2 28 March 1855 (letter from James Cowan); HFR New Series Vol. I p.82 (1857)

59 HFR New Series Vol. I p.82

60 HFR New Series Vol. III p.32 (1859)

61 Lawson (Croft History) p.8; Seton p.55. Malcolm MacQueen remembered how 'one Donald McKinnon, a native of the island, whom Dr MacDonald of Ferintosh had taken away and sent to College', was his teacher for a while and at the same time was 'Factor' [i.e. 'sub-tacksman', ground officer or equivalent]. MacKinnon, he said, 'married the daughter of a schoolmaster who was in Harris'; but he and Rev. Neil MacKenzie 'did not get on very well' and the people 'placed their faith in the minister'. There was complaint about his 'factorship' and 'he was moved away' [MacQueen p.16]. MacKinnon was precentor in the

Harris parish church by about 1847 [see Rev. Roderick MacDonald's letter p.398 and n.25 above]. Also while in Harris he signed some 'Harris birth registers', and reminiscences of a descendant record how he settled on a croft at Obbe in 1840 'where he practised, both as a missionary and a "veterinary", aided by his daughter Janet, a lay midwife'. It was at this croft house that St Kilda women gave birth [Holohan (1985) pp.50-53].

62 This account of Muir's visit is derived from T S Muir: <u>Characteristics of Old Church Architecture etc. in the Mainland and Western Isles of Scotland</u> Edinburgh 1861 pp.208-224.

63 W P Anderson: <u>Silences that Speak – Records of Edinburgh's Ancient Churches and burial grounds with biographical sketches of the notables who rest there</u> Edinburgh 1931 pp.465-466

64 <u>HFR</u> New Series Vol. III p.32

65 <u>HC</u> CH3/983/1 pp.230, 245, 254

66 <u>JHM</u> (1860) [KBP 15/1]; <u>DC</u> Section 2 637/2/2 Memorandum regarding the origin and management of the St Kilda Fund. Unless otherwise stated the following account of Maxwell's visit to St Kilda in 1860 is taken from the journal. For the story of the Maxwells of Dargavel, and the Halls of Fulbar, see A H Millar: <u>The Castles and Mansions of Renfrewshire and Buteshire</u> Glasgow 1889. While in Edinburgh John Hall Maxwell and his family lived at 6 Albyn Place, where his household included 6 children, a governess, and 7 miscellaneous servants, among them a butler and a coachman [Census 1861]. In 1861 Maxwell's age was given as 48. He died in 1866.

The HASS papers relating to the Kelsall Bequest (St Kilda Fund) are at present held in the offices of the National Trust for Scotland, Edinburgh, where they have been catalogued in draft. References here are to the handlist produced by the Trust.

67 <u>HC</u> CH3/983/1 p.259

68 <u>HC</u> CH3/983/1 pp.259, 261, 269. An account of Mrs Thomas's benevolent works in Harris is given in <u>Scottish Home Industries</u> (N.D) pp.71, 73-76. See also J & E.R Pennell: <u>Our Journey to the Hebrides</u> London 1889 pp.115-116, 123, 130.

69 For the letters and observations of the Duke and Duchess of Athole, see <u>Atholl Archives</u>, Blair Castle Box 58 Bundle 28 nos.5, 6, 8-10; <u>JHM</u> (1860) [KBP 15/1] (They crossed the Clyde by steamer).

70 For a description of one of the 'men' in Sutherland see C R Weld: <u>Two Months in the Highlands, Orcadia, and Skye</u> London 1860 pp.245-252.

71 Old Parish Registers (Assynt, Lochbroom)

72 St Kilda Register of Baptisms, Marriages and Deaths [see Part 4 n.63]

73 <u>KBP</u> 7/3

74 For Maxwell's 'census', and Otter's, see appendix to this part.

75 Otter, Letter Book OD365 Hydrographic Data Centre, The United Kingdom Hydrographic Office, Taunton.

76 J E Morgan: 'The Falcon among the Fulmars; or, Six Hours at St. Kilda' in <u>MacMillan's Magazine</u> Vol. III (1861) pp.104-111. According to Seton (p.26) Morgan was at the time 'tutor in the family of the late Mr Rainy of Raasay'.

77 Thomas's visit took place apparently two weeks after the *Porcupine's* previous voyage with Maxwell, in late June. The surname 'Sharbau' is often thought to be 'Sharban', the last letter being difficult to distinguish from the signature on his plan of the St Kilda settlement [KBP 16/1]. In articles by Thomas the name occurs in both spellings, but 'Sharbau' seems to be a little more frequent. In the census of 1851 Effy MacCrimmon's age was given as 71; she had been a weaveress and cottar, and was a 'landless spinster'. In 1861 she was recorded as 'Effy McCrimon', aged 82. For the photograph of Effy see also Thomas papers <u>NMS</u> M.28.

78 <u>The Inverness Courier and General Advertiser</u> Vol. XLI nos.2238-2241 (4-25 October 1860) for descriptions of the storm and its effects, with special reference to St Kilda. Also article in <u>North British Daily Mail</u> 15 October 1860 [<u>KBP</u> 11/3]

79 <u>KBP</u> 4/6. Kennedy's 'statement' [<u>KBP</u> 4/6 3 October 1860]:

'The damage done in this island by the last night storm cannot be calculated at less than 80 bolls of barley and 80 bolls of oats as the whole barley and corn crops were out – the barley shorn and the corn not shorn and were all swept away or destroyed. The boat which was most useful was broken to pieces and all the houses are destroyed there is no remembrance in the island of an equal storm and the inhabitants of the island are in great danger except relief be sent to them without much delay'

80   JHM (1863) [KBP 15/2]

81   KBP 1/1-60

82   JHM (1863) [KBP 15/2]

83   DC Section 2 637/2/2; KBP 2/1-3

84   Seton pp.61, 59; MacKenzie Papers GD403/50/3 Note of Crew. In a letter of 22 May 1863 the proprietor said that he did not think shortage of meal occasioned the unfortunate voyage. He added:

'There were in the lost boat seven men and one woman – The men all in the prime of life, and such as the island could worst spare. The woman was Betty Scott, whose letter to Captain Otter you will remember, - not a native of St. Kilda. She appears to have left her husband and two children on the island. The poor woman whose grief seems to have found a vent against poor McRaild lost her husband in the boat. They had no child. McRaild understands that between money and goods there was not less in value than £100 in the boat. The main object of the trip he believes to have been to get representations made through which they might obtain the immediate enjoyment of a portion of the large sum destined for their use which they believe to be in your hands.' [KBP 3/17]

Another reason for Betty Scott's departure was given later: 'She..proved unfaithful, and deserted her husband, but fate overtook her in her attempt to reach the mainland' [MacDiarmid p.11].

85   Seton p.60; Sands (1878) pp.66-67 (The incident is attributed, mistakenly, to 1874); JHM (1863) [KBP 15/2]

86   HC CH3/983/1 pp.363, 367, 388, 392, 396, 401, 410

87   JHM (1863) [KBP 15/2] The account of Maxwell's second visit to St Kilda is from this journal unless otherwise stated.

88   Captain Otter noted a list of 'Pilots' for this area in 1858 – 'the best men to be procured'. They included four from Obbe, all of whom spoke Gaelic: Donald McLeod, seaman; [?] McLeod, (Over) seaman; Murdoch Ferguson, seaman; Hugh McLeod, 'No Seaman'. Donald McLeod spoke Gaelic only. In addition there were John McCaskill, seaman, Berneray, and Alexander McDonald, (Over) seaman, Boreray. Both had English as well as Gaelic. [Hydrographic Data Centre OD365]

89   FCMR New Series no.14 (1 December 1863) The illustration may be compared with that given by Seton (pl.V opp. p.84).

90   FCMR New Series no.29 (1 December 1864)

91   As n.90 above.

92   FCMR (1 August 1863) p.305

Appendix to Part 5

1. John Hall Maxwell's 'census' of 1860 [JHM KBP 15/1]

'With a view to a fair and appropriate distribution of what the Duke and I had brought, one of my first cares was to obtain from the Catechist, the names and numbers of the different families, and before proceeding farther I may here insert the census of the Island.

1	Lachlan McKinnon	wife and 5 children			7
		children dead		4	
2	John McDonald	wife	2 children		4
				5	
3	Finlay Gillies	wife	6 do.		8
				8	
4.	Neill Ferguson	wife	2 do.		4
				8	
5.	Finlay Ferguson	wife,	sister in law 1 child		4
				5	
6.	Roderick Gillies	wife,	1 child		3
				2	
7.	John McDonald	wife	3 children		5
				6	
8.	Malcolm McDonald	wife	2 children		4
				12	
9.	Donald McQuien	Mother, wife	2 children		5
				12	
10.	John Gillies	wife	5 children		7
				6	
11.	Norman Gillies	wife	3 children		5
				5	
	Malcolm McKinnon	Mother	0		2
12.	Donald Gillies	wife	2 children		4
				8	
	Angus McDonald	wife	0		2
13.	Widow Gillies		4 children		5
				3	
14.	Widow McDonald		1 child		2
15.	Widow McCrimmon		1 child		2

466

Roderick Gillies	old Bachelor	
Effie McCrimmon	unmarried	
Christina McLeod	Idiot	3

'There are only two single heads of families unmarried one of them an old Bachelor – 1 Idiot – Christina McLeod, and it will be observed that as against 40 Children alive – 84 have died.'

2. <u>Captain Henry C Otter's 'census'</u>: Families in St Kilda June 1860
[<u>Hydrographic Data Centre –</u> Letter Book Captain Otter]

	<u>Present number in each family</u>	<u>Children dead</u>
Finlay Gillies	8	8
Lachlan McKinnon	7	4
Roderick Gillies	1	
John Macdonald	4	5
Neil Ferguson	4	8
Finlay Ferguson	4	5
Roderick Gillies	3	2
John Macdonald	5	6
Malcolm Macdonald	4	12
Ann McCrimmon	2	
Donald McQueen	5	12
John Gillies	7	6
Norman Gillies	5	5
Malcolm McLennan	2	
Widow Gillies	5	3
Donald Gillies	4	8
Angus McDonald	2	
Donald McDonald	2	1
Christy McLoed	1	
Effie McCrimmon	<u>1</u>	<u>–</u>
	76	85

—————— PART VI ——————

TOURISTS AND JOURNALISTS
Pressure on St Kilda from the
'Outside World'

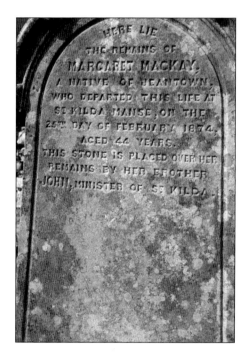

The possibility of deserting St Kilda and emigrating to the mainland or abroad was almost continually in the air after 1850. An assortment of visitors came by yacht, by government ships and by one or other of the west coast steamers such as the *Dunara Castle* that ventured on trips out beyond Uist and Harris, and in their books and newspaper articles remarked on the economic sense of removing the population and leaving the place to the birds. The only disadvantage of this would have been the disappearance of a major tourist attraction if there was no group of 'natives' to look at.

The more the islanders depended on outside aid from remote organisations and individuals the less it appeared that they could survive on their own independent efforts. The Free Church, first with the catechist Kennedy and then with John Mackay, minister in St Kilda for twenty-four years, had to deal with the various forms of outside interest which invaded St Kilda while it was still inhabited. It was therefore an essential intermediary between the steamer parties, naturalists, yachtsmen and officials, and the island people eager as they were to take advantage of the gifts and goods brought to them, whether needed or not, and because of that ready to question the merits of their minister as their representative in these worldly matters. The difficult relationship between St Kilda and the outside world was highlighted by the journalistic John Sands whose personal views and prejudices as expressed in his books and in letters to the press were the cause of extended dispute with the proprietor, Macleod of Macleod, and his sister Emily over the marketing of island produce. While Emily looked for means to make it easier for the people to live in St Kilda by establishing a nurse and a teacher and arranging a sufficient kind of communication, others persisted in the view that evacuation was the only answer.

CHAPTER 1

Alexander Carmichael and Effie MacCrimmon meet
about island traditions, and Rev. John Mackay arrives

When Alexander Cameron went to St Kilda in 1863 neither the Free Church nor any other religious body held that broad authority over the people that had characterised former years. Various kinds of loss had already diminished both the numbers and the collective nature of the community. Perhaps no period in the island's history had been without change, but the arrival of John MacDonald and evangelical preaching in the 1820s had begun a process, scarcely perceptible at first, of gradual fragmentation which saw the departure of Donald Mackinnon, at MacDonald's instance, to become a catechist and precentor, and in due course the emigration of 1852. To this movement away can be added other individual cases of migration to some of the larger islands in the Outer Hebrides and eventually to the mainland. The loss of the *Dargavel* can only have undermined what little confidence there was left in the ability of the people to survive as a distinct island population.

While the islanders were necessarily bound by circumstances to work together and organise their activities by unified consent evangelical religion had helped to set apart individuals as leaders with influence over the rest, a development which was both reinforced and slightly upset by the presence on the island of Betty Scott, a strong personality from the mainland who married into an island family and must have introduced an independent way of thinking. Her husband and son became exceptionally prosperous, while her daughter, as housekeeper to the minister, also held a position of unusual importance. But more disruptive than any of these variations from the traditional unity were the interventions of total strangers, many of whom never even saw St Kilda from a distance. Certainly there were those who actually visited - Acland, the *Vulcan*'s passengers, T S Muir - but, like the public subscriptions and other philanthropic gestures of 1860 and afterwards, more remote agencies of 'help' for the poor people began to appear, as for instance the 'Ladies' associations in mainland towns and cities.

When therefore the Kelsall Bequest funds came into the hands of the HASS in 1857 they greatly increased public interest and a general realisation among the inhabitants of St Kilda that material assistance from 'outside' was available. External aid, when it arrived, resulted in further reliance upon it, and it came in all shapes and sizes, ranging from presents given by rich parties on board steam yachts to government ships responding to apparent distress. With the impact of these unexpected resources greater changes still occurred. Religion, while remaining central to daily life, could do nothing by way of bringing in the means of material advancement which the islanders now hoped for; the people themselves learned to look more eagerly - greedily some said - for the gifts and free supplies that seemed so great a contrast to the harsh trading arrangements made by the steward or factor for so long; and the proprietor became a person of more doubtful relevance by comparison with Admiralty officers and journalists.[1]

The years after 1863 thus brought an array of odd arrivals to the St Kilda scene, serving only to confuse and disturb a small group of inhabitants, who, though called 'St Kildans', 'St Kildians', 'St Kildites', and other inappropriate names, no longer seemed to be a coherent island community but rather a disparate remnant, maintaining some traditions but waiting for some kind of rescue or solution. Surprisingly perhaps, their story had not quite reached its inevitable conclusion, and the church was still to play a part in prolonging their deep attachment to their 'rock' in the ocean.

*

Charles Kelsall and his bequest could have inspired two other gentlemen to express a concern for the welfare of Hebridean people. Both may have already had leanings towards the Free Church, and both were especially interested in remoter islands, including Barra and those lesser isles scattered southwards. In November 1857 the Edinburgh Ladies Highland Schools Association (ELHSA) heard that Duncan Cowan Esq. of Beeslack near Penicuik had been financially supporting a school 'in the dark and Popish island of Barra' and was ready to add a further £20 in aid of another school, possibly to be situated in Berneray, sometimes called Barra Head after the main cliff and headland with its lighthouse, but more probably in Barra itself. Some months after, in the spring of 1858, the ELHSA committee, having been informed by the 'Lighthouse Authority' that it could not give any grant of money to help in maintaining a teacher on Berneray, found itself unable to pay the whole salary itself and so could do nothing for the people of 'this remote island'. Later in the same year, however, it appeared that a 'Mr McKerrol of Bath' had promised £20 or £25 for three years to support a school but 'from the inaccessible nature of the place it had been found impossible to get arrangements made to open a school there before Spring'. A school was duly opened in 1859, but it was on Mingulay rather than Berneray, and an account of events was presented to the ELHSA's general meeting at the end of November:

'Great difficulty was experienced in the case of Barrahead, in which W. McKerrol, Esq., Great Malvern, felt so much interest as to offer £25 a year for a school there. The lighthousekeeper, expecting to be removed, withdrew his offer of aid, and most of the people were removed to the adjacent island of Mingulay, where nobody could be found to make any

471

preparation for the teacher, or to promise to encourage or aid him. It was felt to be a very perilous and difficult experiment to send a young man to so remote a place, where nobody could read, and all were Roman Catholics, and where the only mode of communication was a small packet to Barra, - itself a very inaccessible place, - once a fortnight. However, a young man being found willing to make the trial, he was sent in May last, and was so well received, that in a few weeks he had a flourishing school of about sixty scholars, was lodged by the people as comfortably as they could; and in August, when the barn was required in which the school had been taught, they offered to build a new house, if a little aid could be given them for timber for the roof and windows, for which they had to send a boat to Fort-William. The progress the children have made has been very encouraging, and this arduous enterprise has hitherto succeeded beyond the most sanguine expectations.'[2]

The ELHSA teachers in Barra and Mingulay saw next to no visitors over several years 'and little could be known of them except from the teachers themselves,' a remark that was reminiscent of those made regarding the St Kilda missionary more than a century earlier. At its 1865 AGM the ELHSA committee recorded its gratitude for 'the diligence and faithfulness of their solitary and unaided labours in these most inaccessible regions'. During the year 'very encouraging letters' had arrived from both stations, 'the teachers there having met with more encouragement there than in any former years'. The tireless Dr McLauchlan had been to some of the remotest schools, 'and his details of visits to Barra and Mingalay must surely awaken increased sympathy for the teachers, who are so completely shut out from the privileges of society and means of grace'. The language again seems as much suited to St Kilda as to Mingulay or Barra: 'It is very rarely that such islands as Mingalay can be reached, the voyage there being one of great danger, except in the fine calm weather of part of the last summer; and cheerless indeed would be the lot of the inhabitants of these remote islands without the education which this association has been the means of bringing within their reach.' Perhaps the Free Church ladies had the impression that one of their teachers in a totally Catholic community was far more cut off than one on the Free Church island of St Kilda, as indeed to some degree he was.[3]

The young man who was the ELHSA teacher in Mingulay was John Finlayson, whose subsequent somewhat erratic career on the island is better known for its involvement in natural history than for its educational success. He came from Lochcarron where the family was of well-known Free Church persuasion, and his residence of around forty years as teacher among the Catholic population of the island, with his marriage to Jane Campbell, is among the more unusual episodes in recent Outer Hebrides history. His teaching in the early years seems to have been effective but he was faced with various problems and from time to time left for unknown reasons. In 1868 he was away for a while but was back by May 1869 when £3 was ordered to be sent to 'Mr John Finlayson teacher Mingalay to be divided between the woman who nursed his Substitute through the fever of which he died, and her nephew who carried on the School till Mr Finlayson's return'. There is a tradition that his apparent contentment in a Catholic community did not meet with the approval of the Free Church, and this may explain the letters that were read by the ELHSA on 14 October 1870. They contained 'an unsatisfactory account of the School at Mingalay' and recommended 'that it should be suspended for the winter and a new Teacher sent there in Spring'. The suggestion was made by Rev. Robert Ross in South Uist and was accepted, but with the Education Act of 1872 the ELHSA's connection with Mingulay ceased and Finlayson stayed. Less than ten years later the ladies revived their interest in education at St Kilda, where schooling had been always rather fitful and substitutes were virtually unheard of.[4]

*

Publicity such as that given by the publication in October 1860 of Captain Otter's letter about the storm, and possible communication between benefactors like Kelsall and Cowan, attracted ever greater attention to distant islanders, especially to those in St Kilda. For the most part, however, this meant interest by a wide variety of individuals rather than by tourist crowds who were as yet without means of reaching the extreme west and in any case knew nothing about it. Yachtsmen, having their own transport, made the island the highlight of a northern cruise, as when the Irishman William Power included it in his round-Britain expedition. He arrived in the St Kilda bay one June afternoon in the early 1860s and saw the gathering of the inhabitants at the shore where they directed him to the landing place. The factor was there, and so too was a clergyman who could have been either Duncan Kennedy or, less likely, Alexander Cameron but was unnamed in Power's log:

'Walking up towards the village, the natives following, we were met by the minister who received us very kindly and invited us into his house, a two storied building rather dilapidated as to slates. Whiskey and bread and cheese and milk was put before us. The minister's two daughters nice looking ladylike girls waited upon us - they would not sit down while we were eating. The minister however eat and drank with us, and took large quantities of snuff, he was very deaf, however he smiled most cheerfully at everything we said, indeed all the St Kildieans seemed to be perpetually on the broad grin. While we were eating they had collected outside the window and kept peering in to see how the strangers conducted themselves, not rudely staring in, but vanishing as soon as they were observed. Having wound up with a cup of tea, the ladies retired, and we observed them outside surrounded by an eager crowd anxious to learn something about the new arrivals in St Kilda. They held forth and seemed to have much authority with the natives. The ministers parlour was not very cheerful, few panes of glass being left in the windows and but little plaster remaining on the roof and walls, the result of heavy gales in the spring.'

The minister invited his guests to stay for the night, but with the wind blowing straight in from the east they had to leave, 'the minister promising to breakfast with us next morning, after which he would show us the island, and we should see the natives descending the cliffs by ropes'. Two of the visitors, 'Bob and Andy', were 'much disgusted with the general appearance of St Kilda', and the yacht departed with no one on board particularly wishing ever to return.[5]

Another kind of interested individual was Alexander Carmichael, who went to the island not to collect taxes but to see the place with the eyes of one who wished to learn and preserve what he could of the traditions and songs. He set out from Lochmaddy on 22 May 1865, travelling by Royal Navy ship perhaps commanded by Captain, later Admiral, Otter. The ship left at 4.30 a.m. on a fine morning with a few light showers and reached St Kilda at noon. Carmichael went ashore in the first boat and spent the majority of his time, but not all of it, like an average visitor as he recorded in revealing notes: 'Was at Manse. Poorly furnished but good house. Cameron the missionary oldish and common looking. St Kildeans good looking ..fellows with pale complexions. Women good looking and ruddy complexions, and bad ankles and feet. Beautiful white teeth. Enunciation peculiar and lisping.' He was rather disappointed with the behaviour of the islanders – 'People seem to be spoiled. Not polite.' He bought 10¼ yards of cloth for 14s and a bottle of fulmar oil for 1s. Then he kissed 'a St Kilda Lassie. A little beauty with dark brown eyes and fresh complexion about ten or eleven years. Kissed her so as to have to say that I kissed a St Kilda lassie.' Like a tourist too he climbed a slope at the back of the houses and watched men 'going in rocks'. But at some point, quite unlike a tourist, he spent a while recording compositions 'from the recitation of Eibhrig Nic Cruimein, Euphemia MacCrimmon, cottar, aged eighty-four years, who had many old songs, stories, and traditions of the island'. This was the old lady who had given some of her store to Anne Kennedy only two or three years earlier, and she was clearly something an exception among the St Kilda people. Carmichael was rather frustrated by the inconvenient circumstances at his meeting with Euphemia:

'I would have got more of these had there been peace and quiet to take them down, but this was not to be had among a crowd of naval officers and seamen and St Kilda men, women and children, and, even noisier than these, St Kilda dogs, mad with excitement and all barking at once. The aged reciter was much censured for her recital of these songs and poems, and the writer for causing the old woman to stir the recesses of her memory for this lore; for the people of St Kilda have now discarded songs and music, dancing, folklore, and the stories of the foolish past.'

One story he heard was of a visit made to North Uist for corn seed. The eighteen men in the boat were taken to the farm of Balranald where they were supplied with what they needed, and then they started out on their return voyage, during which they were overwhelmed by the sea and all drowned. Carmichael noted that their visit to Balranald was long remembered: 'If a question were asked of one of them, all the eighteen men would reply simultaneously, with one voice and one accord.' Mrs MacDonald at the farm asked whether they had marriages and baptisms in St Kilda. 'Oh my dear beloved, no, we have no marriages or baptisms, rather we are dying out. How shall we marry and baptize, did not the "bramach-innilt" die? and we cannot have children, and we are, my dear, like to die out.' 'What is the "bramach-innilt"?' 'It is, my dear, the female who attends to the woman who is sending children into the world.'[6]

The 1850s in St Kilda were a period of no marriages and, with high infant deaths, few baptisms, and it may be that the voyage to Uist was that of the *Dargavel* when disaster was narrowly avoided. Certainly the loss of eighteen island men is not otherwise recorded as it surely would have been if it had happened. But the interesting thing about the conversation at Balranald is the comment by the island crew, if indeed it was genuine, that the St Kilda population was 'dying out'. Was this a real feeling among the people? With the emigration in 1852, the deaths of children, the lack of marriages, and the absence of regular spiritual and medical care, it would not be surprising if the community did look upon its future with pessimism. And, while it may have cheered the people up a little, the appearance of a successor to Alexander Cameron in 1865 soon after Carmichael's visit was to prove less of a comfort than might have been expected.

*

Alexander Cameron sent no more than one or two messages by way of report to the Free Church Highlands committee which had appointed him. In November 1864 the committee read a letter from him stating that no deputies had visited the island over the last three years and confirming the desirableness of having there such a person as himself, an ordained probationer. His stay on St Kilda had already been extended for a second period of twelve months, and perhaps he would have liked to continue under a permanent or long-term arrangement, but on 17 May 1865 the presbytery of Skye and Uist sent notice to the committee that it was seeking the Free Church General Assembly's permission to take a probationer 'on trials' for ordination with a view to his being appointed on a regular basis to St Kilda. A week or so later the committee agreed that it would quickly recall Cameron and in his place send Mr John MacKay.[7]

John MacKay, born in Inverness about 1816, was the son of a Lochcarron fisherman, also John MacKay, who lived in a small thatched cottage at the west end of the long village known sometimes as Jeantown. The family attached itself to the Free Church, probably soon after 1843, just as the Finlaysons of the same place did. No doubt John Finlayson and John MacKay came to know each other well before their respective departures to Mingulay and St Kilda. Like Finlayson and like many other young men who were to make the church their career MacKay seems to have begun as a teacher and was nearly fifty at the time of his commitment to St Kilda. It appears that the salary, previously an obstacle that had prevented an earlier appointment of an ordained missionary, was less of a problem in 1865 because 'through the effective appeals of Dr. McLauchlan, convener of the Highland committee, a sum of £500 was raised as an endowment, which, added to the other allowances, enabled the Church to send a minister, and on 13th August 1865, Mr John MacKay was ordained by the Presbytery of Skye and Uist as missionary to St. Kilda'. On 19 August the committee considered a letter from the presbytery clerk, Rev. James Reid, already met in the company of Captain Otter in 1860, enquiring as to the amount MacKay would in fact receive should the proceeds of the endowment be added to the existing £60 per annum. The convener replied that indeed the proceeds would be added, even though there had been no proper agreement between the presbytery and the committee over MacKay's ordination.[8]

John MacKay was already in St Kilda before the committee was able to deal with Alexander Cameron's letter telling members that though his appointment came to an end on 1 September 1865 he would not be able to leave until 1 October when Mackay was expected to arrive. The letter also contained application for further employment, but the committee, meeting on 16 January 1866, while agreeing to pay him for the extra month on the island, delayed consideration of the request for a job.[9]

The new missionary's first move after his arrival was to write to say that the windows of the church and manse needed repair. The Highlands committee, however, decided merely to keep this work in view as it could do nothing about it until at least the following spring, and by then the weather had taken a hand again. At the same January meeting a letter from Rev. Alexander McColl, Dunvegan, was read with some concern. A severe gale had just swept over St Kilda and McColl wished to bring to the committee's attention 'the probable effects of the late storm upon the houses of the people and the Church buildings'. Having the example of the help given by Otter and the *Porcupine* before him he suggested that an application should be made to the Admiralty 'to ask that one of their vessels in the vicinity should call in and see the state of the people'. It was agreed that the convener should write seeking the assistance of 'one of the Government steamers' in the area, which might be ordered to call at the island for this purpose. Within the next month H.M.S. *Jackal* visited St Kilda in response, and 'best thanks' were conveyed to the Admiralty and to the ship's commanding officer, Captain Dyer, for prompt and generous attention to the islanders' assumed needs. It appears that although the press had announced that the people were suffering from famine the situation was in fact not nearly so serious, but repairs to the buildings were certainly necessary. Damage had been done to both Church and manse. When McColl wrote again in May 1866 to say that the factor Norman MacRaild had undertaken to procure materials and ensure that the 'church' repairs were carried out by the mason already working there for the proprietor the Free Church accepted responsibility for the expense.[10]

Almost since the building of the church and manse it had been evident that from time to time repairs would be necessary and that the islanders themselves would not be able to carry these out because, even if they had the skills, they lacked the materials. Thus the very presence of the buildings added to the community's dependence upon outside assistance, as would a constructed landing place and any other similar feature introduced by the proprietor or by government. The newly-erected cottages were reckoned to be a great improvement, providing better living conditions than those to be found in much more accessible islands, but they illustrated the plain fact that attempts to bring the poor people of St Kilda into such an advanced state as might encourage them to stay had economic implications far beyond the means of those people, whatever their level and variety of produce, and might, by making them look ever more frequently to the external world, achieve exactly the opposite of the effect intended. The proprietor and his factor were no longer the only source of relief after crop failure or storms; now, following the precedent set by the *Porcupine*, Admiralty vessels were called upon, at whatever embarrassment to the proprietor, to bring supplies in seasons of distress.

In due course John MacKay was to become more immediately involved in such points of crisis, as was H.M.S. *Jackal*, but in his first winter on the island he was more concerned with the condition of his own house. After the initial disturbance by the January storm he was able to apply himself to his duties and to establish a programme of religious activity consistent with the usual arrangements made by a permanently resident Free Church minister anywhere in the Highlands and islands, while his employers, greatly satisfied at having secured an incumbent for their remotest and, to many, most unappealing outpost, devoted themselves to raising funds in support of further appointments to difficult stations. They were to some extent frustrated. Issue no. 60 of the Monthly Record, dated 1 July 1867, noted that 'The sums contributed to aid the Endowment Scheme for the last year have been very small. This is cause of great regret, seeing how much depends upon it. There are several charges throughout the Highlands which could not now be enjoying the services of a settled ministry were it not for this scheme. The case of St Kilda alone is sufficient to prove its value, the poor people of that island having now a settled minister, after a delay of upwards of twenty years.' John MacKay remained 'settled' in St Kilda until 1889, living in a fairly uncomfortable manse but looked after perhaps by his sister Margaret and certainly by Betty Scott's daughter, Ann MacDonald, his servant and later housekeeper.[11]

Nearly three years after his move to St Kilda MacKay met Henry John Elwes, a sturdy, whiskered gentleman who had been educated at Eton and was a captain in the Scots Guards. Elwes, to whom 'Ornithology was certainly his first love', had spent part of his childhood collecting eggs and firing at birds with a catapult, an excellent apprenticeship for becoming an ornithologist in Victorian times, and a kind of training for the later ornithological pursuits which formed the main occupation and purpose of his tour among the Hebrides in the 'unusually stormy' spring and summer of 1868. He had made arrangements for a smack to take him to St Kilda during this period but in view of the poor weather 'I should have failed in the expedition if it had not been for the kindness of Captain Bell, of H.M.S. *Harpy*, a paddle-steamer, which was going to see how the St. Kildans were faring, since they had been cut off from communication with the other islands for nearly nine months'. So, in the early morning of 22 May 1868 the *Harpy* took him out past Gaisgeir into the Atlantic. No landing was possible on Boreray as had been the plan owing to 'the tremendous swell', and the steamer made for the bay, where, almost immediately, 'the people began to appear', and some men came out 'in a large, clumsy boat, the only one they have in which to go to the adjacent isles'. Down to the shore too came John MacKay.[12]

In his subsequent account of the visit Elwes gave the impression that MacKay was pleased to see him although there was nothing whatsoever in common between the Etonian soldier and the Free Church minister, not even an interest in birds. 'On landing we were met by the minister, Mr. Mackay, who appeared very glad to see anyone, as may well be imagined. Strange to say, he did not seem to take any interest in, or to know much about the birds, though he has been two years among people whose thoughts are more occupied by birds than anything else, and who depend principally on them for their living.' There was of course nothing strange about this as, being resident among them, MacKay would take the presence and usefulness of birds for granted and had more important aspects of life to think about. When he showed a picture of the probably extinct great auk to the people, perhaps in the hope that someone would say that he saw one yesterday, Elwes achieved very little response, 'and though Mr. Mackay promised to take down any stories or information about the bird that he could collect' it seems that he never did. At the time the islanders 'were so excited by the arrival of strangers that it was impossible to get them to say more about it', and the great auk would have to wait till they calmed down. But by then Elwes and the *Harpy* were gone.

Before his departure Elwes climbed Conachair and himself collected fulmar eggs by descending the cliff on a rope. He 'got one of the natives to go down to show us his way of catching birds' and by this means added fulmar to his 'spoils'. He returned to the houses and walked along the 'street'. 'After visiting a few of the houses, and examining all the objects of interest, I returned to the *Harpy* to deposit my birds and eggs, and found most of the older men collected on board begging for tobacco, sugar and other things, though they did not seem very anxious to give us anything in exchange.' Some of the ship's crew had been busy collecting eggs themselves, but this 'excited the indignation of the older men, who considered it in the light of stealing their property'. To quieten them down they were given small presents of the tobacco and sugar they were asking for. The *Harpy* remained long enough for a ship's boat to be launched to land Elwes and some islanders on Dun where the former took some puffin eggs and the latter 'every fulmar and every egg they could get' in the short time they were there. But darkness was coming on, the wind was rising quickly, and they left in a hurry, having difficulty in returning to the boat owing to the increasing swell. Elwes was very sorry to leave the place without visiting all the islands but, unlike the Duke of Athole, he had no wish to be left in St Kilda for a month or more, and 'the weather looked so threatening that Captain Bell was very unwilling to remain longer'. Soon a gale was blowing from the south-east, and a further landing at St Kilda was to prove impossible during the next five weeks.

Visits by individuals like Elwes were still not very common in the 1860s, but it presumably took an ornithologist of his kind to introduce the idea to St Kilda that money might be made out of selling birds' eggs and possibly birds, especially the fulmar which was then found nowhere else in Britain. The great auk, had it been available, would have been a really valuable commodity. After 1870 the urge to collect specimens was a regular part of the naturalist's intention in visiting bird colonies of the Hebrides, and mingled with it was the pleasure the sportsman derived from shooting birds and animals with his gun and rifle. Not far removed from this form of fun was the cannon-firing and whistle-blowing by vessels passing near Boreray with the aim of entertaining passengers who would wonder at the sight of the startled gannets taking off and filling the sky above them. Birds, it seems, were as much a recreation as a view of the St Kilda natives - and their minister.

John MacKay might have expected Free Church deputies from Lewis, Skye or the mainland to appear occasionally around midsummer but none

479

came, partly because MacKay was settled minister in the island and there was no need for them, and partly because there was no eagerness among ministers to make the long and often uncomfortable journey. A few went, out of a sense of duty or of curiosity, to some other isolated places. Rev. Sutherland of Inverness, for instance, serving as a deputy, made his way in 1866 to the Shetland island of Foula which he called 'the St. Kilda of the Northern seas'. On his approach in a ship named the *Nelson* the 'worthy catechist' there, James Manson, came out in a boat, 'and great was his delight to find a Free Church deputy on board'. It might have been John MacKay greeting a long-awaited visitor; but no such delight brightened the life of that isolated missionary if he needed one.

Sutherland's dealings with Manson were similar to those of a deputy visiting a catechist in St Kilda:

'I instructed him to proceed to the school-house, announce my coming, and despatch three of the swiftest-footed in the school to the two or three hamlets that include the population, and apprise them of a sermon at the school-house at 4 o'clock. Meanwhile, I slowly wended my way to the school-house, where I found a most interesting group of children. I examined them in the ordinary branches, more especially in Bible history and the Shorter Catechism, and most admirably did they answer. Thereafter, I preached a short sermon to the children; and towards its close all the adults, male and female, on the island at the time had assembled ... The services were somewhat protracted - nearly three hours in duration - but they were *manifestly* and *demonstratively* appreciated by young and old. After the interesting meeting, I distributed tracts and suitable books, which were highly prized; and I handed the remainder to your worthy catechist, to whose excellent and acceptable services Mr. Cheyne - the schoolmaster, son of the late worthy teacher at Fair Isle, belonging to the S.P.C.K. - bore the most willing testimony.'

Sutherland left the island and its 'interesting people' with much reluctance, but, as so often at St Kilda, the ship's captain was keen to depart although the evening was gloriously calm. 'I believe,' reported the minister, not about St Kilda but of Foula, 'that amongst them, though poor in regard to this world, and far remote, there are those who are "rich in faith", and "near to the Lord".'[13]

The rarity or absence of deputy visits to the distant, often inaccessible island stations left the missionaries of the Free Church in St Kilda and Foula feeling abandoned, but they may not have been so much at risk as those teachers and catechists placed in the Catholic islands of Eriskay, Mingulay and even Barra. In Eriskay and Barra, wrote Mr Fullartown of Grantown who went there as a deputy in 1870, '*Popery holds almost unbroken sway*'. Of over 400 people on the former island only two or three were not Catholic, and, as the Free Church man saw it, 'Nothing is being done for poor Eriskay and its 400 perishing souls but what the male and female teachers employed by the Glasgow ladies do.' Meanwhile on Barra nothing was being done for the 2000 perishing souls there 'except what is done by Mr Norman McLean'. Mr McLean was the catechist, 'labouring diligently and successfully, building up the adherents of the Free Church .., giving them the gospel of the grace of God from week to week', and gaining 'the respect of the Roman Catholics and Established Church people', even though there was no available spot for a meeting place. 'Is this Scotland, one feels inclined to ask, where people who would worship God can find no place to meet even on the sea-shore, and who, when they move inland, can find no field but what is owned by an adherent of the Church of Rome?'[14]

Catholicism and Catholic places certainly presented a great challenge but they were not exactly the threat they had been to the Protestant church a century and more earlier. Isolation, neglect, shortage of funds and of men as always, and, above all, a changing world, were much more troublesome problems for the Free Church. This Church was fortunate in having a Gaelic-speaking minister in St Kilda. Elsewhere the lack of men able to preach in Gaelic meant many vacant charges and extra demands upon limited resources in order to support and encourage Gaelic-speaking students in their years at university. In 1871 Dr McLauchlan told the Free Church Assembly that 'after a long vacancy of twenty-seven years' a minister had been at last 'planted' in the 'Popish' island of South Uist, but this had only been possible because 'kind friends' had produced an endowment of £1000 for the charge. The appeal for further donations to endow ministers was a regular feature of each year's programme, accompanied as it was by the equally well established Sustentation Fund for which congregations had to 'exert themselves'. In addition to these financial burdens there were other, more general concerns that might endanger any 'flock' that was not properly looked after, 'For it is not reasonable to suppose that those whom the Church does not care for will be able to withstand the corrupting influences of the World'. These 'influences' were, in the opinion of the Free Church, uncomfortably near, and as things turned out not even a settled Free Church missionary was able to defend the people of St Kilda against them:

'It is absolutely certain that a critical time for the Highlands is approaching. The land is passing out of the hands of the old proprietors into the possession, in many instances, of wealthy Englishmen who have made money by trade. The iron horse also is finding his way into the glens, and the loneliest mountain crags have been startled with the shriek of the railway whistle. And immense and increasing shoals of tourists are pouring all the summer through along its highways. That all this must tell upon the character of the people is obvious.'[15]

The lesser threat of rival activity was also observed in the behaviour of 'the busy Convener of the Home Mission Scheme of the Establishment' who 'has this summer been visiting the Isles, and trying to bring back some of the lost sheep to the fold'.

Despite its remoteness, or rather because of it, St Kilda was, as from one point of view or another it had always been, at least as much at risk from 'influences' as anywhere else in the north-west. With the publicity given by writers and lecturers and the now customary eagerness among the inhabitants to pick up gifts from visiting ships, the island was already at the mercy of the encroaching world outside. Railways might be a long way off, but the steamer full of tourists was soon to make up for that, and the relationship of 'the World' to John MacKay's Free Church 'influence' would then become a matter of great importance to continued life in St Kilda. All of a sudden the Free Church, as much as any other denomination open to accusations of being a corrupting influence, might find itself in the position of being an upholder of tradition, custom and values amid a rapidly changing atmosphere and economy. How would it react? Would it become more 'worldly' or would it stiffen its resolve? And in his island fastness would John MacKay or his successor respond to any changes of attitude occurring in far-away committees?

CHAPTER 2

The steamer Dunara Castle begins its regular visits with tourists, St Kilda returns to the Macleods of Macleod, and Norman MacRaild is replaced as factor by John T Mackenzie

Throughout their history the people of St Kilda were described by strangers whose personal experience of the island varied in length from many years to none at all. Until the ministry of Neil MacKenzie ending in 1844 most accounts were written by visitors who spoke Gaelic and could therefore communicate directly with the islanders, but subsequently the record is almost entirely composed of recollections by English-speaking tourists and officials who depended upon the information supplied by missionaries. There were exceptions, but it has to be borne in mind that the later picture of life in St Kilda is largely the work of non-native people, often journalists or contributors to newspapers, whose approach was not objective but influenced by their own prejudices and misconceptions. This is especially the case after 1870 when the little community experienced the 'shoals' of sightseers forecast and feared by the Free Church Monthly Record.

Anyone wishing to see St Kilda for himself, or for that matter other strange attractions in the west like Staffa or possibly Mingulay, depended of course on transport by sea. Until the 1870s fishing boats, private yachts and Admiralty vessels were the most likely means available, although it might be possible to reach St Kilda in a hired boat or by accompanying the estate factor on one of his visits in a smack. But steamer services, then expanding throughout the islands, were adding passenger to cargo facilities and becoming increasingly popular. Cargo steamers, leaving from Glasgow and Oban, arranged their routes in a very accommodating manner. In the summer of 1873 for instance the steamer – *Clydesdale* or *Clansman* - setting out from Oban to Stornoway called at Craignure, Lochaline, Salen, Armadale, Glenelg, Balmacara, Kyleakin, Broadford, 'and any other place that may be agreed upon'. Goods and some adventurous passengers were thereby delivered to many a remote settlement on the mainland and island shores.[16]

New vessels were advertised with a flourish if not always with immediate relevance to a passenger's comfort, as when the *St Clair of the Isles* appeared in July 1873:

> 'We are glad to announce to our friends in the west, that a new steamer, the "St Clair of the Isles", has just begun to ply between the Clyde and the Western Isles. The "St Clair" is a fine paddle steamer, with splendid saloon accommodation, and berths, etc., for forty cabin passengers. Her figurehead is a Highlander in full costume – blue bonnet with feather, dark-green jacket, Stewart tartan plaid fastened at the shoulder with a

gold brooch, his right hand is brought across his breast as if in the act of making for his claymore, on which his left hand is laid, and his face looks as if he were in earnest.'[17]

It may be that many of the forty passengers nervously looked forward to seeing such an earnest 'Highlander' emerge from a cave or thatched cottage in Morvern, Skye and Lewis, but even if fancy and ignorance did not extend that far the St Clair's fine figurehead must have played its part in strengthening the extraordinary 'Scottish Highlander' image that persisted for so long.

Sailing on schedule 'unless prevented by some unforeseen occurrence', the St Clair of the Isles promised much for the tourist trade. But three weeks after her first voyage she struck a rock and had to retire for repairs, while her owners, the Western Isles Steam Packet Company, had to look for a temporary replacement. On 16 August 1873 news from Barra included sympathy for the injured vessel which had been expected in Castlebay. 'We hope the company will not be discouraged for a moment; let them only persevere and they need not fear of success. The traffic to and from the Western Isles has of late years so immensely increased, and is still increasing, that there is ample room for two weekly steamers at the least.' In the same month the Earl of Shaftesbury, not trusting to steamers, went to St Kilda 'in a steam-yacht, taking with him a large quantity of tea and sugar, etc., and a large number of Bibles for distribution amongst the St Kildeans.'[18]

The people of North Uist looked forward to the return of the St Clair of the Isles as they considered her scale of charges 'reasonable' compared with 'the exorbitant charges of the other steamers'. And she was soon in action once again; in mid November 1873 she arrived in the Clyde after calls at Barra, Uist and elsewhere, unloading at the Broomielaw 70 head of cattle including 2 horses and 2 'fine Highland bulls', 83 pigs, 10 tons of cheese, dried fish, lobsters, wool, and 87 passengers. On 6 December the launch of a consort for her was announced in the shape of the Lady Ambrosine: 'She is an iron vessel, propelled by a screw, and is to have compound surface condensing engines of the newest description.'[19]

The following year, 1874, began roughly with several 'disastrous storms', but the two ships, 'started for the patriotic purpose of stimulating the industries and supplying the wants of the Western Isles', acquitted themselves well in the conditions. On 19 March Lady Ambrosine left with a large cargo for Tiree and other ports of call; 'and, by the way, we should mention that the proprietors are projecting a special trip to St Kilda, in June'. This proposal intended as a good advertisement for the company, was supported by the Highlander newspaper that reported it:

'In regard to this, we must put our readers on their guard, lest they should lose the chance. Unless a certain number shall have made application for passages by the 15th of May, there is no certainty that the

August 1821 by the trustees to John MacPherson MacLeod. The sale to Norman Macleod of Macleod was completed on 20 May 1871, when, in return for £3000, the several islands and 'insulated rocks' of St Kilda 'on which the sea fowls are in use to breed' became the property of Norman who, as part of his acquisition, received 'power to build milns and other machinery' there for grinding corn or any other purpose and rights to 'minerals and fossils'. No sooner had this transaction taken place than Macleod of MacLeod had to give consideration to various difficulties, great and small, relating to his exceptional property.[28]

His father had left debts amounting to £46460, and Norman, sinking even further into financial trouble, would have been well advised not to spend money on purchasing an island which was inevitably going to be an added burden on his virtually nonexistent resources. In these circumstances he let the castle of Dunvegan and, leaving his sister Emily Macleod to look after affairs at home, he went to London where he was at first junior clerk in the civil service and in time became head of the Science and Arts department at what was then called the South Kensington Museum.[29]

From a distance therefore he had to familiarise himself with the nature of St Kilda, its sixteen holders of land lots and four or five elderly inhabitants without lots, the amount of rent each of them paid, arrears if any, and its future economic potential. For information of this kind he had initially to rely on Norman MacRaild, who had looked after the island for such a long time and whose records for the early 1870s showed what the produce then was - wool from the proprietor's sheep on Soay and Dun, oil, 'white blanketing', tweed cloth, tallow, cheese, black and grey feathers, and a few cattle - and what happened to it when sold. MacRaild also supplied a list and estimated valuation of articles on St Kilda which had belonged to Sir John MacPherson MacLeod prior to the sale. They included approximately 360 sheep on Soay and Dun, some simple furniture and instruments which must have been in the house built for the factor or 'bailie', and a barometer and encyclopaedia of unknown value in the manse. Whatever the usefulness of his knowledge and experience, however, by April 1873 MacRaild knew that he was no longer needed. 'As I understand by your letter of the 5th Instant my service as Steward of St Kilda is at an end,' he wrote from Colbost; and he was to be replaced by John T MacKenzie, who kept the post office at Dunvegan. 'I am at a loss,' MacRaild went on, 'what disliking the people of St Kilda could have of me as I never went be-yound my instructions, besides I made more for their comfort this 31 years past (through the aid of my employer) in my manual labour etc. that [i.e.than] any of my predecessors.' Thus MacRaild retired from duties which had often been both arduous and dangerous, leaving the proprietor and his appointed factor to face up to a number of unexpected challenges.[30]

There was a minor problem to do with the Free Church. When Sir John MacPherson MacLeod came to sell St Kilda the fate of Alexander MacLeod's mortification was an issue still unresolved. On 6 June 1870 John W Tawse, secretary to the SSPCK, sent a memorandum showing the unchanged position of the Society in relation to the island to Donald MacDonald of Tormore and asked him if he 'could suggest any means by which our funds could be made available.' The obstacle to the use of the money lay in the fact that it would have to be given to the Free Church, and Tawse was looking for a way round this:

> 'It seems to be of no earthly consequence for the People of a Place like St Kilda if the Gospel is preached to them whether it is by a member of the Established Church Free Church or U.P. since if the Free Church will take it up, and send a stated missionary good and well, if not they should hand the Island over to us so that our fund for a missionary may be made available.'

The memorandum was passed by MacDonald to MacLeod of MacLeod who in turn sent it to Rev. John S MacPhail at Knock in Sleat. MacPhail studied it and gave his opinion to the new proprietor in October 1871. He first reviewed briefly the circumstances of the mortification from the beginning, noting that after the Disruption 'the Funds belonging to St Kilda could not be made available by the Society in the ordinary way' because the people joined the Free Church and would only accept 'a religious Instructor' of that persuasion. It was also evident, in MacPhail's interpretation, 'That Mr. Tawse labours under a misapprehension as to what has been done by the Free Church since the responsibility of supplying St. Kilda with Christian ordinances has been laid upon her. All that could possibly be done for some years after the Disruption, was to send a deputation of ministers, now and again, to instruct the people and to administer ordinances. Several ministers of the Free Church did thus visit them - one as often as 5 times. Then as soon as the late Proprietor consented to give the use of the church and manse in St.Kilda to the Free Church, an efficient Catechist, Mr Kennedy, was at once sent to the Island, and I can personally testify as to his diligence and the religious intelligence of the people under his instructions. On Mr. Kennedy's removal in 1863 a Probationer was sent who laboured in the Island for a year and a half and in 1865 an ordained missionary was sent to the Island who has been labouring there ever since. So that Mr. Tawse's statement is not correct when he says "that the people are growing up and dying without religious ordinances." For the last ten years or more the religious wants of the people have been attended to and that they were not attended to earlier arose from the fact that the accommodation on the Island was not open to the Free Church.'

What therefore should be done with the mortification funds?

'It must be plain to anyone acquainted with the case - as you are - that it is vain to attempt to send a minister or catechist of the Established Church there as long as the people continue of their present mind. If the Society desire to make their funds available it can only be, in the meantime by a Free Church agency. And it remains with the Society to consider whether they may not employ a Free Church agency in St. Kilda. I confess that I can see no great difficulty in the case. Mr. Tawse admits in his Letter, that if the Gospel is preached, it is of no consequence, whether it is by a minister of the Established Church or Free Church – that is if the work is done for which the money was given, the Free Church may do it as well as the Established Church. Why then might not Mr. Tawse hand over, year after year, to the Highland Committee of the Free Church, who takes charge of St. Kilda, the Interest of the 6000 merks funded, in order to help in paying the Salary of the missionary? Say that the Interest amounts to £30 - this would pay the half of the salary at present given by the Free Church to the missionary. By this arrangement the work would be done - the funds left would be made available, in doing it - whilst the Society would still retain the capital to be employed in connection with the Established Church, if the people should, at some future time, alter their mind. In any arrangement of this sort, I think it would be right that the Society should feel satisfied that the missionary employed by the Free Church, be a suitable and satisfactory one and that the payment of the annual Interest should depend on their being thus satisfied. I do not see too why, in the case of a new appointment to St. Kilda the person appointed by the F.C. Highland Committee, might not be sent to a Committee of the Society for Prop. Christian Knowledge to satisfy them as to his qualifications.'

MacLeod probably thought that MacPhail's proposal was very sensible, and he wrote to Tawse on the matter, but the latter's reply, of 6 January 1872, presented a completely different solution:

'I regret very much the situation of the Inhabitants of St Kilda but I think you will find it stated in the memorandum which you received from Mr Macdonald that the Society is prohibited by its charter as well as by a decision of the Supreme Court from employing any Schoolmaster Missionaries or Catechists except such as are members or adherents of the Church of Scotland.

'It seems a matter of moonshine whether the Inhabitants of St Kilda belong to the Church of Scotland or Free Church so that they have the Gospel preached to them, and as we cannot give our funds to a Free Church man it would be well if they could be persuaded to take a missionary from us, and probably you might have some influence with them in this way by explaining that it is not a matter of Choice the employment of a Church of Scotland Missionary but of necessity on the part of the Directors.'[31]

Before answering MacLeod got in touch with Sir Charles Trevelyan, a civil servant in India when Sir John MacPherson MacLeod was there and a close friend of Lord Macaulay. Trevelyan and MacLeod of MacLeod had worked in association around 1850 on measures to bring relief to the Highlands and islands where, as in Ireland, destitution was often 'solved' by emigration. MacLeod now let Sir Charles see what John MacPhail had suggested and sought his advice, to which the response was that MacPhail's idea seemed 'moderate and reasonable' and that the SSPCK should agree to it. Trevelyan imagined that Alexander MacLeod 'would not have approved of the people in whom he took so much interest being left without any benefit from his endowment unless they joined in the profession of opinions which they did not really hold'. When that endowment was made there was only one 'kirk of Scotland', and if Alexander had been living in 1872 'there can be little doubt as to which side he would support'. It appeared that Trevelyan had little sympathy for religious arguments:

> 'There is something unexpressibly melancholy in these simple Islanders living on the utmost verge of our civilization, and detached from all communication with us during the greater part of the year, being made the victims - and that in their highest of all interests - of the controversies which amuse the leisure of the more cultivated and better provided population of the mainland. The St Kildans are children in mind and character, as might be predicated from their isolated situation and the narrow range of their ideas - but of the fact several striking examples might be given. I will mention one within my own observation. When we worked together, after the great famine, to relieve the congested population of the Western Highlands and Islands, by sending a large number of entire families to Australia, a large proportion of the population of St Kilda arrived at Liverpool in H. M. Ship Hercules on their way to the Southern Hemisphere. The Docks at Liverpool were the first specimen of the world these good people had ever seen outside St Kilda, and what they observed was in the highest degree astonishing to them. In a Letter which Sir J. M. MacLeod or your Sister (I forget which) shewed me, they said they could compare the multitude of people there to nothing but the last assemblage of all nations at the day of judgement.

> 'It will be extremely gratifying to me if our intercession should obtain a favorable hearing for them on this occasion also.'[32]

MacLeod then replied to Tawse's letter in April 1872, expressing some uncertainty as to which 'side' of the kirk Alexander MacLeod would have supported but quoting Trevelyan's views at length and accordingly recommending that since the SSPCK could not administer the mortification nor put it to use 'it should divest itself of the Fund and convey it to those who can'. As for using his influence, as Tawse had hoped, to persuade the people of St Kilda back into the fold of the established church, MacLeod said: 'I can exercise none in such a matter and I am assured that if I attempted it I would not succeed.' The situation in the island was no longer as it had been about 1850 when 'settled' pastoral care had been wanting for several years and the people, with less definite beliefs of their own, were still as easily persuaded as they had always been. The consequence, therefore, of the discussion by correspondence was to confirm that the SSPCK would have nothing more to do with St Kilda and to clear that particular issue from the path of the proprietor.[33]

At the same time MacLeod learned from the almost as new secretary of the HASS, Fletcher N Menzies, that the Kelsall Fund now stood at £379.3s.7d. This money would continue to be available apart from any contributions to the welfare of the island that MacLeod might make over and above his method of management, and therefore the HASS secretary as well as the landlord and his factor could be held immediately responsible for failure to respond to the islanders' needs in ordinary circumstances or, more especially, in emergency. Shortages, prices, communications, landing-place, these were just some of the old persistent problems at St Kilda; but within a few years the most serious of the unexpected challenges to confront those who in many ways controlled life there, including the missionary, appeared, not with another storm or shipwreck but in the personality and arguments of that disturbing visitor of the mid 1870s, Mr John Sands.[34]

*

A succession of yacht visits to St Kilda began in 1873 with the arrival of the *Nyanza* owned by a Mr Young who took with him four members of his own family and several friends including Dr R Angus Smith. Smith duly published an account of the trip in two parts in the *Good Words* volume for 1875 and again, with some alterations, as an independent work in 1879. The party was met on landing by a crowd of inhabitants who struck them as looking remarkably prosperous: 'How happy these men looked! How bright-eyed, how fat and comfortable, and well-fed! We expected scenes of misery, where have they gone? - surely such men live in happy homes.' When the minister, John MacKay, was asked by these 'happy' inhabitants to seek the help of the strangers in doing 'something for the poor people of this island' the request aroused no ready willingness to assist them as '"Amongst all the working people we have seen, we have observed none that looked so sleek and well fed, or more comfortably clad"'. Though presents were distributed requests multiplied, and 'If we had supposed that our journey was to cause us to undertake the social regeneration of St. Kilda, or the increase of wealth, we should have hesitated to come'. Long lines and small lines for the fishing were needed, as was 'a nine-ton boat in order to cross to Harris', and Mr Young went away with at least the latter in mind by way of positive response.[35]

With the minister as guide the visitors walked on to see the houses, most of which were now those built in the 1860s and were not as comfortable to live in as their outward appearance promised. In one of his articles *Maolan* who, from what he wrote, could have been a member of Mr Young's party, or of his crew, observed of the zinc plates with which the slates on each house had been replaced that they were 'by far too short' and not watertight, 'for no sooner does it rain outside … than it directly drops through the roofs, and although the drops are not so black as tar, as they used to be in the old houses, they are, nevertheless, equally disagreeable'. On this subject Smith quoted the minister, who said that the zinc plates were a failure, '"since it rained inside whenever it rained outside"'. Two of the older dwellings were still inhabited, and to Dr Smith these were just the same as the generality of houses in rural Lewis and Harris. After visiting one of them and watching a demonstration of the traditional distaff and spindle method of spinning, Smith and his friends enquired into the island's economy, watched a fowling display, and noted 'a poor and damp-looking church' and the schoolhouse, 'well enough built, but unused', in which MacKay tried to educate a few children on two days of the week. Before long a flag hoisted on the yacht summoned the shore party and they left in haste, watched by the minister through 'his new double-eyed field glass' which had just been given to him.[36]

A year later, in the evening of 25 August 1874, the steam-yacht *Griffin* departed from Loch Nevis, just north of Mallaig, with 'a party of sixteen, besides servants', intent upon taking advantage of fine weather to view St Kilda. Many visitors by yacht merely entered brief notes in their diaries or kept up the ship's log but this time the writer aboard was Lady Baillie of Polkemmet who sent her account to *The Church of Scotland Home and Foreign Missionary Record*.[37]

A successful landing was made by means of 'our life-boat', but 'So few of the inhabitants made their appearance at first that we feared they were not going to give their usual welcome to strangers'. Gradually however the people emerged, 'after dressing themselves in their best attire', and the minister came to shake hands:

> 'He looked pale and delicate, and, to our eyes, somewhat unclerical. He spoke English fairly, and seemed truly glad to see and converse in his own native tongue with the Highland clergyman who accompanied us. Mr Mackay comes from Loch Carron. He had not been to the mainland for eight years, which seems hardly considerate on the part of those who are liberal enough to keep him there. A very little more would give him

a holiday year by year, and return him strengthened to instruct, cheer, and civilise his people. His salary is £80; and he acts as magistrate, doctor, and schoolmaster.'

MacKay was supplied with newspapers which would bring him a little more up to date with what was going on in other parts of the world, and of course presents were handed out among the people 'as fairly as we could, considering the anxiety to get them'. The houses and crops drew comment, as did the church, adjoining schoolhouse and 'comfortable manse'. The visiting party was then rowed to Boreray to look at the rocks and birds, after which everyone returned to the yacht and made ready to leave. For the first time, wrote Lady Baillie, two large steam-yachts were anchored in the bay at the same time when *The Calder* arrived to pay a brief call and lay near *Griffin*. Both vessels left, the latter at least spending a wet and foggy night trying to reach the right point on the mainland. After a somewhat erratic course *Griffin* eventually reached the Sound of Sleat from off Ardnamurchan, and made her way into Loch Nevis. 'We left the shores of St Kilda, probably never to return, but the inhabitants will not be forgotten by us; and I would be truly glad if this little narrative would induce others who have the means of visiting them to do so.'

Lady Baillie was one of those writers who managed to make even the word 'they' alone sound as if it denoted a primitive tribe. It is not therefore surprising to find that she thought the 1830s dwellings, now between the more recent cottages, were 'more like Indian wigwams than anything else', that she, unlike other strangers, noticed 'too much of the simple look of cretins among them', presumably as a result of unavoidable intermarriage, and that, in her opinion, the whole community should be forcibly removed:

> 'It would be much to the advantage of these poor people were they removed from their lonely island home, and houses and work for a time provided for them on the mainland. The fowlers might be sent to St Kilda for a few months during the breeding season, with sufficient provisions and suitable appliances for taking the birds. This arrangement would certainly be the most humane and benevolent in the end, though the people might rebel against it in the first instance.'

The lady's views were not so much a useful source of information about the people as a sign that the accounts of occasional yachtsmen and other casual visitors, including some journalists, usually lacked sympathy, understanding and any valuable perceptions of island character. Yet those same unsympathetic versions of St Kilda and its 'natives', combined with the ever increasing reliance on outside support, helped to form mainland and even government attitudes towards the island and so in the end hastened on the day of evacuation. Although still largely in control of ordinary domestic life the church, in these circumstances, became, for the most part, irrelevant to the fate of a community which it had until quite recently led, once as an instrument of government, and new persuasive influences were now at work. Nothing highlighted all these developments more strongly than the arrival on the island of John Sands in the summer of 1875. He might have been just another Lady Baillie, or perhaps a Captain Otter, but he was in fact quite different - though having a touch of both about him - and his St Kilda adventure deserves a detailed description.

CHAPTER 3
John Sands and the start of his dispute with Macleod

John Sands was born at Arbroath in 1827. His grandfather was Robert Sands, 'radical extremist and political martyr', and his father, John Sim Sands, practised as a solicitor but spent much of his time composing political and satirical poems, writing outspoken letters to the press, and editing the *Arbroath Argos*, a monthly paper which he had founded. Whatever he inherited from this side of the family John Sands would probably have chosen a sea-faring career had not several of his mother's kin and his own brother been lost at sea. Instead he too trained as a solicitor. In the mid 1850s he spent three years in America, travelling, farming and teaching, and out of this experience he eventually wrote a novel called *Frank Powderhorn,* an adventure story for boys, illustrated from sketches made by Sands himself of American scenes, people and incidents. On returning to Scotland he stayed for a while with a married sister near Edinburgh but was never at home there for long. He moved to East Lothian, where he may have lived at Ormiston, from which place he wrote letters in 1876 and 1877, but by 1880 he resided with his mother and two sisters at Bankhead between Tranent and Prestonpans. When here he took up the cause of local coal miners and published a series of rather biased and eccentric essays under the title of *Sketches of Tranent in the Olden Time*. Long after his death it was said of him that he 'took a particular delight in frequenting out-of-the-way corners, and spent lengthy periods, living more or less as a recluse, at Tiree in the Inner Hebrides, Vaila, Foula and Papa Stour in Shetland'. He also visited the Faroe Islands, where people later remembered his interests in archaeology and folklore. For much of his life Sands fought against injustice and oppression in areas he came to know well. When in Shetland he championed 'the cause of the Foula folk in their struggle against landlordism, and the pernicious system of truck that prevailed'. One of his weapons was writing to newspapers, another the production of cartoons, some of which were contributed to Punch. One cartoon represented Foula as a beautiful maiden. 'Entwined round the body was an ugly boa-constrictor, its deadly fangs poised over the maiden's head as if it were about to strike. The serpent was labelled "Landlordism".' In 1875 he took his views and hostilities with him to St Kilda.[38]

Variously described as 'An aspiring politician', 'the M.P. and journalist', 'a wandering Scottish artist', and 'an artist with a love for solitude and for out-of-the-way experiences', he was really none of these, though he certainly had a love for wild places - and for playing the bagpipes. That he was, as some people seem to have believed, an M.P. seems to be a fiction arising from his references to the people of St Kilda as his 'distressed' and 'poor constituents', and from a misreading of facetious remarks by a subsequent writer that, given his adopted position of 'representative of the island' in matters relating to the landlord and to a possible mail service, 'we may expect to find a sixty-first representative for that part of her Majesty's dominions called Scotland - another "friend of the people" in the person of John Sands, Esquire, M. P. for St Kilda'.[39]

A month before *Dunara Castle's* maiden voyage John Sands set off for the island, reaching Dunvegan on 20 May 1875, in the belief that the smack which had been chartered by the proprietor to take the factor and in which he had arranged to go would depart the following day. Unfortunately for him it was away on 'a cruise' and he had to wait until 1 June for the *Janet* as the smack was named to come into the loch. When it did it was seen to be towing the boat made and gifted to the people of St Kilda in accordance with the request to Mr Young, owner of the *Nyanza,* in 1873. The factor's servant and another man had to sail and steer the boat 'so as to make her as little of a drag on the smack as possible'.[40]

Being a keen piper Sands was interested in the MacCrimmons, and as the *Janet* neared a cliff where one of them 'used to practise his immortal piobrachd' he paid his respects: 'I lifted my bonnet as we passed the sacred spot.' The weather was none too settled and in the early morning of 3 June, after two uncomfortable nights, he was glad to find that the smack was almost at its destination. Then, 'it being a dead calm four of us took the presentation boat, and towed the smack into the bay'. This was achieved by rowing the boat a distance that proved to be greater than Sands had at first thought. Either because it was very early or because the people knew that the factor had arrived there was no immediate response from the houses. When at last some occupants emerged Sands saw that the women, as of old, made off up the hill at the back while a few men gathered at the landing place. He recollected too that 'The figure of Mr Mackay, the minister, could also be distinguished sauntering from the manse'.

Once he was ashore Sands met MacKay, 'who, sitting down on a stone, and waving his hand to another for me to sit on, told me he had lived for eight years on the island, and had not seen a newspaper for as many months'. Then while the islanders turned their attention to producing their rents the 'lover of solitude' set up his home in the factor's own house where, not having made any arrangements for leaving, he was to remain until 19 July when a chance yacht called *Crusader* turned up and agreed to take him away. During the six weeks of his stay he spent the time sketching, viewing the island people and events, and 'apparently practising for his own solace' on his pipes. Every now and again he had further encounters with the minister and formed what seemed to be a good impression of the island spokesman, the one man there who could converse in English. The only other person who was fluent in English was 'a woman from Ross-shire', Isabella Ross Munro, a cousin of John MacKay, who had come to St Kilda, perhaps with the minister, and in 1869 had married Neil MacDonald, son of Malcolm MacDonald and Betty Scott and brother to Ann, MacKay's housekeeper.[41]

Less than two days after he had settled in Sands attended the funeral of a child at the graveyard. As a necessary preliminary 'two little boxes' were 'disinterred to make room for the new one', the sight of which sad task may well have returned in his memory when a year later he visited 'a churchyard situated on an island called St Colme' in Loch Erisort south of Stornoway. Here he noted that 'the people persist in interring the dead within the ancient limits' and that 'piling the coffins one on the top of the other' had produced a turf-covered heap ten feet high. In St Kilda too it appears that the same confined burial area had been used for centuries, though no great mound had come into existence. The deaths of infants aroused interest and concern in Sands, who formed the opinion that island children were the subject of unusually fond attention. He recorded other observations, on the size of the population, the sufferers from mental or physical handicap, and island features such as good teeth and minds of wit and intelligence: 'Their minds are wonderfully acute considering their contracted experience, which, in the most of cases, has been confined to the rock on which they have been born.' Not all visitors would have agreed with him, but Sands had a natural sympathy with the 'poor people' and was already preparing to take up their cause even though the people themselves may not have thought that they had one.[42]

When it approached, the yacht *Crusader*, owned and apparently skippered by a tall gentleman who 'proved to be a baronet', excited the usual attention among the islanders. 'On the shore stood Mr Mackay, in his best rig, watching the motions of the stranger through an opera-glass that made you see double for the time, and gave you a squint for some minutes afterwards.' Sands hurriedly packed up his bagpipes and was being given parting gifts by the women when suddenly the baronet, and the minister, arrived in his room. While the yachtsman made for the cliffs to watch the fowling demonstration Sands went aboard and, being given a 'snug state-room', found himself abruptly 'in the midst of luxury' like a long-term camper having a hot bath. The yacht left slowly on an almost windless afternoon and reached Gourock after a long journey by Barra Head, Skerryvore, and Rathlin Island. Its unexpected passenger then took the train to Glasgow, 'dressed in a suit of the native cloth' from St Kilda and, judging from the behaviour of ladies in the carriage, still giving off that 'strong and peculiar odour which adheres tenaciously to everything in Hirta'. The baronet, Sir Patrick Keith Murray, no doubt after reflection on his voyage and on what his passenger had told him during the return journey, 'sent two clocks to the island, the first that had ever been there, and other useful articles', including the two wooden chandeliers, each with three sheep tallow candles, which were hung from the ceiling of the church.[43]

*

A few weeks after Sands left on the *Crusader*, at the beginning of August 1875, a small group 'engaged upon a business cruise in the western seas' landed at St Kilda. The members had little good to say about the place. On talking with 'the Free Church clergyman' and 'a woman who had come from Tain' they learned that medical treatment was urgently required for the people, and so one of the group who happened to be 'a famous doctor' spent most of his time ashore giving appropriate attention to the sick while the rest climbed a hill for the sake of the view. The visitors did think highly of Rev. MacKay:

> 'The Free Church has behaved handsomely and well with this melancholy place. It has sent there a very sensible and intelligent clergyman, to whom we gave (besides the aforesaid medicines for the body) all the periodicals and books we could spare. The last time he saw a new book was two years ago, when a certain nobleman called at the island and left him a few books. The clergyman has out of his salary of £79 to buy the medicines which the dyspeptic people need.'

Aside from the merits of MacKay as a leader of the community there was not much else to say in its favour. Cultivation was sparse and insufficient, and fishing was carried on 'in a kind of scrambling way' without energy and determination. Isolation had led to laziness, and a failure on the part of the proprietor's agent, John T MacKenzie, to send salt for curing ling had merely added to the people's lethargy. In fact 'The continued existence of people upon such an island is a mistake', and the example of Fair Isle should be followed. There a subscription raised 'for conveying away one-half of the population to Canada' had been successful in relieving the over-peopled island, and now 'A similar subscription should be got up for the removal of these seventy-two persons from their lazy, stupid, and dirty life in the island of St Kilda'. In their place goats and sheep should be introduced.[44]

This party, like that including the Baillies of Polkemmet, evidently saw no reason ever to return to 'the dreary hills' of St Kilda, and John Sands claimed that he had 'no intention of going there again'. During the autumn he set to work on writing an account of the island and the resulting book was published speedily in the spring of 1876. It immediately led to some correspondence in the *Spectator*, the *Scotsman* and elsewhere, involving one or two incidental contributors but chiefly Norman MacLeod of MacLeod as the island's proprietor and Sands himself. The topics discussed included communication and infant mortality, and it became clear from the letters, all in the latter half of April 1876, that Sands was already set on making a second visit. A private exchange also began at this time between MacLeod and Sands when the former wrote, on 24 April, to ask for a copy of Sands's book and to point out the difficulties which would confront the St Kilda people if they were encouraged to make journeys in a boat of their own to sell their produce. In his reply, sent along with the required book, Sands showed that he now fancied himself a voice on behalf of the people, a more provocative and challenging protester than the minister who at this stage merely communicated between the islanders and any person or parties who could not speak Gaelic. A mutually hostile tone crept in beneath the outward politeness of the proprietor and his opponent.[45]

Sands said he did not trust the factor, John MacKenzie, who, he was convinced, 'has an interest in keeping things as they are'. He then put forward his argument against the prevailing system of management, and in so doing he expressed, within his own terms, a criticism or complaint which might have been made at more or less any time over St Kilda's known history:

> 'When I was on the island last Summer the men came several times to me and requested me to try and get them a boat large enough to carry a crew and cargo to the Lewis. After a time I began to feel for them and to see that there was some reason in their request and I promised to let their position be known. I thought it was hard that 73 people should be kept prisoners on a rock, without any means of seeing or intermingling with their fellow creatures in other places and compelled to trade with a factor on any terms that he chose. I found that their produce was valuable and that no working people would be better off than they if they could only get to a market where they could enjoy the benefit of competition. Such a reform too I believed would be for the benefit of the landlord. On my return I began to enquire the prices of their commodities and found that their grievance was greater than I had at first imagined. I fulfilled my promise to them by writing a letter to the "Scotsman", explaining how they were situated and how much they wished for a boat. As this letter had no practical effect I was induced to start a subscription to raise a fund to buy a boat …I believe the people will never be contented until they get to the market themselves and even should the boat fail other means might be found of enabling them to conduct their own trade.'

The main assertion that Sands made was that if the proprietor would convert the rents from produce to money and if there was a sufficient boat at the island the people could trade on their own account, cut out the factor or 'middle man', and free themselves from the unwelcome grip of the landlord who, according to Sands in a further letter to the *Spectator*, 'has never had his foot on the Island'. On the other side MacLeod responded with a defence of his own attitude and of his factor and proclaimed the economic benefits for the islanders in the existing monopoly market arrangements and of the present means of communication:

'In your book .. and in your Letters you have certainly endeavoured to convey an as unfavorable an Impression as possible of the owner of St Kilda. Your leading idea seems to have been that I as proprietor of the Island take no interest whatever in the people, and that it had therefore become necessary for a stranger to step in and remedy the ills under which they are supposed [to] suffer. With this object in view you suggest that I should "kindly agree" to accept money instead of produce for the Rents, and that I would "have the goodness to approve of the steps that are being taken to improve their Condition". You also offer "to inform the people when you again go to them, that I feel interested in their welfare". In referring to these expressions I do not wish you to suppose that I resent your Interference between me and my tenants. I have no feeling of that kind. At the same time I think that in assuming as you have done that I am indifferent and careless about the people of St Kilda, and putting yourself forward as the redresser of their wrongs, you have assumed a very serious responsibility and as I think you can scarcely have realised the full extent of it, it is right I should give you the result of much careful and anxious Consideration on the subject of these Islanders. My belief is that the people never can and never will be independent of outside aid. No vessel of any kind can remain at anchor in the Bay. No boat sufficiently large to carry men and Cattle can be hauled up on the rocks. My opinion is that if the people try to use the Boat you propose to give them they will lose their lives. If she is shallow as you describe her to be she cannot carry cattle, or any quantity of other goods in safety. But supposing that the Boat, its crew and freight should succeed in reaching Harris or the Lews have you considered that their market being Glasgow they are very far from it still? They must transship their goods into a larger sailing vessel, or into a steamer. Arrived in Glasgow I can tell them from experience that they will find their feathers, their oil and their cloth extremely difficult of sale. There for the supplies they must buy the empty Oil casks for next years oil, the bags for feathers, the oatmeal, and their other many wants, and convey them by steamer to some port on the East Coast of Harris or the Lews, either Roudil, Tarbet or Lochmaddy where Steamers occasionally call. Then comes the return voyage in the boat, the waiting for suitable weather, and the risk of damage to goods, and remember also that to carry all the produce of the Island the expedition which I have described must be repeated at least six times as the boat is so small. I have said nothing about the expenses, but I think you will perceive that they must be very considerable, probably far exceeding those incurred by me, heavy tho' they are.

'I have entered into this detail in order to show you what difficulties will attend the plan which appears to you so simple. After much

Consideration of the subject my belief is that the people of St Kilda will always be obliged to continue to rely on their proprietor, as they have done in past times, for Communications with the outer world. I wish sincerely it were otherwise, as I would much rather they were able to manage their own affairs. They may perhaps try your boat, but I hope they will have more sense than to do so. If they make the attempt I shall watch with very great anxiety, for I am confident they will be lost, as they were when they tried the same experiment [before]. It would go hard with the little community, if they lose their youngest and best lives. Under any Circumstances I shall this year send my vessel as usual, with the customary supplies of meal and other Commodities. The people must then determine, whether they will in future give all their produce to me or sell it all themselves, for if they ship any of their produce away in their boat, I could not undertake to send a vessel at a great expense for half a cargo, or perhaps none at all, and I cannot send meal and other supplies which they perhaps may not require, and may decline to take.'

On 12 May Sands replied at equal length and was not deflected from his purpose. 'If the St.Kildians can get to the Lewis in a boat of their own,' he wrote, 'I have no doubt they will get supplies for themselves at about half the price you charge for them and I also calculate that they will get a great deal more for their produce … I see no necessity for the people being dependent on the proprietor. If the present system continues the whole population will be improved off the face of the earth. In twenty years or less the numbers will be so diminished that enough will not be left to work the island - and the remnant will be sent off by subscription, or at the public expense, to Canada (as has already been proposed) and the island which might support 500 happy natives, and be a good investment to the proprietor, will be handed over to the fulmars as a Xmas gift. I know no place or people with greater capabilities.' Sands openly blamed MacLeod for running a monopoly and for failing to take any steps to find a cure for the 'distemper' that killed the children – 'I think this omission alone shews a wonderful indifference to the welfare of your tenantry.' He even blamed the landlord for the intermarriage in the island by preventing the people from having communication with other places.

On receiving this letter MacLeod denied all the accusations it contained and sharply closed the correspondence. But he did not leave matters there. Within the next four days he despatched 'To the St. Kilda People' a letter, and to the minister another letter with two enclosures, relating to the very issues that he and Sands had just been disputing. These letters contained information that showed the proprietor had been seriously touched if not wounded by Sands's arguments and they mark yet another important stage in the course upon which the hapless islanders were set. MacLeod's address to the people of St Kilda presented them with a choice that might determine their future survival on the island but which was certainly beyond their power as a whole community to make:

'I am informed by Mr J Sands a gentleman who was for some weeks in St Kilda last year that you complained to him of the prices allowed for your produce, and also of the prices charged against you for meal and other goods; and that you told him you wished to have a boat in which you might take your produce to market, and bring back your own Supplies. If you really did say all this I assure you that I should be very glad for you to manage your own affairs and that nothing would give me greater satisfaction than that you should sell and buy for yourselves. I have acted for you only because I beleive you to be so situated that you cannot transact your own business, but if you think you can, I certainly will put no difficulty in your way.

'I must however point out to you that if you determine to manage your own affairs it will be impossible for me to do what I have hitherto done, and send a vessel to St Kilda twice a year, because there will be nothing for her to take or bring away. A passage to and from St Kilda is so uncertain that a vessel charges high and either she must have a sufficient Cargo, or it will not pay to send her at all. I wish you to understand that I shall be glad for you to manage your own business, but if you do any of it, you must do it all, and in that Case I will appoint someone either at Dunvegan, or in Harris or the Lews to receive the Rents which one of you can bring over. If on the other hand you wish me to continue sending a vessel twice a year I will do so, but there must be no more grumbling and you must accept my assurance that I charge you only what is necessary.

'I understand that Mr J Sands has got a boat which he is to send to you. From the description I have of her I do not beleive she is fit to carry either men or goods in safety. It is right therefore I should caution you not to trust yourselves in her unless you are quite satisfied that she is a proper boat for the work. It is for you however to judge, and I hope you will not run any foolish risk.

'This Letter will be delivered to you by Mr MacKenzie. Altho you did not send last year a List of the things you expected to want this year we have determined to send the usual supplies which you can take or not as you like. You will tell Mr MacKenzie whether you wish me to send again in August as usual or whether you will use the boat, and in either case you will sign a paper putting to it the names of all the tenants.'

The minister, John MacKay, would probably have to read this out to them, translating and explaining as he went. The message to him presented the options, and in effect asked him to arrange that the people choose the alternative they preferred and sign the appropriate paper. They could put their names to either of the enclosed sentences: 'We the Inhabitants of St Kilda are quite satisfied to rely on our Proprietor for the sale of our produce, and for the supply of the goods we require and we unanimously request he will continue to send a vessel to us twice a year as he has hitherto done' or 'We the Inhabitants of St Kilda have unanimously agreed, that we will in future carry the produce of the Island to market ourselves or otherwise dispose of the same and obtain our own supplies and that therefore it will be unnecessary for our Proprietor to send to us twice a year as he has hitherto done, and we hereby agree that his Rents shall be paid in Cash to any person whom he may appoint to receive the same either at Dunvegan or at some place in Harris or the Lews to be hereafter determined.'[46]

*

John Sands had indeed promised the St Kilda people that he would try to procure a better boat than that sent out by Mr Young which 'was more suitable for the Clyde than for the strong seas between St Kilda and the main[land?].' He believed that a purpose-built craft was essential, and so launched an appeal for funds which raised between £50 and £60. This amount was more than sufficient, and he did not delay in employing a man at Ardrishaig who had been at St Kilda to carry out the work, which was completed, with sails included, for £40. The surplus he intended to spend on a compass, anchor, rope, chart and other equipment, leaving a sum to cover the cost of taking the boat to St Kilda. 'I intend to go out in her myself, but will require to employ three of a crew. She is twenty-six feet by ten feet, and is shallow in proportion to her breadth. She is small enough for the seas she may have to encounter, but as there is no harbour in St Kilda, and as it will be necessary to pull her up the rocky shore, a larger and heavier craft would have been of no use. I feel, of course, a deep interest in the experiment, and hope, before the summer is over, to see the factor's monopoly abolished and free-trade established.' A month later he was on his way.[47]

On 30 May 1876 Sands went to Lochgilphead to collect the boat, arranging for two men to take her by the Crinan canal to Oban. 'Here the men got drunk and extortionate, and I dismissed them.' The boat and Sands both went on board the *Clansman* on 2 June and departed for Stornoway. 'Although the steamer was full of ministers returning from the Assemblies, we arrived without any accident at Stornoway on the 3rd.' Unless some prejudice against the church be seen as an excuse he offered no explanation as to why a company of ministers might have caused an accident or delayed arrival. In Stornoway he met Captain MacDonald, of the fishery cruiser *Vigilant*, and hoped that MacDonald would take man and boat on to St Kilda, but this proved impossible, and as a result Sands spent more than a week visiting places like Loch Erisort. On 13 June however he travelled by the *Vigilant* to the island of Scalpay, 'where I wanted to be left for a change', and there he passed four days, at the end of which the *Vigilant* moved him and his boat to Obbe. He found the factor's smack, 'my old friend the Janet', waiting for the weather to improve, and there were two women from St Kilda who, after giving birth in what were judged to be the healthier surroundings of Harris, were anxious to return home. Lodging in the inn Sands stayed a further five days in Obbe, where he had the pleasure of listening to an expert piper in 'one of the huts' and managed to engage two men 'to work the boat to St Kilda' for £8. The skipper of the *Janet* agreed to take these two back to Harris.

With an easterly wind Sands and his two men left, all three in the new boat, 'and a rope connecting us with the smack'. Sands claimed that he would have liked to sail independently, and subsequently he remarked that being taken in tow 'was no great favour', particularly as 'MacLeod cast it in my teeth afterwards'. They arrived safely in the evening of 22 June, one of the St Kilda women holding up her infant 'in a triumphant manner' as they approached the island. Two days later, when the *Janet* left, Sands was established as a lodger in the house of Neil MacDonald and his wife Isabella Ross Munro where he stayed for two or three weeks before moving to a house of his own, little knowing that he would not find a way of leaving the island for eight months.

Soon after landing from the smack the factor presented the islanders with the landlord's alternatives, known to the minister after delivery of the letter to him at the same time. According to Sands the reaction of the people was to be definitely inclined 'to trade for themselves', but at the crucial moment Rev. MacKay expressed his view in favour of MacLeod:

> 'the minister (who the previous year had been grumbling at the prices charged for supplies as much as anyone, and wishing the islanders had a boat large enough to go to the market in) interfered, and persuaded the men to sign the paper. I was not pleased at this, as the boat, although she was found useful in making excursions to Boreray and Soa, had been got on purpose that the islanders might have an opportunity of trading with Harris. I saw that all my labour - and it had been great - in collecting subscriptions, and all the money I had collected from benevolent people, had, through the uncalled for interference of this reverend gentleman, been thrown away.'

So the campaign against the proprietor suffered a setback. The people followed their minister's advice, and as there was therefore no possibility of a journey to Harris Sands was forced to wait for a chance yacht or, at the latest, the return of the factor's smack in the autumn. He had sufficient food for three months, and spent the days 'in wandering about the island, in making excursions with the men in the boats, in playing the pipes, in sketching, taking notes, and trying to learn Gaelic'. He occasionally went to church. No yacht came, nor, to his deep annoyance, did the promised smack with its essential supplies and opportunity to escape his unintended isolation.

Fine weather in September passed without a visit from any kind of craft. Lack of food became a real possibility. The shoes worn every day fell into 'a shocking state', so that one of the men had to be asked to make a pair of 'brogan tiondadh'. During his visit in 1875 Sands had observed that 'The brogan are sewed with thongs of sheep-skin. The brog tiondadh or turned shoe, so called because it is sewed on the wrong side, and then turned inside out, was in vogue until quite recently... It is made to fit either foot'. With these he was able to get about, while with the aid of a fulmar oil lamp, meal and salt mutton, he maintained a somewhat deprived existence indoors. He had to face the fact that winter was at hand when for several dark months no boat would even be worth looking for.

One evening in early October there came an excited report of 'strangers in the glen' - or at least of 'a loud whistle... several times repeated'. Search was made for the strangers without success, but 'Next morning a steamer was seen making away from the island, and it was no doubt her fog-whistle that had startled the village'. Sands explained that he had recorded this incident 'to show how easily the people of St Kilda are excited, especially if the object of alarm is connected with the mysterious world outside'. The relationship between the St Kilda community and 'outside', always an uncertain and delicate one, was soon to be set on edge by another episode, this time involving shipwreck, of which the people had experience over centuries, and more importantly having consequences that introduced to Sands's thinking the already familiar idea of abandoning the island as a place to live.

Since he had sprained his ankle Sands spent part of December making a 'miniature ship' by which he planned to communicate with some other part of the world. He 'put a letter in her hold, in the hope that she might reach some place where there was a post-office, being anxious to let my friends know that I was alive, and also to let the public know that MacLeod had broken his promise to send provisions to the people, and that we were all in want'. It was launched into the ocean and nine months later was found by a boy in Norway, from which country the letter was sent to its address in Edinburgh.[48]

Another month passed. Then, on 17 January 1877, 'the most remarkable event occurred that had happened in St Kilda for many years'. Most of the islanders had just gone to church when Sands, to his amazement, saw a boat in the bay. It contained nine men 'all in sou'-westers and oil-skins'. Sands shouted in vain from the shore, a woman ran to tell the church congregation, and soon everyone was helping to bring the strangers in through the surf. 'In a few minutes their boat was knocked to pieces on the rocks, and they were prisoners like myself.' The shipwrecked men were taken into the manse where dry clothes were brought to them, and the captain who happened to be one of those rescued told of how when about eight miles west of St Kilda he and his companions had abandoned their ship, the *Peti Dubrovacki,* still with seven men aboard who had refused to leave. Once they had changed the strangers, all Austrians, were housed by the islanders, 'the minister keeping the captain, and every two families taking charge of one man'. Food was the severest problem. Nine extra men to feed meant that grain set aside for seed had to be ground for meal, only one illustration of the extent to which their hosts put themselves out in order to look after the unexpected guests. 'This hospitable conduct,' said Sands, '..is all the more commendable when one considers that their guests were all foreigners and Papists, whom they had been taught to hold in horror.'[49]

At the end of January Sands was busy again, this time shaping out of a log a canoe in order to send another message reporting the plight in which he and those who had been shipwrecked found themselves:

> 'I had written a letter and put it into her hold, enclosed in a pickle bottle. The captain begged me to write a note for him addressed to the Austrian Consul, Glasgow, and to put it in another bottle. The sailors, glad of anything in the shape of work, helped me to rig her and put the iron ballast right, and to caulk the deck. We delayed launching her until the wind should blow from the N.W., which we hoped would carry her to Uist or other place where there is a post. A small sail was put on her, and with a hot iron I printed on her deck, "*Open this*".'

This canoe, four feet long, was set adrift on 5 February and three weeks later was found at Poolewe near Gairloch by a Mr John MacKenzie who posted the letters it contained. But even better progress was made by a bottle attached to a lifebuoy which the Austrian captain had saved from his lost ship. It had been thrown into the sea on 30 January 'and, strange to say, reached Birsay in Orkney, and was forwarded to Lloyd's agent in Stromness on the 8th February, having performed the passage in nine days'.[50]

Knowing nothing of the outcome of their experiments Sands and the captain grew more and more desperate, the Austrian offering money for a lift to Harris in the boat Sands had brought. Lots were drawn among the island men for a crew to face the dangers of February seas and weather. It was determined, against the captain's wishes, that Sands himself should go to 'represent the condition of the island to the public, and try and get provisions sent'. Generosity was not universal on this occasion however, for Isabella

MacDonald, with whom Sands had stayed, had developed, for good reason, a resentment against her former lodger:

'The Ross-shire woman (who was indebted to my good word for a clock, and the largest stock of carpenters tools ever seen or heard of in the island, besides many gifts out of my own pocket) suggested that I should be made to pay for my passage in the boat I had been the means of getting for them, - a degree of ingratitude with which I was highly amused. The men, however, would not listen to this; and all was settled but the weather.'

While they were waiting for wind and sea to subside the situation was taken out of their hands. On the morning of 22 February, with Sands still in his bed, 'the shriek of a steam whistle' startled everybody. A vessel was in the bay. Sands packed his trunk, hastened to the shore, and immediately stepped into a boat. He had with him 'a mandate, written in Gaelic by the minister, and signed by him and by all the men who could write', authorising him to do his best to arrange for a twice-yearly mail service to St Kilda; and he had been asked also to arrange for provisions and seed corn to be sent. He agreed to do his best, 'but the minister, now jealous of his authority as dictator, pushed on board of the steamer (which I saw was H.M.S. *Jackal*), and explained the state of the island to the commander, who telegraphed the fact to the Admiralty, who took no notice of it'. The captain of the *Jackal* pacified the minister with some tobacco, and left a quantity of biscuits and oatmeal. It was then that Sands discovered that the *Jackal* had left Rothesay on 12 February, in response to the lifebuoy message found at Birsay only four or five days previously.

Thus Sands and the Austrians were conveyed happily to the mainland. On arrival at Oban the press gathered round, and 'the destitute condition of St Kilda' became known to the whole country. The scene was repeated on 26 February at Gourock, 'where a crowd of newspaper reporters were waiting our arrival, and to whom I communicated a full, true, and particular account of my eight months' experience, in the belief that the more light that was thrown upon the condition of St Kilda, the greater was the hope of its being ameliorated'. The story appeared in the papers on the morning of 26 February 1877 as H.M.S. *Jackal* was about to tie up at Gourock. One or two details emerged that were intended either to reflect to Sands's credit or merely to amuse readers; for instance, it appeared that Sands had suggested the lifebuoy with a bottle and small sail soon after the Austrians had come ashore, that this invention had been put in the sea on 22 January but returned by the waves two days later, and that the buoy sent off on 30 January was a different one, 'lighter rigged'. 'From other resources', said one paper mysteriously, 'we hear that there were seven young unmarried women of marriage age, and only two young unmarried men' on the island. The implications of this unnecessary and unconnected remark were obvious, but the paper needed more: 'We may also mention that an attachment sprung up between one of the Austrian seamen and one of the young women of the island, and, although not understanding the language of each other, they seemed to have understood the universal language of love, and at parting there was quite a scene.' People in Glasgow who read this might well have pictured that scene in much the same way as they would have visualised a separation between a Glaswegian and an Indian squaw in North America.[51]

A day on, and the 'Arrival of the St Kilda Castaways' was reported with some different details and questionable accuracy. H.M.S. *Jackal's* port in the Clyde varied. Mr Sands, 'the tourist', had gone on to Edinburgh after giving a lengthy account of his recent stay and of his previous one in '1865'. There were not seven but thirteen unmarried young women and the two eligible young men were already engaged. 'No wonder,' concluded the *Highlander*, 'that an attachment should have sprung up between the forlorn St Kilda lasses and the Austrians, for some of the foreign seamen were rather handsome looking fellows.' The St Kilda people were no longer just curiosities; they were also amusing. The Austrians having reached Glasgow where they 'were comfortably housed in the Seaman's Home', Basilio Chersonaz, captain of the *Peti Dubrovacki,* wrote a letter of thanks mentioning all who had helped the shipwrecked men to survive:[52]

CHAPTER 4

John Sands, Emily Macleod, and John MacDiarmid's
visit for the Highland and Agricultural Society

Apart from the return of the marooned men to the mainland an additional and equally remarkable source of interest and publicity emerged in a curious episode that occurred towards the end of 1875. This was the ghostly reappearance of the lost *Dargavel* crew, or rather of one of them. Drawing upon what John Sands was able to say upon his arrival with H.M.S. *Jackal* the *Scotsman* told the story briefly:

> 'A letter was received by a Harris clergyman from a firm engaged at the South African goldfields mentioning that a man, whose parentage they gave, had died there, leaving property to the value of about £40. The letter was forwarded to St Kilda, and it turned out that the individual referred to was one of the crew of the boat which had never been heard of. No mention as to how the man got to Africa was contained in the letter, and the islanders are now more puzzled about the matter than ever. Instead of believing that their relatives were murdered, they argue that if one man was saved why not all, and they have got vague and terrifying notions about a passing ship bearing off the occupants of the boat to a savage clime. Such is the story as told by the islanders, and keeping in view the fact that they have little education, no opportunities of mixing with the rest of mankind, no one can wonder at the simplicity of their reasoning, or the dread they have of the outer world of which they have had so unpleasant an experience.'[53]

The letter from South Africa received by the post office at Obbe in Harris was addressed to 'Mr Lachlan Macinnon, Island of St Kilda, by Stornoway, Scotland'. Lachlan was the brother of Donald MacKinnon, catechist, the precentor in the established church of Harris, and he was the father of the Donald MacKinnon lost with the *Dargavel* in 1863. The precentor Donald was consulted about the letter and, with no possibility of sending it on to the island for several months, opened it. He found that the man who seemed to be his nephew had died of fever at 'Delego Bay, Gold Coast, Natal', and with the letter were enclosed 'a lock of the deceased's hair, and a cutting from a local newspaper, giving an account of his death and funeral'. It happened that when dying the man had spoken much of his parents in St Kilda. Donald MacKinnon at Obbe asked the minister of Harris, Charles MacLean, to write to Natal, and in due course there came 'a satisfactory reply'. The proceeds of the dead person's effects were forwarded to a bank at Stornoway, but the mystery of the supposed survivor of the *Dargavel* remained. 'There can be no question,' it was said in April 1876, 'but that the Donald Macinnon who died of fever at Delego Bay in 1875, was the same Donald Macinnon who left St Kilda in the boat …twelve years before.' How had he escaped drowning? Why did he not write home? Suspicion fell upon the three English vessels that reported the loss of the *Dargavel* to St Kilda, and it was guessed that these boats had 'carried the hapless St Kildians into captivity, somewhere abroad'.[54]

By May 1877 it was accepted by South African authorities that a mistake had been made and that the deceased Donald MacKinnon had been a native of Lewis and not of St Kilda, although the evidence for this change of view was not forthcoming. However in January 1878 John Sands wrote to the *Highlander* with further news on 'The St Kilda "Mystery"':

'I have just received a copy of the Otago Times, which contains the following letter addressed by the minister of St Kilda to the Commissioners of the Emigration Company, Dunedin:-

'"Gentlemen, - I wish to bring before your serious consideration a very mysterious affair, viz. Donald McKinnon, unmarried; Angus Macdonald, married; Donald Gillies, married; Mrs Malcolm Macdonald, or Betty Scott; Alexander Gillies, unmarried; Donald Macdonald, married; Ewen Gillies, unmarried, all from St Kilda. The above-named seven men and the woman went in the spring of 1863 in a boat for some commodity for their families to Harris, but of whom no traces could be found. It was then and since thought that they were all drowned in crossing the channel: but it now turns out by an account received of Donald McKinnon, St Kilda, who died of a fever at Transvaal Republic, South-East Africa, that they were taken away by some bad captain of a ship which met them in the bay, and had disposed of them into different parts of the world. It seems that they bound themselves by an oath, that they would never declare how they had been dealt with. Mr George W. Bancroft says that Donald McKinnon went to Dunedin, Australia [i.e. New Zealand?], in 1863, and that he and some other acquaintances of his came back in the same ship with him from Australia to Transvaal Republic. He says those who are interested in the matter could easily cause inquiries to be made in Dunedin, Otago, New Zealand, where a list of ships and passengers for the year 1863 would be easily procurable. I hope, gentlemen, you will examine your lists of passengers for the year thus mentioned, to see if you will find any person or persons named from St Kilda, N. Britain, in your list of passengers for the year 1863. I am etc. John McKay, St Kilda Manse, July 10th 1877."'

'The subject is of the utmost interest to the inhabitants of St Kilda, and it will be an act of charity to publicise it. I believe the Donald Mackinnon who died in Africa in 1875 and left property to the value of £37, which was remitted to Lachlan Mackinnon, St Kilda, on the supposition that the deceased was his long-lost son, was a native of the Lews, and not of St Kilda; but Mr Mackay has evidently received further information on the subject. This resurrection, as it were, from the dead occasioned the St Kildians inexpressible distress during all the time I was amongst them, and they are still doomed to suffer "the hope that keeps alive despair". The servant of the minister is a daughter of Betty Scott, who was in the lost boat, and her continued lamentations for her mother would have driven the strongest mind distracted - Mr Mackay's feelings seem to have been worked upon until he became as credulous as his congregation.'[55]

So ended the extended story of the *Dargavel.* Nothing more seems to have been heard of the mysterious Donald MacKinnon, and the people were left, once again, to their unappeased distress.

*

To the people of St Kilda the fate of Donald Mackinnon, like that of other islanders lost before and since, was of a deep emotional significance unappreciated by mainland readers of the papers who were far more interested in the controversy being stirred up by John Sands. The day after he reached his home at Ormiston, on 28 February 1877, Sands added to the fame he had already achieved in speaking to the reporters at Oban and Glasgow by writing a letter to the *Scotsman,* in which he set out his opinions on the state of things at St Kilda. He referred to the boat which he had taken with him and which, being 'got by subscription', he had in a sense to defend against critics: 'The natives were resolved to make a trip in her, but were persuaded by the minister to sign a document agreeing to accept supplies from the proprietor for another year, which supplies never arrived.' Unless a steamer could be sent twice a year with mail and provisions 'free-trade would never be established there':

> 'I have no doubt, if the inhabitants could obtain fair prices for their produce, and get supplies at a moderate rate, that they could well afford to pay for a steamer. At present the trade is a monopoly, and a profit (sometimes exorbitant) is charged on what is bought and what is sold. As an example, 3d is paid for feathers worth, I was informed in Glasgow, 1s per pound; and MacLeod of MacLeod charges the poor girls at the rate of 2s.8d for lozenges, which are almost a necessary article of food in St Kilda, where there is no seasoning.'

Sands also suggested that when, by the arrival of the Austrians, the people were compelled to use up their seed corn there might have been a real gain, as there had been no change [of seed] for sixty years at least, and the crops in consequence had become 'wretched'. Meal and potatoes, as well as the seed corn, were urgently needed, and though there had been no shortage of meat - mutton and fulmars - during his long stay he had tasted no tea, sugar or bread. The Austrians had been hospitably treated, but 'I think that people who are so generous to those in misfortune are worthy of all sympathy when in misfortune themselves'.[56]

Such public pronouncements drew a prompt response. An open meeting was called in Edinburgh 'by advertisement and circular' for 5 March 1877, its purpose being 'to consider the present position of the Islanders, and if anything can be done by Public Subscription or otherwise to assist them in present emergencies'. Rev. Dr Thomas McLauchlan, of the Free Church, proposed that the meeting express sympathy and resolve 'that an appeal be made to the public for funds to assist them in their necessitous circumstances'. If enough money was raised it should, if possible, be applied to some item of permanent benefit. Two more proposals were made, one by Rev. Dr. James Begg, also of the Free Church, the other by William Ferguson of Kinmundy. Begg suggested that a committee be appointed to enquire into any existing funds held for the benefit of the islanders - by which was meant principally the Kelsall Bequest fund - and how best to apply the money, while Ferguson proposed that government should be approached with a view to the establishment of a regular postal system and possibly a lighthouse. All three proposals were, after some discussion, unanimously agreed, and the committee which came into existence must have included most of those present though it omitted all of the ladies. Among its members were the Free Church leaders McLauchlan and Begg, the inevitable John Sands who had not attended the meeting, and, interestingly, Fletcher N Menzies of Menzies, secretary to the Highland and Agricultural Society.

The meeting was reported in some detail in the following day's *Scotsman*. There had been a letter from Sands asserting that Menzies was keeping the Kelsall Fund a secret and emphasising the importance of a postal service with at least two steamer visits a year. Dr John Ferguson, St Peter's Place, Edinburgh, who thought it was discourteous to call the meeting without consulting MacLeod of MacLeod, questioned the truth of several of Sands's statements. It was, for instance, not true that seed corn had not been introduced for over 60 years, since Ferguson knew there had been a delivery in the 1840s, and Rev. McLauchlan said there had been another in or about 1861. 'This whole story of destitution on the island, was, he affirmed, a got-up story, and could not be maintained.'

Perhaps the most startling feature of the discussion was the support given by Menzies to the principle for which Sands chiefly fought:

'Nothing better .. could be done than to allow the islanders to trade for themselves. As far as he could make out, the main thing for the island was to get free trade introduced to it. (Hear, hear.) At present, the islanders were in the hands of the proprietor's factor - he said "factor" because he did not believe the proprietor of the island knew what was going on there - but he had not the least doubt that a system of usury was going on at St Kilda which was thoroughly disgraceful.'

Menzies, making it clear that there was nothing secret about the Kelsall Bequest, considered that a fund should be organised to enable 'the outside steamer that went up by Long Island' to call at St Kilda four times a year. Moreover 'He could tell them some strange facts as to the prices of things bought and sold there, but that might be considered beyond the scope of the meeting. ("No, no," and "Go on.")' He had learned that salt, sold in Lewis at £1.6s or £1.10s a ton, was sold by the factor to St Kilda at £3.10s a ton, while sugar, until recently available in Edinburgh at 3d a pound, was sold in St Kilda at twice that amount. Sweeties, which some found an amusing subject, were 'a sort of Necessity' at St Kilda, where 'the quantity of fresh sea-fowl which the islanders eat rendered it necessary for them to take something to give the stomach a tone'. Menzies quoted other price differences; and he said that in 1863, after the loss of the *Dargavel*, it had been judged that the islanders were such bad sailors that the idea of a replacement large boat was given up.

The two Free Church ministers took a broadly similar approach to the matter of communicating with the proprietor. McLauchlan thought that MacLeod should be contacted before any further practical steps were taken, and he urged that whatever was done should indeed be for the permanent benefit of the islanders, 'and not a mere present exhibition of charity towards making them more dependent than they were before'. He also noticed that Sands appeared to believe that the Free Church harassed the people of St Kilda by making them pay £10 to the Sustentation Fund. He was certain 'that the Free Church never asked one sixpence of that £10 from the islanders', recalling that when he was at St Kilda many years ago, at a time when there was no minister or teacher there, he had determined to raise an endowment, and that this still existed, producing £60 per annum towards a salary for John MacKay, who 'not only administered ordinances, but taught the children to read and write'. Dr Begg approved of consultation with the proprietor, but he did not agree with Dr Ferguson that MacLeod should have been consulted before the meeting was called. 'They did not in this country,' he said, 'hold the feudal idea about the proprietor that the people of St Kilda were his, and that no one should meddle or do any good to them without his permission.'[57]

Further letters to the papers immediately followed the Edinburgh meeting. Dr Ferguson wrote to complain of Sands's 'inaccuracies and misstatements', blaming these for the 'severe remarks' made by Menzies, and then saying 'I must decline a newspaper correspondence'. Sands certainly did not decline one, and replied straightaway, declining instead membership of the Edinburgh committee and preferring to battle on independently. March 1877 was indeed awash with views in the press supporting or criticising one side or the other in what became a wrangle between Sands and the MacLeod family, so that even by 6 March F G Buchanan wrote from Dunvegan that 'So much is being written and said about St Kilda and the above gentleman [Sands] that people here are beginning to wonder if it has changed hands again, and Mr Sands become proprietor, as he seems to be taking so great an interest in the spiritual and temporal affairs of the inhabitants'.[58]

On 6 March also John Sands wrote to Fletcher Menzies. He told him what the islanders needed by way of supplies and asked if he could be allowed a passage to St Kilda in the vessel that would convey the goods. 'I could explain to the people who are the donors and also testify on my return that the provisions and seed-corn were delivered. I should like the people to know that I have done my duty in letting their position be known. As the Minister and I did not part the best of friends (for I had made a sketch of him without permission) he may forget to mention my name in the matter.' Sands thought that a Gaelic-speaker should go 'so that he may hear the sentiments of the people without the aid of an interpreter'. At this stage he and Menzies were on reasonably friendly terms in spite of the accusations about secrecy, and he told the secretary that he liked 'the tone of your speech' as it was reported in the *Scotsman* that day. About a week later he wrote again, anxious to learn what was happening and ready to look for transport by yacht if the requested passage was not permitted.[59]

Provoked to annoyed impatience, even to anger, by the implications of the articles and correspondence, the former often passed from one publication to another, and by the report of the Edinburgh meeting, Norman MacLeod of MacLeod was forced to participate from the distance of his London residence at 33, Cadogan Place. The publicity following the *Jackal's* 'rescue' of Sands and the Austrians had already created a widespread, perhaps mistaken, impression that the proprietor and his factor were in the wrong, ignoring the plight of the diminishing number of islanders, overcharging and underpaying them, restricting their freedom, and treating them as 'serfs'. There was a tendency, too, on the part of the press to support Sands, the 'eccentric but warm-hearted Scottish artist' who had been stranded on 'the remote and romantic Hebridean rock' for eight months and with his bottle message had found a way of making his own predicament, and that of the Austrians, known to the world. The first edition of his book, together with his personal narrative, enabled the press to circulate extraordinary and nonsensical descriptions of an island where people were 'almost as primitive as Antipodean aborigines', living in 'circular dwellings, often with underground cellars or vaults, built in a fashion which probably prevailed in the island before the historic period'. Their hard life was 'a strange feature in English ethnography', and as for their religion, 'the St.

Kildians have never been a pleasant people to live amongst. After the Reformation they indulged in horrid pagan rites and sacrifices. Now they profess Presbyterianism of a peculiarly narrow type.' Their spiritual guide was 'a well-intentioned man - but with very Puritanical ideas of what is good for his subjects. He has no books, and never sees a newspaper for eight months at a time. It is not, therefore, surprising to find that he is of the Free Kirk persuasion.' In fact the papers were none too fond of the Free Church in its dealings with the St Kilda people: 'How they manage to raise their annual tribute of £20 a year to the Sustentation Fund of the Free Church is a mystery. It is a grim satire on the argument that Church Establishments are kept for the benefit of the poor.' And the proprietor was, in at least one column, a despot.[60]

During the summer of 1876, when Sands was in the midst of his prolonged stay on St Kilda, MacLeod wrote to the *Spectator* to say what he thought of the unauthorised visitor:

'As a sequel to previous correspondence it may interest some of your Readers to know, that Mr Sands has carried out his intention of conveying a boat to the Island of St Kilda. My vessel having on board Stores for the Islanders had been lying at Obe in Harris for a fortnight, watching for suitable weather, when about the middle of June the Boat arrived there by a Steamer. Mr Sands engaged two Harris men to go over with him and my vessel and his boat started together, but they had not gone far, before those in the boat were compelled to ask for assistance, and she was towed by my vessel the whole way to the Island. My Agent immediately on landing gave the Inhabitants a Letter from me to the effect, that they were perfectly free to sell and buy where they pleased, and that I would keep up the communication with them or not according to their wish. Notwithstanding very unjustifiable Interference on the part of Mr Sands the people unanimously authorized a paper to be signed on their behalf begging me to continue to act for them, as I have hitherto done. My Agent offered Mr Sands a passage back, but he declined the offer and remains on the Island, where he will probably endeavor to create as much discontent and illwill as he can. I think however the people have too much good sense to listen to him, and I am sure they will not venture to risk their lives in his boat.'[61]

The speech by Fletcher Menzies at the Edinburgh meeting moved MacLeod to resume his own defence by letter. On 8 March 1877 he wrote to the *Scotsman* objecting once again to all of Sands's various observations and stating that the boat taken or rather towed out to St Kilda in 1876 was quite useless; and on 9 March he wrote to Menzies to question his remarks on 'a System of Usury' and his quoted prices of feathers, sugar, salt and sweeties.

Had Sands been the source of that information, and, if so, had it been verified?[62]

A letter in the *Scotsman* from MacLeod was sufficient to draw from Sands immediate and lengthy replies, in the course of which he took the opportunity to dismiss 'such mosquitoes and gadflies as Dr Ferguson, etc.' One or two anonymous 'gadflies' had ideas on possible uses for St Kilda – 'It would be a capital place for a State establishment for dipsomaniacs' or a lighthouse and meteorological station. Others preferred evacuation: 'the right course would be, not to get up subscriptions for them from time to time, or to influence the Government to send a steamer several times a-year at great expense to ascertain how it fares with them, but to induce them to leave their isolated barren rock altogether'. But Sands himself principally concentrated upon his favourite criticisms, directed as most of them were against the proprietor, and his letters were now more blunt and direct: 'He wants to keep them chained to that rock that his factor may feed upon their entrails'; 'It is dangerous to trust to him'; 'He may leave the people to starve, and excuse himself again by blaming the weather'. There were however two other targets also - the Edinburgh committee, and the managers of the Kelsall Bequest fund who appeared to be doing little or nothing to relieve the 'destitution' which Sands said he had left behind him.[63]

*

After MacLeod of MacLeod had written to Menzies and the latter had responded it was not long before the objects of Sands's disapproval began to work together. They agreed that accurate, impartial information was lacking, although in mid March a copy of the report by the *Jackal's* commanding officer, Lieutenant Commander W. Digby, submitted to the Admiralty from Portree on 23 February 1877, reached MacLeod and was found to contain a factual account of the vessel's hurried visit to St Kilda the day before, and its rough return in 'a strong gale from N.W. with furious squalls and a remarkably high and heavy sea'. The report certainly expressed the islanders' indignation at the failure of the proprietor's smack to arrive in autumn, but it did not precisely describe the degree of 'destitution' they were suffering as a consequence. Everybody accepted that a vessel with provisions ought to go to the island, but there was confusion over who would send it. MacLeod gave directions to John MacKenzie his agent at Dunvegan 'to send some meal seedcorn and potatoes as quickly as he could', but on 14 March he 'countermanded' that instruction because he had just learned that the Highland and Agricultural Society (HASS) had obtained the use of the *Jackal* for this purpose so there was no need for him to send any. A few days later Menzies wrote to MacLeod to say that he had been told by the Admiralty that as MacLeod was arranging a smack to St Kilda the *Jackal* would not be going.

To solve this problem MacLeod then renewed the order to MacKenzie that his smack or sloop, *Robert Hadden,* should sail at once. MacKenzie accordingly set off on or about 21 March, and though he himself went only as far as Obbe there were men on board who would give a fair description of the situation in the island. Three attempts were made to reach and land the supplies, and the last was successful, yet the mission had taken a month to accomplish and it was the evening of 20 April when the battered *Robert Hadden* came in to Dunvegan with its news.[64]

MacLeod's concern over the reflections upon his reputation as a caring proprietor was shared by his sister Emily. Unlike her brother, whose remoteness in the south from the St Kilda issue and apparent lack of knowledge of the island and its people did not help his cause, she lived at Dunvegan and felt more immediately involved. Her reaction was not to join in the newspaper correspondence but to write to Menzies following what the MacLeods saw as his unfortunate remarks to the Edinburgh committee, of which she did not hear anything until 16 March. She was disappointed that her 'old friend' Menzies had repeated the supposed falsehoods and exaggerations coming from John Sands, and she claimed that the factor, MacKenzie, was 'a most respectable man, and quite incapable of wronging the St. Kildians or anyone else'. It was her understanding that the islanders were 'far better off than in our villages here', that they were 'better instructed also, (for their minister has taught every man, woman and child to read the Bible in Gaelic)', and that they had long been 'very religious moral and well conducted' although now 'they have a little worldly wisdom too, and have made a very good thing of complaining to yachts of their want of boats etc. (they have always had two)'. She had been told that when 'the last tourist-contributed boat arrived, they were heard to say in Gaelic "this is a nice boat; when the other comes we can sell it in Stornoway"'. Some years previously she had thought of staying on the island for several months 'to see if I could be of use' but had been so satisfied by reports of conditions there that she remained at home.[65]

Emily MacLeod naturally supported her brother. For her too the real trouble was not the system of management but John Sands:

'The saddest part is that the long residence of such a man must have done the people infinite harm in many ways. He is known to have passed a night in drinking with a common sailor, and his conduct to the girls has been highly objectionable. The ignorant people thought he was going to marry one of them. He himself said when he first came that they were particularly modest and well-conducted. If what report says is true of his conduct during his first visit some of them no longer deserve that character - Poor things! One cannot publish this, as one does not exactly know what has taken place, but it is very hard that such a man should be turned loose among a primitive people who imagine he is a gentleman and look up to him as a supposed benefactor.

'He has not only set the people against their proprietor, but against their good minister, who though he may be narrow-minded perhaps, has proved himself a real benefactor to them.'[66]

Having told Menzies off for accepting at face value the tales from Sands Emily clearly expected him to accept her own, which were of course intended to portray Sands as a dangerous and damaging interloper, and to an extent she succeeded in bringing the HASS secretary over to the MacLeod side. As Norman MacLeod said to him, 'when you come to know Mr Sands better you will not attach so much value to what he says'; and even though neither Norman and his sister nor Menzies had met the offender there was soon a united hostility towards him. The result was that Sands never received an answer telling him whether or not he was to be given a lift in any supply vessel that might go on behalf of the HASS, and Menzies was able to reassure MacLeod that 'I have never put faith in Mr Sands, and he has been showing himself off by Letters in the papers which I think have quite opened the eyes of the Public to him … Mr Sands is attacking me now because I will not send him to St Kilda. My opinion of him is such that I think he should <u>if possible</u> be kept out of the Island.'

Gradually Emily came to the view that it would be useful after all if she did pay a visit to St Kilda:

'I think of going to St.Kilda myself the next time my brother sends there, probably about the end of May or June. I should like to see what is really going on, and would remain for some weeks. We have perfect confidence in Mr. Mackenzie's personal integrity, but he is much attached to my brother, and I am not without a suspicion, that, with the view of making the best of an unprofitable property, he may not have charged more of the expense of carriage to the islanders than he need have done. No doubt carriage is very expensive, but the lion's share should be borne by the proprietor. I also think it more than probable that my brother scarcely looked at Mr. Mackenzie's accounts and knew nothing about them.'[67]

With these belated and private admissions she made her plans for the expedition during April 1877, while Sands was still keeping up his campaign by letter and article. She was no doubt keen to form her own conclusions with regard to the numerous contradictory reports on the island in the press, so many indeed that 'there appears some danger lest the three score and ten inhabitants of St Kilda may ultimately wish to be saved from their friends, and allowed to pursue their isolated existence in peace'. But it was now too late for this. Interest in the island was so great, and government involvement frequent enough, that the 'poor people' there, who had never really controlled their own destiny, were not in a position to wish to be left alone. The outside intervention, with all sorts of ideas, was what mattered:

> 'By some it is asserted that they are in periodical danger of starvation and need regular succour; by others that they are better off than many peasants in the north of Scotland - two statements, by the way, not absolutely inconsistent. Some advocate the maintenance of this primitive community intact, while others declare that, unless it is recruited by new blood, disease and idiocy among its members will lead to its speedy extinction. According to one view, something ought to be done for the island at once; according to another, it is nobody's business but the proprietor's; while a third party would try to induce or compel the inhabitants to emigrate and abandon the place to the sea gulls.'[68]

There was no doubt that, either of her own accord or under pressure of public opinion, Emily Macleod was one of those who thought the St Kilda community needed help, and so too was the HASS secretary Fletcher Menzies who, in spite of the *Robert Hadden*'s recent visit, went ahead with arrangements for a supply of 'seed and other necessaries' to be delivered by an Admiralty vessel. Emily told Menzies about the damage suffered by the *Robert Hadden* in stormy conditions and of how 'the people were begging her to fly, even before she had landed all her cargo, for they said "If you are wrecked no one will ever dare to come near us again"'. Further news about the troublesome John Sands had also been brought back by the factor and his crew: 'It seems the minister and Mr. Sands had a great quarrel - the minister having remonstrated about his conduct. It is said that Mr. Sands has promised to return in the summer and marry one of the girls.' This possibility alarmed Emily a good deal. 'I don't think it is likely he will do that,' she wrote, 'but I should like to know if he really means to go there, for I intend to be there if possible for some weeks, and should not wish to meet him.'[69]

In spite of her dislike and disapproval of Sands and his public statements Emily Macleod responded positively to at least three of his accusations. She looked into the matter of prices, she reflected on the problem of communication, and she was determined to go to an island upon which her proprietor brother had never set foot. Her idea about an improved communication method was interesting in itself: 'What would you think,' she asked Menzies, 'of the benevolent Public hiring a steam yacht from April to September, going to St. Kilda as often as required, and paying themselves during the intermediate times by letting her out to Cockney tourists who abound at that season. If stationed at Harris, they might be taken to see the

Princess of Thule's bay and islands which would delight them. It might not be a bad speculation.' She must also have realised that the Free Church minister, John MacKay, was an important figure when it came to communication, at a different level, between the island and all those, like herself, who were now devoting so much attention to the inhabitants.

Like his predecessor Duncan Kennedy Rev. MacKay, however reluctant he might have been and however much he tried to confine himself to spiritual matters, found himself unavoidably caught up in the arguments over conditions in St Kilda and in the unfamiliar world of Admiralty ships and tourism. As minister, and as a speaker and writer of English, he had involuntarily become the voice of the people, asked to advance their material as well as their religious welfare. His rather quaint and clumsy letters in the spring of 1877 to Fletcher Menzies dealt with the need for provisions over and above those delivered by the *Robert Hadden* and commented rather variably on John Sands. 'Be Kind enough,' he wrote in one, 'as to give no instructions, orders, or directions, of any Kind whatever relating to St Kilda to a certain person called Mr Sands. I have seen enough of him already.' But only five days later he was rather less antagonistic:

> 'Since I wrote you yesterday, a steamer from Arisaig called in here, and the Captain of the steamer says, that Mr Sands and MacLeod of MacLeod were writing against each other in the Newspapers. Mr Sands is right in giving a full and accurate account of the state of the Island - As the people here are somewhat fond of him, for advocating their cause, I think it better, that you should only keep with yourself what I have said about his Character. I am rather for peace. Ignorant people will do, and say any thing, for the sake of their bellies.

> 'I write you this in a private way, I do not wish to bring myself into trouble with Mr Sands. I hope you will send the supplies at once.'[70]

Evidently the minister had suddenly realised he might appear in one of Sands's newspaper contributions, and soon he was to discover that his new-found caution had not saved him from just such a fate.

Following the arrival of the Kelsall Fund, the assistance provided by Captain Otter and the *Porcupine*, the visits by yacht parties, and, especially, the publicity deliberately courted by John Sands, St Kilda experienced the outcome of being invaded by several varieties of benevolence. Sir John MacPherson MacLeod, perhaps aware of the possible consequences, had tried to deter at least a good proportion of outside 'help', but with the change of ownership and a new proprietor living just as far away as the old one interest and interference in island affairs quickly got out of control. The Free Church, as the established church before it, slipped from its once dominant position further into the background, and its St Kilda missionary, whether he liked it or not, had to respond rather than govern in circumstances where outside influences and 'benevolent' assistance occupied so much of his time. What did the islanders think of a minister in this position? They were no longer, if they ever had been, meek victims of their religious instructor, accepting dutifully everything he said. They now had to judge his qualities as an intermediary in worldly as well as in spiritual matters, so that preaching lengthy sermons and teaching islanders to read the bible in Gaelic were not sufficient in themselves to justify the minister's presence and labours in his 'station'. Emily MacLeod summed up this fundamental aspect of the St Kilda community in April 1877 as she contemplated her forthcoming voyage:

> 'I fear it will now be impossible to prevent their asking for aid. Since yachts began to go there about 20 years ago, they have fancied themselves objects of compassion and are always urging their minister to speak for them. One of them said lately "Our minister is too old and stupid now - we want a cleverer man to speak for us. We should get much more if he was <u>smart</u> in speaking." Have you seen Mr. Sands caricature of the minister in the Graphic of the 7th.'[71]

There was something reminiscent of Alexander Buchan and perhaps too of other religious leaders of St Kilda in this picture of MacKay. A deep respect for religion, and for tradition, could be maintained at the same time as there was little or none for the missionary 'labourer' except when he was laying down the law as taught by the church to which the people happened to adhere.

*

Philanthropic interest in St Kilda went on increasing, stimulated by such occurrences as the gift in mid April 1877 by a grateful Austrian government of £100 'to be disposed of for the benefit of the hospitable islanders'. With John Sands still a terrier at his heels Menzies had supplies from the HASS loaded onto 'Her Majesty's gunboat Flirt', normally attached to H.M.S. *Aurora*, and early on 9 May - without a word to Sands - a junior clerk of the HASS, John MacDiarmid, left with the gunboat, commanded by Lieutenant O'Rorke, to superintend the delivery and the distribution of goods believed to be desperately needed.[72]

The supplies on board had been financed partly from the Kelsall Fund and partly by using the Austrian money. They were procured and assembled by Mr David Cross, of Argyll Street in Glasgow, 'whose kindness and willingness in getting everything ready for despatch so promptly, and on such short notice, shows the warm interest he takes in the welfare of these remote islanders'. Large quantities of oats, bere, potatoes and oatmeal were sent, along with flour, sugar, horse mane and tail hair for ropes, brandy, sherry and port 'for medicinal use', leather for shoes, tea, 20 pounds of 'sweeties', and turnip seed donated by Mr Cross himself. A special allocation of seed oats, potatoes, tea and sugar, together with a parcel forwarded by Walker & Sons of Aberdeen, was addressed to Rev. MacKay.[73]

After a rough passage round Kintyre and northward the *Flirt* reached Portree on Friday 11 May. Setting off again early on Saturday the gunboat passed through the Sound of Harris in the middle of the day and, helped by a good stern breeze, came in to the bay at St Kilda about 9.15 that evening. 'The natives' were eagerly watching, 'and a boat manned by four active young St Kilda men was soon alongside, and in a twinkling landed us safely on the rocky shore, where we received the very hearty greetings and kindly blessings of these simple-minded people'. A 'wail' of relief arose when it was learned that supplies had been brought, and combined with the howling of dogs and 'the hollow murmuring sound of the Atlantic waves' the 'weird din' deeply impressed MacDiarmid and his companions.

Conditions were suitable for unloading and the visitors decided that this should be done immediately with the help of the islanders and their boats. Opportunities for such movement between sea and shore being rare Lieutenant O'Rorke wished to seize the moment without delay. 'But here came a hitch in the proceedings: the old men shook their heads, and gathered around their minister in solemn conclave; the minister thrust his hands deep into his trouser pockets, and cast his eyes upon the ground in pensive meditation; eager, anxious women and amazed children stood with bated breath awaiting the result of the deliberation.' The old men, among them the elders, and the minister were evidently in command on this late Saturday evening, and their decision would be final. Soon it was announced that 'as it was now drawing near the Sunday, and as the people must be prepared for the devotions of the morrow, they could not think of encroaching on the Sabbath by working at the landing of the goods'. Religious sensitivities had clearly been disregarded in planning the visit but the response from the *Flirt* was understandable in the circumstances. If it had to wait till Monday the vessel could be in grave danger. But no amount of pleading, even 'though uttered in the hardest Gaelic', could bring about a change of heart, 'and as for reasoning with them upon its being a work of necessity, such a conception seemed to have no place in their creed'. Rather than bring the supplies ashore during the Sabbath the people were prepared to go to Harris for them if the *Flirt* had to leave before Monday dawned. O'Rorke tried unsuccessfully to land a few bags with his own boats through the surf but was eventually forced to accept the minister's advice and wait out in the bay. As if to confirm the approval of Providence a calm prevailed throughout Sunday and 'the ship lay as still as if in harbour'. MacDiarmid himself spent Saturday night as Rev. MacKay's guest in the manse.

The belief that Saturday evening should be spent in preparation for the Sabbath was, and to an extent still is, widespread among Highland and island Protestant communities, so that there was nothing either unique to St Kilda or even unusual about the decision by the minister and old men. One consequence was that it enabled MacDiarmid with some of the ship's officers and passengers to attend the first of the three Sunday services, begun at 11 a.m. and, like the others at 2 and 6 p.m., 'conducted in the same form as in other Free churches'. The curious visitors were able to note details of dress and appearance while trying to follow the proceedings. Most of the inhabitants were present. 'They seemed very earnest and attentive to the discourse, and now and then heaved a long deep sigh, as if by way of response. The singing baffles description.' At the end of the service, of which the visitors can have understood very little, the men all sat down and allowed the women to depart first.[74]

Some might have thought the restraint of the islanders remarkable. They had been anxiously waiting for further provisions since the departure of the *Robert Hadden* and were believed to be desperate. The day before the *Flirt* left Greenock 'three of the stoutest and hardiest men on the island set out in an open boat .. in search of seed and meal'. They were apparently making for Harris, but owing to contrary winds were forced to return home, 'having unsuccessfully combated the winds and waves for three days, and at the risk of their lives'. MacDiarmid had good reason to think it unduly Sabbatarian of 'the natives' to risk the possibility of missing out on their supplies and of having to venture once again on the hazardous crossing, yet nothing outweighed the religious code which these 'simple-minded' people observed.

The truth, however, seemed to be that the islanders were not really very desperate. MacDiarmid considered that they still had plenty of salted meat, meal and potatoes following upon the factor's visit a month previously, and there was sufficient seed for sowing the 1877 crop. 'Judging from outward appearance,' he said, 'I cannot believe the St Kildians suffered much from want of food.' They seemed to him to be healthy enough, several women giving him the impression of being 'more than ordinarily stout'. The main interest, as usual, was in tobacco: 'Tobacco was what they invariably asked for, and among the first questions put by the minister was, if I had brought any tobacco, and when I had unfortunately to answer in the negative, I perceived he felt far from happy.'

Though on the island for not much more than a day, and that day Sunday, MacDiarmid made notes on the people, their houses, their occupations, the land, rents, boats, means of landing, and other essential features of life there. He entered the dwellings and former houses turned into byres, and paid special attention to the manse and church, describing these buildings in a much kinder way than Sands did in his book:

'The minister's house is neat and commodious, and is enclosed on one side by a very high wall for shelter. It is a one-storeyed building, of four apartments and a porch. In front of it is an enclosed bit of tilled land, in which some rhubarb was growing, and in which was also set a rain-gauge. Immediately behind the manse is the church - a good, substantial edifice, with four windows, and a door. The minister can enter the church by a small door on the end next his house, and which opens on a landing beside the pulpit. It has a slated roof, but no flooring; and the seats consist of plain deal benches. Two enclosed pews flank the pulpit – one for the elders, the other reserved for visitors; and there is the usual box for the precentor.'

More than one copy of the Gaelic bible was to be seen in every house, but not much else in the way of reading material except at the manse where were such demanding works as 'Smith's Moral Sentiments, Butler's Fifteen sermons, Hervey's Meditations, works of John Owen, D.D., Select Works of Dr Chalmers, Baxter's Call, Sir John Herschell's Astronomy, all appropriate to a Free Church minister's library', and all in keeping with the kind of books that had mouldered away in St Kilda since the days of Buchan. The glebe, next to the manse, consisted chiefly of 'an acre of tilled land', but the minister also kept a cow and a few sheep, 'for which, I presume, he pays nothing'. The minister himself, John MacKay, was, said MacDiarmid incorrectly, a native of Lochalsh, and perhaps more accurately was described as 'an unmarried man between fifty and sixty years of age, of kindly disposition, fair intelligence, but far from robust-looking, and apparently rather deficient in vigour and action'.

It occurred to MacDiarmid that the minister 'must have much spare time, which could be profitably employed in teaching English to the young'. It seemed that the people were eager to learn both English and arithmetic, and that young and old would probably pick up at least the language very quickly since they readily learned English names and words, although 'our captain's name proved rather a puzzler to them, and invariably stuck in their throats'. In the absence of a regular schoolteacher the minister could step in to help and if of an evangelical turn of mind he might do so enthusiastically. 'Indeed I cannot conceive that anything could be a greater pleasure to the minister than to train up the dozen lambs of his flock in the knowledge of the English tongue and the simplest rules of arithmetic, and an acquaintance with their own situation in respect to their country, etc.' The long-established principle of combining religious and ordinary education under one man, catechist or missionary, could be followed yet again in the St Kilda of the 1870s.

After a walk over to Glen Mor and some thought on the promising nature of the hill pasture MacDiarmid took a look at the four boats on the shore, two of them almost new but, 'though excellent boats of their kind .. scarcely strong enough built to withstand long the rough usage of having to be hauled over the rocks when landing'. The further boat which the Government was supposed to be providing on the recent recommendation of Lieutenant Commander Digby of the *Jackal* would be 'of very little use to them', and though one built specially at Stornoway 'after the style of the herring-boats common there' would be much more appropriate the problem of that vital step between sea and dry shore remained, for 'The want of a proper landing-place is a great drawback to the island, and causes incalculable toil and great danger to the inhabitants'. With a safe haven, MacDiarmid felt, and with a fishing smack, the people 'could find their way to and from the mainland …The people are, in my opinion, fearless sailors'. An adequate fuel source in place of 'the present disastrous system' of stripping the turf from the pasture and a good landing or harbour were the two most urgent improvements required, but neither could be introduced by the islanders alone.

While the energetic MacDiarmid was exploring the island Staff-Surgeon Scott from the *Flirt* was busy attending to the diseased leg of one islander and examining at least a score of others who were 'clamouring for a cure for their various ailments'. His medical report was handed to MacDiarmid who then seemed to have all the information he was likely to get on what, in St Kilda, was the wrong day for asking questions: 'I quite failed in getting any approximation to the quantity of exports. Had I been there on a week-day, I might have prevailed upon each to try and draw upon his memory, and give me a list of what he gave the factor every year; but most unfortunately it was Sunday, and the people were extremely reticent. If any questions were asked them, they would either move away, or tell me plainly they would not answer such inquiries on the Sabbath.' An hour after midnight the visiting party, who had not been to bed, called out the islanders, boats were launched, and the landing of supplies began. A scheme for division into equal shares was drawn up and a copy left with Rev. MacKay. By 7.30 that Monday morning the work was finished, the island women had, as was customary, helped to draw up the boats out of the water, and the *Flirt* left 'amidst the cheering of the St Kildians and their hearty good wishes'. Soon the ship disappeared from view into 'the wide expanse of ocean'.[75]

At a meeting of the HASS directors in February 1878 the board, on the recommendation of Mr Walker of Bowland, chairman of the Board of Supervision, awarded a gold medal to John MacDiarmid for his report and £10 from the Kelsall Fund for taking charge of the distribution of the goods sent to the island.[76]

*

At about the time of the *Flirt*'s return John Sands was preparing a second edition of his book on St Kilda. He may well have prided himself on having instigated the visits to the island of both the *Robert Hadden* and the *Flirt*, and he seems to have been moved by a genuine concern for the island people:

'To break open the door of MacLeod's prison was the object of my second visit ...To liberate the poor serfs who had been so long incarcerated and cruelly used, and to bring them into communication with the rest of the world, was my mission ...I felt as if I had had a Divine call to perform the work, and must proceed at any cost, and despite of any opposition. Providence often selects strange instruments with which to execute His purposes, - instruments that would seem altogether unsuitable to Doctors Begg and McLauchlan.'[77]

But the merit of his attempts, through writing, to have 'immediate relief sent out to my distressed constituents, and afterwards to get a mail steamer to call twice a year' was marred in the public view by his attacks on the proprietor and by what proved to be valid accusations of exaggeration and scaremongering. MacDiarmid's investigation showed that tales of extreme destitution were unfounded and that the proprietor's arguments were reasonable even if not the full story. Claims that MacLeod was respected and well liked by the islanders were really rather hollow since the two had never met.[78]

The efforts made by Sands, whether favourably received or not, led inevitably to greatly increased interest in St Kilda and were therefore the very means by which any further campaigning on his part was rendered unnecessary. With the island turned into an object of tourist curiosity rather than being merely the home of a dwindling community struggling to survive, Sands may have come to regret the publicity he had thought would bring help to the people. Nevertheless he revised his book apparently with the purpose of self-justification and of pursuing his vendetta against a proprietor whose 'breach of contract' in failing to send his supply vessel in the autumn of 1876 was 'little short of culpable homicide'.

When the second edition appeared, possibly before 1 November 1877 though dated 1878, it contained, even more than the first, information which resulted in what may be called St Kilda myths. Real feeling and genuine observations tended to make the whole work seem reliable, but that did not mean that all impressions derived from it were equally fair and accurate. Remarks on the landlord's behaviour, or that of his factor, may be so expressed as to permit an entirely misleading picture to emerge, even though based on fact; and to Sands may be traced popular but hardly just interpretations of certain features of the community in the mid 1870s.

There was, for instance, the daily meeting of St Kilda men to talk over any matter of interest and discuss what needed to be done. This meeting, closely related to the long-established practice of acting as one in nearly all circumstances, was an integral part of the nature of island existence, one of those uniting essentials that enabled people to survive in a place at the mercy of the seasons and the elements. As a traditional feature it was far more important than the treatment it has received at the hands of numerous writers and in popular anecdote. It was the 'common assembly of the male population' noticed by Atkinson in 1831, the 'kind of senate' mentioned in 1863, and in course of time it came to be thought a speciality of St Kilda, even uniquely associated with the island. Yet it had its counterpart, perhaps less formalised, in many other Hebridean communities, where the business of the day was settled and anything that could be debated was.

Rev. Dr. Thomas McLauchlan, recollecting his own visit 'with some friends' to St Kilda, was of the opinion that the island's morning assembly was a relic of ancient government. In St Kilda, he rashly declared, 'is a purely Celtic population, retaining many of the earlier customs of the race'. In his remarks he contributed to the existing impression among many mainland people that the St Kilda 'natives' might be compared to a tribe, and promoted the false picture of a primitive 'council' gathering, still to be seen 'far out among the waves of the Atlantic' but no longer found elsewhere: 'The men of the island, as often as needs be, meet in a certain spot, and there, as round the Indian council fire, settle the affairs of the nation.' Sands, on the other hand, treated the matter more lightheartedly, almost trivialising it:

'The men of St Kilda are in the habit of congregating in front of one of the houses almost every morning for the discussion of business. I called this assembly the Parliament, and with a laugh they adopted the name. When the subject is exciting the members talk with loud voices and all at one time …Some of the men may be seen reclining on the top of the wall of an old hut, others leaning against it, while two or three stride backwards and forwards with their hands in their pockets and their beards in the air, bawling at the full pitch of their powerful voices, and even rising on tip-toe when the debate becomes vehement. You may hear them half a mile off. A stranger would fancy they were about to come to blows; but nothing is farther from their thoughts. Shall we go to catch solan geese, or ling, or mend the boat? or hunt sheep? are examples of the subjects that occupy the house. Although exceedingly disputatious, they work in perfect harmony when once the question is settled.'[79]

The lack of seriousness in the manner with which Sands treated the meeting of the St Kilda men was apparent in his description of island religion and especially of the minister. In the first edition of his book he expressed some admiration for MacKay, seeing him as 'not only an earnest and honest man, but a kind-hearted one withal, whom those of any or of no persuasion would respect'. The Free Church pastor struck him as an isolated figure:

'There, posted like a sentinel on a rocky bank close to the sea, his whole aim is to keep the devil out of the island. Absorbed in this duty, he forgets the loneliness of his situation, and is deaf to the roaring of the waves that rage before his sentry-box during the long winter, and blind to the desolate aspect of the hills that tower steeply around, their lofty tops enveloped in drifting fogs. He is contented with plain fare and drinks none, is attentive to the infirm, and shares in a stealthy way what luxuries he has with them. Although an educated man, he has no books and no newspapers to enliven his solitude. Who so anxious as he when the boats happened to be caught by a storm? Methinks I see him now, wandering restlessly on the shore, watching the waves outside the bay lashed into foam by the strong north wind, until the boats came round the rocky point. And when the crews told him they had lost their lines, I still hear him muttering: 'Lost their lines! I'm sorry for that, - very sorry for that!'

'Although a bachelor, who, according to the vulgar creed, ought to have no tenderness for the young, he is seldom to be seen without a rosy-cheeked urchin - a lamb of his flock - hanging on to his breeches' pocket and following him like a dog. Personally I am indebted to him for numberless acts of friendship, - kindness continued from first to last. He pressed me to live in his house, and when, preferring freedom and the bagpipes, I declined his invitation, he did his utmost to render me comfortable in my own quarters. Take him for all in all, the Free Kirk has few soldiers she has more reason to feel proud of.'[80]

Here was a worthy man indeed, far different from the tyrannical zealot of subsequent popular myth. But it appears that something happened to change Sands's mind, for in the second edition of his book the passages quoted above were omitted, and scattered through the pages instead were less respectful remarks and a good deal less than respectful portrait sketch. From this altered version of MacKay comes the uncomplimentary impression of him still current today.[81]

The remarks related to religious practices, mainly with the purpose of illustrating the regime supposedly prevailing under the minister and of revealing his personality. Sands thought the church itself 'very plain - not to say ugly' and 'an ugly modern building'. In winter it was 'a miserable place', with mould on the walls, worm-eaten backless benches and the cold ground for a floor. There were three meetings on a Sunday, two of them probably equivalent to the morning service and afternoon Sunday school or 'Bible-class' mentioned by Alexander Cameron. The weekly prayer meeting on a Wednesday evening was still a regular event, conducted by the elders, and on the first Tuesday of each month a further meeting was held 'to return thanks

The uncomplimentary caricature by John Sands of Rev. John Mackay (pub. 1878)

*The picture of Rev. John Mackay in D W Logie's
account of his visit to St Kilda in 1889*

for the preservation of Captain Otter of H.M.S.Porcupine'. Sands said; 'This was instituted at the request of the now deceased Captain, who brought them supplies in a season of dearth, and who attempted a number of improvements which have proved abortive.' He was of the opinion that the Otter meeting 'savours of Popery', a remark calculated to cause unease among the Free Church Highlands committee members.[82]

As for the people attending the services, 'I had never,' wrote Sands, 'although familiar with the meeting-houses of the backwoods and prairies, seen a humbler church or congregation'. He was impressed by the 'more than ordinary development of the religious instinct' which seemed to characterise the population in general, but what struck him most was a depressing atmosphere which accompanied the arrival of each Sabbath and which was so pervading as to leave no room for ordinary social contact:

> 'The Sabbath is indeed a day of intolerable gloom.At the clink of the bell the whole flock hurry to the church, with sorrowful looks, and eyes bent upon the ground. It is considered sinful to look to the right hand or to the left. They do not appear like good people going to listen to glad tidings of great joy, but like a troop of the damned whom Satan is driving to the bottomless pit. Surely this is not the proper deportment for good Christians - surely religion, with its promises of remission of sins and everlasting life beyond the grave, should make true believers more cheerful and not more miserable than benighted heathen, who have no such consolations ..

'No one speaks above a whisper or visits another on the seventh day.'[83]

Added to the Sunday and other services was family worship, 'held in every house morning and evening' every day. On occasions when groups of men and women were away on another island worship was conducted as usual, both there and at home, and 'Every meal is preceded by a grace, nor will they take a drink of milk or water without uncovering the head'.

Intense devotion, quietness, limitations on visiting, grace before refreshment, are features not confined to the St Kilda of 1876. Proper or not, this was the 'deportment' of the 'good Christians' of the island and of other places throughout the Highlands, a pattern of religious practice to which the people had been gradually accustomed over the previous thirty years, and even the length of Sabbath church time - said by Sands to have amounted to 'six hours and a half' - cannot be considered exceptional, although in circumstances of bare feet and damp, uncomfortable surroundings the comment clearly carried overtones of disapproval. There is no real evidence for attributing the quite usual and widespread kind of religious programme witnessed by Sands and other visitors in St Kilda to peculiarities in Rev. MacKay's character or conduct.

It was however the minister himself who became the subject of some of the sharpest and more critical observations in the second edition of Sands's book. He was no longer the pleasant if lonely person of the first edition. 'The minister acts as schoolmaster, and teaches, in a desultory way, the six or seven children who are of the proper age for instruction. But the man is old' -in fact, about 58 – 'and has a disordered liver, and perhaps does not see the importance of giving the young a better secular education.' This was the man whom Sands had seen with a child 'following him like a dog' out of affection, but now dismissed as a dull, rambling teacher and, presumably, preacher who had apparently picked up an old ministerial joke: 'if any woman, say, happens to drop asleep, she is immediately aroused with a "Lachlan, duisg a bhean; cha bhi cadal an Ifrinn - Lachlan, awaken your wife; she wont sleep much in hell, I think !" which causes Lachlan to stick his elbow into his wife's ribs immediately. The minister then indulges in a low chuckle, mingled with coughing and inarticulate sounds, and waits patiently until the woman is thoroughly aroused.'[84]

Both MacKay and his housekeeper Ann MacDonald were pictured in a roundabout way, Sands now giving space to his feelings in a manner that was quite contrary to the favourable view he had formerly expressed:

> 'The best resident ruler, "guide, philosopher, and friend", for St Kilda would be a sensible, firm, and good-tempered old sailor, able to work and repair a boat, to teach the three R's and a little English to the young, and to scrape a reel on the fiddle for the girls to dance to; and the worst home ruler would be a well-meaning but feeble-minded, irresolute, yet domineering fanatic, whose servant would lead him by the nose, and get him to preach at any woman to whom she had a spite, who would be obliged to sit and listen in silence, however innocent. This latter character is, of course, entirely supposititious, but it is quite possible that the Free Church might send such a representative to St Kilda, to sit like an incubus on the breast of the community. In that sequestered island, beyond the supervision of Sessions and Presbyteries, he might, by working on the religious prejudices of his flock, retain his grasp, and exercise a tyranny which would never be tolerated in other places.'

Whatever the motives behind the two different descriptions there may have been some truth in both of them. The reason for the change from the one to the other must surely have been MacKay's intervention in the matter of the alternatives sent to the island by the proprietor and his obstruction, as Sands saw it, of the proposed direct trading between St Kilda and Harris in the new boat. Sands had hoped that this boat would have freed the islanders from dependence on the proprietor and his agent, and so, frustrated, he took his revenge on the minister and increased his hostility towards MacLeod. But the second edition was too late to achieve very much apart from perpetuating an unfair image of MacKay as a Free Church villain who helped to bring about the demise of St Kilda's community.

On 9 April 1877, only just over five weeks after his return in the *Jackal*, John Sands addressed the Society of Antiquaries on the antiquities of St Kilda. He might have hoped this event would have attracted more useful public attention, and probably it did, but it was also an indication of his interest in a subject not confined to the island. Five years later, in 'Notes on the Antiquities of the Island of Tiree', he wrote again of his explorations in the history, folklore and ancient remains of one of the Hebrides but without the emotional involvement in the living population that had coloured his record of St Kilda. By 1885 his pursuits may have included ornithology, as on 10 June that year J A Harvie Brown wrote to 'J. Sands' from the steam yacht *Eunice* in Stornoway harbour about records of the migration and distribution of birds. Harvie Brown had heard 'casually' that 'you are forming a collection of Birds and eggs in the Long Island'. Whether or not it was owing to this particular activity's having been broadened in scope Sands then spent time in Shetland where in 1888 he was living when his book of poems, *King James' Wedding and other Rhymes*, was published in Arbroath. In the 1890s he retired to Bowriefauld, near Letham in Angus, and in March 1909 was buried at Dunnichen.[85]

It is easy to understand and to have some sympathy for the views of a writer whose account of St Kilda is informative, largely accurate, and often sincerely felt. But of course there were many who were offended by his observations and his aims, and who thought that his work should have avoided indulgence in prejudice and remained within the limits of innocuous description. Among those who disapproved but at the same time took advantage of the widespread interest which Sands had aroused was George Seton, 'Advocate, M.A. Oxon., etc.', whose book *St Kilda Past and Present* was published in 1878.

CHAPTER 5

*Emily Macleod in St Kilda, George Seton's book,
and 'The "Curse" of Gaelic'*

A copy of the report due from John MacDiarmid was eagerly awaited by Emily MacLeod who had arranged to travel to St Kilda with Lord and Lady MacDonald in their steam yacht *Lady of the Isles*. She planned to stay for a month and come back by the *Dunara Castle* 'which is advertised to make a trip there on the 28th June', but delay in getting away from Skye cut short that period by a week or more. She was particularly anxious to learn from MacDiarmid whether John Sands was on the island. She expected him to go on the *Dunara Castle* but feared that he might be already there and that she would have to meet the man whose accusations had indirectly led to her proposed visit: 'I have a list now,' she wrote to Menzies, 'of the names characters and circumstances of all the people, so I shall hope to find out whether there are, or not, any real grievances and shall at all counts do what I can to allay any bad feeling, Mr. Sands may have aroused. I hear there is a large party against him, but my information may come from a prejudiced source.' In the event her worries proved groundless.[86]

The steam yacht, with the MacDonalds, Rev. Archibald McNeill minister of Sleat, and the experienced Donald MacDonald of Tormore, at last arrived at Dunvegan to pick up Emily in the afternoon of 13 June, and at 10 a.m. the next morning the party was met by a comfortingly 'hearty and friendly reception' in St Kilda. Miss MacLeod made herself at home in one of the rooms of the factor's house and within a day had reached some conclusions regarding the character of the inhabitants. She found them 'very nice and friendly [and] not a bit shy', and she was 'struck by their well-to-do and comfortable appearance'. On the other hand they seemed greedy, since they were not contented with the 10s Lord MacDonald gave them for a fulmar-catching demonstration, even though he produced some tobacco and his wife some dresses.

During her residence of nearly three weeks Emily wrote a letter almost every day on the chance that some vessel would call and take one or several away. There were all sorts of things to write about. She mentioned the blind man to whom she read who did not appreciate the stories but 'was never tired listening to little sermons'. A girl asked her for a copy of Thomas Boston's *Fourfold State*, the one on the island being 'torn to pieces with much reading', and most people wanted nothing but similarly heavy religious works. Prices were investigated and explained, the episodes of the *Dargavel* and of the shipwrecked Austrians were recorded, and the departure to sale of island cattle described – 'the women get very fond of their cows, and when the minister, having three, sent away the eldest, the parting between her and his servant was quite touching'. Special attention was paid to the women, among whom were several Mrs Ferguson: 'when I told them that my sister was Mrs Ferguson who sent them the scissors and knives, they were much delighted …they are exactly like the people ..[in Skye] when I was young - before they were contaminated by Glasgow.' For the most part all the people were busy and cheerful, particularly the women. 'They are much more full of life and fun than Highlanders in general,' thought Emily, and they were inclined to mimicry. 'The women told me that they had never seen a drunken man till a doctor came to vaccinate them … One began to mimic the ways of a tipsy man, he must have drunk himself into a fit for she kicked and screamed, but when they found what was the matter, though they were kind at first, thinking he was dying, they were much disgusted.' Isabella Ross Munro was something of an exception, being rather ill-tempered, and so too was Ann MacDonald. 'I went to call on the minister just now,' Emily wrote. 'His servant came in sat down and talked as if she had been his daughter, joining in my conversation with him.' Ann was not particularly gloomy but she was serious and rather domineering.[87]

Since there was a new baby on the island Emily heard a good deal about the infant mortality and of how expectant mothers 'sometimes go to Harris to be confined', although they had to be away from September to the following June and did not like Harris life: '"It is a poor place" one said "nothing to eat but bread and tea no fulmar, no mutton"'. Emily had her own theory on the cause of the deaths and was certain that the 'real want of this island is a well-educated nurse for the old woman who acts as such is thoroughly ignorant'. Brother Norman and his wife would surely send one out.

The minister kept some medicine supplied by Mrs MacLeod, and this was in accordance with the rather vague assumption existing since at least the time of Neil MacKenzie that the missionary would serve as doctor although totally unskilled. Emily seems to have quite enjoyed the Sabbath under John MacKay's guidance:

'Sunday was very quiet - they begin it on Saturday at 6 P.M. No one works after that hour. All can read Gaelic well and are thoroughly well-versed in Scripture. The minister gave a good Gaelic sermon - his manner very earnest and quaint. He wished to prove that works are required to shew your faith and repeated acts! acts! acts! six times, then came a peculiar Gaelic "Ugh" very long, ending with an interrogation as much as to say "Ah! have you any acts to shew?" Silence for a minute, and then an answering groan from the people. All the children go to church, even 2 year olds and four of these roared several times. When the service ends, all the women go out first, then all the men in single file and so they walk each alone to their houses. This is to avoid foolish talking. In the evening there was school in the church and all the young people from 35 downwards said hymns and chapters, each in their own seat without any shyness. Not a sound was heard all day but on Monday morning, the village woke to its usual laughing and talking liveliness.'

Despite the obsession with religious books Emily soon discovered that the islanders entertained themselves in other ways. One beautiful, fine evening 'all were sitting on the low wall before their doors'. She wandered along and sat down too. 'A good many gathered round me and began telling stories of long ago.' She heard the tale of Fearchar and Dugan and 'tried to make them date this story and several others, but could get nothing nearer than "hundreds of years ago".' Among the other tales were incidents handed down through not many generations:

'A man of 60 said that in his Father's time, a vessel arrived on Sunday, and made them gather their lambs and all their best possessions, which were carried off, and the strange sailors put swords to the throats of every man who refused to deliver them up. The St. Kildans seemed to feel the having been forced to work on Sunday more than the loss of their goods. They say the island was repeatedly plundered at that time. I think it may perhaps have been during the 2nd American war in 1814 and that the pirates were Americans - perhaps Paul Jones himself. They also said that once a man swam ashore, pursued by other men out of a large ship - that they sheltered the fugitive, and put him in a secret cave. Then numbers of furious men landed with swords and guns and said if they did not give the man up, they would cut the throat of every St. Kildan and set fire to their houses. I said surely they did not give him up? Yes they did - they could not help it, and the poor fellow was taken on board and tied to the mast and beaten till he fainted - there was no skin left on his back, and they heard his screams and saw it all, for the ship was close to the shore and they were on the hill above … They told many other stories, and finally thinking I should be afraid said "Oh this was long ago, no bad ships come here now".'

One day Emily looked into 'a little black hut' which, she heard, had housed Lady Grange, and this reminded her that back in Skye it had always been said of St Kilda 'that it was used as a convict settlement, and that when people at Dunvegan were not bad enough to be hanged at Beallach na Croiche, and yet were troublesome, that they were sent here'.

Perhaps her chief pursuit however, at least initially, was collecting gossip about John Sands, and the results clearly gave her some satisfaction. The disgruntled Isabella Ross Munro, Neil MacDonald's wife, was the probable source of most of what she gathered. 'I now see who is the culprit as to grumbling to tourists. It is Bell, the Loch Carron woman, and who being the only person who speaks English is always brought forward, and makes a very good thing of it. She gets heaps of presents.' Isabella told Emily that Sands had lodged with her for about a month. 'She fed him with mutton, milk, fish, the best of all she had, washed his clothes and supplied fuel - he gave her 5s -!! But she said she did not wish to complain for he had got Sir Patrick Murray to give her husband a box of tools worth £5. No doubt Sands told Sir P. that he was a poor man, whereas he is one of the richest in the island with lots of sheep. What a shameful way of paying private debts.' It seems likely that Isabella was not the most reliable provider of information; certainly some of the stories about Sands were not true.

One of the Austrians was reported to have formed an attachment to a St Kilda girl, but more interesting to Emily was the reasonably sound report on the island that Sands himself had gone a stage further:

> 'Marion Gillis, to whom Mr. Sands promised marriage, has been very handsome. She is 33 and looks more - there is something very nice about her. She is quite devoted to him. Some say he is 60 and grey, and others think he is an old 45. I don't suppose he will marry her. Indeed it was reported that he is a married man. It is also said that he was a bankrupt photographer, and ran away from his creditors. He must be clever for he could not have chosen a better place than this. He quarrelled with the factor during his first visit and vowed to be revenged. Hence all his letters to the newspapers.'[88]

St Kilda was divided on the matter of Sands. Some were against him and believed the worst of the stories about him, and some were his friends and against MacLeod. In his favour it can at least be said that he was not already married when proposing to Marion.

> 'The anti-Sands party here say that Mr. S. used very strong language against both proprietor and factor. "I'll trample him under foot, I'll take the island from him". I have very little doubt from what they say, that his plan was, by making the row he did, to provoke him into selling it. Mr. S. had got benevolent people in Edinburgh, headed by a Mr. Stewart W. S., ready to buy it and to give him the management at a salary of £50 a year. They were to keep a steamer for him to go to Glasgow twice a year to sell their feathers etc. I fear the poor benevolents would have a large outlay, with very little coming in, but the penniless Mr. S. would do well. He must be very poor, which is the only excuse for his conduct. The only thing he has ever given them (though he lived six weeks on them during his first visit and was supplied with food, fuel and service for eight months on the second occasion) was half a lb of peppermint lozenges to each family!'[89]

Rev. MacKay was of course involved in the marriage question but at this stage opposed to Sands:

'The minister still declares he will not marry one of his flock to that bad man so there will be a row when he comes by Dunara. I don't think it would be right to refuse to marry them if they leave this, for of course if he got her away, he never would marry her. I have scarcely seen her, all the other people come to me very often, but I suppose she is anti-MacLeod, for neither she nor any of her people have come.'

Then, as the day of the *Dunara Castle*'s arrival approached, one of that family did meet Emily:

'Marion Gillis' mother came to-day, to ask for a private interview with me. She began at once to ask if I knew any thing of Mr. Sands. She said the minister had so bad an opinion of him that he had refused to marry him to her daughter saying he had heard a report that he was already married, and that he feared he was only going thro' the ceremony that he might live with her while here, and then that he would go and leave her. She added that Mr. S. had lately written a Gaelic letter that he would come by the first opportunity, that he had asked leave to come by the Flirt but that the Captain no doubt influenced by the proprietor, had refused a passage. She fully expected he would be here on Monday. She feared the minister would not marry him but that Marion was so much attached to him, she would go away with him and trust to being married on the main-land. He had said he would have a nice house for her near Edinburgh and keep a Gaelic servant for her. I said I feared he was not able to do so for he was said to be very poor, and it looked like being true, as he had never given anyone here any payment for his food etc. She said, He had left his purse here by mistake that there was £2 in it, and perhaps he meant to give them that. "Even if he did," I answered "it was absurdly little for all he had had". She said He had taken away many dozens of stockings to sell for them in Edinburgh - perhaps he would pay them when he had sold them … She concluded by saying that she and her husband had made up their minds to let Marion go with Mr. S. if he came. I said if they chose to let them marry no one else had a right to speak, but I entreated her not to allow Marion to leave the island <u>without marriage</u> for <u>her </u>sake, and so the interview ended. I then went to the minister, and he quite saw that if Marion was really resolved to go with him, that for her sake he had better give in and marry them. The poor man was in a dreadful state of mind at the prospect of Mr. S's return. He walked up and down the room muttering "he is the ruin of the people".'

The visit of the *Dunara Castle* had been arranged for Monday 2 July. The day before John MacKay 'preached an earnest sermon on the dangers of bad companionship', and as no one on the island could be called a bad companion everyone recognised that 'Mr. Sands must have been on his brain'. The minister delivered his warning: 'Some of you like amusing companions even if they are bad. You will have a bad companion in the next world - even the devil, and you will be very tired of each other in the long weeks of eternity.' And with these words in their minds the whole island population waited anxiously to see what Monday morning would bring - none more anxiously than Marion.

At 6 a.m., the Sabbath past, the ship was sighted and three hours later she was at anchor in the bay. Boats set off towards the shore. Emily watched. 'Tourist after tourist landed and spread themselves over the place.' Then, with the utmost relief - but to Marion's utter disappointment - 'No Mr. Sands!!'

Emily quickly gathered her belongings together, entered an island boat which was nearly swamped with tourists, and went on board the steamer which soon took her away. As the *Dunara Castle* left the tourists 'all talked of the great advantage it would be to the people to have regular post and communication with Glasgow'. Emily did not agree. 'I cannot but dread what the effect would be. Even that day, some of the steamer people got hold of two of the natives, offered them whiskey, brandy and wine. Both men accepted one glass, but nothing could induce them to take more, adding that they did not think it right.' But she knew that resistance would not last, for 'Glasgow contamination' would overcome the people as it had done in Skye where 'As soon as children grow up, away they go - boys and girls of 16 and 17, delighted to throw off parental control, off to Glasgow where they spend their wages in selfish indulgence, and leave their parents to the parish.' Regular communication she was sure would just be damaging to the islanders:

> 'If so called civilisation reaches St. Kilda, I fear the effect would be the same, and I should mourn to see the simple happy, Christian people sink in the lowest Gorbals of Glasgow. As to post, no one but the minister can read or write English, and not one has a relation or friend they would wish to write to if they could out of the Island. All their interests are centred in it. I earnestly hope that no schemes of improvement will be attempted. They are much better people and better Christians than the generality of their would-be improvers, and why not let well alone?'

So Emily MacLeod went home, with fond memories of her 'long-wished for visit to St Kilda'. Back in Skye she contemplated the fundamental contradictions at the heart of improvement, having already witnessed, that final morning in St Kilda, contamination at work.

*

The first voyage to St Kilda of the *Dunara Castle*, on Monday 2 July 1877, intended 'To afford an opportunity to Tourists of visiting this Island', was a great success. Still under the command of Captain McEwan, who with Mr Donald the clerk or purser 'did everything in their power to insure an enjoyable expedition', she put ashore her party of sightseers and brought them back to Greenock without mishap. The number of tourists varied in different accounts. The Edinburgh advocate, George Seton, who was one of them, said there were about forty, while the *Highlander* newspaper reported around sixty. They were a miscellaneous crowd, which included the procurator fiscal from Lochmaddy, Captain MacDonald of the *Vigilant* fishery cruiser, Rev. John Macrae of North Uist, and Mr W. M. Wilson probably from Ayrshire.[90]

One newspaper stated that the captain had 'found the inhabitants in a comfortable condition' and briefly outlined what had happened during the visit:

> 'About fifty passengers landed, and the natives showed them the mode of bird-catching and all the other wonders of their island home. Many of the passengers made purchases of calves, dogs, fowls, birds, etc. The natives were delighted with the excursionists, who remained about three hours on the island.'[91]

Immediately after reaching home W. M. Wilson set about writing nine weekly articles for the *Ayr Observer* on his trip 'Round the Hebrides and Saint Kilda'. He was well into article V before the steamer 'dropped her anchor in the bay, about a gunshot from the beach', and already the characteristically facetious style of the tourist become journalist was in full flight. Soon after passing through the Sound of Harris the passengers had made a collection of half-crowns, totalling about £4.10s, for rewarding St Kilda cliff climbers, and having approached the island their programme was fixed. 'It speedily reduced itself into four heads: A view of the natives, and of their social economy; an exhibition by the Cragsmen of their celebrated feats of fowling; a ramble over the Island; and a tour round the entire St Kildian group.' An experienced adviser was at hand in the captain of the *Vigilant*, and Miss Emily MacLeod was there to help: 'The venerable lady who does good by stealth, and would blush to find it fame, had incurred voluntary exile in this remote corner of the world, for the luxury of doing good, and the peace that passeth all understanding.' There too was 'the Bishop of the Isles, the unmitred Mr Mackay, available on shore in case of emergency'. The rest of Wilson's information was presented in the same manner.[92]

Captain MacDonald warned the party before landing that care should be taken with money. 'Don't be profuse. The men will be at their work. I'm afraid the mistaken kindness of yachting people will demoralise the Islanders. If you scatter your money carelessly, those who come next will pay for your extravagance.' Rev. MacKay would distribute £2, a liberal amount, with fairness, and more could be spent on buying produce. In this way the visitors' programme was begun, purchases were made, and aspects of the island and its inhabitants noted. Much space in the articles was given to quotations from other authors, especially perhaps from MacDiarmid whose report, in pamphlet form, was published at the beginning of July, but there were a few original remarks, such as one on the minister and education:

> 'Mr Mackay, besides preaching in the Church twice on Sunday, and holding a prayer meeting during the week, maintains a daily visitation and supervision of his flock. He also teaches the children English two hours a day on three days a week. For it seems the School Board of the parish of Harris, in which St Kilda lies, have either not yet discovered the necessity or do not perceive the legality of planting a Board School on the Island.'

The main conclusion reached in Wilson's story was that those who supported the Sands arguments were completely mistaken and that the idea of a government vessel making special calls at St Kilda three or four times a year 'to supply the islands with necessaries at cost price' was ridiculous – 'Surely all this is philanthropy and sentiment run mad'. Unfortunately very little sound reasoning lay behind this conclusion, based as it was on such evidence as the 'character' of MacLeod, of his sister Emily, and of the factor, and on the views of 'That fine old seaman' the captain of the *Vigilant*, 'That genial old gentleman and scholar' Roderick MacDonald former minister of Harris, and those 'men of the world' Captain McEwan and Mr Donald of the *Dunara Castle*. Moreover how could anyone be so foolish as to 'gainsay the corroborative testimony of the clergy, and lawyers, and doctors, and civil engineers, and artists, and merchants, and travellers, the passengers of the Dunara Castle', after three or four hours spent on the island? All these people, said Wilson, had 'landed with minds open to the truth'; some who had Gaelic – probably McEwan and his crew members – 'entered freely into personal communication with the islanders, and had their confidence'; and in the end everyone left 'with the intelligent conviction that presumption, probability, experience and fact were all in favour of Macleod of Macleod', and that 'never was public agitation more delusive and mischievous than that based upon the fictitious oppression and misery of the poor islanders of Saint Kilda!'

Wilson's account illustrates the way in which the St Kilda people and the realities of their existence there had become in some quarters a subject for public entertainment and extraordinary discussions which, failing to deal with such essentials as the significance of infant mortality, limitation of marriage opportunity, and cultural tradition, promoted misleading superficiality, inaccuracy, and perhaps a strain of falsehood to be found in a whole sequence of subsequent writing about not only St Kilda but the Hebrides in general.The distance between writer and subject is apparent in the book which another passenger on the steamer, George Seton, was soon to publish. Meanwhile, so successful had its first voyage to St Kilda been that the *Highlander* of 21 July 1877 announced:'We hope to hear of the "Dunara Castle" making another trip there before the harvest is over.'[93]

*

After her weeks in St Kilda Emily MacLeod was convinced that she knew what would be of the greatest benefit to the people:

> 'The real want of the island is a good educated sick-nurse, and if we can persuade one of the women to come and get a regular course of instruction, my brother and his wife will arrange for the expense. It would be hopeless to expect an active competent Lowland nurse to banish herself, but I have great hopes of getting one there - Her Father objected but the woman herself [is] very willing … With an educated nurse and a little judicious starvation, I think we shall hear no more of baby mortality.'[94]

To further the project she enlisted the aid of Rev. John MacKay, either through having spoken to him when she was on the island or by writing to him later. MacKay was seen by the MacLeods as an ally, although this opinion of him was not to last for very long. His being in favour was chiefly owing to the fact that he had spoken in support of the proprietor when in 1876 the islanders were given the choice of how to market their produce, and MacLeod had then said:'Mr McKay behaved in a manner which raises him greatly in my esteem'. Towards the end of Emily's visit the minister had earned further approval when he wrote to tell MacLeod that he was on the proprietor's side. No one on the island, he claimed, blamed MacLeod for the failure of the *Robert Hadden* to appear with supplies in the previous autumn, and in any case 'The people under your guardianship .. are pretty well off'. The same letter had begun positively also – 'I am glad you have not parted with St Kilda on account of Sands' slanders. I am sure I have suffered more from him than you have done.' But it ended rather hesitantly: 'I hope you will Keep your ground and that you will not part with St Kilda. Sands will at once then say that he had got the better of you.'[95]

It is evident that John MacKay was now, whether he wanted to be or not, deeply involved in the new world of St Kilda which had developed since the visits of John Hall Maxwell and had advanced rapidly with the stir caused by John Sands.There are signs that he was rather pleased by the importance of his role in this area of community affairs, although it cannot be said that he had much influence on the people outside his ministerial duties. Nevertheless he did from time to time sway opinion, and was the one person on the island who might have been able to assist Emily in finding an islander who could be persuaded to train as a nurse. He was however unsuccessful:

'I have spoken to some women here, asking them if any of them would be willing to go to Skye as suggested by the Honourable Mrs MacLeod of MacLeod, in order to be educated and trained for a nurse, and midwife, but none of them is willing to undertake such a responsible charge. You had better try, to see, if you can find any person, about you at Duirinish, as the women there are more bold and courageous, to leave home than the St Kildian women, who are so much attached by long usage to their native place. I am highly obliged to the Honourable Mrs MacLeod of MacLeod for the canister of gooseberries, which she has sent to me.'[96]

In October 1877 Emily MacLeod, having had no luck with Rev. MacKay, wrote to Fletcher Menzies on the same subject.

'I think I told you that my brother's wife had authorised me to write to the St. Kildians and offer to take charge of any one of their women who was willing to learn the duties of a nurse - to keep her here till she had learned English and then to send her to Edinburgh with the view of getting a first-rate medical education. I wrote them a Gaelic letter, and one to the minister in English, but alas! they write they are afraid! ! to come. Is it not sad, and yet the autumn vessel has brought back the news that another pretty young woman and her baby have died since I was there. It is quite nonsense to expect that any competent person will go and live there so that to educate one of themselves is the only plan. I intend going as early as possible next year and will insist on bringing one away <u>with</u> me ..'[97]

It was necessary therefore to set aside the hunt for a nurse for the time being, and in any case Emily had another worry on her mind. She had received a letter, probably in October, from George Seton, who was 'requesting notes or any information I can give him about St. Kilda, in which he appears to take great interest'. As she knew nothing of him except that he had introduced himself to her when on the island she was afraid he might be another Sands, and she asked Menzies 'whether the book he is publishing is likely to be well written and whether it is adviseable to tell him anything'. Menzies must then have assured her that Seton's book would be 'well written', that is, not in the least objectionable to the proprietor in a Sands-like manner, for she supplied the author with copies of her letters written from St Kilda and other useful information.

Seton's book, *St Kilda Past and Present,* came out early in 1878. Some five years later Richard Barrington, a naturalist who spent three weeks in St Kilda, commented that 'Seton's is entirely a scissors book - he was only four hours on the island'. By this he meant that Seton, having little personal experience of the place and the people, had assembled his book by extracting passages from other works and using information without acknowledging the sources. While this observation was no doubt true it was rather unkind as the 'scissors' approach in relation to St Kilda has never been avoided, and Seton's work was at the time a most valuable and comprehensive collection of relevant material. R A Smith's verdict that 'to Mr Seton we owe a history of the island so far as it seems possible to obtain it' was perhaps a little too hasty but it reflected a feeling that Seton had searched a wider range of record, written and oral, than anyone else. When Emily MacLeod had read her copy she found very little to complain about: 'I have finished reading your book and could not resist congratulating you on its complete success. It is wonderful that you could find so much that is really interesting to say about an island that has neither history nor tradition.'[98]

Her sweeping dismissal of St Kilda's cultural background, typical of a certain attitude towards the Gaelic areas of Scotland since long before Dr Johnson's time, did not deter Seton from returning thanks for Emily's 'most interesting letter', and, he added, 'I am glad to learn that you approve of my book'. He promised to send her a copy for MacKay in the hope she would be able to take it with her when she went to the island again in the coming May or June. Seton also remarked that his nephew was 'an enthusiastic collector of Birds, which he stuffs most beautifully'. This nephew wanted good specimens of St Kilda birds, together with their eggs: 'I daresay my worthy little friend McKay would endeavour to procure a few for him and that you would kindly be the bearer of them as far as Dunvegan.' Had he known of this description of him Rev. MacKay might have ignored the request, and he was not ready to be used by advocates and naturalists.[99]

St Kilda Past and Present was partly a reaction to the second edition of Sands's book and the publicity that followed it. Seton took exception, as did W. M. Wilson and other passengers on the *Dunara Castle*, to what he saw as prejudiced and improper accusation against the landlord. Yet Seton himself was not free of prejudice on other matters, one in particular being not the history, nor the tradition, but the language of the St Kilda people.

John MacDiarmid in his published report suggested that the minister of St Kilda should be schoolteacher as well, and the *Highlander* in its account of the *Dunara Castle's* visit said that 'Mr John McKay, Lochalsh, is both minister and teacher'. One of the two main purposes, as MacDiarmid envisaged them, of this combined office was to educate the islanders in speaking and possibly reading English, a long-standing if never achieved aim since the time of Alexander Buchan. In 1877 it might well have seemed to those concerned on the mainland that the arrival of tourists such as those on the *Dunara Castle* and the probable repetition of that popular trip in the future made knowledge of English more evidently useful. The more contact there was between St Kilda and the English-speaking 'outside world' the less sensible it was, from an increasingly widespread point of view, that the few islanders, understood as having no worthwhile culture and traditions, should continue to use Gaelic. This was a new form of the old doctrine that Gaelic needed to be eradicated in order to civilise the natives, and it now appeared towards the end of Seton's book on a page headed 'The "Curse" of Gaelic'.

> 'Even in more important islands than St Kilda, the all but exclusive maintenance of the Gaelic language ... is much to be regretted. An intelligent and accomplished Lowlander, whose official duties imply a residence in one of the largest of the Western Islands, very recently informed me that, after a good many years' experience of the locality, he had been forced to the conclusion that the people among whom he lived were afflicted by two "curses" - one of which I forbear to mention in the present connection, the other being the perpetuation of the Gaelic tongue. Probably, however, its knell has been sounded even in St Kilda ...'[100]

These unsympathetic comments had apparently been stimulated by an article, signed 'W.C.', in *Chambers's Journal*. The issue of 3 November 1877 began with a piece entitled 'The Gaelic Nuisance', in which 'W.C.', presumably William Chambers, expressed his concern at the existence of minority languages: 'It is not a very creditable fact that after centuries of national consolidation, there should be communities within the British Islands who use different vernacular tongues and are ignorant of English.' Those who belonged to these linguistically isolated groups were deprived of all the advantages which English-speaking brought: they 'can neither send nor intelligibly receive letters'; being 'Cut off from English books and newspapers, a correct knowledge of history, of science and art, and of passing events is scarcely possible'; and so 'Theirs is a life of stagnation and impoverishment, in the spot where they were born'. Gaelic-speakers languished 'amidst vague legends and superstitions'. If only they knew English all would be well.

The author of the article continued his argument through almost three packed pages. He had been to Barra where 'We seemed to step back twelve hundred years' and where his opinion of the people was that 'they belonged to a far-back age'. This was the fault of language:

> 'There they are, for anything we can see, unimprovable. Speaking Gaelic and nothing else, they, in their dismal isolation, are left behind in all ordinary means of advancement. Who has not heard of the institutions plausibly and benevolently set on foot to enlighten the aborigines of the

Highlands and Islands? Well, here, after all that is done, things are much as they were in the era of St Columba - people living almost like savages, without the ability to hold intercourse with strangers, or the power to improve their circumstances, in consequence of knowing no other tongue than Gaelic. That language is their bane. It keeps them poor, it keeps them ignorant..'

To maintain Gaelic as a living language, in this writer's view, was 'an error to be lamented and abandoned'. By all means let it become a subject for academic study at universities but steer it away from everyday use. There was too much sentiment. 'For example, we see it fervently argued that Highlanders should be able to understand and relish the ancient Gaelic poetry, as if an acquaintanceship with a few old songs and ballads were a primary concern in life. Poor people nailed to a sterile soil by their hereditary ignorance of English, are to be congratulated for their knowledge of some poem which the world at large never heard of, and does not care about.' Even Highlanders themselves, said 'W.C.', quoting one of them from a Glasgow newspaper, thought Gaelic should be given up. And if Barra was 'still in a singularly primitive condition', what of St Kilda?

'A melancholy case of a rigid adherence to Gaelic, is that of the extremely remote island of St Kilda. Here, as was described a few months ago by Mr J. Sands in our pages, the natives speak Gaelic and nothing else; in Gaelic they are preached to by a minister originally from the mainland; he and his wife being the only individuals who know English. Of course the natives can hold no epistolary correspondence with the exterior world, on whose sympathy they are forced to rely. A present of English books would be valueless, for they could not read them. They could not emigrate unless accompanied by an interpreter … We ask, Is that a position in which any of Her Majesty's subjects should continue to be placed through the effect of custom or prejudice? Such an afflicting condition of affairs is little better than a national disgrace.'[101]

This argument, in which some might recognise an understandable and familiar attitude, was of course at times inaccurate - Gaelic poetry and culture consisted of rather more than 'a few old songs and ballads' and Rev. MacKay was not married - and in general arrogant, misdirected and expressed with that inability to see and accept anyone else's point of view which was a characteristic of many 'outside world' pronouncements. However it had no difficulty in appealing to a man like Seton, whose book gives the impression that he thought St Kilda a curiosity, an anachronism comparable with the version of Barra presented by 'W.C.'. In this case what fate could be imagined for the island and its people other than becoming a mere tourist attraction of a rather unusual kind? A genuine perception of the value of the Gaelic language and culture, apparent in much of the contemporary Alexander Carmichael's researches, was entirely missing, as it always seemed to be with observers travelling through the Hebrides by steamer.

Seton devoted several pages to mocking John Sands and to explaining the seeming injustice of the latter's condemnations of the St Kilda proprietor. His defence of MacLeod is scarcely relevant, inasmuch as it largely consisted of disagreeing with Sands on the basis of MacDiarmid's report and a letter from MacLeod himself. He would have had to admit, however, that Sands had achieved a good deal in making St Kilda a subject of public concern. During 1877 'reforms and improvements' had been discussed at length, and Seton supported such suggestions as the conversion of the island into 'a penal settlement'. He did not think that St Kilda deserved a system of 'telegraphic communication' since there were only 76 inhabitants, none of whom except perhaps the minister was interested in keeping up with the news, but he reckoned that 'no reasonable person' would object to 'a limited amount of postal communication'. For this two mail steamers a year would be appropriate; they might transport the factor, and possibly convey 'scientific men and tourists' in the summer 'unless, indeed, special provision should be made by the advancing enterprise of Messrs Cook and Sons!' A landing place to serve the steamers would be essential; two more boats would be 'a great boon'; some 'stalwart Orcadians' to teach seamanship and introduce new blood would be highly satisfactory; and a supply of coal to prevent 'the disastrous practice of stripping the precious turf as a substitute for the peat' would be equally helpful.

As for religion and education it was clear that Seton was no Free Church enthusiast:

> 'One of my fellow-passengers in "the Dunara Castle" was the bearer of some perfectly unobjectionable Gaelic song-books, and on his presenting them to the islanders, they were immediately submitted to the censorship of the minister, who decided that as they were "neither psalms nor spiritual hymns," they could not be accepted!'

Unaware of what people might wish to read Seton had brought 'fairy tales and other picture-books' which he distributed among the children and, to his relief, saw that the '"holy father"' of St Kilda made no sign of disapproval. Quoting from Sands he hoped that since 'the Endowment Committee of the Church of Scotland' was 'no doubt keeping its eye upon the sea-girt isle' it would not be long before 'the "swallows" will peaceably resume possession of their former nests!' In other words, the Free Church would be displaced by the returning established church.[102]

The 'most beneficial influence that could be brought to bear upon the St

Kildans' would be educational, the introduction of 'a systematic course of instruction in English', so that the people could enjoy 'the vast benefits which would inevitably ensue'. While they were ignorant 'of the language of the United Kingdom' they could not possibly enjoy 'the means of enlarging their minds and subverting their prejudices, by the perusal of English literature'. So far was Seton lacking in understanding of the realities of Gaelic culture and island life that he could obviously think and approve of a St Kilda 'native' sitting down to read Shakespeare on the low wall outside his house; and to lend weight to his opinion he referred to the 'admirable article' by 'W.C.' which he would recommend to 'all who are interested in the future welfare of the inhabitants of St Kilda'.[103]

It was now the turn of William Chambers to respond to Seton. In March 1878 he produced a second article under the same title of *The Gaelic Nuisance*. In it he re-stated his views, asserting this time that fostering Gaelic was a form of cruelty in that it encouraged 'the practice of rearing, or allowing to grow up, groups of children with a knowledge of no other language ..', thus condemning them to a life of poverty and ignorance. After giving a description of the educationally deprived children in the Lewis parish of Barvas taken from the *Scotsman* he went on to a revised version of his comments on St Kilda:

'The island of St Kilda, to which we called attention, exhibits a small population with no means of learning English, and who for religious instruction in Gaelic are wholly dependent on the Rev. John McKay, a minister appointed by the Free Church. This worthy individual, who is a bachelor of advanced age [60], and whom, by mistake, we spoke of as being married, can speak and read English; but with the exception of the imported wife of one of the natives, he is the only individual on the island who can do so, and acts as a general interpreter on the occasion of visits from strangers. There is no school in the island, nor is there any attempt to teach English. Is this a condition of things which commends itself to philanthropists?'

The whole of this passage was the outcome, not of extended personal acquaintance or experience but of reading 'a handsomely printed and illustrated work, St Kilda Past and Present, by George Seton, Advocate'. The two writers flattered each other, 'W.C.' quoting the very words with which Seton expressed approval of the first *Gaelic Nuisance* article and then thanking Seton 'for this acknowledgment of the correctness of our views'.

Sadder, however, than any of his own remarks were the instances given by 'W.C.' in support of his argument from the Gaelic-speaking areas themselves. In order, perhaps, to appear fashionably educated, up-to-date and un-primitive, certain people in the Highlands and islands behaved and expressed views in a manner that they had picked up from the English 'centre' of modern life. First, there was a reference by 'W.C.' to a note from 'a sheriff-substitute in a Highland county' who said: 'I have resided here for several years, and am convinced that the civilisation of the Highlands is impossible so long as Gaelic continues to be the language of the common people. I hope your article will open the eyes of common-sense people to the necessity of abolishing Gaelic as a spoken language, by the substitution of English.' This was followed by mention of 'A gentleman connected by heritage with one of the outer Hebrides', as 'W.C.' put it, who stated that 'We Highlanders are determined to adopt the current language, just as we have adopted the current coin of the realm'. And a 'Western Highlander' had written to say: 'if our much-loved language has become an impediment rather than a gain, why, let it go. We shall remain good Highlanders regardless of any particular mode of speech.' Whether these correspondents were real or invented for the purposes of making his case, 'W.C.' certainly illustrated the genuine existence of those who gave the impression of betraying the Gaelic inheritance from within. The future human occupation of St Kilda and other Hebridean islands was thus threatened not only by internal difficulties like diminishing numbers but also by a variety of alien influences ranging from the impact of material assistance to attacks on culture and language and leading to a sense of inferiority.[104]

*

From 1877 onwards measures taken or contemplated for improvement at St Kilda were often the subject of consideration by the Edinburgh committee, whose firm intention was to provide assistance to the island financially through the HASS Kelsall Bequest fund and persuasively through lobbying government offices. It also sought to raise subscriptions towards the establishment of a regular communication and mail service. George Seton noted that a correspondent of the *Edinburgh Courant*, 'in commenting on the Edinburgh St Kilda Committee assuming the guardianship of the islanders, suggests that they ought to have asked the Board of Supervision for the Relief of the Poor to allow their visiting inspector to proceed to the island, with the view of investigating the condition of the inhabitants'. Seton was none too keen on this idea since he did not approve of adding yet another collection of unfortunate people to the roll of those receiving poor relief, even though St Kilda was already a victim of outside help in one form or another. Setting this possibility aside, the committee approached the Home Office with a request that it consider the construction of a safe landing place and shelter for small boats and at the same time the introduction of intermittent postal communication between the island and 'the nearest mainland' - perhaps Harris or North Uist. The overall purpose was still to achieve permanent improvements for the islanders.[105]

In mid June 1878 the *Dunara Castle* set off again on a trip to St Kilda with around 40 tourist passengers. Leaving Dunvegan at 9 a.m. on Saturday the vessel spent Sunday at Tarbert and departed again in the early hours of Monday morning. 'The announcement ...that the island was in sight brought the passengers on deck en masse', among them being at least four churchmen, and some members of 'the Glasgow Stock Exchange'. On board too was a 'jollyboat', together with its sailing gear and compass, which had been presented by the Admiralty to the island community in response to a request from John Sands and which was transported free of charge by courtesy of Mr Orme. It was lowered into the water to share with a boat from the shore the task of taking the visitors to land for their few hours of exploration. 'Among the first to offer a hearty welcome .. was Mr Mackay, the minister, and a lady, the only other person on the island who could speak English.' Thus received in conventional fashion 'the excursionists at once proceeded to distribute the little luxuries they had brought, principally tobacco and "sweeties", for the latter of which the inhabitants show a decided partiality'. There was then a climb to the top of Conachair to watch 'the best cragesmen' at work, and on return to the houses purchases of eggs, cloth and stockings were made, 'some of the articles being secured for the British Museum'. The tourists spent the rest of their time ashore 'rambling through the hamlet', where they found 'the natives' suitably appreciative of their presence. Once the party had embarked the steamer headed homewards, reaching Greenock on the Wednesday afternoon. All the passengers were of course 'much delighted with their trip', praising the steamer arrangements, the kindness of Mr Orme 'who has the welfare of the Western Islands at heart', and the hospitable nature of the islanders whom they found to be 'well and prosperous' and 'looking so happy and comfortable'. One of the most pleasant recollections was perhaps that the return excursion from Dunvegan had cost each of them just £1.12s.6d.[106]

The safe delivery of the jollyboat and its equipment, and the comforting report of conditions in St Kilda, must have set many an official mind at rest. Emily MacLeod, on the other hand, was aware that children were still dying of tetanus and persisted in her intention of securing a nurse on the island. At the end of May 1878 she wrote to Fletcher Menzies that the factor, John MacKenzie, was searching on her behalf for a woman of Skye, and if he succeeded in finding one 'I shall put off going to St Kilda, as I shall have to look after her English education before she goes to Edinburgh, but I am preparing to go, in case he fails'. She planned to travel with the factor to the island, but it is not clear whether she went with him, or with the *Dunara Castle*, or by some other means, as it seems certain that she did spend more time in St Kilda after the non-appearance of a Skye volunteer. She may have been given a lift by 'Mrs Gamble's steam yacht "Cecile",' which called at the island in July and afterwards made it known that the people were 'in good health, and that their crops were looking well'. In August 1878 'A recent visitor to St Kilda' wrote that 'We left Miss Macleod of Macleod there. She went for the purpose of bringing a woman from the island to be trained as a nurse.' Though she was 'well over sixty' Emily was clearly a woman of character and sympathy. 'Miss Macleod is the soul of sweetness and benevolence, and full of good sense, information and intelligence. *Aingeal De ann an neamh treis an so air thalamh, a ghraidh,* said an old woman at Dunvegan to me. The remark was no less beautiful than appropriate.' Whether or not the people of St Kilda agreed with this picture of her she seems to have gone home again without success in her mission and to have redirected her efforts once more towards finding an answer in Skye or even the mainland.[107]

Meanwhile 'Some good-natured people', presumably members of the Edinburgh committee, were urging forward the necessity of a regular postal communication for St Kilda, and were so far successful, it was reported in October 1878, 'that one of the assistant secretaries of the General Post Office London, actually visited the island in the month of July last', though by what means was not stated. This G.P.O. representative was a Mr Benthall who was already acquainted with appeals for mail service from most of the Hebridean islands. He found that visits by the factor and by the *Dunara Castle* were sufficient for the few letters to be transported. In 1878 Rev. John MacKay wrote, and received, what little correspondence there was.[108]

One other event during the summer of 1878 was of a kind that might have given some satisfaction to William Chambers and George Seton. 'English literature' came to St Kilda in a large vessel of 870 tons put to purposes of pleasure as a yacht. The *Mastiff,* hired by Mr John Burns, had a party of 50 pleasure seekers, including Mrs Hugh Blackburn 'Our Artist' and Anthony Trollope whose account of the voyage contained a brief record of their call at the island. They met the minister, and there too was Emily MacLeod, 'of whose goodness in going among them and remaining with them from time to time it is impossible to speak in terms of too high praise', Presents of tea, sugar and other stores were handed over, and purchases of birds' eggs, stockings and cloth made – 'It is the necessity of their position,' said Trollope, 'that such aid should be essential almost to their existence.' He knew the people were very religious, 'though probably in some things their religion may run towards superstition, as must be the case in so small a community', but he had sympathy with Rev. MacKay whose situation was not an easy one:

'The pastor, whose life here is certainly not to be envied, and who acts as schoolmaster as well as minister, receives £80 per annum from the Scotch Free Church. That also is to be counted among the charities bestowed upon the island, and is bestowed at the cost of great necessary deterioration in the energy and intellectual capacity of the clergyman selected for the purpose. That it should be otherwise is impossible. There is but one person in the island, but himself, a married woman, who can speak a word of English. No books can reach him; hardly a newspaper. To him can come none of that light which we all receive from intellectual conversation..'

'.. he has upon his shoulders and on those of his sister, the onerous task of sustaining by his private means the existence of the community and of relieving their wants. As for the £80, we may say that it goes a very short way in reimbursing him. It is good to find a man who will do this, but it is not good to have a state of things in which such doing is necessary.'

As Trollope and his friends sailed away, 'having seen all that there was to be seen in St Kilda', they thought about the occupants of that 'most picturesque point in the ocean ...an atom of land hardly intended by nature as a habitation for man'. Although the people were 'comely' and 'good,-looking, bearing no outward signs of want'. the visitors could only think it unfortunate that there were inhabitants in such a remote spot. Evacuation seemed a sensible possibility.

'Who shall say that these people ought to be deported from their homes and placed recklessly upon some point of the mainland? I have not the courage so to say. They themselves, if they were consulted, would probably be averse to such deportation. Were they so deported each individually would suffer, at any rate for a time, by the change...

'But yet their existence cannot be good for them, and certainly not for their posterity; - and as far as we can judge a time will come when that posterity must die out unless the people be removed. In the meantime it appeared to me that all is done for them that present kindness can do.'[109]

1   As early as 1847 Rev. Norman MacLeod wrote of a wider trend in the Highlands and islands: 'There is a spirit of insubordination, disregard of authority, and class feeling abroad; demands for free clothes – free Indian meal – free education – free tracts, free Bibles (I mean given gratis) – free passage to Glasgow, - that in short, all the freeness of public munificence towards them have made too many of them lose all self-reliance.' [MacLeod (1898) p.227]
    This was said in 'famine' time, less drastic in St Kilda than in many other places, but outside assistance and loss of self reliance were matters later raised frequently with regard to the island.
2   ELHSA CH3/1428/2 20 November 1857, 9 April 1858, 9 October 1858, with extract from The Witness 1 December 1859. For John Finlayson's career see B Buxton: Mingulay – An Island and Its People Edinburgh 1995 pp.100-112; and his article: 'Mingulay's remarkable schoolteacher turned gamekeeper' in WHFP 21 November 1997 p.21. McKerrol's other interests included the school at 'Ruandunan' in Skye and a sewing school in Scarp. He was known variously as 'of Bath', 'of Great Malvern', and 'of Hillhouse'.
3   ELHSA CH3/1428/3 11 May 1861, 30 June 1865
4   ELHSA CH3/1428/3 5 December 1866; CH3/1428/4 14 October 1870. One explanation for Finlayson's absence in 1868-1869 would be that he was attending the Free Church College as part of his training for the ministry [Buxton p.105], though he never became a minister.
5   W A Power: The Log of the Olivia The Richmond Publishing Company Ltd. 1983. It seems more probable that the minister was Duncan Kennedy, who had a partiality for snuff. One of his 'daughters' might have been his niece Anne, the other perhaps another niece or a St Kilda girl.
6   CWC no.113; CG Vol. IV pp.106-107. Carmichael was especially impressed with stories of a striking St Kilda girl. He was much too late to meet her, but drew upon the descriptions given him by some who had known her. He said she was known as 'Mor Hiorteach – (More correctly) Mor Iorteach', probably after she had left St Kilda for ever. A Mrs MacLeod, Lochmaddy, and others described her to him in February 1869, and he collected some of the songs she had composed. She was believed to have been the girl who attracted the attention of Robert Campbell of Shawfield in 1799.
7   ELHSA CH3/1428/2 pp.28,43,48
8   Information from John MacKenzie, Lochcarron, 30 April 1997; T Brown: Annals of the Disruption New Edition Edinburgh 1893 p.699; FCMR 1 October 1865 p.932; HC CH3/983/2 p.55
9   HC CH3/983/2 p.68
10 HC CH3/983/2 pp.60, 68-70, 82. Seton [p.119] noted that 'A terrific gale took place at St Kilda in January 1866'.
11 FCMR 1 July 1867 p.158
12 E G Hawke (edit.): Memoirs of Travel, Sport, and Natural History by the late Henry John Elwes London 1930 pp.5, 31-36; H J Elwes: 'The Bird-Stations of the Outer Hebrides' in Ibis January 1869 pp.19-37. On 24 May 1868 Elwes wrote in a letter to J A Harvie Brown, 'I have not seen such pleasant good looking, well to do people in any island as the St Kildians, and in the summer it would be a pleasant place to stay for a month. None of them but the minister have any English and I have got the local Gaelic names for most of the birds.' [HB 16/261]
13 FCMR 1 December 1866 pp.16-17
14 FCMR 2 October 1871 pp.204-205
15 FCMR 2 October 1871 p.206
16 The Highlander Vol. I no.7 28 June 1873 p.14
17 The Highlander Vol. I no.8 5 July 1873 p.8. The St Clair of the Isles was built in 1860 and originally named Lisboa [WHS p.115].
18 The Highlander Vol. I no.8 5 July 1873 p.14; no.14 16 August 1873 pp.8, 10
19 The Highlander Vol. I no.19 20 September 1873 p.10; no.27 15 November 1873 p.9; no.30 6 December 1873 p.11

20 The Highlander Vol. I no.45 21 March 1874 p.11
21 The Highlander Vol. III no.105 15 May 1875 p.4; WHS p.129; information from Alasdair Beaton,Totardor, Struan, Skye, and W MacLean, Cladach Vallay, North Uist.
22 The Highlander Vol. III no.112 3 July 1875 p.7; Census Return 1881 (there were at this time five passengers aboard, including Rev. Donald Nicolson, Free Church minister in the parish of Barvas)
23 W M Wilson:'Round the Hebrides and St Kilda' in The Ayr Observer and Galloway Chronicle 24 July 1877; A Smith: A Summer in Skye Edinburgh 1912 pp.419-420
24 For the articles by Maolan see The Highlander Vol. III 6 & 20 February, 13 & 27 March, 26 June, 1875. The first and third articles contain examples of verse composed by John MacDonald of Ferintosh, one of them relating to the arrival of smallpox in the island. A tradition concerning ancestry is recorded in the fourth article:
'After St Kilda was depopulated…it was peopled, says Mr John Morrison of Scalpay, by men imported thither from the adjoining islands of Skye, Uist, and Harris. The Macqueens and Gillies of St Kilda are from Skye, the MacDonalds from Uist, and the McLeods from Harris. The few McKinnons to be found there are also from Skye. They were sent there, says Morrison, for crimes committed in their own countries…They seem to have been an exceedingly simple race of people – easily led astray, and as easily convinced of their error. Iagain, Iain, was the name of a spiritual adviser in St Kilda many years ago. This man well knew the failings of the people over whom he ruled, for he was looked upon as King Supreme; but instead of correcting any false ideas they might possess and improving their minds generally by instruction and example, he seemed only to glory in their simplicity. For example, when a young couple was to be married, the minister placed the bride at one end of the apartment, when the company was assembled, and the bridegroom at the other end, while he himself stood with his back to the wall about the centre of the place. Being thus placed, the parson, if I may apply that title to the individual under consideration, proceeded with the marriage ceremony, by commencing a nonsensical oration, of which the following is part: -
A Mhoiri gun amais, a Mhoiri gun amais,
An a lag a chamais.
As soon as the word chamais was uttered, the young couple approached and met each other on the centre of the floor, and they were directly pronounced man and wife.'
It is not easy to determine when, if ever, the author visited St Kilda. His first article begins 'Having recently had a glimpse of the lonely island' but this could merely mean that he had seen it from a distance. Towards the end of his last article he states that 'St Kilda forms now no part of the Dunvegan property' and that it is still possessed 'by a branch of that stock – a Major Macleod who, about the year 1814.' etc. He must therefore have been writing prior to 1871 or from hearsay, being ignorant of the true circumstances.
25 For the Duke's exclamation see Part 5 n.69
26 Dictionary of National Biography Supplementary Volume (Reprint, Oxford 1998) p.1002. The only evidence for his first visit seems to be that in a letter of 7 August 1860 [KBP 3/2] in which the proprietor wrote of how he ate 'a kind of wild spinage..when I first visited the island now 54 years since'. The second visit, according to Malcolm MacQueen, must have been in the late 1830s or early 1840s, when Malcolm was at school [see Part 5 n.43]
27 A & A MacDonald Vol. III pp.521-522. There is also a 'Tormore Lodge' near Skeabost, Skye. Purchase decisions made by Donald MacDonald, particularly in connection with ropes and two boats for St Kilda, are recorded in three letters from him to F N Menzies in 1869 [KBP 7/22-24], and a letter from him to MacLeod of MacLeod [DC Section 2 637/3].
28 NAS Sasine Abridgements 9.40 Registered 30 June 1870, 13.156 Registered 27 June 1871; Register of Sasines 103/13 ff.156-157 - entry for the new owner was at Whitsunday 1871. A brief account of the sale of St Kilda to Lt. Col. Donald MacLeod, and of the removal in 1805 of William MacNeil from his position as St Kilda tacksman, was given by Charles Fraser-MacKintosh, unfortunately without sources of the information, in his Antiquarian Notes

555

[Second Series Inverness 1897 pp.299-300]. The sale was incorrectly stated to have taken place in 1805.

29   Grant pp.582-586

30   DC Section 2 626/3-7, 627/2, 626/2, 626/1 – MacRaild's letter of 12 April 1873. Four years later MacDiarmid noted of the new factor: 'They have great confidence in Mr McKenzie, who, they say, is just and generous, and easy to deal with, and quite different from Mr McRaild, of whom they don't speak in very complimentary terms' [MacDiarmid p.21].

31   DC Section 2 637/1/2, 637/1/5, 637/1/3

32   DC Section 2 637/1/6

33   DC Section 2 637/1/4 Draft of letter 2 April 1872. The Highlander of 24 October 1879 reported that the Free Church presbytery of Skye and Uist had submitted an overture to the General Assembly seeking the removal of the Court of Session decision in 1846 to restrict the funds of the mortification to the management of the Established Church only, with the consequence, in the Free Church's view, that the St Kilda people were deprived of the benefits.

34   DC Section 2 637/2/1

35   Smith (1879); Smith (1875). See R. Lawson (1902) p.16 with reference to 'Mr Young of Kelly,' and the islanders' 'lack of independence'.

36   Maolan: 'St Kilda' article no.II in The Highlander 20 February 1875 p.3

37   [Lady M Baillie of Polkemmet]: 'Visit to St Kilda – By a Lady' in The Church of Scotland Home and Foreign Missionary Record 1 January 1875 pp.254-257. Seton (p.64) wrote that Sir William Baillie of Polkemmet and the late Mr Baird of Cambusdoon were also members of the party. Lady Baillie recorded the recent purchase price of St Kilda incorrectly as £2000.

38   The 1881 Census implies that 1827 was the year of his birth; an obituary in the Shetland Times (15 September 1909) indicates that the year was 1834. Article headed 'John Sands' in Shetland Times 3 July 1937, and 'The Tailor and the R.N.R.' in Shetland Times 10 July 1937. For a fuller account of John Sands see G Zealand: 'John Sands of Ormiston' in Arbroath Herald Christmas Annual Arbroath 1994, in which the year of his death is given as 1900.

39   Steel p.180; MacLean (1997) p.117; Peeblesshire Advertiser and County Newspaper 10 June 1876 (reprint article from Spectator); Seton pp.65, 319; Sands (1878) pp.130, 141.

40   Unless otherwise stated the following account of Sands's visits to St Kilda is based on the two editions of his book Out of the World; or, Life in St Kilda Edinburgh 1876 and Edinburgh 1878.

41   MacKay had been in St Kilda for nearly ten years; presumably the last newspapers that he saw were those given him by the visitors from the Nyanza in August 1874. It is possible that Isabella Ross Munro had come to St Kilda as housekeeper to the minister, and that when she married Ann MacDonald took over from her. Lady Baillie referred to Isabella when noting: 'Only one woman from Inverness could read or speak English' [Baillie p.255]. She apparently did some dress-making in St Kilda.

42   Sands (1878) p.68

43   Seton pp.64, 115

44   'St Kilda' in the Scotsman 13 August 1875

45   Letter from MacLeod of MacLeod to the Spectator 22 April 1876; draft letter, MacLeod of MacLeod to Sands [DC Section 2 637/4/1 and Section 5/133 (Scrapbook of cuttings, copy letters etc.)]

46   Letter from J Sands to MacLeod of MacLeod 25 April 1876 [DC Section 2 637/4/2]; Letter from Sands to Spectator 29 April 1876 [DC Section 5/133]; DC Section 2 637/4/8. Further letters at this time in DC Section 5/133 include Dr Latham's to the Spectator on infant mortality, reprinted in the Oban Times 13 May 1876, and one also in the Oban Times 27 May 1876 from 'Cabar Feithe' who wrote, with reference to St Kilda, on 'the curious way in which they articulate their words, by often uttering quite the contrary to what they intend to convey'.

47   Letter from Sands to the Spectator 29 April 1876 [DC Section 5/133]

48   Seton p.66

[49] The Scotsman (27 February 1877) made rather more of the islanders' reaction to 'Papists': '…an even worse difficulty presented itself…The sailors were Roman Catholics, and the poor islanders had been accustomed to regard "Papists" with a dread and horror compounded partly of ignorance and partly of instilled prejudice. The exigencies of the situation, however, were such as to leave no room for theological scruples'. This was typical of the inclination of the press at the time to elaborate on and exaggerate Sands's words.

[50] Newspaper cutting pasted in rear of NTS Seton copy; Sands (1878) p.117. The message in the bottle ran as follows: 'St Kilda, January 22, 1877. The Pete Mubrovacki, of Austria, 886 tons, was lost near this island on the 17th inst. The captain and eight of the crew are in St Kilda, and have no means of getting off. Provisions are scarce. Written by J. Sands, who came to the island in the summer, and cannot get away. The finder of this will much oblige by forwarding this letter to the Austrian Consul in Glasgow.' [Newspaper cutting DC Section 5/133]

[51] Newspaper cutting, NTS Seton copy.

[52] Newspaper cutting, NTS Seton copy; The Highlander Vol. IV no.199 3 March 1877 p.7

[53] Scotsman 27 February 1877

[54] The Highlander Vol. IV no.152 8 April 1876 p.8. 'Delego Bay' was later said to be 'Delagoa Bay' [The Highlander Vol. IV no.210 19 May 1877 p.5]. Seton (p.61) said that the letter reported the death of Donald MacKinnon 'at Pilgrim's Rest, Lydenburg gold fields'.

[55] The Highlander Vol. V no.243 January 1878 p.4. On 13 July 1876 MacLeod of MacLeod wrote to his factor enclosing a letter from Rev. MacKay posted in Stornoway, possibly by Sands. 'Sir John MacLeod has read Mr McKays Letter, but he does not believe the imaginative story he has founded on the Remittance from Donald McKinnon. It appears to me probable the Boat was lost, and that Donald McKinnon alone was picked up. He might easily have neglected to write home. If all had been saved surely some one among them would have communicated with their friends' [MacKenzie Papers GD403/50/2].

[56] Scotsman 1 March 1877. At much the same time the 'Echo' reported a shipwreck at Fair Isle in December 1876. 'The same story comes from both islands – the inhabitants suffer from the greed of their proprietors' [DC Section 5/133]

[57] DC Section 5/133; Scotsman 6 March 1877. Mr Walker of Bowland, attending the meeting, had visited St Kilda with John Hall Maxwell in 1863.

[58] Scotsman 8 March 1877; DC Section 5/133

[59] KBP 7/25, 29

[60] Morning Advertiser 21 February 1877, Daily Telegraph 28 February 1877 [DC Section 5/133]

[61] DC Section 2 637/4/10 3 July 1876. The proprietor had long been annoyed by Sands's presence on the island: 'I am surprised Mr Sands should have decided to remain, and I think it is to be regretted he should have done so, but it could not be helped, and I should rather conceive, that the more the people see of him the less they will like him' [MacKenzie Papers GD403/50/1 Letter 3 July 1876]. Now that he was 'marooned' Sands became an even greater source of irritation. A series of letters between MacLeod and his factor related to the failure of the Robert Hadden to visit St Kilda in the autumn of 1876 and to the eventual rescue of Sands and the shipwrecked Austrians. Of Sands MacLeod wrote (13 February 1877): 'The fact of his being unable to get away proves how absurd it was of him to think that his boat would be used by the St Kilda people for the establishment of a traffic. I dare say however when he does leave the Island he will have plenty to say against us, and will accuse us of having purposely kept away' [MacKenzie Papers GD403/50/4-10, 51/1-5].

[62] DC Section 5/133 Letter of 8 March 1877 to Scotsman 10 March 1877; KBP 7/27

[63] DC Section 5/133 (Scotsman 10, 12 & 13 March 1877)

[64] DC Section 5/133. Thomas Gray, Board of Trade, wrote to MacLeod on 10 March 1877 enclosing copy of Digby's report. The Robert Hadden was said by Seton (p.137) to be 'a craft of 62 tons', which visited St Kilda three times in 1875 and once in 1876. In 1877 a further three visits seemed probable. MacKenzie the factor usually went only once a year. It may be that the Janet was hired when the Robert Hadden was not available.

[65] KBP 6/1; DC Section 5/133. MacLeod himself told Dr Ferguson that 'Mr MacKenzie is a most upright kind-hearted man' and went on: 'You probably know that he acts entirely as my agent in this matter, and while he does what is fair and just by me, he is the last man in the world to put improper pressure on the people or to exact from them a farthing more than they ought to pay…Whatever happens, my opinion is that Mr Sands's visit to St Kilda will prove the greatest misfortune that could possibly have befallen its Inhabitants.' Dr Ferguson wrote a letter under the pseudonym of 'Equity' to the Edinburgh Courant (30 March 1877) in which he attributed to Sands alone the unreliable reports of distress and destitution now circulating and pointed out that a subscription would appear to be unnecessary.

[66] KBP 6/1

[67] DC Section 5/133; KBP 6/2

[68] The Graphic 7 April 1877, The Globe 2 April 1877 [DC Section 5/133]

[69] John o' Groat Journal 10 May 1877 [DC Section 5/133]; KBP 6/6. A letter from MacLeod to MacKenzie of 11 June 1877, just two days before Emily set off for St Kilda, appeared to recommend caution in dealing with Sands:

'I am very sorry to hear how low in price the St Kilda feathers are. By all means make the people aware of the fact. I think you had better stand out for the present. Perhaps by waiting you may get a higher offer. Have you sold the Cattle yet?

'I certainly would give Mr Sands no assistance in getting to the Island, but I do not see how I can prevent his marrying this girl if he wishes it. I cannot for a moment suppose that he would desire to live at St Kilda always. Should he express the wish to do so, we must consider whether he can be allowed.'

[MacKenzie Papers GD403/50/11]

[70] KBP 7/42, 43

[71] KBP 6/3. In The Graphic (7 April 1877) an article based on Sands included the observation: 'It seems very questionable whether such remote islands as these should be left to the mercy of an absentee proprietor, who is both landlord and shopkeeper, and who, having no competitor, buys cheap from the unlucky inhabitants and sells dear to them.'

[72] DC Section 5/133 (Letter in Scotsman 4 May 1877); The Highlander Vol. IV no.210 19 May 1877 p.5

[73] Unless otherwise indicated this account of the Flirt's visit is derived from J MacDiarmid: St Kilda and its Inhabitants Edinburgh 1877. See also The Highlander Vol. IV no.208 5 May p.8 for the Robert Hadden's visit.

[74] Apparently the minister sent round a message on the Saturday evening bidding all the inhabitants to attend the Sunday morning service, though no reason is given for this unusual action. 'All were well dressed – in fact, better dressed than the class in the same position in other parts of the West Highlands' [The Highlander Vol. IV no.210 19 May 1877 p.5].

[75] The Flirt reached Stornoway the same night [The Highlander Vol. IV no.210 19 May 1877 p.5].

[76] The Highlander Vol. V no.249 16 February 1878 p.5

[77] Sands (1878) pp.122-123

[78] Sands (1878) p.130

[79] T McLauchlan: Celtic Gleanings Edinburgh 1857 pp.32-33. McLauchlan's visit was in 1850. Sands (1878) p.32

[80] Sands (1876) pp.27-28

[81] The difference in treatment of the minister was pointed out by Seton in his own book (pp.269-271).

[82] 'Captain Otter, of the Government Survey, did a great deal for the islanders, and is still remembered by them with great gratitude' [Baillie p.255].

[83] The bell was probably that 'saved from a wreck' [Sands (1878) p.15]. The wreck is supposed to have been that of the ship Janet Cowan of Greenock, 831 tons, on a voyage from Calcutta to Dundee with a cargo of jute. For an account of the loss, in April 1864, see Scotsman 2 April

1877 [DC Section 5/133].

84   The 'joke' was known to Dr James Kidd, who is said to have shouted 'Wake up, sir! Wake up!
      There will be no sleeping in Hell' [C MacLean: Going to Church NMS Edinburgh 1997 pp.27-
      28].

85   The Highlander Vol. IV no.206 21 April 1877 p.5; OT 14 April 1877; Sands (1877); Sands
      (1882); HB 41/699. According to Zealand Sands died in 1900 [see n.38 above].

86   Unless otherwise stated this account of Emily MacLeod's visit to St Kilda in 1877 is derived
      from her letters to Menzies [KBP 6/4-6/10], and to 'Mary' (with copies) [DC Section 2
      638/1/1-13/7].

87   Emily MacLeod was particularly impressed with the islanders' recollection of the Dargavel:
      'They cannot, even now, speak of the loss of their own boat about 14 years ago with 8 young
      men and 1 woman without tears.' The inclination to mimic appeared in their account of the
      shipwrecked, Catholic Austrians: 'While telling this, two or three women threw themselves on
      the ground, imitating the act of swimming, and screaming Mary! Mary! They were a good deal
      scandalised by their calling on the Virgin in time of danger' [DC Section 2 638/1/11].
      Presumably the drunken doctor was one of the two doctors who visited the island to
      vaccinate the inhabitants in 1873. These were Dr Webster of Dunvegan and, three months
      later, Dr Murchison of North Harris who went with the Jackal [Seton p.235]. Dr McKellar of
      Obbe was a passenger on the Dunara Castle in 1877 and vaccinated 3 children.

88   In other copies of this letter Marion's age is given as 35 and 36.

89   Emily also wrote: 'They say here that Mr Sands intends to get Norman to sell the island to a
      Company in Edinburgh and that he is to have the management of it and live here. I really
      believe all the row he has made has been with the intention of worrying Norman into getting
      rid of it.' [DC Section 2 638/1/3]

90   Seton p.64; The Highlander Vol.V no.219 21 July 1877 p.8. It was reported by The Highlander
      that 'Miss McLeod made a house to house inspection when there and found the people
      remarkable for their intelligence, in fact superior to those who live in more central situations
      – to the praise of their teacher be it told.'

91   DC Section 5/133

92   The Ayr Observer and Galloway Chronicle 24 July-25 September 1877. The ninth article,
      supposedly in the paper of 2 October 1877, seems to be wanting. The articles were also
      printed in the Cumnock Express at the same time – for Part III only (8 September 1877) DC
      Section 2 641/1/8.

93   The Highlander Vol.V no.219 21 July 1877 p.8. On his way back from St Kilda Seton met the
      precentor Donald MacKinnon at Obbe – 'an intelligent man of about sixty' – who told him of
      the visit to St Kilda of a 'Laird of Islay', supposedly in the 1820s, and of how this 'laird'
      intended to marry an island girl called Marion Morrison (see n.6 above). MacKinnon also
      recounted the story of the wreck at Rockall of the Charlotte of Hull in 1839, after which 18
      crewmen reached St Kilda in a boat and spent about a fortnight on the island where they
      were 'clothed, housed, and fed'. Seton related this incident to one recorded by Neil
      MacKenzie's daughter Mrs McVean in her reminiscences [Seton pp.55-57]. Further
      information derived by Seton from Donald MacKinnon related to a song of St Kilda origin
      [Seton p.279].

94   KBP 6/10

95   MacKenzie Papers GD403/50/1; DC Section 2 637/6/1

96   DC Section 2 637/6/2

97   KBP 6/8

98   HB 3/40 Letter from Barrington to Harvie Brown 4 December 1883; Smith (1879) p.5; DC
      Section 2 638/1/1. At least two long reviews admired the physical appearance of Seton's 'very
      beautiful volume' but were more inappropriately written than many of the newspaper
      articles of the time and, as comments on St Kilda, contributed nothing. That in the Saturday
      Review 9 February 1878 remarked of the Western Isles: 'Things have changed for the better

since the overcrowded population has been thinned by emigration' [DC Section 5/133].
Coinciding with the publication of Seton's book came an unexpected exchange of
correspondence in the Scotsman, which printed in one issue four letters dated within the
first two weeks of March 1878. These were followed in another paper by a letter and
comment on 18 March. Lieutenant Commander Digby of the *Jackal* had reported to the
Admiralty in February 1877 that Sands had been brought back to Greenock from St Kilda. The
Treasury refused to cover the cost of 'the entertainment of Mr Sands on board', amounting to
£2.5s, or 9s a day, which sum Digby was asked to recover from Sands, who, 'being an artist,
who had gone to St Kilda for his own pleasure, cannot be considered as a distressed
shipwrecked person'. Sands refused to pay since in his view he had performed a service to
the government by sending his letter in a bottle, and he pointed out that he was only four
days on the ship so that, if charged anything, the bill should only amount to £1.16s. This
moved an anonymous reader to write that he too had been a guest on board a ship from
Bombay and paid his mess bills as a matter of course. He thought Sands's response 'highly
abusive and insolent'. [DC Section 5/133]

99   DC Section 4/1522 Letter from Seton to Emily MacLeod 12 March 1878.

100   The Highlander Vol.V no.219 21 July 1877 p.8; Seton p.247

101   Chambers's Journal 4th Series no.723 (3 November 1877) pp.689-691

102   Seton pp.319-335

103   Seton pp.335-336

104   Chambers's Journal 4th Series no.740 (2 March 1878) pp.129-132, no.723 p.691

105   The Highlander Vol.V no.248 9 February 1878 p.5; Seton pp.338-339

106   The Highlander Vol. VI no.266 15 June 1878 p.7, no.267 22 June 1878 p.5, no.268 29 June
      1878 p.6; letter from John Sands to the John o' Groat Journal (undated but 1879): 'In 1877 I
      heard that some old service boats were for sale at Plymouth Dockyard, and I sent a petition
      to the Admiralty to let me have one of them' etc. [DC Section 5/133]; The Highlander Vol. VI
      no.272 27 July 1878 p.7

107   KBP 6/9; The Highlander Vol. VI no.272 27 July 1878 p.5, no.276 24 August 1878 p.7

108   The Highlander Vol. VI no.284 19 October 1878 p.4; J A MacKay: Islands Postal History Series
      no.1 Harris and St Kilda Dumfries 1978 p.24; The Highlander Vol. V no.241 22 December
      1877 p.5

109   Anthony Trollope – An Illustrated Autobiography including How the 'Mastiffs' went to Iceland
      Gloucester 1987 pp.261-270. The reference to MacKay's mysterious sister is of interest. Her
      tombstone indicates that Margaret died four years before Trollope's visit.

PART VII

DISPUTES, AND 'DEMORALISING'
THE PEOPLE
John Mackay leaves St Kilda

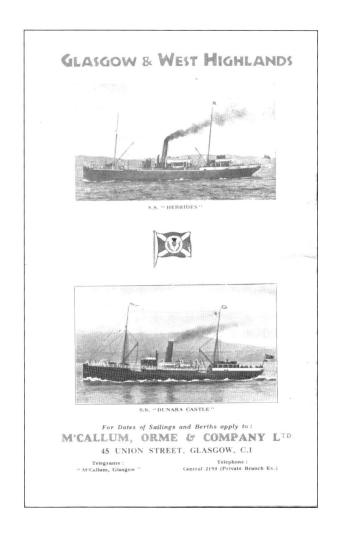

In and after 1880 arguments were often put forward suggesting evacuation as the economic solution to the burden of sustaining an inhabited St Kilda, but though some of the islanders were willing to consider leaving the majority were still too deeply attached to their home. The alternative was to assist them to become 'civilised' through educating them out of the use of Gaelic and helping them to join in the modern world even there, out in their isolated fragment of Britain.

To this end Emily Macleod eventually found a nurse who for a while did some teaching of sewing as well until it was decided far away that Free Church students should be sent, as they were to many parts of the Highlands and islands, as teachers of more general subjects for up to a year and sometimes more. The teacher too served as a guide and interpreter for the companies of visitors who continued to appear as usual, some of them with critical, occasionally hostile views of the island, and some much more friendly and interested. Many became aware of what they called the 'demoralising' impact of the tourists and of mainland sources providing gifts and aid; the proprietor renewed his complaint about independent trade practice; and the 'Napier' Commission and other government or official representatives concluded that improved landing facilities would be essential to the development of fishing and, indeed, to the survival of a viable population. Confused news of distress in St Kilda after storms revived all these issues and drew further naval and less helpful journalist investigation.

The Free Church minister, John Mackay, was involved in many of these matters, but his behaviour and manner of dealing with them, or the personal approach of the leading church elder, aroused religious conflict within the community and in 1889 Mackay was advised to retire. After his many years in St Kilda he and his household then removed to live in Skye.

CHAPTER 1

Teachers in St Kilda – Mrs Ann MacKinlay,
Kenneth Campbell, and their successors

Lady Baillie of Polkemmet did not lose track of her opinions on St Kilda and nearly three years after her visit in 1874 she was still pursuing the idea of evacuation which she had put forward in her article. In March 1877 she wrote to Fletcher Menzies seeking support: 'I want to enlist your sympathy and assistance in letting people be aware that it would be much better to <u>remove</u> the people from the Island and merely to send <u>men</u> there during the summer months to collect the Feathers. It is <u>not</u> a fit place for families to live in ..' The landing place, she thought, was inadequate, with vessels finding it hard to come anywhere near the shore, and the inhabitants were really unattractive: 'The intermarriages are too numerous, consequently the people are weak-minded, and unhealthy looking – and only half Civilised, and greedy.' But not everyone agreed with her, and enforced removal did not strike any authority as a realistic option, especially in view of what seemed to be the islanders' strong attachment to their home. Outside assistance was concentrated instead on making good accidental damage and dealing with emergencies after storms and bad seasons, and, above all, on promoting education, which, taken in conjunction with observations on the benefit of learning English and on the disadvantages of retaining Gaelic, was seen, as it had been for centuries, as the best means of 'civilising' the 'natives' and helping them to participate in the modern world.[1]

The form and purposes of improved education in St Kilda, as in other Hebridean islands, were the product of remote, mainland concepts based on the insufficient accounts of visitors like Lady Baillie and on practice in utterly different areas. It looks as if John Finlayson in Mingulay never knew quite what best to do as far as the matter of language was concerned, even though his work in the 'hovel' of a schoolroom was, theoretically at least, directed and supervised by the local School Board and by inspectors. In 1876 he found, probably not for the first time, that the Gaelic-speaking children had difficulty in acquiring 'the correct pronounciation of the English', but he persisted with his lessons and in getting his pupils to translate from English into Gaelic. Inspectors' reports, which had to be entered in the school logbook by the inspected teacher, are revealing. The second, for 1879, recommended that 'Gaelic should be less used, especially in the higher classes'; but two years later, in a building much better than the previous 'miserable premises', Finlayson recorded: 'The Teacher should make a liberal use of his Gaelic in imparting an intelligent knowledge of the meanings and matter of the lessons and the practice of bi-lingual instruction should be a marked feature of the work.' Then, 'Constant use should be made of the Gaelic language in cultivating an intelligent comprehension of the Reading Lessons' was the message in 1882. By 1884 things had gone too far: 'Owing to the Teacher having reverted to a rather exclusive use of Gaelic in addressing the children, the latter have not made the expected progress in English during the year.' It took until 1886 before poor Finlayson, who no doubt tried to do only what he was told, achieved a balance that satisfied an inspector and would perhaps have pleased even 'W.C.': 'The native language is judiciously and successfully used to promote an intelligent comprehension of English.'[2]

Meanwhile in St Kilda, now deemed to lie within the parish of Harris but for which the Harris School Board took no responsibility, where no inspector called and where no logbook was kept, all teaching, of English and of any other subject thought useful, was left to Rev. John Mackay, whose efforts and success over the years went largely unrecorded and were certainly never impartially judged. In 1881 every islander spoke Gaelic as a matter of course, as did nearly every inhabitant of the Hebrides and much of the Highlands in spite of School Boards and inspectors. According to John MacDiarmid Mackay had been 'a long time schoolmaster at Garve' before he became 'a probationer at Kinlochewe', and spent 'five years in South Uist' as well as 'some time in the island of Eig' before going to St Kilda; but his teaching experience was largely irrelevant to his missionary work and with only a few hours devoted to 'education' each week he probably had no intention of achieving anything other than greater ability in reading the Gaelic bible and perhaps a slightly improved acquaintance with the English version. He had no need to do more as he was not employed in the island as a teacher.[3]

Consequently attempts to find a better means of introducing a language hardly relevant to life in St Kilda were continued elsewhere. When MacDiarmid returned from his visit in May 1877 with the feeling that a proper school was necessary he wrote to Thomas McLauchlan on the subject, and McLauchlan's reply offered the usual solution to the problem of who would run such a school in a place so remote that an impecunious Board could justly claim to have neither the will to do so nor the money to have a suitable building constructed. He said that the Edinburgh Ladies Highland Schools Association (ELHSA) might assume the responsibility: 'The Ladies Association of which Miss Abercrombie 7 Doune Terrace is Secretary do much for Highland Education. But primarily the duty of sending a teacher to St Kilda lies with the School Board of Harris.' However he went on: 'I do not doubt that the ladies would consider an application favourably.'[4]

The experienced Association already supported schools in 'the remote island of Heisker' and in Scarp, and in 1877 opened one in Taransay, and though it may have forgotten its rather vague connection with St Kilda in 1852 it was well acquainted with contemporary conditions in the remoter islands. It was however possessed of limited funds and in 1883 issued a 'Special Statement and Appeal' which, while intended to attract contributions, is of particular interest as a description of the ELHSA's circumstances and purposes:

'The object of this Association is to improve the temporal and spiritual condition of the people in the remote parts of the Highlands and Islands, mainly through the instruction of the young.

'During the last 32 years, it has maintained schools for a longer or shorter period in 130 of the most destitute and inaccessible places in Scotland; and it still has over 70 Teachers (male and female) in its employment.

'The Scholars are taught to read the Bible in Gaelic (their mother-tongue). They also receive a good Elementary Education in English, and the girls are trained in needlework.

'The male Teachers are usually Students preparing for the Ministry, and they engage in mission-work as they have opportunity, visiting the sick, holding prayer-meetings, and conducting Sabbath Schools at their respective stations, many of which are out of reach of the ordinary means of grace. During the five winter months a certain number of the Teachers come to College, leaving substitutes to carry on the work; and this arrangement has enabled a large number of Gaelic-speaking men to complete their studies, to whom the eight years' curriculum in Arts and Theology would otherwise have presented insuperable difficulties.

'Scarce as Gaelic-speaking Ministers still are, we may well ask what would have become of the Highlands, had not some such way been found to increase the supply? There are in connection with the Free Church 183 charges (besides more than 30 preaching stations), in which Gaelic services are required; and as the habitual use of that language has almost died out in the upper and middle classes of society, Ministers for the Highlands must be found among those who have to toil for their education, a class which has produced some of Scotland's noblest sons.

'There are 90 ordained Ministers now in the Free Church who have been teachers in the Ladies' Schools, besides some who have finished their earthly course, and others who have gone to the Colonies or the Mission-field. Let us add, that they often refer to their early labours in connection with this Association as one of the most valuable parts of their training for the work of the Ministry.

'The action of the School Boards has now superseded many of the Ladies' Schools. But it is impossible for School Boards, under present regulations, to provide instruction for all the children in the West Highlands, where there are more than 100 inhabited islands, and where the mainland is so cut up by mountains, lochs, and torrents, that an extraordinary number of schools is required in proportion to the number of scholars.

'....Building is expensive, where skilled labour and much of the material have to be imported from a distance. ....And if we take into account the exceptional poverty that prevails in the West Highlands, the wonder is that School Boards there have done so much from local resources.

'The aim of the Ladies' Association is to supplement their efforts, by carrying instruction into nooks and corners which they cannot provide for; by supplying schools in a few populous districts, for pupils above school age who cannot be accommodated in the public schools, or who have a desire for higher instruction with a view to College; by giving religious teaching to young and old on week days and Sabbath days; by promoting the industrial training of girls, supplying sewing materials, and providing clothing for the most needy.

'The periodical destitution in the Hebrides shows the importance of fitting the people for employment in the Lowlands and in the Colonies, by teaching them English; and the fact that several of the islands are to this day inhabited mainly by Roman Catholics give them a special claim on the sympathy and aid of those more highly favoured.

'Not a few in Barra, S. Uist, Benbecula, and other places are indebted to the Ladies' Schools for the only Bible teaching they have ever enjoyed.

'The Highland Committee now gives a grant of £5 a-year to each of our teachers in respect of his mission work; but, with this exception, the Ladies receive no aid from any of the public funds of the Free Church. Their whole income is collected privately.

'The Association has of late lost several valued friends by death, one of whom long contributed £100 a-year to each of its two branches in Edinburgh and Glasgow, now happily united.

'This appeal is issued in the hope that others may become interested in the work, and may aid it with their contributions and their prayers...'[5]

It seems that no application to the Association was made in 1877, but at their meeting on 10 October 1879 committee members considered a letter from John MacKay in St Kilda 'earnestly requesting the appointment of a female teacher there'. In answer the committee said it would send such a teacher if possible although further enquiries would have to be made first. Moreover 'Miss MacLeod of MacLeod, who had been consulted, expressed her sympathy with the proposal, but felt that there would be much difficulty in inducing a qualified person to go there'. The 'female teacher' was requested perhaps in order to maintain sewing instructions following the death in 1878 of Isabella Ross Munro,

Neil MacDonald's wife, who may have helped in this way for a few years.[6]

Miss Emily MacLeod had been to St Kilda again in the summer of 1879. She was a passenger on board the *Dunara Castle*, on a trip which followed exactly the same course as that of the previous year, and visited the houses on behalf of her brother. This time she certainly did not stay. Having brought herself up to date with the situation in the island she could advise the ELHSA with some confidence, and a letter from her was received after the October meeting to be read at that on 14 November 1879. She stated that in her view there would be 'immense difficulty' in finding a teacher willing to go to the island and 'some difficulty' about her accommodation if she did go. The ladies learned too that 'There were only 4 girls of School age in the Island, and it was customary for the men to do the Sewing there'. Nevertheless, drawing no doubt on her experience in searching for a nurse, Emily MacLeod 'would suggest our making a small grant to a woman of the Island, if one could be found able and willing to teach Sewing, and if the girls consented to learn. She proposed enquiring about a Mrs Donald Ferguson who might perhaps undertake the duty.' Why an island woman would be any more inclined to become a teacher than a nurse was not explained although it might have been because she would not have to leave her home. But even with a St Kilda instructor the introduction, if such it would be, of sewing lessons for girls appeared to be an imposition contrary to traditional practice.[7]

The possible teacher, Rachel Ferguson, was not quite 40 years old and mother of at least four children, one of whom, Alexander, was an exceptionally quick learner. As a member of possibly the most talented and enterprising family on the island Rachel was no doubt a sensible choice, and a salary of £5 a year was offered to her 'if she would engage to do the work'. But when the ELHSA committee discussed the matter again in January 1880 there was disappointing news from Emily MacLeod, who 'expressed the fear that Mrs Donald Ferguson was not in sufficiently good health to teach Sewing to the St Kilda girls'. Miss MacLeod said she expected to return to the island in the spring, and the committee agreed 'to keep the matter open until we learn what arrangement she recommends after seeing the people'.[8]

*

The years 1879 and 1880 at St Kilda saw an increased number of comings and goings. In the second week of May 1879, with snow on the hills of Harris, 'A crew of nine St Kilda men' landed at Tarbert 'and made large purchases in the shops'. Their boat was perhaps the jollyboat brought out by the *Dunara Castle*.'They seemed to be in good condition – physically and financially', and had left Rev. MacKay – 'the Bishop' as he was facetiously called in the report – also in good health. The men said that there had been two or three deaths since the previous summer, including that of the minister's sister, 'the only woman who could speak English, a native of Lochcarron'. Since according to a tombstone in the little St Kilda burial ground the death of MacKay's somewhat shadowy sister Margaret occurred in February 1874 this 'sister' may in fact have been Isabella Munro or MacDonald, often described as the only female English speaker.[9]

The next contact with 'the outside world' took place in June when the *Dunara Castle* arrived with Emily MacLeod among the passengers, and then apart from a possible yacht or two and the visit of the factor that should have been the end of communication for the year. But in early August another steamer, *St Clair,* departed from her regular route up the west coast by extending it to include St Kilda. On board was 'an excursion party of twenty-five ladies and gentlemen who were anxious to visit this now famous island'. She approached at 8 a.m. on Monday 8 August, fired a gun to announce her presence, and anchored close in two hours later. John MacKay naturally welcomed the party ashore. Purchases were made, the islanders offering stockings, socks, homespun clothes, seabirds' eggs and 'wild fowl' at prices 'about twice the value of them'. Not deterred, the tourists bought over sixty pairs of stockings and socks and about fifty yards of cloth. Presumably some acquired eggs and specimens. Leaving in the late evening the ship was back at Greenock by Wednesday afternoon, and as usual everybody thanked the captain, John MacCallum in this instance, and his purser for looking after them so well.[10]

While voyages from St Kilda to Tarbert or to Berneray in the Sound of Harris became rather frequent they were always accompanied by considerable risk. Steamer trips on the other hand, though often in rough seas, were reassuringly safe by comparison. *Dunara Castle,* usually in mid June, and now *St Clair* in early August provided a comfort which did not detract from the exciting sense of adventure that their passengers enjoyed.

In June 1880, when John Sands was still fitfully 'pressing the case of the "lone island" on the attention of the public and the Government' and persisting in his campaign to free the money in the Kelsall Bequest fund from what he saw as unnecessary restrictions, the *Dunara Castle* paid its regular visit under the ever-satisfactory attention of Captain McEwan and his officers. On the way the party of tourists spent the Sunday at Harris, first in attending a service 'held by two clergymen of the company under the awning on quarterdeck' and then 'in walking about that Hebridean wilderness with its picturesque hills'. In St Kilda puffins were sold to the visitors who 'eagerly' bought them at 1s each. On looking with their usual blatant curiosity into the houses they found people confined to bed 'with what is called the visitor's cold', brought this time apparently by the Lewis crews of four 'skiffs' out at the fishing. Of special interest to the island was the presence of clergymen among the passengers, for it may already have been the custom to arrange St Kilda's communion season to coincide with the arrival of the *Dunara Castle* and so enable assisting ministers to attend a service.[11]

Since it was necessary to plan steamer programmes well in advance those who travelled with them had to put up with whatever sea and weather conditions they happened to meet. When the *St Clair* ventured out in August 1880 the weather was unfavourable and it was 'especially rough during the rather long stretch between Skye and the islet.' In spite of this most aboard enjoyed the trip and 'the civility and attention paid to them all .. from Captain McCallum, downwards'. Unfortunately, however, the vessel arrived off St Kilda at a bad moment: 'It so happened that on the very morning of their visit, and also on the day before, a death had occurred on the island, the deceased in both cases being young persons.' A clergyman was inevitably at hand to assist: 'devotional exercises suitable for the occasion, were held by Mr McKay, the resident minister, and by the Rev. Mr. Whitelaw, of Kilmarnock'. It was noticed by the visitors that apparently 'the natives' were 'all in their holiday attire to receive them'; heavy homemade tweed was worn by both men and women, 'the upper garment of the former being a sleeved waistcoat, the [sleeves] and back of which differed from the rest in being white or undyed'. The occasion being a solemn rather than a festive one, the islanders might well have been dressed for a double funeral rather than for a holiday occasion.[12]

Presents of 'sweeties' and tobacco were of course distributed by the *St Clair* party and were welcomed, though it was suggested by whoever reported the trip that 'the cost of these might be more profitably laid out in some more substantially serviceable way, such as, say, coals', for it was apparent that the practice of stripping the turf for fuel was visibly damaging to the pasture. Purchases worth about £30 included ewe-milk cheese along with the more regular tweed and socks. 'One of the excursionists, I should add, an adventurous and roaming spirit, remained on the island; and with his gun and dog is prepared to remain there for a twelvemonth, if he can subsist and cannot get away sooner.' This gentleman was certainly not John Sands, but he may have been Sands-inspired. His identity is unknown, as is the actual length of his stay, but it is likely that he was persuaded to leave then and there with the *St Clair.*

The subject of fuel, or rather the misuse of pasture, had been taken up in 1879 by Professor M. F. Heddle of St Andrews whose letter to Dr R A Smith featured in the latter's *A Visit to St. Kilda in "The Nyanza"*, an extended version of his article in *Good Words* 1875. Smith announced that his book 'speaks of the beginning of a new interest in the island', an interest which he attributed to the efforts of John Sands: 'I suppose that Mr Sand's enthusiasm is the real cause of the great attention given to the place within four or five years. That gentleman has spent weeks upon St. Kilda, and is now closely identified with its progress.' There was comment too on the 'new attempt to give to the inhabitants their own means of independence', an interestingly misleading and inappropriate remark at a time when the islanders were being helplessly drawn ever more quickly to greater dependence. But to a mainland visitor of any kind at the time being independent meant having the means of continued existence on the island even though this were to depend largely on services from elsewhere. What in these circumstances was 'independence'? The people of St Kilda had never been really self-sufficient. They depended upon 'the outside world' for money, relief oatmeal and other goods, boats, education and religion. They had long been subject to educational and religious persuasion, the landlord and his 'Steward' had to a considerable extent controlled their material needs, and John Sands and Miss Emily MacLeod, along with a variety of writers and the G.P.O., were still trying to increase the range of alien influences bearing upon them. Smith, an optimist who used words like 'progress' and 'true' without reserve, said he had left St Kilda 'with much admiration for the minister, who is also, to a large extent, a governor'; and though he did not exactly govern John MacKay was at least as much of an alien influence as any other.[13]

*

Of considerable interest in the account of the *St Clair's* visit in August 1880 was a brief, unexpected observation which had nothing to do with the tourist party: 'Some seven children are at present attending a school on the island under the direction of a female teacher sent out by Miss MacLeod of Dunvegan.' It is clear that after the ELHSA meeting in January Emily MacLeod had been very active in her search for someone to serve as a nurse and another person to be a teacher, but she must have quickly concluded that no island woman would come forward, not even if – and this now seemed a sensible possibility – the two jobs were combined. Following the news that Mrs Donald Ferguson was not fit enough to teach sewing, another letter reached the ELHSA in March 1880. Emily had evidently achieved some success in Skye. She wrote 'approving of the Suggestion that the duties of nurse and Teacher should be combined at St Kilda, and stating that Mrs MacKinlay, who has already been engaged as nurse, was able and willing to teach English and Sewing for the salary of £5 offered by the Ladies'. The 'Ladies' themselves 'decided to accept Mrs MacKinlay's services for one year'; and to have been in 'a school' by the beginning of August she must have reached the island by way of either the factor's smack or the *Dunara Castle*. In October 1880 the ELHSA read yet another letter from Emily 'testifying to the usefulness of our Sewing Teacher at St Kilda'. In this way the wishes of Rev. MacKay and of the proprietor and his sister were answered.[14]

Ann MacLeod, later Mrs MacKinlay, spent her childhood at Bolvean, near Orbost and about four miles from Miss Emily MacLeod's home at Dunvegan. Her father Norman and his wife Janet tried to earn a living from their small piece of land at Bolvean, and Ann often went out with her mother, a midwife, to confinements in the district. Eventually she was able to go on her own. She had a brother John who migrated to Glasgow and received a weekly wage. In or about 1835 she married Murdoch MacKinlay, and almost immediately they set off for Glasgow to stay with John. Ann continued there as a midwife, and Murdoch, who could not secure a full-time employment, made a little out of carrying luggage or goods from the docks to nearby hotels and stores. In 1836

570

their daughter Margaret was born and in 1842 Ann, expecting her second child, returned on her own to Bolvean. Her husband apparently stayed in the city and died after working as a silk-dyer for a while. Then Ann left Skye again and trained in Edinburgh for a diploma in midwifery which she was awarded in 1849. She stayed in Edinburgh as 'Ladies Nurse' in the 1850s but returned home about 1864.[15]

Having chiefly in mind the deaths of infants in St Kilda Emily MacLeod was no doubt delighted at being able to persuade an experienced midwife who spoke Gaelic to go as the island's nurse and even more so at gaining the support of the Ladies' Association. In her later sixties, when she might well have thought of staying in Skye or returning to Edinburgh, Ann MacKinlay was undertaking work of a demanding kind. She occupied the comparatively substantial house used by the factor and may have acted as housekeeper on his visits. In December 1880 the ELHSA confirmed with satisfaction that it had successfully placed female teachers at Skigersta in the Lewis district of Ness and in St Kilda, each of them teaching sewing and instructing in English.[16]

In the first months of 1881 the ELHSA contacted Emily MacLeod on the subject of Mrs MacKinlay's salary as teacher, or more precisely on how to get the salary to her. Miss MacLeod replied, probably in March, 'that a vessel was about to sail for that Island by which she would forward a parcel we sent to her for Mrs MacKinlay, and by the same opportunity she hoped to ascertain if Mrs MacKinlay were willing to continue there another year and what she wishes done with her salary'. In fact Mrs MacKinlay, who may sometimes have come away from the island before winter and certainly had a break in the winter of 1883-84, remained in St Kilda for another seven years but for most of that time as nurse only. The removal of her teaching responsibilities followed a sort of inspectors' visit in June 1883 when Emily MacLeod, accompanied by Mrs Thomas as ELHSA representative and by Rev. William Ross as deputy from the Free Church Highlands committee, again went out with the *Dunara Castle*. 'They found that Mrs MacKinlay, though an excellent .. nurse, was not well qualified for teaching and that there was a great desire for a male Teacher in the Island.' In response to this desire Miss MacLeod was able to tell the ELHSA that Mr MacLeod of MacLeod 'would provide a room and fuel and might perhaps get a grant from Government if this Committee could see its way to send a Teacher next Spring'. The Association committee agreed to keep this in view and try to find a suitable person.[17]

When she heard that the committee had agreed Emily MacLeod was well pleased and let it be known that the boat that usually went to St Kilda in the spring would be likely to leave early in April. She felt it would be ideal if the teacher could go with it. Taking on the rather difficult task of finding someone from among the few Gaelic-speaking college students prepared to isolate himself for an uncertain length of time meant that the ELHSA had put St Kilda on its list of 'regular stations' and this in turn required it to supply teachers. Fortunately for the 'Ladies' much trouble was saved on this first occasion when Kenneth Campbell, who had taught through a winter in Heisgeir and therefore had experience of the island community nearest to St Kilda, volunteered to go out for one year, though whether this was under some persuasive pressure is not clear. Miss MacLeod was glad to hear of his appointment, and the ELHSA secretary was to find out from her whether Campbell 'should have a room exclusively set apart for him'. If Mrs MacKinlay returned to St Kilda after her winter away 'any salary allowed to her by the Ladies for teaching Sewing should be dependent on her cooking and washing for the Teacher, if required to do so'. In reply Emily MacLeod said that Campbell 'was assured of a room free from any interference whatever' and that he would be supplied with coals by the proprietor. Furthermore the elderly Mrs MacKinlay would indeed cook for him and do his washing 'if her salary were continued', which it was. It appears therefore that Mrs MacKinlay continued to teach sewing while giving up to the newly appointed Campbell the instruction in English and any other subject offered.[18]

Mrs Ann MacKinlay, nurse, and Kenneth Campbell, teacher,
pictured with islanders in 1884

Kenneth Campbell began the 'school' in St Kilda on 16 June 1884. Just over six weeks later Miss Rainy and Miss Blackie, leading lights of the ELHSA, visited the island, taking with them 'a nice School desk as a present from Dr Blackie'. They found that sixteen scholars were already enrolled, at least twelve of whom, going by the 1881 census, must have been children. There was no special school building. 'Mr Campbell was teaching them in the room in which he lives, and an adjournment to the church being proposed, it was objected that it would be too cold to work in in winter.' An arrangement was made that the teaching should take place in the church for the present and that a stove would be sent to heat it. According to a later story 'Mr Campbell had them all the winter in the Church', however cold it was.[19]

In March 1885 Campbell's successor had still not been appointed. 'Some conversation took place about the time when Mr Campbell should be relieved by a new Teacher at St Kilda' and the ELHSA committee 'agreed that an appointment for one year should always be made in Spring' so that the new teacher could, as usual, go out 'by the first opportunity'. In April the committee chose Hugh McCallum, and it would have been either by the *Robert Hadden* that month or by the *Dunara Castle* in June that he made the journey. The ELHSA had already decided to place Campbell, when he was available, at Scaliscro in the west of Lewis, a position that was to be kept open for him and in the meantime covered by a substitute. In due course this rearrangement was carried out, so that by the autumn McCallum was well settled in St Kilda and Campbell, with whose work in the island over the previous year Emily MacLeod was most satisfied, in Scaliscro.[20]

A year on, in December 1886, Kenneth Campbell gave a talk about St Kilda in Oban where he was then resident. In spite of a decade of intense curiosity and exchange of information that followed upon the publication of books by Sands and Seton and much communication to newspapers and journals, Campbell had discovered that far from being enlightened about the island and its people the public was still amazingly ignorant. 'Persons have asked me,' he said, 'what language was spoken by the inhabitants, [and] whether they were black or white. Others again had never heard of such a place or at best did not know where it was.' To Campbell this seemed to show 'A state of ignorance only equalled by that of the unsophisticated and untutored St Kildans' who themselves asked such questions as 'Is the manse of the Edinburgh minister near the other houses?', 'Do potatoes grow well in the town of Edinburgh?', and 'Are Glasgow and Edinburgh much larger than Dunvegan?' The difference in the enquiries was that those of St Kilda demonstrated a natural wish to know more, whereas those of the mainland came from persons who ought to have known more.

Campbell, a Skye man by birth, pictured for his audience a typical voyage to St Kilda in the *Robert Hadden* smack, from which those on board could admire the cliffs at the mouth of Loch Dunvegan as they set off and eventually, after the frustrations of an absolute calm on the approach to the Sound of Harris followed by seasickness in the open Atlantic, witness 'eight or nine screaming natives yelling and gesticulating at a furious rate' as, in their own boat, they reached the smack at anchor in the bay. The lecturer was then able to provide what was expected of him – a description of a community conceived by at least some of his listeners to be like a 'savage' tribe in America or Africa:

'.. To know what they are saying or what language they speak is for a time impossible. This exciteability by the way I believe has something to do with what is know[n] there as the visitors' cold. You look at them with some interest and discover that they have good features, have well developed and muscular bodies and most of them about the medium height, Hair either red or dark, Good teeth and fair or dark complexions.

'They wear on their heads a broad Balmoral bonnet and have three folds and a thick woolen cravat round their throats. They leave their jackets at home, choosing to wear on all ordinary occasions vests with white woollen sleeves, dark blue trousers etc. They wear no shoes. As a rule their costume is not complete without having a rope made up in coils hanging from their shoulders.'

Whatever may have been their real thoughts it became apparent, with Kenneth Campbell, that the Free Church college teachers were as inclined as many mainlanders to speak with a rather superior air of the St Kilda people as curiosities.[21]

*

In June 1886 Hugh McCallum left St Kilda and was replaced by George Murray from the parish of Rogart. Murray, an arts student at Aberdeen, had enlisted with the ELHSA in March when he was sitting, with ultimate success, his examinations for his M.A. in classics. He set off from Dunvegan aboard the *Robert Hadden* in the evening of 9 June and reached St Kilda early on Thursday 11 June. Hugh McCallum went away with the same boat on its return voyage to Skye a fortnight later. He was then to serve at Glenroy.[22]

Like his predecessor McCallum too was moved to describe his experience in St Kilda but he left it for 23 years before doing so in an article in *The Caledonian Medical Journal* when he was a minister at Blair Atholl. He had a kinder opinion of the islanders than Campbell and his account concentrated upon the various features of daily life, many of which were now familiar topics dealt with in the ever-increasing sequence of books and articles on the island.

From 'the oldest inhabitant', possibly Neil Ferguson if male, McCallum learned about the changes in housing:

'Over seventy years ago there might be seen a row of huts, which, from inward and outward appearances, were scarcely worthy of the name of human dwelling-houses. Built after the shape of an egg, the walls 3 feet thick and 6 feet high, the roof thatched, and no window save a hole in the roof, which admitted light and air simultaneously. The interior was divided into two by a stone wall, one end kept for the cows the other for the biped, man and beast going out and coming in at the same door. The beds also were of stone, built like little caves, and must have been anything but comfortable.

'In these houses they had a strange habit of storing peat dust and ashes all the year. The ashes from their peat fires, instead of being carried outside, were strewn about the floor. In addition to this, an occasional creel of peat dust was brought home and mixed with the ashes. The level of the floor was in this way gradually raised, an incline being left towards the door. In springtime, my informant told me, they were comfortably near the roof, and when anxious to know the direction of the wind or the state of the weather they could with ease pop out their heads through the hole in the roof from this exalted position. Fortunately, when sowing time came the heap was removed. With all these disadvantages, and in spite of their surroundings, they lived peaceful, contented lives; and on wintry nights, when the wind and the roar of waves mingled in dread harmony outside, they, inside, sat round their cosy fires, which were in the centre of the floor, heedless of the raging elements, and with anything but woebegone faces, though they sat among ashes.

'These houses have disappeared, and all who passed their days in them have fallen asleep. In place of these houses arose well-built ones with more accommodation and improved with windows, though they also have served their day, and are now used as barns and byres. The present abodes are, in structure and comfort, far ahead of many houses one can see in all the Western Isles.'

McCallum also heard 'a number of strange traditions among the people as to how the island came to be inhabited' but recorded only the story of the boat race. For the most part, however, he confined himself to his own observations on matters ranging from the stranger's cold to gannet catching and the discussion meeting held 'as occasion requires'. He mentioned that the St Kilda Gaelic remained 'extremely pure' and avoided introducing English with a Gaelic sound for modern terms: 'For example, instead of calling the funnel of a steamer "funnel," they say *crann teine,* the *"fiery mast."'* As for religious behaviour, he described the marriage ceremony with its accompanying reiteach or betrothal feast and the similar feast in the manse with the minister after the service, when 'Dancing, singing anything but Psalms, even whistling, was strictly prohibited', and then commented more generally:

'For many years the religious needs of the people were entirely neglected. This state of matters came to an end through the repeated visits of the late well-known apostle of the north, Dr Macdonald. A sincere religious interest was awakened, which resulted in the building of a church and manse, and the settlement of a clergyman. There are three services on Sabbath, and though each service lasted two hours, and in winter draughts whistled on all sides, there were few absentees.

Where there is not the spirit, there is a strict adherence to the form of religion. Morning and evening each door in the village is closed at a certain time, and the day is begun and ended with family worship. One night I went with the men to cast lines for ling; after the lines were set it was too late to return to the village, and as the sea was calm we sought shelter for the night in one of the many caves scooped out with the incessant roll of the waves. We dropped anchor in total darkness, and, before stretching ourselves on the hard board to sleep, one of the elders conducted worship. We had no light; he announced the psalm, repeated four verses, we sang; he mentioned a certain chapter in Hebrews, repeated it from end to end; another psalm in the same way, then prayer.'

After his year in St Kilda McCallum concluded that the inhabitants were 'a fine class of people' and 'very kind to strangers', but it was 'with unusual joy' that he saw the vessel coming to take him away.[23]

*

The minutes of the ELHSA committee meetings note the receipt of letters from St Kilda during George Murray's time on the island, 1886-87, and for a while thereafter but say nothing of their content. Instead of giving talks or writing articles Murray kept a diary, extracts from which show that Ann MacKinlay was still present and that the teacher shared the factor's house with her, where in accordance with the rules laid down for continued payment of her salary she helped to look after him. But Mrs MacKinlay, 'my landlady' as Murray called her, was into her seventies and not particularly well. In March 1887 she had a 'swollen and sore foot', and in April she 'turned very ill'. The following day Murray wrote: 'I did not expect she would see this day. She is certainly drawing near her latter end and has little concern about what is before her. May the Holy Spirit awaken her to see that out of Christ there is no safety.' She remained ill in bed and 'very troublesome as she won't allow anyone to attend upon her except two women and myself day and night'. The ELHSA heard of her condition during the summer when she was poorly, but then surprisingly she began to recover: 'Mrs MacKinlay's health had failed very much, so that at one time it was proposed to bring her away from the island. Her health is now improved and Miss McLeod writes that having failed to find a successor for her, there is no recourse but to leave her at her post for some time longer.' It seems that she was able eventually to keep house for Ranald MacDonald who succeeded Murray in 1887, but when it was decided in April 1888 that Murdo Macrae should go as teacher it became clear that she could no longer manage the work: 'As Mrs MacKinlay does not now discharge the duties she undertook at St Kilda for the Association her salary ceases now.' So she left the island, arrived in Skye, and after a while returned to Edinburgh where she died in 1891.[24]

CHAPTER 2

Rev. John Mackay and the Great Auk, the naturalists,
and the Napier Commission

Though the St Kilda community, like that of any other Hebridean island, did not necessarily accept everything that minister, nurse and teacher said, there is no doubt that it recognised any sincere concern for its welfare. One minister or teacher might find it more difficult than another to adjust to the exceptional place and way of life, but having to make a lengthy stay he had the opportunity, whether he took it or not, of showing a genuine interest in island traditions and becoming closely familiar with individuals going about their daily activities, unlike those visitors who were able to spend no more than the few hours ashore allowed by steamers and yachts.

As minister however John MacKay was inevitably set apart from the rest of the people, much as the manse stood at some distance from the other dwellings. He remained the island's spiritual instructor but, aside from his role as intermediary between the Gaelic-speaking inhabitants and the 'English' world of government and tourist, he was no more a leader than the church elders who might well challenge him on religious topics and disagree with his approach to practical issues such as the need for supplies or the location of a pier. In the course of the 1880s MacKay was caught amidst an ever greater number of contrasting tasks and conflicting views, and, perhaps with the onset of declining health, he began to lose the respect formerly paid to him by landlord, islanders, and many visitors. Like Ann MacKinlay he was really kept too long in St Kilda.

A fundamental division was partly responsible for MacKay's dilemma and for a very confusing stage in the island's story. On the one hand a group of native St Kilda people struggled to maintain their customary existence, part of which was now the established acceptance of Free Church religion. This was what by long practice and habit they understood, and in that situation alone the minister's position was clear. On the other hand the abundance of outside and often contradictory influences was now increasingly in control of that existence, disapproving of some things, disregarding or mocking some, and tending all the time to encourage a view that the people should not live in the island anyway. The minister could not defend his flock against this invasion of opinion, especially when it appeared that one or two of the islanders sympathised with it and supported measures not of their own making. He would be out of his depth if he tried.

Nowhere was the variety of invasive and disturbing influence more apparent than in the behaviour and subsequent written or spoken accounts of the miscellaneous band of tourists and journalists who, following in the wake of Sands and Seton, arrived during the years of Ann MacKinlay's work on the island. One of the first to appear during that period was R Scott Skirving, an Edinburgh resident with East Lothian connections. On 24 May 1880 he wrote from Drummond Place, Edinburgh, that 'On the 10th June I am going a trip to St Kilda. I have been at Foula the likest thing to it, but I have always wished to see St Kilda.' He claimed that for many years he had wished to see 'the wonders' of this western island and along with other 'gentlemen' including a Mr Dudgeon of Glasgow and Professor Heddle of St Andrews had tried to charter a steamer independently but had, not surprisingly, found it too expensive and had therefore resorted to booking a place on the *Dunara Castle*. Skirving's record of his trip survives in his journal.[25]

Emily MacLeod – said by Skirving to be 'the grandest old Highland gentlewoman I ever met' – boarded the vessel as usual at Dunvegan, along with her nephew, the son and heir of the St Kilda landlord. It seems likely that Ann MacKinlay was also on board, this being the time of her initial journey to her new post. On leaving Tarbert after the morning quarterdeck service and the walk in 'that Hebridean wilderness' and on entering the open Atlantic 'a strong ocean swell .. disturbed the stomachs of a good many passengers'. Even a steward was 'terribly sick' for twelve hours. Skirving tried to assert his superiority over the elements, but 'Just after sighting St Kilda I felt squemish for about a quarter of an hour'. This did not prevent him from surveying the scene as the *Dunara Castle* came into the bay at 7 o'clock in the morning. He had been told that on the approach he would be awestruck by the sight and astonished by the crowds of gannets, but – feeling superior again – 'Nothing occurred to produce either effect'. It appears to have been consistent with Skirving's attitude in general that he should be impressed by very little.[26]

As no one was on the shore to watch the steamer come in he would have thought that the people 'still slept the sleep of the just – and the lazy', had not Stornoway boats out fishing in the early hours contradicted the popular notion that all Highlanders were perpetually idle.[27] Slowly the St Kilda people drifted down from the eighteen inhabited houses, although many were incapable of doing so because of their suffering the 'visitor's cold'. The latest *Dunara Castle* party landed and distributed their presents which, according to Skirving, included tobacco, tea, oranges, illustrated papers, pictures, and so on. These, he said, were taken 'most unthankfully', and he decided that the mischievous practice of handing out gifts, being out of date and uncalled for, should be discontinued. The display of 'cragsmanship' was then watched and seemed to him 'truly wonderful' and 'the only manly thing the natives of St Kilda are capable of'. A sneering disposition cannot have endeared this particular visitor to the people who were risking their lives to entertain him, and he had little patience with the outcome of their 'cragsmanship':

> 'On bringing the Fulmars to the top the St Kildens showed themselves to be quite civilized so far as the practise of extortion goes. They demanded 2s 6d each for the Petrols but ultimately were glad to get 6d when they found no more could be got. More senseless <u>ruffians</u> I never

saw, as they kept swinging the dead birds about to the destruction of their plumage and seemed not to know that their <u>skins</u> were what was wanted. I wonder if they thought we were going to eat them.'

To a people whose survival depended on birds as a source of food, rent and fuel, the preserving of the skins as specimens in museums and private collections must have been difficult to understand. Skirving evidently fancied himself as an ornithologist and it was this interest that led him to confront the minister.

Inevitably the subject of the garefowl or great auk was raised, it being clearly one of the few things, among birds in general, that stirred Skirving's collector's eagerness if not his imagination. He assumed the authority of an ornithological researcher, asked some 'cragsmen' about the bird, recorded what he was told in his journal and later added further information sent to him from elsewhere:

'They had heard so much of the Great Auk that they took some interest in its history and one and all agreed that an old man still alive and in the Island was the capturer of the now historic Auk secured alive in 1821 and presented, first to the Factor of the Island and by him to the master of a cruser who took it with him in his ship intending to present it to the Edinburgh Museum. Wishing to give it a bath he tied a string to the leg and let it swim from the ship near Arran where it made its escape.

'The man was brought to me, a very little old fellow called [McQueen]. He said he was about 70 but he looked 80 at least. He said the people were wrong when they said he personally caught the Auk. He was one of four young men who caught it. They were in a boat when they saw the Auk on a low ledge of rock on the East side of the Island and they resolved to try to catch it. One man was landed at some distance from the bird and a second as far off on the other side of it. Then the boat was rowed slowly towards the bird and right in front of it, while the two men crawled along the rock towards the last of the Auks. It finally leapt down to the sea just as one of the men got directly under it, and it absolutely sprang into his outstretched arms.

'The old man showed me how his companion clasped it ...'[28]

After prolonging his account of the extraordinary bird with other instances of comparatively recent survivals Skirving returned to the subject of his visit to St Kilda. He had roamed 'over a portion of the chief Island', looked at the church, and met the 'poor wretched specimen of a Free Church Minister'. He had looked into the houses, purchased eggs and other goods, and then returned to go aboard the *Dunara Castle*. 'While doing so a furious altercation took place between the male natives and the crew of the steamer. The subject was trifling about who should put us on board, the ships crew with their boats or the natives in hope of mere gain.' Skirving, as usual, was not impressed, although, since he probably lacked Gaelic, he may not have fully grasped what was going on. 'The steamer had free of expense taken their largest boat off with them last year to get it repaired and had now brought it back to them mended free of expense but the rude mercenary brutal Islanders gave no thanks but furious abuse. The crew of the steamer ultimately drove them off declaring they would thrash every mothers son of them if they were farther provoked.'

Skirving, whose first impression of St Kilda from the sea had not come up to expectations, was if anything disappointed with the place; but his condemnation of 'the rude mercenary brutal Islanders' contrasts strikingly with Emily MacLeod's concern for them, with the 'keen, bright eyes' bespeaking intelligence noticed by MacDiarmid, and with the attentive, hospitable neighbours among whom John Sands had lived only four years previously. As so often with descriptions of St Kilda, and of other islands, the writing reveals more about the writer than about the subject, and such a contrast, by no means unique in St Kilda history, makes it difficult to accept at face value any pronouncements upon the character of the inhabitants. It comes as no surprise therefore that Skirving's final comments, based on an acquaintance with the scene of only a few hours and with individuals of no more than minutes, should be entirely unsympathetic and intolerant:

> 'The inhabitants in everything save their rock exploits are as miserable a set of men as we may meet with in Europe. Poor ignorant ill-natured avaricious creatures, unable to take advantage of the civilization now offered them. They are also the degraded slaves of one of the most contemptible beings I ever saw – their <u>cretin</u> like minister. I asked this man if living in such a remote solitude where wild birds were the most numerous inhabitants, and the chief objects of animated nature he saw around him, did he take any interest in them and he answered "<u>Na</u>".'

Rev. MacKay's answer seems appropriate enough in the circumstances. Even if he had taken a great interest in the birds he might sensibly have responded in the same way. And 'civilization', as manifested in the behaviour of curious visitors, may not always have appeared an attractive prospect.

*

The unattractive R Scott Skirving had not long departed St Kilda's shores when Rev. MacKay requested from Fletcher Menzies of the HASS a supply of oatmeal which, he suggested, could be sent 'by the Dunara steamer to Dunvegan, Skye, care of Mr John MacKenzie, Postmaster, who will bring it here with the other supplies in the latter end of August'. The severe bout of 'visitor's cold' noticed by the *Dunara Castle*'s passengers in June had confined most of the islanders to bed for much longer than usual. 'They have done nothing this summer for their families,' MacKay reported, 'owing to this trying visitation. They say that they can't do much work, owing to their weakness and want of strength.' When the landlord heard of this request he did not at first believe that there was a real need for the meal, since the people were in his view 'by far the richest of their class in the whole of the Highlands'. Unnecessary aid, he said, merely demoralised its recipients, and 'the people of St Kilda are I am sorry to say in a state of rapid deterioration'. On what evidence he was able to state this is not clear but presumably it was the accounts of the place given by visitors and particularly by the factor MacKenzie. Two weeks later he seems to have changed his mind as he then asked Menzies to write to the minister and tell him to give a double share of the meal to 'old Donald McQuien, who is really an object of Charity', though the rest of the community had plenty. At about this time old Donald died, taking with him his memories of how he helped to capture the last garefowl of St Kilda.[29]

An interest in birds, plants and cliff climbing brought another naturalist of a kind rather different from Skirving to the island in 1881. As it was the minister's task to receive visitors with a handshake as they landed it may be assumed that John MacKay welcomed ashore Richard M Barrington from County Wicklow. Barrington had some acquaintance with island communities. In 1879 he had been to the Blasket islands where the people 'speak hardly any English but are friendly and hospitable when taken rightly – though they pelted our boats with stones from the cliffs last year thinking <u>at first</u> we might be process servers'. Soon the mistake was realised. 'Poor people they nearly embraced us afterwards when we gave them some tobacco.' In reaching St Kilda he enjoyed the comforts of the *Dunara Castle* but he could only make one of the voyages with her as he stayed in the island for three weeks. Writing to his friend J A Harvie Brown in July 1911 he recollected that early adventure in the steamer: 'Dont I know the Dunara Castle, well, god bless me – is she alive still – for she took me to St Kilda 30 years ago – or from it – I forget which. Old David McBrayne was alive then – and offered to send her to St Kilda for me specially – if "marooned" – for £30 from Obbe.'[30]

While there Barrington explored a great deal, getting to 'Soa', 'Borrera', 'the Doon' and 'all the neighbouring Stacks' except for 'Stack a-Lii and Stack-an-Narmin'. He is reputed to have been the first person to camp in St Kilda and in Rona, but the weather was not suitable for that way of staying on the former and 'the floor of the tent after three weeks walking on it was a puddle'. His greatest achievement was his climbing, in the company of two islanders, an extremely difficult rock tower in the channel below Soa: 'Stack-a-Biorach I climbed being the great feat of St Kilda – and never shall I forget its difficulty or the <u>guillimots</u> on its summit.' Such expeditions were not easy to arrange. 'I found the natives sluggish and difficult to rouse from their own ways – to undertake boating expeditions on my account.' There was of course no reason why 'the natives' should be eager to launch a boat and risk the dangers of currents, tides and changeable weather, but reluctantly or not they did help him. On the main island as elsewhere 'I scaled the cliffs in company with the natives and caught the birds as they did', and he took Leach's petrels and their eggs from the huts on Borera and from Dun, but in spite of spending three or four days trying to shoot St Kilda wrens for specimens he failed to get any. Three decades later he told Harvie Brown of his attempts to reach fulmars: 'On St Kilda they preferred ledges on Conacher (1400 feet) which were projecting and were 2 or 3 feet wide. I went over this face on various occasions – with the natives in 1881.' His conclusion regarding his relationship with the people was markedly different from many others: 'after a time we became great friends'.[31]

The exploits of naturalists – Elwes, Skirving, Barrington and numerous others after them – formed one of the means by which attention was shifted away from the reality of community life on St Kilda towards whatever there was about the island to satisfy the wider interests and curiosity of the 'outside world'. The church, with its concentration on the spiritual and moral condition of the people, had for good or ill claimed a central position in the progress of the island and had kept eyes focused on 'the natives' themselves until at least the years of Neil MacKenzie's ministry. Now in the 1880s, so far as dominating influences and most descriptions were concerned, everything had changed, and it had become far more difficult to recognise the main concerns of the islanders lying beyond the intentions and impressions of those who came to look with wonder and astonishment at their climbing performances on the cliffs or to shoot razorbills and wrens.

New experiences for the St Kilda people now seemed to happen every year, varying in kind but each one adding a slender thread of dependence and attachment to realms over the sea. The island was now no prison. News reached it even if late and tourists keen to see an imagined relic of primitive society must have been disappointed to find that there were more inhabitants of thatched houses in other islands and on the mainland than in St Kilda. Perhaps there was disappointment too in the discovery that the 'simple natives' were not ready to give their tweed and birds' eggs away for nothing. From steamer crews, Lewis fishermen and Harris shopkeepers information was received in the island without visitors and writers being aware of it, and the enduring islanders moved ahead of the outsider's imagined picture of them.

In 1881 the steamer *St Clair* was replaced by the *Hebridean* which, like the *Dunara Castle*, made two trips to St Kilda each summer. In 1882 the *Hebridean* went three times. With the factor's boat also calling twice the people now enjoyed up to six deliveries of mail within four months, but then there were none for the rest of the year. Few letters were sent or received, and communication by steamer did not necessarily occur at times of most need so that it was still occasionally the case that a St Kilda boat had to make an emergency voyage to Tarbert or Dunvegan. Often enough after a long rough journey out to the island it was impossible to land and boats and steamers had either to wait out in open waters or turn and go back. Neither Malcolm Ferguson nor any of his fellow-passengers on the *Dunara Castle* could land in June 1882 owing to the stormy conditions which almost swamped an island boat that put out to meet the steamer. John MacKenzie the factor, 'with several tradesmen who were to remain on the island for a time, to do some repairs on the cottages, etc.', along with the church and manse damaged by severe weather the previous November, had to return without achieving anything. The Marquis of Ailsa, 'dressed in a plain light Tweed suit', who had arrived at Tarbert by yacht and spent Sunday in the hotel, insisted that he was going to land and along with an English gentleman managed to get into the island boat 'against the advice and entreaties of their friends', but had to return without success. Seemingly put off by bad weather at Dunvegan, Emily MacLeod, who had boarded the ship there 'with a lot of luggage' as she intended to remain in St Kilda for some time, disembarked almost immediately, but with her friend Miss Ashley crossed the Minch in a steam yacht and joined the *Dunara Castle* again at Tarbert. Miss Ashley proved to be the only passenger who was not seasick. She 'continued busy sketching the whole time we were about the islands, an active nice-looking young lady, who, I understand, spends a good deal of her time in her steam yacht'. Both these ladies also had to give up hopes of landing, and Ferguson himself was especially disappointed as he was aware that he 'had a considerable number of namesakes among the St.Kildans … and was curious to find out if any of them were distant kinsmen'. It was one of innumerable such frustrating situations, but of much greater importance and risk to the island crew who were out in a rough sea and for a time unable to reach the shore.[32]

*

Though she was unable to land in St Kilda in 1882 Emily MacLeod managed to send Rev. MacKay a note from 'the Dunara Steamer', letting him know that in response to a letter from him in May the HASS had agreed to arrange for the construction of a boat to replace the one lost at the island during the gale in November 1881. The island men, said MacKay, 'are longing much to get a sight of their new boat, rigged with jib, and mainsail', which was to be sent, like the meal, to Mr MacKenzie, factor, at Dunvegan. In due course it arrived with the *Hebridean*, but the young men were greatly disappointed, as the minister wrote to the HASS secretary, Fletcher Menzies:

'They are much indebted to you, for the agreeable manner by which you answer their letters, when applied to you, in needful cases, which they appreciate much in a gentleman of quality, such as you are. But they are sorry to say, that the boat is far from being suitable for the Island'.

It was too shallow and too small.

'They have boats enough for going to the adjacent Islands for birds and fishing about the Island, but they especially wanted this boat for going to the mainland, in cases of emergency. They would have gone to the mainland in April last, for a supply of Provisions, had they a boat to serve the purpose. Now, my dear Sir, I hope this will not cause any difference between you, and the poor people on this solitary Island. I must honestly say, that this boat is quite useless to the people for the purpose intended by them.'[33]

At the same time the factor and his employer were beginning to lose patience with the islanders and their minister. MacKenzie, along with his tradesmen and building material, returned to St Kilda with the *Dunara Castle* on her second trip to the island on 27 July 1882. 'I was much annoyed to find on my arrival there,' he reported to MacLeod, '... that the people had sold all their cattle to a Harris man who went there for the purpose, and gave an advance of 2s or 3s a head over last year; (as he might well do). If the stupid people had only waited I would have given them an advance of 10s a head.' Perhaps this was written in self-defence; but MacKenzie suggested that a message from MacLeod as landlord, rather like that six years previously, might be worthwhile:

'Your letter to the Ground Officer some time ago having had such a beneficial effect, I have been thinking it might be advisable that you should write to the Tenants now, expressing surprise at their selling their cattle to a man who had no interest whatever in their welfare beyond his own personal gain, and who took their cattle at less than (this years) market value, thus injuring themselves and breaking their agreement with you at the same time.'

A lack of return from island produce generally also put the factor out of temper, and he probably found the excuse for dealing with the Harris man somewhat irritating:

'This season the cloth has not been selling so well. The feathers were lost, and the cattle were put past us, so that the oil and a small quantity of fish is all we have to look to.

'The letting of the Castle [at Dunvegan] which they learned from the passengers on board the "Hebridian" appears to have had an injurious effect upon the Islanders. When I questioned them about selling their cattle they answered at great length, all to the effect that they thought as the Castle was let matters must have gone wrong, that I would not be sent there any more, and that they would be forgotten and neglected, but at the same time I could see with a forlorn hope that under the circumstances of being thus overlooked the Island might through some unaccountable cause ultimately fall to themselves. I left, assuring them, that their ideas were altogether erroneous.'[34]

The complications of managing St Kilda were again evident. Monopoly control, reliance upon supplies from the factor or landlord, freedom to trade, size of boats, an adequate landing place, ability to fish out at sea, all matters that had been fiercely raised by John Sands, were now accompanied by the effect of steamers and tourists on the island economy and what this might mean for rent levels and prices. These were issues which were really none of the minister's business but because they were of the utmost importance to the community and because the minister's position was also central Rev. John MacKay was involved, and where formerly he had tended to take the side of the landlord he now began to change his attitude.

Only a few days after his previous communication on his visit to St Kilda in late July MacKenzie wrote again to MacLeod, even more upset. This time there were two subjects for complaint:

'I am really at my "Wits ends" as to how those people can best be managed.

'Public interference hampers firm measures, while too much indulgence as in our case is imposed upon. In my former letter I suggested that the people should be written to, offering to bring the existing agreement to a termination; casting before them the fact that they prefer giving the benefits of their produce to others rather than to their proprietor. And at the same time it would be as well to write to the Ground Officer to say that if the tenants of St Kilda made up their minds to deal with outsiders instead of their proprietor that his services as G.O. would no longer be required. Also that whoever took the feathers and fish, or rather whoever used the store for preserving those commodities would be charged £5 or perhaps £10 a year of rent. That they might if they liked have Dune at a rent of 1s a sheep, but Soa you would keep for yourself.

'They are most anxious to get hold of Soa, only they wont pay rent for it, because it is so unaccessable they think it will fall to themselves if they make it unprofitable through neglect.

'I am afraid too, - that of late the minister has been playing a double game.

'For some time past I have been noticing that he has been losing ground with the people, and to recover his influence with them he has all of a sudden taken up the position of pleader and sympathizer, and he has become just as low, and as great a beggar as any of them, that the people like and admire.

'The passengers on board the "Dunara" were very much disgusted with him, and I am sure none of them would lose more by a change of arrangements than he would, and on that account he might perhaps be written to also.

'The people are so elated with the number of trips the steamers have made to the Island this year that they are difficult to hold.'[35]

The proprietor was in Austria when he received this second letter. In reply he sent MacKenzie copies of the messages he had immediately addressed to the islanders, including the ground officer, and, apparently, to the minister. Part of the latter contained a firm request:

'As it thus appears that these foolish men have no trust in their proprietor, let them try, if they can do better without him. You will please tell them [that] when they enter into an engagement it is their Christian duty to keep it, that I am very much displeased and that unless they express their regret for their conduct, I will only send once a year to collect the Rent and take no further Interest in their welfare. I shall also feel obliged if you will read to them the Letter I have addressed to them and to the ground officer.'

The letter to 'my people of St Kilda' – as if he owned them as well as the land – played upon their feelings of insecurity and isolation, and recalled, with threatening overtones, the communication read by MacKay in the presence of Sands:

'I am greatly surprised and annoyed to hear, that you have sold all your Cattle to a Harris man, who has no interest in you except for his own profit, and who has given you less than this years market Value. You have not only done this foolish thing to your own loss, but you have broken your engagement to me. You promised to keep the produce of the Island for my Vessel, which goes there for your advantage, and I only send her on condition, that the whole of the produce is kept for her. I was informed lately by my sister, that you had acknowledged gratefully my kindness to you and also that of Mr MacKenzie, and this is the return we get. It would serve you quite right, if I were to leave you to find a market for [the sale?] not of your Cattle only, but your cloth, and your oil and feathers which it is extremely difficult to sell. You know quite well that unless your Proprietor takes an Interest in you, nobody else will, except to visit you sometimes for their own profit. Situated as you are you may rest assured, that you must have some one who is specially interested in your welfare but at the same time if you wish as would seem to be the Case, to sell your own produce I give you free leave to do so in future but it must be the whole. In that Case those who require the store for storing their produce will pay yearly £10 for its use. You can have the Dune at the rate of 1s per sheep, and Soay will remain in my own hands unless you agree to pay an adequate Rent for it. Let me hear what you decide that I may know whether to send to you next spring or not.

'The ground officer at St Kilda is informed that if the tenants there make up their minds to sell the produce of the Island without my assistance, and buy what they want themselves, his services as ground officer will no longer be required, and those who use the store for feathers oil or fish will have to pay a duty of £10 for it.'[36]

Composed by MacLeod as if he were a sort of commercial clan chief lecturing his children, the letter, it would seem, had the desired effect; and, apart from reading it out, Rev. MacKay featured no further in the dispute. When, in the following June, the 'Crofters Commission' came to St Kilda, Donald MacDonald, one of the island crofters and fishermen, was asked among other things about cattle. It was clear that the proprietor, through his factor, was the sole purchaser. The price paid, said MacDonald, varied; it was fixed by MacKenzie who would add a shilling or so sometimes 'when we are complaining'. Possibly the sale to the Harris man had such a beneficial result for the islanders.[37]

*

On Saturday 2 June 1883 at 6 a.m. HMS *Lively* steamed out of West Loch Tarbert bound for St Kilda. On board were six Royal Commissioners of Inquiry, who were in the midst of their task of investigating the condition and circumstances of crofters and cottars in the Highlands and islands. Two days earlier, when they had been busy taking evidence in Harris, the weather had been so rough 'as almost to induce the Commissioners to abandon the idea of visiting the island', but there was a great improvement on Friday 'and the voyage was an exceedingly pleasant one to those who were not rendered uncomfortable by the long, rolling swell of the Atlantic'.[38]

The commanding officer, Captain Parr, brought his vessel to anchor in the bay at 12.30 p.m. and soon afterwards the commissioners, led by their chairman, Lord Napier and Ettrick, went ashore where they were greeted by the minister and a number of islanders. It was immediately decided that a meeting should be held in the church, and 'after a short preliminary talk over the election of delegates' – much to the surprise of the St Kilda people who knew nothing about the Commission and had received no warning of the party's approach – Rev. MacKay opened proceedings with a prayer. He was also a delegate, the first to be questioned, which was only to be expected in the case of a man who had long been accepted as an island spokesman. But the commissioners were not contented with the minister alone.

MacKay was able to make brief, often positive but sometimes rather incomplete and evasive, comments in response to most of the questions put to him. He remarked on communications, or the lack of them, and on a wide range of St Kilda topics about which the commissioners must have learned something before they came. The school was kept up regularly 'by a woman, Miss McKinlay', who was also nurse. Pupils were making good progress in learning English under her guidance, and MacKay himself continued to instruct the class every Sunday evening in reading the Gaelic bible. The people were, in his opinion, better off both materially and morally than they were when he arrived in the island eighteen years previously, but they were often set a bad example by some of the visitors and did not much like strangers. 'When the steamers come here do they do any mischief by the sale of liquors or any other way?' asked the chairman. 'I don't think it. Some of these passengers are very loose in their character, and some of them are drunk when they come ashore, but the people avoid them as far as they can.' Did the visits do any other harm? Well, said the minister, they were 'very annoying' when they delivered tourists who stayed on the island through the Sabbath. 'What do they do?' 'They go about the hills, and go seeing through the windows and striking the dogs and one thing and another.'

John MacKay told how in April 1883 some of the men 'had to go to Skye in a small boat, or fishing-boat, which they got from Mr Young' for food supplies. But for the most part he left practical matters of that kind to the two other delegates, young St Kilda men in their mid thirties called Donald MacDonald and Angus Gillies. They answered questions on rents, fishing, fowling, boats, the need for a pier; and Gillies spoke of how, following the deprivations of the recent winter and spring, 'We went in that little boat I have mentioned to the factor at Dunvegan, and he sent over a vessel with meal for us. We could not bring it in the little boat ourselves. I believe there were very few people in any of the Western Islands that would have undertaken the risk we did.' It seems probable that MacDonald and Gillies were chosen to represent the community because they were more fluent than others in speaking English. Neither of them knew anything about a certain 'movable cross' that had existed in St Kilda in ages past.

It is to some extent surprising that the commissioners should have ventured out for their afternoon of examination in such a remote place. Their questions reveal that they already had in mind one or two possible solutions to what they had heard were the island's problems. No mention was made of emigration except for a question about the 1852 episode. There might perhaps be a means of conveying mail during the eight months when no steamer or other vessel was scheduled to call. A pier would surely be a great improvement, as it would allow an extension to the fishing, and a new, larger, half-decked boat could then be useful. By this stage of their whole Inquiry the commissioners were accustomed to hearing complaints, as one of them, Sheriff Nicolson, indicated: 'We have had complaints laid before us in Skye, and the other islands we have been in, as to the smallness of the quantity of land that is in the hands of the crofters. Have you any such complaint?' The answer was probably obvious enough before it was uttered. 'We have none, because the proprietor can give us no more than we have except the little island which he has for his sheep.' The little island was probably Soay, but even though the islanders wanted it there was no complaint about that nor about prices or anything else.[39]

The investigation over, the commissioners then behaved like tourists and so suddenly appeared less odd. There was time for them to visit the houses, distribute a large quantity of gifts including tea, tobacco, gaily-coloured handkerchiefs and shawls, and sweeties, and buy stockings, cloth and other 'native produce'. They even went up the hill and sat at the edge of a cliff to watch 'the mode in which the sea birds are taken'. Then they had to hurry back to the *Lively* and at 9 p.m. the vessel 'started on her return voyage, making, however, a trip round the island before finally taking leave of it, so as to afford a glimpse of the wild and beetling crags by which it is engirdled'. At around 4 o'clock on Sunday morning they came into West Loch Tarbert whence they had left less than 24 hours earlier, pleased as much by the entertaining sights as by the business success of their expedition.[40]

A short while later the St Kilda factor, John MacKenzie, read the evidence given to Lord Napier and his colleagues and submitted a few comments. He noted especially two omissions by those examined. Rev. MacKay had not mentioned that he was in charge of a medicine chest 'and that he himself is possessed of some skill in the proper dispensing of those medicines', while Angus Gillies had failed to state that, in addition to meal, flour, seed oats and potatoes had been recently supplied, the last, 'by Miss McLeod's special orders', provided at half price or 5s a barrel, 'she undertaking to pay the other half out of her own private means'. MacKenzie was convinced that, given the provision of the right facilities and the existence of the appropriate determination, 'Prosperity lies before the St Kildeans in the fishing occupation'.[41]

CHAPTER 3
The impact of the 'outside world'

In 1857 F W L Thomas, lieutenant in command of the survey vessel *Woodlark* and working along the coast of Harris, went ashore when time allowed to explore the nearer antiquities and to take photographs of places and people; at St Kilda in 1860 he pursued the same interests and was possibly the first to use a camera on the island. Some twenty years later, in the mid 1880s, professional photographers with improved though still cumbersome equipment made a fuller record of the St Kilda scene. From these early pictures, some of them now very familiar, island faces look out, the history of thought and feeling behind them hidden today and the inherited traditions and songs, long submerged beneath biblical devotion, mostly lost for ever. However interesting they may be the photographs also bring to mind the intrusive curiosity with which the tourist went around 'seeing through windows' and gazing at the 'natives'.

Alexander Ross, an Inverness architect, made a visit to St Kilda in June 1884, taking with him 'Mr McWhirter, R.A., and Mr Whyte, photographer, Inverness'. They travelled there on the steam yacht owned by Henry Evans, a gentleman who used to call at the island frequently and formed his own lively opinions about what he found there. On this occasion the yacht was greeted from a distance by the usual crowd, including the minister and the newly-appointed teacher. Four men came out in one of the island boats, and, with one of them on board as a pilot, the visitors then set off to wonder at and photograph the cliffs. Outside the bay there was more obvious movement in the sea so that 'some doubt was expressed as to our being able to do much', especially when Mr Whyte began to feel seasick. 'However, by a strong effort, he conquered, and set to work in right earnest.' A balancing mechanism to offset the motion of the yacht was brought into action, the tripod fixed, and soon 'view after view was taken with great facility'. After four hours sailing they anchored in 'the East Bay' for the night. Ross was adept at the old habit of inventing or using English placenames which were not even translations of Gaelic originals. He wrote of 'the Dun(e) Island', 'South Bay', 'North Bay', 'East Bay', 'High Street', 'Amazon Glen' and 'the West Glen', all as foreign to the island as Mr Whyte's photographic equipment.[42]

Next morning the party landed and climbed to a vantage point from which, Ross recorded, 'Mr McWhirter made some lovely drawings, Mr Whyte photographed, while I made my geological notes and collections, occasionally indulging in a water colour or pencil sketch'. Then Whyte and McWhirter went on 'a second cruise' while Ross, like an explorer in Africa, 'determined to see something of the interior and people'.

He visited the houses first of all, remarking on wooden locks, diet, marriage, and 'the iron and zinc roofs, which remain till this day, an eyesore and a disfigurement to the island'. He next 'struck up the face of Oschival, accompanied by Mr Kenneth Campbell, schoolmaster, a very intelligent and obliging young gentleman, who has volunteered to stay and teach the young St Kildians during the ensuing winter'. They crossed over Conachair into the glen and back by 'the shoulder of Mullach More'.

On Campbell's invitation Ross witnessed eight boys and nine girls 'at their lessons in school'. When the time for buying island 'curiosities' arrived Ross acquired 'an old St Kilda lamp of stone' and Whyte 'one of their copper brooches', the latter article made by hammering out a penny or halfpenny.

Five months after their visit, on 17 December 1884, Ross and Whyte gave an illustrated lecture to the Inverness Scientific Society and Field Club. Whyte projected his photographs 'by means of the oxy-hydrogen light', and the audience enjoyed seeing them: 'Most of these views were very fine and clear, marvellously beautiful and effective to have been taken, as they were, on board the yacht, and therefore on a surface never quite free from motion.' When the talk was eventually published as a paper in the Society's transactions two of Ross's sketches appeared, showing the islands of the group, and two of Whyte's photographs, one with men, women and children posed outside a house in the 'street', the other a more distant view, from the east, of the store, manse, church and line of houses below the steep hillslopes. Writing in November 1884 the yacht owner, Henry Evans, expressed his admiration for the quality of Whyte's pictures of Skye scenes, presumably taken on the same expedition: 'I have just received Whytes Skye photographs. They are splendid and you would appreciate them ..' Evans also received a letter from Ross on the subject of St Kilda geology which had been the architect's principal interest when in the island. Today, unfortunately, few of Whyte's negatives or photographs taken prior to 1890 seem to survive, many having been destroyed and buried underground. However, his picture of Ann MacKinlay 'in a group with some St Kildans and the Schoolmaster of that year – Mr Campbell', along with those published with the lecture, is a welcome exception.[43]

Skirving had dismissed the people of St Kilda as rude, mercenary and brutal; Ross four years later saw them, on an equally limited acquaintance, as 'good-looking, healthy, and intelligent'. Similarly, messages of distress or food shortages from the island contrasted with Ross's impression that 'On the whole, the people live well' and his quotation of a ridiculous remark from an improbable Skye man 'who had been often on the island for various lengths of time': '"They are the best fed people in creation. I speak the truth, master."' Such contradictions or differences of opinion, reflecting the limitations of the observer rather than those of the observed, mostly show that statements from visitors in this period can rarely be taken as a certain guide to the actual situation. On the other hand another of Ross's conclusions regarding the state of the islanders may be rather more accurate regarding changes occurring in the 1880s. He remarked that 'the people have learned the value of money, and to enjoy many of the luxuries of civilized life ... they are learning to depend too much on their visitors, and really look on as their rights what the kindness of yachtsmen may lead them to give them'. Ross was probably right here. 'Indeed,' he added, 'they run a great risk of being spoiled by the visitors who go there in considerable numbers annually.' MacLeod of MacLeod, writing to Lord Napier on 29 October 1884, disapproved of a proposed gift to St Kilda of a boat and herring nets for this reason: 'I really think they will have boats enough. It is quite right they should have herringnets, but they are well able to pay for them themselves. The many gifts they receive have already quite demoralized them!' But no one seemed to weigh up what 'spoiling' or 'demoralizing' the people might mean or what the significance for the future might be.[44]

*

Messages from St Kilda caused the greatest stir over the next two years and aroused an interest and concern which was reminiscent of the Sands commotion ten years earlier. They began with a letter to the landlord, MacLeod of MacLeod, from the tenants of the island. Three tenants, Donald MacDonald, Malcolm MacKinnon and Neil MacKinnon, allowed their names to appear as signatures 'in name and by appointment' of the rest alongside their marks, the whole communication being evidently written by Rev. John MacKay who added a covering note. The arrival of the factor on 3 June 1885, the day before this letter was written, seems to have been the occasion of the appeal made in it for what amounted to a reduction in rent. It was claimed that too much was being paid for sheep and 'that the land has become so unfruitful' that as a consequence 'we have to buy more meal for our families' while potato crops were 'almost a perfect failure'. The letter also drew attention to a genuine problem now apparent in the balance of the population: 'the old men on the island can do nothing for themselves, they are only assisted by the young men. The most of the men on the island are from 60 to 80 years of age. Two of the young men who were wont to be fishing with us are talking of going to Australia and an old man which will be a great loss to us as we are already short of able bodied men.' In his accompanying note to MacLeod Rev. MacKay emphasised the implication intended in the possible emigration: 'I hope you will be good enough to grant to your poor tenants their humble request, and that you will not allow them to be scattered to the four winds of Heaven.' But MacLeod was not persuaded and in his reply dismissed the appeal to his generosity:

'I have just received your Letter of the 4th of June and also that which

592

you have written for the St Kilda people. From the purport of the latter it is evident that Hugh Gillis has done his best to raise a discontented spirit in the Island which I very much regret. You appear to think, that the people should have a deduction of Rent. I can assure you however that the present Rent is ridiculously low, and you may believe me, that with such a discontented spirit any Rent at all would be more than they would like to pay. As to the poor people being scattered to the four winds it is with no wish of mine that some of them seem inclined to seek their fortune in other lands. I suppose it must be that they are acting on the advice of Hugh Gillis but if they choose to go I cannot prevent them. They are free to do what they please. Hoping that you will use your Influence in favor of the existence of kindly feelings between the tenants and myself.'

At the same time as he wrote these observations to John MacKay MacLeod also responded directly 'To the people of St Kilda'. He commented on payment for sheep, on the right to take birds from the cliffs, and on the prices charged for various supplies taken to the island. 'It is not difficult to see,' he said, 'that some foolish and ignorant person has been trying to set you all against your Proprietor, and there is no doubt it must be Hugh Gilles. May God forgive him for such wickedness.' Agreeing that the shortage of young men was indeed regrettable but pointing out that it was 'a circumstance I cannot help', MacLeod concluded his message with a declaration and piece of advice: 'my desire is to do everything in my power for your advantage, and pray do not listen to any person who wants to sow discord between you and me.'[45]

From the proprietor's point of view this reply to the three St Kilda men who had signed on behalf of the community, including its appeal to God's forgiveness, seemed to achieve its intended effect, just as his previous letters of disapproval had done, and presumably the minister felt it wise not to pursue the issue further with MacLeod. But the islanders were not satisfied, and in two months raised the rent matter again in different quarters. However, there was no renewed threat of going to Australia, and the apparently troublesome Gillies became the island's most unpopular individual, apart, perhaps, from the minister's housekeeper.

MacLeod's 'Hugh Gillis', more commonly known as Ewen Gillies, was one of those who emigrated to Australia in 1852 and survived. During his subsequent erratic career and many travels, nothing of which can have inspired confidence in the worthwhileness of removing to the southern hemisphere, he returned to St Kilda twice, but in the end he went to Canada for the last years of his life.

*

Information came again from St Kilda in August 1885 with another newspaper article which was not in the least disturbing though it helped to maintain public interest in the place.[46]

Dunara Castle left Greenock on the evening of 23 July 1885 for her usual journey north through the islands and out to St Kilda. She called at Colonsay, belonging to Sir John MacNeil 'of Soudan fame', Oban, Tobermory, Coll and Tiree, then crossed to Barra and South Uist, came in to Skye, and reached Tarbert in Harris where she tied up for the Sabbath. Warning that the steamer was about to visit had been given to the St Kilda people by a yacht party a week before, and they had expected her arrival almost immediately. The passengers managed six hours ashore, and after their safe return to the Clyde one of them, J A Clarke, became the author of what now seems the inevitable newspaper account describing their adventure. He came to the conclusion that no one who wished to enjoy the wild scenery of the west could do better than take a trip in 'the steady sea-going and admirably managed steamer the Dunara Castle'.

Clarke's article, containing an independence of opinion not always apparent in such writing, was full of familiar detail, much of which came from Hugh McCallum who had been on the island for just over a month and who on this occasion acted as 'our guide and interpreter'. There was also in it an evident but unacknowledged reliance upon the work of John Sands. The visitors found that only three people could speak English fluently, the minister, Mrs McKinlay, and McCallum himself – a 'young man acting in the capacity of teacher'. There was as well 'a native youth' who could manage to make himself understood in English. In general the inhabitants seemed healthy, much more so than expected, 'so close has been the intermarrying amongst them'; many were 'rather pleasant-looking' but though 'some of the younger women are even pretty, with sparkling eyes and expressive countenances', a few of the older people 'did not impress one so favourably'.

From the women purchases were made of cloth, stockings, socks, eggs, live and dead birds, and 'a curious native brooch made out of a halfpenny beaten thin'. A performance by 'the cragsmen' followed, some of the birds caught were sold to the onlookers, and then the climbers 'asked that a collection be made by way of payment for the exhibition of daring of which we had just been witnesses'. It was thus obvious to the strangers that the islanders 'are speedily acquiring the customs of the inner world' – that is, the outer, mainland world from which good things for the island were supposed to come. Variable sums were asked for the brooch; one was sold for 2d, another for 6d, and in a third case 1s was asked by 'an old dame, who rather overdid the thing, and thus lost her would-be customer'. This interest in making a sale rather surprised the writer. 'An impression prevails in the minds of many,' he noted with some sympathy, 'that the St Kildians know not the value of money, and that they would be just as well pleased to receive a penny as a shilling; but from personal experience we can positively affirm the contrary.' It was indeed difficult for a visitor to see what use could be made of money, but 'we were told that there was a collection at church every Sunday, that they gave £8 yearly to foreign missions (!!), and that they gave no less than £30 yearly to the Sustentation Fund – from which fund comes their pastor's stipend – besides, they like to have a little cash in the hands of their banker, the minister, for the proverbial rainy day, we suppose'. An interest in money, at least as old as the early eighteenth century, was connected also with the sale of produce, the purchase of stock and supplies, and the levels of rent; and the *Dunara Castle*'s passengers heard something of the recent appeal to the landlord: 'Whether the crofters' agitation of the neighbouring islands has reached St Kilda we cannot say, but we were told that the factor had experienced some difficulty this year in getting his rent.' The outcome of the petition for a rent reduction was as yet as unknown on board the steamer as the state of possible crofting unrest.[47]

The buildings, from church to cottages, attracted Clarke's attention. He thought them all 'comfortless in the extreme' and utterly different from what he was accustomed to. He was especially interested in the church: 'People living in such a city as Glasgow can form no idea of what the St. Kildian church is like internally from anything they have seen of a similar nature around their own doors, the poorest looking mission church in Glasgow being almost a palace in comparison ..' In spite of the inhospitable interior, however, all the people, except for infants, the very old and the infirm, attended every service, which meant the three Sunday meetings, the Wednesday prayer meeting and the extra monthly Otter celebration. 'All the people are very religious, many of them truly pious. They have family worship in their homes every morning and evening, and when the men go to the fishing they take their Bibles with them, and always make a point of returning in time for the Wednesday's prayer meeting, and on Saturday evening to allow plenty of time for preparation for the Sabbath.' The 'plain stone and slated cottage' occupied by Rev. MacKay was not much more comfortable than the church, and was 'presided over by a somewhat self-important, strong-willed housekeeper, who perhaps, next to the minister, is the most important personage upon the island'. Clarke probably did not have the time to meet the elders.

He did meet John MacKay and formed a favourable impression of him:

'It is but right and proper ... that our attention should first be directed to the guide, philosopher, and friend of the St Kildians, the minister, the Rev. Mr. MacKay. He is a stoutish, short-set man, evidently about 60 years of age. He is a bachelor, and this, coupled with the secluded life that he leads, must have much to do with the peculiarity in his manner. It is 20 years since Mr Mackay came to the island, and for 18 years he has not been away from it. The minister made himself very free with the visitors, shaking hands with each and all, and did his best to make our stay agreeable. Mr Mackay is a strict Sabbatarian, and as Sabbath begins with him at 6 p.m. on Saturday and does not end till 12 p.m. on Sabbath, those who should visit the island between these hours find the minister almost inaccessible. He does not show himself, and it is only by calling upon him and as a special favour that he will give an audience to anyone. Luckily for us our visit was paid on a week-day, and thus as we did not encroach upon his Sabbath we found him all that we could wish.'

The return voyage in 'splendid weather' left Clarke with pleasant recollections of his trip, and he was neither a journalist nor a writer who looked to stir up controversy. But the relatively peaceful atmosphere of his visit was not to last, for in the autumn came disturbances which again raised doubts about the future of the St Kilda community.

*

On Saturday 12 September 1885 yet another in the unending line of Atlantic storms passed over the island. As its effects subsided Alexander Ferguson, about 12 or 13 years old at the time, tore a page out of a school exercise book and wrote a letter to his former teacher, Kenneth Campbell, now working in the west of Lewis:

'My Dear Sir – I am now going to write you a letter and sending her in one of the little ships in which we were sailing on the shore as you know to let you know all the knews. the men were building a house just a little house for the cows a great storm came on and all the corn and barley were swept away by the storm and one of the boats was swept away by the sea the men of St Kilda is nearly dead with the hunger. They send two boats from St Kilda to go to Haries not the fishing boats but little piece of wood like the little one which I send. I sent my best loves unto you – I am yours truly..'

The letter was addressed to 'Mr Kenneth Campbell, teacher, Uig, Lews, by Stornoway' and pushed into a small bottle, which in turn was placed in a wooden boat of the kind apparently invented by John Sands. By an extraordinary coincidence 'one of the rural letter-carriers in the Uig district of Lews' happened to pick up this little craft, which could have gone to Orkney or Norway, on a beach near Aird Uig and took it to the postmaster at Miavaig who forwarded a copy for publication to the *Northern Chronicle*. Presumably the original reached Kenneth Campbell.[48]

596

In due course Alexander Ferguson's letter appeared in print and aroused a response from the factor, John T MacKenzie, who tried to set minds at rest by questioning the real value of the 'Distressing Message from St Kilda'. He said first that only very recently 'the usual quantity of supplies, consisting of oatmeal, flour, groceries, salt, coals, and other commodities sufficient, with the crop of the island, to last the people till the month of April' had been safely delivered by the *Robert Hadden*, and that 'if the story of their corn being swept away is true' these supplies might run out about the end of the coming January. He then added:

> 'I have to remark that there is not a grown up person at St Kilda called "Alexander Ferguson" - there may be a boy of that name, but I am surprised that a boy should be employed to despatch such an important message, when there is a minister, a schoolmaster, and a ground officer in the island to look after the interest and welfare of its inhabitants, and they are all aware that a communication addressed to me would receive immediate attention.'[49]

Whatever its disastrous effects, the September storm seems to have presented to some of the people of St Kilda an opportunity to revive the complaint about rent. A petition, signed by a number of the inhabitants, was sent to the County or Land Assessor, its argument being that unfair charges were made 'for grazing for sheep which we do not possess' and for the birds caught 'in steep and high rocks at great danger to our lives'. When it came to be considered no one appeared to represent the islanders and so the appeal was dismissed. The *Inverness Courier* printed both the petition and the letter from Alexander Ferguson on 1 October 1885, and as a consequence MacLeod of MacLeod, no doubt after discussion with his factor, sought to defend himself as the proprietor once more. He admitted that the inhabitants might now have been charged for sheep they had lost, 'and as I always treat exceptionally these lonely people, surrounded as they are by the melancholy main, I shall certainly comply with the wish they have expressed'. But he stated that he had never asked the people 'to pay a penny' for either the birds themselves or the rocks on which they were caught.[50]

These attempts to allay public concern might have succeeded and the rent and storm have been forgotten had the petition and the message from the schoolboy been the only communications. This turned out not to be the case. On 16 September Rev. John MacKay wrote two letters, virtually identical in wording for the most part, in which he recorded how 'a great storm' had destroyed the crops of corn, barley and potatoes, and how one of the boats had been lost. He may have given them to the teacher for putting in the bottles, which were 'enclosed in a little boat made of a piece of plank'. One letter was addressed to Rev. Alexander MacColl, Free Church minister at

Lochalsh, the other to Dr Robert Rainy, principal of the Free Church College in Edinburgh. The boat was launched and was carried off by the currents and a strong westerly wind. Within two weeks it was found on the island of Taransay, from which the teacher there, Alexander Sutherland, sent the letters on to their intended recipients. On 29 September Sutherland had written a covering letter for each, the words being almost the same:

'I have just received the enclosed letter from one of the inhabitants of this island, and although apparently it was the writer's simple desire that the letter should be posted, I think it right that it should be known how the letter has reached the Post-office at this time of the year, as it has been sent off in a very unusual way.

'It was found yesterday (28th) by an old man while walking along the beach, and has evidently come from St Kilda, as it was carefully put into a little boat made of a thick plank about a yard in length, on which were the words cut deep into the wood – "St Kilda, Please open – Hugh Macallum".

'On opening a small hatch two bottles were found, in each of which was a letter, the enclosed being one. The little boat must have come in a very short time during the western gales of last week, as there was a sail set, and a heavy piece of iron nailed to the bottom, so that it could not be upset.

'The letter will be posted the first opportunity, though I fear a few days may elapse before a boat leaves our island'.

There cannot have been much delay, as both communications were received in only a week. MacColl despatched his letters to the *Inverness Courier*, asking for them to be inserted in the first possible issue thereafter. Rainy on the other hand promptly sent copies to Fletcher Menzies, the HASS secretary, in the hope of some helpful response. His letter to Menzies was dated 8 October 1885:

'I beg to enclose copies of two letters which reached me today by post.

'Both writers are known to me and the letters are undoubtedly genuine. Sutherland is a teacher in the service of the F.C. Ladies Association, and Mr MacKay is the resident minister.

'I am informed that the H. and A. Society have or lately had funds at their disposal applicable to St Kilda. May I ask you to submit to your Directors the question whether the emergency now described is not one in which those funds, if I am rightly informed as to their existence might be drawn upon to help the islanders.

'I have forwarded the original letters to the Home Secretary.'[51]

Once again the people of St Kilda had turned to their minister as the accepted means of communicating their sense of distress or discontent. The schoolboy's letter seems to have been by way of an extra. There is no sign that Rainy was upset by the directness of MacKay's, for the phrasing of which the island's elderly pastor was soon to be publicly criticised. 'You will be kind enough', MacKay had written to 'Rev. and Dear Dr' Rainy, 'to apply to Government in order to send us a supply of corn seen, barley, and potatoes.' He had visited all 'the 16 Crofts in the island in order that I might be able to judge for myself as to the extent of the loss of the crops... I can honestly say that I never saw anything that could come near to it'. The letter was evidently well-meant, and ended 'I sincerely hope you are well. I am afraid this will not reach you.'

Rainy treated the news from St Kilda very seriously, recognising that with winter approaching quickly there would be little or no chance to deliver emergency supplies before the existing store was exhausted. On 12 October he wrote again to the HASS secretary to say that he had been discussing the situation with the Glasgow businessman Sir William Collins 'who had previously consulted one or two persons qualified to advise' and who 'has had great experience of such cases in connection with more than one period of destitution'. As Sir William was 'extremely exact and businesslike' and 'knows the whole Hebrides, having been all round them in his own steam yacht', Rainy suggested to Menzies that he set aside a sum from the Kelsall Bequest fund and entrust it to Collins or authorise him to spend an equivalent amount, so that assistance could be given to St Kilda as soon as possible. It had been discovered that the steamer *Hebridean* would sail in three days for the islands and would call at Loch Roag in the west of Lewis, 'one of the nearest points to St Kilda'. From here she would try to land any cargo of supplies, an opportunity that ought not be neglected; besides, it was important that the people in St Kilda should know that the message had been delivered, otherwise they might risk their lives in trying to reach Harris or Lewis in one of their remaining small boats.[52]

Although the government and the proprietor had been informed of the apparent problem at St Kilda, Rainy and Collins, acting urgently on their own initiative and in conjunction with the HASS, were much the quicker with their response. Trusting to 'the charitable public' to assist in covering the costs, they arranged the supplies and got them on board the *Hebridean*, which was specially chartered to go out to the island as a 'relief ship' with quantities of oats, oatmeal, potatoes, tea and sugar. On Thursday 15 October the vessel left Glasgow. It was as usual in the charge of Captain McKechnie, but the owner, Captain McCallum, was also there, and so too was a 'special correspondent' of the *Glasgow Herald* called Robert Connell, to whom a remote and small population without communication for two thirds of the year was a total mystery:'It seems incredible that we should have such men for countrymen'.[53]

CHAPTER 4

The 'Special Correspondent', Robert Connell, and Rev. John Mackay

The chartered part of the *Hebridean's* voyage was permitted on condition that the weather was good enough, and so, in spite of the late season, it turned out to be. At first it was undecided 'when we should make the bold dash for St Kilda', and Captain McKechnie was a cautious man, but soon 'the smart little steamer darted out on the billows of the broad Atlantic', achieving her fourth and easiest trip to the island during 1885. The vessel arrived on the afternoon of the Sabbath and relief, in the shape of the various supplies, had to wait until after midnight. There was time therefore for the visitors to wander along 'inspecting the crofters' cottages' and 'learning many facts about the social economy of this singular community'. They were then able to accept the minister's rather surprising invitation to tea. Once the work started the task of unloading and transferring the goods to the shore was completed by 3 a.m., after which some of the islanders went aboard the *Hebridean* and in their turn inspected the interior fittings. 'The obliging master and officers did everything in their power,' wrote Connell, 'to make the poor people feel at home.'[54]

As the 'relief expedition' steamed back up the Clyde H.M.S. *Jackal* was leaving Rothesay Bay on yet another visit to St Kilda. In response to Dr Rainy's communication to the Home Secretary the government had resolved that the gunboat, in the charge of Commander Osborne, should leave at the earliest opportunity. With MacLeod away in Paris telegrams had been sent from Whitehall to the factor asking whether any action was being taken by the proprietor to alleviate distress, and from MacKenzie's reply it appeared that the matter was for the time being left in the hands of Sir William Collins who intended 'sending a steamer' shortly. MacKenzie also received a letter from Angus MacLeod, Commander R.N., of H.M.S. *Excellent* at Portsmouth. It was dated 16 October 1885 when Rainy and Collins were busy arranging for relief:

'I only heard this morning of the storm and destruction of crops in St Kilda, by means of a letter from Mr McKay, found at Barra in a bottle, and had seen nothing about it in the papers. I thought MacLeod of MacLeod owned the Island, but from a remark made in the "Standard" almost fancied it might now belong to some one else.

'Hearing of the likelihood of a steamer going across this week I took the liberty of telegraphing to commission you to buy five pounds worth of articles for their benefit leaving to your better judgement what would help them most, and I hope I have not presumed too much. It struck me that they want present help to be of any good, and I expect the Government and MacLeod are sending real help. I only wish I could do more.

'Any particulars you can give me will be welcome, and specially what regular provision there is for supplying their wants in distress or bad years. It is a delicate matter asking how people are treated, but in this case I am sure I have good cause for asking, as my grand-father was the minister there and my father was born on the Island.

'If the steamer has not sailed, kindly send the enclosed to Mr McKay: if she has, will you take care of it till opportunity offers.'

Mackenzie forwarded the £5 to Sir William Collins who acknowledged receipt, explained how funds from the public had been spent, and hinted that if more money was donated it might be advisable to spend it on a new boat to replace the one apparently lost.[55]

Travelling with the *Jackal* and Commander Osborne was another significant passenger, Malcolm McNeill, former secretary to the Crofters Commission and now, as Inspecting Officer of the Board of Supervision, commissioned by the government to report on the condition of the St Kilda people. He had experience of the island and was clearly well able to form a reasonably accurate picture of the situation there.

McNeill and Osborne landed on the morning of 22 October 1885, the day after Connell's account of his visit appeared in the Herald. They immediately went to the manse where 'a prolonged conference' took place in which 'the minister, the schoolmaster, and the resident ground officer' participated. After it was over McNeill discussed some matters with the islanders and in the end was satisfied with the information he received. He heard about the severe storm in mid September and of how it had destroyed the crops of oats and barley but not of potatoes. No damage had been done to stock or to buildings, and the loss of a boat turned out to be that of an old one which McNeill had noted as unseaworthy on previous occasions. There were still 'four excellent boats (one of these of large size and nearly new)' which had survived unharmed. So far as food and seed for next year's planting were concerned the people seemed to have more than enough; there was plenty of tea, sugar and tobacco which had either been given by tourists or bought from the factor. At least 200 tourists had visited during the recent summer, buying cloth, birds' eggs, bird skins and other wares, so that each islander had earned some money from the sales. 'I have thus no doubt,' McNeill concluded, 'that the inhabitants of St. Kilda are amply – indeed luxuriously – supplied.'

McNeill also remarked on the desire, and existing proposals, for an improved landing place, and he commented, perhaps more importantly, on the unsettling reappearance of the emigrant Ewen Gillies, his words suggesting a need to weigh the worthwhileness of a better landing with its costs against the possibility that before long the island might be abandoned:

'During the year 1884 a former emigrant from St. Kilda to Australia returned, and resided for some months in the Island; this person seems to have occupied himself in spreading discontent among the people, and in striving to place them in antagonism with their indulgent landlord. But his teaching has produced an effect which probably he did not anticipate, for within the past 18 months a strong desire to emigrate has sprung up and, with the exception of one or two old men, I found none who were not anxious to be transferred either to the mainland or to Australia.

'It may well be worth consideration by Her Majesty's Government whether, in view of this disposition of the people, it may not be wise and in the end economical, to assist them in attaining their object, and thus to avoid a recurrence of the anxieties which their isolated position must periodically produce.'

Two days after his enquiries at St Kilda McNeill was back in Edinburgh writing up his report, which was not to be laid before Parliament until March 1886. It was then quickly published and those who read it discovered that the calls for help sent in bottles from St Kilda the previous September had been at least false alarms and possibly deliberate deception.[56]

*

Connell's article in the *Glasgow Herald* of 21 October 1885, written and printed without the benefit of McNeill's report, gave an account of the *Hebridean*'s voyage and the circumstances leading to it but was not at all clear as to the supposed deprivations likely to be suffered by the islanders over the following months. As he was about to leave St Kilda the people asked him 'to state that the provisions sent would hardly be sufficient to carry them through the winter, and that they would require at least 30 bolls or more of oatmeal'. On other aspects of his visit little was said, apart from comments on what were seen as the 'peculiar views' of the inhabitants 'about the observance of the day of rest', on the minister, and on emigration. The last was a topic about which Connell thought the people evenly divided, though Rev. MacKay's domineering housekeeper 'declared that St Kilda was the biggest prison in all the world'. MacKay himself was more discreet, and when told that 'the Rev. Dr Gordon, of Glasgow, and other gentlemen, had suggested in letters to the Glasgow Herald, that the Island of St Kilda ought to be abandoned finally, with all convenient speed, and the people transplanted in a body to some other island of the Outer Hebrides, or to the mainland', he answered that while the idea seemed reasonable it was for the people themselves to give an opinion and not for him.[57]

There were one or two prompt responses to the article in the correspondence columns of the same paper. The first recollected a conversation with a young woman who had emigrated from St Kilda in 1852 and was met by chance in Melbourne two years later. Perhaps a cheerful story from such a person might encourage the remaining islanders to emigrate as well. But a letter in reply stated that the 1852 emigration 'experiment' was not successful, and told how those who had then left St Kilda 'expressed with strong emotion their sorrow at leaving their beloved lonely isle'. When however the *Jackal* returned on Saturday 24 October it was learned that the people were well supplied for the present after the *Hebridean*'s delivery and even 'in comparatively comfortable circumstances', so that public concern was set at rest.[58]

The official picture which emerged from the report submitted by Malcolm McNeill seemed to confirm that the messages of probable distress originally conveyed by wind and sea from St Kilda were indeed inaccurate to say the least. Both the *Glasgow Herald* and the *Scotsman* of 7 April 1886 were severely critical of what one called 'this unpleasant case'. The islanders were accused of having 'played a successful game of imposture, by which they have materially increased their basket and their store at the cost of the unsuspecting benevolence of the mainland'. They had assumed that the government would be bound to help and their behaviour 'vividly illustrates the social effect of recent agitation' in the Highlands and islands and 'of the consideration that has been shown to agitators and inventors of grievances'. The *Scotsman*, hostile to such people and supporter of the establishment, was disappointed that the inhabitants of St Kilda had fallen from grace in this way: 'It might have been thought that their home lay far enough away in the ocean, and was sufficiently isolated, to escape the demoralisation that has overtaken so many of their class in the Western Isles and elsewhere. But they, too, have caught the idea that they have a right to look to the Government for the supply of all their wants, real and imaginary.' No recognition of the changing position in which the islanders were placed by population decline and outside influence was shown by the paper, nor any realisation that the 'benevolent' mainland had contributed to such demoralisation as may have occurred. All that could be seen was undesirable dependence: 'A Western crofter or fisherman of these days seems to think that if he is not sufficiently happy, all he has to do is to make out a statement of his desires, and put in his claim against the Government.'

Even more at fault, however, was the minister, whose letter to Dr Rainy had apparently not told the truth and who seemed to have been made the instrument of the people in their 'little game'. He had, too, written to Rainy using words inappropriate in a subordinate: 'The Free Church minister of St Kilda does not pray, or beg, or even request. He makes an intimation and conveys instructions. He makes a claim of right on the Government, and he instructs Principal Rainy in the language of a superior to present it.' Rainy's own letter to the Duke of Richmond, Secretary for Scotland, was quoted as an example of how these things should be done. In effect the papers accused Rev.Mackay of lying about the crops and the boat, and there would have to be punishment – 'Principal Rainy will no doubt see that the Presbytery to which St Kilda belongs shall investigate the conduct of the Rev. John McKay'. It seems probable that the investigation never took place but the minister was certainly upset and deeply hurt by this public condemnation when he eventually heard of it.[59]

The indefinite nature of Robert Connell's association with journalism and with the *Glasgow Herald* became still more evident with events in early 1886. Even after the appearance of McNeill's report and its reassuring portrait of the St Kilda community with its plentiful stores of food and better housing 'some anxiety', according to Connell, 'was manifested regarding the condition of the islanders by the numerous people interested in their welfare'. Who these 'numerous people' were was not explained, nor what combination of them decided that he should return to the island. If it was expected that the welfare of the St Kilda people would be assisted by a second visit then Connell was not the person to choose for that purpose. Nevertheless, 'in order to ascertain precisely how matters stood, it was arranged .. that I should again visit St Kilda on the first opportunity'. The identity of those who asked or arranged for him to go is also unknown; but on 8 June 1886 the *Robert Hadden* slowly left Dunvegan pier in an absolute calm with two John MacKenzies – father and son – as factor and future factor, Connell himself, and George Murray the new teacher. Connell was again the *Herald*'s 'Special Correspondent'. They reached St Kilda two mornings later, anchored at 7 a.m., and were welcomed by barking dogs and, after some time, by the people who were initially cautious of meeting the 'Sassenach' who, as Connell put it, 'only presents himself to them in the shape of gunboats and tipsy tourists and charity oatmeal'.[60]

In many ways Connell was a typical tourist, full of moral superiority and understanding very little of what he saw in St Kilda. To him the people, about whose 'welfare' he pretended to be concerned, were 'those strange islanders', dirty, ignorant of the world, unskilled sailors, and speaking discordantly 'their Gaelic gibberish'. They were a nuisance with their eagerness for charity and their urgent enquiries about 'the Crofter question' – at that time a subject of immense importance throughout the Highlands and islands – when all Connell was interested in was his breakfast. They were rude and unthinking enough to have eight of the most active men and a woman away on Boreray barbarously 'tearing the fleece' off the sheep's back when they should all have been present to unload the smack. They were so greedy and cunning that 'some of the people declined to sit to a photographer without being first paid for their services', and it was customary for them now to besiege a visiting vessel, 'proposing to relieve you of everything you are simple-minded enough to part with, from a smoke of tobacco or a lead pencil to a hamper of wines'.

Ashore, 'the begging nuisance becomes intensified' and the recipients of charity were ungrateful. 'All this,' concluded Connell, 'betrays the unfortunate lack of independence and self-respect which has come to be identified with the nature of these poor islanders ... Yachtsmen and tourists by the Glasgow steamers have contributed to the result.' And so too, if what Connell said was true, had journalists.

Instead of laying most of the blame on visitors he laid it firmly on the minister: 'the man mainly responsible is the head of the community, who appears to discourage the unfortunate proclivities of the people by neither precept nor example'. Having little or no knowledge of the Free Church and certainly no sympathy with its principles and teaching Connell merely made fun of religious figures, practice and feeling, as in the case of the expedition to Boreray which so irritated him. The party had, as usual, taken a church elder with them, which to Connell meant only frustration:

> 'The elder is a sort of ornamental man, carried not so much for the purpose of assisting in snaring birds or plucking sheep as for conducting the services on Sunday, without which no St. Kildian would feel half happy. As the stereotyped length of the day's services is six hours, I am surprised that they have been able to find even so many as three men in St. Kilda qualified for the eldership. When, therefore, we learned that the party who had gone to Boreray included an elder, we had to make up our minds, however reluctantly, for a prolonged stay on the island.'

The 'Special Correspondent' here showed no awareness of the weather conditions required for a landing on Boreray and for leaving again, no recognition of the hard and dangerous work involved in catching sheep there, no grasp of the qualifying process by which a man might become an elder, and no realisation that an elder could be an expert catcher of birds or plucker of fleeces. What he did reveal however was a readiness to mock a way of life which in all sincerity gave religion, for better or worse, a pre-eminent place, and so there is no surprise in the fact that Rev. John MacKay, by no means 'the head of the community', was the target for most of Connell's worst exaggerations and most unkind and prejudiced descriptions.

Failing to see any welcoming group as he arrived on his first visit by the *Hebridean* Connell had been puzzled until he pretended to remember that the islander had 'peculiar views' about Sabbath observance. There was in fact nothing especially peculiar about their views since, like most people in the Outer Hebrides from North Uist northwards and like many in the Highlands, they observed the day of rest as a day of rest. Again, Connell attributed their non-appearance to the minister, for, as he said, 'it was a matter of common report, known to all on board, that the worthy pastor of the island added one other to his many virtues of head and heart in the supreme wealth of his

Sunday fare, which as a rule entertained the good people ..from early morn to dusk'. This was of course not the reality since the normal sequence of the three Sabbath services amounted in all to five and a half or six hours and was also typical of many island and mainland areas.

The anticipation with which Connell had imagined 'the figure of the Rev. John MacKay' had been fuelled by 'the well known picture' of him drawn by John Sands and published by him in his book and in the illustrated journal called *The Graphic*. This uncomplimentary portrait formed for Connell his introduction to the man he believed was 'head' of the island people and so his mind was already made up when he was confronted by 'the reverend gentleman himself' and the refusal to bring goods ashore until after midnight. Even the invitation to tea did nothing to change Connell's opinion. Detached from up to date sources of information on what was happening in the rest of the world, MacKay's range of questions relating to the cholera outbreak in Europe and his lack of interest in the British general election of that year, which indeed had no immediate relevance to the voteless islanders, seemed to Connell to be nothing but amusing and faintly ridiculous. Considering that 'this Hebridean Rip Van Winkle', his watch two hours fast, was unwilling to talk about worldly matters on Sundays, he tried to challenge the minister into conversation by raising the subject of emigration but received only a terse response which must have disappointed the insistent correspondent.

*

Connell's second stay was a good deal longer than the first, but not because he wished it to be so. Although the party on Boreray was blamed for holding things up, the fortnight spent at St Kilda was probably the convenient period for the factor, who usually needed some time to carry out his business there. Connell had less to do, and consequently paid undue and inappropriate attention to matters on which he expanded at great length in his subsequent article.

Within twenty four hours of landing he paid a visit to the manse, finding Rev. MacKay crowned with 'his chimney pot hat' and filling 'a short clay pipe' amid the simple furnishing of his main room. The domestic events that followed were described at extravagant length in words that failed to capture the reality of the situation. The minister apparently complained about a newspaper article that he had found objectionable, while Ann MacDonald was a restless listener: 'It was not reassuring to observe the stalwart housekeeper flitting in and out of the room in an excited manner, and hissing between her closed teeth what sounded to my Sassenach ear like swearing in Gaelic.' MacKay was troubled by the accusation in the article - probably that in the *Scotsman* - that he had been deliberately misleading in his letter to Dr Rainy. In his view, without the *Hebridean*'s call the islanders would have certainly

607

been desperately short of supplies, especially oatmeal and seed corn, during the winter months, and Malcolm McNeill, whose report he found generally fair, had overestimated the amount of stored food on the island.

That evening MacKay went out 'to look at plans for a proposed harbour which the factor had prepared'. Next day he was unwell. For some reason Connell attended him in his sick room along with what he called 'A blubbering crowd of women', the housekeeper being the loudest in her wailing. In the company was a mystery woman, mentioned to no obvious purpose other than that of entertaining readers: 'Among the others present was a poor old, broken-hearted looking creature whom I had not seen before, and whom we were told was the minister's sister.' The account of Rev. MacKay's indisposition seems also to have been intended to amuse. It took up disproportionate space and was written in a manner to emphasise the primitive nature of the people; the housekeeper concocted a medicine of oatmeal and port wine as if on the occasion of a birth, and the women who had crowded into the manse kitchen 'were squatted like squaws upon the cold clay floor'. With a typically unsuitable attempt to be humorous Connell said that 'Every one was protesting that the newspapers had killed their parson'. But far from being in his last hours John MacKay began to recover, and all the onlookers were distracted by yet another visit from Henry Evans in his steam yacht with a gift of herring nets.

The minister may have looked older than he really was since he was regularly described, at this period, as an old man, yet however physically disabled he may have been he was still active of mind, carrying out his duties, taking an interest in news from the mainland, and, with the help of 'a rain-gauge in the manse garden', sending weather statistics to the secretary of the Scottish Meteorological Society. He seems to have had his peculiarities of manner and eccentricities, and Connell clearly disapproved of him heartily. Sands's hostile opinions of MacKay were quoted, and in a passage full of phrases intended to apply uniquely to the minister but which happen, perhaps also intentionally, to condemn features seen as characteristic of the whole Free Church Connell expressed extreme and unsympathetic hostility:

'There can be no manner of doubt that for much of the unhealthy moral atmosphere pervading the island at present the ecclesiastical authority in the person of Mr. Mackay is mainly responsible. The weak-minded pope and prime-minister rolled into one who rules the destinies of the island has reduced religion into a mere hypocritical formalism, finding no place in his creed for self-reliance or any of the manlier virtues. Men are enjoined to two hours devotions every week day, and eight on Sunday, when they must also wear a sad face and speak an octave under their usual voice. Whistling and singing are at all times tabooed, and not to comply is to be accounted an infidel, and worse than a heathen. The apostle of this novel evangel has no stomach for the common affairs of life. He has enervated the islanders by arrogating to himself all the power, temporal as well as spiritual, and with this influence, which might have been directed to the most useful ends, Mr. Mackay has only sought to enforce a fantastical sacerdotalism. It is nothing to Mr. Mackay whether the poor people starve their crofts or neglect the fishing so long as his own silly fads are observed. There is no use blinking the fact that during the twenty years the Reverend gentleman has held the island in his firm grip no useful public work of any kind has been executed. We know something of what he might have succeeded in doing. At every point in the island one comes upon evidences of the practical usefulness of a former minister, the Rev. Neil Mackenzie, under whose beneficent guidance the St. Kildians appear to have put forth some energy to improve their condition. That, however, was in the good old days of cakes and ale, before the Disruption, when whistling was not as yet a sin, and when fiddling and piping, and even dancing, were not unknown in St. Kilda.'

Whatever its merits as an attack on the Free Church this lengthy onslaught on Rev. MacKay is largely unfair and even nonsensical. Many of the statements are simply not true and betray a lack of understanding of island behaviour, religious and otherwise. The passage raises further suspicions about Connell's motive in coming again to St Kilda and about those who instigated his visit. The absurd reference to 'cakes and ale' times before the Disruption is partly intended to show that 'useful public work' might have been a more suitable task for MacKay than enforcing 'fantastical sacerdotalism', whatever that might mean, but it may be wondered what possible public works Connell had in mind. The community already had houses judged to be better than most equivalent dwellings in the rest of the Hebrides. An improved landing or 'harbour' had been under discussion for some time, and MacKay was at least interested in the factor's proposals. The problem of communication was one that far exceeded any minister's ability to deal with. The island's fuel resources were inadequate but the minister, who complained at the price he had to pay for a ton of coal, was not in the position to solve that difficulty on behalf of the 'poor people'. Connell did not mention the landlord's or factor's responsibilities in these matters, and his one suggestion was the total abandonment of St Kilda as a place to live.

If undermining Rev. MacKay's position in the island was Connell's principal aim it was almost matched by his support for the emigration idea. 'The problem of what is to be done with the St. Kildians,' he wrote, 'is one that now exercises every thoughtful person who feels any interest in the island. It is only within a comparatively recent period that the problem has pressed itself for solution on the public mind.' The period to which he referred happened to be that in which Sands wrote and steamers began their regular calls. The 'problem', if the fate of the islanders was conceived as one, did not 'press itself', it was pressed by people like Sands on readers of all kinds. It could never be claimed that the origins of that 'problem' lay no further back in time than around 1875, but the clamour of concern that arose in the decade that followed Sands's visit and was brought to a climax by the *Herald* article of June 1886, together with rumours of destitution in bad seasons, led 'many sensible people', according to Connell, 'to think that the only way of solving it satisfactorily is to abandon the island'. McNeill's report gave a degree of official backing to this view. But that anything should be 'done with the St. Kildians' was a recent development of thinking which tended to make impressions of Rev. MacKay irrelevant; and as soon as a minister's presence could be seen as an irrelevance, excepting only his task as spiritual guide, then the moving influence of the church in St Kilda had ceased to exist.

*

The difference between St Kilda and the mainland as Connell saw it was much the same as it had been seen two centuries earlier. It was a matter of civilisation, and the old story of the Celtic, Gaelic-speaking barbarian was still very much alive. 'The average civilised man would not feel happy if he had the accumulated letters of eight months handed in to him of a morning, but the civilised man is a being with whom the St. Kildian has little in common.' This was all very well if the kind of civilisation represented by a daily mail delivery – and by 'tipsy tourists' – was in every respect a good thing. To many of those who did not live in St Kilda it was, but 'the accumulated letters of eight months' for a single St Kilda family might only have numbered one or two and Connell, like many other commentators on the Hebridean scene, generally estimated the island's needs by standards not common among those who did live there.

Civilisation, therefore, implied to Connell the necessity of leaving the island for ever. A few of the islanders came to share this view, having in mind recollections of the departure for Australia by so many in 1852 and increasing awareness of the numerous benefits which 'civilisation' brought. The *Hebridean*, visiting on 22 June 1885, had taken away 'several of the natives, who are about to emigrate to the colonies', among them Ewen Gillies, who had come home, annoyed MacLeod of MacLeod from a distance, taken a second wife, and being restless had left again '*en route* for their new home' before MacLeod wrote to complain about him. A year later Connell remarked that, after discussion following the return of the Boreray party during his second visit, three couples resolved to emigrate to Australia and that 'The opinion in favour of emigration was almost unanimous, the only dissentients being one or two old men, whom it would be folly to ask to go to a new settlement at their time of life'. The old men's families had no wish to go either.[61]

The thought of emigration was certainly in the air in 1886. Connell was in no doubt that 'many of the people could readily be induced to go' to Australia, provided that they were given assisted passages, and that anyone left behind would soon follow. Nothing was said about what would happen to the old men. But what if nearly everyone chose to stay? Connell, having no doubt talked with the factor and his son on the subject, recommended a harbour, built by local labour 'paid only moderate wages' so that the people would learn to do things for themselves - as if they had never done anything before. With a good, sheltered recess for boats a fishing station could be developed. The idea was nearly two hundred years old. 'But when all has been said in favour of making the island a fishing station, the fact remains that the most effectual way of benefiting the St. Kildians is to enable them to settle in one or other of our colonies.' In that way they would be no longer 'St. Kildians' and the economic bother that the island and its people caused would be removed.

The articles contributed by Connell to the *Glasgow Herald* in October 1885 and June 1886, 'to some extent re-written and considerably expanded', were published again in book form in 1887 under the title *St.Kilda and the St. Kildians*.The author's hope was that his work would 'help to keep before the public mind the absolute necessity of something being done to ameliorate the condition of the St. Kildians', and in this he was a second Sands. Parts of the book have a flavour of fiction about them, and, along with the exaggerations, unnecessary and frivolous descriptions, and unsympathetic approach, call into question its value as a source of information. Connell drew heavily upon Sands and may even have enlarged upon ideas suggested by his predecessor, as in the case of the uncomplimentary attitude adopted towards the minister and the Free Church.Added to this, unacknowledged debts to previous publications are particularly troublesome when the substance is mere impression and prejudice. Misunderstandings, wrong information and unreliable views are thereby transmitted and repeated so that what was composed many years ago emerges again in the latest work as if it were new, original and contemporary. At first sight, for instance, Alexander Ross's paper to the Inverness Scientific Society about his visit to St Kilda in 1884 seems to have been delivered in its entirety in December of that year but it was not published until 1893, by which time extensive and largely unacknowledged extracts from 'the correspondent to the Glasgow Herald', that is, Robert Connell, had been incorporated within it. Not surprisingly it was Connell who recorded the Skye man's words on the St Kilda diet, and Connell who described the odd procedure at 'the Lover's or Mistress' Stone'. These and other instances of 'borrowing' - accounts of 'the stranger's cold' and of the church - filled out Ross's paper when eventually it appeared in print, even though there were certain distinct differences of approach between the two authors. Ross liked the islanders and thought the minister 'a very worthy old man'; Connell gave a mocking picture of a primitive and simple community ridiculously out of place in the modern British world.

CHAPTER 5

George Murray, teacher, and island troubles

After nearly two weeks out at St Kilda the *Robert Hadden* left with the MacKenzies and Connell, taking away too Hugh McCallum who had completed his year as teacher and was to move on to Paisley. The crossing to the Sound of Harris was rough but without mishap and 'We cast anchor at Dunvegan on Friday morning, June 25.'

Connell's second 'excellent and exhaustive' article contributed to the *Herald* was enough to encourage another 'Correspondent' to make a trip of his own only a month later, in July 1886. This anonymous writer determined to spend a week of his holidays 'in viewing the magnificent scenery of the West Coast, and in inspecting .. the habits and habitations of the primitive race peopling the lonely Island of St Kilda', since to 'the mature civilised mind' the island 'has become almost as alluring as the tropical home of Robinson Crusoe to the awakening intelligence of the schoolboy'. So off he went on the *Hebridean* along with several others 'intent, like myself, on personally acquainting themselves with the drawbacks of St Kilda life'. Evidently there was a distinct connection between publications and bookings on the west coast steamers.[62]

The visitors landed, beat off the dogs with their sticks, and shook hands with the inhabitants. Inevitably the minister was standing there, looking as if he had just emerged from the columns of Connell's article or as Sands's cartoon figure:

> 'I then made my way to where the Rev. Mr Mackay was. He has improved very much in health, but what a frail and feeble old man. A bloodless and pallid face, bleared eyes, lips slightly turned up like a negro's, stooping shoulders, a satin hat, the date of whose manufacture can only be relegated to the dim and distant past; a capacious Highland cloak, possibly coeval with the former – such is the portrait of the Mikado of St Kilda.'

John MacKay was still complaining about the *Scotsman*'s criticism of him and he maintained his attack until 'one of the party mollified him by assuring him that the whole country was on his side'. Another 'enthusiastic passenger' interested in 'the crofter question' then took him away to look at the cultivated land, while the writer and his friends walked to the sparsely furnished manse where they received 'a right hearty welcome from a buxom, fresh-looking woman … with superb teeth, like rows of pearls, and a tongue which galloped and rattled like the paddles of a steamboat'. This was Ann MacDonald, the housekeeper, the description of whom by Connell – 'a

Portrait of the teacher in St Kilda (1886-87),
George Murray, in his later years

remarkable woman, standing about six feet high, and proportionately well built, who is the terror of the whole island' – had led the visitors to imagine a dominating tyrant. But she proved to be 'not the tall virago I had pictured to myself'. In fact Captain McCallum of the *Hebridean* was 'a great favourite with her' and while she coyly sat on his knee he 'playfully attempted to kiss her'. Reflection on the trip after the steamer returned led to the conclusion that 'life would indeed be a burden imprisoned in such a place'; and it was not really surprising that an application to government had been made 'for assistance to aid a few, at least, in emigrating'. In a novel St Kilda might be made to appear fascinating, 'but that it actually exists and that in a state of precarious uncertainty should arouse our interest and win our sympathy'.

One other person on the island was briefly mentioned. This was the new schoolmaster, George Murray, who had just replaced Hugh McCallum. 'He has been only a month on the island, and so has not become fossilised. His felt hat, his fashionably-cut coat, bespoke a St Kildan of quite recent growth.' As soon as he arrived Murray started to his duties as teacher and began the diary in which he sought to make a record of daily routine and events. By the time his year on St Kilda was over that record was nearly as interesting as a revelation of his own character as it was as an account of what happened around him.[63]

Murray was quickly involved in the major incidents of St Kilda life, being present at the funeral of old Finlay Gillies, aged eighty yet a member of the crew that went to Soay for puffins at the end of July, and attending the monthly prayer meeting on 3 August when 'the Revd. Mr McKay drew the attention of the people to the Irish question'. Two days later the *Hebridean* came in with many passengers, among them Miss Rainy of the ELHSA 'who shortly after landing examined the school and was well pleased with the way in which the scholars acquitted themselves'.[64]

Apart from 'holding school' for what were rather variable lengths of time Murray, like those teachers before him, participated as a young, active man in bird catching on the cliffs and helped out with safer activities such as reading and writing letters on behalf of the islanders, few of whom were yet able to do these things for themselves even though the number of people who could speak English was increasing. On 3 September 1886: 'Had no school as I had no less than 23 letters to read for myself besides some through the village. All my relatives and acquaintances are well, which cheers my heart.' Communication with his friends was very important to him as he felt the isolation keenly. When the *Robert Hadden* reached the island on Sunday 24 September those on board did not come ashore until 4 a.m. on Monday morning, 'when I got up to get news and read letters'. Contrary winds delayed the smack's departure until the Wednesday night, and 'I spent the most of the time in writing and bidding farewell to my friends in the world. I could not help feeling sad I could not get more news from home for the next eight or nine months.'

Although both minister and teacher were strictly 'Free Church' appointments they did not necessarily agree or get on well with each other. Within a month or so of his arrival George Murray had formed a rather poor opinion of the minister's sermons. When he called on MacKay one afternoon to discuss Malcolm McNeill's report he first of all had to listen to 'what I hold as gross superstition, the greatest rubbish of tales'. He did not, unfortunately, explain what it was he heard; the superstition and tales might have been anything from versions of St Kilda traditions to views on contemporary island gossip or on Glasgow and Edinburgh newspapers. On a Sunday in October he attended church service twice as usual, 'but I must confess that I make very little of the sermons I hear. It is poor feeding for the people or, rather, good food spoiled in the serving out. Ecclesiastically matters are asleep.' Yet the diary had variable and seemingly contradictory entries reflecting the writer's mood at the time. The Sunday after he was at least awake himself as he 'Listened with more than usual attention to Mr. McKay's afternoon sermon', and the following evening he was 'entertained kindly' when he visited the manse. Perhaps after more than twenty years in St Kilda the delivery, if not the content, of the minister's sermons had grown a little dull and stale; or Murray, whose reading matter included Hugh Miller's *My Schools and Schoolmasters*, Dr MacDonald's *Gaelic Poems*, Whewell's *Moral Philosophy*, Higgin's *Solar System*, Froude's *Oceana*, and so on, may have felt that MacKay was now lacking in intellectual and spiritual vigour. On 1 November he noted: 'The Sabbaths I do not feel as I used. The preaching is dry and monotonous. The old man is doubtless at his best.'

Murray's reaction to the nature of Rev. MacKay's preaching and conversation was possibly that of a sensitive personality deprived of immediate contact with his own family and friends. He certainly responded very strongly to gossip and rows among the people:

'This morning I am told that few on the island saw such a night as there was last night. An old woman of eighty fighting with her daughter, a married woman. It came to blows. Others got entangled in the row, and a son of the old woman with his family left the house where he stayed with his mother. This was about midnight. It is terrible to think upon the like. She is a wicked old woman. May God in mercy visit her in her old age.

'This has been a terrible day. After breakfast I went up the hill for a walk. I had not gone far when I saw the people removing furniture from one house to another. A family removed in consequence of the row. No sooner was this finished than another wicked woman began with her evil tongue speaking scandalous things about a married young man whom she declares had something to do with herself. He flatly denies the charge laid against him. She is and has been a dangerous woman and yet I understand she is a great favourite at the Manse. May God put down the evil that exists in our midst.'

Rev. MacKay apparently attempted to quieten the situation on the Sabbath when in his sermons he made reference to the disturbance amongst the people and prayed that 'the Lord would in mercy visit the old woman'.

Further entries in the diary give the impression that Murray was a serious and somewhat humourless young man. 'From what transpired within the last few days and the reports current about certain persons in the island,' he wrote, 'one cannot help coming to the conclusion that morality is at low tide in St. Kilda.' His own experience of the island so far was insufficient to equip him with the evidence for such a conclusion, nor is it clear why he should have been certain that 'A great change for the worse has come over the island during the last thirty or forty years.' Morality reminiscences, like recollections of past summers, might easily be inaccurate, and 'lawlessness' as Murray thought of it was not necessarily a recent and present condition only. He also found indelicate those seasonal enquiries as to how rams were getting on among the ewes, and when he met a young girl who said 'she was putting the sheep and rams together' he considered that 'Things would look better and leave a better impression upon a stranger, were the fair sex to leave these things to the opposite sex ... There is a great want of modesty still clinging to the rocks of St. Kilda.' It may be doubted that 'modesty' was ever a characteristic of island, or indeed mainland rural, life, while rows almost inevitably were.

Apart from a sequence of nine sermons on 'the Prodigal Son', which seemed to Murray to be rather excessive, the minister's services drew no more criticism from the schoolteacher. School books and the master's desk were removed to the factor's house at the beginning of November, 'as the church is now getting very cold' and to hold classes there seemed no longer possible. Singing lessons of some kind were introduced once a week. Illness and superstitious behaviour increased with the onset of winter but on the whole time passed fairly peacefully until trouble arose over peats for the school fire.

It was customary for country children in many parts of Scotland to take a peat each day for the school stove or open fire. St Kilda's 'scholars' in 1886-87 were no exception, although the practice had most probably been introduced by one of his two predecessors or by Murray himself. On 19 November Murray recorded that he was upset over the refusal of one family to send peats 'as they ought', a reasonable objection from people whose supply of peat or turf was extremely limited. He did not know then that this was the beginning of the first of three disturbances which were of rather greater significance than earlier 'rows'. The refusing family was that of Donald Ferguson, whose actions were likely to set an example for others to follow since he was one of the elders and in effect ground officer.

To begin with 'the peat difficulty' was dealt with peaceably, but on the night of 1 December 'war was waged between D. F. Elder and myself about the peats'. The boys, presumably Donald's sons Alexander and Neil, persisted in not bringing them to school and Murray went to see the parents. At the house he was confronted by the father, 'in a most furious rage about speaking to his boys about peats'. They argued for a while and Murray returned to his lodging with the feeling that he had 'triumphed' but determined not to have more to do with Ferguson until an apology was received. No apology was made and on 4 January 1887 trouble threatened again: 'Last night I heard that the Elder ... is watching me like a tiger for his prey. Tomorrow the Xmas prizes are to be distributed amongst the Scholars and if his children do not get what he thinks proper, I will get a "supper" (i.e. I will get from his tongue what will suffice for a supper). He did not spare the other two [Campbell and McCallum], the latter of whom he brought to tears with his language. Of this he boasts. Poor man, I'm sorry for him. Should he commence on me, which he very likely will, I am resolved not to open my mouth and so silence him with silence. I have conscientiously awarded the prizes to the deserving parties and

I care not should he or any other roar about them … I am sorry indeed to see that such a man is an elder in a Church.'

The heat seems to have left this issue, but another soon arose. It involved the 'wild man' who left his mother's house towards the end of October after great rows there. This man was apparently Ewen Gillies, not long back once more from foreign lands, and since his mother is said to have died about fifty years earlier the house he left with his family may have been that of his mother-in-law. They removed to the dwelling 'above us' as Murray expressed it, near enough to hear sounds coming from the factor's house on a quiet evening. Murray gathered that Ewen 'was just on the point of coming down to us on Monday night to see what noise were we making'. Such noise as there was came from conversation between the teacher, Mrs MacKinlay and the minister's servant Ann MacDonald, and from the breaking of coals for the fire. A week later Murray was at the manse 'talking over the business' of the 'row' with Gillies when Mrs Gillies arrived. 'She there maintained strongly before us that there [was] something unusual in our kitchen on the Monday night … The minister's servant said there was not.' And Murray, rather excitedly, told Mrs Gillies 'that she had not the truth and so should be quiet and that it was as great a lie as ever a man made', whereupon she marched out 'and in going she told her husband that I lifted my hand to her face'. Along came Ewen to the factor's house and abused Murray. 'I wished him to go to the manse, where I had three witnesses that I did not lift my hand to her', but Gillies replied 'that he would not take the minister for a witness'. After he had left, Murray, having heard stories of his opponent's brutality when abroad, was too afraid to go to bed. Report of the 'row' reached everybody. In one house 'the wife was taking the part of Gillies and his wife, and the man was on the minister's and mine', and so great was the difference between the couple that the wife went off with her children to her father's house. It happened that the husband was Neil MacDonald, Ann's brother.

The third disturbance occurred at the manse. Visiting the minister one evening as he often did Murray 'was told that extraordinary elder [Donald Ferguson] … had been giving the minister a doing up for something he said on Wednesday at the prayer meeting and which the elder took to himself'. In 'a terrible rage' Ferguson had confronted Rev. MacKay demanded an explanation. 'Really he is a terrible man – yes terrible and dangerous. Strong words to use about any elder.' Then there was an unexpected interlude. In his role as elder Ferguson made peace between Neil MacDonald and his wife, and after a prayer meeting came to tell Murray, with whom he seemed to be reconciled, that 'he is out on the minister through the servant and that he does not intend going to Church unless he put away the servant'. It appeared to be a quarrel over a trifling matter, but Murray had reservations: 'there is certainly too much gossip carried into and conducted in the manse. That I cannot deny. Kind as they are to me I must speak the truth.' A further 'scene' after a

Wednesday meeting brought the affair to a conclusion, at least for a while. Someone had also said that the manse was too frequently a place of gossip:

> 'This made a terrible noise and the servant went at once to where the Elder was and asked what he had against her. He told her that he had nothing against her but against the minister. How he reconciles that statement with what he told me is rather difficult for me to see. Next day the minister went to his house and, with difficulty, I understand, came to an understanding. The elder is now going again to church after absenting himself and all his family one Sabbath and one prayer meeting evening.'

Rows of one sort or another went on occurring, the elder and the minister's servant apparently having a part in many of them. These disputes upset Murray exceedingly and therefore made his life in St Kilda more miserable than it might have been if he had been less sensitive to them. Had Rev. MacKay been a younger and fitter man he could possibly have kept firmer control with his advice and prevented petty dissensions arising. As it was the strong-willed Ann MacDonald and the equally touchy Donald Ferguson, both of them in their different positions having considerable influence in religious affairs, opposed each other and disrupted an island life that was otherwise more agreeable than Murray conceived it. The remaining agent of disturbance was of course Ewen Gillies, who was encouraged by his fellow islanders not to stay.

*

George Murray's diary came to an end in June 1887, the last entries – for example, 6 June: 'This is terrible. No vessel yet.' – showing how impatient he was to be away. He was replaced by Ranald MacDonald, whose appointment for the year 1887-88 had been fixed in April, and he reached the mainland long before the ELHSA committee heard the news contained in one of his last letters to the ladies from the island. Read at a meeting on 14 October 1887 Murray's communication and another from his successor MacDonald were found to convey 'distressing intelligence' about which the Association showed an almost motherly concern. Mrs MacKinlay's health had deteriorated. 'One of our little girl pupils had died. Another met with a very serious accident by falling over a cliff.' The first little girl was Annie Ferguson, aged only ten, who had suffered for two weeks the pains of 'the Lock-jaw, which works such havoc amongst the St. Kildians', and who had died on 10 March. The second was the subject of a letter from Ranald MacDonald to Captain McCallum of the *Hebridean* and published in the *Glasgow Herald* of 24 August 1887: 'I am sure you will be sorry to learn that Annie, Norman Gillies's daughter, went over the rocks. Her body was got. We thought she was dead, but life was in her.

We took her home, and she is lying between life and death. I hope you will have a doctor on board the next time you come. The girl's head is badly cut and bruised. I wish you could bring something for healing.' Before the *Hebridean* could leave, however, a steamer called *Holly*, used by the Highland Fisheries Company for carrying mails to the Outer Hebrides in earlier years, reached St Kilda three days after the accident, and on board there happened to be 'several medical students', two of whom offered assistance. Their help was refused by the tradition-loving islanders but they left instructions for treatment. The minister was found to be in good health himself, 'and it is only fair to state that the reverend gentleman was opposed to the absurd scruples of his flock'.[65]

The Free Church Monthly Magazine of 1 August 1888 on its front page presented once more the picture of the pyramidal rock which may have been Levenish but which was captioned 'St. Kilda'. This time it illustrated the opening article, 'An Outlying Congregation', which began with a description intended to rid readers of misconceptions: 'St. Kilda is not a fairly level island which the inhabitants can cross from side to side. It is simply a rock [as in the picture] rising abruptly from the sea, furnishing a most natural resting-place and home to innumerable sea-birds, but offering shelter to its human tenants only in one small bay.' Here there were 'less than eighty souls' in better care under the Free Church than they would have been under the established church, for 'No Establishment has ever been, or will ever be, so complete and comprehensive as to meet the necessities of isolated handfuls'. The article then went on to set out the virtues of the sustentation fund, with the support of which 'ordinances are maintained in a poor and isolated island', and 'as our brethren there are unable to make adequate provision for themselves, it is in entirest accord with the genius of our system that we should cheerfully give them help, and that they should, without any loss of self-respect, frankly accept of it'. By this means St Kilda enjoyed the benefit of both minister and teacher, a provision which some much less remote places lacked.[66]

That the St Kilda community could contribute anything at all to the sustentation fund remained to many people a surprise and a puzzle. Sands had discovered that in 1874 £20 was given – 'which must have cost them an enormous effort'. In 1885 the total contribution amounted to £30 a year. Any income from tourists would have proved very useful, perhaps essential, since the collection of the fund was one of the very few occasions when actual money was required from the 'poor people' of the island. Like other Free Church congregations the islanders no doubt gave what they could and appreciated that in return they received the guidance of a minister and, through the ELHSA, a teacher whose services were now much more valued than they used to be. The presence of a nurse was a different matter.[67]

Mrs MacKinlay, elderly and none too well, having returned to Skye in the summer of 1888, was replaced after a short while by Mrs Urquhart who was certainly in St Kilda by the beginning of October. It has become a popular belief that the nurses of this period had a difficult time in the face of island opposition to outside ideas and that consequently little medical progress was made. Connell was perhaps responsible for furthering this notion when he wrote that from her arrival in 1880 'the nurse [Mrs MacKinlay] had the deep-rooted prejudices of the islanders to fight against'. A prejudice against change was, as already said, characteristic of rural communities, and some urban ones, throughout Scotland, and his other remarks about 'the old system and the old nurse' were made without reference to anything but unspecified hearsay. Nevertheless Connell noted what, without means of comparison, he saw as some improvement, there being 'no more of the disgusting practices which used to disgrace the island'.[68]

If Mrs MacKinlay had indeed managed to introduce a few beneficial changes Miss Emily MacLeod could take some of the credit for the apparent success of her efforts; and although there were perhaps problems of the kind suggested by Connell the determined Emily did not hesitate to look for a second person to continue the good work. The result was described by her brother, Norman MacLeod of MacLeod, who must have read Connell's book. Writing in the autumn of 1890 about the nurses he told how Miss Emily had maintained one on the island at her own expense for nearly eleven years, and now 'has had at last to give up hope of every satisfying the people owing to their peculiar customs and prejudices'. For nine of these years, according to MacLeod, nurse MacKinlay struggled on 'and succeeded after great fighting with the customs and Prejudices of the people in saving with one or two exceptions all the Children born while she was there'. When at last she left, owing to 'many unpleasantnesses' to which she had been subjected, Emily had tried again to find an island woman to train in Glasgow but had again failed. She then persuaded 'Miss Urquhart' to go to St Kilda for at least a year. The new nurse was just as successful as her predecessor 'but was not well received by the people', so that when the boats of 1889 arrived she took the opportunity to leave. Thereafter Emily said to the islanders that 'if they wanted another nurse, to try and provide one for themselves' and that 'as they were in comfortable Circumstances they ought to pay her Salary and cease to be dependent on others for her Remuneration'. The ELHSA, whose interest in nursing provision to the Highlands and islands developed a little as its responsibilities for education ever more rapidly diminished, was given no reports of the 'unpleasantnesses' supposedly inflicted upon Mrs MacKinlay and Mrs Urquhart, and it seems possible that MacLeod's account contained rather misleading and exaggerated information on the circumstances surrounding the appointment and subsequent island life of each nurse.[69]

When Mrs Urquhart went away in 1889, possibly along with Murdo Macrae, schoolmaster for the past year, only the latter's successor had been found. This was John Ross, like George Murray before him a native of the parish of Rogart in Sutherland. Ross, whose father was also John, was born in 1867. In 1881 the family was living at Achafrish, a little to the north of Lairg, where the elder John, a farm servant, worked for a year or two before moving with his wife Phoebe and their six daughters to Kingsburgh in the Trotternish district of Skye. In the spring of 1889 the younger John Ross, then aged 22, was employed by the ELHSA as a substitute teacher at Eriboll in north Sutherland. On 8 March he was asked to go to St Kilda, and he accepted the appointment. It was arranged that he should travel by the *Dunara Castle* which would be leaving Glasgow on 6 June, and that one of his sisters should go with him to serve as the sewing mistress. There is no sign that she was expected to serve as nurse as well.[70]

*

One Monday afternoon in July, the year unspecified, the *Hebridean* left the Clyde on yet another of its voyages to the Hebrides as far as St Kilda. It could have been in 1884, though not earlier, but that is unlikely, and somewhere in the later 1880s, probably when George Murray was teacher, seems more probable. On board was a tourist with a literary inclination, the sort of passenger who would have kept a journal, and eventually he published a little book describing the 'cruise' with a substantial part devoted to the call at St Kilda. It contained many elaborate and fanciful statements which tended to obscure some interesting observations, though it is difficult to decide whether the latter were made during the visit or, since the book did not appear until 1891, added in later. As a result the work can only be of value as again an imprecise and general impression formed by one person after a brief holiday.[71]

The author, Robert Thomson, from Kinning Park in Glasgow, had an inventive turn of mind, stimulated perhaps by Robert Connell whose book he was to recommend to all interested in St Kilda and its inhabitants, and he was prepared for features of the island that had already received much attention, in particular the minister. In resolving to write his own book about his experience he was faced with difficulties of selection – 'for every Glen, Mountain, Loch, and Castle in the Western Hebrides, have records of Clans and Clan Feuds, Love and War, Hatred and Revenge, and are boundless in tales and legends of historical incident, as well as teeming with objects of attraction to the Geologist, the Antiquarian, and the Artist, and interesting to every Scotchman'. Amid this company of capital letters St Kilda would surely have pride of place, both as one of the 'Western Hebrides' and, though perhaps lacking some of those items listed, as an 'object of attraction' in itself.

Following a tour through Dunvegan Castle the *Hebridean*'s passengers were given a grand farewell. Thanks for the kindness and courtesy of 'the MacLeod and his lady' having been expressed, the lady 'wished the visitors, and the good ship *Hebridean*, a safe and pleasant voyage to St Kilda ... Three hearty cheers were then given, and her ladyship waving adieu we all once more got into marching order, the piper again in front, playing "Hieland Laddie" and other well known and inspiriting airs, till the boat was reached'. The crossing to Loch Eport in North Uist was calm and warm, 'the heavings of the mighty ocean' after leaving Pabbay behind were less welcome. A form of mascot, similar to the new mothers who returned home with the factor's smack in 1876, was usefully available: 'On board we had as passenger an aged native of St. Kilda, returning from Glasgow, where he had been undergoing a surgical operation, and to those who could speak Gaelic – of which language I am unfortunately ignorant – he recounted many reminiscences of his lonely island home, and the condition of life there.' A wet fog cut off the unrecorded stories; then it cleared, and 'the old native ... was getting a bit excited' as the ship neared its destination. Like any island person coming back after some lengthy time away 'He kept creeping nearer and nearer to the boat's bow, until he stood there all alone in an attitude of expectancy, looking eagerly for the first glimpse of his island home'. Thomson, astray in matters of language at least, had no doubt that 'the words of that beautiful and expressive song, "Home, Sweet Home" would be in his mind'. As the fog lifted 'the old man shouted, Land! Land!' and 'there was observed a small speck, just on the horizon'. Then the fog came over again and the captain had to edge the steamer cautiously towards an anchorage 'because lying in the bay was a brigantine which had been sunk, her mast only being just visible above the water'. There was no warning light 'and it would not have been pleasant for our propeller to have got foul of the sunken spars and rigging'.[72]

The arrival was excitingly mysterious. Dogs were heard to bark, oars to splash, people to shout; and 'then a boat shoots out from the mist manned by several natives'. The old man was greeted with enthusiastic pleasure. 'On the voyage out,' Thomson remembered, 'I often wondered what it could be that made the old man so happy as we neared that cold and lonely island; whatever it was it seemed to quicken his pulse and bring a look of rapture to his face. Surely it was something better, brighter, and holier than the glare, and glitter, and tinsel show of a pleasure loving world, for *that* he could not have in St. Kilda.' Compared with 'the sacred associations twined around his island home' what would the old man have felt about emigration as recommended by Connell and McNeill?

On this occasion the islanders were urgently in need of a doctor as that day a boy had been born to the old man's daughter, a grandson who was to survive for only six days. While the man went ashore the tourists stayed on board for the night but by 5 a.m. most of them were shaking 'not very clean' hands, distributing presents, and, 'since we were anxious to get all the information possible', accepting invitations to enter houses. Even this manner of intrusion was accepted now. After paying respects to the minister Thomson and his companions 'peeped in at the schoolhouse, where we noticed a lady, the sister of a well-known Edinburgh divine, (she had joined us at Dunvegan), busy holding a school examination'. Ignorant of the Free Church connection Thomson could only add that 'she was acting on behalf of some committee or other which looks after the scholastic and spiritual welfare of these islanders'. In attendance at the examination was the schoolmaster (Murray):

> 'The teacher we found to be a young man who had not been many weeks on the island, but who was wearying terribly already, and as he and the minister were not getting on well together, he thought of leaving. No wonder he had that intention, his surroundings were far from comfortable, and his opportunities for social enjoyment were few and very restricted. He was a nice, pleasant, intelligent, young man, but it was expected that he would remain for one year.'

The question of who and what to believe crops up repeatedly. The remarks of the later teacher John Ross after leaving the island contrast with Thomson's, but both men were evidently victims of their reading in Connell's book, as well as being acquainted with some of the earlier accounts. Whatever his recollection of Rev. John MacKay Ross took away strong feelings of affection for the islanders, of whom he wrote: 'they are as nice civil kind and honest a people to live amongst as can be found anywhere ... although ... at first sight one is apt to form a different opinion of them owing to their strange behaviour when under excitement as they always are when anything unusual occurs.' The landing of unknown strangers still caused a great disturbance, and so too did the arrival of a steamer. Some years previously, according to Ross, visitors 'used to scatter money right and left', and now 'the poor natives expect that it should run a little more freely' so that their eager gathering round a group of *Dunara Castle*'s or *Hebridean*'s passengers 'makes them actually look greedy and when money is concerned that is only a failing common to many people'. It was a failing however that was 'more noticeable in such a small community especially when a number of eyes are eagerly watching to find some fault or other to report'.[73]

Thomson seemed ready to find fault. He found the place of the examination unattractive – 'the church is the school, and the school is the church, one and the same,' he said, as if making a neat observation on the long-prevailing connection between religion and education. There was nothing to soften the school's bleak accommodation, with its uncomfortable 'high backed forms', about twelve of which stood on each side of a central space, now with a 'rough coating of some kind of cement' looking like a pathway across the otherwise earthen floor. 'The whole place was cold and damp, and smelling like a vault', 'a bare barn-like building ... adjoining an ugly looking barn-like structure for a manse', certainly not a place to linger. So Thomson moved on to the row of houses which looked alright from the outside but within were 'not at all suitable for dainty ladies with high-heeled boots'.

Apparent greed depressed Thomson even more. 'The trail of the serpent in this and various ways is seen in St. Kilda, where one would expect to find every inhabitant pure and good, and the village a little heaven below, without stain or sin.' Unfortunately this ideal picture was no more attainable on the island than it was anywhere else, and the disappointed visitor concluded that 'it is one of the most miserable, lonely, and desolate places in the British Isles', ready for a change of direction. 'I think the Government should step in and take possession of this island, either as a Refuge for Inebriates, or a Convict Settlement; in that way it might be of some benefit to the Empire, as it is at present, it is useless.' There were nevertheless compensations and, unlike Connell and McNeill, Thomson did not think that emigration was absolutely necessary. The people in general seemed healthy, and 'one is astonished to meet so refined a lot of women in such an outlandish place'. One of these was 'a nice, pleasant, fresh coloured young woman', aged around 25, who conducted him through the settlement. At some point he discovered that she was known as 'the Queen', though this may have happened after his departure when the subject of 'the Queen's wedding' drew the attention of the press. The 'Queen' was Ann Ferguson, daughter of Donald Ferguson, the elder, and sister of Alexander who was 'said to be far and away the best scholar on the island' but had not yet made the decision to leave the island for Glasgow.

Alexander might still have chosen to stay at home, an option which Thomson was in no doubt he should reject. 'Their life is not a case of living, it is merely vegetating, coming into the world, sleeping through it, half-starving while doing so, then shuffling off, without even having attempted or done anything to advance mankind.' Not only was this a misconception of existence on St Kilda, it was also the extreme, mainland, colonialist view which usually failed to acknowledge that life could be led in any way but its own, which believed that the only valid reason for existence was usefulness to the empire, and which conducted its affairs with assumptions, principles and purposes not always consistent with Hebridean conditions. However, since through developments for which the islanders themselves were scarcely responsible St Kilda had come to rely heavily on the mainland it was an understandable view. The possibility that Alexander Ferguson might decide to go to Glasgow suggested an example of worthy enterprise. 'When questioned about Emigration, the majority expressed themselves as being content with their lot, if they could get quit of rent paying, and had no desire to leave their island home.' This would mean a continuing resident population which might show enterprise as well. What it needed, and in this Thomson was imitating Sands, was 'a good, clever Medical Missionary' with a 'practical knowledge of Mechanics' who could help to achieve improvements in social conditions and treatment of illness, whatever he did by way of spiritual guidance. 'I feel confident that the men, if they were roused, are intelligent enough to be taught various handicrafts, so as to earn an ordinary comfortable living on land or sea for themselves and families, and become useful members of the commonwealth. The women could be taught various domestic and household duties, necessary to everyday life, and all could be pure, good, happy and true, so that St. Kilda would be a perfect Utopia.' But why, it might be asked, remain in St Kilda, when the benefits of handicrafts, industry and 'an ordinary comfortable living' could be far more easily achieved elsewhere? Robert Thomson was but the latest in a line of visitors and writers who, on the basis of their few hours or days ashore, were unable to realise and understand the implications of the conflict between a deeply traditional way of life, with all its 'sacred associations' and its brutalities, and the enticement of modern comforts and rewards. It was a conflict by no means confined to St Kilda's dwindling community or to the late nineteenth century, and under such circumstances greed and cunning seem to be entirely consistent with the generous, kindly, credulous nature of a remote island people.

The mist prevented the customary demonstration of 'cragsmanship' and none of the visitors climbed up the hills. Instead they returned to the 'school' where the examination had finished, leaving the lady examiner 'expressing herself as fairly well pleased with the attainments of the youngsters'. Some of the party entered the building, which they now treated as the church it really was, and there 'sung the hundredth psalm, and indulged in a few minutes' silent prayer'. Though they thought this was a harmless exercise they had intruded without asking permission and were unaware of the feelings likely to be aroused. 'Several of the natives looked in at the Church door while the grand old tune was being sung, they however did not join in, rather looked displeased. We afterwards found that we had taken an unwarrantable liberty, which they looked upon as almost sacrilege.' Fortunately the steamer's whistle called its passengers back and soon a bell sounded to warn 'all natives who were on board' to go ashore. The *Hebridean* then departed, without the 'aged native' but with 'a young native' who was 'going to Glasgow to push his fortune'. To Thomson's later dismay a fortnight in the city proved too much and the young man went back home.

As other visitors before him Thomson looked upon the St Kilda community as a kind of show. The 'cragsmen' could not perform because of the mist; the natives came out 'gesticulating, and jabbering', and 'a short palaver' followed; and the minister behaved as if he were an offended ringmaster or sulking tribal chief. Writing up the story of his adventures from his recollections and influenced by Sands and Connell Thomson made it clear that he thought MacKay had a lot to do with the uninspired state of the people.

CHAPTER 6

Disagreements, discord, and the departure of
John Mackay with his household

When the steamer headed out of the Sound of Harris into the open Atlantic, often at night, the tourists on board paid little regard to the islands they were leaving behind. Berneray, Pabbay, Ensay, Killegray, Taransay and Scarp were all inhabited but not one became the subject of a book; St Kilda, however, continued to be the occasion of an ever-increasing number of special studies, articles and books which gave the island a fame matched only perhaps by that of Skye or Iona. Quantities of detail were provided about 'primitive' life on 'Hirta', virtually nothing was said about such life on most other islands in the Outer Hebrides. One consequence of this attention was that St Kilda's little group of inhabitants was made to seem quite different from every other Hebridean community, and in this context Rev. John MacKay himself was treated as if he too was exceptional, perhaps even unique.

Tourist presence could be, in these circumstances, both demeaning and flattering. One family might be offended by having its house examined by strangers, another might be delighted at the interest the house aroused. Some individuals might hide from a photographer, others might deliberately pose with pleasure. The people of St Kilda seem to have responded through the centuries with excitement to the event or visitor bringing some variety to enliven the usual routine of their existence, though the unknown or unexpected usually meant the excitement of fear. The sight of a ship under sail looming out of the mist or driving rain was at first unwelcome and frightening, just as the mysterious strangers who occasionally came to Rona were terrifying to the few inhabitants there. The usual reaction to a vessel approaching across the great plains of ocean was a hurried retreat into remote caves and secret hiding places, especially by the women and children. But human intervention, especially in later years, was for the most part peaceful and offered an opportunity to pick up news and talk about something different. A lone and temporary visitor, even though a journalist, was met with more than ordinary curiosity and often an exceptionally hospitable welcome.[74]

Residents in St Kilda who were not native to the island, ranging from Betty Scott to the minister and the teacher, must have appreciated more than most the presence, however brief, of someone who might make up a little for lack of contact with home or could understand their peculiar problems and concerns. For John MacKay, whose stay on the island was as long as that of Alexander Buchan, there were sporadic visits by Free Church deputies, but he had to put up with long intervals when no direct personal communication from his employers took place. Deprivation of this kind was as keenly felt by

626

a teacher although appointments for one year only were very different from MacKay's seemingly endless 'sentence'. In Catholic districts the social problem facing Free Church representatives heightened their sense of isolation – unless they were like John Finlayson – as the ELHSA noted in December 1868: 'Some of the teachers in Popish districts especially – as at Arisaig, where a promising school has lately been opened; at Barra and Mingalay, where the Bible has been taught for many years to the children of Roman Catholics – would most gladly welcome a visitor, whose sympathy would cheer and encourage them in their difficult work.' And in view of stories about the ignorance in St Kilda of things which to mainlanders were simple and everyday and which were taken for granted it is interesting to come across a reminder that the island was not unusual in this respect. In the late 1860s a west Highland expedition to various schools was made by Miss Bird, 'an English lady, already well known by her writings on Latin Hymnology and other subjects', who walked around Wester Ross and Skye, 'examining schools with the thoroughness of a Government Inspector'. She chose 'those most out of the way of ordinary visitors', including Melvaig, 'where there is no road within seven miles, … where a bad exposed beach renders communication by boat difficult', and where 'The younger children had <u>never seen a horse or cart</u>!' This school, twelve miles from the nearest church, was easily accessible compared with that at Kalnakill between Lonbain and Cuaig on the coast north of Applecross. Miss Bird reached it by a curious route, walking from Ardheslaig on Loch Torridon over the hills to Applecross, from which she was then taken in a boat 'rowed by eight young men from the Callikilli school'. What followed bears some resemblance to what might have happened if she had gone to St Kilda:

> 'This is one of the most inaccessible of your schools. It is twelve miles from a road, and has such an "awful beach", that it can only be approached by water under the most favourable circumstances. In addition to this, there is no accommodation at all for visitors. Every one told me it was impossible for a lady to reach Callikilli; but circumstances were favourable, and had the difficulties been ten times greater than they were, I would willingly have encountered them for the sake of the interest at the end. The people had been much disappointed at the non-arrival of other expected visitors, and they were out on the rocks four miles from Callikilli, to see if I had really come. The rowers hoisted a flag as a signal, and when I reached the rocks below the school, there was a great bonfire on the brae above, and the population of the three villages assembled. Although it was a dead calm, the sound of the swell upon the beach all night was like Niagara. The boulders of rough rock of which it is composed are worn round and smooth, by being perpetually pounded together.

'Remote and inaccessible as it is, religion flourishes among the people. I have never heard of a population so universally under its influence. You would have been delighted to see the school-house next morning decorated with bog-myrtle, heather, and meadow-sweet, and crowded with the scholars, and a number of the mothers in clean white caps. Sixty pupils were present, fully half the number being between sixteen and thirty; all so earnest and intent, though, of course, only beginners in English. I spent two hours in this most interesting school, and found it quite difficult to get away from the warm-hearted, generous people, who in many different methods sought to express their gratitude to the Association. I should think there is no place in the Highlands where a school is more needed and valued. Mr McInnes, the teacher, has his whole heart in his work, and the people are already devoted to him. They provide him with milk, fish, and potatoes daily, besides giving him cheese and butter. They ran four miles along the coast when I came away, waving shawls and handkerchiefs, and begging me to convey their gratitude and blessings to the Association.'

At about the same time, in 1867, two ELHSA schools on the Harris shores of Loch Seaforth at Molinginish and 'Renigidil' were in a similar situation, though even the brave Miss Bird did not reach them.

'Of all secluded and inaccessible corners known to me either in the highlands or islands, these two inhabited spots are the most inaccessible … We may form some idea of the extreme remoteness of this place by the panic occasioned by the appearance of a quadruped common enough in civilized regions. "Not one of these children had ever seen a horse before" (they encountered it on their way to school), "and on beholding the strange apparition, in one simultaneous fit of terror the poor children fled pell-mell, rushing out upon a small beach up to their waists in the sea, and raising the cry of terror."'

So wrote Dr MacKay in Harris who had maintained the Renigadale school for the past three years at his own expense. It may be noted that children in remote areas of Wester Ross and Harris at this time, and for many years to come, saw even fewer strangers than those on St Kilda and probably therefore did not have their eager enthusiasm dampened by frequent arrivals of unattractive visitors.[75]

*

During the first fifteen years of his labours in St Kilda, when he was teacher as well as minister, Rev. MacKay received no deputies from the Free

Church Highlands Committee. He knew nothing of the letter written in March 1872 by MacLeod of MacLeod, then the new proprietor of the island, asking the committee whether some arrangement could be made whereby the annual interest (£25) of the old mortification could be used to increase the minister's salary. It was not until a letter from MacKay was read on 18 July 1882, reporting the extensive damage done to the church and manse by the storm on 22 November 1881 and requesting repairs, that the committee gave real attention to their remote missionary. There was a short-lived flurry of response. Rev. Roderick MacKenzie of Tarbert in Harris was sent to the island to see how things were, and in September 1882 he gave an account of 'the religious condition of the people', which he found to be 'of an encouraging character', and of the damage done by the severe weather of the previous winter. As Rev. MacKenzie was probably at St Kilda in advance of the factor's second attempt at the end of July to land workmen to carry out the repairs the committee undertook in the autumn responsibility for those needed to church and manse, and when another letter came from John MacKay the following May asking about them they were promptly authorised. Rev. William Ross, Rothesay, visited in June 1883, perhaps to launch the repairs workmen to their task, and when he reported in July he suggested that Rev. MacKenzie should make a second trip as deputy, but it seems that nothing of that sort took place.[76]

John Sands's uncomplimentary comments, with drawing, on Rev. MacKay drew no response from the Free Church Highlands Committee which perhaps knew something of the background. The Napier Commission's visit in 1883 gave the committee no cause for concern, and it would have been pleased to hear Alexander Ross's observation after his visit in 1884 that the islanders were 'ministered to by a very worthy old man, Mr Mackay'. Remarks to the effect that the Sabbath was strictly a day of worship and rest would not have surprised members, nor would descriptions of serious Sabbath quietness and length of services, and no heed was paid to the fact that MacKay was now aged around 67 and not in the best of health. The authors of the late 1870s and the 1880s, being no admirers of the Free Church, had little time for what one called 'the results of those unhappy influences which have unfortunately prevailed on the north side of the Tweed' and condemned them in St Kilda as if they were especially peculiar features of that island's life. Only Malcolm Ferguson, who in 1882 preferred to spend a fine, bright, sunny Sunday in Tarbert at church, revealed a wider knowledge of ecclesiastical practice and problems:

'On making enquiries about churches, we soon ascertained that the Parish Church [at Scarista] was close on 20 miles off, and that there was only one church – a Free – in the village, a circumstance which, I believe, ought to be regarded as a special boon and blessing by the villagers and people in the immediate district; because any one visiting many districts in the north of Scotland, Skye, etc., can hardly fail to observe that church affairs are one of the chief and most engrossing topics that permeate the whole social fabric, and the direct cause of a large amount of unfriendly feeling and bitter strife amongst, in many cases, poor uneducated Highlanders, encouraged and embittered, I have been told, in not a few cases by illiberal narrow-minded ministers, who profess to preach the glorious gospel message of peace, goodwill, and brotherly love amongst professing Christians. A number of us went to the Free Church, and heard a very long, dreich, dreary discourse – the sermon alone lasted an hour and a-half – and I never remember seeing such evident and unmistakeable signs of weariness and impatience on the part of a congregation, a considerable number of whom came from Scalpa.'[77]

Disagreements and discord were characteristic of a kind of religion that had no time for decorative ritual formalities and placed the greatest emphasis upon an individual's spiritual state. Lacking adherents of any differing denomination to argue with, a small community such as St Kilda's with a minister who had been in charge for over twenty years might have been as unlikely to be disturbed by religious disputes as it was to be touched by the crofters' unrest prevailing in many Hebridean islands, yet there was an atmosphere of unease, heightened a little by discussion of possible emigration following McNeill's report; and the publication of Connell's book, highlighting in a journalistic manner every possible instance of dispute, did nothing to reduce the tension. Soon after the presentation of the McNeill report before parliament in March 1886 the Highlands committee contemplated sending a deputation to the island during the summer and referred the matter to its convener on 2 June, but there is no sign that any deputy went to see what was happening in St Kilda before 1889.[78]

That there was definite dissension between the minister and the people of St Kilda for several years there is no doubt. It spoiled the last stages of John MacKay's long incumbency. Unfortunately its prevalence and explanation are only known through Connell's writing, and the facetious and demeaning tale told by him in both articles and book cannot be relied upon as presenting a faithful version of events and personalities. Nevertheless Connell's record has been used as if it were an authoritative and accurate source, and as a consequence MacKay, the Free Church, and St Kilda's religion through the second half of the nineteenth century, all have suffered from exaggerated and generalised disapproval and been treated as major agents in the move towards the eventual desertion of the island. According to one author 'the stern faith of the Free Church, in the manner of its application and of its acceptance, made slaves of the people of St Kilda'. Further criticism followed. 'The damage that was done in little over half a century of Free Church rule was to prove too great for the repairing zeal of latter-day missionaries ..'Yet this was to misjudge the effect of the Free Church and of Rev. MacKay on the island and to underestimate greatly the ability of the people to manage their own affairs. Easily persuaded they may have been, but to say that 'The St Kildans themselves never once voiced a complaint against the clergyman sent to their island, or against the dogma they were asked to accept', was certainly untrue. In the late 1880s, and not for the first time, they took exception to the minister's words and behaviour, but there is no clear evidence for concluding, as popular belief still has it, that MacKay or his church had anything to do with the ultimate 'death' of St Kilda's community.[79]

*

St Kilda in Revolt ran a headline in the *Oban Times* of 20 April 1889. The series of events that lay behind these eye-catching words implied disturbance in the island at an unprecedented level and readers of the Oban paper could not get the detailed story they wanted. For this they would have had to turn to the work of a familiar figure – Robert Connell once again.

When Connell was in the midst of his second visit to St Kilda in 1886 two 'natives' substituted for the unwell minister in church on the Sabbath. The first was Donald MacDonald, one of the two islanders questioned by the Napier Commission and while apparently not an elder still 'the most intelligent and sensible man on the island'; the second was Donald Ferguson, the elder who had just returned from Boreray and was probably acting as ground officer in place of his father Neil. There were already signs of disagreement between Rev. MacKay and Ferguson, who, as Connell wrote, had recently taken it upon himself 'to tell poor Mr. Mackay that unless he was going to make better sermons he had better look out for another job', to which MacKay, not surprisingly, had reacted angrily. MacKay was the island's registrar and kept the records carefully; 'if he was only equally successful at sermon-making', said Connell, 'he would have fewer squabbles with the triumvirate of elders'. Ferguson seems to have been the most forceful of these three, perhaps as 'ruling elder', and evidently took the lead in most disputes, George Murray, the schoolmaster, describing the various quarrels in which he was involved during the winter of 1886-87.[80]

Though the quality of his sermons was not publicly questioned again, so far as is known, Rev. MacKay certainly had arguments with his leading elder, and before long the whole of the community was affected. If sermons were not the real issue then the cause of division had to be discovered elsewhere, and though Murray had portrayed Ferguson as a quarrelsome and overbearing individual blame could not be laid solely upon him. When members of the Free Church presbytery of Uist met on 2 April 1889 they regretted 'to find from letters that have come from that island that matters are not in a satisfactory state between the missionary and the people, and that owing to disagreements between him and the congregation, Mr McKay's ministry is almost deserted'. Without minuting the details of these 'disagreements' the presbytery 'appointed Mr McLean Tarbert and Mr Morrison, Bernera to visit St Kilda, and to enquire and to report'. The clerk was asked to write to MacKay immediately and tell him that the presbytery was of opinion 'that, in the present circumstances of St Kilda, and considering Mr McKay's advanced age, he should retire and leave the field to a younger man, and that in the event of his doing so, they will strongly recommend his case to the Highland Committee, in the hope that they may provide a suitable retiring allowance for him'. The presbytery also decided to send an extract of the minutes to the committee, along with remarks on a replacement if MacKay were indeed to retire.[81]

Clearly there was some impression that all was not well in the manse, and such differences as there had been in 1886 had equally clearly developed into a more disturbing situation through the intervening two years or so. During the rough winter of 1888-89 someone or some group in St Kilda had despatched more sea-borne bottle messages with news that the islanders appeared to have a sufficient quantity of supplies but that 'St Kildian society had been shaken to its centre and completely disorganised by a grave ecclesiastical revolution'. Word of the bottle letters and their contents, and perhaps too of the presbytery meeting, seems to have reached the newspapers, and a familiar figure, the 'Special Correspondent', was soon busy investigating St Kilda affairs again for the *Glasgow Herald*. An article on 15 April 1889 reported the condition of the people at the end of the winter and claimed to give full details of the 'religious conflict' there. From the tone and style of the writing the author was almost certainly Robert Connell. He had visited the island only the previous week and brought himself fully up to date with the situation.

In the course of the recent winter the factor's smack *Robert Hadden* had come 'to grief during a gale .., and is at present at the bottom of Dunvegan Loch'. Feeling it advisable nevertheless to take out seed corn and potatoes prior to the season's sowing John MacKenzie, the factor, looked for means of transport and chartered the smaller smack, the *Janet*, from its owner, Peter McLean, merchant at Dunvegan. He set out on 4 April, having with him as sole passenger the 'Special Correspondent'. The aims were to deliver the goods and letters – perhaps including the communication to MacKay from the presbytery clerk - to confirm that the 'material welfare' of the people was satisfactory, and to find out more about the 'social chaos' supposed to have resulted from the reported 'split in the church'.

The visitors landed in the evening of Saturday 6 April and 'got a warm welcome from one or two, particularly from Mr Macrae, the young teacher, who has been out since last summer, and felt deeply the want of home news'.

Once properly ashore the first step was a call at the manse, where the minister was already going through the mail. 'He greeted us' – presumably the correspondent and the factor – 'very kindly, and ordered tea to be prepared for us at once. He was not looking well, and in reply to inquiries about his health said that the disturbed state of the people during the winter had told seriously on him.' For a while his place in the conversation was taken by the housekeeper, Ann MacDonald, and her brother, both of whom held forth 'on the cruelty to which the minister had been subjected during winter by the erring members of his congregation'. In the meantime someone described as the minister's sister, 'according to invariable custom, was kept in the background', though who this person actually was and the nature and purpose of the custom remain unexplained.

Accommodation for the visiting party was naturally available in the building known as 'the factor's house', where Mr Macrae and Mrs Urquhart, 'the trained nurse sent out .. by Miss McLeod of Dunvegan', were already in residence. The latter was particularly welcoming for while the teacher had friends at the manse she had lacked any friend to talk to during her months in St Kilda and now 'looked upon our arrival as the first glimpse of social sunshine' she had enjoyed. Her only companion, a cheerful but noisy one, was 'a splendid cockatoo' which she had brought with her. In response to enquiries both teacher and nurse gave their views on the material and spiritual state of the island. Though seed corn and potatoes had indeed been wanting the general circumstances of the community were not such 'as to cause any concern to the public or the Government', and so the discussion was largely devoted to the drama of religious controversy, of which the informants were able to give an independent and objective impression even though each had fallen victim to it.[82]

The letters sent in the winter had apparently contained an outline of two main events, around which other minor complaints had circulated. One related to the manse household:

> 'All the families except three took the side of the ruling elder in a dispute he had with the minister's housekeeper. They left the church in the first week of November, and since then a deplorable amount of scandal and gossip has increased the feeling of bitterness to such an extent that they declare now they will not again sit under the present minister although a deputation of thirty ministers of the Free Church should visit St Kilda to settle the dispute.'

A rather more lurid version of the incident told how in the afternoon of 5 November, reckoned by the correspondent to be a suitable date for explosive occurrences, Donald Ferguson was seen leaving the manse 'with an inflamed countenance and waving his arms about his head'. Intensely excited he came to the factor's house and 'announced in language more vigorous than pious, that he would never darken the door of the church while Rev. Mr MacKay officiated in the pulpit or his housekeeper held sway in the manse kitchen'.

The second reason given for the 'war of faith' concerned the minister himself:

> '..the Rev. John Mackay .. had refused to baptise a child until the father of the child should undergo Church discipline for some offence which he had committed. This the man declined to do, and he was supported by a near relation, a ruling elder, and a man of light and leading in the congregation. The progress and details of the dispute were not made very clear in the letters received, but it appeared to culminate in a disruption in which the elder "came out," followed by most of the congregation, leaving three families in the fold of the pastor.'

The complaints amounted to almost one and the same objection to the behaviour of the housekeeper, and so there had emerged opposing groups, the great majority of islanders under the influence of Donald Ferguson, and 'the manse party' consisting of the minister, his housekeeper, and three families including that of Neil MacDonald. As he continued to attend church Macrae was seen to belong to the minister's side and so became unpopular, with the result that when Mrs Urquhart, who seems to have remained impartial, received 'any small luxury' it was brought to her 'with the condition that no share should be given to the teacher'. Furthermore Mrs Urquhart had initially won favour with the majority when, before the 'disruption' took place, she ceased to attend church services. Everyone thought that it was because she objected to 'the manse government', whereas in reality it was owing to the loss of her only hat which was blown away by a gust of wind:

> 'She was therefore in high favour, and was receiving from one family a regular supply of milk. On New Year's Day, which was about two months after the St Kilda disruption, a special service was, according to custom, held in the church, and Mrs Urquhart determined to begin the new year better than she had closed the old one. With all the resources at her command, which were a piece of cloth cut from a dress and an old straw hat from which the cockatoo had in his idle moments removed the front, Mrs Urquhart, with female deftness of finger, put together a respectable, if not a fashionable, headgear and attended divine service. Such backsliding from the islanders' point of view could not be overlooked, and the supply of milk was cut off immediately. She continued to attend church regularly after that, and the minister, who during all her absence had never condescended to inquire as to the reason annexed, graciously

accepted the explanation about the bonnet, and received her back into the fold. The islanders have not yet been enlightened as to the real circumstances of the case, and attribute Mrs Urquhart's return to the church to a sad want of resolution.'

On Sunday the morning and afternoon services and the evening prayer were attended only by the manse party, though there was apparently more general support for the Sabbath school. Monday morning would have been the first opportunity to unload the rest of the provisions from the smack, but the sea was too rough, and so a further visit was paid to the minister, who was reluctant to pass any comment on the cause of controversy.

'He alluded to the difference of opinion that had arisen about giving baptism to the child of a man who had been guilty of some grave errors, but had been supported by the elders of the congregation, and he wondered what kind of conscience an elder could have that would recommend such a man. As I discovered this baptism controversy to be one of at least two years' standing, I suggested that something must have occurred more recently to excite the people to the step they had taken. The people, he said, had always been bad, but never so bad as this winter, and it was his belief that gossip was the cause of the whole of it. It was after a good deal of circumlocution that I ventured to mention the housekeeper as a possible element in the case, and Mr MacKay then said that on the day in November already alluded to there had been a somewhat violent discussion in the manse kitchen between the housekeeper and Donald Ferguson, the elder. The origin of the quarrel was, as usual, some gossip in the place. The minister went into the kitchen and got involved in the discussion, when the elder actually declared that he cared no more for the minister's preaching than for the bleating of a sheep. He then left the kitchen, vowing that he would never attend the church again.'

At a meeting of the rebellious majority held in his house that afternoon, attended by the principal men, several women, and the *Janet's* skipper, Donald Ferguson,'very forcibly and with wonderful brevity for a Gaelic elder', laid the blame firmly on the housekeeper whose careful reporting of 'scandal' to the minister had been going on for years. She had, it was said, been conducting herself as if she were minister. She was always believed, 'had therefore the power of getting Church privileges denied or censure administered to anyone who offended her', and had gone beyond all reasonable bounds in this regard. It was considered that the minister had the duty of trying to settle the quarrel, and since various other faults were to be found with Rev. MacKay they expected the matter to be raised at the Free

Church General Assembly. 'They considered the Assembly was bound to send them another minister, and if not they would apply to the Established Church. If the Established Church would not assist them they would communicate with Mr Spurgeon or with any Christian Church that would send them a minister.'

The manse party denied the validity of the meeting's accusations, stating instead that the main cause of the dispute was 'the overweening ambition of Donald Ferguson .. who ever since Mr MacKay came to the island had tried to get the upper hand'. Ferguson's opponents were prepared to prove that he was not fit to be an elder, and at another interview in the manse Ann MacDonald, 'weeping copiously', showed her great distress.

By this stage of the special correspondent's visit it must have occurred to several in the community that an appeal to the press was a good idea and 'documents' had been drawn up, some of them by 'a very intelligent lad' who the previous year had spent time in Glasgow but being homesick had returned to the island. Other papers had come from a man who had long been a disruptive influence:

'Another batch of documents, and the most original of the whole, had been prepared by the most remarkable St Kildian to be met with – a man who had the enterprise to leave the place when he was 26 years of age and push his way in the world. He was several times round the world, and lived a great part of his life in Australia and California. He is now over 60 years of age and living in St Kilda, to which he had a fancy to return when he had earned a competency. He is, however, far from happily situated in the community, and attributed this to his state of civilisation being too advanced for St Kilda. In politics he is an Advanced Radical, and declares that his attempts to enlighten the people get him into disfavour with the powers that be. He was the first to protest against the autocratic style of the manse government, and left the church some time before the others. His attempt to teach the natives the ways and laws of the world also proved a signal failure, as he shared the fate usually assigned to a prophet in his own country. The result is that he is on equally unpleasant terms with all parties, and does not hold a high opinion of the social tone which pervades St Kildian society. He has married a young and comely St Kildian girl, and when summer comes he intends to carry his young wife away with him to Canada, where he expects to find a more congenial atmosphere for a man of his intelligence and enlightenment … In one document concerning the disruption in the island he says: - "If the Free Church will not look better after this poor island we must look somewhere else. We can say we were better off in the Old Church than we are here in the Free Church now. We are hoping the sun will rise on us yet, and we are getting in need of it. We are like sheep without a shepherd, and what is to come if we gain the whole world and lose our own souls. The Lord will look after his own, and St Kilda is as near to the Lord as any other place."[83]

*

The factor and the special correspondent left after a stay of four days during which each accomplished what he had set out to do. Nothing very startling had emerged, even in the accusations against the minister, about which there was something very old-fashioned. Refusal of baptism was not uncommon in the history of the evangelical church; a late instance of it was thought to have been one reason why Malcolm MacDonald and Murdo MacKay 'exiled' themselves to Rona in 1884. And reporting matters held to be scandalous, usually the task of the elders, was once a traditional feature of parish life throughout Scotland. Perhaps the most interesting discovery was the renewed activity of Ewen Gillies, who, having returned home once more, was busy as ever upsetting everybody. It might even be that he was the primary cause of the whole trouble on the island.

Rev. Mackay had said that he would be writing to Robert Rainy and other leading Free Church people to explain his case, but whether he did or not is doubtful. There was not, of course, very much to explain. But distance, which made communication so much more difficult, helped to magnify an issue which many would see as trivial, and without easy means of getting the dispute in proportion most of the islanders were excessively upset. Their experience of the church through much of the nineteenth century had, if anything, increased the need they felt for religious guidance, and if the provision was insufficient or lacking altogether as it had sometimes been in the previous century under the established church and seemed now to be again under the Free Church a small population in a world of its own for most of the time was left in a sad and pathetic state of uncertainty and confusion. This condition, heightened by contact with visitors who had read newspaper reports, might have been less unhappy if something like the long-departed 'papist' framework of symbolic and linguistic references had existed within the structure of the Free Church, or if a strong body of traditional tales, customs and entertainments had been vigorously maintained. But these things, for better or worse, were missing, the people were at a loss where to turn for a pastor, and the Free Church seemed to be failing to supply the necessary direction and purpose for a people who had come to depend on it, so that Glasgow, Australia or Canada might have offered to some as promising a future as their own island home. It was, in some respects, a repetition of the uncertainties and possibilities around 1850.

On 16 April 1889, the day after it could have read the latest article in the *Herald* from its special correspondent, the Free Church Highlands Committee considered the extract sent by the Uist presbytery, and after some deliberation it was fully convinced that a change of missionary minister in St Kilda was essential. It decided to ask John MacKay to leave the island. Terms for a retirement allowance would be arranged, and the Free Church General Assembly, preoccupied with its own future direction, would be requested to allow the presbytery to ordain a new missionary on terms also to be considered. A letter received by the committee soon afterwards from Rev. John MacLean in Harris, one of the deputies appointed to St Kilda by the presbytery, suggested that the committee should add a deputy of its own and this was agreed, the choice falling upon Rev. Duncan McNicol of Dunoon. Meanwhile Rev. MacKay was already planning to leave the island in the summer, 'and it is understood that the housekeeper and her relatives will accompany him'. On 25 May the *Oban Times* announced that a mail for St Kilda would be 'made up' at the post office on 11 June, on which day the steamer *Clydesdale* would leave Oban for a special trip to St Kilda with Captain MacEachnie, 'who is a thorough master of the difficult navigation of the Island Route', comfortingly in command. It was expected that MacKay, 'whose connection with his parishioners have been somewhat strained of late', would take advantage of the visit to return to the mainland.[84]

Having heard from the Assembly and from a subcommittee the Highlands committee met on 5 June 1889, duly reflected on 'the long and devoted services of Mr McKay for 24 years in the island', and resolved to allow him £40 per annum 'on condition of his leaving the island'. The matter of a new missionary was delayed until the report of the deputies was available but a 'temporary supply or ordinances' would be arranged. The following day the *Dunara Castle* departed with a party of tourists, the three Free Church deputies or 'Commissioners', and the new teacher, John Ross, who it appears had his sister with him after all. The crew of a Harris fishing boat had already told MacKay of the General Assembly's decision to investigate the case of 'the clerical dispute' in St Kilda, and the minister immediately took to his bed. When the deputies arrived they found him 'a good deal distressed' but he was said to have given them a warm and hospitable reception. Having landed on the afternoon of Saturday 8 June they stayed, presumably in the manse, until the following Wednesday when the *Clydesdale* came in with its forty passengers and, the investigation being complete, took them away. From the passengers came an account of how the deputies had satisfactorily settled with the minister:

'Mr Mackay expressed his determination to leave as soon as possible, and when the resolution of the Highland Committee regarding a retiring allowance was made known to him, he expressed his gratitude, at the same time stating that he hoped to be able to leave ... on the 26th of this month. After Mr Mackay leaves, a successor will be appointed, and with this arrangement the St Kildans, with very few exceptions, are quite satisfied. At the same time they expressed their great regard for Mr Mackay, and gratification with the provision made for him in his old age.'

The housekeeper, who '"bosses" the island and the minister', was still seen as the cause of trouble whereas MacKay himself remained loyal to her and blamed the people. He was believed to be 'heartily glad' that he was going to leave St Kilda. 'In future the spiritual needs of St Kilda will be attended to by an unordained minister.'[85]

The deputies – Messrs McNicol, MacLean and Morrison – duly submitted their report to the Highlands Committee which found the contents 'very interesting' and 'quite satisfactory as regards the arrangements made for the retirement of the Rev. John McKay, our ordained missionary, after a lengthened period of service in the island'. The report confirmed that MacKay had 'cordially acquiesced' in the proposals for his retirement, and Rev. MacLean was appointed 'moderator of Session' for the island until the successor was in place.[86]

After so long a connection with St Kilda the minister's departure, apparently without any sister, was an important as well as sad occasion. With him went his stalwart and faithful housekeeper, Ann MacDonald, a woman of the island though the object of complaint. John Ross watched them both leave, sympathising especially with MacKay 'whose last words before entering the boat which was to separate him perhaps for ever from his home of the last twenty four years were "I think it is time I was leaving them now"'. Recollection of that eventful period, which had coincided with such momentous change in the life of the community, must have haunted the minds of those who were going and those who watched them go. Of course the minister had no relatives there to mourn his leaving, though all onlookers were well acquainted with the lonely inscribed stone and accompanying willow tree in the graveyard preserving the memory of Margaret MacKay. 'But I am sorry to say,' Ross remembered, 'there was much more ado made for his housekeeper .. than for himself as I saw clearly.'[87]

The occupants of the manse left, as intended, on the *Hebridean* which indeed called on 26 June:

'The s.s. Hebridean, from St Kilda, called at Lochmaddy on Thursday last, and put ashore nine persons from that island, consisting of the Rev. Mr MacKay, the late minister, his sister, his nephew, and his housekeeper, two women respectively named Mary MacQueen and Christina MacKinnon, Neil MacKinnon, and a man called Gillies, along with his wife. The women, Mary MacQueen and Christina MacKinnon, with the man Neil MacKinnon, their brother, intend proceeding to Skye to consult a doctor there regarding the disease of cancer which these women are supposed to suffer from. They intend returning to St Kilda with the first steamer going there. The man Gillies and his wife intend to emigrate to America immediately … Mr MacKay and the members of his household were to leave next day for Dunvegan, where it is understood Mr MacKay is to stay meantime.'[88]

The journey was continued to Dunvegan where the little manse group went to live near Peter MacLean's store in 'Dr. MacDonald's Cottage', almost opposite to the Dunvegan Hotel. Not long after they had settled in some English tourists heading for St Kilda on the *Hebridean* in the middle of August 1889 took advantage of cargo loading at Dunvegan's pier to call on them uninvited, out of sheer curiosity. The housekeeper introduced MacKay and there was a brief conversation, but even the presence on the steamer of three islanders going home to St Kilda could not persuade him to venture outside, and the visitors soon had no choice but to say goodbye to 'the worthy gentleman'. In 1891 Ann MacDonald, whose age was given as 42, was described as a 'Relative' of the retired minister, and so too was 'John Ross MacDonald', a young man of 19, who had lived in the St Kilda manse for a long time and now worked as a labourer. The actual relationship between the three was not made clear. In 1895, Dr Roderick MacDonald having died, MacKay moved to a house in Kilmuir, Dunvegan, belonging to John Macaskill who farmed at Ullinish, and then a year later he left, apparently going to Lochcarron where he died on 9 April 1901.[89]

A column-long obituary in the Free Church Monthly Record paid tribute to John MacKay's qualities, one of which was his ability to isolate himself for 'thirty years' in a remote island. 'The solitude was to him a cause of no complaint – of no miserable whining for the excitement that begets the ennui of modern life.' His eccentricities were noted as well as his religious devotion:

'As might be expected of one so long absorbed in the contemplation of the Eternal unaffected by modern thought or environment of books and daily literature, he was strangely original and quaint in his expression of religious experience. There was a peculiar, and, indeed, fascinating old world touch about all he said, which could not fail to impress us. His prayers were fervent and unctuous, and his love for his Master was ever on his lips. Never did we see, and we may probably never see again, one who came so near to living in full compliance with the Apostolic injunction – "Pray without ceasing." As he lived so he died, a Free Churchman full of hope and confidence.'[90]

1   KBP 7/28. Writing in 1881 Dr J Brydon, of Hawick, gave his opinion on the people: 'They are sallow-faced, generally dark-haired, and their eyes are dark grey, with a peculiar pensive sadness about their expression, especially those of the young women. It conveys an idea of something approaching to vacancy, just as if they were listlessly gazing away towards some object in the far distant.' [Brydon]

2   Mingulay School Logbook 15 & 29 February 1876, 12 December 1876, pp.54, 77-79, 90-91, 101, 111-112

3   Seton p.246; MacDiarmid p.15

4   KBP 7/60

5   ELHSA CH3/1428/4 4 June 1875, /5 9 May 1877, /7

6   ELHSA CH3/1428/5 10 October 1879

7   The Highlander Vol. VII no.319 20 June 1879 p.8 – when Emily MacLeod arrived 'the minister and all the inhabitants – men, women, and children – were on shore, and there was a hearty shaking of hands'; ELHSA CH3/1428/5 14 November 1879

8   ELHSA CH3/1428/5 9 January 1880

9   The Highlander Vol. VI no.314 16 May 1879 p.8. [For Isabella Ross Munro's death in 1878 see Part 6 n.107]

10 The Highlander Vol. VII no.328 22 August 1879 p.7. In 1881 Dr Brydon wrote: 'with John McCallum & Co.'s splendid steamer The Hebridean, the visit is rendered comparatively safe and certainly very pleasant. Without a doubt, the trip – John McCallum is both principal of the firm and captain – to St Kilda is the most enjoyable six days' sailing that can be found in the waters of the United Kingdom' [Brydon]. For an obituary notice of Dr John Brydon see The Hawick Advertiser 9 June 1905 p.4

11 The Highlander Vol. VII no.328 22 August 1879 p.7 quoting letter to The Spectator, Vol. VIII no.372 23 June 1880 p.8, Vol. VII no.369 4 June 1880 p.5 – 'He [Sands] calls his efforts a game of "Freedom or Feudalism". That is it. He urges that herring as well as cod fishing may be prosecuted at St Kilda.'

12 The Highlander Vol. VIII no.379 11 August 1880 p.2

13 Smith (1879) pp.5, 70, 75. Smith had extensive thoughts on island fuel (pp.57-69). He had been disturbed by the use of turf with the consequent destruction of good pasture land, and was pleased to receive a sympathetic letter (14 July 1879) on the subject from Professor Heddle. Heddle had visited St Kilda in 1879 with the *Dunara Castle* and had met Emily MacLeod who agreed that the prevalent system was extremely damaging. Rev. MacKay seemed to share their views but appeared to accept the people's claim that there was no peat available. Heddle explored the hills and found a modest depth of rather poor quality peat on Mullach Mor. He was disappointed to learn that though fish was taken up to dry in cleitean situated high on the slopes no one was willing to bring peats down much the same distance, and one man, who seemed 'to overawe the rest', said he would rather leave the island than carry peats. Heddle told Emily that the man should indeed leave since he was 'an active instrument for evil', a phrase which was translated for the object of disapproval himself by the minister.

The 'independence' of islanders was a subject for comment by A A MacGregor in more recent times [A A MacGregor: The Western Isles London 1949 pp.231-232]. The people enjoy the independence gained from crofting and fishing. 'This one could admire in them, were they also to assert their independence in other ways – were it not that so many of them are now largely maintained in their so-called independence by a variety of public subsidies and gratuities.' MacGregor suggested a 'drastic curtailment of public expenditure' upon the islands: 'Nowhere in Britain has so much been spent with so little to show for it.' This was the outcome of 'an emotional and sentimental attitude' towards the islands rather than of 'a courageous and realistic policy'. Such a policy, if it had been applied promptly to St Kilda, might have led to the evacuation of the people in the 1880s in spite of their status as a tourist attraction.

14 ELHSA CH3/1428/5 12 March 1880, /6 8 October 1880

15 The census of 1881 notes that Mrs McKinlay was born in the parish of Bracadale. Mrs McKinlay's experiences gave rise to a few tales about St Kilda, e.g.

'In the hard days on the Island, Ann made brose for the men and boys by pouring hot water on oatmeal and stirring it up. On asking how they liked it, she was told it would have been better made with oil (fulmars). Their staple diet being sea-birds, their tastes were more used to oily foods.

'The sheep dogs on St Kilda were very numerous and half wild. Each man owned six or so and visitors were used to being armed with a stick to stop them jumping up. On returning to Skye, Ann went visiting in the pony and trap. When she was about to get down at the croft, she asked the driver for "the stick for the dogs" and apparently everyone there fell about laughing at this.'

The typescript 'Story' states that Emily MacLeod persuaded Mrs McKinlay to go to St Kilda in 1884 but this is evidently incorrect. Attached to the typescript is a reproduction copy of the diploma signed by Dr John Thatcher, lecturer in midwifery etc., and dated at Edinburgh 4 April 1849. [NLS McKinlay ff.32-38]

16 The Highlander Vol. VIII no.396 8 December 1880. Dr Brydon, in 1881, was impressed by Mrs McKinlay and admired her hat: 'the next most distinguished head-gear [after the minister's], the only lady's bonnet, which belongs to the midwife, and I should think, covers the best head in the island. She is a very superior person altogether; studied under Dr Thatcher at Edinburgh; and, with better prospects abandoned, has allowed herself to be exiled to this Patmos, with a true missionary spirit urging her on to deny self and do what she could for these lonely outcasts.' Perhaps he never saw the minister's 'head-gear': 'It is said that there is only one tall crowned hat in the island, the property of the minister. It is reported to be of great altitude, and only entered by its occupant on extraordinary state occasions, such as burials and bridals.' [Brydon]

17 ELHSA CH3/1428/6 8 April 1881, 12 October 1883

18 ELHSA CH3/1428/6 9 November 1883, 11 January 1884, 8 February 1884, 4 March 1884; CH3/1428/7 11 April 1884

19 ELHSA CH3/1428/7 10 October 1884; Murray p.26

20 ELHSA CH3/1428/7 13 March 1885, 28 April 1885, 9 October 1885. McCallum most probably went to St Kilda with the Robert Hadden.

21 CWC no.395

22 ELHSA CH3/1428/7 19 January 1886, 30 March 1886, 14 May 1886; Murray: introduction

23 H MacCallum: 'St. Kilda' in The Caledonian Medical Journal Vol. VII (1909) pp.18-24. When McCallum was teaching in St Kilda there were several people still alive who had lived in the pre-1830s houses. In 1909 he was a minister at Blair Atholl, and was still there in 1913 when he gave a lecture on the island 'illustrated with limelight views' [The Celtic Monthly Vol. XXI (1913) p.19].

24 Murray pp.12, 25, 28; ELHSA CH3/1428/7 14 October 1887, 8 April 1887, 13 April 1888; NLS McKinlay f.38

25 HB 43/734; SOC MS Journal of R Scott Skirving, from which most of the following account of his visit is taken.

26 For the Sunday service and walk at Tarbert, Harris, see p.568 and n.11 above.

27 The words 'and the lazy' were later deleted.

28 The name 'McQueen' (i.e. Donald MacQueen) was entered in pencil.

29 KBP 8/1, 3, 4

30 HB 3/40, 3/43

31 HB 3/40, 3/45

32 NC (Evidence) p.865; Ferguson pp.10, 14-15, 21-23

33 KBP 8/5, 6

34 DC Section 2 637/5/3 The tradesmen were to work on the storehouse.

35 DC Section 2 637/5/4

36 DC Section 2 637/4/11

37 NC (Evidence) p.871

38 DC Section 5/133 Newspaper cutting 5 June 1883: 'The Crofters' Commission visit to St Kilda'

39 NC (Evidence) Vol. II pp.864-875

40 See n.38

41 NC (Report) Appendix A no. XII pp.38-39

42 Ross (1893). The account is largely based on this article. Henry Evans passed various comments on St Kilda in his letters. For instance, two letters to Miss [Emily?] MacLeod contain the following remarks:

'...everyone appears contented and they are quite pleased to be rid of that Californian lunatic. His last "threat" was to return next summer and take away every soul from the island. Probably they will end by putting him in the sea and no harm either, for surely the law does not reach here! I did suggest that course to the minister.'

'The new school-master [MacCallum] appears to be a nice douce sensible young fellow, I took him round the islands in [the] yacht yesterday and had a good deal of conversation with him.' [20 July 1885 DC Section 2 638/2/4]

'My opinion, whatever it is worth, is, that the St. Kilda people are very well off, far better than people of the same kind of standing in Harris for example, and much better housed.

'Of their mode of life and its drawbacks I say nothing, no two people would think the same about it. I have always thought them a happy, prosperous, and affectionate people and think so still. For these artificial megrains they have been suffering from are surely like the morning dew.'

[8 October 1885 DC Section 2 638/2/5]

Evans seems to have used a Harris man as 'pilot' through the Sound of Harris, for Ross mentioned that the intended pilot at Obbe was 'an old pilot' called 'Johnnie Macrae'. Unfortunately he had gone off to Tarbert, so in his place they found his cousin, reputed to be efficient and with experience of St Kilda. It was arranged that he arrive at 6 a.m. but he did not turn up till 7.30, 'not from any special cause, but from the inveterate habit of the natives in the district, who are bad early risers' [Ross (1893) p.73].

43 DC Section 2 638/2/1 & 2; McKinlay f.35
44 DC Section 4 1380/4
45 DC Section 2 637/6/4, 637/4/12
46 North British Daily Mail 18 August 1885; newspaper cuttings, NTS Seton copy
47 One visitor got a live puffin for 3d, others for 1s. Stockings cost 2s, socks 1s 6d a pair, 'native cloth' 3s a yard.
48 Northern Chronicle (date?): letter 8 September 1885 – but this date should perhaps be 18 September in view of the storm being 12-14 September [DC Section 5/133. See n.50 below]
49 Northern Chronicle (date?): letter 2 October 1885
50 Inverness Courier no.4072 1 October 1885 – petition dated 15 September 1885. The assessor was Mr Balderston; Inverness Courier no.4076 10 October 1885 – letter from MacLeod of MacLeod 5 October 1885.
51 Inverness Courier no.4077 13 October 1885 – letter from Rev. MacKay 16 September 1885 and letter from Alexander Sutherland 29 September 1885; KPB 8/7 letter from Rainy 8 October 1885, including letters from MacKay to Rainy and MacColl.
52 KBP 8/10
53 'Relief of St Kilda' etc. in Glasgow Herald 21 October 1885. At much the same time a report from the Northern Isles stated: 'it seems that the poor people in Foula are in as bad a condition as the people of St Kilda' [HN Vol. III no.108 2 November 1885].
54 See n.53
55 'The Island of St Kilda – Visit of Her Majesty's Ship Jackal' in Glasgow Herald 26 October 1885; MacKenzie Papers GD403/52/1-3 telegrams, /4 letter from Angus MacLeod, /5 letter from Sir William Collins
56 McNeill pp.4-11; HN Vol. III no.108 2 November 1885 – article 'The Distress at St Kilda'
57 Glasgow Herald 21 October 1885
58 Glasgow Herald 23, 24 & 26 October 1885
59 Two weeks after the Scotsman article of 7 April 1886 Emily MacLeod received a letter, dated 16 April 1886, from her brother Norman MacLeod of MacLeod, then in Paris, in which he wrote: 'The "Scotsman" also came today. I am not sorry Mr McKay should get a check. He is too apt to write what the people ask for, and to commit himself to it. The St Kilda men are cunning. They think they have only to demand something and they get it. To be sure they have been successful hitherto, but as the article says they may cry "Wolf" too often' [DC Section 4 1461/49].
60 'News from St Kilda' in Glasgow Herald 28 June 1886. The following account of Connell and St Kilda is largely derived from this article and from his book. As for payment in return for photographs see also O G Pike: Through Birdland Byways London N D pp.51-54
61 HN Vol. II no.91 29 June 1885
62 'Notes on a Trip to St Kilda' in Glasgow Herald 15 July 1886

[63] Murray p.3

[64] The following account is based on Murray's diary. That Finlay Gillies was able to hunt puffins on Soay at the age of 80 need cause no surprise. 'As an instance of the hardihood of the islanders, one of the rowers happened to be the oldest inhabitant, and although his age was just eighty, he pulled the whole distance [from Hirt to Boreray] without once stopping, although his younger companions twice changed oars' [O G Pike: Through Birdland Byways London N D p.153].

[65] ELHSA CH3/1428/7 8 March 1889. 'Mr Murray' was to go as teacher to Lochboisdale and according to John Ross he then went to Eriboll. Glasgow Herald 24 & 25 August 1887; WHS p.62

[66] FCM 1 August 1888 pp.225-226

[67] Sands (1878) p.30. Around 1886-1887 the annual contribution seems to have been about £18 [FCM 1 June 1888 p.187.] Clarke, whose reference to £30 may have been an exaggeration, also mentioned a St Kilda contribution of £8 a year to 'foreign missions' [See n.46].

[68] ELHSA CH3/1428/7 9 October 1888; Connell p.109

[69] Nurses at St Kilda NAS AF57/1 letter 20 September 1890

[70] Census 1881, 1891; ELHSA CH3/1428/7 8 March 1889, 10 May 1889. After leaving St Kilda Macrae seems to have gone to Ardow near Tobermory [J Ross].

[71] R Thomson: A Cruise in the Western Hebrides or a Week on Board The S.S Hebridean Glasgow 1891. Thomson's description of the teacher indicates that the latter was indeed George Murray, that the inspecting lady was Miss Rainy, and that therefore the year was 1886.

[72] Dr Archibald Campbell of Glasgow also recorded this wreck in his account of 'A Trip to St Kilda' [OT 13 April 1889]. He was describing his 'cruise' on the Dunara Castle in the summer of 1888. 'We arrived in the east bay, opposite which is the landing place of the island, and the spot where all the inhabitants have their houses, and anchored within a short distance of the shore. Immediately inside where we anchored was the wreck of a schooner, her masts being visible. It was stated that she had sprung a leak, and tried to run for shore, but settled down before getting far enough in.'

[73] J Ross: Journal

[74] News, possibly unsubstantiated, of a pirate ship off St Kilda, was received as late as the beginning of February 1900: 'Stories ran from mouth to mouth about the last time a pirate was seen in these waters, and it was said the men, the masts, and the deck were covered with blood.' Signalling with flags from the shore failed to arouse a response. 'The effect of the scare, however, was that a good many of the islanders left their houses, and took to the hills behind the village, and remained hidden in the clefts of the rocks all night.' The inspector in charge of building the pier with difficulty persuaded them to emerge and return to work. A mundane and reasonable explanation of this story was offered; and Alexander Ferguson, writing from Glasgow, said that the whole thing was 'a splendid piece of fabrication'. [OT 10 & 17 February 1900]

[75] FCMR no.77 (1 December 1868) pp.276-277; FCMR no.87 (1 October 1869) p.228 - 'A teacher has perseveringly laboured for many years in the remote island of Mingalay, himself the only Protestant on the island, which is so very difficult of access that scarcely any stranger ever visits it'. FCMR no.62 (2 September 1867) pp.201-202

[76] HC CH3/989/3 pp.311, 317, 355, 362, 366

[77] Ross (1893) p.89; Seton p.272; Ferguson p.14

[78] HC CH3/983/4 p.54

[79] Steel pp.92, 102

[80] Connell p.85

[81] FCPU CH3/596/1 p.27 (2 April 1889)

[82] Mrs Urquhart went to St Kilda with the Dunara Castle which left Greenock on 26 July 1888. Dr Archibald Campbell wrote, somewhat inaccurately: 'I may here mention that among our passengers was a lady nurse or midwife sent out by Miss MacLeod of MacLeod, the first who has ever been on the island, although Miss MacLeod offered to send one about ten or twelve years ago, but the natives did not see any necessity for it, as Mr MacKay the minister seems to act their medical as well as spiritual adviser. This nurse also brought with her a cockatoo which caused some amusement to the islanders, but I think it extremely unlikely that the bird will survive the winter if it is at all severe.' ['A Trip to St Kilda' Part II OT 13 April 1889] The Glasgow Herald article of 15 April 1889 shows that the bird had indeed survived [see n.83

below].

83   This account of the controversy is chiefly derived from the special correspondent's article in the <u>Glasgow Herald</u> of 15 April 1889 with its variety of headings: 'Visit to St Kilda. Condition of Islanders during Winter. Full Details of Religious Conflict. Statements by the Minister and the People.'

84   <u>HC</u> CH3/983/4 pp.140, 148; 'News from St Kilda – The Split in the Church' in <u>OT</u> 20 April 1889, also 25 May 1889.

85   <u>HC</u> CH3/983/4 pp.149-150; 'The Free Church Commissioners Visit to St Kilda' in <u>OT</u> 15 June 1889, also 22 June 1889

86   <u>FCM</u> 1 October 1889 p.294; <u>HC</u> CH3/983/4 pp.152-153

87   J Ross: Journal

88   'Arrival of the St Kilda Minister at Lochmaddy' in <u>OT</u> 6 July 1889

89   J Ross: Journal; Logie pp.16-17; Census 1891; Inverness-shire Valuation Rolls 1895-1897. In 1890 MacKay asked for an increase of £10 to his pension but this was refused [<u>HC</u> CH3/983/4 p.187]. Dr Roderick MacDonald died 1894-1895.

90   <u>FCM</u> May 1901 p.85

PART VIII

THE BEGINNING OF THE END
St Kilda without Angus Fiddes

Visitors in the closing years of the nineteenth century, and long after, prolonged the uncomplimentary caricature-like impression of John Mackay launched by John Sands, and a further dispute between minister and elder, each with his supporting faction, led to the departure of the last ordained churchman. Previously there had been agreement between them over several important matters, in particular their shared objection to the tourist attempt to make a showpiece of the island community on the occasion of a wedding. They also agreed on the necessity of a proper means of landing and of harbouring larger island boats.

Events around 1900 were to demonstrate how useful the minister could be in helping to advance the material as well as spiritual welfare of the inhabitants. With the aid of Angus Fiddes, the last minister to reside in St Kilda, the notorious infant mortality was at last prevented, education was extended and a school building added to the church. A landing pier was constructed by 'outside' engineers and an island workforce (an example of cooperation which might have been repeated in the future) in the face of inclement weather and of more calls for evacuation or emigration. A kirk session minute book was begun. None of these achievements, however, prevented the criticisms and disagreements to which the minister, at whatever period, had long been subject on matters of attitude, mainland intervention, and, latterly, biblical or philosophical interpretation. The rather mysterious and perhaps trivial dispute that closed the career of Angus Fiddes in St Kilda seemed to be the outcome of external influences channelled through him and allowed a strong elder to lead opposition against him rather than against the source of the trouble. In this way the church, not for the first time, found itself involuntarily the rather surprising means whereby the 'outside world' had its impact on the islanders.

After Fiddes was gone missionary teachers served for short periods until the population left in 1930. They dealt with troubles of all kinds from medical problems to disturbing talk about imminent evacuation. They were visited annually by 'deputies', now from the United Free Church, who performed the duties lying outwith the scope of missionary work. Yet, in spite of all the interventions, distractions and changes of religious teaching over the centuries, there lingered among the people to the final years of occupation and long afterwards that sense of attachment, that peculiar knowledge of St Kilda custom and devotion to tradition which seemed to go back beyond the visitors, the sermons of John Macdonald, the struggles of Alexander Buchan, beyond the lost crucifix and the Reformation, to those shadowy 'natives' contemporary with Brendan and Columba and possibly even to their distant forebears.

CHAPTER 1

Mackay's reputation, John Ross the teacher, and the St Kilda 'wedding'

It would have been pleasing had the picture of Rev. John MacKay drawn by John Sands and writers that followed him been allowed to fade on his leaving St Kilda but this was not to happen. Because Robert Thomson's book, when published in 1891, consisted of recollections from four or five years earlier it revived in readers' minds the period when MacKay was minister on the island and was of course far from complimentary in its references to him. On landing there Thomson and his companions had been 'anxious to get all the information possible' about the place and therefore were eager to visit the people in their houses. But as if he had already decided that MacKay was an object of mockery Thomson had thought that a call on the minister was necessary first of all:

'As we moved along we saw at the outside of his manse, and were introduced to his small kingship, the Rev. Mr McKay, who had been minister *and more* for a long period of years; but from his looks and manner, he must have had a bad billious attack the night before, as he seemed in anything but a pleasant frame of mind, and did not show any warmth of welcome to the strangers, or appear grateful for their coming so far to see, and thereby take an interest in the island over which he ruled. He seemed anxious for news, but he would not inquire about the outside world, in case it would be considered too much condescension on his part, yet he could not keep his curiosity entirely under control, but the moment any questions were asked of him, he retired into his shell, and would not give any information whatever, in fact it was only by the process vulgarly known as pumping, that he could be got to speak, and then only in monosyllables. We were beginning to get tired of the process, when one of our party with all due formality presented his reverence with a large cake of golden gem tobacco, which seemed to give satisfaction and to mollify him a bit, but his highness was so unmannerly as to grab at it in a half shamefaced way just as a child would, and quickly deposited in his trouser pocket before the donor had done speaking, he then grunted out some words which were supposed to be thanks, but it may have been anything else for all we knew, and gave a sickly kind of smile, half satisfied, half pettish as a spoiled child might do, but at the same time, by turning away, he distinctly showed us that we were unwelcome, at least so far as he was concerned. Indeed he was altogether the most ungracious, uncommunicative, and uninteresting person it had ever been my misfortune to meet on my holidays. As we could not tolerate his arrogance, we did not trouble ourselves to solicit his favour, therefore we considered it best to accept the invitation so kindly given to us by some of the natives, and get what information we could about the island from them, so we left his reverence alone with his stalwart *premier*, who was of the *feminine gender*, and first favourite at his court; she was quite able to *boss* the whole show, his priestly kingship included.'[1]

This long paragraph, relying upon an already popular view of MacKay as a ridiculous figure, was as absurd as it was rude and did no credit to the author, whose own intrusive arrogance scarcely deserved the minister's monosyllabic answers, but it helped to perpetuate the poor reputation of a man now retired and resident in Skye. Further similar remarks, exaggerated and inaccurate, were made on the length of sermons and the severe regime which MacKay was said to have imposed, until, moving on to the developments of 1889, Thomson was able to write: 'I am pleased to learn, for the sake of the islanders, that he was been forced to retire.'

Speaking, as it were, from the future, some years after his own few hours at St Kilda, Thomson assumed an unsubstantiated position of authority and associated MacKay with what he considered the least attractive side of the Free Church; he looked forward with the hope that the successor, a Mr Fiddes, would be a great improvement:

'The people themselves could be taught to be more self-reliant and industrious, but at present they have no backbone, every independent sentiment, and aspiration after self-culture, has been ruthlessly crushed out of them, by a narrow dogmatic system of dictatorship, both spiritual and temporal, which has held up God the supreme giver of all good, not as a loving Father, who pitieth his children, and would that not one should be lost, but as a cruel, relentless, tyrannical, exacting, vengeful God; consequently the majority of the people have become morose, and very narrow in thought. However, it is sincerely hoped that on the change now accomplished, they will revive again, and that Mr Fiddes will be successful in his labours, but had they continued long in the conditions they were in at our visit I believe they would soon have been completely demoralised, and depending for a living only on the charity of a sympathetic public.'[2]

It is quite possible that Thomson was stirred to produce his account by reading a similar record of a visit to St Kilda, also with the *Hebridean*, in 1889. D W Logie's 'week' was 12-17 August, and his story first appeared in the *Stirling Sentinel* three days afterwards. The two articles were then run together in book form and published the same year.[3]

Logie and his friends, including two ministers and two ex-bailies of

Stirling, took a train to Oban where they joined the steamer and found themselves, like Thomson, fortunate in their company: 'I learned from one of the passengers that there were three St Kildans on board – a man, his wife, and a girl. Naturally I went in search of them'. Having approached the three he found that only the girl could speak and understand English. It seems likely that the islanders were Neil MacKinnon, Christina MacKinnon, and Mary MacQueen, who had been leaving St Kilda on the *Hebridean* at the same time as Rev. MacKay.

> 'The girl told me that she had been unwell, and had left St Kilda about seven weeks ago to go to the Edinburgh Infirmary, where she had been under medical treatment ever since. She also told me that the man and woman were her uncle and aunt, and that they had left St Kilda about three weeks ago – the aunt being ill also ... The form of the aunt's face, and her sallow appearance, along with a peculiarity about the eyes, gave a downcast look, as if she had been struck by a sudden light. This was not so marked in the face of the girl, through her not having so sallow a countenance, nor so long as her aunt's .. Still, she had a slight appearance of the peculiarity of the eyes ... They were of medium height, and seemed intelligent, though evidently lazy, and of a dependent and sneaking nature. It was somewhat difficult to keep up a conversation with them. I got from them, however, that on no account would they prefer to live anywhere else than at St Kilda. Even the girl expressed this.'[4]

The extraordinary assumption after only a brief conversation on the *Hebridean* that these three islanders were lazy, dependent and sneaking is a clear sign that Logie was going on his trip with the usual baggage of prejudice and preconception; but in spite of his approach and perhaps because he believed that laziness and other 'faults' were the marks of a truly primitive people he still intended to 'get' information from any inhabitant he happened to meet during his few hours of opportunity. Like other collectors he gave no indication that he was grateful for anything he 'got'.

After calls at Tobermory and Tiree the steamer reached Dunvegan, and here three English passengers went off to impose themselves on Rev. MacKay while the three going home to St Kilda paid no attention to their former minister and chose to 'visit a farmhouse nearby'. There followed a pleasant crossing to Loch Eport, where in the sheltered waters a kind of musical evening took place:

> 'Shortly after the vessel was anchored, the three St Kildans entertained us by singing several of their hymns, which they executed with considerable taste. They sang these hymns in Gaelic, so that I am unable

to name them. The first was sung to an old Gaelic measure, the second was sung to "Coleshill", and the third to "Martyrdom" – all of them slow measures – and all executed with great taste. The man read two lines, and then raised the tune, followed by the two female voices. In the still grey twilight of this magnificent Highland Loch it had really a charming effect – an effect which, in its quaintness, no music in any church could equal.'[5]

The singers may not have thought of their 'performance' as either entertaining or quaint, words which in the quiet setting of calm Loch Eport might have been more appropriately applied to the next 'turn': 'Afterwards our English friends – Miss E. E. Blyth, Miss Coward, Mr Charles Oldham, Mr C. G. Coward, and Mr Alfred Coward, entertained the company with song and recitation.'

At St Kilda there was the usual affectionate welcome for those returning home, 'and', said Logie, 'the flow of gibberish was something overpowering'.[6] Using the girl as an interpreter he ordered two live young fulmars and a wren for taking away with him but was told that it would be impossible to catch a wren in mid August. Then, after the visit to the houses, they met the new missionary:

'The present clergyman on the island – the Rev. Angus Fiddes, with whom we had some conversation on our visit in regard to the inhabitants, informed us that he had for many years officiated as a clergyman in the Highlands, but that nowhere where he had been stationed had he found, as he found in St Kilda, that in each house the song was raised in family worship. He had only been, he said, about six weeks on the island, and spoke highly of the religious fervour and piety of the inhabitants.'

The Stirling tourists also met John Ross, 'the young and intelligent teacher' of about 17 children, and thought he was named Macfarlane. They concluded that 'Macfarlane', 'having been employed by a few benevolent ladies in Edinburgh to go to St Kilda and teach the children the various branches of education', would soon 'make English the language of the island'. Ross, officially replaced by Rev. Fiddes as teacher, was carrying on his duties until the end of August, at which time it was intended that Fiddes would take over and the ELHSA responsibility would be much, though not entirely, reduced. Fiddes, however, 'informed us that in all likelihood he also would leave the island early next spring' as the arrangement did not allow for him to continue beyond that time.[7]

As the *Hebridean* began its homeward journey it passed close to Boreray and, in accordance with the unfortunate custom of visiting vessels, blew its steam whistle off Stack Lee to make the gannets fly up and astonish the passengers. On the way back one of Logie's live fulmars hanged itself in the loose string supplied by Rev. Fiddes to tether it in the cabin. The other one was fed on bits of raw fish which it ate greedily 'and now and again squirted out of his beak fully a teaspoonful of foul-smelling oil'. Logie himself enjoyed the well-managed facilities of the steamer and came to the conclusion that a fishing station and landing place should be constructed at St Kilda, the islanders doing all the work.

Ross, watching the party go, had his own thoughts on both the people of St Kilda and those who came to look at them. He had been given the impression before his arrival that the islanders were unattractive and difficult to get on with, and perhaps there were problems, but as he discovered 'the better one gets acquaint[ed] with them the more one is convinced that at heart they are a well enough meaning people'; to which he was to add, on leaving:

'.. The people were exceedingly kind to me quite a different character they had to what was represented to me on my landing. One has to stay some time amongst them to know them thoroughly.

'One can have no idea of a St. Kilda[n] by paying him a flying visit and I know by my short stay with him that although he like other men has his shortcombings he has many good points to balance. And the way he treats a stranger depends greatly on the stranger himself. What else could one expect from the inhabitants of such an isolated island?'

Frequently the opinions of outsiders were mistaken, for 'Parties are very often if not always led to take a wrong view of St. Kildan character during a stay of a few hours'.[8]

*

With Angus Fiddes coming as teacher as well as minister John Ross had no more than three months in St Kilda, during which time there were brief visits from one or two steamer groups and the rather more extended presence of a botanist, Alexander Gibson, who was on the island when Logie arrived. The new minister was rather more energetic than his predecessor and took part in island activities. Ross, Gibson and Fiddes accompanied an expedition for fulmars to Dun, although Fiddes went fishing with men left in charge of the boat and Gibson spent some time looking for plant specimens. On another occasion Ross and Gibson tried hunting puffins. The teacher was a careful observer and recorder, with the result that after he had left the island he wrote up an account of the place in which he covered nearly every possible subject that would serve to remind him of his experience and be of interest to others.

He commented of course on the school, regularly held in the church; all the older children, he claimed, could now speak English fluently, as well as learning some grammar, geography, history and arithmetic. 'I asked them once whether they would like to leave the island and the majority were decidedly in favour of doing so.'

In fact Ross was probably one of those who thought that the young should leave and 'push' their way in the world, something which would have meant the whole population soon abandoning its home. As it was he was quite glad to leave himself, thereby avoiding 'the perhaps terrible experience of a winter in St. Kilda', although he regretted parting from the people and especially from the children. On 31 August 1889 he wrote his last letter from the island, in which he said, as if in haste, 'I am going by the *Clydesdale* just now'; and by 5 September he was at home with his parents at Kingsburgh. In his thoughts was Angus Fiddes, whom he had last seen all alone but who had quickly acquired 'an old housekeeper' from Lewis 'to look after his temporal wants', and teach sewing. This lady was Catherine MacLennan from Carloway, who, Ross speculated, had probably been a minister's servant or housekeeper before.[9]

While in St Kilda Ross had been in communication with James Gall Campbell of Sunderland who, rather like Charles Kelsall forty years earlier, took the island to heart and became another of its 'benefactors'. He sent marbles for the children though they 'had not the slightest idea of what to make of them' until Ross showed them how to play games, and, just as Ross was leaving, some books arrived which were, with the approval of the ELHSA, the first of what would be a St Kilda library, donated by Campbell and looked after by Rev. Fiddes. In return Campbell asked for eggs of wild birds, a request which Ross left with Alexander Ferguson to deal with.[10]

When he reached Kingsburgh Ross already knew that his next 'port' as he called it would be in Uist and in mid September he received a letter from Miss Rainy of the ELHSA telling him he was to go to Gramisdale on the north coast of Benbecula and that his sister was to accompany him. By this time he was aware that Campbell and his wife were planning a long stay on St Kilda in the summer of 1890, and it seems to have been this that encouraged him to gather his notes into a 'monstrous book' Campbell had sent him. Once at Gramisdale Ross continued to write to Campbell with information about St Kilda and about Benbecula. He also reported on progress made in the book and when the account was finished it was apparently sent to Campbell for his interest and amusement. Before the end of November the purpose of Campbell's proposed expedition was clear. He was certainly expecting to take the rest of the library; but he was also assembling a tourist party to attend the forthcoming marriage of the so-called 'Queen' of St Kilda, Ann Ferguson, to John Gillies, known as 'Ian Ban'. Of this rather doubtful event Ross wrote in his 'Notes':

'The only marriageable man is to marry the Queen of St. Kilda and who would blame him. They would have been married before we left but unfortunately the minister did not get a sufficiently comprehensive licence to meet the requirements of a place as St. Kilda and so we had to forego the honour of "getting the Queens wedding".

'But it may create more stir as it is for she herself told me that they were going (D.V.) to Glasgow next summer for that very purpose and one important enough I think.

'But it must be a sight worth seeing as neither party ever left St. Kilda before and the young man is rather a bashful and excitable fellow although [he] had the experience of passing through the marriage ceremony once already."In short" he is a widower.'[11]

These words may have had something to do with Campbell's idea of making the wedding a public show, just as cliff-climbing had long been, with presents as reward. If not for this reason the event was certainly re-located at some stage from Glasgow to St Kilda, and Campbell made arrangements for John Ross and his sister to join the visiting party which would travel to the island in May. With the promise of the great number of presents the visitors would bring, it was expected that the wedding would be fixed at a time to suit the arrival of the steamer at the end of the month. One of the gifts would be the wedding-dress, ready made on the assumption that the 'Queen' was an average, fairly thickset, St Kilda woman, and this would mean smartening up the bridegroom. 'The Queen to be dressed up in the height of fashion', wrote Ross, 'and her Consort strutting at her side in Blanket sleeves would make rather an odd figure.'[12]

As the early months of 1890 passed Campbell grew ever more enthusiastic. He asked for details about the couple down to the size of the Queen's foot and was perhaps slightly troubled by the fact that neither bride nor groom could speak English, but the only real concern was whether the guests would be able to land and so it was thought safer that the steamer's arrival should be a day or two before that of the ceremony. Towards the end of April, when the weather had become threateningly stormy, the wedding presents were mounting ever higher and included 'Digestive Syrup' and Bovril as well as some silver teaspoons.[13]

Campbell had wanted to pay a visit prior to the wedding in order to check on arrangements but this proved not to be possible. A letter from Ross to Campbell of 2 May 1890 indicated as much: 'I am sorry you are not getting out before the wedding but I have no doubt things will be all right.' It was a pity, given all the effort and anticipation: 'The wedding preparations must really have been very expensive to you wasting both time and money. But I do hope they will be appreciated which I know from the spirit in which you have carried them on from the beginning is the return that would be most pleasing to you. You have done for them Sir what they cannot sufficiently appreciate. You have led the way and that well in bringing St. Kilda into true civilization and making it part of Great Britain.' The bridegroom's measurements were included in this letter though it is not clear how they were obtained. Nearly a fortnight later a revised list of presents had been drawn up and it seemed to Ross that 'you will have a perfect ship load going out with you'. On board would be 'the "American Organ"' which Ross was sure 'will be a cause of great astonishment if it does not be eclipsed totally by the Brides cake'. He had seen a sketch of the cake, 'a perfect mass of great beauty and undoubtedly of great excellence for the wedding'. There were still hopes that Ross and his sister would be able to join in, but what Rev. Fiddes thought of the whole extraordinary affair was not known and the 'Queen' and her 'Consort' had never been asked either. On 14 February the ELHSA had announced 'that the Clydesdale was to leave Oban for St Kilda on the 27th May' and that Mr Campbell had collected books for a library there and would welcome 'additional donations thereto'. Now the great day had come and on 28 May 1890 the steamer *Clydesdale* entered the bay at St Kilda with Campbell, his books, and his company of wedding guests.[14]

*

The Free Church presbytery of Uist having recommended the appointment of an unordained missionary to St Kilda as a temporary measure, and suggesting that in addition to his responsibility for the spiritual welfare of the islanders he should also 'conduct work in the school hitherto carried on by the Agent of the Ladies' Association', the Highlands committee had accepted this arrangement and authorised an allowance of travelling expenses for whoever would fill the post.[15]

Angus Fiddes, the person chosen, was from Easter Ross. He was born in the parish of Tarbat in or about 1843. At the age of 8 he was living at Petley with his widowed mother Jane Fiddes and attended a local school. He had at least four brothers and one sister, all of whom were considerably older; and Jane, as well as three of her sons, worked as a labourer, perhaps on a nearby farm. Angus too may have spent his first working days in the same way, but he entered upon his career in the church some years before his appointment to St Kilda and in the summer of 1887 he was a Free Church probationer in Torridon. The presbytery of Uist had hopes that through the presence on St Kilda of a preacher and teacher, probably for a year, 'harmony may be restored in the congregation', and Fiddes evidently gave this matter some necessary thought. On 16 July 1889 the Highlands committee was pleased to report that everything had fallen into place:

'For carrying on the work in the meantime the acting Convener stated that steps had been taken to secure the services of Rev. Angus Fiddes, probationer, who after fully considering the case had indicated his willingness to undertake the work. It was resolved that he should sail by the Steamer from Glasgow on the 25th Inst., that the engagement should be for nine months, and that the Salary should be £80 Sterling for that period, vizt. £70 from the funds of this Committee and £10 expected to be given by the Ladies' Association.'[16]

Accommodation was naturally in the manse where three rooms were to be furnished 'in a plain and comfortable way', the furniture of course remaining the property of the church, and after only a little over two months it was 'already clear to the Committee they could not have made a better selection'. It appears that Fiddes, a Gaelic speaker, was immediately well received, except by Neil MacDonald, the former housekeeper's brother, who with his family had belonged to John MacKay's 'manse party'.[17]

'The manse, which was in a bad state of repair, he has thoroughly renovated, and as the Committee sent furniture for a parlour and bedroom, along with needed kitchen utensils, he is comfortably settled down for the winter. The people gave him a most cordial welcome, and, with the exception of one family, are most regular in their attendance on his services.

'The islanders appreciate highly the kindness of the Church in thus providing for their spiritual interests. Mr Fiddes was commissioned to send by the last mail their contributions to some of the schemes of the Church ... He thinks a local mail boat may be launched from the island, as on former occasions, about the beginning of the year. At the date of writing (August 31), the health of the island was good, and there seemed to be sufficient provision for the winter. It is quite cheering to read the account Mr Fiddes gives of his surroundings and of his prospects for the coming months.'[18]

In the third week of April 1890 the Highlands committee agreed to correspond with Fiddes, 'when the communication with St Kilda opens for the season', on the subject of summer arrangements, which would include the date of the annual communion and the fate of the missionary. But before that Fiddes had to cope with the proposed wedding.[19]

On 24 May, only four days before the arrival of the *Clydesdale*, Fiddes wrote to Mrs MacLeod of MacLeod with 'all the news of your people'. He was glad to say there were no scandals to report and, for the moment, 'peace and happiness' prevailed. But it was necessary to explain his fears about the visit of the steamer, and in particular about J G Campbell:

'Now with respect to the Gentleman from Sunderland who is getting up a Free Library for this Island I have grave doubts as to the sincerity of his motives. He is by profession a Publisher of that town and as far as I can make out the proprietor of a newspaper called the "Daily Echo" of that town.

'In the Oban Telegraph he is represented as a "Tourist-Conductor" and that in January last [he] came to Oban to make arrangements for his annual Tour in the West Highlands. He is advertised to come here on the 28th inst with a party of 50 from Sunderland to marry Ann Ferguson and for this end has obtained through advertisement in his own and other publications so many presents for the wedding.

'A certain Revd. Mr. Rae one of the party is to perform the ceremony. I learn that he has been making no small amount of stirr to accomplish his purpose in the south.

'I have materials in my possession, his own letters, to prove him an impostor. All this is being done for mercenary purposes, the gratification or amusement of his party and make this affair the occasion for the publication in a book form with photographic views of the event and of the people. In the first place to give sport to his party at the expense of the simplicity of the people and secondly to publish a record of the event and other things he can gather together and colour the materials with truth and falsehoods in such a taking manner as will command a ready sale in the market.

'This is my own personal conviction which a perusal of his letters conveys. I have warned all parties here against him and his proposals, more especially the parties waiting to be united and their parents and got them to agree that no such ceremony shall take place for the purpose of sport or publication.

'I have written to Revd. Mr. MacLean Tarbert, Harris, Moderator of Session here and enclosed all the communication I received from this Campbell and also another Gentleman in Oban to watch the interests of this Island and people lest we might be imposed upon but the weather is so calm and the wind contrary that there is no prospect of dispatching letters before Sunday to reach parties in time before the 28th inst the date fixed for the Clydesdale being here.

'This Campbell says that he has collected 400 Vols for this Island. In another letter [he] says a great many of these are promised. In one letter he says, that he has a suit for the Bridegroom, in another that he was in communication with the owners of the Hebridean to know what they would charge from Harris to this Island – his purpose being to get the measure of the Bridegroom for a marriage suit and pair of boots, but the fare sought £25 was such that he could not afford it so wrote me to get the measures required and the consent of parties.

'In short he thought he could play his tricks on me as he has done upon the simple and believing public, but he has found his match.

'Now as to the books this Campbell is gathering for this Island it is simple folly bringing so many here to rot upon one another with damp. And many of whom will be of questionable authority owing to the sources and the manner of procuring them.

'The people prefer Gaelic books and the best thing we can do is to put into their hands the best Gaelic standard books that can be had. They have a good many books already and those you and Miss Rainy has so Kindly sent from time to time is still doing duty but they are getting done with time and damp. The people as a whole are not given to reading.'[20]

Campbell had no idea what was waiting for him when he landed.

*

The *Clydesdale,* decorated with bunting and blowing its whistle cheerfully, anchored in the afternoon. There was no immediate matching response on shore, but after some time a boat put out and soon there climbed aboard the steamer Donald Ferguson, the bride's father and the ruling elder who, it was now understood, had 'successfully headed the revolt against the authority of the Rev. Mr Mackay' the previous year. With him was his son Alexander, 'an intelligent and well-educated youth', who straightaway let it be known that his sister was not going to be married and that there would be no wedding.[21]

At this disconcerting news it was resolved to send a deputation ashore to talk over the matter, and J. G. Campbell, Rev. Rae, and John Ross 'who had been brought over from Lochboisdale to act as interpreter', accompanied by 'several professional and amateur photographers, an artist, and several newspaper reporters', were all landed on the rocks near the manse. The islanders naturally thought this an ideal opportunity to sell their wares. When a reporter asked Donald Ferguson about the wedding the answer was: 'What business have you with a wedding? When we want a wedding, we can arrange it for ourselves.'

After a short while Campbell came across the 'Queen' busy selling eggs and stockings. He had with him a selection of wedding rings and started trying them on while other women watched. One of the rings fitted, but Ann Ferguson said nothing, and the possible husband-to-be, John Gillies, 'looked on quite unconcernedly at the arrangements that were being made for his happiness'. Since there was no more positive response to the ring than this the deputation went off to see Angus Fiddes in the manse where its members were received politely but to no greater effect. Campbell, sounding a little annoyed, asked why there was to be no wedding, to which Fiddes replied that he was only a missionary, that he had nothing to do with the matter, and that Rev. John MacLean in Harris, as 'Moderator of Session', was the only one who could give an answer. Indeed MacLean might be coming to St Kilda in June and the wedding could take place then. Fiddes thanked Campbell for bringing books, and the deputation left the manse none the happier. To make up a little for their disappointment Fiddes gave the reporters an account of the general state of the island and showed them the improvements he had made to the garden.

It appeared that Campbell had been defeated by the joint effort of Fiddes and the ruling elder. His intentions, whatever they really were, had come to nothing, and his expenditure on wedding dress, steamer transport, and so on had been wasted. There stacked on board the *Clydesdale* to no purpose were the dress and veil, the groom's suit, the cake 'and all the "trimmings" of a wedding feast', fireworks 'to let off at night', and a huge quantity of wedding presents including an inscribed silver teapot for the 'Queen', the American organ, two dozen microscopes, three dozen pairs of spectacles, feeding bottles, paint boxes, balls, and a range of articles 'designed to make the "Queen" of St Kilda the medium of advertising'. These consisted of cough syrups, ointments, pills, magic cleansers, hair restorers and corn cures; 144 fly-catchers had been promised but never materialised. The sum total of gifts was estimated to amount to about seven hundredweight.

While the consultation was proceeding in the manse the rest of the steamer's passengers, most of whom were the 'North of England Whitsuntide holiday-makers' invited by Campbell, had landed and were surprised to learn that their journey had been in vain and that there was to be no wedding. The only thing they could do was to transform themselves into an ordinary tourist party and follow the usual routine of exploring the houses and watching 'cragmanship'. They heard that the people had objected to making sport for 'the Philistines' and were not prepared to amuse unwanted guests by laying on a wedding. Though Campbell persevered, unsuccessfully, in his efforts to persuade Fiddes and others to change their minds, Rev. Rae decided that the whole affair had better be abandoned. On making one final attempt to secure the missionary's consent the deputation members 'were met in the door by one of the steamboat stewards, who said that he had been instructed to inform them that Mr Fiddes was not in'.

That evening some of the islanders visited the *Clydesdale*, passing on their way several 'strongly-bound boxes' dumped on the rocks near the landing place and then almost forgotten. So Campbell's collection of books for the 'St Kilda Library' lay there, in its way as useless a contribution as the presents piled on the steamer. Only Neil MacDonald, of the former 'manse party', was impressed by the pile to the extent of saying that it was a pity that with so many gifts available the wedding had not come off. After the *Clydesdale* left on its return voyage Campbell was faced with the difficult task of returning the gifts to the respective donors. Anyone who still felt well-disposed towards him would say that the whole fruitless episode had been a well-meant attempt to hasten on and celebrate a marriage day which was said to have been delayed by the ruling elder, Donald Ferguson, who was believed to have been unhappy at the prospect of losing his daughter. On the other hand Campbell's preparations, in which John Ross played a surprisingly inappropriate part, were made without the knowledge of the people most closely involved and could easily be condemned as an intolerable intrusion of the kind Angus Fiddes described in his letter.[22]

CHAPTER 2

Rev. Angus Fiddes, last Free Church minister in St Kilda, and his work

The unsuccessful Campbell excursion was one of five major events in which Angus Fiddes participated during his thirteen years as missionary minister of St Kilda, and in some ways it was the most significant. In spite of the temptation offered by the great heap of gifts the island community, under the leadership and influence of the missionary and the dominating elder, objected at last to what was probably the most blatant instance in the long sequence of mainland patronising and asserted its right to do things in its own way. In this the part played by the two leaders was of the first importance, and it is easy to imagine that the rest of the people just left the decision to them. Fiddes showed an awareness of worldly issues and suspect motives which suitably accompanied his practical abilities, and Donald Ferguson was, as the newspaper expressed it, 'a man of great force of character, and in his own small community a potentate whom it is safe to have on your side when there is any quarrelling to be done'. The united resistance of the two men showed not only that some measure of 'harmony' had been, at least temporarily, restored in St Kilda, but also that apart from the necessarily negative character of resistance the island church had the capacity to be positive and constructive as well. In the person of Angus Fiddes it was both of these.[23]

Fiddes was most probably already on the island when Thomson wrote that 'a good, clever Medical Missionary' was needed there. The new missionary certainly had an interest in the health care required by the people and had taken with him a quantity of medicines. In the spring of 1890 he recommended two islanders suffering from rheumatism 'to try the mineral wells of Strathpeffer' and had treated many others who were ailing during the winter. All this made him strongly aware of the value of a nurse, Mrs Urquhart having left and the people not being immediately willing to take up Emily MacLeod's suggestion and pay for one themselves. Two men, Donald MacQueen and Neil MacKinnon, came to him and said they would need the services of a nurse before harvest. 'I said well I said are you ready to procure a house and keep if you get one. They said our houses are small and we have no house on the Island where we can give her accommodation – besides it is only a few families that require the services of such a person and the rest will not undertake to help us.' Fiddes, faced with this difficulty, thought of employing a nurse as housekeeper but would have preferred to see her accommodated independently in somewhere like the seldom used factor's house and put the idea to the proprietor's wife.[24]

Only a week or two after J. G. Campbell and his friends had gone Rev. John MacLean, Tarbert, and Rev. Angus Stewart, Whiting Bay, were picked as the 1890 deputies to go to St Kilda, their principal tasks being to dispense the communion and to report on the work and conduct of Angus Fiddes as missionary and teacher. Whether Rev. MacLean actually went on this occasion is not certain; he probably did but it was Rev. Stewart who officiated at the communion and provided a report on his return. The Highlands committee considered this report on 22 July. It was stated that the people of St Kilda were 'greatly pleased' with the services of their probationer 'who had been labouring among them for nearly a year', and they earnestly wished that he would continue with them as an ordained missionary. The committee expressed its satisfaction with the deputy's communication and it was decided that Fiddes should if possible be reappointed. Presumably he was willing to stay, and as always it would have proved difficult to find a replacement if he had not been. So the committee respectfully recommended that he be ordained by the Uist presbytery and that his annual salary be raised to at least £100 on the understanding that he would continue to teach the children in the school until some other arrangement was made. It was also agreed to assign £10 for various necessary outlays on the church and manse, with the hope that the sum might be recovered 'through a notice in the "Monthly"'.[25]

At the end of June 1890 Fiddes left St Kilda for Edinburgh and on 5 July he was staying at the Waverley Temperance Hotel from which he wrote to the longstanding HASS secretary, Fletcher Menzies. 'A storm of uncommon violence', his letter began, 'burst upon the Island of St Kilda on Tuesday of last week which carried off and smashed the only boat the natives had for crossing to Boreray Isle ..' Fiddes said that he had been 'commissioned' by the islanders to approach Menzies with a view to soliciting his assistance, with the resources of the St Kilda fund, in providing a new boat. To support his case he told the story of how in early spring a crew had been forced by a storm to take refuge on Dun while their boat was broken to bits. As a consequence of the two losses the people were left with only one boat, and that an old one acquired fifteen years previously and 'unseaworthy and untrustworthy'. Almost a week later Fiddes sent a further letter from Inverness – he had been staying in the Nairn manse with Rev. Lees – to say that he was very pleased to hear that money for a secondhand boat would be forthcoming. He concluded:

'I beleive these losses would have been in a great measure prevented provided there was a harbour or slip erected where they could land them in safety. There is one place right below the F C manse very suitable for such a harbour and could be made at very little expense. No one visiting the Island but sees the absolute need there is for such a landing place. Now that the Fishery Board are in possession of Funds for such purposes I beleive a few influential friends combining together and approaching them for this object who can tell but they might be successful.

'I cannot however dwell at large here and now on this matter but the men has been appealing in vain for years to get some slip or harbour erected with parties in the south and otherwise.'[26]

Fiddes was still at Nairn on 21 July but expected to be again in Edinburgh before 15 August when he hoped to return to St Kilda. He was on his way back a day or two before that as he attended a meeting of the Uist presbytery in the Free Church at Clachan, North Uist, on 14 August. Here the prescribed trials for ordination were heard and sustained, and were followed by the ordinary ordination procedure. The officer of the court was told to go to 'the most patent door' of the church and proclaim three times that if anybody had any objection to the life and doctrine of Angus Fiddes he should now substantiate the same before the presbytery. No one did. Rev. Murdo Morrison, Berneray, then preached from Romans I and 16, and at the end of the public service he asked Fiddes the questions 'put to ministers on these occasions'. The answers were deemed satisfactory, and the 'formula' being signed in the presence of presbytery and congregation Rev. Morrison as moderator then ordained Fiddes by solemn prayer and imposition of hands. The meeting concluded with the formal reception of Fiddes as ordained missionary to St Kilda by the presbytery members who all extended to him the 'right hand of fellowship'.[27]

Home again in St Kilda Rev. Fiddes, on behalf of the population of 79 persons, then composed a memorial or petition to Queen Victoria, seeking a royal contribution to the cost of maintaining a nurse on the island: 'Any sum Your Majesty may see proper to give either as an endowment or to be paid annually ... will be gratefully received by Messrs John McCallum and Sons, Religious Institution Rooms, 181 Buchanan Street, Glasgow.' Adding his concern for the mortality of mothers and of children from tetanus to his medical responsibilities Fiddes had spent part of his holiday on the mainland looking for a nurse and as a result 'a fully qualified person has been provided through The Higginbottoms Institute, Sauchiehall Street, Glasgow, in the person of Mrs Chisnhall'. Nurse Jessie Chisnhall, a widow, born in Stratherrick, spoke both English and Gaelic, and when the petition was sent already resided on the island in the manse as a sort of extra housekeeper along with Catherine MacLennan.[28]

The search by Fiddes for a nurse to fill the gap left by Mrs Urquhart seems to have been chiefly related to his wish to find a cure for the infantile tetanus which had been a scourge in St Kilda for so long. The story of the disease there and to a lesser extent in other islands was the subject of articles before and during Fiddes's years as missionary but with his evidently successful efforts to eradicate the trouble it came to a surprisingly sudden end. Some might claim that his achievement was of greater importance than his dealings with Campbell over the wedding; it was certainly more striking.

According to Dr G. A. Turner's presidential address to the Glasgow Obstetrical and Gynaecological Society in January 1895 Fiddes, while on the mainland in the summer of 1890, had applied to the Glasgow Sick-poor and

Private Nursing Association for one of their nurses, 'he promising to pay her expenses out of funds collected by him for the purpose'. Nurse Chisnhall agreed to go, spent ten months on the island, and went back to the mainland in June 1891. Three children were born during this period, the only one who lived being the baby born to the 'Queen', Ann Ferguson, after her marriage, mercifully unattended by J. G. Campbell and company, to John Gillies. After a month away Mrs Chisnhall returned in July 1891, but during that month she and Rev. Fiddes, who had again left in pursuit of medical guidance, met Professor W. L. Reid in Glasgow. He outlined a form of treatment which he thought would be successful, and the outcome confirmed his opinion as the two children treated in the recommended way both lived.[29]

Unfortunately Mrs Chisnhall was not popular. Fiddes told Mrs MacLeod of MacLeod that though the nurse had been busy among the people 'giving them medicines and attending to them' her services were not appreciated. A rival had emerged in the form of Mrs Rachel Ferguson, Donald's wife and Ann's mother, who some ten years earlier had not been well enough to teach sewing. Two mothers had preferred her to Mrs Chisnhall 'on account of a groundless feeling' aroused against the latter. 'Its the old story', said Fiddes:

'Some of them would find fault with the most skilful person. Some of them threaten not to employ her over the winter which is very hard upon me after taking her to the Island for to Keep them at home and be not under the necessity of going to Harris to get attended to.

'The nurse thinks that I ought to use my authority and put a stop to Mrs Ferguson for interfering with her work. I said to her that it was not Mrs F who was so much to blame as those who employed her and that I could not force them to use her offices when they hated her.

'But if there were any requiring and sending for her that she would not suffer on that account, so that I am placed between two fires as you can understand.

'I hope however with more prudence and tact and patience she may be able to secure their confidence and by the help of providence do some good among the people.

'She is very hasty in temper and somewhat too ready to Express her own opinions which is the only fault they have against her.'[30]

For these reasons it was not possible to apply as widely as was desirable the treatment which it was hoped would lead to the eradication of tetanus among the infants, and nurse Chisnhall, after spending a second frustrating winter in the island, was glad to leave for Glasgow in June 1892. She did not go back to St Kilda again, and no further Gaelic-speaking nurse could be found when Fiddes himself went to Glasgow in search of one during the same summer. However he contacted Dr Turner who supplied him with more detailed instructions as to 'the careful antiseptic treatment of the cord' after birth, and on 6 August 1894 the missionary, once more in Glasgow, was able to report the total success of his own nursing methods based upon what Reid and Turner had told him. He seems to have won the support and approval of the islanders, perhaps by enlisting the aid of Rachel Ferguson and ensuring that she had 'everything about herself clean and free of any impurities'. Fiddes returned to St Kilda on 10 August after a short visit to Tiree and continued the application of a treatment to which Turner made only minor corrections after reading an account of the steps taken so far.[31]

*

The record of Angus Fiddes's labours in St Kilda mainly consists of his material achievements, and it is clear that, so far as the outside world at least was concerned, his spiritual success was definite but unremarkable and routine. It could hardly have been otherwise for much of the time, since the islanders were apparently content with their Free Church position and such disturbances as the Free Presbyterian secession in 1893 and disagreement over possible union with the United Presbyterian Church were still too remote to trouble the island's own religious leaders. Fiddes himself no doubt gave thought to such matters, but his influence was seen most obviously in his school teaching, his requests for supplies, and his ultimately successful attempts to procure an improved landing place. The impact of the church upon the progress of St Kilda through the centuries had, without its being admitted, always depended upon the support of other bodies in sustaining a population there, and, except for men like Neil MacKenzie and Angus Fiddes who contributed to the material welfare of the people where they could, the evangelical church of the nineteenth century, in confining its concern to the spiritual state of the island's community, had perhaps even less relevance than its predecessors to the future of practical human existence in St Kilda.

On his return to 'this wild and forbidding Island' with Mrs Chisnhall in July 1891 Rev. Fiddes wrote almost immediately to Menzies to say that the men of St Kilda were sending 'one of their own boats about six years old' to the factor at Dunvegan for repair, and that he thought this would cost about £8. He also said that the potato crop had apparently suffered from northerly gales, and he evidently hoped that Menzies would be able to assist by meeting the cost of both boat and potato supplies out of the Kelsall Bequest fund. No less concerned about such regular requirements than about the health of the people Fiddes, with some tact and politeness, chose to maintain the minister's role as intermediary between the island and the increasing number of outside

665

interests bearing upon it. His letter to the HASS secretary of 6 June 1895, written shortly before he left for a holiday at Portmahomack in his home country of Easter Ross, contained his thoughts on contemporary difficulties. As usual it began with his 'commission':

'I am requested by the men of St. Kilda to ask you how much you can afford to give them of the Interest of their money for this year as they will be requiring some meal this year and to give me notice of the amount at your earliest opportunity ..

'I may tell you the reason for this application by the natives. Factor McKenzie of Dunvegan failed to supply some of those in arrears with the usual quantity of meal. They surmise that he will repeat it and therefore it is they make the present request.

'The result of that move at Dunvegan is that the St. Kildians are to make a counter movement and strike against the ruling and dictation of their superior by sending for the Crofters Commission. The point of the grievance is as follows: that their superior has been getting hitherto the produce of these Islands that his profits are large while they only get the merest fraction in return for their goods; that the result is they are annually falling into arrears to such an extent as to be totally unable now to clear his claims upon them.

'Seven families are involved to the extent of £200 and upwards.

'I had to provide some of them with meal from Glasgow out of my own pocket last season and since you have money of theirs I see no reason why I should be the loser of the amount.

'In case any should think that I was the means of leading on the St. Kildians to take the Steps in which they are now moving, allow me to say that I am perfectly free from any blame in the matter. It originated entirely with themselves.

'I have been at great pains with them and their children imparting education. What the result will be time will tell. For the present, at any rate an English education has an uphill work here. It is an invasion upon the Gaelic and it fills the mind of the young with the desire to leave for to win bread, butter and cheese elsewhere which their sires do not wish. Hence it is that they place obstacles in the way of progress and advancement. I have been very successful in overcoming the ninth-day sickness among the infants of St. Kilda. I have not lost a single child since I began operations. Hence the death scourge among the infants has been Knocked on the head. If any will be lost afterwards the fault lies with the mothers.'[32]

There are hints in this letter that Fiddes was becoming a little impatient with people and circumstances in the island and beyond, and not much had changed the following year when, after his customary stay on the mainland, he wrote again to convey, this time, the islanders' request for 32 barrels of potatoes to replace the year's crop said to have been almost entirely destroyed by disease. Fiddes himself, having made 'a casual visit' to the fields, could find 'no trace of the disease among the small plots I saw' and suggested that the HASS treasurer take the request 'with a grain of salt'. Seed potatoes next spring would do instead.

'I may also tell you that I have been approached with an appeal for 32 tons of coals; but when they heard the possible cost of conveyance in bags by the Steamer from Glasgow to St.Kilda they withdrew their application.

'The reason they offered to me for making that demand on the Fund at your disposal, viz. that the season was so wet for their ordinary fuel to dry which consists of turf as to leave many of the families without the usual quantity of it, therefore they said we are compelled to get some coals – if you be kind enough to apply for us to the Treasurer of our Fund in Edinburgh, it will help us to tide over the severities of the coming winter.'[33]

With communication ever more frequent and tourist visitors ever more numerous, renewed press interest and more publications were an unsurprising consequence. Angus Fiddes served on the island in a period of unprecedented development and corresponding contact with both official agencies and unexpected trippers, naturalists and would-be authors. A remnant of support came from the ELHSA well after its involvement with the island school had declined. Members sent packages of what they imagined would be useful items. At the AGM in December 1894 they were reminded of how for six years they had provided teachers: 'The Rev.Mr Fiddes now taught the children besides ministering to the congregation in holy things. As the population was very small, that could easily be accomplished.' But even so, though their assistance in matters of ordinary school teaching was no longer needed, they 'continued to send a box annually with a few requisites and prizes', and gave some attention to the supply of sewing instruction. In the mid 1890s the men were still the makers of the women's clothes, but two or three years later 'a schoolmistress was sent up ... to teach the girls to sew, and to relieve the minister from his scholastic duties for a time'. This unfortunate lady could not speak Gaelic yet in spite of this 'it certainly would have been difficult to find a more suitable person'. She took some furniture with her for rooms in the factor's house but she found that it was not available and 'was wandering disconsolate on the shore' for a time before she was taken in to the manse. She was perhaps the Miss Fenton who spent part of the 1899 summer in St Kilda. Earlier that year the ELHSA noted 'that those interested in St Kilda, were anxious to send a woman thither to teach sewing for the summer months', and in the following October Rev. D Macphail produced a report 'telling that Miss Fenton had taught the girls sewing there for two months'. There must have been some realisation of her predicament in the island as 'it was intended in future to employ a male teacher for nine months, under Mr Fiddes' superintendence.' Had Fiddes been married, or had a sister with him, the problem would not have existed.[34]

*

The summer of 1896 saw the usual invasion of visitors. The Kearton brothers, naturalist and photographer, arrived with the *Dunara Castle* in June and stayed in the factor's house. They were accompanied by 'our friend', the younger John MacKenzie, who had taken over from his father as factor, and by 'our friend', Mr John Young, another naturalist, while home on holiday was Alexander Ferguson, son of the elder and ground officer, 'who a year or two back forsook the lone crags of St. Kilda for the more lucrative and less adventurous life of a Glasgow commercial house.' Also present were two Glasgow journalists, enticed to the island by the expectation of finding sixteen shipwrecked Spanish sailors whose fate was described in a bottle message found in the spring on the west coast of Skye. Meeting no Spaniard they left disappointed, compensated only with statistics provided by Rev. Fiddes, news of the recent death of Lachlan MacKinnon, believed to have been 'nearer 100 than 90' but in reality perhaps a mere 88, and information on the 'school':

> 'The work of education is being rigorously prosecuted by Mr Fiddes, who has an assistant student, a young man named George Matheson, from South Harris, and the school underwent official examination on Saturday by Mr Strachan, sub-inspector, who joined the Dunara Castle at Obbe. There are complaints as to irregular attendance, and a lack on the part of some parents of all interest whatever in the education of their children, a few of whom are not so far advanced as they should be.'[35]

As in the days of John Ross Rev. Fiddes went fishing with the Keartons and they attended his Sunday morning service, to which all were summoned by 'an old ship's bell, erected on the top of a wall near the church'. This was the bell from the wrecked *Janet Cowan*, as opposed to the handbell, donated in 1832 by Peter Ewing of Glasgow, which was now used to call the children to school. The Keartons believed that the ancient and what they saw as the courteous practice of letting women leave the church before any man moved was a praiseworthy custom, but then they learned 'that it is a lingering relic of Roman Catholicism which is still in force on the Continent'. They also discovered that far from looking like Sands's 'troop of the damned' those who attended the service were cheerful and quite ready to chat on the way back to the houses. Cheerfulness, however, did not seem to extend far into the ordinary lives of the children:

> 'I innocently asked the minister one day what kind of games the children played. The old man smiled good-naturedly at my ignorance, and answered: "None whatever; their parents would consider it frivolity to have them taught anything except climbing rocks, catching sheep, and such other things as will become necessary to them in after-life." The austerity of the doctrine inculcated by the Free Kirk of Scotland has been blamed for this gloomy strictness; and, whilst acquitting the minister of any bigoted abuse of reason, I am willing to believe a deal in the way of religious intolerance on the part of the terribly earnest body he represents ..'[36]

The *Hebridean* left Greenock with another group of tourists in the evening of Monday 10 August 1896. On reaching Dunvegan on Wednesday it was learned that the funeral was taking place of Emily MacLeod, who had died three days before. 'The late Miss McLeod is said to have been a most charitable lady and a warm friend and benefactor to the poor people of the locality. She had reached the ripe age of 85 and died full of years and honours, sincerely mourned by all who knew her.' Out of respect the tourists refrained from looking round Dunvegan castle and instead set out across the Minch to the tune of 'Over the sea to Skye', sung by the purser and with the passengers joining in the chorus. A conventional call at St Kilda ended with a visit to the steamer by the 'old man', Angus Fiddes, aged then around 53, 'along with another lady and gentleman who were staying at his house as summer visitors'. Fiddes delivered 'a short address on his work among the people', claiming that it was 'his love of the work' and his wish to improve living conditions that kept him there. Describing the trip later in a newspaper article a visitor stated, without hesitation, that 'The key to the hearts of the people here is the Gaelic tongue', although by that time, after sixteen years of deliberate instruction, most of the children and the younger adults were able to use English freely. Further information on George Matheson and his contribution was lacking, but it seems that he and, a little later, Miss Fenton were not the only assistants to help Rev. Fiddes and to stand in for him when he went away for his summer holiday.[37]

In February 1897 St Kilda became once again the subject of an illustrated article in the *Free Church Monthly* magazine. Again too there was a far from accurate and impartial outline of the island's religious history, the main intention of which was to solicit contributions towards repairs to church and manse. Since it was more than sixty years since they had been built the *Monthly* was not surprised that repairs were needed: 'The roof of each has, on several occasions, been partly stripped by the wind, and quite recently the church suffered so severely that the falling *debris* destroyed some of the pews.' Rev. Fiddes had explained to his distant employers the ferocity of the elements which the buildings had to withstand – 'and, indeed, from time to time there is danger of the roof of the church being lifted from its place and swept off bodily into the sea'. In the damp manse the minister's books and furniture were damaged, and his own health had suffered from the same cause.[38]

Even in the 1890s one account of the island could contradict another. From a visitor in 1894, who strongly objected to 'the filthy habit of spitting all about the church floor' during the service, came this version of the Sunday timetable:

'Theirs is the Free Church, and all are great church-goers; some of the congregation, the minister informed me, could repeat word for word many chapters of the Bible. I never noticed less attend at church than a congregation of sixty out of a possible seventy-three. Their services are extremely long, especially when one does not understand a word of Gaelic, but you are expected to attend, and the hours are as follows: 8 to 9.30, again 11.30 to 3; one Sunday this was extended to 4.20. Then they gave an English service from 6 to 8, which we were obliged also to attend, being the only two who did not understand Gaelic, otherwise they never preach in English. After this a Gaelic service is continued till 9.30.'[39]

Such hours in church under Angus Fiddes would have put John MacKay's Sabbath regime in the shade. But the outline presented in 1897 was markedly different and perhaps more accurate. News had come from Fiddes by way of a letter in which he reported on the state of the island over the past year:

'the account he gives of his flock is that "they are a serious and devout people, who regularly wait on the means of grace, observing strictly the fourth commandment, and, so far as I am aware, free from scandal." The provision made for their spiritual wants is as complete as that which is enjoyed in our best-equipped congregations. On the Sabbath there are two services, at 11 and 6, with a Sabbath school at 4.30, attended by 22 children; and a Welfare of Youth class. There is a prayer-meeting every Wednesday evening, and on the first Monday of every month there are special gatherings for fellowship or business. It must also be borne in mind that Mr. Fiddes is the week-day schoolmaster as well as the minister, and that his school is regularly inspected by H. M. Inspector. The school is taught in the church, which is most undesirable ..'[40]

Since the latter description bears some comparison with normal Free Church practice today it may be the more realistic. Only the 'Otter' meeting had been given up.

Angus Fiddes had quickly earned a reputation as one 'who has, both spiritually and materially, done so much to improve the condition of the natives on the lonely isle'. His small failures, as in the case of his attempt to introduce a calendar, were nothing compared to his success in eradicating tetanus. He usually received a favourable hearing when in communication with mainland authorities, and when he made known his concern at the lack of a schoolroom the response was immediate and helpful. Making its first call of 1898 on Saturday 11 June the *Dunara Castle* 'probably caused more excitement than any similar event since the famous expedition to marry the "Queen" of St. Kilda'. This was because the steamer had on board a team of eleven workmen, including the foreman, Mr MacDonald, who were expected to remain for three months. 'The Highland Committee of the Free Church .. have determined to practically rebuild the church and to add a new school. The contract for the work is in the hands of Mr Bain, of Carnan, who had, of course, to take out with him the whole of the building material, with the exception of the stone ..' As the workmen took their supplies ashore by means of a hastily constructed raft, Mr Robertson, H. M. Inspector of Schools, visited Rev. Fiddes and examined the children, while Dr Robertson, medical officer of South Harris, treated what genuine ailments he could find. At midnight, if not before, the islanders refused 'to lend the slightest aid' to any further unloading as it would encroach upon the Sabbath and 'got perfectly frantic at the bare suggestion that they should'. They went off to their houses, leaving the contractor and his men to finish the work which was completed at 4 a.m. on the Sunday morning.[41]

The workmen, and ten others including some tourists and the factor, were left behind when the steamer departed, 'so that the population of St. Kilda is at this present moment considerably greater than it has been for many a year'. Accommodation proved something of a problem, the workmen spending that Sunday morning sleeping in the open air. Fiddes had made arrangements for them subsequently to lodge with the islanders, but how this would turn out after he went off for his holiday on the mainland was a matter of great uncertainty. Those 'excursionists' who returned with the *Dunara Castle* much appreciated the sight of 'myriads of various kinds of seabirds' flying up in alarm when the ship's siren blasted them from the cliffs.[42]

Among the company on shore were Norman Heathcote and his intrepid sister Evelyn, who, being related to the proprietor, were able to stay in the factor's house for ten days, during which time they attended the laying of the foundation stone of the new school building. Norman made a short speech

671

but Fiddes 'managed to talk for half-an-hour about the history of education in St. Kilda'. Nevertheless the Heathcotes had some sympathy for the minister whose life seemed to them a lonely one – 'Nine weary months out of every year without a chance of exchanging a word with an educated person'. They found him even-tempered and his sermons, like his speech, too long. It would be an improvement, they thought, if the system of appointing ministers to the island and other remote stations were altered, and they suggested that St Kilda should be treated as a place for missionaries sent on a short-term tour of duty. The idea heralded actuality in years to come.

Norman Heathcote was struck by a predominant characteristic of the community: 'I should say they are the most truly religious people I have ever come across, not merely because they go to church a great deal and have daily prayers in their houses morning and evening, but because they seem really devout and honestly believe their religion to be the most important part of their life. Can this be said of any other community?' In the Hebrides it could, without difficulty, but perhaps the nature of St Kilda made it more apparent. He was also impressed by more worldly changes. So far as he could make out 'The advent of steamers and tourists has shown them the value of money and taught them to be discontented with their lot'. Conversation in English with strangers, official reports and 'greater facilities for leaving the island' had further promoted the possibility of emigration in the people's minds, although most of them, Heathcote found, would prefer to stay where they were, and in this he agreed with them. The answer, in his view, was 'some plan that would tend to make them more self-reliant and independent'. There was nothing new about such a proposal, and he did not know exactly what form it might take unless it might possibly be the direct marketing of their cloth to Glasgow and the conversion of their rents to money. But there were risks, 'and I doubt whether the spirit of good fellowship and community of interests which are now to be found amongst them would survive the trial'. [43]

In view of the work to be done to church and manse, and for a new schoolroom, it was remarkable that not long after the Heathcotes had gone it was well advanced, and that all appeared to be completed when Messrs MacCallum and Co.'s new steamer *Hebrides*, which would in due course replace the *Hebridean*, made her first ever voyage to St Kilda in late July 1898, only a short time after she was built and launched. The weather was exceptionally fine and the party of passengers was 'the largest that ever visited the island'. It was reported that the schoolroom had been erected, that the church had been lined with wood, 'giving it a most comfortable appearance', and that the steamer 'embarked the workmen who had been engaged in the renovation of the church'. Up rose the birds again in response to another siren blast from the *Hebrides*, which, in addition to its sightseers had brought to the island the returning Rev. Fiddes, busy in his mind with thoughts of an improvement more significant than the schoolroom. [44]

CHAPTER 3

The building of the pier and possible evacuation

For the steamer passengers the landing at St Kilda posed an obstacle that only the more agile could overcome with anything like ease, and those aboard the *Dunara Castle* in June 1898 were no less troubled by it than the parties of previous years:

> 'The island must .. remain isolated for a large part of the year unless something is done to provide some kind of a pier where goods might be landed and taken aboard with safety. There are no insuperable mechanical difficulties to the construction of such a landing stage, though, of course, it would be a matter of considerable expense, as the pier would require to be of a very substantial character. Certain representations by the natives are to be made on this subject with a view to interesting the Fishery Board in the matter. There can be no doubt that the formation of such a pier would prove an enormous boon to the islanders. It would enable them to take advantage of the almost illimitable fishing resources at their door, at present scarcely tapped by them. It would remove one of the reasons why steamers will not call during the greater part of the year, and it would enable the natives to send their fish and other produce direct to market, thus abolishing the antiquated and not altogether satisfactory system at present existing, by which the proprietor becomes the purchaser of the entire produce and the seller of the food supplies. The matter is one entirely of money, and it is not to be expected that either the proprietor or the Government will be in any hurry to comply with the desire of the natives.'[45]

Rev. Fiddes pursued the subject of a pier on behalf of the islanders during his short holiday in June and July 1898, when he 'laid the necessity of a harbour before a number of influential gentlemen, who are stated to have taken the matter up in such a manner that Mr Fiddes is confident that next year's visitors will be landed at a pier'. His confidence was rather too optimistic, but 1899 was indeed to see a start made on the long-awaited 'harbour' facilities that were supposed to provide the solution to the problem of the island's economic future. The recorded history of St Kilda's landing place stretched back at least two hundred years, and now, only thirty years before evacuation of the remaining population, no project seemed to some people more vital and to others more futile.[46]

The old landing place was once an ordinary, accepted part of everyday existence. Martin Martin said it was a 'low Rock, called the Saddle', slightly sloping and so slippery with seaweed that islanders who gathered to welcome visitors ashore wore 'on their Feet the usual dress on such occasions, i.e. Socks of old Rags sowed with Feathers instead of Thread'. In calm weather the island *Birlin* or Boat' was brought up to the side of the rock, 'upon which all the Inhabitants of both Sexes are ready to join their united Force to hale her through this Rock, having for this end a Rope fastned to the Fore-part; a competent Number of them are also employed on each side; both these are determined by a Cryer, who is employed on purpose to warn them all at the same Minute, and he ceases when he finds it convenient to give them a breathing'. On or near this rock, and presumably high up out of reach of most spring tides, was a hollow into which the boat was drawn and called by Martin 'the Gallies Dock'. In spite of its distance from the waves the sea during a severe storm pushed large boulders into it. A summer alternative to the rock landing was the beach, 'though extremely dangerous, and for that reason seldom attempted, unless the weather be very favourable'. Here the men on shore would rush into the water, form themselves into two lines with 'the two ablest men .. each in front of his own little corps', and the rest 'clung fast to those immediately before them'. Everyone then took hold of the boat, ropes from the bow and stern were passed to the women and children on the beach, and with a great heave the boat, with its contents, was pushed and hauled well clear of the sea's reach.[47]

For an unknown number of centuries the curiously-named 'Saddle', a combined slipway and jetty, served as the one customary access to the island. Regularly used by islanders and visitors alike it was hazardous in most weathers, and when in 1860 Captain Otter set about his attempt to create an improved landing he soon discovered what damage the sea could do on that part of the shore. His plan was to take four masons from Portree 'who understand blasting', put them to work for two months from early August to late September, employ two islanders as labourers at 10s a week, and thereby clear a 'small bay' to serve as a safe landing place when the weather was reasonable. He also intended to install a crane with which boats could be hoisted up above the reach of waves and swell. In the event he secured three 'first rate Invernessmen' who were reckoned to be more intelligent and reliable than the cheaper masons he had expected to employ in Skye, and these workers, led by one Campbell 'the head blaster', had the daily assistance, at least in theory, of eight St Kilda labourers who were allowed £16 as an overall wage to share out among themselves. Fowling expeditions were a legitimate excuse for not turning up to work, but at least three of the eight had always to be present.[48]

As the great storm approached at the beginning of October 1860 the 'harbour' was finished and a crane was in position, but the destruction of the large island boat by the gale showed that however promising the 'harbour' had seemed to be it was not sufficient to withstand extreme conditions and soon it became useless. It remained necessary to use the Saddle, that ancient and invaluable natural landing place having apparently been unharmed by Otter's 'blasters'; and when MacDiarmid came to the island in 1877 he found the lack of a proper landing 'causes incalculable toil and great danger to the inhabitants'. Otter's scheme struck him as being half finished: 'He intended to have cleared away the rock in front, and then make a cutting into the bank to the right front of the minister's house for about 40 or 50 yards, and let the sea run in at high water.' This he thought would have been a safe arrangement for landing and for mooring a smack all winter. Much rock had already been removed, and 'the natives' could do the work of cutting further into the bank if carefully supervised. Once complete it would be an unsurpassed improvement, enabling the people not only to keep a smack but to 'find their way to and from the mainland'. Some visitors, naval and otherwise, considered that St Kilda crews were no good at handling a boat, but MacDiarmid, with greater understanding of conditions, thought differently: 'The people are, in my opinion, fearless sailors.'[49]

Thinking about the improvement methods was determined by economic expectations as well as by weather and sea. If a 'harbour' existed probably the principal advantage in many outsiders' minds was that it would enable the islanders to fish more extensively because they could have one or two large smacks, and this in turn would lessen the burden of care for the people borne by the proprietor, the government and the public. But most of those who went to study the conditions at St Kilda were not convinced that any useful improvement in means of landing could be achieved.

In July 1878 the commanding officer of the *Jackal*, Lieutenant Commander Digby, wrote to the Secretary of the Admiralty with his opinion on the St Kilda landing, although he had been at the island for no more than an hour when taking off John Sands and the Austrians. He was certain 'that no landing place or pier could be built out from the shore that would stand against the winter gales unless built of very large blocks of concrete and at an enormous expense'. Even if this were done no vessel could be moored there for 'the squalls strike down on the Bay with terrific force tearing up the water and making it dangerous for open boats'. He too suggested that a 'basin' might be blasted out of the rock but, doubting that it would be sufficiently safe, preferred the idea of something similar to the Saddle. 'What I believe would be practicable and of great service to the Islanders would be a slip cut out of the rock at the place they now use for hauling up their boats which is the only site that would do for any sort of landing place. This would give them a chance of running their boats up at once clear of the seas over a smooth surface instead of over the rough rocks where they get continually damaged.' The appeal of this proposal would be its much smaller cost, but its recognition of the fact that it would allow no real possibility of introducing larger boats such as fishing in the open sea required might not have been so welcome. Unlike MacDiarmid Digby was one of those who believed that the islanders 'are not seamen', and therefore that they would not be very successful at fishing; on the other hand in 1882 Malcolm Ferguson saw a St Kilda boat with five men coming out of the bay in rough sea: 'I had often both read and heard of the St. Kildans being indifferent boatmen or sailors, but I have formed quite a different opinion as to their prowess in this direction. I never before saw a boat handled with such rare pluck and skill; indeed, I never saw a boat venture out in such a sea.' If the islanders were reluctant fishermen it was because they had nowhere to shelter adequate boats and no safe means of passing between shore and ocean.[50]

With the arrival of the Napier Commission in June 1883 Rev. John MacKay found himself questioned on this all-important matter. 'We have always heard, and we felt to-day, there was a difficulty in landing. Do you think a pier could be erected at comparatively little expense, which would make it convenient for passengers to come ashore?' The minister, not being an expert in this field, hesitated. 'Well, I think so.' When asked further if he thought it would be an improvement worth having he surprisingly was not sure until he had consulted 'with the people', after which he was able to say that 'It would improve the place very much.' More immediate and definite answers were provided by the St Kilda spokesmen.

'Would you like to have a pier?'

'Certainly we would be the better off of a pier.'

'How would you be?'

'If you saw some of the days when we have to land here you would understand then what need we have of it.'

Would the pier be most useful for the island fishermen or for the landing of people and goods from the steamers? The reply was that it would benefit the fishing. 'Two boats go out to fish now. We are fallen off in able-bodied men.'[51]

Of two proposals put forward in the 1880s that of the factor was ambitious and on the lines of Captain Otter's attempt twenty years previously. In his letter of 12 August 1882 MacKenzie told the proprietor that he had looked more extensively into the matter. He thought a 'Dock' would be suitable, 40 yards long, 6 yards wide and 6 yards deep, the cutting out of which he calculated would cost £288, with additional expenses for cement to be used in paving the rock on one side as a quay and in purchasing a crane which would have to be worked either by hand or by steam.[52]

The other idea came from the commander of the gunboat *Jackal*, Mr Pricket[t], who, on the order of the Admiralty, visited St Kilda in the summer of 1884 and 'held an inquiry as to the possibility of making a small harbour or safe landing-place at the island for boats'. As in the case of the Napier Commission, two of 'the natives' and 'a catechist' - Rev. John MacKay - were examined, after which a 'minute personal examination' of the relevant piece of coastline was made, all leading to the conclusion that 'the formation of a harbour was impracticable'. Instead Pricket proposed to present the Admiralty with a scheme to enable boats to land with greater safety than hitherto, relying upon the availability of money from the Kelsall Bequest fund.[53]

Pricket's investigation had been instigated by Lord Napier himself who had acted upon the information he had gathered in 1883. Along with the *Jackal* went Malcolm McNeill, formerly secretary to the Crofters' Commission and in 1886 the writer of a report on St Kilda's apparently fictitious destitution. Their scheme envisaged 'the enlargement of a sort of creek or fissure in the rocks' where visitors customarily landed and 'the construction of a sloping timber stage or slide on which the boats could be run with safety and rushed up to a point beyond the reach of the Surf'. Most significantly, there seemed to be 'no possibility of forming a regular boat Shelter with a masonry pier at which boats could lie in the water even at high tides'. The estimated cost was about £600, well beyond the resources of the fund in the hands of the HASS.

It was not thought that the proprietor should or could bear the whole expense, and as the government would probably 'not recognize any obligation' it was believed that the only way the work could be paid for would be by public subscription. Nevertheless MacLeod of MacLeod's approval would be essential, leave being necessary for 'access, encampment, and the appropriation of a portion of the soil .. to make a road from the shore to the Store house'. On receiving permission the Admiralty would be asked to grant 'Superintendence, skilled labour, and some materials and explosives'. The islanders might supply unskilled labour for nothing or for very little.[54]

At the end of October 1884 MacLeod thanked Lord Napier for his informative letters and for a copy of Commander Pricket's report to the Admiralty. He was rather annoyed that the *Jackal* had gone to St Kilda on a definite mission without his knowledge and he was of the opinion that Pricket's plan was 'not quite the best'. If it were carried out the money would 'probably be thrown away'. The old Otter scheme seemed better, especially as 'improved upon' by the factor. MacLeod objected to a public subscription as he did to Napier's intention of buying a boat and herring net for the islanders. In effect this meant that permission for the work was refused, and so far as the boat and net were concerned, 'they are well able to pay for them themselves'.[55]

Napier wrote a polite reply to MacLeod's comments, reaffirming that the sum of £600 or £800 could only be found by subscription 'among sympathizing people in Glasgow and elsewhere, by government assistance and by assistance from other sources, or funds'. He judged that the only real difference between the several plans stemming from Otter, MacKenzie and Pricket was 'simply one of local adaptation'. The first two proposed an almost right-angled turn in the approach to a dock, Pricket a straight run to it which

Napier thought more reasonable. It was still hoped that MacLeod would sanction the undertaking in whatever was decided the best manner. 'Little wonder,' wrote John Ross in 1889, 'that the St. Kildan is not a better seaman under such circumstances and that he does not wish to go much to sea. Nature alone has been at work in the construction of their landing place and it is not at all suitable for the encouragement of a sea faring life.' What an advantage it would be, he added, 'were some one to take in hand to make a landing place into which they might safely enter when running before the storm'. If nothing were done, 'the sooner St. Kilda is cleared off the better for all concerned', since dependence on public charity and little else meant that the inhabitants would 'come to grief sooner or later'.[56]

*

No progress was made in 1884, and another fifteen years went by before anything was done about the new landing place. Old notions on a 'basin' harbour challenged those in favour of a pier, and the whole subject became entangled with suggestions on emigration. Would it not be better to spend public money on removing all the islanders to Skye or the mainland than on a construction to serve a population which would probably have to emigrate anyway? Malcolm McNeill had raised this issue in the report of his visit in 1885. In his view schemes for a landing place put forward by Pricket and by the factor John MacKenzie appeared to be excellent but were very expensive, and so he recommended initial blasting work only to remove loose boulders in 'the small creek' which was the one place where anything like a harbour or dock could be conceived. Perhaps this would be sufficient. Yet, more importantly, he remarked at the same time on the unsettling reappearance of the emigrant Ewen Gillies, his words hinting at the need to balance the worthwhileness of a better landing with its costs against the possibility that before long, whether at Ewen's suggestion or not, the island might be abandoned.[57]

As usual, thought of emigration seemed to occur among the people in response to questions put to them by a visitor rather than spontaneously from within the community. But the same thought remained in the official mind of government as long as requests for the use of public funds to help the islanders continued to arrive. Eventually, however, in June 1899, the Congested Districts Board for Scotland, which had been constituted only two years earlier, sent its engineer, Captain Andrews, to study the situation in the island and report. Andrews travelled by steamer in the company of MacLeod of MacLeod and was thus able to talk over the problem while there. 'He came to the conclusion .. that the best way would be to form a small dock protected by a pier or wall leading to a ramp, up which the inhabitants could haul their boats by a capstan. In forming the dock and clearing the boulders, materials will be gained which will go towards construction of the protecting pier.'[58]

This proposal was accepted, and a plan and specification were prepared. To have contracted out the work would, it was understood, have been prohibitively expensive, and so it was suggested by Colonel J Gore Booth, consulting engineer to the Secretary of State for Scotland under the Department of Agriculture, that 'a Supervisor experienced in such work and accustomed to the use of explosives' should be appointed with a weekly pay of £3. He would employ some island men to labour 'at fair wages', and he would be accommodated in the furnished factor's house at no further cost. It was also thought that this supervisor should try 'to communicate by flashing light with the Monach Islands lighthouse', the keepers of which would receive directions to watch at stated times'. No emergency system was arranged for periods of bad weather or poor visibility, but 'I need hardly point out what a great boon this would be to the inhabitants'. Malcolm McNeill now thought the construction would be very useful and offered no objection, although he considered it would prove very expensive – 'if it is thought worthwhile to incur the cost for the sake of 70 inhabitants, I shall offer no opposition'. Only a year before he had stated that St Kilda 'ought not to be inhabited'.[59]

There were inevitably doubts as to whether the threatened expenditure of over £1000 was sensible, and an alternative 'scheme of migration to the MacLeod Estates in Skye' was contemplated and indeed preferred by the pier project's opponents. 'I would sooner vote £2000 to transport them to Skye or elsewhere,' said one, 'than £1000 to help them in St Kilda.' Perhaps MacLeod of MacLeod should be informed that the Congested Districts Board (CDB) might give substantial help 'if he saw his way to migrating the St. Kildians'. The secretary said that the removal of the people had not been put before the Board, but even so notice of the discussion reached both Norman MacLeod of MacLeod and his brother Reginald and the latter drew up a memorandum on the possible migration and its consequences:

'The Proprietor has certainly no object in maintaining the existing population in the Island. He has nothing but anxiety and loss. His answer can be obtained to the question whether, if the people were removed from the Island and started in new houses at the cost of and under the management of the C.D.B., he would provide suitable land for them on the MacLeod Estate in Skye.

'Assuming his consent the following difficulties suggest themselves.

1. In St Kilda
   a. Would the general consent of the people be obtained? No good would be done unless all left, for the position of a few remaining families –

especially if – as is probable – they were the least competent – would be worse and more anxious than at present.

b. On leaving what would be done with their stock and other small possessions? It would be utterly useless to the Proprietor and he could not be expected to take it over. It could not be brought to Skye for it is of a quality and character most unsuited to successful farming. If removed and sold off for what it would fetch the value received would be very small.

2. In Skye
It is certain the habits of the people have not fitted them for making their way as Crofters. Their real skill is as fowlers for which there would be no opening; as fishermen they have shown no aptitude. The younger men might make their way but the older men would hardly do more than a little desultory work on some small allotment.

They would practically have to be maintained by somebody and unless this were provided on a Scale very superior to that common to crofters in Skye they would be very ill pleased with the change.

My own belief is that some day, perhaps a generation hence, the people will insist upon leaving and that it is possible they would be willing to go now if the suggestion were put before them as emanating from C.D.B.

But the C.D.B. and the Proprietor would have to provide for the difficulties attendant on a desertion of the Island and practically to maintain a considerable proportion of the population for the rest of their life.'[61]

With a copy of this memorandum before him Norman MacLeod wrote to the Board secretary on 14 July 1899:

'I have received through my brother a copy of memoranda by members of C.D.Board regarding the proposed improvement to the landing place at St.Kilda, on which I beg to make the following observations.

1. If the Congested Districts Board can persuade the St. Kildans to migrate, I have no objection to offer, and will do my best to find a suitable location for them on my property in Skye, but I do not think they will consent to migrate under [any] circumstances. About 20 years ago, my Father offered to remove the whole population to Skye, which offer they unanimously rejected. In June this year, when I visited St. Kilda, I made enquiries on this point, and found they were strongly opposed to migration. I think it will

be a very long time before the people of St. Kilda wish to remove altogether from the island.

2. If the present population were moved to Skye, I do not consider they would be capable of maintaining themselves under the altered circumstances.

3. If they remain in St. Kilda, where I think they are very happy, (and here I might point out that the population has slightly increased in the last few years), I consider it is of great importance to make the landing easier, safer, and less destructive to boats than it is at present. I do not think that any smaller scheme than that proposed by Col. Gore Booth would be of sufficient advantage to be worth undertaking at all, but I think that the people themselves may fairly be asked to contribute towards the cost of undertaking which is entirely for their benefit, in the shape of free labour. I think that in their original petition they offered this themselves, I, also, as proprietor of the island, am willing to contribute towards the cost, provided the Scheme as proposed by Col. Gore Booth is carried out. Perhaps the Congested Districts Board might see their way to sanctioning the proposed scheme, which appears to me to be the best thing to do, taking all the circumstances into consideration, provided the usual proportion of the cost of such work one fifth could be raised locally in free labour by the people, and a subscription from the proprietor.'[61]

*

The Board went ahead with the pier as suggested by Captain Andrews and Colonel Gore Booth, the latter being given the responsibility of directing the project. An experienced supervisor, W E Wookey, and an assistant engineer, E Matthews, as foreman were specially employed to conduct the works on the island, and a sum of £1500 was set aside to cover the cost. 'We took advantage of this opportunity', the Board reported in 1900, 'to bring St. Kilda as far as possible into communication with the outer world. Supervisor Wookey took with him a flagstaff and a set of mercantile code signalling flags to communicate with passing vessels, and, by the kindness of the owners of steam line-fishing boats, frequent calls are made with and for letters. Our Engineer has also been enabled to send many newspapers to the island, which were kindly sent to him by the public for the purpose.' Quite sensibly, signalling to fishing and other passing vessels was reckoned to be a more reliable means of communication than trying to attract the attention of Monach lighthousekeepers by flashing lights.[62]

Wookey and Matthews and his wife went aboard the *Hebridean* at Glasgow, taking with them, in addition to the flagstaff and flags, provisions for a year, cement, drills, explosives, and two lifeboats purchased by Matthews in Greenock. After calls at Oban, Tobermory and Dunvegan the steamer reached St Kilda on 18 August 1899 – 'it was rather a shock to be dumped down on an island, miles from anywhere … with no ships calling, and with the knowledge that you are there marooned for a period of at least ten months'. Work started promptly, with seventeen able-bodied St Kilda men employed as labourers at a rate of 3d per hour and providing free labour for a modest proportion of the time, while five boys earned a little by helping to remove 'Stores from Rocks'. After several months satisfactory progress had been made: 'The Islanders are not accustomed to labour of this nature, but, on the whole, they have done well.'[63]

The Board's information on the project as it proceeded came from reports sent in as regularly as possible by Wookey, who also kept a diary of more general interest. The report of 28 October 1899 was one of the less cheerful:

'There has not been much progress this week. On Monday and Tuesday all the men were away catching sheep. On Wednesday they started work in the morning but only worked 1½ hours when the weather not being good they went to their sheep. On Thursday they were again at their sheep but as the Trawler (189 F.D.) came in I got them to come down and launch a boat to land ladder etc. and take off letters. On Friday 9½ hours was worked quarrying in basin and Dock and on Saturday 5 hours clearing Dock. I hope next week to make more progress as they do not want to go away to their sheep again.'

In fact the following week was hampered by stormy weather with a succession of gales:

'On Wednesday the sea was making a clear sweep over the whole site and everything had to be removed. A quantity of the split boulders which had been deposited about ten feet above H.W. were carried back into the Bason. We cleared them out again on Thursday and Friday but on Saturday night the sea came over the whole of the site again with such force as to take the boulders from the bottom of the bank on North Side of Ramp leaving the bank overhanging to such an extent that about 10 feet of the bank will have to be taken down. The large boulders which have been on the rocks on South Side of Basin were carried into the Basin. These boulders have been on the rocks for generations. The tops of the rocks themselves were torn up wherever a joint occurred and thrown into Basin which is choked with them. According to Mr Fiddes and the natives this is the worst storm for 30 years. Large pieces of rock were also taken down from North end of Basin. The damage done will take three weeks to make good.'

Fiddes, like the missionaries before him, served as an interpreter and intermediary. When one evening the labourers told Matthews that 'they intended to start work at 9 a.m. next morning and work only seven hours', a decision that may have had something to do with the limited daylight in November, Wookey 'got Mr Fiddes to call them together in the Schoolhouse where I addressed them after which they agreed to work as asked'. Occasionally the men were absent on work of their own such as rescuing sheep from the cliffs, so that Wookey and Matthews had to continue without help, but in general attendance was good and in periods of better weather construction advanced well. In late November the working hours each day were 'from 8 a.m. to 12 noon and from 1 p.m. to 5 p.m.' Copies of Wookey's reports were sent to MacLeod from the Consulting Engineer's office in Edinburgh on 12 December 1899, by which time the work force had been reduced by one man:

> 'The incident referred to by Wookey regarding Donald McQuien arose from the fact that in October last, the old man was knocked down by a plank, and had to be carried off. Mr Fiddes examined him and found he had been more frightened than hurt. However as he is really too old for this kind of work and was a source of danger to the other men Colonel Gore Booth agreed that he should not again be allowed on the works. He appears aggrieved at not being allowed to work but we must not endanger the lives of the others.'[64]

This seems to be the only recorded accident during an operation which had reached an advanced stage by the spring of 1900. Norman Heathcote, whose book about his visits to St Kilda in 1898 and 1899 came out in 1900, heard shortly before publication 'that the pier has made substantial progress, and though not yet completed has already been of material assistance to the islanders'. During the recent winter, when caught in a storm, a crew and its boat had been able to reach land when it would previously have been impossible; and 'the new shelter' had enabled the *Dunara Castle*, on her first trip of 1900, 'to land goods and passengers in spite of a south-easterly gale'. Wookey and Matthews left the island in June 1900, the former bringing at least the St Kilda part of his diary to an end when the steamer taking them away arrived at Greenock on 27 June, and the C.D.B.'s report for 1900-1901 stated that work would resume in May 1901.[65]

The supervisor's diary contained comments on most aspects of island life seen from an outsider's point of view, although like other accounts by visitors over the years its accuracy varied according to the extent of the writer's knowledge.[66]

'St. Kilda proved to be very interesting, (if nothing else) no trees, no shops, no Doctors nor any sign of civilization except a deeply religious feeling of a primitive kind, which consisted of every person praying before they left the house every morning and then assisting themselves to my coal.'

'The staple food is the Fulmer Petrel, an evil smelling bird, the feathers of which are given to the Landlord … for rent, the flesh is salted for food and the oil is either drunk with the oatmeal porridge or used as oil for the cruse, (lamp). Vegetables are unknown here but the oil appears a suitable substitute. The church is interesting having for a bell one that was thrown up from a wreck Janet Cowan 1842. The Church Service commences at 10.30 a.m. and concludes at 2.30 p.m. (no cooking being allowed to break the Sabbath). I felt tired upon arrival and did not go to Church but the Natives refused to work for an Heathen which compelled me to suffer every Sunday for the Service was in Gaelic, and the smell of Fulmar oil is detestable. The singing (sitting down) reminding one of a lament on the Bagpipes .. An organ was offered to them but they do not care for innovations and would not worship the Lord by machinery. A Magic Lantern lecture was also given by the Minister but the old folks condemned it saying it was the work of the Evil One which could n't be shown in daylight and threatening to put him off the island if he dared to show it again.'.[67]

There were brief mentions of dress, the homemade mail boats, surnames, and the graveyard, 'a circular enclosure full of weeds etc.' When Wookey told the people it should be cleaned up 'they replied they would not disturb the dead'. As for the labouring, they learned quickly and for the most part applied themselves to it willingly:

'Before starting work in the morning family prayers must be attended to, after which the men set out in a circle and hold Parliament on the proposed days work. If it starts to rain they knock off for the day. They are like a lot of sheep; if one starts work the whole start. I often had to coax the old man down when the others would follow ..'

'They proved very good pupils (exceedingly strong) fixing casing to rock, mixing and depositing concrete, fixing ring bolts, cranes 2 etc.'

Angus Fiddes was helpful too:

'The Minister was very handy. He sharpened all the drill[s] twice daily but he was not appreciated by the natives. He built a stone wall round his garden. They pulled it down saying he was getting too worldly.'

On 12 December 1899 Mrs Matthews made and cooked a dumpling – 'quite a luxury'. The minister was invited to the meal: 'he is a fine old man and, always pleased to have a chat with Mainlanders, remained till 2 a.m. I said good-night to him 4 times. He liked the Music Hall songs the best. (Sentimental Ones).'

A heavy fall of snow on 25 December caused the men to refuse to work. They said it was too cold. Wookey tried unsuccessfully to persuade them to change their mind, but 'They told me to go home and have a sleep'. There was a church service on the last day of the year, and at midnight the *Janet Cowan* bell rang 'the old year out and the new one in'. The first day of the twentieth century was celebrated with dinner in the manse. Two chickens formed the main fare, and afterwards Matthews presented prizes to the children –'Speeches given by all'.[68]

At the end of May 1901 Wookey went back to St Kilda with the *Hebrides*, which was making 'The opening run of the century to the lonely and isolated island'. His task was to supervise the work still required to finish the 'boatslip' beside the pier. Its completion would 'facilitate immensely the landing of visitors, and be of much service to the natives, who are beginning to realise that the fishing industry will prove more beneficial than the tweed industry carried on by men as well as women for some time back'. In about two months the end was in sight, and 'Surveyor Challis, of the Scottish Office, .. made an official inspection of the pier and works at St Kilda now nearing completion'. On 24 August 1901 it was announced that 'The St. Kildians have sent a letter of thanks to the Congested Districts Board and Colonel Gore Booth for the generous treatment received both during the erection of the pier at the island and in the presentation of boats, tools, etc.' This expression of their gratitude was presumably arranged by Rev. Fiddes and marked the conclusion of an undertaking which had extended over two years and which, in the event, made no real difference to fishing at all.[69]

'Landing stores at St. Kilda' at the 'pier' completed in 1901

CHAPTER 4

Achievements of Angus Fiddes,
the United Free Church, and further disputes

The construction of the concrete landing place was the climax of material development at St Kilda, and although it did not amount to a great deal the minister could justly claim some credit for a real improvement as he could for previous achievements such as the eradication of tetanus among children. In other minor ways he sought to better the general condition of the islanders. By 1900 he had become 'anxious to provide a library for the natives to wile away the long winter months', and in June wrote a letter of thanks on behalf of the people for parcels of illustrated newspapers sent by well-wishers. On 5 April 1901 the gunboat *Bellona*, which had on board Mr Gibson come to take the census and a ship's surgeon who 'was of some help to many of the inhabitants', brought a parcel of books and magazines from a young man in Greenock. In thanking him Fiddes said that 'We are living in a very isolated district, and your gift of literature removes the mystery and tension of what is taking place in the outside world'. Nothing was said about J G Campbell's boxes of 400 books which Fiddes did not want and which were last heard of lying on the shore.[70]

The *Bellona's* commanding officer reported that 'Attempts are being made by Mr Fiddes to introduce new systems of carding and weaving which would obviate the laborious methods now in use'; and he pointed out that it was only through 'the Minister's private benevolence' that there was a 'supply of simple medicines' available. This latter situation was unsatisfactory. While in St Kilda Rev. Fiddes, like the missionaries before him, did his best to give medical treatment when needed, but nearly every time a steamer or other official vessel called there was a cry for the services of a doctor, and, if one was present, he would then have to deal with every kind of ailment, serious, trivial or imagined, presented to him. When Dr Brydon visited in 1881, along with another doctor, the two of them 'exercised our functions on about a third of the population' even though it was Sunday. Brydon noticed that the people, having hardly ever seen a doctor before and been unimpressed by those they had seen, crowded around him with complaints that were not serious and when treated relaxed their Sabbatarian strictness and showed off querns, looms, salted fulmars and other objects of interest to the strangers. In 1889 Rev. MacKay asked Dr Archibald Campbell to see a few cases of supposed ailments, 'but in a short time I found nearly every one in the island had some real or imaginary disease', and this general clamour for the attention of a visiting medical man usually occupied most of that individual's limited time ashore. Certain fears remained, as a kind of tradition, among the people, especially their dread of smallpox. Hearing in 1901 of an epidemic on the mainland and on the continent they asked Fiddes to help in procuring the services of a doctor who would take preventive measures. Fiddes accordingly communicated with the proprietor who 'sent' Dr MacKenzie from North Uist to vaccinate them, but as he could not stay for a week to see the results the children were not allowed to be given the necessary protection. The same happened the following year when Dr Fraser of Harris joined the *Hebrides* at Obbe for the trip to St Kilda and had to leave without vaccinating anyone. Dr John MacNab, who had been medical officer in South Harris for fourteen years, described in July 1902 how he had been expected to visit the island twice a year 'for vaccination and sanitary purposes', but he did not claim that he had actually done so. Regular visits certainly took place, mostly from North Uist, apparently at the expense of the proprietor, but as these happened not much more often than once a year it could scarcely be argued that the provision was adequate.[71]

Also in June 1900 a sub post office was established in St Kilda with Rev. Fiddes, who had long distributed what mail there was, as sub postmaster. One of his duties was to put the outgoing mail bag on board whichever vessel was to take it away. In summer this was usually a tourist steamer, and one of the passengers on a visit in 1901 witnessed the event: 'The only use I could see for the bag was to bring away the correspondence of the passengers, many of whom had been busy on Saturday and Sunday writing Postcards, etc., from St Kilda and posting them when they got there'. It was stated that same year that 'The Rev. Mr Fiddes is untiring in his energies to promote the welfare of those people with whom he has cast his lot to remain for the present.'[72]

*

Like blowing drizzle in autumn an uneasy atmosphere of decline spoiled any appearance of progress and success there might have been in the introduction of pier and post office. Although the level of population was holding steady and even slightly rising talk of emigration was still in the air, MacLeod of MacLeod, whatever his sentiments, had little to gain from his ownership of the island, the Harris School Board had at last assumed responsibility for education facilities, and the church, apart from its comforting persistence as spiritual guide to the people, was no longer a central influence upon the progress of their daily life. Intervention and administration by the 'outside world' had taken over, and there was no likelihood that an inhabited St Kilda could make economic sense in the changed 'modern' setting any more than it had done in the past.

The question of whether rates should be paid by and for St Kilda highlighted most of the troublesome circumstances surrounding the island in 1900. It is probable that neither the minister nor the church participated in the discussion for the issue was one that chiefly concerned the people themselves, the proprietor and the county authorities. In the 1890s MacLeod, deriving little benefit from his remote and often isolated possession, considered that any demand for payment of rates was unjustified. The matter was raised following a query in December 1893 from the Harris District Committee of the Inverness-shire County Council. The committee observed that although the owner and occupiers of St Kilda had been annually assessed for road and public health rates since the passing of the 'Local Government Act' in 1889 no payment had ever been received. What should be done?[73]

In December 1894 MacLeod's factor, John MacKenzie, stirred by another Act just passed, wrote to Thomas Wilson, solicitor and district rates collector at Lochmaddy:

'I beg to lodge an appeal against the County Assessment charged to the Island of St Kilda, on the ground that St Kilda is an exceptional community, living and maintained entirely within itself – is in every way isolated from the rest of Scotland, and under certain Acts of Parliaments exempt from interference – it lays no claim to the funds or rates of Harris or of any other parish – it participates in none of the benefits to which it is asked to contribute – and there are districts in Scotland, and even in Inverness-shire where the rates are left uncollected as a set off to their claim for roads. It would only be right and just that St Kilda, which has stronger reasons, should be afforded the same privilege. There is neither rent nor profit got from the Island, its exports do not meet its imports, it is only a matter of sentiment and moral duty to have it in hand at all. Therefore be good enough to lay this letter before the Meeting to be held at Lochmaddy on the 28th current, in the hope that the matter will be so favourably considered that the claim will be abandoned.'[74]

A sympathetic Wilson replied that an appeal had already been made for exemption and that he thought it 'ridiculous' to assess St Kilda at all – 'I will do my utmost to procure exemption'. He served as clerk to the Harris District Committee, which, at its meeting in the hotel at Tarbert on 3 April 1895, discussed MacKenzie's appeal and recommended exemption. This decision was naturally supported by Wilson, who in a letter of 19 April stated: 'The St Kilda people derive no benefit whatever from the District Rates.' The county collectors admitted that MacKenzie had for some time declined to pay on grounds that 'MacLeod of MacLeod had an arrangement with the parish of Harris by which it was agreed that the parish should pay all rates due on St Kilda on condition that MacLeod of MacLeod would make no claim upon them for purposes for which those rates were levied'. However the collectors considered that this was a private arrangement only and so looked for payment of £5.18s.11d, the amount now due.[75]

Nothing was paid, and in September 1896 Mackenzie sent a letter to the county clerks, the second half of which repeated the content of his appeal to Wilson in 1894. The first half explained the nature of the agreement with Harris:

> 'Many years ago an arrangement was entered into between The MacLeod of MacLeod and the Parish of Harris (in which St Kilda is situated) that so long as St Kilda paupers made no claim on Harris for relief, no poor rate would be asked. When the Education Act of 1872 came into operation the arrangement made previously in regard to poor rates was extended to schools, St Kilda undertaking to provide education for its own children, which it did, and still continues to do, without aid from Harris; but when the Local Government Act was passed, assessment under that Act began to be levied, and payment demanded. The Parish of Harris was again approached, and application made to it to have the old arrangement respecting poor and school rates to include the Local Government rates as well. To this proposal the Harris Parish Council very considerably acquiesced, and referred us to the County Council, who, I hope, will take the matter into consideration, and agree with Harris, that so long as St Kilda makes no claim, and does not participate in any of the funds to which it is asked to contribute, it should be allowed to go free.'[76]

A number of aspects of life in St Kilda during the nineteenth century may be clarified by this communication. It suggests, for instance, that by the agreement on the non-payment of poor rates, which would have been the responsibility of the proprietor, the poorest of the inhabitants, all of whom were poor, received no poor relief. It has been remarked that in Scotland 'the able-bodied had no right to any relief unless disabled from work by illness, or, in the case of women, the need to care for young children'. In St Kilda many of the people were able-bodied, but they were and had always been forced by circumstance to struggle for a living and there was no work for them other than that involved in their own efforts to survive and produce their rents. If any became disabled in some way this made no difference, and it appears that, in avoiding payment of poor rates, the proprietor shared the rather reluctant attitude towards the poor general throughout the country and for this reason among others repeated the common adage about the demoralising effect of outside help. This did not mean, however, that he did not make his own contributions to the care of those in special need. A second point in the letter was the undertaking, again to avoid payment of rates, that St Kilda would provide its own education system. This was the reason why the Harris School Board was not bound in its earlier days to build a school and supply a teacher and why John MacKay and Angus Fiddes had to teach as well as preach except in periods covered by ELHSA or other schoolmasters. Thirdly, only where roads and public health were concerned did it seem fully justifiable to refuse rates, since neither service could be supplied in St Kilda on a permanent basis. It may be guessed too that discussion on rates, at least as old as 1872, helped to confirm the attachment for administrative as well as ecclesiastical purposes of St Kilda to the parish of Harris.[77]

The argument over whether local authority rates should or should not be paid for St Kilda came to depend on two circumstances, the value of the property to the landowner and the conditions under which collection of payments by the islanders might be conducted. In November 1897 MacKenzie replied to an enquiry by the county clerks about the former. He sent them a copy of the 1896 accounts, showing 'in a nutshell' how there was a loss to the proprietor. Expenses, including cost of stores and supplies taken to the island, fares and other management costs, and income tax, amounted to £200.19s, while the value of produce and cash received from tenants came to only £184.11s.6d. MacKenzie also said:

> 'The accumulated debts, or rather outlays by the proprietor for the comfort of the people was at Whitsunday 1896 £271.16s.10d for which he does not expect to get paid, and this sum is exclusive of a new fishing boat he gifted to them not very long ago. In addition to that, he expended £40 in repairing some of their houses.'

Thinking this picture might relate to one year only the clerks asked whether the St Kilda rents were fixed amounts or estimates, to which MacKenzie answered that 'the rent is a fluctuating one, depending on the stock each tenant keeps', but that it had been paid only in part until 1890, and now was nothing.[78]

The ability of the St Kilda people to pay rent meant that, in theory at least, some of them might have been able to pay rates and that the proprietor could make some profit from the island, but the sums involved would have been very small and the islanders were often in arrears. Moreover the case could still be argued that they enjoyed none of the benefits for which rates were demanded. What brought the matter to an eventual conclusion seems to have been, in the first place, the signed statement by Thomas Wilson to the county clerks of 29 December 1897, in which he showed that, irrespective of their ability to pay, any attempt to collect rates from the islanders would have been a nonsense.[79]

Every year since 1890 Wilson had sent to the 'St Kildians' a demand notice for rates about which Rev. Fiddes had presumably expressed an opinion. The collector had never received anything, and he had never gone to St Kilda to hold a collection as he considered the expense of a visit unjustified even if payment was indeed made. He detailed the costs of a voyage with the *Dunara Castle* on the assumption that payment was not only forthcoming but so prompt as to allow him to return with the steamer on the same visit. The round trip would mean his going aboard at Lochmaddy, returning to Tarbert and waiting a day for the boat back to North Uist, food on the steamer and lodging in Tarbert for one night – a total cost of £2.13s. However if he did hold a collection he would not receive anything; if he then took steps to make the people pay by 'Distraint Warrants' he would have to go to the island with a sheriff's officer specially employed for the purpose, with two 'concurrents' also specially employed. To make the journey he would have a choice of three ways. He could charter a steamer, spend two or three days at St Kilda to allow for distraint and diligence – that is confiscating possessions for sale – and since no islander would buy the articles a day would have to be spent in loading them onto the steamer for sale elsewhere. 'There is also the risk,' said Wilson, 'that having reached St Kilda by special Steamer a landing could not be effected (quite a common occurrence); or having landed, the weather changed, and we could not get off again for several days.' The steamer could not be procured nearer than Oban, if even from there, and would cost at least £70 and probably more. The sheriff's officer would expect £5 at the minimum and the 'concurrents' £2.10s each, thus making a sum of probably more than £80. A second method of going to the island would be by hiring a sailing smack for £15 or £20. Time required would be even less certain, the officer and 'concurrents' would need twice the pay, and the total would be around £40. It would also be possible, for much the same cost as by a smack, to go out with the *Dunara Castle* on her 'first pleasure excursion there' and wait five or six weeks for her to come back.

'By whatever method carried out the cost would be enormously out of proportion to the amount of the Assessments; to cover that cost it would be necessary to distrain the greater part of the goods and chattels in St Kilda, and when knocked down for want of a purchaser, I doubt very much whether these could be removed except under Police protection. But assuming these chattels successfully removed to the mainland, they would not there realize as much as it would cost to sell them, so that the whole expedition would result in any cost from £50 to £100 for nothing.'

And as if this was not enough, Wilson continued:

'I may add that I am not certain that the St Kildians would afford shelter and hospitality to such a Party, in which event a tent, and a good supply of provisions, with "a drappie speerits" while tenting out, would require to be taken with the Party. I have not dealt with whether my own remuneration as Collector would not require to be remodelled if the duties covered by it included an annual visit to St Kilda with a Sheriff's Officer and party, but I have no objections whatever to going there provided I am specially ordered to go, and that the expenses disbursed by me reasonably, are paid. I however wish to place it on record that I do not think those Assessments can be recovered, and that it is utter folly wasting public monies in making the attempt.'

The 'utter folly' of the whole idea of collection must have been realised by the authorities as Wilson was authorised 'to strike off the St Kilda occupiers rates as irrecoverable'. He still had to apply for the proprietor's payments, although he agreed that it was 'a great hardship upon him' that he should have to pay anything, and he suggested that the island should be put down at 'a nominal rental, which he could justly do, for I understand he really has no rental worth speaking about from St Kilda'. Eventually the whole business was conveniently forgotten.[80]

*

With his views on the importance of relating the islanders to the rest of the world very much in mind Rev. Fiddes made a point of communicating to the people national news, now more frequently brought to the island and thus more up to date than formerly. When Colonel Gore Booth came to inspect the pier work in June 1900 he conveyed 'the official message' from Lord Roberts announcing his entry into Pretoria, a significant event in the war in South Africa. The reaction to this sort of information on the part of the St Kilda 'natives' may be guessed, but it was no doubt Fiddes who arranged a meeting 'in support of the fund for the relief of the widows and orphans of those who have fallen'. Fiddes himself presided, and he explained 'that they had met with the object of showing their sympathy for and condolence with those who had sacrificed their lives in the defence of the interests of their country, and to give their moral and material support to those who had been left behind'. A resolution was 'carried with acclamation', to the effect that the residents of St Kilda were delighted with the latest success of the British army and looked forward to the day when the Orange Free State and the Transvaal would be made 'a Crown colony, where the different races may live in unity, love and peace under the British flag'. So long used to being the supposed beneficiaries of outside religious, political and philanthropic interest, the islanders, familiar now with resources called funds and having some money of their own, were in a position to contribute to something vaguely like the Free Church's sustentation fund. 'Close on £3 was subscribed at the close of the meeting, and will be forwarded to the proper quarter.'[81]

It was not long before the British flag literally flew in St Kilda. Newspapers saw that some public entertainment could be derived from the contrast between great national events and the daily existence of St Kilda's small population. In the past the ignorance of the people through lack of communication had provided the amusement, but in 1900 it was the response of those still called 'primitive' to comparatively recent occurrences reported to them by fishermen, tourists, official visitors and their sub postmaster that seemed worth telling. Individuals or groups seemed to think that it would be great fun to be present on the island when special occasions were celebrated there or unusual news announced, and as result it was generally the visiting party rather than the inhabitants who appeared ridiculous, just as J G Campbell's Sunderland group had done in 1890.

The succession of King Edward VII upon the death of his mother Queen Victoria in 1901 was announced to the island by the *Bellona's* captain, whose party of 'marines and bluejackets' presented arms in front of the islanders and was large enough to produce a band which played 'God Save the King'. The change of monarch proved to be both a stimulant to a group of mainly Yorkshire enthusiasts and an excellent reason for a newspaper to interest its readers once again with an account of St Kilda affairs. Under the heading 'The King and St.Kilda' a report of 14 June 1902 stated:

> 'A party of Bradford gentlemen who are to visit St. Kilda have obtained this Majesty's consent to present the inhabitants with a Union Jack. The King said it would be an inconvenient precedent for him to present Coronation medals, but he expresses the hope that the St. Kildians will have a good season at fulmar catching.

> 'Sir Theophilus and Lady Peel, Bradford, will give medals, and also the flag.'

This was followed up on 28 June with 'The King and the St. Kildians', an account of the visit by the *Hebrides* and its 'large party of excursionists' to celebrate the coronation on St Kilda. Among them was Dr Charles Forshaw of Bradford, 'who is going to the island by command of His Majesty the King' as the bearer of the message about fulmar-catching. The King had been unable to allow Forshaw to present 'a royal standard' but the union jack was on its way instead, and to compensate for the absence of medals Queen Alexandra had 'voluntarily sent to Dr Forshaw large and beautifully executed photographs of their Majesties, each bearing the inscription, "A gift to the St. Kildians from Her Majesty the Queen with her good wishes .." ' To these gifts 'Sir F. Peel, Bart., High Sheriff of Yorkshire, and Lady Peel' added a flag and, for each child on the island, 'a bronze medal which had been submitted to the King and received his approval'. The children were also sent 'parcels of suitable illustrated literature' by the publisher Sir George Newnes, and the minister of the island had not been forgotten, for 'the Rev. F. St John Corbett, M.A., rector of Long Marton, Carlisle, has sent for him a volume of his original sermons, besides a parcel of other literature'. Further presents included two dozen enamel 'beakers' sent by Sir Tristram Tempest, Bart., Tong Hall, Yorkshire, and some 'bound volumes and publications' from Newnes. Over and above all this was a 'large consignment of miscellaneous goods .. sent from the Hebrides for distribution', and the 'Royal messages', by which was presumably meant those relating to fulmars, were printed at the expense of the Mayor of Bradford so that each islander could have a copy. The remarkable collection, delivered by Dr Forshaw, must have bemused as well as pleased the St Kilda people, who, it was thought, 'are likely to be in clover for a considerable time to come'.

The actual arrival of the *Hebrides* was described a week later. The steamer reached St Kilda at 2 a.m. on Thursday 26 June and the inhabitants, peacefully asleep, were wakened abruptly by the blast of her foghorn. In the course of the voyage a message had reached the ship that the King had become unwell and that the coronation had been postponed, but this made no difference to what had been planned for St Kilda as 'the opportunity might not occur again'. Sixty one passengers landed in the morning at a sensible hour to participate in Dr Forshaw's attempt 'to assist the islanders in suitably celebrating the Coronation'. The union jack from the High Sheriff of Yorkshire was accordingly hoisted by Dr Mitchell of Ballater and the Misses Fenton of Edinburgh to the singing of the national anthem by at least some of the assembled company. Dr Forshaw read the several messages, which were translated into Gaelic by one of the islanders - perhaps rather by a temporary teacher - and they were greeted 'with great cheering' by the visitors 'to the no small wonder of the natives, who are not given to expressing their feelings in that way, and did not appear to the English visitors to have a proper appreciation of the distinction conferred on them'.

The gifts were then distributed, each adult receiving a copy of the photograph, a beaker and a medallion, each of 19 children a medal. There was no demand or welcome for about half a ton of literature delivered, but 'numerous packets of sweets' were a great success. One of the Misses Fenton, perhaps the teacher of 1899, assisted with the handing out of gifts, and Finlay MacQueen, one of the 'natives', produced specimens of birds and eggs as a return present for the King and Queen along with a plea for better medical care: 'if the authorities should think of appointing a lady medical schoolmistress or missionary it would be a great boon'. Since the whole absurd occasion seemed in many ways a repetition, this time by Yorkshire, of the intended marriage celebration twelve years earlier it is not in the least surprising that the visitors were 'much struck with the strong commercial instinct exhibited by the islanders, who seemed much more interested in the sale of their eggs, socks, and other wares than in the ceremonies they were asked to witness'.

The minister, Angus Fiddes, was not present, being, as it was believed, on his usual mainland holiday.[82]

*

Whenever Rev. Fiddes came back from his annual holiday – 'a much-needed period of recreation' which John MacKay, perhaps involuntarily, had done without but which his successor enjoyed in each of his years at St Kilda – he brought back, as a matter of course and sometimes of importance to the island, news of all kinds. After 1896 or thereabouts he was replaced during the period of his absence and often for several weeks more by a temporary relief. In 1900, for instance, Fiddes left with 'Inspector Matthews' and his wife on the *Hebrides* at the end of June but in his stead there was a 'relief female teacher sent by the Ladies' Highland Association'. She had arrived with the same steamer and would stay until 'the end of the season'. This seemed to be the usual arrangement, under which Miss Fenton had come the year before, and was made possible by the frequency of visits by steamers and other vessels during the summer and early autumn. The last steamer call marked the season's end and was likely to be the occasion of the relief teacher's departure. It happened that the news carried to the island by Fiddes on his return in 1900 was of particular significance both to the people and to the employers of the teachers.[83]

During his absence Fiddes undoubtedly learned more of the internal dissension once again disturbing the Free Church. The great majority of ministers moved towards union with the United Presbyterian Church, and in the autumn the final step was taken when on 31 October the Uniting Act was signed and the United Free Church was founded with Robert Rainy as moderator. Since the opponents of union were mostly in the Highlands and islands and formed the core of a Free Church somewhat marginalised by the change that had taken place there was considerable uncertainty in this area as to which Protestant denomination – Free, United Free, Free Presbyterian or Established – would prevail in any particular district.[84]

In response to the new loyalties of Angus Fiddes it seemed as though St Kilda would choose to support the union. The United Free Church at first retained possession of the buildings, the churches and manses which had belonged to the pre-union Free Church, and would probably have no difficulty in doing so at St Kilda. But following the construction of the pier it seemed at the time that a fishing industry might be based on the island and might require the land presently occupied by the old manse and church. The proprietor's factor, John MacKenzie, therefore had to contemplate the possible grant of a feu to the United Free Church for the purpose of building a different manse and perhaps church. He thought that a manse site would have to be clear of the well generally used by the islanders and would be best located above the main pathway past the houses, as 'some day all the ground presently occupied by the Minister will be required for the Fishing industry, which I think is bound to develop'. He favoured a position 'above the burying ground' for the manse, and, since it would probably have to be moved as well, for the church also. But since he was considering these matters less than a month after the Uniting Act he had to be prepared for the possibility that the St Kilda people might refuse to join the United Free Church and so he recommended that nothing should be done for the time being. It is evident that MacKenzie shared what may have been a widespread belief that the proposed fishing industry would be started and run by an outside company, whose requirements would indeed include a large area of land.[85]

A fleet of fishing boats at St Kilda (c1900)

As it turned out no fishing industry materialised, no new manse and church were necessary, and the St Kilda community adhered to the United Free Church apparently without hesitation or protest. This last attachment seems to have been owing to the persuasive powers of Angus Fiddes, who, according to a report on 8 June 1901, 'some time ago explained to them the nature of the union, and seemingly they hailed it with satisfaction'. Since they understood church issues with 'a fair amount of intelligence' there was no doubt that all was then well: 'Ecclesiastically, they are very pleased with the union of the Churches.' Arriving with the *Hebrides* on 29 May 1901 Rev. Beaton from Muir of Ord, one of the many ministers who accepted the union, had stayed behind, in the ordinary way at communion time, 'to dispense the annual sacrament with Mr Fiddes on Sunday' and helped no doubt to confirm the St Kilda communicants in their attachment to the new church.[86]

One of the passengers on the *Dunara Castle* which visited St Kilda on Sunday 23 June 1901 wrote a journal of his trip. Sabbath observance had changed, probably as a consequence of all the contact with the 'outside world' over the past few years and perhaps because Rev. Fiddes had less regard for extremes of strictness:

'We cast anchor in St Kilda Bay at 12.30 p.m. and shortly afterwards we saw the people flock out of the Church. They had just finished their Gaelic Service and were about to begin the English one when they saw our ship entering the bay. They soon gathered along the shore and on the pier and in a short time two boats put out to visit us. Our ladder was put down over the side, and the Islanders came on board.

'That was a funny meeting: they looked at us doubtless as the American Indians gazed at Columbus when he first touched American soil, and we looked at them with a like curiosity. They were St Kildans, inhabitants of that lonely island of which so many strange stories had been told and which we had come so far to see. We expected something wonderful. I do not think we would have been surprised if we had found them dressed like Choctaw Indians in paint and feathers.'

The writer, representative of those numerous tourists who looked upon inhabitants of Hebridean islands as primitive tribesmen, was almost disappointed to find the St Kilda people 'much more civilized' and wearing a British style of clothes and ordinary boots.

Though it was Sunday the usual transactions were made at the head of the new pier, the visitors handing out sweets, tobacco, Gaelic tracts and copper coins, all of which were seized eagerly. It seemed that education had reverted to the system operated before Fiddes came to the island:

'Our party was taken in hand by the Schoolmaster who gave us much interesting information. He was not a St Kildan himself, he belonged to Harris and had been stationed on St Kilda for nine months, he was leaving the Island by our boat, his place being taken by another teacher during the ensuing winter. (I may mention by the way that the Schoolmaster wore a pair of trousers made of cloth woven entirely by himself in his spare time.) He showed us the Church, the Schoolhouse with the Library, the Church bell (an old ship's bell hung outside on a cross beam of wood) and the Church notice board.'

The purpose of the noticeboard baffled the visitors, as the islanders already knew the information on it, and strangers only arrived on Sundays twice a year at the most.

The St Kilda teacher, James Mackenzie, about to ring the bell outside the church and new school (see Part VIII n.93)

The unnamed schoolmaster took his party to the houses, and showed off antiquities including the nettle-filled graveyard where were 'three upright stones with names carved on them'. Eventually they met one of the engineers – perhaps W E Wookey – working on the pier who said that 'the work tended to elevate the Islanders, they were not so lazy now as when he came, and they were beginning to be proud of getting their wages on Saturdays'. The engineer then guided some of the visitors on a walk to view the cliffs and caves, showing how it was best to go down steep places in socks. At midnight the *Dunara Castle* prepared to leave, and a group of island men went on board to make a last-minute sale of dead birds and eggs now that the Sabbath was over. The cargo for the island was taken ashore, the last boatload of islanders disappeared into the darkness, the sound of oars getting fainter and fainter, 'and St Kilda was again cut off from the outside world'.

Much of the time these tourists were on the island Rev. Fiddes was busy conducting business with the 'laird'. MacLeod had come aboard at Stein in Skye. As in the case of the figurehead ornamenting the *St Clair of the Isles* in 1873 visitor imagination had been at work: 'some of us were expecting to see a gentleman dressed in tartan array .., a Claymore by his side, and a skean dhu at his knee, but he was only dressed in a very plain suit of St Kilda tweeds and he carried in his hand a small Kodak camera'. In fact it was easier to look on him as an American tourist than as a Highland chief, and the spectators were disillusioned. When at last Fiddes appeared he was asked to hold an English service for the steamer's passengers but he refused, suggesting only that one of them should take a children's service in the afternoon in place of the usual Sunday school. No one attended until the ship's bell was rung; then the children arrived, and there was sermon and singing. 'They sang the usual children's hymns from the Free Church Hymn Book, and the children sang very well.'[87]

Because they saw so little of Fiddes the visitors heard or sensed nothing like discontent on the island, but when, only two weeks later, the *Hebrides* called again, differences must have been emerging within the community. Angus Fiddes went off on his holiday and with him several islanders left, 'enticed southwards' by word of the great Glasgow exhibition. Some had never been away from the island before, and when they came back in the *Hebridean* a month afterwards they were welcomed home 'with characteristic effusiveness'. The minister probably returned by the same steamer, and before the end of August was deeply involved in a dispute not unlike that which had accompanied the last days as St Kilda's minister of Rev. John MacKay.[88]

Rumour reached the mainland that Fiddes had fallen out with his congregation:

'In connection with the recent strained relations existing between the inhabitants of the island of St. Kilda and their minister, the Rev. Angus Fiddes, which culminated the other day in the refusal of the islanders to land the minister's winter's supplies, a clergyman of the United Free Church has been sent out by the Rev. Alexander Lee, Secretary and Mission Superintendent for the Highlands and Islands. The mediator sailed on Monday by the steamer Hebrides on her last run this season to the island.

'It is not expected that the effort to effect a reconciliation or induce the rebellious flock to land their minister's supplies will prove effectual.

'In some quarters it is supposed that the cause of the friction is the position taken up by Mr Fiddes on the Church union question, but it is believed that local differences between the minister and natives play a considerable part in the squabble.'[89]

Reports of the dispute continued to appear. The 'natives' and their minister had certainly quarrelled, 'and unless the sternness of the former relaxes the rev. gentleman may have an anxious time during the winter'. The supply of provisions for the manse was still on board the *Hebrides* when it made its last call for the season at the beginning of September but again 'the natives refused to allow it to be transported from the steamer', and so it returned to Obbe where Rev. Lee tried to arrange for a boat and crew to take everything back to St Kilda once more. Neither boat nor crew turned up. A rather unreliable newspaper, the Glasgow *Weekly Mail*, elaborated on the episode and gave what seemed to be a false picture of attitudes and motives. It stated that the people had 'a soft place in their hearts still for the minister who has been with them so long, and whom they regard as a good man who has taken the wrong road'. One of the islanders, it was said, had 'confided in an interviewer, who in turn has made haste to publish it to all the world, that they did not intend to let him starve altogether, though how near starvation he may be brought before they relent is not disclosed'. This form of behaviour showed 'how much alive the ways of the Celtic people who are opposed to the Union are'.[90]

The *Weekly Mail* left no doubt that the argument was over the recent union of the churches, and that force, not reason, was the natural weapon of isolated 'Celtic' communities like that of St Kilda against opponents. It was assumed that the islanders wanted a Free Church minister, not one attached to the United Free, but there was now a lack of Free Church preachers, and 'it may be that they will have to be content with the preaching and the pastoral work of Mr Fiddes through the winter, though they regard him as one who has gone wrong upon the Union'. The winter closed in, and no one 'outside' knew what was going on in the remote island until the third week of May 1902.[91]

*

The *Hebrides* arrived in cold but favourable weather at 12.20 a.m. After horn blasts and the barking of dogs a boat with four young men came out to take ashore the mails and 'a young St. Kildian resident in Glasgow'. Later in the morning it was learned that the ecclesiastical situation was unchanged except for one important difference: 'The people, with but few exceptions, are as strenuous as ever in their opposition to the minister, but say that whatever steps they may finally take they do not blame the Union of the Churches for their present attitude.' The *Weekly Mail* was therefore entirely, and perhaps wilfully, misleading; and Rev. Fiddes had survived the winter.[92]

Another voyage by the *Hebrides* in June 1902 took a United Free Church deputation to St Kilda to investigate the causes of difference, and a missionary was left on the island 'to supply the pulpit in the absence of the Rev. Mr Fiddes who embarked .. for the South', while several passengers chose to remain for a short stay 'in pursuit of the study of natural history'. The general impression must have been that Fiddes had once more departed on holiday, and all the islanders were used to having a substitute in the form of a young teacher, but this time the presence of the missionary as well as the teacher seemed to suggest at least a change in the usual summer arrangements. Two weeks later, when the 'Coronation' party from Yorkshire came, 'a young lady teacher' landed to take the place of Mr Roderick Campbell, schoolmaster. Roderick

Campbell had succeeded the teacher who had been the helpful guide to the *Dunara Castle* group in 1901 and who, having then completed nine months on the island, was possibly the first to serve instead of Rev. Fiddes through the winter. In 1902 therefore teachers were no surprise to the islanders; a missionary was something new.[93]

Fiddes did not return in July, and at the end of that month he resigned his post as minister in St Kilda, to the regret of those who 'take a keen interest in the spiritual welfare of the little community'. On Saturday 9 August he was interviewed by a reporter who described him as 'a middle-aged man with iron-grey hair and moustache, a kindly and strong face, and .. the last representative of an old family, who were said to be religious refugees from England in the 17th century'. The interview inevitably began with questions about the dispute between minister and islanders and, probably, whether it had driven him to resign:

'Mr Fiddes was very reticent regarding the dispute which for some time caused a feeling of estrangement between himself and the people. Fortunately, it has been lived down, and no one regrets his departure more than the islanders. The real cause of the trouble has been greatly exaggerated and misrepresented. Mr Fiddes acted with discretion in face of peculiar and delicate circumstances.

'Mr Fiddes has acted as minister, doctor, and schoolmaster on the island for twelve years, and during that time the younger portion of the inhabitants have made great progress. Their education was attended with great difficulties.

' "Everything," said Mr Fiddes, "has to be represented on the blackboard. The young folks have never seen a tree, a horse, or a train, and the simplest things in life are great mysteries to them. Last season there were 25 scholars on the roll; this year there will be 19. The report of His Majesty's Inspectors has been very favourable."

' "Did you at times feel the island solitude hard to bear?" he was asked.

' "When I saw the last steamer leave the island for the year," he replied, "a lump came in my throat. I was shut off from the world, and from all those who were near and dear to me. And then, when the long dreary winter was over, and news came from the mainland, I would hear that a brother or sister had months before sickened, and died, and while I was thinking of them as still in life, they were under the sod." '[94]

On the Monday after this interview, 11 August 1902, Rev. Fiddes joined the

Hebrides at Glasgow for one last journey to St Kilda. He was only going for the purpose of tidying up the manse and removing his small possessions. The young lady teacher was apparently there for the summer months only and would soon leave the missionary on his own. Meanwhile reflections on Fiddes's career in the island were prepared for the press and proved complimentary:

> 'Mr Fiddes has been engaged in the island for the last twelve years, and has done his utmost for the temporal as well as the spiritual welfare of the people. For a time he acted as schoolmaster in addition to his work as missionary, but latterly teachers have been appointed under the Harris School Board. The school is examined annually by Mr Robertson, H.M.Inspector of Schools, and last year's report was more favourable than any hitherto presented. During the winter months the school is taught by an ex-pupil teacher, and in the summer months a lady teacher from the mainland gives lessons in cookery and domestic economy. Mr Fiddes's labours on behalf of the people have been very successful. He was largely instrumental in getting the Congested Districts Board to erect a pier at the landing-place, behind which the boats of the islanders can enter in safety. He has now, however, severed his connection with the island. Last month he placed his resignation in the hands of the Highland Committee of the United Free Church; and the Committee, being satisfied with the reasons he assigned for taking this step, resolved to accept it, at the same time acknowledging the valuable services he has rendered for so many years. Mr Fiddes will be employed as a missionary on the mainland, and will be succeeded on the island by Mr Lachlan MacLean, a man who is believed to have special qualification for the duties he will be called upon to undertake. He is a native of Tiree, and received his training at the Glasgow Bible Training Institute.'

Making a safe landing Angus Fiddes took his last leave of the islanders. The postponed actual Coronation Day was being celebrated at the same time and in St Kilda was 'fittingly observed'. The flag was hoisted 'approximately at the hour the King was crowned', and Fiddes prayed for his Majesty in Gaelic before delivering an 'oration' also in Gaelic. A St Kilda enthusiast, Major Colquhoun, who said that he had visited the island four times since 1894, 'led off the National Anthem, which was heartily sung'. The missionary, Lachlan MacLean, who had been in St Kilda since the day in June when Fiddes first went south, embarked with his predecessor for a break on the mainland 'presumably to fortify himself for the nine months' isolation awaiting him', but he was away only a short time as a yacht party, which landed soon after the last of the season's steamers, the *Hebridean*, had gone in late August, 'made a tour of inspection through the quaint little township under the kind guidance of Mr MacLean, the missionary'.[95]

It was not just Angus Fiddes that left St Kilda that mid-August day in 1902. With him faded the remaining glimmers of a Protestant fire, never a bright one, which was lit so hopefully two hundred years before, and in his person departed the last of the ministers ordained solely to serve the 'poor people' of that lonely Hebridean island. Almost submerged under the flood of events, useful or ridiculous, those islanders who stayed at home for a few more years became almost incidental to the interests of the 'outside world'. Like the 'wedding' and 'coronation' parties visitors tended increasingly to impose their own aims and pursuits upon surroundings that, instead of being the real and natural setting of a Gaelic-speaking island community, were now treated as if they were there for photographing, writing about, studying, and to satisfy mere curiosity still. The little company of human inhabitants were objects, primitive relics rather than the people about whose inner selves few but the church had shown any concern.

After Fiddes had gone one question remained unanswered, that to which he had discretely said nothing. Why had he resigned his charge? Perhaps it has never been answered. Major Colquhoun thought he provided an explanation in an article or letter contributed to the *North Star* and reprinted in the *Aberdeen Daily Journal* of Saturday 17 January 1903. If what he wrote was true then it shows that the minister ran out of patience with the triviality which was often the essence of St Kilda arguments. Certainly Colquhoun, stating that he was 'intimately acquainted with the facts of the case in all its stages' because he had lived on the island for weeks at a time, claimed that the reason for the dispute related to 'the final withdrawal' of Rev. Fiddes. He told how two persons 'not now on the island' orchestrated a 'disgraceful campaign' against their pastor, and how some of the natives 'invaded the manse in a body and gave the minister "what for" to his face'. Refusal to land his stores and coals after three separate attempts to deliver them was followed by the permitted landing from a Fleetwood trawler of supplies sufficient only for one person and not enough for the three occupants of the manse. A ton of coal was also brought. With these limited resources Fiddes, the manse servant, and the schoolmaster, Mr Roderick Campbell, 'a young man who acquitted himself with much credit in his scholastic duties' and probably a friend of the minister, had to make do for nine months until relief came in June.

'An official inquiry had been intimated, but none was held. The agents of the church went back by the steamer in which they came, same time as the writer, taking the minister along with them! Thereafter, until the middle of August, when Mr Fiddes finally returned to remove his stuff, the writer, as an interested spectator of events, remained in the manse; having brought with him, besides provisions, his own bedding and furniture. The most remarkable episode of that time was undoubtedly the unannounced return of the Rev. W. Ross, who, as it appeared by and by from an indifferently illustrated article by himself, in the United Free Church Record, had enjoyed "a good time" among the natives; the absent minister was never mentioned!'[96]

Retribution, as Colquhoun saw it, for the islanders' unkind behaviour swiftly followed. Having denied the minister coals, one of them sent off a plea for 'a few tons of coals to help through the long and cold winter'. The urgent message, launched into the sea around 20 October 1902, fetched up on the Shetland island of Unst where none other than Angus Fiddes happened to be at the time. Furthermore Colquhoun believed that the St Kilda people deserved any hardship that might follow for though industrious and intelligent they were crafty and 'demoralised' as well:

'There has been, however, throughout, no question of religion, nor any Church question involved in the persecution of their late minister. They simply wanted to be free from the irksome supervision of their benefactor, the saviour of their race. They "wanted the island for themselves," and they have got it; for even "The MacLeod," the nominal proprietor, can scarcely now further interfere with them. What they further want, as, to them, the richer "harvest of the sea," is the harvest of the tourist season and of "personally conducted tours" on and around the island by field naturalists and others with long purses and with no "Manse" further to interfere with them. They have shown themselves to be ungrateful, greedy and mercenary. They seem in reality to care as little for the United Free Church of Scotland as now they care for the Church of their ancestors, the ruins of whose forgotten chapels have crumbled from their hillsides.'

Whether or not this explanation and the accompanying condemnation of the islanders were accepted as fair, history and the impact of the 'outside world' would have to bear some of the blame for any undesirable behaviour. Only sympathy was felt for Angus Fiddes, whose services on the island were not considered to have lacked 'prudence' and understanding but were praised by, among others, the Highlands committee of the United Free Church although apparently not rewarded in any other way:

'It is not too much to say that in addition to his faithful preaching of the Gospel, he had done more for the education of the young, and the amelioration of the social conditions of the whole community, than any other man who ever lived among them.'

It was perhaps only just, from Major Colquhoun's point of view, that he should finish his account of Rev. Fiddes's final departure on a level of absurdity. When leaving Fiddes wished to assign possession of the cow he had grazed on the glebe to his servant who had always looked after the animal. Even though she was to continue as servant to Lachlan MacLean the people refused to allow either her or the missionary to keep the cow, which had to leave the island along with Fiddes:

'The "inwardness" of this was to be found in crafty preparation for confiscation of the glebe, so long coveted for its grass. The "coming man", if any, is warned he can have "No cow!" The hint is intended for the Church authorities, as drawing their attention to the undoubted fact that their power in St Kilda on modified conditions, is now a feeble one.'[97]

CHAPTER 5
Missionary teachers and the survival of tradition

It would not be fair to give the impression that with the departure of Rev. Angus Fiddes in 1902 the effective presence of the Protestant church in St Kilda had come to an end. Its powerful influence upon the people may have diminished but its support remained with the succession of missionaries and teachers who served the island through the last three decades of the community's existence.

Like its predecessor the United Free Church maintained interest in the island after Fiddes had left. Before he did so, during the 1890s, the Free Church Highlands Committee sent the occasional deputy. In June 1892, when in the aftermath of John MacKay's retirement religious harmony had not been fully restored, there was a report that the state of the congregation 'urgently required the visit of a deputation', and Rev. John MacLean of Tarbert was appointed to go along with Rev. John S MacPhail of Benbecula in order to establish peace once more. Presumably they succeeded as there were no further concerns of that kind expressed and the deputies who visited regularly thereafter found time to comment on material as well as spiritual needs. Rev. D. J. MacKay, Free Church minister in Tiree, wrote in October 1893 of the anxiety of the people 'to have a visit from one of H.M. Gunboats during this year and as soon as possible' in the hope that it would 'convey a truss from Mr MacKenzie, the factor at Dunvegan to a man in St Kilda who had a rupture'. No gunboat did go; but in September of the following year H.M.S. *Starling* was willing to take out 'any provisions that may be required for the island' even though the proprietor claimed that he had already sent out necessary stores himself and all that was left at Dunvegan was a ton of coal for the island's minister. A still more worldly role for St Kilda's pastor was apparent by 1898 when, in view of 'a growing desire on the part of tourists to reside for several days on the island', and since 'this in the early part of the summer is quite possible by going by one line and returning by another', lodging was made available in the manse.[98]

The sequence of visiting ministers around 1900 was as varied as the matters claiming their attention. In 1895 Rev. Roderick MacKenzie, Maryburgh, was the deputy, and in 1901 Rev. Archibald Beaton, of Urray, submitted a satisfactory report of an 'encouraging' nature after his 'deputational' call at St Kilda. The Highlands Committee secretary went there, and to other islands, with Rev. William Ross in 1902 during the quarrel with Fiddes, and that autumn Ross, described as 'evangelist', gave an account of their expedition. Subsequent deputies, always one a year now, included Rev. James Johnstone, Strathpeffer, in 1903, Rev. Alexander MacKay, Glenurquhart, in 1904, Rev. James MacLeod, Munlochy, in 1905, Rev. Allan Munn, Kirkhill, in 1906, and Rev. Donald MacAlister, Glenorchy, in 1907. Apart from reporting on the state of religion and any other island issues that attracted his attention the deputy's main tasks were as usual the dispensing of communion and the conducting of marriages and baptisms, all the more important after the replacement of the last ordained minister, Angus Fiddes, by missionary teachers who were not allowed to perform such major duties. And so the series of visiting ministers, who usually appeared by a steamer in July, persisted to the end, the last being Rev. John MacKinnon from Paisley in 1929.[99]

Apart from appointing deputies the Highlands Committee, whether Free Church or United Free, also had the usual incidental matters to deal with such as acknowledging with due gratitude occasional grants and donations intended to benefit either the St Kilda people or their missionaries. Towards the close of 1900 there was discussion relating to the possible necessity of building a new manse for United Free Church use and Dr MacPhail said that he had already prepared an appeal for funds signed by Dr Rainy and Mr Lee, but of course in the event this did not happen. Then with Fiddes leaving the committee had to give urgent consideration to future arrangements for the island and this inevitably involved thoughts on education provision. Members had to decide whether teaching and preaching might, as Norman Heathcote had partly suggested in his book, be combined under one missionary sent out for a short period or perhaps be treated as work to be shared by a married couple.[100]

A new pattern of religious and educational supply therefore gradually emerged, taking slightly different forms as it did so. When Angus Fiddes came to St Kilda the presence of a teacher employed by the ELHSA and of a Free Church minister had been the regular arrangement for five years. Fiddes then took over both tasks until perhaps 1896 in which year George Matheson arrived to assist with the teaching. The experienced elder Donald Ferguson could fill in on the side of religion, and so it became possible for Fiddes to continue having a summer break away on the mainland. Further relief from his duties came with the annual appointment of a young female sewing instructor during two or three summer months, probably beginning with Miss Fenton in 1899. These two valuable supports seem to have been at first intermittent for during the Heathcotes' stay in 1898 there was apparently no assistant teacher and in 1899 only Miss Fenton was there although there were plans for a male teacher to serve through the winter 'under Mr Fiddes' superintendence'. In 1900 the ELHSA's 'relief female teacher' arrived and soon afterwards the 'male teacher' in the shape of James MacKenzie, about both of whom the school inspector, Mr Robertson, now to be a regular visitor each year, wrote: 'Since my last visit the efficiency of the school has risen greatly, and it is clear that the teacher of the ordinary branches and the special teacher of needlework have taught diligently and with creditable success.' In 1901 MacKenzie was replaced by Roderick Campbell, and on 25 June that year the Highlands

Committee was informed that Miss Johanna Stewart was going to St Kilda as 'Female Teacher' for two months. When Lachlan MacLean succeeded Fiddes as missionary in the summer of 1902 the committee secretary reported on 30 September that, as lay missionary, he was appointed 'to carry on the mission' in the island for the winter and spring period and that, with the consent and approval of Mr Robertson, he had undertaken to teach the school over the same months, efforts to secure a former pupil teacher having failed and Mary C MacKenzie having completed her 'interim' stay of just under two months as rather more than just sewing instructor, especially in mid August when Fiddes had gone for good and MacLean was away for a brief holiday.[101]

In September 1903 John Fraser came to St Kilda as missionary from the Ross of Mull, exchanging places with Lachlan MacLean, whose teaching duties were taken over by Donald MacDonald from Benbecula. Unlike his predecessor Fraser remained for more than the nine months of his original appointment and in fact spent three years in the island. During this period a succession of winter and summer teachers followed each other, appointed for about nine months and two months respectively. Of the former kind Donald MacDonald was succeeded by another MacDonald in 1904, and he in turn by Donald MacAskill in 1905. At the same time the sewing teachers were Edith Findlay, 'Central School', Inverness, who left 'after a most pleasant stay of seven weeks', Kathleen Kennedy from Inverness Academy who 'enjoyed a very happy time in St Kilda' in 1904, and Miss K W Gollan, of Glenfintaig School, Invernessshire, who also enjoyed her stay. There then came a complete change when in 1906 after the customary consultation with the Schools Inspector the Highlands committee secretary was asked to confer with Rev. Peter MacLauchlan, preacher at Garve in Rossshire, and his wife over the possibility of their taking up the posts of both missionary and teacher in St Kilda. Before the end of June the MacLauchlans had been approached and had agreed to go to the island for one year. When they arrived they found the manse, which had been the subject of plans for additions and alterations in 1903, in serious disrepair, and the building was still unimproved a year later. A contractor at Lochmaddy, W Bain in 1903 and John Bain in 1907, was prepared to carry out the work, which was possibly much delayed as Mrs MacLauchlan noted the arrival of 'Bain, Contractor and his man' in 1908, or had to be repeated more than once.[102]

*

In 1906, when John Fraser was in his last weeks as missionary, St Kilda was visited by ' A Medical Inspector' who wrote an account of his experiences.[103] He had to stay for two weeks between steamer calls and his main purpose seems to have been to vaccinate as many islanders as he could. It struck him that both missionary and teacher must have had a beneficial influence in this regard, because, unlike the reaction to previous medical visits, almost all the young people attended for the vaccination and even some men, who 'passed the ordeal' and laughed at the 'paltryness' of the scratches.

The doctor had something to say about aspects of island life, though his comments were not free of conventional bias. He learned that one of the older men had an ancient vaccination lancet which he used, as his father had before him, to let blood. 'As the lancet was greasy, and not overclean, I suggested that he should always boil it before use. In the true St Kildian manner, he retorted that as the instrument was forty years old, he thought it was time someone presented him with a new one, and suggested that I should buy him one and send it on.' As far as work in general was concerned, the doctor held similar preconceptions:

> 'They do little fishing, and make nothing of their grant of a three miles limit. Their crofts are slovenly tilled, and they make no attempts at improvements. The numerous cleits and stone dykes on the island are the work of more industrious generations in the past. Women and men alike are said to work well when once set agoing; but they dawdle and gossip away the golden hours just the same as wet ones. They have not yet grasped the rudiments of independence. They accept gifts with gratitude, but with no sense of obligation to repay. They are emotional, easily offended, easily depressed; courageous enough, though careful, in bird catching on the rocks ..'

He did not really approve of either the place or the people – 'The bleak and lonely aspect of the island, and the isolation and seeming poverty of its inhabitants, have of late years excited more public sympathy than the case demands' – but although transference of the whole population to the mainland had been offered in a gesture of sympathy it had been declined. On the credit side however, he was impressed by the religious situation. During the first week of his visit Fraser 'had to preside at five religious services – three times on Sunday, a prayer meeting on Monday forenoon, and another on Wednesday evening', in fact the usual programme. Partly as a consequence, in the doctor's opinion, the people were happily 'permeated with the doctrine of Christian faith', and while at the moment 'diligence in business, original thought, discontent, ambition, energising' were 'yet in embryo' much might be achieved through sensible teaching towards securing what he believed was the most desirable outcome: 'Nothing can be expected from the older generation, but with proper attention from our education department the virgin soil may in time realise such possibilities, and the lone shores of Hirta will then be abandoned to their true aborigines, the sea birds.'

The MacLauchlans must have been aware of such attitudes towards their isolated community, none of them new but serving to move the people inevitably towards the ultimate evacuation. Perhaps they even came to share the same views. Yet in spite of the somewhat fatalistic atmosphere the missionary and his wife, and their successors, had to maintain their enthusiasm and faithfully carry out routine daily tasks which ranged from keeping the school register, apparently introduced in Fiddes's last year or two, to supporting bereaved families and seeking ways of improving communication. The usual time for leaving school was on reaching the age of 14, but this could in practice vary when the reason given for leaving was to 'help Parents with home Industries', and there were occasional abrupt misfortunes when a child had to be taken away to hospital or when in October 1906 young Norman Gillies was drowned. Such a disaster seemed to depress everyone, and Mrs MacLauchlan herself was no exception. After three men were lost at Dun in 1909 she wrote: 'This is an awful place.'[104]

Ministers and missionaries through the ages led a twofold life. For some of the time they felt themselves part of the community, while on occasion they knew they were isolated individuals different from the rest of the inhabitants. The missionary of later years who was allowed to accompany a fowling party on a night raid to Stack Lee must have been pleased to join in to such a traditional venture, but when, after climbing up and being told not to utter the least sound, a gannet nearly severed a finger and he could not hold back a groan of pain, the words of a nearby companion brought the isolation flooding back: 'What are you shouting for?' And having bound the finger with a piece of shirt he was told on the return journey to keep his hand hidden when taking the service on Sunday, 'otherwise the women will laugh at you'. Whoever was missionary, or teacher, from time to time was overwhelmed with an awareness not only of the isolation and deprivation to which he or she had been, often willingly, committed but also of the pathetic nature of the people in their forlorn struggle to survive. A sensitive person such as George Murray would suffer greatly in these circumstances, particularly in the winter, while others, like Hugh McCallum, might be better able to endure, and later even recollect the experience with some pleasure. It may have been Lachlan MacLean who found the task beyond him. F. G. Rea, who recorded his reminiscences as a schoolmaster in South Uist during the period 1890 to 1913, wrote of an occasion when the *Dunara Castle* had called on her way back south:

'She had that week put into our port with a missionary from St Kilda on board, but he was quite insane. At the boat's last St Kilda visit, some nine months before, he, a young ecclesiastical student, had landed there as missionary, schoolmaster, registrar and postmaster. As he could not speak Gaelic, imagination only can give any idea of what that young man had been through.'[105]

The church in St Kilda became more organised after 1900. In earlier years there had been elders, a rather indefinite and irregular kirk session, and a register of baptisms, marriages and deaths, but it appears that no session minute book was kept until the United Free Church assumed responsibility for the island's religious welfare in 1901-1902. A Communicants Roll Book was begun in July 1902 when Rev. William Ross was making his visit as deputy and entries continued until 1929. Records of some deaths were included, as were the names of the missionaries. In July 1906, when John Fraser was reaching the end of his term as missionary and Rev. Allan Munn was present as deputy, a session minute book was begun in regular fashion, although the first entry was an account of the constitution of a kirk session on 22 August 1898 with Donald Ferguson and Norman Gillies as elders. Rev. Alexander MacDonald of Ardclach was deputy then, and 'As no Record of the transactions of the Kirk-Session has been hitherto kept it was decided to Record that the Revd. Angus Fiddes was ordained by the Free Presbytery of Uist to the oversight of the Congregation'. The session met once a year at communion time, and business included revision of the communicants roll, detailing the daily sequence of meetings over the communion period with a note of who did what, and recording baptisms and occasionally deaths. In 1910, for example, the communion days occupied the last week of July, with Rev. M MacLennan from Edinburgh in attendance as deputy, the other session members being the missionary, Dougal MacLean, and the elder, Donald Ferguson. Special services of preparation began on Monday evening and continued till Wednesday, from Thursday till Monday there were early morning prayer meetings, while ordinary preparatory services took place at noon and at 6.30 p.m. On Friday the usual fellowship meeting was at noon, when William MacDonald gave out the question ('the Ceisd') from 2 Corinthians VII.10, and it was 'spoken to' by seven of the men and the missionary. Two services on Saturday, together with the distribution of tokens to the would-be communicants, led to the communion service on Sunday at 11 a.m. when the whole population attended except for three 'who happened to be from home on necessary business'. The 'solemn service', with twenty-nine 'at the table' among whom were four for the first time, was followed by a short service at 4 p.m. for the 'young people', 'and the day's work was brought to a close by a service at 6.30' conducted by the missionary. Two baptisms succeeded the thanksgiving service on Monday, and it was concluded that the event 'gave much cheer to us all' and was 'attended with heartiness by much the greater portion of old and young'.

A whole crowd of visiting ministers and other 'friends from the South' attended communion in 1914. In July 1916, after a year in which there had been no communion celebration and no deputy 'owing to the unsettled state of the country on account of the war with Germany', in addition to the usual matters the session had to deal with one of the minor upsets which sometimes interrupted the peaceful state of the community. William MacDonald, a church member, and Mary Ann MacQueen, an 'adherent', had to appear before the session because Mary Ann had accused William of 'using unbecoming language towards her about six weeks ago to the effect that She had not the good manners of a dog – Cha neil modha' Choin agad'. William maintained that he had actually said 'Cha neil modha' Choin na'd theangaidh', which did not seem to make much difference to the argument, but he admitted that these were not proper words to use and that he ought not to have uttered them. Perhaps seeing that the case was a distinctly old-fashioned one and rather trivial the session decided to take no action and hoped the two would soon be reconciled.[106]

There was often little difference between the communicants roll book, the session minutes, and a third record in the form of congregational returns made irregularly between 1907 and 1929. These too contained numbers of communicants, numbers attending school, occasional baptisms and deaths, and changes of missionary, adding thereby a little more detail to the picture of island religion but, like the other two records, containing almost nothing about the various events of a more worldly kind that certainly claimed the attention and the interest of the missionaries. Frequently whalers, based in Harris, put in at St Kilda, and whales were collected in the bay where they were moored to a buoy until taken to Bunaveneader for processing. Emergency 'relief' was sent to the island in 1912, a short-lived radio communication system was introduced in 1913, and in 1918 a German submarine bombarded the settlement. Less dramatically tourists continued to arrive by yacht and steamer with cameras and notebooks at the ready to record the material for use in journals and letters.[107]

In August 1910 J A Smith, writing from Aberdeen and enclosing four photographs taken in St Kilda, outlined his impressions of the people and noted that 'two policemen from Lewis who had been on the island a fortnight under the sheep dipping order told me that the sheep would never have been dipped at all if they (the policemen) had not done it themselves. They were sent to see it done and had to do it personally in order to get away.' These were not the first officers of the law to visit St Kilda nor were they the last. In July 1889 the Lochmaddy police inspector, who had to go to the island to investigate a case of alleged sheep stealing, seems to have been the first, 'and it would appear that the distant isle is now to have the benefits of such modern forms of civilisation'. Sheep dipping supervision was evidently the main reason for police attendance in later years, but a policeman's presence was otherwise unnecessary and the kirk session provided such moral control as was needed.[108]

News of the 'plight' of the St Kilda people was brought in May 1912 by a trawler skipper. After a severe winter they were once again short of food supplies. The islanders now relied on the 'provision steamer' which usually made a call in August before the onset of bad weather and another in April after winter was supposedly past, but this time severe storms had twice prevented the landing of much needed goods. The *Daily Mirror* rather than the *Glasgow Herald* immediately organised a vessel, the tug *Victor*, to take out essentials, and at the same time H.M.S *Achilles* was instructed to do likewise. In support of the newspaper's initiative Sir Thomas Lipton, on board his yacht *Shamrock* at Southampton, sent a 'splendid telegram' in which he said: 'Delighted to be of any service to starving inhabitants of St. Kilda. I will supply at my own personal expense your tug of mercy with the provisions you require.' The tug, with a doctor on board, promptly fulfilled its mission, though it seemed that the *Achilles* had arrived and left 'just before us'. At the sight of all this help 'Men and women burst into tears, while Donald Ferguson, now an octogenarian islander, burst out into improvised poetry in Gaelic', and the *Mirror's* reporter was assured that the composition 'was as beautiful in its sentiment as it was musical to the ear'. The missionary, Dougal MacLean again, who, according to the captain of the *Achilles*, was 'more or less, the head authority in the island', told of 'some touching instance of privations' including the situation in the manse where 'the diet since the beginning of March has consisted of nothing but tea, bread and butter – three times a day for three months'. A photograph of Sir Thomas Lipton was shown to the islanders who cheered it, the women pressing it 'to their hearts by way of thanks', and all were greatly upset when photographs of the *Titanic* loss were needlessly produced and explained. A more detached view of the whole episode was given in a letter from Captain Stanhope Hawke of the *Achilles* who had handed over a request in writing to 'the Minister, Postmaster and Precentor' that they should see to the even distribution of the supplies. The captain excused himself for including tea and tobacco which might have been considered non-essential luxuries but which seemed worthwhile, the second after he had learned that one man 'had cut his waistcoat pocket where he generally kept his tobacco and had used it to chew after the last of the tobacco in the island had run out'. He concluded: 'At present there seems to be no one responsible for the island, or, if there is, nothing much is done, and everything is left to chance.'[109]

At the end of January 1914 Nurse Robertson, from Edinburgh, was given the unenviable task of paying a short visit to St Kilda in the middle of winter. Since the days of Nurse Chisnhall in 1892 there seems to have been no regular nursing care in the island, the only medical attention available being either that provided by the very occasional doctor or the limited skills of the missionary and his wife. Otherwise islanders in need of treatment had to find a way of reaching Glasgow or Aberdeen. Nurse Robertson's visit, presumably in response to a radio call, was made in order to examine widow MacDonald's leg ulcer. The journey was, almost inevitably, in very rough conditions, involving a steamer crossing from Kyle of Lochalsh to Stornoway by the *Sheila*, and then a voyage from Breascleit to St Kilda by the lighthouse vessel *Polestar*; and time spent on the island amounted to no more than 1¹/₂ hours as the weather would not allow the *Polestar* to linger in the bay. As it turned out the nurse was unable to improve on the treatment of the ulcer already being given, 'as they were dressing it as well as I could'. She met, and perhaps shared the feelings of, a young man who had been in the island for over a month repairing 'the wireless installation' and who was now able to leave by the *Polestar*. 'I never saw such joy in my life as in that boy's face when he got off the island.' That same summer, on 21 May, Nurse McLellan arrived along with the deputy, Rev. Alexander MacDonald, who had come to introduce the new missionary, Alexander MacKinnon, and his wife. Thereafter until the evacuation of the remaining population the medical responsibilities of the missionary passed to a series of resident nurses.[110]

Alexander MacKinnon wrote to the island's proprietor, MacLeod of MacLeod, on 15 May 1918 to report that 'today about 10 a.m. we have been bombarded by a German Submarine', which had come as far as the outer limits of the bay and fired around 70 shells. 'The nurse's cottage is uninhabitable. Neil MacKinnon's, Finlay McQueen's are badly damaged, both wall, and roof. The church is very badly damaged, but the Manse escaped fairly well, with the exception of windows.' Submarines were often seen and the missionary thought it would be worth having a gun with which to retaliate. In due course the gun arrived, too late to be useful, and began a long period of rusting and decay. Not until two years later, in October 1920, was a claim submitted to the Board of Trade for the damages done by the shelling on the basis of the following costs: the church £440.3s.9d, the storehouse £412.4s.10d, Neil MacKinnon's house £286.7s.11d, Finlay MacQueen's house £9.11s, and William MacDonald's house £1, amounting in all to £1149.7s.6d. Apparently a 'stereotyped acknowledgement' was the only response, and MacLeod wrote in October 1921 that while the United Free Church had spent £440 on repairs to the church he still expected compensation of £372 for the loss of the store and £296 for the damage to the houses.[111]

At this stage, in spite of the professed reluctance of the islanders ever to abandon their home, notions of evacuation were again circulating, more strongly perhaps than for many years; and at the same time MacLeod was contemplating the sale of St Kilda. The two possible courses of action were closely linked, because the proprietor was now eager to rid himself of a costly and unrewarding possession.

The projected sale was a subject of discussion between MacLeod and his factor John MacKenzie in 1920 and 1921. One possible buyer was Lord Leverhulme, who, it was said later, 'was anxious to move the whole population to Leverburgh', and the sum suggested was £6000 although 'it might be modified to the extent of throwing in the Soay sheep stock, which can only be realised at much expense and with great difficulty'. If Leverhulme offered £5000 'as a definite proposition' it would be worth considering, and 'Selling the island now would in no way prejudice your claim [for damages] as far as I can see'. The operator of the whaling station in Harris, Carl Herlofsen, would also have liked to buy St Kilda, 'but,' said MacKenzie, 'he told me that lack of funds <u>at present</u> prevented his coming forward'. MacKenzie was ready to put in a small offer himself: 'Would you before making any arrangement for sale be disposed to feu the Factor's Cottage and the croft on which it stands to me, and if so, at what rate per annum? I am fond of the place and would enjoy an occasional visit to the Island after our connection was severed.' In due course a Mr Norman Robertson visited the island with regard to the Leverhulme interest 'and found everyone willing to leave, but when the actual detailed arrangements were about to be made, sentimental ties held them to the island and the Scheme dropped'.[112]

Thoughts tending towards evacuation or emigration persisted thereafter. In the summer of 1928 Rev. Finlay MacQueen, minister of East Kew presbyterian church in Melbourne, Australia, and son of Calum who emigrated from St Kilda in 1852, was in Britain and had a conversation with MacLeod 'about getting the population...away from the Island'. MacLeod apparently agreed that this was a good idea, particularly if government assistance were available, but the fate of the evacuated people presented a problem. Some might be placed in Skye, possibly on land owned by MacLeod or on 'holdings under the Board of Agriculture', but many of the older inhabitants and even several of the younger might be unwilling to move. The Australian authorities were not thought likely to assist in any way, but there was a possibility that families might be allowed into that country to lodge with Scottish households already in Victoria and elsewhere. 'With regard to the older people, it would seem to me that the best way of dealing with their case would be to try and get relatives in Scotland to take them away from the Island to live with them in Glasgow or elsewhere, rather than to consider migration to a distant and strange land.' On his return to Melbourne Rev. MacQueen would look for 'openings' for families there and report. An alternative destination might be Canada, 'if there is any hitch in regard to Australia', but 'the Scottish Delegation from Australia (of which Mr. MacQueen was a member) were given a strong hint by their organisers not to talk too much about migration while in the Highlands'.[113]

The factor's reaction to the letter on removal possibilities was negative: 'I have given this subject very careful consideration, and have come to the conclusion that it would be unwise to take up the question of removing the inhabitants. Such action on your part would undoubtedly be misconstrued, and I think the wisest course to pursue is to wait until the people themselves have made the first move.' The large MacKinnon family was already willing to leave, and would have made for Canada if assistance had been available for them all, but there were two handicapped children and no aid for them was permitted, so the family was still on the island. 'As regards the other people, the most of them would oppose emigration, but perhaps one family of the name of Gillies might be induced to leave…I remember they asked MacQueen what wages they would get if they went to Australia, and when he told them, they showed no enthusiasm – rather the other way about.'[114]

Within two years the last missionary, Dougal Munro, had drawn up the petition for evacuation assistance and all the remaining people were gone, under circumstances and to destinations already well described elsewhere.

*

More than twenty years ago Robin Fox wrote his book about a people of the Celtic fringe on Tory Island off the north west coast of Donegal. He intended his work 'to be, in some small way, a memorial to this unique and remarkable people who may not be able to survive the worst devastation of all: progress'. Later in the same book he elaborated on this: 'After years of subtle resistance based on isolation, the very isolation has turned against them. When they could be left to their subsistence and ignored, they could survive. Now, along with the crofters of Scotland and the outporters of Newfoundland, they are being sucked into the welfare state which, paradoxically, cannot let them live in their culture of relative poverty but must, because it cannot tolerate their poverty, destroy their culture. With the very best of intentions.' So St Kilda too had its culture destroyed and its shores emptied by progress and the pressure from 'outside', and there must be a lesson here for other island communities of the Celtic fringe. Caught up in the inevitable materialist flood tide the islanders themselves, to an extent, contributed to the destruction, but if the church was involved it was only through the personal views and actions of individual missionaries and not as a consequence of doctrine or policy.[115]

What influence the church, in any of its forms, had upon the character of a St Kilda inhabitant it is not easy to say. Throughout the period for which some reasonably detailed record survives, about 450 years, the people were always inclined towards beliefs and practices that might be called religious, although the significance of these is blurred by the presumptions of the commentators who described them. Many thought the 'natives' conspicuous for their genuine hospitality to strangers yet at the same time remarked on their suspicion and greed when it came to relations with non-native parties or individuals. Contradictions seem always to have been a feature of island behaviour; to Martin the islanders were an extremely virtuous race who could at times be anything but virtuous, while less than twenty years later Alexander Buchan was apparently one of many to find them generous and sympathetic in spite of their expecting payment for simple things like the loan of a pot. In

716

Protestant times at least there was a tendency to see what missionaries and others considered the better qualities of the people as the consequence of religious preaching and of an education almost entirely dominated by religion. It is therefore difficult to judge the worth of such a comment as that made by Dr Norman MacLeod in the time of Rev. Neil MacKenzie's ministry.

On 2 August 1838 Dr MacLeod wrote a letter to a friend in which he set out his feelings on returning from his trip with Dr David Dickson to St Kilda where he had landed on Saturday 28 July and seen the distribution of furnishings for the new houses. He had, he said, enjoyed every minute of the excursion.

'Staffa made us forget the Giant's Causeway, the Spar Cave and Coruisg almost drove Staffa out of our minds, but the noble St Kilda obliterated the recollection of them all.

'I consider St. Kilda the most extraordinary island connected with Great Britain; the situation of the place, the genius and manners of the inhabitants, the constitution of the little commonwealth, the amazing dexterity with which they manage the most important branches of their calling, the marvellous courage with which they encounter dangers unsurmountable to any other race of men, and their happy ignorance, which renders them absolute strangers to those extravagant desires and endless pursuits which keep the great world in a constant agitation, - all these and other extraordinary circumstances taken together render this island singularly and intensely interesting.'

The scenery was of course 'fearful and sublime' and could not be adequately described, and the community remarkable:

'I shall say nothing about the poor people at present - they are far, far behind in the more ordinary arts of life; their huts are not better than those of the Kaffirs, but their moral and spiritual condition is the most marvellous feature in their history. I believe that there are not of their number more holy persons on earth. As to the Sabbath day, it was one to be had in remembrance. I thank God I was there. I have not passed a sweeter day on earth. Poor people – farewell – God bless them; we have added much to their comfort, and I hope to add more.'[116]

Though this could be considered an unrealistic impression from an outsider with somewhat romantic views on the primitive 'natives' there can be no doubt that, living in hardship and poverty as they did, the people of St Kilda derived some comfort from the religious instruction provided by the priests, the 'Impostor', and by even the least effective of the missionary ministers who guided them after 1700. If in later years the congregation's attention was usually directed by preachers towards a spiritual state elsewhere it cannot be said that the ordinary day-to-day material world was entirely neglected, even though there was little the people could do about it on their own by way of improvement. Perhaps the ministers and missionaries were led to show concern for the mundane difficulties of existence on the island by the very fact that they too suffered the effects of isolation, absence of medical care, severe weather, shortages of food and so on. Hardly one resident Protestant pastor enjoyed his period of exile, having to put up with opposition, inadequate payment, ill-health, and apparent neglect, even hostility, from his employers; and judging from the problems faced by the Franciscan missionaries in the islands during the seventeenth century the conditions endured by the priests of earlier times can only have been worse. It is as well to remember Alexander Buchan's hardships, Roderick MacLennan's finally disordered mind, the poor health and erratic attendance of the MacLeods, the influence felt by Neil MacKenzie and the two murders of which he heard, Peter McEwan's illness, and the apparent insanity of, perhaps, Lachlan MacLean, before accepting Dr MacLeod's picture of life in St Kilda. To the poor people issues that might be considered insignificant by a mainlander were often of great importance, and it would not be surprising if, as it appears, the departures of Duncan Kennedy and Angus Fiddes were indeed hastened by what each might have called a trivial dispute over a cow.

Much has been said here about the opinions of visitors on the nature and characteristics of the St Kilda people, and here too, as elsewhere, these opinions have been frequently criticised as lacking in sufficient background knowledge, understanding and sympathy. Yet in some respects they contained a good deal of objective truth in spite of the preconceptions and attitudes which lay behind them. However appealing the people were to Rev. Dr Norman MacLeod and others, in some ways those who saw them, for instance, as 'children' in moral behaviour, such as Rev. Neil MacKenzie, might not have considered the observations of a visiting bird photographer around 1910 as anything other than accurate comment on a less attractive side of the St Kilda 'natives'. Reminiscent of the story of the missionary on Stack Lee was the treatment of wild creatures:

'I cannot understand how it is that a people who are so devoutly religious should be so cruel to animals. The way they treat the birds and sheep is enough to make one's blood boil. I have seen some of the most desperate torture inflicted on birds, and when one remonstrates with them they simply laugh and say, "Oh! It's only a bird!" The young birds are taken from their nests and given to the children to play with, and these youngsters, too young to know what they are doing, are most intensely cruel to these small creatures. I have seen a full-grown Puffin taken from its nest, where it had young; its two wings were tied together, and its sharp beak was also tied so that it could not bite, and then it was given to the children as a toy. They chased this bird about for hours, beating it with sticks...I have seen the natives cutting out the fleshy part of the back of young Gannets and then leaving the wriggling bodies lying on the cliffs in the hot sun! One cannot imagine men who profess to be so good doing acts like this, and I should like to suggest to those who have the teaching of them, to remember that one of the first elements of religion is to learn to be kind to dumb animals. All the praying and church-going and singing of psalms will not make a man good when he treats God's creatures in this inhuman manner.'

The sheep on Soay, or Boreray, suffered too:

'On another island there was a large number of wild sheep, and one day most of the men of the island went off to capture some of them. We did think of going with them, but I am glad we did not, as it was bad enough to see them on our return. There was a boatload of the poor sheep, and each of them had its four feet tied up close together with thin cord that cut into the flesh. These helpless sheep were handled and thrown about as if they were sacks of corn instead of live animals. While they were lying on the jetty, I noticed some of the very small children amusing themselves by hitting the creatures' eyes with their fingers. Here the sheep were left for about two hours; then they were carried up to a stone shed about one hundred yards above the jetty, the cords were cut from their feet and all were bundled in. There they remained until the next morning, and I will not attempt to describe the awful scene of amateur butchery that took place there.'

Selfishness, stealing, greed, maltreatment of animals, and in later days unwillingness to help visitors, were quite possibly naturally accepted forms of behaviour which only visitors saw as faults and interpreted in what they considered appropriate terms, but this does not mean that they did not really exist. The later presence of wooden locks on doors of houses or outbuildings suggests lack of neighbourly trust, though here too it may be necessary to qualify similar 'outside' interpretations of them. Certainly resident teachers and ministers or missionaries as well as visitors were upset at times by St Kilda habits and practices, but they apparently had to learn to live with them in spite of seeing them as obstacles to a 'civilising' education and religion.[117]

Despite all the drawbacks and difficulties the priests and the ministers exercised some control over the islanders through the authority they possessed in matters of religion, and though they have been described as men of limited ability they nevertheless played a useful part in communicating with all the external agencies having an interest in St Kilda. This was still true of the latter-day missionaries, so much so that on his visit in 1912 with the tug *Victor* Dr Charles Taylor formed the impression that the people could scarcely have survived if deprived of their services: 'What St. Kilda would do without Mr. and Mrs. [Dougal] McLean I do not know, for they are everything to the islanders.'[118]

*

One fine day in June 1928 the naturalist and author Seton Gordon went aboard a boat at St Kilda's concrete jetty built thirty years earlier and left on a crossing to Boreray. The open sea was calm.

'Every few minutes the rowers called for a burst. "Ho ro," they cried in unison, and their strong oars made music which blended with the swish of the water at the bow. What a setting the scene would have made for an *iorram* or old Gaelic rowing song! The crew were questioned. It was found that Finlay MacQuien had in earlier days sung an *iorram*. In vain John MacKenzie [the factor] and his brother boatmen persuaded him to try his voice. His islesfolk coaxed him and teased him, but to no purpose, and so the boat was urged forward without music, but with periodic shouts of "Ho ro; ho ro," so that the well-tried timbers of the old craft strained and protested at each vigorous stroke of the oars.'

A hundred years previously the song raised when rowing had been commonplace, accompanying most expeditions whether between the Sound of Harris and St Kilda or on short excursions to Boreray or Soay. Now, only two years before St Kilda was finally abandoned by its inhabitants, it had faded away almost to nothing. But it was still known to Finlay MacQueen and some consciousness of it seemed to well up in the other members of the crew. Moreover, when visiting Soay, Gordon and his companions heard the story of Fearchar and Dugan, a tale which many of the islanders recounted long after the evacuation; and the visitors also discovered that tradition was alive in smaller ways for they learned of various strange practices such as that associated with the opening of the 'puffin season' on Soay: 'The first puffin caught was plucked, all except tail and wings. It was then liberated in sorry plight. Unless this were done the people believed that bad fortune would follow.'[119]

Twenty years later, in March 1948, Seton Gordon was corresponding with a Frank Mackereth, who lived in Sussex and who had visited St Kilda in June 1928, only about ten days before Gordon's own trip there. Mackereth had travelled aboard the *Hebrides*, on which Rev. Finlay MacQueen from Australia had also been a passenger, and going to his old home by the same vessel was

John Ferguson, who had served for three years in the Glasgow police. Ferguson agreed to introduce Mackereth and two companions to lesser known features of the island. On arrival therefore a group led by Ferguson went up through the houses to the burial ground where the guide remarked that the stones stood in places used over and over again, '"when the body beneath was no longer within the memory of the living."' Soon they came to a heap of stones where Ferguson said in a matter-of-fact voice, '"That is where the Fairy lived who stole the little girl."' None of the visiting party had met a person who believed in fairies, so Mackereth asked, '"What was her name?"' Ferguson said he would find out when they returned to the houses, and he added that there was great difficulty in getting the girl back. The walk then continued up to the edge of the cliff.

> 'John Ferguson went over the edge, climbed down several yards, put his foot on a fulmar petrel, stooped, picked up the bird with its egg, walked back over the top. I remember that he held the bird by the legs in one hand and the egg in the other, that the bird disgorged its quota of oil, and after being put down, had difficulty in getting air-borne, but eventually got away. We had stood watching this performance in the wind when he pointed to a place further to the west and remarked that it was the last place where Fairies had been seen. He went on to tell us that one night when McQuien…was bird catching, the Fairies appeared and danced around him in a ring. I asked "What did he do?" Ferguson said, quite calmly and seriously, "He said the Lord's Prayer and they went away".'[120]

On more than one occasion it has been stated that the Protestant church in St Kilda taught the islanders to abandon the songs, dancing, stories and superstitions that had long been an essential part of their inheritance. This opinion, to a large extent based on a reading of John MacDonald's preaching in the island in the 1820s and on John MacKay's answers to the Napier Commission, is evidently a mistaken one, exaggerating and over-simplifying a situation in which missionary teaching going back beyond Neil MacKenzie to at least John MacDonald certainly concentrated upon religious practice and behaviour but did not prevent the people from maintaining an undercurrent of traditional and probably ancient beliefs. Had ministers and missionaries been successful in eradicating what they are said to have thought undesirable Captain Thomas would have received nothing to interest him from Euphemia MacCrimmon, the teacher John Ross in 1889 would not have heard the story of the fairy woman and her gift of milk nor that of the well which vanished, and Mrs Alice MacLauchlan would not have been able to write, of Donald MacQueen's visit to the manse, 'Donald was in great form and was telling us heaps of stories about the island – pirates etc.' She was frustrated at her inability to record them properly: 'I wished I had had more Gaelic to understand him better. He told us of men falling over the rocks at Soay – boys being stolen away from Boreray and robbers coming to the island. His gestures were so funny and if any of the others dared to dispute anything he said he almost devoured them.' And if traditional beliefs had indeed been wiped out by religion the 'Warrant Telegraphist' in charge of the naval detachment at St Kilda in 1918 would not have reckoned Finlay MacQueen to have been 'the most interesting character' he met because 'It was from him that I heard the tales of the past, sitting with his family in the glow of the peat fire, his daughter Christina translating from the Gaelic, his arms as well as his black beard gesticulating.' One of these tales recalled the old island fear of mysterious ships with unpleasant dogs on the deck, and the 'Warrant Telegraphist' was able to give an outline:

> 'One morning the islanders awoke to find a large ship anchored in the bay. She appeared to be armed but yet not a man o' war. There was considerable activity aboard, and also what was very alarming to the St. Kildeans was that there were a number of big black dogs aboard. It appeared that the ship's company were preparing to land an armed party. However, suddenly a man who was probably the Master came on deck and a long argument started with another. This discussion seemed to be getting very heated – arms waving, etc. However, as a result the vessel got her anchor out of the water and sailed away, much to the relief of the islanders.'

Another of Finlay's tales dealt with the discovery of old earthenware 'around which fairies were involved' and with how it was sent to MacLeod at Dunvegan.[121]

As placenames and stories associated with them are handed down not as superstition but as a form of useful history so traditions of a superstitious kind survived on St Kilda in a manner that demonstrated reconciliation with a religion that did tend to diminish the strength and enthusiasm with which they were retained. The story told by John Ferguson, a member of that family which had led the island community for over a century and had provided ruling elders in doing so, had recorded how Finlay MacQueen used the Lord's Prayer to make the fairies go away, a fine illustration of how two leading and, some might say, opposing aspects of St Kilda life came to exist side by side. Later in the twentieth century Donald John Gillies, Donald MacDonald and Donald Ferguson were islanders who, with the encouragement of the missionaries, themselves became churchmen and who in their last years were happy to tell with sincerity about Fearchar and Dugan and about the fairies that used to lurk behind the houses in which they were born.

[1] Thomson pp.57-58

[2] Thomson pp.60-61, 69-70

[3] Logie: Stirling Sentinel 20 & 27 August 1889

[4] For the sallow countenance and peculiarity of the eyes see Part 7 n.1 (Brydon)

[5] See Part 7 p.640 for this visit to MacKay. In 1881 Dr Brydon listened to singing while in the church on St Kilda: 'After sermon they sang. The tune was Coleshill, and really the ring about it, the monotonous melody, strongly reminded us of the American jubilee singers. They have good voices, have had them considerably trained, and go into the exercise with a will.' Brydon's party found other aspects of the service unpleasant, the more so because the proceedings had already begun when the visitors arrived. 'On entering the sacred edifice, each worshipper felt his nose the most prominent member he possessed. On further experience, and after some deliberation, this was decided not to emanate from the building, but its occupants. Indeed, the odour of the St Kildans is a sensation which, once experienced, can never be forgotten.' It was composed of 'the effluvia of turf reek, tobacco smoke, fulmar oil, and a general abstemiousness from soap and water'. [Brydon]

[6] By this time 'gibberish' – applied to Gaelic – was as familiar a term as 'Hottentot' had been in reference to the cluster of older houses [see e.g. R Carruthers: The Highland Note-Book or Sketches and Anecdotes New edition Inverness 1887 pp.399-400: 'Their huts are of the most wretched description, resembling, from a little distance, a Hottentot kraal']. Dr Brydon wrote: 'The service is in Gaelic, and the audience is most devout. Up on his vantage ground, the minister leans with his right arm on a small Bible, and thumps away on the pulpit with his left fist; but to our ignorant ears his ejaculations are simply gibberish. Like all the Gaelic, his oratory strikes the Sassenach as being monotonous.' [Brydon]

[7] In a letter of 18 September 1889 from Kingsburgh John Ross said that he had written to 'Mr McFarlane Stirling' – which may explain the misunderstanding, Logie himself being from Stirling [J Ross: Journal].

[8] J Ross: Journal

[9] J Ross: Journal; Census 1891

[10] J Ross: Journal

[11] J Ross: Journal; ELHSA CH3/1428/7 11 October 1889: 'the Highland Committee having appointed Mr Fiddes to be both minister and teacher in the island Mr Ross had left shortly after Mr Fiddes's arrival and goes to Gramsdale for the winter'. J Ross: Journal. Dr Campbell, in St Kilda in 1888, referred to the 'Queen' – 'a very modest and attractive girl' ['A Trip to St Kilda' (Part II) in OT 13 April 1889].

[12] J Ross: Journal

[13] J Ross: Journal

[14] J Ross: Journal; ELHSA CH3/1428/7 14 February 1890

[15] HC CH3/983/4 pp.152-153

[16] Census 1851 (Tarbat); HN Vol. IV no.196 2 July 1887; FCPU CH3/596/1 p.34; HC CH3/983/4 pp.152-153

[17] FCM 1 October 1889

[18] FCM 1 October 1889

[19] HC CH3/983/4 p.181

[20] DC Section 2 639/6/1 letter 24 May 1890

[21] For this account of the 'wedding' events: The Scotsman 30 May 1890. The article as cutting NAS AF57/1. For his comment on the occasion see Kearton pp.51-52.

[22] James Gall Campbell was born in Sunderland in 1837. He lived in Foyle Street, a well-to-do part of the town, and supported the Free Church, having, as a small boy, witnessed 'the historic procession of ministers through the streets' of Edinburgh at the Disruption. His working life was spent in the printing business, but he was also known as an 'excursion agent', especially in Oban. His enthusiasm for Scotland, in particular the west coast, and his generosity were described in the Sunderland Echo obituary (11 July 1902), while the Oban Times, in two reports, concentrated on his local connections:
'The deceased, who was a genial and kindly-dispositioned man, had been engaged in conducting summer excursion parties which he had organised from the north of England to Oban and the West Coast for a considerable number of years. While in Oban in May last, he recorded the fact that that was the sixty-seventh time in his northern journeys that he and his party had put up at the Balmoral Hotel, which he invariably made his headquarters' [19

July 1902].

'Hundreds, of course, have heard of Mr Campbell as 'the printer', but thousands knew him as the man who ran the excursions to the West Highlands. He had gone something like ninety times, but the beauties never faded. And what anecdotes of past trips! Hear him tell of the famous Sunderland Alderman, now at rest, who in the Crinan Canal suggested to Mr Campbell that he "reckoned they were now in the Solway Firth." Then the saloon parties, the coach parties, the merry teas at the Balmoral in Oban, with my friend as the inspiration of them all!' [26 July 1902, quoting a correspondent of the 'Sunderland Daily Echo']

23 Scotsman 30 May 1890
24 DC Section 2 639/6/1 letter 24 May 1890. The factor's house had of course previously accommodated Mrs McKinlay and Mrs Urquhart, as well as the ELHSA teachers
25 HC CH3/983/4 pp.187, 191
26 KBP 8/19, 20
27 KBP 8/24; FCPU CH3/596/1 pp.55-56
28 DC Section 2 639/6/2 letter from I M Dodds 13 September 1890 with copy of petition; Census 1891
29 Turner; R A Collacott: 'Neonatal tetanus in St Kilda' in Scottish Medical Journal Vol.26 (1981) pp.224-227
30 DC Section 2 639/6/4
31 Turner pp.167-168
32 KBP 8/25. That the six years old boat existed seems to contradict the statement in his letter of the previous year that the only boat left on the island was at least fifteen years old. The boat sent to Dunvegan was apparently repaired by John MacNeill, boatbuilder at Colbost. Fiddes also wrote to Robert Rainy as convener of the Free Church Highlands Committee asking that £44, due to the Glasgow Sick Poor Association in return for the services of nurse Chisnhall, be paid by the Committee. A contribution of £20 or £25 might be made by the HASS out of the Kelsall Bequest fund. It seemed to Rainy that Fiddes had engaged the nurse in the belief that money would be found to pay for her services from some source or other [KBP 8/27]. KBP 8/28
33 KBP 8/29
34 ELHSA CH3/1428/7 15 June 1892, /8 14 December 1894; Kearton pp.18-19; Heathcote pp.76-77; ELHSA CH3/1428/9 14 April and 16 October 1899. Norman Heathcote, writing a book published in 1900, says (p.76) that the teacher was sent 'last summer' but that she could not use the factor's house because the Heathcotes (Norman and his sister) were already in possession. Their second visit was in 1899.
35 Kearton pp.84-85. Part of Kearton's general description of St Kilda was printed in the Quiver, from which it was extracted and printed again by the Oban Times (9 July 1898) under the title of 'A Sunday on St Kilda'. A column headed 'News from St Kilda - Agrarian Difficulties in the Island' in the Glasgow Herald (15 June 1896) stated that an increase in the number of wrens 'and other ornithological matters appertaining to the island will be fully investigated within the next week or two by the Messrs Kearton, from Cassells's publishing house, who are joint authors of "British Birds' Nests".'
    Lachlan MacKinnon may have been the person to whom Elliott referred in 1894: 'When we were on the island one of the oldest inhabitants was still living who helped in the slaughter of one of the last birds [Great Auk] ever seen there, and probably one of the last specimens ever obtained' [Elliott (Part II) p.130].
36 Kearton p.36. Elliott, after his visit to St Kilda in 1894, helped to perpetuate the notion that Rev. John MacKay had been responsible for the suppression of entertainment and recreation: 'Music is now unknown to them having been stamped out by the late minister, whom I believe they have to thank for many such ridiculous notions. Whistling is never indulged in; to watch their expression when you are amusing yourself with some lively tune in their company is very laughable. They regard it as most frivolous – yes, and even sinful' [Elliott p.120].
    Elliott, however, had evidently read Connell's book.
37 'The Hebrides and St Kilda' in The Dalkeith Advertiser 1 & 8 October 1896. There is mention in this article of the notice board outside the church. A lengthy and flattering account of Emily MacLeod was given by the former Inspector of Schools, John MacLeod, in his Reminiscences [Elgin 1910 pp.121-127]. Details of her stay on St Kilda were derived from her

letters, and John Sands is called 'An Edinburgh scamp'.

38 FCM 1 February 1897 pp.40-41

39 Elliott p.119

40 FCM 1 February 1897 pp.40-41

41 'Latest News from St Kilda' in OT 5 February 1898.
'The minister has the only timepiece on the island, likewise a calendar. He informed me he took the trouble to make a copy of his own for every household for the year, which they kindly returned to him again, saying they would sooner keep to the old way of cutting a nick in a stick for each day that passed. This process is carried on by two of the women. They informed the minister that they could not very well tell when their cows would calve by his way. I might mention that in last year's counting of the nicks they found the previous year was composed of 363 days only' [Elliott pp.119-120].
In similar fashion Malcolm MacDonald and Murdo MacKay on Rona in 1884-1885 noted the passing of each day by cutting a notch in the edge of a board.
'Visit to St Kilda' in OT 18 June 1898.
On 7 February 1898 Principal Rainy, on behalf of the Highlands Committee of the Free Church, wrote to MacLeod regarding the school. He said that Mr Lee had submitted the project of adding to the church in St Kilda 'a small hall, sufficient to serve as a schoolroom for the children', since at present school was held in the church which was considered unsuitable and uncomfortable. The church itself was in need of repair, and the whole work would be very costly. Since the church legally belonged to the proprietor Rainy said: 'It would relieve our difficulty…if you saw your way to give us an expression of your intention to allow us to occupy the buildings as heretofore so long as your tenants in St Kilda continue to adhere to us.' It was hoped that MacLeod would not wish to disturb the existing circumstances of possession [DC Section 2 639/1/1].
In his reply of 12 February MacLeod asked Rainy to inform the committee that 'as long as the people of St Kilda wish to have a Free Church Minister among them, I should never think of disturbing the Free Church in their possession of the Church or any other buildings erected by them'. He was grateful for the work done by the Free Church and would always be pleased to assist [DC Section 2 639/1/2].
Regarding the contractor Mrs Alice MacLauchlan's St Kilda diary (p.46 11 June 1908) records that '"Hebrides" came in alright at 10 o' clock, bringing Bain, Contractor and his man.' [Also p.1 (2 August 1908)]

42 'Visit to St Kilda' in OT 18 June 1898; Heathcote p.9

43 Heathcote pp.43, 65, 69, 80, 96-97, 202, 226-227

44 WHS pp.124-125; 'Visit to St Kilda' in OT 30 July 1898. Rev. R Lawson travelled to St Kilda with the Hebrides in July 1902. He called it 'a fair-sized steamer, with fairly good accommodation'. About sixty passengers meant that every berth was occupied. 'The chief drawback to sailing in these small steamers, in my opinion, is the poor character of the sleeping accommodation. There were eight berths in one cabin, arranged in two storeys round a very small room (I wonder what a Dean of Guild Court would say to it as an over-crowded lodging-house?).' Fortunately the whole group was 'a very pleasant one'. It consisted of about 40 men, including more than half a dozen ministers, and 20 women – 'which makes, generally speaking, a good blend on an occasion like this is'. Open-air games and evening deck concerts ('when the men did most of the singing') helped pass the time [R Lawson (1902) pp.3-4].

45 OT 18 June 1898

46 OT 30 July 1898

47 Martin (1698) pp.10-11, 17-18, 19, 116; MacAulay pp.15-16

48 KBP 4/2, /4

49 The lack of damage done to the Saddle by Otter's men is indicated by Kearton who said that 'so long have the people hauled their boats up in one particular spot that the rock is grooved by the grinding of innumerable keel-plates' [Kearton pp.43-44]; MacDiarmid pp.25-26

50 NAS AF57/5; Ferguson p.20

51 NC (Evidence) Vol. II pp.870-871

52 DC Section 2 637/5/3

53 HN Vol. I no.52 29 September 1884

54 DC Section 4 1380/2

55 DC Section 4 1380/4

56 DC Section 4 1380/3; J Ross: Journal

57 McNeill

58 OT 16 June 1900

59 DC Section 2 639/3/2 Typescript copy of correspondence exchange June-July 1899

60 DC Section 2 639/2 Memorandum 1899

61 DC Section 2 639/3/1

62 CDB Second Report 1 January 1899-31 March 1900 Glasgow 1900 p.xxiii

63 Matthews p.292; DC Section 2 639/5/8. It was reported in June 1900: 'The natives were to supply the labour, giving one day of the week free, and being paid half a crown a day for the other five days. The arrangement has, on the whole, worked satisfactorily, for, though the natives are quite unaccustomed to working continuously at labour of this kind, they submitted to the task with tolerable complaisance' [OT 16 June 1900]

64 DC Section 2 639/5/1-8 Extracts from 1899 Engineers reports; DC Section 2 639/5/1

65 Heathcote p.41; CDB Third Report Glasgow 1901 Appendix VII p.25

66 Wookey, from which extracts follow.

67 Matthews p.293: 'We once showed a magic lantern, thinking to please them, but after the show they smashed it to pieces, assuming that it was the work of the Devil, because it could not be shown in daylight.'

68 At the celebrations at 'New Year' of the new century Rev. Fiddes 'gave a treat to the school children', Mrs Matthews sang 'Scots Wha' Hae' to the 'great pleasure of the natives', and Wookey gave a short address on the advantage of education. Sweets were then distributed to the children. [OT 10 February 1900]

69 'St Kilda Visited' in OT 8 June 1901; 'News from St Kilda' in OT 10 August 1901; OT 24 August 1901

70 OT 16 June 1900, 25 May 1901

71 NAS AF57/1/6 Extract of letter from H G Dalton; Brydon; OT 13 April 1889, 8 June 1901, 5 July 1902, 2 August 1902

72 J A MacKay: Islands Postal History Series no.1 Harris and St Kilda Dumfries 1978 p.25; Rutherford p.34; OT 8 June 1901, 16 June 1900. A tourist, James Wood, wrote: 'I had a very interesting talk with the postmaster [at Lochmaddy], who tells me that he has twenty-one sub-offices under him, St. Kilda being, of course, the farthest off. He also tells me that every trip this season [1903] there has been posted at St. Kilda an average of 600 pictorial post cards. These post cards of St. Kilda were for sale on the steamer and nearly all the passengers have them written ready for posting.' ['A Trip to St Kilda' in Innerleithen Standard 23 September 1903]. Wood never reached St Kilda owing to bad weather.

73 IA HRA/R13/K4 The Act appears to be that establishing County Councils in place of Commissioners of Supply (1889)

74 IA HRA/R13/K4; NAS AF57/1/4 Copy letter 11 September 1896. The second Act is probably that setting up the Local Government Board in place of the Board of Supervision (1894).

75 IA HRA/R13/K4 Wilson's letter 26 December 1894. The only two members of the Harris District Committee present at the meeting were R F Matheson, chairman, and Rev. Donald MacLean.

76 IA HRA/R13/K4 11 September 1896; NAS AF57/4

77 M A Crowther: 'Poverty, Health and Welfare' in W H Fraser & R J Morris (edits.): People and Society in Scotland Vol. II (1830-1914) Edinburgh 1990 p.270

78 IA HRA/R13/K4 13 & 20 November 1897

79 IA HRA/R13/K4 29 December 1897

80 IA HRA/R13/K4 12 & 16 January 1898

81 OT 16 June 1900

82 The Bellona left some old naval uniforms for the island men who thereafter wore them on special occasions – 'semi naval costumes' with brass buttons as a visitor described them. [Steel p.34; Rutherford pp.23-24] For an account of this episode see OT 14 & 28 June 1902, 5 July 1902.

The King's wish that the islanders would have a good fulmar-catching seems to have led to the sending of a fulmar to him as a present. A letter came from Buckingham Palace to Dr Forshaw, dated 3 July 1902: 'I am sure the King will be happy to accept a specimen of the bird (the fulmar) to which you allude.' Eggs were sent to the Queen and enjoyed by Prince Edward and Prince Albert. It seems that Forshaw planned a history of the 'St Kildians' with a dedication to 'the Princess of Wales' [OT 26 July 1902].

The half ton of books was probably the donation from Glasgow reported by 'A Medical Inspector' in May 1907: 'Some years ago, Mrs Coats, of Paisley, gifted a library of some three or four hundred volumes to the island. But they hibernate on the shelves of the manse parlour; in the past year not one has been asked for.' The author also remarked that 'On Communion Sundays some of the elders have appeared lately in blue frock coats and white ties, and one of them at least can take his stand in the pulpit, and give a rousing discourse.' ['The Life of St Kilda' in Scotsman 18 May 1907]. It would therefore appear that exotic dress had become a temporary badge of eldership.

On 16 June 1900 the Oban Times reported improved ability to signal with flags and flare, even to the Monach lighthouse:

'In order to bring the island into more direct communication with the mainland all the year round, Colonel Gore Booth has had erected a flagstaff and sent out naval code flags, by which means communication can be held with passing vessels. A flare-up signal has also been provided, which can be seen from the lighthouse in the Sound of Harris [i.e. Monach], so that in the event of any emergency a gunboat could be sent at any moment.'

Presumably someone taught 'the natives' how to use the flags and flare, but at least the latter would require clear weather to be effective.

In or about 1908 a visitor wrote: 'On the Sabbath all the natives don their best clothes – a few of the men had remarkable clothes. I saw one in a rather ancient cut of frock-coat and a captain's cast-off peak-cap, and it was really one of the funniest combinations of clothes I have ever seen' [O G Pike: Through Birdland Byways London N D pp.50-51].

During his few hours ashore in July 1902 Rev. R Lawson noticed in the houses 'the photographs of King Edward and Queen Alexandra, which were sent by the Queen as a coronation present, nailed against the wall without any frame whatever' [R Lawson (1902) p.14].

83   OT 30 June 1900

84   Ansdell p.196

85   DC Section 2 637/5/7

86   OT 8 June 1901

87   Rutherford pp.22-30. Dr Brydon in 1881 heard 'the jingling of an old crack pot bell' summoning people to church. 'The bell has a separate wooden erection at the back of the kirk for itself, gibbet-form, consisting of one horizontal and two perpendicular beams. It hangs only about four feet above the ground, has no rope attached to it, and only a very small tongue; but there is a big stick lying near, and probably the ringing of the bell is done gong-wise.' [Brydon]

88   OT 13 July 1901, 10 August 1901

89   OT 31August 1901

90   OT 7 September 1901. Views of the Celtic people were not uncommon in considerations of the state and future prospects of the Highlands. The following is one example:

'It is a subject of regret, that any good work or scheme, public or private, for the benefit of the Highlanders, or any man taking a prominent part in promoting it, too often calls forth from sundry quarters a spirit of depreciation, detraction, and hidden opposition, arising apparently from vanity, love of notoriety, or ignorance. This spirit is, of course, not uncommon in other regions, but it is the besetting sin of the modern Celt.' [MacLeod (1898) p.90]

91   OT 7 September 1901, including a letter from a 'Free Church Islander', of 29 August 1901, in which a picture was provided of how the 'staunch Free Church men' of St Kilda had been deceived by the Unionists and since the 'truth' was out they were angry. The writer promised they would get Free Church supply 'after a little time'. There was of course no substance to the letter or the promise.

92   OT 31 May 1902

93   OT 14 June 1902, 5 July 1902. The 'deputation' was apparently Rev. William Ross of Cowcaddens, Glasgow, who stayed to assist at the island communion. The union jack flag was, in a rather unnecessary gesture, hoisted to signal a holiday while the steamer was present [OT 19 July 1902].

The teacher in early 1901 was James MacKenzie [St Kilda School Logbook, Western Isles Libraries, Stornoway]. The Oban Times (5 July 1902) called the 'young lady teacher' Miss MacKay, but later (18 October 1902) reported that Rev. Ross, having visited St Kilda as a deputy during the past summer, thought that 'Miss MacKenzie has done admirably and deserves all credit for her work' in the school. The paper added: 'Miss M C MacKenzie is well-known in Inverness, having been assistant art and music teacher in the Royal Academy, Inverness, for a considerable number of years.' On 26 June 1902 Miss MacKenzie wrote her first entry in the St Kilda school logbook: 'I arrived by the S S "Hebrides" to act as interim teacher. Mr Campbell, who has been in charge since August 1901 left by the same steamer.' On 14 August she wrote her last entry: 'Today, I leave by the S.S. "Hebrides" much regretting my departure as I have been most happy in my work here…The School will remain closed for a fortnight as the new Teacher is not expected until the 28th August.'

At his arrival in St Kilda Roderick Campbell was aged 19. He belonged to Bragar in Lewis. He wrote an interesting account of his stay in three articles which were published in the Stornoway Gazette (25 July, 1 & 8 August 1961). In these he described the quarrel between Fiddes, whose photography and joinery skills were noted, and some of the islanders; and he mentioned 'a Col. Colquhoun of Luss' who lodged in the manse for three months and took 'many hundreds of pictures', later giving 'many scores' to Campbell. Occasionally Campbell has been given the initial D, presumably for Donald, but this is clearly a mistake.

Teachers in St Kilda at this stage were appointed by the Harris School Board, the island being treated as a 'Side School' dependent on the school at Obbe [Note to initial inspector's report, St Kilda School Logbook].

Rev. R Lawson, arriving a little later in July 1902, had a brief conversation with Rev. Ross:

'The minister who had been sent over to dispense the Communion was the Rev. Mr. Ross, formerly of the Cowcaddens United Free Church, Glasgow. He told me that he had preached every day for the fortnight he had been there; while on each of the four days before and after the Communion, he had preached three times. "How many attended the services?" I asked. "Every man, woman and child on the island." "Did you preach in English at all?" "Yes; once to the children, being the only time English had ever been preached there." ' [R Lawson (1902) pp.12-13]

[94] OT 16 August 1902. It was said that John Fiddes, an ancestor of Hugh Miller, stone mason, author, and 'a redoubtable champion of the Free Church', was 'a kinsman' of Angus Fiddes [W G Blaikie: After Fifty Years London 1893 p.143].

[95] OT 23 August 1902

[96] Aberdeen Daily Journal 17 January 1903; also as file cutting NAS AF57/7

Rev. R Lawson's rather free, hearsay version of Fiddes's last days in St Kilda included reference to John MacKay's ministry:

'Some years ago, there was an old minister of the Free Church, named MacKay, who presided over the people. He preached on Sundays, taught what children could be induced to come to school twice a week, and ruled all things with a rod of iron, while he himself was ruled by a stalwart housekeeper he had. But at last the people got tired of him; declared that their elders could preach better than he, and that if his preaching did not improve they would cease attending the church. This brought matters to a head, and a new minister was sent out. This man, however, apparently lacked prudence; and some coals which had been sent specially for his use, having disappeared one night, he said the thieves must be on the island, and that it behoved them to find out who they were. The result was that nobody would come to hear him, and he, too, has had to go. At present, the elders, along with a lay missionary, take turns at the preaching, and an ordained minister is sent over at the Communion time, while a female teacher opens the School for certain months in the year; and this is perhaps as good an arrangement as could be come to meanwhile.' [R Lawson (1902) pp.14-15]

Fiddes, who was on holiday when Lawson visited, did not seem to lack 'prudence' and had of course achieved much for the island over the years he had lived there.

[97] OT 29 November 1902. It may be noted that in 1907 and 1908 Rev. Angus Fiddes was back in the Outer Hebrides, where he was 'missionary' at North Bay in Barra [HC CH3/983/5 pp.471, 86].

[98] HC CH3/983/4 p.249; NAS AF57/2; OT 27 August 1898 'St Kilda as a Tourist Resort'.

[99] HC CH3/983/4 p.337; CH3/983/5 pp.204, 241, 248, 316; UFC CH3/275/1 14 July 1929. Rev. William Ross was, as has been mentioned, an evangelist. 'Himself a Highlander, a master of the Gaelic language, deeply versed in Celtic studies, and having all his life the liveliest interest in all that pertained to the welfare of his kinsmen according to the flesh, his removal leaves a great blank.' He died in 1904. [HC CH3/983/5 p.316 (26 April 1904)]

[100] HC CH3/983/4 pp.221, 256, 310; CH3/983/5 p.176

[101] St Kilda School Logbook; HC CH3/983/5 pp.201. 248

[102] HC CH3/983/5 pp.288, 368, 277, 309, 361, 396, 401, 430, 450, 281, 454; St Kilda School Logbook pp.17, 10, 16, 26; Quine (1988) pp.54-55; MacLauchlan Diary. The MacLauchlans (MacLachlans – the form 'MacLauchlan' is that used regularly in the Highlands Committee minutes) were to receive a salary of £80, with a grant of £50 from 'the Highland Trust' as well as a government grant [HC CH3/983/5 p.401].

[103] Scotsman 15 & 18 May 1907

[104] St Kilda School Register; MacLauchlan Diary

[105] Late Rev. Donald J Gillies; F G Rea: A School in South Uist – Reminiscences of a Hebridean Schoolmaster, 1890-1913 Edited with introduction by J L Campbell London 1964 p.51. Lachlan MacLean seems to be the only person who fits Rea's description, if correct, of 'missionary, schoolmaster, registrar and postmaster'. Fiddes, who came before MacLean, and Fraser, who came after, were in St Kilda for much longer than nine months, and no missionary served as postmaster after Peter MacLauchlan handed over that office to Neil Ferguson in 1906. It might be possible to calculate from other information in Rea's account the exact year in which the Dunara Castle put in with the invalid; but there is of course a chance that his memory was inaccurate and misplaced the event.

[106] UFC CH3/275/2 19 July 1902; CH3/275/1 introduction, pp.8-11, 17-18

[107] UFC CH3/275/3; MacLauchlan Diary

[108] KBP 9/15; OT 6 July 1889; IA HRA/R79/Di/703 (7)

[109] NAS AF57/10 Daily Mirror 20 & 23 May 1912, Letter of Proceedings 21 May 1912. For the reminiscences of the doctor, Charles Taylor, see his article 'St Kilda' in The British Medical Journal Vol. I (1912) pp.1249-1251, in which he wrote:'I had to rely for my information upon the minister, Mr. McLean, who attends to the bodily as well as the spiritual needs of the islanders, and combines these offices with that of magistrate.'

[110] NAS AF57/15 Nurse Robertson's Narrative. She learned that the missionary was a Mr McArthur. UFC CH3/275/1 p.15; J Mathieson:'St Kilda' in The Scottish Geographical Magazine Vol. XLIV (1927) pp.65-90. Among the other nurses were nurses Littlejohn, MacKenzie, Flett and Barclay. UFC CH3/275/2

[111] DC Section 2 639/10; MacKenzie Papers GD403/53/1, 2; unsourced newspaper cutting 'The Bombardment of St Kilda' and MacKenzie's letter 4 October 1921

[112] MacKenzie Papers GD403/53/1 13 November 1920 MacKenzie explained the calculation of £5000:'The late MacLeod paid Sir John £3000, while the Government laid out £1500 on the jetty, making the value £4500. You may yet have to pay the half of the jetty, which we agreed to do, when being proposed. An additional £500 for the stock is not much, but it brings the value of the subject to £5000.' NAS AF57/26 Report by G Henderson 20 May 1930

[113] MacKenzie Papers GD403/53/4-9 Letter from S MacLeod to MacLeod of MacLeod 14 September 1928

[114] MacKenzie Papers GD403/53/10 5 December 1928

[115] Fox pp.10, 192

[116] MacLeod (1898) pp.160-167

[117] O G Pike: Farther Afield in Birdland London N.D. pp.65-67, 89-90

[118] C Taylor:'St Kilda' in The British Medical Journal Vol. I (1912) pp.1249-1251

[119] S Gordon: Islands of the West London 1933 pp.108, 116-117; A Stewart:'The St Kilda Maid's Song' in The Gael Vol. 6 (April 1877) p.125

[120] Information kindly supplied by Raymond Eagle, biographer of Seton Gordon.

[121] MacLauchlan Diary (1 April 1908); S H V Abbott's Recollections of St Kilda

ABBREVIATIONS

DC   Dunvegan Castle - MacLeod Muniments
EUL   Edinburgh University Library (Special Collections):
HASS [Royal] Highland and Agricultural Society of Scotland - see NTS
IA   Inverness Archives (The Highland Council) Inverness Library
NAS   National Archives of Scotland
NC   New College, Edinburgh
NLS   National Library of Scotland
NMS   National Museums of Scotland
NTS   National Trust for Scotland
PRO   Public Record Office
RS   Royal Society
SCA   Catholic Archives, Edinburgh
SOC   Scottish Ornithologists Club

Manuscript Collections

EUL: CWC   Carmichael Watson Collection
NC: Kirkwood Kirkwood Collection
NAS: ELHSA   Minutes of the Edinburgh Ladies Highland Schools
               Association
               (Association for the religious improvement of the remote
               Highlands and Islands in connexion with the Free Church of
               Scotland) CH3/1428
      FCPU   Minutes of the Free Church Presbytery of Uist and Skye
               CH3/596
      GA   General Assembly Papers, including some of RB CH1
      HC   Minutes of the Free Church (and United Free Church)
               Committee for the Highlands [Highlands Committee]
               CH3/983
      PA   Minutes of the Presbytery of Abertarff CH2/7
      PC   Minutes of the Presbytery of Caithness CH2/47
      PE   Minutes of the Presbytery of Edinburgh CH2/121
      PL   Minutes of the Presbytery of Lewis - CH2/473
      PS   Minutes of the Presbytery of Skye - CH2/330
      PT   Minutes of the Presbytery of Tongue - CH2/508
      PU   Minutes of the Presbytery of Uist - CH2/361
      RB   Register [Minutes] of the Actings and Proceedings of the
               Royal Bounty Committee, included under GA and EUL Laing
               MSS
      SA   Minutes of the Synod of Argyll - CH2/557
      SG   Minutes of the Synod of Glenelg - CH2/568
      SSPCK   Society in Scotland for the Propagating of Christian
               Knowledge - Records of GD 95
      UFC   Minutes of the [United] Free Church, St Kilda - CH3/275/1;

Communicants Roll Book, St Kilda – CH3/275/2;
Congregational Returns, St Kilda – CH3/275/3

NLS:	Chalmers	Chalmers Collections Adv. MSS (1) 21.1.5, (2) 29.1.1 vii 'A politicall whim concerning St Kilda one of the Western Isles of Scotland writen in the year 1735' (ff.169-172)
	DP	Delvine Papers MS 1389
	McKinlay	'The Ann McKinlay Story' (Typescript copy) MS 14952
	ML	MacPherson – MacAulay Correspondence – MS 2958
	Sibbald	Sibbald Collections, including Balfour papers Adv. MSS 15.1.1, 31.2.6, 33.2.27, 33.3.16, 33.3.20, 33.5.15
NMS:	HB	Harvie Brown Collection
NTS	KBP	Kelsall Bequest Papers, possessed by HASS but handlisted and presently housed by NTS, including
	JHM	Journals of visits to St Kilda by HASS Secretary, John Hall Maxwell, in 1860 and 1863
	John Ross	Account of St Kilda 1889

Newspapers

HN	Highland News
OT	Oban Times
WHFP	West Highland Free Press

Printed Works

CSP	Calendar of State Papers relating to Scotland
RMS	Register of the Great Seal of Scotland
RPC	Register of the Privy Council of Scotland

BD	R C Macleod: The Book of Dunvegan 2 Vols Aberdeen 1938-1939
CDB	Congested Districts Board for Scotland – Reports etc.
CRA	Collectanea de Rebus Albanicis Iona Club Edinburgh 1847
DN	Dictionary of National Biography
EB	Encyclopaedia Britannica Sixth edition (Vol.XI) Edinburgh 1823
EE	Edinburgh Encyclopoedia, - conducted by David Brewster, LL.D. (18 vols) Edinburgh 1830
ESSGS	Edinburgh Society for the Support of Gaelic Schools – annual reports
ESSH	A O Anderson: Early Sources of Scottish History AD 500-1286 2 Vols Reprint Stamford 1990
Fasti	H Scott: Fasti ecclesiae Scoticanae New edition Edinburgh 1915-1928
FCM[R]	Free Church Monthly [Record]
HFR	The Home and Foreign Record of the Free Church of Scotland Edinburgh 1851 etc.
IR	Innes Review
McNeill	Report of Malcolm McNeill, Esq., Inspecting Officer of the Board of

Supervision, on the Alleged Destitution in the Island of St. Kilda in October, 1885, with supplementary reports by Lieutenant Osborne, R.N., commanding officer, and by the medical officer of H.M.S. "Jackal", and copy correspondence relative thereto [presented to Parliament in March 1886] London 1886

MGC   A Mitchell(edit.): Geographical Collections relating to Scotland made by Walter MacFarlane SHS (Vols LI-LIII) 3 Vols Edinburgh 1906-1908

MM   D MacKinnon & A Morrison: The MacLeods – The Genealogy of a Clan (in 5 'Sections') Edinburgh n.d.

NCE   [Napier Commission] Evidence taken by Her Majesty's Commissioners of Inquiry into the Condition of the Crofters and Cottars in the Highlands and Islands of Scotland Edinburgh 1884

NCR   [Napier Commission] Report of Her Majesty's Commissioners etc. With Appendices Edinburgh 1884

NQS   Notes and Queries of the Society of West Highland and Island Historical Research

NSA   New [Second] Statistical Account

OPS   C Innes (edit.): Origines Parochiales Scotiae Edinburgh 1851

PB   F A Pottle & C H Bennett (edits.): Boswell's Journal of a Tour to the Hebrides with Samuel Johnson, LL.D 1773 Melbourne 1963

PHB   P Hume Brown: Scotland before 1700 from Contemporary Documents Edinburgh 1893

PSAS   Proceedings of the Society of Antiquaries of Scotland

RCAHMC   The Royal Commission on Ancient and Historical Monuments and Constructions of Scotland: Ninth Report with Inventory of Monuments and Constructions in the Outer Hebrides, Skye and the Small Isles Edinburgh 1928

SHS   Scottish History Society

SRS   Scottish Record Society

SSPCK   Case for the Society in Scotland ... and Opinion of Counsel thereon Edinburgh 1843

TGSI   Transactions of the Gaelic Society of Inverness Inverness 1872-

TI   Theophilus Insulanus: Treatises on The Second Sight Glasgow 1819

TISSFC   Transactions of the Inverness Scientific Society and Field Club Vols I-IX (1875-1925)

BIBLIOGRAPHY

Only those sources used for this book are included. Reference has also been made in general to M Harman's <u>An Isle Called Hirte</u> (Isle of Skye 1997) which serves as a useful guide through the intricacies of the St Kilda story.

Manuscript sources
Atholl Archives, Blair Castle

EUL: CWC   Carmichael Watson Collection
              Laing MSS
              Letters from T Jameson Torrie – General 1996/8/7-9
              Letters preserved in the British Museum and copied from the originals – DC.8.35
              Rev. Colin Campbell Collection

NAS: ELHSA   Minutes of the Edinburgh Ladies Highland Schools Association (Association for the religious improvement of the remote Highlands and Islands in connexion with the Free Church of Scotland) – CH3/1428
     FCPU   Minutes of the Free Church Presbytery of Uist and Skye – CH3/596
     GA   General Assembly Papers, including some of RB –CH1
     HC   Minutes of the Free Church (and United Free Church) Committee for the Highlands [Highlands Committee] – CH3/983
              MacKenzie Papers – GD 403
              Miscellaneous Accessions relating to St Kilda in GD 1, including A L M Cook: A Family Saga – GD 1/980
     PA   Minutes of the Presbytery of Abertarff – CH2/7
     PC   Minutes of the Presbytery of Caithness – CH2/47
     PE   Minutes of the Presbytery of Edinburgh – CH2/121
     PL   Minutes of the Presbytery of Lewis – CH2/473
     PS   Minutes of the Presbytery of Skye – CH2/330
     PT   Minutes of the Presbytery of Tongue – CH2/508
     PU   Minutes of the Presbytery of Uist – CH2/361
     RB   Register [Minutes] of the Actings and Proceedings of the Royal Bounty Committee, included under GA and EUL Laing MSS
              Register of Sasines
              Sasine Abridgements
     SA   Minutes of the Synod of Argyll – CH2/557
     SG   Minutes of the Synod of Glenelg – CH2/568
              Minutes of the Kirk Session of the Parish of Thurso – CH2/414
     SSPCK   Society in Scotland for the Propagating of Christian Knowledge, Records of – GD 95
     UFC   Minutes of the [United] Free Church, St Kilda – CH3/275/1;
              Communicants Roll Book, St Kilda – CH3/275/2;
              Congregational Returns, St Kilda – CH3/275/3

Campbell of Stonefield Papers – GD 14
Warrand of Bught Papers – GD 23
Letter from James Wilson, of Woodville, to Miss Sym – RH1/2/862
Government Files – AF57

NLS: Chalmers Chalmers Collections Adv. MSS (1) 21.1.5, (2) 29.1.1 vii 'A politicall whim concerning St Kilda one of the Western Isles of Scotland – writen in the year 1735' (ff.169-172)

DP Delvine Papers MS 1389
  Lundie Letters MS 1675

McKinlay 'The Ann McKinlay Story' (Typescript copy) – MS 14952

ML MacPherson – MacAulay Correspondence – MS 2580
  [Robert Campbell of Shawfield] Journal: 'An Account of the Island of St Kilda and Neighbouring Islands, Visited August 1799' – MS 3051

Sibbald Sibbald Collections, including Balfour papers – Adv. MSS 15.1.1, 31.2.6, 33.2.27, 33.3.16, 33.3.20, 33.5.15
  Stevenson Papers – Dep.216/97

NMS HB Harvie Brown Collection
  F W L Thomas Papers – notes, photographs etc.

NTS KBP Kelsall Bequest Papers, possessed by HASS but handlisted and presently housed by NTS, including

JHM Journals of visits to St Kilda by HASS Secretary, John Hall Maxwell, in 1860 and 1863

John Ross Account of St Kilda 1889

SOC McWilliam Collection
  R Scott Skirving: MS Journal of a visit to St Kilda 1881

Hydrographic Data Centre, The United Kingdom Hydrographic
  Office, Taunton:
  Letter Books and Sailing Directions (H C Otter)
  Sailing Directions (F W L Thomas)
  Photographs and Illustrations

Western Isles Libraries, Stornoway:
  Mingulay School Logbook
  St Kilda School Logbook
  St Kilda Register of Baptisms, Marriages and Deaths (microfilm copy)

In private possession:
  S H V Abbott: Recollections of St Kilda
  G C Atkinson: Journal – 'A few Weeks' Ramble among the Hebrides in the summer of 1831' (Typescript copy – also NTS)
  A MacLauchlan: Diary 1906-1909 (Typescript copy – also NTS)

G Murray: Diary 1886-1887 (Typescript copy - also NTS)
A Rutherford: Our Trip to St Kilda
W E Wookey: St Kilda Diary

Newspapers, newspaper cuttings etc.
Aberdeen Daily Journal
Arbroath Herald (Christmas Annual)
Ayr Observer and Galloway Chronicle
Cumnock Express
Daily Mirror
Daily Telegraph
Glasgow Free Press
Glasgow Herald
Globe
Graphic
Highland News
Highlander
Innerleithen Standard
Inverness Courier and General Advertiser
John O' Groat Journal
Morning Advertiser
North British Daily Mail
Northern Chronicle
Oban Times
Peeblesshire Advertiser and County Newspaper
Scotsman
Shetland Times
Spectator
Stirling Sentinel
Sunderland (Daily) Echo
West Highland Free Press

Printed Sources

Calendar of the State Papers of Ireland 1615-1625
CSP   Calendar of State Papers relating to Scotland
RMS   Register of the Great Seal of Scotland
RPC   Register of the Privy Council of Scotland

A Acland: A Devon Family - The Story of the Aclands London 1981
R J Adam: Papers on Sutherland Estate Management 1802-1816 2 vols SHS
               Fourth Series Vols 8 & 9 Edinburgh 1972
W P Anderson: Silences that Speak - Records of Edinburgh's Ancient Churches
               and burial grounds with biographical sketches of the notables
               who rest there Edinburgh 1931
D Ansdell: The People of the Great Faith - The Highland Church 1690-1900
               Stornoway 1998

P F Anson:	Underground Catholicism in Scotland 1622-1878 Montrose 1970
H Armet (edit):	Extracts from the Records of the Burgh of Edinburgh 1701-1718 Edinburgh & London 1967
G C Atkinson:	'A Notice of the Island of St Kilda, on the North-west Coast of Scotland' in Transactions of the Natural History Society of Northumberland, Durham and Newcastle Vol.II 1838
M Baillie:	'Visit to St Kilda – By a Lady' [Lady Baillie of Polkemmet] in The Church of Scotland Home and Foreign Missionary Record 1 January 1875
A Beith:	A Highland Tour 2nd edition Edinburgh 1874
R Black:	'Colla Ciotach' in TGSI Vol.48 (1972-1974
J Blaeu:	Atlas Novus Amsterdam 1654
W G Blaikie:	After Fifty Years London 1893
O Blundell:	The Catholic Highlands of Scotland – The Western Highlands and Islands Edinburgh 1917
J Boswell:	The Journal of a Tour to the Hebrides, with Samuel Johnson, LL.D. London 1785
[H Brougham]:	The Life and Times of Henry Lord Brougham – by himself 2 vols Edinburgh & London 1871
T Brown:	Annals of the Disruption New edition Edinburgh 1893
S Bruce:	'Social change and collective behaviour: the revival in eighteenth century Ross-shire' in The British Journal of Sociology Vol.XXXIV no.4
J Brydon:	'A Glimpse of St Kilda' – newspaper cutting (between 24 September and 7 November 1881) in SOC McWilliam Collection
[A Buchan]:	A Description of St.Kilda, The Most remote Western Isle of Scotland Edinburgh 1727
[A Buchan]:	A Description of St.Kilda by Mr Alexander Buchan late minister there Edinburgh 1774 (added to Monro's Description of the Western Isles and printed in 1773). Reprinted separately under same title Glasgow 1818
J L Buchanan:	Travels in the Western Hebrides from 1782 to 1790 London 1793
D Budge:	Jura – an island of Argyll Glasgow 1960
C Burns (edit):	Calendar of Papal Letters to Scotland of Clement VII of Avignon 1378-1394 SHS Fourth Series Vol.12 Edinburgh 1976
B Buxton:	Mingulay – An Island and Its People Edinburgh 1995
B Buxton:	'Mingulay's remarkable schoolteacher turned gamekeeper' in WHFP 21 November 1997
A T Campbell:	'A Trip to St Kilda' (Parts 1-4) in OT 16 March – 27 April 1889
J F Campbell (edit):	Leabhar na Feinne Vol.I (Gaelic Texts) London 1872
J L Campbell:	'The Catholic Church in the Hebrides 1560-1760' in The Tablet Vol. 206 (31 December 1955)
J L Campbell:	Gaelic Words and Expressions from South Uist and Eriskay collected by Rev. Fr. Allan McDonald Dublin 1958
J L Campbell (edit):	Tales from Barra Told by the Coddy Edinburgh 1960
J L Campbell (edit):	A Collection of Highland Rites and Customs copied by Edward Lhuyd from the Manuscript of the Rev. James Kirkwood (1650-1709 and annotated by him with the aid of the Rev. John Beaton

	Folklore Society 1975
J L Campbell:	A Very Civil People – Hebridean Folk, History and Tradition (edit. H Cheape) Edinburgh 2000
J L Campbell & C Eastwick:	'The MacNeils of Barra in the Forty-Five' in IR Vol.17 (1966)
A Carmichael:	Carmina Gadelica Edinburgh 1900 (Vols 1 & 2) 1928-1971 (Vols 1-6)
A Carmichael:	'Grazing and Agrestic Customs of the Outer Hebrides' in NC (Report) Appendix A
I Carmichael:	Lismore in Alba Perth n.d.
R Carruthers:	The Highland Note-Book or Sketches and Anecdotes New Edition Inverness 1887
W & R Chambers:	'The Story of Lady Grange' in Chambers' Edinburgh Journal New Series no.114 7 March 1846
[W Chambers]:	'The Gaelic Nuisance' in Chambers' Journal Fourth Series nos.723 (3 November 1877), 740 (2 March 1878)
H Cockburn:	Circuit Journeys 1837-1854 Edinburgh 1888
R A Collacott:	'Neonatal tetanus in St Kilda' in Scottish Medical Journal Vol.26 (1981) Collections and Observations methodiz'd; concerning the worship, discipline, and government of the Church in Four Books Edinburgh 1709
R Connell:	St Kilda and the St Kildians London 1887 Correspondence from July, 1846, to February, 1847, relating to The Measures Adopted for the Relief of the Distress in Scotland London 1847
I B Cowan:	The Parishes of Medieval Scotland SRS Edinburgh 1967
I B Cowan:	The Medieval Church in Scotland (edit. J Kirk) Edinburgh 1995
J W Croker (edit):	Boswell's Life of Johnson Second Edition London 1835
M A Crowther:	'Povert, Health and Welfare' in W H Fraser & R J Morris (edits): People and Society in Scotland Vol.II (1830-1914) Edinburgh 1990
C L Duckworth & G E Langmuir:	West Highland Steamers Fourth Edition Glasgow 1987
V E Durkacz:	The Decline of the Celtic Languages Edinburgh 1983 Edinburgh Commissariot – Register of Testaments 1701-1800
J S Elliott:	'St Kilda and the St. Kildans' in Journal of the Birmingham Natural History and Philosophical Society Vol.I (March 1895)
H J Elwes:	'The Bird-Stations of the Outer Hebrides' in Ibis January 1869
M Ferguson:	Rambles in Skye, with sketch of A Trip to St. Kilda Irvine 1885
J Fergusson:	Argyll in the Forty-Five London 1951
R Fox:	The Tory Islanders – A people of the Celtic fringe Cambridge 1978
C Fraser-MacKintosh:	Antiquarian Notes Second Series Inverness 1897
C Giblin:	Irish Franciscan Mission to Scotland 1619-1646 Dublin 1964
S Gordon:	Islands of the West London 1933
I F Grant:	The MacLeods – The History of a Clan 1200-1956 London 1959
D Gregory:	The History of the Western Highlands and Isles of Scotland, from A.D.1493 to A.D.1625 Second Edition London 1881
J Hamilton:	Memoirs of the Life of James Wilson of Woodville London 1859
E G Hawke (edit):	Memoirs of Travel, Sport, and Natural History by the late Henry

	John Elwes London 1930
R A Hay:	Genealogie of the Hayes of Tweeddale (Appendix IV: John Chiesly of Dalry; Appendix V: An Account of the Misfortunes of Mrs Erskine of Grange, commonly known as Lady Grange, taken from The Scots Magazine November 1817) Edinburgh 1835
N Heathcote:	St Kilda London 1900
G Henderson (edit):	Dain Iain Ghobha – The Poems of John Morison Second Edition 2 Vols Glasgow & Edinburgh 1896
	Historical Manuscripts Commission 11th Report Appendix Part IV The MSS of the Marquess of Townshend p.361 Postscript to letter of 30 September 1746
A M Holohan:	'St Kilda: Childbirth and the women of Main Street' in Scottish Medical Journal Vol. 30/1 (1985)
A M Holohan:	'St Kilda: Emigrants and Disease' in Scottish Medical Journal Vol. 31/1 (1986)
S Johnson:	A Journey to the Western Islands of Scotland London 1775
R Kearton:	With Nature and a Camera London 1898
J Kennedy:	The Days of the Fathers in Ross-shire Edinburgh 1867
J Kennedy:	The Apostle of the North – The Life and Labours of the Rev. John MacDonald, D.D., of Ferintosh New Edition Inverness 1932
J Kinsley:	Alexander Carlyle – Anecdotes and Characters of the Times London 1973
J Knox:	A Tour through the Highlands of Scotland, and the Hebride Isles, in 1786 London 1787 Ladies Association in Support of Gaelic Schools
D Laing:	'An Episode in the Life of Mrs Rachel Erskine, Lady Grange' etc. in PSAS Vol.XI Part II (1876); also 'Lady Grange, in Edinburgh, 1730' etc. in PSAS Vol.XII Part I (1877)
R Lawson:	A Flight to St Kilda in July, 1902 Paisley 1902
W M Lawson:	'Families of St Kilda' in St Kilda Mail No.5 (1981)
W M Lawson:	St Kilda and its Church Northton 1993
W M Lawson:	Croft History – Isle of St Kilda Northton 1993
J L[eyden]:	'Specimens of the Poetry of St Kilda' in Scots Magazine Vol.64
E R Lindsay & A I Cameron (edits):	Calendar of Scottish Supplications to Rome 1418-1422 SHS Third Series Vol.23 Edinburgh 1934
D W Logie:	An Account of a trip from Stirling to St Kilda in S.S. Hebridean of Glasgow 12th-17th August Stirling 1889
[D McAllum]:	Remains of the late Rev. Daniel McAllum, M.D., With a memoir including the journal of an Excursion to the Shetland Isles London 1829
H MacCallum:	'St Kilda' in The Caledonian Medical Journal Vol.VII 1909
D MacArthur:	'The Breadalbane 1844-1853 and her work for the Highland Destitution Committee' in TGSI Vol.LV (1986-1988) 1989
K MacAulay:	The History of St Kilda London 1764
J MacCulloch:	The Highlands and Western Isles of Scotland 4 Vols London 1824
J MacDiarmid:	St Kilda and its Inhabitants Edinburgh 1877

A & A MacDonald: The Clan Donald 3 Vols Inverness 1896-1904

F A MacDonald: 'Irish Priests in the Highlands – Judicial Evidence from Argyll' in IR Vol. LXVI No.1 (Spring 1995)

J MacDonald: General View of the Agriculture of the Hebrides or Western Isles of Scotland Edinburgh 1811

K MacDonald: Social and Religious Life in the Highlands Edinburgh 1902

N MacDonald (edit): The Morrison Manuscript – Traditions of the Western Isles by Donald Morrison, Cooper, Stornoway National Society Daughters of Founders and Patriots of America 1975

J MacGillivray: 'Account of the Island of St Kilda, chiefly with reference to its Natural History; from Notes made during a Visit in July 1840' in Edinburgh New Philosophical Journal Vol.32 (1842)

A A MacGregor: The Western Isles London 1949

M McHugh: 'The religious Condition of the Highlands and Islands in the mid-eighteenth Century' in IR Vol.35 (1984)

J Macinnes: 'A Folktale from St Kilda' in Scottish Studies Vol.5 Part 2 (1961)

J Mackay: The Church in the Highlands or the progress of Evangelical Religion in Gaelic Scotland 563-1843 London [1914]

J A MacKay: Islands Postal History Series No.1 Harris and St Kilda Dumfries 1978

M M MacKay: The Rev. Dr. John Walker's Report on the Hebrides of 1764 and 1771 Edinburgh 1980

W MacKay (edit): Chronicles of the Frasers – The Wardlaw Manuscript entitled 'Polichronicon seu Policrata Temporum, or, The True Genealogy of the Frasers' 916-1674 by Master James Fraser SHS Vol.XLVII Edinburgh 1905

W R MacKay: 'Early St Kilda – A Reconsideration' in NQS No.26 April & August 1985

A MacKenzie: History of the MacDonalds Inverness 1881

C MacKenzie: Catholicism and Scotland London 1936

J B MacKenzie (edit): Episode in the Life of the Rev. Neil MacKenzie at St Kilda From 1829 to 1843 Privately Printed 1911

O H MacKenzie: A Hundred Years in the Highlands London 1921

W MacKenzie: 'The Gaelic Incantations and Charms of the Hebrides' in TGSI Vol.XVIII (1891-1892) 1894

W C MacKenzie: History of the Outer Hebrides Paisley 1903

W C MacKenzie: The Highlands and Islands of Scotland – A Historical Survey Edinburgh & London 1937

D MacKillop: 'The Place Names of Berneray – A Manuscript by Mr John Ferguson, Berneray' in TGSI Vol.LIII (1982-1984) 1985

J M MacKinlay: Ancient Church Dedications in Scotland – Scriptural Dedications: Edinburgh 1910; Non-Scriptural Dedications: Edinburgh 1914

D MacKinnon: 'Education in Argyll and the Isles 1638-1709' in Records of the Scottish Church History Society Vol.6 (1938)

D MacKinnon: 'The MacPhersons of Skye' in The Scottish Genealogist I: 2-3; also III: nn.171, 217

T McLauchlan: Celtic Gleanings Edinburgh 1857

A MacLean: 'Notes on South Uist Families' in TGSI Vol.LIII (1982-1984) 1985

C MacLean:	Going to Church NMS Edinburgh 1997
L MacLean:	Sketches of the island of St Kilda Glasgow 1838
[D] McLeod:	'Notices on the Present State of St Kilda – by Lieut. Col. McLeod, the Proprietor' in Scots Magazine and Edinburgh Literary Magazine December 1814
J MacLeod:	Reminiscences Elgin 1910
J N MacLeod:	Memorials of The Rev. Norman MacLeod, Senr. etc. Edinburgh 1898
M MacLeod:	'Gaelic in Highland Education' in TGSI Vol.XLIII (1960-1963) 1966
R MacLeod:	'The Bishop of Skye' in TGSI Vol.LIII (1982-1984) 1985
R C MacLeod:	The MacLeods – Their History and Traditions Edinburgh [1929]
J R N MacPhail (edit):	Highland Papers (SHS Second Series Vols.5, 12, 20; Third Series Vol.22) Vols.1-4 Edinburgh 1914-1934
K & E G McQueen (edits):	St Kilda Heritage – Autobiography of Callum MacCuithinn (Malcolm MacQueen) The Scottish Genealogy Society Edinburgh 1995
A MacRae:	Revivals in the Highlands and Islands in the 19th Century Stirling n.d.
D C MacTavish (edit):	Minutes of the Synod of Argyll (SHS Third Series Vol.XXXVII 1639-1651, Vol.XXXVIII 1652-1661) 2 Vols Edinburgh 1943-1944
J Maidment (edit):	Kay's Edinburgh Portraits – A Series of Anecdotal Biographies Chiefly of Scotchmen, mostly written by James Paterson 2 Vols London 1885
J Marsden:	Sea Road of the Saints – Celtic Holy Men in the Hebrides Edinburgh 1995
M Martin:	A Late Voyage to St. Kilda, the Remotest of all the Hebrides, or Western Isles of Scotland London 1698
M Martin:	A Description of the Western Islands of Scotland London 1703
W Matheson:	'Notes on Mary MacLeod – (1) Her Family Connexions; (2) Her Forgotten Songs' in TGSI Vol.XLI (1951-1952) 1953
J Mathieson:	'St Kilda' in The Scottish Geographical Magazine Vol.XLIV (1927)
E Matthews:	'St Kilda – An Odd Engineering Job' in The Sapper June 1933
D E Meek:	'Gaelic Bible, revival and mission – the spiritual rebirth of the nineteenth century Highlands' in J Kirk (edit): The Church in the Highlands Scottish Church History Society Edinburgh 1998
A H Millar:	The Castles and Mansions of Renfreshire and Buteshire Glasgow 1889
W M E Milner:	'Some Account of the people of St Kilda, and of the Birds in the Outer Hebrides' in The Zoologist Vol.6 (1848)
J E Morgan:	'The Falcon among the Fulmars; or, Six Hours at St. Kilda' in MacMillan's Magazine Vol.III (1861)
A Morrison:	'The Contullich Papers, 1706-1720' in TGSI Vol.XLIV (1964-1966) 1967
A Morrison:	'The Island of Pabbay' in Clan MacLeod Magazine Vol.6 No.34 1969
A Morrison:	'The Accounts of a Doer – Alexander MacLeod the "Advocat" ' in

	TGSI Vol.L (1976-1978) 1979
A Morrison:	'Eilean Phabaidh – Eachdraidh, Sgeulachdan, Taibhsearachd agus Bardachd' in TGSI Vol.LV (1986-1988) 1989
T S Muir:	Characteristics of Old Church Architecture etc. in the Mainland and Western Isles of Scotland Edinburgh 1861
J Munro:	The British Fisheries Society 1786-1893 Edinburgh 1978
J & R W Munro (edits):	Acts of the Lords of the Isles 1336-1493 SHS Fourth Series Vol.22 Edinburgh 1986
R W Munro (edit):	Monro's Western Isles of Scotland and Genealogies of the Clans 1549 Edinburgh 1961
R W Munro:	'Profusion of Pabbays' in NQS No.XVI September 1981
R W Munro:	'Hirta or Harris?' in NQS No.18 October 1982
T M Murchison:	'Lord Macaulay and the Scottish Highlanders' in TGSI Vol.XLIII (1960-1963) 1966
T Nicol:	By Mountain, Moor and Loch To the Dream Isles of the West Stirling 1931
D O' Donoghue (edit):	Lives and Legends of Saint Brendan the Voyager Reprint Felinfach 1994
	Oliver & Boyd's Scottish Tourist Edinburgh 1852
W Otter (edit):	The Life and Remains of Edward Daniel Clarke Second Edition 2 Vols London 1825
H Palsson & P Edwards (trans):	The Book of Settlements (Landnamabok) Winnipeg 1972
H Palsson:	'Towards a Glossary of Norse Place Names in Lewis and Harris' in Scottish Gaelic Studies Vol.XVII (Special Volume) University of Aberdeen 1996
H Palsson (2):	'Aspects of Norse Place Names in the Western Isles' in Northern Studies Vol.31 Edinburgh 1996
H Paton (edit):	The Lyon in Mourning or a collection of speeches letters journals etc. relative to the affairs of Prince Charles Edward Stuart by the Rev. Robert Forbes 1746-1775 (SHS Vols.XX-XXII) 3 Vols Edinburgh 1895
J & E R Pennell:	Our Journey to the Hebrides London 1889
	Philosophical Transactions of the Royal Society of London
O G Pike:	Through Birdland Byways with Pen and Camera London n.d.
O G Pike:	Farther Afield in Birdland London n.d.
L F Powell:	'The History of St Kilda' in Review of English Studies 16 (1940)
W A Power:	The Log of the Olivia The Richmond Publishing Company Ltd. 1983
M Purcell:	The Story of the Vincentians All Hallows College Dublin 1973
D A Quine:	St Kilda Portraits [Privately Printed] 1988
R Ralph (edit):	William MacGillivray – A Hebridean Naturalist's Journal 1817-1818 Stornoway 1996
F G Rea:	A School in South Uist – Reminiscences of a Hebridean Schoolmaster, 1890-1913 (edit. J L Campbell) London 1964
	Register of Marriages for the Parish of Edinburgh 1701-1750

	(SRS) Report to the Board of Supervision by Sir John McNeill on the Western Highlands and Islands Edinburgh 1851
E Richards (1):	'The Decline of St Kilda – Demography, Economy and Emigration' in Scottish Economic and Social History Vol.XII (1992)
E Richards (2):	'St Kilda and Australia – Emigrants at Peril, 1852-1853' in Scottish Historical Review Vol.LXXI 1:2 Nos. 191/2 April & October 1992
M Robson:	Rona – The Distant Island Stornoway 1991
M Robson:	A Desert Place in the Sea Ness 1997
	Roll of Edinburgh Burgesses and Guild Brethren 1701-1841 (SRS)
A Ross:	'A Visit to the Island of St Kilda' in TISSFC Vol.III (1883-1888) Inverness 1893
D R[oss]:	'Thoughts on the Beneficial Effects of Gaelic Schools, and on the Present State of Religion in the Isle of Skye' in The Edinburgh Christian Instructor No.LXXXII (May 1817) Vol.XIV No.V 'St Kilda Poetry' in The Edinburgh Magazine and Literary Miscellany March 1818
J Sands:	Out of the World; or, Life in St Kilda Edinburgh [1876]
J Sands:	Out of the World; or, Life in St Kilda Second Edition Edinburgh 1878
J Sands:	'Notes on the antiquities of the island of St Kilda' in PSAS Vol.XII Part 1 Edinburgh 1877
J Sands:	'Notes on the antiquities of the Island of Tiree' in PSAS Vol.XVI Edinburgh 1882
	Scottish Home Industries n.d.
	Scottish Studies
G Seton:	St Kilda Past and Present Edinburgh 1878
W F Skene:	Celtic Scotland – A History of Ancient Alban 3 Vols Edinburgh 1880
W F Skene (edit):	John of Fordun's Chronicle of the Scottish Nation 2 Vols Reprint Felinfach 1993
A Smith:	A Summer in Skye 2 Vols Edinburgh 1865
A Smith:	A Summer in Skye Edinburgh 1912
R A Smith:	'A Visit to St Kilda in 1873' in Good Words 1875
R A Smith:	A Visit to St Kilda in "The Nyanza" Glasgow 1879
T Steel:	The Life and Death of St Kilda Glasgow 1975
D Stevenson:	Alasdair MacColla and the highland Problem in the Seventeenth Century Edinburgh 1980
A Stewart:	'The St Kilda Maid's Song' in The Gael Vol.6 (April 1877)
A B Taylor:	'The Norsemen in St Kilda' in Saga Book Viking Society for Northern Research, University College, London Vol.XVII Parts 2-3 (1967-1968)
A B Taylor:	'The Name "St Kilda" ' in Scottish Studies Vol.13 (1969)
C Taylor:	'St Kilda' in The British Medical Journal Vol.I (1912)
F W L Thomas:	'Letter from St Kilda' in PSAS Vol.X (1872-1874)
R Thomson:	A Cruise in the Western Hebrides or a Week on Board The S.S. Hebridean Glasgow 1891

[A Trollope]:	An Illustrated Autobiography including How the 'Mastiffs' went to Iceland Gloucester 1987
G A Turner:	'The successful preventive treatment of the scourge of St Kilda (tetanus neonatorum), with some considerations regarding the management of the cord in the new-born infant' in The Glasgow Medical Journal Vol.43 No.III (March 1895)
J C Watson:	Gaelic Songs of Mary MacLeod Scottish Gaelic Texts Society Edinburgh 1965
R W S Watson:	'The Strange Story of Lady Grange' in History Vol.XVI (1931)
W J Watson:	The History of the Celtic Place-Names of Scotland Edinburgh & London 1926
D E R Watt:	'Bishops in the Isles before 1203: Bibliography and Biographical Lists' in IR Vol.XLV No.2 (Autumn 1994)
J Watts:	Scalan - The Forbidden College, 1716-1799 East Linton 1999
B Webster (edit):	Regesta Regum Scottorum Vol.VI - The Acts of David II, King of Scots 1329-1371 Edinburgh 1982
C R Weld:	Two Months in the Highlands, Orcadia and Skye London 1860
J Wiglesworth:	St Kilda and its Birds - A lecture delivered before the Liverpool Biological Society, on an ornithological expedition to the island in the summer of 1902 Liverpool 1903
N M Wilby:	'The "Encrease of Popery" in the Highlands 1714-1747' in IR Vol.17 (1966)
J Wilson:	A Voyage round the Coasts of Scotland and the Isles 2 Vols Edinburgh 1842
W M Wilson:	'Round the Hebrides and St Kilda' in The Ayr Observer and Galloway Chronicle 24 July-25 September 1877
J Wood:	'A Trip to St Kilda' in Innerleithen Standard 9, 16 & 23 September, 7 October, 1903
G Zealand:	'John Sands of Ormiston' in Arbroath Herald Christmas Annual Arbroath 1994

INDEX

A selective index, chiefly of persons but also with some places and other relevant subjects. Aspects of St Kilda life (e.g. fowling, fishing) are not included. Where subjects involve larger groups of pages these are given only in the relevant Parts.

A

B

C

Cachaileith na Beatha 11
Caithness – presbytery of 185-188, 190-192
Calum Mor Cleireach (Lismore) 198
Cameron, Rev. Alexander 449, 455, 457, 470, 473-476
Campbell, Rev. Alexander (Portree) 250, 265
Campbell, Dr Archibald 644, 686
Campbell, Roderick – teacher in St Kilda 700, 703, 728
Campbell, Rev. Daniel (Kilmichael,Glassary) Part II
Campbell, Donald - tacksman of Scalpay 196
Campbell, Rev. James (Kilbrandon) 130, 140-141, 144
Campbell, James Gall 653-661, 723-724
Campbell, Rev. John (Harris) 53-55, 59-62, 64, 66-68, 70, 75, 93, 134, 149, 157
Campbell, Katharine – wife of Rev. Alexander Buchan Part II , 161
Campbell, Kenneth – teacher in St Kilda 23-24, 26, 572-574, 591, 596
Campbell, Margaret – wife of Rev. John MacAulay 197-198, 261
Campbell, Murdo (St Kilda) 104, 111-114, 116, 160, 176
Campbell, Robert –of Shawfield 244-246
Canisbay – parish of 186-189
Canna, Isle of 40, 135, 162-163, 167, 272, 359
Caolas Hirt 9, 70-71
Carmichael, Mr – catechist in St Kilda 386-387, 389
Carmichael, Alexander 5-6, 260, 290, 365, 474-475
Casey (Cahassy), John (missionary) 50
Causamul 30
Chapels in St Kilda 23, 25-26, 28, 37, 75, 285, 357
Charles Edward, Prince 195-197, 260-261
Chisnhall, Jessie – nurse in St Kilda 663-665
Church Bell 308, 329, 348, 429, 668, 684-685, 727
Church, W H 329
Cill Eiseam (Berneray, Harris) 11, 71
Clarke, Edward Daniel 236-242
Clarke, J A 594-596
Clerk, Rev. Archibald (Duirinish) 178
'Clydesdale' (steamer) 653, 655-656, 658-660
Coishletter (Harris) 324, 372
Coll Ciotach [MacDonald] 35-36, 38, 157, 240
Collins, Sir William (Glasgow) 599, 601-602
Colquhoun, Major 702-704, 728
Columba (Colum Cille) 12-16, 20, 22-23, 26, 28, 39-40, 363
Committee of the General Assembly for the Reformation of the Highlands and Islands of
    Scotland and for Managing His Majesty's Bounty [Royal Bounty] Parts II & III, 272
Communion token 430
Con (Coan, Conn), Cornelius 50, 57, 74
Congested Districts Board for Scotland [CDB] 678-681, 683
Connell, Robert –Special Correspondent 600-603, 605-612, 620-622, 630-637
Corbett, Rev. George 449
Corriechatachan (Corrie, Corry) 219, 290, 301-302, 314-315, 323
'Corronach' 44-45, 64, 160
Couper (Cooper), Rev. Alexander (North Uist) 51, 68, 74
Cowan, Duncan (Beeslack, Penicuik) 471
Crawford, Elizabeth – wife of Rev. Neil MacKenzie 314, 320, 327, 346, 348
Crawford, James 321, 327, 345, 348, 352-353
Crofters Commission 587-589
Cross (crucifix) 4, 62-63, 160, 430
'Crusader' (yacht) 498-500

D

Dargavel (Bishopton) 425-426, 450
'Dargavel' (Boat) 446-449, 451, 465, 470, 511-513, 515, 559

Davidson, Rev. Alexander (Manish, Harris) 417-419
Davidson, Peter (? Missionary to St Kilda) 311
Dewar, Rev. Dr Daniel (Tron, Glasgow, & Principal, Marischal College, Aberdeen) 311-313, 408-409, 411
Dewar, James – schoolmaster 143-145
Dickson, Dr Part IV.
Doctors for or at St Kilda 500, 559, 686-687
Drink in St Kilda 30, 238, 243
Duggan, Dermot 48-49
'Dunara Castle' (steamer) Parts VI, VII, 671, 683, 697
Dunbar, Rev. David (Olrig) 190
Dunbar, James 186
Dunvegan 498, 504-505, 518, 535, 545, 550, 605, 621, 633, 640, 650, 665-666, 668
Duror – 'Government' church at 368, 385
Dwyer (Devoyer), James (Missionary) 50

E

Early ownership of St Kilda 21-22
'Earth Houses' (South Uist) 28
Edderachilis – parish of 185
Edinburgh Bible Society 312
Edinburgh Encyclopaedia 251
Edinburgh Ladies Highland Schools Association (ELHSA – Free Church) 412-414, 417, 471-473, Part VII, 651, 653, 655, 667-668, 695
Edinburgh – presbytery of 98, 108, 110, 183-184
Edinburgh Society for the Support of Gaelic Schools (ESSGS) 269-272, 294-297, 300, 412
Education and Schools Parts I-VIII, 261, 463, 725, 728
Eigg, Isle of 11, 20, 39-40, 134-135, 162, 167, 359
Elders in St Kilda 352, 386, 405, 407, 418, 452, 456, 524, 606, 617, 631, 633-634, 711, 727
Elwes, Henry John 478-479
Emigration and Evacuation from St Kilda Parts V, VI, VII, VIII, 462
Ensay, Isle of 51, 55, 225-226, 278-279, 282, 306
Eriskay, Isle of 480
Evacuation – see Emigration
Evans, Henry 590-591, 608

F

Farr – parish of 185-186, 270
'Fearchar and Dugan' – tale of 24-26, 49, 395, 442, 537, 720
Female teachers in St Kilda 418, 453, 566-567, 570-571, 667-668, 694, 700, 702, 707-708, 728
Ferguson, Alexander (St Kilda) 596-599, 624, 658, 668
Ferguson, Ann ('Queen', St Kilda) 624, 653-655, 657-659
Ferguson, Annie (St Kilda) 618
Ferguson, Donald (St Kilda) 616-618, 624, 631, 633-635, 658, 660, 713
Ferguson, Rev. Donald (St Kilda) 722
Ferguson, Finlay 466-467
Ferguson, John (1) (St Kilda) 281, 325, 366, 462
Ferguson, John (2) (St Kilda) 721-722
Ferguson, Malcolm 583, 629-630
Ferguson, Neil (1) (St Kilda) 418, 452-454, 466-467, 631
Ferguson, Neil (2) (St Kilda) 616
Ferguson, Rachel (St Kilda – Mrs Donald Ferguson) 567, 570, 664
Festivals in St Kilda 42, 73, 263-264
Fiddes, Rev. Angus Part VIII, 728
Fife Adventurers 32, 34
Findlater, Rev. 414, 416-417
Finlayson, John – teacher in Mingulay 472-473, 476, 563
Flannan Isles 9, 13-14, 25, 335
Foula, Isle of 480, 497, 643

748

M

MacIver, Murdoch (catechist, Harris) 225
MacKay, Rev. John 6, Parts VI, VII, 643, 648-650, 658, 676
MacKay, Margaret – sister of Rev. John 478, 560, 568
MacKenzie of Seaforth 35, 48
MacKenzie, Alexander – builder in Stornoway 301, 307-309
MacKenzie, Alexander – teacher in St Kilda Part IV, 412
MacKenzie, Colin – of 'Kildin' (Kildun) 167
MacKenzie, Rev. Colin (Lochs)135
MacKenzie, Sir George – of Coul 250, 357
MacKenzie, Rev. James (Laggan) 132
MacKenzie, Rev. James B, son of Rev. Neil MacKenzie 394-395
MacKenzie, Jane, daughter of Rev. Neil MacKenzie 327
MacKenzie, John Tolmie, and son John – factors to MacLeod of MacLeod for St Kilda 489, 501,
    504, 518-520, 551, Parts VII, VIII
MacKenzie, Lady Mary – of Gairloch 413-414
MacKenzie, Mary, daughter of Rev. Neil MacKenzie 327
MacKenzie, Murdoch, nephew of Murdoch MacKenzie, surveyor 201-202
MacKenzie, Nathaniel, son of Rev. Neil MacKenzie 319
MacKenzie, Rev. Neil Part IV, 385-386, 390-395, 401, 403, 407, 483
MacKenzie, Rev. Roderick (Tarbert, Harris) 629
Mackereth, Frank 720-721
McKerrol, W (Great Malvern & Bath) 471, 554
MacKinlay, Mrs Ann – nurse and teacher in St Kilda 570-572, 576-578, 588, 591, 617-620, 641-642
MacKinnon, Donald (St Kilda – precentor etc. in Harris) 346, 419, 463-464, 470, 511, 559
MacKinnon, Donald – lost with 'Dargavel' 447, 511-513, 557
MacKinnon, Lachlan (St Kilda) 511, 513, 668
MacKinnon, Lachlan – of Corrie (Corry) 301-302, 304, 306, 315
MacKinnon, Malcolm (St Kilda) 434, 592
MacKinnon, Margaret, wife of Angus MacLeod 229
MacKinnon, Neil (St Kilda) 592
MacKinnon, Rev. Neil (Skye & Small Isles) 39
McLachlan, John, of Kilbride 79
MacLauchlan (MacLachlan), Peter and his wife – missionary and teacher in St Kilda 708-710
MacLauchlan, Rev. Thomas 403-405, 456-457, 472, 481, 514-515, 529, 564
MacLean of Boreray 35-36
MacLean, Allan (catechist & teacher, North Uist) 163
MacLean, Hector - of Coll 165, 167
MacLean, Rev. John (North Uist) 135
MacLean, Lachlan 345-346, 348-349
MacLean, Lachlan – missionary in St Kilda 702, 708, 729
MacLean, Lauchlan (probationer in South Uist) 195
MacLean, Marion – wife of Rev. Lachlan MacLeod 248, 253
MacLean, Norman – catechist in Barra 481
MacLean, Peter – merchant at Dunvegan 632
MacLean, Rev. Roderick (South Uist) 257
MacLellan, Murdoch – tacksman of Scalpay and St Kilda, and of Milton Part IV, 387-389, 461
MacLennan, Catherine (Carloway) 653
MacLennan, Daniel – son of Rev. Roderick MacLennan 191
MacLennan, John (itinerant preacher, Kilmallie) 200
MacLennan, Murdo (Lochaber) 186
MacLennan, Rev. Roderick Part III, 259
MacLeod of Harris and Dunvegan Parts I, VI, VII, VIII, 116, 174, 180, 182, 195, 211, 226-227
MacLeod of MacLeod – see MacLeod of Harris and Dunvegan
MacLeod, Alexander (advocate) 95, 97, 111, 116, 119-120, 128, 167, 174-175, 179, 184, 288,
    385-386
MacLeod, Captain Alexander – of Harris 226-227, 231, 233, 247
MacLeod, Alexander Hume – of Harris 247, 255, 488
MacLeod, Alexander – elder and catechist in Bracadale, missionary to St Kilda 204, 212, 221,
    229, 264

McQueen, Rev. Archibald (Sleat) 137, 151
McQueen, Rev. Daniel (Small Isles) 166
MacQueen, Rev. Donald (North Uist) 390
MacQueen, Finlay (St Kilda) 694, 720-722
MacQueen, Rev. Finlay (Australia) 715, 720
MacQueen, Rev. James (North Uist) 270
MacQueen, Malcolm (St Kilda) 413, 462-463, 555
MacPhail, Rev. John S (Sleat) 490-492
McRae, Rev. Donald 406
MacRae, Rev. Finlay (North Uist) 257, 311
MacRae, Murdo - teacher in St Kilda 576, 620, 632-633
MacRaild, Norman - factor for St Kilda 358, 386, 389, 395, 400-404, 408, 416-417, 419-420, 422-423, 448, 465, 489, 556
MacSueen, Charles 178, 260
Maitland, Brigadier (at Fort William) 69, 168
Manse in St Kilda 116, 238, 243-244, 250, 256, Parts IV, V, 474, 476-478, 575, 583, 595, 617-618, 623, 629, 634-635, 656, 659, 669-670, 672, 695, 708, 713-714
Manson, James - catechist on Foula 480
'Maolan' (J McLennan) 487-488, 494, 555
Maoldomhnaich (Ludovick, Lewis) 59-60, 75
Maolrubha 13-14, 358
Marriage and wedding 62-63, 238, 304, 332, 429, 432, 434, 653-660
Martin, Martin 52-67, 69, 74-75, 82, 119, 139-140, 156-157, 215-216, 673
'Mary Jane' (steamer) 391
Matheson, George - teacher in St Kilda 668-669
Matthews, E - engineer 681-685, 726
Maxwell, John Hall (HASS) 421-432, 434-436, 439-440, 444-454, 464, 466-467
Mealasta - Lewis 447
Meldrum, Professor George 93, 95-98
'Men' 427, 464
Menzies, Fletcher N (HASS) 493, 514-523, 535, 544, 551, 563, 580, 583, 598, 662, 665
Milner, W M E 391-394
Milton (South Uist) 315, 387
Mingulay, Isle of 471-473, 480
Molinginish - school at 628
Moluag 11-14, 22, 71
Monro, Archdeacon Donald 29-31
Morgan, Dr John E 441
Morison, Rev. Alan (North Uist & Ness) 51, 68
Morison, Rev. Daniel (Stornoway) 135
Morison, William - teacher at Ratagan and Stroma 191-192
Morison, Rev. William (Tiree & Coll) 135
Morrison, Donald (Daniel)- catechist at Stornoway 163, 173
Morrison, John - catechist in Harris 163
Morrison, John - catechist at Barvas 163
Morrison, John (Ian Gobha - Harris) 278, 360
Mortification (bequest by Alexander MacLeod advocate)159-160, 174-175, 179-180, 242, 244, 256, 288, 371, 385-386, 411, 456, 489-493, 556
Moulin (Pitlochry) 360
Muck, Isle of 135, 162-163, 167
Muir, Thomas S 418-420, 470
Munro, Donald - teacher in Taransay 270
Munro, Isabella Ross (St Kilda) 498-500, 506, 508-509, 536-537, 551-552, 566, 568
Murray, George - teacher in St Kilda 574, 576, 605, 613-618, 620-621, 623, 631, 644
Music 64, 111

N

Ness - Lewis 365, 571
Nicolson, Rev. Alexander 296